Organizational Behaviour

Concepts, Controversies, Applications

Seventh Canadian Edition

Organizational Behaviour

Concepts, Controversies, Applications

Seventh Canadian Edition

Nancy Langton
University of British Columbia

Stephen P. Robbins
San Diego State University

Timothy A. Judge
University of Notre Dame

With contributions by
Katherine Breward, Ph.D.
University of Winnipeg

Toronto

Vice-President, CMPS: Gary Bennett
Editorial Director: Claudine O'Donnell
Acquisitions Editor: Carolin Sweig
Marketing Manager: Jessica Saso
Program Manager: Karen Townsend
Project Manager: Jessica Hellen
Manager of Content Development: Suzanne Schaan
Developmental Editor: Jennifer Murray
Media Editor: Keriann McGoogan
Media Developer: Kelli Cadet
Compositor: Cenveo® Publisher Services
Production Editor: Claudia Forgas
Permissions Project Manager: Joanne Tang
Photo Permissions Research: Steve Merland, Lumina Datamatics
Text Permissions Research: Jen Roach, PMG
Cover and Interior Designer: Alex Li
Cover Image: Jamie Farrant/Digital Vision Vectors/Getty Images

10 9 8 7 6 5 4 3 [CKV]

Library and Archives Canada Cataloguing in Publication

Robbins, Stephen P., 1943-, author Organizational behaviour : concepts, controversies, applications / Nancy Langton (University of British Columbia), Stephen P. Robbins (San Diego State University), Timothy A. Judge (University of Notre Dame) ; with contributions by Katherine Breward, Ph.D. (University of Winnipeg). – Seventh Canadian edition.

Includes bibliographical references and index.
ISBN 978-0-13-359178-1 (bound)

1. Organizational behavior—Textbooks. 2. Management—Textbooks. I. Langton, Nancy, author II. Judge, Tim, author III. Breward, Katherine, author IV. Title.

HD58.7.R62 2015 658 C2014-907198-1

ISBN 978-0-13-359178-1

BRIEF CONTENTS

CONTENTS

PART 5   Reorganizing the Workplace   454

CHAPTER 13   Organizational Structure   454

MyManagementLab™: Improves Student Engagement Before, During, and After Class

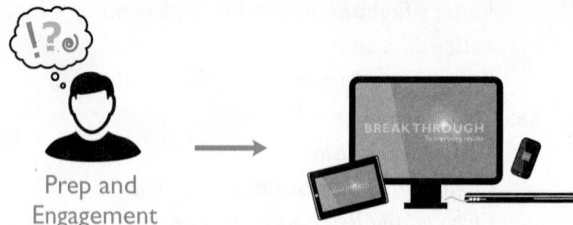

Prep and Engagement

- **Video exercises** – engaging videos that bring business concepts to life and explore business topics related to the theory students are learning in class. Quizzes then assess students' comprehension of the concepts covered in each video.

- **Learning Catalytics** – a "bring your own device" student engagement, assessment, and classroom intelligence system helps instructors analyze students' critical-thinking skills during lecture.

- **Dynamic Study Modules (DSMs)** – through adaptive learning, students get personalized guidance where and when they need it most, creating greater engagement, improving knowledge retention, and supporting subject-matter mastery. Also available on mobile devices.

- **Business Today** – bring current events alive in your classroom with videos, discussion questions, and author blogs. Be sure to check back often, this section changes daily.

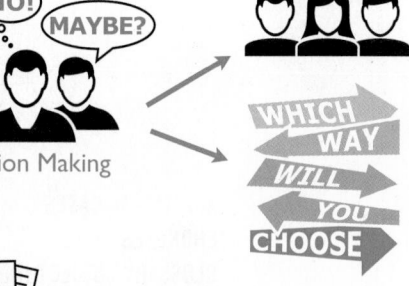

- **Simulations** – place your students in the role of a key decision-maker. The simulation will change and branch based on the decisions students make, providing a variation of scenario paths. Upon completion of each simulation, students receive a grade, as well as a detailed report of the choices they made during the simulation and the associated consequences of those decisions.

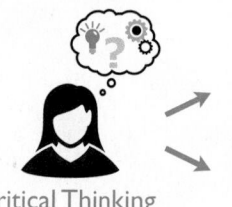

Decision Making

Critical Thinking

- **Writing Space** – better writers make great learners—who perform better in their courses. Providing a single location to develop and assess concept mastery and critical thinking, the Writing Space offers automatic graded, assisted graded, and create your own writing assignments, allowing you to exchange personalized feedback with students quickly and easily.

  Writing Space can also check students' work for improper citation or plagiarism by comparing it against the world's most accurate text comparison database available from **Turnitin**.

- **Additional Features** – included with the MyLab are a powerful homework and test manager, robust gradebook tracking, comprehensive online course content, and easily scalable and shareable content.

http://www.pearsonmylabandmastering.com

PEARSON

PREFACE

Welcome to the seventh Canadian edition of *Organizational Behaviour*. Since its arrival in Canada, *Organizational Behaviour* has enjoyed widespread acclaim across the country for its rich Canadian content and has quickly established itself as the leading text in the field.

Organizational Behaviour, Seventh Canadian edition, is truly a Canadian product. While it draws upon the strongest aspects of its American cousin, it expresses its own vision and voice. It provides the context for understanding organizational behaviour (OB) in the Canadian workplace and highlights the many Canadian contributions to the field. Indeed, it goes a step further than most OB texts prepared for the Canadian marketplace.

Specifically, it asks, in many instances:

- How does this theory apply in the Canadian workplace of today?

- What are the implications of the theory for managers and employees working in the twenty-first century?

- What are the implications of the theory for everyday life? OB, after all, is not something that applies only in the workplace.

This text is sensitive to important Canadian issues. Subject matter reflects the broad multicultural flavour of Canada and also highlights the roles of women and visible minorities in the workplace. Examples reflect the broad range of organizations in Canada: large, small, public and private sector, unionized and non-unionized.

Organizational Behaviour continues to be a vibrant and relevant text because it's a product of the Canadian classroom. It is used in Canada by the first author and her colleagues. Thus, there is a "front-line" approach to considering revisions. We also solicit considerable feedback from OB instructors and students throughout the country. While we have kept the features of the previous edition that adopters continue to say they like, there is also a great deal that is new.

Our Pedagogical Approach in Writing the Text

- *Relevance.* The text reminds both teacher and student alike that we must contend with a new paradigm of work that is more globally focused and competitive, relies more heavily on part-time and contract jobs, and places a higher premium on entrepreneurial skills, either within the traditional workplace structure, as an individual seeking out an alternative job, or as the creator of your own new business. Today's younger employees can expect to hold many more jobs, and possibly be self-employed more and longer than their parents.

  From its beginning, this text was the first to emphasize that OB is for everyone, from the bottom-rung employee to the CEO, as well as to anyone who has to interact with others to accomplish a task. We continue to emphasize this theme. We remind readers of the material's relevance beyond a "9-to-5" job by concluding each chapter with a summary that out-lines the implications not only for the workplace and managers, but also for individuals in their daily lives. We also include the feature **OB in the Street**, which further emphasizes how OB applies outside the workplace.

- *Writing style.* Clarity and readability are the hallmarks of this text. Our reviewers find the text "conversational," "interesting," "student-friendly," and "very clear and understandable." Students say they really like the informal style and personal examples.

- *Examples, examples, examples.* From our teaching experience, we know that students may not remember a concept, but they will remember an example. This text is packed full of recent real-world examples drawn from a variety of organizations: business and not-for-profit, large and small, and local and international. We also use examples taken from the world at large, to illustrate the broader applicability of OB material.

- *Comprehensive literature coverage.* This text is regularly singled out for its comprehensive and up-to-date coverage of OB from both academic journals as well as business periodicals. The latest research can be found in sections marked "Research Findings" and "Focus on Research."

- *Skill-building emphasis.* Each chapter's **OB at Work** section is full of exercises to help students make the connections between theories and real-world applications. Exercises at the end of each chapter reinforce critical thinking, self-analysis, behavioural analysis, and team building.

Highlights of the Seventh Edition

The seventh edition was designed to evolve with today's students. There are more relevant examples, updated theory coverage, and a continued emphasis on providing the latest research findings. Based on reviews from numerous instructors and students across Canada, we have found that many potential users want chapters that have the right balance of theory, research, and application material, while being relevant to student learning. To accomplish this, we have:

- Continued to highlight the importance of Learning Outcomes as a "road map" leading to focused reading and increased learning comprehension. Learning Outcomes appear initially as an enumerated list on the chapter-opening page and then the numbered outcomes appear throughout the chapter again in the margins to direct readers to the section where the Learning Outcome is addressed. Finally, the numbered outcomes are linked to review questions at the end of the chapter so that students can test whether they have achieved these outcomes.

- Continued to feature current and topical chapter-opening vignettes as well as the subsequent references back to the vignettes that appear throughout the chapter, at the start of most major sections.

- At the beginning of each chapter, a "Big Idea" item appears in the margin which is meant to give readers a big picture view of the topic at hand. Then, at the end of the chapter a "Lessons Learned" appears in the margin to recap the key takeaways for the chapter.

- Continued to integrate a series of relevant and helpful questions throughout the chapters (look for questions that are set in a square design) to encourage students to think about how OB applies to their everyday lives and engage students in their reading of the material. These questions first appear as bullet lists at the bottom of the chapter opener, under the heading "OB Is for Everyone," and then appear throughout each chapter.

- Updated the boxed features throughout the text, including **OB in Action, OB in the Street, OB in the Workplace, Focus on Research, Focus on Ethics,** and **Focus on Diversity** boxes.

- Continued to address and highlight how OB principles vary across cultures in the **Global Implications** sections. Chapters now conclude with references to the cultural differences that exist within and between countries. Until recently, most OB research was conducted in Western countries. That is changing, however, and we are now in a much better position to answer the question "How does what we know about OB vary based on culture?" Some OB principles vary little across cultures, while others vary a great deal.

- Continued to include the popular **For You** feature at the end of each chapter, to highlight the relevance of the chapter to one's everyday life.

- Reflected the ever-changing world of organizational behaviour through a series of new end-of-chapter case incidents.

- Included four new comprehensive cases in the **Additional Cases**. Case 1: The Personality Problem deals with the topics of personality, organizational culture, and work attitudes; Case 4: Bad Faith Bargaining? Government Power and Negotiations with the Public Service covers power and politics, conflict and negotiation, and ethics; Case 7: Promotion from Within covers motivation, work attitudes, communication, and politics. Case 9: Boundaryless Organizations deals with organizational structure and boundaryless organizations, organizational culture, diversity and teams, organizational socialization, and organizational change. In addition, a new table was added at the beginning of the Additional Cases to show the chapters that apply to the major topic areas addressed in each case for easy reference.

- Continued to include our **OB on the Edge** feature, which highlights what's new and hot in OB. OB on the Edge, which is unique to the Canadian edition, provides an opportunity to explore challenging issues and encourages students to read more about these hot topics. In this edition, we cover four topics in this innovative feature: *Stress at Work*; *Trust*; *Workplace Bullying*; and *Spirituality in the Workplace*.

Chapter-by-Chapter Highlights: What's New

In this seventh edition, we have made a concerted effort to thoroughly update the text. Taken together, the changes we made render this text the leader in the market and the undisputed pioneer vis-à-vis meaningful application of OB concepts and theories. Each chapter offers new examples, the latest cutting-edge research, discussions of current issues, and a wide variety of application material. The key *changes* are listed below.

Chapter 1: What Is Organizational Behaviour?

- New *Opening Vignette* about Lululemon Athletica

- New section: "Big Data"

- New exhibit: "Employment Options"

- New major section: "Challenges and Opportunities in the Canadian Workplace"

- New *Focus on Diversity*: "SaskTel Is a Top Diversity Employer"
- New major section: "Coming Attractions: Developing an OB Model"
- New exhibit: "A Basic OB Model"
- New exhibit: "The Plan of the Book"
- New *Point/Counterpoint*: "Lost in Translation?"
- New *Ethical Dilemma*: "Jekyll and Hyde"
- New *Case Incident*: "Apple Goes Global"
- New *Case Incident*: "Era of the Disposable Worker?"

Chapter 2: Perception, Personality, and Emotions

- New *Opening Vignette* about Matthew Corrin, the CEO of the restaurant Freshii
- New *Research Findings*: "Stereotyping"
- New section: "The Dark Triad"
- New exhibit: "Jobs in Which Certain Big Five Personality Traits Are More Relevant"
- New exhibit: "Does Business School Make You Narcissistic?"
- New *Focus on Research*: "First Impressions Count"
- New research and discussion on emotional intelligence
- New exhibit: "A Cascading Model of Emotional Intelligence"
- New *Focus on Ethics*: "An Ethical Choice"
- New *Focus on Research*: "Smile, and the Work World Smiles with You"
- New section: "Emotion Regulation"
- New *Research Findings*: "Emotion Regulation"
- New *OB in the Workplace*: "Affective Computing: Reading Your State of Mind"
- New exhibit: "Emotional States Cross-Culturally"
- New *Point/Counterpoint*: "Millennials Are More Narcissistic"
- New *Experiential Exercise*: "Who Can Catch a Liar?"
- New *Ethical Dilemma*: "Happiness Coaches for Employees"
- New *Case Incident*: "On the Costs of Being Nice"
- New *Case Incident*: "Can You Read Emotions from Faces?"

Chapter 3: Values, Attitudes, and Diversity in the Workplace

- New *Opening Vignette* about Corus Entertainment partnering with TD Bank to help a program designed to aid Aboriginal children achieve literacy through summer camps
- New *Research Findings*: "Hofstede"
- Updated exhibit: "Hofstede's Cultural Values by Nation"

- New exhibit: "Dominant Work Values in Today's Workforce"
- New *Research Findings*: "Generational Differences"
- New *OB in the Street*: "Generation Z: Coming to Your Workplace Soon"
- New research in "Francophone and Anglophone Values"
- Updated major section: "Attitudes"
- New exhibit: "The Components of an Attitude"
- New exhibit: "The Worst Jobs for Job Satisfaction, 2013"
- New exhibit: "Relationship between Average Pay in Job and Job Satisfaction of Employees in That Job"
- New section: "Perceived Organizational Support"
- New research and discussion in "Employee Engagement"
- New *OB in the Workplace*: "Minding Manners, Helping Customers"
- Updated exhibit: "Practices Used by a Selected Sample of Canada's Most Welcoming Places to Work"
- New exhibit: "Average Levels of Employee Job Satisfaction by Country"
- Updated section with new research: "Are Employees in Western Cultures More Satisfied with Their Jobs?"
- New *Point/Counterpoint*: "Employer–Employee Loyalty Is an Outdated Concept"
- New *Experiential Exercise*: "Feeling Excluded"

OB on the Edge: Stress at Work

- New research in "Consequences of Stress"
- New discussion of personality in "Why Do Individuals Differ in Their Experience of Stress?"
- New research and discussion in "Organizational Approaches"
- Updated the list of "The Most and Least Stressful Jobs"

Chapter 4: Theories of Motivation

- New *Opening Vignette* about how motivation influenced Olympic snowboarder Mark McMorris to win a medal just weeks after fracturing a rib
- New *OB in the Workplace*: "Stock Analyst Recommendations and Valence"
- Updated section: "The Importance of Providing Performance Feedback"
- Updated *Research Findings*: "The Effects of Goal Setting"
- Updated section: "Reinforcement Theory"
- Updated section: "Fair Process and Treatment"
- New *Point/Counterpoint*: "Goals Get You to Where You Want to Be"
- New *Experiential Exercise*: "Organizational Justice"

- New *Ethical Dilemma*: "Grade Inflation"
- New *Case Incident*: "Equity and Executive Pay"

Chapter 5: Motivation in Action

- New *Opening Vignette* about how high-growth social media start-up Hootsuite manages to keep its workforce engaged and productive
- New research in "What to Pay: Establishing a Pay Structure"
- Updated section: "Merit-Based Pay"
- New research in "Flexible Benefits: Developing a Benefits Package"
- New *Focus on Research*: "The Reward for Helping Others at Work"
- New *OB in the Street*: "Rewarding Gym Attendance While Wanting Weight Loss"
- Updated exhibit: "Examples of High and Low Job Characteristics"
- New section: "Relational Job Design"
- New research in "Flextime"
- Updated *Research Findings*: "Telecommuting"
- New research in "Variable Pay"
- New *Point/Counterpoint*: "'Face-Time' Matters"
- Updated *Ethical Dilemma*: "Are CEOs Paid Too Much?"
- New *Case Incident*: "Motivation for Leisure"
- New *Case Incident*: "Attaching the Carrot to the Stick"

Chapter 6: Groups and Teamwork

- New research in "Self-Managed Teams"
- New research in "Virtual Teams"
- New *Focus on Ethics*: "Virtual Teams Leave a Smaller Carbon Footprint"
- New section: "Multiteam Systems"
- New *OB in the Workplace*: "Turning Around a Losing Team"
- New *Focus on Diversity*: "Developing Team Members' Trust across Cultures"
- New research in "(Team) Composition"
- Updated section: "Diversity of Members"
- New *Point/Counterpoint*: "To Get the Most Out of Teams, Empower Them"
- New *Case Incident*: "Tongue-Tied in Teams"

OB on the Edge: Trust

- Revised section: "What Determines Trust?"
- New box: "What Are the Consequences of Trust?"
- New discussion in "Basic Principles of Trust"

Chapter 7: Communication

- New *Opening Vignette* about how the two young entrepreneurs who launched Palette, a mechatronics company, use communication to find investors for their new invention and to stay connected
- Updated major section: "Barriers to Effective Communication"
- New research in "Downward (Communication)"
- New exhibit: "Allocation of Time at Work for Managers and Professionals"
- New *OB in the Workplace*: "Asleep in Paris, Busy Working in Toronto"
- Updated section: "Social Media"
- Updated section: "A Cultural Guide"
- New *Point/Counterpoint*: "Employees' Social Media Presence Should Matter to Managers"
- New *Ethical Dilemma*: "The Pitfalls of Email"
- New *Case Incident*: "Using Social Media to Your Advantage"
- New *Case Incident*: "PowerPoint Purgatory"

Chapter 8: Power and Politics

- New *Opening Vignette* about former Toronto mayor Rob Ford
- Updated major section: "Bases of Power"
- New major section: "How Power Affects People"
- New *OB in the Workplace*: "It's Not About the Affair, It's About the Coverup"
- New research in "Sexual Harassment"
- New *Focus on Ethics*: "Sex at Work"
- Updated *Research Findings*: "Politicking"
- New *Focus on Research*: "Powerful Leaders Keep Their (Fr)Enemies Close"
- Updated *Research Findings*: "Impression Management Techniques"
- New section: "The Ethics of Behaving Politically"
- New *Point/Counterpoint*: "Everyone Wants Power"
- New *Ethical Dilemma*: "How Much Should You Defer to Those in Power?"
- New *Case Incident*: "Delegate Power, or Keep It Close?"
- New *Case Incident*: "Barry's Peer Becomes His Boss"

Chapter 9: Conflict and Negotiation

- New *Opening Vignette* on the BC Teachers' Federation strike
- New section: "Types of Conflict"
- New section: "Loci of Conflict"
- Updated *Research Findings*: "The Constructive Effects of Conflict"

- New research and discussion in "Personality Traits in Negotiation"
- New *Focus on Ethics*: "Using Empathy to Negotiate More Ethically"
- New research in "Moods/Emotions in Negotiation"
- New research and discussion in "Gender Differences in Negotiation"
- New major section: "Third-Party Negotiations"
- New *Ethical Dilemma*: "The Lowball Applicant"
- New *Case Incident*: "Choosing Your Battles"
- New *Case Incident*: "The Pros and Cons of Collective Bargaining"

OB on the Edge: Workplace Bullying

- New research and discussion in "Workplace Violence"
- New section: "Legislation to Prevent Bullying"
- New statistics on workplace bullying

Chapter 10: Organizational Culture

- New *Opening Vignette* about how the Calgary Stampede's organizational culture helped it deal with an unexpected crisis
- New discussion in "Definition of *Organizational Culture*"
- New *OB in the Workplace*: "WestJet Brings on the Fun"
- New section: "The Ethical Dimension of Culture"
- New research in "Strong vs. Weak Cultures"
- New *OB in the Workplace*: "Making Culture Work"
- New research and discussion in "Socialization"
- New research and discussion in "Barrier to Mergers and Acquisitions"
- New discussion in major section: "Changing Organizational Culture"
- New research in "Creating an Ethical Organizational Culture"
- New *Point/Counterpoint*: "Organizations Should Strive to Create a Positive Organizational Culture"
- New *Ethical Dilemma*: "A Bankrupt Culture"
- New Case Incident: "Google and P&G Swap Employees"

Chapter 11: Leadership

- New *Opening Vignette* about Bryce Williams and the leadership issues faced by the young chief of the Tsawwassen First Nation
- New *Research Findings*: "Behavioural Theories of Leadership"
- Updated *Research Findings*: "Path-Goal Theory"
- Updated *Research Findings*: "Transformational Leadership"
- New research in "Mentoring"

- New research and discussion in "Ethical Leadership"
- New section: "Servant Leadership"
- New *Point/Counterpoint*: "Heroes Are Made, Not Born"
- New *Ethical Dilemma*: "Undercover Leaders"
- New *Case Incident*: "Leadership by Algorithm"

Chapter 12: Decision Making, Creativity, and Ethics

- New *Opening Vignette* about Billy-Joe Nachuk, a military veteran who suffered discrimination by three police officers due to their poor decision making
- New discussion in "Bounded Rationality in Considering Alternatives"
- New *Focus on Research*: "Putting Intuition to Work in the Workplace"
- New research in "Escalation of Commitment"
- New *OB in the Street*: "Groupthink at Target Canada"
- New exhibit: "Three-Stage Model of Creativity in Organizations"
- New section: "Creative Behaviour"
- New section: "Causes of Creative Behaviour"
- New discussion in "Creative Potential"
- New section: "Creative Outcomes (Innovation)"
- New discussion in "Four Ethical Decision Criteria"
- New *Focus on Research*: "Why People Cheat"
- New research and discussion in "Making Ethical Decisions"
- New *OB in the Workplace*: "The Ethics of Fostering a 'Culture of Shortcuts'"
- New *Global Implications* section: "Creativity"
- New *Point/Counterpoint*: "People Are More Creative When They Work Alone"
- New *Case Incident*: "The Youngest Female Self-Made Billionaire"

OB on the Edge: Spirituality in the Workplace

- New definition of *workplace spirituality*
- New discussion in "Why Spirituality Now?"
- New section: "Spirituality and Mindfulness"
- New research and discussion in "Characteristics of a Spiritual Organization"
- New section: "Achieving a Spiritual Organization"

Chapter 13: Organizational Structure

- New *Opening Vignette* about how the nonprofit Revitalization Saint-Pierre owes its success to embedding community participation in its organizational structure
- New research and discussion in "Centralization and Decentralization"

- New *OB in the Workplace*: "The World Is My Corporate Headquarters"

- New research and discussion in "The Virtual Organization"

- New research and discussion in "The Boundaryless Organization"

- New research and discussion in "The Leaner Organization: Organization Downsizing"

- New *Focus on Research*: "Working from Home"

- New *Global Implications* section: "Culture and the Impact of Downsizing"

- New *Point/Counterpoint*: "The End of Management"

- New *Case Incident*: "Creative Deviance: Bucking the Hierarchy?"

Chapter 14: Organizational Change

- New *Opening Vignette* about the organizational changes that the Hudson's Bay has undergone to stay relevant and profitable in a competitive marketplace

- New research in "Overcoming Resistance to Change"

- New *OB in the Workplace*: "Habitat for Humanity and Rockwood Institution Partner to Change Lives"

- New *Ethical Dilemma*: "Changes at the Television Station"

- New *Case Incident*: "Starbucks Returns to Its Roots"

- New *Case Incident*: "When Companies Fail to Change"

Pedagogical Features

The pedagogical features of *Organizational Behaviour: Concepts, Controversies, Applications,* Seventh Canadian edition, are designed to complement and reinforce the textual material. This text offers the most complete assortment of pedagogy available in any OB book on the market.

- The text is developed in a "story-line" format that emphasizes how the topics fit together. Each chapter opens with a list of learning outcomes related to a main example that threads through the chapter. The opening vignette is carried throughout the chapter to help students apply a real-life example to the concepts they are learning. The learning outcome questions appear in the margin of the text, to indicate where they are addressed. In "For Review" at the end of each chapter, students can discover whether they have achieved these learning outcomes.

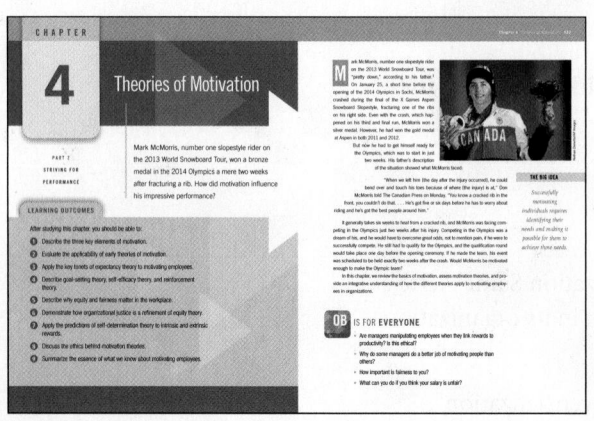

- **OB Is for Everyone** in the chapter-opener highlights the integrated questions that students will encounter throughout each chapter. Right from the start, these questions encourage students to think about how OB applies to everyday lives.

- A "Big Idea/Lessons Learned" feature appears at the beginning and end of each chapter. These resources are designed to work hand-in-hand. At the beginning of the chapter, a "Big Idea" item appears in the margin which is meant to give readers a big-picture view of the topic at hand. Then, at the end of the chapter a "Lessons Learned" appears in the margin to recap the key takeaways from the chapter.

- Exclusive to the Canadian edition, **OB in the Street**, **OB in the Workplace**, **Focus on Ethics**, **Focus on Diversity**, and **Focus on Research** help students see the links between theoretical material and applications.

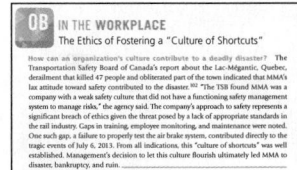

- **OB in Action** features provide tips for using the concepts of OB in everyday life, such as Managing Virtual Teams, Choosing Strategies to Deal with Conflicts, Social Networking Responsibly, and Reducing Biases and Errors in Decision Making.

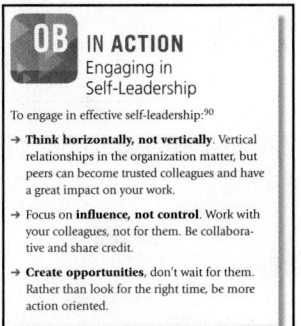

- To help instructors and students readily spot significant discussions of **Research Findings**, we have included a research icon to indicate where these discussions appear. **Focus on Research** provides additional links to related research. Marking research discussions so clearly helps emphasize the strong research foundation that underlies OB.

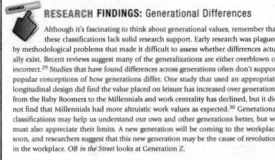

- We have continued to integrate a series of relevant and helpful questions throughout the chapters to encourage students to think about how OB applies to their everyday lives and engage students in their reading of the material. These questions first appear as a bullet list in the chapter opener, under the heading **OB Is for Everyone,** and then appear throughout each chapter.

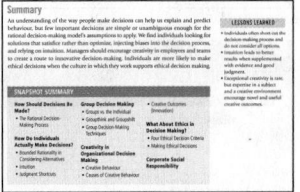

- The **Global Implications** section addresses and highlights how OB principles vary across cultures.

- **Summary** provides a review of the key points of the chapter, while the **Snapshot Summary** provides a study tool that helps students to see the overall connections among concepts presented within each chapter.

- Each chapter concludes with **OB at Work**, a set of resources designed to help students apply the lessons of the chapter. Included in **OB at Work** are the following features:

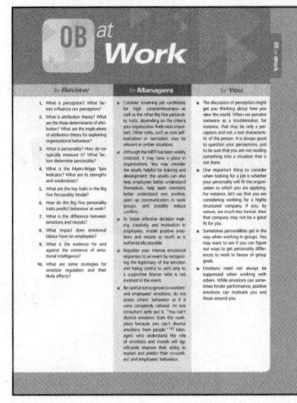

  - **For Review** poses a series of questions that are linked to the learning outcomes identified in the chapter opener.

  - New **For Managers** outlines ways that managers can apply OB in the workplace.

  - **For You** outlines how OB can be used by individuals in their daily lives.

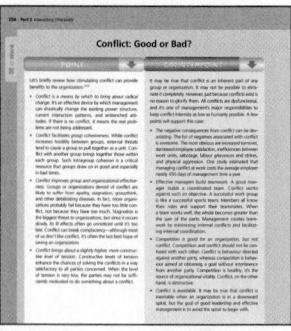

- **Point/Counterpoint** promotes debate on contentious OB issues. This feature presents more focused arguments.

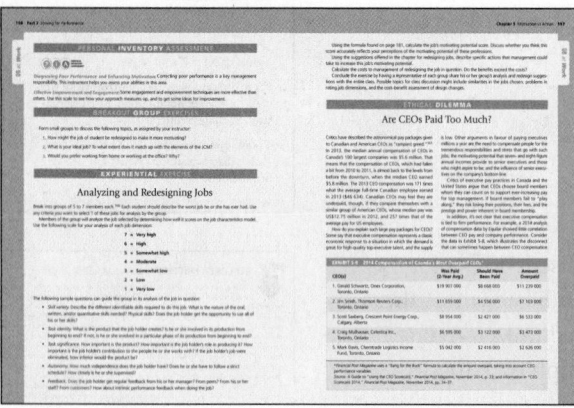

- New **Personal Inventory Assessment (PIA)** is a collection of online exercises designed to promote self-reflection and engagement in students, enhancing their ability to connect with the concepts taught in the text. PIA marginal icons appear throughout the text.

- **Breakout Group Exercises**, **Experiential Exercise**, and **Ethical Dilemma** are valuable application exercises for the classroom. The many new exercises included here are ones that we have found particularly stimulating in our own classrooms. Our students say they like these exercises *and* they learn from them. Additional exercises can be found on MyManagementLab.

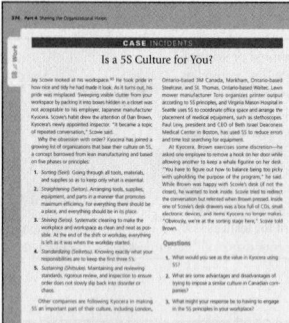

- **Case Incidents** (two per chapter) deal with real-world scenarios and require students to exercise their decision-making skills. Each case enables an instructor to quickly generate class discussion on a key theme within the chapter.

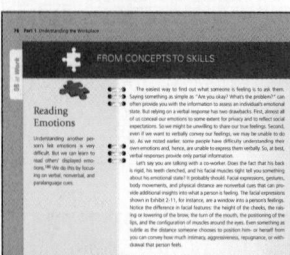

- **From Concepts to Skills** provides a wide range of applications for students. The section begins with a practical set of tips on topics such as reading emotions, setting goals, and solving problems creatively, which demonstrate real-world applications of OB theories. These tips are followed by the features *Practising Skills* and *Reinforcing Skills*. *Practising Skills* presents an additional case or group activity to apply the chapter's learning outcomes. *Reinforcing Skills* asks students to talk about the material they have learned with others, or to apply it to their own personal experiences.

- Exclusive to the Canadian edition, **OB on the Edge** (following each part) takes a close look at some of the hottest topics in the field: work-related stress, trust, behavioural pathologies that can lead to workplace bullying, and spirituality in the workplace. Since this is a stand-alone feature, these topics can be introduced at the instructor's discretion.

- Our reviewers have asked for more cases, and more comprehensive and integrated cases. To address this request, we have included 10 **Additional Cases** that feature a variety of challenges and organizations. All of these cases require students to apply material from a variety of chapters.

Supplements

MyManagementLab

We have created an outstanding supplements package for *Organizational Behaviour*, Seventh Canadian edition. In particular, we have provided access to MyManagementLab, which provides students with an assortment of tools to help enrich and expedite learning. MyManagementLab is an online study tool for students and an online homework and assessment tool for faculty. MyManagementLab lets students assess their understanding through auto-graded tests and assignments, develop a personalized study plan to address areas of weakness, and practise a variety of learning tools to master management principles. New and updated MyManagementLab resources include the following:

- *New Personal Inventory Assessment (PIA)*. Students learn better when they can connect what they are learning to their personal experience. PIA is a collection of online exercises designed to promote self-reflection and engagement in students, enhancing their ability to connect with concepts taught in principles of management, organizational behaviour, and human resource management classes. Assessments can be assigned by instructors, who can then track students' completions. Student results include a written explanation along with a graphic display that shows how their results compare to the class as a whole. Instructors will also have access to this graphic representation of results to promote classroom discussion.

- *New Personalized Study Plan*. As students work through MyManagementLab's new Study Plan, they can clearly see which topics they have mastered—and, more importantly, which they need to work on. Each question has been carefully written to match the concepts, language, and focus of the text, so students can get an accurate sense of how well they've understood the chapter content.

- *New Business Today Videos*. Business Today is a dynamic and expanding database of videos covering the disciplines of management, business, marketing, and more. Instructors will find new videos posted monthly, which makes Business Today the ideal resource for up-to-date video examples that are perfect for classroom use.

- *New Learning Catalytics*. Learning Catalytics is a "bring your own device" student engagement, assessment, and classroom intelligence system. It allows instructors to engage students in class with a variety of question types designed to gauge student understanding.

- *Assignable Mini-Cases and Video Cases*. Instructors have access to a variety of case-based assessment material that can be assigned to students, with multiple-choice quizzes or written-response format in MyManagementLab's new Writing Space.

- *eText*. Students can study without leaving the online environment. They can access the eText online, including videos and simulations. The interactive eText allows students to highlight sections, bookmark pages, or take notes electronically just as they might do with a traditional text. Instructors can also add their own notes to the text and then share them with their students.

- *Glossary Flashcards*. This study aid is useful for students' review of key concepts.

- *Simulations*. Simulations help students analyze and make decisions in common business situations; the simulations assess student choices and include reinforcement quizzes, outlines, and glossaries.

Most of the following materials are available for download from a password-protected section of Pearson Canada's online catalogue (www.pearsoncanada.ca/highered). Navigate to your text's catalogue page to view a list of those supplements that are available. Contact your local sales representative for details and access.

- *Instructor's Resource Manual with Video Guide.* Each chapter of the Instructor's Resource Manual with Video Guide includes a chapter outline, learning outcomes, chapter synopsis, study questions, suggested teaching plan, annotated lecture outlines, answers to questions found under OB at Work's *For Review,* a summary and analysis of *Point/Counterpoint* features, comments on end-of-chapter exercises and notes on the *Case Incidents, From Concepts to Skills,* and key terms.

- *Computerized Test Bank.* The Test Bank contains over 1800 items, including multiple choice, true/false, and discussion questions that relate not only to the body of the text but to *From Concepts to Skills, Point/Counterpoint,* and case materials. For each question we have provided the correct answer, a reference to the relevant section of the text, a difficulty rating, and a classification (recall/applied). Pearson's computerized test banks allow instructors to filter and select questions to create quizzes, tests, or homework. Instructors can revise questions or add their own, and may be able to choose print or online options. These questions are also available in Microsoft Word format.

- *PowerPoint Presentation.* A ready-to-use PowerPoint slideshow designed for classroom presentation. Use it as is, or edit content to fit your individual classroom needs.

- *Image Gallery.* This package provides instructors with images to enhance their teaching.

CourseSmart. CourseSmart goes beyond traditional expectations—providing instant, online access to the texts and course materials you need at a lower cost for students. And even as students save money, you can save time and hassle with a digital eText that allows you to search for the most relevant content at the very moment you need it. Whether it's evaluating texts or creating lecture notes to help students with difficult concepts, CourseSmart can make life a little easier. See how when you visit www.coursesmart.com/instructors.

Pearson Custom Library. For enrollments of at least 25 students, you can create your own text by choosing the chapters that best suit your own course needs. To begin building your custom text, visit www.pearsoncustomlibrary.com. You may also work with a dedicated Pearson Custom editor to create your ideal text—publishing your own original content or mixing and matching Pearson content. Contact your local Pearson Representative to get started.

Learning Solutions Managers. Pearson's Learning Solutions Managers work with faculty and campus course designers to ensure that Pearson technology products, assessment tools, and online course materials are tailored to meet your specific needs. This highly qualified team is dedicated to helping schools take full advantage of a wide range of educational resources, by assisting in the integration of a variety of instructional materials and media formats. Your local Pearson Education sales representative can provide you with more details on this service program.

Acknowledgments

A number of people worked hard to give this seventh Canadian edition of *Organizational Behaviour* a new look.

I received incredible support for this project from a variety of people at Pearson Canada. The three people who worked hardest to keep this project on track were Jennifer Murray, Developmental Editor, Claudia Forgas, Copy Editor and Production Editor, and Jessica Hellen, Project Manager. All three were extremely supportive and helpful. Jennifer supplied a number of great ideas for examples and vignettes, never complained when I was late with chapters, and she provided much needed cheerfulness at some of the most difficult parts of this project. I can't thank her enough for her dedication to the task.

Claudia Forgas was the Copy Editor and Production Editor for the project. Claudia has worked on a number of my projects and still continues to amaze for how well she makes sure everything is in place and written clearly. Claudia provided a wealth of support, great ideas, and goodwill throughout the production process. Turning the manuscript into the text you hold in your hands could not have happened without her inspired leadership. She was extremely diligent about checking for consistency throughout the text and performed a number of helpful fact-checking activities. Her keen eyes helped to make these pages as clean as they are. I am grateful for the opportunity to work with her again.

There are a variety of other people at Pearson who also had a hand in making sure that the manuscript would be transformed into this book and then delivered to you. To all of them I extend my thanks. I know the Pearson sales team will do everything possible to make this book successful.

I also want to acknowledge my divisional secretary, Nancy Tang, who helps keep me on track in a variety of ways. I could not ask for a better, more dedicated, or more cheerful assistant. She really helps keep things together.

In our continuing effort to improve the text, we have conducted many reviews to elicit feedback over the years and editions. Many thanks to several students from the Northern Alberta Institute of Technology (NAIT) who provided us with suggestions for improving the text. The students are Barb Kosak, Prudence Musinguzi, Andres Sarrate, and Robert Tucci. Student input helps keep the material fresh and alive.

Finally, I want to acknowledge the many reviewers of this text for their detailed, helpful comments. I appreciate the time and care that they put into their reviewing. The reviewers include Ian Anderson (Algonquin College), Julia Dotson (Confederation College), Patricia Fitzgerald (Saint Mary's University), Judith Hunter (Sheridan Institute of Technology and Advanced Learning), Martha Reavley (University of Windsor), and Yanelia Yabar (Red Deer College).

Nancy Langton received her Ph.D. from Stanford University. Since completing her graduate studies, Dr. Langton has taught at the University of Oklahoma and the University of British Columbia. Currently a member of the Organizational Behaviour and Human Resources division in the Sauder School of Business, UBC, she teaches at the undergraduate, MBA, and Ph.D. levels and conducts executive programs on attracting and retaining employees, time management, family business issues, as well as women and management issues. Dr. Langton has received several major three-year research grants from the Social Sciences and Humanities Research Council of Canada, and her research interests have focused on human resource issues in the workplace, including pay equity, gender equity, and leadership and communication styles. Her articles on these and other topics have appeared in such journals as *Administrative Science Quarterly*, *American Sociological Review*, *Sociological Quarterly*, *Journal of Management Education*, and *Gender, Work and Organizations*. She has won Best Paper commendations from both the Academy of Management and the Administrative Sciences Association of Canada.

Dr. Langton routinely wins high marks from her students for teaching. She has been nominated many times for the Commerce Undergraduate Society Awards, and has won several honourable mention plaques. She has also won the Sauder School of Business's most prestigious award for teaching innovation, The Talking Stick. The award was given for Dr. Langton's redesign of the undergraduate organizational behaviour course as well as the many activities that were a spin-off of these efforts. She was also part of the UBC MBA Core design team that won the Alan Blizzard award, a national award that recognizes innovation in teaching. More recently, she was acknowledged by the Sauder School of Business for her development of the Sauder Africa Initiative, which took her to Kenya with UBC students to help young people in the slums of Nairobi write business plans.

In Dr. Langton's "other life," she engages in the artistry of quiltmaking, and one day hopes to win first prize at *Visions*, the juried show for quilts as works of art. More recently, she has been working at mastering the art of photography, creating abstract art using segments of real objects. When she is not designing quilts or taking photographs, she is either reading novels recommended by her book club colleagues or studying cookbooks for new ideas. All of her friends would say that she makes the best pizza from scratch in all of Vancouver, and one has even offered to supply venture capital to open a pizza parlour.

Stephen P. Robbins

Education

Ph.D., University of Arizona

Professional Experience

Academic Positions: Professor, San Diego State University, Southern Illinois University at Edwardsville, University of Baltimore, Concordia University in Montreal, and University of Nebraska at Omaha.

Research: Research interests have focused on conflict, power, and politics in organizations; behavioural decision making; and the development of effective interpersonal skills.

Books Published: World's best-selling author of textbooks in both management and organizational behaviour. His books have sold more than 5 million copies and have been translated into 20 languages; editions have been adapted for Canada, Australia, South Africa, and India, such as these:

- *Essentials of Organizational Behavior*, 12th ed. (Prentice Hall, 2014)

- *Management*, 12th ed. with Mary Coulter (Prentice Hall, 2014)

- *Fundamentals of Human Resource Management*, 10th ed., with David DeCenzo (Wiley, 2010)

- *Prentice Hall's Self-Assessment Library 3.4* (Prentice Hall, 2010)

- *Fundamentals of Management*, 8th ed., with David DeCenzo and Mary Coulter (Prentice Hall, 2013)

- *Supervision Today!* 7th ed., with David DeCenzo and Robert Wolter (Prentice Hall, 2013)

- *Training in Interpersonal Skills: TIPS for Managing People at Work*, 6th ed., with Phillip Hunsaker (Prentice Hall, 2012)

- *Managing Today!* 2nd ed. (Prentice Hall, 2000)

- *Organization Theory*, 3rd ed. (Prentice Hall, 1990)

- *The Truth About Managing People*, 2nd ed. (Financial Times/Prentice Hall, 2008)

- *Decide and Conquer: Make Winning Decisions and Take Control of Your Life* (Financial Times/Prentice Hall, 2004).

Other Interests

In his "other life," Dr. Robbins actively participates in masters' track competition. After turning 50 in 1993, he won 18 national championships and 12 world titles. He is the current world record holder at 100 metres (12.37 seconds) and 200 metres (25.20 seconds) for men 65 and over.

Timothy A. Judge

Education

Ph.D., University of Illinois at Urbana-Champaign

Professional Experience

Academic Positions: Franklin D. Schurz Chair, Department of Management, Mendoza College of Business, University of Notre Dame; Visiting Distinguished Adjunct Professor of King Abdulaziz University, Saudi Arabia; Visiting Professor, Division of Psychology & Language Sciences, University College London; Matherly-McKethan Eminent Scholar in Management, Warrington College of Business Administration, University of Florida; Stanley M. Howe Professor in Leadership, Henry B. Tippie College of Business, University of Iowa; Associate Professor (with tenure), Department of Human Resource Studies, School of Industrial and Labor Relations, Cornell University; Lecturer, Charles University, Czech Republic, and Comenius University, Slovakia; Instructor, Industrial/Organizational Psychology, Department of Psychology, University of Illinois at Urbana-Champaign.

Research: Dr. Judge's primary research interests are in (1) personality, moods, and emotions; (2) job attitudes; (3) leadership and influence behaviours; and (4) careers (person–organization fit, career success). Dr. Judge has published more than 145 articles on these and other major topics in journals such as *Journal of Organizational Behavior, Personnel Psychology, Academy of Management Journal, Journal of Applied Psychology, European Journal of Personality*, and *European Journal of Work and Organizational Psychology*.

Fellowship: Dr. Judge is a fellow of the American Psychological Association, the Academy of Management, the Society for Industrial and Organizational Psychology, and the American Psychological Society.

Awards: In 1995, Dr. Judge received the Ernest J. McCormick Award for Distinguished Early Career Contributions from the Society for Industrial and Organizational Psychology. In 2001, he received the Larry L. Cummings Award for mid-career contributions from the Organizational Behavior Division of the Academy of Management. In 2007, he received the Professional Practice Award from the Institute of Industrial and Labor Relations, University of Illinois. In 2008, he received the University of Florida Doctoral Mentoring Award. And in 2012, he received the Editorial Board of the *European Journal of Work and Organizational Psychology* (EJWOP) best paper of the year award.

Other Books Published: H. G. Heneman III, T. A. Judge, and J. D. Kammeyer-Mueller, *Staffing Organizations*, 7th ed. (Madison, WI: Mendota House/Irwin, 2012)

Other Interests

Although he cannot keep up (literally!) with Dr. Robbins' accomplishments on the track, Dr. Judge enjoys golf, cooking and baking, literature (he's a particular fan of Thomas Hardy and is a member of the Thomas Hardy Society), and keeping up with his three children, who range in age from 24 to 10.

CHAPTER 1

What Is Organizational Behaviour?

PART 1

UNDERSTANDING

THE WORKPLACE

How can people skills help you run a successful business?

LEARNING OUTCOMES

After studying this chapter, you should be able to:

1. Define *organizational behaviour* (OB).

2. Demonstrate the importance of interpersonal skills in the workplace.

3. Identify the major behavioural science disciplines that contribute to OB.

4. Understand the value of systematic study to OB.

5. Demonstrate why few absolutes apply to OB.

6. Identify workplace challenges that provide opportunities to apply OB concepts.

7. Describe the three levels of analysis in this book's OB model.

Vancouver-based Lululemon Athletica is known for its fashionable yoga wear, as well as its promotion of yoga.[1] Founded in 1998 by Chip Wilson, the company has grown rapidly, although not without some stumbles.

The company originally manufactured all of its clothing in Canada, but by 2007 only 50 percent of its factories were in Canada, and by 2014 only 3 percent of its factories were in Canada. By locating so much of its manufacturing in other countries, Lululemon no longer has complete control over the production of its clothing. This became embarrassingly clear when black yoga pants had to be pulled off the shelves in 2012 because they were too sheer to be worn. Christine Day, the former CEO, said at the time that Lululemon had given too much control over production to its overseas partners rather than staying personally involved. "If there were 10 technical specs," she said, "we were probably controlling four. Every single factory has all the same patterns now."

THE CANADIAN PRESS/Jonathan Hayward

Lululemon has acquired cult-brand status, with sales of $1.37 billion in 2012. Wilson no longer heads the company, although he worries that the board of directors has lost sight of what Lululemon is about. He also believes the board is focused on short-term goals, to the detriment of the overall vision of the company.

The challenges that organizations such as Lululemon face illustrate several concepts you will find as you study the field of organizational behaviour. Let's take a look, then, at what organizational behaviour is.

THE BIG IDEA

OB helps managers and employees make sense of the workplace and also applies to work in groups of all kinds.

 **IS FOR EVERYONE**

- Why do some people do well in organizational settings while others have difficulty?

- Do you know what a "typical" organization looks like?

- Does job satisfaction really make a difference?

- What people-related challenges have you noticed in the workplace?

- Why should you care about understanding other people?

- Are you ready to take on more responsibility at work?

Defining Organizational Behaviour

1 Define *organizational behaviour* (OB).

Organizational behaviour (often abbreviated as *OB*) is a field of study that looks at the impact that individuals, groups, and structure have on behaviour within organizations for the purpose of applying such knowledge toward improving an organization's effectiveness. Because the organizations studied are often business organizations, OB is often applied to topics such as jobs, work, absenteeism, employment turnover, productivity, human performance, and management. OB also examines the following core topics, although debate exists about their relative importance:[2]

- Motivation
- Leader behaviour and power
- Interpersonal communication
- Group structure and processes
- Attitude development and perception
- Change processes
- Conflict and negotiation

Much of OB is relevant beyond the workplace. The study of OB can cast light on the interactions among family members, students working as a team on a class project, the voluntary group that comes together to do something about reviving the downtown area, the parents who sit on the board of their children's daycare centre, or even the members of a lunchtime pickup basketball team.

> Why do some people do well in organizational settings while others have difficulty?

What Do We Mean by *Organization*?

An **organization** is a consciously coordinated social unit, composed of a group of people, that functions on a relatively continuous basis to achieve a common goal or set of goals. Manufacturing and service firms are organizations, and so are schools, hospitals, churches, military units, retail stores, police departments, volunteer organizations, start-ups, and local, provincial, and federal government agencies. Thus, when we use the term *organization* in this book, we are referring not only to large manufacturing firms but also to small mom-and-pop stores, as well as to the variety of other forms of organization that exist. Small businesses with less than 100 people made up 98 percent of the employers in Canada in 2012, and they employed 69.7 percent of the private sector workforce. Only 14 percent of businesses have more than 500 employees, and they employ 46 percent of the workforce. Most of these large organizations are in the public sector.[3]

organizational behaviour A field of study that investigates the impact of individuals, groups, and structure on behaviour within organizations; its purpose is to apply such knowledge toward improving an organization's effectiveness.

organization A consciously coordinated social unit, composed of a group of people, that functions on a relatively continuous basis to achieve a common goal or set of goals.

The examples in this book present various organizations so that you can gain a better understanding of the many types of organizations that exist. Although you might not have considered this before, the college or university you attend is every bit as much a "real" organization as is Lululemon Athletica, Air Canada, or the Vancouver Canucks. A small for-profit organization that hires unskilled workers to renovate and build in the inner city of Winnipeg is as much a real organization as is London, Ontario-based EllisDon, one of North America's largest construction companies. Therefore, the theories we cover should be considered in light of the variety of organizations you may encounter. We try to point out instances where the theory may be less applicable (or especially

> Do you know what a "typical" organization looks like?

David and Penny Chapman understand the importance of organizational behaviour and treating employees well. When Markdale, Ontario-based Chapman's Ice Cream factory burned down in September 2009, many employees feared that they had lost their jobs. However, the owners quickly put together plans with senior managers on rebuilding the factory and keeping ice cream production going by working with other nearby ice cream producers. Not one employee lost a paycheque, although many had to be bussed to jobs at other locations or put up in hotels.

applicable) to a particular type of organization. For the most part, however, you should expect that the discussions in this book apply across the broad spectrum of organizations. Throughout, we highlight applications to a variety of organizations in our feature *OB in the Workplace*.

OB Is for Everyone

It might seem natural to think that the study of OB is for leaders and managers of organizations. However, many organizations also have informal leadership opportunities. In organizations in which employees are asked to share in a greater number of decision-making processes rather than simply follow orders, the roles of managers and employees are becoming blurred.[4] For instance, employees in some retail operations are asked to make decisions about when to accept returned items rather than defer the decision to the manager.

OB is not just for managers and employees. Entrepreneurs and self-employed individuals may not act as managers, but they certainly interact with other individuals and organizations as part of their work. OB applies equally well to all situations in which you interact with others: on the basketball court, at the grocery store, in school, or in church. In fact, OB is relevant anywhere that people come together and share experiences, work on goals, or meet to solve problems. To help you understand these broader connections, you will find a feature called *OB in the Street* throughout the book.

The Importance of Interpersonal Skills

Until the late 1980s, business school curricula emphasized the technical aspects of management, focusing on economics, accounting, finance, and quantitative techniques.

 Demonstrate the importance of interpersonal skills in the workplace.

Course work in human behaviour and people skills received minimal attention. Over the past three decades, however, business school faculty have come to realize the significant role that understanding human behaviour plays in determining organizational effectiveness; required courses on people skills have been added to many curricula. Employers are looking for people skills as well. In a 2012 survey, executives said that employees lack "communication, collaboration, critical thinking and creative skills."[5] In a recent survey, 34 percent of Canadian chief financial officers said that a job applicant's people skills were more important than industry experience and software proficiency. Five years earlier, only 1 percent cared about interpersonal skills.[6]

Does job satisfaction really make a difference?

Organizations that invest in the development of employees' interpersonal skills are more likely to attract and keep high-performers. Regardless of labour market conditions, outstanding employees are always in short supply.[7] Companies known as great places to work in 2014—such as Toronto-based Royal Bank of Canada (RBC), Woodstock, New Brunswick-based Xplornet Communications, Dartmouth-based Jazz Aviation, Winnipeg-based Aboriginal Peoples Television Network, Regina-based SaskTel, Calgary-based Agrium, and Vancouver-based Mountain Equipment Co-op[8]—have been found to generate superior financial performance.[9] A recent survey of hundreds of workplaces, and more than 200 000 respondents, showed that the social relationships among co-workers and supervisors were strongly related to overall job satisfaction. Positive social relationships also were associated with lower stress at work and lower intentions to quit.[10] Having managers with good interpersonal skills is likely to make the workplace more pleasant, and research indicates that employees who know how to relate to their managers well with supportive dialogue and proactivity find that their ideas are endorsed more often, further improving workplace satisfaction.[11] Creating a pleasant workplace appears to make good economic sense, particularly because wages and benefits are not the main reasons people like their jobs or stay with an employer.[12] Partially for these reasons, universities have begun to incorporate social entrepreneurship education into their curricula in order to train future leaders to address social issues within their organizations with interpersonal skills.[13] This is especially important because there is a growing awareness of the need for understanding the means and outcomes of corporate social responsibility.[14]

Succeeding in the workplace takes good people skills. This book has been written to help managers and employees develop those people skills. To learn more about the kinds of people skills needed in the workplace, see the *Experiential Exercise* on page 29 and *From Concepts to Skills—Developing Interpersonal Skills* on pages 32–35.

OB: Making Sense of Behaviour in Organizations

When Lululemon Athletica faced the sheer yoga pants issue, company CEO Christine Day said that it was an isolated issue, thus making light of customer complaints.[15] The supplier was then blamed, although the supplier responded by saying that the product had been made to specification and that the problem was "a gap between Lululemon's expectations and reaction from the market."

Founder Chip Wilson offered another explanation: Women were buying the wrong size yoga pants, and this was causing them to stretch out. Eventually the company decided to pull the product off its shelves and offered refunds to those who had bought the defective product, but not before creating much customer dissatisfaction with the company.

About six months later, customers again started complaining about some of the yoga pants, noting that they were pilling. Wilson, in an interview with Bloomberg News, blamed it on women's thighs, not the pants themselves. "It's really about the rubbing through the thighs, how much pressure is there. I mean over a period of time, and how much they use it," he said. What can Lululemon learn from OB to do a better job of managing customer satisfaction and engaging in better communication?

In this next section, we consider the discipline of OB, looking first at the fields of study that have contributed to it. We then discuss the fact that OB is a scientific discipline based on careful research that is conducted to test and evaluate theories.

The Building Blocks of OB

OB emerged as a distinct field in the 1940s in the United States.[16] It is an applied behavioural science that builds upon contributions from a number of behavioural disciplines: mainly psychology, social psychology, sociology, and anthropology. Psychology's contributions have been primarily at the individual, or micro, level of analysis, while the other three disciplines have contributed to our understanding of macro concepts, such as group processes and organization. Exhibit 1-1 presents an overview of the major contributions of behavioural science to the study of OB.

3 Identify the major behavioural science disciplines that contribute to OB.

EXHIBIT 1-1 Toward an OB Discipline

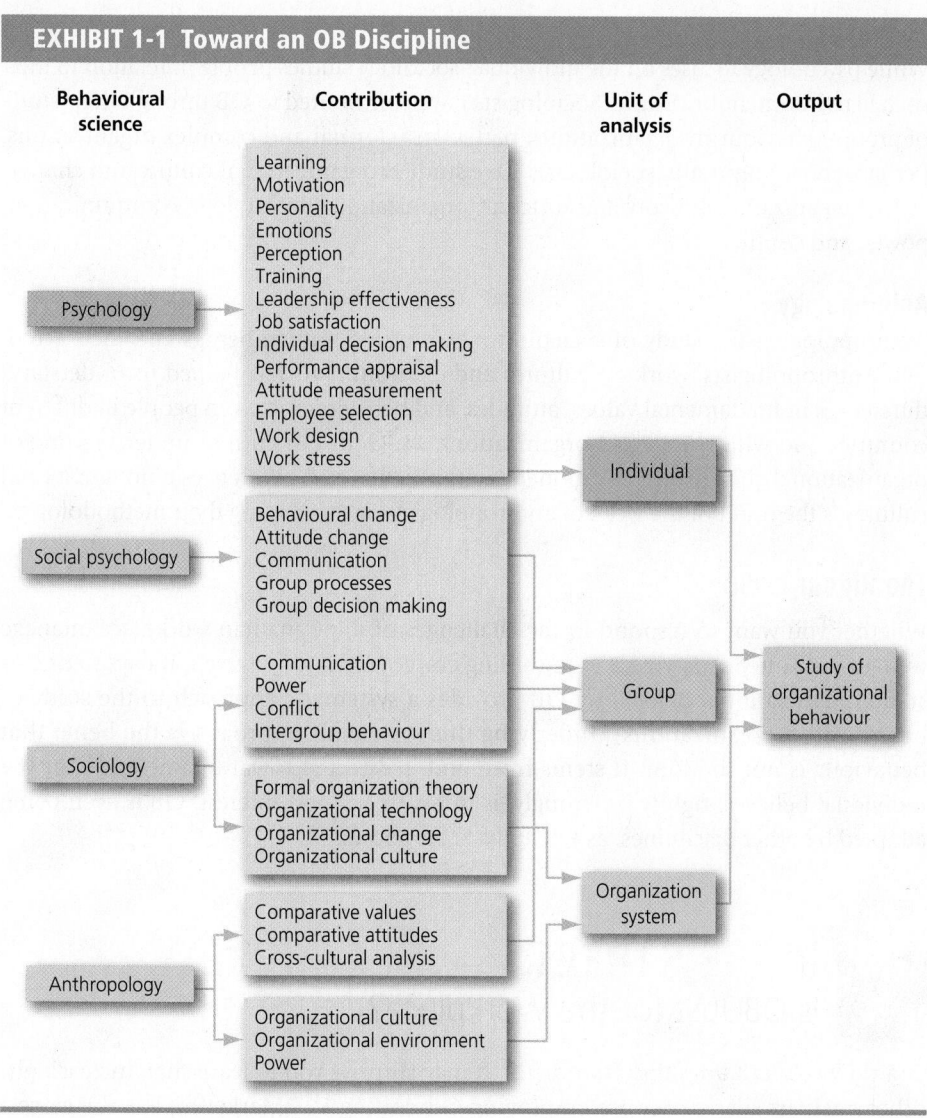

Psychology

Psychology seeks to measure, explain, and sometimes change the behaviour of humans and other animals. Those who have contributed and continue to add to the knowledge of OB are learning theorists, personality theorists, counselling psychologists, and, most important, industrial and organizational psychologists.

Early industrial and organizational psychologists studied the problems of fatigue, boredom, and other working conditions that could impede efficient work performance. More recently, their contributions have been expanded to include learning, perception, personality, emotions, training, leadership effectiveness, needs and motivational forces, job satisfaction, individual decision making, performance appraisal, attitude measurement, employee selection techniques, work design, and work stress.

Social Psychology

Social psychology, generally considered a branch of psychology, blends concepts from both psychology and sociology to focus on people's influence on one another. One major study area is *behavioural change*—how to implement it and how to reduce barriers to its acceptance. Social psychologists also contribute to measuring, understanding, and changing attitudes; identifying communication patterns; and building trust. Finally, they have made important contributions to our study of communication, intergroup behaviour, power, and conflict.

Sociology

While psychology focuses on the individual, sociology studies people in relation to their social environment or culture. Sociologists have contributed to OB through their study of group behaviour in organizations, particularly formal and complex organizations. Perhaps most important, sociologists have studied organizational culture and change, formal organizational theory and structure, organizational technology, communication, power, and conflict.

Anthropology

Anthropology is the study of societies to learn about human beings and their activities. Anthropologists' work on cultures and environments has helped us understand differences in fundamental values, attitudes, and behaviour between people in different countries and within different organizations. Much of our current understanding of organizational culture, organizational environments, and differences among national cultures is the result of the work of anthropologists or those using their methodologies.

The Rigour of OB

Whether you want to respond to the challenges of the Canadian workplace, manage well, or guarantee satisfying and rewarding employment for yourself, it pays to understand organizational behaviour. OB provides a systematic approach to the study of behaviour in organizations. Underlying this systematic approach is the belief that behaviour is not random. It stems from and is directed toward some end that the individual believes, rightly or wrongly, is in his or her best interest. OB is even being adopted by other disciplines, as *OB in the Street* shows.

IN THE **STREET**
Is OB Just for the Workplace?

Can finance learn anything from OB? It may surprise you to learn that, increasingly, other business disciplines are employing OB concepts.[17] Marketing has the closest overlap with OB. Trying to predict consumer behaviour is not that different from trying to predict employee behaviour. Both require an understanding of the dynamics and underlying causes of human behaviour, and there is a lot of correspondence between the disciplines.

What is perhaps more surprising is the degree to which the so-called hard disciplines are making use of soft OB concepts. Behavioural finance, behavioural accounting, and behavioural economics (also called *economic psychology*) all have grown in importance and interest in the past several years.

On reflection, the use of OB by these disciplines should not be so surprising. Your common sense will tell you that humans are not perfectly rational creatures, and in many cases, our actions don't conform to a rational model of behaviour. Although some elements of irrationality are incorporated into economic thought, finance, accounting, and economics, researchers find it increasingly useful to draw from OB concepts.

For example, investors have a tendency to place more weight on private information (information that only they, or a limited group of people, know) than on public information, even when there is reason to believe that the public information is more accurate. To understand this phenomenon, finance researchers use OB concepts. In addition, behavioural accounting research might study how feedback influences auditors' behaviour, or the functional and dysfunctional implications of earnings warnings on investor behaviour.

The point is that while you take separate courses in various business disciplines, the lines between them are increasingly being blurred as researchers draw from common disciplines to explain behaviour. We think that this is a good thing because it more accurately matches the way managers actually work, think, and behave. _____

OB Looks at Consistencies

Certainly there are differences among individuals. Placed in similar situations, all people don't act exactly alike. However, there are certain fundamental consistencies underlying the behaviour of most individuals that can be identified and then modified to reflect individual differences.

◉ Watch on MyManagementLab

Herman Miller

These fundamental consistencies are very important because they allow predictability. When you get into your car, you make some definite and usually highly accurate predictions about how other people will behave. In North America, for instance, you predict that other drivers will stop at stop signs and red lights, drive on the right side of the road, pass on your left, and not cross the solid double line on mountain roads. Your predictions about the behaviour of people behind the wheels of their cars are almost always correct. Obviously, the rules of driving make predictions about driving behaviour fairly easy.

What may be less obvious is that rules (written and unwritten) exist in almost every setting. Therefore, it can be argued that it's possible to predict behaviour (undoubtedly, not always with 100 percent accuracy) in supermarkets, classrooms, doctors' offices, elevators, and in most structured situations. For instance, do you turn around and face the doors when you get into an elevator? Almost everyone does. Is there a sign inside the elevator that tells you to do this? Probably not! Just as we make predictions about drivers, where there are definite rules of the road, we can make predictions about the behaviour of people in elevators, where there are few written rules. This example supports a major point of this book: Behaviour is generally predictable, and the *systematic study* of behaviour is a means to making reasonably accurate predictions.

OB Looks Beyond Common Sense

Each of us is a student of behaviour. Whether or not you have explicitly thought about it before, you have been "reading" people almost all your life, watching their actions and trying to interpret what you see and predict what people might do under different

 4 Understand the value of systematic study to OB.

conditions. Unfortunately, the casual or common sense approach to reading others can often lead to erroneous predictions. However, you can improve your predictive ability by supplementing intuition with a more systematic approach.

The systematic approach used in this book uncovers important facts and relationships and provides a base from which to make more accurate predictions of behaviour. Underlying this systematic approach is the belief that behaviour is not random. Rather, we can identify certain fundamental consistencies underlying the behaviour of all individuals and modify them to reflect individual differences.

These fundamental consistencies are very important. Why? Because they allow predictability. Behaviour is generally predictable, and the *systematic study* of behaviour is a means to making reasonably accurate predictions. When we use the phrase **systematic study**, we mean looking at relationships, attempting to attribute causes and effects, and basing our conclusions on scientific evidence—that is, on data gathered under controlled conditions and measured and interpreted in a reasonably rigorous manner. Exhibit 1-2 illustrates the common methods researchers use to study topics in OB.

Evidence-based management (EBM) complements systematic study by basing managerial decisions on the best available scientific evidence. We would want doctors to make decisions about patient care based on the latest available evidence, and EBM argues that managers should do the same, becoming more scientific in how they think about management problems. For example, a manager might pose a managerial question, search for the best available evidence, and apply the relevant information to the question or case at hand. You might think it's difficult to argue against this (what manager would say that decisions should not be based on evidence?), but the vast majority of management decisions are still made "on the fly," with little or no systematic study of available evidence.[18]

EXHIBIT 1-2 Research Methods in OB

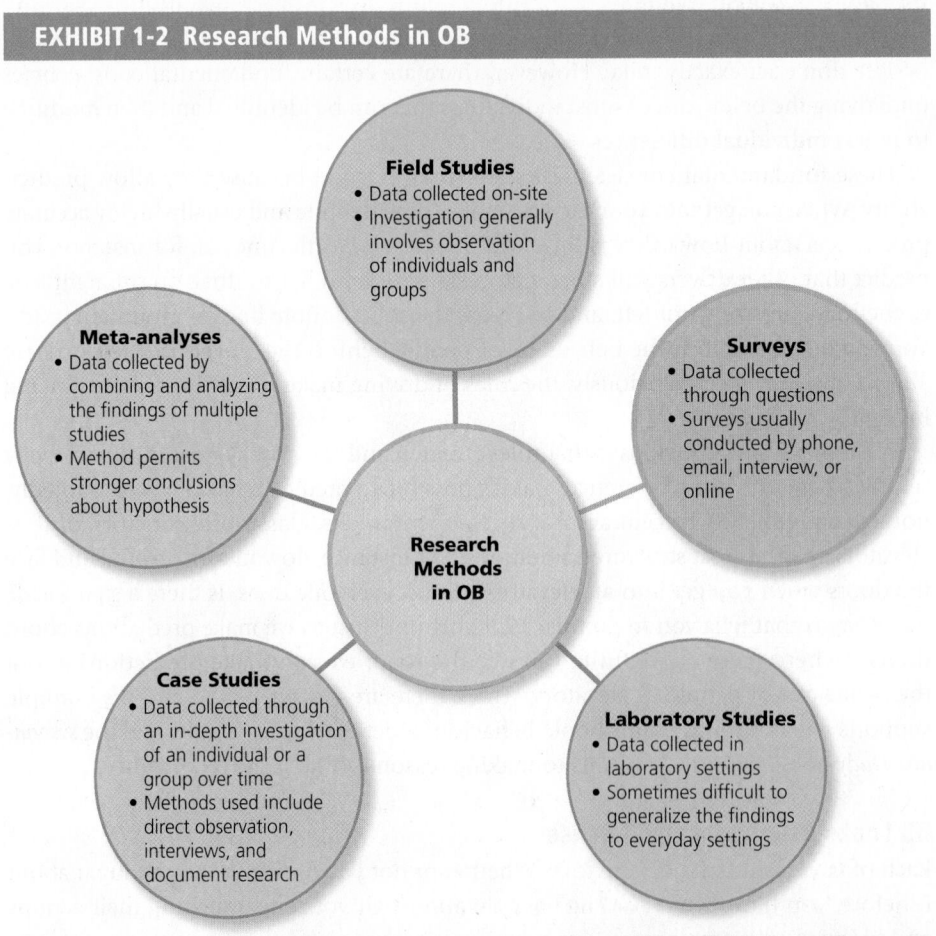

systematic study Looking at relationships, attempting to attribute causes and effects, and drawing conclusions based on scientific evidence.

evidence-based management (EBM) Basing managerial decisions on the best available scientific evidence.

Systematic study and EBM add to **intuition**, or those "gut feelings" about what makes others (and ourselves) "tick." Of course, the things you have come to believe in an unsystematic way are not necessarily incorrect. Jack Welch (former CEO of GE) noted, "The trick, of course, is to know when to go with your gut."[19] If we make all decisions with intuition or gut instinct, we are likely working with incomplete information—imagine making an investment decision with only half the data about the potential for risk and reward.

Relying on intuition is made worse because we tend to overestimate the accuracy of what we think we know. Surveys of human resources managers have also shown that many managers hold "common sense" opinions regarding effective management that have been flatly refuted by empirical evidence.

We find a similar problem in looking to the business and popular media for management wisdom. The business press tends to be dominated by fads. As a writer for the *New Yorker* put it, "Every few years, new companies succeed, and they are scrutinized for the underlying truths they might reveal. But often there is no underlying truth; the companies just happened to be in the right place at the right time."[20] Although we try to avoid it, we might also fall into this trap. It's not that the business press stories are all wrong; it's that without a systematic approach, it's hard to know the truth.

Big Data   It is good news for the future of business that researchers, the media, and company leaders have identified the potential of data-driven management and decision making. While "big data"—the extensive use of statistical compilation and analysis—has been applied to many areas of business, increasingly it is applied to making effective decisions (which we cover in Chapter 12) and managing human resources. Online retailers may have been the first to notice and act upon information on customer preferences that was newly available through Internet shopping, information far superior to data gathered in simple store transactions. This information enabled online retailers to create more targeted marketing strategies than ever before.

The bookselling industry is a case in point: Before online selling, brick-and-mortar bookstores could collect data about book sales only to make their projections about consumer interests and trends. With the advent of Amazon, suddenly a vast array of information about consumer preferences became available for tracking: what customers bought, what they looked at, how they navigated the site, and what they were influenced by (such as promotions, reviews, and page presentation). The challenge for Amazon then was to identify which statistics were *persistent*, giving relatively constant outcomes over time, and *predictive*, showing steady causality between certain inputs and outcomes. The company used these statistics to develop algorithms that let it forecast which books customers might like to read next. Amazon then could base its wholesale purchase decisions on the feedback customers provided, both through these passive methods and through solicited recommendations for upcoming titles, by which Amazon could continuously perfect its algorithms.

The success of Amazon has revolutionized bookselling—and even retail industries—and has served as a model for innovative online retailers. It also illustrates what big data can do for other businesses that can capitalize on the wealth of data available through virtually any Internet connection, from Facebook posts to sensor readings to GPS signals from cellphones. Savvy businesses use big data to manage people as well as technology. A 2012 study of 330 companies found that data-driven companies were 5 percent more productive and 6 percent more profitable than their competitors. These may seem like small percentage gains, but they represent a big impact on economic strength and measurable increases in stock market evaluations for these companies, which are in the top third of their industries.[21] Another study of 8000 firms in 20 countries confirms that constant measuring against targets for productivity and other criteria is a hallmark of well-run companies.[22]

intuition A gut feeling not necessarily supported by research.

The use of big data for managerial practices is a relatively new area but one that holds promise. In dealing with people, leaders often rely on hunches and estimate the influence of information that they have heard most recently, that has been frequently repeated, or that is of personal relevance. Obviously, this information is not always the best because all managers (all people) have natural biases. Managers who use data to define objectives, develop theories of causality, and test those theories can determine which employee activities are most relevant to their business objectives.[23]

We are not advising that you throw your intuition, or all the business press, out the window. Nor are we arguing that research is always right. Researchers make mistakes, too. What we are advising is to use evidence as much as possible to inform your intuition and experience. That is the promise of OB.

Throughout this book, the *Focus on Research* feature will highlight some of the careful studies that form the building blocks of OB. We have also marked major research findings in every chapter with an icon (shown in the margin) so that you can easily see what the research says about various concepts we cover.

If understanding behaviour were simply common sense, we would not observe many of the problems that occur in the workplace, because managers and employees would know how to behave. Unfortunately, as you will see from examples throughout this book, many employees and managers exhibit less than desirable behaviour in the workplace. With a stronger grounding in OB, you might be able to avoid some of these mistakes.

OB Has Few Absolutes

FOCUS ON RESEARCH

5 Demonstrate why few absolutes apply to OB.

Laws in the physical sciences—chemistry, astronomy, physics—are consistent and apply in a wide range of situations. They allow scientists to generalize about the pull of gravity or to confidently send astronauts into space to repair satellites. But as one noted behavioural researcher aptly concluded, "God gave all the easy problems to the physicists."

Social scientists study human problems—and human beings are complex. Because people are not all alike, our ability to make simple, accurate, and sweeping generalizations is limited. Two people often act very differently in the same situation, and the same person's behaviour changes in different situations. Not everyone is motivated by money, and people may behave differently at a religious service than they do at a party.

OB Takes a Contingency Approach

Just because people can behave differently at different times does not mean, of course, that we cannot offer reasonably accurate explanations of human behaviour or make valid predictions. It does mean, however, that OB must consider behaviour within the context in which it occurs—a strategy known as a **contingency approach**. In other words, OB's answers depend upon the situation. For example, OB scholars would avoid stating that everyone likes complex and challenging work (the general concept). Why? Because not everyone wants a challenging job. A job that is appealing to one person may not be to another, so the appeal of the job is contingent on the person who holds it. OB theories mirror the subject matter with which they deal. People are complex and complicated, and so too must be the theories developed to explain their actions.

Consistent with the contingency approach, *Point/Counterpoint* debates are provided in each chapter. These debates are included to highlight the fact that within OB there are disagreements. Through the *Point/Counterpoint* format, you will gain the opportunity to explore different points of view, discover how diverse perspectives complement and oppose each other, and gain insight into some of the debates currently taking place within the OB field. *Point/Counterpoint* on page 28 debates the quality of evidence offered by popular books and academic research studies on organizational behaviour.

contingency approach An approach taken by OB that considers behaviour within the context in which it occurs.

Challenges and Opportunities in the Canadian Workplace

Lululemon's approach to developing its employees is to encourage them to work on themselves first.[24] "What we try to do is work on the self first. You'll see that with personal responsibility, with the opportunity to attend (personal development workshops at) Landmark as a choice, with setting a vision for all aspects of our life. That's actually the core of it," explained Margaret Wheeler, senior vice-president of Human Resources.

All employees are expected to develop their "vision-and-goals" and to pay attention to their vision and goals daily. The goals have specified timelines, and employees are expected to review their goals twice a year. They are posted on cubicle walls and are meant to be discussed with other employees, including management. Managers and other employees help each person be accountable to their goals.

Some new employees face culture shock because of these expectations. For some employees, "to bring your whole self [to the organization], that just feels weird," goals coach Chloe Gow-Jarrett said.

Lululemon is committed to being a good employer, with enthusiastic, goal-oriented employees. Will "vision-and-goals" be enough? What factors affect good teamwork? How can Lululemon managers motivate employees to perform well in their jobs?

6 Identify workplace challenges that provide opportunities to apply OB concepts.

Understanding OB has never been more important for managers. Take a quick look at the dramatic changes in organizations. The typical employee is getting older; more women and members of visible minorities are in the workplace; corporate downsizing and the heavy use of temporary workers are severing the bonds of loyalty that tied many employees to their employers; and global competition requires employees to become more flexible and cope with rapid change. The global recession has brought to the forefront the challenges of working with and managing people during uncertain times, as *Case Incident—Era of the Disposable Worker?* on page 31 shows.

As a result of these changes and others (for example, the rising use of technology), new employment options have emerged. Exhibit 1-3 details some of the types of options individuals may find offered to them by organizations or for which they would like to negotiate. Under each heading in the exhibit, you will find a grouping of options from which to choose—or combine. For instance, at one point in your career you may find yourself employed full-time in an office in a localized, non-union setting with a salary and bonus compensation package, while at another point you may wish to negotiate for a flextime, virtual position and choose to work from overseas for a combination of salary and extra paid time off.

In short, today's challenges bring opportunities for managers to use OB concepts. In this section, we review some of the most critical issues confronting managers for which OB offers solutions—or at least meaningful insights toward solutions.

Simulate on **MyManagementLab**

What Is Management?

What people-related challenges have you noticed in the workplace?

Responding to Economic Pressures

When the US economy plunged into a deep and prolonged recession in 2008, virtually all other large economies around the world followed suit. Canada fared much better than the United States, but still faced widespread layoffs and job losses, and those who survived the axe were often asked to accept pay cuts. When times are bad, managers are on the front lines with employees who must be fired, who are asked to make do with less, and who worry about their futures. The difference between good and bad management can be the difference between profit and loss or, ultimately, between survival and failure.

EXHIBIT 1-3 Employment Options

Categories of Employment	Types of Employment	Places of Employment	Conditions of Employment	Compensation for Employment
Employed	Full-time	Anchored (office/cubicle)	Local	Salary
Underemployed/ underutilized	Part-time	Floating (shared space)	Expatriate	Hourly
Re-employed	Flextime	Virtual	Short-term assignee	Overtime
Unemployed/jobless	Job share	Flexible	Flexpatriate	Bonus
Entrepreneur	Contingent	Work from home	International business traveller	Contract
Retired	Independent contractor		Visa employee	Time off
Job seeking	Temporary		Union/non-union employee	Benefits
Furloughed	Reduced hours			
Laid off	Intern			

Employed: an individual working for a for-profit or nonprofit company, organization, or for another individual, either for money and/or benefits, with established expectations for performance and compensation

Underemployed/underutilized: an individual working in a position or with responsibilities that are below his or her level of education or experience, or an employee working less than full-time who wants full-time employment

Re-employed: an individual who was either dismissed by a company and rehired by the same company or who left the workforce (was unemployed) and found new employment

Unemployed/jobless: an individual who is currently not working; may be job seeking, either with or without government benefits/assistance, either with or without severance pay from the previous job, either new to the workforce or terminated from previous employment, either short-term unemployed (months) or long-term/chronic unemployed (years)

Entrepreneur: an individual who runs his or her own business, either as a sole worker or as the founder of a company with employees

Retired: an individual who has ended his or her career in a profession, either voluntarily by choice or involuntarily by an employer's mandate

Job seeking: an individual who is unemployed but actively looking for a job; either with or without government benefits from the previous job or from disability/need, either with or without severance pay from previous job, or either new to the workforce or terminated from previous employment

Furloughed: similar to a layoff; an employer-required work stoppage, temporary (weeks up to a month, usually); pay is often suspended during this time, although the individual retains employment status with the company

Laid off: sometimes a temporary employer-required work stoppage (usually without pay), but more often a permanent termination from the company in which the employee is recognized to be not at fault

Full-time: hours for full-time employment established by companies, generally more than 30 hours per week in a set schedule, sometimes with salary pay and sometimes with hourly pay, often with a benefits package greater than that for the part-time employment category

Part-time: hours for part-time employment established by companies, generally less than 30 hours per week in a set schedule, often with hourly pay, often with a benefits package less than that for the full-time employment category

Flextime: an arrangement where the employee and employer create nonstandard working hours, which may be a temporary or permanent schedule; may be an expectation for a number of hours worked per week

Job share: an arrangement where two or more employees fill one job, generally by splitting the hours of a full-time position that do not overlap

Contingent: an outsourced employee (e.g., individual from a professional service firm, specialized expert, or business consultant) who is paid hourly or by the job and does not generally receive any company benefits and is not considered as part of the company; a contingent worker may also be a temporary employee or independent contractor

Independent contractor: an entrepreneur in essence, but often a specialist professional who does not aspire to create a business but who provides services or goods to a company

Temporary: an individual who may be employed directly by the organization or through an employment agency/temporary agency; hours may be fixed per week or vary, the employee does not generally receive any company benefits and is not considered as part of the company; a temporary employee is employed for a short duration or as a trial for a position

(Continued)

Reduced hours: a reduction in the normal employee's work schedule by the employer, sometimes as a measure to retain employees/reduce layoffs in economic downturns (as in Germany's Kurzarbeit program, which provides government subsidies to keep workers on the job at reduced hours); employees are only paid for the time they work

Intern: an individual employed for a short (often fixed) term; the position is designed to provide practical training to a preprofessional, either with or without pay

Anchored: an employee with an assigned office, cubicle, or desk space

Floating: an employee with a shared-space workplace and no assigned working area

Virtual: an employee who works through the Internet and is not connected with any office location

Flexible: an employee who is connected with an office location but may work from anywhere

Work from home: an employee who is set up by the company to work from an office at home

Local: an employee who works in one established location

Expatriate: an employee who is on extended international work assignments with the expectation that he or she will return (repatriate) after an established term, usually a year or more; either sent by corporate request or out of self-initiated interest

Short-term assignee: an employee on international assignment longer than business trips yet shorter than typical corporate expatriate assignments, usually 3 to 12 months

Flexpatriate: an employee who travels for brief assignments across cultural or national borders, usually for 1 to 2 months

International business traveller: an employee who takes multiple short international business trips for 1 to 3 weeks

Visa employee: an employee working outside of his or her country of residence who must have a work visa for employment in the current country

Union/non-union employee: an employee who is a member of a labour union, often by trade, and subject to its protections and provisions, which then negotiates with management on certain working condition issues; or an employee who works for a non-union facility or who sometimes elects to stay out of membership in a unionized facility

Salary: employee compensation based on a full-time workweek, where the hours are generally not kept on a time clock but where it is understood that the employee will work according to job needs

Hourly: employee compensation for each hour worked, often recorded on time sheets or by time clocks

Overtime: for hourly employees, compensation for hours worked that are greater than the standard workweek and paid at an hourly rate determined by law

Bonus: compensation in addition to standard pay, usually linked to individual or organizational performance

Contract: prenegotiated compensation for project work, usually according to a schedule as the work progresses

Time off: negotiated time off (either paid or unpaid according to the employment contract) including vacation time, sick leave, personal days, and/or time allotted by management as compensation for time worked

Benefits: advantages other than salary typically stated in the employment contract or the human resources employee handbook; they may include health insurance plans, savings plans, retirement plans, discounts, and other options available to employees at various types of employment

---

Sources: J. R. Anderson, "Action Items: 42 Trends Affecting Benefits, Compensation, Training, Staffing and Technology," *HR Magazine*, January 2013, p. 33; M. Dewhurst, B. Hancock, and D. Ellsworth, "Redesigning Knowledge Work," *Harvard Business Review*, January–February 2013, pp. 58–64; E. Frauenheim, "Creating a New Contingent Culture," *Workforce Management*, August 2012, pp. 34–39; N. Koeppen, "State Job Aid Takes Pressure off Germany," *Wall Street Journal*, February 1, 2013, p. A8; and M. A. Shaffer, M. L. Kraimer, Y.-P. Chen, and M. C. Bolino, "Choices, Challenges, and Career Consequences of Global Work Experiences: A Review and Future Agenda," *Journal of Management*, July 2012, pp. 1282–1327.

Managing employees well when times are tough is just as hard as when times are good—if not harder. But the OB approaches sometimes differ. In good times, understanding how to reward, satisfy, and retain employees is at a premium. In bad times, issues such as stress, decision making, and coping come to the fore.

Responding to Globalization

Organizations are no longer constrained by national borders. Burger King is in the process of buying Tim Hortons and moving to Canada. McDonald's sells hamburgers in more than 100 countries on six continents. New employees at Finland-based cellphone maker Nokia are increasingly being recruited from India, China, and other developing countries—non-Finns now outnumber Finns at the company's renowned research centre in Helsinki. And all major automobile makers now manufacture cars outside their borders; Honda builds cars in Alliston, Ontario, Ford in Brazil, Volkswagen in Mexico, and both Mercedes and BMW in South Africa. Apple has also moved almost all of its manufacturing overseas, as discussed in *Case Incident—Apple Goes Global* on page 30.

In recent years, businesses in Canada have faced tough competition from those in the United States, Europe, Japan, and China, as well as from other businesses within our borders. To survive, they have had to reduce costs, increase productivity, and improve quality. A number of Canadian companies have found it necessary to merge in order to survive. For instance, Rona, the Boucherville, Quebec-based home improvement store, bought out Lansing, Revy, and Revelstoke in recent years to defend its turf against the Atlanta, Georgia-based Home Depot. As a result, in 2014, after some ups and downs, Rona was still holding its own against chief rivals Home Depot and recent entrant Lowes.[25]

Some employers have outsourced jobs to other countries where labour costs are lower to remain profitable. For instance, Toronto-based Dell Canada's technical service lines are handled by technicians working in India. Toronto-based Wall & Associates, a full-service chartered accounting and management consulting firm, outsources document management to Uganda. Employees in Uganda are willing to work for $1 an hour to sort and record receipts. While these wages might seem low, on average, Ugandans make only $1 a day.

Twenty or 30 years ago, national borders protected most firms from foreign competitive pressures. This is no longer the case. Trading blocs such as the North American Free Trade Agreement (NAFTA) and the European Union (EU) have significantly reduced tariffs and barriers to trade, and North America and Europe no longer have a monopoly on highly skilled labour. The Internet has also enabled companies to become more globally connected by opening up international sales and by increasing the opportunities to carry on business across borders. Even small firms can bid on projects in different countries and compete with larger firms via the Internet.

As multinational corporations develop operations worldwide, as companies develop joint ventures with foreign partners, and as employees increasingly pursue job opportunities across national borders, managers and employees must become capable of working with people from different cultures. To be successful, managers and employees need to know the cultural practices of the workforce in each country where they do business. For instance, in some countries a large percentage of the workforce enjoys long holidays. Country and local regulations must be taken into consideration, too. Managers of subsidiaries abroad need to be aware of the unique financial and legal regulations applying to "guest companies" or else risk violating them, which can have economic and even political consequences. Such violations can have implications for their operations in that country and also for political relations between countries. As well, managers need to be cognizant of differences in regulations for their competitors in that country; many times, the laws will give national companies significant financial advantages over foreign subsidiaries. The ever-changing global competitive environment means that not only individuals but also organizations have to become increasingly flexible by learning new skills, new ways of thinking, and new ways of doing business.

Understanding Workforce Diversity

workforce diversity The mix of people in organizations in terms of gender, race, ethnicity, disability, sexual orientation, age, and demographic characteristics such as education and socio-economic status.

An important challenge for organizations is *workforce diversity*, a concept that recognizes the heterogeneous nature of employees in the workplace. Whereas globalization focuses on differences among people from different countries, workforce diversity addresses differences among people within given countries. **Workforce diversity** acknowledges that the workforce consists of women and men; many racial and ethnic groups; individuals with a variety of physical or psychological abilities; and people who differ in age, sexual orientation, and demographic characteristics. We discuss workforce diversity in Chapter 3.

Nicholo Groom/Landov

Dallas, Texas-based Pizza Hut has responded to globalization by expanding its restaurants and delivery services worldwide. The company considers mainland China to be the primary market for new restaurant development because of the country's enormous growth potential. Currently, Pizza Hut is the number one Western casual dining brand in China, with over 1200 restaurants in 305 cities and an additional 200 Pizza Hut Home Service units in 26 cities.[26]

One workforce diversity challenge in Canadian workplaces is the mix of generations—members of the Baby Boomer, Generation X, and Millennial groups—who work side by side. Due to their very different life experiences, they bring different values and different expectations to the workplace.

> Why should you care about understanding other people?

We used to assume that people in organizations who differed from the stereotypical employee would somehow simply fit in. We now recognize that employees don't set aside their cultural values and lifestyle preferences when they go to work. The challenge for organizations, therefore, is to accommodate diverse groups of people by addressing their different lifestyles, family needs, and work styles.[27]

The *Focus on Diversity* feature found throughout this book highlights diversity matters that arise in organizations. Our first example looks at Regina-based SaskTel, which values having a diverse workforce.

FOCUS ON DIVERSITY SaskTel Is a Top Diversity Employer

Does workforce diversity make business sense? Regina-based SaskTel was named one of Canada's Best Diversity Employers in 2014 because of its commitment to diversity.[28] It has diversity programs for women, people with disabilities, visible minorities, and Aboriginal people. While the company received this award for a number of reasons, its work with Aboriginal people is particularly outstanding. Aboriginal people are well represented in the SaskTel workplace: 10 percent of its employees and 8.1 percent of its managers are Aboriginal. Aboriginal people currently represent 15 percent of the Saskatchewan population, and that number is expected to grow to 21 to 24 percent in 20 years.

The number of Aboriginal employees at SaskTel speaks to the effectiveness of the company's Aboriginal recruitment strategy, which was intended to increase the number of Aboriginal employees and address the chronic labour shortages of information and communications technologies workers it faced. SaskTel partners with First Nations bands, tribal councils, and Aboriginal employment agencies.

SaskTel also keeps a database of Aboriginal-owned and operated businesses, which it consults when it is looking for new suppliers and partners.

SaskTel is not just a good employer. It also tries to be a good community member. Several years ago it started an initiative to bring Internet and wireless coverage to the 28 First Nations communities in Saskatchewan. "We have always believed in the importance of all Saskatchewan people benefitting from having access to the most powerful and extensive communications network available," said Don McMorris, Minister Responsible for SaskTel. "With increased access to technology, residents of these communities will be able to take advantage of numerous educational and business opportunities that were not available to them before."

SaskTel strives to have a workforce that is as diverse as its customers—a goal the company finds makes good sense not only for the community but also for the future of the company.

Improving Customer Service

Today, the majority of employees in developed countries work in service jobs, including 78 percent in Canada.[29] Service employees include technical support representatives, fast-food counter workers, sales clerks, nurses, automobile repair technicians, consultants, financial planners, and flight attendants. The shared characteristic of their jobs is substantial interaction with an organization's customers. OB can increase the success of these interactions by showing how employee attitudes and behaviour influence customer satisfaction.

Many an organization has failed because its employees failed to please customers. Management needs to create a customer-responsive culture. OB can provide considerable guidance in helping managers create such cultures—in which employees are friendly and courteous, accessible, knowledgeable, prompt in responding to customer needs, and willing to do what is necessary to please the customer.[30]

Improving People Skills

Throughout the chapters of this book, we will present relevant concepts and theories that can help you explain and predict the behaviour of people at work. You will also gain insights into specific people skills that you can use on the job. For instance, you will learn how to design motivating jobs, improve your listening skills, and create more effective teams.

Working in Networked Organizations

Networked organizations allow people to communicate and work together even though they may be thousands of kilometres apart. Independent contractors can telecommute via computer to workplaces around the globe and change employers as the demand for their services changes. Software programmers, graphic designers, systems analysts, technical writers, photo researchers, book and media editors, and medical transcribers are just a few examples of people who can work from home or other nonoffice locations.

The manager's job is different in a networked organization. Motivating and leading people and making collaborative decisions online requires different techniques than when individuals are physically present in a single location. As more employees do their jobs by linking to others through networks, managers and employees must develop new skills. OB can provide valuable insights to help with honing those skills.

Jan Woitas/Landov

Richard Branson, CEO of Virgin Group, thinks that "the customer is only right sometimes" more accurately reflects how customers should be treated. Instead, he believes that by recognizing the value of employees, who are the ambassadors of the organization, they will give great customer service.

Enhancing Employee Well-Being at Work

Employees are increasingly complaining that the line between work and nonwork time has become blurred, creating personal conflicts and stress.[31] At the same time, however, today's workplace presents opportunities for workers to create and structure their own roles. And even if employees work at home or from half a continent away, managers need to consider their well-being at work.

One of the biggest challenges to maintaining employee well-being is the new reality that many workers never get away from the virtual workplace. Communication technology allows employees to do their work at home, in their cars, or on the ski slopes at Whistler—but it also means many feel like they never really get a break. Another challenge is that organizations are asking employees to be available in off-work hours via cellphones and email. According to a recent study, one in four employees show signs of burnout, partially as a result of longer work hours, and two in three report high stress levels and fatigue.[32] These findings may actually underestimate how common employee burnout is because many employees maintain "always on" access for their managers through email and texting. Finally, employee well-being is challenged by heavy outside commitments. Millions of single-parent households and employees with dependent parents have even more significant challenges in balancing work and family responsibilities, for instance.

As a result of their increased responsibilities in and out of the workplace, employees want more time off. Recent studies suggest that employees want jobs that give them flexibility in their work schedules so they can better manage work–life conflicts.[33] In fact, 56 percent of men and women in a recent study reported that work–life balance was their definition of career success, more than money, recognition, and autonomy.[34] Most college and university students say that attaining a balance between personal life and work is a primary career goal; they want "a life" as well as a job. Organizations that don't help their people achieve work–life balance will find it increasingly difficult to attract and retain the most capable and motivated employees. As you will see in later chapters, the field of OB offers a number of suggestions for designing workplaces and jobs that can help employees deal with work–life conflicts. *OB in the Workplace* looks at how Habañero helps its employees manage work–life balance.

 ## IN THE **WORKPLACE**
Habañero's Employees Help Set Policies

What do empowered employees do? Steven Fitzgerald, president of Vancouver-based IT firm Habañero Consulting Group, believes in empowering his employees.[35] Employees share human resources duties by mentoring each other, encouraging career development, and making sure everyone understands their jobs.

Fitzgerald knows that an "all work and no play" ethic is not a good way to define the business. As a result, he gives his employees autonomy, telling them they will be "judged on the quality of their work—not the number of hours they put in." Habañero allows telecommuting and flextime, and does not track sick days.

More recently, Fitzgerald's employees noted that Habañero's invoicing model, which was based on a target number of billable hours per month, contradicted the company's commitment to work–life balance. The employees worked with management to develop a new model of project-based billing that was more consistent with a truly flexible workplace, while still maintaining profitability. Fitzgerald is pleased with how empowerment has worked for Habañero. He says that knowing what employees want and acting on that knowledge can help you "attract people who are engaged for the right reasons."

Creating a Positive Work Environment

Although competitive pressures on most organizations are stronger than ever, some organizations are trying to realize a competitive advantage by encouraging a positive work environment. Sometimes they do this by creating pleasing physical environments with attractive modern workstations, workplace "perks" such as Google's free lunches, or a shared commitment to environmental sustainability initiatives such as recycling.[36] But, more often, employees perceive a work environment as positive or negative in terms of their work experiences with other employees, rather than in the quality of its physical surroundings. For example, Jeff Immelt and Jim McNerney, both disciples of Jack Welch (former CEO of GE), have tried to maintain high performance expectations (a characteristic of GE's culture) while also encouraging a positive work environment in their organizations (GE and Boeing, respectively). "In this time of turmoil and cynicism about business, you need to be passionate, positive leaders," Immelt recently told his top managers.[37]

A real growth area in OB research is **positive organizational scholarship** (also called *positive organizational behaviour*), which studies how organizations develop human strengths, foster vitality and resilience, and unlock potential. Researchers in this area argue that too much of OB research and management practice has been targeted toward identifying what is wrong with organizations and their employees. In response, they try to study what is *good* about organizations.[38] Some key independent variables in positive OB research are engagement, hope, optimism, and resilience in the face of strain.

Positive organizational scholars have studied a concept called "reflected best-self"—asking employees to think about situations in which they were at their "personal best" to understand how to exploit their strengths. The idea is that we all have things at which we are unusually good, yet too often we focus on addressing our limitations and too rarely think about how to exploit our strengths.[39]

Although positive organizational scholarship does not deny the negative (such as critical feedback), it does challenge researchers to look at OB through a new lens and pushes organizations to think about how to use their employees' strengths rather than dwell on their limitations.

Improving Ethical Behaviour

In an organizational world characterized by cutbacks, expectations of increasing productivity, and tough competition, it's not surprising that many employees feel pressured to cut corners, break rules, and engage in other forms of questionable practices. Increasingly they face **ethical dilemmas and ethical choices**, in which they are required to identify right and wrong conduct. Should they "blow the whistle" if they uncover illegal activities taking place in their company? Do they follow orders with which they don't personally agree? Should they give an inflated performance evaluation to an employee they like, knowing that such an evaluation could save that employee's job? Do they allow themselves to "play politics" to advance their careers?

Ethics is the study of moral values or principles that guide our behaviour and inform us whether actions are right or wrong. Ethical principles help us "do the right thing," such as not padding expense reports, or not phoning in sick to attend the opening of *Avengers 2: Age of Ultron*.

As we show in Chapter 11, the study of ethics does not come with black and white answers. What constitutes good ethical behaviour has never been clearly defined, and, in recent years, the line differentiating right from wrong has blurred. Nonetheless, individuals who strive hard to create their own set of ethical values will more often do the right thing. Moreover, companies that promote a strong ethical mission encourage employees to behave with integrity, and provide strong ethical leadership that can influence employee decisions to behave ethically.[40] The *Ethical Dilemma* on page 29 asks you to consider whether it's ever appropriate to lie about salary expectations. It

positive organizational scholarship An area of OB research that concerns how organizations develop human strength, foster vitality and resilience, and unlock potential.

ethical dilemmas and ethical choices Situations in which individuals are required to define right and wrong conduct.

ethics The study of moral values or principles that guide our behaviour and inform us whether actions are right or wrong.

also asks you whether you should consider the ethical reputation of a company before becoming one of its employees.

Throughout this book, you will find references to ethical and unethical behaviour. The *Focus on Ethics* feature will provide you with thought-provoking illustrations of how ethics is treated in various organizations.

Coming Attractions: Developing an OB Model

We conclude this chapter by presenting a general model that defines the field of OB, stakes out its parameters, and identifies inputs, processes, and outcomes. The result will be "coming attractions" of the topics in the remainder of this book.

7 Describe the three levels of analysis in this book's OB model.

An Overview

A **model** is an abstraction of reality, a simplified representation of some real-world phenomenon. Exhibit 1-4 presents the skeleton on which we will construct our OB model. It proposes three types of variables (inputs, processes, and outcomes) at three levels of analysis (individual, group, and organizational). The model proceeds from left to right, with inputs leading to processes and processes leading to outcomes. Notice that the model also shows that outcomes can influence inputs in the future.

Inputs

Inputs are the variables like personality, group structure, and organizational culture that lead to processes. These variables set the stage for what will occur in an organization later. Many are determined in advance of the employment relationship. For example, individual diversity characteristics, personality, and values are shaped by a combination of an individual's genetic inheritance and childhood environment. Group structure, roles, and team responsibilities are typically assigned immediately before or after a group is formed. Finally, organizational structure and culture are usually the result of years of development and change as the organization adapts to its environment and builds up customs and norms.

EXHIBIT 1-4 A Basic OB Model

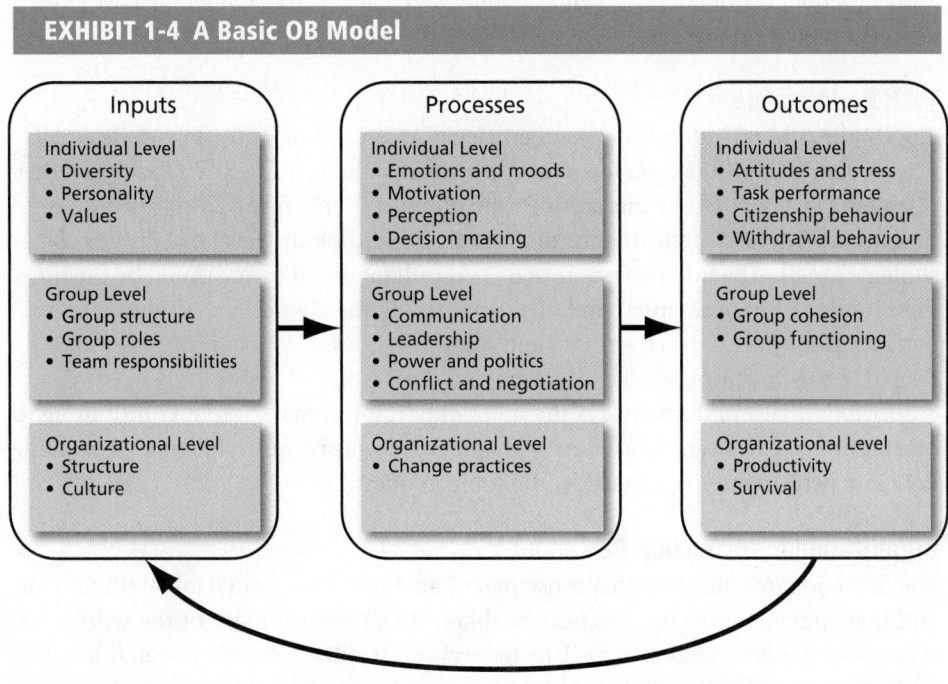

model An abstraction of reality. A simplified representation of some real-world phenomenon.

input Variables that lead to processes.

Processes

If inputs are like the nouns in organizational behaviour, processes are like the verbs. **Processes** are actions that individuals, groups, and organizations engage in as a result of inputs and that lead to certain outcomes. At the individual level, processes include emotions and moods, motivation, perception, and decision making. At the group level, they include communication, leadership, power and politics, and conflict and negotiation. Finally, at the organizational level, processes include change practices.

Outcomes

Outcomes are the key variables that you want to explain or predict, and that are affected by some other variables. What are the primary outcomes in OB? Scholars have emphasized individual-level outcomes such as attitudes and stress, task performance, citizenship behaviour, and withdrawal behaviour. At the group level, cohesion and functioning are the dependent variables. Finally, at the organizational level, we look at overall profitability and survival. Because these outcomes will be covered in all the chapters, we will briefly discuss each here so you can understand what the "goal" of OB will be.

Attitudes and Stress

Employee **attitudes** are the evaluations employees make, ranging from positive to negative, about objects, people, or events. For example, the statement, "I really think my job is great," is a positive job attitude, and "My job is boring and tedious" is a negative job attitude. **Stress** is an unpleasant psychological process that occurs in response to environmental pressures.

Some people might think that influencing employee attitudes and stress is purely soft stuff and not the business of serious managers, but as we will show, attitudes often have behavioural consequences that directly relate to organizational effectiveness. The belief that satisfied employees are more productive than dissatisfied employees has been a basic tenet among managers for years, although only now has research begun to support it. Ample evidence shows that employees who are more satisfied and treated fairly are more willing to engage in the above-and-beyond citizenship behaviour so vital in the contemporary business environment. For more information on the causes and consequences of stress as well as coping mechanisms, see *OB on the Edge—Stress at Work* on pages 118–125.

Task Performance

The combination of effectiveness and efficiency at doing your core job tasks is a reflection of your level of **task performance**. If we think about the job of a factory worker, task performance could be measured by the number and quality of products produced in an hour. The task performance of a teacher would be the level of education that students obtain. The task performance of a consultant might be measured by the timeliness and quality of the presentations they offer to the client firm. All these types of performance relate to the core duties and responsibilities of a job and are often directly related to the functions listed on a formal job description.

Obviously task performance is the most important human output contributing to organizational effectiveness, so in every chapter we devote considerable time to detailing how task performance is affected by the topic in question.

Organizational Citizenship Behaviour

The discretionary behaviour that is not part of an employee's formal job requirements, and that contributes to the psychological and social environment of the workplace, is called **organizational citizenship behaviour (OCB)**.[41] Recent research has also looked at expanding the work on OCB to team behaviour.[42]

⊙ Watch on **MyManagementLab**

East Haven Fire Department: Managing Stress

---

processes Actions that individuals, groups, and organizations engage in as a result of inputs and that lead to certain outcomes.

outcomes Key factors that are affected by some other variables.

attitudes Evaluations individuals make about objects, people, or events.

stress An unpleasant psychological process that occurs in response to environmental pressures.

task performance The combination of effectiveness and efficiency at doing your core job tasks.

organizational citizenship behaviour (OCB) Discretionary behaviour that is not part of an employee's formal job requirements, but that nevertheless promotes the effective functioning of the organization.

Successful organizations need employees who will do more than their usual job duties—who will provide performance that is *beyond* expectations. In today's dynamic workplace, where tasks are increasingly performed by teams and flexibility is critical, employees who engage in "good citizenship" behaviours help others on their team, volunteer for extra job activities, avoid unnecessary conflicts, respect the spirit as well as the letter of rules and regulations, and gracefully tolerate the occasional work-related impositions and nuisances.

Toronto-based BBDO Canada, one of the country's leading creative agencies, encourages an entrepreneurial spirit as a way of inspiring organizational citizenship behaviour. The agency's president and CEO, Gerry Frascione, notes that a team leader on the Campbell Soup account overheard a Campbell's representative musing about a program that would launch Campbell Soup ads when the temperature dipped. "Instead of waiting to get approvals, she acted very entrepreneurially and took it upon herself and made the whole thing happen in one week," says Frascione. "She went back to the client, analyzed the situation, fleshed out the opportunity, came up with an integrated communication plan, came up with a budget, and it was all done within five days."[43]

Organizations want and need employees who will do those things that are not in any job description. Evidence indicates that organizations that have such employees outperform those that don't.[44] As a result, OB is concerned with organizational citizenship behaviour.

> Are you ready to take on more responsibility at work?

Withdrawal Behaviour

We have already mentioned behaviour that goes above and beyond task requirements, but what about behaviour that in some way is below task requirements? **Withdrawal behaviour** is the set of actions that employees take to separate themselves from the organization. There are many forms of withdrawal, ranging from showing up late or failing to attend meetings to absenteeism and turnover.

Employee withdrawal can have a very negative effect on an organization. The cost of employee turnover alone has been estimated to run into the thousands of dollars, even for entry-level positions. Absenteeism also costs organizations significant amounts of money and time every year. For instance, a recent survey found the average direct cost to employers for absenteeism in Canada is $16.6 billion.[45] In Sweden, an average of 10 percent of the country's workforce is on sick leave at any given time.[46]

It's obviously difficult for an organization to operate smoothly and attain its objectives if employees fail to report to their jobs. The workflow is disrupted, and important decisions may be delayed. In organizations that rely heavily on assembly-line production, absenteeism can be considerably more than a disruption; it can drastically reduce the quality of output or even shut down the facility. Levels of absenteeism beyond the normal range have a direct impact on any organization's effectiveness and efficiency. A high rate of turnover can also disrupt the efficient running of an organization when knowledgeable and experienced personnel leave and replacements must be found to assume positions of responsibility.

All organizations, of course, have some turnover. If the "right" people are leaving the organization—the marginal and submarginal employees—turnover can actually be positive. It can create an opportunity to replace an underperforming individual with someone who has higher skills or motivation, open up increased opportunities for promotions, and bring new and fresh ideas to the organization.[47] In today's changing world of work, reasonable levels of employee-initiated turnover improve organizational flexibility and employee independence, and they can lessen the need for management-initiated layoffs.

So why do employees withdraw from work? As we will show later in the book, reasons include negative job attitudes, emotions and moods, and negative interactions with co-workers and supervisors.

withdrawal behaviour The set of actions employees take to separate themselves from the organization.

Group Cohesion

Although many outcomes in our model can be conceptualized as individual level phenomena, some relate to how groups operate. **Group cohesion** is the extent to which members of a group support and validate one another at work. In other words, a cohesive group is one that sticks together. When employees trust one another, seek common goals, and work together to achieve these common ends, the group is cohesive; when employees are divided among themselves in terms of what they want to achieve and have little loyalty to one another, the group is not cohesive.

Ample evidence shows that cohesive groups are more effective.[48] This result is found both for groups that are studied in highly controlled laboratory settings and also for work teams observed in field settings. This finding fits with our intuitive sense that people tend to work harder in groups that have a common purpose. Companies attempt to increase cohesion in a variety of ways ranging from brief icebreaker sessions to social events such as picnics, parties, and outdoor adventure team retreats. Throughout the book we will try to assess whether these specific efforts are likely to result in increases in group cohesiveness. We will also consider ways that picking the right people to be on the team in the first place might be an effective way to enhance cohesion.

Group Functioning

In the same way that positive job attitudes can be associated with higher levels of task performance, group cohesion should lead to positive group functioning. **Group functioning** refers to the quantity and quality of a group's work output. In the same way that the performance of a sports team is more than the sum of individual players' performance, group functioning in work organizations is more than the sum of individual task performances.

What does it mean to say that a group is functioning effectively? In some organizations, an effective group is one that stays focused on a core task and achieves its ends as specified. Other organizations look for teams that are able to work together collaboratively to provide excellent customer service. Still others put more of a premium on group creativity and the flexibility to adapt to changing situations. In each case, different types of activities will be required to get the most from the team.

Productivity

The highest level of analysis in OB is the organization as a whole. An organization is productive if it achieves its goals by transforming inputs into outputs at the lowest cost. Thus **productivity** requires both **effectiveness** and **efficiency**.

A hospital is *effective* when it successfully meets the needs of its clientele. It is *efficient* when it can do so at a low cost. If a hospital manages to achieve higher output from its present staff by reducing the average number of days a patient is confined to bed or increasing the number of staff–patient contacts per day, we say the hospital has gained productive efficiency. A business firm is effective when it attains its sales or market share goals, but its productivity also depends on achieving those goals efficiently. Popular measures of organizational efficiency include return on investment, profit per dollar of sales, and output per hour of labour.

Service organizations must include customer needs and requirements in assessing their effectiveness. Why? Because a clear chain of cause and effect runs from employee attitudes and behaviour to customer attitudes and behaviour to a service organization's productivity. Sears has carefully documented this chain.[49] The company's management found that a 5 percent improvement in employee attitudes leads to a 1.3 percent increase in customer satisfaction, which in turn translates into a 0.5 percent improvement in revenue growth. By training employees to improve the employee–customer interaction, Sears was able to improve customer satisfaction by 4 percent over a 12-month period, generating an estimated \$200 million in additional revenues.

group cohesion The extent to which members of a group support and validate one another while at work.

group functioning The quantity and quality of a work group's output.

productivity The combination of the effectiveness and efficiency of an organization.

effectiveness The degree to which an organization meets the needs of its clientele or customers.

efficiency The degree to which an organization can achieve its ends at a low cost.

EXHIBIT 1-5 The Plan of the Book

The Individual	The Group	The Organization
Inputs • Personality (Ch. 2) • Values (Ch. 3) • Diversity in Organizations (Ch. 3)	**Inputs** • Group structures (Ch. 6) • Group roles (Ch. 6) • Team responsibilities (Ch. 6)	**Inputs** • Culture (Ch. 10) • Structure (Ch. 13)
Processes • Perception (Ch. 2) • Emotions and moods (Ch. 2) • Motivation (Ch. 4 and 5) • Decision making (Ch. 6)	**Processes** • Communication (Ch. 7) • Power and politics (Ch. 8) • Conflict and negotiation (Ch. 9) • Leadership (Ch. 11)	**Processes** • Change practices (Ch. 14)
Outcomes • Attitudes (Ch. 3) • Stress (OB on the Edge: Stress at Work) • Task performance (all) • Citizenship behaviour (all) • Withdrawal behaviour (all)	**Outcomes** • Group cohesion (Ch. 6) • Group functioning (Ch. 6)	**Outcomes** • Profitability (Ch. 1) • Survival (Ch. 1 and 10)

Survival

The final outcome we will consider is **organizational survival**, which is simply evidence that the organization is able to exist and grow over the long term. The survival of an organization depends not just on how productive the organization is, but also on how well it fits with its environment. A company that is very productively making goods and services of little value to the market is unlikely to survive for long, so survival factors in things like perceiving the market successfully, making good decisions about how and when to pursue opportunities, and engaging in successful change management to adapt to new business conditions.

Having reviewed the input, process, and outcome model, we are going to change the figure up a little bit by grouping topics together based on whether we study them at the individual, group, or organizational level. As you can see in Exhibit 1-5, we will deal with inputs, processes, and outcomes at all three levels of analysis, but we group the chapters as shown here to correspond with the typical ways that research has been done in these areas. It is easier to understand one unified presentation about how personality leads to motivation, which leads to performance, than to jump around levels of analysis. Because each level builds on the one that precedes it, after going through them in sequence you will have a good idea of how the human side of organizations functions.

Summary

Organizational behaviour (OB) investigates the impact that individuals, groups, and organizational structure have on behaviour within an organization, and it applies that knowledge to make organizations work more effectively. Specifically, OB focuses on how to improve productivity; reduce absenteeism, turnover, and deviant workplace behaviour; and increase organizational citizenship behaviour and job satisfaction. The essential points of OB that you should keep in mind as you study this topic are listed in Exhibit 1-6.

LESSONS LEARNED

• OB is for everyone.
• OB draws upon a rigorous multidisciplinary research base.

organizational survival The degree to which an organization is able to exist and grow over the long term.

EXHIBIT 1-6 The Fundamentals of OB

- OB considers the multiple levels in an organization: individual, group, and organizational.

- OB is built from the wisdom and research of multiple disciplines, including psychology, sociology, social psychology, and anthropology.

- OB takes a systematic approach to the study of organizational phenomena. It is research-based.

- OB takes a contingency approach to the consideration of organizational phenomena. Recommendations depend on the situation.

SNAPSHOT SUMMARY

Defining Organizational Behaviour
- What Do We Mean by *Organization*?
- OB Is for Everyone
- The Importance of Interpersonal Skills

OB: Making Sense of Behaviour in Organizations
- The Building Blocks of OB
- The Rigour of OB

Challenges and Opportunities in the Canadian Workplace
- Responding to Economic Pressures
- Responding to Globalization
- Understanding Workforce Diversity
- Improving Customer Service
- Improving People Skills
- Working in Networked Organizations

- Enhancing Employee Well-Being at Work
- Creating a Positive Work Environment
- Improving Ethical Behaviour

Coming Attractions: Developing an OB Model
- An Overview
- Inputs
- Processes
- Outcomes

MyManagementLab

Study, practise, and explore real business situations with these helpful resources:

- **Study Plan:** Check your understanding of chapter concepts with self-study quizzes.
- **Online Lesson Presentations:** Study key chapter topics and work through interactive assessments to test your knowledge and master management concepts.
- **Videos:** Learn more about the management practices and strategies of real companies.

P I A PERSONAL INVENTORY ASSESSMENT

- **Simulations:** Practise management decision-making in simulated business environments.

OB at Work

for **Review**

1. What is organizational behaviour (OB)?
2. What is the importance of interpersonal skills in the workplace?
3. What are the major behavioural science disciplines that contribute to OB?
4. Why is systematic study of value to OB?
5. Why do few absolutes apply to OB?
6. What workplace challenges provide opportunities to apply OB concepts?
7. What are the three levels of analysis in this book's OB model?

for **Managers**

- Resist the inclination to rely on generalizations; some provide valid insights into human behaviour, but many are erroneous.
- Use metrics and situational variables rather than "hunches" to explain cause-and-effect relationships.
- Work on your interpersonal skills to increase your leadership potential.
- Improve your technical skills and conceptual skills through training and staying current with organizational behaviour trends such as big data.
- OB can improve your employees' work quality and productivity by showing you how to empower your employees, design and implement change programs, improve customer service, and help your employees balance work–life conflicts.

for **You**

- As you journey through this course in OB, bear in mind that the processes we describe are as relevant to you as an individual as they are to organizations, managers, and employees.
- When you work together with student teams, join a student organization, or volunteer time to a community group, know that your ability to get along with others has an effect on your interactions with the other people in the group and the achievement of the group's goals.
- If you are aware of how your perceptions and personality affect your interactions with others, you can be more careful in forming your initial impression of others.
- By knowing how to motivate others who are working with you, how to communicate effectively, and when to negotiate and compromise, you can get along in a variety of situations that are not necessarily work-related.

OB *at Work*

Lost in Translation?

POINT

Walk into your nearest major bookstore. You will undoubtedly find a large section of books devoted to management and managing. Consider the following recent titles:

- *Hardcore Leadership: 11 Master Lessons from My Airborne Ranger Uncle's "Final Jump"* (CreateSpace, 2013)
- *Half-Naked Interview* (Amazon Digital, 2013)
- *The Chimp Paradox: The Mind Management Program to Help You Achieve Success, Confidence, and Happiness* (Tarcher, 2013)
- *Four Dead Kings at Work* (SlimBooks, 2013)
- *Monopoly, Money, and You: How to Profit from the Game's Secrets of Success* (McGraw-Hill, 2013)
- *The Tao of Rice and Tigers: Taoist Leadership in the 21st Century* (Publius Press, 2013)
- *Nothing to Lose, Everything to Gain: How I Went from Gang Member to Multimillionaire Entrepreneur* (Portfolio Trade, 2013)
- *Ninja Innovation: The Ten Killer Strategies of the World's Most Successful Businesses* (William Morrow, 2013)
- *Giraffes of Technology: The Making of the Twenty-First-Century Leader* (CreateSpace, 2013)

Popular books on OB often have cute titles and are fun to read, but they make the job of managing people seem much simpler than it is. Most are based on the author's opinions rather than substantive research, and it is doubtful that one person's experience translates into effective management practice for everyone. Why do we waste our time on "fluff" when, with a little effort, we can access knowledge produced from thousands of scientific studies on human behaviour in organizations?

OB is a complex subject. Few, if any, simple statements about human behaviour are generalizable to all people in all situations. Should you really try to apply leadership insights you got from a book about giraffes or Tony Soprano?

COUNTERPOINT

Organizations are always looking for leaders, and managers and manager-wannabes are continually looking for ways to fine-tune their leadership skills. Publishers respond to this demand by offering hundreds of titles that promise insights into managing people. Books like these can provide people with the secrets to management that others know about. Moreover, isn't it better to learn about management from people in the trenches, as opposed to the latest esoteric musings from the "Ivory Tower"? Many of the most important insights we gain from life aren't necessarily the product of careful empirical research studies.

It is true there are some bad books out there. But do they outnumber the esoteric research studies published every year? For example, a few recent management and OB studies were published in 2013 with the following titles:

- *Market Segmentation, Service Quality, and Overall Satisfaction: Self-Organizing Map and Structural Equation Modeling Methods*
- *The Effects of Performance Rating, Leader–Member Exchange, Perceived Utility, and Organizational Justice on Performance Appraisal Satisfaction: Applying a Moral Judgment Perspective*
- *Nonlinear Moderating Effect of Tenure on Organizational Identification (OID) and the Subsequent Role of OID in Fostering Readiness for Change*
- *Examining the Influence of Modularity and Knowledge Management (KM) on Dynamic Capabilities*

We don't mean to poke fun at these studies. Rather, our point is that you cannot judge a book by its cover any more than you can a research study by its title.

There is no one right way to learn the science and art of managing people in organizations. The most enlightened managers are those who gather insights from multiple sources: their own experience, research findings, observations of others, and, yes, business press books, too. If great management were produced by carefully gleaning results from research studies, academicians would make the best managers. How often do we see that?

Research and academics have an important role to play in understanding effective management. But it is not fair to condemn all business books by citing the worst (or, at least, the worse-sounding ones).

PERSONAL **INVENTORY** ASSESSMENT

Learn about yourself with the PIA collection of online exercises. Designed to promote self-reflection and engagement, these assessments will enhance your ability to connect with the key concepts of organizational behaviour. Go to MyManagementLab to access the assessments.

BREAKOUT **GROUP** EXERCISES

Form small groups to discuss the following topics, as assigned by your instructor.

1. Consider a group situation in which you have worked. To what extent did the group rely on the technical skills of the group members vs. their interpersonal skills? Which skills seemed most important in helping the group function well?

2. Identify some examples of "worst jobs." What conditions of these jobs made them unpleasant? To what extent were these conditions related to behaviours of individuals?

3. Develop a list of "organizational puzzles," that is, behaviour you have observed in organizations that seemed to make little sense. As the term progresses, see if you can begin to explain these puzzles, using your knowledge of OB.

EXPERIENTIAL EXERCISE

Interpersonal Skills in the Workplace

This exercise asks you to consider the skills outlined in the Competing Values Framework on pages 32–34 to develop an understanding of managerial expertise. Steps 1–4 can be completed in 15–20 minutes.

1. Using the skills listed in the Competing Values Framework, identify the 4 skills that you think all managers should have.

2. Identify the 4 skills that you think are least important for managers to have.

3. In groups of 5–7, reach a consensus on the most-needed and least-needed skills identified in steps 1 and 2.

4. Using Exhibit 1-8, determine whether your "ideal" managers would have trouble managing in some dimensions of organizational demands.

5. Your instructor will lead a general discussion of your results.

ETHICAL **DILEMMA**

Jekyll and Hyde

Let's assume that you have been offered a job by Jekyll Corporation, a company in the consumer products industry. The job is in your chosen career path.

Jekyll Corporation has offered you a position that would begin two weeks after you graduate. The job

responsibilities are appealing to you, make good use of your training, and are intrinsically interesting. The company seems well positioned financially, and you have met the individual who would be your supervisor, who assures you that the future prospects for your position and career are bright. Several other graduates of your program work at Jekyll Corporation, and they speak quite positively of the company and promise to socialize and network with you once you start.

As a company, Jekyll Corporation promotes itself as a fair-trade and sustainable organization. Fair trade is a trading partnership—based on dialogue, transparency, and respect—that seeks greater equity in international trade. It contributes to sustainable development by offering better trading conditions to, and securing the rights of, local producers and businesses. Fair-trade organizations are actively engaged in supporting producers and sustainable environmental farming practices, and fair-trade practices prohibit child or forced labour.

Yesterday, Gabriel Utterson—a human resources manager at Jekyll Corporation—called you to discuss the initial terms of the offer, which seemed reasonable and standard for the industry. However, one aspect was not mentioned: your starting salary. Gabriel said Jekyll is an internally transparent organization—there are no secrets. While the firm very much wants to hire you, there are limits to what it can afford to offer, and before it makes a formal offer, it was reasonable to ask what you would expect. Gabriel wanted you to think about your salary expectation and call back tomorrow.

Before calling Gabriel, you thought long and hard about what it would take to accept Jekyll Corporation's offer. You have a number in mind, which may or may not be the same number you give Gabriel. What starting salary would it take for you to accept Jekyll Corporation's offer?

Questions

1. What starting salary will you give Gabriel? What salary represents the minimum offer you would accept? If these two numbers are different, why? Does giving Gabriel a different number than your "internal" number violate Jekyll Corporation's transparent culture? Why or why not?

2. Assume that you have received another offer from Hyde Associates. Like the Jekyll job, this position is on your chosen career path and in the consumer products industry. Assume, however, that you have read in the news that "Hyde Associates has been criticized for unsustainable manufacturing practices that may be harmful to the environment." It has further been criticized for unfair trade practices and for employing underage children. Would these criticisms change whether you would be willing to take the job? Why or why not?

3. These scenarios are based on studies of corporate social responsibility (CSR) practices that show consumers generally charge a kind of rent to companies that do not practice CSR. In other words, they generally expect a substantial discount in order to buy a product from Hyde rather than from Jekyll. For example, if Jekyll and Hyde sold coffee, people would pay a premium of $1.40 to buy coffee from Jekyll and demand a discount of $2.40 to buy coffee from Hyde. Do you think this preference would affect your job choice decision? Why or why not?

CASE INCIDENTS

Apple Goes Global

It was not long ago that products from Apple, perhaps the most recognizable name in electronics manufacturing around the world, were made entirely in the United States.[50] This is not so anymore. Now, almost all of the approximately 70 million iPhones, 30 million iPads, and 59 million other Apple products sold yearly are manufactured overseas. This change represents more than 20 000 jobs directly lost by US workers, not to mention more than 700 000 other jobs and business given to foreign companies in Asia, Europe, and elsewhere. The loss is not temporary. As the late Steve Jobs, Apple's iconic co-founder, told US President Obama, "Those jobs aren't coming back."

Vancouver-based Lululemon Athletica has also transferred many jobs out of Canada to countries such as

Cambodia and Bangladesh. When the company first started in 1998, all of its factories were located in Canada. By 2007, only 50 percent of the factories were in Canada and now that figure is only 3 percent.

At first glance, the transfer of jobs from one workforce to another would seem to hinge on a difference in wages, and that certainly is one of the reasons for the move to overseas factories. Rather, and of more concern, Apple's leaders believe the intrinsic characteristics of the labour force available to them in China—which they identify as flexibility, diligence, and industrial skills—are superior to those of the North American labour force. Apple executives tell stories of shorter lead times and faster manufacturing processes in China that are becoming the stuff of company legend. "The speed and flexibility is breathtaking," one executive said. "There's no American plant that can match that." Another said, "We shouldn't be criticized for using Chinese workers. The U.S. has stopped producing people with the skills we need."

The perception of an overseas advantage might suggest that the North American workforce needs to be better led, better trained, more effectively managed, and more motivated to be proactive and flexible. If Canadian and US workers are less motivated and less adaptable, it's hard to imagine how that does not spell trouble for the future of the North American workforce.

There is an ongoing debate whether companies such as Lululemon and Apple serve as examples of the failure of North America to maintain manufacturing plants at home or whether these companies should best be viewed as examples of global ingenuity.

Questions

1. What are the pros and cons for local and overseas labour forces for companies going global? What are the potential political implications for country relationships?

2. How could managers use increased worker flexibility and diligence to increase the competitiveness of their manufacturing sites? What would you recommend?

Era of the Disposable Worker?

The great global recession has claimed many victims.[51] In many countries, unemployment is at near-historic highs, and even those who have managed to keep their jobs have often been asked to accept reduced work hours or pay cuts. Another consequence of the current business and economic environment is an increase in the number of individuals employed on a temporary or contingent basis.

The statistics on temporary workers are grim. Increases in layoffs mean that many jobs formerly considered safe have become "temporary" in the sense that they could disappear at any time with little warning. Forecasts suggest that the next 5 to 10 years will be similar, with small pay increases, worse working conditions, and low levels of job security. As Peter Cappelli of the University of Pennsylvania's Wharton School notes, "Employers are trying to get rid of all fixed costs. First they did it with employment benefits. Now they're doing it with the jobs themselves. Everything is variable."

We might suppose that these corporate actions are largely taking place in an era of diminishing profitability. However, data from the financial sector are not consistent with this explanation. Among *Fortune* 500 companies, 2009 saw the second-largest jump in corporate earnings in the list's 56-year history. Moreover, many of these gains don't appear to be the result of increases in revenue. Rather, they reflect dramatic decreases in labour costs. One equity market researcher noted, "The largest part of the gain came from lower payrolls rather than the sluggish rise in sales . . ." Wages also rose only slightly during this period of rapidly increasing corporate profitability.

Some observers suggest that the very nature of corporate profit monitoring is to blame for the discrepancy between corporate profitability and outcomes for workers. Some have noted that teachers whose evaluations are based on standardized test scores tend to "teach to the test," to the detriment of other areas of learning. In the same way, when a company is judged primarily by the single metric of a stock price, executives naturally try their best to increase this number, possibly to the detriment of other concerns such as employee well-being or corporate culture. On the other hand, others defend corporate actions that increase the degree to which they can treat labour flexibly, noting that in an increasingly competitive global marketplace, it might be necessary to sacrifice some jobs to save the organization as a whole.

The issues of how executives make decisions about workforce allocation, how job security and corporate loyalty influence employee behaviour, and how emotional reactions come to surround these issues are all core components of OB research.

Questions

1. To what extent can individual business decisions (as opposed to economic forces) explain deterioration in working conditions for many workers?

2. Do business organizations have a responsibility to ensure that employees have secure jobs with good working conditions, or is their primary responsibility to shareholders?

3. What alternative measures of organizational performance, besides share prices, do you think might change the focus of business leaders?

FROM CONCEPTS TO SKILLS

Developing Interpersonal Skills

We note in this chapter that having a broad range of interpersonal skills to draw on makes us more effective organizational participants. So what kinds of interpersonal skills does an individual need in today's workplace?

Robert Quinn, Kim Cameron, and their colleagues have developed a model known as the "Competing Values Framework" that can help us identify some of the most useful skills.[52] They note that the range of issues organizations face can be divided along two dimensions: an internal-external and a flexibility-control focus. This idea is illustrated in Exhibit 1-7. The internal–external dimension refers to the extent that organizations focus on one of two directions: either inwardly, toward employee needs and concerns and/or production processes and internal systems; or outwardly, toward such factors as the marketplace, government regulations, and the changing social, environmental, and technological conditions of the future. The flexibility–control dimension refers to the competing demands of organizations to stay focused on doing what has been done in the past vs. being more flexible in orientation and outlook.

Because organizations face the competing demands shown in Exhibit 1-7, it becomes obvious that managers and employees need a variety of skills to help them function within the various quadrants at different points in time. For instance, the skills needed to operate an efficient assembly-line process are not the same as those needed to scan the external environment or to create opportunities in anticipation of changes in the environment. Quinn and his colleagues use the term *master manager* to indicate

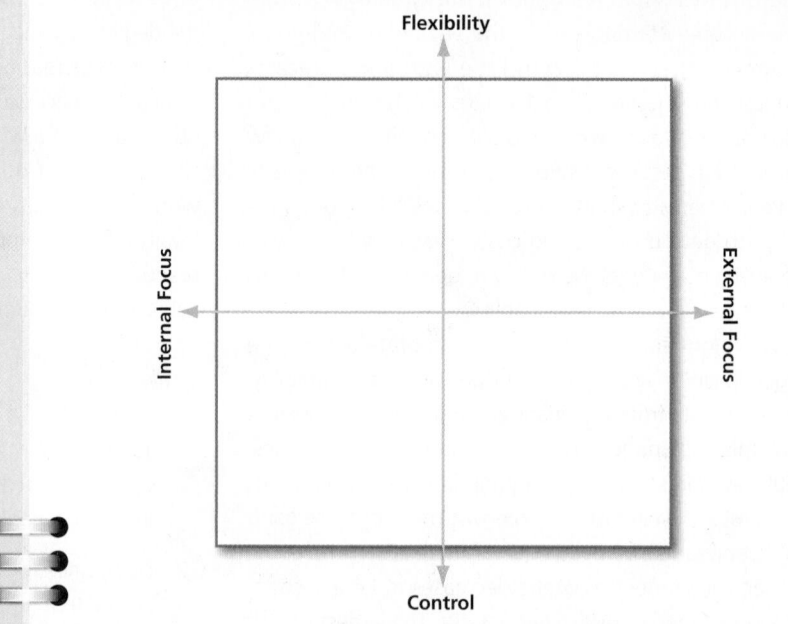

EXHIBIT 1-7 Competing Values Framework

Source: Adapted from K. Cameron and R. E. Quinn, Diagnosing and Changing Organizational Culture: Based on the Competing Values Framework, 2006, ISBN: 9780787982836, Fig 3.1, pg. 35. Copyright © John Wiley & Sons.

OB *at* **Work**

that successful managers learn and apply skills that will help them manage across the range of organizational demands; at some times moving toward flexibility, at others moving toward control, sometimes being more internally focused, sometimes being more externally driven.[53]

As organizations increasingly cut their layers, reducing the number of managers while also relying more on the use of teams in the workplace, the skills of the master manager apply as well to the employee. In other words, considering the Competing Values Framework, we can see that both managers and individual employees need to learn new skills and new ways of interpreting their organizational contexts. Continuing to use traditional skills and practices that worked in the past is not an option. The growth in self-employment also indicates a need to develop more interpersonal skills, particularly for anyone who goes on to build a business that involves hiring and managing employees.

Exhibit 1-8 outlines the many skills required of today's manager. It gives you an indication of the complex roles that managers and employees fill in the changing workplace. The skills are organized in terms of four major roles: maintaining flexibility, maintaining control, maintaining an external focus, and maintaining an internal focus. Identifying your own strengths and weaknesses in these skill areas can give you a better sense of how close you are to becoming a successful manager.

On the flexibility side, organizations want to inspire their employees toward high-performance behaviour. Such behaviour includes looking ahead to the future and imagining possible new directions for the organization. To do these things, employees need to think and act like mentors and facilitators. It is also important to have the skills of innovators and brokers.

EXHIBIT 1-8 Skills for Mastery in the New Workplace

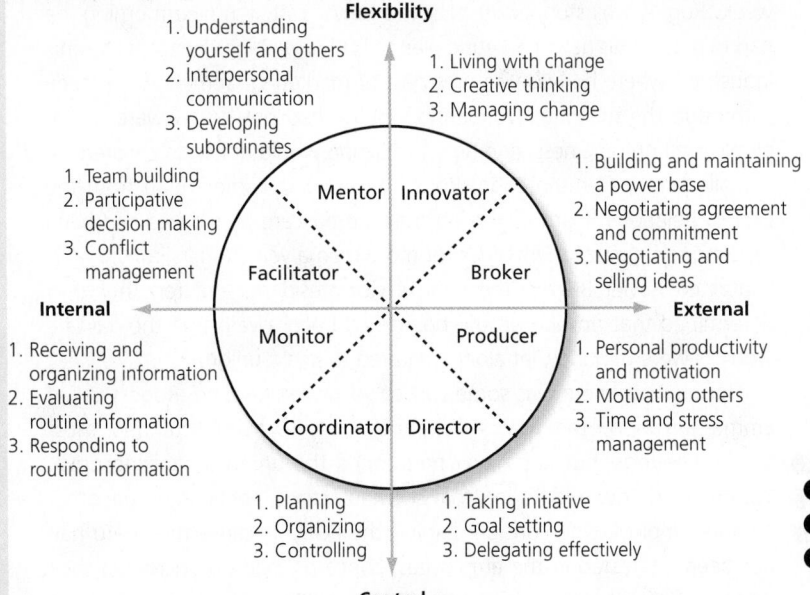

Source: R. E. Quinn, *Beyond Rational Management* (San Francisco: Jossey-Bass, 1988), p. 86. Copyright © John Wiley & Sons.

On the control side, organizations need to set clear goals about productivity expectations, and they have to develop and implement systems to carry out the production process. To be effective on the production side, employees need to have the skills of monitors, coordinators, directors, and producers. The *Experiential Exercise* on page 29 helps you better understand how closely your views on the ideal skills of managers and leaders match the skills needed to be successful in the broad range of activities that managers and leaders encounter.

At this point, you may wonder whether it's possible for people to learn all of the skills necessary to become a master manager. More important, you may wonder whether we can change our individual style, say from more controlling to more flexible. Here is what Peggy Kent, chair, former president, and CEO of Century Mining Corporation (a mid-tier Canadian gold producer), said about how her managerial style changed from controlling to more flexible over time: "I started out being very dictatorial. Everybody in head office reported to me. I had to learn to trust other executives so we could work out problems together."[54] So, while it is probably true that each of us has a preferred style of operating, it is also the case that we can develop new skills if that is something we choose to do.

Practising Skills

As the father of two young children, Marshall Rogers thought that serving on the board of Marysville Daycare would be a good way to stay in touch with those who cared for his children during the day.[55] But he never dreamed that he would become involved in union–management negotiations with daycare-centre employees.

Late one Sunday evening, in his ninth month as president of the daycare centre, Rogers received a phone call from Grace Ng, a union representative of the Provincial Government Employees' Union (PGEU). Ng informed Rogers that the daycare employees would be unionized the following week. Rogers was stunned to hear this news. Early the next morning, he had to present his new marketing plan to senior management at Techtronix Industries, where he was vice-president of marketing. Somehow he made it through the meeting, wondering why he had not been aware of the employees' unhappiness, and how this action would affect his children.

Following his presentation, Rogers received documentation from the Labour Relations Board indicating that the daycare employees had been working to unionize themselves for more than a year. Rogers immediately contacted Xavier Breslin, the board's vice-president, and together they determined that no one on the board had been aware that the daycare workers were unhappy, let alone prepared to join a union.

Hoping that there was some sort of misunderstanding, Rogers called Emma Reynaud, the Marysville supervisor. Reynaud attended most board meetings, but had never mentioned the union-organizing drive. Yet Reynaud now told Rogers that she had actively encouraged the other daycare employees to consider joining the PGEU because the board had not been interested in the employees' concerns, had not increased their wages sufficiently over the past two years, and had not maintained communication channels between the board and the employees.

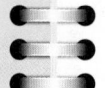

All of the board members had full-time jobs elsewhere, and many were upper- and middle-level managers in their own companies. They were used to dealing with unhappy employees in their own workplaces, although none had experienced a union-organizing drive. Like Rogers, they had chosen to serve on the board of Marysville to stay informed about the day-to-day events of the centre. They had not really thought of themselves as the centre's employer, although, as board members, they represented all the parents of children enrolled at Marysville. Their main tasks on the daycare-centre board had been setting fees for the children and wages for the daycare employees. The board members usually saw the staff members several times a week, when they picked up their children, yet the unhappiness represented by the union-organizing drive was surprising to all of them. When they met at an emergency board meeting that evening, they tried to evaluate what had gone wrong at Marysville.

Questions

1. If you were either a board member or a parent, how would you know that the employees taking care of your children were unhappy with their jobs?

2. What might you do if you learned about their unhappiness?

3. What might Rogers have done differently as president of the board?

4. In what ways does this case illustrate that knowledge of OB can be applied beyond your own workplace?

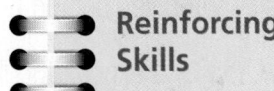 

Reinforcing Skills

1. Talk to several managers you know and ask them what skills they think are most important in today's workplace. Ask them to specifically consider the use of teams in their workplace, and what skills their team members most need to have but are least likely to have. How might you use this information to develop greater interpersonal skills?

2. Talk to several managers you know and ask them what skills they have found to be most important in doing their jobs. Why did they find these skills most important? What advice would they give a would-be manager about skills worth developing?

2

Perception, Personality, and Emotions

Can a manager with a hard-driving personality attract employees who have the same kind of drive?

LEARNING OUTCOMES

After studying this chapter, you should be able to:

1. Define *perception*, and explain the factors that influence it.

2. Explain attribution theory, and list the three determinants of attribution.

3. Describe personality, the way it is measured, and the factors that shape it.

4. Describe the Myers-Briggs Type Indicator personality framework and its strengths and weaknesses.

5. Identify the key traits in the Big Five Personality Model.

6. Demonstrate how the Big Five personality traits predict behaviour at work.

7. Differentiate between emotions and moods.

8. Show the impact of emotional labour on employees.

9. Contrast the evidence for and against the existence of emotional intelligence.

10. Identify strategies for emotion regulation and their likely effects.

Matthew Corrin is CEO of Freshii, a rapidly expanding chain of restaurants that feature fresh ingredients from organic and local farms.[1]

After graduating from Western University and interning in New York City for a few years, Corrin started Freshii in Toronto. Today, the company has more US than Canadian restaurants, is headquartered in Chicago, and has expanded into Austria, China, Colombia, Switzerland, and the United Arab Emirates.

Corrin started Freshii from his parents' house when he was 23; now 32, he runs a company whose annual revenues approach $100 million. His unusual personality may explain much of his early and rapid success. Corrin is known for his outsized ambitions; in fact, he intends to have 1000 restaurants in the next few years and wants to create a "global, iconic brand" as ubiquitous as Starbucks. Asked to describe his philosophy in hiring managers, Corrin commented, "Merely 'good' managers need not apply. You will only fit into our organization if you're a 'super-achiever.'"

Corrin is also known for his hard-driving ways. He demands the best from others— "failure is not an option," he says—and is not afraid to do what it takes to succeed. He also says: "I think the traditional restaurant mantra is, 'If you build it, they will come.' I think that is just so old school. So our philosophy is build it and then guerilla market the hell out of it to make them come."

Corrin might be described as somewhat narcissistic. He expects those around him to adapt to his personality. He also enjoys being the centre of attention and likes being recognized. In fact, some might perceive him as a media hog. He loves rubbing elbows with celebrities: Ryan Seacrest and Ashton Kutcher attended one of Freshii's grand openings in New York.

All of our behaviour is somewhat shaped by our perceptions, personalities, emotions, and experiences. In this chapter, we consider the role that perception plays in affecting the way we see the world and the people around us. We also consider how personality characteristics affect our attitudes toward people and situations. We then consider how emotions shape many of our work-related behaviours.

> ### THE BIG IDEA
>
> *Individual differences can have a large impact on how groups and organizations function.*

 **IS FOR EVERYONE**

- What causes people to have different perceptions of the same situation?
- Can people be mistaken in their perceptions?
- Whom do you tend to blame when someone makes a mistake? Ever wonder why?
- Have you ever misjudged a person? Do you know why?
- Can perception really affect outcomes?
- Are people born with their personalities?
- Ever wonder why the grocery clerk is always smiling?

Perception

❶ Define *perception*, and explain the factors that influence it.

Perception is the process by which individuals organize and interpret their impressions to give meaning to their environment. However, what we perceive can be substantially different from objective reality. We often disagree about what is real.

Perception is important to organizational behaviour (OB) because people's behaviour is based on their perception of what reality is, not on reality itself. *The world as it is perceived is the world that is behaviourally important.* A recent study of political behaviour suggests that once individuals hold particular perceptions, it can be difficult to change their minds, even if they are shown contrary evidence.[2]

Factors That Influence Perception

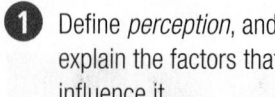

Orpheus Group Casting: Social Perception and Attribution

A number of factors shape and sometimes distort perception. These factors can reside in the *perceiver*; in the object, or *target*, being perceived; or in the *situation* in which the perception is made. Exhibit 2-1 summarizes the factors that influence perception.

> What causes people to have different perceptions of the same situation?

The Perceiver

When you ("the perceiver") look at a target, your interpretation of what you see is heavily influenced by your personal characteristics—attitudes, motives, interests, past experiences, and expectations. For instance, if you expect police officers to be authoritative, you may perceive them as such, regardless of their actual traits. A recent study found that people's perceptions of others reveal a lot about the people themselves.[3] People with positive perceptions of others tended to describe themselves (and be described by others) as "enthusiastic, happy, kind-hearted, courteous, emotionally stable and capable." Negative perceptions of others were related to increased narcissism and antisocial behaviour.

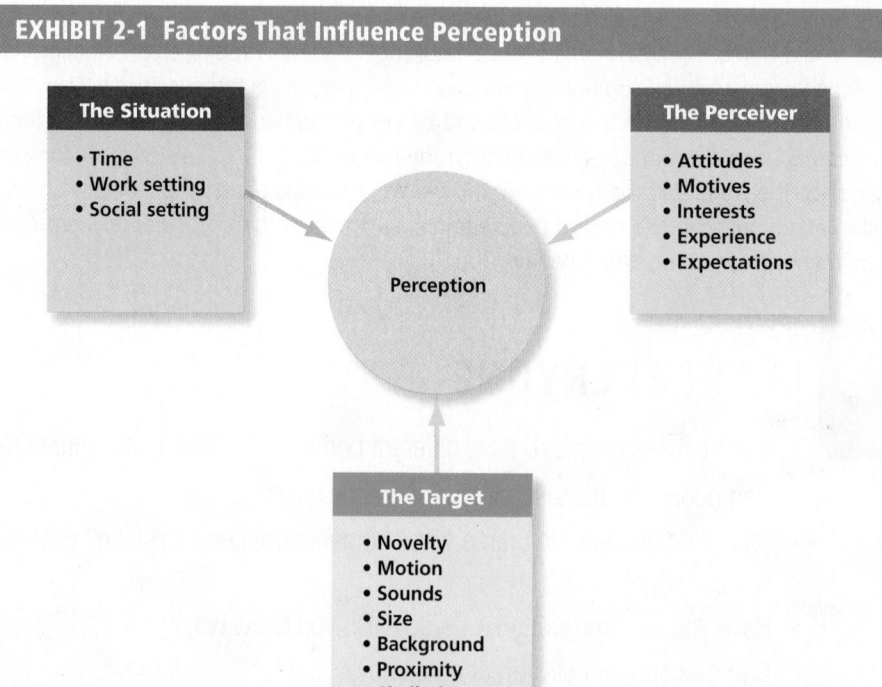

EXHIBIT 2-1 Factors That Influence Perception

The Situation
- Time
- Work setting
- Social setting

The Perceiver
- Attitudes
- Motives
- Interests
- Experience
- Expectations

Perception

The Target
- Novelty
- Motion
- Sounds
- Size
- Background
- Proximity
- Similarity

perception The process by which individuals organize and interpret their impressions in order to give meaning to their environment.

The Target

A target's characteristics also affect what we perceive. Loud people are more likely to be noticed in a group than are quiet ones. So too are extremely attractive or unattractive individuals. Novelty, motion, sounds, size, and other characteristics of a target shape the way we see it.

Because we don't look at targets in isolation, the relationship of a target to its background influences perception. For instance, we often perceive women, Aboriginal people, Asians, or members of any other group that has clearly distinguishable characteristics as alike in other, unrelated ways as well.

The Situation

Context matters too. The time at which we see an object or event can influence attention, as can location, light, heat, or any number of situational factors. For example, at a nightclub on Saturday night, you may not notice someone "decked out." Yet that same person so attired for your Monday morning management class would certainly catch your attention. Neither the perceiver nor the target changed between Saturday night and Monday morning, but the situation is different.

Perceptual Errors

Perceiving and interpreting why others do what they do takes time. As a result, we develop techniques to make this task more manageable. These techniques are frequently valuable—they allow us to make accurate perceptions rapidly and provide valid data for making predictions. However, they are not foolproof. They can and do get us into trouble. Some of the errors that distort the perception process are attribution theory, selective perception, halo effect, contrast effects, projection, and stereotyping.

> Can people be mistaken in their perceptions?

Attribution Theory

Attribution theory tries to explain the ways we judge people differently, depending on the meaning we attribute to a given behaviour.[4] Basically, the theory suggests that when we observe what seems like atypical behaviour by an individual, we try to make sense of it. We consider whether the individual is responsible for the behaviour (the cause is internal), or whether something outside the individual caused the behaviour (the cause is external). *Internally* caused behaviours are those an observer believes to be under the personal behavioural control of another individual. *Externally* caused behaviours are what we imagine the situation forced the individual to do. For example, if a student is late for class, the instructor might attribute his lateness to partying into the wee hours of the morning and then oversleeping. This would be an internal attribution. But if the instructor assumes that a major automobile accident tied up traffic on the student's regular route to school, he or she is making an external attribution. In trying to determine whether behaviour is internally or externally caused, we rely on three rules about the behaviour: (1) distinctiveness, (2) consensus, and (3) consistency. Let's discuss each of these in turn.

> Whom do you tend to blame when someone makes a mistake? Ever wonder why?

2 Explain attribution theory, and list the three determinants of attribution.

Distinctiveness **Distinctiveness** refers to whether an individual acts similarly across a variety of situations. Is the student who arrives late for class today also the one who is always goofing off in team meetings and not answering urgent emails? What we want to know is whether this behaviour is unusual. If it is, we are likely to give it an external attribution. If it's not, we will probably judge the behaviour to be internal.

attribution theory The theory that when we observe what seems like atypical behaviour by an individual, we attempt to determine whether it is internally or externally caused.

distinctiveness A behavioural rule that considers whether an individual acts similarly across a variety of situations.

Consensus If everyone who is faced with a similar situation responds in the same way, we can say the behaviour shows **consensus**. The tardy student's behaviour would meet this criterion if all students who took the same route to school were also late. From an attribution perspective, if consensus is high, you would probably give an external attribution to the student's tardiness. But if other students who took the same route made it to class on time, you would attribute the cause of lateness for the student in question to an internal cause.

Consistency Finally, an observer looks for **consistency** in a person's actions. Does the person respond the same way over time? If a student is usually on time for class, being 10 minutes late will be perceived differently from the student who is late almost every class. The more consistent the behaviour, the more we are inclined to attribute it to internal causes.

> Have you ever misjudged a person? Do you know why?

Exhibit 2-2 summarizes the key elements in attribution theory. It illustrates, for instance, how to evaluate an employee's behaviour on a new task. To do this, you might note that employee Emma generally performs at about the same level on other related tasks as she does on her current task (low distinctiveness). You see that other employees frequently perform differently—better or worse—than Emma does on that current task (low consensus). Finally, if Emma's performance on this current task is consistent over time (high consistency), you or anyone else who is judging Emma's work is likely to hold her primarily responsible for her task performance (internal attribution).

How Attributions Get Distorted One of the more interesting findings from attribution theory is that there are errors or biases that distort attributions. When we judge the behaviour of other people, we tend to underestimate the influence of external factors and overestimate the influence of internal, or personal, factors.[5] This **fundamental attribution error** can explain why a sales manager attributes the poor performance of his or her sales agents to laziness rather than acknowledging the impact of the innovative

consensus A behavioural rule that considers whether everyone faced with a similar situation responds in the same way.

consistency A behavioural rule that considers whether the individual has been acting in the same way over time.

fundamental attribution error The tendency to underestimate the influence of external factors and overestimate the influence of internal factors when making judgments about the behaviour of others.

EXHIBIT 2-2 Attribution Theory

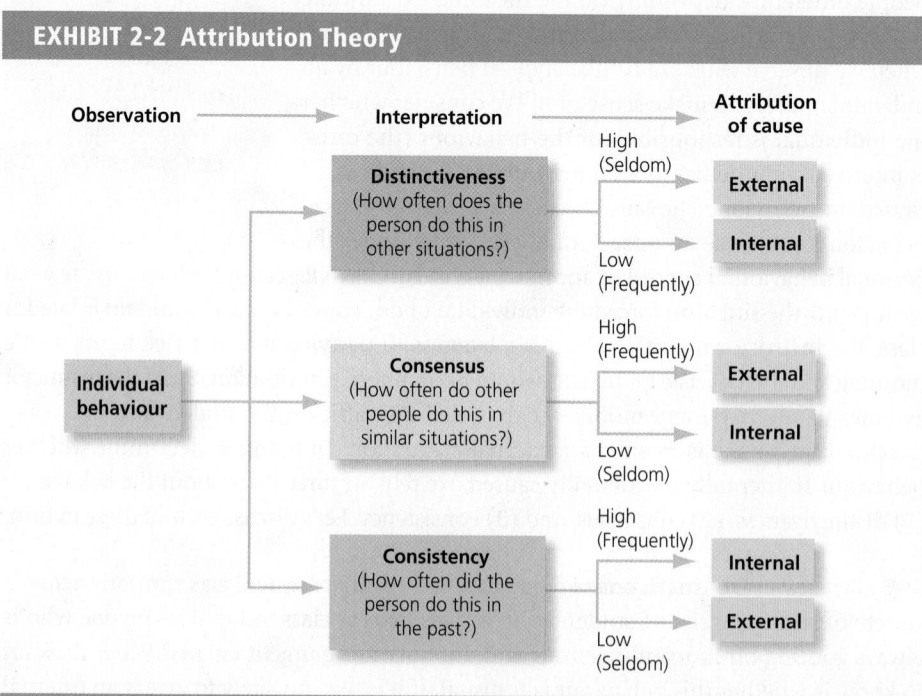

EXHIBIT 2-3 Percentage of Individuals Rating Themselves Above Average on Each Attribute

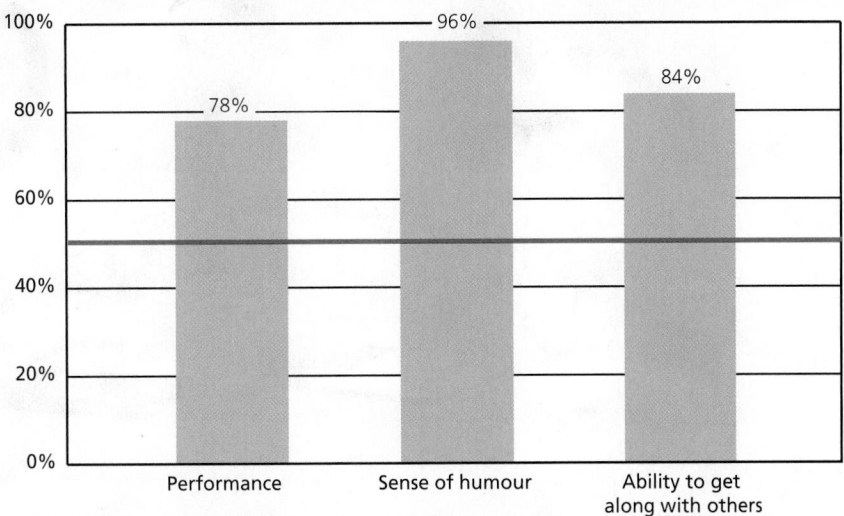

Source: Based on C. Merkle and M. Weber, *True Overconfidence—The Inability of Rational Information Processing to Account for Overconfidence* (March 2009). Available at SSRN: http://ssrn.com/abstract=1373675.

product line introduced by a competitor. A 2011 study suggests that this same error occurs when we judge leaders as charismatic, based on limited information.[6] For instance, Steve Jobs, Apple's co-founder, gave spellbinding presentations that led him to be considered a charismatic visionary. What the audience did not see were "the ten hours of practice Jobs [committed] to every ten minute pitch," without which he might have looked less charismatic.[7]

We use **self-serving bias** when we judge ourselves, however. This means that when we are successful, we are more likely to believe it was because of internal factors, such as ability or effort. When we fail, however, we blame external factors, such as luck. In general, people tend to believe that their own behaviour is more positive than the behaviour of those around them. Research suggests, however, that individuals tend to overestimate their own good behaviour, and underestimate the good behaviour of others.[8] Exhibit 2-3 illustrates this point.

Selective Perception

Because it's impossible for us to see everything, any characteristic that makes a person, object, or event stand out will increase the probability that it will be perceived. Thus you are more likely to notice cars that look like your own. It also explains why some people may be reprimanded by their manager for doing something that goes unnoticed when other employees do it. Since we cannot observe everything going on about us, we engage in **selective perception**.

How does selectivity work as a shortcut in judging other people? Since we cannot take in all that we observe, we take in bits and pieces. But we do not choose randomly; rather, we select according to our interests, background, experience, and attitudes. Selective perception allows us to speed-read others, but not without the risk of coming to an inaccurate conclusion. Because we see what we want to see, we can draw unwarranted conclusions from an ambiguous situation. Selective perception led the Law Society of BC to discriminate against lawyers who suffer from a mental illness, as *Focus on Diversity* shows.

self-serving bias The tendency for individuals to attribute their own successes to internal factors while putting the blame for failures on external factors.

selective perception People's selective interpretation of what they see based on their interests, background, experience, and attitudes.

Monkey Business Images/Shutterstock

The behaviours that both women and men engage in can affect the perceptions that others have about their ability to become senior managers. A recent study found that assertiveness and independence were top qualities to exhibit, and individuals who did not do so were deemed less suited to be CEOs.[9] Those judging the suitability were engaging in selective perception.

FOCUS ON DIVERSITY

Law Society's Question About Mental Health Challenged

Should employees be required to reveal that they have a mental illness? In July 2011, the BC Human Rights Tribunal ruled that the Law Society of BC had discriminated against a lawyer with a mental disability.[10] The lawyer, Peter Mokua Gichuru, was awarded almost $100 000 by the tribunal.

Gichuru's problems started when he began applying for work as an articling student and had to fill out a law society admission program form with the following question: "Have you ever been treated for schizophrenia, paranoia, or a mood disorder described as a major affective illness, bipolar mood disorder, or manic depressive illness?" He answered "yes."

Gichuru had been suffering from bouts of depression for almost five years and was on antidepressants when he was faced with the law society's question. He felt that his articles were delayed because he answered truthfully about his mental health. He also felt that his difficulties in keeping his articling positions and finding others were a result of his answer to the question.

In making its determination, the tribunal found that the law society, while acting in good faith, went beyond what was necessary to determine the fitness of someone to practise law. The law society changed the question related to mental health history on the admission form as a result of Gichuru's appeal. It now reads:

> Based upon your personal history, your current circumstances or any professional opinion or advice you have received, do you have any existing condition that is reasonably likely to impair your ability to function as a lawyer or articled student? If the answer is "yes" to the question above, please provide a general description of the impairment.

Those who answer "yes" to this new question are followed on a case-by-case basis, but the information is kept confidential and is not disclosed to potential employers. While Gichuru still has some concerns about the use of the information, he testified that it "is a dramatic improvement . . . and that on its face it does not discriminate between so-called physical and mental illnesses."

Halo Effect

When we draw a general impression of an individual on the basis of a single characteristic, such as intelligence, likeability, or appearance, a **halo effect** operates.[11] If you are a critic of Prime Minister Stephen Harper, try listing 10 things you admire about him. If you are an admirer, try listing 10 things you dislike about him. No matter which group describes you, odds are that you will not find this an easy exercise! That is the halo effect: Our general views contaminate our specific ones.

The reality of the halo effect was confirmed in a now classic study in which subjects were given a list of traits and asked to evaluate the person to whom those traits applied.[12] When trait terms such as *intelligent*, *skillful*, *practical*, *industrious*, *determined*, and *warm* were used, the person was judged to be wise, humorous, popular, and imaginative. When *cold* was substituted for *warm*, subjects had a completely different set of perceptions, although otherwise the list was identical. Clearly, the subjects were allowing a single trait to influence their overall impression of the person being judged.

Contrast Effects

There is an old saying among entertainers: "Never follow an act that has children or animals in it." Why? Audiences love children and animals so much that you will look bad in comparison.

This example demonstrates how **contrast effects** can distort perceptions. We don't evaluate a person in isolation. Our reaction to one person is often influenced by other people we have recently encountered.

In a series of job interviews, for instance, interviewers can make distortions in any given candidate's evaluation as a result of his or her place in the interview schedule. The candidate is likely to receive a more favourable evaluation if preceded by mediocre applicants, and a less favourable evaluation if preceded by strong applicants.

Projection

It's easy to judge others if we assume that they are similar to us. For instance, if you want challenge and responsibility in your job, you assume that others want the same. Or you are honest and trustworthy, so you take it for granted that other people are equally reliable. This tendency to attribute our own characteristics to other people is called **projection**.

Winnipeg Boyz – Charlie Fettah and John C. Photo by Thosh Collins

Aboriginal hip-hop artists, led by Winnipeg Boyz (pictured here), have created a coalition against the negative stereotyping of Indigenous rappers by the mainstream media. This initiative is an opportunity for Indigenous hip hop to define itself in a sustainable and healthy manner for the future. Aboriginal musician Jarrett Martineau says that hip hop is popular with Aboriginal youth because it deals with oppression and dispossession and because First Nations culture has a strong tradition of storytelling.[13]

halo effect Drawing a general impression of an individual on the basis of a single characteristic.

contrast effects The concept that our reaction to one person is often influenced by other people we have recently encountered.

projection Attributing one's own characteristics to other people.

People who engage in projection tend to perceive others according to what they themselves are like, rather than perceiving others as they really are. Because they always judge people as being similar to themselves, when they observe someone who is actually like them, their perceptions are naturally correct. But when they observe others who are not like them, their perceptions are not as accurate. Managers who engage in projection compromise their ability to respond to individual differences. They tend to see people as more homogeneous than they really are.

Stereotyping

When we judge someone on the basis of our perception of the group to which he or she belongs, we are using the shortcut called **stereotyping**.

We rely on generalizations every day because they help us make decisions quickly. They are a means of simplifying a complex world. It's less difficult to deal with an unmanageable number of stimuli if we use **heuristics** (judgment shortcuts in decision making) or stereotypes. For example, it does make sense to assume that Tre, the new employee from accounting, is going to know something about budgeting or that Allie from finance will be able to help you figure out a forecasting problem. The problem occurs, of course, when we generalize inaccurately or too much. In organizations, we frequently hear comments that represent stereotypes based on gender, age, race, religion, ethnicity, and even weight:[14] "Women will not relocate for a promotion," "men are not interested in child care," "older workers cannot learn new skills," "Asian immigrants are hard-working and conscientious," "overweight people lack discipline." Stereotypes can be so deeply ingrained and powerful that they influence life-and-death decisions. One study showed that, controlling for a wide array of factors (such as aggravating or mitigating circumstances), the degree to which black defendants in murder trials looked "stereotypically black" essentially doubled their odds of receiving a death sentence if convicted.[15]

One of the problems of stereotypes is that they *are* widespread and often useful generalizations, despite the fact that they may not contain a shred of truth when applied to a particular person or situation. So we constantly have to check ourselves to make sure we are not unfairly or inaccurately applying a stereotype in our evaluations and decisions. Stereotypes are an example of the warning, "The more useful, the more danger from misuse." Stereotypes can lead to strong negative reactions, such as prejudice, which we describe below.

michaeljung/Shutterstock

stereotyping Judging someone on the basis of one's perception of the group to which that person belongs.

heuristics Judgment shortcuts in decision making.

Muslim women in Canada often experience discrimination in being hired, or how their co-workers treat them, when they wear a hijab. In some cases, co-workers of Muslim women have been surprised when they returned to work following maternity leave. The co-workers assumed that Muslim women would be expected by their husbands to stay at home to raise children rather than work.

RESEARCH FINDINGS: Stereotyping

A variety of recent studies show that even today we believe Germans are better workers, Italians and African Americans are more loyal, Jews and Chinese are more intelligent, and Japanese and English are more courteous.[16] What is surprising is that positive stereotypes are not always positive.

Men are commonly believed to have stronger math abilities than women. One study shows that when this stereotype is activated before men take a math test, their performance on the test actually goes down. Another study found that the belief that white men are better at science and math than women or visible minorities caused white men to leave science, technology, engineering, and math majors. Finally, a study used basketball to illustrate the complexity of stereotypes. Researchers provided evidence to one group of undergraduates that whites were better free throw shooters than blacks. Another group was provided evidence that blacks were better free throw shooters than whites. A third group was given no stereotypical information. The undergraduates in all three groups then shot free throws while observers watched. The people who performed the worst were those in the negative stereotype condition (black undergraduates who were told whites were better and white undergraduates who were told blacks were better). However, the positive stereotype group (black undergraduates who were told blacks were better and white undergraduates who were told whites were better) also did not perform well. The best performance was turned in by those in the no stereotypical information group. In short, we are more likely to "choke" when we identify with positive stereotypes because they induce pressure to perform at the stereotypical level.

Prejudice **Prejudice** is the dislike of a person or group based on preconceived and unfounded opinions. For instance, an individual may dislike people of a particular religion or state that they do not want to work with someone of a particular ethnicity. Prejudice can lead to negative consequences in the workplace and, in particular, to discrimination. For instance, an individual of a particular ethnic group might be passed over for a management position because of the belief that employees might not see that person as a good manager. In another instance, an individual in his 50s who is looking for work but cannot find a job may be discriminated against because of the belief that younger workers are more appealing than older workers. Prejudice generally starts with stereotypes and then has negative emotional content added. Prejudice is harmful to the person who is the target of the behaviour. A 2011 study by researchers from the University of Toronto found that Asian women are more likely to take racism more personally than sexism and were more negatively affected by racism.[17]

Why Do Perception and Judgment Matter?

People in organizations are always judging one another. Managers must appraise their employees' performances. We evaluate how much effort our co-workers are putting into their jobs. When a new person joins a work team, the other members immediately "size her up." Individuals even make judgments about people's virtues based on whether they exercise, as a recent study by McMaster University professor Kathleen Martin Ginis showed.[18] In many cases, judgments have important consequences for the organization. A recent study found that in organizations that did not seem to value innovation, employees who wanted to see change were often afraid to speak out, due to fear of negative perceptions from co-workers who valued the status quo.[19] Another recent study found that positive employee perceptions of an organization have a positive impact on

> Can perception really affect outcomes?

prejudice The dislike of a person or group based on preconceived and unfounded opinions.

retention, customer loyalty, and financial outcomes.[20] A 2011 study noted that individuals who misperceive how well they have done on a task (positively or negatively) tended to prepare less and to perform poorly in subsequent tasks.[21]

Let's briefly look at a few of the most obvious applications of judgment shortcuts in the workplace: employment interviews, performance expectations, and performance evaluations.

Employment Interviews

It's fair to say that few people are hired without undergoing an interview. But interviewers make perceptual judgments that are often inaccurate[22] and draw early impressions that quickly become entrenched. Research shows we form impressions of others within a tenth of a second, based on our first glance.[23] A 2013 study indicates that our individual intuition about a job candidate is not reliable in predicting job performance, but that collecting input from multiple independent evaluators can be predictive.[24] Most interviewers' decisions change very little after the first four or five minutes of an interview. As a result, information that comes out early in the interview carries greater weight than information that comes out later, and a "good applicant" is probably characterized more by the absence of unfavourable characteristics than by the presence of favourable ones.

Performance Expectations

People attempt to validate their perceptions of reality even when they are faulty.[25] The terms **self-fulfilling prophecy** and *Pygmalion effect* describe how an individual's behaviour is determined by others' expectations. If a manager expects big things from her people, they are not likely to let her down. Similarly, if she expects only minimal performance, they will likely meet those low expectations. Expectations become reality. The self-fulfilling prophecy has been found to affect the performance of students, soldiers, and even accountants.[26]

Performance Evaluations

Performance evaluations very much depend on the perceptual process.[27] An employee's future is closely tied to the appraisal—promotion, pay raises, and continuation of employment are among the most obvious outcomes. Although the appraisal can be objective (for example, a salesperson is appraised on how many dollars of sales are generated in his territory), many jobs are evaluated subjectively. Subjective evaluations, although often necessary, are problematic because all the errors we have discussed thus far—selective perception, contrast effects, halo effect, and so on—affect them. Ironically, sometimes performance ratings say as much about the evaluator as they do about the employee!

As you can see, perception plays a large role in how people are evaluated. Personality, which we review next, is another major factor affecting how people relate to and evaluate one another in the workplace.

Personality

3 Describe personality, the way it is measured, and the factors that shape it.

Matthew Corrin, CEO of Freshii, is a risk-taker.[28] In 2005, he opened his first Lettuce Eatery restaurant in Toronto, with make-your-own salad offerings. Over several years, the number of Lettuce Eateries expanded. Then Corrin decided that he wanted to open up a similar style restaurant in Chicago, although he planned to expand the menu to include rice bowls and burritos. Lettuce Eateries was no longer a good name, because it did not represent the full menu selection available. So when he opened up his first restaurant in Chicago, he named it Freshii.

Being Freshii in the United States and Lettuce Eateries in Canada did not really make long-term sense to Corrin, as it caused confusion in branding. So overnight, he changed the name of the Canadian stores to Freshii as well, knowing he could easily lose customers who became confused by the name change. In the end it worked out for him, but it was a risky manoeuvre.

self-fulfilling prophecy A concept that proposes a person will behave in ways consistent with how he or she is perceived by others.

Corrin can take these risks because he is open to experiences, one of the Big Five personality traits that we discuss below. When a franchise manager brings Corrin new ideas for menu items, he lets the manager try them in his or her store. Corrin's view is to "launch fast, fail fast, iterate faster." He does not feel that ideas have to be right, but that it's important to test the ideas and learn from them. As he explains, "If it sells great, we'll scale it, and if it doesn't, then we'll take it away. But we've only done it in a very small testing environment." How do one's personality attributes influence OB?

Understanding the impact of individual personalities on OB is important. Why are some people quiet and passive, while others are loud and aggressive? Are certain personality types better adapted to certain job types? Before we can answer these questions, we need to address a more basic one: What is personality?

What Is Personality?

When we speak of someone's personality, we don't mean the person has charm or is constantly smiling. As organizational behaviourists, we are describing a dynamic concept of the growth and development of a person's personality.

Gordon Allport produced the most frequently used definition of *personality* more than 70 years ago. He said personality is "the dynamic organization within the individual of those psychophysical systems that determine his unique adjustments to his environment."[29] For our purposes, we define **personality** as the stable patterns of behaviour and consistent internal states that determine how an individual reacts to and interacts with others. It's most often described in terms of measurable traits that a person exhibits.

Measuring Personality

The most important reason managers need to know how to measure personality is that research has shown that personality tests are useful in hiring decisions. Scores on personality tests help managers forecast who is the best fit for a job.[30] The most common means of measuring personality is through self-report surveys, with which individuals evaluate themselves on a series of factors, such as "I worry a lot about the future." Although self-report measures work when well constructed, the respondent might lie to create a good impression. When people know that their personality scores are going to be used for hiring decisions, they rate themselves as about half a standard deviation more conscientious and emotionally stable than if they are taking the test just to learn more about themselves.[31] Another problem is accuracy: A candidate who is in a bad mood when taking the survey may have inaccurate scores.

Observer ratings provide an independent assessment of personality. Here, a co-worker or another observer does the rating (sometimes with the subject's knowledge and sometimes without). Although the results of self-reports and observer ratings are strongly correlated, research suggests that observer ratings are a better predictor of success on the job.[32] However, each can tell us something unique about an individual's behaviour in the workplace. An analysis of a large number of observer-reported personality studies shows that a combination of self-reports and observer-reports predicts performance better than any one type of information. The implication is clear: Use both observer ratings and self-report ratings of personality when making important employment decisions.

Personality Determinants

An early argument in personality research centred on whether an individual's personality is predetermined at birth or the result of the individual's environment. Clearly, there is no simple answer. Personality appears to be a result of both; however, research tends to support the importance of heredity over the environment. In addition, today we recognize a third factor—the situation. Thus, an adult's personality is now generally

Watch on **MyManagementLab**

CH2MHill: Ability and Personality

personality The stable patterns of behaviour and consistent internal states that determine how an individual reacts to and interacts with others.

considered to be made up of both hereditary and environmental factors, moderated by situational conditions.

Heredity refers to those factors that were determined at conception. Physical stature, facial attractiveness, gender, temperament, muscle composition and reflexes, energy level, and biological rhythms are characteristics that are generally considered to be either completely or substantially influenced by your biological parents' biological, physiological, and inherent psychological makeup. The heredity approach argues that the ultimate explanation of an individual's personality is a person's genes.

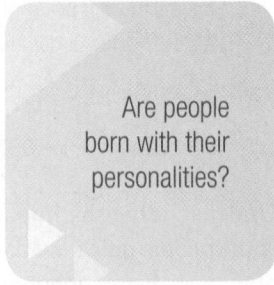

Are people born with their personalities?

Researchers in many different countries have studied thousands of sets of identical twins who were separated at birth and raised apart.[33] If heredity played little or no part in determining personality, you would expect to find few similarities between separated twins. Researchers have found, however, that genetics accounts for about 50 percent of the personality similarities between twins and more than 30 percent of the similarities in occupational and leisure interests. One set of twins, who had been separated for 39 years and raised 70 kilometres apart, were found to drive the same model and colour car, chain-smoke the same brand of cigarette, own dogs with the same name, and regularly vacation within three blocks of each other in a beach community 2000 kilometres away. Several 2014 studies confirmed these results. Identical twins were much more likely to have similar drawing abilities than fraternal twins.[34] A related study found that the correlation between literacy and mathematical ability was genetically linked.[35]

Interestingly, twin studies have suggested that parents don't add much to our personality development. The personalities of identical twins raised in different households are more similar to each other than to the personalities of siblings with whom the twins were raised. Ironically, the most important contribution our biological parents may make to our personalities is giving us their genes.

Does personality change over one's lifetime? Most research in this area suggests that while some aspects of our personalities do change over time, the rank orderings do not change very much. For example, people's scores on measures of conscientiousness tend to increase as they get older. However, there are still strong individual differences in conscientiousness, and despite the fact that most of us become more responsible over time, people tend to change by about the same amount, so that the rank order stays roughly the same.[36] For instance, if you are more conscientious than your sibling now, that is likely to be true in 20 years, even though you both should become more conscientious over time. Consistent with the notion that the teenage years are periods of great exploration and change, research has shown that personality is more changeable in adolescence and more stable among adults.[37]

Personality Traits

◄●┤Simulate on MyManagementLab

Individual Behaviour

The early work in the structure of personality revolved around attempts to identify and label enduring characteristics that describe an individual's behaviour. Popular characteristics include shy, aggressive, submissive, lazy, ambitious, loyal, and timid. Those characteristics, when they are exhibited in a large number of situations, are called **personality traits**.[38] The more consistent the characteristic and the more frequently it occurs in diverse situations, the more important that trait is in describing the individual.

A number of early research efforts tried to identify the *primary* traits that govern behaviour.[39] However, for the most part, they resulted in long lists of traits that were difficult to generalize from and provided little practical guidance to organizational decision makers. Two exceptions are the Myers-Briggs Type Indicator and the Big Five Personality Model, the dominant frameworks for identifying and classifying personality traits.

personality traits Enduring characteristics that describe an individual's behaviour.

Keep in mind that each of us reacts differently to personality traits. This is partially a function of how we perceive those traits.

The Myers-Briggs Type Indicator

The **Myers-Briggs Type Indicator (MBTI)** is the most widely used personality-assessment instrument in the world.[40] It's a 100-question personality test that asks people how they usually feel or act in particular situations. On the basis of their answers, individuals are classified as extraverted or introverted (E or I), sensing or intuitive (S or N), thinking or feeling (T or F), and judging or perceiving (J or P). These terms are defined as follows:

- *Extraverted/introverted.* Extraverted individuals are outgoing, sociable, and assertive. Introverts are quiet and shy. E/I measures where we direct our energy when dealing with people and things.

- *Sensing/intuitive.* Sensing types are practical and prefer routine and order. They focus on details. Intuitives rely on unconscious processes and look at the "big picture." This dimension looks at how we process information.

- *Thinking/feeling.* Thinking types use reason and logic to handle problems. Feeling types rely on their personal values and emotions.

- *Judging/perceiving.* Judging types want control and prefer their world to be ordered and structured. Perceiving types are flexible and spontaneous.

These classifications together describe 16 personality types. To illustrate, let's look at three examples:

- *INTJs are visionaries.* They usually have original minds and great drive for their own ideas and purposes. They are skeptical, critical, independent, determined, and often stubborn.

- *ESTJs are organizers.* They are realistic, logical, analytical, decisive, and have a natural head for business or mechanics. They like to organize and run activities.

- *ENTPs are conceptualizers.* They are innovative, individualistic, versatile, and attracted to entrepreneurial ideas. They tend to be resourceful in solving challenging problems, but may neglect routine assignments.

The MBTI has been widely used by organizations including Apple, AT&T, Citigroup, GE, 3M, many hospitals and educational institutions, and even the US Armed Forces. Evidence is mixed as to whether the MBTI is a valid measure of personality, however much of the evidence is against it.[41] One problem is that the model forces a person into either one type or another (that is, you are either introverted or extraverted). There is no in-between, although people can be both extraverted and introverted to some degree. The best we can say is that the MBTI can be a valuable tool for increasing self-awareness and providing career guidance. But because results tend to be unrelated to job performance, managers probably should not use it as a selection test for job candidates.

The Big Five Personality Model

The MBTI may lack valid supporting evidence, but an impressive body of research supports the **Big Five Personality Model**. The model proposes that five basic personality dimensions underlie all others and encompass most of the significant variation in human personality.[42] Test scores of these traits do a very good job of predicting how people behave in a variety of real-life situations.[43] The Big Five personality traits are as follows:

- **Extraversion**. This dimension captures a person's comfort level with relationships. Extraverts tend to be gregarious, assertive, and sociable. Introverts tend to be reserved, timid, and quiet.

4 Describe the Myers-Briggs Type Indicator personality framework and its strengths and weaknesses.

5 Identify the key traits in the Big Five Personality Model.

Myers-Briggs Type Indicator (MBTI) A personality test that taps four characteristics and classifies people into 1 of 16 personality types.

Big Five Personality Model A personality assessment model that taps five basic dimensions.

extraversion A personality factor that describes the degree to which a person is sociable, talkative, and assertive.

- **Agreeableness**. This dimension refers to a person's propensity to defer to others. Highly agreeable people are cooperative, warm, and trusting. People who score low on agreeableness are cold, disagreeable, and antagonistic.

- **Conscientiousness**. This dimension is a measure of reliability. A highly conscientious person is responsible, organized, dependable, and persistent. Those who score low on this dimension are easily distracted, disorganized, and unreliable.

- **Emotional stability**. This dimension—often labelled by its converse, *neuroticism*—taps into a person's ability to withstand stress. People with positive emotional stability tend to be calm, self-confident, and secure. Those with high negative scores tend to be nervous, anxious, depressed, and insecure.

- **Openness to experience**. The final dimension addresses a person's range of interests and fascination with novelty. Extremely open people are creative, curious, and artistically sensitive. Those at the other end of the openness category are conventional and find comfort in the familiar.

Researchers at the University of Toronto have recently created a "fake proof" personality test to measure the Big Five personality traits.[44] Professor Jordan Peterson, one of the researchers, noted that it is common for people to try to "make themselves look better than they actually are on these questionnaires. . . . This sort of faking can distort the predictive validity of these tests, with significant negative economic consequences. We wanted to develop a measure that could predict real-world performance even in the absence of completely honest responding."[45]

Exhibit 2-4 shows the characteristics for the high and low dimensions of each Big Five personality trait.

agreeableness A personality factor that describes the degree to which a person is good-natured, cooperative, and trusting.

conscientiousness A personality factor that describes the degree to which a person is responsible, dependable, persistent, and achievement-oriented.

emotional stability A personality dimension that characterizes someone as calm, self-confident, and secure (positive) vs. nervous, depressed, and insecure (negative).

openness to experience A personality factor that describes the degree to which a person is imaginative, artistically sensitive, and curious.

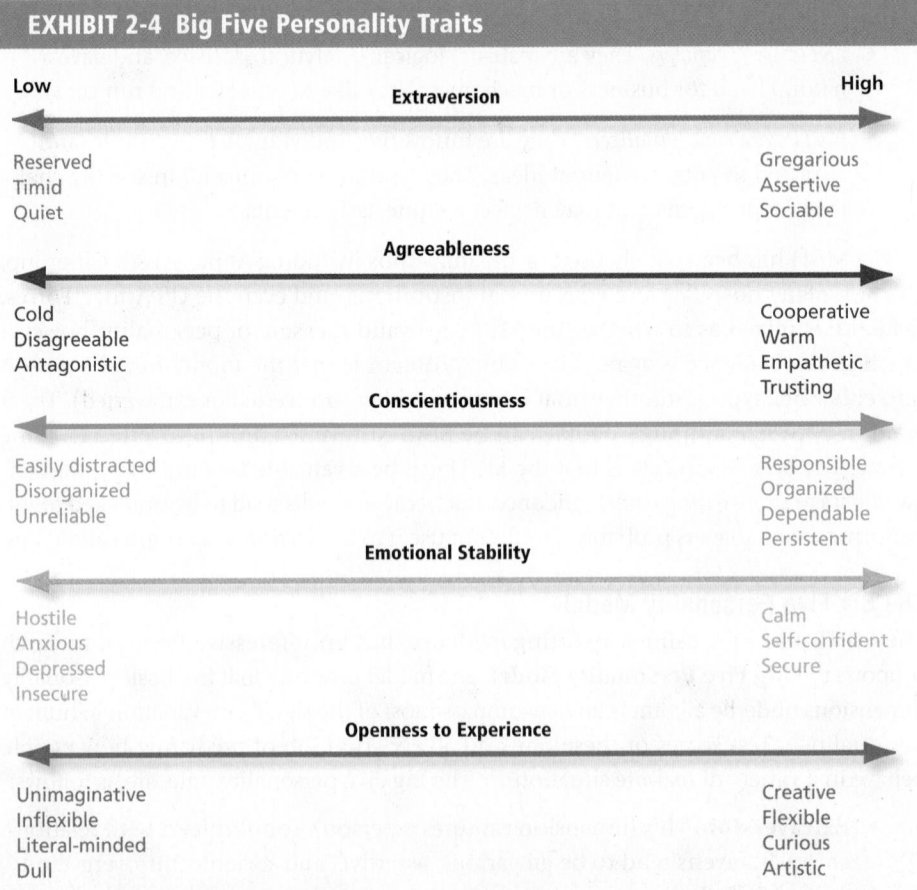

EXHIBIT 2-4 Big Five Personality Traits

Low	Extraversion	High
Reserved Timid Quiet		Gregarious Assertive Sociable

	Agreeableness	
Cold Disagreeable Antagonistic		Cooperative Warm Empathetic Trusting

	Conscientiousness	
Easily distracted Disorganized Unreliable		Responsible Organized Dependable Persistent

	Emotional Stability	
Hostile Anxious Depressed Insecure		Calm Self-confident Secure

	Openness to Experience	
Unimaginative Inflexible Literal-minded Dull		Creative Flexible Curious Artistic

RESEARCH **FINDINGS:** The Big Five

Research on the Big Five has found a relationship between the personality dimensions and job performance.[46] As the authors of the most-cited review observed, "The preponderance of evidence shows that individuals who are dependable, reliable, careful, thorough, able to plan, organized, hardworking, persistent, and achievement-oriented tend to have higher job performance in most if not all occupations."[47] Employees who are more conscientious provide better service.[48] Employees who score higher in conscientiousness develop higher levels of job knowledge, probably because highly conscientious people learn more (a review of 138 studies revealed that conscientiousness was related to grade point average).[49] Higher levels of job knowledge then contribute to higher levels of job performance.[50] Conscientious individuals who are more interested in learning than in just performing on the job are also exceptionally good at maintaining performance in the face of negative feedback.[51] There can be "too much of a good thing," however, as extremely conscientious individuals typically do not perform better than those who are simply above average in conscientiousness.[52]

Interestingly, conscientious people live longer; they take better care of themselves and engage in fewer risky behaviours such as smoking, drinking, drugs, and risky sexual or driving behaviour.[53] They don't adapt as well to changing contexts, however. They are generally performance oriented and may have trouble learning complex skills early in the training process because their focus is on performing well rather than on learning. Finally, they are often less creative than less conscientious people, especially artistically.[54]

The Big Five have also been found to be related to characteristics needed for specific jobs. This is illustrated in Exhibit 2-5.

Although conscientiousness is the trait most consistently related to job performance, the other Big Five personality traits also have some bearing. Let's look at the implications of these traits, one at a time. (Exhibit 2-6 summarizes the discussion.)

Emotional stability. People who score high on emotional stability are happier than those who score low. Of the Big Five personality traits, emotional stability is most strongly related to life satisfaction, job satisfaction, and low stress levels. This is probably true because high scorers are more likely to be positive and optimistic in their

6 Demonstrate how the Big Five personality traits predict behaviour at work.

EXHIBIT 2-5 Jobs in Which Certain Big Five Personality Traits Are More Relevant

Detail Orientation Required	Social Skills Required	Competitive Work	Innovation Required	Dealing with Angry People	Time Pressure (Deadlines)
Jobs scoring high (the traits listed below should predict behaviour in these jobs)					
Air traffic controller	Clergy	Coach/scout	Actor	Correctional officer	Broadcast news analyst
Accountant	Therapist	Financial manager	Systems analyst	Telemarketer	Editor
Legal secretary	Concierge	Sales representative	Advertising writer	Flight attendant	Airline pilot
Jobs that score high make these traits more relevant to predicting behaviour					
Conscientiousness (+)	Extraversion (+) Agreeableness (+)	Extraversion (+) Agreeableness (−)	Openness (+)	Extraversion (+) Agreeableness (+) Neuroticism (−)	Conscientiousness (+) Neuroticism (−)

Note: A plus (+) sign means individuals who score high on this trait should do better in this job. A minus (−) sign means individuals who score low on this trait should do better in this job.

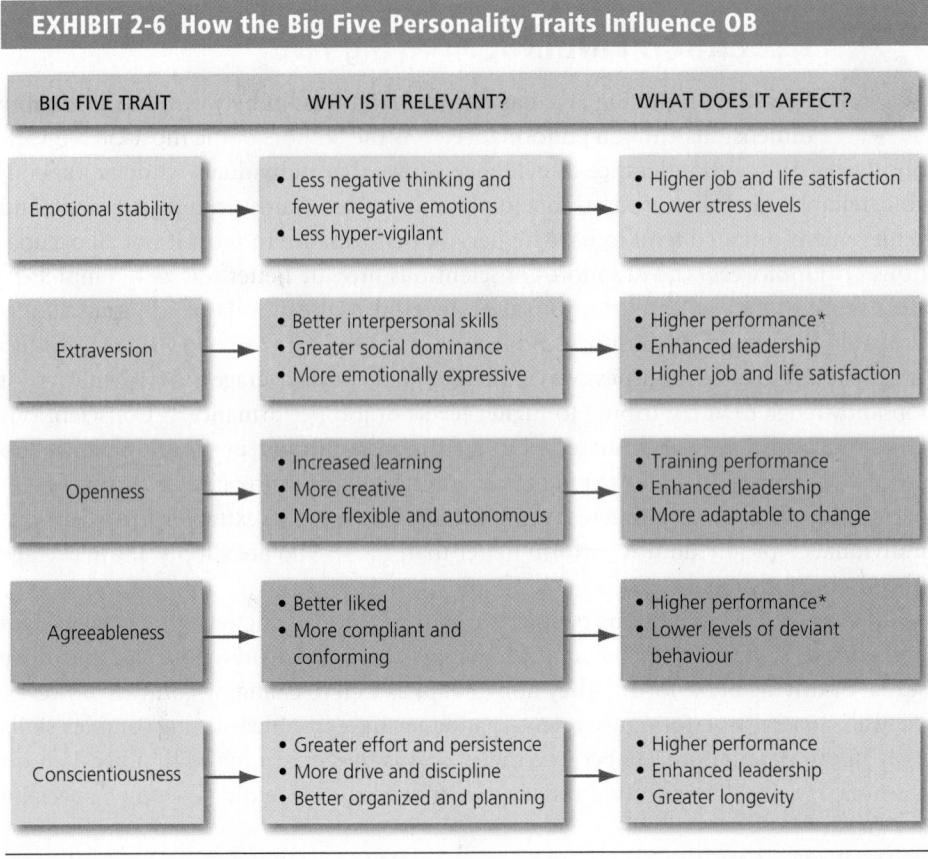

EXHIBIT 2-6 How the Big Five Personality Traits Influence OB

BIG FIVE TRAIT	WHY IS IT RELEVANT?	WHAT DOES IT AFFECT?
Emotional stability	• Less negative thinking and fewer negative emotions • Less hyper-vigilant	• Higher job and life satisfaction • Lower stress levels
Extraversion	• Better interpersonal skills • Greater social dominance • More emotionally expressive	• Higher performance* • Enhanced leadership • Higher job and life satisfaction
Openness	• Increased learning • More creative • More flexible and autonomous	• Training performance • Enhanced leadership • More adaptable to change
Agreeableness	• Better liked • More compliant and conforming	• Higher performance* • Lower levels of deviant behaviour
Conscientiousness	• Greater effort and persistence • More drive and discipline • Better organized and planning	• Higher performance • Enhanced leadership • Greater longevity

*In jobs requiring significant teamwork or frequent interpersonal interactions.

thinking and experience fewer negative emotions. People low on emotional stability are hyper-vigilant (looking for problems or impending signs of danger) and are especially vulnerable to the physical and psychological effects of stress.

Extraversion. Extraverts tend to be happier in their jobs and in their lives as a whole. They experience more positive emotions than do introverts, and they more freely express these feelings. They also tend to perform better in jobs that require significant interpersonal interaction, perhaps because they have more social skills—they usually have more friends and spend more time in social situations than introverts. Finally, extraversion is a relatively strong predictor of leadership emergence in groups; extraverts are more socially dominant, "take charge" sorts of people, and they are generally more assertive than introverts.[55] Extraverts are more impulsive than introverts; they are more likely to be absent from work and engage in risky behaviour such as unprotected sex, drinking, and other impulsive or sensation-seeking acts.[56] One study also found that extraverts were more likely than introverts to lie during job interviews.[57]

Openness to experience. Individuals who score high on openness to experience are more creative in science and in art than those who score low. Because creativity is important to leadership, open people are more likely to be effective leaders. They are also more comfortable with ambiguity and change than are those who score lower on this trait. As a result, open people cope better with organizational change and are more adaptable in changing contexts.[58] Recent evidence also suggests, however, that they are especially susceptible to workplace accidents.[59]

Agreeableness. You might expect agreeable people to be happier than disagreeable people, and they are, but only slightly. When people choose romantic partners, friends, or organizational team members, agreeable individuals are usually their first choice.

Learn About Yourself
Tolerance of Ambiguity Scale

It's unusual for two people to share the CEO role, but Ronnen Harary (left) and Anton Rabie (right), co-CEOs of Toronto-based toy company Spin Master (pictured with executive vice-president Ben Varadi), like the arrangement. Rabie is an extravert, while Harary is an introvert. The childhood friends feel their personalities complement each other, making an ideal management team.

Thus, agreeable individuals are better liked than disagreeable people, which explains why they tend to do better in interpersonally oriented jobs such as customer service. They are also more compliant and rule abiding and less likely to get into accidents and more satisfied in their jobs. They contribute to organizational performance by engaging in citizenship behaviour[60] and are less likely to engage in organizational deviance. Agreeableness is associated with lower levels of career success (especially earnings). For an interesting look at the upside and downside of agreeableness in the workplace, read *Case Incident—On the Costs of Being Nice* on page 74.

The Dark Triad

With the exception of neuroticism, the Big Five personality traits are what we call socially desirable, meaning that we would be glad to score high on them. Researchers have found that three other socially *undesirable* traits, which we all have in varying degrees, are relevant to organizational behaviour: Machiavellianism, narcissism, and psychopathy. Owing to their negative nature, researchers have labelled these three traits the **Dark Triad**—although, of course, they do not always occur together.[61]

Machiavellianism

Hao is a young bank manager in Shanghai. He has received three promotions in the past four years and makes no apologies for the aggressive tactics he has used to propel his career upward. "My name means clever, and that's what I am—I do whatever I have to do to get ahead," he says. Hao would be termed Machiavellian.

The personality characteristic of **Machiavellianism** (often abbreviated to *Mach*) is named after Niccolò Machiavelli, who wrote in the sixteenth century on how to gain and use power. An individual high in Machiavellianism is pragmatic, maintains emotional distance, and believes that ends can justify means. "If it works, use it" is consistent with a high-Mach perspective. A considerable amount of research has found that high Machs manipulate more, win more, are persuaded less, and persuade others

Dark Triad A group of negative personality traits consisting of Machiavellianism, narcissism, and psychopathy.

Machiavellianism The degree to which an individual is pragmatic, maintains emotional distance, and believes that ends can justify means.

more than do low Machs.[62] They are more likely to act aggressively and engage in other counterproductive work behaviours as well. A 2012 review of the literature revealed that Machiavellianism does not significantly predict overall job performance.[63] High-Mach employees, by manipulating others to their advantage, win in the short term, but they lose those gains in the long term because they are not well-liked.

The effects of Machiavellianism depend somewhat on the context. The reason, in part, is that individuals' personalities affect the situations they choose. One 2012 study showed that high-Mach job seekers were not positively affected by knowing that a potential employer engaged in a high level of corporate social responsibility (CSR).[64] Another 2012 study found that Machs' ethical leadership behaviours were less likely to translate into followers' work engagement because followers "see through" these behaviours and realize it is a case of surface acting.[65]

Narcissism

Sabrina likes to be the centre of attention. She often looks at herself in the mirror, has extravagant dreams, and considers herself a person of many talents. Sabrina is a narcissist. The trait is named for the Greek myth of Narcissus, a youth so vain and proud he fell in love with his own image. In psychology, **narcissism** describes a person who has a grandiose sense of self-importance, requires excessive admiration, has a sense of entitlement, and is arrogant. Evidence suggests that narcissists are more charismatic than others.[66] Both leaders and managers tend to score higher on narcissism, suggesting that a certain self-centredness is needed to succeed. Narcissists also reported higher levels of work motivation, job engagement, and life satisfaction than others. A 2012 study of Norwegian bank employees found that those scoring high on narcissism enjoyed their work more.[67] Some evidence suggests that narcissists are more adaptable and make better business decisions than others when the decision is complex.[68]

While narcissism seems to have little relationship with job performance, it is fairly strongly related to increased counterproductive work behaviours and is linked to other negative outcomes. A study found that while narcissists thought they were *better* leaders than their colleagues, their supervisors rated them as *worse*. In highly ethical contexts, narcissistic leaders are likely to be perceived as ineffective and unethical.[69]

Special attention has been paid to the narcissism of CEOs. An Oracle executive described that company's CEO Larry Ellison as follows: "The difference between God and Larry is that God does not believe he is Larry."[70] A study of narcissistic CEOs revealed that they make more acquisitions, pay higher premiums for those acquisitions, respond less clearly to objective measures of performance, and respond to media praise by making even more acquisitions.[71] Research using data compiled over 100 years has shown that narcissistic CEOs of baseball organizations generate higher levels of manager turnover, although members of external organizations see them as more influential.[72]

Narcissism and its effects are not confined to CEOs or celebrities. Narcissists are more likely to post self-promoting material on their Facebook pages.[73] Like the effects of Machiavellianism, those of narcissism vary by context. A study of Swiss Air Force officers found that narcissists were particularly likely to be irritated by feeling under-benefited, meaning that when narcissists don't get what they want, they are more stressed by that than others.[74]

Does business school reinforce narcissism in the classroom? The results of a 2012 study that compared the level of narcissism in Millennial business and psychology students appear in Exhibit 2-7. The *Point/Counterpoint* on page 72 considers whether Millennials are more narcissistic than other generations.

Psychopathy

Psychopathy is part of the Dark Triad, but in OB, it does not connote insanity. In the OB context, **psychopathy** is defined as a lack of concern for others and a lack of guilt or remorse when one's actions cause harm.[75] Measures of psychopathy attempt to assess

narcissism The tendency to be arrogant, have a grandiose sense of self-importance, require excessive admiration, and have a sense of entitlement.

psychopathy The tendency for a lack of concern for others and a lack of guilt or remorse when one's actions cause harm.

EXHIBIT 2-7 Does Business School Make You Narcissistic?

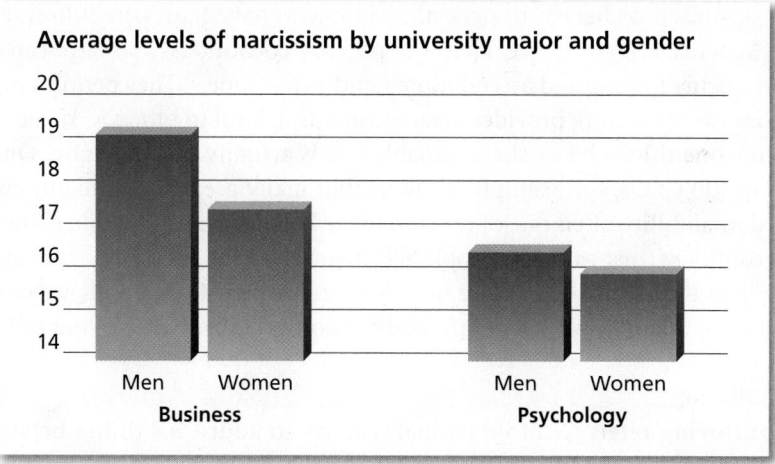

Average levels of narcissism by university major and gender

Source: Based on J. W. Westerman, J. Z. Bergman, S. M. Bergman, and J. P. Daly, "Are Universities Creating Millennial Narcissistic Employees? An Empirical Examination of Narcissism in Business Students and Its Implications," *Journal of Management Education* 36 (2012), pp. 5–32.

the person's motivation to comply with social norms; willingness to use deceit to obtain desired ends and the effectiveness of those efforts; impulsivity; and disregard, that is, lack of empathetic concern, for others.

The literature is not consistent about whether psychopathy or other aberrant personality traits are important to work behaviour. One review found little correlation between measures of psychopathy and job performance or counterproductive work behaviours.[76] A 2013 study found that antisocial personality, which is closely related to psychopathy, was positively related to advancement in the organization but unrelated to other aspects of career success and effectiveness.[77] Still other recent research suggests that psychopathy is related to the use of hard influence tactics (threats, manipulation) and bullying work behaviour (physical or verbal threatening).[78] The cunning displayed by people who score high on psychopathy may thus help them gain power in an organization but keep them from using that power toward healthy ends for themselves or their organizations.

Other Personality Attributes That Influence OB

The Big Five personality traits have proven highly relevant to OB, and the Dark Triad promises to be the subject of much future research, but they don't exhaust the range of traits that can describe someone's personality. Now we will look at other, more specific attributes that are powerful predictors of behaviour in organizations: core self-evaluation, self-monitoring, and proactive personality. We briefly introduce these attributes and summarize what we know about their ability to explain and predict employee behaviour.

Core Self-Evaluation

People who have positive **core self-evaluations** like themselves and see themselves as effective, capable, and in control of their environment. Those with negative core self-evaluations tend to dislike themselves, question their capabilities, and view themselves as powerless over their environment.[79]

People with positive core self-evaluations perform better than others because they set more ambitious goals, are more committed to their goals, and persist longer at attempting to reach these goals. For example, one study of life-insurance agents found that core self-evaluations were critical predictors of performance. In fact, this study

core self-evaluation The degree to which an individual likes or dislikes himself or herself, whether the person sees himself or herself as capable and effective, and whether the person feels in control of his or her environment or powerless over the environment.

showed the majority of successful salespersons did have positive core self-evaluations.[80] In life-insurance sales, 90 percent of sales calls end in rejection, so an agent has to believe in himself or herself to persist. People who have high core self-evaluations provide better customer service, are more popular co-workers, and have careers that begin on a better footing and ascend more rapidly over time.[81] They perform especially well if they feel their work provides meaning and is helpful to others.[82] What happens when someone thinks he or she is capable but is actually incompetent? One study of *Fortune* 500 CEOs, for example, showed that many are overconfident, and their perceived infallibility often causes them to make bad decisions.[83] While many people are overconfident, just as many people sell themselves short and are less happy and effective than they could be because of lack of confidence. If we decide we cannot do something, for example, we will not try, and not doing it only reinforces our self-doubts.

Learn About Yourself
Core Self-Evaluation Scale

Self-Monitoring

Self-monitoring refers to an individual's ability to adjust his or her behaviour to external, situational factors.[84] High self-monitors show considerable adaptability in adjusting their behaviour to external situational factors. They are highly sensitive to external cues and can behave differently in varying situations, sometimes presenting striking contradictions between their public personae and their private selves. Low self-monitors cannot disguise themselves in the same way. They tend to display their true dispositions and attitudes in every situation. High behavioural consistency exists between who they are and what they do.

Learn About Yourself
Self-Awareness Assessment

Research suggests that high self-monitors tend to pay closer attention to the behaviour of others and are more capable of conforming than are low self-monitors.[85] High self-monitoring managers tend to be more mobile in their careers and receive more promotions (both internal and cross-organizational) and are more likely to occupy central positions in an organization.[86] High self-monitors also receive better performance ratings, are more likely to emerge as leaders, and show less commitment to their organizations.[87]

According to research, we can accurately judge others' personalities a few seconds after meeting them, as *Focus on Research* shows.

FOCUS ON RESEARCH

First Impressions Count

How accurate are first impressions of people's personalities? Research indicates that individuals can accurately appraise others' personalities only a few seconds after first meeting them.[88] This "zero acquaintance" approach shows that regardless of the way in which people first meet someone, whether in person or online, their first judgments about the other's personality have validity. In one study, for example, individuals were asked to introduce themselves, on average, in 7.4 seconds. Observers' ratings of those individuals' extraversion were significantly correlated with the individuals' self-reported extraversion.

While some factors make these first impressions, or "thin slices," more accurate, they have only a modest effect. For example, some traits like extraversion are easier to perceive than others upon initial acquaintance, but less obvious traits like self-esteem and emotional stability are also often judged fairly accurately by others. Even being forced to make intuitive, quick judgments rather than deliberate evaluations does not seem to undermine the accuracy of the appraisals.

The moderate accuracy of "thin slices" helps explain the moderate validity of employment interviews. Specifically, research shows that interviewers make up their minds about candidates within two minutes of first meeting them. While this is hardly an ideal way to make important employment decisions, the research on personality also shows that these judgments do have some level of validity.

self-monitoring A personality trait that measures an individual's ability to adjust behaviour to external, situational factors.

Proactive Personality

Did you ever notice that some people actively take the initiative to improve their current circumstances or create new ones? These people have a **proactive personality**.[89] People with a proactive personality identify opportunities, show initiative, take action, and persevere until meaningful change occurs. Not surprisingly, proactives have many behaviours that organizations desire. They also have higher levels of job performance and career success.[90]

Other actions of proactives can be positive or negative, depending on the organization and the situation. Proactives are more likely to challenge the status quo or voice their displeasure when situations are not to their liking.[91] If an organization requires people with entrepreneurial initiative, proactives make good candidates; however, they are also more likely to leave an organization to start their own business.[92] As individuals, proactives are more likely to achieve career success.[93] They select, create, and influence work situations in their favour. Proactives are more likely to seek out job and organizational information, develop contacts in high places, engage in career planning, and demonstrate persistence in the face of career obstacles.

Emotions

Matthew Corrin, CEO of Freshii, had to learn to manage his emotions when he first started to build his business.[94] He says of his early days in running the business "I fell in love too fast. And I'd make hiring decisions that ultimately didn't last more than 12 months, and that's expensive." He learned that he had to take more time to make the right hiring decisions and not rely on his first impression of "love." To make sure he can trust his emotions before having someone work for his company, Corrin often provides a probationary period, even for senior partners, to get to know them better.

Another way that Corrin manages his emotions is by knowing when to pick his battles. As he explains, "sometimes you need to know when to roll over and just sort of roll with it. And sometimes you need to know when to fight back and be aggressive, whether it's negotiating a lease, or a new contract, or doing something with an employee." Can managing one's emotions really help make for a better workplace?

Each of us has a range of personality characteristics, but we also bring with us a range of emotions. Given the obvious role that emotions play in our everyday life, it might surprise you to learn that, until very recently, the topic of emotions was given little or no attention within the field of OB.[95] Why? We offer two possible explanations.

First is the *myth of rationality*.[96] Until very recently, the protocol of the work world kept a damper on emotions. A well-run organization did not allow employees to express frustration, fear, anger, love, hate, joy, grief, or similar feelings thought to be the antithesis of rationality. Although researchers and managers knew emotions were an inseparable part of everyday life, they tried to create organizations that were emotion-free. Of course, that was not possible.

The second explanation is that many believed emotions of any kind were disruptive.[97] Researchers looked at strong negative emotions—especially anger—that interfered with an employee's ability to work effectively. They rarely viewed emotions as constructive or contributing to enhanced performance.

Certainly some emotions, particularly when exhibited at the wrong time, can reduce employee performance. But employees do bring their emotions to work every day, and no study of OB would be complete without considering their role in workplace behaviour.

proactive personality A person who identifies opportunities, shows initiative, takes action, and perseveres until meaningful change occurs.

What Are Emotions and Moods?

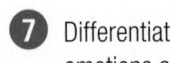 **7** Differentiate between emotions and moods.

Let's look at three terms that are closely intertwined: *affect, emotions,* and *moods.* **Affect** is a generic term that covers a broad range of feelings people experience, including both emotions and moods.[98] **Emotions** are intense feelings that are directed at someone or something.[99] **Moods** are less intense feelings than emotions and often (although not always) arise without a specific event acting as a stimulus.[100]

Most experts believe emotions are more fleeting than moods.[101] For example, if someone is rude to you, you would likely feel angry. That intense emotion probably comes and goes fairly quickly, maybe even in a matter of seconds. When you are in a bad mood, however, you can feel bad for several hours.

Emotions are reactions to a person (seeing a friend at work may make you feel glad) or an event (dealing with a rude client may make you feel frustrated). You show your emotions when you are "happy about something, angry at someone, afraid of something."[102] Moods, in contrast, are not usually directed at a person or an event. But emotions can turn into moods when you lose focus on the event or object that started the feeling. And, by the same token, good or bad moods can make you more emotional in response to an event. So when a colleague criticizes how you spoke to a client, you might show emotion (anger) toward a specific object (your colleague). But as the specific emotion starts to go away, you might just feel generally dispirited. You cannot attribute this feeling to any single event; you are just not your normal self. You might then overreact to other events. This affect state describes a mood. Exhibit 2-8 shows the relationships among affect, emotions, and moods.

First, as the exhibit shows, *affect* is a broad term that encompasses emotions and moods. Second, there are differences between emotions and moods. Some of these differences—that emotions are more likely to be caused by a specific event, and emotions are more fleeting than moods—we just discussed. Other differences are subtler. For example, unlike moods, emotions such as anger and disgust tend to be more clearly revealed by facial expressions. Also, some researchers speculate that emotions may be more action oriented—they may lead us to some immediate action—while moods may be more cognitive, meaning that they may cause us to think or brood for a while.[103]

Finally, the exhibit shows that emotions and moods are closely connected and can influence each other. Getting your dream job may generate the emotion of joy, which can put you in a good mood for several days. Similarly, if you are in a good or bad mood, it might make you experience a more intense positive or negative emotion than

affect A broad range of feelings that people experience.

emotions Intense feelings that are directed at someone or something.

moods Feelings that tend to be less intense than emotions and that lack a contextual stimulus.

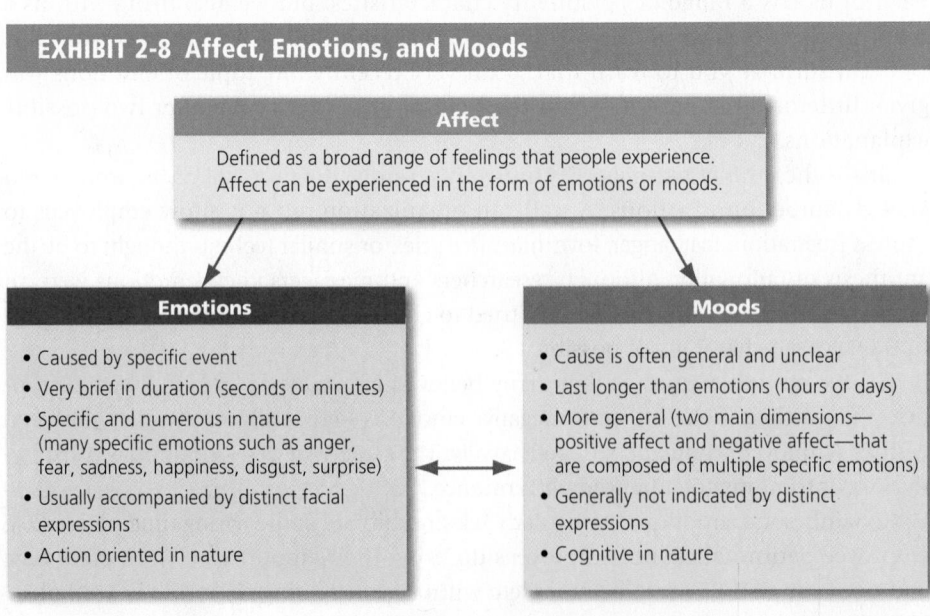

EXHIBIT 2-8 Affect, Emotions, and Moods

Affect

Defined as a broad range of feelings that people experience. Affect can be experienced in the form of emotions or moods.

Emotions	**Moods**
• Caused by specific event	• Cause is often general and unclear
• Very brief in duration (seconds or minutes)	• Last longer than emotions (hours or days)
• Specific and numerous in nature (many specific emotions such as anger, fear, sadness, happiness, disgust, surprise)	• More general (two main dimensions—positive affect and negative affect—that are composed of multiple specific emotions)
• Usually accompanied by distinct facial expressions	• Generally not indicated by distinct expressions
• Action oriented in nature	• Cognitive in nature

otherwise. In a bad mood, you might blow up in response to a co-worker's comment that would normally have generated only a mild reaction.

Affect, emotions, and moods are separable in theory; in practice the distinction is not always crystal clear. In some areas, researchers have studied mostly moods, in other areas mainly emotions. So, when we review the OB topics on emotions and moods, you may see more information about emotions in one area and about moods in another. This is simply the state of the research. *OB in the Street* discusses how our perception of emotions can affect our romantic relationships.

OB IN THE **STREET**
How Perception Causes Fights in Relationships

What happens if you think your partner is neglecting you?   A 2011 study found that how people perceive the emotions of their romantic partner during a conflict affected their overall view of and reactions to the conflict.[104] The researchers studied the arguments that 105 university students had during an eight-week period. They looked at two types of emotions: "hard" (asserting power) and "soft" (expressing vulnerability). They also looked at two types of perceptions: "perceived threat" (perception that the partner is being hostile, critical, blaming, or controlling) and "perceived neglect" (perception that the partner does not seem committed to or invested in the relationship).

The researchers found that when a person sees his or her partner react with hard emotion, that person perceives a threat to control, power, and status in the relationship. When a person sees his or her partner show little emotion, or less soft emotion than desired, that person perceives partner neglect. The perceived threat and neglect increase the person's own hard and soft emotions.

One of the study's co-authors explained the results as follows: "[W]hat you perceive your partner to be feeling influences different types of thoughts, feelings and reactions in yourself, whether what you perceive is actually correct. . . . If a person perceives the other as angry, they will perceive a threat so they will respond with a hard emotion like anger or blame. Likewise, if a person is perceived to be sad or vulnerable, they will perceive a neglect and will respond [with] either flat or soft [emotions]." _____

Choosing Emotions: Emotional Labour

If you have ever had a job working in retail sales or waiting on tables in a restaurant, you know the importance of projecting a friendly demeanour and smiling. Even though there were days when you did not feel cheerful, you knew management expected you to be upbeat when dealing with customers. So you faked it. Every employee expends physical and mental labour by putting body and mind into the job. But jobs also require **emotional labour**, an employee's expression of organizationally desired emotions during interpersonal transactions at work.[105]

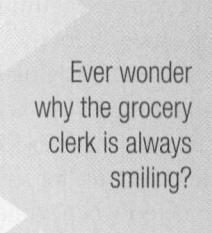

Ever wonder why the grocery clerk is always smiling?

8 Show the impact of emotional labour on employees.

The concept of emotional labour emerged from studies of service jobs. Airlines expect their flight attendants, for instance, to be cheerful; we expect funeral directors to be sad; and we expect doctors to be emotionally neutral. But really, emotional labour is relevant to almost every job. Your managers expect you, for example, to be courteous, not hostile, in interactions with co-workers. The true challenge arises when employees have to project one emotion while simultaneously feeling another.[106] This difference is **emotional dissonance**, and it can take a heavy toll on employees. Bottled-up feelings of frustration, anger, and resentment can eventually lead to emotional exhaustion

emotional labour When an employee expresses organizationally desired emotions during interpersonal interactions.

emotional dissonance Inconsistency between the emotions an individual feels and the emotions he or she shows.

and burnout.[107] It is because of emotional labour's increasing importance in effective job performance that an understanding of emotion has gained heightened relevance within the field of OB.

Emotional labour creates dilemmas for employees. There are people with whom you have to work that you just don't like. Maybe you consider their personality abrasive. Maybe you know they have said negative things about you behind your back. Regardless, your job requires you to interact with these people on a regular basis. So you are forced to pretend to be friendly.

It can help you, on the job especially, if you separate emotions into *felt* or *displayed* emotions.[108] **Felt emotions** are an individual's actual emotions. In contrast, **displayed emotions** are those that the organization requires employees to show and considers appropriate in a given job. They are not natural; they are learned. Similarly, most of us know that we are expected to act sad at funerals, regardless of whether we consider the person's death to be a loss, and to pretend to be happy at weddings, even if we don't feel like celebrating.

Effective managers have learned to be serious when giving an employee a negative performance evaluation and to hide their anger when they have been passed over for promotion. A salesperson who has not learned to smile and appear friendly, regardless of his true feelings at the moment, is not typically going to last long on most sales jobs. How we *experience* an emotion is not always the same as how we *show* it.[109]

Displaying fake emotions requires us to suppress real ones. **Surface acting** is hiding one's inner feelings and emotional expressions in response to display rules. For example, when an employee smiles at a customer even when he does not feel like it, he is surface acting. **Deep acting** is trying to modify one's true inner feelings based on display rules. A health care provider trying to genuinely feel more empathy for her patients is deep acting.[110] Surface acting deals with one's *displayed* emotions, and deep acting deals with one's *felt* emotions. Research in the Netherlands and Belgium indicated that surface acting is stressful to employees, while mindfulness (learning to objectively evaluate our emotional situation in the moment) is beneficial to employee well-being.[111] Displaying emotions we don't really feel is exhausting, so it is important to give employees who engage in surface acting a chance to relax and recharge. A study that looked at how cheerleading instructors spent their breaks from teaching found those who used the time to rest and relax were more effective after their breaks.[112] Instructors who did chores during their breaks were only about as effective after their break as they were before. Another study found that in hospital work groups where there were heavy emotional display demands, burnout was higher than in other hospital work groups.[113] Although much of the research on emotional labour shows negative consequences for those displaying false positive emotions, a 2011 study suggests that as people age, engaging in positive emotions and attitudes, even when the circumstances warrant otherwise, actually enhances emotional well-being.[114] *Case Incident—Can You Read Emotions from Faces?* on page 75 considers whether facial expressions reveal our true emotions. Meanwhile, the *Experiential Exercise* on page 73 asks you whether you can detect when someone is lying.

felt emotions An individual's actual emotions.

displayed emotions Emotions that are organizationally required and considered appropriate in a given job.

surface acting Hiding one's inner feelings to display what is expected.

deep acting Trying to modify one's true inner feelings to match what is expected.

Why Should We Care About Emotions in the Workplace?

Research is increasingly showing that emotions are actually critical to rational thinking.[115] We must have the ability to experience emotions to be rational. Why? Because our emotions provide important information about how we understand the world around us. Would we really want a manager to make a decision about firing an employee without regarding either his or the employee's emotions? The key to good decision making is to employ both thinking *and* feeling in our decisions.

There are other reasons to be concerned about understanding emotions in the workplace.[116] People who know their own emotions and are good at reading others'

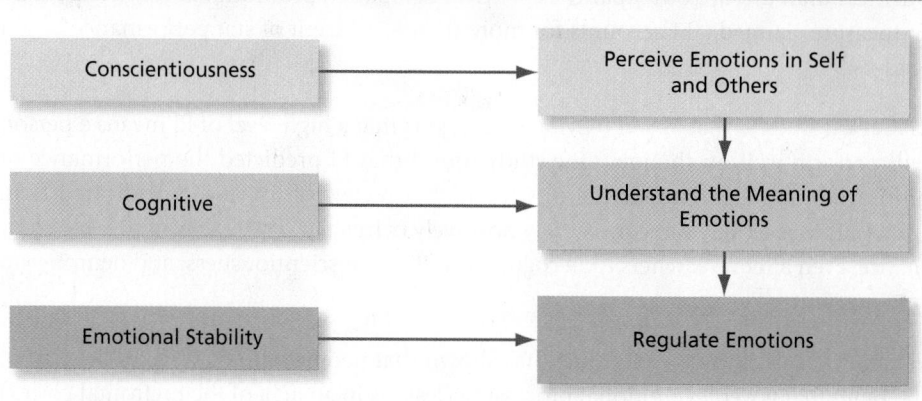

EXHIBIT 2-9 A Cascading Model of Emotional Intelligence

Conscientiousness → Perceive Emotions in Self and Others

Cognitive → Understand the Meaning of Emotions

Emotional Stability → Regulate Emotions

emotions may be more effective in their jobs. That, in essence, is the theme underlying contemporary research on emotional intelligence. The entire workplace can be affected adversely by negative workplace emotions, another issue we consider below. Finally, we consider emotion regulation and how it affects work performance.

Emotional Intelligence

Diane is an office manager. Her awareness of her own and others' emotions is almost zero. She is moody and unable to generate much enthusiasm or interest in her employees. She does not understand why employees get upset with her. She often overreacts to problems and chooses the most ineffectual responses to emotional situations.[117] Diane has low emotional intelligence. **Emotional intelligence (EI)** is a person's ability to (1) perceive emotions in the self and others, (2) understand the meaning of these emotions, and (3) regulate one's emotions accordingly in a cascading model, as shown in Exhibit 2-9. People who know their own emotions and are good at reading emotional cues—for instance, knowing why they are angry and how to express themselves without violating norms—are most likely to be effective.[118]

A 2011 comprehensive study reviewed and analyzed most of the previous studies on EI and concluded that EI is strongly and positively correlated with job performance—emotionally intelligent people are better workers.[119] One study that used functional magnetic resonance imaging (fMRI) technology found executive MBA students who performed best on a strategic decision-making task were more likely to incorporate emotion centres of the brain into their choice process. The students also de-emphasized the use of the more cognitive parts of their brains.[120]

Some researchers argue that EI is particularly important for leaders.[121] One simulation study also showed that students who were good at identifying and distinguishing among their own feelings were able to make more profitable investment decisions.[122]

EI has been a controversial concept in OB. It has supporters and detractors. In the following sections, we review the arguments for and against the effectiveness of EI in OB. *From Concepts to Skills* on pages 76–77 gives you some insight into reading the emotions of others.

The Case for EI

The arguments in favour of EI include its intuitive appeal, the fact that EI predicts criteria that matter, and the idea that EI is biologically based.

Intuitive Appeal   Intuition suggests that people who can detect emotions in others, control their own emotions, and handle social interactions well will have a powerful leg up in the business world.[123] As just one example, partners in a multinational consulting

9 Contrast the evidence for and against the existence of emotional intelligence.

PERSONAL INVENTORY ASSESSMENT

Learn About Yourself
Emotional Intelligence Assessment

emotional intelligence (EI) The ability to detect and to manage emotional cues and information.

firm who scored above the median on an EI measure delivered $1.2 million more in business than did the other partners.[124] One company's promotional materials for an EI measure claimed, "EI accounts for more than 85 percent of star performance in top leaders."[125]

EI Predicts Criteria That Matter   Evidence suggests that a high level of EI means a person will perform well on the job. One study found that EI predicted the performance of employees in a cigarette factory in China.[126] A review of 59 studies indicated that, overall, EI was weakly but consistently positively correlated moderately with job performance, even after researchers took cognitive ability, conscientiousness, and neuroticism into account.[127]

EI Is Biologically Based   One study has shown that people with damage to the part of the brain that governs emotional processing (lesions in an area of the prefrontal cortex) scored no lower on standard measures of intelligence than people without similar damage. Nevertheless, they scored significantly lower on EI tests and were impaired in normal decision making, as demonstrated by their poor performance in a card game with monetary rewards. This study suggests that EI is neurologically based in a way that is unrelated to standard measures of intelligence.[128] There is also evidence EI is genetically influenced, further supporting the idea that it measures a real underlying biological factor.[129]

The Case Against EI

For all its supporters, EI has just as many critics. Its critics say that EI is vague and impossible to measure, and they question its validity.

EI Researchers Do Not Agree on Definitions   It seems as though researchers are unclear on what EI is because researchers use different definitions of the concept.[130] Some have focused on tests with right and wrong answers from which we can infer someone's ability to recognize and control emotions, which is the ability-based perspective on EI. Other researchers have viewed EI as a broad variety of ideas that we can measure by self-reports and that are connected primarily by the fact that none of them are the same as cognitive intelligence. Not only are these two definitions different, but the measures used by each perspective are barely correlated with one another.[131]

EI Cannot Be Measured   Many critics have raised questions about measuring EI. Because EI is a form of intelligence, they argue, there must be right and wrong answers about it on tests. Some tests do have right and wrong answers, although the validity of some questions is doubtful. One measure asks you to associate particular feelings with specific colours, as if purple always makes us feel cool and not warm. Other measures are self-reported, meaning that there is no right or wrong answer. For example, an EI test question might ask you to respond to the statement "I'm good at 'reading' other people," and have no right or wrong answers. The measures of EI are diverse, and researchers have not subjected them to as much rigorous study as they have measures of personality and general intelligence.[132]

EI Is Nothing but Personality with a Different Label   Some critics argue that because EI is so closely related to intelligence and personality, once you control for these factors, EI has nothing unique to offer. There is some foundation to this argument. EI appears to be correlated with measures of personality, especially emotional stability.[133] If this is true, then biological markers such as brain activity and heritability are attributable to other well-known and much better researched psychological variables. To some extent, researchers have resolved this issue by noting that EI is a construct partially determined by traits like cognitive intelligence, conscientiousness, and neuroticism, so it makes sense that EI is correlated with these characteristics.[134]

Although the field is progressing in its understanding of EI, many questions have not been answered. EI is wildly popular among consulting firms and in the popular press, but it's still difficult to validate this construct with the research literature. Thus, assessing exactly how EI should be used in the workplace is unclear, as *Focus on Ethics* shows.

FOCUS ON ETHICS

An Ethical Choice

Should managers use emotional intelligence tests? Should EI tests be used to select the best job candidate?[135] Here are some ethical considerations:

- *No commonly accepted test exists.* For instance, researchers have recently used the Mayer-Salovey-Caruso Emotional Intelligence Test (MSCEIT), the Trait Emotional Intelligence Questionnaire, and the newly developed Situational Judgment Test of Emotional Intelligence (SJT of EI) in studies. Researchers feel EI tests may need to be culturally specific because emotional displays vary by culture; thus, the interpretation of emotional cues differs. A recent study in India comparing the EI scores for Indian and North American executives using the Emotional Competence Inventory (ECI-2) test found the results similar but not the same, suggesting the need for modification.
- *Applicants may react negatively to taking an EI test in general, or to parts of it.* The face recognition test, for example, may seem culturally biased to some if the subject photos are not diverse. Also, participants who score high on EI tests tend to consider them fair; applicants who score lower may not perceive the tests to be fair and can thus consider the hiring organizations unfavourably—even if they score well on other assessments.
- *EI tests may not be predictive of performance for all types of jobs.* In a study of 600 Romanian participants, results indicated that EI was valid for salespeople, public servants, and CEOs of public hospitals, but these were all roles requiring significant social interaction. EI tests may need to be tailored for each position category or not be used when the position description does not warrant.
- *It remains somewhat unclear what EI tests are actually measuring.* They may reflect personality or intelligence, in which case other measures might be better.
- *Not enough research exists on how EI affects counterproductive or desirable work behaviours.* It may not be prudent to test and select applicants who are rated high on EI when we are not yet certain that everything about EI leads to desired workplace outcomes.

These concerns suggest that EI tests should be avoided in hiring decisions. However, because research has indicated that EI does predict job performance to some degree, managers should not be too hasty to dismiss the tests. Rather, those wishing to use EI in hiring decisions should be aware of these issues to make informed and ethical decisions about not only whom to hire but also how to hire.

Negative Workplace Emotions

Negative emotions can lead to a number of deviant workplace behaviours. Anyone who has spent much time in an organization realizes that people often engage in voluntary actions that violate established norms and threaten the organization, its members, or both. These actions are called **employee deviance**.[136] Deviant actions fall into categories such as production (leaving early, intentionally working slowly); property (stealing, sabotage); political (gossiping, blaming co-workers); and personal aggression (sexual harassment, verbal abuse).[137]

Many of these deviant behaviours can be traced to negative emotions. For instance, envy is an emotion that occurs when you resent someone for having something you don't, and strongly desire—such as a better work assignment, larger office, or higher salary.[138] It can lead to malicious deviant behaviours, such as hostility, "backstabbing,"

employee deviance Voluntary actions that violate established norms and threaten the organization, its members, or both.

and other forms of political behaviour that negatively distort others' successes and positively distort your own accomplishments.[139] Angry people look for other people to blame for their bad mood, interpret other people's behaviour as hostile, and have trouble considering others' points of view.[140] It's not hard to see how these thought processes, too, can lead directly to verbal or physical aggression. Evidence suggests that people who feel negative emotions, particularly those who feel angry or hostile, are more likely than others to engage in deviant behaviour at work.[141]

Managing emotions in the workplace becomes important both to ward off negative behaviour and to encourage positive behaviour in those around us. Some managers have even hired happiness coaches for their employees, as discussed in *Ethical Dilemma* on page 74.

Focus on Research looks at the issue of whether smiles are infectious. You may be surprised to learn the extent to which your mood can affect the mood of others. Once aggression starts, it's likely that other people will become angry and aggressive, so the stage is set for a serious escalation of negative behaviour.

FOCUS ON RESEARCH

Smile, and the Work World Smiles with You

Can you make another person smile? It is true that a smile usually creates an unconscious return smile from the person smiled at.[142] However, anyone who has ever smiled at an angry manager knows that a smile does not always have a positive effect. In truth, the giving and withholding of smiles is an unconscious power play of office politics.

New research on the "boss effect" suggests that the amount of power and status a person feels over another person dictates who will smile. Subordinates generally smile more often than their bosses smile back at them. However, the perception of power is complex and varies by national culture: in a recent study, Chinese workers reflexively smiled only at bosses who had the power to give them negative job evaluations, while US participants smiled most to managers perceived to have higher social power. Other researchers found that when individuals felt powerful, they usually did not return even a high-ranking individual's smile. Conversely, when people felt powerless, they returned everyone's smiles.

While we think of smiling as a choice, smiling (or concealing a smile) is often unconscious. Researchers are finding that social pressure affects neurobiology. "It shapes your neural architecture," said cognitive neuroscientist Sook-Lei Liew. Smile reactions are, therefore, partially involuntary; when smiling is a product of our attitudes, it can become an unconscious process. Thus, "your feelings about power and status seem to dictate how much you are willing to return a smile to another person," cognitive neuroscientist Evan Carr affirmed.

Emotion Regulation

10 Identify strategies for emotion regulation and their likely effects.

Have you ever tried to cheer yourself up when you are feeling down or calm yourself when you are feeling angry? If so, you have engaged in *emotion regulation*, which is part of the EI literature but is increasingly being studied as an independent concept.[143] The central idea behind emotion regulation is to identify and modify the emotions you feel. Recent research suggests that emotion management ability is a strong predictor of task performance for some jobs and organizational citizenship behaviours.[144]

Researchers of emotion regulation often study the strategies people may employ to change their emotions. One strategy we have discussed in this chapter is surface acting, or literally "putting on a face" of appropriate response to a given situation. Surface acting does not change emotions, though, so the regulation effect is minimal. Perhaps due to the costs of expressing what we don't feel, a recent study suggested that individuals who vary their surface-acting response may have lower job satisfaction and higher levels of work withdrawal than those who consistently use surface acting.[145] Deep acting, another strategy we have covered, is less psychologically costly than surface acting because the employee is actually trying to experience the emotion. Deep acting, although less "false" than surface acting, still may be difficult because it represents acting nonetheless.

Organizational behaviour researchers are looking to understand strategies people may employ that yield the results of acting (such as showing appropriate emotions) but mitigate the effects of acting (such as emotional exhaustion and workplace withdrawal). The goal is to give employees and managers tools to monitor and modify their emotional responses to workplace situations.

Although the research is ongoing, studies indicate that effective emotion regulation techniques include acknowledging rather than suppressing our emotional responses to situations, and re-evaluating events after they occur.[146] A 2013 study illustrates the potentially powerful effect of cognitive reappraisal. Of the Israeli participants who were shown anger-inducing information on the Israeli–Palestinian conflict, those who were primed to reappraise the situation showed more willingness to consider conciliatory measures toward Palestine and less support for aggressive tactics than the control group, not just immediately after the study but up to five months later. This finding suggests that cognitive reappraisal techniques may allow people to change their emotional responses, even when the subject matter is as highly emotionally charged as the Israeli–Palestinian conflict.[147]

Another technique with potential for emotion regulation is venting. Research shows that the open expression of emotions can be helpful to the individual, as opposed to keeping emotions "bottled up." Caution must be exercised, though, because venting, or expressing your frustration outwardly, touches other people. In fact, whether venting emotions helps the "venter" feel better depends very much upon the listener's response. If the listener does not respond (many refuse to respond to venting), the venter actually feels worse. If the listener responds with expressions of support or validation, the venter feels better. Therefore, if we are going to vent to a co-worker, we need to choose someone who will respond sympathetically. Venting to the perceived offender rarely improves things and can result in heightening the negative emotions.[148]

As you might suspect, not everyone is equally good at regulating his or her emotions. Individuals who are higher in the personality trait of neuroticism have more trouble doing so and often find their moods are beyond their ability to control. Individuals who have lower levels of self-esteem are also less likely to try to improve their sad moods, perhaps because they are less likely than others to feel they deserve to be in a good mood.[149]

While it might seem in some ways desirable to regulate your emotions, research suggests there is a downside to trying to change the way you feel. Changing your emotions takes effort, and as we noted when discussing emotional labour, this effort can be exhausting. Sometimes attempts to change an emotion actually make the emotion stronger; for example, trying to talk yourself out of being afraid can make you focus more on what scares you, which makes you more afraid.[150] From another perspective, research suggests that avoiding negative emotional experiences is less likely to lead to positive moods than does seeking out positive emotional experiences.[151] For example, you are more likely to experience a positive mood if you have a pleasant conversation with a friend than if you avoid an unpleasant conversation with a hostile co-worker.

RESEARCH FINDINGS: Emotion Regulation

While emotion regulation techniques can help us cope with difficult workplace situations, research indicates that the effect varies. A 2013 study in Taiwan found that participants who worked for abusive supervisors reported emotional exhaustion and work withdrawal tendencies, but to different degrees based on the emotion regulation strategies they employed. This finding suggests that more research

Watch on **MyManagementLab**

East Haven Fire Department: Emotions and Moods

on the application of techniques needs to be done to help employees.[152] Thus, while there is much promise in emotion regulation techniques, the best route to a positive workplace is to recruit positive-minded individuals and to train leaders to manage their moods, job attitudes, and performance.[153] The best leaders manage emotions as much as they do tasks and activities. Although with computers now being programmed to read emotions, as *OB in the Workplace* indicates, it may be harder to hide emotions at work in the future.

OB IN THE **WORKPLACE**
Affective Computing: Reading Your State of Mind

Can computers really recognize a user's emotions? The Massachusetts Institute of Technology (MIT) Media Lab is currently programming computers to use 24 facial points from which they can infer an emotion.[154] What if computers could be made emotionally intelligent to help a person get past frustration into productivity? What if managers could automatically receive reports on virtual employees' emotions? What if sensors could help employees stay well by providing feedback on their emotional reactions to stress?

Affective computing can provide managers with in-the-moment help. At MIT's lab, a tiny traffic light, visible only to the wearer, flashes yellow when a listener's face indicates lack of engagement in the conversation and red for complete disengagement. These cues could help a manager who is delivering important safety information to an employee, for instance. The MIT team has also developed wristbands that sense emotional states and activity levels. They could help managers work with employees who are on the Asperger's or autism spectrum. "With this technology in the future, we'll be able to understand things . . . that we weren't able to see before, things that calm them, things that stress them," said Rosalind Picard, the team's director.

With this possibility comes responsibility, of course. Obvious ethical issues will only grow with the technology's increasing sophistication. Employees may not want computers to read their emotions either for their managers' use or for automatic feedback. "We want to have some control over how we display ourselves to others," said Nick Bostrom of the University of Oxford's Future of Humanity Institute.

Organizations will eventually have to decide when it is appropriate to read employees' emotions, as well as which emotions to read. In the meantime, according to affective computing experts, people are still the best readers of emotions from facial cues. Perhaps managers can get to know their employees' state of mind by paying closer attention to those cues.

GLOBAL **IMPLICATIONS**

In considering potential global differences in this chapter's concepts, let's look at the four areas that have attracted the most research: (1) perception, (2) attributions, (3) personality, and (4) emotions.

Perception

Several studies have examined how people observe the world around them.[155] In one study, researchers showed East Asians and US subjects a photo with a focal object (like a train) with a busy background and tracked their eye movements. They found that the

US subjects were more likely to look at the focal object, whereas the East Asian subjects were more likely to look at the background. Thus, the East Asians appeared to focus more on the context or environment than on the most important object in it. As one of the researchers concluded, "If people are seeing different things, it may be because they are looking differently at the world."[156]

Perceptual differences across cultures have been found to be rooted in the brain's architecture. Using an fMRI device to scan subjects' brains, one researcher found that when Singaporeans were shown pictures where either the foreground or background was varied, their brains were less attuned to new foreground images and more attuned to new background images than those of US subjects.[157] This finding suggests that perception is not universal, and that the cultural tendency to focus on either an object/person or a context is part of the "hard wiring" of our brains.

Finally, culture affects what we remember as well. When asked to remember events, US subjects recall more about personal details and their own personal characteristics, whereas Asians recall more about personal relationships and group activities.[158]

As a set, these studies provide striking evidence that Eastern and Western cultures differ in one of the deepest aspects of organizational behaviour: how we see the world around us.

Attributions

The evidence on cultural differences in perception is mixed, but most studies suggest that there *are* differences across cultures in the attributions people make.[159] One study also found Korean managers less likely to use the self-serving bias—they tended to accept responsibility for group failure "because I was not a capable leader" instead of attributing failure to group members.[160] On the other hand, Asian managers are more likely to lay blame on institutions or whole organizations, whereas Western observers are more likely to believe individual managers should be the focus of blame or praise.[161] That probably explains why US newspapers prominently report the names of individual executives when firms do poorly, whereas Asian media provide more coverage of how the firm as a whole has failed. This tendency to make group-based attributions also explains why individuals from Asian cultures are more likely to make group-based stereotypes.[162] Attribution theory was developed largely based on experiments with US and Western European workers. But these studies suggest caution in making attribution theory predictions in non-Western societies, especially in countries with strong collectivistic traditions.

These differences in attribution tendencies don't mean that the basic concepts of attribution and blame completely differ across cultures, though. Self-serving biases may be less common in East Asian cultures, but evidence suggests that they still operate across cultures.[163] Studies suggest that Chinese managers assess blame for mistakes using the same distinctiveness, consensus, and consistency cues Western managers use.[164] They also become angry and punish those who are deemed responsible for failure, a reaction shown in many studies of Western managers. This finding means that the basic process of attribution applies across cultures but that it takes more evidence for Asian managers to conclude someone else should be blamed.

Personality

The five personality traits identified in the Big Five model appear in almost all cross-cultural studies.[165] These studies have included a wide variety of diverse cultures—such as China, Israel, Germany, Japan, Spain, Nigeria, Norway, Pakistan, and the United States. Differences tend to be in the emphasis on particular dimensions and whether countries are predominantly individualist or collectivist. For example, Chinese managers use the dimension of conscientiousness more often and agreeableness less often than do US managers. The Big Five appear to predict behaviour more accurately in individualistic cultures than collectivistic cultures.[166] However, a surprisingly high amount of agreement exists among researchers that the Big Five variables are useful predictors, especially among individuals from developed countries. A comprehensive review of studies covering people from what was then the 15-nation European Community found conscientiousness to be a valid predictor of performance across jobs and occupational groups.[167] US studies have reached the same conclusion.

With respect to proactive personality, a 2013 study of 231 Flemish unemployed individuals found that proactive personality was negatively related to persistence in job searching; proactive individuals abandoned their job searches sooner. However, it may be that proactivity includes knowing when to step back and reconsider alternatives in the face of failure.[168]

A 2013 study of 95 R & D teams in 33 Chinese companies revealed that teams with high-average levels of proactive personality were more innovative.[169] Like other traits, proactive personality is affected by the context. A 2012 study of bank branch teams in China found that if a team's leader is not proactive, the benefits of the team's proactivity will lie dormant or, worse, be suppressed by the leader.[170]

Emotions

People vary in the degree to which they experience emotions. In China, for example, people report experiencing fewer positive and negative emotions than people in other cultures, and the emotions they experience are less intense than what other cultures report. Compared with mainland Chinese, Taiwanese are more like Canadian

EXHIBIT 2-10 Emotional States Cross-Culturally

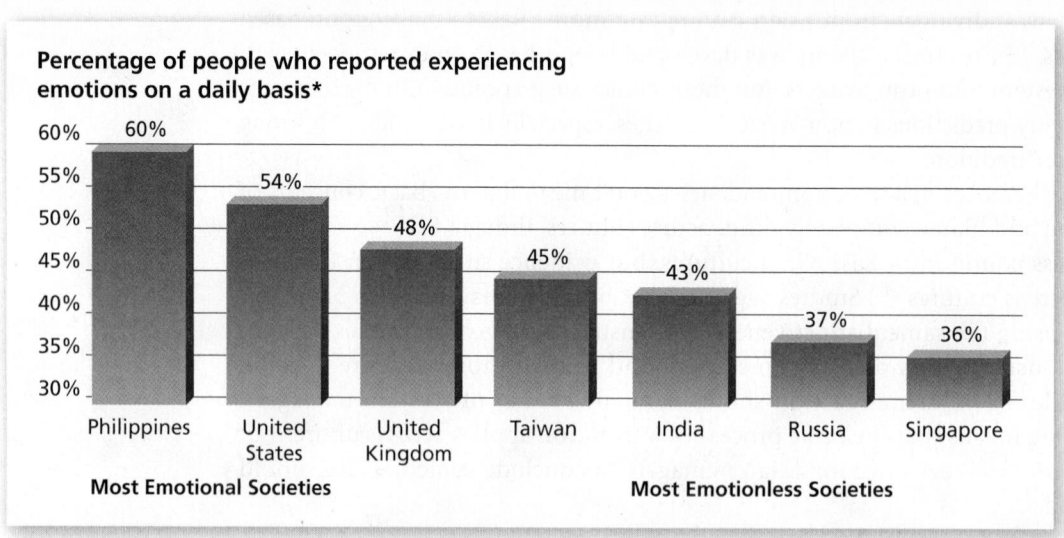

Percentage of people who reported experiencing emotions on a daily basis*

Most Emotional Societies: Philippines 60%, United States 54%, United Kingdom 48%, Taiwan 45%

Most Emotionless Societies: India 43%, Russia 37%, Singapore 36%

*Respondents in 150+ countries worldwide over two years were asked whether they experienced five positive emotions (well-rested, treated with respect, enjoyment, smiling and laughing, learning or doing something interesting) and five negative emotions (anger, stress, sadness, physical pain, worry) daily.

Source: J. Clifton, "Singapore Ranks as Least Emotional Country in the World," *Gallup World*, November 21, 2012, http://www.gallup.com/poll/158882/singapore-ranks-least-emotional-country-world.aspx.

employees in their experience of emotions: On average, Taiwanese report more positive and fewer negative emotions than their Chinese counterparts.[171] People in most cultures appear to experience certain positive and negative emotions, but the frequency of their experience and their intensity varies to some degree.[172] Exhibit 2-10 illustrates the percentage of people who experience emotions on a daily basis across cultures.

Despite these differences, people from all over the world interpret negative and positive emotions in much the same way. We all view negative emotions, such as hate, terror, and rage, as dangerous and destructive. And we all desire positive emotions, such as joy, love, and happiness. However, some cultures value certain emotions more than others. For example, Americans value enthusiasm, while the Chinese consider negative emotions to be more useful and constructive. In general, pride is seen as a positive emotion in Western, individualistic cultures such as the United States, but Eastern cultures such as China and Japan tend to view pride as undesirable.[173]

Recent research has suggested that **negative affect** actually has many benefits. Visualizing the worst-case scenario often allows people to accept present circumstances and cope, for instance.[174] Negative affect can allow managers to think more critically and fairly, other research indicates.[175]

The norms for the expression of emotions vary by culture as well. For example, some fundamentalist Muslims see smiling as a sign of sexual attraction, so women have learned not to smile at men so as not to be misinterpreted.[176] And research has shown that in collectivistic countries, people are more likely to believe that the emotional displays of another have something to do with their own relationship with the person expressing the emotion, while people in individualistic cultures don't think that another's emotional expressions are directed at them.[177] Evidence indicates that in Canada a bias exists against expressing emotions, especially intense negative emotions. French retail clerks, in contrast, are infamous for being surly toward customers (a report from the French government itself confirmed this).[178] Reports also indicate that serious German shoppers have been turned off by Walmart's friendly greeters and helpful personnel.[179]

Summary

Individuals base their behaviour not on the way their external environment actually is, but rather on the way they see it or believe it to be.

Personality matters to OB. It does not explain all behaviour, but it sets the stage. Emerging theory and research reveal how personality matters more in some situations than others. The Big Five Personality Model has been a particularly important advancement, although the Dark Triad and other traits matter as well. Moreover, every trait has advantages and disadvantages for work behaviour. No perfect constellation of traits is ideal in every situation. Personality can help you understand why people (including yourself!) act, think, and feel the way we do, and the astute manager can put that understanding to use by taking care to place employees in situations that best fit their personality.

Emotions and moods are similar in that both are affective in nature. They are also different—moods are more general and less contextual than emotions. And events do matter. The time of day, day of the week, stressful events, social activities, and sleep patterns are some of the factors that influence emotions and moods. Emotions and moods have proven relevant for virtually every OB topic we study, and they have implications for managerial practice.

negative affect A mood dimension that consists of emotions such as nervousness, stress, and anxiety at the high end and relaxation, tranquility, and poise at the low end.

SNAPSHOT SUMMARY

Perception
- Factors That Influence Perception
- Perceptual Errors
- Why Do Perception and Judgment Matter?

Personality
- What Is Personality?
- Measuring Personality

- Personality Determinants
- Personality Traits
- The Dark Triad
- Other Personality Attributes That Influence OB

Emotions
- What Are Emotions and Moods?

- Choosing Emotions: Emotional Labour
- Why Should We Care About Emotions in the Workplace?

MyManagementLab

Study, practise, and explore real business situations with these helpful resources:

- **Study Plan:** Check your understanding of chapter concepts with self-study quizzes.
- **Online Lesson Presentations:** Study key chapter topics and work through interactive assessments to test your knowledge and master management concepts.
- **Videos:** Learn more about the management practices and strategies of real companies.
- **Simulations:** Practise management decision-making in simulated business environments.

P I A PERSONAL INVENTORY ASSESSMENT

OB at **Work**

for **Review**

1. What is perception? What factors influence our perception?

2. What is attribution theory? What are the three determinants of attribution? What are the implications of attribution theory for explaining organizational behaviour?

3. What is personality? How do we typically measure it? What factors determine personality?

4. What is the Myers-Briggs Type Indicator? What are its strengths and weaknesses?

5. What are the key traits in the Big Five Personality Model?

6. How do the Big Five personality traits predict behaviour at work?

7. What is the difference between emotions and moods?

8. What impact does emotional labour have on employees?

9. What is the evidence for and against the existence of emotional intelligence?

10. What are some strategies for emotion regulation and their likely effects?

for **Managers**

■ Consider screening job candidates for high conscientiousness—as well as the other Big Five personality traits, depending on the criteria your organization finds most important. Other traits, such as core self-evaluation or narcissism, may be relevant in certain situations.

■ Although the MBTI has been widely criticized, it may have a place in organizations. You may consider the results helpful for training and development; the results can also help employees better understand themselves, help team members better understand one another, open up communication in work groups, and possibly reduce conflicts.

■ To foster effective decision making, creativity, and motivation in employees, model positive emotions and moods as much as is authentically possible.

■ Regulate your intense emotional responses to an event by recognizing the legitimacy of the emotion and being careful to vent only to a supportive listener who is not involved in the event.

■ Be careful not to ignore co-workers' and employees' emotions; do not assess others' behaviour as if it were completely rational. As one consultant aptly put it, "You can't divorce emotions from the workplace because you can't divorce emotions from people."[180] Managers who understand the role of emotions and moods will significantly improve their ability to explain and predict their co-workers' and employees' behaviour.

for **You**

■ The discussion of perception might get you thinking about how you view the world. When we perceive someone as a troublemaker, for instance, that may be only a perception and not a real characteristic of the person. It is always good to question your perceptions, just to be sure that you are not reading something into a situation that is not there.

■ One important thing to consider when looking for a job is whether your personality will fit the organization to which you are applying. For instance, let's say that you are considering working for a highly structured company. If you, by nature, are much less formal, then that company may not be a good fit for you.

■ Sometimes personalities get in the way when working in groups. You may want to see if you can figure out ways to get personality differences to work in favour of group goals.

■ Emotions need not always be suppressed when working with others. While emotions can sometimes hinder performance, positive emotions can motivate you and those around you.

OB *at Work*

Millennials Are More Narcissistic

Those in university and college today have many good qualities: They are more technologically savvy, more socially tolerant, and more balanced in their work and family priorities than previous generations.[181] Thus, those poised to enter the workforce today do so with some important virtues. Humility, however, is not one of them.

A 2014 study comparing Millennials with Generation Xers found that Millennials expect faster promotions, change jobs every two years, and are confident they will achieve their career goals. Jason Kipps, managing director for Toronto-based Universum Canada, in another 2014 study, concluded that Millennial university students are saying, "I want to get out there, and I want to kill it. And I want to make lots of money."

Studies measuring narcissism suggest that scores are rising, especially among younger generations. For example, by presenting a choice between two statements—"I try not to be a show-off" vs. "I will usually show off if I get the chance"—psychologists have found that narcissism has been growing since the early 1980s.

Another recent study found that compared with Baby Boomers and Generation X, students entering college and university today are more likely to emphasize extrinsic values (money, image, fame) and less likely to value intrinsic ones (concern for others, charity, jobs that contribute to society).

These findings do not paint a pretty picture, but data do not lie: The sooner we admit it, the sooner we can begin to address the problem in families, in education, and at work.

"THE YOUTH OF TODAY ARE LOST!" This argument is like a broken record that seems to play over and over: Every generation tends to think the new generation is without values, and the new generation thinks the older one is hopelessly judgmental and out of touch. Didn't the supposed "Me generation" occur a generation ago? Let's send the broken record to the recycling bin and review the evidence.

Another study offered an interesting explanation for why people *think* Millennials are more narcissistic. Specifically, young people in general are more self-focused, but as people age, they become more "other" focused. So we think young people are different when in fact they are just the way older folks were when they were younger. As these authors conclude, "Every generation is Generation Me." Our level of narcissism appears to be one of the many things that change as we get older.

In fact, this idea raises an important point: Values change over time as we age, but we should not confuse that change with generational effects. One large-scale review of the literature revealed that during college and university years, we place more weight on intrinsic values, and as we progress in our careers and start families, extrinsic values increase in importance.

Other research has found that people think that generations differ in their values much more than they in fact do. One study found that of 15 work values, in every case the perceived differences among Baby Boomers, Generation Xers, and Millennials were greater than the actual ones.

More broadly, narcissistic folks exist in every generation. We need to be careful when generalizing about entire groups (whether one sex, one race, one culture, or one generation). While generalizations have caused no small amount of trouble, we still like to simplify the world, sometimes for good reason. In this case, however, the good reason is not there, especially considering the latest evidence.

Tolerance of Ambiguity Scale: Some people are much more tolerant of ambiguity than others, which may impact career preferences. Use this scale to determine your own tolerance of ambiguity.

Core Self-Evaluation Scale: Understanding your own personality can help you select the types of roles that are right for you. Use this scale to learn more about how you view yourself and your confidence levels in specific situations.

Self-Awareness Assessment: This self-assessment is designed to help you gain insight into yourself and efforts you can make to increase your self-awareness.

Emotional Intelligence Assessment: Emotional intelligence can help people communicate more effectively and can assist in the management of conflict. Use this scale to learn more about your personal emotional intelligence.

BREAKOUT **GROUP** EXERCISES

Form small groups to discuss the following topics, as assigned by your instructor. Each person in the group should first identify 3–5 key personal values.

1. Think back to your perception of this course and your instructor on the first day of class. What factors might have affected your perceptions of what the rest of the term would be like?

2. Describe a situation where your perception turned out to be wrong. What perceptual errors did you make that might have caused this to happen?

EXPERIENTIAL EXERCISE

Who Can Catch a Liar?

We mentioned earlier in the chapter that emotion researchers are highly interested in facial expressions as a window into individuals' emotional worlds.[182] Research has also studied whether people can tell someone is lying based on signs of guilt or nervousness in their facial expressions. Let's see who is good at catching liars, but first consider this: How good you are at detecting lies by others is related to your own mood. You are actually less likely to correctly detect a lie if you are in a happy mood. *Hint:* If you are in a negative mood, concentrate mostly on the message itself (Does it seem plausible?); if you are in a positive mood, read the nonverbal cues (such as fidgety or calm behaviour) more.

Split up into teams and follow these instructions.

1. Randomly choose someone to be the team organizer. Have this person write down on a piece of paper "T" for truth and "L" for lie. If there are, say, six people in the group (other than the organizer), then three people will get a slip with a "T" and three a slip with an "L." It's important that all team members keep what is on their paper a secret.

2. Each team member who holds a T slip needs to come up with a true statement, and each team member who holds an L slip needs to come up with a false statement. Try not to make the statement so outrageous that no one would believe it (for example, "I have flown to the moon").

3. The organizer will have each member make his or her statement. Group members should then examine the person making the statement closely to try to determine whether he or she is telling the truth or lying. Once each person has made his or her statement, the organizer will ask for a vote and record the tallies.

4. Each person should now indicate whether the statement was the truth or a lie.

5. How good was your group at catching the liars? Were some people good liars? What did you look for to determine whether someone was lying?

ETHICAL **DILEMMA**

Happiness Coaches for Employees

We know there is considerable spillover from personal unhappiness to negative emotions at work.[183] Moreover, those who experience negative emotions in life and at work are more likely to engage in counterproductive behaviours with customers, clients, or fellow employees.

Increasingly, organizations such as American Express, UBS, and KPMG are turning to happiness coaches to address this spillover from personal unhappiness to work emotions and behaviours.

Srikumar Rao is a former college professor who has the nickname "the happiness guru." Rao teaches people to analyze negative emotions to prevent them from becoming overwhelming. If your job is restructured, for example, Rao suggests avoiding negative thoughts and feelings about it. Instead, he advises, tell yourself it could turn out well in the long run, and there is no way to know at present.

Beyond reframing the emotional impact of work situations, some happiness coaches attack the negative emotional spillover from life to work (and from work to life). A working mother found that a happiness talk by Shawn Actor helped her stop focusing on her stressed-out life and instead look for chances to smile, laugh, and be grateful.

In some cases, the claims made by happiness coaches seem a bit trite. Jim Smith, who labels himself "The Executive Happiness Coach," asks: "What if I told you that there are secrets nobody told you as a kid—or as an adult, for that matter—that can unlock for you all sorts of positive emotional experiences? What if the only thing that gets in the way of you feeling more happiness is—YOU?! What if you can change your experience of the world by shifting a few simple things in your life, and then practicing them until they become second nature?"

If employees leave their experiences with a happiness coach feeling happier about their jobs and their lives, is that not better for everyone? Says one individual, Ivelisse Rivera, who felt she benefited from a happiness coach, "If I assume a negative attitude and complain all the time, whoever is working with me is going to feel the same way."

But what if you cannot afford a happiness coach and your employer does not want to foot the bill? Recent research suggests a do-it-yourself opportunity to increase your good mood at home. The key is to lend a helping hand. If you help others at work, you may find that later at home, after you have had a chance to relax and reflect, your mood will be improved.

Questions

1. Do you think happiness coaches are effective? How might you assess their effectiveness?

2. Would you welcome happiness training in your workplace? Why or why not?

3. Under what circumstances—if any—is it ethically appropriate for a supervisor to suggest a happiness coach for a subordinate?

CASE INCIDENTS

On the Costs of Being Nice

Agreeable people tend to be kinder and more accommodating in social situations, which you might think could add to their success in life.[184] However, one downside of agreeableness is potentially lower earnings. Recent research has shown the answer to this and other puzzles; some of them may surprise you.

First, and perhaps most obvious, agreeable individuals are less adept at a type of negotiation called distributive bargaining. As we discuss in Chapter 9, distributive bargaining is less about creating win–win solutions and more about claiming as large of a share of the pie as possible. Because salary negotiations are generally distributive, agreeable individuals often negotiate lower salaries for themselves than they might otherwise get.

Perhaps because of this impaired ability to negotiate distributively, agreeable individuals have lower credit scores.

Second, agreeable individuals may choose to work in industries or occupations that earn lower salaries, such as the "caring" industries of education or health care. Agreeable individuals are also attracted to jobs both in the public sector and in nonprofit organizations.

Third, the earnings of agreeable individuals also may be reduced by their lower drive to emerge as leaders and by their tendency to engage in lower degrees of proactive task behaviours, such as coming up with ways to increase organizational effectiveness.

While being agreeable certainly does not appear to help one's pay, it does provide other benefits. Agreeable individuals are better liked at work, are more likely to help others at work, and generally are happier at work and in life.

Nice guys—and gals—may finish last in terms of earnings, but wages themselves do not define a happy life, and on that front, agreeable individuals have the advantage.

Questions

1. Do you think employers must choose between agreeable employees and top performers? Why or why not?

2. Often, the effects of personality depend on the situation. Can you think of some job situations in which agreeableness is an important virtue, and some in which it is harmful to job performance?

3. In some research we have conducted, we have found that the negative effect of agreeableness on earnings is stronger for men than for women (that is, being agreeable hurt men's earnings more than women's). Why do you think this might be the case?

Can You Read Emotions from Faces?

Some researchers—psychologist Paul Ekman may be the best known—have studied whether facial expressions reveal true emotions.[185] These researchers have distinguished real smiles (so-called Duchenne smiles, named after French physician Guillaume Duchenne) from "fake" smiles. Duchenne found genuine smiles raised not only the corners of the mouth (easily faked) but also cheek and eye muscles (much more difficult to fake). So, one way to determine whether someone is genuinely happy or amused is to look at the muscles around the upper cheeks and eyes—if the person's eyes are smiling or twinkling, the smile is genuine. Ekman and his associates have developed similar methods to detect other emotions, such as anger, disgust, and distress. According to Ekman, the key to identifying real emotions is to focus on micro-expressions, or those facial muscles we cannot easily manipulate. Recent research indicates that people cannot accurately infer emotions in others from their facial expressions.

Dan Hill has used these techniques to study the facial expressions of CEOs and found they vary dramatically not only in their Duchenne smiles but also in the degree to which they display positive versus negative facial expressions. The accompanying table shows Hill's analysis of the facial expressions of some prominent male executives:

Jeff Bezos, Amazon	51% positive
Warren Buffett, Berkshire Hathaway	69% positive
Michael Dell, Dell Computers	47% positive
Larry Ellison, Oracle	0% positive
Bill Gates, Microsoft	73% positive
Phil Knight, Nike	67% positive
Donald Trump, The Trump Organization	16% positive

It's interesting to note that these individuals, all of whom are successful in various ways, have such different levels of positive facial expressions. It also raises the question: Is a smile from Larry Ellison worth more than a smile from Bill Gates?

Questions

1. Most research suggests that we are not very good at detecting fake emotions, and we think we are much better at it than we are. Do you believe training would improve your ability to detect emotional displays in others?

2. Do you think the information in this case could help you tell whether someone's smile is genuine?

3. Is your own impression of the facial expressions of the seven business leaders consistent with what the researcher found? If not, why do you think your views might be at odds with his?

FROM CONCEPTS TO SKILLS

Reading Emotions

Understanding another person's felt emotions is very difficult. But we can learn to read others' displayed emotions.[186] We do this by focusing on verbal, nonverbal, and paralanguage cues.

The easiest way to find out what someone is feeling is to ask them. Saying something as simple as "Are you okay? What's the problem?" can often provide you with the information to assess an individual's emotional state. But relying on a verbal response has two drawbacks. First, almost all of us conceal our emotions to some extent for privacy and to reflect social expectations. So we might be unwilling to share our true feelings. Second, even if we want to verbally convey our feelings, we may be unable to do so. As we noted earlier, some people have difficulty understanding their own emotions and, hence, are unable to express them verbally. So, at best, verbal responses provide only partial information.

Let's say you are talking with a co-worker. Does the fact that his back is rigid, his teeth clenched, and his facial muscles tight tell you something about his emotional state? It probably should. Facial expressions, gestures, body movements, and physical distance are nonverbal cues that can provide additional insights into what a person is feeling. The facial expressions shown in Exhibit 2-11, for instance, are a window into a person's feelings. Notice the difference in facial features: the height of the cheeks, the raising or lowering of the brow, the turn of the mouth, the positioning of the lips, and the configuration of muscles around the eyes. Even something as subtle as the distance someone chooses to position him- or herself from you can convey how much intimacy, aggressiveness, repugnance, or withdrawal that person feels.

EXHIBIT 2-11 Facial Expressions and Emotions

Each picture portrays a different emotion. Try to identify them before looking at the answers.

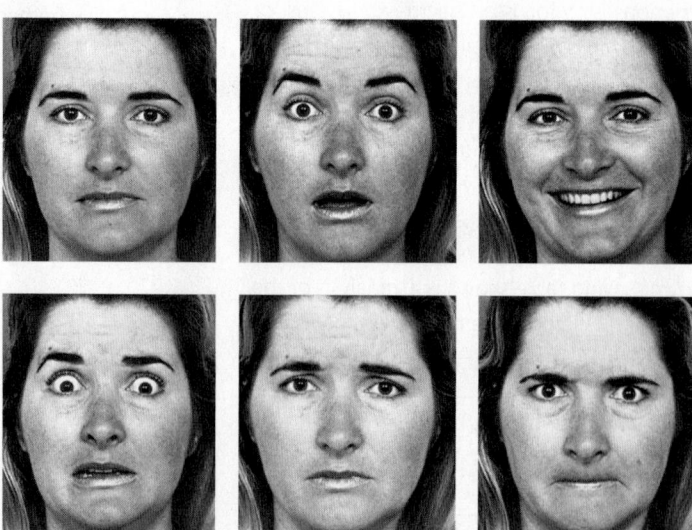

Top, left to right: neutral, surprise, happiness. Bottom: fear, sadness, anger.

Source: Paul Ekman, PhD/Paul Ekman Group, LLC.

When you speak with someone, you may notice a sharp change in the tone of her voice and the speed at which she speaks. You are tapping into the third source of information on a person's emotions—paralanguage. This is communication that goes beyond the specific spoken words. It includes pitch, amplitude, rate, and voice quality of speech. Paralanguage reminds us that people convey their feelings not only in what they say, but also in how they say it.

Practising Skills

Part A. Form groups of 2. Each person is to spend a couple of minutes thinking of a time in the past when he or she was emotional about something. Examples might include being upset with a parent, sibling, or friend; being excited or disappointed about an academic or athletic achievement; being angry with someone over an insult or slight; being disgusted by something someone has said or done; or being happy because of something good that happened. Do not share this event with the other person in your group.

Part B. Now you will conduct 2 role plays. Each will be an interview. In the first, 1 person will play the interviewer and the other will play the job applicant. The job is for a summer management internship with a large retail chain. Each role play will last no longer than 10 minutes. The interviewer is to conduct a normal job interview, except you are to continually rethink the emotional episode you envisioned in part A. Try hard to convey this emotion while, at the same time, being professional in interviewing the job applicant.

Part C. Now reverse positions for the second role play. The interviewer becomes the job applicant and vice versa. The new interviewer will conduct a normal job interview, except that he or she will continually rethink the emotional episode chosen in part A.

Part D. Spend 10 minutes analyzing the interview, with specific attention focused on these questions: What emotion(s) do you think the other person was conveying? What cues did you pick up? How accurate were you in reading those cues?

Reinforcing Skills

1. Watch the actors in an emotion-laden film, such as *Death of a Salesman* or *12 Angry Men*, for clues to the emotions they are exhibiting. Try to determine the various emotions projected and explain how you arrived at your conclusion.

2. Spend a day specifically looking for emotional cues in the people with whom you interact. Did paying attention to emotional cues improve communication?

Values, Attitudes, and Diversity in the Workplace

Corus Entertainment has a strong set of core values. How do these values affect the company's workplace?

LEARNING OUTCOMES

After studying this chapter, you should be able to:

1. Contrast Rokeach's terminal and instrumental values.

2. Describe Hofstede's value dimensions for assessing cultures.

3. Identify unique Canadian values.

4. Understand the three components of an attitude.

5. Describe key attitudes that affect organizational performance.

6. Summarize the main causes of job satisfaction.

7. Identify the main consequences of job satisfaction.

8. Identify four employee responses to job dissatisfaction.

9. Describe how organizations can manage diversity effectively.

10. Identify the benefits of cultural intelligence.

Toronto-based Corus Entertainment decided to partner with TD Bank in summer 2014 to support a program designed to aid Aboriginal children achieve literacy through summer camps.[1] The program, Frontier College, provides summer literacy camps to Aboriginal children in 80 communities across Canada. John Cassaday, president and CEO of Corus, explains that the company values "the healthy development and well-being of Canadian children."

Corus, a media and entertainment company that creates, broadcasts, and licenses content around the world (for example, Cartoon Network (Canada), HBO Canada, and TELETOON), has five core values:

Hand-out/FRONTIER COLLEGE/Newscom

- *Accountability:* We do what we say we will do—no excuses.
- *Knowledge:* We believe in continuous learning and the sharing of our insights and ideas.
- *Initiative:* We empower employees to make great things happen.
- *Innovation:* We are committed to creative thinking that leads to breakthrough ideas and superior results.
- *Teamwork:* We believe that the greatest value is realized when we work together.

Corus also values having a diverse workforce. In fact, it was named one of Canada's Best Diversity Employers in 2014 and one of Greater Toronto's Best Employers that same year.

Generally, we expect that an organization's stated values, like those of an individual, will be reflected in its actions. For example, if a company states that it values environmental responsibility but has processes that are not environmentally friendly, we would question whether that value is really important to the company.

In Corus' case, the company backs up its value statements with concrete policies and actions to show support for its values. Does having strong values make for a better workplace?

In this chapter, we look carefully at how values influence behaviour and consider the relationship between values and attitudes. We also examine two significant issues that arise from our discussion of values and attitudes: how to enhance job satisfaction and manage workforce diversity.

 **IS FOR EVERYONE**

- How do countries differ in their values?
- Are Millennials really different from their elders?
- What can you learn about OB from Aboriginal culture?
- What would you need to know to set up a business in Asia?

Values

👁 Watch on **MyManagementLab**

Honest Tea—Ethics—Company
Mission and Values

Is capital punishment right or wrong? Is a person's desire for power good or bad? The answers to these questions are value-laden.

Values represent basic convictions that "a specific mode of conduct or end-state of existence is personally or socially preferable to an opposite or converse mode of conduct or end-state of existence."[2] They contain a judgmental element in that they carry an individual's ideas as to what is right, good, or desirable. Values have both content and intensity attributes. The content attribute says a mode of conduct or end-state of existence is *important*. The intensity attribute specifies *how important* it is. When we rank an individual's values in terms of their intensity, we discover that person's **value system**. All of us have a hierarchy of values according to the relative importance we assign to values such as freedom, pleasure, self-respect, honesty, obedience, and equality.[3]

Values tend to be relatively stable and enduring.[4] Most of our values are formed in our early years—with input from parents, teachers, friends, and others. As children, we were told that certain behaviours or outcomes are *always* desirable or *always* undesirable. There were few grey areas. It is this absolute or "black-or-white" characteristic of values that more or less ensures their stability and endurance.

Below we examine two frameworks for understanding values: Milton Rokeach's terminal and instrumental values, and Kent Hodgson's general moral principles.

Rokeach Value Survey

① Contrast Rokeach's terminal and instrumental values.

Milton Rokeach created the Rokeach Value Survey (RVS), which consists of two sets of values, each containing 18 individual value items.[5] One set, called **terminal values**, refers to desirable end-states of existence. These are the goals that individuals would like to achieve during their lifetime. They include

- A comfortable life (a prosperous life)
- An exciting life (a stimulating, active life)
- A sense of accomplishment (lasting contribution)
- Equality (brotherhood, equal opportunity for all)
- Inner harmony (freedom from inner conflict)
- Happiness (contentedness)[6]

The other set, called **instrumental values**, refers to preferred modes of behaviour, or means for achieving the terminal values. They include

- Ambitious (hard-working, aspiring)
- Broad-minded (open-minded)
- Capable (competent, effective)
- Courageous (standing up for your beliefs)
- Imaginative (daring, creative)
- Honest (sincere, truthful)[7]

Each of us places value on both the ends (terminal values) and the means (instrumental values); a balance between the two is important. Which terminal and instrumental values are especially key vary by the person.

Hodgson's General Moral Principles

Ethics is the study of moral values or principles that guide our behaviour and inform us whether actions are right or wrong. Thus, ethical values are related to moral judgments about right and wrong.

values Basic convictions that a specific mode of conduct or end-state of existence is personally or socially preferable to an opposite or converse mode of conduct or end-state of existence.

value system A hierarchy based on a ranking of an individual's values in terms of their intensity.

terminal values Goals that individuals would like to achieve during their lifetime.

instrumental values Preferable ways of behaving.

ethics The study of moral values or principles that guide our behaviour and inform us whether actions are right or wrong.

In recent years, there has been concern that individuals are not grounded in moral values. It is believed that this lack of moral roots has resulted in a number of business scandals, such as those at WorldCom, Enron, Hollinger International, and even in the sponsorship scandal of the Canadian government. We discuss the issue of ethics further in Chapter 12.

Management consultant Kent Hodgson has identified seven general moral principles that individuals should follow when making decisions. He calls these "the Magnificent Seven" and suggests that they are universal values that managers should use to make *principled*, *appropriate*, and *defensible* decisions.[8] They are presented in *OB in Action—The Magnificent Seven Principles*.

Assessing Cultural Values

Corus Entertainment is committed to valuing diversity in its workplace,[10] which reflects a dominant value of Canada as a multicultural country. The approach to diversity is very different in the United States, which considers itself a melting pot with respect to different cultures. Corus' core values (accountability, knowledge, initiative, innovation, and teamwork) also guide employees. What do you know about the values of people from other countries? What values make Canadians unique?

OB IN ACTION
The Magnificent Seven Principles

→ *Dignity of human life.* The lives of **people are to be respected**.

→ *Autonomy.* All persons are **intrinsically valuable** and have the **right to self-determination**.

→ *Honesty.* **The truth should be told** to those who have a right to know it.

→ *Loyalty.* **Promises**, **contracts**, and **commitments** should be **honoured**.

→ *Fairness.* **People should be treated justly**.

→ *Humaneness.* Our **actions ought to accomplish good**, and we should **avoid doing evil**.

→ *The common good.* Actions should accomplish **the greatest good for the greatest number** of people.[9]

In Chapter 1, we noted that managers have to become capable of working with people from different cultures. Thus, it is important to understand how values differ across cultures.

Hofstede's Framework for Assessing Cultures

One of the most widely referenced approaches for analyzing variations among cultures was developed in the late 1970s by Geert Hofstede.[11] He surveyed more than 116 000 IBM employees in 40 countries about their work-related values, and found that managers and employees vary on 5 value dimensions of national culture:

- *Power distance.* **Power distance** describes the degree to which people in a country accept that power in institutions and organizations is distributed unequally. A high rating on power distance means that large inequalities of power and wealth exist and are tolerated in the culture, as in a class or caste system that discourages upward mobility. A low power distance rating characterizes societies that stress equality and opportunity.

- *Individualism vs. collectivism.* **Individualism** is the degree to which people prefer to act as individuals rather than as members of groups and believe in individual rights above all else. **Collectivism** emphasizes a tight social framework in which people expect others in groups of which they are a part to look after them and protect them.

- *Masculinity vs. femininity.* Hofstede's construct of **masculinity** is the degree to which the culture favours traditional masculine roles, such as achievement, power, and control, as opposed to viewing men and women as equals. A high masculinity rating indicates the culture has separate roles for men and

2 Describe Hofstede's value dimensions for assessing cultures.

power distance A national culture attribute that describes the extent to which a society accepts that power in institutions and organizations is distributed unequally.

individualism A national culture attribute that describes the degree to which people prefer to act as individuals rather than as members of groups.

collectivism A national culture attribute that describes a tight social framework in which people expect others in groups of which they are a part to look after them and protect them.

masculinity A national culture attribute that describes the extent to which the culture favours traditional masculine work roles of achievement, power, and control. Societal values are characterized by assertiveness and materialism.

⏴⊙⏵ Simulate on MyManagementLab

Human Resources and Diversity

women, with men dominating the society. A high **femininity** rating means the culture sees little differentiation between male and female roles and treats women as the equals of men in all respects.

- *Uncertainty avoidance.* The degree to which people in a country prefer structured over unstructured situations defines their uncertainty avoidance. In cultures that score high on uncertainty avoidance, people have an increased level of anxiety about uncertainty and ambiguity, and use laws and controls to reduce uncertainty. Cultures low on **uncertainty avoidance** are more accepting of ambiguity and are less rule-oriented, take more risks, and more readily accept change.

- *Long-term vs. short-term orientation.* This more recent addition to Hofstede's typology measures a society's long-term devotion to traditional values. People in a culture with **long-term orientation** look to the future and value thrift, persistence, and tradition. In a culture with **short-term orientation**, people value the here and now; they accept change more readily and don't see commitments as impediments to change.

More recently, Hofstede has added a sixth dimension, based on studies he has conducted over the past 10 years.[12]

- *Indulgence vs. restraint.* This newest addition to Hofstede's typology measures society's devotion (or lack thereof) to indulgence. Cultures that emphasize **indulgence** encourage "relatively free gratification of basic and natural human desires related to enjoying life."[13] Those that favour **restraint** emphasize the need to control the gratification of needs.

How do different countries score on Hofstede's dimensions? Exhibit 3-1 shows the ratings for the countries for which data are available. For example, power distance is higher in Malaysia than in any other country. Canada is tied with the Netherlands as one of the top five individualistic countries in the world, falling just behind the United States, Australia, and Great Britain. Canada also tends to be short term in orientation and is low in power distance (people in Canada tend not to accept built-in class differences among people). Canada is also relatively low on uncertainty avoidance, meaning that most adults are relatively tolerant of uncertainty and ambiguity. Canada has a much higher score on masculinity in comparison with Sweden and Norway, although its score is lower than that of the United States.

You will notice regional differences. Western and Northern nations such as Canada and the Netherlands tend to be more individualistic. Poorer countries such as Mexico and the Philippines tend to be higher on power distance. South American nations tend to be higher than other countries on uncertainty avoidance, and Asian countries tend to have a long-term orientation.

> How do countries differ in their values?

Hofstede's cultural dimensions have been enormously influential on OB researchers and managers. Nevertheless, his research has been criticized. First, Hofstede's original work is over 40 years old and was based on a single company (IBM). Thus, people question its relevance to today. However, the work was updated and reaffirmed by a Canadian researcher at the Chinese University of Hong Kong (Michael Bond), who conducted research on values in 22 countries on 5 continents during the 1980s.[14] Between 1990 and 2002, the work was updated again by Hofstede and his colleagues with six major studies that each included a minimum of 14 countries.[15] These more recent studies used a variety of subjects: elites, employees and managers of corporations other than IBM; airline pilots; consumers; and civil servants. Hofstede notes that the more recent studies are consistent with the results of his original study. Second, few researchers have read the details of Hofstede's

femininity A national culture attribute that sees little differentiation between male and female roles; women are treated as the equals of men in all respects.

uncertainty avoidance A national culture attribute that describes the extent to which a society feels threatened by uncertain and ambiguous situations and tries to avoid them.

long-term orientation A national culture attribute that emphasizes the future, thrift, and persistence.

short-term orientation A national culture attribute that emphasizes the past and present, respect for tradition, and fulfillment of social obligations.

indulgence A national culture attribute that emphasizes the gratification of basic needs and the desire to enjoy life.

restraint A national culture attribute that emphasizes the importance of controlling the gratification of needs.

EXHIBIT 3-1 Hofstede's Cultural Values by Nation

Country	Power Distance Index	Power Distance Rank	Individualism versus Collectivism Index	Individualism versus Collectivism Rank	Masculinity versus Femininity Index	Masculinity versus Femininity Rank	Uncertainty Avoidance Index	Uncertainty Avoidance Rank	Long- versus Short-Term Orientation Index	Long- versus Short-Term Orientation Rank
Argentina	49	35–36	46	22–23	56	20–21	86	10–15		
Australia	36	41	90	2	61	16	51	37	31	22–24
Austria	11	53	55	18	79	2	70	24–25	31	22–24
Belgium	65	20	75	8	54	22	94	5–6	38	18
Brazil	69	14	38	26–27	49	27	76	21–22	65	6
Canada	39	39	80	4–5	52	24	48	41–42	23	30
Chile	63	24–25	23	38	28	46	86	10–15		
Colombia	67	17	13	49	64	11–12	80	20		
Costa Rica	35	42–44	15	46	21	48–49	86	10–15		
Denmark	18	51	74	9	16	50	23	51	46	10
Ecuador	78	8–9	8	52	63	13–14	67	28		
El Salvador	66	18–19	19	42	40	40	94	5–6		
Finland	33	46	63	17	26	47	59	31–32	41	14
France	68	15–16	71	10–11	43	35–36	86	10–15	39	17
Germany	35	42–44	67	15	66	9–10	65	29	31	22–24
Great Britain	35	42–44	89	3	66	9–10	35	47–48	25	28–29
Greece	60	27–28	35	30	57	18–19	112	1		
Guatemala	95	2–3	6	53	37	43	101	3		
Hong Kong	68	15–16	25	37	57	18–19	29	49–50	96	2
India	77	10–11	48	21	56	20–21	40	45	61	7
Indonesia	78	8–9	14	47–48	46	30–31	48	41–42		
Iran	58	29–30	41	24	43	35–36	59	31–32		
Ireland	28	49	70	12	68	7–8	35	47–48	43	13
Israel	13	52	54	19	47	29	81	19		
Italy	50	34	76	7	70	4–5	75	23	34	19
Jamaica	45	37	39	25	68	7–8	13	52		
Japan	54	33	46	22–23	95	1	92	7	80	4
Korea (South)	60	27–28	18	43	39	41	85	16–17	75	5
Malaysia	104	1	26	36	50	25–26	36	46		
Mexico	81	5–6	30	32	69	6	82	18		
The Netherlands	38	40	80	4–5	14	51	53	35	44	11–12
New Zealand	22	50	79	6	58	17	49	39–40	30	25–26
Norway	31	47–48	69	13	8	52	50	38	44	11–12
Pakistan	55	32	14	47–48	50	25–26	70	24–25	0	34
Panama	95	2–3	11	51	44	34	86	10–15		
Peru	64	21–23	16	45	42	37–38	87	9		
Philippines	94	4	32	31	64	11–12	44	44	19	31–32
Portugal	63	24–25	27	33–35	31	45	104	2	30	25–26
Singapore	74	13	20	39–41	48	28	8	53	48	9
South Africa	49	35–36	65	16	63	13–14	49	39–40		
Spain	57	31	51	20	42	37–38	86	10–15	19	31–32
Sweden	31	47–48	71	10–11	5	53	29	49–50	33	20
Switzerland	34	45	68	14	70	4–5	58	33	40	15–16
Taiwan	58	29–30	17	44	45	32–33	69	26	87	3
Thailand	64	21–23	20	39–41	34	44	64	30	56	8
Turkey	66	18–19	37	28	45	32–33	85	16–17		
United States	40	38	91	1	62	15	46	43	29	27
Uruguay	61	26	36	29	38	42	100	4		
Venezuela	81	5–6	12	50	73	3	76	21–22		
Yugoslavia	76	12	27	33–35	21	48–49	88	8		
Regions:										
Arab countries	80	7	38	26–27	53	23	68	27		
East Africa	64	21–23	27	33–35	41	39	52	36	25	28–29
West Africa	77	10–11	20	39–41	46	30–31	54	34	16	33

Scores range from 0 = extremely low on dimension to 100 = extremely high.

Note: 1 = highest rank. LTO ranks: 1 = China; 15–16 = Bangladesh; 21 = Poland; 34 = lowest.

Source: Geert Hofstede, Gert Jan Hofstede, Michael Minkov, "Cultures and Organizations, Software of the Mind," Third Revised Edition, McGrawHill 2010, ISBN 0-07-166418-1.

methodology closely and are therefore unaware of the many decisions and judgment calls he had to make (for example, reducing the number of cultural values to just five). Despite these concerns, many of which Hofstede refutes,[16] he has been one of the most widely cited social scientists ever, and his framework has left a lasting mark on OB.

RESEARCH FINDINGS: Hofstede

Recent research across 598 studies with more than 200 000 respondents has investigated the relationship of Hofstede's cultural values and a variety of organizational criteria at both the individual and national level of analysis.[17] Overall, the five original cultural dimensions were equally strong predictors of relevant outcomes, meaning that researchers and practising managers need to think about culture holistically and not just focus on one or two dimensions. The researchers also found that measuring individual scores resulted in much better predictions of most outcomes than assigning all people in a country the same cultural values. In sum, this research suggests that Hofstede's value framework may be a valuable way of thinking about differences among people, but we should be cautious about assuming that all people from a country have the same values.

The GLOBE Framework for Assessing Cultures

Begun in 1993, the Global Leadership and Organizational Behavior Effectiveness (GLOBE) research program is an ongoing cross-cultural investigation of leadership and national culture. Using data from 825 organizations in 62 countries, the GLOBE team identified nine dimensions on which national cultures differ.[18] Some—such as power distance, individualism/collectivism, uncertainty avoidance, gender differentiation (similar to masculinity vs. femininity), and future orientation (similar to long-term vs. short-term orientation)—resemble the Hofstede dimensions. The main difference is that the GLOBE framework added dimensions, such as humane orientation (the degree to which a society rewards individuals for being altruistic, generous, and kind to others) and performance orientation (the degree to which a society encourages and rewards group members for performance improvement and excellence).

Which framework is better? That is hard to say, and each has its adherents. We give more emphasis to Hofstede's dimensions here because they have stood the test of time and the GLOBE study confirmed them. For example, a review of the organizational commitment literature shows that both the Hofstede and GLOBE individualism/collectivism dimensions operated similarly. Specifically, both frameworks showed that organizational commitment (which we discuss later in the chapter) tends to be lower in individualistic countries.[19] This study shows that too often we make false assumptions about different cultures. Ultimately, both frameworks have a great deal in common, and each has something to offer.

The *Ethical Dilemma* on page 115 asks you to consider when something is a gift and when it is a bribe. Different cultures take different approaches to this question.

Values in the Canadian Workplace

3 Identify unique Canadian values.

Studies have shown that when individual values align with organizational values, the results are positive. Individuals who have an accurate understanding of the job requirements and the organization's values adjust better to their jobs, and have greater levels of satisfaction and organizational commitment.[20] In addition, shared values between the employee and the organization lead to more positive work attitudes,[21] lower turnover,[22] and greater productivity.[23]

Individual and organizational values do not always align. Moreover, within organizations, individuals can have very different values. Two major factors lead to a potential clash of values in the Canadian workplace: generational differences and cultural differences.

EXHIBIT 3-2 Dominant Work Values in Today's Workforce

Cohort	Entered the Workforce	Approximate Current Age	Dominant Work Values
Baby Boomers	1965–1985	Mid-40s to mid-60s	Success, achievement, ambition, dislike of authority; loyalty to career
Generation Xers	1985–2000	Late 20s to early 40s	Work–life balance, team-oriented, dislike of rules; loyalty to relationships
Millennials	2000 to present	Under 30	Confident, financial success, self-reliant but team-oriented; loyalty to both self and relationships

Let's look at the findings and implications of generational and cultural differences in Canada.

Generational Differences

Research suggests that generational differences exist in the workplace among the Baby Boomers (born between the mid-1940s and the mid-1960s), Generation Xers (born between the mid-1960s and the late 1970s), and the Millennials (born between 1979 through 1994).[24] Exhibit 3-2 highlights the different work values of the three generations, and indicates when each entered the workforce. Because most people start working between the ages of 18 and 23, the eras also correlate closely with employee age.

Generation Xers are squeezed in the workplace between the much larger Baby Boomer and Millennial groups. With Millennials starting to climb the ladder in organizations,

Courtesy of Rona Inc.

When Robert Dutton, former president and CEO of Boucherville, Quebec-based Rona, started working at the company, senior managers often were his grandfather's age, while he was a young Baby Boomer. After working over 30 years at Rona, Dutton noticed that Millennials were starting to make up a larger portion of Rona's dealers. Dutton started the group Young Rona Business Leaders to help develop the Millennial talent that will be the future of Rona.[25]

while Boomers are continuing to hold on to their jobs rather than retire, the impact of having these two large generations—one younger and one older—in the workplace is gaining attention. Bear in mind that our discussion of these generations presents broad generalizations, and you should certainly avoid stereotyping individuals on the basis of these generalizations. There are individual differences in values. For instance, there is no law that says a Baby Boomer cannot think like a Millennial. Despite these limitations, values do change over generations.[26] We can gain some useful insights from analyzing values this way to understand how others might view things differently from ourselves, even when they are exposed to the same situation.

Baby Boomers

Baby Boomers (or *Boomers* for short) are a large cohort born after World War II, when veterans returned to their families and times were good. Boomers entered the workforce from the mid-1960s through the mid-1980s. They brought with them the "hippie ethic" and distrust of authority. But they placed a great deal of emphasis on achievement and material success. Pragmatists who believe ends can justify means, they work hard and want to enjoy the fruits of their labours. Boomers see the organizations that employ them merely as vehicles for their careers. Terminal values such as a sense of accomplishment and social recognition rank high with them.

Generation X

The lives of Generation Xers (or *Xers* for short) have been shaped by globalization, two-career parents, MTV, AIDS, and computers. They value flexibility, life options, and the achievement of job satisfaction. Family and relationships are very important to this cohort. Xers are skeptical, particularly of authority. They also enjoy team-oriented work. In search of balance in their lives, Xers are less willing to make personal sacrifices for the sake of their employer than previous generations were. They rate high on the terminal values of true friendship, happiness, and pleasure.

THE CANADIAN PRESS/Larry MacDougal

When Sean Durfy announced that he was resigning as CEO of Calgary-based WestJet in 2011, he said it was for "family reasons." While that has often been code for "being let go," in Durfy's case it was more likely the truth. His wife had been ill for four years, and the couple has young children. Instead, there was talk that Durfy's announcement was the start of what might be expected from other Generation Xers, who "work to live rather than live to work." Baby Boomers were expected to sacrifice their family to climb the corporate ladder. But this may no longer be true of younger generations.

Millennials

The most recent entrants to the workforce, the Millennials, grew up during prosperous times. They have high expectations and seek meaning in their work. Millennials have life goals more oriented toward becoming rich (81 percent) and famous (51 percent) than do Xers (62 percent and 29 percent, respectively), but they also see themselves as socially responsible and are at ease with diversity. Millennials are the first generation to take technology for granted. More than other generations, they tend to be questioning, electronically networked, and entrepreneurial. At the same time, some have described Millennials as entitled and needy. They grew up with parents who watched (and praised) their every move. They may clash with other generations over work attire and communication. They also like feedback. An Ernst & Young survey found that 85 percent of Millennials want "frequent and candid performance feedback," compared with only half of Boomers.[27]

Are Millennials really different from their elders?

The Generations Meet in the Workplace

An understanding that individuals' values differ but tend to reflect the societal values of the period in which they grew up can be a valuable aid in explaining and predicting behaviour. Baby Boomers currently dominate the workplace, but their years of being in charge are limited. In 2013, half of them were at least 55 and 18 percent were over 60.[28]

RESEARCH FINDINGS: Generational Differences

Although it's fascinating to think about generational values, remember that these classifications lack solid research support. Early research was plagued by methodological problems that made it difficult to assess whether differences actually exist. Recent reviews suggest many of the generalizations are either overblown or incorrect.[29] Studies that have found differences across generations often don't support popular conceptions of how generations differ. One study that used an appropriate longitudinal design did find the value placed on leisure has increased over generations from the Baby Boomers to the Millennials and work centrality has declined, but it did not find that Millennials had more altruistic work values as expected.[30] Generational classifications may help us understand our own and other generations better, but we must also appreciate their limits. A new generation will be coming to the workplace soon, and researchers suggest that this new generation may be the cause of revolution in the workplace. *OB in the Street* looks at Generation Z.

IN THE STREET
Generation Z: Coming to Your Workplace Soon

Will the next generation of employees be radically different from their older siblings? Ann Makosinski, just 16 years old and from Victoria, is already trying to start her own company.[31] A friend from the Philippines was having trouble getting homework done and failed a grade, because she did not have access to electricity to study at night. Makosinski won Google's annual international science fair in 2013 with her battery-free "Hollow Flashlight," which is powered by body heat.

Makosinski is part of Generation Z, the group that comes after the Millennials, and was born starting in 1995. The oldest are 19, and just starting to enter the workplace. Makosinski's cohort is described by researchers as "educated, industrious, collaborative and eager to build a better planet," exactly what she is already doing.

Sparks & Honey, a New York City advertising agency, found that 60 percent of Gen Zers want jobs that had a social impact compared with 31 percent of Millennials. They are the first generation to have digital access from the crib, making them extremely comfortable in that world. While their parents feel anxious about how multitasking might affect thinking, Gen Zers see it as a natural action.

It's probably too early to define where Gen Z will go, but Makosinski is representative of her generation thus far. "I'm just very glad I've been able to inspire a few people," she says. "I think that's what really changed my life, now I'm more conscious of my actions and how I spend my time."

Cultural Differences

Canada is a multicultural country: In 2011, 20.6 percent of its population was foreign-born.[32] This figure compares with 12.9 percent for the United States.[33] In 2011, 46 percent of Toronto's population, 40 percent of Vancouver's population, and 22.6 percent of Montreal's population were made up of immigrants.[34] The 2011 Census found that 20 percent of Canada's population spoke a language other than the country's two official languages at home. In Vancouver and Toronto, this rate was 31 percent and 32 percent, respectively, so nearly one-third of the population of those two cities does not speak either English or French as a first language.[35] In Canada, of those who speak other languages, the dominant languages are Punjabi, Chinese (not specified), Cantonese, and Spanish.[36] These figures indicate the very different cultures that are part of the Canadian fabric of life.

PERSONAL INVENTORY ASSESSMENT

Learn About Yourself
Intercultural Sensitivity Scale

Although we live in a multicultural society, some tension exists among people from different races and ethnic groups. In a recent poll, 68 percent of Canadians reported having heard a racist comment in the past year. About 31 percent reported witnessing a racist incident. Young people aged 18 to 24 were more likely to report having heard racist comments (81 percent) and having witnessed racist incidents (50 percent).[37]

Canadians often define themselves as "not Americans" and point out differences in the values of the two countries. Ipsos Reid recently conducted a national survey of Americans and Canadians, ages 18 to 34, and found a number of differences between the two countries' young adults. Both groups rated health care, education, and employment as their top concerns. "When we compare the lifestyles of young adults in the United States and Canada, one could describe the Americans as more 'traditional' and more 'domestic' in their values and focus, whereas Canadians are more of the 'free-spirit' type," said Samantha McAra, senior research manager with Ipsos Reid.[38] Exhibit 3-3 shows some of the other differences between Canadian and American young adults.

Next, we identify a number of cultural values that influence workplace behaviour in Canada. Be aware that these are generalizations, and it would be a mistake to assume that everyone coming from the same cultural background acts similarly. Rather, these overviews are meant to encourage you to think about cultural differences and similarities so that you can better understand people's behaviour.

Francophone and Anglophone Values

Quebec is generally seen as culturally, linguistically, politically, and legally distinct from the rest of Canada.[39] French, not English, is the dominant language in Quebec, and Roman Catholicism, not Protestantism, is the dominant religion. Unlike the rest of Canada, where the law is based on English common law principles, Quebec's legal system is based on the French civil code. From time to time, Quebec separatists threaten that the province will leave Canada. Thus, it will be of interest to managers and employees in Canadian firms to be aware of some of the potential cultural differences when managing in francophone environments compared with anglophone environments.

EXHIBIT 3-3 Differences between Canadian and American Young Adults, 18 to 34

	Canada	United States
Text messages per week (sent and received)	78.7	129.6
Online social media	Facebook: 81% had registered a profile MySpace: 23% had registered a profile	Facebook: 57% had registered a profile MySpace: 54% had registered a profile
Married	25%	39%
Domestic partnerships	18%	7%
Own a home	35%	45%
Employed on a full- or part-time basis or self-employed	62%	64%
Some post-secondary education	76%	68%
Actively participate in a recycling program	88%	72%
Use public transportation once a week or more often	33%	20%
Favourite sport	NHL hockey (58%)	NFL football (57%)

Source: Based on Ipsos Reid, *A Check-up on the Habits and Values of North America's Young Adults (Part 1)* (Calgary: Ipsos Reid, 2009), http://www.ipsos-na.com/news-polls/pressrelease.aspx?id=4532.

A number of studies have shown that English-speaking Canadians and French-speaking Canadians have distinctive value priorities. In general, Canadian anglophone managers are seen to be more individualistic than Canadian francophone managers,[40] although more recent research finds greater similarity between anglophone and francophone middle managers in terms of their individualistic–collectivistic orientation.[41] Francophones have also been shown to be more concerned about the interpersonal aspects of the workplace than task competence.[42] They have also been found to be more committed to their work organizations.[43] Earlier studies suggested that anglophones took more risks,[44] but more recent studies have found that this point has become less true and that French-speaking Canadians had the highest values for "reducing or avoiding ambiguity and uncertainty at work."[45]

Canadian anglophone business people have been found to use a more cooperative negotiating style when dealing with one another, compared with Canadian francophone business people.[46] However, Canadian francophones are more likely than Canadian anglophones to use a more cooperative approach during cross-cultural negotiations.[47] Other studies indicate that anglophone managers tend to value autonomy and intrinsic job values, such as achievement, and thus are more achievement-oriented, while francophone managers tend to value affiliation and extrinsic job values, such as technical supervision.[48] A recent study conducted at the University of Ottawa and Laval University suggests that some of the differences reported in previous research may be decreasing.[49] Another study suggests that anglophones and francophones are not very different personality-wise.[50] Yet another study indicates that French Canadians have become more like English Canadians in valuing autonomy and self-fulfillment.[51] These studies are consistent with a recent study that suggests there are few differences between francophones and anglophones.[52]

Professor Carolyn Egri of the business school at Simon Fraser University led a cross-cultural study on the attitudes of managers toward different influence strategies.[53] The study found that Canadian anglophone and francophone managers tend to favour somewhat different influence strategies. Specifically, Canadian anglophone managers consider behaviour that is beneficial to the organization first and foremost as more acceptable than do Canadian francophone managers. By contrast, Canadian francophone managers favour behaviour that is beneficial to their own interests first. They also consider the following behaviours more acceptable than do Canadian anglophone managers: "destructive legal behaviours" (what the authors term a "get out of my way or get trampled" approach) and "destructive illegal behaviours" (what the authors term a "burn, pillage and plunder" approach). The study also found that Mexican managers score higher than Canadian francophone managers on their acceptance of destructive behaviours. Both American and Canadian anglophone managers consider destructive behaviours to be less acceptable. The results of this study suggest that Canadian francophone managers might serve as a bridge between Mexican managers at one end and American and Canadian anglophone managers on the other because of their level of acceptance of the different influence styles studied. The study's authors concluded that Canadian francophones would do well in "joint ventures, business negotiations, and other organizational interactions that involve members of more divergent cultural groups. For example, a national Canadian firm may find it strategically advantageous to utilize Canadian francophones in negotiating business contracts with Mexican firms."[54]

Despite some cultural and lifestyle value differences, both francophone and anglophone managers today would have been exposed to more of the same types of organizational theories during their training in post-secondary school, which might also influence their outlooks as managers. Thus we would not expect to find large differences in the way that firms in francophone Canada are managed, compared with those in the rest of Canada.

Aboriginal Values

Entrepreneurial activity among Canada's Aboriginal peoples has been increasing at the same time that there are more partnerships and alliances between Aboriginal and non-Aboriginal businesses. Because of these business interactions, it's important to examine the types of differences we might observe in how each culture manages its businesses. For instance, sustainability is an important value in Aboriginal logging companies. Chilanko Forks, BC-based Tsi Del Del, a logging company, received the 2011 Aboriginal Forest Products Business Leadership Award because of the substantial amount of revenues the company put into education.[55] For every cubic metre harvested, the Alexis Creek First Nations–owned company puts 50 cents into a post-secondary educational fund. The fund is used to train the next generation of loggers. Andrew Gage, vice-president of the Forest Products Association of Canada, says that it's a wise investment for the company. "You are not going to find a group of people that are more committed to sustainable harvesting. They share those values that our industry has been trying to get to for the last decade or so."[56]

> What can you learn about OB from Aboriginal culture?

Aboriginal values "are usually perceived [by non-Aboriginals] as an impediment to economic development and organizational effectiveness."[57] These values include reluctance to compete, a time orientation different from the Western one, and an emphasis on consensus decision making.[58] Aboriginal people do not necessarily agree that these values are business impediments, however.

Specifically, although Canadian businesses and government have historically assumed that "non-Native people must teach Native people how to run their own organizations," the First Nations of Canada are not convinced.[59] They believe that traditional culture, values, and languages do not have to be compromised in the building of a self-sustaining economy. Moreover, they believe that their cultural values may actually be a positive force in conducting business.[60]

In recent years, Canadian businesses facing Native land claims have met some difficulties in trying to accommodate demands for appropriate land usage. In some cases, accommodation can mean less logging or mining by businesses until land claims are worked out. Cliff Hickey and David Natcher, two anthropologists from the University of Alberta, collaborated with the Little Red River Cree Nation in northern Alberta to develop a new model for forestry operations on First Nations land and achieve better communication between businesses and Native leaders.[61] The anthropologists sought to balance the Native community's traditional lifestyle with the economic concerns of forestry operations. *OB in Action— Ground Rules for Developing Business Partnerships with Aboriginal People* outlines several of Hickey and Natcher's recommended ground rules, which they say could be used in oil and gas developments as well. Johnson Sewepegaham, chief of the Little Red River Cree, said his community would use these recommendations to resolve difficulties on treaty lands for which Vernon, BC-based Tolko Industries and Vancouver-based Ainsworth jointly hold forest tenure. The two companies presented their general development plan to the Cree in fall 2008.[62] In 2009, the Cree were effective in persuading Tolko to revise its tree harvesting activities in a way that recognizes and respects the First Nations' ecological and cultural needs.[63]

OB IN ACTION
Ground Rules for Developing Business Partnerships with Aboriginal People

→ Modify management operations to **reduce negative impact on wildlife species**.

→ Modify operations to **ensure community access** to lands and resources.

→ **Protect** all those **areas identified by community members** as having biological, cultural, and historical significance.

→ **Recognize and protect Aboriginal and treaty rights** to hunting, fishing, trapping, and gathering activities.

→ **Increase** forest-based **economic opportunities** for community members.

→ **Focus feedback** on **performance**, not personalities.

→ **Increase** the **involvement of community members** in decision making.[64]

Lindsay Redpath of Athabasca University has noted that Aboriginal cultures are more collectivist in orientation than are non-Aboriginal cultures in Canada and the United States.[65] Aboriginal organizations are much more likely to reflect and advance the goals of the community. There is also a greater sense of family within the workplace, with greater affiliation and loyalty. Power distance in Aboriginal cultures is smaller than in non-Aboriginal cultures of Canada and the United States, and there is an emphasis on consensual decision making. Aboriginal cultures are lower on uncertainty avoidance than non-Aboriginal cultures in Canada and the United States. Aboriginal organizations and cultures tend to have fewer rules and regulations. Each of these differences suggests that businesses created by Aboriginal people will differ from non-Aboriginal businesses, and both research and anecdotal evidence support this conjecture.[66] For instance, Richard Prokopanko, director of government relations for Vancouver-based Alcan, says that shifting from handling issues in a generally legalistic, contract-oriented manner to valuing more dialogue and collaboration has helped ease some of the tension that had built up over 48 years between Alcan and First Nations people.[67]

Asian Values
The largest visible minority group in Canada are the Chinese. Over 1 million Chinese live in Canada, representing 26 percent of the country's visible minority population.[68] The Chinese in this country are a diverse group; they come from different countries, speak different languages, and practise different religions. The Chinese are only one part of the entire East and Southeast Asian population that influences Canadian society. It's predicted that by 2017 almost one-half of all visible minorities in Canada will come from two groups, South Asian and Chinese, and that these groups will be represented in almost equal numbers.[69] As well, many Canadian organizations, particularly those in

British Columbia, conduct significant business with Asian firms. Asian cultures differ from Canadian culture on many of the GLOBE dimensions discussed earlier. For instance, Asian cultures tend to exhibit greater power distance and greater collectivism. These differences in values can affect individual interactions.

What would you need to know to set up a business in Asia?

Professor Rosalie Tung of Simon Fraser University and her student Irene Yeung examined the importance of *guanxi* (personal connections with the appropriate authorities or individuals) for a sample of North American, European, and Hong Kong firms doing business with companies in mainland China.[70] They suggest that their findings are also relevant in understanding how to develop relationships with firms from Japan, South Korea, and Hong Kong.

"*Guanxi* refers to the establishment of a connection between two independent individuals to enable a bilateral flow of personal or social transactions. Both parties must derive benefits from the transaction to ensure the continuation of such a relationship."[71] *Guanxi* relations are based on reciprocation, unlike Western networked relationships, which may be characterized more by self-interest. *Guanxi* relationships are meant to be long-term and enduring, in contrast with the immediate gains sometimes expected in Western relationships. *Guanxi* also relies less on institutional law, and more on personal power and authority, than do Western relationships. Finally, *guanxi* relations are governed more by the notion of shame (that is, external pressures on performance), while Western relations often rely on guilt (that is, internal pressures on performance) to maintain agreements. *Guanxi* is seen as extremely important for business success in China—more than such factors as the right location, price, or strategy, or product differentiation and quality. For Western firms wanting to do business with Asian firms, an understanding of *guanxi* and an effort to build relationships are important strategic advantages.

Our discussion about differences in cross-cultural values should suggest to you that understanding other cultures matters. When Canadian firms develop operations across Canada, south of the border, or overseas, employees need to understand other cultures to work more effectively and get along with others.

PERSONAL INVENTORY ASSESSMENT

Learn About Yourself
Multicultural Awareness Scale

Attitudes

4 Understand the three components of an attitude.

Attitudes are evaluative statements—either positive or negative—about objects, people, or events. They reflect how we feel about something. When I say, "I like my job," I am expressing my attitude about work. Typically, researchers have assumed that attitudes have three components: cognition, affect, and behaviour.[72] Let's look at each.

The statement "My pay is low" is the **cognitive component** of an attitude—a description of or belief in the way things are. It sets the stage for the more critical part of an attitude—its **affective component**. Affect is the emotional or feeling segment of an attitude and is reflected in the statement "I'm angry over how little I'm paid." Finally, affect can lead to behavioural outcomes. The **behavioural component** of an attitude describes an intention to behave in a certain way toward someone or something—to continue the example, "I'm going to look for another job that pays better."

Viewing attitudes as having three components—cognition, affect, and behaviour—is helpful in understanding their complexity and the potential relationship between attitudes and behaviour. Keep in mind that these components are closely related, and cognition and affect in particular are inseparable in many ways. For example, imagine that you realized someone has just treated you unfairly. You are likely to have feelings about that, occurring virtually instantaneously with the realization. Thus, cognition and affect are intertwined.

Exhibit 3-4 illustrates how the three components of an attitude are related. In this example, an employee did not get a promotion he thought he deserved; a co-worker got it instead. The employee's attitude toward his supervisor is illustrated as follows:

attitudes Positive or negative feelings about objects, people, or events.

cognitive component The opinion or belief segment of an attitude.

affective component The emotional or feeling segment of an attitude.

behavioural component An intention to behave in a certain way toward someone or something.

EXHIBIT 3-4 The Components of an Attitude

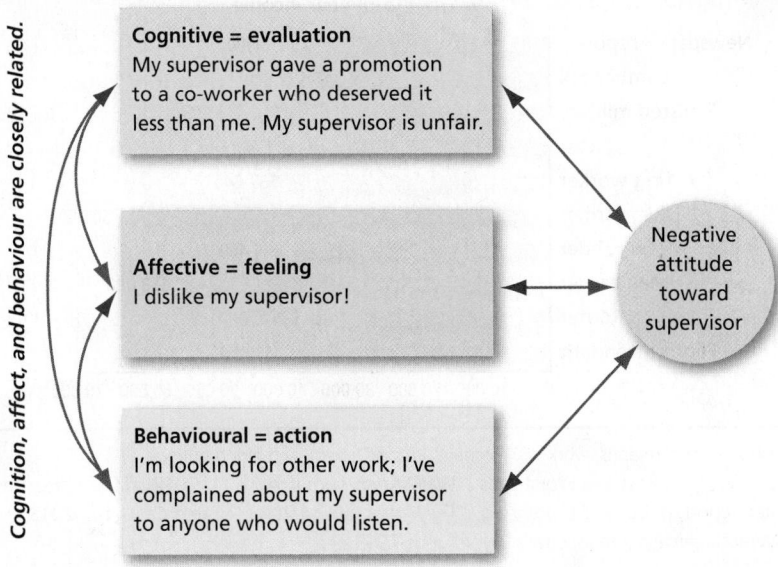

Cognition, affect, and behaviour are closely related.

Cognitive = evaluation
My supervisor gave a promotion to a co-worker who deserved it less than me. My supervisor is unfair.

Affective = feeling
I dislike my supervisor!

Behavioural = action
I'm looking for other work; I've complained about my supervisor to anyone who would listen.

Negative attitude toward supervisor

The employee thought he deserved the promotion (cognition), he strongly dislikes his supervisor (affect), and he has complained and taken action (behaviour). As we have noted, although we often think cognition causes affect, which then causes behaviour, in reality these components are difficult to separate.

In organizations, attitudes are important because they affect job behaviour.[73] Employees may believe, for example, that supervisors, auditors, managers, and time-and-motion engineers are all conspiring to make them work harder for the same or less money. This may then lead to a negative attitude toward management when an employee is asked to stay late for help on a special project.

Employees may also be negatively affected by the attitudes of their co-workers or clients. *From Concepts to Skills* on page 116 looks at whether it's possible to change someone's attitude, and how that might happen in the workplace.

A person can have thousands of attitudes, but OB focuses our attention on a limited number of work-related attitudes that tap positive or negative evaluations that employees hold about aspects of their work environments.[74] Below we consider five important attitudes that affect organizational performance: job satisfaction, organizational commitment, job involvement, perceived organizational support, and employee engagement.

5 Describe key attitudes that affect organizational performance.

Job Satisfaction

Our definition of **job satisfaction**—a positive feeling about a job resulting from an evaluation of its characteristics—is clearly broad.[75] A survey conducted by Mercer in 2011 found that Canadians are not all that satisfied: 36 percent said they were thinking about leaving their employers and another 20 percent were ambivalent about staying or going.[76]

What Causes Job Satisfaction?

Think about the best job you have ever had. What made it so? Chances are you liked the work you did and the people with whom you worked. Interesting jobs that provide training, variety, independence, and control satisfy most employees.[77] A recent European study indicated that job satisfaction is positively correlated with life satisfaction, in that your attitudes and experiences in life spill over into your job approaches and experiences.[78] Interdependence, feedback, social support, and interaction with co-workers outside the workplace are strongly related to job satisfaction even after accounting for

6 Summarize the main causes of job satisfaction.

job satisfaction A positive feeling about a job resulting from an evaluation of its characteristics.

EXHIBIT 3-5 The Worst Jobs for Job Satisfaction, 2013*

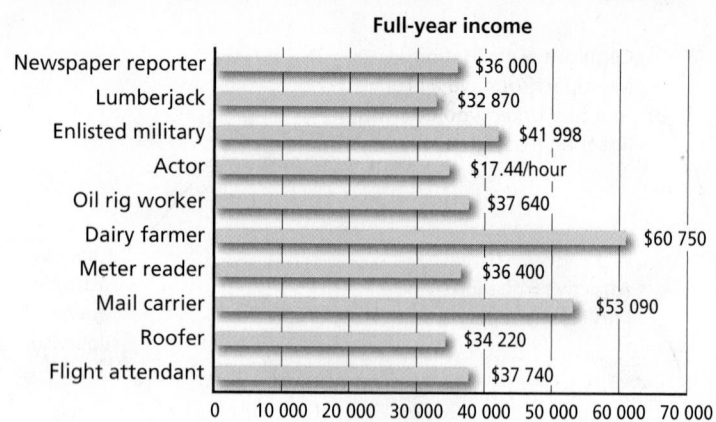

Full-year income

Job	Income
Newspaper reporter	$36 000
Lumberjack	$32 870
Enlisted military	$41 998
Actor	$17.44/hour
Oil rig worker	$37 640
Dairy farmer	$60 750
Meter reader	$36 400
Mail carrier	$53 090
Roofer	$34 220
Flight attendant	$37 740

*Based on physical demands, work environment, income, stress, and hiring outlook.
Sources: L. Weber, "Best and Worst Jobs," *Wall Street Journal*, April 11, 2012, in the CareerCast.com Jobs Rated report, p. B6; and K. Kensing, "The Worst Jobs of 2013," *CareerCast.com*, 2013, http://www.careercast.com/jobs-rated/worst-jobs-2013.

characteristics of the work itself.[79] A look at the list of worst jobs for job satisfaction (Exhibit 3-5) may give you some indications of what people consider bad jobs.

You have probably noticed that pay comes up often when people discuss job satisfaction. For people who are poor (for example, living below the poverty line) or who live in poor countries, pay does correlate with job satisfaction and overall happiness. But once an individual reaches a level of comfortable living (in Canada, that occurs at about $40 000 a year, depending on the region and family size), the relationship between pay and job satisfaction virtually disappears. People who earn $80 000 are, on average, no happier with their jobs than those who earn close to $40 000.[80] Take a look at Exhibit 3-6. It shows the relationship between the average pay for a job and the average level of job satisfaction. As you can see, not much of a relationship exists

EXHIBIT 3-6 Relationship between Average Pay in Job and Job Satisfaction of Employees in That Job

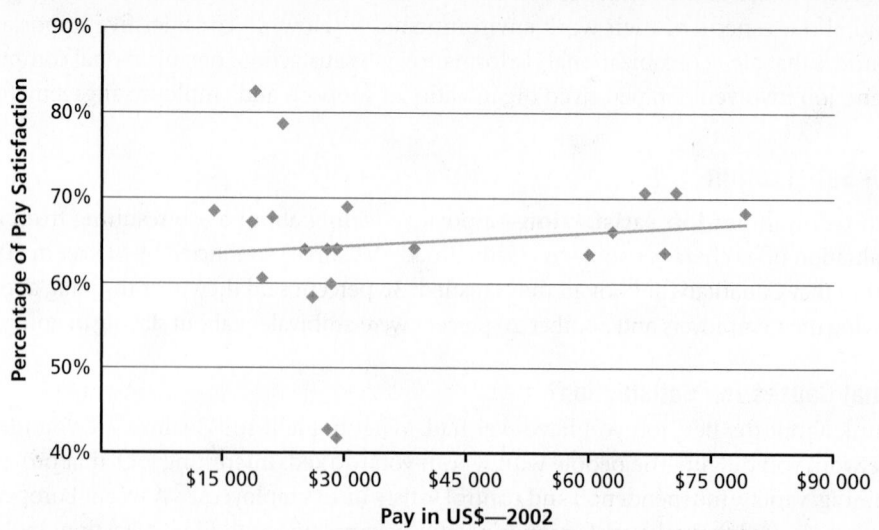

Source: T. A. Judge, R. F. Piccolo, N. P. Podsakoff, J. C. Shaw, and B. L. Rich, "Can Happiness Be 'Earned'? The Relationship between Pay and Job Satisfaction," working paper, University of Florida, 2005.

Britta Kasholm-Tengve/Getty Images

When asked "On a scale of 1 (not at all) to 7 (completely) how satisfied are you with your life?" *Forbes* magazine's "richest Americans" averaged 5.8 and an East African Maasai tribe, who engage in traditional herding and lead nomadic lives, averaged 5.7. The results of this study suggest that money does not buy life satisfaction.[81]

between pay and job satisfaction. One researcher even found no significant difference when he compared the overall well-being of the richest people on the *Forbes* 400 list with that of Maasai herders in East Africa.[82] *Case Incident—Thinking Your Way to a Better Job* on page 116 considers the effect state of mind has on a person's job satisfaction.

Money does motivate people, as we will discover in Chapter 4. But what motivates us is not necessarily the same as what makes us happy. A recent study found that people who work for companies with fewer than 100 employees, who supervise others, whose jobs include caregiving, who work in a skilled trade, and who are not in their 40s are more likely to be happy in their jobs.[83]

Job satisfaction is not just about job conditions. Personality also plays a role. Research has shown that people who have positive **core self-evaluations** (see Chapter 2)—who believe in their inner worth and basic competence—are more satisfied with their jobs than those with negative core self-evaluations. Not only do they see their work as fulfilling and challenging, they are more likely to gravitate toward challenging jobs in the first place. Those with negative core self-evaluations set less ambitious goals and are more likely to give up when they confront difficulties. Thus, they are more likely to be stuck in boring, repetitive jobs than those with positive core self-evaluations.[84]

So what are the consequences of job satisfaction? We examine this question below.

Job Satisfaction and Productivity

The authors of that review even labelled it "illusory." As several studies have concluded, happy workers are more likely to be productive workers. Some researchers used to believe the relationship between job satisfaction and job performance was a myth. But a review of more than 300 studies suggested the correlation between job satisfaction and job performance is quite strong, even across international contexts.[85] This conclusion also appears to be generalizable across international contexts. The correlation is higher for complex jobs that provide employees with more discretion to act on their attitudes.[86] As we move from the individual to the organizational level, we also find support for the satisfaction–performance relationship.[87] When we gather satisfaction and productivity data for the organization as a whole, we find organizations with more satisfied employees tend to be more effective than organizations with fewer.

 7 Identify the main consequences of job satisfaction.

core self-evaluation The degree to which an individual likes or dislikes himself or herself, whether the person sees himself or herself as capable and effective, and whether the person feels in control of his or her environment or powerless over the environment.

Matt Stroshane/Hong Kong Disneyland/AP Images

Employees waving to guests at Hong Kong Disneyland are committed to the company and its goal of giving visitors a magical and memorable experience. Through careful hiring and extensive training, Disney ensures that employees identify with its priority of pleasing customers by serving them as special guests.

Job Satisfaction and Organizational Citizenship Behaviour

In Chapter 1, we defined **organizational citizenship behaviour (OCB)** as discretionary behaviour that is not part of an employee's formal job requirements, and is not usually rewarded, but that nevertheless promotes the effective functioning of the organization.[88] Individuals who are high in OCB will go beyond their usual job duties, providing performance that is beyond expectations. Examples of such behaviour include helping colleagues with their workloads, taking only limited breaks, and alerting others to work-related problems.[89] More recently, OCB has been associated with the following workplace behaviours: "altruism, conscientiousness, loyalty, civic virtue, voice, functional participation, sportsmanship, courtesy, and advocacy participation."[90] OCB is important, as it can help the organization function more efficiently and more effectively.[91]

It seems logical to assume that job satisfaction should be a major determinant of an employee's OCB.[92] Satisfied employees would seem more likely to talk positively about an organization, help others, and go beyond the normal expectations in their jobs because they want to reciprocate their positive experiences.[93] Consistent with this thinking, evidence suggests that job satisfaction is moderately correlated with OCB; people who are more satisfied with their jobs are more likely to engage in OCB.[94] Why? Fairness perceptions help explain the relationship.[95] Those who feel their co-workers support them are more likely to engage in helpful behaviours, whereas those who have antagonistic relationships with co-workers are less likely to do so.[96] Individuals with certain personality traits are also more satisfied with their work, which in turn leads them to engage in more OCBs.[97] Finally, research shows that when people are in a good mood, they are more likely to engage in OCBs.[98]

Job Satisfaction and Customer Satisfaction

As we noted in Chapter 1, employees in service jobs often interact with customers. Because service organization managers should be concerned with pleasing customers, it's reasonable to ask: Is employee satisfaction related to positive customer outcomes?

organizational citizenship behaviour (OCB) Discretionary behaviour that is not part of an employee's formal job requirements, but that nevertheless promotes the effective functioning of the organization.

For front-line employees who have regular contact with customers, the answer is yes. Satisfied employees increase customer satisfaction and loyalty.[99]

A number of companies are acting on this evidence. The first core value of online retailer Zappos, "Deliver WOW through service,"[100] seems fairly obvious, but the way in which Zappos does it is not. Employees are encouraged to "create fun and a little weirdness" and are given unusual discretion in making customers satisfied; they are encouraged to use their imaginations, like sending flowers to disgruntled customers. Zappos offers a $2000 bribe to quit the company after training (to weed out the half-hearted).

Job Satisfaction and Absenteeism and Turnover

We find a consistent negative relationship between job satisfaction and absenteeism, but it is moderate to weak.[101] While it certainly makes sense that dissatisfied employees are more likely to miss work, other factors affect the relationship. Organizations that provide liberal sick leave benefits are encouraging all their employees—including those who are highly satisfied—to take days off. You can find work satisfying yet still want to enjoy a three-day weekend if those days come free with no penalties. When numerous alternative jobs are available, dissatisfied employees have high absence rates, but when there are few they have the same (low) rate of absence as satisfied employees.[102]

The relationship between job satisfaction and turnover is stronger than between job satisfaction and absenteeism.[103] Recent research suggests that managers looking to determine who might be likely to leave should focus on employees' job satisfaction levels over time, because levels do change. A pattern of lowered job satisfaction is a predictor of possible intent to leave. Job satisfaction has an environmental connection too. If the climate within an employee's immediate workplace is one of low job satisfaction, there will be a "contagion effect." This research suggests managers should consider the job satisfaction patterns of co-workers when assigning new workers to a new area for this reason.[104]

The satisfaction–turnover relationship also is affected by alternative job prospects. If an employee is presented with an unsolicited job offer, job dissatisfaction is less predictive of turnover because the employee is more likely leaving in response to "pull" (the lure of the other job) than "push" (the unattractiveness of the current job). Similarly, job dissatisfaction is more likely to translate into turnover when employment opportunities are plentiful because employees perceive it is easy to move. Also, when employees have high "human capital" (high education, high ability), job dissatisfaction is more likely to translate into turnover because they have, or perceive, many available alternatives.[105] Finally, employees' embeddedness in their jobs and communities can help lower the probability of turnover, particularly in collectivistic cultures.[106]

How Employees Can Express Dissatisfaction

Job dissatisfaction and antagonistic relationships with co-workers predict a variety of behaviours organizations find undesirable, including unionization attempts, substance abuse, stealing at work, undue socializing, and tardiness. Researchers argue that these behaviours are indicators of a broader syndrome called *deviant behaviour in the workplace* (or *counterproductive behaviour* or *employee withdrawal*).[107] If employees don't like their work environment, they will respond somehow, although it's not always easy to forecast exactly *how*. One worker might quit. Another might use work time to surf the Internet or take work supplies home for personal use. In short, workers who don't like their jobs "get even" in various ways—and because those ways can be quite creative, controlling only one behaviour, such as with an absence control policy, leaves the root cause untouched. To effectively control the undesirable consequences of job dissatisfaction, employers should attack the source of the problem—the dissatisfaction—rather than try to control the different responses.

Exhibit 3-7 presents a model—the exit-voice-loyalty-neglect framework—that can be used to examine individual responses to job dissatisfaction along two dimensions:

8 Identify four employee responses to job dissatisfaction.

EXHIBIT 3-7 Responses to Job Dissatisfaction

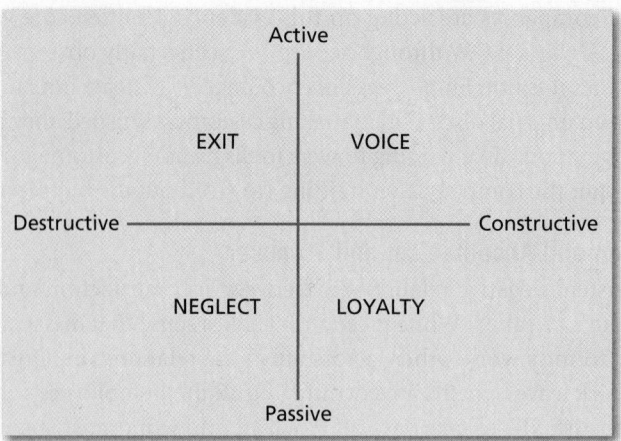

Source: "When Bureaucrats Get the Blues: Responses to Dissatisfaction among Federal Employees" by Caryl Rusbult, David Lowery. *Journal of Applied Social Psychology 15*, no. 1, p. 83. Copyright © 1985, John Wiley and Sons.

whether they are constructive or destructive and whether they are active or passive. Four types of behaviour result:[108]

- **Exit**. Actively attempting to leave the organization, including looking for a new position as well as resigning. This action is destructive from the point of view of the organization. Researchers study individual terminations and *collective turnover*, the total loss to the organization of employee knowledge, skills, abilities, and other characteristics.[109]

- **Voice**. Actively and constructively attempting to improve conditions, including suggesting improvements, discussing problems with superiors, and some forms of union activity.

- **Loyalty**. Passively but optimistically waiting for conditions to improve, including speaking up for the organization in the face of external criticism and trusting the organization and its management to "do the right thing."

- **Neglect**. Passively allowing conditions to worsen, including chronic absenteeism or lateness, reduced effort, and increased error rate. This action is destructive from the point of view of the organization.

Exit and neglect behaviours reflect employee choices of lowered productivity, absenteeism, and turnover in the face of dissatisfaction. But this model also presents constructive behaviours such as voice and loyalty that allow individuals to tolerate unpleasant situations or to work toward satisfactory working conditions. It helps us understand situations, such as those we sometimes find among unionized workers, where low job satisfaction is coupled with low turnover.[110] Union members often express dissatisfaction through the grievance procedure or through formal contract negotiations. These voice mechanisms allow them to continue in their jobs while convincing themselves that they are acting to improve the situation.

Managers Often "Don't Get It"

Given the evidence we have just reviewed, it should come as no surprise that job satisfaction can affect the bottom line. One study by a management consulting firm

exit Dissatisfaction expressed by actively attempting to leave the organization.

voice Dissatisfaction expressed by actively and constructively attempting to improve conditions.

loyalty Dissatisfaction expressed by passively waiting for conditions to improve.

neglect Dissatisfaction expressed by passively allowing conditions to worsen.

separated large organizations into high morale (where more than 70 percent of employees expressed overall job satisfaction) and medium or low morale (fewer than 70 percent). The stock prices of companies in the high morale group grew 19.4 percent, compared with 10 percent for the medium or low morale group. Despite these results, many managers are unconcerned about employee job satisfaction. Still others overestimate how satisfied employees are with their jobs, so they don't think there is a problem when there is. In one study of 262 large employers, 86 percent of senior managers believed their organization treated its employees well, but only 55 percent of the employees agreed.[111] Another study found 55 percent of managers thought morale was good in their organization, compared with only 38 percent of employees.[112] Managers first need to care about job satisfaction, and then they need to measure it rather than just assume that everything is going well.[113]

Organizational Commitment

In **organizational commitment** an employee identifies with a particular organization and its goals, and wishes to remain a member.[114] Most research has focused on emotional attachment to an organization and belief in its values as the "gold standard" for employee commitment.[115]

Professor John Meyer at the University of Western Ontario and his colleagues have identified and developed measures for three types of commitment:[116]

- **Affective commitment**. An individual's emotional attachment to an organization and a belief in its values. For example, a PetSmart employee may be affectively committed to the company because of its involvement with animals.

- **Normative commitment**. The obligation an individual feels to stay with an organization for moral or ethical reasons. An employee spearheading a new initiative may remain with an employer because she feels she would "leave the employer in the lurch" if she left.

- **Continuance commitment**. An individual's perceived economic value of remaining with an organization. An employee may be committed to an employer because she is paid well and feels it would hurt her family to quit.

A positive relationship appears to exist between organizational commitment and job productivity, but it is a modest one.[117] A review of 27 studies found that the relationship between commitment and performance is strongest for new employees, and considerably weaker for more experienced employees.[118] Interestingly, research indicates that employees who feel their employers fail to keep promises to them feel less committed, and these reductions in commitment, in turn, lead to lower levels of creative performance.[119] And, as with job involvement, the research evidence demonstrates negative relationships between organizational commitment and both absenteeism and turnover.[120]

Different forms of commitment have different effects on behaviour. One study found managerial affective commitment more strongly related to organizational performance than was continuance commitment.[121] Another study showed that continuance commitment was related to a lower intention to quit but an increased tendency to be absent and lower job performance. These results make sense in that continuance commitment is not really a commitment at all. Rather than an allegiance (affective commitment) or an obligation (normative commitment) to an employer, a continuance commitment describes an employee "tethered" to an employer simply because nothing better is available.[122]

Point/Counterpoint on page 113 considers whether employer–employee loyalty is still relevant today.

organizational commitment The degree to which an employee identifies with a particular organization and its goals, and wishes to maintain membership in the organization.

affective commitment An individual's emotional attachment to and identification with an organization, and a belief in its values.

normative commitment The obligation an individual feels to stay with an organization.

continuance commitment An individual's calculation to stay with an organization based on the perceived costs of leaving the organization.

Katsumi Kasahara/AP Images

A major focus of Nissan Motor Company's Diversity Development Office in Japan is helping female employees develop their careers. Nissan provides women such as the assembly-line workers shown here with one-on-one counselling services of career advisers and training programs to develop applicable skills. Women can also visit Nissan's corporate intranet to read interviews with "role models," women who have made substantial contributions to the company. Nissan believes that hiring more women and supporting their careers will contribute to the company's competitive edge.

Job Involvement

◉-⎡Watch on **MyManagementLab**

Gawker Media: Attitudes and Job Satisfaction

Related to job satisfaction is **job involvement**,[123] which measures the degree to which people identify psychologically with their job and consider their perceived performance level important to self-worth.[124] Employees with a high level of job involvement strongly identify with and really care about the kind of work they do. Another closely related concept is **psychological empowerment**, employees' beliefs in the degree to which they influence their work environment, their competence, the meaningfulness of their job, and their perceived autonomy.[125] One study of nursing managers in Singapore found that good leaders empower their employees by fostering their self-perception of competence—through involving them in decisions, making them feel their work is important, and giving them discretion to "do their own thing."[126] Another study found, however, that for teachers in India, the self-perception of competence does not affect innovative behaviour, which would be a desired outcome. This research suggests that empowerment initiatives need to be tailored to the culture and desired behavioural outcomes.[127]

job involvement The degree to which a person identifies with a job, actively participates in it, and considers performance important to self-worth.

psychological empowerment Employees' belief in the degree to which they affect their work environment, their competence, the meaningfulness of their job, and their perceived autonomy in their work.

perceived organizational support (POS) The degree to which employees believe an organization values their contribution and cares about their well-being.

Perceived Organizational Support

Perceived organizational support (POS) is the degree to which employees believe the organization values their contributions and cares about their well-being. An excellent example has been related by R & D engineer John Greene of salesforce.com. When Greene was diagnosed with leukemia, CEO Marc Benioff and 350 fellow salesforce.com employees covered all out-of-pocket costs for his care, staying in touch with him throughout his recovery. No doubt stories like this one are part of the reason salesforce.com is on *Fortune*'s 100 Best Companies to Work For list.[128]

Research shows that people perceive their organization as supportive when rewards are deemed fair, when employees have a voice in decisions, and when employees view their supervisors as supportive.[129] Employees with strong POS perceptions have been found to engage in higher levels of organizational citizenship behaviour, exhibit lower levels of tardiness, and offer better customer service.[130] These outcomes seem to hold true mainly in countries where power distance is lower. In such countries, including Canada, people are more likely to view work as an exchange rather than a moral obligation. This is not to say that POS cannot be a predictor of work behaviours anywhere on a situation-specific basis. Although little cross-cultural research has been done, one study found that POS predicted only the job performance and organizational citizenship behaviour of untraditional or low power-distance Chinese employees—in short, those more likely to think of work as an exchange rather than a moral obligation.[131]

Employee Engagement

A recent concept that comes out of the work on job involvement is **employee engagement**, an individual's involvement with, satisfaction with, and enthusiasm for the work he or she does. To evaluate employee engagement, we might ask employees whether they have access to resources and the opportunities to learn new skills, whether they feel their work is important and meaningful, and whether their interactions with co-workers and supervisors are rewarding.[132] Highly engaged employees have a passion for their work and feel a deep connection to their company; disengaged employees have essentially "checked out"—putting time but not energy or attention into their work.[133] Calgary-based Vista Projects, an engineering procurement and construction management firm, consults with its employees for engagement ideas. Doing so has resulted in educational initiatives, opportunities for company ownership, and time off for religious holidays.[134] To encourage engagement, the president of Charlottetown, PEI-based Holland College visits the college's 13 sites routinely to give employees an opportunity to raise concerns.[135]

Engagement is a real concern for most organizations because surveys indicate that few employees are highly engaged by their work. A 2012 survey of Canadians conducted by the Canadian Management Centre and Ipsos Reid found that "only 27 percent of employees are highly engaged and one in five are not engaged at all."[136] Engagement is highest in BC and Alberta, at 33 percent. Engagement is lowest for Millennials (24 percent) and Generation Xers (22 percent). Engagement is higher for Baby Boomers (29 percent), and Traditionalists (those 64 years or older) are the most engaged (49 percent). These numbers are consistent with the United States, but much higher than other countries. A 2013 survey by Gallup, conducted in 142 countries, found that only 13 percent of employees worldwide are engaged at work.[137] Most are disengaged: 63 percent are not engaged, and 24 percent are actively disengaged.

Toronto-based Molson Coors Canada found that engaged employees were five times less likely to have safety incidents, and when one did occur, it was much less serious, and less costly for the engaged employee than for a disengaged one ($63 per incident vs. $392). Molson proudly reported that its engagement went up in 2013 from 2012, reaching a high of 57 percent, compared with 51 percent in 2012.[138] Oakville, Ontario-based Ford Canada recently contracted with Charles "the Butler" MacPherson to help its employees develop more engaged customer service relationships, as *OB in the Workplace* illustrates.

OB IN THE **WORKPLACE**
Minding Manners, Helping Customers

Can a butler help salespeople engage more with their customers? Ford Canada recently hired Charles "the Butler" MacPherson to provide customer service training sessions to employees.[139] His first stop was Ottawa, and then 23 more Ford locations across Canada.

employee engagement An individual's involvement with, satisfaction with, and enthusiasm for the work he or she does.

MacPherson's role is to help employees in Ford's service departments engage more with their customers so that customers receive more personalized service. MacPherson explained why he was comfortable helping salespeople: "Whether you're serving food or whether you're presenting someone a proposal on a repair in the car, you still have to be able to do it in the same way about making sure that you're at ease, that we're listening to you, that you're able to speak your thoughts."

Ford Canada's national consumer experience manager, Gemma Giovinazzo, is enthusiastic about developing more engaged employees. "We know, based on statistical research, that a highly engaged employee will lead to a highly engaged customer. Highly engaged employees will bend over backwards for the company and its customers. In such a culture, there is no 'this is just my job; I am only going to do that.'"

Ford believes its investment in employees will also lead to more loyal customers. ____

PERSONAL INVENTORY ASSESSMENT

Learn About Yourself
Flourishing Scale

Managers and scholars have become interested in facilitating employee engagement, believing something deeper than liking a job or finding it interesting drives performance. Studies attempt to measure this deeper level of commitment. However, the concept is relatively new and still generates active debate about its usefulness. Part of the reason for this debate is the difficulty of identifying what creates job engagement. For instance, the top two reasons for job engagement that participants gave in one recent study were (1) having a good manager they enjoy working for and (2) feeling appreciated by their supervisor.[140] Another study found that engagement is linked to an employee's belief that he or she is engaged in meaningful work. This belief is partially determined by job characteristics and access to sufficient resources to work effectively.[141] Another factor is a match between the individual's values and those of the organization.[142] Leadership behaviours that inspire workers to a greater sense of mission also increase employee engagement.[143]

Recent research on engagement has set out to clarify the dimensions of employee engagement. For instance, a 2012 Australian study found that emotional intelligence is linked to job satisfaction, well-being, and employee engagement.[144] Another 2012 study suggested that engagement fluctuates partially due to daily challenge-seeking and demands.[145] This work has demonstrated that engagement is distinct from job satisfaction and job involvement and incrementally predicts job behaviours after we take these traditional job attitudes into account.[146] Moreover, engagement questionnaires usually assess motivation and absorption in a task, quite unlike job satisfaction questionnaires. Engagement may also predict important work outcomes better than traditional job attitudes.[147]

Some critics note that engagement may have a "dark side," as evidenced by positive relationships between engagement and work–family conflict.[148] Individuals might grow so engaged in their work roles that family responsibilities become an unwelcome intrusion. Further research exploring how engagement relates to these negative outcomes may help clarify whether some highly engaged employees might be getting "too much of a good thing."

Managing Diversity in the Workplace

Corus Entertainment was recognized as one of Canada's Best Diversity Employers in each year from 2009 to 2014.[149] It was also recognized as one of Greater Toronto's Top Employers in 2010, 2011, 2013, and 2014. Corus uses a wide variety of strategies to focus managers and employees on diversity issues. The company has an equity plan, a diversity and inclusion policy, and an equity and diversity committee that includes employees from a variety of ranks. Corus is committed to developing leadership talent in its female employees, creating the "Corus Women's Leadership Network" (CWLN) with training and social networking events.

Corus supports the development of female managers and managers from visible minorities: 43.7 percent of its managers are women, and 11.83 percent of its managers are visible minorities. The company also has diversity programs for employees in the following groups: women, disabilities, visible minorities, and Aboriginal people. Why does managing diversity well make a difference?

Organizations increasingly face diversity concerns as workplaces become more heterogeneous. **Biographical characteristics** such as age, gender, race, disability, and length of service are some of the most obvious ways employees differ. Others include length of service (tenure), religion, sexual orientation, and gender identity. There is also diversity in **ability**, an individual's current capacity to perform the various tasks in a job. Earlier in the chapter, we discussed cultural and generational differences and their implications in the Canadian workplace.

Many organizations have attempted to incorporate workforce diversity initiatives into their workplaces to improve relations among co-workers. Toronto-based Corus Entertainment is one such company. Corus' policy on diversity states the following:

> Corus is committed to promoting an equitable work environment based on the merit principle. Corus is also committed to conducting business and providing services in the communities where we operate in a manner that respects the dignity and independence of all employees and customers, including those with varying abilities.
>
> Our collective commitment to respect and nurture a diverse and accessible work environment promotes Accountability, Innovation, Initiative, Teamwork and Knowledge across the organization.[150]

Corus' statement on diversity is typical of statements found in company annual reports and employee information packets to signal corporate values to those who interact with the company. Some corporations choose to signal the value of diversity because they think it is an important strategic goal. Other organizations recognize that the purchasing power of diverse groups is substantial.

When companies design and then publicize statements about the importance of diversity, they are essentially producing value statements. The hope, of course, is that the statements will influence the behaviour of members of the organization, particularly since preference for people who are ethnically like ourselves may be ingrained in us at an early age. For example, in a study published in 2011, researchers from Concordia University and the University of Montreal found that Asian Canadian and French Canadian preschoolers preferred to interact with kids of their own ethnic group.[151]

Little research indicates that values can be changed successfully.[152] Because values tend to be relatively stable, workplaces try to address diversity issues through education aimed at changing attitudes.

Effective Diversity Programs

Joan Vogelesang, who was CEO of Montreal-based animation software company Toon Boom, says that Canadian companies don't make use of the diversity in the employees they have. She thinks Canadian companies need to look beyond imperfect English and cultural customs when hiring. When she worked at Toon Boom, most of her executive team were first-generation immigrants. Her employees could speak 20 languages among them. "Two . . . staff members [could] speak Japanese. You can hardly do business in Japan if you don't speak it," she says.[153]

Vogelesang's description of diversity as a competitive advantage speaks to the need for effective diversity programs that have three distinct components. First, they should teach people about the legal framework for equal employment opportunity

 Describe how organizations can manage diversity effectively.

biographical characteristics
Personal characteristics—such as age, gender, race, and length of tenure. These characteristics are representative of surface-level diversity.

ability An individual's capacity to perform the various tasks in a job.

◉⃞[Watch on **MyManagementLab**

Verizon Diversity

and encourage fair treatment of all people, regardless of their demographic character-istics. Second, they should teach people how a diverse workforce will be better able to serve a diverse market of customers and clients. Third, they should foster personal development practices that bring out the skills and abilities of all workers, acknowl-edging how differences in perspective can be a valuable way to improve performance for everyone.[154] A 2011 study by researchers at the University of Toronto Scarborough found that focusing on the positive benefits of diversity, rather than telling people what they should and should not do, was more likely to reduce people's prejudices toward other groups.[155] The *Experiential Exercise* on page 114 considers what it feels like to be targeted or excluded based on demographic status.

Much concern about diversity has to do with fair treatment.[156] Most negative reac-tions to employment discrimination are based on the idea that discriminatory treatment is unfair. Regardless of race or gender, people are generally in favour of diversity-oriented programs if they believe the policies ensure everyone has a fair opportunity to show their skills and abilities.

A major study of the consequences of diversity programs came to what might seem a surprising conclusion.[157] Organizations that provided diversity training were not consistently more likely to have women and minorities in upper management positions than organizations that did not. On closer examination, though, these results are not surprising. Experts have long known that one-shot training sessions without strategies to encourage effective diversity management back on the job are not likely to be very effective. Some diversity programs, such as those of Toronto-based Corus Entertainment, Ottawa-based Health Canada, Regina-based Information Services Corporation, and Brampton, Ontario-based Loblaw Companies, are truly effective in improving represen-tation in management. They include strategies to measure the representation of women and visible minorities in managerial positions, and they hold managers accountable for achieving more demographically diverse management teams.

Toon Boom

Joan Vogelesang, former CEO of Montreal-based animation software company Toon Boom, says that Canadian companies do not make use of the diversity in employees they have. She thinks Canadian com-panies need to look beyond imperfect English and cultural customs when hiring. When she worked at Toon Boom, most of her executive team were first-generation immigrants. Her employees could speak 20 languages among them. She is pictured with Francisco Del Cueto, CTO (left), and Steven Chu, COO (right).

EXHIBIT 3-8 Practices Used by a Selected Sample of Canada's Most Welcoming Places to Work

Company (Location)	Industry	Number of Employees	Diversity Activities
Jazz Aviation (Dartmouth, NS)	Aviation	4708	Launched a dedicated Aboriginal employee group and invited an Aboriginal elder to help develop the group's mission statement
Cameco Corp. (Saskatoon)	Mining	3169	Works with Women in Mining and the Mining Human Resource Council to research employment barriers faced by women in the mining industry
BC Hydro (Vancouver)	Electric utility (Crown Corporation)	4909	Maintains an in-house multicultural society as well as a cultural buddy program to provide support to employees from all walks of life
Canadian Imperial Bank of Commerce (Toronto)	Commercial bank	34 418	Maintains "WorkAbility," an employee network for persons with disabilities, and hosts an annual "Abilities Marketplace" event that offers services for persons with disabilities
Standard Aero (Winnipeg)	Aerospace industry	1425	Company's employment equity committee meets on a quarterly basis to review its employment equity plan
Ontario Public Service (OPS) (Toronto)	Government support	61 037	Manages the OPS Pride Network to support LGBT employees and allies
Sodexo Canada (Burlington, ON)	Food services	5943	Launched the "Willow Bean Café" in partnership with Vancouver Coastal Health and the Canadian Mental Health Association to provide employment opportunities and work experience to persons with mental health issues
Northwest Territories Government (Yellowknife)	Government services	5269	Created a government-wide Traditional Knowledge Policy to ensure that Aboriginal knowledge, values and experience are handed down from generation to generation
Newalta Corp. (Calgary)	Recycling and industrial waste management	1820	Established the Women's Leadership Network to support the advancement of female employees

Source: Based on "The Year's Most Inspiring Workplace Inclusiveness Stories: Canada's Best Diversity Employers for 2014 Announced Today," February 10, 2014, http://www.newswire.ca/en/story/1302795/the-year-s-most-inspiring-workplace-inclusiveness-stories-canada-s-best-diversity-employers-for-2014-announced-today; and http://www.canadastop100.com/diversity/.

Organizational leaders should examine their workforce to determine whether the **protected groups** covered by Canada's Employment Equity Act (women, people with disabilities, Aboriginal people, and visible minorities) have been underutilized. If groups of employees are not proportionally represented in top management, managers should look for any hidden barriers to advancement. They can often improve recruiting practices, make selection systems more transparent, and provide training for those employees who have not had adequate exposure to necessary work-related experiences in the past. Exhibit 3-8 presents examples of what some of the leading companies are doing as part of their diversity initiatives.[158]

protected groups The four groups designated by the Employment Equity Act as the beneficiaries of employment equity (women, people with disabilities, Aboriginal people, and visible minorities).

Management should also clearly communicate the company's diversity policies and their rationale to employees so they can understand how and why certain practices are followed. Communications should focus as much as possible on qualifications and job performance; emphasizing that certain groups need more assistance could well backfire.

To ensure the top-level management team represents the diversity of its workforce and client base, Safeway implemented the Retail Leadership Development (RLD) program, a formal career development program. This program is open to all employees, so it is inclusive, but women and underrepresented racial or ethnic groups are particularly encouraged to participate. Interested individuals take tests to determine whether they have management potential. Safeway managers are charged with providing promising RLD participants with additional training and development opportunities to ensure they have the skills needed for advancement, and are given performance bonuses if they meet concrete diversity goals. The RLD program has increased the number of white women store managers by 31 percent since its inception, and the number of women-of-colour store managers by 92 percent.[159] *OB in the Street* looks at what corporate boards in Canada can do to recruit more diverse members.

OB IN THE STREET
Adding Diversity to Boards of Directors

Why should corporate boards pay more attention to diversity? The Canadian Board Diversity Council together with KPMG recently published a study on the boards of 450 of the *Financial Post* 500 (FP500) companies.[160] The study found that women held 15 percent of board seats on the FP500 companies; visible minorities held 5.3 percent; persons with disabilities held 2.9 percent; and Aboriginal people (including First Nations, Inuit, and Métis) held 8 percent. With the exception of Aboriginal representation, the numbers were far fewer than the representation of these categories in society at large. Pamela Jeffery, founder and president of the council, called the results "disappointing."

Does the lack of diversity hurt the bottom line? Accounting firm Ernst & Young found that the lack of diversity on boards can make it difficult for companies to innovate. Directors who sat on FP500 boards that had more women, visible minorities, or Aboriginal diversity believed that the boards made better decisions because the diversity led to better discussions with more perspectives. Board members expressed some frustration about finding new directors and reported that "their own networks are almost exclusively made up of white men."

The council does not favour using quotas to change the situation. Instead, it recommends that with the large wave of retirements from boards expected in the next several years, FP500 boards should use rigorous, transparent recruiting processes "to replace one of every three retiring directors with a director of a diverse background." _____

Just because a company's managers value diversity does not mean that all employees will share that value. Consequently, even if they are required to attend diversity training, employees may exhibit negative attitudes toward individuals because of their gender or ethnicity. Additionally, what attitudes are appropriately displayed outside of the workplace may be questioned by some employers, as you will discover in *Case Incident—You Cannot Do That* on page 115.

Finally, the workplace is not the only place where people's attitudes toward racial diversity are displayed, underscoring that the responsibility for education about reacting to diversity goes beyond employers. In September 2011, at an exhibition game between the Philadelphia Flyers and the Detroit Red Wings played in London, Ontario, someone from the audience threw a banana at Flyers' player Wayne Simmonds, one of the few black players in the NHL. Retired Montreal Canadiens forward Georges Laraque, when asked to comment on the incident, noted that "throughout [my] career, [I] had to endure the 'N' word a number of times."[161]

Cultural Intelligence

Are some individuals better than others at dealing with people from different cultures? Management professors Christopher Earley of the London School of Business and Elaine Mosakowski of the University of Colorado at Boulder have recently introduced the idea of **cultural intelligence (CQ)**, to suggest that people vary in how they deal with other cultures. CQ is defined as "the seemingly natural ability to interpret someone's unfamiliar and ambiguous gestures in just the way that person's compatriots and colleagues would, even to mirror them."[162]

Earley and Mosakowski suggest that CQ "picks up where emotional intelligence leaves off." Those with CQ try to figure out whether a person's behaviour is representative of all members of a group or just that person. Thus, for example, a person with high CQ who encounters two German engineers would be able to determine which of the engineers' conduct is explained by the fact of being an engineer, by being German, and by behaviour that is simply particular to the individual. A recent study found that CQ is particularly helpful to expatriates on international assignment because the ability to be confident about and interested in being in new cultural environments makes it easier to adjust to the demands of foreign assignments.[163]

10 Identify the benefits of cultural intelligence.

RESEARCH FINDINGS: Cultural Intelligence

According to researchers, "cultural intelligence resides in the body [the physical] and the heart [the emotional/motivational], as well as the head [the cognitive]."[164] Individuals who have high *cognitive* CQ look for clues to help them identify a culture's shared understandings. Specifically, an individual does this by looking for consistencies in behaviours across a variety of people from the same cultural background. Individuals with high *physical* CQ learn the customs and gestures of those from other cultures and therefore act more like them. This increases understanding, trust, and openness between people of different cultures. One study found that job candidates who used some of the mannerisms of recruiters who had different cultural backgrounds from themselves were more likely to receive job offers than those who did not do so.[165] Those with high *emotional/motivational* CQ believe that they are capable of understanding people from other cultures, and will keep trying to do so, even if faced with difficulties in doing so.

Based on their research, Earley and Mosakowski have discovered that most managers fall into the following CQ profiles:[166]

- *Provincial.* They work best with people of similar background, but have difficulties working with those from different backgrounds.

- *Analyst.* They analyze a foreign culture's rules and expectations to figure out how to interact with others.

- *Natural.* They use intuition rather than systematic study to understand those from other cultural backgrounds.

- *Ambassador.* They communicate convincingly that they fit in, even if they do not know much about the foreign culture.

cultural intelligence (CQ) The ability to understand someone's unfamiliar and ambiguous gestures in the same way as would people from that person's culture.

EXHIBIT 3-9 Measuring Your Cultural Intelligence

Rate the extent to which you agree with each statement, using the following scale:

    1 = strongly disagree
    2 = disagree
    3 = neutral
    4 = agree
    5 = strongly agree

_____ Before I interact with people from a new culture, I ask myself what I hope to achieve.
_____ If I encounter something unexpected while working in a new culture, I use this experience to figure out new ways to approach other cultures in the future.
_____ I plan how I'm going to relate to people from a different culture before I meet them.
_____ When I come into a new cultural situation, I can immediately sense whether something is going well or something is wrong.

Total _____ ÷ 4 = **Cognitive CQ**

_____ It's easy for me to change my body language (for example, eye contact or posture) to suit people from a different culture.
_____ I can alter my expression when a cultural encounter requires it.
_____ I modify my speech style (for example, accent or tone) to suit people from a different culture.
_____ I easily change the way I act when a cross-cultural encounter seems to require it.

Total _____ ÷ 4 = **Physical CQ**

_____ I have confidence that I can deal well with people from a different culture.
_____ I am certain that I can befriend people whose cultural backgrounds are different from mine.
_____ I can adapt to the lifestyle of a different culture with relative ease.
_____ I am confident that I can deal with a cultural situation that is unfamiliar.

Total _____ ÷ 4 = **Emotional/motivational CQ**

Interpretation: Generally, an average of less than 3 would indicate an area calling for improvement, while an average of greater than 4.5 reflects a true CQ strength.

Source: P. C. Earley and E. Mosakowski, "Cultural Intelligence," _Harvard Business Review_ 82, no. 10 (October 2004), pp. 139–146. Reprinted by permission of _Harvard Business Review_.

- _Mimic._ They control actions and behaviours to match others, even if they do not understand the significance of the cultural cues observed.

- _Chameleon._ They have high levels of all three CQ components. They could be mistaken as being from the foreign culture. According to research, only about 5 percent of managers fit this profile.

Exhibit 3-9 can help you assess your own CQ.

GLOBAL IMPLICATIONS

Although a number of topics were covered in this chapter, we review only three in terms of their application beyond Canada and the United States. First, we consider whether job satisfaction is simply a US concept. Second, we examine whether employees in Western cultures are more satisfied with their jobs than people from other cultures. Finally, we look at international differences in how diversity is managed.

Is Job Satisfaction a US Concept?

Most of the research on job satisfaction has been conducted in the United States. So, is job satisfaction a US concept? The evidence strongly suggests it is *not*; people in other cultures can and do form judgments of job satisfaction. Moreover, similar factors seem to cause, and result from, job satisfaction across cultures: We noted earlier that pay is positively, but relatively weakly, related to job satisfaction. This relationship appears to hold in other industrialized nations as well.

Are Employees in Western Cultures More Satisfied with Their Jobs?

Although job satisfaction appears relevant across cultures, that does not mean that no cultural differences exist in job satisfaction. Evidence suggests that employees in Western cultures have higher levels of job satisfaction than those in Eastern cultures.[167] Exhibit 3-10 provides the results of a global study of job satisfaction levels of employees in 15 countries. As the exhibit shows, the highest levels appear in Mexico and Switzerland. Do employees in these cultures have better jobs? Or are they simply more positive (and less self-critical)? Conversely, the lowest score in the study was for South Korea. South Korean culture tends to be conformist, and businesses tend to be rigidly hierarchical. Do these factors make for low job satisfaction?[168] It is possible, but low job satisfaction does not seem to translate into poor overall performance. South Korea is viewed as an economic success story, able to adapt to change quickly.

The amount of exposure the culture gets to diverse ways of life may affect job satisfaction in South Korea. The country has the highest percentage of wireless Internet broadband subscriptions of any country (100 percent, or 100 subscriptions per every 100 people), which indicates that people have access to worldwide contemporary business practices. South Korean employees may therefore know about autonomy, merit-based rewards, and benefits for workers in other countries that are unavailable to them. In contrast, Mexico, which has one of the highest job satisfaction scores, has

EXHIBIT 3-10 Average Levels of Employee Job Satisfaction by Country

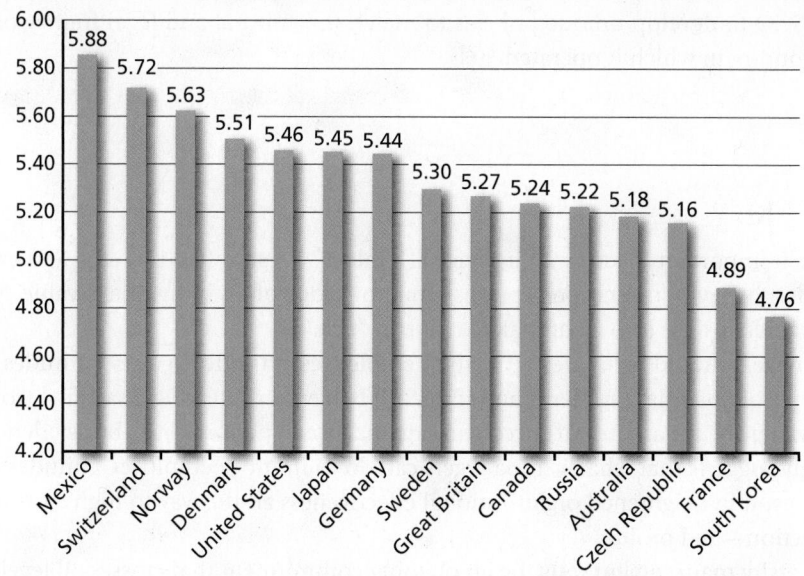

Source: Based on J. H. Westover, "The Impact of Comparative State-Directed Development on Working Conditions and Employee Satisfaction," *Journal of Management & Organization*, July 2012, pp. 537–554.

the lowest percentage of Internet subscriptions (7.7 percent).[169] The higher job satisfaction rate in Mexico could still indicate that it has better jobs or that employees are more satisfied in lesser jobs because there is not as much opportunity for exposure to outside contemporary influences. As you can see, higher job satisfaction may somewhat reflect employee acceptance of the culture's business practices, whether the practices are traditional or cutting-edge contemporary. There are also many other potential contributing factors.

Does organizational commitment vary cross-nationally? A recent study explored this question and compared the organizational commitment of Chinese employees with that of Canadian and South Korean employees.[170] Although results revealed that the three types of commitment—normative, affective, and continuance—are present in all three cultures, they differ in importance. In addition, the study found that Canadians and South Koreans are closer to each other in values than either is with the Chinese. Normative commitment (an obligation to remain with an organization for moral or ethical reasons) and affective commitment (an emotional attachment to the organization and belief in its values) were highest among Chinese employees. Continuance commitment (the perceived economic value of remaining with an organization) was *lower* among Chinese employees than among Canadian, British, and South Korean employees.

Is Diversity Managed Differently across Cultures?

Besides the mere presence of diversity in international work settings, international differences exist in how diversity is managed. Each country has its own legal framework for dealing with diversity, and these frameworks are a powerful reflection of the diversity-related concerns of each country. Many countries require specific targets and quotas for achieving employment equity goals, whereas the legal framework in Canada specifically forbids their use. The types of demographic differences considered important for diversity management also vary across countries. For example, in India the nondiscrimination framework includes quotas and set-aside programs for individuals from lower castes.[171] A case study of the multinational Finnish company TRANSCO found that it was possible to develop a consistent global philosophy for diversity management. However, differences in legal and cultural factors across nations forced TRANSCO to develop unique policies to match the cultural and legal frameworks of each country in which it operated.[172]

Summary

Why is it important to know an individual's values? Values often underlie and explain attitudes, behaviours, and perceptions. So knowledge of an individual's value system can provide insight into what makes a person "tick."

Managers should be interested in their employees' attitudes because attitudes give warnings of potential problems and influence behaviour. Creating a satisfied workforce is hardly a guarantee of successful organizational performance, but evidence strongly suggests that whatever managers can do to improve employee attitudes will likely result in heightened organizational effectiveness all the way to high customer satisfaction—and profits.

Diversity management must be an ongoing commitment that crosses all levels of the organization. Policies to improve the climate for diversity can be effective, so long as they are designed to acknowledge all employees' perspectives.

SNAPSHOT SUMMARY

Values
- Rokeach Value Survey
- Hodgson's General Moral Principles

Assessing Cultural Values
- Hofstede's Framework for Assessing Cultures
- The GLOBE Framework for Assessing Cultures

Values in the Canadian Workplace
- Generational Differences
- Cultural Differences

Attitudes
- Job Satisfaction
- Organizational Commitment
- Job Involvement

- Perceived Organizational Support
- Employee Engagement

Managing Diversity in the Workplace
- Effective Diversity Programs
- Cultural Intelligence

MyManagementLab

Study, practise, and explore real business situations with these helpful resources:

- **Study Plan:** Check your understanding of chapter concepts with self-study quizzes.
- **Online Lesson Presentations:** Study key chapter topics and work through interactive assessments to test your knowledge and master management concepts.
- **Videos:** Learn more about the management practices and strategies of real companies.
- **Simulations:** Practise management decision-making in simulated business environments.

P I A PERSONAL INVENTORY ASSESSMENT

OB at Work

for Review

1. What is the difference between Rokeach's terminal and instrumental values?

2. What are Hofstede's value dimensions for assessing cultures?

3. What values are unique to Canadian culture?

4. What are the three components of an attitude? Are these components related or unrelated?

5. What are the key attitudes that affect organizational performance? In what ways are these attitudes alike? What is unique about each?

6. What causes job satisfaction? For most people, is pay or the work itself more important?

7. What outcomes does job satisfaction influence? What implications do the consequences of job satisfaction have for management?

8. What are the four employee responses to job dissatisfaction?

9. How do organizations manage diversity effectively?

10. What are the benefits of cultural intelligence?

for Managers

■ Pay attention to your employees' job satisfaction levels as determinants of their performance, turnover, absenteeism, and withdrawal behaviours.

■ Measure employee job attitudes objectively and at regular intervals in order to determine how employees are reacting to their work.

■ To raise an employee's job satisfaction, evaluate the fit between the employee's work interests and the intrinsic parts of his/her job to create work that is challenging and interesting to the employee.

■ Consider the fact that high pay alone is unlikely to create a satisfying work environment.

■ Understand your organization's anti-discrimination policies thoroughly and share them with your employees.

■ Look beyond readily observable biographical characteristics and consider the individual's capabilities before making management decisions.

■ Fully evaluate what accommodations a person with disabilities will need and then fine-tune a job to that person's abilities.

■ Seek to understand and respect the unique biographical characteristics of your employees; a fair but individual-oriented approach yields the best performance.

for You

■ You will encounter many people who have values different from yours in the classroom and in various kinds of activities in which you participate, as well as in the workplace. Try to understand value differences, and to figure out ways to work positively with people who are different from you.

■ We indicated that a moderate number of Canadians are very satisfied with their jobs, and we mentioned the sources of some of the satisfactions. We also identified some of the reasons people are dissatisfied with their jobs. This information may help you understand your own feelings about whether you are satisfied with your job.

■ You may be able to use some of the information on attitudes to think about how to better work with people from different cultures. An understanding of how cultures differ may provide insight when you observe people doing things differently from the way you do them.

OB *at* **Work**

Employer–Employee Loyalty Is an Outdated Concept

POINT

The word *loyalty* is horribly outdated.[173] Long gone are the days when an employer would keep an employee for life, as are the days when an employee would work for a single company for his or her entire career.

Workplace guru Linda Gratton says, "Loyalty is dead—killed off through shortening contracts, outsourcing, automation and multiple careers. Faced with what could be 50 years of work, who honestly wants to spend that much time with one company? Serial monogamy is the order of the day." Everyone agrees; in a recent study, only 59 percent of employers reported they felt very loyal to their employees, while a mere 32 percent believed their employers were loyal to them.

The commitment on each side of the equation is weak. For example, Renault ended the 31-year career of employee Michel Balthazard (and two others) on false charges of espionage. When the wrongness of the charges became public, Renault halfheartedly offered the employees their jobs back and a lame apology: "Renault thanks them for the quality of their work at the group and wishes them every success in the future."

As for employees' loyalty to their employers, that is worth little nowadays. One manager with Deloitte says that the current employee attitude is "I'm leaving, I had a great experience, and I'm taking that with me." An expectation of loyalty is not there. In fact, only 9 percent of recent college graduates would stay with an employer for more than a year if they did not like the job, research showed.

The sooner we see the employment experience for what it is (mostly transactional, mostly short to medium term), the better off we will be. The workplace is no place for fantasies.

COUNTERPOINT

Some employers and employees show little regard for each other. That each side can be uncaring or cavalier is hardly a revelation. No doubt such cynical attitudes are as old as the employment relationship itself.

But is that the norm? And is it desirable? The answer to both of these questions is no.

Management guru Tom Peters says, "Bottom line: loyalty matters. A lot. Yesterday. Today. Tomorrow." University of Michigan's Dave Ulrich says, "Leaders who encourage loyalty want employees who are not only committed to and engaged in their work but who also find meaning from it."

It is true that the employer–employee relationship has changed. For example, (largely) gone are the days when employers provide guaranteed payout pensions to which employees contribute nothing. But is that such a bad thing? There is a big difference between asking employees to contribute to their pension plans and abandoning plans altogether (or firing without cause).

Moreover, it's not that loyalty is dead, but rather that employers are loyal to a different kind of employee. Gone are the days when an employer would refuse to fire a long-tenured but incompetent employee. But is that the kind of loyalty most employees expect today anyway? Companies are loyal to employees who do their jobs well, and that too is as it should be. Constantly training new employees wears down morale and profitability.

In short, employees still expect certain standards of decency and loyalty from their employers, and employers want engaged, committed employees in return. That is a good thing—and not so different from yesterday. Says workplace psychologist Binna Kandola, "Workplaces may have changed but loyalty is not dead—the bonds between people are too strong."

OB at Work

Intercultural Sensitivity Scale: Cultural sensitivity can minimize conflict and tension in the workplace. Use this scale to better understand how culturally sensitive you are. Sensitivity levels can be improved with education, contact with other cultures, and effort.

Multicultural Awareness Scale: Understanding other cultures is especially important in Canadian workplaces, since the Canadian workforce is extremely diverse. Use this scale to see how well you understand other cultures and their business practices.

Flourishing Scale: Flourishing is an indicator of well-being connected to engagement, job satisfaction, and life satisfaction. Use this scale to get a sense of your current level of well-being.

BREAKOUT **GROUP** EXERCISES

Form small groups to discuss the following topics, as assigned by your instructor. Each person in the group should first identify 3 to 5 key personal values.

1. Identify the extent to which values overlap in your group.

2. Try to uncover with your group members the source of some of your key values (for example, parents, peer group, teachers, church).

3. What kind of workplace would be most suitable for the values that you hold most closely?

EXPERIENTIAL EXERCISE

Feeling Excluded

This 6-step exercise takes approximately 20 minutes.

Individual Work (Steps 1 and 2)

1. All participants are asked to recall a time when they have felt uncomfortable or targeted because of their demographic status. Ideally, situations at work should be used, but if no work situations come to mind, any situation will work. Encourage students to use any demographic characteristic they think is most appropriate, so they can write about feeling excluded on the basis of race, ethnicity, gender, age, disability status, religion, or any other characteristic. They should briefly describe the situation, what precipitated the event, how they felt at the time, how they reacted, and how they believe the other party could have made the situation better.

2. The instructor asks the students to then think about a time when they might have either deliberately or accidentally done something that made someone else feel excluded or targeted because of their demographic status. Once again, they should briefly describe the situation, what precipitated the event, how they felt at the time, how the other person reacted, and how they could have made the situation better.

Small Groups (Steps 3 and 4)

3. Once everyone has written their descriptions, divide the class into small groups of not more than 4 people. If at all possible, try to compose groups that are somewhat demographically diverse, to avoid intergroup conflicts in the class review discussion. Students should be encouraged to discuss their situations and consider how their experiences were similar or different.

4. After reading through everyone's reactions, each group should develop a short list of principles for how they personally can avoid excluding or targeting people in the future. Encourage them to be as specific as possible, and also ask each group to find solutions that work for everyone. Solutions should focus on both avoiding these situations in the first place and resolving them when they do occur.

Class Review (Steps 5 and 6)

5. Members of each group are invited to provide a very brief summary of the major principles of how they have felt excluded or targeted, and then to describe their groups' collective decisions regarding how these situations can be minimized in the future.

6. The instructor should lead a discussion on how companies might be able to develop comprehensive policies that will encourage people to be sensitive in their interactions with one another.

ETHICAL **DILEMMA**

Is It a Bribe or a Gift?

The Corruption of Foreign Public Officials Act prohibits Canadian firms from making payments to foreign government officials with the aim of gaining or maintaining business.[174] But payments are acceptable if they don't violate local laws. For instance, payments to officers working for foreign corporations are legal. Many countries don't have such legal guidelines.

Bribery is a common way of doing business in many underdeveloped countries. Government jobs there often don't pay very well, so it's tempting for officials to supplement their income with bribes. In addition, in many countries, the penalties for demanding and receiving bribes are few or nonexistent.

You are a Canadian who works for a large European multinational computer manufacturer. You are currently working to sell a $5-million system to a government agency in Nigeria. The Nigerian official who heads up the team that will decide who gets this contract has asked you for a payment of $20 000. He said this payment will not guarantee you get the order, but without it he could not be very encouraging. Your company's policy is very flexible on the issue of "gifts" to facilitate sales. Your boss says that it's okay to pay the $20 000, but only if you can be relatively assured of the order.

You are not sure what you should do. The Nigerian official has told you specifically that any payment to him is not to be mentioned to anyone else on the Nigerian team. You know for certain that three other companies are also negotiating, but it's unconfirmed that two of those companies have turned down the payment request.

What would you do?

CASE INCIDENTS

You Cannot Do That

Paul Fromm is a high school teacher employed in one of the most ethnically diverse school districts in Canada.[175] He is an excellent teacher, and receives high ratings from his students.

During weekends and summer holidays, when he is not working, he participates in conferences held by white supremacists and anti-Semitic groups. For instance, he attended a conference at which swastikas were waving, and individuals gave Nazi salutes. Fromm also attended a celebration of Adolf Hitler's birthday.

Though it's known that Fromm attends these conferences, he has never expressed racist views in the classroom or discriminated against any student. "I am here to teach English, not to make a political statement. This is my job, that's what I do. And I do it very well," he says.

The school board and some of the teachers are upset with Fromm's behaviour. They feel that what he does, even though outside of work time, is not consistent with the school board's values of encouraging multicultural diversity. Some suggest that he should be fired.

Questions

1. What, if anything, should the school board do in this instance?

2. Should Fromm consider not going to further conferences of this sort?

OB *at Work*

Thinking Your Way to a Better Job

You have probably been dissatisfied with a job at one time or another in your life.[176] When faced with a dissatisfying job, researchers and job holders alike usually think in terms of job satisfaction: Ask for more pay, take control over your work, change your schedule, minimize contact with a toxic co-worker, or even change jobs. While each of these remedies may be appropriate in certain situations, increasingly researchers are uncovering an interesting truth about job satisfaction: It is as much a state of mind as a function of job conditions.

Here, we are not talking about the dispositional source of job satisfaction. It's true that some people have trouble finding any job satisfying, whereas others cannot be brought down by even the most onerous of jobs. However, by state of mind, we mean changeable, easily implemented ways of thinking that can affect your job satisfaction. Lest you think we have gone the way of self-help gurus Deepak Chopra and Wayne Dyer, think again. Some solid, albeit fairly preliminary, evidence supports the notion that our views of our job and life can be significantly impacted by changing the way we think.

One main area where this "state of mind" research might help you change the way you think about your job (or life) is in gratitude. Researchers have found that when people are asked to make short lists of things for which they are grateful, they report being happier, and the increased happiness seems to last well beyond the moments when people made the list.

Indeed, gratitude may explain why, when the economy is in bad shape, people actually become more satisfied with their jobs. One survey revealed that, from 2007 to 2008, when the economy slid into recession, the percentage of people reporting that they were "very satisfied" with their jobs increased to a whopping 38 percent (from 28 percent). When we see other people suffering, particularly those we see as similar to ourselves, it often leads us to realize that, as bad as things may seem, they can always be worse. As *Wall Street Journal* columnist Jeffrey Zaslow wrote, "People who still have jobs are finding reasons to be appreciative."

Questions

1. So, right now, make a short list of things about your job and life for which you are grateful. Now, after having done that, do you feel more positively about your job and your life?

2. Now try doing this every day for a week. Do you think this exercise might make a difference in how you feel about your job and your life?

FROM CONCEPTS TO SKILLS

Changing Attitudes

Can you change unfavourable employee attitudes? Sometimes! It depends on who you are, the strength of the employee's attitude, the magnitude of the change, and the technique you choose to try to change the attitude.

People are most likely to respond to changes suggested by someone who is liked, credible, and convincing. If people like you, they are more apt to identify and adopt your message. Credibility implies trust, expertise, and objectivity. So you are more likely to change someone's attitude if that person views you as believable, knowledgeable about what you are saying, and unbiased in your presentation. Finally, successful attitude change is enhanced when you present your arguments clearly and persuasively.

It's easier to change a person's attitude if he or she is not strongly committed to it. Conversely, the stronger the belief in the attitude, the harder it is to change it. Also, attitudes that have been expressed publicly are more difficult to change because doing so requires admitting having made a mistake.

It's also easier to change attitudes when the change required is not very significant. To get a person to accept a new attitude that varies greatly from his or her current position requires more effort. It may also threaten other deeply held attitudes.

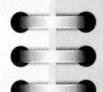

Practising Skills

All attitude-change techniques are not equally effective across situations. Oral persuasion techniques are most effective when you use a positive, tactful tone; present strong evidence to support your position; tailor your argument to the listener; use logic; and support your evidence by appealing to the person's fears, frustrations, and other emotions. But people are more likely to embrace change when they can experience it. The use of training sessions where employees share and personalize experiences, and practise new behaviours, can be a powerful stimulant for change. Consistent with self-perception theory, changes in behaviour can lead to changes in attitudes.

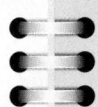

Form groups of 2. Person A is to choose any topic that he or she feels strongly about and state his or her position on the topic in 30 words or less. Person B's task will be to try to change Person A's attitude on this topic. Person B will have 10 minutes to make his or her case. When the time is up, the roles are reversed. Person B picks the topic and Person A has 10 minutes to try to change Person B's attitude.

Potential topics (you can choose either side of a topic) include the following: politics; the economy; world events; social practices; or specific management issues, such as that organizations should require all employees to undergo regular drug testing, there is no such thing as organizational loyalty any more, the customer is always right, and layoffs are an indication of management failures.

Questions

1. Were you successful at changing the other person's attitude? Why or why not?

2. Was the other person successful at changing your attitude? Why or why not?

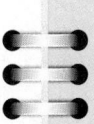

3. What conclusions can you draw about changing the attitudes of yourself and others?

Reinforcing Skills

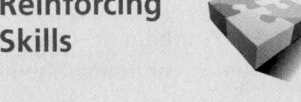

1. Try to convince a friend or relative to go with you to see a movie or play that you know he or she does not want to see.

2. Try to convince a friend or relative to try a different brand of toothpaste.

Lawson and Creamer

Stress @Work

Nathalie Godbout, a partner at Saint John, New Brunswick-based Lawson Creamer since 2006 has a hectic work and family schedule.[1] She has two small children (ages two and five), and her job often starts at 6 a.m.

Godbout is very active in her community. She sits on a variety of boards and is currently the chair of the Mental Health Tribunal for southern New Brunswick.

To balance all of these activities, Godbout has to manage her work and family schedule. Because she works long, intensive days, she is able to take off a week from work about every six-and-a-half weeks. Her husband is a stay-at-home parent, which helps mitigate all of the time Godbout spends at work.

Godbout has also learned to be pragmatic about her work, and sets an auto-reply for her email to let people know that her responses may be delayed. "The universe is kept at bay because they're told that I respond to things at a certain time," she said.

Managers need to be sensitive to stress at work, especially in workplaces in which employees are driven to perform. When Janie Toivanen, a long-time employee of Vancouver-based Electronic Arts (EA) Canada with a track record of superior performance, was diagnosed with severe depression, she asked her employer for indefinite stress leave. Instead, just days later, she was fired. After working there for six years, she "felt like she had been thrown away." Toivanen could not believe EA would not do anything to help her as she struggled to overcome her illness. She subsequently filed a complaint with the BC Human Rights Tribunal and was awarded, among other things, $20 000 for injury to her dignity, feelings, and self-respect and $19 744 in severance pay.

Are We Overstressed?

Stress appears to be a major factor in the lives of many Canadians. A 2013 survey conducted by Statistics Canada found that Canadians experience a great deal of stress, with those from Quebec topping the list.[2] The survey also found that women were more stressed than men. The inset *Stressed Quite a Lot, 2013* reports the findings.

The impact of stress on the Canadian economy is huge, costing an estimated $33 billion a year in lost productivity in 2013,[3] and considerably more than that in medical costs.

Shannon Wagner, a clinical psychologist and a specialist in workplace stress research at the University of Northern British Columbia, notes that changes in the nature of jobs may be increasing the levels of stress in the workplace. While many jobs are not as physically demanding, they are often more mentally demanding. "A lot of people now are identifying techno-stress and the 24/7 workday, which we didn't have even 10 or 15 years ago, this feeling of being constantly plugged in, of checking email 500 times a day."[4]

An additional problem is that employees are working longer hours than ever, according to Professor Linda Duxbury of Carleton University's Sprott School of Business and Professor Chris Higgins of the Richard Ivey School of Business at the University of Western Ontario. Their 2012 survey of more than 24 000 Canadians found that almost two-thirds of Canadians work more than 45 hours a week, a significant increase from 20 years ago.[5] Canadian businesses have cut the number of employees over time, but not the amount of work. Duxbury notes that "Organizations are fooling themselves if they think they're getting increased productivity by expecting those who they have left to do more."[6]

Jobs and Stress Levels

How do jobs rate in terms of stress? The inset *The Most and Least Stressful Jobs* on page 120 shows how selected occupations ranked in an evaluation of 250 jobs. Among the criteria used in the rankings were overtime, quotas, deadlines, competitiveness, physical demands, environmental conditions, hazards encountered, initiative required, stamina required, win–lose situations, and working in the public eye.

Stress is not something that can be ignored in the workplace. A recent poll by Ipsos Reid found that 66 percent of the CEOs surveyed said that "stress, burnout or other physical and mental health issues" have a negative effect on productivity.[8] A study conducted in 15 developed countries found that individuals who report that they are stressed in their jobs are 25 percent more likely to quit and 25 percent more likely to miss days of work.[9] Canadian, French, and Swedish employees reported the highest stress levels. In Canada, 41 percent of employees noted that they "often" or "always" experience stress at work, while only 31 percent of employees in Denmark and Switzerland reported stress levels this high.[10]

What Is Stress?

Stress is a dynamic condition in which an individual is confronted with an opportunity, demand, or resource related to what the individual desires and for which the outcome is perceived to be both uncertain and important.[11] This definition is complicated. Let's look at its components more closely.

Stress is not necessarily bad in and of itself. Although stress is typically discussed in a negative context, it also has a positive value.[12] In response to stress, your nervous system, hypothalamus, pituitary, and adrenal glands supply you with stress hormones to

Stressed Quite a Lot, 2013[7]

	Males (%)	Females (%)
Canada	**21.3**	**24.6**
Newfoundland and Labrador	13.7	16.5
Prince Edward Island	12.8*	22.7
Nova Scotia	18.7	20.6
New Brunswick	19.3	20.8
Quebec	23.8	27.1
Ontario	21.6	25.5
Manitoba	19.3	20.9
Saskatchewan	19.1	20.1
Alberta	18.7	23.6
British Columbia	21.1	23.1
Yukon	16.9	23.8
Northwest Territories	12.6*	21.0

*Use with caution.

Note: Population aged 15 and older who reported experiencing quite a lot or extreme stress most days of their lives.

cope. Your heartbeat and breathing accelerate to increase oxygen, while your muscles tense for action.[13] This response is an opportunity when it offers potential gain. Consider, for example, the superior performance that an athlete or stage performer gives in "clutch" situations. Such individuals often use stress positively to rise to the occasion and perform at or near their maximum. Similarly, many professionals see the pressures of heavy workloads and deadlines as positive challenges that enhance the quality of their work and the satisfaction they get from their job. However, when the situation is negative, stress is harmful and may hinder your progress by elevating your blood pressure uncomfortably and creating an erratic heart rhythm as you struggle to speak and think logically.[14]

Recently, researchers have argued that *challenge stressors*—or stressors associated with workload, pressure to complete tasks, and time urgency—operate quite differently from *hindrance stressors*—or stressors that keep you from reaching your goals (red tape, office politics, confusion over job responsibilities). Early evidence suggests that challenge stressors produce less strain than hindrance stressors.[15]

Researchers have sought to clarify the conditions under which each type of stress exists. It appears that employees who have a stronger affective commitment to their organization can transfer psychological stress into greater focus and higher sales performance, whereas employees with low levels of commitment perform worse under stress.[16] And when challenge stress increases, those with high levels of organizational support have higher role-based performance, but those with low levels of organizational support do not.[17] More typically, stress is associated with *demands* and

The Most and Least Stressful Jobs

How do jobs rate in terms of stress? According to 2014 research by CareerCast.com, the top 10 most and least stressful jobs are as follows:[18]

Ten Most Stressful Jobs
1. Enlisted military personnel
2. Military general
3. Firefighter
4. Airline pilot
5. Event coordinator
6. Public relations executive
7. Senior corporate executive
8. Newspaper reporter
9. Police officer
10. Taxi driver

Ten Least Stressful Jobs
1. Audiologist
2. Hair stylist
3. Jeweller
4. Tenured university professor
5. Seamstress/tailor
6. Dietician
7. Medical records technician
8. Librarian
9. Multimedia artist
10. Drill-press operator

resources. Demands are responsibilities, pressures, obligations, and even uncertainties that individuals face in the workplace. Resources are things within an individual's control that can be used to resolve the demands. For example, when you take a test, you feel stress because you confront opportunities and performance pressures. To the extent that you can apply resources to the demands on you—such as being prepared for the exam—you will feel less stress.

Under the demands–resources perspective, having resources to cope with stress is just as important in offsetting it as demands are in increasing it.[19]

Causes of Stress

Workplace stress can arise from a variety of factors:[20]

- *Environmental factors.* Uncertainty is the biggest reason people have trouble coping with organizational changes.[21] Three common types

of environmental uncertainty are economic, political, and technological. Changes in the business cycle create *economic uncertainties*. When the economy is contracting, for example, people become increasingly anxious about their job security. *Political uncertainties* don't tend to create stress among North Americans as they do for employees in countries such as Haiti or Venezuela. The obvious reason is that the United States and Canada have stable political systems, in which change is typically implemented in an orderly manner.[22] Because innovations can make an employee's skills and experience obsolete in a very short time, computers, robotics, automation, and similar forms of *technological change* are also a threat to many people and cause them stress.

- *Organizational factors.* There is no shortage of factors within an organization that can cause

stress. Pressures to avoid errors or complete tasks in a limited time, work overload, a demanding and insensitive boss, and unpleasant co-workers are a few examples. We have categorized these factors around task, role, and interpersonal demands.[23]

- *Task demands* relate to a person's job. They include the design of the individual's job (autonomy, task variety, degree of automation), working conditions, and the physical work layout. Assembly lines can put pressure on people when they perceive the line's speed to be excessive. Working in an overcrowded room or in a visible location where noise and interruptions are constant can increase anxiety and stress.[24] As customer service grows ever more important, emotional labour becomes a source of stress.[25] Do you think you could put on a happy face when you are having a bad day?

- *Role demands* relate to pressures placed on a person as a function of the particular role he or she plays in the organization.

- *Interpersonal demands* are pressures created by other employees. Lack of social support from colleagues and poor interpersonal relationships can cause stress, especially among employees with a high social need. A rapidly growing body of research has also shown that negative co-worker and supervisor behaviours, including fights, bullying, incivility, racial harassment, and sexual harassment, are especially strongly related to stress at work.[26]

- *Personal factors.* The typical individual works about 40 to 50 hours a week. But the experiences and problems that people encounter in the other 120-plus nonwork hours can spill over to the job. Our final category, then, encompasses factors in the employee's personal life: family issues, personal economic problems, and personality characteristics.

- National surveys consistently show that people hold *family* and personal relationships dear. Marital difficulties, the breaking off of a relationship, caring for elderly parents, and discipline troubles with children create stress employees often cannot leave at the front door when they arrive at work.[27]

- Regardless of income level—people who make $100 000 per year seem to have as much trouble handling their finances as those who earn $20 000—some people are poor money managers or have wants that exceed their earning capacity. The *economic* problems of over-extended financial resources create stress and take attention away from work.

- Studies in three diverse organizations found that participants who reported stress symptoms before beginning a job accounted for most of the variance in stress symptoms reported nine months later.[28] The researchers concluded that some people may have an inherent tendency to accentuate negative aspects of the world in general. If this is true, then stress symptoms expressed on the job may actually originate in the person's *personality*.[29]

When we review stressors individually, it's easy to overlook that stress is

an additive phenomenon—it builds up.[31] Each new and persistent stressor adds to an individual's stress level. A single stressor may seem relatively unimportant in and of itself, but if it is added to an already high level of stress, it can be "the straw that breaks the camel's back."

Consequences of Stress

Stress manifests itself in a number of ways, such as high blood pressure, ulcers, irritability, difficulty in making routine decisions, loss of appetite, accident proneness, and the like. These symptoms can be placed under three general categories: physiological, psychological, and behavioural symptoms.[32]

- *Physiological symptoms.* Most early research concerned with stress was directed at physiological symptoms because most researchers in this area were specialists in the health and medical sciences. Their work led to the conclusion that stress

could create changes in metabolism, increase heart and breathing rates, increase blood pressure, cause headaches, and induce heart attacks. Evidence now clearly indicates that stress may have harmful physiological effects. One study linked stressful job demands to increased susceptibility to upper respiratory illnesses and poor immune system functioning, especially for individuals with low self-efficacy.[33] A long-term study conducted in the United Kingdom found that job strain was associated with higher levels of coronary heart disease.[34] Still another study conducted with Danish human services workers found that higher levels of psychological burnout at the work-unit level were related to significantly higher levels of sickness absence.[35] Many other studies have shown similar results linking work stress to a variety of indicators of poor health.

- *Psychological symptoms.* Job dissatisfaction is an obvious cause of stress. But stress also shows itself in other psychological states—for instance, tension, anxiety, irritability, boredom, and procrastination. For example, a study that tracked physiological responses of employees over time found that stress due to high workloads was related to higher blood pressure and lower emotional well-being.[36] Jobs that make multiple and conflicting demands or in which there is a lack of clarity as to the person's duties, authority, and responsibilities increase stress and dissatisfaction.[37] Similarly, the less control people have over the pace of their work, the greater their stress and dissatisfaction. Jobs that provide a low level of variety, significance, autonomy, feedback, and identity create stress

and reduce satisfaction and involvement in the job.[38] Not everyone reacts to autonomy in the same way, however. For those with an external locus of control, increased job control increases the tendency to experience stress and exhaustion.[39]

- *Behavioural symptoms.* Research on behaviour and stress has been conducted across several countries and over time, and the relationships appear relatively consistent. Behaviourally related stress symptoms include reductions in productivity, absence, and turnover, as well as changes in eating habits, increased smoking or consumption of alcohol, rapid speech, fidgeting, and sleep disorders.[40] More recently, stress has been linked to aggression and violence in the workplace.

Why Do Individuals Differ in Their Experience of Stress?

Some people thrive on stressful situations, while others are overwhelmed by them. What differentiates people in terms of their ability to handle stress? What individual difference variables moderate the relationship between *potential* stressors and *experienced* stress? At least four variables—perception, job experience, social support, and personality—are relevant.

- *Perception.* Individuals react in response to their *perception* of reality rather than to reality itself. Perception, therefore, moderates the relationship between a potential stress condition and an employee's reaction to it. Layoffs may cause one person to fear losing his job, while another sees an opportunity to get a large severance allowance and start her own business.[41] So stress

potential does not lie in objective conditions; instead it lies in an employee's interpretation of those conditions.

- *Job experience.* Experience on the job tends to be negatively related to work stress. Two explanations have been offered.[42] First is selective withdrawal. Voluntary turnover is more probable among people who experience more stress. Therefore, people who remain with the organization longer are those with more stress-resistant traits or those who are more resistant to the stress characteristics of their organization. Second, people eventually develop coping mechanisms to deal with stress. Because this takes time, senior members of the organization are more likely to be fully adapted and should experience less stress.

- *Social support.* Collegial relationships with co-workers or supervisors can buffer the impact of stress.[43] This is among the best-documented relationships in the stress literature. Social support helps ease the negative effects of even high-strain jobs. Outside the job, involvement with family, friends, and community can provide the support if it is missing at work.

- *Personality.* Workaholism is a personality characteristic related to stress levels. Workaholics are people obsessed with their work; they put in an enormous number of hours, think about work even when not working, and create additional work responsibilities to satisfy an inner compulsion to work more. In some ways, they might seem like ideal employees. That is probably why when most people are asked in interviews what their greatest weakness is, they reflexively say, "I just work too hard." However,

working hard is different from working compulsively. Workaholics are not necessarily more productive than other employees, despite their extreme efforts. The strain of putting in such a high level of work effort eventually begins to wear on the workaholic, leading to higher levels of work–life conflict and psychological burnout.[44]

How Do We Manage Stress?

Below we discuss ways that individuals can manage stress, and the programs organizations use to help employees manage stress.

Individual Approaches

An employee can take personal responsibility for reducing his or her stress level. Individual strategies that have proven effective include time-management techniques, physical exercise, relaxation techniques, and a close social support network.

- *Time-management techniques.* Many people manage their time poorly. The well-organized employee, like the well-organized student, can often accomplish twice as much as the person who is poorly organized. So, understanding and using basic time-management principles can help individuals cope better with tensions created by job demands.[45] A few of the more well-known time-management principles are (1) making daily lists of activities to be accomplished; (2) prioritizing activities by importance and urgency; (3) scheduling activities according to the priorities set; (4) knowing your daily productivity cycle and handling the most demanding parts of your job during the high part of your cycle, when you are

most alert and productive; and (5) avoiding electronic distractions like frequently checking email, which can limit attention and reduce efficiency.[46] These time-management skills can help minimize procrastination by focusing efforts on immediate goals and boosting motivation even in the face of tasks that are less desirable.[47]

- *Physical activity.* Physicians have recommended noncompetitive physical exercise, such as aerobics, walking, jogging, swimming, and riding a bicycle, as a way to deal with excessive stress levels. These activities increase lung capacity, lower resting heart rate, and provide a mental diversion from work pressures, effectively reducing work-related levels of stress.[48]

- *Relaxation techniques.* Individuals can teach themselves to reduce tension through relaxation techniques such as meditation, hypnosis, and deep breathing. The objective is to reach a state of deep relaxation, in which you focus all your energy on release of muscle tension.[49] Deep relaxation for 15 or 20 minutes a day releases tension

and provides a pronounced sense of peacefulness, as well as significant changes in heart rate, blood pressure, and other physiological factors. A growing body of research shows that simply taking breaks from work at routine intervals can facilitate psychological recovery and reduce stress significantly and may improve job performance, and these effects are even greater if relaxation techniques are employed.[50]

- *Social support.* Having friends, family, or colleagues to talk to provides an outlet when stress levels become excessive. Expanding your social support network provides you with someone to listen to your problems and to offer a more objective perspective on the situation.

The inset *Tips for Reducing Stress* offers additional ideas for managing stress.

Organizational Approaches

Brantford, Ontario-based The Williamson Group, a benefits consulting and financial services firm, has a comprehensive wellness program for its employees.[51] The company

Tips for Reducing Stress

- At least two or three times a week, spend time with supportive friends or family.
- Ask for support when you are under pressure. This is a sign of health, not weakness.
- If you have spiritual or religious beliefs, increase or maintain your involvement.
- Use a variety of methods to reduce stress. Consider exercise, nutrition, hobbies, positive thinking, and relaxation techniques such as meditation or yoga.[52]

has an in-house running program for employees. It also pays the entry fee for employees and their family members who run in the annual 5 kilometre or 10 kilometre Brantford Rotary Classic Run. As well, the company has Fibre Fridays to promote better nutrition by providing employees with trays of fruits and vegetables. The company's wellness also features an annual health assessment of employees and an employee assistance program. Noel MacKay, group practice leader at the company, believes The Williamson Group's wellness program increases job satisfaction and lowers turnover. "We have people who've been with us for 25 years, and almost 40 per cent of the staff has been here 10 years or more. Wellness programming is something we intuitively know helps us," he said.[53]

Most firms that have introduced wellness programs have found significant benefits. A recent joint study conducted by Sun Life Financial and the Richard Ivey School of Business found that in companies with wellness programs, employees missed 1.5 to 1.7 fewer days due to absenteeism. This resulted in estimated savings of $251 per employee per year.[54] While many Canadian businesses report having wellness initiatives, only 24 percent have "fully implemented wellness strategies" (which includes multi-year goals and an evaluation of results), according to a recent survey.[55]

So what can organizations do to reduce employee stress? In general, strategies to reduce stress include improved employee selection, placement of employees in appropriate jobs, realistic goal setting, designing jobs with employee needs and skills in mind, increased employee involvement, improved organizational communication, offering employee sabbaticals, and, as mentioned, establishment of corporate wellness programs.

Certain jobs are more stressful than others, but individuals also differ in their response to stress situations. We know, for example, that individuals with little experience or an external locus of control tend to be more prone to stress. Selection and placement decisions should take these facts into consideration. Although management should not restrict hiring to only experienced individuals with an internal locus of control, such individuals may adapt better to high-stress jobs and perform those jobs more effectively.

Individuals perform better when they have specific and challenging goals and receive feedback on how well they are progressing toward them.[56] Goals can reduce stress as well as provide motivation.[57] Specific goals that are perceived as attainable clarify performance expectations. Additionally, goal feedback reduces uncertainties as to actual job performance. The result is less employee frustration, role ambiguity, and stress.

Redesigning jobs to give employees more responsibility, more meaningful work, more autonomy, and increased feedback can reduce stress because these factors give the employee greater control over work activities and lessen dependence on others. Of course, not all employees want jobs with increased responsibility. The right design for employees with a low need for growth might be less responsibility and increased specialization. If individuals prefer structure and routine, more structured jobs should also reduce uncertainties and stress levels.

Role stress is detrimental to a large extent because employees feel uncertain about goals, expectations, how they will be evaluated, and the like. By giving these employees a voice in the decisions that directly affect their job performance, management can increase employee control and reduce role stress. So managers should

consider *increasing employee involvement* in decision making because evidence clearly shows that increases in employee empowerment reduce psychological strain.[58]

Increasing formal organizational communication with employees reduces uncertainty by lessening role ambiguity and role conflict. Given the importance that perceptions play in moderating the stress-response relationship, management can also use effective communication as a means to shape employee perceptions. Remember that what employees categorize as demands, threats, or opportunities at work are merely interpretations, and those interpretations can be affected by the symbols and actions communicated by management.

Some employees need an occasional escape from the frenetic pace of their work. In recent years, companies such as American Express, Intel, General Mills, Microsoft, Morningstar, DreamWorks Animation, and Adobe Systems have begun to provide extended voluntary leaves.[59] These *sabbaticals*—ranging in length from a few weeks to several months—allow employees to travel, relax, or pursue personal projects that consume time beyond normal vacation weeks. Proponents say that these sabbaticals can revive and rejuvenate workers who might be headed for burnout.

Our final suggestion is to offer organizationally supported wellness programs. These typically provide workshops to help people quit smoking, control alcohol use, lose weight, eat better, and develop a regular exercise program; they focus on the employee's total physical and mental condition.[60] A study of 36 programs designed to reduce stress (including wellness programs) showed that interventions to help employees reframe stressful situations and use active coping strategies appreciably

When organizations provide on-site daycare facilities, they are filling a needed role in parents' lives, and making it easier for parents to attend to their job demands rather than worry about child-care arrangements.

When employees expect organizations to provide child care, they are shifting their responsibilities to their employers, rather than keeping their family needs and concerns private. Moreover, it is unfair to offer child-care benefits when not all employees have children.

YOUR PERSPECTIVE

1. Think of all the technical avenues enabling employees to be connected 24/7 to the workplace: email, texting, company intranets. A generation ago, most employees could go home after a day at work and not be "on call." What are the positive benefits of this change? What are the downsides? As an employee facing the demand to "stay connected" to your workplace, how would you try to maintain a balance in your life?

2. How much responsibility should individuals take for managing their own stress? To what extent should organizations become involved in the personal lives of their employees when trying to help them manage stress? What are the pros and cons for whether employees or organizations take responsibility for managing stress?

reduced stress levels.[61] Most wellness programs assume that employees need to take personal responsibility for their physical and mental health and that the organization is merely a means to that end. The inset *Toward Less Stressful Work* offers additional ideas.

RESEARCH EXERCISES

1. Look for data on stress levels in other countries. How do these data compare with the Canadian data presented in the Factbox?

Are the sources of stress the same in different countries? What might you conclude about how stress affects people in different cultures?

2. Find out what three Canadian organizations in three different industries have done to help employees manage stress. Are there common themes in these programs? Did you find any unusual programs? To what extent are these programs tailored to the needs of the employees in those industries?

WANT TO KNOW MORE?

If you are wondering how stressed you are, take the Canadian Heart & Stroke Stress Test at **www.heartandstroke.on.ca/ site/c.pvI3leNWJwE/b.4010337/k.5AF9/ Heart_Disease_Stress_Test_How_ fit_are_you_when_it_comes_to_ managing_stress.htm**. The site also offers tips on reducing stress. You can also take a work–life balance quiz at the Canadian Mental Health Association website (**www .cmha.ca/mental_health/work-life-balance-quiz/**) and read more on the effects of mental illness and stress.

Toward Less Stressful Work

- Avoid high-stress jobs—such as stockbroker, customer service/ complaint worker, police officer, waiter, medical intern, secretary, and air traffic controller—unless you are confident in your ability to handle stress.

- If you do experience stress at work, try to find a job that has plenty of control (so you can decide how to perform your work) and supportive co-workers.

- Lack of money is the top stressor reported by people under age 30, so pursue a career that pays you well but does not have a high degree of stress.[62]

4

Theories of Motivation

Mark McMorris, number one slopestyle rider on the 2013 World Snowboard Tour, won a bronze medal in the 2014 Olympics a mere two weeks after fracturing a rib. How did motivation influence his impressive performance?

LEARNING OUTCOMES

After studying this chapter, you should be able to:

1 Describe the three key elements of motivation.

2 Evaluate the applicability of early theories of motivation.

3 Apply the key tenets of expectancy theory to motivating employees.

4 Describe goal-setting theory, self-efficacy theory, and reinforcement theory.

5 Describe why equity and fairness matter in the workplace.

6 Demonstrate how organizational justice is a refinement of equity theory.

7 Apply the predictions of self-determination theory to intrinsic and extrinsic rewards.

8 Discuss the ethics behind motivation theories.

9 Summarize the essence of what we know about motivating employees.

THE CANADIAN PRESS/Nathan Denette

Mark McMorris, number one slopestyle rider on the 2013 World Snowboard Tour, was "pretty down," according to his father.[1] On January 25, a short time before the opening of the 2014 Olympics in Sochi, McMorris crashed during the final of the X Games Aspen Snowboard Slopestyle, fracturing one of the ribs on his right side. Even with the crash, which happened on his third and final run, McMorris won a silver medal. However, he had won the gold medal at Aspen in both 2011 and 2012.

But now he had to get himself ready for the Olympics, which was to start in just two weeks. His father's description of the situation showed what McMorris faced: "When we left him [the day after the injury occurred], he could bend over and touch his toes because of where [the injury] is at," Don McMorris told The Canadian Press on Monday. "You know a cracked rib in the front, you couldn't do that. . . . He's got five or six days before he has to worry about riding and he's got the best people around him."

It generally takes six weeks to heal from a cracked rib, and McMorris was facing competing in the Olympics just two weeks after his injury. Competing in the Olympics was a dream of his, and he would have to overcome great odds, not to mention pain, if he were to successfully compete. He still had to qualify for the Olympics, and the qualification round would take place one day before the opening ceremony. If he made the team, his event was scheduled to be held exactly two weeks after the crash. Would McMorris be motivated enough to make the Olympic team?

In this chapter, we review the basics of motivation, assess motivation theories, and provide an integrative understanding of how the different theories apply to motivating employees in organizations.

THE BIG IDEA

Successfully motivating individuals requires identifying their needs and making it possible for them to achieve those needs.

 IS FOR **EVERYONE**

- Are managers manipulating employees when they link rewards to productivity? Is this ethical?
- Why do some managers do a better job of motivating people than others?
- How important is fairness to you?
- What can you do if you think your salary is unfair?

What Is Motivation?

 Describe the three key elements of motivation.

Motivation is one of the most frequently researched topics in organizational behaviour (OB).[2] A 2013 Gallup poll suggests that employees are not motivated. Seventy percent of Canadian employees are not engaged in their work, and another 14 percent are actively disengaged.[3] In a 2014 survey, 89 percent of employees reported wasting time at work every day, and 62 percent said they waste between 30 and 60 minutes each day. How? Surfing the Internet came in first with 26 percent of respondents (Google, Facebook, and LinkedIn were the most popular time distractors); "too many meetings/conference calls and dealing with annoying coworkers tied for second place with 24% each."[4]

Motivation is the process that accounts for an individual's intensity, direction, and persistence of effort toward reaching a goal.[5]

The three key elements in our definition are intensity, direction, and persistence. *Intensity* describes how hard a person tries. This is the element most of us focus on when we talk about motivation. However, high intensity is unlikely to lead to favourable job-performance outcomes unless the effort is channelled in a *direction* that is beneficial. Therefore, we consider the quality of effort as well as its intensity. Finally, the effort requires *persistence*. This measures how long a person can maintain effort. Motivated individuals stay with a task long enough to achieve their goal.

Many people incorrectly view motivation as a personal trait—something some people have and others don't. Along these lines, Douglas McGregor proposed two distinct views of human beings. **Theory X**, which is basically negative, suggests that employees dislike work, will attempt to avoid it, and must be coerced, controlled, or threatened with punishment to achieve goals. **Theory Y**, which is basically positive, suggests that employees like work, are creative, seek responsibility, and will exercise self-direction and self-control if they are committed to the objectives.[6]

Our knowledge of motivation tells us that neither theory alone fully accounts for employee behaviour. What we know is that motivation is the result of the interaction of the individual and the situation. Certainly, individuals differ in their basic motivational drive. But the same employee who is quickly bored when pulling the lever on a drill press may enthusiastically pull a slot machine lever in Casino Windsor for hours on end. You may read the latest bestseller at one sitting, yet find it difficult to concentrate on a textbook for more than 20 minutes. It's not necessarily you—it's the situation. So as we analyze the concept of motivation, keep in mind that the level of motivation varies both *among* individuals and *within* individuals at different times.

You should also realize that what motivates people will also vary among individuals and situations. Motivation theorists talk about **intrinsic motivators** and **extrinsic motivators**. Extrinsic motivators come from outside the person and include such things as pay, bonuses, and other tangible rewards. Intrinsic motivators come from a person's internal desire to do something, due to such things as interest, challenge, and personal satisfaction. Individuals are intrinsically motivated when they genuinely care about their work, look for better ways to do it, and are energized and fulfilled by doing it well.[7] The rewards the individual gets from intrinsic motivation come from the work itself rather than from external factors such as increases in pay or compliments from the boss.

Are individuals primarily intrinsically or extrinsically motivated? Theory X suggests that people are almost exclusively driven by extrinsic motivators. However, Theory Y suggests that people are more intrinsically motivated. This view is consistent with that of Alfie Kohn, author of *Punished by Rewards*, who suggests that it's only necessary to provide the right environment, and people will be motivated.[8] We discuss his ideas further in Chapter 5.

Intrinsic and extrinsic motivation may reflect the situation, however, rather than individual personalities. For example, suppose that your mother has asked you or your brother to take her to a meeting an hour away. You may be willing to drive her, without any thought of compensation, because it will make you feel good to do something for her.

PERSONAL INVENTORY ASSESSMENT

Learn About Yourself
Work Motivation Indicator

motivation The intensity, direction, and persistence of effort a person shows in reaching a goal.

Theory X The assumption that employees dislike work, will attempt to avoid it, and must be coerced, controlled, or threatened with punishment to achieve goals.

Theory Y The assumption that employees like work, are creative, seek responsibility, and will exercise self-direction and self-control if they are committed to the objectives.

intrinsic motivators A person's internal desire to do something, due to such things as interest, challenge, and personal satisfaction.

extrinsic motivators Motivation that comes from outside the person and includes such things as pay, bonuses, and other tangible rewards.

That is intrinsic motivation. But if you have a love–hate relationship with your brother, you may insist that he buy you lunch for helping out. Lunch would then be an extrinsic motivator—something that came from outside yourself and motivated you to do the task. Later in the chapter, we review the evidence regarding the significance of extrinsic vs. intrinsic rewards, and also examine how to increase intrinsic motivation. Meanwhile, you might consider whether you can motivate yourself through self-talk, an idea considered in *Focus on Research*.

FOCUS ON RESEARCH

Talking to Yourself Can Be a Powerful Self-Motivator

How does internal dialogue affect our motivation? In the children's book *The Little Engine That Could*, the title character says, "I think I can, I think I can," motivating himself to do the job through positive self-talk. In a 2010 study, researchers examined whether this type of talk is the best way to motivate one's self, or whether it is better to ask "Can I do this?"[9]

Subjects were asked to spend one minute either "wondering whether they would complete a task or telling themselves they would." Then they were asked to complete some puzzles. Subjects who asked themselves whether they would complete the task were more successful than those who said they would. Several similar studies were conducted, and the results of each of them indicate that intrinsic motivation increased when subjects asked themselves a question about performance.

These findings suggest that asking yourself whether you will go to the gym three times next week will be more effective than telling yourself that you will go to the gym three times next week. One of the authors of the study summarized the results as follows: "The popular idea is that self-affirmations enhance people's ability to meet their goals. It seems, however, that when it comes to performing a specific behaviour, asking questions is a more promising way of achieving your objectives."

Needs Theories of Motivation

Theories of motivation generally fall into two categories: needs theories and process theories. *Needs theories* describe the types of needs that must be met to motivate individuals. *Process theories* help us understand the actual ways in which we and others can be motivated. There are a variety of needs theories, including Maslow's hierarchy of needs, Herzberg's motivation–hygiene theory (sometimes called the *two-factor theory*), and McClelland's theory of needs. We briefly review these to illustrate the basic properties of needs theories.

Needs theories are widely criticized for not standing up to scientific review. However, you should know them because (1) they represent a foundation from which contemporary theories have grown, and (2) practising managers still regularly use these theories and their terminology in explaining employee motivation.

Maslow's Hierarchy of Needs Theory

The best known theory of motivation is Abraham Maslow's **hierarchy of needs**.[10] Maslow hypothesized that within every human being there exists a hierarchy of five needs:

- *Physiological.* Includes hunger, thirst, shelter, sex, and other bodily needs.

- *Safety.* Includes security and protection from physical and emotional harm.

- *Social.* Includes affection, belongingness, acceptance, and friendship.

2 Evaluate the applicability of early theories of motivation.

hierarchy of needs theory
A hierarchy of five needs—physiological, safety, social, esteem, and self-actualization—in which, as each need is substantially satisfied, the next need becomes dominant.

EXHIBIT 4-1 Maslow's Hierarchy of Needs Applied to the Workplace

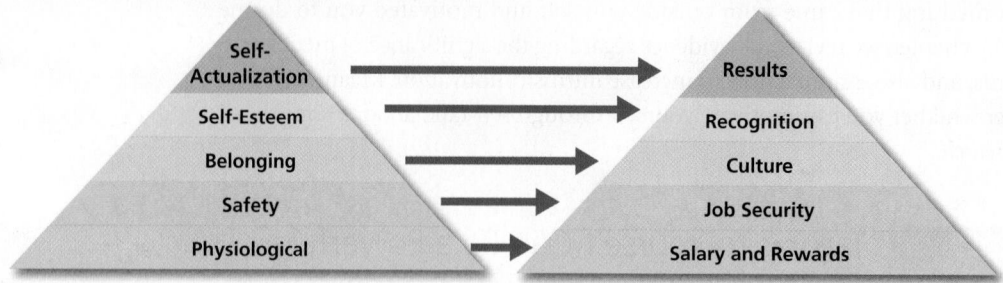

Source: C. Conley, *Peak: How Great Companies Get Their Mojo From Maslow* (San Francisco: Jossey-Bass, 2007). ISBN: 978-0787988616. Copyright © John Wiley & Sons.

Watch on **MyManagementLab**

Joie de Vivre Hospitality: Employee Motivation

- *Esteem.* Includes internal esteem factors such as self-respect, autonomy, and achievement; and external esteem factors such as status, recognition, and attention.

- *Self-actualization.* Includes growth, achieving one's potential, and self-fulfillment. This is the drive to become what one is capable of becoming.

Although no need is ever fully met, a substantially satisfied need no longer motivates. Thus, as each need becomes substantially satisfied, the next need becomes dominant. This is what Maslow means by moving up the steps of the hierarchy. So if you want to motivate someone, according to Maslow, you need to understand what level of the hierarchy that person is currently on and focus on satisfying needs at or above that level. Exhibit 4-1 identifies Maslow's hierarchy of needs on the left, and then illustrates how these needs are applied in the workplace.[11]

Maslow separated the five needs into higher and lower orders. Physiological and safety needs, where people start, are **lower-order needs**, and social (belonging), self-esteem, and **self-actualization** are **higher-order needs**. Higher-order needs are satisfied internally (within the person), whereas lower-order needs are mainly satisfied externally (by rewards such as pay, union contracts, and tenure).

Maslow's theory has received wide recognition, particularly among practising managers. It's intuitively logical and easy to understand, even though little research supports the theory. Maslow himself provided no empirical evidence, and few studies have been able to validate it.[12] One 2011 study differs in its findings, however. Using data from 123 countries, the study found that Maslow's needs are universally related to individual happiness, but that the order of need fulfillment had little bearing on life satisfaction and enjoyment. Lower-order needs were related to positive life evaluation, while higher-order needs were linked to enjoying life. The researchers concluded that the findings overall supported Maslow's theory.[13]

Some researchers have attempted to revive components of the need hierarchy concept, using principles from evolutionary psychology.[14] They propose that lower-level needs are the chief concern of immature animals or those with primitive nervous systems, whereas higher needs are more frequently observed in mature animals with more developed nervous systems. They also note distinct underlying biological systems for different types of needs.

lower-order needs Needs that are satisfied externally, such as physiological and safety needs.

self-actualization The drive to become what a person is capable of becoming.

higher-order needs Needs that are satisfied internally, such as social (belonging), self-esteem, and self-actualization needs.

Motivation–Hygiene Theory

Believing that an individual's relationship to work is basic and that attitude toward this work can very well determine success or failure, Frederick Herzberg wondered, "What do people want from their jobs?" He asked people to describe, in detail, situations in which they felt exceptionally *good* or *bad* about their jobs. The replies people gave when

EXHIBIT 4-2 Comparison of Satisfiers and Dissatisfiers

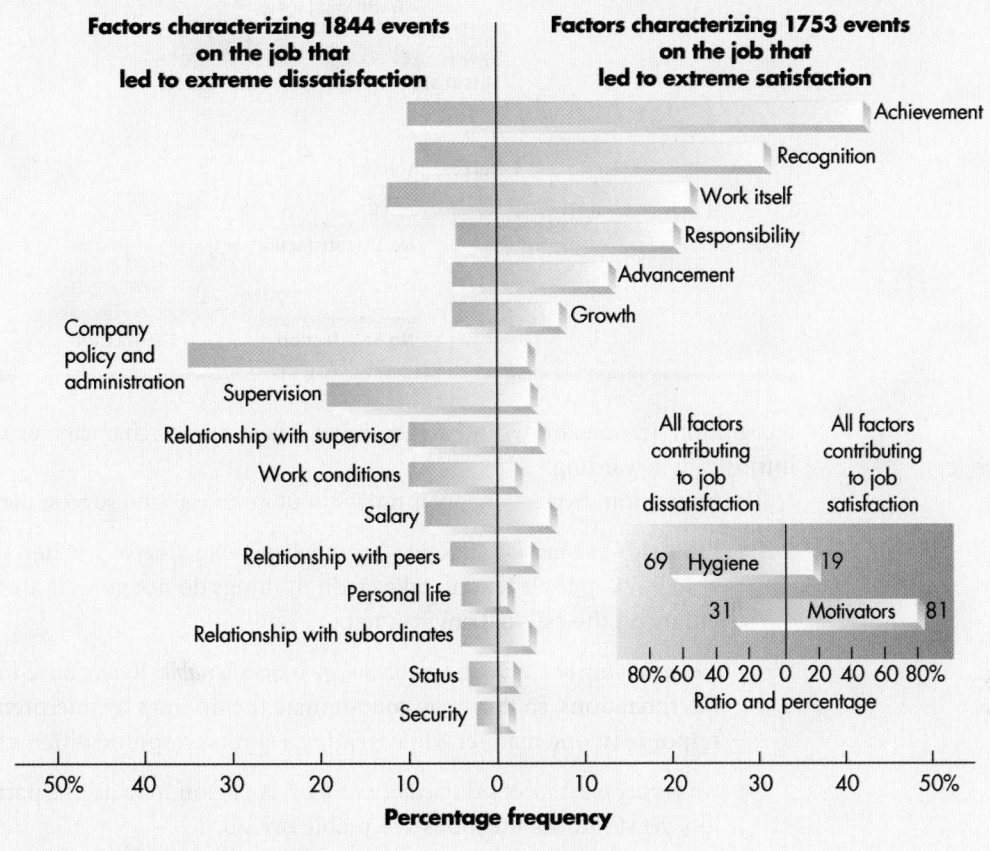

Source: Harvard Business Review. An exhibit from Frederick Herzberg, "One More Time: How Do You Motivate Employees?" *Harvard Business Review* 81, no. 1 (January 2003), p. 90.

they felt good about their jobs significantly differed from when they felt bad, which led Herzberg to his **two-factor theory**—also called *motivation–hygiene theory.*[15]

As Exhibit 4-2 shows, intrinsic factors, such as achievement, recognition, the work itself, responsibility, advancement, and growth, seem to be related to job satisfaction. Respondents who felt good about their work tended to attribute these characteristics to themselves. On the other hand, dissatisfied respondents tended to cite extrinsic factors, such as company policy and administration, supervision, interpersonal relations, and work conditions.

To Herzberg, the data suggest that the opposite of satisfaction is not dissatisfaction, as was traditionally believed. Removing dissatisfying characteristics from a job does not necessarily make the job satisfying. As illustrated in Exhibit 4-3, Herzberg proposed a dual continuum: the opposite of "Satisfaction" is "No Satisfaction," and the opposite of "Dissatisfaction" is "No Dissatisfaction."

According to Herzberg, the factors that lead to job satisfaction (motivators) are separate and distinct from those that lead to job dissatisfaction (hygiene factors). Therefore, managers who seek to eliminate factors that create job dissatisfaction may bring about peace but not necessarily motivation. They will be placating rather than motivating their employees. As a result, Herzberg characterized conditions such as quality of supervision, pay, company policies, physical working conditions, relationships with others, and job security as **hygiene factors**. When they are adequate, people will not be dissatisfied; but neither will they be satisfied. If we want to *motivate* people in their jobs, Herzberg suggested emphasizing factors associated with the work itself or with outcomes directly derived from it, such as promotional opportunities, personal growth opportunities,

two-factor theory A theory that relates intrinsic factors to job satisfaction and associates extrinsic factors with dissatisfaction. Also called the *motivation–hygiene theory.*

hygiene factors Factors—such as company policy and administration, supervision, and salary—that, when adequate in a job, placate employees. When these factors are adequate, people will not be dissatisfied.

EXHIBIT 4-3 Contrasting Views of Satisfaction and Dissatisfaction

recognition, responsibility, and achievement. These are the characteristics people find intrinsically rewarding.

The motivation–hygiene theory is not without its critics, who suggest the following:[16]

- *Herzberg's methodology is limited by its reliance on self-reports.* When things are going well, people tend to take credit. If things do not go well, they blame failure on the external environment.

- *The reliability of Herzberg's methodology is questionable.* Raters have to make interpretations, so they may contaminate the findings by interpreting one response in one manner while treating a similar response differently.

- *No overall measure of satisfaction was used.* A person may dislike part of their job, yet still think the job is acceptable overall.

- *Herzberg assumed that a relationship exists between satisfaction and productivity.* But he looked only at satisfaction. To make his research relevant, one must assume that a strong relationship exists between satisfaction and productivity.[17]

Regardless of these criticisms, Herzberg's theory has been widely read, and few managers are unfamiliar with his recommendations.

McClelland's Theory of Needs

You have one beanbag, and five targets are set up in front of you, each farther away than the last. Target A sits almost within arm's reach. If you hit it, you get $2. Target B is a bit farther out, but about 80 percent of the people who try can hit it. It pays $4. Target C pays $8, and about half the people who try can hit it. Very few people can hit Target D, but the payoff is $16 for those who do. Finally, Target E pays $32, but it's almost impossible to achieve. Which target would you try for? If you selected C, you are likely to be a high achiever. Why? Read on.

McClelland's theory of needs was developed by David McClelland and his associates.[18] The theory focuses on three needs, defined as follows:

- **Need for achievement (nAch)** is the drive to excel, to achieve in relation to a set of standards, and to strive to succeed.

- **Need for power (nPow)** is the need to make others behave in a way that they would not have behaved otherwise.

- **Need for affiliation (nAff)** is the desire for friendly and close interpersonal relationships.

McClelland and subsequent researchers focused most of their attention on nAch. High achievers perform best when they perceive their probability of success as

McClelland's theory of needs Achievement, power, and affiliation are three important needs that help explain motivation.

need for achievement (nAch) The drive to excel, to achieve in relation to a set of standards, and to strive to succeed.

need for power (nPow) The need to make others behave in a way that they would not have behaved otherwise.

need for affiliation (nAff) The desire for friendly and close interpersonal relationships.

0.5—that is, a 50–50 chance.[19] They dislike gambling with high odds because they get no achievement satisfaction from success that comes by pure chance. Similarly, they dislike low odds (high probability of success) because then there is no challenge to their skills. They like to set goals that require stretching themselves a little.

Relying on an extensive amount of research, we can predict some relationships between achievement need and job performance. First, when jobs have a high degree of personal responsibility, feedback, and an intermediate degree of risk, high achievers are strongly motivated. They are successful in entrepreneurial activities such as running their own businesses, for example, and managing self-contained units within large organizations.[20] Second, a high need to achieve does not necessarily make someone a good manager, especially in large organizations. People with a high achievement need are interested in how well they do personally and not in influencing others to do well. High-nAch salespeople do not necessarily make good sales managers, and the good general manager in a large organization does not typically have a high need to achieve.[21] Third, needs for affiliation and power tend to be closely related to managerial success. The best managers are high in their need for power and low in their need for affiliation.[22] In fact, a high power motive may be a requirement for managerial effectiveness.[23]

McClelland's theory has had the best research support of the different needs theories. Unfortunately, it has less practical effect than the others. Because McClelland argued that the three needs are subconscious—we may rank high on them but not know it—measuring them is not easy. In the most common approach, a trained expert presents pictures to individuals, asks them to tell a story about each, and then scores their responses in terms of the three needs. However, the process is time consuming and expensive, and few organizations have been willing to invest in measuring McClelland's concept.

Alexandra Greenhill, co-founder and CEO of myBestHelper is a high achiever. She was named one of Vancouver's Top 40 under 40 winners in December 2013. myBestHelper is a website where people who need care providers (such as nannies, tutors, or babysitters) can connect with people who are looking to provide care. Greenhill, who was writing computer code at an early age, is also a family physician and has helped the BC Medical Association with its work on electronic medical records. She envisions that myBestHelper will be in every major city in Canada within five years.

Summarizing Needs Theories

The needs theories we have just reviewed all propose a similar idea: Individuals have needs that, when unsatisfied, will result in motivation. For instance, if you have a need to be praised, you may work harder at your task in order to receive recognition from your manager or other co-workers. Similarly, if you need money and you are asked to do something (within reason) that offers money as a reward, you will be motivated to complete that task.

Where needs theories differ is in the types of needs they consider and whether they propose a hierarchy of needs (where some needs have to be satisfied before others) or simply a list of needs. Exhibit 4-4 illustrates the relationship among the three needs

EXHIBIT 4-4 Relationship of Various Needs Theories

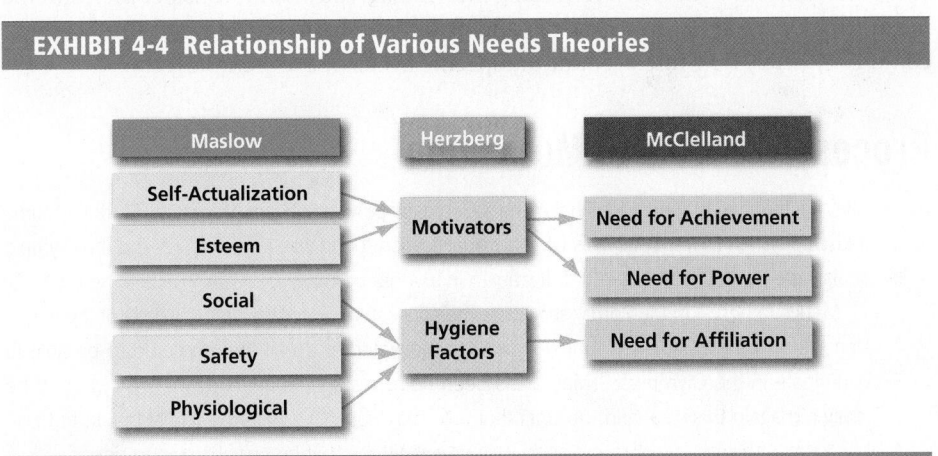

EXHIBIT 4-5 Summarizing the Various Needs Theories

Theory	Maslow	Herzberg	McClelland
Is there a hierarchy of needs?	The theory argues that lower-order needs must be satisfied before one progresses to higher-order needs.	Hygiene factors must be met if a person is not to be dissatisfied. They will not lead to satisfaction, however. Motivators lead to satisfaction.	People vary in the types of needs they have. Their motivation and how well they perform in a work situation are related to whether they have a need for achievement, power, or affiliation.
What is the theory's impact/contribution?	The theory enjoys wide recognition among practising managers. Most managers are familiar with it.	The popularity of giving employees greater responsibility for planning and controlling their work can be attributed to this theory (see, for instance, the job characteristics model in Chapter 5). It shows that more than one need may operate at the same time.	The theory tells us that high-need achievers do not necessarily make good managers, since high achievers are more interested in how they do personally.
What empirical support/criticisms exist?	Research has not validated the hierarchical nature of needs. However, a 2011 study found that the needs are universally related to individual happiness.	It is not really a theory of motivation: It assumes a link between satisfaction and productivity that was not measured or demonstrated.	It has mixed empirical support, but the theory is consistent with our knowledge of individual differences among people. Good empirical support exists on needs achievement in particular.

theories that we discussed, and Exhibit 4-5 indicates whether the theory proposes a hierarchy of needs, and the contribution of and empirical support for each theory.

What can we conclude from needs theories? We can safely say that individuals do have needs, and that they can be highly motivated to achieve those needs. The types of needs, and their importance, vary by individual, and probably vary over time for the same individual as well. When rewarding individuals, you should consider their specific needs. Obviously, in a workplace, it would be difficult to design a reward structure that could completely take into account the specific needs of every employee.

Process Theories of Motivation

After fracturing a rib during the final of the X Games Aspen Snowboard Slopestyle, Mark McMorris had 12 days to recover before his Olympic qualification round was to be held.[24] And the Olympic finals were just two days after that. It was an injury that normally takes six weeks to heal.

Mark's father, Don McMorris, served as the spokesperson for the first few days of the injury. Don told anyone who asked that his son was motivated to do all that he could to be able to participate in the Olympics. "[Mark] has been riding as well as anybody in the world and he really did again this weekend, up until that fall," Don said. "This is a bit of a setback, but I do know that in his mind and in his heart he'll do everything that he possibly can to ride."

Mark's older brother, Craig, was asked to describe him. "If Mark gets it in his head that he's going to do a trick, he's going to do that trick until he gets it, or hurts himself," he said. Both brothers snowboarded competitively for a provincial team in Saskatchewan. However, by the time Mark was 15, he had outgrown the provincial team and started competing internationally. Burton, Red Bull, and Oakley stepped in to sponsor him. Mark was so committed to becoming a professional snowboarder that he dropped out of school after grade 10.

Mark McMorris is motivated by a mix of intrinsic and extrinsic motivation. Like any talented athlete, he wants to be number one. But he also gets joy out of snowboarding as well. What makes someone like McMorris show up at the slope, day after day, practising his tricks?

Process theories go beyond individual needs and focus on the broader picture of how one motivates one's self and others. Process theories include expectancy theory, goal-setting theory (and its application, management by objectives), self-efficacy theory, and reinforcement theory.

Expectancy Theory

One of the most widely accepted explanations of motivation is Victor Vroom's **expectancy theory**.[25] Although it has its critics, most of the evidence supports the theory.[26]

Expectancy theory says that employees will be motivated to exert a high level of effort when they believe the following:

- That the effort will lead to good performance

- That good performance will lead to organizational rewards, such as salary increases and/or intrinsic rewards

- That the rewards will satisfy employees' personal goals

The theory focuses on the three relationships (expectancy, instrumentality, and valence) illustrated in Exhibit 4-6 and described in the following pages. This exhibit also provides an example of how you might apply the theory.

Effort–Performance Relationship

The effort–performance relationship is commonly called **expectancy**. It answers the question: *If I give a maximum effort, will it be recognized in my performance appraisal?* For many employees, the answer is no. Why? Their skill level may be deficient, which means that no matter how hard they try, they are not likely to be high performers. The organization's performance appraisal system may be designed to assess nonperformance factors such as loyalty, initiative, or courage, which means more effort will not

3 Apply the key tenets of expectancy theory to motivating employees.

expectancy theory The theory that individuals act based on their evaluation of whether their effort will lead to good performance, whether good performance will be followed by a given outcome, and whether that outcome is attractive.

expectancy The belief that effort is related to performance.

EXHIBIT 4-6 How Does Expectancy Theory Work?

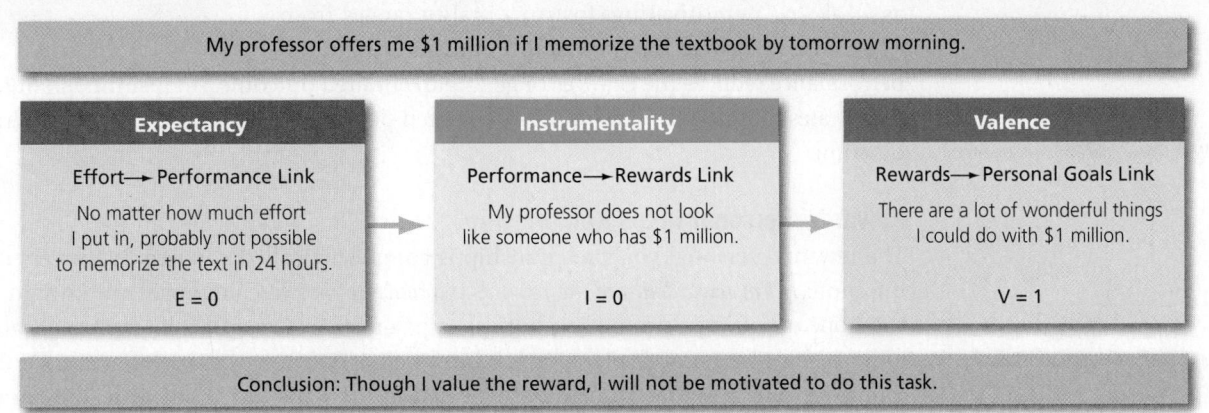

My professor offers me $1 million if I memorize the textbook by tomorrow morning.

Expectancy	Instrumentality	Valence
Effort → Performance Link	Performance → Rewards Link	Rewards → Personal Goals Link
No matter how much effort I put in, probably not possible to memorize the text in 24 hours.	My professor does not look like someone who has $1 million.	There are a lot of wonderful things I could do with $1 million.
E = 0	I = 0	V = 1

Conclusion: Though I value the reward, I will not be motivated to do this task.

THE CANADIAN PRESS/AP/Kevork Djansezian

Using employee performance software, convenience-store retailer 7-Eleven measures the efforts of store managers and employees at its 8700 North American stores. The company ties employee compensation to performance outcomes based on 7-Eleven's five fundamental strategic initiatives—product assortment, value, quality, service, and cleanliness—as well as meeting goals set for new products. Many other companies reward simply on sales, which does not capture the full range of value-added services that employees provide.

necessarily result in a higher evaluation. Another possibility is that employees, rightly or wrongly, think the boss does not like them. As a result, they expect a poor appraisal, regardless of effort. These examples suggest that people will only be motivated if they perceive a link between their effort and their performance. Expectancy can be expressed as a probability, and ranges from 0 to 1. To further provoke your thoughts on this matter, the *Ethical Dilemma* on page 161 asks you to consider how grade inflation has affected the meaning of grades.

Performance–Rewards Relationship

The performance–rewards relationship is commonly called **instrumentality**. It answers the question: *If I get a good performance appraisal, will it lead to organizational rewards?* Many organizations reward things besides performance. When pay is based on factors such as having seniority, being cooperative, or "kissing up" to the boss, employees are likely to see the performance–rewards relationship as weak and demotivating. Instrumentality ranges from –1 to +1. A negative instrumentality indicates that high performance reduces the chances of getting the desired outcome. An instrumentality of 0 indicates that no relationship exists between performance and receiving the desired outcome.

> Are managers manipulating employees when they link rewards to productivity? Is this ethical?

Rewards–Personal Goals Relationship

The rewards–personal goals relationship is commonly called **valence**. It answers the question: *If I'm rewarded, are the rewards attractive to me?* The employee works hard in the hope of getting a promotion but gets a pay raise instead. Or the employee wants a more interesting and challenging job but receives only a few words of praise. Or the employee puts in extra effort to be relocated to the Paris office but instead is transferred to Singapore. Unfortunately, many managers are limited in the rewards they

◉—Watch on **MyManagementLab**

The Work Zone Role Plays—Motivation

instrumentality The belief that performance is related to rewards.

valence The value or importance an individual places on a reward.

China Photos/Getty Images

The performance–reward relationship is strong at Mary Kay Cosmetics, which offers a rewards and recognition program based on the achievement of personal goals set by each salesperson. These independent consultants are posing in front of Mary Kay Career Cars, one of many rewards that motivate Mary Kay's salesforce.

can distribute, which makes it difficult to tailor rewards to individual employee needs. Moreover, some managers incorrectly assume that all employees want the same thing. They overlook the motivational effects of differentiating rewards. In either case, employee motivation may be lower because the specific need the employee has is not being met through the reward structure. Valence ranges from −1 (very undesirable reward) to +1 (very desirable reward). *OB in the Workplace* shows that valence can drive stock analysts to place more buy ratings than sell ratings.

> Why do some managers do a better job of motivating people than others?

 # IN THE **WORKPLACE**
Stock Analyst Recommendations and Valence

Could rewards obscure making accurate recommendations? Stock analysts make their living trying to forecast a stock's future price; the accuracy of their buy, sell, and hold recommendations is what keeps them in work or gets them fired.[27] Nevertheless, analysts place few sell ratings on stocks, although in a steady market, by definition, as many stocks are falling as are rising.

Expectancy theory provides an explanation: Analysts who place a sell rating on a company's stock have to balance the benefits they receive by being accurate against the risks they run by drawing that company's ire. What are these risks? They include public rebuke, professional blackballing, and exclusion from information. Their valence for this is −1. When analysts place a buy rating on a stock, they face no such trade-off because, obviously, companies love it when analysts recommend that investors buy their stock. Expectancy theory suggests that the expected rewards and their desirability is higher for buy ratings than sell ratings, and that is why buy ratings vastly outnumber sell ratings.

EXHIBIT 4-7 Steps to Increasing Motivation, Using Expectancy Theory

Improving Expectancy	Improving Instrumentality	Improving Valence
Improve the ability of the individual to perform.	Increase the individual's belief that performance will lead to reward.	Make sure that the reward is meaningful to the individual.
• Make sure employees have skills for the task. • Provide training. • Assign reasonable tasks and goals.	• Observe and recognize performance. • Deliver rewards as promised. • Indicate to employees how previous good performance led to greater rewards.	• Ask employees what rewards they value. • Give rewards that are valued.

Expectancy Theory in the Workplace

Does expectancy theory work? Although it has its critics,[28] most of the research evidence supports the theory.[29] Research in cross-cultural settings has also indicated support for expectancy theory.[30]

Exhibit 4-7 gives some suggestions for what a manager can do to increase the motivation of employees, using insights from expectancy theory. To appreciate how expectancy theory might apply in the workplace, see this chapter's *Case Incident—Wage Reduction Proposal* on page 162 for an example of what happens when expected rewards are withdrawn.

The Importance of Providing Performance Feedback

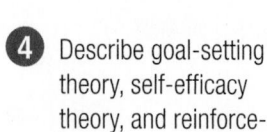

4 Describe goal-setting theory, self-efficacy theory, and reinforcement theory.

People do better when they get feedback on how well they are progressing toward their goals because it helps identify discrepancies between what they have done and what they want to do—that is, feedback guides behaviour. But all feedback is not equally potent. Self-generated feedback—with which employees are able to monitor their own progress or receive feedback from the task process itself—is more powerful than externally generated feedback.[31] Recent research has also shown that people monitor their progress differently depending on how close they are to goal accomplishment. When they have just begun pursuing a goal, they derive motivation from believing that the goal is attainable, so they exaggerate their level of progress in order to stay motivated. However, when they are close to accomplishing their goal, they derive motivation from believing a discrepancy still exists between where they are currently and where they would like to be, so they downplay their progress to date to signal a need for higher effort.[32]

Effective feedback—where the employee perceives the appraisal as fair, the manager as sincere, and the climate as constructive—can lead the employee to respond positively and become determined to correct his or her performance deficiencies.[33] Thus, the performance review should be more like a counselling activity than a judgment process, allowing the review to evolve out of the employee's own self-evaluation. For more tips on performance feedback, see *OB in Action—Giving More Effective Feedback*.

IN **ACTION**
Giving More Effective Feedback

Managers can use the following tips to give more effective feedback:

→ Relate feedback to existing performance **goals** and clear **expectations**.

→ Give **specific** feedback tied to observable behaviour or measurable results.

→ Channel feedback toward **key result areas**.

→ Give feedback as **soon** as possible.

→ Give positive feedback for **improvement**, not just final results.

→ Focus feedback on **performance**, not personalities.

→ Base feedback on **accurate** and **credible** information.[34]

Goal-Setting Theory

You have heard the phrase a number of times: "Just do your best. That's all anyone can ask for." But what does "do your best" mean? Do we ever know whether we have achieved that vague goal? Might we do better with specific goals? Research

Toby Melville/Reuters

Co-founders Anthony Thomson (left) and Vernon Hill (right) launched their first Metro Bank in London, England, with a long-term goal of adding 200 new branches and capturing up to 10 percent of London's banking market. Metro Bank challenges employees to reach this high goal by giving customers exceptionally friendly, convenient, and flexible service.

on **goal-setting theory** in fact reveals the impressive effects of goal specificity, challenge, and feedback on performance.

The research on goal setting theory by Edwin Locke and his colleague, Professor Gary Latham at the University of Toronto, shows that intentions to work toward a **goal** are a major source of work motivation.[35] Goals tell an employee what needs to be done and how much effort is needed.[36] *Point/Counterpoint* on page 159 considers the benefits of goal setting.

How do managers make goal-setting theory operational? That's often left up to the individual. Some managers set aggressive performance targets—what General Electric called "stretch goals." Some senior executives, such as Procter & Gamble's former CEO Robert McDonald and Best Buy's president and CEO Hubert Joly, are known for demanding performance goals. But many managers don't set goals. When asked whether their job had clearly defined goals, only a minority of employees in a survey said yes.[37]

A more systematic way to utilize goal setting is with **management by objectives (MBO)**, which emphasizes participatively set goals that are tangible, verifiable, and measurable.[38] Progress on goals is periodically reviewed, and rewards are allocated on the basis of this progress.

How Does Goal Setting Motivate?

According to Locke, goal setting motivates in four ways (see Exhibit 4-8):[39]

- *Goals direct attention.* Goals indicate where individuals should direct their efforts when they are choosing among things to do. For instance, recognizing that an important assignment is due in a few days, goal setting may encourage you to say no when friends invite you to a movie this evening.

- *Goals regulate effort.* Goals suggest how much effort an individual should put into a given task. For instance, if earning a high mark in accounting is more important to you than earning a high mark in organizational behaviour, you will likely put more effort into studying accounting.

goal-setting theory A theory that says that specific and difficult goals, with feedback, lead to higher performance.

goal What an individual is trying to accomplish.

management by objectives (MBO) An approach to goal setting in which specific measurable goals are jointly set by managers and employees; progress on goals is periodically reviewed, and rewards are allocated on the basis of this progress.

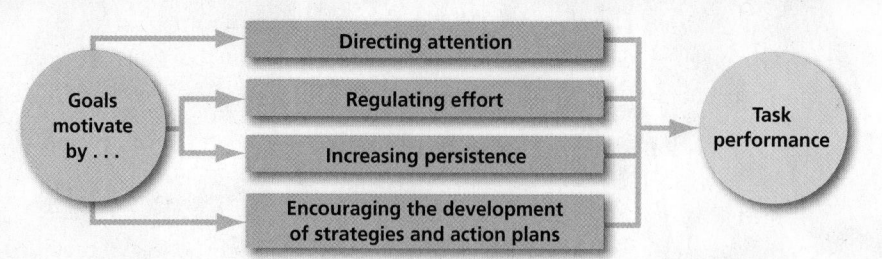

EXHIBIT 4-8 Locke's Model of Goal Setting

Goals motivate by . . .
- Directing attention
- Regulating effort
- Increasing persistence
- Encouraging the development of strategies and action plans

→ Task performance

Source: Adapted from E. A. Locke and G. P. Latham, *A Theory of Goal Setting and Task Performance* (Englewood Cliffs, NJ: Prentice Hall, 1980).

- *Goals increase persistence.* Persistence represents the effort spent on a task over time. When people keep goals in mind, they will work hard on them, even in the face of obstacles.

- *Goals encourage the development of strategies and action plans.* Once goals are set, individuals can develop plans for achieving those goals. For instance, a goal to become more fit may include plans to join a gym, work out with friends, and change eating habits.

In order for goals to be effective, they should be "SMART." SMART stands for

- **S**pecific: Individuals know exactly what is to be achieved.

- **M**easurable: The goals proposed can be tracked and reviewed.

- **A**ttainable: The goals, even if difficult, are reasonable and achievable.

- **R**esults-oriented: The goals should support the vision of the organization.

- **T**ime-bound: The goals are to be achieved within a stated time.

From Concepts to Skills on pages 162–163 presents additional ideas on how to effectively engage in goal setting.

RESEARCH FINDINGS: The Effects of Goal Setting

Locke and his colleagues have spent considerable time studying the effects of goal setting in various situations. The evidence strongly supports the value of goals. More to the point, we can say the following:

- *Specific goals increase performance, under certain conditions.* In early research, specific goals were linked to better performance.[40] However, other research indicates that specific goals can lead to poorer performance in complex tasks. Employees may be too goal-focused on complex tasks, and therefore not consider alternative and better solutions to such tasks.[41]

- *Difficult goals, when accepted, result in higher performance than do easy goals.* Research clearly shows that goal difficulty leads to positive performance for the following reasons.[42] First, challenging goals get our attention and thus tend to help us focus. Second, difficult goals energize us because we have to work harder to attain them. Third, when goals are difficult, people persist in trying to attain them. Finally, difficult goals lead us to discover strategies that help us perform the job or task more effectively. If we have to struggle to solve a difficult problem, we often think of a better way to go about it. However, this relationship does not hold when employees view the goals as impossible, rather than just difficult.[43]

- *Feedback leads to higher performance.* Feedback allows individuals to know how they are doing, relative to their goals.[44] Feedback encourages individuals to adjust their direction, effort, and action plans if they are falling short of their goals. Self-generated feedback—with which employees are able to monitor their own progress—has been shown to be a more powerful motivator than externally generated feedback.[45]

- *Goals are equally effective whether participatively set, assigned, or self-set.* Research indicates that how goals are set is not clearly related to performance.[46] In some cases, participatively set goals yielded superior performance; in others, individuals performed best when assigned goals by their boss. But a major advantage of participation may be that it increases acceptance of the goal as a desirable one toward which to work.[47] Commitment is important. If participation is not used, then the individual assigning the goal needs to clearly explain its purpose and importance.[48]

- *Goal commitment affects whether goals are achieved.* Goal-setting theory assumes that an individual is committed to the goal and is determined not to lower or abandon it. In terms of behaviour, the individual (1) believes he or she can achieve the goal and (2) wants to achieve it.[49] Goal commitment is most likely to occur when goals are made public, when the individual has an internal locus of control (that is, considers that control over one's life resides within the individual), when the goals are self-set rather than assigned, and when goals are based at least partially on individual ability.[50] Goals themselves seem to affect performance more strongly when tasks are simple rather than complex, well learned rather than novel, independent rather than interdependent, and are on the high end of achievable goals.[51] On interdependent tasks, group goals are preferable. Paradoxically, goal abandonment following an initial failure is more likely for individuals who self-affirm their core values, possibly because they internalize the implications of failure.[52]

Although goal setting has positive outcomes, it's not unequivocally beneficial. For example, some goals may be *too* effective.[53] When learning something is important, goals related to performance may cause people to become too focused on outcomes and ignore changing conditions. In this case, a goal to learn and generate alternative solutions will be more effective than a goal to perform. In addition, some authors argue goals can lead employees to focus on a single standard and exclude all others. A goal to boost short-term stock prices may lead organizations to ignore long-term success and even to engage in unethical behaviour such as "cooking the books" to meet those goals. Other studies show that employees low in conscientiousness and emotional stability experience greater emotional exhaustion when their leaders set goals.[54] Finally, individuals may fail to give up on an unattainable goal, even when it might be beneficial to do so. Despite differences of opinion, most researchers do agree that goals are powerful in shaping behaviour. Managers should make sure goals are aligned with company objectives.

Research has found that people differ in the way they regulate their thoughts and behaviours during goal pursuit.[55] Generally, people fall into one of two categories, although they could belong to both. Those with a **promotion focus** strive for advancement and accomplishment and approach conditions that move them closer toward desired goals. Those with a **prevention focus** strive to fulfill duties and obligations and avoid conditions that pull them away from desired goals. Although both strategies work toward goal accomplishment, the manner in which they get there is quite different. As an example, consider studying for an exam. You could engage in promotion-focused activities such as reading class materials and notes, or you could engage in prevention-focused activities such as refraining from things that would get

promotion focus A self-regulation strategy that involves striving for goals through advancement and accomplishment.

prevention focus A self-regulation strategy that involves striving for goals by fulfilling duties and obligations.

in the way of studying, such as playing video games or going out with friends. Or, you could do both activities.

You may ask, "Which is the better strategy?" Well, the answer to that question depends on the outcome you are striving for. While a promotion (but not a prevention) focus is related to higher levels of task performance, organizational citizenship behaviour, and innovation, a prevention (but not a promotion) focus is related to safety performance. Ideally, it's probably best to be both promotion *and* prevention oriented.[56]

Goal-setting theory is consistent with expectancy theory. The goals can be considered the effort–performance link—in other words, the goals determine what must be done. Feedback can be considered the performance–reward relationship, where the individual's efforts are recognized. Finally, the implication of goal setting is that the achievement of the goals will result in intrinsic satisfaction (and, of course, may be linked to external rewards).

Self-Efficacy Theory

The basic premise of **self-efficacy theory**, also known as *social cognitive theory* or *social learning theory*, is that individuals' beliefs in their ability to perform a task influence their behaviour.[57] The higher your self-efficacy, the more confidence you have in your ability to succeed in a task. So, in difficult situations, people with low self-efficacy are more likely to lessen their effort or give up altogether, while those with high self-efficacy will try harder to master the challenge.[58] Self-efficacy can create a positive spiral in which those with high efficacy become more engaged in their tasks and then, in turn, increase performance, which increases efficacy further.[59] Changes in self-efficacy over time are related to changes in creative performance as well.[60] Individuals high in self-efficacy also seem to respond to negative feedback with increased effort and motivation, while those low in self-efficacy are likely to lessen their effort after negative feedback.[61] How can managers help their employees achieve high levels of self-efficacy? By bringing goal-setting theory and self-efficacy theory together.

Goal-setting theory and self-efficacy theory don't compete: they complement each other. As Exhibit 4-9 shows, employees whose managers set difficult goals for them will have a higher level of self-efficacy, and set higher goals for their own performance. Why? Setting difficult goals for people communicates your confidence in them. For example,

EXHIBIT 4-9 Joint Effects of Goals and Self-Efficacy on Performance

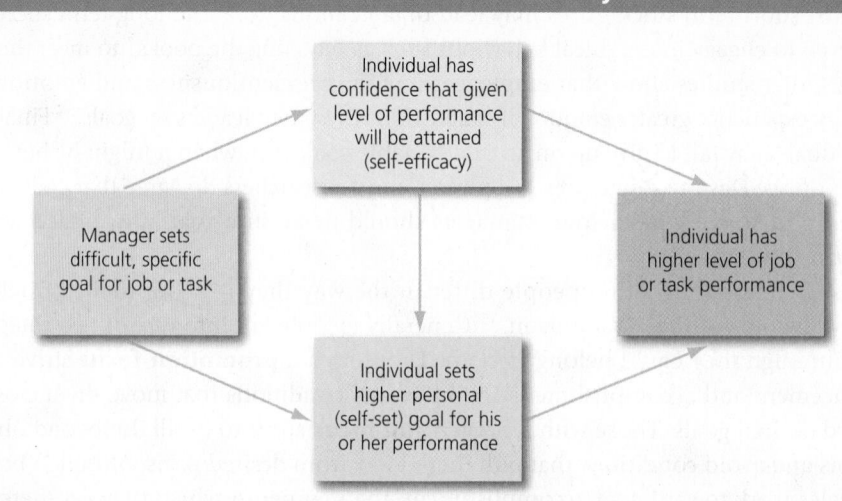

Source: Based on E. A. Locke and G. P. Latham, "Building a Practically Useful Theory of Goal Setting and Task Motivation: A 35-Year Odyssey," *American Psychologist*, September 2002, pp. 705–717.

self-efficacy theory Individuals' beliefs in their ability to perform a task influence their behaviour.

imagine that your boss sets a higher goal for you than for your co-workers. How would you interpret this? As long as you did not feel you were being picked on, you would probably think, *Well, I guess my boss thinks I'm capable of performing better than others.* This idea sets in motion a psychological process in which you are more confident in yourself (higher self-efficacy) and set higher personal goals, performing better both in the workplace and outside it.

The researcher who developed self-efficacy theory, Albert Bandura, proposes four ways self-efficacy can be increased:[62]

- *Enactive mastery.* Gaining relevant experience with the task or job. If you have been able to do the job successfully in the past, then you are more confident that you will be able to do it in the future.

- *Vicarious modelling.* Becoming more confident because you see someone else doing the task. For example, if your friend loses weight, then it increases your confidence that you can lose weight, too. Vicarious modelling is most effective when you see yourself as similar to the person you are observing.

- *Verbal persuasion.* Becoming more confident because someone convinces you that you have the skills necessary to be successful. Motivational speakers use this tactic.

- *Arousal.* An energized state, so the person gets "psyched up" and performs better. But if the task is something that requires a steady, lower-key perspective (say, carefully editing a manuscript), arousal may in fact hurt performance.

The best way for a manager to use verbal persuasion is through the *Pygmalion effect* or the *Galatea effect.* The Pygmalion effect is a form of self-fulfilling prophecy in which believing something can make it true. For example, sailors who were told convincingly that they would not get seasick while out at sea were in fact much less likely to do so.[63] In another example, teachers were told their students had very high IQ scores when, in fact, they spanned a range from high to low. Consistent with the Pygmalion effect, the teachers spent more time with the students they *thought* were smart, gave them more challenging assignments, and expected more of them—all of which led to higher student self-efficacy and better grades.[64] Self-fulfilling prophecies have also been used to improve productivity in the workplace.[65]

What are the OB implications of self-efficacy theory? Well, it's a matter of applying Bandura's sources of self-efficacy to the work setting. Training programs often make use of enactive mastery by having people practise and build their skills. In fact, the reason training works is because it increases self-efficacy.[66] Individuals with higher levels of self-efficacy also appear to reap more benefits from training programs and are more likely to use their training on the job.[67] Intelligence and personality are absent from Bandura's list but they can increase self-efficacy.[68] People who are intelligent, conscientious, and emotionally stable are so much more likely to have high self-efficacy that some researchers argue that self-efficacy is less important than prior research would suggest.[69] They believe it is partially a by-product in a smart person with a confident personality. Although Bandura strongly disagrees with this conclusion, more research is needed.

Reinforcement Theory

Goal-setting is a cognitive approach, proposing that an individual's purposes direct his or her actions. **Reinforcement theory**, in contrast, takes a behaviouristic view, arguing that reinforcement conditions behaviour. The two theories are clearly at odds philosophically. Reinforcement theorists see behaviour as environmentally caused. You need not be concerned, they would argue, with internal cognitive events; what controls behaviour is reinforcers—any consequences that, when immediately following responses, increase the probability that the behaviour will be repeated.

reinforcement theory A theory that says that behaviour is a function of its consequences.

Reinforcement theory ignores the inner state of the individual and concentrates solely on what happens when he or she takes some action. Because it does not concern itself with what initiates behaviour, it is not, strictly speaking, a theory of motivation. But it does provide a powerful means of analyzing what controls behaviour, and this is why we typically consider it in discussions of motivation.[70]

Operant conditioning theory, probably the most relevant component of reinforcement theory for management, argues that people learn to behave to get something they want or to avoid something they don't want. Unlike reflexive or unlearned behaviour, operant behaviour is influenced by the reinforcement or lack of reinforcement brought about by its consequences. Therefore, reinforcement strengthens a behaviour and increases the likelihood it will be repeated.[71]

B.F. Skinner, one of the most prominent advocates of operant conditioning, argued that creating pleasing consequences to follow specific forms of behaviour would increase the frequency of that behaviour. He demonstrated that people will most likely engage in desired behaviours if they are positively reinforced for doing so; that rewards are most effective if they immediately follow the desired behaviour; and that behaviour that is not rewarded, or is punished, is less likely to be repeated. We know a professor who places a mark by a student's name each time the student makes a contribution to class discussions. Operant conditioning scholars would argue that this practice is motivating because it conditions a student to expect a reward (earn class credit) each time he or she demonstrates a specific behaviour (speaking up in class). The concept of operant conditioning was part of Skinner's broader concept of **behaviourism**, which asserts that behaviour follows stimuli in a relatively unthinking manner. Skinner's form of radical behaviourism rejects feelings, thoughts, and other states of mind as causes of behaviour. In short, people learn to associate stimulus and response, but their conscious awareness of this association is irrelevant.[72]

You can see illustrations of operant conditioning everywhere that reinforcements are contingent on some action on your part. Your instructor says that if you want a high grade in the course, you must supply correct answers on the test. A commissioned salesperson who wants to earn a high income must generate high sales in her territory. Of course, the linkage can also teach individuals to engage in behaviours that work against the best interests of the organization. Assume that your boss says that if you will work overtime during the next three-week busy season, you will be compensated for it at the next performance appraisal. However, when performance appraisal time comes, you find that you are given no positive reinforcement for your overtime work. The next time your manager asks you to work overtime, you will probably decline! Your behaviour can be explained by operant conditioning: If a behaviour fails to be positively reinforced, the probability that it will be repeated declines.

Methods of Shaping Behaviour

Behaviour can be shaped in four ways: through positive reinforcement, negative reinforcement, punishment, and extinction.

Following a response with something pleasant is called *positive reinforcement*. Following a response with the termination or withdrawal of something unpleasant is called *negative reinforcement*. *Punishment* is causing an unpleasant condition in an attempt to eliminate an undesirable behaviour. Eliminating any reinforcement that is maintaining a behaviour is called *extinction*. Exhibit 4-10 presents examples of each type of reinforcement. Negative reinforcement should not be confused with punishment: Negative reinforcement strengthens a behaviour because it takes away an unpleasant situation.

Schedules of Reinforcement

While consequences have an effect on behaviour, the timing of those consequences or reinforcements is also important. The two major types of reinforcement schedules are *continuous* and *intermittent*. A **continuous reinforcement** schedule reinforces the

behaviourism A theory that argues that behaviour follows stimuli in a relatively unthinking manner.

continuous reinforcement A desired behaviour is reinforced each and every time it is demonstrated.

EXHIBIT 4-10 Types of Reinforcement

Reinforcement Type	Example
Positive reinforcement	A manager praises an employee for a job well done.
Negative reinforcement	An instructor asks a question and a student looks through her lecture notes to avoid being called on. She has learned that looking busily through her notes prevents the instructor from calling on her.
Punishment	A manager gives an employee a two-day suspension from work without pay for showing up drunk.
Extinction	An instructor ignores students who raise their hands to ask questions. Hand-raising becomes extinct.

desired behaviour each and every time it is demonstrated. Take, for example, the case of someone who has historically had trouble arriving at work on time. Every time he is not tardy, his manager might compliment him on his desirable behaviour. In an intermittent schedule, on the other hand, not every instance of the desirable behaviour is reinforced, but reinforcement is given often enough to make the behaviour worth repeating. Evidence indicates that the intermittent, or varied, form of reinforcement tends to promote more resistance to extinction than does the continuous form.[73]

An **intermittent reinforcement** schedule can be of a ratio or interval type. Ratio schedules depend on how many responses the subject makes. The individual is reinforced after giving a certain number of specific types of behaviour. Interval schedules depend on how much time has passed since the previous reinforcement. With interval schedules, the individual is reinforced on the first appropriate behaviour after a particular time has elapsed. A reinforcement can also be classified as fixed or variable. When these factors are combined, four types of intermittent schedules of reinforcement result: **fixed-interval schedule**, **variable-interval schedule**, **fixed-ratio schedule**, and **variable-ratio schedule**.

Exhibit 4-11 summarizes the five schedules of reinforcement and their effects on behaviour.

EXHIBIT 4-11 Schedules of Reinforcement

Reinforcement Schedule	Nature of Reinforcement	Effect on Behaviour	Example
Continuous	Reward given after each desired behaviour	Fast learning of new behaviour but rapid extinction	Compliments
Fixed-interval	Reward given at fixed time intervals	Average and irregular performance with rapid extinction	Weekly paycheques
Variable-interval	Reward given at variable time intervals	Moderately high and stable performance with slow extinction	Pop quizzes
Fixed-ratio	Reward given at fixed amounts of output	High and stable performance attained quickly but also with rapid extinction	Piece-rate pay
Variable-ratio	Reward given at variable amounts of output	Very high performance with slow extinction	Commissioned sales

intermittent reinforcement A desired behaviour is reinforced often enough to make the behaviour worth repeating, but not every time it is demonstrated.

fixed-interval schedule The reward is given at fixed time intervals.

variable-interval schedule The reward is given at variable time intervals.

fixed-ratio schedule The reward is given at fixed amounts of output.

variable-ratio schedule The reward is given at variable amounts of output.

Although reinforcers such as pay can motivate people, the process is much more complicated than stimulus–response. In its pure form, reinforcement theory ignores feelings, attitudes, expectations, and other cognitive variables known to affect behaviour. Reinforcement is undoubtedly an important influence on behaviour, but few scholars are prepared to argue that it's the only one. The behaviours you engage in at work and the amount of effort you allocate to each task are affected by the consequences that follow. If you are consistently reprimanded for outproducing your colleagues, you will likely reduce your productivity. But we might also explain your lower productivity in terms of goals, inequity, or expectancies.

Responses to the Reward System

5 Describe why equity and fairness matter in the workplace

Olympic sports that are judged rather than timed are sometimes criticized for what appears to be arbitrariness by the judges.[74] Mark McMorris, one of the top-ranked slopestylers in the world, had spent nearly two weeks trying to recover from a fractured rib and thought he turned in a good performance during his Olympic qualification round. Then, he saw that the posted score did not match his expectations. With a score of 89.25, he was ranked seventh, which meant that he would have to compete in the semifinals to be able to make it to the finals of the slopestyle event.

He was not happy with his score or the outcome. "It's pretty ridiculous," said McMorris afterward. "It's a judged sport; what can you do?"

McMorris eventually went on to win the first Olympic medal for Canada at the Sochi Olympic Games—a bronze. While he was excited to have won a medal, he was also surprised that his teammates Max Parrot and Sebastien Toutant, who made it to the final, did not. The Canadian slopestylers had dominated the sport for several years. However, this was the first time the event was held in the Olympics.

"It's hard to wrap your head around what (the judges) really wanted to see," McMorris said. Kerry Gillespie, a reporter for the *Toronto Star*, wrote that "there are no defined criteria on how to score any of [the slopestyle performance], or any way to parse out an athlete's achievement on the individual elements. There are three rail sections and three jumps on the Olympic course. The score is simply the judges' overall impression."

Generally, individuals want to know how they will be judged, so that they know when and if they will be rewarded. The slopestylers are not pushing for clear standards in judging, however. They want to continue to be part of a creative sport, not one where the snowboarders simply copy one another to just do a movement better. Still, outcomes that are not clear can make the system seem unfair, with individuals giving the best performances not getting the highest marks. When individuals encounter unfairness in rewards systems, how do they respond?

To a large extent, motivation theories are about rewards. The theories suggest that individuals have needs and will exert effort in order to have those needs met. The needs theories specifically identify those needs. Goal-setting and expectancy theories portray processes by which individuals act and then receive desirable rewards (intrinsic or extrinsic) for their behaviour.

Three additional process theories ask us to consider how individuals respond to rewards. Equity theory suggests that individuals evaluate and interpret rewards. Fair process goes one step further, suggesting that employees are sensitive to a variety of fairness issues in the workplace that extend beyond the reward system but also affect employee motivation. Self-determination theory examines how individuals respond to the introduction of extrinsic rewards for intrinsically satisfying activities.

Equity Theory

Ainsley is a university student working toward a bachelor's degree in finance. In order to gain some work experience and increase her marketability, she has accepted a summer internship in the finance department at a pharmaceutical company. She is quite pleased with the pay: $15 an hour is more than other students in her cohort were receiving for their summer internships. At work she meets Josh, a recent graduate of the same university working as a middle manager in the same finance department. Josh makes $30 an hour.

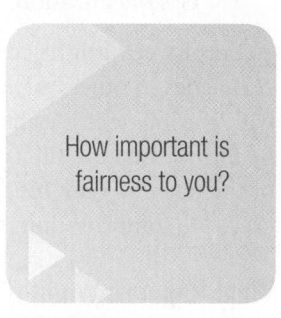

How important is fairness to you?

On the job, Ainsley could be described as a go-getter. She is engaged, satisfied, and always seems willing to help others. Josh is quite the opposite. He often seems disinterested in his job and even has thoughts about quitting. When pressed one day about why he is unhappy, Josh cites his pay as the main reason. Specifically, he tells Ainsley that, compared with managers at other pharmaceutical companies, he makes much less. "It isn't fair," he complains. "I work just as hard as they do, yet I don't make as much. Maybe I should go work for the competition."

How could someone making $30 an hour be less satisfied with his pay than someone making $15 an hour and be less motivated as a result? The answer lies in **equity theory** and, more broadly, in principles of organizational justice. According to equity theory, employees compare what they get from their job (their "outcomes," such as pay, promotions, recognition, or having the corner office) to what they put into it (their "inputs," such as effort, experience, and education). They take the ratio of their outcomes to their inputs and compare it to the ratio of others, usually someone similar, such as a co-worker or someone doing the same job. This idea is illustrated in Exhibit 4-12. If we believe our ratio to be equal to those with whom we compare ourselves, a state of equity exists and we perceive the situation as fair. J. Stacy Adams proposed that this negative state of tension provides the motivation to do something to correct it.[75]

To Whom Do We Compare Ourselves?

The referent that an employee selects when making comparisons adds to the complexity of equity theory.[76] There are four referent comparisons that an employee can use:

- *Self-inside.* An employee's experiences in a different position inside his or her current organization.

- *Self-outside.* An employee's experiences in a situation or position outside his or her current organization.

EXHIBIT 4-12 Equity Theory

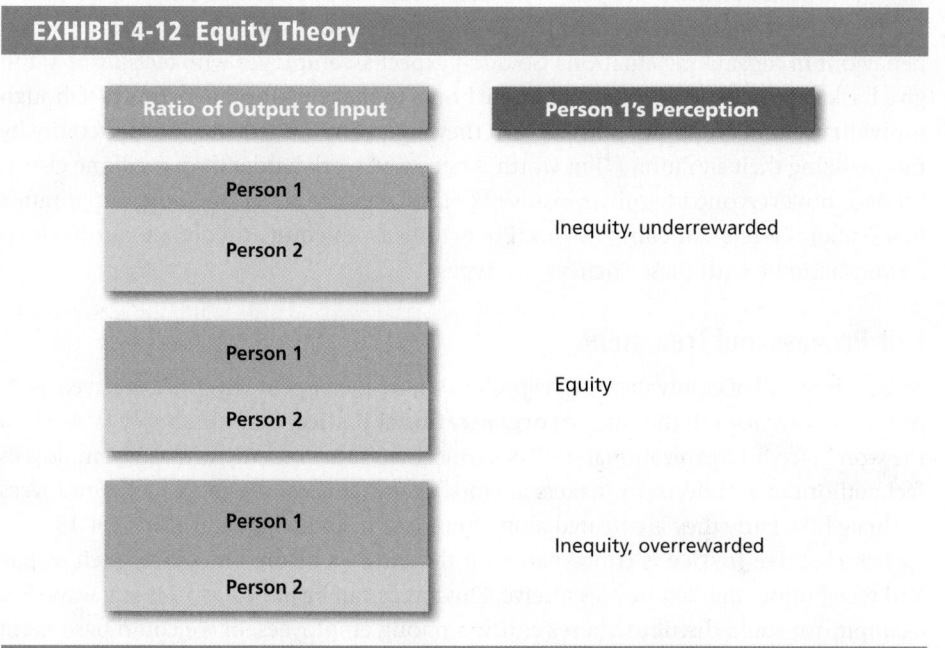

Ratio of Output to Input	Person 1's Perception
Person 1 / Person 2	Inequity, underrewarded
Person 1 / Person 2	Equity
Person 1 / Person 2	Inequity, overrewarded

equity theory A theory that asserts that individuals compare their job inputs and outcomes with those of others and then respond to eliminate any inequities.

Simulate on MyManagementLab

Motivation

- *Other-inside.* Another individual or group of individuals inside the employee's organization.

- *Other-outside.* Another individual or group of individuals outside the employee's organization.

Employees might compare themselves with friends, neighbours, co-workers, colleagues in other organizations. Alternatively, they might compare their present job with previous jobs they have had. Which referent an employee chooses will be influenced by the information the employee holds about referents, as well as by the attractiveness of the referent. *Case Incident—Equity and Executive Pay* on page 161 considers whether executive compensation is equitable when compared with the pay of the average worker.

What Happens When We Feel Treated Inequitably?

Based on equity theory, employees who perceive an inequity will make one of six choices.[77]

- *Change their inputs* (exert less effort if underpaid, or more if overpaid).

- *Change their outcomes* (individuals paid on a piece-rate basis can increase their pay by producing a higher quantity of units of lower quality).

- *Adjust perceptions of self* ("I used to think I worked at a moderate pace, but now I realize I work a lot harder than everyone else.")

- *Adjust perceptions of others* ("Mike's job isn't as desirable as I thought.")

- *Choose a different referent* ("I may not make as much as my brother-in-law, but I'm doing a lot better than my Dad did when he was my age.")

- *Leave the field* (quit the job).

> What can you do if you think your salary is unfair?

RESEARCH FINDINGS: Inequitable Pay

Some of these propositions have been supported, but others have not.[78] First, inequities created by overpayment do not seem to significantly affect behaviour in most work situations. So don't expect an employee who feels overpaid to give back part of her salary or put in more hours to make up for the inequity. Although individuals may sometimes perceive that they are overrewarded, they restore equity by rationalizing their situation ("I'm worth it because I work harder than everyone else"). Second, not everyone is equity-sensitive.[79] A few actually prefer outcome–input ratios lower than the referent comparisons. Predictions from equity theory are not likely to be very accurate with these "benevolent types."

Fair Process and Treatment

Although not all of equity theory's propositions have held up, the hypothesis served as an important precursor to the study of **organizational justice**, or more simply fairness, in the workplace.[80] Organizational justice is concerned more broadly with how employees feel authorities and decision-makers at work treat them. For the most part, employees evaluate how fairly they are treated along four dimensions, shown in Exhibit 4-13.

Distributive justice is concerned with the fairness of the outcomes, such as pay and recognition, that employees receive. Outcomes can be allocated in many ways. For example, we could distribute raises equally among employees, or we could base them on which employees need money the most. However, as the earlier discussion on equity

6 Demonstrate how organizational justice is a refinement of equity theory.

organizational justice An overall perception of what is fair in the workplace, composed of distributive, procedural, informational, and interpersonal justice.

distributive justice Perceived fairness of the amount and allocation of rewards among individuals.

EXHIBIT 4-13 Model of Organizational Justice

Distributive Justice

Definition: perceived fairness of outcome

Example: I got the pay raise I deserved.

Procedural Justice

Definition: perceived fairness of process used to determine outcome

Example: I had input into the process used to give raises and was given a good explanation of why I received the raise I did.

Informational Justice

Definition: perceived truthfulness of explanations for decisions

Example: The raise I received was lower than I had hoped, but my manager explained that department cutbacks were the reason.

Interpersonal Justice

Definition: perceived degree to which one is treated with dignity and respect

Example: When telling me about my raise, my supervisor was very nice and complimentary.

Organizational Justice

Definition: overall perception of what is fair in the workplace

Example: I think this is a fair place to work.

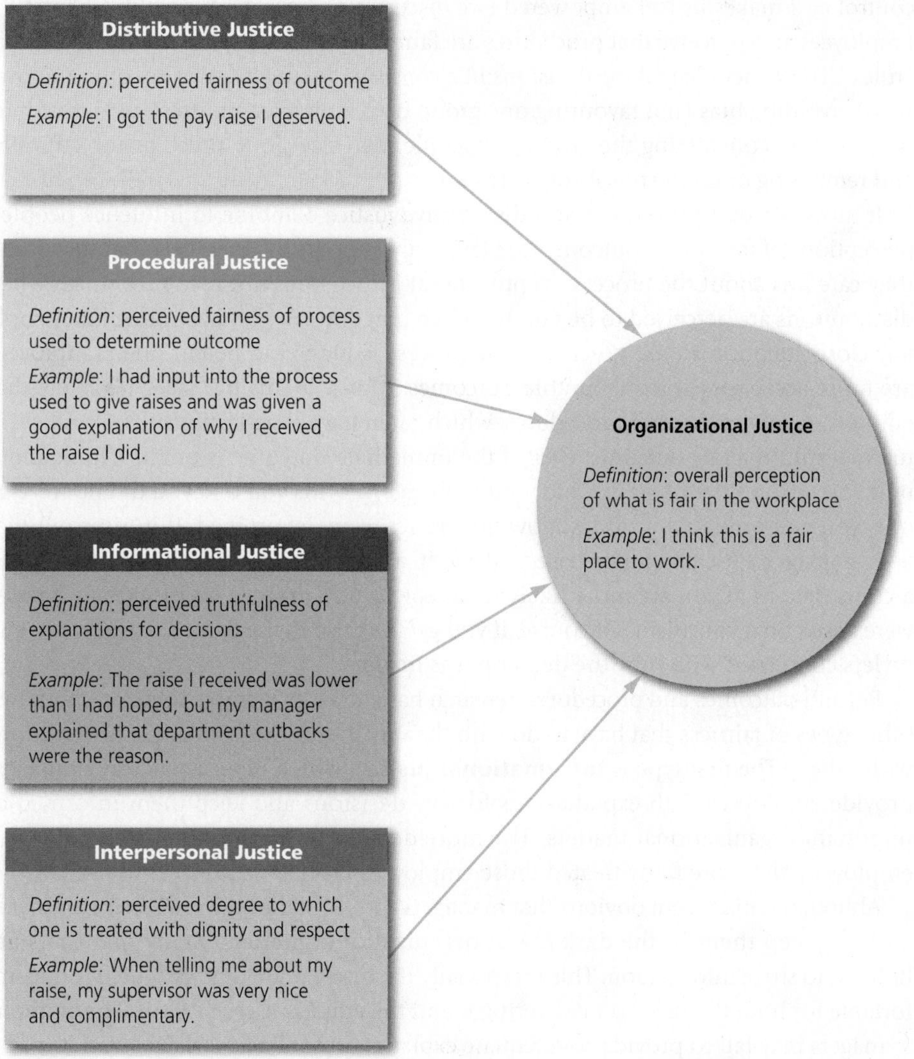

theory suggests, employees tend to perceive their outcomes are fairest when they are distributed equitably.

Does the same logic apply to teams? At first glance, it would seem that distributing rewards equally among team members is best for boosting morale and teamwork—that way, no one is favoured more than another. A recent study of National Hockey League teams suggests otherwise. Differentiating the pay of team members on the basis of their inputs (how well they performed in games) attracted better players to the team, made it more likely they would stay, and increased team performance.[81]

The way we have described things so far, it would seem that distributive justice and equity are gauged in a rational, calculative way as individuals compare their outcome–input ratios to others. But the experience of justice, and especially injustice, is often not so cold and calculated. Instead, people base distributive judgments on a feeling or an emotional reaction to the way they think they are being treated relative to others, and their reactions are often "hot" and emotional as well.[82]

Although employees care a lot about *what* outcomes are distributed (distributive justice), they also care a lot about *how* outcomes are distributed. While distributive justice looks at *what* outcomes are allocated, **procedural justice** examines *how* outcomes are allocated.[83] What makes procedures more or less fair? There are several factors. For one, employees perceive that procedures are fairer when they are given a say

procedural justice The perceived fairness of the process used to determine the distribution of rewards.

in the decision-making process. Having direct influence over how decisions are made, or at the very least being able to present your opinion to decision makers, creates a sense of control and makes us feel empowered (we discuss empowerment more in Chapter 8). Employees also perceive that procedures are fairer when decision makers follow several "rules." These include making decisions in a consistent manner (across people and over time), avoiding bias (not favouring one group or person over another), using accurate information, considering the groups or people their decisions affect, acting ethically, and remaining open to appeals or correction.

It turns out that procedural and distributive justice combine to influence people's perceptions of fairness. If outcomes are favourable and individuals get what they want, they care less about the process, so procedural justice does not matter as much when distributions are perceived to be fair. It's when outcomes are unfavourable that people pay close attention to the process. If the process is judged to be fair, then employees are more accepting of unfavourable outcomes.[84] Why is this the case? It's likely that employees believe that fair procedures, which often have long-lasting effects, will eventually result in a fair outcome, even if the immediate outcome is unfair. Think about it. If you are hoping for a raise and your manager informs you that you did not receive one, you will probably want to know how raises were determined. If it turns out that your manager allocated raises based on merit, and you were simply outperformed by a co-worker, then you are more likely to accept your manager's decision than if raises were based on favouritism. Of course, if you get the raise in the first place, then you will be less concerned with how the decision was made.

Beyond outcomes and procedures, research has shown that employees care about two other types of fairness that have to do with the way they are treated during interactions with others. The first type is **informational justice**, which reflects whether managers provide employees with explanations for key decisions and keep them informed of important organizational matters. The more detailed and candid managers are with employees, the more fairly treated those employees feel.

Although it may seem obvious that managers should be honest with their employees and not keep them in the dark about organizational matters, many managers are hesitant to share information. This is especially the case with bad news, which is uncomfortable for both the manager delivering it and the employee receiving it. For example, managers may fail to provide an adequate explanation for bad news such as a layoff or temporary pay cut out of a fear of being blamed, worries about making the situation worse, or concerns about triggering legal action.[85] In fact, research has linked the *absence* of explanations to increased litigation intentions by employees who have been laid off.[86] Explanations for bad news are beneficial when they take the form of post hoc excuses ("I know this is bad, and I wanted to give you the office, but it wasn't my decision") rather than justifications ("I decided to give the office to Sam, but having it isn't a big deal").[87]

The second type of justice relevant to interactions between managers and employees is **interpersonal justice**, which reflects whether employees are treated with dignity and respect. Compared with the three other forms of justice we have discussed, interpersonal justice is unique in that it can occur in everyday interactions between managers and employees.[88] This quality allows managers to take advantage of (or miss out on) opportunities to make their employees feel fairly treated. Many managers may view treating employees politely and respectfully as too "soft," choosing more aggressive tactics out of a belief that doing so will be more motivating. Although displays of negative emotions such as anger may be motivating in some cases,[89] managers sometimes take this too far.

How much does justice really matter to employees? A great deal, as it turns out. When employees feel fairly treated, they respond in a number of positive ways. All four types of justice discussed in this section have been linked to higher levels of task performance and organizational citizenship behaviours (such as helping co-workers) as well as lower levels of counterproductive behaviours (such as shirking job duties). Distributive and procedural justice are more strongly associated with task performance,

PERSONAL INVENTORY ASSESSMENT

Learn About Yourself
Workplace Discipline Indicator

informational justice The degree to which employees are provided truthful explanations for decisions.

interpersonal justice The degree to which employees are treated with dignity and respect.

while informational and interpersonal justice are more strongly associated with organizational citizenship behaviour. Even more physiological outcomes, such as how well employees sleep and the state of their health, have been linked to fair treatment.[90] Why does justice have these positive effects? First, fair treatment enhances commitment to the organization and makes employees feel it cares about their well-being. In addition, employees who feel fairly treated trust their supervisors more, which reduces uncertainty and fear of being exploited by the organization. Finally, fair treatment elicits positive emotions, which in turn prompts behaviours like organizational citizenship behaviour.[91] The *Experiential Exercise* on page 160 helps you understand how managers can foster fairness in the workplace based on the four types of organizational justice.

Studies suggest that managers are indeed motivated to foster employees' perceptions of justice because they wish to ensure compliance, maintain a positive identity, and establish fairness at work.[92] To enhance perceptions of justice, they should realize that employees are especially sensitive to unfairness in procedures when bad news has to be communicated (that is, when distributive justice is low). Thus, it's especially important to openly share information about how allocation decisions are made, follow consistent and unbiased procedures, and engage in similar practices to increase the perception of procedural justice. However, it may be that managers are constrained in how much they can affect distributive and procedural justice because of formal organizational policies or cost constraints. Interpersonal and informational justice are less likely to be governed by these mechanisms, because providing information and treating employees with dignity are practically "free." In such cases, managers wishing to promote fairness could focus their efforts more on informational and interpersonal justice.[93]

Despite all attempts to enhance fairness, perceived injustices are still likely to occur. Fairness is often subjective; what one person sees as unfair, another may see as perfectly appropriate. In general, people see allocations or procedures favouring themselves as fair.[94] So, when addressing perceived injustices, managers need to focus their actions on the source of the problem. In addition, if employees feel they have been treated unjustly, having opportunities to express their frustration has been shown to reduce their desire for retribution.[95]

Self-Determination Theory

 7 Apply the predictions of self-determination theory to intrinsic and extrinsic rewards.

"It's strange," said Marcia. "I started work at the Humane Society as a volunteer. I put in 15 hours a week helping people adopt pets. And I loved coming to work. Then, three months ago, they hired me full-time at $11 an hour. I'm doing the same work I did before. But I'm not finding it nearly as much fun."

Does Marcia's reaction seem counterintuitive? There is an explanation for it. It's called **self-determination theory**, which proposes that people prefer to feel they have control over their actions, so anything that makes a previously enjoyed task feel more like an obligation than a freely chosen activity will undermine motivation.[96] Much research on self-determination theory in OB has focused on **cognitive evaluation theory**, which hypothesizes that extrinsic rewards will reduce intrinsic interest in a task. When people are paid for work, it feels less like something they *want* to do and more like something they *have* to do. Self-determination theory also proposes that in addition to being driven by a need for autonomy, people seek ways to achieve competence and positive connections to others. A large number of studies support self-determination theory.[97] Its major implications relate to work rewards.

self-determination theory A theory of motivation that is concerned with the beneficial effects of intrinsic motivation and the harmful effects of extrinsic motivation.

cognitive evaluation theory Offering extrinsic rewards (for example, pay) for work effort that was previously rewarding intrinsically will tend to decrease the overall level of a person's motivation.

Extrinsic vs. Intrinsic Rewards

Historically, motivation theorists have generally assumed that intrinsic motivators are independent of extrinsic motivators. That is, the stimulation of one would not affect the other. But cognitive evaluation theory suggests otherwise. It argues that when extrinsic rewards are used by organizations as payoffs for superior performance, the intrinsic rewards, which are derived from individuals doing what they like, are reduced.

When organizations use extrinsic rewards as payoffs for superior performance, employees feel they are doing a good job less because of their own intrinsic desire to excel than because that is what the organization wants. Eliminating extrinsic rewards can also shift an individual's perception of why she works on a task from an external to an internal explanation. If you are reading a novel a week because your contemporary literature instructor requires you to, you can attribute your reading behaviour to an external source. However, if you find yourself continuing to read a novel a week when the course ends, your natural inclination is to say, "I must enjoy reading novels, because I'm still reading one a week!"

Studies examining how extrinsic rewards increase motivation for creative tasks suggest that we might need to place cognitive evaluation theory's predictions into a broader context.[98] Goal setting is more effective in improving motivation, for instance, when we provide rewards for achieving the goals. The original authors of self-determination theory acknowledge that extrinsic rewards such as verbal praise and feedback about competence can improve intrinsic motivation under specific circumstances. Deadlines and specific work standards do, too, if people believe they are in control of their behaviour.[99]

Making extrinsic rewards specifically contingent on creative performance, rather than more broadly on routine performance, can enhance rather than undermine creativity. Again, like deadlines and specific work standards, the benefits of extrinsic rewards for creativity seem to hold only if individuals have control over the task or the reward.[100] These findings are consistent with the central theme of self-determination theory: Rewards and deadlines diminish motivation if people see them as coercive or controlling.

What does self-determination theory suggest for providing rewards? If a senior sales representative really enjoys making the deal, a commission indicates she has been doing a good job and increases her sense of competence by providing feedback that could improve intrinsic motivation. On the other hand, if a computer programmer values writing code because she likes to solve problems, a reward for working to an externally imposed standard she does not accept, such as writing a certain number of lines of code every day, could feel coercive, and her intrinsic motivation would suffer. She would be less interested in the task and might reduce her effort.

A recent outgrowth of cognitive evaluation research is **self-concordance**, which considers how strongly people's reasons for pursuing goals are consistent with their interests and core values.[101] If individuals pursue goals because of intrinsic interest, they are more likely to attain their goals, and are happy even if they do not attain them. Why? Because the process of striving toward them is fun. In contrast, people who pursue goals for extrinsic reasons (money, status, or other benefits) are less likely to attain their goals and are less happy even when they do achieve them. Why? Because the goals are less meaningful to them.[102] OB research suggests that people who pursue work goals for intrinsic reasons are more satisfied with their jobs, feel like they fit into their organizations better, and may perform better.[103] Research also suggests that in cases where people do *not* enjoy their work for intrinsic reasons (those who work because they feel obligated to do so) can still perform well, although they experience higher levels of strain as a result.[104]

What does all of this mean? For individuals, it means choose your job for reasons other than extrinsic rewards. For organizations, it means managers should provide intrinsic as well as extrinsic incentives. They need to make the work interesting, provide recognition, and support employee growth and development. Employees who feel that what they do is within their control and a result of free choice are likely to be more motivated by their work and committed to their employers.[105]

self-concordance The degree to which a person's reasons for pursuing a goal are consistent with the person's interests and core values.

Increasing Intrinsic Motivation

Our discussion of motivation theories and our discussion of how to apply motivation theories in the workplace has focused more on improving extrinsic motivation. Professor Kenneth Thomas of the Naval Postgraduate School in Monterey, California, developed a model of intrinsic motivation that draws from the job characteristics model (see Chapter 5) and cognitive evaluation theory.[106] He identified four key rewards that increase an individual's intrinsic motivation:

- *Sense of choice.* The opportunity to select what one will do and perform the way one thinks best. Individuals can use their own judgment to carry out the task.

- *Sense of competence.* The feeling of accomplishment for doing a good job. Individuals are more likely to feel a sense of accomplishment when they carry out challenging tasks.

- *Sense of meaningfulness.* The opportunity to pursue worthwhile tasks. Individuals feel good about what they are doing and believe that what they are doing matters.

- *Sense of progress.* The feeling of accomplishment that one is making progress on a task, and that it is moving forward. Individuals feel that they are spending their time wisely in doing their jobs.

Thomas also identified four sets of behaviours managers can use to build intrinsic rewards for their employees:

- *Leading for choice.* Empowering employees and delegating tasks.

- *Leading for competence.* Supporting and coaching employees.

- *Leading for meaningfulness.* Inspiring employees and modelling desired behaviours.

- *Leading for progress.* Monitoring and rewarding employees.

Exhibit 4-14 describes what managers can do to increase the likelihood that intrinsic rewards are motivational.

EXHIBIT 4-14 Building Blocks for Intrinsic Rewards

Leading for Choice	Leading for Competence
• Delegated authority	• Knowledge
• Trust in workers	• Positive feedback
• Security (no punishment) for honest mistakes	• Skill recognition
• A clear purpose	• Challenge
• Information	• High, noncomparative standards
Leading for Meaningfulness	**Leading for Progress**
• A noncynical climate	• A collaborative climate
• Clearly identified passions	• Milestones
• An exciting vision	• Celebrations
• Relevant task purposes	• Access to customers
• Whole tasks	• Measurement of improvement

Source: From Intrinsic Motivation at Work: Building Energy and Commitment. Copyright © K. Thomas. 1997. Berrett-Koehler Publishers Inc., San Francisco, CA. All rights reserved. www.bkconnection.com.

Motivation for Whom?

8 Discuss the ethics behind motivation theories.

An ongoing debate among organizational behaviour scholars is, Who benefits from the theories of motivation?[107] Some argue that motivation theories are only intended to help managers get more productivity out of employees, and are little concerned with employees beyond improvements in productivity. Thus, needs theories, process theories, and theories concerned with fairness could be interpreted not as ways to help employees get what they want or need, but rather as means to help managers get what they want from employees. In his review of "meaningful work" literature, professor Christopher Michaelson of New York University Stern finds that researchers propose that organizations have a moral obligation to provide employees with "free choice to enter, honest communication, fair and respectful treatment, intellectual challenge, considerable independence to determine work methods, democratic participation in decision making, moral development, due process and justice, nonpaternalism, and fair compensation."[108]

Michaelson suggests that scholars concerned with meaningful work should focus on the conditions of the workplace and improving those conditions. He also suggests that researchers have a moral obligation to make workplaces better for employees. While productivity may be a by-product of better work conditions, the important thing is for employers to treat employees well, and to consider the needs of employees as an end in itself. By contrast, he argues, mainstream motivation theory does not consider the moral obligation of employers to their employees, but it does consider ways to ensure employees are more productive.

While this debate is not easily resolved, and may well guide the elaboration of motivation theories in years to come, it does inspire a provocative analysis of why employers provide the workplace conditions they do.

Putting It All Together

9 Summarize the essence of what we know about motivating employees.

While it's always dangerous to synthesize a large number of complex ideas into a few simple guidelines, the following suggestions summarize the essence of what we know about motivating employees in organizations:

- *Recognize individual differences.* Employees have different needs and should not be treated alike. Managers should spend the time necessary to understand what is important to each employee and then align goals, level of involvement, and rewards with individual needs.

- *Use goals and feedback.* Employees should have challenging, specific goals, as well as feedback on how well they are doing in pursuit of those goals.

- *Allow employees to participate in decisions that affect them.* Employees should contribute to a number of decisions that affect them: setting work goals, choosing their own benefits packages, solving productivity and quality problems, and the like. Doing so can increase employee productivity, commitment to work goals, motivation, and job satisfaction.

- *When giving rewards, be sure that they reward desired performance.* Rewards should be linked to the type of performance expected. It's important that employees perceive a clear linkage. How closely rewards are actually correlated to performance criteria is less important than the perception of this relationship. If individuals perceive this relationship to be low, the results will be low performance, a decrease in job satisfaction, and an increase in turnover and absenteeism.

- *Check the system for equity.* Employees should be able to perceive rewards as equating with the inputs they bring to the job. At a simplistic level, this means that experience, skills, abilities, effort, and other obvious inputs should explain differences in performance and, hence, pay, job assignments, and other obvious rewards.

GLOBAL IMPLICATIONS

Most current motivation theories were developed in the United States and Canada.[109] Goal-setting and expectancy theories emphasize goal accomplishment as well as rational and individual thought—characteristics consistent with Canadian and American culture. Let's look at several motivation theories and consider their cross-cultural transferability.

Needs Theories

Maslow's needs theory says people start at the physiological level and progress up the hierarchy to safety, social (belonging), self-esteem, and self-actualization needs. This hierarchy, if it applies at all, aligns with Canadian and US culture. In Japan, Greece, and Mexico, where uncertainty-avoidance characteristics are strong, security needs would be on top of the hierarchy. Countries that score high on nurturing characteristics—Denmark, Sweden, Norway, the Netherlands, and Finland—would have social needs on top.[110] Group work will motivate employees more when the country's culture scores high on the nurturing criterion.

The view that a high achievement need acts as an internal motivator presupposes two cultural characteristics—willingness to accept a moderate degree of risk (which excludes countries with strong uncertainty avoidance characteristics) and concern with performance (which applies to countries with strong achievement characteristics). This combination is found in Anglo-American countries such as the United States, Canada, and Great Britain[111] and much less so in Chile and Portugal.

Goal Setting

Setting specific, difficult, individual goals may have different effects in different cultures. Most goal-setting research has been done in the United States and Canada, where individual achievement and performance are most highly valued. To date, research has not shown that group-based goals are more effective in collectivistic than in individualistic cultures. There is evidence that in collectivistic and high power-distance cultures, achievable moderate goals can be more highly motivating than difficult ones.[112] Finally, assigned goals appear to generate greater goal commitment in high rather than low power-distance cultures.[113] Much more research is needed to assess how goal constructs might differ across cultures.

Equity Theory and Fairness

Equity theory has gained a strong following in Canada and the United States because the reward systems assume that employees are highly sensitive to equity in reward allocations and equity is meant to closely tie pay to performance.

Meta-analytic evidence shows individuals in both individualistic and collectivistic cultures prefer an equitable distribution of rewards over an equal division (everyone gets paid the same regardless of performance).[114] Across nations, the same basic principles of procedural justice are respected, and workers around the world prefer rewards based on performance and skills over rewards based on seniority.[115] However, in collectivistic cultures employees expect rewards to reflect their individual needs as well as their performance.[116] Other research suggests that inputs and outcomes are valued differently in various cultures.[117] Some cultures emphasize status over individual achievement as a basis for allocating resources. Materialistic cultures are more likely to see cash compensation and rewards as the most relevant outcomes of work, whereas relational cultures will see social rewards and status as important outcomes. International managers must consider the cultural preferences of each group of employees when determining what is "fair" in different contexts.

Intrinsic and Extrinsic Motivation

A recent study found interesting differences in managers' perceptions of employee motivation.[118] The study examined managers from three distinct cultural regions: North America, Asia, and Latin America. The results of the study revealed that North American managers perceive their employees as being motivated more by extrinsic factors (for example, pay) than intrinsic factors (for example, doing meaningful work). Asian managers perceive their employees as being motivated by both extrinsic and intrinsic factors, while Latin American managers perceive their employees as being motivated by intrinsic factors.

Even more interesting, these differences affected evaluations of employee performance. As expected, Asian managers focused on both types of motivation when evaluating their employees' performance, and Latin American managers focused on intrinsic motivation. Oddly, North American managers, though believing that employees are motivated primarily by extrinsic factors, actually focused more on intrinsic factors when evaluating employee performance. Why the paradox? One explanation is that North Americans value uniqueness, so any deviation from the norm—such as being perceived as being unusually high in intrinsic motivation—is rewarded.

Latin American managers' focus on intrinsic motivation when evaluating employees may be related to a cultural norm termed *simpatía*, a tradition that compels employees to display their internal feelings. Consequently, Latin American managers are more sensitized to these displays and can more easily notice their employees' intrinsic motivation.

Cross-Cultural Consistencies

Don't assume that there are *no* cross-cultural consistencies. The desire for interesting work seems important to almost all employees, regardless of their national culture. In a study of 7 countries, employees in Belgium, Britain, Israel, and the United States ranked work number 1 among 11 work goals, and employees in Japan, the Netherlands, and Germany ranked it either second or third.[119] In a study comparing job-preference outcomes among graduate students in the United States, Canada, Australia, and Singapore, growth, achievement, and responsibility had identical rankings as the top three.[120] Meta-analytic evidence shows that individuals in both individualistic and collectivistic cultures prefer an equitable distribution of rewards (the most effective employees get paid the most) over an equal division (everyone gets paid the same regardless of performance).[121] Across nations, the same basic principles of procedural justice are respected, and employees around the world prefer rewards based on performance and skills over rewards based on seniority.[122]

Summary

The motivation theories in this chapter differ in their predictive strength. Maslow's hierarchy of needs, Herzberg's two-factor theory, and McClelland's theory of needs focus on needs. None of these theories has found widespread support, although support for McClelland's is the strongest, particularly regarding the relationship between achievement and productivity. Expectancy theory can be helpful, but it assumes that employees have few constraints on decision making, such as bias or incomplete information, which limits its applicability. Goal-setting theory can be helpful but does not cover absenteeism, turnover, or job satisfaction. Reinforcement theory can be helpful, but not regarding employee satisfaction or the decision to quit. Equity theory's strongest legacy is that it provided the spark for research on organizational justice, which has more support in the literature. Self-determination theory and cognitive evaluation theory have merits to consider.

LESSONS LEARNED

- Recognize individual differences.
- Goals and feedback help motivate individuals.
- Rewards signal what is important to the employer (or leader).

SNAPSHOT SUMMARY

What Is Motivation?

Needs Theories of Motivation
- Maslow's Hierarchy of Needs Theory
- Motivation–Hygiene Theory
- McClelland's Theory of Needs
- Summarizing Needs Theories

Process Theories of Motivation
- Expectancy Theory
- Goal-Setting Theory
- Self-Efficacy Theory
- Reinforcement Theory

Responses to the Reward System
- Equity Theory
- Fair Process and Treatment
- Self-Determination Theory
- Increasing Intrinsic Motivation

Motivation for Whom?
- Putting It All Together

MyManagementLab

Study, practise, and explore real business situations with these helpful resources:

- **Study Plan:** Check your understanding of chapter concepts with self-study quizzes.
- **Online Lesson Presentations:** Study key chapter topics and work through interactive assessments to test your knowledge and master management concepts.
- **Videos:** Learn more about the management practices and strategies of real companies.
- **Simulations:** Practise management decision-making in simulated business environments.

OB at

for **Review**

1. What are the three key elements of motivation?

2. What are some early theories of motivation? How applicable are they today?

3. What are the key tenets of expectancy theory?

4. What are the key principles of goal-setting theory, self-efficacy theory, and reinforcement theory?

5. Why do equity and fairness matter in the workplace?

6. How is organizational justice a refinement of equity theory?

7. How do the predictions of self-determination theory apply to intrinsic and extrinsic rewards?

8. What are some of the ethical issues with motivation theories?

9. What is the essence of what we know about motivating employees?

for **Managers**

- Consider goal-setting theory: Clear and difficult goals often lead to higher levels of employee productivity.

- Consider how reinforcement theory applies to the quality and quantity of work, persistence of effort, absenteeism, tardiness, and accident rates.

- Consult equity theory to help you understand productivity, satisfaction, absence, and turnover variables.

- Expectancy theory offers a powerful explanation of performance variables such as employee productivity, absenteeism, and turnover.

for **You**

- Don't think of motivation as something that should be done for you. Think about motivating others and yourself as well. How can you motivate yourself? After finishing a particularly long and dry chapter in a text, you could take a snack break. Or you might buy yourself a new album once that major accounting assignment is finished.

- Be aware of the kinds of things that motivate you, so you can choose jobs and activities that suit you best.

- When working in a group, keep in mind that you and the other members can think of ways to make sure everyone feels motivated throughout the project.

Goals Get You to Where You Want to Be

POINT

Of course this is a true statement.[123] Goal-setting theory is one of *the* best-supported theories in all the motivation literature. Study after study has consistently shown the benefits of goals. Want to excel on a test, lose a certain amount of weight, obtain a job with a particular income level, or improve your golf game? If you want to be a high performer, merely set a specific, difficult goal and let nature take its course. That goal will dominate your attention, cause you to focus, and make you try harder.

All too often, people are told by others to simply "do their best." Could anything be more vague? What does "do your best" actually mean? Maybe you feel that your "best" on one day is to muster a grade of 50 percent on an exam, while your "best" on another day is an 80. But if you were given a more difficult goal—say, to score a 95 on the exam—and you were committed to that goal, you would ultimately perform better.

Edwin Locke and Gary Latham, the researchers best known for goal-setting theory, put it best when they said: "The effects of goal setting are very reliable." In short, goal-setting theory is among the most valid and practical theories of motivation in organizational psychology.

COUNTERPOINT

Sure, a lot of research has shown the benefits of goal setting, but those studies ignore the harm that is often done by it. For one, how often have you set a "stretch" goal, only to see yourself later fail? Goals create anxiety and worry about reaching them, and they often create unrealistic expectations as well. Imagine those who had set a goal to earn a promotion in a certain period of time (a specific, difficult goal), only to find themselves laid off once the recession hit. Or how about those who envisioned a retirement of leisure yet were forced to take on a part-time job or delay retirement altogether in order to continue to make ends meet. When too many things are out of our control, our difficult goals become impossible.

Consider this: Goals can lead to unethical behaviour and poorer performance. How many reports have you heard over the years about teachers who "fudged" students' test scores in order to achieve educational standards? Another example: When Ken O'Brien, a professional quarterback for the New York Jets, was penalized for every interception he threw, he achieved his goal of fewer interceptions quite easily—by refusing to throw the ball even when he should have.

In addition to this anecdotal evidence, research has directly linked goal setting to cheating. We should heed the warning of Professor Maurice E. Schweitzer—"Goal-setting is like a powerful medication"—before blindly accepting that specific, difficult goal.

OB at **Work**

Work Motivation Indicator: Motivation levels can be situational depending on whether you consider your occupation a job, a career, or a calling. Use this scale to see how your current occupation ranks.

Workplace Discipline Indicator: Not all forms of discipline are effective. This instrument helps you identify areas in which you may struggle when disciplining subordinates.

BREAKOUT **GROUP** EXERCISES

Form small groups to discuss the following topics, as assigned by your instructor:

1. One of the members of your team continually arrives late for meetings and does not turn drafts of assignments in on time. Choose one of the available theories and indicate how the theory explains the member's current behaviour and how the theory could be used to motivate the group member to perform more responsibly.

2. You are unhappy with the performance of one of your instructors and would like to encourage the instructor to present more lively classes. Choose one of the available theories and indicate how the theory explains the instructor's current behaviour. How could you as a student use the theory to motivate the instructor to present more lively classes?

3. Harvard University recently changed its grading policy to recommend to instructors that the average course mark should be a B. This was the result of a study showing that more than 50 percent of students were receiving an A or A– for coursework. Harvard students are often referred to as "the best and the brightest," and they pay over $36 000 (US) per academic year for their education, so they expect high grades. Discuss the impact of this change in policy on the motivation of Harvard students to study harder.

EXPERIENTIAL EXERCISE

Organizational Justice

Task Purpose

This exercise will highlight the four primary sources of organizational justice and help you understand what managers can do to ensure fairness in the workplace.

Time

Approximately 20 to 30 minutes.

Instructions

• Break into groups of 3 or 4.

1. Each person should recall an instance in which he or she was (a) treated especially fairly and (b) treated especially unfairly. Work-related instances are preferable, but nonwork examples are fine too.

2. Spend several minutes discussing whether the instance was more distributive, procedural, informational, or interpersonal in nature. What was the source of the fair/unfair treatment? How did you feel, and how did you respond? Was it easier to remember the fair or the unfair instance, and why do you think that is?

3. Each group should develop a set of recommendations for handling the unfair situations in a fairer manner. Select a leader for your group who will briefly summarize the unfair instances, along with the group's recommendations for handling them better. The discussion should reflect the four types of justice discussed in this chapter (distributive, procedural, informational, and interpersonal).

ETHICAL **DILEMMA**

Grade Inflation

Oscar-nominated actor James Franco made headlines when he received a D in "Directing the Actor II," a graduate-level class at New York University.[124] The subsequent firing of his professor, José Santana, which prompted a wrongful-termination lawsuit, raised questions about grade inflation. Grade inflation is of particular concern in graduate programs, where it's not uncommon for 75 percent of grades to be A's. Of course, along with grade inflation we have seen tuition inflation, and educators have commented about a possible link between the two. As Professor Santana commented, "There's pressure to retain students."

Questions

1. James Franco missed all but two of his classes in Professor Santana's course. Is that grounds for a D? What would constitute grounds for failure?

2. If around 75 percent of grades in graduate programs are A's, are grades now meaningless?

3. Provincial funding of many colleges and universities has decreased dramatically over the years, increasing pressure on administrators to generate revenue through tuition increases and other means. How might this pressure create ethical tensions between the need to generate revenue, student retention, and grading?

CASE INCIDENTS

Equity and Executive Pay

Few topics in the business press grab headlines and ignite the public like the compensation packages received by top management, which continue to rise.[125] CEOs in Canada's 100 largest companies earned a median compensation of $5.6-million in 2013, a level of compensation just under that received before the economic downturn.

How do compensation committees set executive compensation? In many cases, it comes down to equity theory and depends on the referent others to which the CEO is compared. To determine a "fair" level of pay for a given CEO, members of a compensation board find out how much CEOs with similar levels of experience in similar firms (similar inputs) are being paid and attempt to adjust compensation (outcomes) to be similar. So, CEOs in large tech firms are paid similarly to CEOs in other large tech firms, CEOs in small marketing companies are paid similarly to CEOs in other small marketing companies, and so forth. Proponents of this practice consider it to be "fair" because it achieves equity.

However, critics of high CEO pay want to change the perspective by comparing the CEO's pay to the pay of the average employee. For example, Canada's 100 highest paid CEOs are paid 171 times more than the average employee. From this perspective, CEO pay is grossly inequitable and thus "unfair."

In response, many CEOs, such as Mark Zuckerberg of Facebook and Larry Page of Google, have taken $1 annual salaries, though they still earn substantial compensation by exercising their stock options. In addition, shareholders of some companies, such as Verizon, are playing a greater role in setting CEO compensation by reducing awards when the company underperforms.

Questions

1. How does the executive compensation issue relate to equity theory? Who do you think should be the comparative others in these equity judgments? How should we determine what is a "fair" level of pay for top executives?

2. Can you think of procedural justice implications related to the ways pay policies for top executives have been instituted? Do these pay-making decisions follow the procedural justice principles outlined in the chapter?

OB *at* **Work**

Wage Reduction Proposal

The following proposal was made to employees of Montreal-based Quebecor's Vidéotron cable division:[126]

Employees are asked to increase the number of hours worked per week to 40 from 35, while receiving the same pay as working the shorter work week. In addition, they are asked to accept less paid holiday time.

Quebecor spokesman Luc Lavoie justified the request made to the employees by saying, "They have the richest work contract in the country, including eight weeks of holiday and high absenteeism."

The company made it clear that if this proposal were not accepted, it would sell its cable television and Internet installation and repair operations to Entourage Technology Solutions.

The employees, members of Canadian Union of Public Employees (CUPE) Local 2815, were reluctant to agree to these conditions. If they accepted, 300 to 400 employees were likely to be laid off, and the company could still consider outsourcing the work later.

Questions

1. Analyze this proposal in terms of motivation concepts.

2. As an employee, how would you respond if you received this proposal?

3. If you were the executive vice-president of the company, and a number of your non-unionized employees asked you for a holiday cash gift, would you have responded differently? Why or why not?

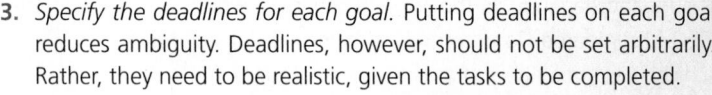

FROM CONCEPTS TO SKILLS

Setting Goals

You can be more effective at setting goals if you use the following eight suggestions:[127]

1. *Identify your key tasks.* Goal setting begins by defining what it is that you want to accomplish.

2. *Establish specific and challenging goals for each key task.* Identify the level of performance expected. Specify the target toward which you will work.

3. *Specify the deadlines for each goal.* Putting deadlines on each goal reduces ambiguity. Deadlines, however, should not be set arbitrarily. Rather, they need to be realistic, given the tasks to be completed.

4. *Allow the employee to participate actively.* When employees participate in goal setting, they are more likely to accept the goals. However, it must be sincere participation. That is, employees must perceive that you are truly seeking their input, not just going through the motions.

5. *Prioritize goals.* When you have more than one goal, it's important for you to rank the goals in order of importance. The purpose of prioritizing is to encourage you to take action and expend effort on each goal in proportion to its importance.

6. *Rate goals for difficulty and importance.* Goal setting should not encourage people to choose easy goals. Instead, goals should be rated for their difficulty and importance. When goals are rated, individuals can be given credit for trying difficult goals, even if they don't fully achieve them.

7. *Build in feedback mechanisms to assess goal progress.* Feedback lets you know whether your level of effort is sufficient to attain the goal. Feedback should be frequent and recurring.

8. *Link rewards to goal attainment.* Linking rewards to the achievement of goals will help motivate you.

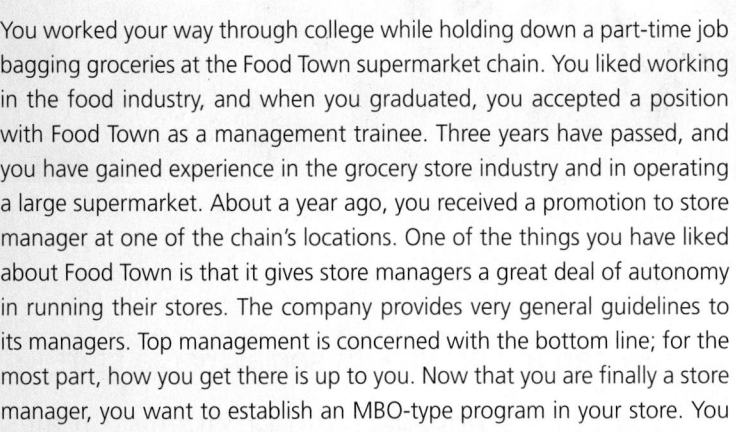

Practising Skills

You worked your way through college while holding down a part-time job bagging groceries at the Food Town supermarket chain. You liked working in the food industry, and when you graduated, you accepted a position with Food Town as a management trainee. Three years have passed, and you have gained experience in the grocery store industry and in operating a large supermarket. About a year ago, you received a promotion to store manager at one of the chain's locations. One of the things you have liked about Food Town is that it gives store managers a great deal of autonomy in running their stores. The company provides very general guidelines to its managers. Top management is concerned with the bottom line; for the most part, how you get there is up to you. Now that you are finally a store manager, you want to establish an MBO-type program in your store. You like the idea that everyone should have clear goals to work toward and then be evaluated against those goals.

Your store employs 70 people, although except for the managers, most work only 20 to 30 hours per week. You have 6 people reporting to you: an assistant manager; a weekend manager; and grocery, produce, meat, and bakery managers. The only highly skilled jobs belong to the butchers, who have strict training and regulatory guidelines. Other less-skilled jobs include cashier, shelf stocker, maintenance worker, and grocery bagger.

Specifically describe how you would go about setting goals in your new position. Include examples of goals for the jobs of butcher, cashier, and bakery manager.

Reinforcing Skills

1. Set personal and academic goals you want to achieve by the end of this term. Prioritize and rate them for difficulty.

2. Where do you want to be in five years? Do you have specific five-year goals? Establish three goals you want to achieve in five years. Make sure these goals are specific, challenging, and measurable.

5

Motivation in Action

How can a high-growth social media start-up keep its workforce engaged and productive? It all starts with community.

LEARNING OUTCOMES

After studying this chapter, you should be able to:

1 Demonstrate how the different types of variable-pay programs can increase employee motivation.

2 Show how flexible benefits turn benefits into motivators.

3 Identify the motivational benefits of intrinsic rewards.

4 Describe the job characteristics model and the way it motivates by changing the work environment.

5 Compare the main ways jobs can be redesigned.

6 Explain how specific alternative work arrangements can motivate employees.

7 Describe how employee involvement programs can motivate employees.

8 Describe how knowledge of what motivates people can be used to make organizations more motivating.

R yan Holmes is CEO of Hootsuite, a highly successful company offering social media marketing and social media management services to corporate clients.[1] In a single year, his business grew from 60 employees to 200. As of 2013 he had 350 employees and the company was experiencing quarterly revenue growth of 300 percent. In this high-growth atmosphere, Holmes knew it was incredibly important to keep his employees motivated and engaged. "People aren't as productive or passionate when they feel like separate cogs in a machine. Being social and building communities is what makes us thrive at work," says Holmes. "This is as true in a company like ours as in a multinational with 100,000 employees scattered across multiple continents. The goal is always to find positive and effective ways that let people meet, interact, and collaborate."

Ward Perrin/Vancouver Sun

So how does Holmes create the motivational team environment that he seeks? First of all he makes recognition a cornerstone of the corporate culture. The company's online performance management system allows anyone in the company to publicly recognize a colleague for excellence in areas such as teamwork, growth, passion, or entrepreneurial spirit. The company also funds monthly theme parties. The only rule is that each party must be organized by two departments that don't normally work together. This rule helps create a sense of engagement and community between groups that would otherwise rarely interact. In addition, the parties themselves provide a great opportunity to have fun together and create the warm social atmosphere that helps this social media company thrive.

In this chapter, we focus on how to apply motivation concepts. We review a number of reward programs and consider whether rewards are overrated. We also discuss how to create more motivating jobs and workplaces, both of which have been shown to be alternatives to rewards in motivating individuals.

THE BIG IDEA

Organizations can use piece-rate wages, merit-based pay, bonuses, stock options, and employee stock ownership plans to motivate employees. More effective, however, is making jobs themselves more motivating.

OB IS FOR EVERYONE

- Ever wonder why employees do some strange things?

- Are rewards overrated?

- When might job redesign be most appropriate?

- Do employers really like flexible arrangements?

- Would you find telecommuting motivating?

- How do employees become more involved in the workplace?

From Theory to Practice: The Role of Money

The most commonly used reward in organizations is money. As one author notes, "Money is probably the most emotionally meaningful object in contemporary life: only food and sex are its close competitors as common carriers of such strong and diverse feelings, significance, and strivings."[2] A recent survey of Canadian employees found that overall, 46 percent believe they are underpaid. More employees in Quebec think they are underpaid (54 percent) than those in Ontario (38 percent). The survey's results are similar to a poll conducted in the United States, in which 45 percent felt they were underpaid.[3]

The motivation theories we have presented only give us vague ideas of how money relates to individual motivation. For instance, Theory X suggests that individuals need to be extrinsically motivated. Money is certainly one such extrinsic motivator. According to Maslow's hierarchy of needs, individuals' basic needs must be met, including food, shelter, and safety. Generally, money can be used to satisfy those needs. Herzberg's motivation–hygiene theory, on the other hand, suggests that money (and other extrinsic motivators) are necessary but not sufficient conditions for individuals to be motivated. Process theories are relatively silent about the role of money specifically, indicating more how rewards motivate, without specifying particular types of rewards. Expectancy theory does note that individuals need to value the reward, or it will not be very motivational.

Despite the importance of money in attracting and retaining employees, and rewarding and recognizing them, not enough research has been done on this topic.[4] With respect to job satisfaction, one recent study found that pay level was only moderately correlated, and concluded that a person could be satisfied with his or her pay level, and still not have job satisfaction.[5] Another study concluded that "money leads to autonomy but it does not add to well-being or happiness."[6] Supporting this idea, recent research suggests that money is not the sole motivator for Millennial and Baby Boomer employees. Both generations find having "a great team, challenging assignments, a range of new experiences, and explicit performance evaluation and recognition" as important as money.[7] Exhibit 5-1 illustrates the key differences and similarities of what the two generations value in addition to money.

A number of studies suggest that there are personality traits and demographic factors that correlate with an individual's attitude toward money.[8] People who highly value money score higher on "attributes like sensation seeking, competitiveness, materialism, and control." People who desire money score higher on self-esteem, and need for achievement. Men seem to value money more than women, who value recognition for doing a good job more.[9]

EXHIBIT 5-1 What Baby Boomers and Millennials Value as Much as Compensation

Baby Boomers	Millennials
High-quality colleagues	High-quality colleagues
An intellectually stimulating workplace	Flexible work arrangements
Autonomy regarding work tasks	Prospects for advancement
Flexible work arrangements	Recognition from one's company or boss
Access to new experiences and challenges	A steady rate of advancement and promotion
Giving back to the world through work	Access to new experiences and challenges
Recognition from one's company or boss	

Source: Based on S. A. Hewlett, L. Sherbin, and K. Sumberg, "How Gen Y & Boomers Will Reshape Your Agenda," *Harvard Business Review*, July/August 2009, p. 76.

What these findings suggest is that when organizations develop reward programs, they need to consider very carefully the importance to the individual of the specific rewards offered. The *Ethical Dilemma* on page 197 gives you an intriguing look at the amount of money needed to motivate some Canadian CEOs.

Creating Effective Reward Systems

At Hootsuite, being social and part of a healthy community is all part of the job.[10] CEO Ryan Holmes believes that "human nature is to make connections and build upon commonalities. And we're a social media company, so there are simply no excuses to not be social." He fosters that community spirit with incentives and perks that reinforce the culture. One example is the onsite gym and the associated lunch hour workout club. An employee named Gerald reports that "the noon workout is a great break for me as it forces me to get away from my desk. I work out with a great team. It's the team aspect that is really important. You always show up so you don't let each other down, you plan your meals around it and even go to bed earlier the night before." Other incentives include team performance-based bonuses, stock options, and the opportunity to get financial support for pet projects that help to improve the lives of other employees or support the broader community. Holmes also ensures that the work atmosphere stays friendly by providing stress release options such as rooftop gardens, nap rooms, and 20 friendly therapy dogs who work each day alongside the human employees. These stress-busting tools help people cope with anxiety and overloading that might otherwise come out in the form of interpersonal conflict.

At all of these actions signal to employees that they are valued as important contributors to the company's success. What else can a company do to make sure its employees feel valued?

As we saw in Chapter 3, pay is not a primary factor driving job satisfaction. However, it does motivate people, and companies often underestimate the importance of pay in keeping top talent. A recent study found that although only 45 percent of employers thought that pay was a key factor in losing top talent, 71 percent of top performers called it a top reason.[11]

Given that pay is so important, will the organization lead, match, or lag the market in pay? How will individual contributions be recognized? In this section, we consider (1) what to pay employees (which is decided by establishing a pay structure); (2) how to pay individual employees (for example, through variable-pay programs); (3) what benefits to offer, especially whether to offer employees choice in benefits (flexible benefits); and (4) how to construct employee recognition programs.

What to Pay: Establishing a Pay Structure

There are many ways to pay employees. The process of initially setting pay levels entails balancing *internal equity*—the worth of the job to the organization (usually established through a technical process called *job evaluation*)—and *external equity*—the external competitiveness of an organization's pay relative to pay elsewhere in its industry (usually established through pay surveys). Obviously, the best pay system pays the job what it is worth (internal equity) while also paying competitively relative to the labour market.

Some organizations prefer to pay above the market, while some may lag the market because they cannot afford to pay market rates, or they are willing to bear the costs of paying below market (namely, higher turnover as people are lured to better-paying jobs). Some companies who have realized impressive gains in income and profit margins have done so partially by holding down employee wages, such as Walmart.[12]

Pay more, and you may get better-qualified, more highly motivated employees who will stay with the organization longer. A study covering 126 large organizations found employees who believed that they were receiving a competitive pay level had higher morale and were more productive, and customers were more satisfied as well.[13] But pay is often the highest single operating cost for an organization, which means paying too much can make the organization's products or services too expensive. It's a strategic decision an organization must make, with clear trade-offs.

In the case of Walmart, it appears that its strategic decision to keep wages low has not been working as of late. Sales at Canadian stores open for more than a year, an important barometer of retail health known as same-store sales, fell 1.3 percent and customer traffic at those stores declined 1.8 percent in 2013.[14] One of Walmart's larger competitors, Costco, had a 5 percent increase in sales in the same period. The average employee at Costco makes approximately two and a half times what the average employee at Walmart earns. Costco's strategy is that they will get more if they pay more—higher wages are resulting in increased employee productivity and reduced turnover.

How to Pay: Rewarding Individuals through Variable-Pay Programs

① Demonstrate how the different types of variable-pay programs can increase employee motivation.

"Why should I put any extra effort into this job?" asks a frustrated grade 4 teacher. "I can excel or I can do the bare minimum. It makes no difference. I get paid the same. Why do anything above the minimum to get by?" Similar comments have been voiced by schoolteachers (and some other unionized employees) for decades because pay increases are tied to seniority.

A number of organizations are moving away from paying people based solely on credentials or length of service. Piece-rate wages, merit-based pay, bonuses, gainsharing, profit-sharing plans, stock options, and employee stock ownership plans are all forms of a **variable-pay program**, which bases a portion of an employee's pay on some individual, group, and/or organizational measure of performance. Earnings therefore fluctuate up and down with the measure of performance,[15] as Jason Easton, director of Strategy and Business Transformation at Toronto-based GM Canada, explains: "In any given year the variable pay can actually be zero, below the target or above the target, depending on how the company has performed."[16] When GM Canada gave performance-based bonuses to its salaried employees, it generated discontent among union employees who had no such provision in their collective agreement.[17]

Burnaby, BC-based TELUS and Hamilton, Ontario-based ArcelorMittal Dofasco are just a couple of examples of companies that use variable pay with rank-and-file employees. About 10 to 15 percent of the base pay of ArcelorMittal Dofasco's blue-collar workers is subject to variable compensation, while more than half of the CEO's compensation is based on variable pay.[18] GM Canada gave performance-based bonuses to its salaried employees in 2011, generating discontent among union employees who had no such provision in their collective agreement.[19]

Variable-pay plans have long been used to compensate salespeople and executives. Recently they have begun to be applied to other employees. A recent international survey by Hewitt Associates of large organizations in 46 countries found that more than 80 percent offered variable pay. In Canada, 9.6 percent of the payroll, on average, goes to variable pay.[20]

The fluctuation in variable pay is what makes these programs attractive to management. It turns part of an organization's fixed labour costs into a variable cost, thus reducing expenses when performance declines. When the economy falters, such as in 2008, companies with variable pay are able to reduce their labour costs much faster than others.[21] When pay is tied to performance, the employee's earnings recognize contribution rather than become a form of entitlement. Low performers find, over time, that their pay stagnates, while high performers enjoy pay increases commensurate with their contributions.

variable-pay program A pay plan that bases a portion of an employee's pay on some individual and/or organizational measure of performance.

Individual-Based Incentives

There are four major forms of individual-based variable-pay programs: piece-rate wages, merit-based pay, bonuses, and skill-based pay.

Piece-Rate Wages The **piece-rate pay plan** has long been popular as a means for compensating production employees with a fixed sum for each unit of production completed. A pure piece-rate plan provides no base salary and pays the employee only for what he or she produces.

Ball park workers selling peanuts and soft drinks frequently are paid this way. If they sell 40 bags of peanuts at $1 each for their earnings, their take is $40. The harder they work and the more peanuts they sell, the more they earn. The limitation of these plans is that they're not feasible for many jobs. Surgeons earn significant salaries regardless of their patients' outcomes. Would it be better to pay them only if their patients fully recover? It seems unlikely that most would accept such a deal, and it might cause unanticipated consequences as well (such as surgeons avoiding patients with complicated or terminal conditions). So, although incentives are motivating and relevant for some jobs, it is unrealistic to think they can constitute the only piece of some employees' pay.

Merit-Based Pay **Merit-based pay plans** pay for individual performance based on performance appraisal ratings. A main advantage is that people thought to be high performers can get bigger raises. If designed correctly, merit-based pay plans let individuals perceive a strong relationship between their performance and their rewards.[22]

Most large organizations have merit-based pay plans, especially for salaried employees. Merit pay is slowly taking hold in the public sector. Most government employees are unionized, and the unions that represent them have usually demanded that pay raises be based solely on seniority.

The thinking behind merit pay is that people who are high performers should be given bigger raises. For merit pay to be effective, however, individuals need to perceive a strong relationship between their performance and the rewards they receive.[23] Unfortunately, the evidence suggests that this is not the case.[24]

A move away from merit pay is coming from some organizations that don't feel it separates high and low performers enough. "There's a very strong belief and there's evidence and academic research that shows that variable pay does create focus among employees," said Ken Abosch, a compensation manager at human-resource consulting firm Aon Hewitt. Even those companies that have retained merit pay are rethinking the allocation.[25]

Although you might think a person's average level of performance is the key factor in merit pay decisions, recent research indicates that the projected level of future performance also plays a role. One study found that National Basketball Association players whose performance was on an upward trend were paid more than their average performance would have predicted. The upshot? Managers may unknowingly be basing merit pay decisions on how they *think* employees will perform, which may result in overly optimistic (or pessimistic) pay decisions.[26]

Despite the intuitive appeal of paying for performance, merit-based pay plans have several limitations. One is that they are typically based on an annual performance appraisal and thus are only as valid as the performance ratings. Another limitation is that the pay raise pool fluctuates based on economic or other conditions that have little to do with an individual employee's performance. One year, a colleague at a top university who performed very well in teaching and research was given a pay raise of $300. Why? Because the budget for pay raises was very small. Yet that is hardly pay for performance. Unions typically resist merit-based pay plans and prefer seniority-based pay, where all employees get the same raises. Relatively few teachers are covered by merit pay for this reason. Instead, seniority-based pay, where all employees get the same raises, predominates.

Finally, merit pay systems may result in gender and racial discrimination in pay. A recent study found that when organizations have merit-based cultures, managers tend to favour male employees over female employees, with men getting larger monetary rewards. The researchers conclude that there may be "unrecognized risks behind certain organizational efforts used to reward merit."[27]

piece-rate pay plan An individual-based incentive plan in which employees are paid a fixed sum for each unit of production completed.

merit-based pay plan An individual-based incentive plan based on performance appraisal ratings.

Chinese Internet firm Tencent Holdings rewards employees with attractive incentives that include cash bonuses for lower-ranking employees. The young men shown here were among 5000 employees who received a special bonus tucked in red envelopes and personally handed out by Tencent's CEO and co-founder Pony Ma.

Bonuses   An annual **bonus** is a significant component of total compensation for many jobs.[28] Bonuses reward employees for recent performance rather than historical performance and are one-time rewards rather than ongoing entitlements. They are used by such companies as Hydro One, the Bank of Montreal (BMO), and Molson Coors Brewing Company. The incentive effects of performance bonuses should be higher because, rather than paying for performance that may have occurred years ago (and was rolled into their base pay), bonuses reward only recent performance. Moreover, when times are bad, firms can cut bonuses to reduce compensation costs. The cuts can happen unevenly within a firm as well. Even though Canada's six largest banks posted healthy profits for 2013, not all aspects of banking did as well. Thus bankers who worked in wealth management, and helped raise bank profits, expected to see larger bonuses than those who worked in capital market units, because the number of mining and energy deals slumped.[29]

Bonuses are not free from organizational politics (which we discuss in Chapter 8), and they can sometimes result in employees engaging in negative behaviours to ensure they will receive bonuses. *Focus on Ethics* raises the possibility that part of the US financial crisis that began in September 2008 was due to the way bonuses were awarded to executives.

FOCUS ON ETHICS

Huge Bonuses, Disastrous Results for the United States

Did bonuses help fuel a financial meltdown?   During a two-week period in September 2008, the American economy almost looked to be in free fall.[30] The US government bought up the assets of mortgage insurers Freddie Mac and Fannie May. Global financial services firm Merrill Lynch, founded in 1914, agreed to be bought by Bank of America for very little money. Global financial services firm Lehman Brothers, founded in 1850, went into bankruptcy. Morgan Stanley was in merger discussions. Major American insurance corporation AIG received an $85-billion bailout from the US government. Independent investment banks Goldman Sachs, founded in 1869, and Morgan Stanley, founded in 1935, announced that they would become bank holding companies. Investment banks

bonus An individual-based incentive plan that rewards employees for recent performance rather than historical performance.

issue and sell securities and provide advice on mergers and acquisitions. By becoming bank holding companies, the two companies are now subjected to greater regulation than they were previously.

There is no simple answer to why all of these corporations faced collapse or near collapse all at once, but the role that bonuses played in the financial meltdown has been raised. The trigger for the economic crisis was the collapse of many subprime mortgages during 2007 and 2008. In the preceding years, numerous Americans had been given mortgages for homes, even though they had no down payments, and sometimes did not even have jobs. The loan payments were low at the beginning, but eventually many of those given subprime mortgages started to default on their loans.

Why would someone give out a loan to an individual who did not have a job or did not provide clear evidence of earnings? The banking industry rewarded mortgage brokers for making loans, giving out bonus payments based on the size of loans. The loans were then bundled together to make new financial instruments. These resulted in commissions and bonuses for those packaging the instruments. Several Wall Street CEOs who lost their jobs because of the fallout from subprime loans earned "tens of millions in bonuses during the heady days of 2005 and 2006."

The collapse of so many financial institutions at once suggests that rewarding individuals based on financial measures can cause problems.

Recent research has shown that the way bonuses and rewards are categorized also affects people's motivation. Dividing rewards and bonuses into multiple categories—even if those categories are meaningless—makes people work harder. Why? Because they are more likely to feel as if they "missed out" on a reward if they don't receive one from each category. Although admittedly a bit manipulative sounding, taking rewards and bonuses and splitting them into categories may increase motivation.[31]

Skill-Based Pay   **Skill-based pay** (also called *competency-based* or *knowledge-based pay*) is an alternative to job-based pay and bases pay levels on the basis of how many skills employees have or how many jobs they can do.[32] For employers, the lure of skill-based pay plans is increased flexibility of the workforce: Staffing is easier when employee skills are interchangeable. Skill-based pay also facilitates communication across the organization because people gain a better understanding of one another's jobs. One study found that across 214 different organizations, skill-based pay was related to higher levels of workforce flexibility, positive attitudes, membership behaviours, and productivity.[33] Another study found that over five years, a skill-based pay plan was associated with higher levels of individual skill change and skill maintenance.[34] These results suggest that skill-based pay plans are effective in achieving their stated goals.

What about the downside? People can "top out"—that is, they can learn all the skills the program calls for them to learn. This can frustrate employees after they have been challenged by an environment of learning, growth, and continual pay raises. Plus, skill-based plans don't address the level of performance, but only whether someone can perform the skill.

Group-Based Incentives
There is one major form of group-based pay-for-performance program: gainsharing.

Gainsharing   **Gainsharing** is a formula-based group incentive plan that uses improvements in group productivity from one period to another to determine the total amount of money to be shared.[35] For instance, if last month a company produced 1000 items using 10 000 person hours, and this month production of the same number of items was produced with only 9000 person hours, the company experiences a savings of 1000 person hours, at the average cost per hour to hire a person. Productivity savings can be divided between the company and employees in any number of ways, but 50-50 is fairly typical.

skill-based pay An individual-based incentive plan that sets pay levels on the basis of how many skills employees have or how many jobs they can do.

gainsharing A group-based incentive plan in which improvements in group productivity determine the total amount of money to be shared.

Gainsharing differs from profit sharing, discussed below, in tying rewards to productivity gains rather than profits, so employees can receive incentive awards even when the organization is not profitable. Because the benefits accrue to groups of employees, high-performers pressure weaker performers to work harder, improving performance for the group as a whole.[36] Whole Foods uses gainsharing as one way of motivating employees. Individual stores develop monthly budgets, and if a store comes in under budget for the month, the surplus is added to the annual sum paid out to employees. Whole Foods explains the rationale: "We strive to create a company-wide consciousness of 'shared fate' by uniting the interests of team members as closely as possible with those of our shareholders."[37]

Organizational-Based Incentives

There are two major forms of organizational-based pay-for-performance programs: profit-sharing and stock option plans, which include employee stock ownership plans.

Profit-Sharing Plans A **profit-sharing plan** distributes compensation based on some established formula designed around a company's profitability. The plan can distribute direct cash outlays or stock options. Facebook's Mark Zuckerberg, who accept a $1 salary in 2012, made a whopping $2.3 billion after cashing out 60 000 stock options.[38] Although senior executives are most likely to be rewarded through profit-sharing plans, employees at any level can be recipients. Burlington, Ontario-based O.C. Tanner Canada pays all of its employees' bonuses based on profits, twice a year.

Profit-sharing plans do not necessarily focus employees on the future, because employees and managers look for ways to cut costs today, without considering longer-term organizational needs. They also tend to ignore factors such as customer service and employee development, which may not be seen as having a direct link to profits. Employees can see inconsistent rewards with such a plan. Employees working under profit-sharing plans have a greater feeling of psychological ownership.[39]

Employee Stock Ownership Plans and Stock Options An **employee stock ownership plan (ESOP)**[40] is a company-established benefit plan in which employees acquire stock as part of their benefits. Stock options give employees the right to buy stocks in the company at a later date for a guaranteed price. In either case, the idea is that employees will be more likely to think about the consequences of their behaviour on the bottom line if they own part of the company.

Canadian companies lag far behind the United States in the use of ESOPs because Canada's tax environment is less conducive to such plans. Nevertheless, Edmonton-based PCL Constructors, the sixth-largest construction firm in North America, has been owned by its employees since 1977, with 90 percent of the firm's 3500-plus full-time salaried staff owning shares. "PCL's unique employee-ownership model is one of the keys to the company's success," notes PCL president and CEO Paul Douglas.[41] Toronto-based I Love Rewards and Edmonton-based Cybertech are other examples of companies that have employee stock ownership plans.

profit-sharing plan An organization-wide incentive plan in which the employer shares profits with employees based on a predetermined formula.

employee stock ownership plan (ESOP) A company-established benefit plan in which employees acquire stock as part of their benefits.

RESEARCH FINDINGS: ESOPs

The research on ESOPs indicates that they increase employee satisfaction and innovation.[42] But their impact on performance is less clear. A study by the Toronto Stock Exchange found positive results for public companies with ESOPs:[43]

- Five-year profit growth was 123 percent higher.

- Net profit margin was 95 percent higher.

- Productivity, measured by revenue per employee, was 24 percent higher.

- Return on average total equity was 92.3 percent higher.
- Return on capital was 65.5 percent higher.

For ESOP plans to be successful, employees need to psychologically experience ownership.[44] That is, in addition to their financial stake in the company, they need to be kept regularly informed on the status of the business and have the opportunity to influence it in order to significantly improve the organization's performance.[45]

ESOP plans for top management can reduce unethical behaviour. CEOs are more likely to manipulate firm earnings reports to make themselves look good in the short run when they don't have an ownership share, even though this manipulation will eventually lead to lower stock prices. However, when CEOs own a large amount of stock, they report earnings accurately because they don't want the negative consequences of declining stock prices.[46]

RESEARCH FINDINGS: Variable-Pay Programs

Do variable-pay programs increase motivation and productivity? Studies generally support the idea that organizations with profit-sharing plans have higher levels of profitability than those without them.[47] Profit-sharing plans have also been linked to higher levels of employee affective commitment, especially in small organizations.[48] One study found that although piece-rate pay-for-performance plans stimulated higher levels of productivity, this positive effect was not observed for risk-averse employees. Thus, American economist Ed Lazear generally seems right when he says, "Workers respond to prices just as economic theory predicts. Claims by sociologists and others that monetizing incentives may actually reduce output are unambiguously refuted by the data."[49] However, that does not mean everyone responds positively to variable-pay plans.[50]

Flexible Benefits: Developing a Benefits Package

Alain Boudreau and Yasmin Murphy have very different needs in terms of employee benefits. Alain is married and has three young children and a wife who is at home full time. Yasmin, too, is married, but her husband has a high-paying job with the federal government, and they have no children. Alain is concerned about having a good dental plan and enough life insurance to support his family in case it's needed. In contrast, Yasmin's husband already has her dental needs covered on his plan, and life insurance is a low priority for both Yasmin and her husband. Yasmin is more interested in extra vacation time and long-term financial benefits such as a tax-deferred savings plan.

A standardized benefits package for all employees at an organization would be unlikely to satisfactorily meet the needs of both Alain and Yasmin. Some organizations, therefore, cover both sets of needs by offering flexible benefits.

Consistent with expectancy theory's thesis that organizational rewards should be linked to each individual employee's personal goals, **flexible benefits** individualize rewards by allowing each employee to choose the compensation package that best satisfies his or her current needs. They replace the traditional "one-benefit-plan-fits-all" programs designed for a male with a wife and two children at home that dominated organizations for more than 50 years.[51] The average organization provides fringe benefits worth approximately 40 percent of an employee's salary. Flexible benefits can be uniquely tailored to accommodate differences in employee needs based on age, marital status, spouse's benefit status, number and age of dependants, and the like.

The three most popular types of benefits plans are modular plans, core-plus plans, and flexible spending accounts.[52] *Modular plans* are predesigned packages of benefits, with each module put together to meet the needs of a specific group of employees. A module designed for single employees with no dependants might include only essential benefits. Another, designed for single parents, might have additional life insurance, disability insurance, and expanded health coverage. *Core-plus plans* consist of a core

2 Show how flexible benefits turn benefits into motivators.

flexible benefits A benefits plan that allows each employee to put together a benefits package individually tailored to his or her own needs and situation.

of essential benefits and a menu-like selection of other benefit options from which employees can select. Typically, each employee is given "benefit credits," which allow the "purchase" of additional benefits that uniquely meet his or her needs. *Flexible spending accounts* allow employees to set aside pretax dollars up to the dollar amount offered in the plan to pay for particular benefits, such as eye care and dental premiums. Flexible spending accounts can increase employee take-home pay because employees don't pay taxes on the dollars they spend out of these accounts.

A 2009 survey of 211 Canadian organizations found that 60 percent offer flexible benefits, up from 41 percent in 2005.[53] And they're becoming the norm in other countries, too. Almost all major corporations in the United States offer flexible benefits. A survey of firms in the United Kingdom found that nearly all major organizations were offering flexible benefits programs, with options ranging from private supplemental medical insurance to holiday trading, discounted bus travel, and child-care vouchers.[54]

Intrinsic Rewards: Employee Recognition Programs

3 Identify the motivational benefits of intrinsic rewards.

⊙ Watch on **MyManagementLab**

Rudi's Bakery: Motivation

Laura makes only $10.00 per hour working at her fast-food job, and the job is not very challenging or interesting. Yet Laura talks enthusiastically about the job, her boss, and the company that employs her. "What I like is the fact that Guy [her supervisor] appreciates the effort I make. He compliments me regularly in front of the other people on my shift, and I've been chosen Employee of the Month twice in the past six months. Did you see my picture on that plaque on the wall?"

Organizations are increasingly recognizing what Laura knows: Important work rewards can be both intrinsic and extrinsic. Rewards are intrinsic in the form of employee recognition programs and extrinsic in the form of compensation systems. In this section, we deal with ways in which managers can reward and motivate employee performance. Expectancy theory tells us that a key component of motivation is the link between performance and rewards (that is, having your behaviour recognized). Employee recognition programs range from a spontaneous and private "thank you" on up to widely publicized formal programs in which specific types of behaviour are encouraged and the procedures for attaining recognition are clearly identified.[55] Some research suggests financial incentives may be more motivating in the short term, but in the long run it's nonfinancial incentives that are motivating.[56]

A recent study found that recognition programs are common in Canadian firms.[57] An obvious advantage of recognition programs is that they are inexpensive because praise is free![58] As companies and government organizations face tighter budgets, nonfinancial incentives become more attractive.

Brian Scudamore, CEO of Vancouver-based 1-800-GOT-JUNK? understands the importance of showing employees that they are appreciated. "I believe that the best way to engage someone is with heartfelt thanks. We have created a culture of peer recognition, and 'thank yous' have become contagious. Whether it's a card, kudos at the huddle or basic one-on-one thanks, gratitude goes a long way toward building team engagement, loyalty and, of course, happiness."[59] Scudamore says that actions like these keep the company growing, and employees having fun.

A survey of Canadian firms found that 34 percent of companies recognize individual or group achievements with cash or merchandise.[60] For example, Toronto-based software developer RL Solutions developed a formal program for employees to recognize co-workers who go above and beyond in working with clients or in other aspects of their work. Those recognized by their co-workers receive cash and/or other rewards. Employees are also recognized with bonuses when they refer good job candidates to the company.[61]

Other ways of recognizing performance include sending employees personal thank-you notes or emails for good performance, putting employees on prestigious committees, sending employees for training, and giving an employee an assistant for a day to help clear backlogs. Recognition and praise, however, need to be meaningful.[62]

EXHIBIT 5-2 Management Reward Follies

We hope for …	But we reward …
Teamwork and collaboration	The best team members
Innovative thinking and risk-taking	Proven methods and not making mistakes
Development of people skills	Technical achievements and accomplishments
Employee involvement and empowerment	Tight control over operations and resources
High achievement	Another year's effort
Long-term growth; environmental responsibility	Quarterly earnings
Commitment to total quality	Shipping on schedule, even with defects
Candour; surfacing bad news early	Reporting good news, whether it's true or not; agreeing with the manager, whether or not (s)he's right

Sources: Constructed from S. Kerr, "On the Folly of Rewarding A, While Hoping for B," *Academy of Management Executive* 9, no. 1 (1995), pp. 7–14; and "More on the Folly," *Academy of Management Executive* 9, no. 1 (1995), pp. 15–16. Copyright © Academy of Management, 1990.

Beware the Signals That Are Sent by Rewards

Perhaps more often than we would like, organizations engage in what has been called "the folly of rewarding A, while hoping for B"[63]; in other words, managers may hope employees will engage in one type of behaviour, but they reward another. Expectancy theory suggests that individuals will generally perform in ways that raise the probability of receiving the rewards offered. Exhibit 5-2 provides examples of common management reward follies. By signalling what gets rewarded, organizations implicitly determine whether employees engage in organizational citizenship behaviour, as *Focus on Research* shows.

> Ever wonder why employees do some strange things?

FOCUS ON RESEARCH

The Reward for Helping Others at Work

Is there a payoff to being a good citizen at work? We discussed in Chapter 1 how employers like employees to engage in organizational citizenship behaviour (OCB). But do employees get rewarded for engaging in OCB?

Research suggests that "it depends." In some organizations, employees are evaluated more on *how* their work gets done. If they possess the requisite knowledge and skills, or if they demonstrate the right behaviours on the job (for example, always greeting customers with a smile), they are determined by management to be motivated, "good" performers. In these organizations, actions targeted toward task performance goals and actions targeted toward "citizenship" goals (for example, helping a co-worker in need) are evaluated positively, which then motivates employees to continue their OCB.

However, in other organizations, employees are evaluated more on *what* gets done. Here, employees are determined to be "good" performers if they meet objective goals such as billing clients a certain number of hours or reaching a certain sales volume. When managers overlook employee OCB, frown on helpful behaviours, or create an overly competitive organizational culture, employees are not motivated to engage in helpful actions.

There may be a trade-off between being a good performer and being a good citizen. In organizations that focus more on behaviours, following your motivation to be a good citizen can lead to positive outcomes for your career. However, in organizations that focus more on objective outcomes, you may need to consider the cost.

Research suggests that there are three major obstacles to ending these follies:[64]

1. *Individuals are unable to break out of old ways of thinking about reward and recognition practices.* Management often emphasizes quantifiable behaviours to the exclusion of nonquantifiable behaviours; management is sometimes reluctant to change the existing performance system; and employees sometimes have an entitlement mentality (they don't want change because they are comfortable with the current system for rewards).

2. *Organizations often don't look at the big picture of their performance system.* Consequently, rewards are allocated at subunit levels, with the result that units often compete against each other.

3. *Both management and shareholders often focus on short-term results.* They don't reward employees for longer-range planning.

Organizations would do well to ensure that they do not send the wrong message when offering rewards. When organizations outline an organizational objective of "team performance," for example, but reward each employee according to individual productivity, this does not send a message that teams are valued. When a retailer tells commissioned employees that they are responsible for monitoring and replacing stock, those employees will nevertheless concentrate on making sales. Employees motivated by the promise of rewards will do those things that earn them the rewards they value.

Gordon Nixon, CEO of the Royal Bank of Canada (RBC), highlights changes RBC made to be sure it was rewarding the right things: "We constantly reinforce the values of the organization and ensure it is living up to those values by the way we respect people, the way we compensate and promote people, the way we recognize [them]. We changed our review process to ensure there is alignment with respect to values and culture—that there is alignment between our values and how people are recognized and rewarded."[65] *OB in the Street* offers additional evidence that what is rewarded guides people's focus of activity.

OB IN THE STREET
Rewarding Gym Attendance While Wanting Weight Loss

Will offering incentives for going to the gym prevent first-year university students from gaining weight?   University students are notorious for gaining several kilograms in their first year, as they adjust to living away from home and being more responsible for food choices, while trying to keep up with their studies.[66] Researchers wondered if providing monetary incentives for students to go to the gym would help them keep off weight.

Students were assigned to experimental or control groups. In the experimental group, students were paid between $10 and $38.75 weekly if they met the goals researchers set for going to the fitness centre. Student activity was monitored through ID cards used to check in and check out of the centre.

The monetary incentives did make a difference in whether students went to the fitness centre weekly: 63 percent of those receiving incentives met the weekly goals on average, while only 13 percent of those in the control group did so. However, the rate of quitting going to the fitness centre dropped off at about the same rate for both the control and incentive groups. While the control group gained a bit more weight than did the group receiving incentives for going to the fitness centre, the difference was not significant.

The results indicate that the monetary rewards did in fact increase the likelihood that students would meet their weekly goals for going to the fitness centre. However, the students were not given rewards for maintaining or losing weight over the same period. The researchers had assumed that a link existed between going to the fitness centre and weight fluctuations. The students might have been more successful at minding their weight had the researchers rewarded weight loss rather than going to the fitness centre.

Can We Eliminate Rewards?

Alfie Kohn, in his book *Punished by Rewards*, argues that "the desire to do something, much less to do it well, simply cannot be imposed; in this sense, it is a mistake to talk about motivating other people. All we can do is set up certain conditions that will maximize the probability of their developing an interest in what they are doing and remove the conditions that function as constraints."[67] For an additional discussion on whether incentives are truly motivating, see *Case Incident—Attaching the Carrot to the Stick* on page 198.

Are rewards overrated?

Based on his research and consulting experience, Kohn proposes a number of actions that organizations can take to create a more supportive, motivating work environment.

Abolish Incentive Pay Pay employees generously and fairly so they don't feel exploited. They will be more able to focus on the goals of the organization, rather than have their paycheque as their main goal.

Re-evaluate Evaluation Instead of making performance appraisals look and feel like a punitive effort—who gets raises, who gets promoted, who is told they are performing poorly—structure the performance evaluation system more like a two-way conversation to trade ideas and questions. The discussion of performance should not be tied to compensation. "Providing feedback that employees can use to do a better job ought never to be confused or combined with controlling them by offering (or withholding) rewards."[68]

Create the Conditions for Authentic Motivation A noted economist summarized the evidence about pay for productivity as follows: "Changing the way workers are *treated* may boost productivity more than changing the way they are *paid*."[69] There is some consensus about what the conditions for authentic motivation might be: helping employees rather than putting them under surveillance; listening to employee concerns and thinking about problems from their viewpoint; and providing plenty of feedback so they know what they have done right and what they need to improve.[70]

Encourage Collaboration People are more likely to perform better in well-functioning groups where they can get feedback and learn from one another.[71] Therefore, it's important to provide the necessary supports to create well-functioning teams.

Enhance Content People are generally the most motivated when their jobs give them an opportunity to learn new skills, provide variety in the tasks that are performed, and enable them to demonstrate competence. Some of this can be fostered by carefully matching people to their jobs, and by giving them the opportunity to try new jobs. It's also possible to increase the meaningfulness of many jobs, as we discuss later in this chapter.

But what about jobs that don't seem inherently interesting? One psychologist suggests that in cases where the jobs are fundamentally unappealing, the manager might acknowledge frankly that the task is not fun, give a meaningful rationale for why it must be done, and then give people as much choice as possible in how the task is completed.[72] One sociologist studying a group of garbage collectors in San Francisco discovered that they were quite satisfied with their work because of the way it was organized: Relationships among the crew were important, tasks and routes were varied to provide interest, and each worker owned a share of the company, and thus felt "pride of ownership."[73]

Provide Choice   "We are most likely to become enthusiastic about what we are doing—and do it well—when we are free to make decisions about the way we carry out a task."[74] Extrinsic rewards (and punishments) remove choice, because they focus us on rewards, rather than on tasks or goals. Research suggests that burnout, dissatisfaction, absenteeism, stress, and coronary heart disease are related to situations where individuals did not have enough control over their work situations.[75] By *choice* we do not mean lack of management, but rather, involving people in the decisions that are to be made. A number of studies indicate that participative management, when it includes full participation by everyone, is successful.[76]

It would be difficult for many organizations to implement these ideas immediately and expect that they would work. Managers would need to relinquish control and take on the job of coach. Employees would need to believe that their participation and input mattered. Nevertheless, these actions, when implemented, can lead to quite a different workplace than what we often see. Moreover, Kohn suggests that sometimes it's not the type or amount of rewards that makes a difference as much as whether the work itself is intrinsically interesting.

Below we examine how to create more motivating jobs and workplaces in order to make work itself more intrinsically rewarding for employees. You might consider whether Starbucks is moving in the right direction to create an intrinsically motivating workplace after you read *OB in the Workplace*.

OB IN THE **WORKPLACE**
Starbucks Aims for Better Coffee

Can management make operations too efficient?   Starbucks recently revised coffee-making procedures after complaints from customers suggested that the chain's coffee was too mechanized.[77] In a bid to bring back the perception of better coffee at its stores, Starbucks told its baristas to focus on making no more than two drinks at a time, rather than multiple drinks at once.

Starbucks studied how baristas make coffee, trying to get the routine down to the least amount of time possible in order to "eliminate wasteful activity and speed up service." For instance, beans are no longer stored below the counter because it wastes time to bend over to scoop beans.

Baristas were also told to steam just enough milk for one drink at a time, not a whole pitcher to be used for several drinks. The corporation envisions a more efficient operation, but employees fear longer lines. They also do not think the new rules make sense: "While I'm blending a frappuccino, it doesn't make sense to stand there and wait for the blender to finish running, because I could be making an iced tea at the same time," barista Tyler Swain says.

Starbucks says that the baristas just need to get comfortable with the new method, and all will be well. If a customer does need to wait longer, baristas should simply let the customer know. While the operation may be more efficient, employees complain about the lack of autonomy they have in preparing orders. _____

4 Describe the job characteristics model and the way it motivates by changing the work environment.

job design The way the elements in a job are organized.

Motivating by Job Redesign

Increasingly, research on motivation focuses on approaches that link motivational concepts to changes in the way work is structured. Research in **job design** suggests that the way the elements in a job are organized can increase or decrease effort and also suggests what those elements are. We will first review the job characteristics model and then discuss some ways jobs can be redesigned. Finally, we will explore alternative work arrangements.

EXHIBIT 5-3 Examples of High and Low Job Characteristics

Skill Variety

High variety	The owner-operator of a garage who does electrical repair, rebuilds engines, does body work, and interacts with customers
Low variety	A body shop worker who sprays paint eight hours a day

Task Identity

High identity	A cabinet maker who designs a piece of furniture, selects the wood, builds the object, and finishes it to perfection
Low identity	A worker in a furniture factory who operates a lathe solely to make table legs

Task Significance

High significance	Nursing the sick in a hospital intensive care unit
Low significance	Sweeping hospital floors

Autonomy

High autonomy	A salesperson who schedules his or her own work each day, and decides on the sales approach for each customer without supervision
Low autonomy	A salesperson who is given a set of leads each day and is required to follow a standardized sales script with potential customers

Feedback

High feedback	A factory employee who assembles iPads and tests them to see whether they operate properly
Low feedback	A factory employee who assembles iPads and then routes them to a quality-control inspector for testing and adjustments

Source: Based on G. Johns, *Organizational Behavior: Understanding and Managing Life at Work*, 4th ed. Copyright © 1997. Adapted by permission of Pearson Education, Inc. Upper Saddle River, NJ.

The Job Characteristics Model

Developed by OB researchers J. Richard Hackman from Harvard University and Greg Oldham from the University of Illinois, the **job characteristics model (JCM)** says we can describe any job in terms of five core job dimensions:[78]

- **Skill variety**. The degree to which the job requires a variety of different activities so the employee can use specialized skills and talents.

- **Task identity**. The degree to which the job requires completion of a whole and identifiable piece of work.

- **Task significance**. The degree to which the job has an impact on the lives or work of other people.

- **Autonomy**. The degree to which the job provides the employee freedom, independence, and discretion in scheduling work each day and determining the procedures for carrying it out.

- **Feedback**. The degree to which carrying out work activities generates direct and clear information about the employee's performance.

Jobs can be rated as high or low on these dimensions. Examples of jobs with high and low ratings appear in Exhibit 5-3.

Exhibit 5-4 presents the job characteristics model (JCM). Note how the first three dimensions—skill variety, task identity, and task significance—combine to create meaningful work the incumbent will view as important, valuable, and worthwhile. A 2014 study found that religious workers, social workers, counsellors, and medical professionals rated their jobs as highly meaningful, while those who held jobs as food

job characteristics model (JCM) A model that proposes that any job can be described in terms of five core job dimensions: skill variety, task identity, task significance, autonomy, and feedback.

skill variety The degree to which the job requires a variety of different activities.

task identity The degree to which the job requires completion of a whole and identifiable piece of work.

task significance The degree to which the job has a substantial impact on the lives or work of other people.

autonomy The degree to which the job provides substantial freedom, independence, and discretion to the individual in scheduling the work and determining the procedures to be used in carrying it out.

feedback The degree to which carrying out the work activities required by the job results in the individual obtaining direct and clear information about the effectiveness of his or her performance.

EXHIBIT 5-4 The Job Characteristics Model

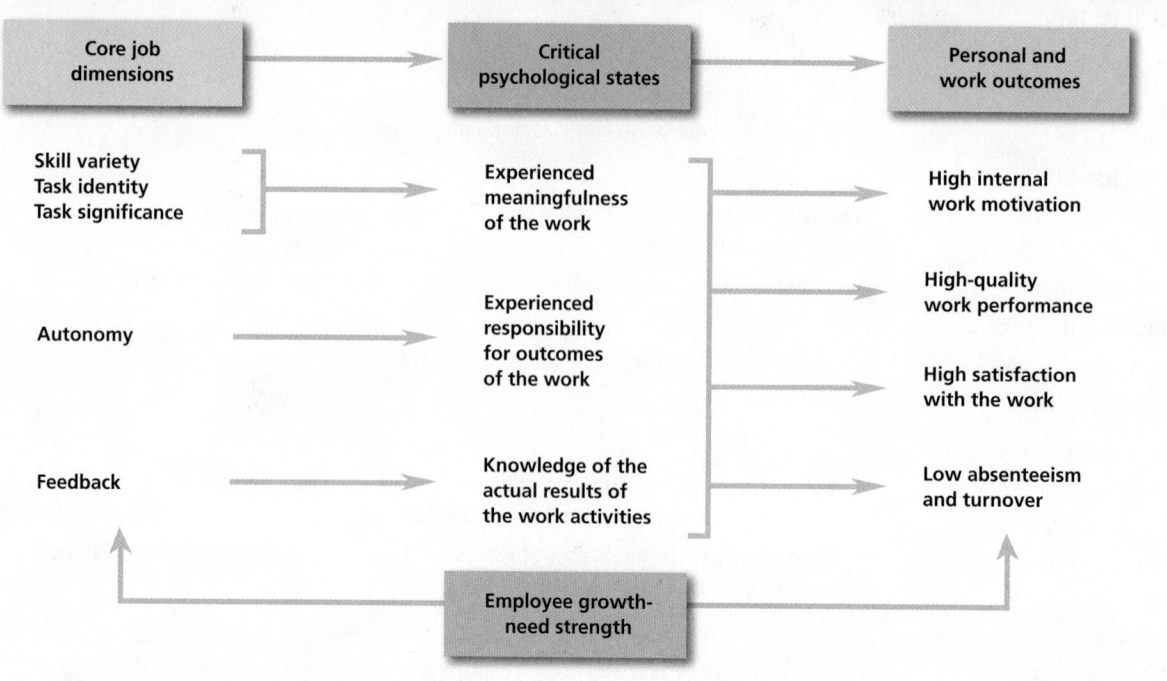

Source: J. R. Hackman, G. R. Oldham, *Work Redesign* (excerpted from pages 78–80). Copyright © 1980 by Addison-Wesley Publishing Co. ISBN: 978-0201027792.

service and hospitality workers rated them as being very low in meaningfulness. Fast food cooks were at the bottom of the list of meaningfulness.[79]

Jobs with high autonomy give incumbents a feeling of personal responsibility for the results; if a job provides feedback, employees will know how effectively they are performing. From a motivational standpoint, the JCM proposes that individuals obtain internal rewards when they learn (knowledge of results) that they personally have performed well (experienced responsibility) on a task they care about (experienced meaningfulness).[80] The more these three psychological states are present, the greater will be employees' motivation, performance, and satisfaction, and the lower their absenteeism and likelihood of leaving. As Exhibit 5-4 also shows, individuals with a high growth need are more likely to experience the critical psychological states when their jobs are enriched—and respond to them more positively—than are their counterparts with a low growth need. Autonomy does not mean the same for every person, as *Focus on Research* shows.

FOCUS ON RESEARCH

Autonomy and Productivity

Can autonomy really make a difference? Research published in 2011 by professors Marylène Gagné and Devasheesh Bhave of Concordia's John Molson School of Business found that every culture values autonomy, and that the perception of autonomy has a positive impact on employees.[81] "However, managers can't simply export North American methods of granting autonomy anywhere and expect them to work. Even in Canada, approaches to giving workers more autonomy need to be constantly rethought as the country becomes more multicultural," says Gagné.

The researchers found that how autonomy is applied makes a difference in how it is perceived. In some cultures, too much freedom in the workplace can be viewed as management disorganization. However, if employees feel they have some control over their activities, they generally show more commitment and productivity, particularly when the work is complex or demands creativity.

Working on a fish-processing line requires being comfortable with job specialization. One person cuts off heads, another guts the fish, a third removes the scales. Each person performs the same task repetitively as fish move down the line. Such jobs are low on skill variety, task identity, task significance, autonomy, and feedback.

A survey of college and university students highlights the underlying theme of the JCM. When the students were asked about what was most important to them as they thought about their careers, their top four answers were as follows:

- Having idealistic and committed co-workers (very important to 68 percent of the respondents)
- Doing work that helps others (very important to 65 percent)
- Doing work that requires creativity (very important to 47 percent)
- Having a lot of responsibility (very important to 39 percent)[82]

Salary and prestige ranked lower in importance than these four job characteristics.

Motivating Potential Score

We can combine the core dimensions into a single predictive index, called the **motivating potential score (MPS)**, which is calculated as follows:

$$\text{Motivating Potential Score (MPS)} = \left[\frac{\text{Skill variety} + \text{Task identity} + \text{Task significance}}{3} \right] \times \text{Autonomy} \times \text{Feedback}$$

To be high on motivating potential, jobs must be high on at least one of the three factors that lead to experienced meaningfulness and high on both autonomy and feedback. If jobs score high on motivating potential, the model predicts motivation, performance, and satisfaction will improve, while absence and turnover will be reduced.

The first part of the *Experiential Exercise* on page 196 provides an opportunity for you to apply the JCM to a job of your choice. You will also calculate the job's MPS. In the second part of the *Experiential Exercise*, you can redesign the job to show how you might increase its motivating potential. *From Concepts to Skills* on pages 199–201 provides specific guidelines on the kinds of changes that can help increase the motivating potential of jobs.

motivating potential score (MPS) A predictive index suggesting the motivation potential in a job.

RESEARCH FINDINGS: JCM

Much evidence supports the JCM concept that the presence of a set of job characteristics—variety, identity, significance, autonomy, and feedback—generates higher and more satisfying job performance and reduces absenteeism and turnover costs.[83] But, we can better calculate motivating potential by simply adding the characteristics rather than using the formula.[84] On the critical issue of productivity, the evidence is inconclusive.[85] In some situations, job enrichment increases productivity; in others, it decreases productivity. However, even when productivity goes down, there does seem to be consistently more conscientious use of resources and a higher quality of product or service.

While many employees want challenging, interesting, and complex work, some people prosper in simple, routinized work.[86] The variable that seems to best explain who prefers a challenging job is the strength of an individual's higher-order needs.[87] Individuals with high growth needs are more responsive to challenging work. Many employees meet their higher-order needs *off* the job. There are 168 hours in a week, and work rarely consumes more than 30 percent of them. That leaves considerable opportunity, even for individuals with strong growth needs, to find higher-order need satisfaction outside the workplace.

> When might job redesign be most appropriate?

Job Redesign in the Canadian Context: The Role of Unions

Labour unions have been largely resistant to participating in discussions with management over job redesign issues. Redesigns often result in loss of jobs, and labour unions try to prevent job loss.[88] Union head offices, however, can sometimes be at odds with their membership over the acceptance of job redesign. Some members value the opportunity for skill development and more interesting work.

Some of the larger unions have been more open to discussions about job redesign. For instance, the Communications, Energy and Paperworkers Union of Canada (CEP) asserted that unions should be involved in the decisions and share in the benefits of work redesign.[89] The CEP believes that basic wages, negotiated through a collective agreement, must remain the primary form of compensation, although the union is open to other forms of compensation as long as they do not detract from basic wages determined through collective bargaining.

While managers may regard job redesign as more difficult under a collective agreement, the reality is that for change to be effective in the workplace, management must gain employees' acceptance of the plan whether or not they are unionized.

How Can Jobs Be Redesigned?

5 Compare the main ways jobs can be redesigned.

Let's look at some of the ways to put JCM into practice to make jobs more motivating.

Job Rotation

If employees suffer from overroutinization, one alternative is **job rotation**, or the periodic shifting of an employee from one task to another with similar skill requirements at the same organizational level (also called *cross-training*). At Singapore Airlines, a ticket agent may take on the duties of a baggage handler. Extensive job rotation is among the reasons Singapore Airlines is rated one of the best airlines in the world.[90] At McDonald's, this approach is used as a way to make sure that the new employees learn all of the tasks associated with making, packaging, and serving hamburgers and other items.

Many manufacturing firms have adopted job rotation as a means of increasing flexibility and avoiding layoffs. Managers at these companies train workers on all

job rotation The periodic shifting of an employee from one task to another.

their equipment so they can move around as needed in response to incoming orders. Although job rotation has often been conceptualized as an activity for assembly line and manufacturing employees, many organizations use job rotation for new managers to help them get a picture of the whole business as well.[91] Employees in technical trades and clerical and administrative positions were more likely to rotate jobs than managerial and professional employees.

The strengths of job rotation are that it reduces boredom, increases motivation, and helps employees better understand how their work contributes to the organization. Research from Italy, Britain, and Turkey shows that job rotation is associated with higher levels of organizational performance in manufacturing settings.[92]

However, job rotation has drawbacks. Training costs increase, and moving an employee into a new position reduces productivity just when efficiency at the prior job is creating organizational economies. Work that is done repeatedly may become habitual and "routine," which makes decision making more automatic and efficient. Job rotation creates disruptions when members of the work group have to adjust to new employees. The manager may have to spend more time answering questions and monitoring the work of the recently rotated employee.

Job Enrichment

Job enrichment expands jobs by increasing the degree to which the employee controls the planning, execution, and evaluation of the work. An enriched job allows the employee to do a complete activity, increases the employee's freedom and independence, increases responsibility, and provides feedback so individuals can assess and correct their own performance.[93]

Some newer versions of job enrichment concentrate more specifically on improving the meaningfulness of work, such as providing employees with mutual assistance programs.[94] Employees who can help one another directly through their work come to see themselves, and the organizations for which they work, in more positive, pro-social terms. This, in turn, can increase employee affective commitment.

The evidence on job enrichment shows that it reduces absenteeism and turnover costs and increases satisfaction, but not all job enrichment programs are equally effective.[95] A review of 83 organizational interventions designed to improve performance management showed that frequent, specific feedback related to solving problems was linked to consistently higher performance, but infrequent feedback that focused more on past problems than future solutions was much less effective.[96] Some recent evidence suggests that job enrichment works best when it compensates for poor feedback and reward systems.[97] One recent study showed that employees with a higher preference for challenging work experienced larger reductions in stress following job redesign than individuals who did not prefer challenging work.[98]

Relational Job Design

While redesigning jobs on the basis of job characteristics theory is likely to make work more intrinsically motivating to people, more contemporary research is focusing on how to make jobs more pro-socially motivating to people. In other words, how can managers design work so employees are motivated to promote the well-being of the organization's beneficiaries? Beneficiaries of organizations might include customers, clients, patients, and users of products or services. This view of job design shifts the spotlight from the employee to those whose lives are affected by the job that the employee performs.[99]

One way to make jobs more pro-socially motivating is to better connect employees with the beneficiaries of their work, for example, by relating stories from customers who have found the company's products or services to be helpful. Medical device manufacturer Medtronic invites people to describe how Medtronic products have improved,

job enrichment The vertical expansion of jobs, which increases the degree to which the employee controls the planning, execution, and evaluation of the work.

or even saved, their lives and shares these stories with employees during annual meetings, providing a powerful reminder of the impact of their work. One study found that radiologists who saw photographs of patients whose scans they were examining made more accurate diagnoses of their medical problems. Why? Seeing the photos made it more personal, which elicited feelings of empathy in the radiologists.[100]

Even better, in some cases managers may be able to connect employees directly with beneficiaries. Researchers found that when university fundraisers briefly interacted with the undergraduates who would receive the scholarship money they raised, they persisted 42 percent longer, and raised nearly twice as much money, as those who did not interact with potential recipients.[101] The positive impact of connecting employees was apparent even when they met with just a single scholarship recipient.

Why do these connections have such positive consequences? There are several reasons. Meeting beneficiaries first-hand allows employees to see that their actions affect a real, live person and that their jobs have tangible consequences. In addition, connections with beneficiaries make customers or clients more accessible in memory and more emotionally vivid, which leads employees to consider the effects of their actions more. Finally, connections allow employees to easily take the perspective of beneficiaries, which fosters higher levels of commitment.

You might be wondering whether connecting employees is already covered by the idea of task significance in the JCM. However, some differences make beneficiary contact unique. For one, many jobs might be perceived to be high in significance, yet employees in those jobs never meet the individuals affected by their work. Second, beneficiary contact seems to have a distinct relationship with pro-social behaviours such as helping others. One study found that lifeguards who read stories about how their actions benefited swimmers were rated as more helpful by their bosses; this was not the case for lifeguards who read stories about the personal benefits of their work.[102] The upshot? There are many ways you can design jobs to be more motivating, and the choice should depend on the outcome or outcomes you would like to achieve.

Alternative Work Arrangements

6 Explain how specific alternative work arrangements can motivate employees.

Beyond redesigning work itself and including employees in decisions, another approach to motivation is to alter work arrangements with flextime, job sharing, or telecommuting. Doing so might address one of Kohn's ideas for increasing motivation that we discussed above: creating better work environments for people. These arrangements are likely to be especially important for a diverse workforce of dual-earner couples, single parents, and employees caring for a sick or aging relative.

Do employers really like flexible arrangements?

Flextime

Flextime is short for "flexible work time." Employees must work a specific number of hours a week, but they are free to vary the hours of work within certain limits. As shown in Exhibit 5-5, each day consists of a common core, usually six hours, with a flexibility band surrounding it. The core may be 9 a.m. to 3 p.m., with the office actually opening at 6 a.m. and closing at 6 p.m. All employees are required to be at their jobs during the common core period, but they may accumulate their other two hours before and/or after the core time. Some flextime programs allow extra hours to be accumulated and turned into a free day off each month.

Canadian employees do not have much access to flextime, however. According to the results of a survey of 25 000 Canadians employed full-time conducted by professor Linda Duxbury of the Sprott School of Business, Carleton University, in 2011–2012,

flextime An arrangement where employees work during a common core period each day but can form their total workday from a flexible set of hours outside the core.

EXHIBIT 5-5 Examples of Flextime Schedules

Schedule 1

Percent Time:	100% = 40 hours per week
Core Hours:	9:00 a.m.–5:00 p.m., Monday through Friday (1 hour lunch)
Work Start Time:	Between 8:00 a.m. and 9:00 a.m.
Work End Time:	Between 5:00 p.m. and 6:00 p.m.

Schedule 2

Percent Time:	100% = 40 hours per week
Work Hours:	8:00 a.m.–6:30 p.m., Monday through Thursday (1/2 hour lunch)
	Friday off
Work Start Time:	8:00 a.m.
Work End Time:	6:30 p.m.

Schedule 3

Percent Time:	90% = 36 hours per week
Work Hours:	8:30 a.m.–5:00 p.m., Monday through Thursday (1/2 hour lunch)
	8:00 a.m.–Noon Friday (no lunch)
Work Start Time:	8:30 a.m. (Monday–Thursday); 8:00 a.m. (Friday)
Work End Time:	5:00 p.m. (Monday–Thursday); Noon (Friday)

Schedule 4

Percent Time:	80% = 32 hours per week
Work Hours:	8:00 a.m.–6:00 p.m., Monday through Wednesday (1/2 hour lunch)
	8:00 a.m.–11:30 a.m. Thursday (no lunch)
	Friday off
Work Start Time:	Between 8:00 a.m. and 9:00 a.m.
Work End Time:	Between 5:00 p.m. and 6:00 p.m.

only 15 percent of employees said they had access to flextime schedules. Employees did report some flexibility in determining some of their work hours, however, with 69 percent indicating high or moderate flexibility for work hours and location.[103] According to a recent survey, a majority (53 percent) of US organizations now offer some form of flextime.[104] In Germany, 73 percent of businesses offer flextime, and such practices are becoming more widespread in Japan as well.[105] In fact, in Germany, Belgium, the Netherlands, and France, by law, employers are not allowed to refuse an employee's request for either a part-time or a flexible work schedule as long as that request is reasonable, such as to care for an infant child.[106]

Most of the evidence stacks up in favour of flextime. Flextime tends to reduce absenteeism and frequently improves employee productivity and satisfaction,[107] probably for several reasons. Employees can schedule their work hours to align with personal demands, reducing tardiness and absences, and they can work when they are most productive. Other research on the impact of flextime on the Canadian workplace has found that employees have positive attitudes toward it and view it as their most preferred work option.[108] Managers are in favour,[109] and women with flextime suffer less stress.[110]

Flextime can also help employees balance work and family life, as is the case at Goodfish Lake, Alberta-based Goodfish Lake Development Corporation (GFLDC). GFLDC is an Aboriginal business that provides dry-cleaning, clothing manufacturing and repair, protective clothing rentals, and bakery services to Fort McMurray. Many of the company's employees are women who have husbands that work full time in Fort McMurray. This can make it difficult for GFLDC's female employees to care for their children, so the company created flexible schedules to help employees balance work and home life.[111]

A 2010 study by University of Toronto researchers found that flextime can lead to longer hours of work overall and more multi-tasking. These effects in turn lead to greater work–life conflict and stress.[112] So the management of flextime is an important issue for employees. Flextime's other major drawback is that it's not applicable to every job or every employee. It works well with clerical tasks where an employee's interaction with people outside his or her department is limited. It's not a viable option for receptionists, salespeople in retail stores, or people whose service jobs require them to be at their workstations at predetermined times. It also appears that people who have a stronger desire to separate their work and family lives are less prone to take advantage of opportunities for flextime.[113] Overall, employers need to consider the appropriateness of both the work and the workers before implementing flextime schedules.

Job Sharing

Job sharing allows two or more people to split a 40-hour-a-week job. One might perform the job from 8:00 a.m. to noon and the other from 1:00 p.m. to 5:00 p.m., or the two could work full but alternate days. While it's popular in Europe, it's not a common arrangement in Canada. About 14 percent of Canadian employers offer this arrangement.[114] The reasons it's not more widely adopted are likely the difficulty of finding compatible partners to share a job and the historically negative perceptions of individuals not completely committed to their jobs and employers.[115]

Job sharing allows the organization to draw upon the talents of more than one individual in a given job. It also opens up the opportunity to acquire skilled employees—for instance, women with young children, retirees, and others desiring flexibility—who might not be available on a full-time basis.[116]

From the employee's perspective, job sharing increases flexibility and can increase motivation and satisfaction for those for whom a 40-hour-a-week job is just not practical. But the major drawback is finding compatible pairs of employees who can successfully coordinate the demands of one job. "Job sharing must be well planned, and needs clear job descriptions," says Julianna Cantwell, HR consultant with Edmonton-based Juna Consulting.[117]

Job sharing can be a creative solution to some organizational problems. For example, Nunavut has had great difficulty finding doctors willing to commit to serving the territory for more than short periods of time.[118] Dr. Sandy MacDonald, director of Medical Affairs and Telehealth for Nunavut, allows doctors to work for three months at a time. "In the past, the government was trying to get some of them to sign up for two or three years, and most people don't want to do that initially, or they would leave positions unfilled because someone would only come for two or three weeks or a month," he says. Meanwhile, doctors working in Nunavut were overworked because there were not enough doctors on call. MacDonald's approach has changed that—now more doctors are available because of the job-sharing solution.

Telecommuting

Telecommuting (sometimes called *teleworking*) might be close to the ideal job for many people. No commuting, flexible hours, freedom to dress as you please, and few or no interruptions from colleagues. Telecommuting refers

job sharing The practice of having two or more people split a 40-hour-a-week job.

telecommuting Working from home at least two days a week on a computer that is linked to the employer's office.

Would you find telecommuting motivating?

to working at home at least two days a week on a computer linked to the employer's office.[119] (A closely related term—*the virtual office*—is increasingly being used to describe employees who work out of their home on a relatively permanent basis.) Telecommuting has been a popular topic lately as a result of companies such as Yahoo! (and Best Buy) eliminating this form of flexible work.[120]

More than 1 billion people worldwide worked remotely at the end of 2010, and more than one-third of all workers were forecast to be mobile by 2013.[121] A 2013 BMO poll found that about 23 percent of Canadian companies offer telecommuting,[122] which was down from about 40 percent of Canadian companies in 2008.[123] At Cisco's downtown Toronto office, there are 200 desks for 500 employees. "Everyone else works remotely and just comes in occasionally for meetings," said Jeff Seifert, chief technology officer for Cisco's Canadian division. An internal survey of Cisco employees found increased productivity and satisfaction due to the telecommuting. It also saved the company $277 million in one year.[124]

What kinds of jobs lend themselves to telecommuting? There are three categories: routine information-handling tasks, mobile activities, and professional and other knowledge-related tasks.[125] Writers, attorneys, analysts, and employees who spend the majority of their time on computers or the phone—telemarketers, customer-service representatives, reservation agents, and product-support specialists—are natural candidates for telecommuting. As telecommuters, they can access information on their computer screens at home as easily as on the company screen in any office.

THE CANADIAN PRESS/Jonathan Hayward

Bob Fortier, president of InnoVisions Canada (a telecommuting and flexible work consulting organization), says, "Mobile work is here to stay." He says that telework [telecommuting] has many benefits: It helps attract employees who are looking for flexible work, reduces turnover, and reduces carbon emissions. However, some managers worry about supervising employees who work off-site. "In an ideal situation, teleworkers work from home or on the road a set number of hours a week, but come into the office to work and interact with managers for the rest of the time. This gives them a healthy balance," says Fortier.[126]

RESEARCH FINDINGS:
Telecommuting

Telecommuting has several potential benefits. They include a larger labour pool, higher productivity, improved morale, and reduced office-space costs. A positive relationship exists between telecommuting and supervisor performance ratings,[127] but any relationship between telecommuting and potentially lower turnover intentions has not been substantiated in research to date.[128] Beyond the benefits to organizations and its employees, telecommuting has potential benefits to society. One study estimates that, in the United States, if people telecommuted half the time, carbon emissions would be reduced by approximately 51 metric tons per year. Environmental savings could also come about from lower office energy consumption, fewer traffic jams that emit greenhouse gases, and fewer road repairs.[129]

The major downside for management is less direct supervision of employees. In today's team-focused workplace, telecommuting may make it more difficult for management to coordinate teamwork and can reduce knowledge transfer in organizations.[130] From the employee's standpoint, telecommuting can offer a considerable increase in flexibility and job satisfaction—but not without costs.[131] For employees with a high social need, telecommuting can increase feelings of isolation and reduce job satisfaction. And all telecommuters are vulnerable to the "out of sight, out of mind" effect.[132] Employees who are not at their desks, who miss meetings, and who don't share in day-to-day informal workplace interactions may be at a disadvantage when it comes to raises and promotions because they are perceived as not putting in the requisite "face-time." *Point/Counterpoint* on page 195 considers whether face-time actually matters.

Finally, a 2011 study by University of Toronto researchers found greater psychological stress for women than men when employees were contacted frequently at home by supervisors, co-workers, or clients. The researchers concluded that women may encounter greater difficulties balancing work and home life while working at home.[133]

The Social and Physical Context of Work

The JCM shows that most employees are more motivated and satisfied when their intrinsic work tasks are engaging. However, having the most interesting workplace characteristics in the world may not always lead to satisfaction if you feel isolated from your co-workers, and having good social relationships can make even the most boring and onerous tasks more fulfilling. Research demonstrates that social aspects and work context are as important as other job design features.[134] Policies such as job rotation, employee empowerment, and employee participation have positive effects on productivity, at least partially because they encourage more communication and a positive social environment.

Some social characteristics that improve job performance include interdependence, social support, and interactions with other people outside of work. Social interactions are strongly related to positive moods and give employees opportunities to clarify their work role and how well they are performing. Social support gives employees greater opportunities to obtain assistance with their work. Constructive social relationships can bring about a positive feedback loop as employees assist one another in a "virtuous circle."

The work context is also likely to affect employee satisfaction. Hot, loud, and dangerous work is less satisfying than work conducted in climate-controlled, relatively quiet, and safe environments. This is probably why most people would rather work in a coffee shop than a metalworking foundry. Physical demands make people physically uncomfortable, which is likely to show up in lower levels of job satisfaction.

To assess why an employee is not performing to his or her best level, look at whether the work environment is supportive. Does the employee have adequate tools, equipment, materials, and supplies? Does the employee have favourable working conditions, helpful co-workers, supportive work rules and procedures, sufficient information to make job-related decisions, and adequate time to do a good job, and the like? If not, performance will suffer.

PERSONAL INVENTORY ASSESSMENT

Learn About Yourself
Diagnosing Poor Performance and Enhancing Motivation

Employee Involvement

One way to foster employee involvement is to simply be available to listen to your employees and hear their ideas.[135] This is something that Hootsuite CEO Ryan Holmes takes very seriously. In addition to the monthly parties, Holmes also finds other ways to make himself accessible. The lunch room, for example, is centrally located, and employees are strongly encouraged to eat together and talk rather than eat at their desks. Holmes participates in this lunchtime ritual as well as in team sports and other recreational activities that are run by and for employees. Casual contact provides opportunities for him to hear good ideas that he might otherwise miss, and his employees are more motivated because they know he will engage with them, listen to them, and when appropriate act on what they tell him.

What other ways can companies encourage employee involvement?

Employee involvement is a participative process that uses employees' input to increase their commitment to the organization's success. The logic is that if we engage employees in decisions that affect them and increase their autonomy and control over their work lives, they will become more motivated, more committed to the organization, more productive, and more satisfied with their jobs. These benefits don't stop with individuals—when teams are given more control over their work, morale and performance increase.[136]

How do employees become more involved in the workplace?

Examples of Employee Involvement Programs

Let's look at two major forms of employee involvement—participative management and representative participation—in more detail.

Participative Management

The distinct characteristic common to all **participative management** programs is joint decision making, in which subordinates share a significant degree of decision-making power with their immediate superiors. Participative management has, at times, been promoted as the solution for poor morale and low productivity. For participative management to be effective, followers must have trust and confidence in their leaders. Leaders should refrain from coercive techniques and instead stress the organizational consequences of decision making to their followers.[137]

Studies of the participation–performance relationship have yielded mixed findings.[138] Organizations that institute participative management do have higher stock returns, lower turnover rates, and higher estimated labour productivity, although these effects are typically not large.[139] A careful review of the research at the individual level shows participation typically has only a modest influence on employee productivity, motivation, and job satisfaction. Of course, this does not mean participative management cannot be beneficial under the right conditions. However, it's not a sure means for improving performance.

Representative Participation

Almost every country in western Europe requires companies to practise **representative participation**, called "the most widely legislated form of employee involvement around the world."[140] Its goal is to redistribute power within an organization, putting labour on a more equal footing with the interests of management and stockholders by letting employees be represented by a small group of employees who actually participate.

The two most common forms are works councils and board representatives.[141] Works councils are groups of nominated or elected employees who must be consulted when management makes decisions about employees. Board representatives are employees who sit on a company's board of directors and represent the employees' interests.

The influence of representative participation on working employees seems to be minimal.[142] Works councils are dominated by management and have little impact on employees or the organization. While participation might increase the motivation and satisfaction of employee representatives, there is little evidence that this effect trickles down to the employees they represent. Overall, "the greatest value of representative participation is symbolic. If one is interested in changing employee attitudes or in improving organizational performance, representative participation would be a poor choice."[143]

employee involvement A participative process that uses the input of employees and is intended to increase employee commitment to an organization's success.

participative management A process in which subordinates share a significant degree of decision-making power with their immediate superiors.

representative participation A system in which employees participate in organizational decision making through a small group of representative employees.

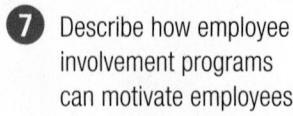

7 Describe how employee involvement programs can motivate employees.

PERSONAL INVENTORY ASSESSMENT

Learn About Yourself
Effective Empowerment and Enagagement

8 Describe how knowledge of what motivates people can be used to make organizations more motivating.

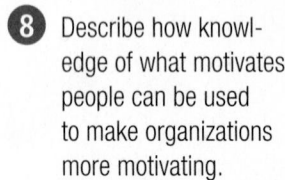

PERSONAL INVENTORY ASSESSMENT

Learn About Yourself
Personal Empowerment Assessment

Linking Employee Involvement Programs and Motivation Theories

Employee involvement draws on a number of the motivation theories we discussed in Chapter 4. Theory Y is consistent with participative management, and Theory X is consistent with the more traditional autocratic style of managing people. In terms of Herzberg's two-factor theory, employee involvement programs could provide intrinsic motivation by increasing opportunities for growth, responsibility, and involvement in the work itself. The opportunity to make and implement decisions—and then see them work out—can help satisfy an employee's needs for responsibility, achievement, recognition, growth, and enhanced self-esteem. Extensive employee involvement programs clearly have the potential to increase employee intrinsic motivation in work tasks. Giving employees control over key decisions, along with ensuring that their interests are represented, can enhance feelings of procedural justice.

Motivation: Putting It All Together

In Chapter 4, we reviewed basic theories of motivation, considering such factors as how needs affect motivation, the importance of linking performance to rewards, and the need for fair process. In this chapter, we considered various ways to pay and recognize people, and looked at job design and creating more flexible workplaces. Three Harvard University professors recently completed two studies that suggest a way to put all of these ideas together to understand (1) what motivates people and (2) how to use this knowledge to make sure that organizational processes motivate.[144]

According to the study authors, research suggests that four basic emotional drives (needs) guide individuals.[145] These are the drive to acquire; the drive to bond; the drive to comprehend; and the drive to defend. People want to acquire any number of scarce goods, both tangible and intangible (such as social status). They want to bond with other individuals and groups. They want to understand the world around them. As well, they want to protect against external threats to themselves and others, and want to ensure justice occurs.

Understanding these different drives makes it possible to motivate individuals more effectively. As the study authors point out, "each drive is best met by a distinct organizational lever." The drive to acquire is met through organizational rewards. The drive to bond can be met by "creat[ing] a culture that promotes teamwork, collaboration, openness, and friendship." The drive to comprehend is best met through job design and creating jobs that are "meaningful, interesting, and challenging." The drive to defend can be accomplished through an organization's performance management and resource allocation processes; this includes fair and transparent processes for managing performance and adequate resources to do one's job. Exhibit 5-6 indicates concrete ways that organizational characteristics can address individual drives.

GLOBAL IMPLICATIONS

Do the motivational approaches we have discussed vary by culture? Because we have covered some very different approaches in this chapter, let's break down our analysis by approach. Not every approach has been studied by cross-cultural researchers, so we consider cross-cultural differences in (1) variable pay, (2) flexible benefits, (3) job characteristics and job enrichment, (4) telecommuting, and (5) employee involvement.

Variable Pay

Globally, around 80 percent of companies offer some form of variable-pay plan. In Latin America, more than 90 percent of companies offer some form of variable-pay

EXHIBIT 5-6 How to Fulfill the Drives That Motivate Employees

DRIVE	PRIMARY LEVER	ACTIONS
Acquire (1)	Reward System	• Sharply differentiate good performers from average and poor performers • Tie rewards clearly to performance • Pay as well as your competitors
Bond (2)	Culture	• Foster mutual reliance and friendship among co-workers • Value collaboration and teamwork • Encourage sharing of best practices
Comprehend (3)	Job Design	• Design jobs that have distinct and important roles in the organization • Design jobs that are meaningful and foster a sense of contribution to the organization
Defend (4)	Performance Management and Resource Allocation Processes	• Increase the transparency of all processes • Emphasize their fairness • Build trust by being just and transparent in granting rewards, assignments, and other forms of recognition

Source: N. Nohria, B. Groysberg, and L.-E. Lee, "Employee Motivation: A Powerful New Model," *Harvard Business Review* 86, no. 7–8 (July–August 2008), p. 82.

plan. Latin American companies also have the highest percentage of total payroll allocated to variable pay, at nearly 18 percent. European and US companies are relatively lower, at about 12 percent.[146] When it comes to executive compensation, Asian companies are outpacing Western companies in their use of variable pay.[147]

Flexible Benefits

Today, almost all major corporations in the United States offer flexible benefits. They are becoming the norm in other countries, too. As mentioned earlier, a recent survey of 211 Canadian organizations found that 60 percent offer flexible benefits.[148] Research in 2013 of companies in the United Kingdom found that only 27 percent have flexible benefits programs in place, up just 8 percent since 2007.[149]

In Exhibit 5-7, we show the link between a country's rating on GLOBE/Hofstede cultural dimensions, which we discussed in Chapter 3, and its preferences for particular types of rewards. Countries that put a high value on uncertainty avoidance prefer pay based on objective measures, such as skill or seniority, because the outcomes are more certain. Countries that put a high value on individualism place more emphasis on an individual's responsibility for performance that leads to rewards. Countries that put a high value on humane orientation offer social benefits and programs that provide work–family balance, such as child care, maternity leave, and sabbaticals.[150] Also, although vacation is an important reward, taking leisure time appears to be more challenging for North American employees as compared with European employees as *Case Incident—Motivation for Leisure* on page 198 shows. Managers who receive overseas assignments should consider a country's cultural orientation when designing and implementing reward practices.

EXHIBIT 5-7 Reward Preferences in Different Countries

GLOBE/Hofstede Cultural Dimension	Reward Preference	Examples
High uncertainty avoidance	Certainty in compensation systems: • Seniority-based pay • Skill-based pay	Greece, Portugal, Japan
Individualism	Compensation based on individual performance: • Pay for performance • Individual incentives • Stock options	Australia, United Kingdom, United States
Humane orientation (Hofstede's masculinity vs. femininity dimension)	Social benefits and programs: • Flexible benefits • Workplace child-care programs • Career-break schemes • Maternity leave programs	Sweden, Norway, the Netherlands

Source: Based on R. S. Schuler and N. Rogovsky, "Understanding Compensation Practice Variations across Firms: The Impact of National Culture," *Journal of International Business Studies* 29, no. 1 (First Quarter 1998), pp. 159–177.

Job Characteristics and Job Enrichment

A few studies have tested the JCM in different cultures, but the results are not very consistent.[151] One study suggested that when employees are "other oriented" (concerned with the welfare of others at work), the relationship between intrinsic job characteristics and job satisfaction is weaker. The fact that the JCM is relatively individualistic (considering the relationship between the employee and his or her work) suggests that job enrichment strategies may not have the same effects in collectivistic cultures as in individualistic cultures (such as Canada and the United States).[152] However, another study suggests that the degree to which jobs have intrinsic job characteristics predicted job satisfaction and job involvement equally well for US, Japanese, and Hungarian employees.[153]

Telecommuting

Does the degree to which employees telecommute vary by nation? Does telecommuting's effectiveness depend on culture? First, one study suggests that telecommuting is more common in the United States than in all the European Union (EU) nations except the Netherlands. In the study, 24.6 percent of US employees engaged in telecommuting, compared with only 13.0 percent of EU employees. Of the EU countries, the Netherlands had the highest rate of telecommuting (26.4 percent); the lowest rates were in Spain (4.9 percent) and Portugal (3.4 percent). What about the rest of the world? Unfortunately, lack of data on telecommuting rates prevents comparison in other parts of the world. Similarly, we don't really know whether telecommuting works better in one country than another. However, the same study that compared telecommuting rates between the United States and the EU determined that employees in Europe appeared to have the same level of interest in telecommuting: regardless of country, interest is higher among employees than among employers.[154]

Employee Involvement

Employee involvement programs differ among countries.[155] A study of four countries, including the United States and India, confirmed the importance of modifying practices to reflect national culture.[156] While US employees readily accepted these programs, managers in India who tried to empower their employees through employee involvement programs were rated low by those employees. These reactions are consistent with India's high power-distance culture, which accepts and expects differences in authority. Similarly, Chinese employees who were very accepting of traditional Chinese values showed few benefits from participative decision making, but employees who were less traditional were more satisfied and had higher performance ratings under participative management.[157] Another study conducted in China, however, showed that involvement increased employees' thoughts and feelings of job security, enhancing their well-being.[158]

Summary

As we have seen in this chapter, the study of what motivates individuals is ultimately the key to organizational performance. Employees whose differences are recognized, who feel valued, and who have the opportunity to work in jobs that are tailored to their strengths and interests will be motivated to perform at the highest levels. Employee participation also can increase employee productivity, commitment to work goals, motivation, and job satisfaction.

LESSONS LEARNED

- Money is not a motivator for all individuals.
- Effective reward systems link pay to performance.
- Jobs characterized by variety, autonomy, and feedback are more motivating.

SNAPSHOT SUMMARY

From Theory to Practice: The Role of Money

Creating Effective Reward Systems
- What to Pay: Establishing a Pay Structure
- How to Pay: Rewarding Individuals through Variable-Pay Programs
- Flexible Benefits: Developing a Benefits Package
- Intrinsic Rewards: Employee Recognition Programs

- Beware the Signals That Are Sent by Rewards
- Can We Eliminate Rewards?

Motivating by Job Redesign
- The Job Characteristics Model
- Job Redesign in the Canadian Context: The Role of Unions
- How Can Jobs Be Redesigned?
- Relational Job Design

- Alternative Work Arrangements
- Flextime
- The Social and Physical Context of Work

Employee Involvement
- Examples of Employee Involvement Programs
- Linking Employee Involvement Programs and Motivation Theories

Motivation: Putting It All Together

MyManagementLab Study, practise, and explore real business situations with these helpful resources:
- **Study Plan: Check your understanding of chapter concepts with self-study quizzes.**
- **Online Lesson Presentations:** Study key chapter topics and work through interactive assessments to test your knowledge and master management concepts.
- **Videos:** Learn more about the management practices and strategies of real companies.
- **Simulations:** Practise management decision-making in simulated business environments.

P I A PERSONAL INVENTORY ASSESSMENT

OB at Work

for Review

1. What is variable pay? What variable-pay programs are used to motivate employees? What are their advantages and disadvantages?

2. How can flexible benefits motivate employees?

3. What are the motivational benefits of intrinsic rewards?

4. What is the job characteristics model? How does it motivate employees?

5. What are the main ways that jobs can be redesigned? In your view, in what situations would one of the methods be favoured over the others?

6. What are the three alternative work arrangements of flextime, job sharing, and telecommuting? What are the advantages and disadvantages of each?

7. What are employee involvement programs? How might they increase employee motivation?

8. How can motivation theories be used to create more motivating work environments?

for Managers

- Recognize individual differences: Spend the time necessary to understand what is important to each employee. Design jobs to align with individual needs and maximize their motivation potential.

- Give employees firm, specific goals, and provide them with feedback on how well they are doing in pursuit of those goals.

- Allow employees to participate in decisions that affect them. Employees can contribute to setting work goals, choosing their own benefits packages, and solving productivity and quality problems.

- Link rewards to performance and ensure that employees perceive the link between the two.

- Check the system for equity. Employees should perceive that experience, skills, abilities, effort, and other obvious inputs explain differences in performance and hence in pay, job assignments, and other obvious rewards.

for You

- Because the people you interact with appreciate recognition, consider including a brief note on a nice card to show thanks for a job well done. Or you might send a basket of flowers. Sometimes just sending a pleasant, thankful email is enough to make a person feel valued. All of these things are easy enough to do, and appreciated greatly by the recipient.

- If you are working on a team or in a volunteer organization, try to find ways to motivate co-workers using the job characteristics model. For instance, make sure that everyone has some tasks over which they have autonomy, and make sure people get feedback on their work.

- When you are working on a team project, think about whether everyone on the team should get the same reward, or whether rewards should be allocated according to performance. Individual-based performance rewards may decrease team cohesiveness if individuals do not cooperate with one another.

OB *at Work*

"Face-Time" Matters

POINT

Although allowing employees to work from home is gaining popularity, telecommuting is a practice that will only hurt them and their employers.[159] Sure, employees say they are happier when their organization allows them the flexibility to work wherever they choose, but who would not like to hang around at home in their pajamas pretending to work? I know plenty of colleagues who say, with a wink, that they are taking off to "work from home" the rest of the day. Who knows whether they are really contributing?

The bigger problem is the lack of face-to-face interaction between employees. Studies have shown that great ideas are born through interdependence, not independence. It's during those informal interactions around the water cooler or during coffee breaks that some of the most creative ideas arise. If you take that away, you stifle the organization's creative potential.

Trust is another problem. Have you ever trusted someone you have not met? Probably not. Again, face-to-face interactions allow people to establish trusting relationships more quickly, which fosters smoother social interactions and allows the company to perform better.

But enough about employers. Employees also would benefit by working hard at the office. If you are out of sight, you are out of mind. Want that big raise or promotion? You are not going to get it if your supervisor does not even know who you are.

So think twice the next time you either want to leave the office early or not bother coming in at all, to "work from home."

COUNTERPOINT

Please. So-called face-time is overrated. If all managers do is reward employees who hang around the office the longest, they are not being very good managers. Those who brag about the 80 hours they put in at the office (being sure to point out they were there on weekends) are not necessarily the top performers. Being present is not the same thing as being efficient.

Besides, there are all sorts of benefits for employees and employers who take advantage of telecommuting practices. For one, telecommuting is seen as an attractive perk companies can offer. With so many dual-career earners, the flexibility to work from home on some days can go a long way toward achieving a better balance between work and family. That translates into better recruiting and better retention. In other words, you will get and keep better employees if you offer the ability to work from home.

Plus, studies have shown that productivity is *higher*, not lower, when people work from home. This result is not limited to the United States. For example, one study found that Chinese call centre employees who worked from home outproduced their "face-time" counterparts by 13 percent.

You say all these earth-shattering ideas would pour forth if people interacted. I say consider that one of the biggest workplace distractions is chatty co-workers. So, although I concede that there are times when "face-time" is beneficial, the benefits of telecommuting far outweigh the drawbacks.

OB *at Work*

Diagnosing Poor Performance and Enhancing Motivation: Correcting poor performance is a key management responsibility. This instrument helps you assess your abilities in this area.

Effective Empowerment and Engagement: Some engagement and empowerment techniques are more effective than others. Use this scale to see how your approach measures up, and to get some ideas for improvement.

Personal Empowerment Assessment: This self-assessment helps you better understand the extent to which you are empowered in a particular role.

BREAKOUT **GROUP** EXERCISES

Form small groups to discuss the following topics, as assigned by your instructor:

1. How might the job of student be redesigned to make it more motivating?

2. What is your ideal job? To what extent does it match up with the elements of the JCM?

3. Would you prefer working from home or working at the office? Why?

EXPERIENTIAL EXERCISE

Analyzing and Redesigning Jobs

Break into groups of 5 to 7 members each.[160] Each student should describe the worst job he or she has ever had. Use any criteria you want to select 1 of these jobs for analysis by the group.

Members of the group will analyze the job selected by determining how well it scores on the job characteristics model. Use the following scale for your analysis of each job dimension:

$$7 = \textbf{Very high}$$
$$6 = \textbf{High}$$
$$5 = \textbf{Somewhat high}$$
$$4 = \textbf{Moderate}$$
$$3 = \textbf{Somewhat low}$$
$$2 = \textbf{Low}$$
$$1 = \textbf{Very low}$$

The following sample questions can guide the group in its analysis of the job in question:

- *Skill variety.* Describe the different identifiable skills required to do this job. What is the nature of the oral, written, and/or quantitative skills needed? Physical skills? Does the job holder get the opportunity to use all of his or her skills?

- *Task identity.* What is the product that the job holder creates? Is he or she involved in its production from beginning to end? If not, is he or she involved in a particular phase of its production from beginning to end?

- *Task significance.* How important is the product? How important is the job holder's role in producing it? How important is the job holder's contribution to the people he or she works with? If the job holder's job were eliminated, how inferior would the product be?

- *Autonomy.* How much independence does the job holder have? Does he or she have to follow a strict schedule? How closely is he or she supervised?

- *Feedback.* Does the job holder get regular feedback from his or her manager? From peers? From his or her staff? From customers? How about intrinsic performance feedback when doing the job?

Using the formula found on page 181, calculate the job's motivating potential score. Discuss whether you think this score accurately reflects your perceptions of the motivating potential of these professions.

Using the suggestions offered in the chapter for redesigning jobs, describe specific actions that management could take to increase this job's motivating potential.

Calculate the costs to management of redesigning the job in question. Do the benefits exceed the costs?

Conclude the exercise by having a representative of each group share his or her group's analysis and redesign suggestions with the entire class. Possible topics for class discussion might include similarities in the jobs chosen, problems in rating job dimensions, and the cost–benefit assessment of design changes.

ETHICAL **DILEMMA**

Are CEOs Paid Too Much?

Critics have described the astronomical pay packages given to Canadian and American CEOs as "rampant greed."[161] In 2013, the median annual compensation of CEOs in Canada's 100 largest companies was $5.6 million. That means that the compensation of CEOs, which had fallen a bit from 2010 to 2011, is almost back to the levels from before the downturn, when the median CEO earned $5.8 million. The 2013 CEO compensation was 171 times what the average full-time Canadian employee earned in 2013 ($46 634). Canadian CEOs may feel they are underpaid, though, if they compare themselves with a similar group of American CEOs, whose median pay was US$12.75 million in 2012, and 257 times that of the average pay for US employees.

How do you explain such large pay packages for CEOs? Some say that executive compensation represents a classic economic response to a situation in which the demand is great for high-quality top-executive talent, and the supply is low. Other arguments in favour of paying executives millions a year are the need to compensate people for the tremendous responsibilities and stress that go with such jobs; the motivating potential that seven- and eight-figure annual incomes provide to senior executives and those who might aspire to be; and the influence of senior executives on the company's bottom line.

Critics of executive pay practices in Canada and the United States argue that CEOs choose board members whom they can count on to support ever-increasing pay for top management. If board members fail to "play along," they risk losing their positions, their fees, and the prestige and power inherent in board membership.

In addition, it's not clear that executive compensation is tied to firm performance. For example, a 2014 analysis of compensation data by Equilar showed little correlation between CEO pay and company performance. Consider the data in Exhibit 5-8, which illustrates the disconnect that can sometimes happen between CEO compensation

EXHIBIT 5-8   2014 Compensation of Canada's Most Overpaid CEOs*

CEO(s)	Was Paid (2-Year Avg.)	Should Have Been Paid	Amount Overpaid
1. Gerald Schwartz, Onex Corporation, Toronto, Ontario	$19 907 000	$8 668 000	$11 239 000
2. Jim Smith, Thomson Reuters Corp., Toronto, Ontario	$11 659 000	$4 556 000	$7 103 000
3. Scott Saxberg, Crescent Point Energy Corp., Calgary, Alberta	$8 954 000	$2 421 000	$6 533 000
4. Craig Mulhauser, Celestica Inc., Toronto, Ontario	$6 595 000	$3 122 000	$3 473 000
5. Mark Davis, Chemtrade Logistics Income Fund, Toronto, Ontario	$5 042 000	$2 416 000	$2 626 000

*Financial Post Magazine uses a "Bang for the Buck" formula to calculate the amount overpaid, taking into account CEO performance variables.
Source: A Guide to "Using the CEO Scorecard," Financial Post Magazine, November 2014, p. 33; and information in "CEO Scorecard 2014," Financial Post Magazine, November 2014, pp. 34–37.

and firm performance. *Financial Post Magazine* uses a "Bang for the Buck" formula to calculate which CEOs were overpaid (or underpaid), based on their company's performance between 2012 and 2013.

Is high compensation of CEOs a problem? If so, does the blame for the problem lie with CEOs or with the shareholders and boards that knowingly allow the practice? Are Canadian and American CEOs greedy? Are these CEOs acting unethically? Should their pay reflect more closely some multiple of their employees' wages? What do you think?

CASE INCIDENTS

Motivation for Leisure

"When I have time I don't have money. When I have money I don't have time," says Glenn Kelman, CEO of Redfin.[162] He is not alone. While many employees find themselves faced with 60-, 70-, or 80-hour weeks (and sometimes more); others who are unemployed can find themselves with too much time on their hands. Take Dennis Lee, a sales associate whose girlfriend is unemployed. She has time to spare, but he says her unemployment makes it "financially impossible for me to support the both of us, even if we just go on a small trip, and get a small hotel and stay for a couple of days."

Yet some argue that individuals choose to be unemployed to take advantage of social safety nets and enjoy a more leisurely lifestyle. Casey Mulligan, a University of Chicago economist, says, "I estimate that half of the drop in the employment-population ratio came from an expansion of the social safety net."

Those who are employed and who may have the financial means to take a vacation often leave those vacation days on the table. The average Canadian employee receives almost 4 weeks of vacation time a year, and 76 percent take their full vacation time. The average US employee gets 2.6 weeks of vacation a year, yet only 43 percent take that time.

The challenge of taking leisure time does not seem to be a problem for employees in many European countries. Take the French, who get 30 days of vacation and say they take all of them. Employees in Spain, Italy, and Germany get about the same time off. Moreover, if you work in the European Union and get sick on vacation, the European Court of Justice states that you are entitled to take a make-up vacation.

Questions

1. Why do you think North American employees are given less vacation time relative to employees in other countries?

2. Why do you think Canadian workers often do not take all of their allotted vacation time? Are these personal choices, or are they driven more by society, or by organizational culture?

3. If many unemployed are spending around two hours/day looking for work as some research indicates, do you think that means they are enjoying a "leisurely" lifestyle? Why or why not? If unemployed, how would you spend your days?

Attaching the Carrot to the Stick

It seems like common sense that people work harder when there are incentives at stake, but many scholars question this premise.[163] Alfie Kohn has long suggested that employees are "punished by rewards" and urges that organizations avoid tying rewards to performance because of the negative consequences that can result. As an alternative to rewards, some experts recommend that managers foster a positive, upbeat work environment in hopes that enthusiasm will translate into motivation.

Although rewards *can* be motivating, they can reduce employees' intrinsic interest in the tasks they are doing. Along these lines, Mark Lepper of Stanford University found that children rewarded for drawing with felt-tip pens no longer wished to use the pens at all when rewards were removed, whereas children who were not rewarded for using the pens were eager to use them. And neuro-imaging researchers found that when incentives reached a certain threshold, the brain's reward centre began to shut down and people became distracted. According to Vikram Chib, the lead researcher on the project, people begin to worry about losing the carrot when the stakes get too high, which leads to failure.

Rewards can also lead to misbehaviour by employees. Psychologist Edward Deci notes, "Once you start making people's rewards dependent on outcomes rather than behaviors, the evidence is people will take the shortest route to those outcomes." Consider factory employees paid purely based on the number of units they produce. Because only quantity is rewarded, they may neglect quality. Executives rewarded strictly on the basis of the quarterly stock price will tend to ignore the long-term profitability and survival of the firm; they might even engage in illegal or unethical behaviour to increase their compensation.

Some rewards may also have legal implications. An increasing number of companies, such as Whole Foods, are providing financial rewards to employees who meet health goals or participate in wellness programs, but such efforts raise concerns about discrimination against those unable to reach the goals. Incentives might not motivate employees to take a more active role in managing their health in any case. As David Anderson, vice-president and chief health officer at StayWell Health Management, says, "An incentive itself doesn't necessarily buy engagement. It buys compliance."

However, the majority of research cited in this and the previous chapter shows that individuals given rewards for behaviour will be more likely to engage in the rewarded behaviours. It's also unlikely that individuals engaged in very boring, repetitive tasks will lose their intrinsic motivation if the task is rewarded because they never had any intrinsic motivation to begin with. The real issue for managers is finding an appropriate way to reward behaviours so that desired behaviour is increased while less-desired behaviour is decreased.

Questions

1. Do you think that, as a manager, you should use incentives regularly? Why or why not?

2. Can you think of a time in your own life when the possibility of receiving an incentive *reduced* your motivation?

3. What employee behaviours do you think might be best encouraged by offering incentive rewards?

FROM CONCEPTS TO SKILLS

Designing Enriched Jobs

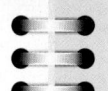

How does management enrich an employee's job? The following suggestions, based on the JCM, specify the types of changes in jobs that are most likely to lead to improving their motivating potential (also see Exhibit 5-9).[164]

1. *Combine tasks.* Managers should seek to take existing and fraction-alized tasks and put them back together to form a new and larger module of work. This increases skill variety and task identity.

2. *Create natural work units.* The creation of natural work units means that the tasks an employee does form an identifiable and mean-ingful whole. This increases employee "ownership" of the work and improves the likelihood that employees will view their work as mean-ingful and important rather than as irrelevant and boring.

3. *Establish client relationships.* The client is the user of the product or service that the employee works on (and may be an "internal

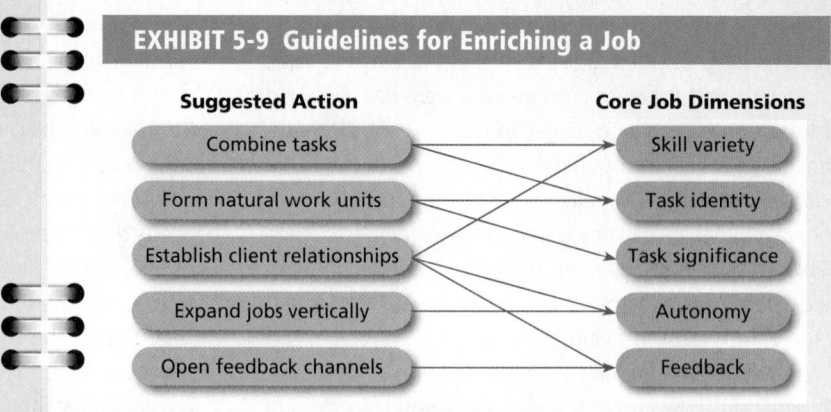

EXHIBIT 5-9 Guidelines for Enriching a Job

Suggested Action	Core Job Dimensions
Combine tasks	Skill variety
Form natural work units	Task identity
Establish client relationships	Task significance
Expand jobs vertically	Autonomy
Open feedback channels	Feedback

Source: J. R. Hackman and J. L. Suttle, eds. *Improving Life at Work* (Santa Monica, CA: Goodyear Publishing, 1977), p. 138.

customer" as well as someone outside the organization). Wherever possible, managers should try to establish direct relationships between employees and their clients. This increases skill variety, autonomy, and feedback for the employee.

4. *Expand jobs vertically.* Vertical expansion gives employees responsibilities and control that were formerly reserved for management. It seeks to partially close the gap between the "doing" and the "controlling" aspects of the job, and it increases employee autonomy.

5. *Open feedback channels.* By increasing feedback, employees not only learn how well they are performing their jobs, but also whether their performance is improving, deteriorating, or remaining at a constant level. Ideally, this feedback about performance should be received directly as the employee does the job, rather than from management on an occasional basis. For instance, at many restaurants you can find feedback cards on the table to indicate the quality of service received during the meal.

Practising Skills

You own and manage Sunrise Deliveries, a small freight transportation company that makes local deliveries of products for your customers. You have a total of nine employees—an administrative assistant, two warehouse personnel, and six delivery drivers.

The drivers' job is pretty straightforward. Each morning they come in at 7:30 a.m., pick up their daily schedule, and then drive off in their preloaded trucks to make their stops. They occasionally will also pick up packages and return them to the Sunrise warehouse, where they will be unloaded and redirected by the warehouse workers.

You have become very concerned with the high turnover among your drivers. Of your current six drivers, three have been working for you less than two months and only one's tenure exceeds six months. This is frustrating because you are paying your drivers more than many of the larger delivery companies like UPS and FedEx. This turnover is getting expensive because you are constantly having to spend time finding and training replacements. It's also hard to develop a quality customer-service program when customers constantly see new faces. When you have asked departing drivers why they are quitting, common complaints include: "There's no room for advancement," "The job is boring," and "All we do is drive." What should you do to solve this problem?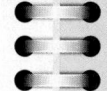

Reinforcing Skills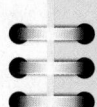

1. Think of the worst job you have ever had. Analyze the job according to the five dimensions identified in the JCM. Redesign the job to make it more satisfying and motivating.

2. Spend one to three hours at various times observing employees in your college dining hall. What actions would you recommend to make these jobs more motivating?

Groups and Teamwork

How can a team come together and perfect a new performance in just a few short months?

Quebec-based Cirque du Soleil is recognized worldwide for the many creative shows it has produced since its start in 1984.[1] The company has 5000 employees, with close to 2000 of them located at its headquarters in Montreal. Its employees represent "more than 50 nationalities and speak 25 different languages," which could present challenges in developing a spirit of teamwork.

Teamwork, however, is what Cirque du Soleil does best. According to Lyn Heward, who was the company's director of creation for many years, "no matter what your product is … your results lie in having a passionate strong team of people. People are the driving force. I think because the Cirque's product is the sum total of people, it's a little more evident." Heward notes the importance of building trust so that everyone can work together interdependently. Guy Laliberté, the founder and majority owner of Cirque, emphasizes that the whole is much bigger than the sum of the parts, as each individual employee is "but a quarter note in a grand symphony."

Cirque assesses 60 to 70 new candidates a year, trying to find individuals who will add to the many talented employees on board. Candidates are evaluated on a number of dimensions, but team skills are important. Specifically, recruiters evaluate whether individuals can effectively work in teams to solve problems and whether they generously share ideas with others.

For teams to excel, a number of conditions need to be met. Effective teams need wise leadership, a variety of resources, and a way to solve problems. Team members need to be dedicated, and they need to build trust. In this chapter, we examine when it's best to have a team, how to create effective teams, and how to deal with diversity on teams.

Images Distribution/Agence Quebec Presse/Newscom

THE BIG IDEA

Effective teams do not simply happen. They require attention to process, team composition, and rewards.

 IS FOR **EVERYONE**

- Ever wonder what causes flurries of activity in groups?

- Should individuals be paid for their "teamwork" or their individual performance?

- Why do some team members seem to get along better than others?

- Why don't some team members pull their weight?

Teams vs. Groups: What Is the Difference?

1 Define *group* and *team*, and identify the different types of teams.

There is some debate whether groups and teams are really separate concepts or whether the two terms can be used interchangeably. We think that there is a subtle difference between the terms. A **group** is two or more people with a common relationship. Thus a group could be co-workers, or people meeting for lunch or standing at the bus stop. Unlike teams, groups do not necessarily engage in collective work that requires interdependent effort.

A **team** is "a small number of people with complementary skills who are committed to a common purpose, performance goals, and approach for which they hold themselves mutually accountable."[2] Groups become teams when they meet the following conditions:[3]

- Team members share *leadership*.
- Both individuals and the team as a whole share *accountability* for the work of the team.
- The team develops its own *purpose* or *mission*.
- The team works on *problem solving* continuously, rather than just at scheduled meeting times.
- The team's measure of *effectiveness* is the team's outcomes and goals, not individual outcomes and goals.

Thus, while not all groups are teams, all teams can be considered groups. Much of what we discuss in this chapter applies equally well to both.

Why Have Teams Become So Popular?

2 Analyze the growing popularity of teams in organizations.

The organization that *does not* use teams has become newsworthy. Teams are everywhere. As organizations have restructured themselves to compete more effectively and efficiently, they have turned to teams as a better way to use employee talents. Management has found that teams are more flexible and responsive to changing events than are traditional departments or other forms of permanent groupings. Teams have the capability to quickly assemble, deploy, refocus, and disband. Teams also can be more motivational. Recall from the job characteristics model discussed in Chapter 5 that having greater task identity is one way of increasing motivation. Teams allow for greater task identity, with team members working on tasks together.

Research suggests that teams typically outperform individuals when the tasks being done require multiple skills, judgment, and experience.[4] However, teams are not necessarily appropriate in every situation. Are teams truly effective? What conditions affect their potential? How do members work together? These are some of the questions we will answer in this chapter.

Types of Teams

3 Contrast the five types of teams.

Teams can make products, provide services, negotiate deals, coordinate projects, offer advice, and make decisions.[5] In this section, first we describe the four most common kinds of teams you are likely to find in organizations:

- Problem-solving (or process-improvement) teams
- Self-managed (or self-directed) teams
- Cross-functional (or project) teams
- Virtual teams

group Two or more people with a common relationship.

team A small number of people who work closely together toward a common objective and are accountable to one another.

EXHIBIT 6-1 Four Types of Teams

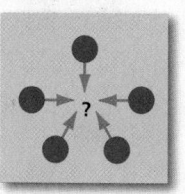 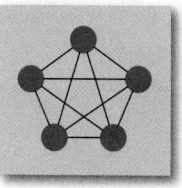 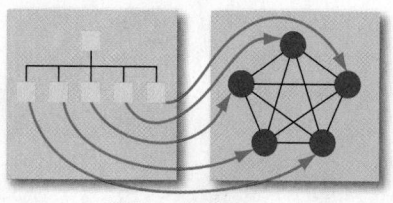 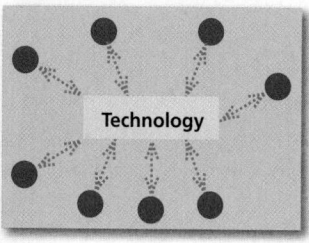

Problem-solving   Self-managed   Cross-functional   Virtual

The types of relationships that members within each team have to one another are shown in Exhibit 6-1. Later in this section, we also describe *multiteam systems*, which use a "team of teams" and are becoming increasingly widespread as work increases in complexity.

Problem-Solving Teams

A **problem-solving (or process-improvement) team** is typically made up of 5 to 12 employees from the same department who meet for a few hours each week to discuss ways of improving quality, efficiency, and the work environment.[6] Such teams can also be planning teams, task forces, or committees that are organized to get tasks done. During meetings, members share ideas or offer suggestions on how to improve work processes and methods. Rarely, however, are these teams given the authority to unilaterally implement any of their suggested actions. Montreal-based Clairol Canada is an exception. When a Clairol employee identifies a problem, he or she has the authority to call together an ad hoc group to investigate, and then define and implement solutions. Clairol presents GOC (Group Operating Committee) Awards to teams for their efforts.

Self-Managed Teams

Problem-solving teams only make recommendations. Some organizations have gone further and created teams that not only solve problems but also implement solutions and take responsibility for outcomes.

A **self-managed (or self-directed) team** is typically made up of 10 to 15 employees. The employees perform highly related or interdependent jobs and take on many of the responsibilities of their managers.[7] Typically, this includes planning and scheduling of work, assigning tasks to members, making operating decisions, taking action on problems, and working with suppliers and customers. Fully self-managed teams even select their own members and leader and have the members evaluate one another's performance. Supervisory positions can take on decreased importance and may even be eliminated.

Research on the effectiveness of self-managed work teams has not been uniformly positive.[8] When disputes arise, members stop cooperating and power struggles ensue, which leads to lower group performance.[9] However, when team members feel confident that they can speak up without being embarrassed, rejected, or punished by other team members—in other words, when they feel psychologically safe—conflict is actually beneficial and boosts performance.[10] In addition, one study of 45 self-managing teams of factory employees found that when team members perceived that economic rewards such as pay were dependent on input from their teammates, performance improved for both individuals and the team as a whole.[11]

Finally, although individuals on teams report higher levels of job satisfaction compared with other individuals, they also sometimes have higher absenteeism and

⊙ Watch on **MyManagementLab**

CH2MHill: Work Teams

problem-solving (or process-improvement) team A group of 5 to 12 employees from the same department who meet for a few hours each week to discuss ways of improving quality, efficiency, and the work environment.

self-managed (or self-directed) team A group of 10 to 15 employees who take on many of the responsibilities of their former managers.

Alexandra Boulat/Corbis

At the Louis Vuitton factory in Ducey, France, all employees work in problem-solving teams, with each team focusing on one product at a time. Team members are encouraged to suggest improvements in manufacturing work methods and processes as well as product quality. When a team was asked to make a test run on a prototype of a new handbag, team members discovered that decorative studs were causing the bag's zipper to bunch up. The team alerted managers, who had technicians move the studs away from the zipper, which solved the problem.

turnover rates. One large-scale study of labour productivity in British establishments found that although using teams in general does improve labour productivity, no evidence supported the claim that self-managed teams performed better than traditional teams with less decision-making authority.[12] Thus, it appears that for self-managing teams to be advantageous, a number of situational factors must be in place. *Point/Counterpoint* on page 234 considers whether empowerment is key to effective teams.

Cross-Functional Teams

Starbucks created a team of individuals from production, global PR, global communications, and marketing to develop its VIA brand of instant coffee. The team's suggestions resulted in a product that would be cost-effective to produce and distribute and that was marketed with a tightly integrated, multifaceted strategy.[13] This example illustrates the use of **cross-functional (or project) teams**, made up of employees from about the same hierarchical level but different work areas, who come together to accomplish a task.

Cross-functional teams are an effective means for allowing people from diverse areas within an organization (or even between organizations) to exchange information, develop new ideas, solve problems, and coordinate complex projects. Of course, cross-functional teams are not easy to manage.[14] Their early stages of development are often time-consuming as members learn to work with diversity and complexity. It takes time to build trust and teamwork, especially among people from varying backgrounds, with different experiences and perspectives.

Virtual Teams

Problem-solving, self-managed, and cross-functional teams do their work face to face. **Virtual teams** use computer technology to tie together physically dispersed members in order to achieve a common goal.[15] They collaborate online—using communication links such as wide-area networks, videoconferencing, instant messaging, and email—whether

cross-functional (or project) team A group of employees at about the same hierarchical level, but from different work areas, who come together to accomplish a task.

virtual team A team that uses computer technology to tie together physically dispersed members in order to achieve a common goal.

Queen's School of Business started an innovative executive MBA program in 2011 that relies on a virtual team of students. While there are three residential sessions during the program, most courses are taught in virtual boardroom sessions with students participating from home. "The program offers the same real-time connectivity and interactivity as our boardroom learning centres, but offers more accessibility to a top-ranked program to participants who wouldn't otherwise have the time or be able to physically be in a boardroom location on weekends," said Gloria Saccon, director of the executive MBA program.[16]

they are only a room away or continents apart. Virtual teams are so pervasive, and technology has advanced so far, that it's probably a bit of a misnomer to call these teams "virtual." Nearly all teams today do at least some of their work remotely.

Despite becoming more widespread, virtual teams face special challenges. They may suffer because there is less social rapport and less direct interaction among members, leaving some feeling isolated. One study showed that team leaders can reduce feelings of isolation, however, by communicating frequently and consistently with team members so none feel unfairly disfavoured.[17] In addition, evidence from 94 studies entailing more than 5000 groups found that virtual teams are better at sharing unique information (information held by individual members but not the entire group), but they tend to share less information overall.[18] As a result, low levels of virtuality in teams results in higher levels of information sharing, but high levels of virtuality hinder it. At the same time, virtual teams can contribute to environmental sustainability, as *Focus on Ethics* shows.

FOCUS ON ETHICS

Virtual Teams Leave a Smaller Carbon Footprint

Should virtual teams be used even more? Despite being in different countries, or even on different continents, many teams in geographically dispersed locations are able to communicate effectively without meeting face-to-face, thanks to technology such as videoconferencing, instant messaging, and email.[19] In fact, members of some of these virtual teams may never meet each other in person. Although the merits of face-to-face versus electronic communication have been debated, there may be a strong *ethical* argument for virtual teams. Keeping team members where they are, as opposed to having them travel every time

IN **ACTION**
Managing Virtual Teams

Establishing trust and commitment, encouraging communication, and assessing team members pose tremendous challenges for virtual team managers. Here are a few tips to make the process easier:

→ Establish **regular times** for group interaction.

→ Set up **firm rules** for communication.

→ Use **visual forms of communication** where possible.

→ **Copy the style of face-to-face teams**. For example, allow time for informal chitchat and socializing, and celebrate achievements.

→ **Give and receive feedback** and offer assistance on a regular basis. Be persistent with people who are not communicating with you or one another.

→ Agree on **standard technology** so all team members can work together easily.

→ Consider using **360-degree feedback** to better understand and evaluate team members.

→ Provide a **virtual meeting room** via an intranet, website, or bulletin board.

→ Note which employees **effectively use email** to build team rapport.

→ **Smooth the way for the next assignment** if membership on the team, or the team itself, is not permanent.

→ **Be available** to employees, but don't wait for them to seek you out.

→ Encourage **informal, off-line conversation** between team members.[21]

they need to meet, may be a more environmentally responsible choice. A very large proportion of airline, rail, and car transport is for business purposes and contributes greatly to global carbon dioxide emissions. When teams are able to meet virtually rather than face-to-face, they dramatically reduce their "carbon footprint."

Here are several ways that virtual teams can be harnessed for greater sustainability:

1. Encourage all team members to think about whether a face-to-face meeting is really necessary and to try to use alternative communication methods whenever possible.
2. Communicate as much information as possible through virtual means, including email, telephone calls, and videoconferencing.
3. When travelling to team meetings, choose the most environmentally responsible methods possible. Also, check the environmental profile of hotels before booking rooms.
4. If the environmental savings are not enough motivation to reduce travel, consider the financial savings. According to a recent survey, businesses spend about 8 to 12 percent of their entire budget on travel. Communicating electronically can therefore result in two benefits: (a) it's cheaper and (b) it's good for the environment.

For virtual teams to be effective, management should ensure that (1) trust is established among team members (one inflammatory remark in a team member email can severely undermine team trust); (2) team progress is monitored closely (so the team does not lose sight of its goals and no team member "disappears"); and (3) the efforts and products of the virtual team are publicized throughout the organization (so the team does not become invisible).[20] For even more tips, see *OB in Action—Managing Virtual Teams*.

Multiteam Systems

The types of teams we have described so far are typically smaller, standalone teams, although their activities relate to the broader objectives of the organization. As tasks become more complex, teams are often made bigger. However, increases in team size are accompanied by higher coordination demands, creating a tipping point at which the addition of another member does more harm than good. To solve this problem, organizations are employing **multiteam systems**, collections of two or more interdependent teams that share a superordinate goal. In other words, multiteam systems are a "team of teams."[22]

To picture a multiteam system, imagine the coordination of response needed after a major car accident. There is the emergency medical services team, which responds first and transports the injured to the hospital. An emergency room team then takes over, providing medical care, followed by a recovery team. Although the emergency services team, the emergency room team, and the recovery team are technically independent, their activities are interdependent, and the success of one depends on the success of the others. Why? Because they all share the higher goal of saving lives.

multiteam system A collection of two or more interdependent teams that share a superordinate goal; a team of teams.

From Individual to Team Member

> Ellie Syracopoulos is the manager of Cirque du Soleil's graphic communications team.[23] Her team works behind the scenes to create promotional materials that make Cirque du Soleil's "charm jump out from the page." To achieve the high-quality production she expects, Syracopoulos emphasizes a work environment that encourages creativity. She finds that "open communication, flexibility and gratitude" form the building blocks for that environment.
>
> She insists that when her team is working, they must be focused on one another and the job at hand, and not be confronted with external distractions. Her basic instructions to her team are as follows:
>
> - "Turn off email notifications
> - Turn down your phone ringer
> - Do not bring your cell phone to a meeting
> - Block off time each day to focus on hot projects, and stick to it!"
>
> How can individual team members actually become a team?

For either a group or a team to function, individuals have to achieve some balance between their own needs and the needs of the group. When individuals come together to form groups and teams, they bring with them their personalities and all their previous experiences. They also bring their tendencies to act in different ways at different times, depending on the effects that different situations and different people have on them.

One way to think of these differences is in terms of possible pressures that individual group members put on one another through roles, norms, and status expectations, as *OB in the Workplace* indicates. As we consider the process of how individuals learn to work in groups and teams, we will use the terms interchangeably. Many of the processes that each go through are the same, with the major difference being that teams within the workplace are often set up on a nonpermanent basis, in order to accomplish projects.

PERSONAL INVENTORY ASSESSMENT

Learn About Yourself
Team Development Behaviours

 IN THE **WORKPLACE**
Turning Around a Losing Team

Can one star performer make a team successful?   The Winnipeg Blue Bombers won three games in 2013 and 9 of 36 from 2012 to 2013.[24] By early August 2014, though, fans thought maybe the team had turned its fate around, with a 5 to 1 winning record on August 6, the best in the West Division.

The Bombers hired quarterback Drew Willy before the 2014 season started, and he received some of the credit for making a difference, earning two CFL Offensive Player of the Week titles playing for the Bombers. With the early winning streak, head coach Mike O'Shea praised Willy for his leadership and his confidence. "He knows he can do it… his belief in himself, his knowledge that he can get the job done spills over to his teammates. They recognize that he believes they are going to get it done."

Willy's skills and leadership were not enough to lead the Bombers to a winning season, however. The team won just one more game after August 6, losing 12 during the season. Despite the dismal record, sportswriter Gary Lawless noted that "Willy is the future in Winnipeg and this off-season will all be about giving him what he needs to succeed." The general view was that Willy had done all that he could do, but he needed a better team. O'Shea noted, as the team was headed into the last game of the season, that even with a losing record, team members were still expected to give their all in the final game. "They need to come and play… . If we've got the right group of guys who love to play football, then this is another opportunity for them to do what they love to do."

Show how role requirements change in different situations.

Roles

Shakespeare once said, "All the world's a stage, and all the men and women merely players." Using the same metaphor, all group members are actors, each playing a **role**. By this term, we mean a set of expected behaviour patterns of a person in a given position in a social unit. The understanding of role behaviour would be dramatically simplified if each of us could choose one role and play it out regularly and consistently. Instead, we are required to play a number of diverse roles, both on and off our jobs.

As we will see, one of the tasks in understanding behaviour is grasping the role that a person is currently playing. For example, on the job a person might have the roles of electrical engineer, member of middle management, and primary company spokesperson in the community. Off the job, there are still more roles: spouse, parent, church member, food bank volunteer, and coach of the softball team. Many of these roles are compatible; some create conflicts. For instance, how does one's religious involvement influence managerial decisions regarding meeting with clients on the Sabbath? We address role conflict below.

Role Conflict

Most roles are governed by **role expectations**, that is, how others believe a person should act in a given situation. For instance, there are certain expectations about how a manager should act while at work. However, if the manager is also a parent, and that manager's child woke up sick in the morning, the manager may be confronted by conflicting role expectations: go to work or remain with the sick child. This dilemma is role conflict. **Role conflict** arises when an individual finds that complying with one role requirement may make it more difficult to comply with another.[25] At the extreme, it can include situations in which two or more role expectations are mutually contradictory! A great deal of research demonstrates that conflict between work and family roles is one of the most significant sources of stress for most employees.[26]

Most employees are simultaneously in occupations, work groups, divisions, and demographic groups, and these different identities can come into conflict when the expectations of one clash with the expectations of another.[27] During mergers and acquisitions, employees can be torn between their identities as members of their original organization and of the new parent company.[28] Organizations structured around multinational operations also have been shown to lead to dual identification, with employees distinguishing between the local division and the international organization.[29]

 Demonstrate how norms exert influence on an individual's behaviour.

Role Ambiguity

Role ambiguity exists when a person is unclear about the expectations of his or her role. In teams, role ambiguity can lead to confusion, stress, and even bad feelings. For instance, suppose two group members each think that the other one is responsible for preparing the first draft of a report. At the next group meeting, neither brings a draft report, and both are annoyed that the other person did not do the work.

Groups benefit when individuals know their roles. Roles within groups and teams should be balanced. Edgar Schein, professor emeritus of the MIT Sloan School of Management, suggests that **role overload** occurs when what is expected of a person "far exceeds what he or she is able to do."[30] **Role underload** occurs when too little is expected of someone, and that person feels that he or she is not contributing to the group.

role A set of expected behaviours of a person in a given position in a social unit.

role expectations How others believe a person should act in a given situation.

role conflict A situation in which an individual finds that complying with one role requirement may make it more difficult to comply with another.

role ambiguity A person is unclear about his or her role.

role overload Too much is expected of someone.

role underload Too little is expected of someone, and that person feels that he or she is not contributing to the group.

Norms

Have you ever noticed that golfers don't speak while their partners are putting on the green, or that employees don't generally criticize their bosses in public? Why? The answer is "norms"!

Norms are acceptable standards of behaviour within a group that are shared by the group's members. All groups have established norms that tell members what they ought and ought not to do under certain circumstances. When agreed to and accepted by the group, norms act as a means of influencing the behaviour of group members, with a minimum of external controls. Norms differ among groups, communities, and societies, but all of these entities have norms.[31]

Formalized norms are written up in organizational manuals that set out rules and procedures for employees to follow. But, by far, most norms in organizations are informal. You don't need someone to tell you that throwing paper airplanes or engaging in prolonged gossip sessions at the water cooler is an unacceptable behaviour when the "big boss from Toronto" is touring the office. Similarly, we all know that when we are in an employment interview discussing what we did not like about our previous job, there are certain things we should not talk about (such as difficulty in getting along with co-workers or our manager). There are other things it's appropriate to talk about (inadequate opportunities for advancement, or unimportant and meaningless work).

Norms can cover virtually any aspect of group behaviour.[32] Some of the most common norms have to do with issues such as

- *Performance.* How hard to work, the level of output, what kind of quality, levels of tardiness

- *Appearance.* Dress codes, when to look busy, when to "goof off," how to show loyalty

- *Social arrangement.* With whom to eat lunch, whether to form friendships on and off the job

- *Allocation of resources.* Pay, assignments, allocation of tools and equipment

OB in Action—Creating a Team Charter presents a way for teams to develop norms when the team first forms.

The "How" and "Why" of Norms

How do norms develop? Why are they enforced? A review of the research allows us to answer these questions.[34]

Norms typically develop gradually as group members learn what behaviours are necessary for the team to function effectively. Of course, critical events in the group might short-circuit the process and quickly prompt new norms. Most norms develop in one or more of the following four ways:

- *Explicit statements made by a group member.* Often, instructions from the group's supervisor or a powerful member establish norms. The team leader might specifically say that no personal phone calls are allowed during working hours or that coffee breaks must be no longer than 10 minutes.

- *Critical events in the group's history.* These set important precedents. A bystander is injured while standing too close to a machine and, from that point on, members of the work group regularly monitor one another to ensure that no one other than the operator gets within two metres of any machine.

- *Primacy.* The first behavioural pattern that emerges in a group frequently sets team expectations. Groups of students who are friends often choose seats near

OB IN ACTION
Creating a Team Charter

When you form a new team, you may want to develop a team charter, so that everyone agrees on the basic norms for group performance. Consider including answers to the following in your charter:

→ What are team members' **names and contact information** (e.g., phone, email)?

→ How will **communication** among team members take place (e.g., phone, email)?

→ What will the **team ground rules** be (e.g., where and when to meet, attendance expectations, workload expectations)?

→ How will **decisions** be made (e.g., consensus, majority vote, leader rules)?

→ What **potential conflicts** may arise in the team? Among team members?

→ How will **conflicts be resolved** by the group?[33]

---

norms Acceptable standards of behaviour within a group that are shared by the group's members.

one another on the first day of class and become upset if an outsider takes "their" seats in a later class.

- *Carry-over behaviours from past situations.* Group members bring expectations with them from other groups to which they have belonged. Thus, work groups typically prefer to add new members who are similar to current ones in background and experience. This is likely to increase the probability that the expectations they bring are consistent with those already held by the group.

Groups don't establish or enforce norms for every conceivable situation, however. The norms that the groups will enforce tend to be those that are important to them.[35] What makes a norm important?

- *It facilitates the group's survival.* Groups don't like to fail, so they seek to enforce any norm that increases their chances for success. This means that groups try to protect themselves from interference from other groups or individuals.

- *It increases the predictability of group members' behaviours.* Norms that increase predictability enable group members to anticipate one another's actions and to prepare appropriate responses.

- *It reduces embarrassing interpersonal problems for group members.* Norms are important if they ensure the satisfaction of their members and prevent as much interpersonal discomfort as possible.

- *It allows members to express the central values of the group and clarify what is distinctive about the group's identity.* Norms that encourage expression of the group's values and distinctive identity help solidify and maintain the group.

Conformity

As a group member, you desire acceptance by the group. Because of your desire for acceptance, you are susceptible to conforming to the group's norms. Considerable evidence shows that the group can place strong pressures on individual members to change their attitudes and behaviours to conform to the group's standard.[36] There are numerous reasons for conformity, with recent research highlighting the importance of a desire to form accurate perceptions of reality based on group consensus, to develop meaningful social relationships with others, and to maintain a favourable self-concept.

The impact that group pressures for **conformity** can have on an individual member's judgment and attitudes was demonstrated in studies by psychologist Solomon Asch.[37] Asch found that subjects gave answers that they knew were wrong, but that were consistent with the replies of other group members, about 35 percent of the time. The results suggest that group norms can pressure us toward conformity. We desire to be one of the group and avoid being visibly different.

Research by University of British Columbia professor Sandra Robinson and colleague Anne O'Leary-Kelly indicates that conformity may explain why some work groups are more prone to antisocial behaviour than others.[38] Individuals working with others who exhibited antisocial behaviour at work were more likely to engage in antisocial behaviour themselves. Of course, not all conformity leads to negative behaviour. Other research has indicated that work groups can have more positive influences, leading to more pro-social behaviour in the workplace.[39]

Overall, research continues to indicate that conformity to norms is a powerful force in groups and teams.

conformity Adjusting one's behaviour to align with the norms of the group.

Stages of Group and Team Development

As Cirque du Soleil's creative team and cast prepared for the spring 2014 opening of Kurios: Cabinet of Curiosities, they faced a number of questions.[40] What was the show's new director, Michel Laprise, going to be like? Would the show capture the same feeling of wonder Laprise says he experienced when he saw Cirque du Soleil as a little boy? How would the 107 people on tour and 150 local hires in every new city learn to work together? What would it be like to produce a show unlike any other that Cirque had done in the past? To build a successful team that produces a high-quality, creative performance, Cirque's cast members had to go through several stages. So what stages do teams go through as they develop?

6 Identify the five stages of group development.

When people get together for the first time with the purpose of achieving some objective, they discover that acting as a team is not something simple, easy, or genetically programmed. Working in a group or team is often difficult, particularly in the initial stages, when people don't necessarily know one another. As time passes, groups and teams go through various stages of development, although the stages are not necessarily exactly the same for each group or team. In this section, we discuss two models of group development. The five-stage model describes the standardized sequence of stages groups pass through. The punctuated-equilibrium model describes the pattern of development specific to temporary groups with deadlines. These models can be applied equally to groups and teams.

⊙ Watch on **MyManagementLab**

Witness.org—Managing Groups and Teams

The Five-Stage Model

As shown in Exhibit 6-2, the five-stage group-development model characterizes groups as proceeding through the distinct stages of *forming, storming, norming, performing,* and *adjourning*.[41] Although we now know that not all groups pass through these stages in a linear fashion, the five-stage model of group development can still help in addressing

⊙ Simulate on **MyManagementLab**

Teams

EXHIBIT 6-2 Stages of Group Development and Accompanying Issues

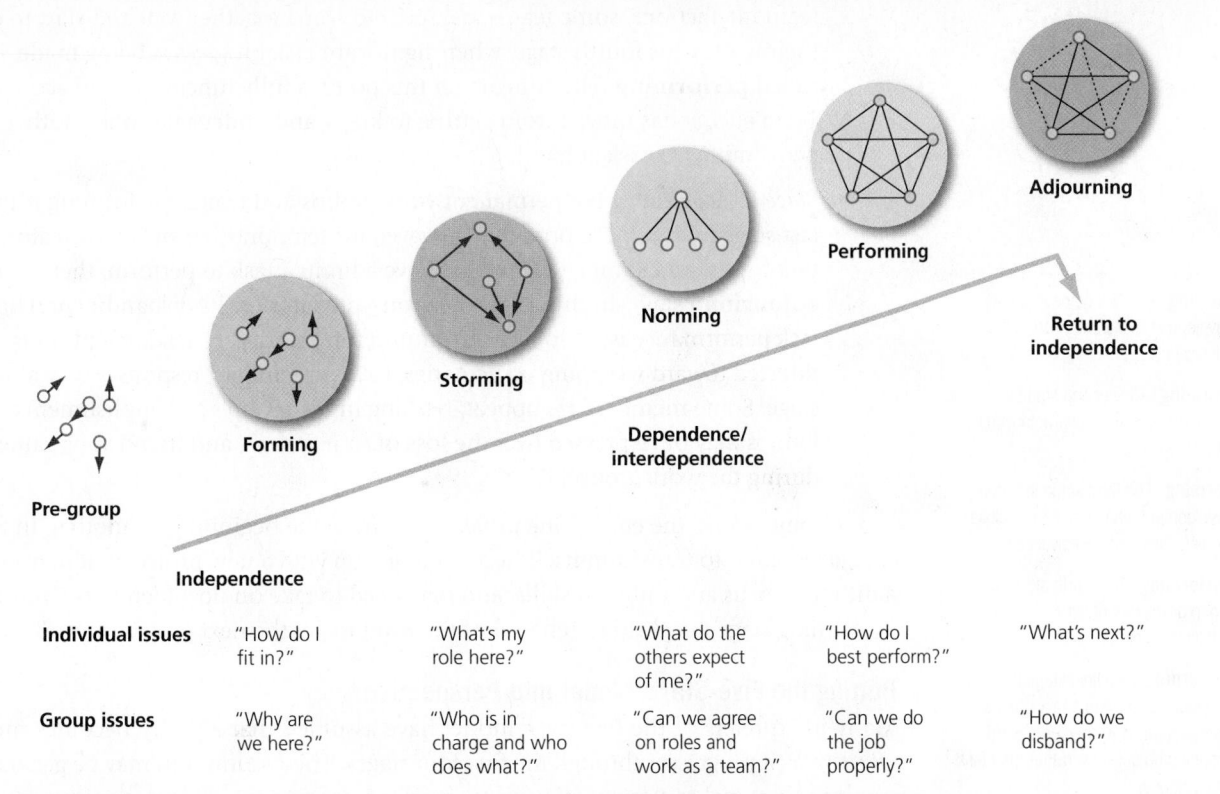

	Forming	Storming	Norming	Performing	Adjourning
Individual issues	"How do I fit in?"	"What's my role here?"	"What do the others expect of me?"	"How do I best perform?"	"What's next?"
Group issues	"Why are we here?"	"Who is in charge and who does what?"	"Can we agree on roles and work as a team?"	"Can we do the job properly?"	"How do we disband?"

any anxieties you might have about working in groups and teams. The model shows how individuals move from being independent to working interdependently with group members.

- *Stage I: Forming.* Think about the first time you met with a new team. Do you remember how some people seemed silent and others felt confused about the task you were to accomplish? Those feelings arise during the first stage of group development, known as **forming**. Forming is characterized by a great deal of uncertainty about the team's purpose, structure, and leadership. Members are "testing the waters" to determine what types of behaviour are acceptable. This stage is complete when members have begun to think of themselves as part of a team.

- *Stage II: Storming.* Do you remember how some people in your team just did not seem to get along, and sometimes power struggles even emerged? These reactions are typical of the **storming** stage, which is one of intragroup conflict. Members accept the existence of the team, but resist the constraints that the team imposes on individuality. Furthermore, there is conflict over who will control the team. When this stage is complete, a relatively clear hierarchy of leadership will emerge within the team.

    Some teams never really emerge from the storming stage, or they move back and forth through storming and the other stages. A team that remains forever planted in the storming stage may have less ability to complete the task because of all the interpersonal problems.

- *Stage III: Norming.* Many teams resolve the interpersonal conflict and reach the third stage, in which close relationships develop and the team demonstrates cohesiveness. There is now a strong sense of team identity and camaraderie. This **norming** stage is complete when the team structure solidifies, and the team has assimilated a common set of expectations of what defines correct member behaviour.

- *Stage IV: Performing.* Next, and you may have noticed this in some of your own team interactions, some teams just seem to come together well and start to do their work. This fourth stage, when significant task progress is being made, is called **performing**. The structure at this point is fully functional and accepted. Team energy has moved from getting to know and understand one another to performing the task at hand.

- *Stage V: Adjourning.* For permanent work groups and teams, performing is the last stage in their development. However, for temporary committees, teams, task forces, and similar groups that have a limited task to perform, there is an **adjourning** stage. In this stage, the group prepares for its disbandment. High task performance is no longer the group's top priority. Instead, attention is directed toward wrapping up activities. Group members' responses vary at this stage. Some members are upbeat, basking in the group's accomplishments. Others may be depressed over the loss of camaraderie and friendships gained during the work group's life.

For some teams, the end of one project may mean the beginning of another. In this case, a team has to transform itself in order to get on with a new project that may need a different focus and different skills, and may need to take on new members. Thus the adjourning stage may lead to renewal of the team to get the next project started.

Putting the Five-Stage Model into Perspective

Many interpreters of the five-stage model have assumed that a group becomes more effective as it progresses through the first four stages. This assumption may be generally true, but what makes a group effective is actually more complex.[42] First, groups proceed

forming The first stage in group development, characterized by much uncertainty.

storming The second stage in group development, characterized by intragroup conflict.

norming The third stage in group development, characterized by close relationships and cohesiveness.

performing The fourth stage in group development, when the group is fully functional.

adjourning The final stage in group development for temporary groups, where attention is directed toward wrapping up activities rather than task performance.

through the stages of group development at different rates. Those with a strong sense of purpose and strategy rapidly achieve high performance and improve over time, whereas those with less sense of purpose actually see their performance worsen over time. Similarly, groups that begin with a positive social focus appear to achieve the "performing" stage more rapidly. Nor do groups always proceed clearly from one stage to the next. Storming and performing can occur simultaneously, and groups can even regress to previous stages.

The five-stage model also ignores organizational context.[43] For instance, a study of a cockpit crew in an airliner found that, within 10 minutes, three strangers assigned to fly together for the first time had become a high-performing team. How could a team come together so quickly? The answer lies in the strong organizational context surrounding the tasks of the cockpit crew. This context provided the rules, task definitions, information, and resources needed for the team to perform. They did not need to develop plans, assign roles, determine and allocate resources, resolve conflicts, and set norms the way the five-stage model predicts.

The Punctuated-Equilibrium Model

Temporary groups with deadlines don't seem to follow the previous model. Studies indicate that temporary groups with deadlines have their own unique sequence of action (or inaction):[44]

- The first meeting sets the group's direction.

- The first phase of group activity is one of inertia.

- A transition takes place exactly when the group has used up half its allotted time.

- This transition initiates major changes.

- A second phase of inertia follows the transition.

- The group's last meeting is characterized by markedly accelerated activity.

This pattern, called the punctuated-equilibrium model, is shown in Exhibit 6-3.[45] It's important for you to understand these shifts in group behaviour, if for no other reason than when you are in a group that is not working well or one that has gotten off to a slow start, you can start to think of ways to help the group move to a more productive phase.

Ever wonder what causes flurries of activity in groups?

EXHIBIT 6-3 The Punctuated-Equilibrium Model

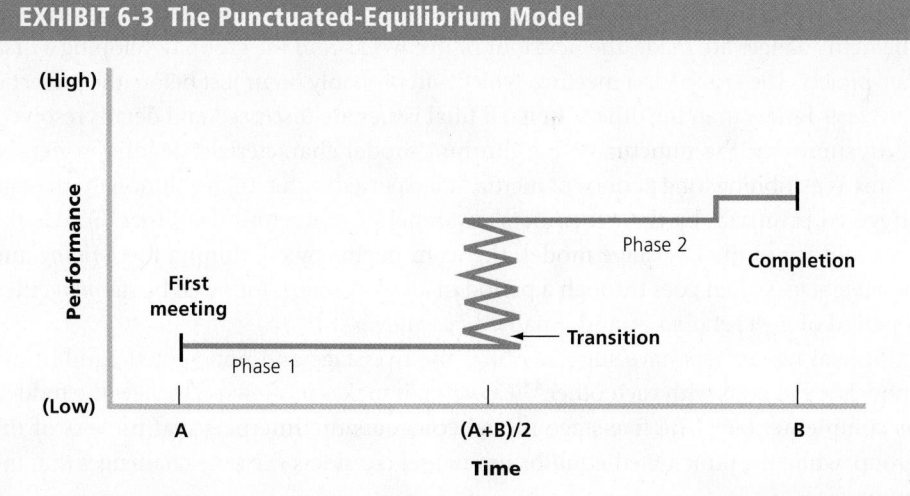

Phase 1

As both a team member and possibly a team leader, it's important that you recognize that the first meeting sets the team's direction. A framework of behavioural patterns and assumptions through which the team will approach its project emerges, sometimes in the first few seconds of the team's life.

Once set, the team's direction becomes "written in stone" and is unlikely to be re-examined throughout the first half of the team's life. This is a period of inertia—that is, the team tends to stand still or become locked into a fixed course of action. Even if it gains new insights that challenge initial patterns and assumptions, the team is incapable of acting on these new insights in Phase 1. You may recognize that in some teams, during the early period of trying to get things accomplished, no one really did his or her assigned tasks. You may also recognize this phase as one where everyone carries out the tasks, but not in a very coordinated fashion. Thus, the team is performing at a relatively low state. This does not necessarily mean that it's doing nothing at all, however.

Phase 2

One of the more interesting discoveries made in work team studies was that teams experienced their transition precisely halfway between the first meeting and the official deadline, whether members spent an hour on their project or six months.[46] The similarity occurred despite the fact that some teams spent as little as an hour on their project, while others spent six months. The midpoint appears to work like an alarm clock, heightening members' awareness that their time is limited and that they need to "get moving." When you work on your next team project, you might want to examine when your team starts to "get moving."

This transition ends Phase 1 and is characterized by a concentrated burst of changes, dropping of old patterns, and adoption of new perspectives. The transition sets a revised direction for Phase 2, which is a new equilibrium or period of inertia. In this phase, the team executes plans created during the transition period. The team's last meeting is characterized by a final burst of activity to finish its work. There have been a number of studies that support the basic premise of punctuated equilibrium, though not all of them found that the transition in the team occurred exactly at the midpoint.[47]

Applying the Punctuated-Equilibrium Model

We can use this model to describe typical experiences of student teams created for doing group term projects. At the first meeting, a basic timetable is established. Members size up one another. They agree they have nine weeks to do their project. The instructor's requirements are discussed and debated. From that point, the group meets regularly to carry out its activities. About four or five weeks into the project, however, problems are confronted. Criticism begins to be taken seriously. Discussion becomes more open. The group reassesses where it has been and aggressively moves to make necessary changes. If the right changes are made, the next four or five weeks find the group developing a first-rate project. The group's last meeting, which will probably occur just before the project is due, lasts longer than the others. In it, all final issues are discussed and details resolved.

In summary, the punctuated-equilibrium model characterizes deadline-oriented teams as exhibiting long periods of inertia, interspersed with brief revolutionary changes triggered primarily by their members' awareness of time and deadlines. To use the terminology of the five-stage model, the team begins by combining the *forming* and *norming* stages, then goes through a period of *low performing*, followed by *storming*, then a period of *high performing*, and, finally, *adjourning*.

Several researchers have suggested that the five-stage and punctuated-equilibrium models are at odds with each other.[48] However, it makes more sense to view the models as complementary: The five-stage model considers the interpersonal process of the group, while the punctuated-equilibrium model considers the time challenges that the group faces.[49]

Creating Effective Teams

Cirque du Soleil has a multicultural workforce, with employees representing over 60 different cultures.[50] The company recognizes that it can use this diversity to its advantage by developing and sharing the cultural assets the employees bring to the workplace. Cirque can draw on Brazilian percussion and capoeira, Australian didgeridoo, Ukrainian and African dancing, Peking opera singing, as well as Kung Fu through the cultural backgrounds of its employees. Diversity can make it harder to be cohesive when teams first develop. Thus, Cirque holds training "boot camps," where new recruits are pushed to their limits. The goal, according to stage director Franco Dragone, is to "turn athletes into artists and form a cohesive team of brothers." What other factors might contribute to the effectiveness of the Cirque du Soleil performers?

7 Identify the characteristics of effective teams.

When we consider team effectiveness, we refer to such objective measures as the team's productivity, managers' ratings of the team's performance, and aggregate measures of member satisfaction. Some of the considerations necessary to create effective teams are outlined next. However, we are also interested in team process. Exhibit 6-4 lists the characteristics of an effective team.

EXHIBIT 6-4 Characteristics of an Effective Team

1. **Clear purpose**	The vision, mission, goal, or task of the team has been defined and is now accepted by everyone. There is an action plan.
2. **Informality**	The climate tends to be informal, comfortable, and relaxed. There are no obvious tensions or signs of boredom.
3. **Participation**	There is much discussion, and everyone is encouraged to participate.
4. **Listening**	The members use effective listening techniques such as questioning, paraphrasing, and summarizing to get out ideas.
5. **Civilized disagreement**	There is disagreement, but the team is comfortable with this and shows no signs of avoiding, smoothing over, or suppressing conflict.
6. **Consensus decisions**	For important decisions, the goal is substantial but not necessarily unanimous agreement through open discussion of everyone's ideas, avoidance of formal voting, or easy compromises.
7. **Open communication**	Team members feel free to express their feelings on the tasks as well as on the group's operation. There are few hidden agendas. Communication takes place outside of meetings.
8. **Clear rules and work assignments**	There are clear expectations about the roles played by each team member. When action is taken, clear assignments are made, accepted, and carried out. Work is distributed among team members.
9. **Shared leadership**	While the team has a formal leader, leadership functions shift from time to time depending on the circumstances, the needs of the group, and the skills of the members. The formal leader models the appropriate behaviour and helps establish positive norms.
10. **External relations**	The team spends time developing key outside relationships, mobilizing resources, and building credibility with important players in other parts of the organization.
11. **Style diversity**	The team has a broad spectrum of team-player types including members who emphasize attention to task, goal setting, focus on process, and questions about how the team is functioning.
12. **Self-assessment**	Periodically, the team stops to examine how well it is functioning and what may be interfering with its effectiveness.

Source: G. M. Parker, *Team Players and Teamwork: The New Competitive Business Strategy* (San Francisco: Jossey-Bass, 1990), Table 2, p. 33. Copyright © 1990 by Jossey-Bass Inc., Publishers. ISBN: 978-1555422578

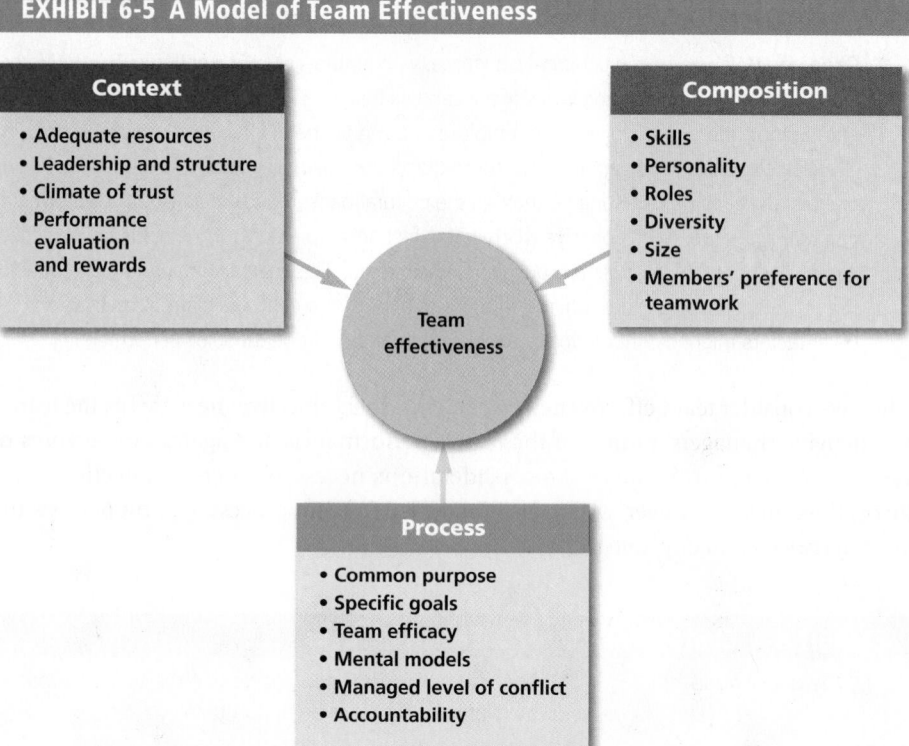

EXHIBIT 6-5 A Model of Team Effectiveness

Context
- Adequate resources
- Leadership and structure
- Climate of trust
- Performance evaluation and rewards

Composition
- Skills
- Personality
- Roles
- Diversity
- Size
- Members' preference for teamwork

Team effectiveness

Process
- Common purpose
- Specific goals
- Team efficacy
- Mental models
- Managed level of conflict
- Accountability

OB IN ACTION
Harming Your Team

→ **Refuse to share** issues and concerns. Team members refuse to share information and engage in silence, avoidance, and meetings behind closed doors where not all members are included.

→ **Depend** too much **on the leader**. Members rely too much on the leader and do not carry out their responsibilities.

→ **Fail to follow through** on decisions. Teams do not take action after decision making, showing that the needs of the team have low priority, or that members are not committed to the decisions that were made.

→ **Hide conflict**. Team members do not reveal that they have a difference of opinion, and this causes tension.

→ **Fail at conflict resolution**. Infighting, put-downs, and attempts to hurt other members damage the team.

→ **Form subgroups**. The team breaks up into smaller groups that put their needs ahead of the team as a whole.[55]

There is no shortage of efforts that try to identify the factors that lead to team effectiveness.[51] However, studies have taken what was once a "veritable laundry list of characteristics"[52] and organized them into a relatively focused model with three general categories summarized in Exhibit 6-5, context, composition, and process.[53]

Keep in mind two caveats as you review the issues that lead to effective teams:

- First, teams differ in form and structure. Since the model we present attempts to generalize across all varieties of teams, you need to be careful not to rigidly apply the model's predictions to all teams.[54] The model should be used as a guide, not as an inflexible prescription.

- Second, the model assumes that it's already been determined that teamwork is preferable over individual work. Creating "effective" teams in situations where individuals can do the job better is equivalent to solving the wrong problem perfectly.

What does *team effectiveness* mean in this model? Typically, it has included objective measures of the team's productivity, managers' ratings of the team's performance, and aggregate measures of member satisfaction. *OB in Action—Harming Your Team* presents activities that can make a team ineffective. You might want to evaluate your own team experience against this checklist to give you some idea of how well your team is functioning, or to understand what might be causing problems for your team. Then consider the factors that lead to more effective teams below. For an applied look at the process of building an effective team, see the *Experiential Exercise* on page 235, which asks you to build a paper tower with teammates and then analyze how the team performed.

Context

The four contextual factors that appear to be most significantly related to team performance are adequate resources, effective leadership, a climate of trust, and a reward system that reflects team contributions.

Wadood Ibrahim (centre), CEO of Winnipeg-based Protegra, a management consulting firm, strongly believes in engaged teams. "We give Protegrans the autonomy and responsibility to do their own work, and as a result, they take on the challenge to do what they need to without strict hierarchical management structures in place."[56]

Adequate Resources

All work teams rely on resources outside the team to sustain them. A scarcity of resources directly reduces the ability of a team to perform its job effectively. As one set of researchers concluded, after looking at 13 factors potentially related to team performance, "perhaps one of the most important characteristics of an effective work group is the support the group receives from the organization."[57] This support includes technology, adequate staffing, administrative assistance, encouragement, and timely information.

Teams must receive the necessary support from management and the larger organization if they are going to succeed in achieving their goals.

Leadership and Structure

Leadership plays a crucial role in the development and success of teams.

Professor Richard Hackman of Harvard University, who is the leading expert on teams, suggests that the role of team leader involves the following:[58]

- Creating a real team rather than a team in name only
- Setting a clear and meaningful direction for the team's work
- Making sure that the team structure will support working effectively
- Ensuring that the team operates within a supportive organizational context
- Providing expert coaching

Leadership is especially important in multiteam systems. Here, leaders need to empower teams by delegating responsibility to them, and they play the role of facilitator, making sure the teams work together rather than against one another.[59] Teams that establish shared leadership by effectively delegating it are more effective than teams with a traditional single-leader structure.[60]

Recent research suggests that women may make better team leaders than men, as *Focus on Research* shows.

A Leader's Gender Can Affect Team Performance

Do men's and women's approaches to team leadership lead to different outcomes? "The more women participating equally in a project, the better the outcome," suggests professor Jennifer Berdahl of the Sauder School of Business at the University of British Columbia.[61] Berdahl's research looked at 169 students enrolled in her organizational behaviour courses. She found that all of the teams started out with

OB IN ACTION
Building Trust

The following actions, in order of importance, help build one's trustworthiness.

→ **Integrity**—built through **honesty** and **truthfulness**.

→ **Competence**—demonstrated by technical and interpersonal **knowledge** and **skills**.

→ **Consistency**—shown by **reliability**, **predictability**, and **good judgment** in handling situations.

→ **Loyalty**—one's willingness to **protect** and **stand up** for another person.

→ **Openness**—one's willingness to **share ideas** and **information** freely.[66]

one person taking a leadership role. However, if the groups were predominantly male, the same person stayed in charge the entire time. In predominantly female teams, women shared leadership roles, and were more egalitarian in how they worked. Male-led teams, whether they were predominantly male groups or mixed-gender groups, received poorer grades on their projects than teams where women shared leadership roles.

Berdahl gives this advice to students: "In a creative project team, it's really important to ensure there is equal opportunity for participation."

A leader, of course, is not always needed. For instance, the evidence indicates that self-managed teams often perform better than teams with formally appointed leaders.[62] Leaders can also obstruct high performance when they interfere with self-managed teams.[63] On self-managed teams, team members absorb many of the duties typically assumed by managers.

Climate of Trust

Members of effective teams trust one another. For team members to achieve a climate of trust, they must feel that the team is capable of getting the task done, and they must believe that "the team will not harm the individual or his or her interests."[64] Interpersonal trust among team members facilitates cooperation, reduces the need to monitor one another's behaviour, and bonds members around the belief that others on the team won't take advantage of them. Team members are more likely to take risks and expose vulnerabilities when they believe they can trust others on their team. Trust allows a team to accept and commit to its leader's goals and decisions. But it's not just the overall level of trust in a team that is important. How trust is dispersed among team members also matters. Trust levels that are asymmetric and imbalanced between team members can mitigate the performance advantages of a high overall level of trust.[65] *OB in Action—Building Trust* shows the dimensions that underlie the concept of trust. *Focus on Diversity* examines how trust varies across cultures.

FOCUS ON DIVERSITY

Developing Team Members' Trust across Cultures

How do you develop trust on multicultural teams? The development of trust is critical in any work situation, but especially in multicultural teams, where differences in communication and interaction styles may lead to misunderstandings, eroding members' trust in one another.[67]

Some studies have shown that overall levels of trust differ across cultures. For example, Germans have been found to be less trusting of people from other countries, such as Mexicans and Czechs. Japanese employees have been found to be more trusting of their North American counterparts than the other way around, but only in long-lasting relationships. Chinese and US employees seem to trust each other equally.

There is some evidence that people from different cultures pay attention to different factors when deciding whether someone is trustworthy. Risk taking appears to be more critical to building trust for US and Canadian employees than for Japanese employees, perhaps reflecting that Canada and the United States are lower in uncertainty avoidance than Japan. Both Chinese and Mexican employees appear to rely more than US employees on emotional cues such as mutual understanding, openness, and social bonding, and less on cognitive cues such as reliability, professionalism, and economic cooperation.

When interacting with others from different cultures, whether in a formal team setting or not, it seems that what drives you to trust your colleagues may differ from what drives your colleagues to trust you, and recognizing these differences can help to facilitate higher levels of trust. _____

For additional information on what leaders can do to improve the climate of trust in their organization, see *OB on the Edge—Trust*, on pages 240–245.

Performance Evaluation and Rewards

How do you get team members to be both individually and jointly accountable? Individual performance evaluations and incentives are not consistent with the development of high-performance teams. So in addition to evaluating and rewarding employees for their individual contributions, management should modify the traditional, individually oriented evaluation and reward system to reflect team performance and focus on hybrid systems that recognize individual members for their exceptional contributions

> Should individuals be paid for their "teamwork" or their individual performance?

and reward the entire group for positive outcomes.[68] Recent research found that when team members did not trust their colleagues' ability, honesty, and dependability, they preferred individual-based rewards rather than team-based rewards. Even when trust improved over time from working together, there was still a preference for individual-based rewards, suggesting that "teams must have a very high level of trust for members to truly embrace group-based pay."[69]

One additional consideration when deciding whether and how to reward team members is the effect of pay dispersion on team performance. Research by Nancy Langton, your Vancouver-based author, shows that when there is a large discrepancy in wages among group members, collaboration is lowered.[70] A study of baseball player salaries also found that teams where players were paid more similarly often outperformed teams with highly paid "stars" and lowly paid "scrubs."[71] How teams are structured and rewarded is the topic of *Focus on Research*.

FOCUS ON RESEARCH

The Impact of Rewards on Team Functioning

Can competitive teams learn to cooperate? Researchers at Michigan State University composed 80 four-person teams from undergraduate business students.[72] In a command-and-control computer simulation developed for the US Department of Defense, each team's mission was to monitor a geographic area, keep unfriendly forces from moving in, and support friendly forces. Team members played on networked computers, and performance was measured by both speed (how quickly they identified targets and friendly forces) and accuracy (the number of friendly fire errors and missed opportunities).

Teams were rewarded either cooperatively (in which case team members shared rewards equally) or competitively (in which case team members were rewarded based on their individual contributions). After playing a few rounds, the reward structures were switched so that the cooperatively rewarded teams were given competitive rewards and the competitively rewarded teams were now cooperatively rewarded.

The researchers found the initially cooperatively rewarded teams easily adapted to the competitive reward conditions and learned to excel. However, the formerly competitively rewarded teams could not adapt to cooperative rewards. It seems teams that start out being cooperative can learn to be competitive, but competitive teams find it much harder to learn to cooperate.

In a follow-up study, researchers found the same results: cooperative teams more easily adapted to competitive conditions than competitive teams did to cooperative conditions. However, they also found competitive teams could adapt to cooperative conditions when given freedom to allocate their roles (as opposed to having the roles assigned). That freedom may lead to intrateam cooperation, and thus the process of structuring team roles helps the formerly competitive team learn to be cooperative. _____

Composition

◉⊣Watch on **MyManagementLab**

The Work Zone Role Plays—Teams

The team composition category includes variables that relate to how teams should be staffed—skills, the ability and personality of team members, the allocation of roles, the diversity of members, the size of the team, and members' preference for teamwork.

Skills

Part of a team's performance depends on the knowledge, skills, and abilities of individual members.[73] It's true that we occasionally read about an athletic team of mediocre players who, because of excellent coaching, determination, and precision teamwork, beat a far more talented group. But such cases make the news precisely because they are unusual. A team's performance is not merely the summation of its individual members' abilities. However, these abilities set limits on what members can do and how effectively they will perform on a team.

Research reveals some insights into team composition and performance. First, when the task entails considerable thought (solving a complex problem such as reengineering an assembly line), high-ability teams—composed of mostly intelligent members—do better than lower-ability teams, especially when the workload is distributed evenly. That way, team performance does not depend on the weakest link. High-ability teams are also more adaptable to changing situations; they can more effectively apply existing knowledge to new problems.

Finally, the ability of the team's leader also matters. Smart team leaders help less-intelligent team members when they struggle with a task. A less intelligent leader can conversely neutralize the effect of a high-ability team.[74]

Exhibit 6-6 identifies some important skills that all team members can apply to help teams function well.

Personality of Members

Teams have different needs, and people should be selected for the team on the basis of their personalities and preferences, as well as the team's needs for diversity and specific roles. We demonstrated in Chapter 2 that personality has a significant influence on individual employee behaviour. This assertion can also be extended to team behaviour.

Many of the dimensions identified in the Big Five Personality Model have been shown to be relevant to team effectiveness. A review of the literature suggests that three of the Big Five traits are especially important for team performance.[75] Specifically, teams that rate higher on mean levels of conscientiousness and openness to experience tend to perform better. Moreover, a 2011 study found that the level of team member agreeableness also matters: Teams did worse when they had one or more highly disagreeable members.[76] Perhaps one bad apple *can* spoil the whole bunch!

Research has provided us with a good idea about why these personality traits are important to teams. Conscientious people are good at backing up other team members,

> Why do some team members seem to get along better than others?

EXHIBIT 6-6 Teamwork Skills

Orients team to problem-solving situation	Assists the team in arriving at a common understanding of the situation or problem. Determines the important elements of a problem situation. Seeks out relevant data related to the situation or problem.
Organizes and manages team performance	Helps team establish specific, challenging, and accepted team goals. Monitors, evaluates, and provides feedback on team performance. Identifies alternative strategies or reallocates resources to address feedback on team performance.
Promotes a positive team environment	Assists in creating and reinforcing norms of tolerance, respect, and excellence. Recognizes and praises other team members' efforts. Helps and supports other team members. Models desirable team member behaviour.
Facilitates and manages task conflict	Encourages desirable and discourages undesirable team conflict. Recognizes the type and source of conflict confronting the team and implements an appropriate resolution strategy. Employs "win-win" negotiation strategies to resolve team conflicts.
Appropriately promotes perspective	Defends stated preferences, argues for a particular point of view, and withstands pressure to change position for another that is not supported by logical or knowledge-based arguments. Changes or modifies position if a defensible argument is made by another team member. Projects courtesy and friendliness to others while arguing position.

Source: G. Chen, L. M. Donahue, and R. J. Klimoski, "Training Undergraduates to Work in Organizational Teams," *Academy of Management Learning & Education* 3, no. 1 (March 2004), p. 40.

and they are also good at sensing when their support is truly needed. One study found that specific behavioural tendencies such as personal organization, cognitive structuring, achievement orientation, and endurance were all related to higher levels of team performance.[77] Open team members communicate better with one another and throw out more ideas, which leads teams composed of open people to be more creative and innovative.[78]

Suppose an organization needs to create 20 teams of 4 people each and has 40 highly conscientious people and 40 who score low on conscientiousness. Would the organization be better off (a) putting all the conscientious people together (forming 10 teams with the highly conscientious people and 10 teams of members low on conscientiousness) or (b) "seeding" each team with 2 people who scored high and 2 who scored low on conscientiousness?

Perhaps surprisingly, the evidence tends to suggest that option (a) is the best choice; performance across the teams will be higher if the organization forms 10 highly conscientious teams and 10 teams low in conscientiousness. The reason is that a team with varying conscientiousness levels will not work to the peak performance of the highly conscientious members. Instead, a group normalization dynamic (or simple resentment) will complicate interactions and force the highly conscientious members to lower their expectations, reducing the group's performance. In such cases, it does appear to make sense to "put all of one's eggs [conscientious team members] into one basket [into teams with other conscientious members]."[79]

Allocation of Roles

Teams have different needs, and members should be selected to ensure all the various roles are filled. A study of 778 major league baseball teams over a 21-year period highlights the importance of assigning roles appropriately.[80] As you might expect, teams with more experienced and skilled members performed better. However, the experience and skill of those in core roles who handle more of the workflow of the team, and who are central to all work processes (in this case, pitchers and catchers), were especially vital. In other words, put your most able, experienced, and conscientious employees in the most central roles in a team.

EXHIBIT 6-7 Roles Required for Effective Team Functioning

	Function	Description	Example
Roles that build task accomplishment	*Initiating*	Stating the goal or problem, making proposals about how to work on it, setting time limits.	"Let's set up an agenda for discussing each of the problems we have to consider."
	Seeking information and opinions	Asking group members for specific factual information related to the task or problem, or for their opinions about it.	"What do you think would be the best approach to this, Jack?"
	Providing information and opinions	Sharing information or opinions related to the task or problems.	"I worked on a similar problem last year and found…"
	Clarifying	Helping one another understand ideas and suggestions that come up in the group.	"What you mean, Sue, is that we could … ?"
	Elaborating	Building on one another's ideas and suggestions.	"Building on Don's idea, I think we could …"
	Summarizing	Reviewing the points covered by the group and the different ideas stated so that decisions can be based on full information.	Appointing a recorder to take notes on a blackboard.
	Consensus taking	Providing periodic testing on whether the group is nearing a decision or needs to continue discussion.	"Is the group ready to decide about this?"
Roles that build and maintain a team	*Harmonizing*	Mediating conflict among other members, reconciling disagreements, relieving tensions.	"Don, I don't think you and Sue really see the question that differently."
	Compromising	Admitting error at times of group conflict.	"Well, I'd be willing to change if you provided some help on …"
	Gatekeeping	Making sure all members have a chance to express their ideas and feelings and preventing members from being interrupted.	"Sue, we haven't heard from you on this issue."
	Encouraging	Helping a group member make his or her point. Establishing a climate of acceptance in the group.	"I think what you started to say is important, Jack. Please continue."

Source: From Ancona / Kochan / Scully / Van Maane. *Managing for the Future*, 1E. © 1996 South-Western, a part of Cengage Learning, Inc. Reproduced by permission. www.cengage.com/permissions

task-oriented roles Roles performed by group members to ensure that the tasks of the group are accomplished.

maintenance roles Roles performed by group members to maintain good relations within the group.

Within almost any group, two sets of role relationships need to be considered: task-oriented roles and maintenance roles. **Task-oriented roles** are performed by group members to ensure that the tasks of the group are accomplished. These roles include initiators, information seekers, information providers, elaborators, summarizers, and consensus makers. **Maintenance roles** are carried out to ensure that group members maintain good relations. These roles include harmonizers, compromisers, gatekeepers, and encouragers.

Effective teams maintain some balance between task orientation and maintenance of relations. Exhibit 6-7 identifies a number of task-oriented and maintenance behaviours in the key roles that you might find in a team.

On many teams, there are individuals who will be flexible enough to play multiple roles and/or complete one another's tasks. This is an obvious plus to a team because it greatly improves its adaptability and makes it less reliant on any single member.[81] Selecting members who themselves value flexibility, and then cross-training them to be able to do one another's jobs, should lead to higher team performance over time. To increase the likelihood team members will work well together, managers need to understand the individual strengths each person can bring to a team, select members with their strengths in mind, and allocate work assignments that fit with members' preferred styles.

Diversity of Members

Group diversity refers to the presence of a heterogeneous mix of individuals within a group.[82] Individuals can be different not only in functional characteristics (jobs, positions, or work experiences) but also in demographic or cultural characteristics (age, race, sex, and citizenship). The degree to which members of a work unit (group, team, or department) share a common demographic attribute, such as age, gender, race, educational level, or length of service in the organization, is the subject of **organizational demography**. Organizational demography suggests that attributes such as age or the date of joining should help us predict turnover. The logic goes like this: Turnover will be greater among those with dissimilar experiences because communication is more difficult and conflict is more likely. Increased conflict makes membership less attractive, so employees are more likely to quit. Similarly, the losers in a power struggle are more apt to leave voluntarily or be forced out.[83]

Many of us hold the optimistic view that diversity should be a good thing—diverse teams should benefit from differing perspectives and do better. Two meta-analytic reviews of the research literature show, however, that demographic diversity is essentially unrelated to team performance overall, while a third review actually suggests that race and gender diversity are negatively related to team performance.[84] One qualifier is that gender and ethnic diversity have more negative effects in occupations dominated by white or male employees, but in more demographically balanced occupations, diversity is less of a problem. Diversity in function, education, and expertise are positively related to group performance, but these effects are quite small and depend on the situation.

Proper leadership can also improve the performance of diverse teams.[85] One study of 68 teams in China found that teams diverse in terms of knowledge, skills, and ways of approaching problems were more creative, but only when their leaders were transformational and inspiring.[86]

We have discussed research on team diversity in race or gender. But what about diversity created by national differences? Like the earlier research, evidence here indicates that these elements of diversity interfere with team processes, at least in the short term.[87]

Size of the Team

Most experts agree that keeping teams small is a key to improving group effectiveness.[88] Generally speaking, the most effective teams have five to nine members. And experts suggest using the smallest number of people who can do the task. Unfortunately, there is a pervasive tendency for managers to err on the side of making teams too large. While a minimum of four or five may be necessary to develop diversity of views and skills, managers seem to seriously underestimate how coordination problems can dramatically increase as team members are added. When teams have excess members, cohesiveness and mutual accountability decline, social loafing increases, and people communicate less. Members of large teams have trouble coordinating with one another, especially under time pressure. When a natural work unit is larger and you want a team effort, consider breaking the unit into subteams if it's difficult to develop effective coordination processes.[89] Uneven numbers in teams may help provide a mechanism to break ties and resolve conflicts, while an even number of team members may foster the need to create more consensus.

8 Explain the implications of diversity for group effectiveness.

9 Show how group size affects group performance.

group diversity The presence of a heterogeneous mix of individuals within a group.

organizational demography The degree to which members of a work unit share a common demographic attribute, such as age, gender, race, educational level, or length of service in an organization, and the impact of this attribute on turnover.

Chen Fei/ZUMA Press/Newscom

Although social loafing is consistent with individualistic cultures, it's not consistent with collectivistic societies such as China. The young employees shown here celebrating the opening of a new KFC restaurant in Shanghai are motivated by ingroup goals and perform better in a group than they do by working individually.

social loafing The tendency for individuals to expend less effort when working collectively than when working individually.

Size and Social Loafing One of the most important findings related to the size of a team has been labelled **social loafing**, the tendency for individuals to expend less effort when working collectively than when working individually.[90] It directly challenges the assumption that the productivity of the team as a whole should at least equal the sum of the productivity of each individual in it. Research looking at teams working on a rope-pulling task showed, the larger the team, the less individual effort expended.[91] One person pulling on a rope alone exerted an average of 63 kilograms of force. In groups of three, per-person force dropped to 53 kilograms. And in groups of eight, it fell to only 31 kilograms per person. Other research supports these findings.[92] Total group performance increases with group size, but the addition of new members has diminishing returns on individual productivity. More may be better in the sense that the total productivity of a group of four is greater than that of one or two people, but the individual productivity of each group member declines.

What causes social loafing? It may be due to a belief that others in the team are not carrying their fair share. If you view others as lazy or inept, you can re-establish equity by reducing your effort. But simply failing to contribute may not be enough to be labelled a "free rider." Instead, the group must believe the social loafer is acting in an exploitive manner (benefiting at the expense of other team members).[93] Another explanation for social loafing is the dispersion of responsibility. Because the results of the team cannot be attributed to any single person, the relationship between an individual's input and the team's output is clouded. In such situations, individuals may be tempted to become "free riders" and coast on the team's efforts. In other words, there will be a reduction in efficiency when individuals believe that their contribution cannot be measured. To reduce social loafing, teams should not be larger than necessary, and individuals should be held accountable for their actions. You might also consider the ideas presented on dealing with shirkers in this chapter's *Ethical Dilemma* on page 236. At the same time, some people who seem to be "free riders" fail to speak up at meetings because they are introverted, as *Case Incident—Tongue-Tied in Teams* on page 236 shows.

THE CANADIAN PRESS/AP/Jae C. Hong

At the Olympic Village for the 2010 Winter Games in Vancouver, teams were housed in apartment buildings. In short order, teams put up their country's flags on balconies in a display of team spirit. The Australian team, however, also put up their boxing Kangaroo flag. The International Olympic Committee asked them to take it down because the flag is a commercial trademark, but the team refused, as they viewed it as their good luck charm. Many Canadians in Vancouver sided with the Australians, and the Australians' iconic flag did not come down.

Members' Preference for Teamwork

Not every employee is a team player. Given the option, many employees will select themselves *out* of team participation. When people who would prefer to work alone are required to team up, there is a direct threat to the team's morale.[94] This suggests that, when selecting team members, individual preferences should be considered, as well as abilities, personalities, and skills. High-performing teams are likely to be composed of people who prefer working as part of a team.

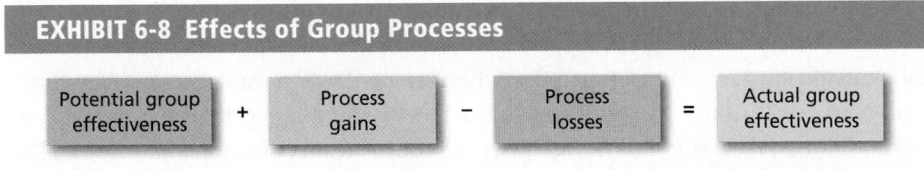

EXHIBIT 6-8 Effects of Group Processes

| Potential group effectiveness | + | Process gains | − | Process losses | = | Actual group effectiveness |

Process

Process variables make up the final component of team effectiveness. The process category includes member commitment to a common purpose, establishment of specific goals, team efficacy, shared mental models, a managed level of conflict, and accountability. These will be especially important in larger teams, and in teams that are highly interdependent.[95]

Why are processes important to team effectiveness? We learned from social loafing that 1 + 1 + 1 does not necessarily add up to 3. When each member's contribution is not clearly visible, individuals tend to decrease their effort. Social loafing, in other words, illustrates a process loss from using teams. But teams should create outputs greater than the sum of their inputs, as when a diverse group develops creative alternatives. Exhibit 6-8 illustrates how group processes can have an impact on a group's actual effectiveness.[96] Scientists often work in teams because they can draw on the diverse skills of various individuals to produce more meaningful research than researchers working independently—that is, they produce positive synergy, and their process gains exceed their process losses.

> Why don't some team members pull their weight?

Common Plan and Purpose

Effective teams begin by analyzing the team's mission, developing goals to achieve that mission, and creating strategies for achieving the goals. Teams that consistently perform better have established a clear sense of what needs to be done and how.[97]

epa european pressphoto agency b.v./Alamy

A study of 23 National Basketball Association teams found that "shared experience"—tenure on the team and time on court—tended to improve turnover and boost win–loss performance significantly. Why do you think teams that stay together longer tend to play better?

Members of successful teams put a tremendous amount of time and effort into discussing, shaping, and agreeing upon a purpose that belongs to them both collectively and individually. This common purpose, when accepted by the team, becomes the equivalent of what GPS is to a ship captain—it provides direction and guidance under any and all conditions. Like a ship following the wrong course, teams that don't have good planning skills are doomed; perfectly executing the wrong plan is a lost cause.[98] Teams should agree on whether their goal is to learn about and master a task or simply to perform the task; evidence suggest that different perspectives on learning versus performance goals lead to lower levels of team performance overall.[99] It appears that these differences in goal orientation produce their effects by reducing discussion and sharing of information. In sum, having all employees on a team strive for the same *type* of goal is important.

Effective teams also show **reflexivity**, meaning that they reflect on and adjust their master plan when necessary. A team has to have a good plan, but it also has to be willing and able to adapt when conditions call for it.[100] Interestingly, some evidence does suggest that teams high in reflexivity are better able to adapt to conflicting plans and goals among team members.[101]

Specific Goals

Successful teams translate their common purpose into specific, measurable, and realistic performance goals. Just as goals can lead individuals to higher performance (see Chapter 4), they can also energize teams. Specific goals facilitate clear communication. They also help teams maintain their focus on achieving results.

Consistent with the research on individual goals, team goals should be challenging. Difficult but achievable goals have been found to raise team performance on those criteria for which they are set. So, for instance, goals for quantity tend to raise quantity, goals for speed tend to raise speed, goals for accuracy tend to raise accuracy, and so on.[102]

Team Efficacy

Effective teams have confidence in themselves. They believe they can succeed. We call this *team efficacy*.[103] Teams that have been successful raise their beliefs about future success, which, in turn, motivates them to work harder. In addition, teams that have a shared knowledge of who knows what within the team can strengthen the link between team members' self-efficacy and their individual creativity because members can more effectively solicit opinions and advice from their teammates.[104]

One of the factors that helps teams build their efficacy is **cohesiveness**—the degree to which members are attracted to one another and are motivated to stay on the team.[105] Although teams differ in their cohesiveness, this factor is important because it's related to team productivity.[106]

Studies consistently show that the relationship of cohesiveness and productivity depends on the performance-related norms established by the group.[107] If performance-related norms are high (for example, high output, quality work, cooperation with individuals outside the group), a cohesive group will be more productive than a less cohesive group. If cohesiveness is high and performance norms are low, productivity will be low. If cohesiveness is low and performance norms are high, productivity increases—but less than in the high cohesiveness–high norms situation. Where cohesiveness and performance-related norms are both low, productivity will tend to fall into the low-to-moderate range. These conclusions are summarized in Exhibit 6-9.

Most studies of cohesiveness focus on socio-emotional cohesiveness, the "sense of togetherness that develops when individuals derive emotional satisfaction from group participation."[108] There is also instrumental cohesiveness: the "sense of togetherness that develops when group members are mutually dependent on one another because they believe they could not achieve the group's goal by acting separately." Teams

PERSONAL INVENTORY ASSESSMENT

Learn About Yourself
Diagnosing the Need for Team Building

reflexivity A team characteristic of reflecting on and adjusting the master plan when necessary.

cohesiveness The degree to which team members are attracted to one another and are motivated to stay on the team.

EXHIBIT 6-9 Relationship among Team Cohesiveness, Performance Norms, and Productivity

	Cohesiveness	
	High	**Low**
High (Performance Norms)	High productivity	Moderate productivity
Low	Low productivity	Moderate to low productivity

need to achieve a balance of these two types of cohesiveness to function well. *OB in Action—Increasing Group Cohesiveness* indicates how to increase both socio-emotional and instrumental cohesiveness.

What, if anything, can management do to increase team efficacy? Two possible options are helping the team to achieve small successes and providing skills training. Small successes build team confidence. As a team develops an increasingly stronger performance record, it also increases the collective belief that future efforts will lead to success. In addition, managers should consider providing training to improve members' technical and interpersonal skills. The greater the abilities of team members, the greater the likelihood that the team will develop confidence and the capability to deliver on that confidence.

mental models Team members' knowledge and beliefs about how the work gets done by the team.

IN **ACTION**
Increasing Group Cohesiveness

To increase socio-emotional cohesiveness:

→ Keep the group relatively **small**.

→ Strive for a **favourable public image** to increase the status and prestige of belonging.

→ Encourage **interaction** and **cooperation**.

→ Emphasize members' **common characteristics** and interests.

→ **Point out environmental threats** (e.g., competitors' achievements) to rally the group.

To increase instrumental cohesiveness:

→ Regularly update and **clarify the group's goal(s)**.

→ Give every group member a **vital "piece of the action."**

→ Channel each group member's special talents toward the **common goal(s)**.

→ **Recognize** and equitably reinforce **every member's contributions**.

→ Frequently remind group members they **need one another** to get the job done.[109]

Mental Models

Effective teams share accurate **mental models**—organized mental representations of the key elements within a team's environment that team members share.[110] If team members have the wrong mental models, which is particularly likely to happen with teams under acute stress, their performance suffers.[111] The similarity of team members' mental models matters, too. If team members have different ideas about how to do things, the teams will fight over how to do things rather than focus on what needs to be done.[112]

Managed Level of Conflict

Conflict on a team is not necessarily bad. As we discuss in Chapter 9, conflict has a complex relationship with performance. *Relationship conflicts*—those based on interpersonal incompatibility, tension, and animosity toward others—are almost always dysfunctional.[113] However, when teams are performing nonroutine activities, disagreements about task content (called *task conflicts*) stimulate discussion, promote critical assessment of problems and options, and can lead to better team decisions. A study conducted in China found that moderate levels of task conflict during the initial phases of team performance were positively related to team creativity, but

IN ACTION
Reducing Team Conflict

→ Work with **more, rather than less, information**, and debate on the basis of facts.

→ Develop **multiple alternatives** to enrich the level of debate.

→ Develop commonly agreed-upon **goals**.

→ Use **humour** when making tough decisions.

→ Maintain a **balanced power** structure.

→ Resolve issues **without forcing consensus**.[118]

both very low and very high levels of task conflict were negatively related to team performance.[114] In other words, both too much and too little disagreement about how a team should initially perform a creative task can inhibit performance.

The way conflicts are resolved can also make the difference between effective and ineffective teams. Effective teams resolved conflicts by explicitly discussing the issues, whereas ineffective teams had conflicts focused more on personalities and the way things were said.[115]

Kathleen Eisenhardt of the Stanford Graduate School of Business and her colleagues studied top management teams in technology-based companies to understand how they manage conflict.[116] Their research identified six tactics that helped teams successfully manage the interpersonal conflict that can accompany group interactions. These are presented in *OB in Action—Reducing Team Conflict*. By handling the interpersonal conflict well, these groups were able to achieve their goals without letting conflict get in the way.

Groups need mechanisms by which they can manage the conflict, however.[117] From the research reported above, we could conclude that sharing information and goals, and striving to be open and get along, are helpful strategies for negotiating our way through the maze of conflict. A sense of humour, and a willingness to understand the points of others without insisting that everyone agree on all points, are also important. Group members should try to focus on the issues, rather than on personalities, and strive to achieve fairness and equity in the group process.

Accountability

As we noted earlier, individuals can engage in social loafing and coast on the group's effort when their particular contributions cannot be identified. Effective teams undermine this tendency by making members individually and jointly accountable for the team's purpose, goals, and approach.[119] Therefore, members should be clear on what they are individually responsible for and what they are jointly responsible for on the team. *From Concepts to Skills* on pages 238–239 discusses how to conduct effective team meetings.

Beware! Teams Are Not Always the Answer

10 Decide when to use individuals instead of teams.

Despite considerable success in the use of teams, they are not necessarily appropriate in all situations. Teamwork takes more time and often more resources than individual work. Teams have increased communication demands, conflicts to be managed, and meetings to be run. So the benefits of using teams have to exceed the costs, and that is not always the case.[120] A study done by Statistics Canada found that the introduction of teamwork lowered turnover in the service industries, for both high- and low-skilled employees. However, manufacturing companies experienced higher turnover if they introduced teamwork and formal teamwork training, compared with not doing so (15.8 percent vs. 10.7 percent).[121]

How do you know if the work of your group would be better done in teams? It's been suggested that three tests be applied to see if a team fits the situation:[122]

- *Can the work be done better by more than one person?* Simple tasks that don't require diverse input are probably better left to individuals.

- *Does the work create a common purpose or set of goals for the people in the group that is more than the sum of individual goals?* For instance, the service departments of many new-car dealers have introduced teams that link customer service personnel, mechanics, parts specialists, and sales representatives. Such teams can better manage collective responsibility for ensuring that customers' needs are properly met.

- *Are the members of the group interdependent?* Teams make sense where there is interdependence among tasks—where the success of the whole depends on the success of each one, *and* the success of each one depends on the success of the others. Soccer, for instance, is an obvious *team* sport because of the interdependence of the players. Swim teams, by contrast, except for relays, rely heavily on individual performance to win a meet. They are groups of individuals performing individually, whose total performance is merely the aggregate summation of their individual performances.

GLOBAL IMPLICATIONS

Research on global considerations in the use of teams is just beginning, but four areas are particularly worth mentioning: the extent of teamwork, self-managed teams, team cultural diversity, and group cohesiveness.

Extent of Teamwork

One study comparing US workers to Canadian and Asian workers revealed that 51 percent of workers in Asian-Pacific countries and 48 percent of Canadian employees report high levels of teamwork. But only 32 percent of US employees say their organization has a high level of teamwork.[123] Thus, Canadians engage in a great deal more teamwork than do Americans.

Self-Managed Teams

Evidence suggests that self-managed teams have not fared well in Mexico, largely due to that culture's low tolerance of ambiguity and uncertainty and employees' strong respect for hierarchical authority.[124] Thus, in countries relatively high in power distance—where roles of leaders and followers are clearly delineated—a team may need to be structured so leadership roles are spelled out and power relationships identified.

Team Cultural Diversity and Team Performance

How do teams composed of members from different countries perform? The evidence indicates that the cultural diversity of team members interferes with team processes, at least in the short term.[125] However, cultural diversity does seem to be an asset for tasks that call for a variety of viewpoints. But culturally heterogeneous team members have more difficulty learning to work with one another and solving problems. The good news is while newly formed culturally diverse teams underperform newly formed culturally homogeneous teams, the differences disappear after about three months.[126] Fortunately, some team performance–enhancing strategies seem to work well in many cultures. One study found that teams in the European Union made up of members from collectivistic and individualistic countries benefited equally from group goals.[127] Read about IBM's use of multicultural project teams in *Case Incident—IBM's Multicultural Multinational Teams* on page 237.

Group Cohesiveness

Researchers studied teams from an international bank with branches in the United States (an individualistic culture) and in Hong Kong (a collectivistic culture) to determine the factors that affected group cohesiveness.[128] Teams were entirely composed of individuals from the branch country. The results showed that, regardless of what culture the teams were from, giving teams difficult tasks and more freedom to accomplish those tasks created a more tight-knit group. Consequently, team performance was enhanced.

However, the teams differed in the extent to which increases in task complexity and autonomy resulted in greater group cohesiveness. Teams in individualistic cultures responded more strongly than did teams in collectivistic cultures, became more united and committed, and, as a result, received higher performance ratings from their supervisors than did teams from collectivistic cultures.

These findings suggest that individuals from collectivistic cultures already have a strong predisposition to work together as a group, so there is less need for increased cohesiveness. However, managers in individualistic cultures may need to work harder to increase team cohesiveness. One way to do this is to give teams more challenging assignments and provide them with more independence.

Summary

Few trends have influenced jobs as much as the massive movement to introduce teams into the workplace. The shift from working alone to working on teams requires employees to cooperate with others, share information, confront differences, and sublimate personal interests for the greater good of the team.

LESSONS LEARNED

- A good team will achieve balance between individual needs and team needs.
- To create effective teams, members should be rewarded for engaging in team behaviour rather than individual behaviour.
- Teams should not be created for tasks that could be better done by individuals.

SNAPSHOT SUMMARY

Teams vs. Groups: What Is the Difference?
- Why Have Teams Become So Popular?
- Types of Teams

From Individual to Team Member
- Roles
- Norms

Stages of Group and Team Development
- The Five-Stage Model
- The Punctuated-Equilibrium Model

Creating Effective Teams
- Context
- Composition
- Process

Beware! Teams Are Not Always the Answer

MyManagementLab

Study, practise, and explore real business situations with these helpful resources:

- **Study Plan:** Check your understanding of chapter concepts with self-study quizzes.
- **Online Lesson Presentations:** Study key chapter topics and work through interactive assessments to test your knowledge and master management concepts.
- **Videos:** Learn more about the management practices and strategies of real companies.
- **Simulations:** Practise management decision-making in simulated business environments.

P I A PERSONAL INVENTORY ASSESSMENT

OB at *Work*

for **Review**

1. Define *group* and *team*. What are the different types of teams?

2. How do you explain the growing popularity of teams in organizations?

3. What are the five types of teams?

4. Do role requirements change in different situations? If so, how?

5. How do group norms influence an individual's behaviour?

6. What are the five stages of group development?

7. What characteristics contribute to the effectiveness of a team?

8. What are the implications of diversity for group effectiveness?

9. How does group size affect group performance?

10. When is work performed by individuals preferred over work performed by teams?

for **Managers**

- Effective teams have common characteristics. They have adequate resources, effective leadership, a climate of trust, and a performance evaluation and reward system that reflects team contributions. These teams have individuals with technical expertise as well as problem-solving, decision-making, and interpersonal skills and the right traits, especially conscientiousness and openness.

- Effective teams also tend to be small—with fewer than 10 people, preferably of diverse backgrounds. They have members who fill role demands and who prefer to be part of a group. The work that members do provides freedom and autonomy, the opportunity to use different skills and talents, and the ability to complete a whole and identifiable task or product. It also has a substantial impact on others.

- Effective teams have members who believe in the team's capabilities and are committed to a common plan and purpose, have an accurate shared mental model of what is to be accomplished, share specific team goals, maintain a manageable level of conflict, and show a minimal degree of social loafing.

- Because individualistic organizations and societies attract and reward individual accomplishments, it can be difficult to create team players in these environments. Try to select individuals who have the interpersonal skills to be effective team players, provide training to develop teamwork skills, and reward individuals for cooperative efforts.

for **You**

- Know that you will be asked to work on teams and groups both during your undergraduate years and later on in life, so understanding how teams work is an important skill to have.

- Think about the roles that you play on teams. Teams need task-oriented people to get the job done, but they also need maintenance-oriented people who help keep people working together and feeling committed to the team.

- Help your team set specific, measurable, realistic goals, as this leads to more successful outcomes.

OB *at* **Work**

To Get the Most Out of Teams, Empower Them

POINT

If you want high-performing teams with members who like one another and their jobs, I have a simple solution.[129] Remove the leash tied to them by management and let them make their own decisions. In other words, empower them. This trend started a long time ago, when organizations realized that creating layers upon layers of bureaucracy thwarts innovation, slows progress to a trickle, and merely provides hoops for people to jump through in order to get anything done.

You can empower teams in two ways. One way is structurally, by transferring decision making from managers to team members and giving teams the official power to develop their own strategies. The other way is psychologically, by enhancing team members' beliefs that they have more authority, even though legitimate authority still rests with the organization's leaders. However, structural empowerment leads to heightened feelings of psychological empowerment, giving teams (and organizations) the best of both worlds.

Research suggests that empowered teams benefit in a number of ways. Members are more motivated. They exhibit higher levels of commitment to the team and to the organization. And they perform much better too. Empowerment sends a signal to the team that it's trusted and does not have to be constantly micromanaged by upper leadership. And when teams get the freedom to make their own choices, they accept more responsibility for and take ownership of both the good and the bad.

Granted, that responsibility also means empowered teams must take the initiative to foster their ongoing learning and development, but teams entrusted with the authority to guide their own destiny do just that. So, do yourself (and your company) a favour and make sure that teams, rather than needless layers of middle managers, are the ones making the decisions that count.

COUNTERPOINT

Empowerment advocates cite the benefits yet neglect the harm that can be done when too much decision-making power is given to teams. They think that, to create effective teams, all you have to do as a leader is nothing because, by empowering teams, you've effectively stepped away as a leader and have lost your authority. Empowerment can do some good in certain circumstances, but it's certainly not a cure-all.

Yes, organizations have become flatter over the past several decades, paving the way for decision-making authority to seep into the lower levels of the organization. But consider that many teams are "empowered" simply because the management ranks have been so thinned that there is no one left to make the key calls. Empowerment is then just an excuse to ask teams to take on more responsibility without an accompanying increase in tangible benefits like pay.

In addition, the organization's leadership already has a good idea of what it would like its teams (and individual employees) to accomplish. If managers leave teams to their own devices, how likely is it that those teams will always choose what the manager wanted? Even if the manager offers suggestions about how the team might proceed, empowered teams can easily ignore that advice. Instead, they need direction on what goals to pursue and how to pursue them. That is what effective leadership is all about.

Consider what happens when decision-making authority is distributed among team members. The clarity of each team member's role becomes fuzzy, and members lack a leader to whom they can go for advice. And finally, when teams are self-managed, they become like silos, disconnected from the rest of the organization and its mission. Simply handing people authority is no guarantee they will use it effectively. So, leave the power to make decisions in the hands of those who have worked their way up the organization. After all, they got to be leaders for a reason.

PERSONAL **INVENTORY** ASSESSMENT

Team Development Behaviours: This self-assessment is designed to help you better understand the contributions you make to building effective teams and teamwork.

Diagnosing the Need for Team Building: Team cohesion is important for optimal team functioning. Use this scale to determine if team-building activities would benefit your group.

Positive Practices Survey: This diagnostic instrument helps you identify the behaviours that are typical of the very highest performing teams and organizations.

BREAKOUT **GROUP** EXERCISES

Form small groups to discuss the following topics, as assigned by your instructor:

1. One of the members of your team continually arrives late for meetings and does not turn drafts of assignments in on time. In general, this group member is engaging in social loafing. What can the members of your group do to reduce social loafing?

2. Consider a team with which you have worked. Was there more emphasis on task-oriented or maintenance-oriented roles? What impact did this have on the group's performance?

3. Identify 4 or 5 norms that a team could put into place near the beginning of its life that might help the team function better over time.

EXPERIENTIAL EXERCISE

The Paper Tower Exercise

Step 1   Each group will receive 20 index cards, 12 paper clips, and 2 marking pens. Groups have 10 minutes to plan a paper tower that will be judged on the basis of 3 criteria: height, stability, and beauty. No physical work (building) is allowed during this planning period.

Step 2   Each group has 15 minutes for the actual construction of the paper tower.

Step 3   Each tower will be identified by a number assigned by your instructor. Each student is to individually examine all the paper towers. Your group is then to come to a consensus as to which tower is the winner (5 minutes). A spokesperson from your group should report its decision and the criteria the group used in reaching it.

Step 4   In your small groups, discuss the following questions (your instructor may choose to have you discuss only a subset of these questions):

   a. What percentage of the plan did each member of your group contribute, on average?

   b. Did your group have a leader? Why or why not?

   c. How did the group generally respond to the ideas that were expressed during the planning period?

   d. To what extent did your group follow the five-stage model of group development?

   e. List specific behaviours exhibited during the planning and building sessions that you felt were helpful to the group. Explain why you found them to be helpful.

OB *at Work*

f. List specific behaviours exhibited during the planning and building sessions that you felt were dysfunctional to the group. Explain why you found them dysfunctional.

Source: This exercise is based on *The Paper Tower Exercise: Experiencing Leadership and Group Dynamics*, by Phillip L. Hunsaker and Johanna S. Hunsaker, unpublished manuscript. A brief description is included in "Exchange," *Organizational Behavior Teaching Journal* 4, no. 2 (1979), p. 49. Reprinted by permission of the authors. The materials list was suggested by Professor Sally Maitlis, Sauder School of Business, University of British Columbia.

ETHICAL **DILEMMA**

Dealing with Shirkers

We have noted that one of the most common problems in groups is social loafing, which means group members contribute less than if they were working on their own. We might call such individuals "shirkers"—those who are contributing far less than other group members.

Most of us have experienced social loafing, or shirking, in groups. And we may even admit to times when we shirked ourselves. We discussed earlier in the chapter some ways of discouraging social loafing, such as limiting group size, holding individuals responsible for their contributions, and setting group goals. While these tactics may be effective, in our experience, many people simply work around shirkers. "We just did it ourselves—it was easier that way," says one group member.

Consider the following questions for dealing with shirking in groups:

1. Do group members have an ethical responsibility to report shirkers to leadership? If you were working on a group project for a class and a group member was social loafing, would you communicate this information to the instructor? Why or why not?

2. Do you think social loafing is always shirking (failing to live up to your responsibilities)? Are there times when shirking is ethical or even justified?

3. Social loafing has been found to be higher in Western, more individualistic nations than in other countries. Do you think this means we should tolerate shirking on the part of North American workers to a greater degree than if it occurred with someone from Asia?

CASE INCIDENTS

Tongue-Tied in Teams

Thirty-one-year-old Robert Murphy has the best intentions to participate in team meetings, but when it's "game time," he chokes.[130] An online marketing representative, Robert cannot be criticized for lack of preparation. After being invited to a business meeting with six of his co-workers and his supervisor, Robert began doing his research on the meeting's subject matter. He compiled notes, arranged them neatly, and walked into the meeting room. As soon as the meeting began, "I just sat there like a lump, fixated on the fact that I was quiet." The entire meeting passed without Robert contributing a word.

Robert is certainly not the first person, nor is he the last, to fail to speak up during meetings. While some employees may actually lack ability, the highly intelligent also freeze. One study found that if we believe our peers are smarter, we experience anxiety that temporarily blocks our ability to think effectively. In other words, worrying about what the group thinks of you makes you dumber. The study also found the effect was worse for women, perhaps because they are more socially attuned.

In other cases, failing to speak up may be attributed to personality. While the extraverted tend to be assertive and assured in group settings, the more introverted prefer to collect their thoughts before speaking—if they speak at all. But again, even those who are extraverted can remain quiet, especially when they feel they cannot contribute.

What to do? Michael Woodward, an organizational psychologist, suggests pairing up with someone more assertive who can pull you into the conversation. Preparation is key, even if it means talking to the person facilitating the meeting beforehand to discuss your thoughts. And finally, the realization that others may be feeling the same anxiety can also help spark the confidence to speak up.

Questions

1. Recall a time when you failed to speak up during a group meeting. What were the reasons for your silence? Are they similar to or different from the reasons discussed here?

2. Beyond the tips provided in this Case Incident, can you think of other strategies that can help the tongue-tied?

3. Imagine that you are leading a team meeting and you notice that a couple of team members are not contributing. What specific steps might you take to try to increase their contributions?

IBM's Multicultural Multinational Teams

As work has become more global, companies are realizing the benefits of composing teams of employees who not only have different cultural backgrounds, but who live in different countries.[131] These multicultural, multinational teams are extremely diverse, allowing companies to leverage widely different points of view about business problems.

One company known for using multicultural, multinational teams is IBM. Although at one time IBM was famous for its written and unwritten rules—such as its no-layoff policy, focus on individual promotions and achievement, expectation of lifetime service at the company, and requirement of suits and white shirts at work—times have changed.

IBM has clients in 170 countries and now does two-thirds of its business outside the United States. As a result, it has overturned virtually all aspects of its old culture. One relatively new focus is on teamwork. To foster appreciation of a variety of cultures and open up emerging markets, IBM sends hundreds of its employees to month-long volunteer project teams in regions of the world where most big companies don't do business. Al Chakra, a software development manager located in Raleigh, North Carolina, was sent to join GreenForest, a furniture manufacturing team in Timisoara, Romania. With Chakra were IBM employees from five other countries. Together, the team helped GreenForest become more computer-savvy to increase its business. In return for the IBM team's assistance, GreenForest was charged nothing. IBM firmly believes these multicultural, multinational teams are good investments, because they help lay the groundwork for uncovering business in emerging economies. IBM is not the only company to use multicul-

tural, multinational teams. Intel Corp., for example, has teams of employees located in the United States, Israel, and Ireland.

To manage these types of teams effectively, leaders must possess certain characteristics. These include obvious factors like openness to cultural diversity and cultural intelligence. According to a survey conducted by Miriam Erez, a faculty member at the Technion-Israel Institute of Technology, it's better for leaders to have a global rather than a cross-cultural perspective. What is the difference? A global perspective means integrating culturally different and geographically different individuals into a single, unified team. Leaders with a global perspective develop a global identity in addition to their local or national identity, while leaders with a cross-cultural perspective do not perceive themselves as belonging to more than one culture.

Questions

1. If you calculate the person-hours devoted to IBM's team projects, they amount to more than 180 000 hours of management time each year. Do you think this is a wise investment of IBM's human resources? Why or why not?

2. Would you like to work on a multicultural, multinational project team? Why or why not?

3. Multicultural project teams often face problems with communication, expectations, and values. How do you think some of these challenges can be overcome?

FROM CONCEPTS TO SKILLS

OB *at Work*

Conducting a Team Meeting

Team meetings have a reputation for inefficiency. For instance, noted Canadian-born economist John Kenneth Galbraith has said, "Meetings are indispensable when you don't want to do anything."

When you are responsible for conducting a meeting, what can you do to make it more efficient and effective? Follow these 12 steps:[132]

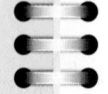

1. *Prepare a meeting agenda.* An agenda defines what you hope to accomplish at the meeting. It should state the meeting's purpose; who will be in attendance; what, if any, preparation is required of each participant; a detailed list of items to be covered; the specific time and location of the meeting; and a specific finishing time.

2. *Distribute the agenda in advance.* Participants should have the agenda sufficiently in advance so they can adequately prepare for the meeting.

3. *Consult with participants before the meeting.* An unprepared participant cannot contribute to his or her full potential. It's your responsibility to ensure that members are prepared, so check with them ahead of time.

4. *Get participants to go over the agenda.* The first thing to do at the meeting is to have participants review the agenda, make any changes, then approve the final agenda.

5. *Establish specific time parameters.* Meetings should begin on time and have a specific time for completion. It's your responsibility to specify these time parameters and to hold to them.

6. *Maintain focused discussion.* It's your responsibility to give direction to the discussion; to keep it focused on the issues; and to minimize interruptions, disruptions, and irrelevant comments.

7. *Encourage and support participation of all members.* To maximize the effectiveness of problem-oriented meetings, each participant must be encouraged to contribute. Quiet or reserved personalities need to be drawn out so their ideas can be heard.

8. *Maintain a balanced style.* The effective group leader pushes when necessary and is passive when need be.

9. *Encourage the clash of ideas.* You need to encourage different points of view, critical thinking, and constructive disagreement.

10. *Discourage the clash of personalities.* An effective meeting is characterized by the critical assessment of ideas, not attacks on people. When running a meeting, you must quickly intercede to stop personal attacks or other forms of verbal insult.

11. *Be an effective listener.* You need to listen with intensity, empathy, and objectivity, and do whatever is necessary to get the full intended meaning from each participant's comments.

12. *Bring proper closure.* You should close a meeting by summarizing the group's accomplishments. Clarify what actions, if any, need to follow the meeting, and allocate follow-up assignments. If any decisions are made, you also need to determine who will be responsible for communicating and implementing them.

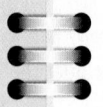

Jameel Saumur is the leader of a five-member project team that has been assigned the task of moving his engineering firm into the booming area of high-speed intercity rail construction. Saumur and his team members have been researching the field, identifying specific business opportunities, negotiating alliances with equipment vendors, and evaluating high-speed rail experts and consultants from around the world. Throughout the process, Tonya Eckler, a highly qualified and respected engineer, has challenged a number of things Saumur said during team meetings and in the workplace. For example, at a meeting two weeks ago, Saumur presented the team with a list of 10 possible high-speed rail projects and started evaluating the company's ability to compete for them. Eckler contradicted virtually all of Saumur's comments, questioned his statistics, and was quite pessimistic about the possibility of getting contracts on these projects. After this latest display of displeasure, two other group members, Bryan Worth and Maggie Ames, are complaining that Eckler's actions are damaging the team's effectiveness. Eckler was originally assigned to the team for her unique expertise and insight. If you had to advise this team, what suggestions would you make to get the team on the right track to achieve its fullest potential?

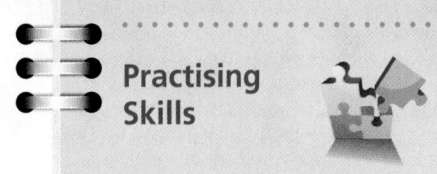

Practising Skills

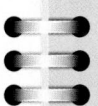

1. Interview three managers at different organizations. Ask them about their experiences in managing teams. Have each describe teams that they thought were effective and why they succeeded. Have each also describe teams that they thought were ineffective and the reasons that might have caused this.

2. Contrast a team you have been in where members trusted one another with another team you have been in where members lacked trust in one another. How did the conditions in each team develop? What were the consequences in terms of interaction patterns and performance?

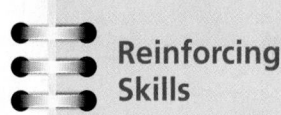

Reinforcing Skills

OB on the EDGE

Paul and Chris Bennett/Environics Communications, Inc./Newscom

Trust

Bruce MacLellan, president and CEO of Toronto-based Environics Communications, finds that building trust in the workplace has a high payoff.[1] In fact, he believes that trust is a crucial element of his public relations firm's success. "Build trust [because] everything you say and do will be watched. . . . Building a stable and trusting atmosphere is essential to other success. People may not always agree, but if they see transparency, consistency and candor, it helps."

Employees (pictured above at a recent company retreat) look forward to the annual ESRA (read it backward) award. The award goes to the person who made the biggest blooper of the year in front of a client or colleague. One employee won for recommending a "suitable" parking spot from which the client got towed. Another employee was caught on a television interview looking like she was falling asleep. "She didn't realize she was on camera and looked like she was falling asleep while our client was speaking," MacLellan says. The award ensures that employees feel safe when they make mistakes and that they can trust their colleagues.

MacLellan also builds trust at Environics by helping employees achieve work–life balance. After working at the firm for four years, Steve Acken, vice-president of digital services, wanted to travel the world and requested four months of unpaid leave. "They held my job for four months and that was everything," said Acken, making him even more committed to the firm.

Trust, or lack of trust, is an increasingly important leadership issue in today's organizations.[2] Trust is fragile. It takes a long time to build, can be easily destroyed, and is hard to regain.[3]

A 2012 survey of Canadians conducted by the Canadian Management Centre and Ipsos Reid found that 61 percent of Canadians don't trust their senior leaders.[4] It's not just senior leaders who get a failing grade for communication. Internal communications are also dissatisfying: only 46 percent of Canadian employees are satisfied.[5]

According to a recent survey by Edmonton-based David Aplin Recruiting, managers and human resources professionals are not aware that a trust deficit exists in the workplace and think that employees quit due to insufficient pay. Likely, this is because employees "aren't going to cite lack of trust as their reason for leaving. It would be experienced by many as burning a bridge on the way out the door," Aplin says.[6]

What Is Trust?

Trust is a psychological state that exists when you agree to make yourself vulnerable to another because you have positive expectations about how things are going to turn out.[7] Trust is a history-dependent process based on relevant but limited samples of experience.[8] It takes time to form, building incrementally and accumulating. Most of us find it hard, if not impossible, to trust someone immediately if we don't know anything about them. At the extreme, in the case of total ignorance, we can gamble, but we cannot trust.[9] But as we get to know someone and the relationship matures, we gain confidence in our ability to form a positive expectation.

There is inherent risk and vulnerability in any trusting relationship. Trust involves making oneself vulnerable, as when, for example, we disclose intimate information or rely on another's promises.[10] By its very nature, trust provides the opportunity for disappointment or to be taken advantage of.[11] But trust is not taking risk per se; rather, it is a willingness to take risk.[12] So when I trust someone, I expect that he or she will not take advantage of me. This willingness to take risks is common to all trust situations.[13]

What Determines Trust?

What are the key characteristics leading us to believe a person is trustworthy? Research has identified three: integrity, benevolence, and ability.[14]

- *Integrity.* Integrity refers to honesty and truthfulness. When 570 white-collar employees were given a list of 28 attributes related to leadership, honesty was rated the most important by far.[15] Integrity also means having consistency between what you do and say.

- *Benevolence.* Benevolence means the trusted person has your interests at heart, even if yours are not necessarily in line with theirs. Caring and supportive behaviour is part of the emotional bond between leaders and followers.

- *Ability.* Ability encompasses an individual's technical and interpersonal knowledge and skills. Even a highly principled person with the best intentions in the world won't be trusted to accomplish a positive outcome for you if you don't have faith in his or her ability to get the job done. Does the person know what he or she is talking about? You are unlikely to listen to or depend upon someone whose abilities you do not believe in.

In addition to these factors, a review of the findings for the effects of leadership on building trust indicates that several characteristics of leadership are most likely to build trust. Leaders who engage in procedural justice (ensuring fair procedures and outcomes) and interactional justice (treating people fairly when procedures are carried out), and who encourage participative decision making and use a transformational leadership style, are most successful at building trust.[16]

Time is another component for building trust. We come to trust people based on observing their behaviour over a period of time.[17] Leaders need to demonstrate they have integrity, benevolence, and ability in situations where trust is important—say, where they could behave opportunistically or let employees down. Trust can be won in the ability domain by demonstrating competence. Recent research with 100 companies around the world suggests that leaders can build trust by shifting their communication style from top-down commands to ongoing organizational dialogue. When leaders regularly create interpersonal conversations with their employees that are intimate, interactive, and inclusive and that intentionally follow an agenda, followers demonstrate trust with high levels of engagement.[18] The inset *What Are the Consequences of Trust* on page 242 illustrates the importance of developing trust in the workplace.

What Are the Consequences of Trust?

Trust between managers and employees has a number of advantages. Here are just a few that research has shown:[19]

- *Trust encourages taking risks.* Whenever employees decide to deviate from the usual way of doing things, or to take their managers' word on a new direction, they are taking a risk. In both cases, a trusting relationship can facilitate that leap.

- *Trust facilitates information sharing.* One big reason employees fail to express concerns at work is that they don't feel psychologically safe revealing their views. When managers demonstrate they will give employees' ideas a fair hearing and actively make changes, employees are more willing to speak out.

- *Trusting groups are more effective.* When a leader sets a trusting tone in a group, members are more willing to help each other and exert extra effort, which increases trust. Members of mistrusting groups tend to be suspicious of each other, constantly guard against exploitation, and restrict communication with others in the group. These actions tend to undermine and eventually destroy the group.

- *Trust enhances productivity.* The bottom-line interest of companies appears to be positively influenced by trust. Employees who trust their supervisors tend to receive higher performance ratings. People respond to mistrust by concealing information and secretly pursuing their own interests.

However, if the transgressor used deception, trust never fully recovers, even when the person deceived is given apologies, promises, or a consistent pattern of trustworthy actions.[23]

- *Mistrusting groups self-destruct.* The corollary to the previous principle is that when group members mistrust one another, they repel and separate. They pursue their own interests rather than the group's. Members of mistrusting groups tend to be suspicious of one another, are constantly on guard against exploitation, and restrict communication with others in the group.

- *Trust increases cohesion.* Trust holds people together.[24] If one person needs help or falters, that person knows that the others will be there to fill in.

- *Mistrust generally reduces productivity.* Leaders who break the psychological contract with workers, demonstrating they are not trustworthy, will find that employees are less satisfied and less committed, have a higher intent toward turnover, engage in less citizenship behaviour, and have lower levels of task performance.[25]

Basic Principles of Trust

Research offers a few principles that help us better understand how trust and mistrust are created:[20]

- *Mistrust drives out trust.* People who are trusting demonstrate their trust by increasing their openness to others, disclosing relevant information, and expressing their true intentions. People who mistrust conceal information and act opportunistically to take advantage of others. A few mistrusting people can poison an entire organization.

- *Trust begets trust.* Exhibiting trust in others tends to encourage reciprocity.

- *Trust can be regained (sometimes).* Leaders who betray trust are especially likely to be evaluated negatively by followers if there is already a low level of leader–member exchange.[21] Once it is violated, trust can be regained, but only in certain situations.[22] If the cause is lack of ability, it's usually best to apologize and recognize you should have done better. When lack of integrity is the problem, apologies don't do much good. Regardless of the violation, saying nothing or refusing to confirm or deny guilt is never an effective strategy for regaining trust. Trust can be restored when the individual observes a consistent pattern of trustworthy behaviours by the transgressor.

What Can Leaders Do to Increase Trust?

Professors Linda Duxbury of Carleton University's Sprott School of Business and Christopher Higgins of the University of Western Ontario's Richard Ivey School of Business found that employees who work in environments characterized by trust and respect report less stress and greater productivity than those who work in environments where trust is lacking.[26]

Increasing Organizational Candour

To develop a culture of candour in your organization, start with yourself and consider these tips.[27]

- *Tell the truth.* Develop a reputation for straight talk.
- *Encourage people to speak truth to power.* People higher up in the organization need to know the truth. Encourage people lower down to be courageous and speak up.
- *Reward contrarians.* Recognize and challenge your own assumptions. Find colleagues to help you do that.
- *Practise having unpleasant conversations.* Deliver bad news kindly so that people do not get hurt unnecessarily.
- *Diversify your sources of information.* Communicate regularly with different groups of employees, customers, and competitors.
- *Admit your mistakes.* If you do so, others will do the same.
- *Build organizational support for transparency.* Hire people who have a reputation for candour elsewhere. Protect whistle-blowers.
- *Set information free.* Share information—unless there is a clear reason not to.

FACT**BOX**

In 2014:

- 53% of Canadians surveyed thought that persons like themselves were credible or extremely credible.
- Only 36% of Canadians surveyed thought that government officials were credible or extremely credible.
- Only 31% of Canadians surveyed thought that information conveyed by CEOs was credible.
- Only 9% of Canadians surveyed said they would trust business leaders to speak the truth, regardless of the complexity or unpopularity of an issue.
- Only 11% of Canadians surveyed said they would trust business leaders to make ethical and moral decisions.[32]

To improve the climate of trust in an organization, it is important to build social capital and build team trust.

Building Social Capital

Maintaining integrity in organizations is a way of building social capital among members of the organization. Scholars use the term *social capital* to refer to strong relationships within organizations that help organizations function smoothly.[28] Social capital is built on trust, and allows deals to move faster, teams to be more productive, and people to perform more creatively.[29]

Some companies seem better able to build social capital than others. The inset *Increasing Organizational Candour* indicates ways that organizations can increase the level of trust available internally.

Building Team Trust

Professor Kurt Dirks of Washington University in St. Louis studied the effect of trust in one's coach on team performance during basketball season for 30 teams in Division I and Division III of the NCAA (National Collegiate Athletic Association).[30] His findings show that basketball players' trust in their coach improves team performance. The two teams with the highest level of trust in their coach had outstanding records for the season he studied. The team with the lowest level of trust won only 10 percent of its games, and the coach was fired at the end of the season.

As these results indicate, team leaders have a significant impact on a team's trust climate. The following points summarize ways to build team trust:[31]

- *Demonstrate that you are working for others' interests, as well as your own.* All of us are concerned with our own self-interest, but if others see you using them, your job, or the organization for your personal goals to the exclusion of your team's, department's, and organization's interests, your credibility will be undermined.

- *Be a team player.* Support your work team both through words and actions. Defend the team and team members when they are attacked by outsiders. Doing so will demonstrate your loyalty to your work group.

- *Practise openness.* Mistrust comes as much from what people don't know as from what they do know. Openness leads to confidence and

trust. So keep people informed, explain your decisions, be candid about problems, and fully disclose relevant information.

- *Be fair.* Before making decisions or taking actions, consider how others will perceive them in terms of objectivity and fairness. Give credit where it's due, be objective and impartial in performance evaluations, and pay attention to equity perceptions in reward distributions.

- *Speak your feelings.* Managers and leaders who convey only hard facts come across as cold and distant. By sharing your feelings, you will encourage others to view you as real and human. They will know who you are, and their respect for you will increase.

- *Show consistency in the basic values that guide your decision making.* Mistrust comes from not knowing what to expect. Take the time to think about your values and beliefs. Then let them consistently guide your decisions. When you know your central purpose, your actions will follow accordingly, and you will project a consistency that earns trust.

- *Maintain confidences.* You trust those you can confide in and rely on. So if people tell you something in confidence, they need to feel assured that you will not discuss it with others or betray that confidence. If people perceive you as someone who "leaks" personal confidences, or someone who cannot be depended upon, you won't be perceived as trustworthy.

- *Demonstrate competence.* Develop the admiration and respect of others by demonstrating technical

The Rules for Trusting Wisely

- *Know yourself.* If you tend to trust the wrong people too quickly, learn to interpret the cues better. If you have difficulty building trusting relationships, learn how to do this.[34]

- *Start small.* Start with small acts of trust, and see if they are reciprocated.

- *Write an escape clause.* Have a plan for how the relationship will end, so that people can trust more fully and with more commitment.

- *Send strong signals.* Signal trustworthiness more clearly and retaliate strongly when your trust is abused.

- *Recognize the other person's dilemma.* The other person is also trying to figure out whether you can be trusted. Reassure that person about whether or how much he or she should trust you.

- *Look at roles as well as people.* A person's role or position can provide some guarantee of his or her expertise and motivation.

- *Remain vigilant and always question.* Do not just engage in due diligence initially. Keep your due diligence up-to-date.

and professional ability and good business sense. Pay particular attention to developing and displaying your communication, team-building, and other interpersonal skills.

- *Work on continuous improvement.* Teams should approach their own development as part of a search for continuous improvement.

High-performance teams are characterized by high mutual trust among members. That is, members believe in the integrity, character, and ability of one another. Since trust begets trust and distrust begets distrust, maintaining trust requires careful attention by leaders and team members.[33] High trust can have a downside, though, if it inspires team members to not pay

attention to one another's work. Team members with high trust may not monitor one another, and if the low monitoring is accompanied by high individual autonomy, the team can perform poorly.[35]

Does Distrust Ever Pay Off?

A recent study by Rotman School of Management professors Nancy Carter and Mark Weber found that people who are more trusting are better able to detect lies in other people.[36] However, Professor Roderick Kramer of the Graduate School of Business at Stanford University suggests that always being completely trusting may not be a desirable strategy. Instead, he offers "tempered trust," which means

to trust wisely and well as a better way for individuals to act. His views are quite contrary to most management literature, which discusses the benefits of trust. Essentially, Kramer argues that distrust can be beneficial.[37]

Kramer believes that we are hard-wired to trust: "trust is our default position; we trust routinely, reflexively, and somewhat mindlessly, across a broad range of social situations."[38] Many times this trust serves us well, but sometimes it lets us down. Witness the many people who were taken in by the charms of New York stock-broker Bernie Madoff and Montreal investment adviser Earl Jones, and lost millions of dollars because of the trust they had in them.

So what does Kramer suggest we do? Start with some *prudent paranoia*. "Prudent paranoia is a form of constructive suspicion regarding the intentions and actions of people and organizations."[39] Kramer argues that such paranoia can be an early warning signal during difficult times. For instance, during times of mergers and acquisitions, employees are naturally distrustful of other departments, and wonder whether they will lose their jobs. Managers may watch out to see who may be threatening their power base. Those with high emotional intelligence are most likely to prac-tise prudent paranoia; after all, one of the signs of emotional intelligence is

F A C E O F F

Trust in others can be dangerous. If you get too close to someone else, that person could take ad-vantage of you, and possibly hurt your chances to get ahead.

Trust improves relationships among individuals. Through trust, produc-tivity can be increased and more creative ideas are likely to come for-ward.

paying attention to one's environment and responding accordingly.

The inset *The Rules for Trusting Wisely* presents some of Kramer's tips for starting on "a lifelong process of learning how to trust wisely and well."[40]

RESEARCH EXERCISES

1. Look for data on the extent to which companies in other coun-tries are trusted by the citizens of those countries. How do they compare with the extent to which Canadians trust companies? Can you draw any inferences about what leads to greater or less trust of corporations?

2. Identify three Canadian organiza-tions that are trying to improve their image to be more trustwor-thy. What effect is this new image having on the organizations' bot-tom lines?

YOUR PERSPECTIVE

1. Why might corporations be will-ing to neglect the importance of trust and instead engage in be-haviours such as those that could lead to corporate scandals?

2. What steps can organizations take to make sure that they are seen as trustworthy by the rest of society?

WANT TO KNOW MORE?

D. DeSteno, "Who Can You Trust?" *Harvard Business Review*, March 2014, pp. 22–23; A. J. C. Cuddy, M. Kohut, and J. Neffinger, "Connect, Then Lead," *Harvard Business Review*, July–August 2013, pp. 54–61; R. M. Kramer, "Rethinking Trust," *Harvard Business Review*, June 2009, p. 71; and J. O'Toole and W. Bennis, "What's Needed Next: A Culture of Candor," *Harvard Business Review*, June 2009, pp. 54–61.

Communication

How can two entrepreneurs best use the web to raise funds for their new invention and stay connected while working in different continents?

LEARNING OUTCOMES

After studying this chapter, you should be able to:

1 Describe the communication process and formal and informal communication.

2 Show how channel richness underlies the choice of communication channel.

3 Identify common barriers to effective communication.

4 Contrast downward, upward, and lateral communication.

5 Compare and contrast formal small-group networks and the grapevine.

6 Show how to overcome the potential problems in cross-cultural communication.

Calvin Chu's fourth-year mechatronics thesis project at the University of Waterloo was the start of a new company, Waterloo-based Palette, which launched in May 2013.[1] Mechatronics combines mechanical systems with electrical/electronic and computer controls to create a complete system. Palette offers buttons, sliders, and dials that allow users to build hardware interfaces for their software. For instance, a DJ might build a controller with dials to adjust music effects, fades, or cue points of songs.

Palette Gear

Chu and classmate Ashish Bidadi, who was a year ahead of Chu at Waterloo, worked together to find funding to get their project off the ground, which meant that they had to be good not only at engineering but also at communicating the value of the idea and the likelihood of its success to potential funders. They took their idea to Kickstarter, a global crowdfunding web-based platform, where a campaign to raise $100 000 ran between November 2013 and January 2014. They went beyond their goal, raising $158 470 in just 45 days.

The two entrepreneurs then applied to be part of HAXLR8R, an accelerator program based in Shenzhen, China, with an office in San Francisco. HAXLR8R provides mentorship, training, and seed funding to entrepreneurs building hardware devices. Most of the successful applicants are from the United States and Europe. Chu and Bidadi were remarkably successful at convincing HAXLR8R that they should be part of the program. One of 10 companies selected in 2013, they were the only team from Canada. Chu and Bidadi recognized that the ability to communicate effectively was key to getting financial support for Palette as well as ensuring the company's viability.

In this chapter, we analyze the power of communication and the ways in which we can make it more effective.

THE BIG IDEA

Real communication requires feedback (both giving it and seeking it).

IS FOR **EVERYONE**

- Does body language really make a difference?
- Ever notice that communicating via email can lead to misunderstandings?
- How can you improve cross-cultural communication?

The Communication Process

① Describe the communication process and formal and informal communication.

Individuals spend nearly 70 percent of their waking hours communicating—writing, reading, speaking, listening—which means that they have many opportunities in which to engage in poor communication. Communication is an important consideration for organizations and individuals alike. Communication is a foundation for many things that happen among groups and within the workplace—from motivating, to providing information, to controlling behaviour, to expressing emotion. Good communication skills are very important to your career success. A recent study of recruiters found that they rated communication skills as *the* most important characteristic of an ideal job candidate.[2]

No group can exist without communication, which is the *transfer* and *understanding* of a message between two or more people. Exhibit 7-1 depicts this **communication process**. The key parts of this model are (1) the sender, (2) encoding, (3) the message, (4) the channel, (5) decoding, (6) the receiver, (7) noise, and (8) feedback. The *sender* initiates a message by encoding a thought. The *message* is the actual physical product of the sender's *encoding*. When we speak, the speech is the message. When we write, the writing is the message. When we gesture, the movements of our arms and the expressions on our faces are the message. The *channel* is the medium through which the message travels. The sender selects it, determining whether to use a formal or informal channel. **Formal channels** are established by the organization and transmit messages related to the professional activities of members. They traditionally follow the authority chain within the organization. Other forms of messages, such as personal or social, follow **informal channels**, which are spontaneous and emerge as a response to individual choices.[3] The *receiver* is the person(s) to whom the message is directed, who must first translate the symbols into understandable form. This step is the *decoding* of the message. *Noise* represents communication barriers that distort the clarity of the message, such as perceptual problems, information overload, semantic difficulties, or cultural differences. The final link in the communication process is a feedback loop. *Feedback* is the check on how successful we have been in transferring our messages as originally intended. It determines whether understanding has been achieved.

The model indicates that communication is both an interactive and iterative process. The sender has to keep in mind the receiver (or audience), and in finalizing the communication may decide to revisit decisions about the message, the encoding, and/or the feedback.

Choosing a Channel

② Show how channel richness underlies the choice of communication channel.

Why do people choose one **channel** of communication over another; for instance, a phone call instead of a face-to-face talk? One answer might be anxiety! An estimated

communication process The steps between a source and a receiver that result in the transfer and understanding of meaning.

formal channels Communication channels established by an organization to transmit messages related to the professional activities of members.

informal channels Communication channels that are created spontaneously and that emerge as responses to individual choices.

channel The medium through which a message travels.

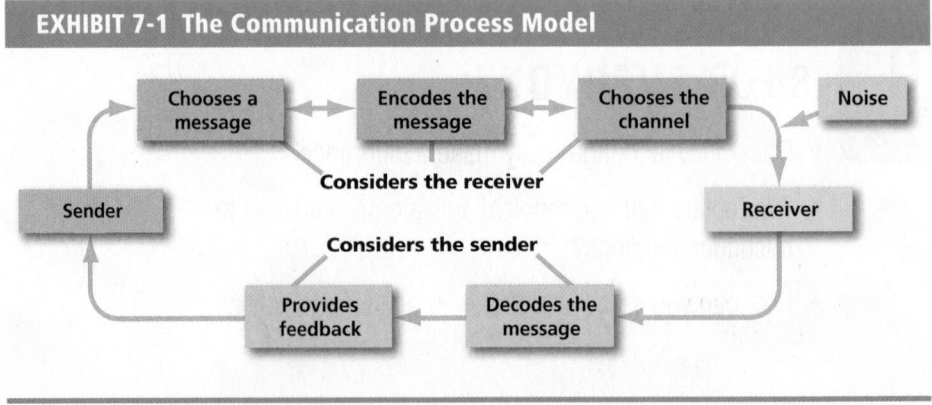

EXHIBIT 7-1 The Communication Process Model

EXHIBIT 7-2 Information Richness of Communication Channels

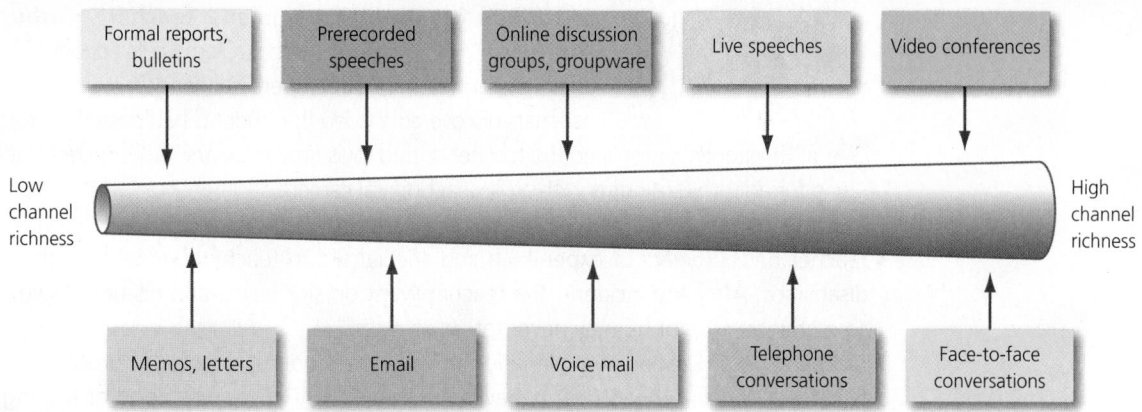

Formal reports, bulletins	Prerecorded speeches	Online discussion groups, groupware	Live speeches	Video conferences

Low channel richness — High channel richness

Memos, letters	Email	Voice mail	Telephone conversations	Face-to-face conversations

Source: R. H. Lengel and R. L. Daft, "The Selection of Communication Media as an Executive Skill," *Academy of Management Executive*, August 1988, pp. 225–232; and R. L. Daft and R. H. Lengel, "Organizational Information Requirements, Media Richness, and Structural Design," *Managerial Science*, May 1996, pp. 554–572. Reproduced from R. L. Daft and R. A. Noe, *Organizational Behavior* (Fort Worth, TX: Harcourt, 2001), p. 311. ISBN: 978-0030316814.

5 to 20 percent of the population[4] suffers from debilitating **communication apprehension**, or anxiety, which is undue tension and anxiety about oral communication, written communication, or both. We all know people who dread speaking in front of a group, but some people may find it extremely difficult to talk with others face to face or become extremely anxious when they have to use the telephone. As a result, they may rely on memos, letters, or email to convey messages when a phone call would not only be faster but also more appropriate.

But what about the 80 to 95 percent of the population who don't suffer from this problem? Is there any general insight we might be able to provide regarding choice of communication channel? A model of media richness has been developed to explain channel selection among managers.[5]

Channels differ in their capacity to convey information. Some are *rich* in that they have the ability to (1) handle multiple cues simultaneously, (2) facilitate rapid feedback, and (3) be very personal. Others are *lean* in that they score low on these three factors. As Exhibit 7-2 illustrates, face-to-face conversations score highest in terms of **channel richness** because they transmit the most information per communication episode—multiple information cues (words, postures, facial expressions, gestures, intonations), immediate feedback (both verbal and nonverbal), and the personal touch of being present. *Focus on Research* explains why face-to-face meetings are so important.

⊙ Watch on MyManagementLab

The Work Zone Role Plays—Communication

⊙ Watch on MyManagementLab

CH2MHill: Communication

FOCUS ON RESEARCH   Communicating in Bad Times

Can communication really make a difference during bad economic times?   A 2011 study found that when economic times are bad, it is particularly important for management to create an atmosphere of trust.[6] They can do this by communicating directly with employees—bulletin boards, intranets, newsletters, and email can all be effective. However, face-to-face communication is the most important way of communicating.

Impersonal written media such as formal reports and bulletins rate lowest in richness. Two students were suspended from class for choosing YouTube, a very rich channel, to distribute their message. Their actions also raised concerns about privacy in the classroom, as *Focus on Ethics* reveals.

communication apprehension
Undue tension and anxiety about oral communication, written communication, or both.

channel richness The amount of information that can be transmitted during a communication episode.

FOCUS ON ETHICS

YouTube's Darker Side

Is it okay for students to post a teacher's outburst on YouTube? Two grade 9 students from École Secondaire Mont-Bleu in Gatineau, Quebec, were suspended from school after teachers discovered a video the students had posted on YouTube.[7] One of the students provoked the teacher during class time while the other secretly taped the scene for about 50 minutes with a compact digital camera.

The students, who have academic problems, were in a special-education class. The teacher had 33 years of experience and specialized in teaching students with learning disabilities. After the incident, the teacher went on sick leave, and his union said, "He is so embarrassed that he may never return to class."

There was no apparent explanation for why the students decided to provoke and then film the teacher. Other students have said that "the teacher was good at helping them improve their grades."

"I think students are just trying to embarrass the teachers they don't like," school board president Jocelyn Blondin said. "In the future, students will have to keep their cellphones in their pockets and use them outside of class," she predicted shortly after the incident.

Teachers and school boards are trying to determine strategies for handling these kinds of events in classrooms. The Gatineau school no longer allows personal electronic devices in the classroom. In Ontario, the Safe Schools Act states that students who engage in online bullying are to be suspended from classes.

The choice of one channel over another depends on whether the message is routine. Routine messages tend to be straightforward and have a minimum of ambiguity. Nonroutine messages are likely to be complicated and have the potential for misunderstanding. Individuals can communicate nonroutine messages more effectively by selecting rich channels. Rob Sobey, president of the Dartmouth, Nova Scotia-based Lawtons Drugs chain, knows that memos do not help in a crisis when staff morale needs

Courtesy of Lawtons Drugs

According to Rob Sobey, president of Lawtons Drugs, a memo never motivates. It can thank and compliment, but in a true crisis, you need to hold a town hall meeting to communicate seminal information. Use of a rich communication channel to communicate a nonroutine message is more likely to be successful.

boosting. "A memo never motivates. A memo can thank and compliment, but you need the town hall meeting [in a true crisis]. You have to put yourself out there in the flesh."[8]

One study found that managers preferred delivering bad news (layoffs, promotion denials, and negative feedback) via email, and that the messages were delivered more accurately this way. However, sending negative information through email is generally not recommended. One of the co-authors of the study noted that "offering negative comments face-to-face is often taken as a sign that the news is important and the deliverer cares about the recipient."[9] In the *Ethical Dilemma* on page 270, it appears that a manager's use of a channel relatively low in richness (email) to convey a nonroutine message caused a lot of embarrassment to the sender.

Channel richness is a helpful framework for choosing your mode of communication. It's not always easy to know when to choose oral rather than written communication, for instance. Experts say oral communication or "face-time" with co-workers, clients, and upper management is key to success. However, if you seek out the CEO just to say hello, you may be remembered as an annoyance rather than a star, and signing up for every meeting on the calendar to increase your face-time is counterproductive to getting the work of the organization done. Your communication choice is worth a moment's thought: Is the message you need to communicate better suited to a discussion, or a diagram?

Barriers to Effective Communication

> As part of their effort to raise money for their business, Palette co-founders Calvin Chu and Ashish Bidadi turned to Kickstarter, a global crowdfunding web-based platform where people introduce projects to potential investors.[10] Palette produces hardware to be used with people's own software, so they had to be able to describe their product effectively to ensure investors would understand the idea. The two also had to convey to others their seriousness and motivation. They did this through posts and pictures placed on their page on the Kickstarter site, creating an impressive story line about Palette. Are there other factors that Chu and Bidadi might have considered to make sure everyone was ready to listen to their pitch for funding?

3 Identify common barriers to effective communication.

PERSONAL INVENTORY ASSESSMENT

Learn About Yourself
Communicating Supportively

A number of factors have been identified as barriers to communication. This section presents the most prominent ones.

Filtering

Filtering refers to a sender's purposely manipulating information so the receiver will see it more favourably. A manager who tells his boss what he feels the boss wants to hear is filtering information.

The more vertical levels in the organization's hierarchy, the more opportunities there are for filtering. But some filtering will occur wherever there are status differences. Factors such as fear of conveying bad news and the desire to please the boss often lead employees to tell their superiors what they think they want to hear, thus distorting upward communications.

Selective Perception

Receivers in the communication process selectively see and hear based on their needs, motivations, experience, background, and other personal characteristics. Receivers also project their interests and expectations into communications as they decode them. An employment interviewer who believes that young people are more interested in spending time on leisure and social activities than working extra hours to further their careers is likely to be influenced by that stereotype when interviewing young job applicants. As we discussed in Chapter 2, we don't see reality; rather, we interpret

filtering A sender's manipulation of information so that it will be seen more favourably by the receiver.

what we see and call it "reality." A 2011 study found that people perceived that they communicated better with people with whom they were close (friends and partners) than with strangers. However, in ambiguous conversations, it turned out that their ability to communicate with close friends was no better than their ability to communicate with strangers.[11]

Information Overload

Individuals have a finite capacity for processing data. When the information we have to work with exceeds our processing capacity, the result is **information overload**. We have seen that dealing with it has become a huge challenge for individuals and for organizations. With emails, phone calls, text messages, meetings, and the need to keep current in one's field, more and more employees are saying that they are suffering from too much information. The information can be distracting as well. A recent study of employees who have tracking software on their computers found that they clicked on their email program more than 50 times in the course of a day, and used instant messaging 77 times. The study also found that, on average, employees visited 40 websites during the workday.[12]

What happens when individuals have more information than they can sort and use? They tend to select, ignore, pass over, or forget. Or they may put off further processing until the overload situation ends. Consider what happens in a poorly planned PowerPoint presentation (see *Case Incident—PowerPoint Purgatory* on page 271). In any case, lost information and less effective communication results, making it all the more important to deal well with overload.

To deal with information overload, it may make sense to connect to technology less frequently, to, in the words of one article, "avoid letting the drumbeat of digital missives constantly shake up and reorder to-do lists."[13] By creating breaks for yourself, you may be better able to prioritize, think about the big picture, and thereby be more effective.[14]

As information technology and immediate communication have become a more prevalent component of modern organizational life, more employees find they are never able to get offline. The negative impacts of these communication devices can spill over into employees' personal lives as well. Both workers and their spouses relate the use of electronic communication technologies outside work to higher levels of work–life conflict.[15] Employees must balance the need for constant communication with their own personal need for breaks from work or they risk burnout from being on call 24 hours a day.

Emotions

You may interpret the same message differently when you are angry or distraught than when you are happy. For example, individuals in positive moods are more confident about their opinions after reading a persuasive message, so well-designed arguments have stronger impacts on their opinions.[16] People in negative moods are more likely to scrutinize messages in greater detail, whereas those in positive moods tend to accept communications at face value.[17] Extreme emotions such as jubilation or depression are most likely to hinder effective communication. In such instances, we are most prone to disregard our rational and objective thinking processes and substitute emotional judgments.

Language

Even when we are communicating in the same language, words mean different things to different people. Age and context are two of the biggest factors that influence such differences.

When business consultant Michael Schiller asked his 15-year-old daughter where she was going with friends, he told her, "You need to recognize your ARAs and measure

information overload A condition in which information inflow exceeds an individual's processing capacity.

against them." Schiller said that in response, his daughter "looked at him like he was from outer space." (For the record, *ARA* stands for accountability, responsibility, and authority.) Those new to corporate lingo may find acronyms such as *ARA*, words such as *deliverables* (verifiable outcomes of a project), and phrases such as *get the low-hanging fruit* (deal with the easiest parts first) bewildering, in the same way parents may be mystified by teen slang.[18]

Our use of language is far from uniform. If we knew how each of us modifies the language, we could minimize communication difficulties, but we usually don't know. Senders tend to incorrectly assume that the words and terms they use mean the same to the receiver as to them.

Silence

It's easy to ignore silence or lack of communication, because it is defined by the absence of information. However, research suggests using silence and withholding communication are common and problematic.[19] One survey found that more than 85 percent of managers reported remaining silent about at least one issue of significant concern.[20] Employee silence means managers lack information about ongoing operational problems. Moreover, silence regarding discrimination, harassment, corruption, and misconduct means top management cannot take action to eliminate this behaviour. Finally, employees who are silent about important issues may also experience psychological stress.

A study looking at the human factors that caused airline accidents found that pilots who had "take charge" attitudes with their crews were more likely to make wrong decisions than pilots who were more inclusive and consulted with their crews before deciding what to do.[21] It was the communication style of the pilot that affected the crew's behaviour. Crew members were not willing to intervene, even when they had necessary information, when they regularly worked under "decisive" pilots. That kind of silence can be fatal. In his book *Outliers*, Malcolm Gladwell noted, "The kinds of

THE CANADIAN PRESS/AP/Gurinder Osan

Call-centre operators at Convergys Corporation in New Delhi, India, speak English in serving their customers from North America and the United Kingdom. But even though the operators and customers speak a common language, communication barriers exist because of differences in the countries' cultures and language accents. To overcome these barriers, the operators receive training in North American and British pop culture so they can make small talk and are taught to speak with Western accents so they can be more easily understood by the calling clients.

errors that cause plane crashes are invariably errors of teamwork and communication. One pilot knows something important and somehow doesn't tell the other pilot."[22]

Silence is less likely where minority opinions are treated with respect, work group identification is high, and high procedural justice prevails.[23] Practically, this means managers must make sure they behave in a supportive manner when employees voice divergent opinions or concerns, and they must take these under advisement. One act of ignoring or belittling an employee for expressing concerns may well lead the employee to withhold important information in the future.

Effective listening skills are discussed in *From Concepts to Skills* on pages 272–273.

Nonverbal Communication

Every time we deliver a verbal message, we also impart a nonverbal message.[24] Sometimes the nonverbal component may stand alone. Anyone who has ever paid a visit to a singles bar or a nightclub is aware that communication need not be verbal to convey a message. A glance, a stare, a smile, a frown, a provocative body movement—they all convey meaning. This example illustrates that no discussion of communication would be complete without a discussion of **nonverbal communication**. This type of communication includes body movements, facial expressions, and the physical distance between the sender and receiver.

> Does body language really make a difference?

It has been argued that every body movement has a meaning and that no movement is accidental.[25] Through body language, we can say such things as, "Help me, I'm confused," or "Leave me alone, I'm really angry." Rarely do we send our messages consciously. We act out our state of being with nonverbal body language, even if we are not aware of doing so. We lift one eyebrow for disbelief. We rub our noses for puzzlement. We clasp our arms to isolate ourselves or to protect ourselves. We shrug our shoulders for indifference, wink one eye for intimacy, tap our fingers for impatience, slap our forehead for forgetfulness.[26]

The two most important messages that body language conveys are (1) the extent to which an individual likes another and is interested in his or her views and (2) the relative perceived status between a sender and receiver.[27] For instance, we are more likely to position ourselves closer to people we like and to touch them more often. Similarly, if you feel that you are of higher status than another, you are more likely to display body movements—such as crossed legs or a slouched seated position—that reflect a casual and relaxed manner.[28]

While we may disagree with the specific meaning of certain movements (and different cultures may interpret specific body movements differently), body language adds to and often complicates verbal communication. For instance, if you read the transcript of a meeting, you do not grasp the impact of what was said in the same way you would if you had been there or had seen the meeting on video. Why? There is no record of nonverbal communication. The *intonations*, or emphasis, given to words or phrases is missing.

The *facial expression* of a person also conveys meaning. A snarling face says something different from a smile. Facial expressions, along with intonations, can show arrogance, aggressiveness, fear, shyness, and other characteristics that would never be communicated if you read a transcript of the meeting.

The way individuals space themselves in terms of *physical distance*, commonly called **proxemics**, also has meaning. What is considered proper spacing is largely dependent on cultural norms. For instance, studies have shown that those from "contact" cultures (for example, Arabs, Latin Americans, southern Europeans) are more comfortable with body closeness and touch than those from "noncontact" cultures (for example, Asians, North Americans, northern Europeans).[29] These differences can lead to confusion. If

nonverbal communication Messages conveyed through body movements, facial expressions, and the physical distance between the sender and receiver.

proxemics The study of physical space in interpersonal relationships.

someone stands closer to you than expected according to your cultural norms, you may interpret the action as an expression of aggressiveness or sexual interest. However, if the person stands farther away than you expect, you might think he or she is displeased with you or uninterested. Someone whose cultural norms differ from yours might be very surprised by your interpretation.

It's important for the receiver to be alert to these nonverbal aspects of communication. You should look for nonverbal cues, as well as listen to the literal meaning of a sender's words. In particular, you should be aware of contradictions between the messages. The manager may say that she is free to talk to you about that raise you have been seeking, but you may see nonverbal signals (such as looking at her watch) that suggest this is not the time to discuss the subject. It's not uncommon for people to express one emotion verbally and another nonverbally. These contradictions often suggest that actions speak louder (and more accurately) than words. The *Experiential Exercise* on page 269 will help you see the value of nonverbal communication in interpersonal relations.

We should also monitor body language with some care. For instance, while it is often thought that people who cross their arms in front of their chest are showing resistance to a message, individuals might also do this if they are feeling cold, regardless of their reaction to a message.

Lying

The final barrier to effective communication is outright misrepresentation of information, or lying. People differ in their definition of a lie. For example, is deliberately withholding information about a mistake a lie, or do you have to actively deny your role in the mistake to pass the threshold? While the definition of a lie befuddles ethicists and social scientists, there is no denying the prevalence of lying. In one diary study, the average person reported telling one to two lies per day, with some individuals telling considerably more.[30] Compounded across a large organization, this is an enormous amount of deception happening every single day. Evidence shows that people are more comfortable lying over the phone than face to face and more comfortable lying in emails than when they have to write with pen and paper.[31]

Can you detect liars? The literature suggests that most people are not very good at detecting deception in others.[32] The problem is that no nonverbal or verbal cues are unique to lying—averting your gaze, pausing, and shifting your posture can also be signals of nervousness, shyness, or doubt. Most people who lie take steps to guard against being detected, so they might look a person in the eye when lying because they know that direct eye contact is (incorrectly) assumed to be a sign of truthfulness. Finally, many lies are embedded in truths; liars usually give a somewhat true account with just enough details changed to avoid detection.

In sum, the frequency of lying and the difficulty in detecting liars makes this an especially strong barrier to effective communication.

Organizational Communication

Calvin Chu and Ashish Bidadi, co-founders of Palette, took on distinct roles in the organization.[33] Chu became CEO, and was initially based in Shenzhen, China, to oversee the production of the parts for Palette. Bidadi became COO, and was based in Waterloo to run the software unit. Working so far away from each other meant that they needed a way to communicate so that both knew exactly what was going on.

"We've worked really hard to make sure [we're] on the same page and that has trickled down to the rest of the team," Mr. Bidadi said. They used Google Hangouts for most of their communication and exchanged emails to "fill the gaps." These mechanisms worked well for the small company, even with the two founders being so geographically far apart. What else can an organization do to make communication more effective?

In this section, we explore ways that communication occurs in organizations, including the direction of communication, formal small-group networks, the grapevine, and electronic communications.

Direction of Communication

4 Contrast downward, upward, and lateral communication.

Communication can flow downward, upward, and/or laterally in organizations.[34] We will explore each of these directional flows and their implications.

Downward

Communication that flows from one level of a group or organization to a lower level is *downward communication*. Group leaders and managers use this approach to assign goals, provide job instructions, inform employees of policies and procedures, identify problems that need attention, and offer feedback.

In downward communication, managers must explain the reasons *why* a decision was made. One study found that employees were twice as likely to be committed to changes when the reasons behind them were fully explained. Although this finding may seem like common sense, many managers feel they are too busy to explain things, or that explanations will "open up a big can of worms." Evidence clearly indicates, though, that explanations increase employee commitment and support of decisions.[35] Although managers might think that sending a message one time is enough to get through to lower-level employees, most research suggests that managerial communications must be repeated several times and through a variety of different media to be truly effective.[36] Moreover, for employees to actually listen to a manager's message, they must believe what is being said. Sentis' 2014 Canadian Employee Benchmark survey found that "40 per cent [of employees] don't believe that their organization's senior leaders communicate honestly with employees."[37] Aware of the importance of open and honest communication, Toronto-based RL Solutions, a health care software developer, shares all of its performance and financial information with employees, so that everyone feels that they are in the loop.[38]

Another problem in downward communication is its one-way nature; generally, managers inform employees but rarely solicit their advice or opinions. Research affirms that employees will not provide input, even when conditions are favourable, if doing so seems against their best interests.[39] A study revealed that nearly two-thirds of employees say their boss rarely or never asks their advice. The study noted, "Organizations are always striving for higher employee engagement, but evidence indicates they unnecessarily create fundamental mistakes. People need to be respected and listened to."[40]

The best communicators explain the reasons behind their downward communications but also solicit communication from the employees they supervise. That leads us to the next direction: upward communication.

Upward

Upward communication flows to a higher level in the group or organization. It's used to provide feedback to higher-ups, inform them of progress toward goals, and relay current problems. Upward communication keeps managers aware of how employees feel about their jobs, co-workers, and the organization in general. Managers also rely on upward communication for ideas on how things can be improved. Port Coquitlam, BC-based Benefits by Design, a benefits administration agency, encourages an open-door policy so that staff members can take their concerns to their managers as soon as possible.[41]

Given that of most managers' job responsibilities have expanded, upward communication is increasingly difficult because managers are overwhelmed and easily distracted. As well, sometimes managers subtly (or not so subtly) discourage employees from speaking up.[42] To engage in effective upward communication, communicate in headlines, support your headlines with actionable items, and prepare an agenda to make sure you use your boss's attention well.[43]

EXHIBIT 7-3 Three Common Small-Group Networks and Their Effectiveness

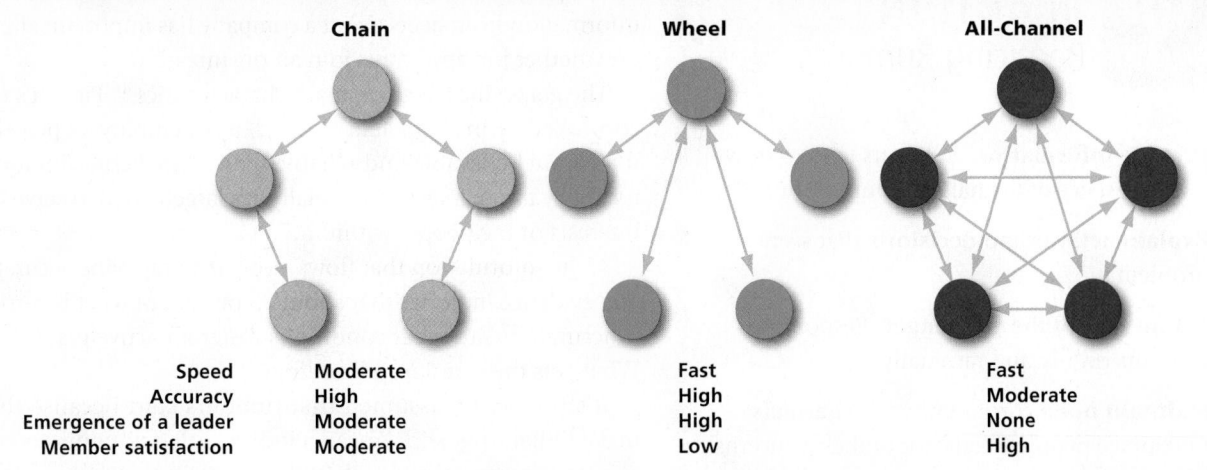

	Chain	Wheel	All-Channel
Speed	Moderate	Fast	Fast
Accuracy	High	High	Moderate
Emergence of a leader	Moderate	High	None
Member satisfaction	Moderate	Low	High

Lateral

When communication occurs among members of the same work group, among members of work groups at the same level, among managers at the same level, or among any horizontally equivalent employees, we describe it as lateral (or horizontal) communication.

Horizontal communication saves time and eases coordination. Some lateral relationships are formally sanctioned. Often, they are informally created to short-circuit the vertical hierarchy and speed up action. So from management's perspective, lateral communication can be good or bad. Because strict adherence to the formal vertical structure for all communications can be inefficient, lateral communication occurring with the knowledge and support of managers can be beneficial. But it can create dysfunctional conflicts when the formal vertical channels are breached, when members go above or around their managers to get things done, or when employers find out that actions have been taken or decisions made without their knowledge.

Small-Group Networks

Formal communication networks can be complicated, including hundreds of people and a half-dozen or more hierarchical levels. To simplify, we have condensed these networks into three common small groups of five people each (see Exhibit 7-3): chain, wheel, and all-channel.

The *chain* rigidly follows the formal chain of command; this network approximates the communication channels you might find in a rigid three-level organization. The *wheel* relies on the leader to act as the central conduit for all group communication; it simulates the communication network you would find on a team with a strong leader. The *all-channel* network permits group members to actively communicate with one another; it's most often characterized in practice by self-managed teams, in which group members are free to contribute and no one person takes on a leadership role.

As Exhibit 7-3 illustrates, the effectiveness of each network depends on the dependent variable that concerns you. For instance, the structure of the wheel network facilitates the emergence of a leader, the all-channel network is best if high member satisfaction is most important, and the chain network is best if accuracy is most important. Thus, we conclude that no single network is appropriate for all occasions.

The Grapevine

The most common **informal communication network** in a group or organization is the **grapevine**.[44] Although rumours and gossip transmitted through the grapevine

5 Compare and contrast formal small-group networks and the grapevine.

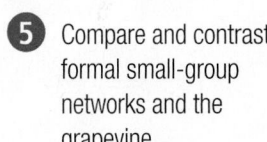

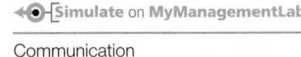
Communication

formal communication networks Task-related communications that follow the authority chain.

informal communication networks Communications that flow along social and relational lines.

grapevine The organization's most common informal network.

OB IN ACTION
Reducing Rumours

→ **Provide information**: Rumours tend to thrive in the absence of formal communication.

→ **Explain actions** and **decisions** that seem problematic.

→ **Do not shoot** the **messenger**: Respond to rumours calmly and rationally.

→ **Maintain open** communication **channels:** Encourage people to talk about their concerns and ideas.[54]

may be informal, it's still an important source of information for employees and candidates. Grapevine or word-of-mouth information from peers about a company has important effects on whether job applicants join an organization.[45]

The grapevine has three main characteristics.[46] First, it's not controlled by management. Second, most employees perceive it as more believable and reliable than formal communiqués issued by top management. Finally, it's largely used to serve the interests of the people within it.

Is the information that flows along the grapevine accurate? The evidence indicates that about 75 percent of what is carried is accurate.[47] But what conditions foster an active grapevine? What gets the rumour mill rolling?

It's frequently assumed that rumours start because they make titillating gossip. Research indicates that rumours emerge as a response to situations that are important to us, where there is ambiguity, and under conditions that arouse anxiety.[48] The secrecy and competition that typically prevail in large organizations around such issues as the appointment of new senior managers, the relocation of offices, and the realignment of work assignments create conditions that encourage and sustain rumours on the grapevine. A rumour will persist until either the wants and expectations creating the uncertainty underlying the rumour are fulfilled or until the anxiety is reduced.

The grapevine is an important part of any group's or organization's communication network.[49] It gives managers a feel for the morale of their organization, identifies issues employees consider important, and helps tap into employee anxieties. The grapevine also serves employees' needs: Small talk creates a sense of closeness and friendship among those who share information, although research suggests it often does so at the expense of those in the "out" group.[50] There is also evidence that gossip is driven largely by employee social networks that managers can study to learn more about how positive and negative information is flowing through the organization.[51] Thus, while the grapevine may not be sanctioned or controlled by the organization, it can be understood.

Can managers entirely eliminate rumours? No. Research indicates that even some forms of gossip provide pro-social motivation.[52] Managers can reduce the negative consequences of rumours by explaining decisions and openly discussing worst-case possibilities.[53] *OB in Action—Reducing Rumours* gives some tips for reducing the negative consequences of rumours.

Electronic Communications

An indispensable—and in about 71 percent of cases, the primary—medium of communication in today's organizations is electronic. Electronic communications—which include email, instant messaging, text messaging, and social media, including blogs—make it possible for you to work, even if you are away from your workstation.

Email

The growth of email's use since its inception nearly 50 years ago has been spectacular, and email is now so pervasive that it's hard to imagine life without it. Recent research found that more than 3.1 billion active email accounts exist worldwide, and corporate employees send and receive, on average, 105 emails each day.[55] Exhibit 7-4 shows the time managers and professionals spend daily on various tasks. Many managers report that they spend too much time on email.

Ever notice that communicating via email can lead to misunderstandings?

EXHIBIT 7-4 Allocation of Time at Work for Managers and Professionals

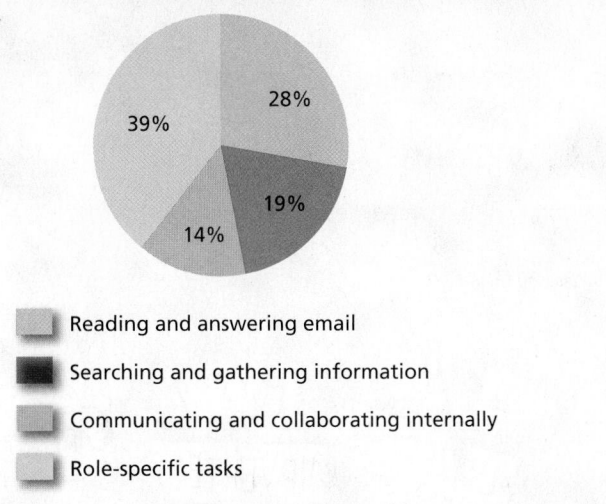

- Reading and answering email
- Searching and gathering information
- Communicating and collaborating internally
- Role-specific tasks

Source: Based on M. Chui et al., "The Social Economy: Unlocking Value and Productivity through Social Technologies," McKinsey & Company, July 2012, http://www.mckinsey.com/insights/high_tech_telecoms_internet/the_social_economy.

Email messages can be quickly written, edited, and stored. They can be distributed to one person or thousands with the same click of a key, although some companies (such as data company Nielsen) have banned the "reply to all" feature.[56] The cost of sending formal email messages to employees is a fraction of the cost of printing, duplicating, and distributing a comparable letter or brochure.[57] Email is not without cost, however. In fact, according to email software company Messagemind, corporations lose $650 billion each year from time spent in processing unnecessary email communication.[58] A recent study also indicated that people focus longer on tasks and are less stressed when they are cut off from checking email.[59] Canadians divert 42 percent of their email directly to "junk mail" folders, according to an Ipsos Reid study.[60] Over one-third of the survey respondents said they had trouble handling all of their email, and only 43 percent thought that email increased efficiency at work. Even though he and his business partner are located many plane hours apart, Damien Veran, co-founder of Slim-Cut Media (with offices in Toronto and Paris) does not think email is the answer for communicating with his co-founder, as *OB in the Workplace* demonstrates.

 IN THE **WORKPLACE**
Asleep in Paris, Busy Working in Toronto

What is the best way to communicate when business partners are on different continents? Toronto-based Damien Veran and Paris-based Thomas Davy launched Slim-Cut Media in 2011.[61] The two, who have been friends since childhood, have only seen each other in person a handful of times since the company launched. To bridge the communication gap, they use the telephone and Skype. "Emails can be tricky," Mr. Veran said. "You need to be careful to make the amount of connecting [in real time] very regular."

Veran is still working hard at 4 p.m. in Toronto, while Davy's day is ending. Veran admits the two sacrifice personal time to keep the communication flowing. "He has to be there for the team at 9 a.m., but he also has to answer my emails from Canada at 11 p.m."

Courtesy of Upverter

Toronto-based Upverter was started by three friends (left to right) Zak Homuth, Stephen Hamer, and Michael Woodworth (shown here at the Maker Faire, an event that showcases grassroots innovation). The three, all trained as electrical engineers, wanted to create a network for online collaboration for hardware designers. They launched a "crowd-sourced library of parts and design tools," and the company took off quickly after they demonstrated the service at DemoFall 2011 in Santa Clara, California.

Focus on Ethics illustrates that employees cannot assume that their email is private.

 **FOCUS ON** ETHICS

Your Email Can Get You Fired

Should your email be safe from your manager's eyes? A recent poll conducted by Environics found that 35 percent of Canadians say they have sent emails from their work-based email address that they worry could come back to hurt them.[62] Even so, about the same percentage of employees believe their employers probably check on email accounts, and 52 percent think their employer has the right to do so. Moreover, 30 percent of Canadians know someone who has been disciplined because of an email sent at work.

While a City of Toronto employee was merely disciplined after sending "inappropriate" pictures using a city computer, Fred Jones (not his real name) was fired from a Canadian company for forwarding dirty jokes to his clients. Until this incident, Jones had been a high-performing employee who sold network computers for his company. Jones thought that he was only sending the jokes to clients who liked them, and assumed that the clients would tell him if they did not want to receive the jokes. Instead, a client complained to the company about receiving the dirty jokes. After an investigation, the company fired Jones. Jones is still puzzled about being fired. He views his email as private; to him, sending jokes is the same as telling them at the water cooler.

Jones was not aware that under current law, employee information, including email, is not necessarily private. Most federal employees, provincial public sector employees, and employees working for federally regulated industries are covered by the federal Privacy Act and Access to Information Act, in place since 1985. Many private sector employees are not covered by privacy legislation, however. _____

Ann Cavoukian, Information and Privacy Commissioner of Ontario, notes that "employees deserve to be treated like adults and companies should limit surveillance to rare instances, such as when there is suspicion of criminal activity or harassment."[63] She suggests that employers use respect and courtesy when dealing with employees' email, and she likens email to office phone calls, which generally are not monitored by the employer. It's clearly important, in any event, that employees be aware of their company's policy on email.

Instant Messaging and Text Messaging

Like email, instant messaging (IM) is usually done via computer. It is a synchronous technology, meaning you need to be there to receive the message. In this way, IM operates like a telephone without an answering machine: If you are present when the IM comes in, you can respond in real time to engage in online typed dialogue. If you miss the incoming IM, you may be alerted when you next log on that a person tried to reach you. However, unlike the case with email, you are not then usually expected to reply.

Text messaging (TM) is similar to instant messaging in that both are synchronous technologies, but text messaging is usually done via cellphone and often as a real-time alternative to phone calls. The guidelines for the business use of texting are still evolving.

Social Media

Nowhere has communication been more transformed than in the rise of social networks like Facebook and LinkedIn, and business is taking advantage of the opportunities these social media present. Many organizations have developed their own in-house social networking applications, known as *enterprise social software*, and most have their own Facebook page and Twitter feeds.[64] According to research advisory firm Gartner Inc., companies that use social media as more than a marketing tool may lead their industries in growth by 2015.[65] Rather than being one huge site, Facebook, with more than 1.11 billion active users per month,[66] is composed of separate networks based on schools, companies, or regions. According to Facebook's 2013 first-quarter earnings report, the lowest numbers of monthly active users are in the United States and Canada; Europe has a larger number of users, and Asia has an even larger number.[67] Users can send public messages to other users either by posting on their walls or through messages or chats. Privacy remains a high concern for many Facebook users.

Unlike many social media venues, LinkedIn was created as an online business network. User profiles on the site are like virtual résumés. Communication is sometimes limited to endorsements of others' skills and establishment of business connections, although direct private communication is available and users can form and belong to groups.

Social media offer potential benefits and drawbacks for organizations, as *Case Incident—Using Social Media to Your Advantage* on page 270 demonstrates.

Blogs   A *blog* (short for web log) is a website about a single person or company. In 2014, over 200 million Tumblr blogs and 75.8 million WordPress blogs existed worldwide.[68]

IN ACTION
Using Social Media Responsibly

→ **Don't write** anything you would be **uncomfortable** having your employer read.

→ Keep in mind that **what you publish** could be public for a **long time**.

→ If you are writing about your company, **be transparent about your role** in the organization.

→ **Get approval** from the organization before posting **private** or internal **conversations**.

→ **Be upfront** about correcting errors and updating previous posts.[71]

And, of course, many organizations and their leaders have blogs that speak for the organization.

Twitter is a hybrid social networking service for users to post "micro-blog" entries of 140 characters to their subscribers about any topic, including work. A 2013 study found that only 5.6 percent of CEOs at the world's largest companies have Twitter accounts, while 68 percent have no social media presence at all.[69] As Harvard professor Bill George noted, "Can you think of a more cost-effective way of getting to your customers and employees?"[70] Having many followers can be an advantage to a firm or a manager, and a huge liability when posts (tweets) are badly written or negative.

Flickr, Pinterest, Google+, YouTube, Wikis, Jive, Socialtext, Snapchat, and Social Cast are just a few of the many public and industry-specific social platforms, with new ones launching daily. Some are designed for only one type of posting: YouTube accepts only videos, for instance, and Flickr only videos and images. Other sites have a particular culture, such as Pinterest's informal posts sharing recipes or decorating tips. There is likely to soon be a social media site tailored to every type of communication. To help you find a balance between your desire to engage in social media and to behave ethically toward the company in which you are employed, *OB in Action—Using Social Media Responsibly* summarizes rules established by IBM.

Should managers care about employees' social media presence? *Point/Counterpoint* on page 268 addresses this question.

GLOBAL IMPLICATIONS

Effective communication is difficult under the best of conditions. Cross-cultural factors clearly create the potential for increased communication problems.

Cultural Barriers to Communication

6 Show how to overcome the potential problems in cross-cultural communication.

Researchers have identified four specific problems related to language difficulties in cross-cultural communication.[72] First, there are *barriers caused by semantics*. As we have noted previously, words mean different things to different people. This is particularly true for people from different cultures. Some words, for instance, don't translate between cultures. The Finnish word *sisu* means something akin to "guts" or "dogged persistence" but is essentially untranslatable in English. Similarly, the new capitalists in Russia may have difficulty communicating with British or Canadian counterparts because English terms such as *efficiency*, *free market*, and *regulation* have no direct Russian equivalents.

Second, there are *barriers caused by word connotations*. Words imply different things in different languages. The Japanese word *hai* translates as "yes," but its connotation may be "yes, I'm listening," rather than "yes, I agree." Western executives may be hampered in their negotiations if they don't understand this connotation.

Third, there are *barriers caused by tone differences*. In some cultures, language is formal; in others, it's informal. In some cultures, the tone changes depending on the context: People speak differently at home, in social situations, and at work. Using a personal, informal style in a situation where a more formal style is expected can be inappropriate.

EXHIBIT 7-5 High- vs. Low-Context Cultures

High
context → Chinese
Korean
Japanese
Vietnamese
Arab
Greek
Spanish
Italian
English
North American
Scandinavian
Low → Swiss
context German

Fourth, there are *differences in tolerance for conflict and methods for resolving conflicts.* Individuals from individualistic cultures tend to be more comfortable with direct conflicts and will make the source of their disagreements overt. Collectivists are more likely to acknowledge conflict only implicitly and avoid emotionally charged disputes. They may attribute conflicts to the situation more than to the individuals and therefore may not require explicit apologies to repair relationships, whereas individualists prefer explicit statements accepting responsibility for conflicts and public apologies to restore relationships.

PERSONAL INVENTORY ASSESSMENT

Learn About Yourself
Communication Styles

Cultural Context

Cultures tend to differ in the degree to which context influences the meaning individuals take from communication.[73] In **high-context cultures** such as China, Korea, Japan, and Vietnam, people rely heavily on nonverbal and subtle situational cues when communicating with others, and a person's official status, place in society, and reputation carry considerable weight. What is *not* said may be more significant than what *is* said. In contrast, people from Europe and North America reflect their **low-context cultures**. They rely essentially on spoken and written words to convey meaning; body language or formal titles are secondary (see Exhibit 7-5).

Contextual differences mean quite a lot in terms of communication. Communication in high-context cultures implies considerably more trust by both parties. What may appear, to an outsider, as a casual and insignificant conversation is important because it reflects the desire to build a relationship and create trust. Oral agreements imply strong commitments in high-context cultures. Also, who you are—your age, seniority, rank in the organization—is highly valued and heavily influences your credibility. But in low-context cultures, enforceable contracts will tend to be in writing, precisely worded, and highly legalistic. Similarly, low-context cultures value directness. Managers are expected to be explicit and precise in conveying intended meaning. It's quite different in high-context cultures, where managers tend to "make suggestions" rather than give orders.

A Cultural Guide

There is much to be gained from business intercultural communications. It is safe to assume that every single one of us has a different viewpoint that is culturally shaped. Because we do have differences, we have an opportunity to reach the most creative solutions possible with the help of others if we communicate effectively.

high-context cultures Cultures that rely heavily on nonverbal and subtle situational cues in communication.

low-context cultures Cultures that rely heavily on words to convey meaning in communication.

Kiyoshi Ota/Bloomberg via Getty Images

Globalization has changed the way Toyota Motor Corporation provides employees with the information they need for decision making. In the past, Toyota transferred employee knowledge on the job from generation to generation through "tacit understanding," a common communication method used in the conformist and subdued Japanese culture. Today, however, as a global organization, Toyota transfers knowledge of its production methods to overseas employees by bringing them to its training centre in Japan, shown here, to teach them production methods by using how-to manuals, practice drills, and lectures.

According to Fred Casmir, a leading expert in intercultural communication research, we often don't communicate well with people outside of our culture because we tend to generalize from only knowing their cultural origin.[74] Doing so can be insensitive and potentially disastrous, especially when we make assumptions based on observable characteristics. Many of us have a richly varied ethnic background and would be offended if someone addressed us according to what culture our physical features might favour, for instance. Also, attempts to be culturally sensitive to another person are often based on stereotypes propagated by the media. These stereotypes usually don't have a correct or current relevance.

> How can you improve cross-cultural communication?

Casmir noted that because there are far too many cultures for anyone to understand completely, and individuals interpret their own cultures differently, intercultural communication should be based on sensitivity and the pursuit of common goals. He found the ideal condition is an ad hoc "third culture" a group can form when they seek to incorporate aspects of each member's cultural communication preferences. The norms this subculture establishes through appreciating individual differences create a common ground for effective communication. Intercultural groups that communicate effectively can be highly productive and innovative.

When communicating with people from a different culture, what can you do to reduce misinterpretations? Casmir and other experts offer the following suggestions:[76]

- *Know yourself.* Recognizing your own cultural identity and biases is critical to then understanding the unique viewpoint of other people.

- *Foster a climate of mutual respect, fairness, and democracy.* Clearly establish an environment of equality and mutual concern. This will be your "third culture" context for effective intercultural communication that transcends each person's cultural norms.

- *Learn the cultural context of each person.* You may find more similarities or differences to your own frame of reference than you might expect. Be careful not to categorize them by culture of origin, however.

- *When in doubt, listen.* If you speak your opinions too early, you may be more likely to offend the other person. You will also want to listen first to better understand the other person's intercultural language fluency and familiarity with your culture.

- *State facts, not your interpretation.* Interpreting or evaluating what someone has said or done, in contrast with describing, is based more on the observer's culture and background than on the observed situation. If you state only facts, you will have the opportunity to benefit from the other person's interpretation. Delay judgment until you have had sufficient time to observe and interpret the situation from the differing perspectives of all the cultures involved.

- *Consider the other person's viewpoint.* Before sending a message, put yourself in the recipient's shoes. What are his or her values, experiences, and frames of reference? What do you know about his or her education, upbringing, and background that can give you added insight? Try to see the people in the group as they really are first, and take a collaborative problem-solving approach whenever potential conflicts arise.

- *Proactively maintain the identity of the group.* Like any culture, the establishment of a common-ground "third culture" for effective intercultural communication takes time and nurturing. Remind members of the group of your common goals, mutual respect, and need to adapt to individual communication preferences.

Old Faithful Shop

Savannah Olsen, a Cree from Saddle Lake, Alberta, is the co-owner of Old Faithful Shop, located in Vancouver's historic Gastown district. She was named the 2013 National Aboriginal Entrepreneur of the Year by the Canadian Council for Aboriginal Business. In giving her the award, the Council noted that her business is a model for helping "Canadians see aboriginal people as net contributors to the Canadian economy and shared prosperity." Because of the store's location, she takes a unique approach to developing her customer base. Olsen says that she "[holds] in-store craft workshops and mini farmers markets featuring growers and other local vendors. These events provide an opportunity to get to know our customers and establish a feeling of neighbourliness."[75]

Summary

You have probably discovered the link between communication and employee satisfaction in this chapter: the less uncertainty, the greater the satisfaction. Distortions, ambiguities, and incongruities between verbal and nonverbal messages all increase uncertainty and reduce effective communication.

LESSONS LEARNED

- Just because something is said, it does not mean that it was heard.
- Communication is rarely "objective." Both the sender's and receiver's reality affects the framing and understanding of the message.
- Information overload is a serious problem for most individuals.

SNAPSHOT SUMMARY

The Communication Process
- Choosing a Channel

Barriers to Effective Communication
- Filtering
- Selective Perception

- Information Overload
- Emotions
- Language
- Silence
- Nonverbal Communication
- Lying

Organizational Communication
- Direction of Communication
- Small-Group Networks
- The Grapevine
- Electronic Communications

MyManagementLab

Study, practise, and explore real business situations with these helpful resources:

- **Study Plan:** Check your understanding of chapter concepts with self-study quizzes.
- **Online Lesson Presentations:** Study key chapter topics and work through interactive assessments to test your knowledge and master management concepts.
- **Videos:** Learn more about the management practices and strategies of real companies.
- **Simulations:** Practise management decision-making in simulated business environments.

P I A PERSONAL INVENTORY ASSESSMENT

OB at Work

for **Review**

1. What are the key parts of the communication process, and how do you distinguish formal from informal communication?

2. How does channel richness underlie the choice of communication channel?

3. What are some common barriers to effective communication?

4. What are the differences among downward, upward, and lateral communication?

5. What are the differences between formal small-group networks and the grapevine?

6. What potential problems underlie cross-cultural communication? How can they be overcome?

for **Managers**

- Remember that your communication mode will partly determine your communication effectiveness.

- Obtain feedback from your employees to make certain your messages—however they are communicated—are understood.

- Remember that written communication creates more misunderstandings than oral communication; communicate with employees through in-person meetings when possible.

- Make sure you use communication strategies appropriate to your audience and the type of message you are sending.

- Keep in mind that culture can be a communication barrier.

for **You**

- If you are having difficulty communicating with someone, you might consider that both you and the other person are contributing something to that breakdown. This tends to be true even if you are inclined to believe that the other person is the party more responsible for the breakdown.

- Often, either selective perception or defensiveness gets in the way of communication. As you work in your groups on student projects, try to observe communication flows more critically to help you understand ways that communication can be improved and dysfunctional conflict avoided.

OB *at Work*

Employees' Social Media Presence Should Matter to Managers

POINT

Everyone uses social media.[77] Well, almost everyone: A recent Pew research study found that the highest percentage of adults who use social networking sites was in Israel at 53 percent, followed by 50 percent in the United States, 43 percent in Russia and Britain, and 42 percent in Spain. Canada was not included in the 20 countries studied.

Business is social, and using employees' social contacts to increase business has always been a facet of marketing. Organizations that don't follow their employees' social media presence are missing an opportunity to expand their business and strengthen their workforce. Employees are key representatives of their companies to the outside world. The Honda employee who once told 30 friends that Honda is best can now tell 300 Facebook friends and 500 Twitter followers about the latest model.

Monitoring employees' social media presence can also strengthen the workforce by identifying the best talent. Managers can look for potential online celebrities—frequent bloggers and Twitter users with many followers—to approach for co-branding partnerships. Scrutiny can also help employers spot problems. For example, consider the employee who is fired one day and turns violent. A manager who had been monitoring the employee's social media posts may have been able to detect warning signs. A human resources department monitoring employees' social media activity may be able to identify a substance abuse problem and provide help for the employee through the company's intervention policies.

A job candidate's social media presence provides one more input to hiring and retention decisions that many companies already take advantage of. In reality, there is no difference between the employee and the person.

Employers that monitor social media can also identify employees who use their platforms to send out bad press or who leak proprietary information. For this reason, managers may someday be *required* to monitor employees' social media postings and to act upon infringements.

Managers should therefore develop enforceable social media policies and create a corporate infrastructure to regularly research and monitor social media activity. The potential increase in business and limit on liability is ample return for dedicating staff and work hours to building a successful monitoring program.

COUNTERPOINT

There is little to be gained and much to be lost when organizations follow candidates' and employees' presence on social media. Managers may be able to learn more about individuals through their online activity, and organizations may be able to catch some good press from employee postings, but the risk of liability for this intrusion on privacy is inescapable. Managers are ill-equipped to monitor, interpret, and act upon employees' social media postings, and few have any experience with relating the medium to business use.

Managers may also easily misinterpret information they find. Few companies have training programs for the proper use of social media; only 40 percent have social media policies of any kind. Those that do are skating on thin ice because monitoring policies can conflict with privacy regulations.

An employee's online image does not reveal much that is relevant to the job, certainly not enough to warrant the time and money a business would spend on monitoring. Most users view social media as a private, recreational venue. In this light, monitoring employees' social media accounts is an unethical violation of their right to privacy.

Equal employment opportunity laws require companies to hire without respect to race, age, religion, national origin, or disability. But managers who check into candidates' social media postings often find out more than the candidate wanted to share, and then there is no way to keep that information from affecting the hiring decision. Searching through social media can, therefore, expose a company to a costly discrimination claim.

Using employees' personal social media presence as a marketing tool through company-supportive postings is unethical from many standpoints. First, it's unethical to expect employees to expand the company's client base through their personal contacts. Second, it's unreasonable to expect them to endorse the company after working hours. And the practice of asking employees for their social media passwords is an obvious intrusion into their personal lives.

In sum, people have a right to a professional and a private image.

PERSONAL **INVENTORY** ASSESSMENT

Communicating Supportively: Supportive communication is a skill that must be practised. Use this scale to find out how well you do at supportive communication now, and get some ideas for future improvement.

Communication Styles: Different people tend to prefer different interpersonal communication styles. Use this scale to determine your communication style, and then think about how variations in style may impact communication effectiveness.

BREAKOUT **GROUP** EXERCISES

Form small groups to discuss the following topics, as assigned by your instructor:

1. What differences have you observed in the ways that men and women communicate?

2. How do you know when a person is listening to you? When someone is ignoring you?

3. Describe a situation in which you ignored someone. What impact did it have on that person's subsequent communication behaviours?

EXPERIENTIAL EXERCISE

An Absence of Nonverbal Communication

This exercise will help you see the value of nonverbal communication in interpersonal relations.

1. The class is to divide into pairs (Party A and Party B).

2. Party A is to select a topic from the following list:
   a. Managing in the Middle East is significantly different from managing in North America.
   b. Employee turnover in an organization can be functional.
   c. Some conflict in an organization is good.
   d. Whistle-blowers do more harm than good for an organization.
   e. An employer has a responsibility to provide every employee with an interesting and challenging job.
   f. Everyone should register to vote.
   g. Organizations should require all employees to undergo regular drug testing.
   h. Individuals who have majored in business or economics make better employees than those who have majored in history or English.
   i. The place where you get your college or university degree is more important in determining career success than what you learn while you are there.
   j. It's unethical for a manager to purposely distort communications to get a favourable outcome.

3. Party B is to choose his or her position on this topic (for example, arguing *against* the view that "an employer has a responsibility to provide every employee with an interesting and challenging job"). Party A now must automatically take the opposite position.

4. The 2 parties have 10 minutes in which to debate their topic. The catch is that individuals can only communicate verbally. They may *not* use gestures, facial movements, body movements, or any other nonverbal communication. It may help for both parties to sit on their hands to remind them of these restrictions and to maintain an expressionless look.

5. After the debate is over, the class should discuss the following:
    a. How effective was communication during these debates?
    b. What barriers to communication existed?
    c. What purposes does nonverbal communication serve?
    d. Relate the lessons learned in this exercise to problems that might occur when communicating on the telephone or through email.

ETHICAL **DILEMMA**

The Pitfalls of Email

While email may be a very useful—even indispensable—form of communication in organizations, it certainly has its limits and dangers.[78] Indeed, email can get you into trouble with more people, more quickly, than almost any other form of communication.

Ask Bill Cochran. Cochran, 44, is a manager at Richmond Group, an advertising agency. As Richmond was gearing up to produce a Super Bowl ad for one of its clients—Bridgestone—Cochran's boss sent an email to 200 people describing the internal competition to determine which ad idea would be presented. Cochran chose the occasion to give a pep talk to his team. Using "locker room talk," he composed an email criticizing the other Richmond teams, naming employees he thought would provide them real competition—and those who would not.

What Cochran did next—hit the Send key—seemed so innocuous. But it was a keystroke he would soon wish he could undo. Shortly after he sent the email, a co-worker, Wendy Mayes, wrote to him: "Oh God . . . Bill. You just hit REPLY ALL!"

Questions

1. After realizing what he had done, how should Cochran have responded to this situation?

2. After the incident, Mayes says of Cochran: "His name soon became synonymous with 'idiotic behavior' such as 'don't pull a Cochran.'" Is it unethical to participate in such ribbing?

3. Kaspar Rorsted, CEO of Henkil, a consumer and industrial products company based in Germany, says that copying others on emails is overused. "It's a waste of time," he said. "If they want to write me, they can write me. People often copy me to cover their back." Do you agree? How can you decide when copying others is necessary vs. "a waste of time"?

CASE INCIDENTS

Using Social Media to Your Advantage

As you know, social media have transformed the way we interact.[79] The transparent, rapid-fire communication they make possible means people can spread information about companies more rapidly than ever.

Do organizations understand yet how to use social media effectively? Perhaps not. Recent findings indicated that only 3 out of 10 CEOs in the *Fortune* 500 have any presence on national social media sites. Many executives are wary of these new technologies because they cannot always control the outcomes of their communications.

However, whether they are directly involved with social media or not, companies should recognize that these messages are out there, so it behooves them to make their voices heard. Some experts say social media tools improve productivity because they keep employees connected to their companies during nonoffice hours. As well, social media can be an important way to learn about emerging trends. André Schneider, chief operating officer of the World Economic Forum, uses feedback from LinkedIn discussion groups and Facebook friends to discover emerging trends and issues worldwide. Padmasree Warrior, chief technology officer of Cisco, has used social media to refine her presentations before a "test" audience.

The first step in developing a social media strategy is establishing a brand for your communications—define what you want your social media presence to express. Experts recommend that companies begin their social media strategy by leveraging their internal corporate networks to test their strategy in a medium that's easier to control. Most companies already have the technology to use social media through their corporate websites. Begin by using these platforms for communicating with employees and facilitating social networks for general information sharing. As social networking expert Soumitra Dutta from Insead notes, "My advice is to build your audience slowly and be selective about your contacts."

Despite the potential advantages, organizations also need to be aware of significant drawbacks to social media. First, it's very difficult to control social media communications. Microsoft found this out when the professional blogger it hired spent more time promoting himself than getting positive information out about the company.

Second, important intellectual capital might leak out. Companies need to establish very clear policies and procedures to ensure that sensitive information about ongoing corporate strategies is not disseminated via social media. Finally, managers should maintain motivation and interest beyond their initial forays into social media. A site that is rarely updated can send a very negative message about the organization's level of engagement with the world.

Questions

1. Do you think organizations need to have a social media presence today? Are the drawbacks sufficient to make you think it's better for them to avoid certain media?

2. What features would you look for in a social media outlet? What types of information would you avoid making part of your social media strategy?

3. What do you think is the future direction of social media? How might emerging technologies change them?

PowerPoint Purgatory

We have all been there, done that: 10 minutes, 20 PowerPoint slides.[80] Whether you have been the harried presenter racing through the slides or the hapless listener choosing between reading the slides or listening to the talk, it's miserable. In all, 350 PowerPoint presentations are given per second worldwide, and the program commands 95 percent of the presentation software market. Why do we do this to ourselves?

The short answer seems to be because we know how, or at least we think we do. Joel Ingersoll of Lorton Data, a Minneapolis database company, said, "You say to yourself, 'I'll start vomiting information I found on my hard drive until I hit, oh, about 20 slides, and then I'll wing the talking-to-people part.'" Bombarding audiences with stark phrases is only one possible pitfall, says Rick Altman, author of *Why Most PowerPoint Presentations Suck*. Another is to overdesign your presentation. Most of us spend 36 percent of our prep time on design, according to a recent study, yet we fail to remember that "less is more." The poor choices that sometimes result (such as using cartoonish typefaces for a serious presentation) can undermine your intended message. Altman cautions against using layer after layer of bullet points to write out what you should say instead,

and he recommends making sparing use of holograms, 3D, and live Twitter feeds that only detract from your message.

Successful talks are about a story and an interaction. "Even if you're a middle manager delivering financials to your department in slides, you're telling a story. A manager is constantly trying to persuade," says Nancy Duarte, owner of a presentation design company. Equally important is the audience. "Everyone is sick of the one-way diatribe," Duarte notes, and Altman recommends engaging people "as if they're in preschool waiting to get picked up by their parents." According to Keith Yamashita, founder of SYPartners communications, this may mean ditching PowerPoint altogether. "There are endless techniques that are more appropriate than PowerPoint," he contends. Like what?

Experts suggest fewer visual aids and more live interaction with the audience. High tech does not guarantee better storytelling. "Pin up butcher paper on the walls, draw a map of your thinking, and hand that out," Yamashita says, or use a white board. The results can amaze you. When sales engineer Jason Jones had trouble launching his two-hour slide presentation to a dozen clients, buddy Dave Eagle stepped in. "All right, I got two presentations for y'all," Eagle told the dozen clients, one where the presentation was "on the wall" with slides, and the other just spoken. The clients chose the latter, and they won the account.

Questions

1. What are some of the ways people misuse Power-Point? What are the potential consequences?

2. Have you used PowerPoint in your school projects or at work? In what presentations did you find PowerPoint most effective in communicating your message? In what presentations did PowerPoint hinder your successful communication?

3. List the pros and cons you see for managers avoiding PowerPoint as a mode of communication.

FROM CONCEPTS TO SKILLS

Effective Listening

Too many people take listening skills for granted.[81] They confuse hearing with listening.

 What is the difference? Hearing is merely picking up sound vibrations. Listening is making sense out of what we hear. That is, listening requires paying attention, interpreting, and remembering sound stimuli.

The average person normally speaks at a rate of 125 to 200 words per minute. However, the average listener can comprehend up to 400 words per minute. This leaves a lot of time for idle mind-wandering while listening. For most people, it also means they have acquired a number of bad listening habits to fill in the "idle time."

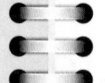 The following eight behaviours are associated with effective listening skills. If you want to improve your listening skills, look to these behaviours as guides:

1. *Make eye contact.* How do you feel when somebody doesn't look at you when you are speaking? If you are like most people, you are likely to interpret this behaviour as aloofness or lack of interest. We may listen with our ears, but others tend to judge whether we are really listening by looking at our eyes.

2. *Exhibit affirmative head nods and appropriate facial expressions.* The effective listener shows interest in what is being said. How? Through nonverbal signals. Affirmative head nods and appropriate facial expressions, when added to good eye contact, convey to the speaker that you are listening.

3. *Avoid distracting actions or gestures.* The other side of showing interest is avoiding actions that suggest your mind is somewhere else. When listening, don't look at your watch, shuffle papers, play with your pencil, or engage in similar distractions. They make the speaker feel that you are bored or uninterested. Maybe more important, they indicate that you are not fully attentive and may be missing part of the message that the speaker wants to convey.

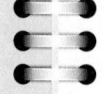

4. *Ask questions.* The critical listener analyzes what he or she hears and asks questions. This behaviour provides clarification, ensures understanding, and assures the speaker that you are listening.

5. *Paraphrase.* Paraphrasing means restating what the speaker has said in your own words. The effective listener uses phrases such as "What I hear you saying is . . ." or "Do you mean . . . ?" Why rephrase what has already been said? Two reasons! First, it's an excellent control device

to check on whether you are listening carefully. You cannot paraphrase accurately if your mind is wandering or if you are thinking about what you are going to say next. Second, it's a control for accuracy. By rephrasing what the speaker has said in your own words and feeding it back to the speaker, you verify the accuracy of your understanding.

6. *Avoid interrupting the speaker.* Let the speaker complete his or her thought before you try to respond. Don't try to second-guess where the speaker's thoughts are going. When the speaker is finished, you will know!

7. *Don't overtalk.* Most of us would rather voice our own ideas than listen to what someone else says. Too many of us listen only because it's the price we have to pay to get people to let us talk. While talking may be more fun and silence may be uncomfortable, you cannot talk and listen at the same time. The good listener recognizes this fact and does not overtalk.

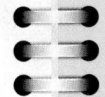

8. *Make smooth transitions between the roles of speaker and listener.* When you are a student sitting in a lecture hall, you find it relatively easy to get into an effective listening frame of mind. Why? Because communication is essentially one-way: The teacher talks and you listen. But the teacher-student dyad is not typical. In most work situations, you are continually shifting back and forth between the roles of speaker and listener. The effective listener, therefore, makes transitions smoothly from speaker to listener and back to speaker. From a listening perspective, this means concentrating on what a speaker has to say and practising not thinking about what you are going to say as soon as you get an opportunity.

. . . .

Practising Skills

Form groups of 2. This exercise is a debate. Person A can choose any contemporary issue. Some examples include business ethics, the value of unions, stiffer grading policies, same-sex marriage, money as a motivator. Person B then selects a position on this issue. Person A must automatically take the counter-position. The debate is to proceed for 8 to 10 minutes, with only one catch. Before each person speaks, he or she must first summarize, in his or her own words and without notes, what the other person has said. If the summary does not satisfy the speaker, it must be corrected until it does. What impact do the summaries have on the quality of the debate?

. . . .

Reinforcing Skills

1. In another class—preferably one with a lecture format—practise active listening. Ask questions, paraphrase, exhibit affirming nonverbal behaviours. Then ask yourself: Was this harder for me than a normal lecture? Did it affect my note taking? Did I ask more questions? Did it improve my understanding of the lecture's content? What was the instructor's response?

2. Spend an entire day fighting your urge to talk. Listen as carefully as you can to everyone you talk to, and respond as appropriately as possible to understand, not to make your own point. What, if anything, did you learn from this exercise?

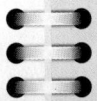

Power and Politics

Can a mayor accused of smoking crack cocaine save his job? Power and politics tell much of the story.

LEARNING OUTCOMES

After studying this chapter, you should be able to:

1. Define *power*.

2. Describe the five bases of power.

3. Explain the role of dependence in power relationships.

4. Identify nine power or influence tactics and their contingencies.

5. Explain what empowerment is, and the factors that lead to it.

6. Show the connection between harassment and the abuse of power.

7. Identify the causes and consequences of political behaviour.

8. Apply impression management techniques.

9. Determine whether a political action is ethical.

In August 2014, Rob Ford, Mayor of Toronto, publicly thanked Deputy Mayor Norm Kelly for taking over after Ford was stripped of his mayoral duties after admitting to smoking crack cocaine.[1] Councillor Joe Mihevc said Ford's words to Kelly were sincere "for that moment."

Ford's problems started when word of a video that allegedly showed him smoking crack was reported in the *Toronto Star* and on the website Gawker in May 2013. For months, Ford denied the accusation that he smoked crack (or that such a video existed). In November, however, Ford admitted using crack, which is when council asked Kelly to take over most of the mayor's duties.

Victor Biro/Alamy

In April 2014, a second video of alleged drug use surfaced, and the *Globe and Mail* agreed to pay its creator $10 000 for six screenshots. As the story went to print, Ford announced that he was going to a rehabilitation facility, and took a leave of absence from the mayor's role for two months.

During much of 2014, Ford's antics were a running joke throughout Canada and even made international headlines. Despite this, he was able to retain his job as mayor until his term ended. Due to illness, he decided not to run for mayor again, but he did run for city councillor and was easily elected to the seat he held for 10 years before he became mayor. Ford has been able to channel his power and politics into getting what he wants—which is making sure that taxpayers' money is spent wisely. So, despite his antics, his constituents believe he has their interests at heart, and that is what matters to them.

In both research and practice, *power* and *politics* have been described as dirty words. It's easier for most of us to talk about sex or money than about power or political behaviour. Power is seductive. People who have power deny it, people who want it try not to look like they are seeking it, and those who are good at getting it are secretive about how they do so.[2]

A major theme in this chapter is that power and politics are a natural process in any group or organization. Although you might have heard the saying "Power corrupts, and absolute power corrupts absolutely," power is not always bad.

Power and politics are realities of organizational life, and they are not going to go away. Understanding how to use power and politics effectively makes organizational life more manageable, because it can help you gain the support you need to do your job effectively.

THE BIG IDEA

Power is not necessarily a zero-sum game. Sharing power may in fact increase everyone's power.

OB IS FOR **EVERYONE**

- Have you ever wondered how you might increase your power?
- What do you need to be truly empowered?
- Why do some people seem to engage in politics more than others?
- In what situations does impression management work best?

A Definition of Power

1 Define *power*.

Watch on **MyManagementLab**

Power and Political Behaviour

Power refers to a capacity that A has to influence the behaviour of B, so that B acts in accordance with A's wishes.[3] This definition implies that there is a *potential* for power if someone is dependent on another. But one can have power and not impose it.

Probably the most important aspect of power is that it's a function of **dependence**. The greater B's dependence on A, the greater A's power in the relationship. Dependence, in turn, is based on the alternatives that B perceives and the importance that B places on the alternative(s) that A controls. A person can have power over you only if he or she controls something you desire. If you are attending college or university on funds totally provided by your parents, you probably recognize the power that your parents hold over you. You are dependent on them for financial support. But once you are out of school, have a job, and are making a good income, your parents' power is reduced significantly. Who among us, though, has not known or heard of the rich relative who is able to control a large number of family members merely through the implicit or explicit threat of "writing them out of the will"?

Within larger organizations, the information technology (IT) group often has considerable power, because everyone, right up to the CEO, is dependent on this group to keep computers and networks running. Since few people have the technical expertise to do so, IT personnel end up being viewed as irreplaceable. This gives them a lot of power within the organization.

Power makes people uncomfortable.[4] People who have power deny it, people who want it try not to look like they are seeking it, and those who are good at getting it are secretive about how they do so.[5] Commenting on a recent study, one researcher noted, "A person's sense of power is an extremely pervasive feeling in everyday life."[6]

Part of the discomfort about power may have to do with how people perceive those in power. A 2011 study found that people who behave rudely—putting their feet up on a chair, ordering a meal brusquely—were believed by those watching this behaviour to be more likely to "get to make decisions" and able to "get people to listen to what [they] say" than people who behave politely. The researchers concluded that "norm violators are perceived as having the capacity to act as they please."[7] As a result, they seem more powerful. Another study found that people who have power judged others much more negatively for speeding, dodging taxes, and keeping a stolen bike than if they engaged in this behaviour themselves. The study also found that those who had legitimate power were even more likely to indulge in moral hypocrisy than those who did not feel personally entitled to their power.[8]

Power should not be considered a bad thing, however. "Power, if used appropriately, should actually be a positive influence in your organization," says professor Patricia Bradshaw of the Schulich School of Business at York University. "Having more power doesn't necessarily turn you into a Machiavellian monster. It can help your team and your organization achieve its goals and increase its potential."[9] *Focus on Research* provides insight into the dynamics of power, choice, and personal control.

FOCUS ON RESEARCH

Power: It's All About Control

Why is choice less important when you have a sense of personal power? A 2011 study examining how people think about power suggests that the desire for power is directly related to control.[10] In one of the experiments that was part of the study, subjects were asked to think about their feelings about being in the role of a boss or an employee after reading a description of the role. Subjects in the employee role read about being in a powerless situation, while those in the boss role read about being in a powerful situation. Afterward, subjects were asked to

power A capacity that A has to influence the behaviour of B, so that B acts in accordance with A's wishes.

dependence B's relationship to A when A possesses something that B requires.

choose whether to "buy eyeglasses or ice cream from a store that had three options or a store that had fifteen options." Subjects in the powerless employee situation chose the scenario with more options, even if it meant driving farther or waiting longer.

In other words, people who have power do not feel the need for as much choice, and people who lack power demand to have more choice. This research suggests that "power satisfies the thirst for choice and choice quenches the desire for power because each replenishes a sense of control."

"People instinctively prefer high to low power positions," says Ena Inesi, one of the researchers from the London Business School. For those in low power positions, "it feels good when you have choice, and it doesn't feel good when choice is taken away." _____

Everyone wants power. Or do they? *Point/Counterpoint* on page 301 considers this question.

Bases of Power

> Rob Ford, formerly the mayor of the largest city in Canada, had legitimate power—power that comes from holding a particular role.[11] This power was called into question, however, when the first crack cocaine video surfaced, and the Toronto city council stripped him of most of his power, giving them to the deputy mayor, Norm Kelly.
>
> Despite his antics, which were widely published in Canada and abroad, many people still sympathized with the mayor. Despite politicians and the media calling for him to step down, many ordinary people did not. As one reporter said, "His regular-guy authenticity still has undeniable appeal. Here is a guy who can make headlines just by talking about his trash-bin face-offs with raccoons (they're getting 'braver and braver')." Ford benefited from another type of power, called referent power. People liked him. What are some other types of power people can have, and how do they use them?

 2 Describe the five bases of power.

Where does power come from? What is it that gives an individual or a group influence over others? We answer by dividing the bases or sources of power into two general groupings—formal and personal—and then breaking each of these down into more specific categories.[12]

Formal Power

Formal power is based on an individual's position in an organization. It can come from the ability to coerce or reward, or from formal authority.

Coercive Power

Coercive power depends on fear of the negative results that might occur if one fails to comply. It rests on the application, or the threat of the application, of physical sanctions such as the infliction of pain, the generation of frustration through restriction of movement, or the controlling by force of basic physiological or safety needs.

At the organizational level, A has coercive power over B if A can dismiss, suspend, or demote B, assuming that B values his or her job. Similarly, if A can assign B work activities that B finds unpleasant or treat B in a manner that B finds embarrassing, A possesses coercive power over B. Coercive power can also come from withholding key information. People in an organization who have data or knowledge others need can make others dependent on them.

Reward Power

The opposite of coercive power is **reward power**. People will go along with the wishes or directives of another if doing so produces positive benefits; therefore,

coercive power Power that is based on fear.

reward power Power that achieves compliance based on the ability to distribute rewards that others view as valuable.

Adeel Halim/Bloomberg via Getty Images

In India, Naina Lal Kidwai is a powerful woman in the banking industry. She derives her power as Chairman of HSBC India. Kidwai's formal power is based on her position at the bank.

someone who can distribute rewards that others view as valuable will have power over those others. These rewards can be either financial—such as controlling pay rates, raises, and bonuses—or nonfinancial, including offering recognition, promotions, interesting work assignments, friendly colleagues, and preferred work shifts or sales territories.[13]

Legitimate Power

In formal groups and organizations, probably the most frequent access to one or more of the bases of power is through a person's structural position. This is called **legitimate power**. It represents the power a person receives as a result of his or her position in the formal hierarchy of an organization.

Legitimate power is broader than the power to coerce and reward. Specifically, it includes acceptance by members of an organization of the authority of a position. We associate power so closely with the concept of hierarchy that just drawing longer lines in an organization chart leads people to infer that the leaders are especially powerful, and when a powerful executive is described, people tend to put the person at a higher position when drawing an organization chart.[14] When school principals, bank presidents, or government department heads speak (assuming that their directives are viewed to be within the authority of their positions), teachers, tellers, and civil servants listen and usually comply.

The *Ethical Dilemma* on page 303 asks you to think about how much you should defer to those in power. The Milgram experiment, discussed in *Focus on Research*, looks at the extremes individuals sometimes go to in order to comply with authority figures.

A Shocking Experiment

Would you shock someone if you were told to do so? A classic experiment conducted by Stanley Milgram studied the extent to which people are willing to obey those in authority.[15] Subjects were recruited for an experiment that asked them to administer electric shocks to a "student" who was supposed to learn a list of words. The experiments were conducted at Yale University, and subjects were assured by the experimenter, who was dressed in a white lab coat, that punishment was an effective way to learn. The subjects were placed in front of an instrument panel that indicated the shocks could go from 15 volts to 450 volts. With each wrong answer, subjects were to administer the next-highest shock level. After the shocks reached a middle level, the "student" started to cry out in pain. The experimenter would instruct the subject to continue administering shocks. What the experimenter was trying to find out was the level at which subjects would stop administering the electric shock. No subject stopped before 300 volts, and 65 percent of the subjects continued to the end of the experiment, even though, at the upper levels, the instrument panel was marked "Danger XXX." It should be noted that subjects were not actually administering shocks, and that the "student" was actually a confederate and was simply acting as if in pain. However, the subjects believed that they were administering electric shocks. This experiment suggests that many people will obey those who appear to have legitimate authority, even in questionable circumstances.

---

legitimate power Power that a person receives as a result of his or her position in the formal hierarchy of an organization.

Personal Power

Many of the most competent and productive chip designers at Toronto-based Celestica have power, but they are not managers and have no formal power. What they have is *personal power*, which comes from an individual's unique characteristics. There are two bases of personal power: expertise and the respect and admiration of others.

👁 Watch on **MyManagementLab**

CH2MHill: Power & Political Behaviour

Expert Power

Expert power is influence based on expertise, special skills, or knowledge. Expertise has become one of the most powerful sources of influence as the world has become more technologically oriented. While it is generally acknowledged that physicians have expertise and hence expert power—most of us follow the advice that our doctor gives us—you should also recognize that computer specialists, tax accountants, economists, and other specialists can have power as a result of their expertise. Young people may find they have increased power in the workplace these days because of their technical knowledge and expertise that Baby Boomer managers may not have.

Referent Power

Referent power develops out of admiration of another and a desire to be like that person. Sometimes teachers and coaches have referent power because of our admiration of them. Referent power explains why celebrities are paid millions of dollars to endorse products in commercials, such as Drake for OVO Jordan Brand sneakers, Eugenie Bouchard for Coca-Cola Canada, Gwen Stefani for L'Oreal, and Justin Timberlake for Sauza tequila. Some people who are not in formal leadership positions nonetheless have referent power and exert influence over others because of their charismatic dynamism, likability, and emotional effects on us.

The *Experiential Exercise* on page 302 gives you the opportunity to explore the effectiveness of different bases of power in changing someone's behaviour.

Evaluating the Bases of Power

Generally, people will respond in one of three ways when faced with those who use the bases of power described above:

- *Commitment.* The person is enthusiastic about the request, and shows initiative and persistence in carrying it out.

- *Compliance.* The person goes along with the request grudgingly, puts in minimal effort, and takes little initiative in carrying out the request.

- *Resistance.* The person is opposed to the request and tries to avoid it with such tactics as refusing, stalling, or arguing about it.[16]

A review of the research on the effectiveness of these forms of power finds that they differ in their impact on a person's performance.[17] Exhibit 8-1 summarizes some of this research. Coercive power leads to resistance from individuals, increased mistrust, and is negatively related to employee satisfaction and commitment. Reward power results in compliance if the rewards are consistent with what individuals want as rewards. Legitimate power also results in compliance, but it does not generally result in increased commitment. In other words, legitimate power does not inspire individuals to act beyond the basic level. Expert and referent powers are the most likely to lead to commitment from individuals and are positively related to employees' satisfaction with supervision, their organizational commitment, and their performance. Ironically, the least effective bases of power for improving commitment—coercive, reward, and legitimate—are the ones most often used by managers, perhaps because they are the easiest to introduce.[18] Research shows that

expert power Influence based on special skills or knowledge.

referent power Influence based on possession by an individual of desirable resources or personal traits.

EXHIBIT 8-1 Continuum of Responses to Power

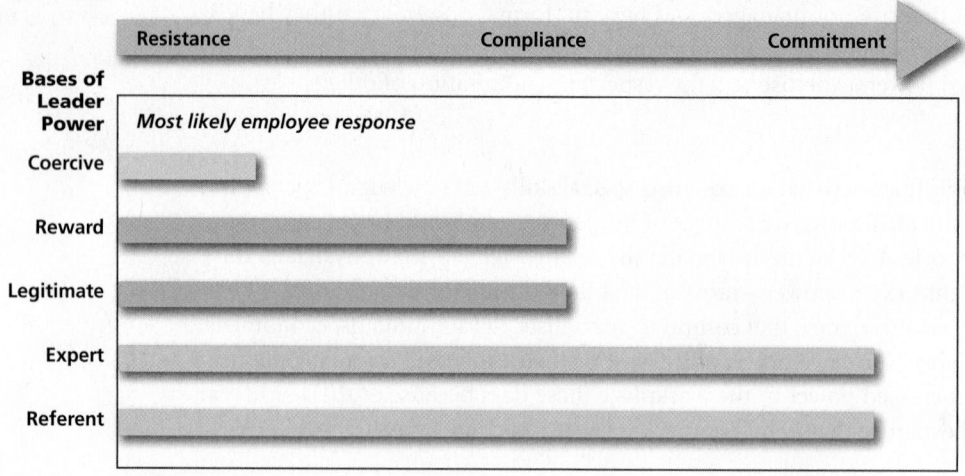

deadline pressure increases group members' reliance on individuals with expert and information power.[19]

Dependency: The Key to Power

3 Explain the role of dependence in power relationships.

> Rob Ford, former mayor of Toronto, ran for election to city council in October 2014 and easily defeated his opponents, receiving almost 3500 more votes than the combined votes of his 13 opponents.[20] Voters in Ward 2 likely think that Ford will be able to help them get things they want for their neighbourhood. When he was their councillor before becoming the mayor, he was known for personally returning phone calls. He vowed after the election that "I'll be taking care of my health and I'll be taking care of the people in Etobicoke North and I'll continue to take care of every taxpayer in this city, like I always have." The voters certainly had alternative candidates to choose from, but they elected Ford. What factors might lead one party (a person or an organization) to have greater power over another?

The most important aspect of power is that it is a function of dependence. In this section, we show how an understanding of dependency is central to furthering your understanding of power itself.

The General Dependency Postulate

Let's begin with a general postulate: *The greater B's dependence on A, the greater the power A has over B.* When you possess anything that others require but that you alone control, you make them dependent upon you and, therefore, you gain power over them.[21] Another way to frame dependence is to think about a relationship in terms of "who needs whom?" The person who has most need is the one most dependent on the relationship.[22]

Dependence is inversely proportional to the alternative sources of supply. If something is plentiful, possession of it will not increase your power. If everyone is intelligent, intelligence gives no special advantage. Similarly, in the circles of the super rich, money does not result in power. But if you can create a monopoly by controlling information, prestige, or anything that others crave, they become dependent on you. Alternatively, the more options you have, the less power you place in the hands of others. This explains, for example, why most organizations develop multiple suppliers rather than give their business to only one.

What Creates Dependence?

Dependence is increased when the resource you control is important, scarce, and cannot be substituted.[23]

Importance

If nobody wants what you have, there is no dependence. To create dependence, the thing(s) you control must be perceived as important. In some organizations, people who control the budget have a great deal of importance. In other organizations, those who possess the knowledge to keep technology working smoothly are viewed as important. What is important is situational. It varies among organizations and undoubtedly also varies over time within any given organization.

> Have you ever wondered how you might increase your power?

Courtesy of Xerox Corporation

Because Xerox Corporation has staked its future on development and innovation, Sophie Vandebroek is in a position of power at Xerox. She is the company's corporate vice president and president of the Xerox Innovation Group, and her group's mission is "to pioneer high-impact technologies that enable us to lead in our core markets and to create future markets for Xerox." Xerox depends on Vandebroek to make that mission a reality.

Scarcity

As noted previously, if something is plentiful, possession of it will not increase your power. A resource must be perceived as scarce to create dependence.

Scarcity can help explain how low-ranking employees gain power if they have important knowledge not available to high-ranking employees. Possession of a scarce resource—in this case, important knowledge—makes those who don't have it dependent on those who do. Thus, an individual might refuse to show others how to do a job or might refuse to share information, thereby increasing his or her importance.

The scarcity–dependence relationship can further be seen in the power of occupational categories. For example, college and university administrators have no problem finding English instructors to staff classes. There are more individuals who have degrees enabling them to work as English instructors than there are positions available in Canada. The market for corporate finance professors, by contrast, is extremely tight, with the demand high and the supply limited. The result is that the bargaining power of finance faculty allows them to negotiate higher salaries, lighter teaching loads, and other benefits.

Nonsubstitutability

The fewer substitutes there are for a resource, the more power comes from control over that resource. At universities with strong pressures on the faculty to publish, the more recognition the faculty member receives through publication, the more mobile he or she is, because other universities want faculty who are highly published and visible. Although tenure can alter this relationship by restricting the department head's alternatives, faculty members with few or no publications have the least mobility and are subject to the greatest influence from their superiors. In another example, when a union goes on strike and management is not permitted to replace the striking employees, the union has considerable control over the organization's ability to carry out its tasks.

People are often able to ask for special rewards (higher pay or better assignments) because they have skills that others don't.

Influence Tactics

④ Identify nine power or influence tactics and their contingencies.

How do individuals translate their bases of power into specific, desired actions? Research has identified nine distinct influence tactics:[24]

1. *Rational persuasion.* Using facts and data to make a logical or rational presentation of ideas.

2. *Inspirational appeals.* Appealing to values, ideals, and goals when making a request.

3. *Consultation.* Getting others involved to support one's objectives.

4. *Ingratiation.* Using flattery, creating goodwill, and being friendly prior to making a request.

5. *Personal appeals.* Appealing to loyalty and friendship when asking for something.

6. *Exchange.* Offering favours or benefits in exchange for support.

7. *Coalitions.* Getting the support of other people to provide backing when making a request.

8. *Pressure.* Using demands, threats, and reminders to get someone to do something.

9. *Legitimacy.* Claiming the authority or right to make a request, or showing that it supports organizational goals or policies.

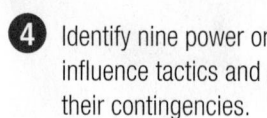

PERSONAL INVENTORY ASSESSMENT

Learn About Yourself
Gaining Power and Influence

PERSONAL INVENTORY ASSESSMENT

Learn About Yourself
Using Influence Strategies

Some tactics are more effective than others. Rational persuasion, inspirational appeals, and consultation tend to be the most effective, especially when the audience is highly interested in the outcomes of a decision process. Pressure tends to frequently backfire and is typically the least effective of the nine tactics.[25] You can also increase your chance of success by using two or more tactics together, as long as your choices are compatible.[26] For instance, using both ingratiation and legitimacy can lessen the negative reactions that might come from appearing to "dictate" outcomes, but only when the audience does not really care about the outcome of a decision process or the policy is routine.[27]

The effectiveness of some influence tactics depends on the direction of influence.[28] Studies have found that rational persuasion is the only tactic that is effective across organizational levels. Inspirational appeals work best as a downward-influencing tactic with subordinates. When pressure works, it's generally only to achieve downward influence. The use of personal appeals and coalitions is most effective with lateral influence attempts. In addition to the direction of influence, a number of other factors have been found to affect which tactics work best. These include the sequencing of tactics, a person's skill in using the tactic, and the culture of the organization.

You are more likely to be effective if you begin with "softer" tactics that rely on personal power such as personal and inspirational appeals, rational persuasion, and consultation. If these fail, you can move to "harder" tactics (which emphasize formal power and involve greater costs and risks), such as exchange, coalitions, and pressure.[29] Interestingly, it has been found that using a single soft tactic is more effective than using a single hard tactic, and that combining two soft tactics or a soft tactic and rational persuasion is more effective than any single tactic or a combination of hard tactics.[30] The effectiveness of tactics depends on the audience.[31] People especially likely to comply with soft power tactics tend to be more reflective and intrinsically motivated; they have high self-esteem and greater desire for control. Those likely to comply with hard power tactics are more action oriented and extrinsically motivated and are more focused on getting along with others than on getting their own way.

People differ in their **political skill**, or the ability to influence others in such a way as to enhance their own objectives. The politically skilled are more effective users of all of the influence tactics. Political skill also appears to be more effective when the stakes are high—such as when the individual is accountable for important organizational outcomes. Finally, the politically skilled are able to exert their influence without others detecting it, which is a key element in being effective (it's damaging to be labelled political).[32] However, these individuals also appear most able to use their political skills in environments marked by low levels of procedural and distributive justice. When an organization is run with open and fairly applied rules, free of favouritism or biases, political skill is actually negatively related to job performance ratings.[33]

Finally, we know that cultures within organizations differ markedly—for example, some are warm, relaxed, and supportive; others are formal and conservative. Some encourage the use of participation and consultation, some encourage reason, and still others rely on pressure. People who fit the culture of the organization tend to obtain more influence.[34] Specifically, extraverts tend to be more influential in team-oriented organizations, and highly conscientious people are more influential in organizations that value working alone on technical tasks. People who fit the culture are influential because they can perform especially well in the domains deemed most important for success. In other words, they are influential because they are competent. Thus, the organization itself will influence which subset of influence tactics is viewed as acceptable for use. The kinds of tactics used have also changed over time.

How Power Affects People

People can use power for a variety of purposes.[35] There is evidence to suggest that while Rob Ford and his brother Doug have done much to serve the people of Etobicoke in their roles as councillors to that city, they have also made use of their positions to benefit themselves and their friends.

The Fords have a family firm, named DECO Labels and Tags. The brothers were accused of helping RR Donnelley, one of the company's US suppliers, to get meetings with city bureaucrats to discuss outsourcing part of city hall printing to them. Meanwhile, DECO was trying to negotiate a better business arrangement with RR Donnelley. While no deals were ever concluded, such behaviour is questionable.

In 2012, then mayor Ford tried to get road work in front of DECO expedited, so that it would be finished before the business' 50th anniversary celebration. City officials directed that public resources be used for this work. When Apollo Health and Beauty Care, a Toronto-based shampoo manufacturer that purchased labels from DECO, was cited for effluent from the manufacturing process getting into the sewer lines, the brothers asked Lou Di Gironimo, the head of Toronto Water, to meet with Apollo representatives to sort out the situation.

In September 2012, Mayor Ford was criticized by a taxpayers' advocacy group for using city staff and equipment to help the Don Bosco Eagles, a youth football team he had coached for many years.

What leads people to use power either selfishly or wisely?

To this point, we have discussed what power is and how it is acquired. But we have not yet answered one important question: Does power corrupt?

Power does appear to have corrupting aspects. For example, power can lead people to place their own interests ahead of those of others. Why does this happen? Interestingly, research suggests that power not only leads people to focus on their self-interests because they can but also liberates people to focus inward, and thus come to place greater weight on their goals and interests. Power also appears to lead individuals to "objectify" others (to see them as tools to obtain their instrumental goals), to value relations with people with less power, and to see relationships as more peripheral.[36]

political skill The ability to influence others in such a way as to enhance one's objectives.

That is not all. Powerful people react (especially negatively) to any threats to their competence. They are more willing to denigrate others. People given power are more likely to make self-interested decisions when faced with a moral hazard (such as when hedge fund managers take more risks with other people's money because they are rewarded for gains but less often punished for losses). Power also leads to overconfident decision making.[37]

So, yes, power does appear to have some important disturbing effects on us. But that is hardly the whole story—it's more complicated than that. Power does not affect everyone in the same way, and there are even positive effects of power. Let's consider each of these in turn.

First, the toxic effects of power depend on one's personality. Research suggests that if we have an anxious personality, power does not corrupt us because we are less likely to think that using power benefits us.[38] Second, the corrosive effect of power can be contained by organizational systems. One 2012 study found, for example, that while power made people behave in a self-serving manner, when accountability of this behaviour was initiated, the self-serving behaviour stopped. Third, forgive the pun, but we have the power to blunt the negative effects of power. One study showed that simply expressing gratitude toward powerful others made them less likely to aggress against us.[39] Finally, remember the aphorism that those with little power grab and abuse what little they have? There appears to be some truth to this in that the people most likely to abuse power are those who are low in status and gain power. Why is this the case? It appears that having low status is threatening, and this fear is used in negative ways if power is given.[40]

As you can see, some factors can ameliorate the negative effects of power. But power can have general positive effects. Power can energize and lead to approach motivation (that is, more motivation to achieve goals). It can also enhance people's motivation to help others (at least certain people). A 2012 study found, for example, that values toward helping others only translated into actual work behaviour when people felt a sense of power.[41]

These studies point to an important insight about power: It's not so much that power corrupts but that it *reveals*. Supporting this line of reasoning, another study revealed that power led to self-interested behaviour only for those with weak moral identities (that is, the degree to which morals are core to one's identity). For those with strong moral identities, power actually enhanced their moral awareness.[42]

Empowerment: Giving Power to Employees

5 Explain what empowerment is, and the factors that lead to it.

Thus far, our discussion has implied—to some extent, at least—that power is something that is more likely to reside in the hands of managers, to be used as part of their interaction with employees. However, in today's workplace, there is a movement toward sharing more power with employees by putting them in teams and also by making them responsible for some of the decisions regarding their jobs. For instance, at Vancouver-based iQmetrix Software Development, employees are part of a results-only workplace, where they are encouraged to make their own decisions.[43] Organizational specialists refer to this increasing responsibility as *empowerment*.

Definition of Empowerment

The definition of *empowerment* that we use here refers to the freedom and the ability of employees to make decisions and commitments.[45] Unfortunately, neither managers nor researchers agree on the definition of empowerment. One study found that executives were split about 50-50 in their definition.[46] One group of executives "believed that empowerment was about delegating decision making within a set of clear boundaries."[47] Empowerment would start at the top, specific goals and tasks would be assigned, responsibility would be delegated, and people would be held accountable for their results. The other group believed that empowerment was "a process of risk taking and personal growth." This type of empowerment starts at the bottom, with considering the employees' needs, showing them what empowered behaviour looks like, building teams, encouraging risk-taking, and demonstrating trust in employees' ability to perform. *Case Incident—Delegate Power or Keep It Close?* on page 304 considers the tension between delegating and remaining in charge.

One difficulty with empowerment is that managers often give lip service to the idea,[48] with organizations telling employees that they have decision-making responsibility, but not giving them the authority to carry out their decisions. The result is a great deal of cynicism in many workplaces, particularly when "empowered" employees are micromanaged. For an employee to be fully empowered, he or she needs access to the information required to make decisions; rewards for acting in appropriate, responsible ways; and the authority to make the necessary decisions. Empowerment means that employees understand how their job fits into the organization and are able to make decisions regarding job action guided by the organization's purpose and mission.

Not every employee appreciates being empowered, however. One study found that sometimes empowerment can make employees ill if they are put in charge at work but lack the confidence to handle their responsibilities.[49]

Robert E. Quinn and Gretchen M. Spreitzer, in their research on the characteristics of empowered people (through both in-depth interviews and survey analysis), found four characteristics that most empowered people have in common:

Discount has a culture of empowerment. As Jay Singer, Discount's president and CEO, notes: "We want a culture where people . . . feel valued every day. We want an environment where they feel their contributions are significant and that their roles truly matter." In 2013, Discount was named one of Canada's 10 Most Admired Corporate Cultures in the Growth & Small Cap category by Waterstone Human Capital. Pictured here are executives David Minas, Susan Ball, Al Nanji, Jay Singer, and Barry Singer.[44]

- Empowered people have a sense of *self-determination* (they feel free to choose how to do their work; they are not micromanaged).

- Empowered people have a sense of *meaning* (they feel that their work is important to them; they care about what they are doing).

- Empowered people have a sense of *competence* (they feel confident about their ability to do their work well; they know they can perform).

- Empowered people have a sense of *impact* (they believe that they can have influence on their work unit; others listen to their ideas).

At Vancouver-based Great Little Box Company (GLBC), which designs and manufactures corrugated containers, employees are given the freedom to do whatever they feel is necessary and appropriate to make customers happy. If a customer is dissatisfied with the product, the employee can say, "OK, I'll bring this product back and return it for you," without having to get prior authorization.

EXHIBIT 8-2 Characteristics of Empowered People

Robert E. Quinn and Gretchen M. Spreitzer, in their research on the characteristics of empowered people (through both in-depth interviews and survey analysis), found four characteristics that most empowered people have in common:

- *Self-determination:* They choose how to do their work (they are not micromanaged).
- *Sense of meaning:* They care about what they do because they consider what they do has an important purpose.
- *Sense of competence:* They believe that they have the ability to perform their work well.
- *Sense of impact:* They believe that their ideas are listened to and that they can influence work outcomes.

Source: Based on R. E. Quinn and G. M. Spreitzer, "The Road to Empowerment: Seven Questions Every Leader Should Consider," *Organizational Dynamics*, Autumn 1997, p. 41.

When employees are empowered, they are expected to act, at least in a small way, as owners of the company, rather than just employees. Ownership is not necessary in the financial sense, but in terms of identifying with the goals and mission of the organization. For employees to be empowered, however, and have an ownership mentality, four conditions need to be met, according to Professor Dan Ondrack at the Rotman School of Management at the University of Toronto:[50]

> What do you need to be truly empowered?

- There must be a clear definition of the values and mission of the company.

- The company must help employees acquire the relevant skills.

- Employees need to be supported in their decision making, and not criticized when they try to do something extraordinary.

- Employees need to be recognized for their efforts.

Exhibit 8-2 outlines what two researchers discovered in studying the characteristics of empowered people.

The Abuse of Power

Studies indicate that when someone is in a position of power, he or she may be more willing to exert that power.[51] *Focus on Research* shows how this idea played out in one particular study.

FOCUS ON RESEARCH

The Cookie Experiment

Who eats the fourth cookie? In a study known as the "cookie experiment," three psychologists instructed teams of three students to write a short paper during a meeting.[52] Two of the team members (the "subordinates") were to do the actual writing, and the third team member (the "boss") was assigned to evaluate the work and determine the pay the two writers would receive. Part way through the meeting, experimenters brought in a plate of five cookies. As expected, no one ate the fifth cookie (rules of etiquette suggest that one should not eat the last item on a plate). The researchers were interested, then, in who ate the fourth cookie, given that it was extra. "Bosses" were far more likely to take the fourth cookie than "subordinates," and were much more likely to chew with their mouths open and scatter crumbs widely, signs that their power enabled them to act in less-inhibited ways.

The authors concluded that people with power behave very differently than those without it. Powerful people are generally less inhibited and sometimes act in counter-normative ways. Powerless people "are more likely to feel negative moods and emotions, to attend to punishment and threat, to make more careful, controlled judgments about others' intentions, attitudes, and actions, and to inhibit their own behaviours and act contingently upon others."

Below we examine ways in which power can be unacceptably exhibited at work.

Harassment in the Workplace

People who engage in harassment in the workplace are typically abusing their power position. The manager–employee relationship best characterizes an unequal power relationship, where position power gives the manager the capacity to reward and coerce. Managers give employees their assignments, evaluate their performance, make recommendations for salary adjustments and promotions, and even decide whether employees retain their job. These decisions give a manager power. Since employees want favourable performance reviews, salary increases, and the like, it's clear that managers control the resources that most employees consider important and scarce.

Although co-workers do not have position power, they can have influence and use it to harass peers. In fact, although co-workers appear to engage in somewhat less severe forms of harassment than do managers, co-workers are the most frequent perpetrators of harassment, particularly sexual harassment, in organizations. How do co-workers exercise power? Most often they provide or withhold information, cooperation, and support.

Some categories of harassment have long been illegal in Canada, including those based on race, religion, and national origin, as well as sexual harassment. Unfortunately, some types of harassment that occur in the workplace are not deemed illegal, even if they create problems for employees and managers. We focus here on two types of harassment that have received considerable attention in the press: workplace bullying and sexual harassment.

Workplace Bullying

Many of us are aware, anecdotally if not personally, of managers who harass employees, demanding overtime without pay or excessive work performance. Further, some of the recent stories of workplace violence have reportedly been the result of an employee feeling intimidated at work. In research conducted in the private and public sector in southern Saskatchewan, Céleste Brotheridge, a professor at the Université du Québec à Montréal, found that bullying was prevalent in the workplace. Forty percent of the respondents noted that they had experienced one or more forms of bullying weekly in the past six months. Ten percent experienced bullying at a much greater level: five or more incidents a week. Brotheridge notes that bullying has a negative effect on the workplace: "Given bullying's deleterious effects on employee health, it is reason for concern."[53]

There is no clear definition of workplace bullying, and Marilyn Noble, a Fredericton-based adult educator, remarks that in some instances a fine line exists between managing and bullying. However, recent research suggests that bosses who feel inadequate or overwhelmed are more likely to bully.[54] As one of the study's co-authors explained: "The

6 Show the connection between harassment and the abuse of power.

combination of having a high-power role and fearing that one is not up to the task … causes power holders to lash out."[55]

The effects of bullying can be devastating. Professors Sandy Hershcovis of the University of Manitoba and Julian Barling of Queen's University found that the consequences of bullying were more harmful to its victims than those who suffered sexual harassment. Bullied employees more often quit their jobs, were less satisfied with their jobs, and had more difficult relationships with their supervisors.[56]

Quebec introduced the first anti-bullying labour legislation in North America on June 1, 2004. The legislation defines psychological harassment as "any vexatious behaviour in the form of repeated and hostile or unwanted conduct, verbal comments, actions or gestures that affect an employee's dignity or psychological or physical integrity and that results in a harmful work environment for the employee."[57] Under the Quebec law, bullying allegations will be sent to mediation, where the accuser and the accused will work with an independent third party to try to resolve the problem. If mediation fails, employers who have allowed psychological harassment can be fined up to $10 000 and ordered to pay financial damages to the victim. WorkSafeBC has also developed occupational health and safety policies to help employers and prevent and address workplace bullying.[58] *OB on the Edge—Workplace Bullying* on pages 340–345 looks at this matter more closely.

Sexual Harassment

Sexual harassment is wrong. It can also be costly to employers. Just ask executives at Walmart, the World Bank, and the United Nations.[59] The Supreme Court of Canada defines **sexual harassment** as unwelcome behaviour of a sexual nature in the workplace that negatively affects the work environment or leads to adverse job-related consequences for the employee.[60] Despite the legal framework for defining sexual harassment, disagreement continues as to what *specifically* constitutes sexual harassment. Sexual harassment includes unwanted physical touching, recurring requests for dates when it is made clear the person is not interested, and coercive threats that a person will lose her or his job if she or he refuses a sexual proposition. The problems of interpreting sexual harassment often surface around some of its more subtle forms— unwanted looks or comments, off-colour jokes, sexual artifacts such as nude calendars in the workplace, sexual innuendo, or misinterpretations of where the line between "being friendly" ends and "harassment" begins.

Most studies confirm that the concept of power is central to understanding sexual harassment.[61] This seems true whether the harassment comes from a supervisor, a co-worker, or an employee. Sexual harassment is more likely to occur when there are large power differentials. The supervisor–employee dyad best characterizes an unequal power relationship, where formal power gives the supervisor the capacity to reward and coerce. Because employees want favourable performance reviews, salary increases, and the like, supervisors control resources most employees consider important and scarce. Thus, sexual harassment by the manager typically creates the greatest difficulty for those being harassed. If there are no witnesses, it's the victim's word against the harasser's. Has this manager harassed others, and, if so, will those others come forward or fear retaliation? Male respondents in one study in Switzerland who were high in hostile sexism reported higher intentions to sexually harass in organizations that had low levels of justice, suggesting that failure to have consistent policies and procedures for all employees might actually increase levels of sexual harassment.[62]

Employers in Canada are expected to protect their employees with sexual harassment policies. Some employers have developed sexual harassment policies, and some go further, either banning workplace romances or requiring them to be reported to management. Lying about a workplace affair got one manager fired, as *OB in the Workplace* shows.

sexual harassment Unwelcome behaviour of a sexual nature in the workplace that negatively affects the work environment or leads to adverse job-related consequences for the employee.

IN THE **WORKPLACE**
It's Not About the Affair, It's About the Coverup

Should an employee be fired for lying about a workplace affair?   Bryan Reichard, a 41-year-old married manager at Kitchener-based Kuntz Electroplating, had an affair with one of the company's administrative assistants.[63] She was single and 26.

In order to prevent sexual harassment lawsuits, Kuntz implemented a non-fraternization policy, which specified that employees in romantic relationships needed to notify their manager. Reichard was repeatedly asked if he was having an affair with the administrative assistant, but he denied it. Kuntz did not forbid office relationships, so Reichard would not have been disciplined for having a workplace affair.

However, Reichard was eventually terminated for lying about the affair. The decision was appealed, and Kuntz's decision to terminate Reichard was upheld. The judge hearing the case gave his reasoning in his December 2011 judgment: "Kuntz had every right to consider that Reichard's wilful misconduct seriously called into question the trust, integrity and honesty required for him to perform his duties as a manager and that Kuntz's lack of trust in Reichard was sufficient to terminate him for cause." _____

In addition to its legal repercussions, sexual harassment obviously has a negative impact on the work environment. Sexual harassment negatively affects job attitudes and leads those who feel harassed to withdraw from the work (for example, avoiding work, failing to attend scheduled meetings). In fact, perceptions of sexual harassment are more likely than workplace bullying to lead to work withdrawal.[64] It also appears that sexual harassment has health consequences. Women exposed to workplace sexual harassment reported psychological distress two years after the harassment occurred.[65]

Workplaces are not the only place where sexual harassment occurs. While nonconsensual sex between professors and students is rape and subject to criminal charges, it's harder to evaluate apparently consensual relationships that occur outside the classroom. There is some argument over whether truly consensual sex is ever possible between students and professors. In an effort to underscore the power discrepancy and potential for abuse of it by professors, in 2009 Yale University implemented a policy forbidding romantic relationships between professors and undergraduate students.[66] Deputy Provost Charles Long explained the university's decision: "I think we have a responsibility to protect students from behavior that is damaging to them and to the objectives for their being here." Most universities have been unwilling to adopt such an extreme stance, and it's not clear that in Canada such a policy would stand up in the courts. Carleton University does not prohibit relationships between individuals in authority and those who are not, but does include the following statement in its sexual harassment policy: "No individual in a position of authority is permitted to grade or supervise the performance of any student, or evaluate an employee or a colleague, with whom they are sexually involved or have been within the past five years."[67]

A recent study found that nearly two-thirds of university students experience some type of sexual harassment, but most of these incidents go unreported.[68] However, much of this harassment comes from student-on-student incidents. Matt Abbott, a student at the University of New Brunswick, says that "certain aspects of sexual violence are almost normal within the dating culture in campus communities." Iain Boekhoff, the editor-in-chief of Western University's Frosh issue of the *Gazette*, came under fire in August 2014 for publishing an article telling first-year students how to sexually harass their teaching assistants (TAs). Boekhoff defended the article as being relatively tame. "Two years ago it was just straight, 'How to have sex with your TA,' as one of the 50 or 100 things to do before you leave Western," he said.[69] Is it any wonder, then, that University of British Columbia student Anoushka Ratnarajah notes that "'the line' with respect to sexual harassment and the issue of consent are still fuzzy for many students"?[70]

Sexual harassment can wreak havoc on an organization, not to mention on the victims themselves. But it can be avoided. A manager's role in preventing sexual harassment is critical. Managers can protect themselves and their employees from sexual harassment in the following ways:

- Make sure an active policy defines what constitutes sexual harassment, informs employees that they can be fired for sexually harassing another employee, and establishes procedures for making complaints.

- Reassure employees that they will not encounter retaliation if they issue a complaint.

- Investigate every complaint and inform the legal and human resource departments.

- Make sure that offenders are disciplined or terminated.

- Set up in-house seminars to raise employee awareness of sexual harassment issues.

Should workplaces ban all forms of sexual behaviour as a way of preventing harassment? *Focus on Ethics* considers this question.

FOCUS ON ETHICS — Sex at Work

Should romantic relationships be prohibited at work? The difficulty in monitoring and defining sexual harassment at work has led some organizations to go beyond discouraging overt sexually harassing behaviours.[71] Companies ranging from Walmart to Staples to Xerox have disciplined employees for workplace romances and upheld policies that ban hierarchical romantic relationships, such as between a supervisor and a subordinate. The idea is that such relationships are so fraught with potential for abuse of power that they cannot possibly be consensual for extended periods of time. Surveys by the Society of Human Resource Management suggest that concerns about both potential sexual harassment and lowered productivity have motivated prohibitions on workplace romances. However, ethicists and legal scholars have thrown some "no romance" policies into question on the grounds they are patronizing or invade employee privacy.

What does organizational behaviour research have to say about *consensual* sexual behaviour at work? One study of more than 1000 respondents found that 40 percent were exposed to sexual behaviour in some form in the past year. Counter to the idea that all sexual behaviour at work is negative, some female and many male respondents reported enjoying the experience. However, exposure to sexual behaviour at work was negatively related to performance and psychological well-being. People may report enjoying it, but it might be hurting their productivity and well-being anyway.

Politics: Power in Action

7 Identify the causes and consequences of political behaviour.

When the stories of the first video purportedly showing Rob Ford smoking crack cocaine surfaced in May 2013, Ford persistently denied both the existence of the video, and that he smoked crack.[72] Not everyone believed his denial, and the story put Toronto's mayor into the international news. Some members of city council, as well as the editorial boards of the *National Post*, *Toronto Sun*, and *Toronto Star*, called for Ford to step down. Ford refused to resign, fired his chief of staff, and faced the resignation of six staff members.

In November 2013, the *Globe and Mail* published photos taken from a second video that showed Ford smoking crack. The police subsequently confirmed the existence of the video. Ford apologized for his actions, claiming he did not really remember them, and announced that he was going into rehab for drug and alcohol abuse. But he adamantly said he would not resign from office, even in the face of some council members suggesting that he do just that.

That Ford did not resign despite this very public scandal indicates that he used his political skills wisely. He made sure that his allies were supportive of him to keep his detractors at bay. How can politics help you save your career?

When people get together in groups, power will be exerted. People want to carve out a niche from which to exert influence, to earn awards, and to advance their careers.[73] When employees in organizations convert their power into action, we describe them as being engaged in politics. Those with good political skills have the ability to use their bases of power effectively.[74] In this section, we look at political behaviour, including the types of political activity people use to try to influence others, and impression management. Political skills are not confined to adults, of course. Even young children are quite adept at waging careful, deliberate campaigns to wear their parents down, so that they can get things that they want.

Definition of Political Behaviour

There is no shortage of definitions for organizational politics. One clever definition of politics comes from Tom Jakobek, Toronto's former budget chief, who said, "In politics, you may have to go from A to C to D to E to F to G and then to B."[75] Essentially, this type of politics focuses on the use of power to affect decision making in an organization, or on self-serving and organizationally unsanctioned behaviours.[76]

For our purposes, we will define **political behaviour** in organizations as those activities that are outside one's formal role and that influence, or attempt to influence, the distribution of advantages and disadvantages within the organization.[77]

When American figure skater Johnny Weir's low scores were announced at the men's 2010 Olympic Figure Skating finals, almost the entire crowd booed the judges in the Vancouver stadium. Some thought that the judges were engaging in politics to send a message to him that his style of artistic skating was not "masculine" enough for the sport. Although he failed to win an Olympic medal, he was asked to be a commentator for NBC for skating events during the 2014 Winter Olympics in Sochi.

THE CANADIAN PRESS/AP/Mark Baker

political behaviour Those activities that influence, or attempt to influence, the distribution of advantages and disadvantages within the organization.

This definition encompasses key elements from what most people mean when they talk about organizational politics. Political behaviour is outside one's specified job requirements. The behaviour requires some attempt to use one's bases of power. Our definition also encompasses efforts to influence the goals, criteria, or processes used for decision making when we state that politics is concerned with "the distribution of advantages and disadvantages within the organization." Our definition is broad enough to include such varied political behaviours as withholding key information from decision makers, joining a coalition, whistle-blowing, spreading rumours, leaking confidential information about organizational activities to the media, exchanging favours with others in the organization for mutual benefit, and lobbying on behalf of or against a particular individual or decision alternative. Exhibit 8-3 provides a quick measure to help you assess how political your workplace is.

EXHIBIT 8-3 A Quick Measure of How Political Your Workplace Is

How political is your workplace? Answer the 12 questions using the following scale:

SD = Strongly disagree

D = Disagree

U = Uncertain

A = Agree

SA = Strongly agree

1. Managers often use the selection system to hire only people who can help them in their future. _____

2. The rules and policies concerning promotion and pay are fair; it's how managers carry out the policies that is unfair and self-serving. _____

3. The performance ratings people receive from their managers reflect more of the managers' "own agenda" than the actual performance of the employee. _____

4. Although a lot of what my manager does around here appears to be directed at helping employees, it's actually intended to protect my manager. _____

5. There are cliques or "in-groups" that hinder effectiveness around here. _____

6. My co-workers help themselves, not others. _____

7. I have seen people deliberately distort information requested by others for purposes of personal gain, either by withholding it or by selectively reporting it. _____

8. If co-workers offer to lend some assistance, it is because they expect to get something out of it. _____

9. Favouritism rather than merit determines who gets ahead around here. _____

10. You can usually get what you want around here if you know the right person to ask. _____

11. Overall, the rules and policies concerning promotion and pay are specific and well-defined. _____

12. Pay and promotion policies are generally clearly communicated in this organization. _____

This questionnaire taps the three salient dimensions that have been found to be related to perceptions of politics: manager behaviour; co-worker behaviour; and organizational policies and practices. To calculate your score for items 1–10, give yourself 1 point for Strongly disagree; 2 points for Disagree; and so forth (through 5 points for Strongly agree). For items 11 and 12, reverse the score (that is, 1 point for Strongly agree, etc.). Sum up the total: The higher the total score, the greater the degree of perceived organizational politics.

Source: G. R. Ferris, D. D. Frink, D. P. S. Bhawuk, J. Zhou, and D. C. Gilmore, "Reactions of Diverse Groups to Politics in the Workplace," *Journal of Management* 22, no. 1 (1996), pp. 32–33.

The Reality of Politics

Why, you may wonder, must politics exist? Isn't it possible for an organization to be politics-free? It's *possible*, but most unlikely. Organizations are made up of individuals and groups with different values, goals, and interests.[78] This sets up the potential for conflict over the allocation of limited resources, such as departmental budgets, space, project responsibilities, and salary adjustments.[79] If resources were abundant, then all constituencies within the organization could satisfy their goals. But because they are limited, not everyone's interests can be satisfied. Furthermore, gains by one individual or group are often *perceived* as coming at the expense of others within the organization (whether they are or not). These forces create real competition among members for the organization's limited resources.

Maybe the most important factor behind politics within organizations is the realization that most of the "facts" that are used to allocate the limited resources are open to interpretation. What, for instance, is *good* performance? What is an *adequate* improvement? What constitutes an *unsatisfactory* job? It's in this large and ambiguous middle ground of organizational life—where the facts *don't* speak for themselves—that politics flourish.

Finally, because most decisions must be made in a climate of ambiguity—where facts are rarely fully objective, and thus are open to interpretation—people within organizations will use whatever influence they can to spin the facts to support their goals and interests. That, of course, creates the activities we call *politicking*. For more about how one engages in politicking, see *From Concepts to Skills* on pages 305–307.

Therefore, to answer the earlier question about whether it is possible for an organization to be politics-free, we can say "yes"—but only if all the members of that organization hold the same goals and interests, organizational resources are not scarce, and performance outcomes are completely clear and objective. However, that does not describe the organizational world in which most of us live.

RESEARCH FINDINGS: Politicking

Individuals who successfully engage in politicking can achieve favourable outcomes. But for most people—who have modest political skills or are unwilling to play the politics game—outcomes tend to be predominantly negative.[80] There is, for instance, very strong evidence indicating that perceptions of organizational politics are negatively related to job satisfaction.[81] The perception of politics also tends to increase job anxiety and stress. This seems to be because of the perception that, by not engaging in politics, a person may be losing ground to others who are active politickers, or, conversely, because of the additional pressures individuals feel because of having entered into and competing in the political arena.[82] Not surprisingly, when politicking becomes too much to handle, it can lead employees to quit.[83]

Researchers have also noted two interesting qualifiers. First, the politics–performance relationship appears to be moderated by an individual's understanding of the "hows" and "whys" of organizational politics. "An individual who has a clear understanding of who is responsible for making decisions and why they were selected to be the decision makers would have a better understanding of how and why things happen the way they do than someone who does not understand the decision-making process in the organization."[84] When both politics and understanding are high, performance is likely to increase because the individual will see political actions as an opportunity. This is consistent with what you might expect among individuals with well-honed political skills. But when understanding is low, individuals are more likely to see politics as a threat, which can have a negative effect on job performance.[85]

Second, perceptions of political behaviour at work influence the extent to which ethical leadership affects organizational citizenship behaviour.[86] One study found that male employees were more responsive to ethical leadership and showed the most organizational citizenship behaviour when levels of both politics and ethical leadership were high. Women, on the other hand, appear most likely to engage in organizational citizenship behaviour when the environment is consistently ethical and *apolitical*.

Types of Political Activity

People engage in a variety of political activities in organizations, including the following:[87]

- *Attacking or blaming others.* Used when trying to avoid responsibility for failure.
- *Using information.* Withholding or distorting information, particularly to hide negative information.
- *Managing impressions.* Bringing positive attention to oneself or taking credit for positive accomplishments of others.
- *Building support for ideas.* Making sure that others will support one's ideas before they are presented.
- *Praising others.* Making important people feel good.
- *Building coalitions.* Joining with other people to create a powerful group.
- *Associating with influential people.* Building support networks.
- *Creating obligations.* Doing favours for others so they will owe you favours later.

Individuals use these political activities for different purposes. Some of these activities (such as attacking or blaming others) are more likely to be used to defend one's position, while other activities (such as building support for ideas and managing impressions) are meant to enhance one's image. Evidence suggests that keeping your enemies close to you makes some sense politically, as *Focus on Research* indicates.

> Why do some people seem to engage in politics more than others?

FOCUS ON RESEARCH

Powerful Leaders Keep Their (Fr)Enemies Close

Is it really wise to keep your enemies close? We have all heard the term "frenemies" used to describe friends who are also rivals or people who act like friends but secretly dislike each other.[88] Some observers have argued that frenemies are increasing at work due to the "abundance of very close, intertwined relationships that bridge people's professional and personal lives."

Recent research based on three experimental studies found that a dominant leader chose to work in the same room with a rival ingroup member, even when instructed that they would probably perform better apart; to sit closer to the rival when working together; and to express an explicit preference to be closer to the rival. The primary reason dominant leaders wanted to be closer to rivals was to monitor the rivals' behaviour and performance and protect their power.

The research also found that the "keeping enemies closer" effect was strong under certain conditions—when a rival was socially dominant, when a dominant leader felt competition from the rival, and when the rewards and ability to serve as a dominant leader were dependent on the rival's performance.

These results suggest that the concept of frenemies is very real and that we choose to keep our rivals close so we can keep an eye on the competition they provide. _____

Impression Management

The process by which individuals attempt to control the impression others form of them is called **impression management**.[89] Being perceived positively by others should have benefits for people in organizations. It might, for instance, help them initially to get the jobs they want in an organization and, once hired, to get favourable evaluations, superior salary increases, and more rapid promotions. In a political context, it might help bring more advantages their way.

Who might we predict will engage in impression management? No surprise here. It's our old friend, the high self-monitor (see Chapter 2).[90] Low self-monitors tend to present images of themselves that are consistent with their personalities, regardless of the beneficial or detrimental effects for them. In contrast, high self-monitors are good at reading situations and moulding their appearances and behaviour to fit each situation.

Keep in mind that when people engage in impression management, they are sending a false message that might be true under other circumstances.[91] Excuses, for instance, may be offered with great sincerity. You may *actually* believe that ads contribute little to sales in your region. But misrepresentation can have a high cost.[92] So the impression manager must be cautious not to be perceived as insincere or manipulative.[93]

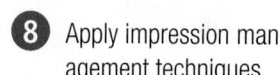

8 Apply impression management techniques.

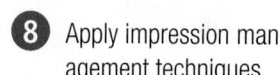

RESEARCH FINDINGS: Impression Management Techniques

Researchers have found that people have mixed reactions when they encounter impression management by others. Participants in a study in Switzerland disliked an experimental confederate who claimed to be a personal friend of the well-liked Swiss tennis star Roger Federer, but they generally liked confederates who just said they were fans.[94] Another study found that when managers attributed an employee's organizational citizenship behaviour to impression management, they actually felt angry (probably because they felt manipulated) and gave subordinates lower performance ratings. When managers attributed the same behaviours to pro-social values and concern about the organization, they felt happy and gave higher performance ratings.[95]

The evidence indicates that most job applicants use impression management techniques in interviews[96] and that, when impression management behaviour is used, it works.[97] In one study, for instance, interviewers felt that applicants for a position as a customer-service representative who used impression management techniques performed better in the interview, and they seemed somewhat more inclined to hire these people.[98] Moreover, when the researchers considered applicants' credentials,

> In what situations does impression management work best?

they concluded that it was the impression management techniques alone that influenced the interviewers. That is, it did not seem to matter if applicants were well or poorly qualified. If they used impression management techniques, they did better in the interview.

Research indicates that some impression management techniques work better in interviews than others. Researchers have compared applicants who used techniques that focused on promoting one's accomplishments (called *self-promotion*) to applicants who used techniques that focused on complimenting the interviewer and finding areas of agreement (referred to as *ingratiation*). In general, applicants appear to use self-promotion more than ingratiation.[99] What is more, self-promotion tactics may be more important to interviewing success. Applicants who work to create an appearance of competence by enhancing their accomplishments, taking credit for successes,

impression management The process by which individuals attempt to control the impression others form of them.

and explaining away failures do better in interviews. These effects reach beyond the interview: Applicants who use more self-promotion tactics also seem to get more follow-up job-site visits, even after adjusting for grade-point average, gender, and job type. Ingratiation also works well in interviews, meaning that applicants who compliment the interviewer, agree with his or her opinions, and emphasize areas of fit do better than those who don't.[100]

In terms of performance ratings, the picture is quite different. Ingratiation is positively related to performance ratings, meaning that those who ingratiate with their supervisors get higher performance evaluations. However, self-promotion appears to backfire: Those who self-promote actually seem to receive *lower* performance evaluations.[101] There is an important qualifier to this general result. It appears that individuals high in political skill are able to translate impression management into higher performance appraisals, whereas those lower in political skill are more likely to be hurt by their attempts at impression management.[102]

What explains these results? If you think about them, they make sense. Ingratiating always works because everyone—both interviewers and supervisors—likes to be treated nicely. However, self-promotion may work only in interviews and backfire on the job because, whereas the interviewer has little idea whether you are blowing smoke about your accomplishments, the supervisor knows because it's his or her job to observe you. Thus, if you are going to self-promote, remember that what works in an interview will not always work once you are on the job.

The Ethics of Behaving Politically

9 Determine whether a political action is ethical.

Although there are no clear-cut ways to differentiate ethical from unethical politicking, there are questions you should consider. For example, what is the utility of engaging in politicking? Sometimes we do it for little good reason. Louis LaPierre, the former head of the New Brunswick Energy Institute, had his Order of Canada taken away from him in June 2014 after it came to light that he had lied about his

Robert Pratta/Reuters

Organizations foster politicking when they reduce resources in order to improve performance. After announcing plans to downsize its global workforce of 100 000 employees to increase its competitiveness, French pharmaceutical firm Sanofi stimulated political activity among employees, who organized protests against the job cuts.

academic record. LaPierre, who had been a professor at the University of Moncton for 30 years, had long claimed he earned a Ph.D. in ecology from the University of Maine, when, in fact, he had earned a Ph.D. in education from Walden University in Minnesota. LaPierre likely had a lot to gain by claiming he had a degree in science, rather than in education.[103] Outright lies like this may be a rather extreme example of impression management, but many of us have at least distorted information to make a favourable impression. One thing to keep in mind is whether it's really worth the risk. For LaPierre, in the end, it really was not. Another question to ask is this: How does the utility of engaging in the political behaviour balance out any harm (or potential harm) it will do to others? Complimenting a supervisor on his or her appearance in order to gain favour is probably much less harmful than grabbing credit for a project that you don't deserve, as *Case Incident—Barry's Peer Becomes His Boss* on page 304 indicates.

Finally, does the political activity conform to standards of equity and justice? Sometimes it's difficult to weigh the costs and benefits of a political action, but its ethicality is clear. The department head who inflates the performance evaluation of a favoured employee and deflates the evaluation of a disfavoured employee—and then uses these evaluations to justify giving the former a big raise and nothing to the latter—has treated the disfavoured employee unfairly.

Unfortunately, powerful people can become very good at explaining self-serving behaviours in terms of the organization's best interests. They can persuasively argue that unfair actions are really fair and just. Our point is that immoral people can justify almost any behaviour. Those who are powerful, articulate, and persuasive are most vulnerable to ethical lapses because they are likely to be able to get away with unethical practices successfully. When faced with an ethical dilemma regarding organizational politics, try to consider whether playing politics is worth the risk and whether others might be harmed in the process. If you have a strong power base, recognize the ability of power to corrupt. Remember that it's a lot easier for the powerless to act ethically, if for no other reason than they typically have very little political discretion to exploit.

GLOBAL IMPLICATIONS

Although culture might enter any of the topics we have covered to this point, three questions are particularly important: (1) Does culture influence views on empowerment? (2) Does culture affect the influence tactics people prefer to use? (3) Does culture influence how people respond to politics in the workplace?

Views on Empowerment

Four US researchers investigated the effects of empowerment on employees of a multinational firm by looking at four of the company's comparable plants: one in the Midwestern United States, one in central Mexico, one in west-central India, and one in the south of Poland.[104] These four locations were chosen because they differed on power distance and individualism (concepts we discussed in Chapter 3). India and Mexico are considered high in power distance, and the United States is considered the lowest in power distance. Mexico and India are high in collectivity, the United States is highly individualistic, and Poland is moderately individualistic.

The findings showed that Indian employees gave their supervisors low ratings when empowerment was high, while employees in the other three countries rated their supervisors favourably when empowerment was high. In both the United States and Mexico, empowerment had no effect on satisfaction with co-workers. However, satisfaction with co-workers was higher when employees were empowered in Poland. In India, empowerment led to lower satisfaction with co-workers.

Similar findings in a study comparing empowerment in the United States, Brazil, and Argentina suggest that in hierarchical societies, empowerment may need to be introduced with care.[105] Employees in those countries may be more used to working in teams, but they also expect their manager to be the person with all the answers. Professor Marylène Gagné of Concordia's John Molson School of Business, who has studied empowerment cross-culturally,[106] notes that "in some cultures, bosses can't ask the opinion of subordinates, because it makes them appear weak. So managers in these environments have to find other ways to make people feel autonomous. There is no simple recipe."[107]

Preference for Influence Tactics

Evidence indicates that people in different countries tend to prefer different influence tactics.[108] A study comparing managers in the United States and China found that US managers prefer rational appeal, whereas Chinese managers prefer coalition tactics.[109] These differences tend to be consistent with the values in these two countries. Reason is consistent with the US preference for direct confrontation and the use of rational persuasion to influence others and resolve differences, while coalition tactics are consistent with the Chinese preference for meeting difficult or controversial requests with indirect approaches. Research also has shown that individuals in Western, individualistic cultures tend to engage in more self-enhancement (such as self-promotion) behaviours than individuals in Eastern, more collectivistic cultures.[110]

A study of Swedish, German, Czech, Polish, and Finnish managers found that Swedish managers saw mere differences in opinion as conflicts, so they adopted a conflict-avoidant strategy that emphasized more passive forms of persuasion.[111] German managers, on the other hand, saw disagreement as a useful opportunity to gain new knowledge and fostered some rational discussion as an influence technique. Finnish managers preferred discussion-oriented influence tactics as well. Czech and Polish managers believed managers were under pressure to halt conflicts quickly when they arose, since conflict resolution is time consuming. Therefore, the Czech and Polish managers switched to more autocratic, power-oriented influence styles.

Are the same influence tactics equally effective across a country? Although researchers usually compare two very different cultures, it is also important to examine differences within a given culture, because those differences can sometimes be greater than differences between cultures. China is a big country with different cultures and traditions. A recent study of mainland Chinese, Taiwanese, and Hong Kong managers explored how the three cultural subgroups differ according to the influence tactics they prefer to use.[112] Although managers from all three places believe that rational persuasion and exchange are the most effective influence tactics, managers in Taiwan tend to use inspirational appeals and ingratiation more than managers from either mainland China or Hong Kong. The study also found that managers from Hong Kong rate pressure as more effective in influencing others than do managers in Taiwan or mainland China. Such differences have implications for business relationships. For example, Taiwanese or mainland Chinese managers may be taken aback by the use of pressure tactics by a Hong Kong manager. Likewise, managers from Hong Kong may not be persuaded by managers from Taiwan, who tend to use ingratiating tactics. Such differences in influence tactics may make business dealings difficult. Companies should address these issues, perhaps making their managers aware of the differences within cultures.

Response to Politics in the Workplace

Almost all our conclusions on employee reactions to organizational politics are based on studies conducted in North America. The few studies that have included other countries suggest some minor modifications.[113] One study of managers in US culture and three Chinese cultures (People's Republic of China, Hong Kong, and Taiwan) found that US managers evaluated "gentle persuasion" tactics such as consultation and inspirational appeal as more effective than did their Chinese counterparts.[114] Other research suggests that effective US leaders achieve influence by focusing on personal goals of group members and the tasks at hand (an analytical approach), whereas influential East Asian leaders focus on relationships among group members and meeting the demands of the people around them (a holistic approach).[115]

Summary

An effective manager accepts the political nature of organizations. Some people are significantly more politically astute than others, meaning that they are aware of the underlying politics and can manage impressions. Those who are good at playing politics can be expected to get higher performance evaluations and, hence, larger salary increases and more promotions than the politically naïve or inept. The politically astute are also likely to exhibit higher job satisfaction and be better able to neutralize job stressors.

Few employees relish being powerless in their job and organization. People respond differently to the various power bases. Expert and referent power are derived from an individual's personal qualities. In contrast, coercion, reward, and legitimate power are essentially organizationally derived. Competence especially appears to offer wide appeal as a political skill.

SNAPSHOT SUMMARY

A Definition of Power Bases of Power
- Formal Power
- Personal Power
- Evaluating the Bases of Power

Dependency: The Key to Power
- The General Dependency Postulate
- What Creates Dependence?

Influence Tactics

How Power Affects People

Empowerment: Giving Power to Employees
- Definition of Empowerment

The Abuse of Power
- Harassment in the Workplace

Politics: Power in Action
- Definition of Political Behaviour
- The Reality of Politics
- Types of Political Activity
- Impression Management
- The Ethics of Behaving Politically

MyManagementLab   Study, practise, and explore real business situations with these helpful resources:

- **Study Plan:** Check your understanding of chapter concepts with self-study quizzes.
- **Online Lesson Presentations:** Study key chapter topics and work through interactive assessments to test your knowledge and master management concepts.
- **Videos:** Learn more about the management practices and strategies of real companies.
- **Simulations:** Practise management decision-making in simulated business environments.

 PERSONAL INVENTORY ASSESSMENT

for **Review**

1. What is power?
2. What are the five bases of power?
3. What is the role of dependence in power relationships?
4. What are the nine most often identified power or influence tactics and their contingencies?
5. What does it mean to be empowered? What factors lead to empowerment?
6. What is the connection between harassment and the abuse of power?
7. What are the causes and consequences of political behaviour?
8. What are some examples of impression management techniques?
9. What standards can you use to determine whether a political action is ethical?

for **Managers**

- As a manager who wants to maximize your power, you will want to increase others' dependence on you. You can, for instance, increase your power in relation to your boss by developing knowledge or a skill she needs and for which she perceives no ready substitute.

- You will not be alone in attempting to build your power bases. Others, particularly employees and peers, will be seeking to increase your dependence on them, while you are trying to minimize it and increase their dependence on you. This push and pull is continual.

- Try to avoid putting others in a position where they feel they have no power.

- An effective manager accepts the political nature of organizations. By assessing behaviour in a political framework, you can better predict the actions of others and use that information to formulate political strategies that will gain advantages for you and your work unit.

- Consider that employees who have poor political skills or are unwilling to play the politics game generally relate perceived organizational politics to lower job satisfaction and self-reported performance, increased anxiety, and higher turnover. Therefore, if you are good at organizational politics, help your employees understand the importance of becoming politically savvy.

for **You**

- Power and politics should not simply be viewed as a win–lose situation. Through power and politics, one builds coalitions to work together effectively. It's possible to make sure that everyone is included.

- There are a variety of ways to increase your power in an organization. As an example, you could acquire more knowledge about a situation and then use that information to negotiate a bonus with your employer. Even if you don't get the bonus, the knowledge may help you in other ways.

- To increase your power, consider how dependent others are on you. Dependency is affected by your importance and substitutability and by the scarcity of options. If you have needed skills that no one else has, you will have more power.

- Politics is a reality of most organizations. Being comfortable with politics is important. Politics is often about making deals with other people for mutual gain.

- Political skills can be developed. Remembering to take time to join in an office birthday celebration for someone is part of developing the skill of working with others effectively.

OB *at* **Work**

Everyone Wants Power

POINT

We don't admit to wanting everything that we secretly want.[116] Money is one example. One psychologist found that few people would admit to wanting money, but they thought everyone else wanted it. They were half right—everyone wants money. And everyone wants power.

Harvard psychologist David McClelland was justifiably famous for his study of underlying motives. McClelland would measure people's motivation for power from his analysis of how people described pictures (called the Thematic Apperception Test, or TAT). Why didn't he simply ask people how much they wanted power? Because he believed that many more people really wanted power than would admit, or even consciously realize. That is exactly what he found.

Why do we want power? Because it's good for us. It gives us more control over our own lives. It gives us more freedom to do as we wish. There are few things worse in life than feeling helpless, and few better than feeling in charge of your destiny.

Research shows that people with power and status command more respect from others, have higher self-esteem (no surprise there), and enjoy better health than those of less stature.

Usually, people who tell you power does not matter are those who have no hope of getting it. Being jealous, like wanting power, is one of those things people just will not admit to.

COUNTERPOINT

Of course it's true that some people desire power—and often behave ruthlessly to get it. For most of us, however, power is not high on our list of priorities, and for some people, power is actually undesirable.

Research shows that most individuals feel uncomfortable when placed in powerful positions. One study asked individuals, before they began work in a four-person team, to indicate what "rank, from 1 [highest] to 4 [lowest], in terms of status and influence within the group, would you like to achieve." You know what? Only about one-third (34 percent) of participants chose the highest rank. In a second study, researchers studied employees participating in Amazon's Mechanical Turk online service. They found that when employees were asked about their reasons for belonging to the three groups (which would be a workplace, a volunteer group, a congregation, etc.) that were most important in their life, the main reason was to gain power to get respect. If they could get respect without gaining power, that is what most preferred. In a third study, the authors found that individuals preferred power only when they had high ability—that is, where their influence helped their groups.

This interesting research suggests that we often confuse the desire for power with other things—like the desire to be respected and to help our groups and organizations succeed. In these cases, power is something most of us seek for more benevolent ends—and only in cases when we think the power does good.

Another study found that the majority of people want respect from their peers, not power. Cameron Anderson, the author of this research, sums it up nicely: "You don't have to be rich to be happy, but instead be a valuable contributing member to your groups," he comments. "What makes a person high in status in a group is being engaged, generous with others, and making self sacrifices for the greater good."

PERSONAL **INVENTORY** ASSESSMENT

Gaining Power and Influence: Power and influence can be gained in many ways, but most people have a preferred style or tactic. Use this scale to determine your preferred power and influence tactics. Are there alternative tactics that may be more effective?

Using Influence Strategies: The ability to influence others is a key component of effective social interaction. This self-assessment helps you identify your preferred approach to exercising influence.

BREAKOUT **GROUP** EXERCISES

Form small groups to discuss the following topics, as assigned by your instructor:

1. Describe an incident where you tried to use political behaviour in order to get something you wanted. What influence tactics did you use?

2. In thinking about the incident described above, were your influence tactics effective? Why?

3. Describe an incident where you saw someone engaging in politics. What was your reaction to observing the political behaviour? Under what circumstances do you think political behaviour is appropriate?

EXPERIENTIAL EXERCISE

Understanding Bases of Power

Step 1: Your instructor will divide the class into groups of about 5 or 6 (making sure there are at least 5 groups).[117] Each group will be assigned 1 of the following bases of power: (1) coercive, (2) reward, (3) legitimate, (4) expert, and (5) referent. Refer to your text for discussion of these terms.

Step 2: Each group is to develop a role play that highlights the use of the power assigned. The role play should be developed using the following scenario:

> You are the leader of a group that is trying to develop a website for a new client. One of your group members, who was assigned the task of researching and analyzing the websites of your client's competition, has twice failed to bring the analysis to scheduled meetings, even though the member knew the assignment was due. Consequently, your group is falling behind in getting the website developed. As leader of the group, you have decided to speak with this team member and to use your specific brand of power to influence the individual's behaviour.

Step 3: Each group should select 1 person to play the group leader and another to play the member who has not done the assignment. You have 10 minutes to prepare an influence plan.

Step 4: Each group will conduct its role play. In the event of multiple groups assigned the same power base, 1 of the groups may be asked to volunteer. While you are watching the other groups' role plays, try to put yourself in the place of the person being influenced, to see whether that type of influence would cause you to change your behaviour.

Immediately after each role play, while the next one is being set up, you should pretend that you were the person being influenced, and then record your reaction using the questionnaire opposite. To do this, take out a sheet of paper and tear it into 5 (or 6) pieces. At the top of each piece of paper, write the type of influence that was used. Then write the letters A, B, C, and D in a column, and indicate which number on the scale (see opposite) reflects the influence attempt.

Reaction to Influence Questionnaire

For each role play, think of yourself as being on the receiving end of the influence attempt described, and record your own reaction.

Type of power used _____

A. As a result of the influence attempt, I will . . .

       definitely not comply   1   2   3   4   5   **definitely comply**

B. Any change that does come about will be . . .

       temporary   1   2   3   4   5   **long-lasting**

C. My own personal reaction is . . .

       resistant   1   2   3   4   5   **accepting**

D. As a result of this influence attempt, my relationship with my group leader will probably be . . .

       worse   1   2   3   4   5   **better**

Step 5: For each influence type, 1 member of each group will take the pieces of paper from group members and calculate the average group score for each of the 4 questions. For efficiency, this should be done while the role plays are being conducted.

Step 6: Your instructor will collect the summaries from each group, and then lead a discussion based on these results.

Step 7: Discussion.

1. Which kind of influence is most likely to immediately result in the desired behaviour?

2. Which will have the most long-lasting effects?

3. What effect will using a particular base of power have on the ongoing relationship?

4. Which form of power will others find most acceptable? Least acceptable? Why?

5. Are there some situations where a particular type of influence strategy might be more effective than others?

ETHICAL **DILEMMA**

How Much Should You Defer to Those in Power?

Although it's not always easy to admit it to ourselves, often we adapt our behaviour to suit those in power.[118] To some degree, it's important for organizational success that we do so. After all, people are in positions of authority for a reason, and if no one paid attention to the rules put in place by these people, chaos would rule.

At other times, however, and more often than we acknowledge, powerful individuals in organizations push our actions into ethical grey areas, or worse.

In Stanley Milgram's famous experiments, most individuals delivered what they thought were severe shocks only because an authority figure directed them to do so.

More recently, managers of restaurants and stores (including McDonald's, Applebee's, Taco Bell, and others) were persuaded to strip search customers or employees when an individual impersonating a police officer phoned in and instructed them to do so.

These powerful examples aside, there are more prosaic ways power persuades us. For example, many stock analysts report pressure from their bosses to promote funds from which the organization profits most (which, in such situations, is not disclosed to their clients).

Few of us are going to deliver electric shocks or perform strip searches. But these examples, as well as the hazing incidents that took place in Dalhousie's men's rugby team and women's hockey team in 2014, highlight the disturbing tendency for many of us to conform to the wishes of those in power.

Questions

1. Do you think people tailor their behaviour to suit those in power more than they admit? Do you?

2. One writer commented that these acts of bending behaviour to suit those in power remind "anyone who is under pressure to carry out orders from 'above' to constantly question the validity and prudence of what they're being asked to do." Why don't we do this more often?

3. Why do some individuals resist the effects of power more strongly than others?

CASE INCIDENTS

Delegate Power, or Keep It Close?

Samantha Parks is the owner and CEO of Sparks, a small agency that develops advertising, promotions, and marketing materials for high-fashion firms.[119] Parks has tended to keep a tight rein on her business, overseeing most projects from start to finish. However, as the firm has grown, she has found it necessary to delegate more and more decisions to her associates. She was recently approached by a hairstyling chain that wants a comprehensive redefinition of its entire marketing and promotions look. Should Samantha try to manage this project in her traditional way, or should she delegate major parts to her employees?

Most managers confront this question at some point in their careers. Some experts propose that top executives need to stay very close to the creative core of their business, which means that even if their primary responsibility is to manage, CEOs should never cede too much control to committees of creative individuals or they can lose sight of the firm's overall future direction. Moreover, executives who do fall out of touch with the creative process risk being passed over by a new generation of "plugged in" employees who better understand how the business really works.

Others offer the opposite advice, saying it's not a good idea for a CEO to "sweat the small stuff" such as managing individual client accounts or projects. These experts advise executives to identify everything they can "outsource" to other employees and to delegate as much as possible. By eliminating trivial tasks, executives will be better able to focus their attention on the most important decision making and control aspects of their jobs, which will help the business and also ensure that the top executive maintains control over the functions that really matter.

These pieces of advice are not necessarily in conflict with one another. The real challenge is to identify what you can delegate effectively without ceding too much power and control away from the person with the unifying vision. That is certainly easier said than done, though.

Questions

1. If you were Samantha Parks, how would you prioritize which projects or parts of projects to delegate?

2. In explaining what makes her decisions hard, Parks said, "I hire good people, creative people, to run these projects, and I worry that they will see my oversight and authority as interfering with their creative process." How can she deal with these concerns without giving up too much control?

3. Should executives try to control projects to maintain their position of authority? Do they have a right to control projects and keep in the loop on important decisions just so they can remain in charge?

Barry's Peer Becomes His Boss

As Barry looked out the window of his office in Toronto, the gloomy October skies obscured his usual view of CN Tower.[120] "That figures," Barry thought to himself—his mood was just as gloomy.

Five months ago, Barry's company, CTM, a relatively small but growing technology company, reorganized itself. Although such reorganizations often imperil careers, Barry felt the change only improved his position. Barry's co-worker, Raphael, was promoted to a different department, which made sense because Raphael had been with the company for a few more years and had worked with the CEO on a successful project. Because Raphael was

OB *at Work*

promoted and their past work roles were so similar, Barry thought his own promotion was soon to come.

However, six weeks ago, Barry's boss left. Raphael was transferred back to the same department and became Barry's boss. Although Barry felt a bit overlooked, he knew he was still relatively junior in the company and felt that his good past relationship with Raphael would bode well for his future prospects.

The past six weeks, however, had brought nothing but disappointment. Although Raphael often told Barry he was doing a great job, drawing from several observations, Barry felt that opinion was not being shared with the higher-ups. Worse, a couple of Barry's friends in the company showed Barry several emails where Raphael had taken credit for Barry's work.

"Raphael is not the person I thought he was," thought Barry.

What was his future in the company if no one saw the outcomes of his hard work? How would it affect his career to work for someone who apparently was willing to do anything to get ahead, even at others' expense? He thought about looking for work, but that prospect only darkened his mood further. He liked the company. He felt he did good work there.

As Barry looked again out his window, a light rain began to fall. The CN Tower was no more visible than before. He just did not know what to do.

Questions

1. Should Barry complain about his treatment by Raphael? To whom? If he did complain, what influence tactics should Barry use?

2. Studies have shown that those prone to complaining or "whining" tend to have less power in an organization. Do you think whining leads to diminished power and influence, or the other way around? How can Barry avoid appearing to be a whiner?

3. Do you think Barry should look for another job? Why or why not?

FROM CONCEPTS TO SKILLS

Politicking

Forget, for a moment, about the ethics of politicking and any negative impressions you may have of people who engage in organizational politics.[121] If you wanted to be more politically adept in your organization, what could you do? The following eight suggestions are likely to improve your political effectiveness:

1. *Frame arguments in terms of organizational goals.* Effective politicking requires camouflaging your self-interest. No matter that your objective is self-serving; all the arguments you marshal in support of it must be framed in terms of the benefits that the organization will gain. People whose actions appear to blatantly further their own interests at the expense of the organization's are almost universally denounced, are likely to lose influence, and often suffer the ultimate penalty of being expelled from the organization.

2. *Develop the right image.* If you know your organization's culture, you understand what the organization wants and values from its employees—in terms of dress; associates to cultivate, and those to avoid; whether to appear risk-taking or risk-averse; the preferred leadership style; the importance placed on getting along well with others; and so forth. Then you are equipped to project the appropriate image. Because the assessment of your performance is not a fully objective process, both style and substance must be addressed.

OB *at* **Work**

3. *Gain control of organizational resources.* The control of organizational resources that are scarce and important is a source of power. Knowledge and expertise are particularly effective resources to control. They make you more valuable to the organization and, therefore, more likely to gain security, advancement, and a receptive audience for your ideas.

4. *Make yourself appear indispensable.* Because we are dealing with appearances rather than objective facts, you can enhance your power by appearing to be indispensable. That is, you don't have to really be indispensable as long as key people in the organization believe that you are. If the organization's prime decision makers believe there is no ready substitute for what you are giving the organization, they are likely to go to great lengths to ensure that your desires are satisfied.

5. *Be visible.* Because performance evaluation has a substantial subjective component, it's important that your manager and those in power in the organization be made aware of your contribution. If you are fortunate enough to have a job that brings your accomplishments to the attention of others, it may not be necessary to take direct measures to increase your visibility. But your job may require you to handle activities that are low in visibility, or your specific contribution may be indistinguishable because you are part of a team endeavour. In such cases, without appearing to be tooting your own horn, you will want to call attention to yourself by highlighting your successes in routine reports, having satisfied customers relay their appreciation to senior executives, being seen at social functions, being active in professional associations, developing powerful allies who speak positively about your accomplishments, and similar tactics. Of course, the skilled politician actively lobbies to get those projects that will increase his or her visibility.

6. *Develop powerful allies.* It helps to have powerful people in your camp. Cultivate contacts with potentially influential people above you, at your own level, and in the lower ranks. They can provide you with important information that may not be available through normal channels. There will be times, too, when decisions will be made in favour of those with the greatest support. Having powerful allies can provide you with a coalition of support if and when you need it.

7. *Avoid "tainted" members.* In almost every organization, there are fringe members whose status is questionable. Their performance and/or loyalty is suspect. Keep your distance from such individuals. Given the reality that effectiveness has a large subjective component, your own effectiveness might be called into question if you are perceived as being too closely associated with tainted members.

8. *Support your manager.* Since he or she evaluates your performance, you will typically want to do whatever is necessary to have your manager on your side. You should make every effort to help your manager succeed, make her look good, and support her if she is under siege, and to spend the time to find out what criteria she will be using to assess your effectiveness. Do not undermine your manager, and do not speak negatively of her to others.

Practising Skills

You used to be the star marketing manager for Hilton Electronics Corporation. But for the past year, you have been outpaced again and again by Sean, a new manager in the design department who has been

accomplishing everything expected of him and more. Meanwhile, your best efforts to do your job well have been sabotaged and undercut by Maria—your and Sean's manager. For example, before last year's international consumer electronics show, Maria moved $30 000 from your budget to Sean's. Despite your best efforts, your marketing team could not complete all the marketing materials normally developed to showcase all of your organization's new products at this important industry show. Also, Maria has chipped away at your staff and budget ever since. Although you have been able to meet most of your goals with less staff and budget, Maria has continued to slice away resources from your group. Just last week, she eliminated two positions in your team of eight marketing specialists to make room for a new designer and some extra equipment for Sean. Maria is clearly taking away your resources while giving Sean whatever he wants and more. You think it's time to do something, or soon you will not have any team or resources left. What do you need to do to make sure your division has the resources to survive and grow?

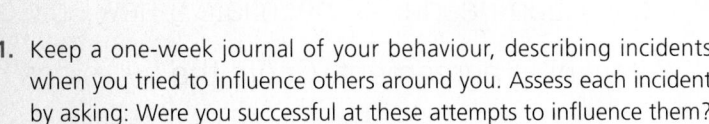

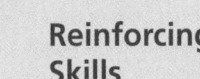

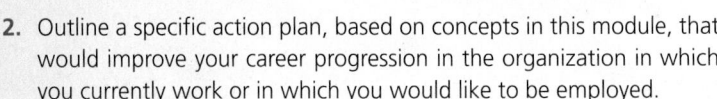

1. Keep a one-week journal of your behaviour, describing incidents when you tried to influence others around you. Assess each incident by asking: Were you successful at these attempts to influence them? Why or why not? What could you have done differently?

Reinforcing Skills

2. Outline a specific action plan, based on concepts in this module, that would improve your career progression in the organization in which you currently work or in which you would like to be employed.

9

Conflict and Negotiation

The BC Government and the BC Teachers'
Federation needed to negotiate a new collective
bargaining agreement. Could the two sides reach
an agreement after years of bitterness?

LEARNING OUTCOMES

After studying this chapter, you should be able to:

1. Define *conflict*.

2. Describe the three types of conflict and the three loci of conflict.

3. Identify the conditions that lead to conflict.

4. Contrast distributive and integrative bargaining.

5. Show how individual differences influence negotiations.

6. Assess the roles and functions of third-party negotiations.

T he BC Teachers' Federation (BCTF), which is the union for public school teachers in BC, and the BC government have a long history of animosity.[1] The union has little admiration for Premier Christy Clarke because in 2002, when she was minister of Education, the BC government effectively tore up the teachers' collective agreement by passing Bills 27, 28, and 29, which eliminated provisions in the collective agreement that dealt with class size and composition, cut support for children with special needs, and took away the rights of teachers to collectively bargain for their working conditions.

These actions outraged the BCTF, which took the government to court over the Bills. In 2007, the Supreme Court of Canada ruled that key parts of Bill 29 were unconstitutional. In 2011, the BC Supreme Court ruled that several sections in Bills 27 and 28 were unconstitutional and gave the government one year to amend those bills. The BC government then introduced Bill 22, which denied teachers the right to negotiate class size and composition. In January 2014, the BC Supreme Court ruled Bill 22 unconstitutional and ordered the government to reinstate the bargaining rights of teachers.

Faced with a government that has passed four bills on teachers' rights since 2002 that have each been declared unconstitutional, the BCTF entered into another round of bargaining with the BC government in spring 2014. Would the parties be able to overcome years of conflict and resolve their differences?

In this chapter, we look at sources of conflict and strategies for resolving conflict, including negotiation.

THE CANADIAN PRESS/Darryl Dyck

THE BIG IDEA

Resolving conflicts and engaging in successful negotiations requires understanding your objectives and the objectives of the other party.

 IS FOR **EVERYONE**

- Is conflict always bad?
- Should you try to win at any cost when you bargain?
- How does anxiety affect negotiating outcomes?
- Ever wonder if men and women negotiate differently?

Conflict Defined

1 Define *conflict*.

Several common themes underlie most definitions of conflict.[2] Conflict must be *perceived* by the parties to it; if no one is aware of a conflict, then it's generally agreed that no conflict exists. Conflict also involves opposition or incompatibility, and interaction between the parties.[3] These factors set the conditions that determine the beginning point of the conflict process. We can define **conflict** broadly as a process that begins when one party perceives that another party has negatively affected or is about to negatively affect something that the first party cares about.[4]

Conflict describes the point when an interaction becomes interparty disagreement. People experience a wide range of conflicts in groups and organizations—incompatibility of goals, differences over interpretations of facts, disagreements based on behavioural expectations, and the like. Our definition covers the full range of conflict levels—from subtle forms of disagreement to overt and violent acts.

Conflict has positive and negative effects, which we will discuss further when we cover functional and dysfunctional conflict. For a discussion of the benefits and drawbacks of conflict, see *Point/Counterpoint* on page 334.

Functional vs. Dysfunctional Conflict

👁 **Watch** on **MyManagementLab**

CH2MHill: Conflict and Negotiation

The general view on conflict is that not all conflict is bad.[5] Some conflicts support the goals of the group and improve its performance; these are **functional**, or constructive, forms of conflict. But some conflicts hinder group performance; these are **dysfunctional**, or destructive, forms of conflict. The criterion that differentiates functional from dysfunctional conflict is group performance. If a group is unable to achieve its goals because of conflict, then the conflict is dysfunctional.

Is conflict always bad?

Stimulating functional conflict can be productive, as *Case Incident—Choosing Your Battles* on page 336 shows.

Types of Conflict

2 Describe the three types of conflict and the three loci of conflict.

One means of understanding conflict is to identify the type of disagreement, or what the conflict is about. Is it a disagreement about goals? Is it about people who just rub one another the wrong way? Or is it about the best way to get things done? Although each conflict is unique, researchers have classified conflicts into three categories: task, relationship, and process.

Task conflict relates to the content and goals of the work. **Relationship conflict** focuses on interpersonal relationships. **Process conflict** is about how the work gets done. Studies demonstrate that relationship conflicts, at least in work settings, are almost always dysfunctional.[6] Why? It appears that the friction and interpersonal hostilities inherent in relationship conflicts increase personality clashes and decrease mutual understanding, which hinders the completion of organizational tasks. Of the three types, relationship conflicts also appear to be the most psychologically exhausting to individuals.[7] Because they tend to revolve around personalities, you can see how relationship conflicts can become destructive. After all, we cannot expect to change our co-workers' personalities, and we would generally take offence at criticisms directed at who we are as opposed to how we behave.

While scholars agree that relationship conflict is dysfunctional, considerably less agreement exists as to whether task and process conflicts are functional. Early research suggested that task conflict within groups was associated with higher group performance, but in 2012 a review of 116 studies found that task conflict was essentially unrelated to group performance. However, the research found that the relationship between conflict and performance depends on a number of mediating factors.[8]

conflict A process that begins when one party perceives that another party has negatively affected or is about to negatively affect something that the first party cares about.

functional conflict Conflict that supports the goals of the group and improves its performance.

dysfunctional conflict Conflict that hinders group performance.

task conflict Conflict over content and goals of the work.

relationship conflict Conflict based on interpersonal relationships.

process conflict Conflict over how work gets done.

One factor is whether the conflict includes top management or occurs at a lower hierarchical level in the organization. Task conflict among top management teams was positively associated with their performance, whereas conflict lower in the organization was negatively associated with their performance. The multi-study review also found that it matters whether other types of conflict are occurring at the same time. If task and relationship conflict occurred together, task conflict was more likely negative, whereas if task conflict occurs by itself, it was more likely positive. Some scholars have argued that the strength of conflict is important—if task conflict is very low, people are not really engaged or addressing the important issues. If task conflict is too high, however, infighting will quickly degenerate into personality conflict. According to this view, moderate levels of task conflict are optimal. Supporting this argument, one study in China found that moderate levels of task conflict in the early development stage increased creativity in groups, but high levels decreased team performance.[9]

Finally, the personalities of team members appear to matter. A recent study demonstrated that teams made up of individuals who are, on average, high in openness and emotional stability are better able to turn task conflict into increased group performance.[10] The reason may be that open and emotionally stable teams can put task conflict in perspective and focus on how the variance in ideas can help solve the problem, rather than letting it degenerate into relationship conflicts.

What about process conflict? Researchers found that process conflicts revolve around delegation and roles. Conflicts over delegation often relate to shirking. Moreover, conflicts over roles can leave some team members feeling marginalized. Thus, process conflicts often become highly personalized and quickly devolve into relationship conflicts. It's also true, of course, that arguing about how to do something takes time away from actually doing it. We have all been part of groups in which the arguments and debates about roles and responsibilities seem to go nowhere.

Loci of Conflict

Another way to understand conflict is to consider its locus, or where the conflict occurs. Here, too, there are three basic types. **Dyadic conflict** is conflict between two people. **Intragroup conflict** occurs within a group or team. **Intergroup conflict** is conflict between groups or teams.

Nearly all of the literature on task, relationship, and process conflict considers intragroup conflict (within the group). That makes sense given that groups and teams often exist only to perform a particular task. However, it does not necessarily tell us about the other loci of conflict. For example, research has found that for intragroup task conflict to influence performance within the team, it's important that the teams have a supportive climate in which mistakes are not penalized and every team member "[has] the other's back."[11] But is this concept useful for understanding the effects of intergroup conflict for the organization? Think about, say, the NHL. For a hockey team to adapt and improve, perhaps a certain amount of task conflict is good for team performance, especially when the team members support one another. But would we care whether members from one team supported members from another team? Probably not. In fact, if teams are competing with one another so that only one team can "win," interteam conflict seems almost inevitable. When is intergroup conflict helpful, and when is it a concern?

One study on intergroup conflict found an interplay between an individual's position within a group and the way that individual managed conflict between groups. Group members who were relatively peripheral in their own groups were better at resolving conflicts between their group and another one. But this happened only when those peripheral members were still accountable to their group.[12] Thus, being at the core

dyadic conflict Conflict that occurs between two people.

intragroup conflict Conflict that occurs within a group or team.

intergroup conflict Conflict between different groups or teams.

of your work group does not necessarily make you the best person to manage conflict with other groups.

Another intriguing question about loci is whether conflicts interact or buffer one another. Assume, for example, that Dana and Alain are on the same team. What happens if they do not get along interpersonally (dyadic conflict) and their team also has high personality conflict? What happens to their team if two other team members, Shawna and Justin, do get along well? It's also possible to ask this question at the intragroup and intergroup level. Intense intergroup conflict can be quite stressful to group members and might well affect the way they interact. A 2012 study found, for example, that high levels of conflict between teams caused individuals to focus on complying with norms within their teams.[13]

Thus, understanding functional and dysfunctional conflict requires not only that we identify the type of conflict; we also need to know where it occurs. It's possible that while the concepts of task, relationship, and process conflict are useful in understanding intragroup or even dyadic conflict, they are less useful in explaining the effects of intergroup conflict.

Thinking about conflict in terms of type and locus helps us realize that it's probably inevitable in most organizations, and when it does occur, we can attempt to make it as productive as possible.

Sources of Conflict

3 Identify the conditions that lead to conflict.

A number of conditions can give rise to conflict. They *need not* lead directly to conflict, but at least one of these conditions is necessary if conflict is to surface. For simplicity's sake, these conditions (which we can also look at as causes or sources of conflict) have been condensed into three general categories: communication, structure, and personal variables.[14]

IBM benefits from the diversity of employees like Greg Labows (left) and Tsegga Medhin, who engage in functional conflict that improves the company's performance. At IBM, diversity drives innovation. For innovation to flourish, IBM relies on the creative tension from different ideas, experiences, perspectives, skills, interests, and thinking.

Chris Seward/MCT/Newscom/Newscom

Communication

As we saw in Chapter 7, communication can be a source of conflict through semantic difficulties, misunderstandings, and "noise" in the communication channels.[15]

A review of the research suggests that differing word connotations, jargon, insufficient exchange of information, and noise in the communication channel are all barriers to communication and potential antecedent conditions to conflict. Research has further demonstrated a surprising finding: The potential for conflict increases when either too little or too much communication takes place. Apparently, an increase in communication is functional up to a point, whereupon it's possible to overcommunicate, with a resultant increase in the potential for conflict.

Structure

Conflicts between two people can be structural in nature; that is, they can be the consequence of the requirements of the job or the workplace more than personality. For instance, it's not uncommon for the sales department to be in conflict with the production department, if sales perceives that products will be delivered late to customers. The term *structure* in this context includes variables such as size of the group, degree of specialization in the tasks assigned to group members, composition of the group, jurisdictional clarity, reward systems, leadership style, goal compatibility, and the degree of dependence between groups.

A review of structural variables that can lead to conflict in the workplace suggests the following:[16]

- *Size, specialization, and composition* of the group act as forces to stimulate conflict. The larger the group and the more specialized its activities, the greater the likelihood of conflict. The potential for conflict tends to be greatest where group members are younger and where turnover is high.

- *The greater the ambiguity* in precisely defining where responsibility for actions lies, the greater the potential for conflict to emerge. Such jurisdictional ambiguities increase intergroup fighting for control of resources and territory.

- *Reward systems* create conflict when one member's gain is at another's expense. Similarly, the performance evaluation process can create conflict when individuals feel that they are unfairly evaluated, or when managers and employees have differing ideas about the employees' job responsibilities.

- *Leadership style* can create conflict if managers tightly control and oversee the work of employees, allowing employees little discretion in how they carry out tasks.

- *The diversity of goals* among groups is a major source of conflict. When groups within an organization seek diverse ends, some of which are inherently at odds—such as when the sales team promises products that the development team has not yet finalized—opportunities for conflict increase.

- *If one group is dependent on another* (in contrast to the two being mutually independent), or if interdependence allows one group to gain at another's expense, opposing forces are stimulated.

Personal Variables

Have you ever met people to whom you take an immediate dislike? You disagree with most of their opinions. The sound of their voice, their smirk when they smile, and their personality annoy you. We have all met people like that. When you have to work with such individuals, there is often the potential for conflict.

Our last category of potential sources of conflict is personal variables, which include personality, emotions, and values. People high in the personality traits of disagreeableness, neuroticism, or self-monitoring are prone to tangle with other people more often, and to react poorly when conflicts occur.[17] Emotions can also cause conflict even when they are not directed at others. An employee who shows up to work irate from her hectic morning commute may carry that anger into her workday and result in a tension-filled meeting.[18] People are furthermore more likely to cause conflict when their values are opposed.

Conflict Resolution

During spring 2014, both the BC government and the province's teachers tried to gain public approval for their approach to bargaining.[19] At the time, public opinion sided more with the teachers (with 43 percent of support) than the government (with 28 percent of support). In late August, a week before classes were to resume (and no one believed that they would), 36 percent of those polled supported the teachers and 35 percent supported the government.

In an effort to restart the stalled negotiations and get the schools opened on time, the minister of Education recommended that both sides enter into mediation and suspend strike and lockout activities for two weeks while mediation carried on. The parties began meeting with mediator Vince Ready a day before the Labour Day weekend was to begin, although the teachers had not yet decided whether to call off their strike. What other approaches might parties use to try to resolve a conflict?

Conflict in the workplace can affect the effectiveness of individuals, teams, and the entire organization.[20] One study found that 20 percent of managers' time is spent managing conflict.[21]

Once conflict arises, what can be done to resolve it? The way a conflict is defined goes a long way toward establishing the sort of outcomes that might settle it. For instance, if I define our salary disagreement as a zero-sum or *win–lose situation*—that is, if you get the increase in pay you want, there will be just that amount less for me—I am going to be far less willing to look for mutual solutions than if I frame the conflict as a potential *win–win situation*. So individual attitudes toward a conflict are important, because attitudes typically define the set of possible settlements.

Learn About Yourself
Strategies for Handling Conflict

Conflict Management Strategies Based on Dual Concern Theory

Conflict researchers often use *dual concern theory* to describe people's conflict management strategies.[22] Dual concern theory considers how one's degree of *cooperativeness* (the degree to which one tries to satisfy the other person's concerns) and *assertiveness* (the degree to which one tries to satisfy one's own concerns) determine how a conflict is handled.[23] The five conflict-handling strategies identified by the theory are as follows:

Learn About Yourself
Managing Interpersonal Conflict

- *Forcing.* Imposing one's will on the other party.

- *Problem solving.* Trying to reach an agreement that satisfies both one's own and the other party's aspirations as much as possible.

- *Avoiding.* Ignoring or minimizing the importance of the issues creating the conflict.

- *Yielding.* Accepting and incorporating the will of the other party.

- *Compromising.* Balancing concern for oneself with concern for the other party in order to reach a solution.

Forcing is a win–lose solution, as is yielding, while problem solving seeks a win–win solution. Avoiding conflict and pretending it does not exist, and compromising,

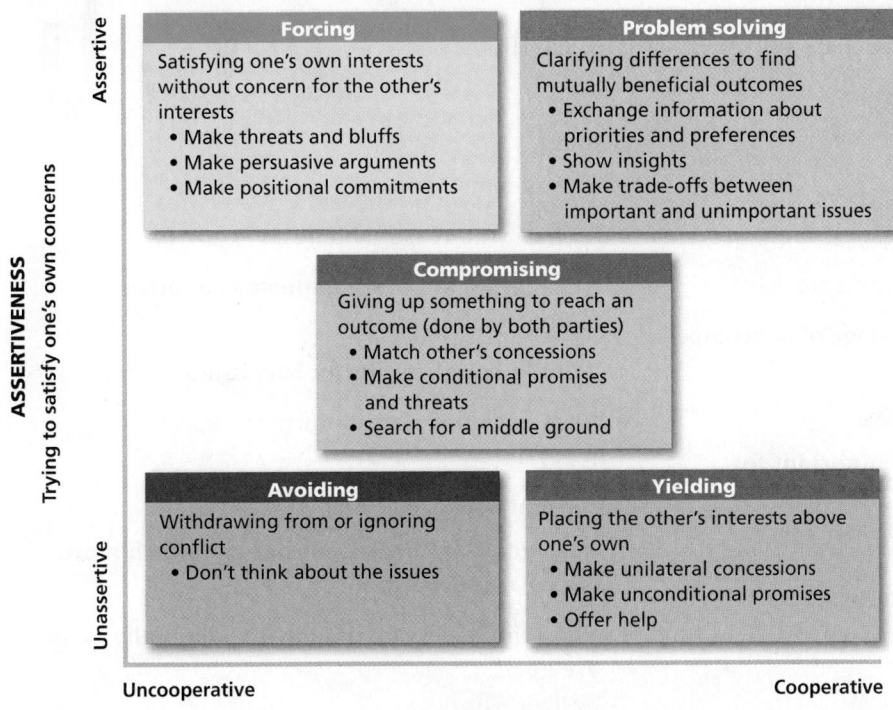

EXHIBIT 9-1 Conflict-Handling Strategies and Accompanying Behaviours

Forcing

Satisfying one's own interests without concern for the other's interests
- Make threats and bluffs
- Make persuasive arguments
- Make positional commitments

Problem solving

Clarifying differences to find mutually beneficial outcomes
- Exchange information about priorities and preferences
- Show insights
- Make trade-offs between important and unimportant issues

Compromising

Giving up something to reach an outcome (done by both parties)
- Match other's concessions
- Make conditional promises and threats
- Search for a middle ground

Avoiding

Withdrawing from or ignoring conflict
- Don't think about the issues

Yielding

Placing the other's interests above one's own
- Make unilateral concessions
- Make unconditional promises
- Offer help

Assertive / Unassertive

ASSERTIVENESS
Trying to satisfy one's own concerns

Uncooperative / Cooperative

COOPERATIVENESS
Trying to satisfy the other person's concerns

Sources: Based on K. W. Thomas, "Conflict and Negotiation Processes in Organizations," in *Handbook of Industrial and Organizational Psychology*, vol. 3, 2nd ed., ed. M. D. Dunnette and L. M. Hough (Palo Alto, CA: Consulting Psychologists Press, 1992), p. 668; C. K. W. De Dreu, A. Evers, B. Beersma, E. S. Kluwer, and A. Nauta, "A Theory-Based Measure of Conflict Management Strategies in the Workplace," *Journal of Organizational Behavior* 22, no. 6 (September 2001), pp. 645–668; and D. G. Pruitt and J. Rubin, *Social Conflict: Escalation, Stalemate and Settlement* (New York: Random House, 1986).

so that neither person gets what they want, can yield lose–lose solutions. Exhibit 9-1 illustrates these five strategies, along with specific actions that one might take when using them.

Choosing a particular strategy for resolving conflict depends on a variety of factors. Research shows that while people may choose among the strategies, they have an underlying disposition to handle conflicts in certain ways.[24] In addition, some situations call for particular strategies. For instance, when a small child insists on trying to run into the street, a parent may need a forcing strategy to restrain the child. Co-workers who are having a conflict over setting deadlines to complete a project on time may decide that problem solving is the best strategy to use.

OB in Action—Choosing Strategies to Deal with Conflicts indicates the situations in which each strategy is best used.

What Can Individuals Do to Manage Conflict?

Individuals can use a number of conflict resolution techniques to try to defuse conflict inside and outside of the workplace. These include the following:[25]

- *Problem solving.* Requesting a face-to-face meeting to identify the problem and resolve it through open discussion.

- *Developing overarching goals.* Creating a shared goal that requires both parties to work together, and motivates them to do so.

Watch on **MyManagementLab**

Gordon Law Group: Conflict and Negotiation

OB IN ACTION
Choosing Strategies to Deal with Conflicts

Forcing

→ In **emergencies**

→ On **important** but unpopular **issues**

→ On **vital issues** when you know you are right

→ Against **people who take advantage** of noncompetitive behaviour

Problem solving

→ If both sets of concerns are **too important for compromise**

→ To **merge different perspectives**

→ To **gain commitment** through a consensus

→ To **mend a relationship**

Avoiding

→ When an issue is **trivial**

→ When your **concerns won't be met**

→ When potential **disruption outweighs the benefits** of resolution

→ To let people **cool down** and regain perspective

Yielding

→ When you find **you are wrong**

→ To show your **reasonableness**

→ When **issues are more important to others** than yourself

→ To **build social credits** for later issues

→ When **harmony and stability** are especially important

Compromising

→ When **goals are important but not worth more assertive approaches**

→ When opponents are committed to **mutually exclusive goals**

→ To achieve **temporary settlements** to complex issues

→ To arrive at **expedient solutions** under time pressure[26]

- *Smoothing.* Playing down differences while emphasizing common interests with the other party.

- *Compromising.* Agreeing with the other party that each will give up something of value to reach an accord.

- *Avoiding.* Withdrawing from or suppressing the conflict.

The choice of technique may depend on how serious the issue is to you, whether you take a win–win or a win–lose approach, and your preferred conflict management style.

When the conflict is specifically work-related, there are additional techniques that might be used:

- *Expansion of resources.* The scarcity of a resource—say, money, promotion opportunities, office space—can create conflict. Expansion of the resource can create a win–win solution.

- *Authoritative command.* Management can use its formal authority to resolve the conflict and then communicate its desires to the parties involved.

- *Altering the human variable.* Behavioural change techniques such as human relations training can alter attitudes and behaviours that cause conflict.

- *Altering the structural variables.* The formal organization structure and the interaction patterns of conflicting parties can be changed through job redesign, transfers, creation of coordinating positions, and the like.

Resolving Personality Conflicts

Personality conflicts are an everyday occurrence in the workplace. A 2011 study found that Canadian supervisors spend about 16 percent of their time handling disputes among employees.[27] A variety of factors lead to personality conflicts at work, including the following:[28]

- Misunderstandings based on age, race, or cultural differences

- Intolerance, prejudice, discrimination, or bigotry

- Perceived inequities

- Misunderstandings, rumours, or falsehoods about an individual or group

- Blaming for mistakes or mishaps (finger-pointing)

Personality conflicts can result in lowered productivity when people find it difficult to work together. The individuals experiencing the conflict may seek sympathy from other members of the work group, causing co-workers to take sides. The ideal solution would be for the two people having a conflict to work it out between themselves, without involving others, but this does not always happen. *OB in Action—Handling Personality Conflicts* suggests ways of dealing with personality conflicts in the workplace.

Resolving Intercultural Conflicts

While some personality conflicts may be stimulated by cultural differences, it's important to consider intercultural conflicts as a separate form of conflict. Canada is a multicultural society, and its organizations increasingly interact in a global environment, setting up alliances and joint ventures with partners from other parts of the world. Greater contact with people from other cultures can lead to greater understanding, but it can also lead to misunderstanding when individuals ignore the different perspectives that might result from cultural differences.

OB IN ACTION
Handling Personality Conflicts

Tips for employees having a personality conflict
→ **Communicate directly** with the other person to resolve the perceived conflict (emphasize problem solving and common objectives, not personalities).

→ **Avoid dragging** co-workers into the conflict.

→ If dysfunctional conflict persists, **seek help** from direct supervisors or human resource specialists.

Tips for third-party observers of a personality conflict
→ **Do not take sides** in someone else's personality conflict.

→ **Suggest the parties work things out** themselves in a constructive and positive way.

→ If dysfunctional conflict persists, **refer the problem** to parties' direct supervisors.

Tips for managers whose employees are having a personality conflict
→ **Investigate and document** conflict.

→ If appropriate, **take corrective action** (e.g., feedback or behaviour shaping).

→ If necessary, **attempt informal dispute resolution**.

→ **Refer difficult conflicts** to human resource specialists or hired counsellors for formal resolution attempts and other interventions.[29]

RESEARCH FINDINGS: Cultural Views on Conflict

Across cultures, people have different ideas about the appropriateness and effects of conflict. For instance, Mexicans expect conflict to be kept private, while Americans expect conflict to be dealt with directly and openly.[30] We suggest in Exhibit 9-2 that there is an optimal level of conflict in the workplace to maximize productivity, but this is decidedly a North American viewpoint. Many Asian cultures believe that conflict almost always has a negative effect on the work unit.[31]

Collectivistic cultures value harmony among members more than individualistic cultures do. Consistent with this idea, research shows that those from Asian cultures show a preference for conflict avoidance, compared with Americans and Britons.[32] Research also shows that Chinese and East Asian managers prefer compromising as a strategy,[33] even though from a North American perspective, this might be viewed as suboptimal. Compromise may be viewed as a way of saving face, so that each party gets to preserve pride and dignity.[34]

EXHIBIT 9-2 Conflict and Unit Performance

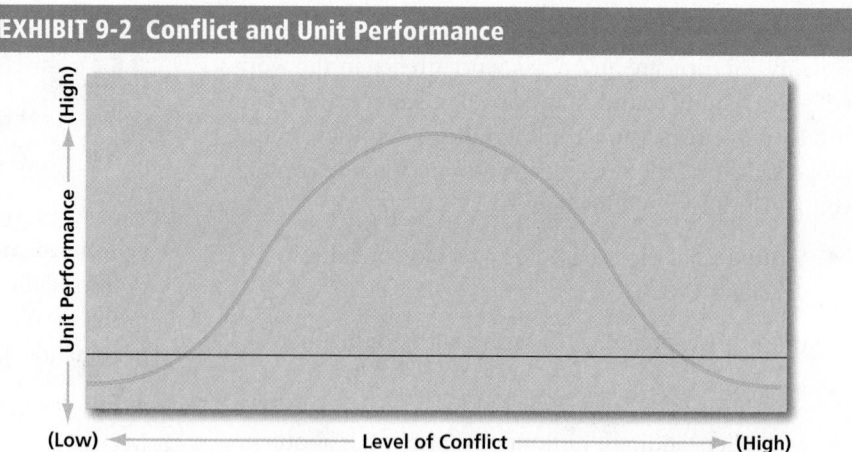

Studies show that North Americans prefer a problem-solving approach to conflicts, because this presents both parties with a win–win solution.[35] Win–win solutions are less likely to be achieved in Asian cultures, however. East Asian managers tend to ignore conflict rather than make it public,[36] and more often than not, Japanese managers tend to choose nonconfrontational styles.[37] Chinese managers prefer compromising and avoiding to manage conflict.[38] These preferences make it difficult to negotiate a win–win solution. In general, Westerners are more comfortable with competition, which may explain why research finds that Westerners are more likely to choose forcing as a strategy than are Asians.[39]

Taken together, these research findings suggest the importance of being aware of cultural differences with respect to conflict. Using one's own culture's conflict resolution strategies may result in even greater conflict.[40] Some individuals and some cultures prefer harmonious relations over asserting themselves, and they may not react well to the confrontational dynamics more common among North Americans. Similarly, North Americans expect that negotiations may lead to a legal contract, whereas Asian cultures rely less on legal contracts and more on relational contracts.

Conflict Outcomes

One of the unfortunate side effects of the dispute between the BC government and the BC Teachers' Federation has been a loss of mutual trust.[41] The teachers were particularly livid that the government, instead of accepting the decision by the BC Supreme Court that Bill 22 was unconstitutional, asked the teachers to set aside grievances arising from that decision while the provincial government appeals the ruling, which could take many years. From the teachers' perspective, the judge had ordered the province to reinstate clauses that it had previously removed from the contract illegally, and the government should follow the judge's directive. Is there a way to minimize negative outcomes when conflict becomes inevitable?

The action–reaction interplay between conflicting parties creates consequences that are *functional*, if the conflict improves the group's performance, or *dysfunctional*, if it hinders performance.

Conflict is constructive when it improves the quality of decisions, stimulates creativity and innovation, encourages interest and curiosity among group members, provides the medium for problems to be aired and tensions released, and fosters self-evaluation and change. Conflict can prevent groupthink (discussed in Chapter 12). It does not allow the group passively to "rubber-stamp" decisions that may be based on weak assumptions, inadequate consideration of relevant alternatives, or other problems.

Conflict challenges the status quo and supports the creation of new ideas, promotes reassessment of group goals and activities, and increases the probability that the group will respond to change. An open discussion focused on higher-order goals can make functional outcomes more likely. Groups that are extremely polarized do not manage their underlying disagreements effectively and tend to accept suboptimal solutions, or they avoid making decisions altogether rather than working out the conflict.[42]

Dean Tjosvold of Lingnan University in Hong Kong suggests three desired outcomes for conflict:[43]

- *Agreement.* Equitable and fair agreements are the best outcome. If agreement means that one party feels exploited or defeated, this will likely lead to further conflict later.

- *Stronger relationships.* When conflict is resolved positively, this can lead to better relationships and greater trust. If the parties trust each other, they are more likely to keep the agreements they make.

- *Learning.* Handling conflict successfully teaches one how to do it better next time. It gives an opportunity to practise the skills one has learned about handling conflict.

Below we examine what research tells us about the constructive effects of conflict.

RESEARCH FINDINGS:
The Constructive Effects of Conflict

Research studies in diverse settings confirm that conflict can be functional and improve productivity. Team members with greater differences in work styles and experience also tend to share more information with one another.[44]

These observations lead us to predict benefits to organizations from the increasing cultural diversity of the workforce. And that is what the evidence indicates, under most conditions. Heterogeneity among group and organization members can increase creativity, improve the quality of decisions, and facilitate change by enhancing member flexibility.[45] Researchers compared decision-making groups composed of all-Caucasian individuals with groups that also contained members from Asian, Hispanic, and Black ethnic groups. The ethnically diverse groups produced more effective and more feasible ideas, and the unique ideas they generated tended to be higher quality than the unique ideas produced by the all-Caucasian group.

The above research findings suggest that conflict within a group can lead to strength rather than weakness. However, factors such as personality, social support, and communication moderate how well groups can deal with internal conflict. At an individual level, both a person's personality (agreeableness) and his or her level of social support influence that person's response to conflict. Agreeable employees and those with lower levels of social support respond to conflict more negatively.[46]

Open communication is important to resolving conflict. Group members who discuss differences of opinion openly and are prepared to manage conflict when it arises resolve conflicts successfully.[47] Group members with cooperative conflict styles and a strong underlying identification to the overall group goals are more effective than those with a more competitive style.[48] Managers need to emphasize shared interests in resolving conflicts, so group members who disagree with one another don't become too entrenched in their points of view and start to take the conflicts personally.

Unfortunately, not all conflict results in positive outcomes. A substantial body of literature documents how dysfunctional conflict can reduce group effectiveness.[49] Among the undesirable outcomes are poor communication, reduced group cohesiveness, and subordination of group goals due to infighting among members. All forms of conflict—even the functional varieties—appear to reduce group member satisfaction and trust.[50] When active discussions turn into open conflicts between members, information sharing between members decreases significantly.[51] At the extreme, conflict can bring group functioning to a halt and potentially threaten the group's survival.

Negotiation

4 Contrast distributive and integrative bargaining.

The dispute between the BC Teachers' Federation and the BC government ended on September 16, 2014, two weeks after what should have been the first day of classes.[52] Throughout the previous summer, it was not clear how the dispute would end. The province assured everyone that it would not legislate the teachers back to work (a tactic the government had used in the past). The teachers said they were not going to call off their strike in order for classes to start on time.

Both parties had spoken occasionally with mediator Vince Ready, to see if he could somehow help them arrive at an agreement. In the spring, Ready had said he did not have time to mediate the dispute. In August, Ready said the parties were too far apart. But in mid-September, Ready found that the parties might be ready to actually engage in collective bargaining and, if that were true, then maybe he could help them through mediation.

As in any collective bargaining situation, it's rare for either party to get everything they want. Compromise is part of negotiation, and both sides hope to get some part of what it wants. In the settlement obtained with the help of Ready, teachers likely felt that the deal offered in mediation was better than what they would get should the province decide instead to legislate the teachers back to work. The province, however, recognized that legislating the teachers back to work would not be popular and would likely lead to a court case. So the province made a somewhat better financial offer, and the teachers agreed to accept less than what they were initially hoping for.

In the end, the teachers voted 86 percent in favour of the new contract. BCTF president Jim Iker explained, "We all know that this deal isn't perfect, but it does provide gains for teachers, it protects our charter rights, it increases support for our students," he said. "There will be more classroom and specialist teachers in schools to help our students; our teachers on call will get fair pay for a day's work and all our members will get a salary increase." How do perceptions of fairness influence the negotiation process?

Earlier in the chapter, we reviewed a number of conflict resolution strategies. One well-developed strategy is to negotiate a resolution. Negotiation permeates the interactions of almost everyone in groups and organizations: Labour bargains with management; managers negotiate with employees, peers, and senior management; salespeople negotiate with customers; purchasing agents negotiate with suppliers; employees agree to cover for one another for a few minutes in exchange for some past or future benefit. In today's loosely structured organizations, in which members work with colleagues over whom they have no direct authority and with whom they may not even share a common boss, negotiation skills are critical.

We define **negotiation** as a process in which two or more parties try to agree on the exchange rate for goods or services they are trading.[53] Note that we use the terms *negotiation* and *bargaining* interchangeably.

Within a negotiation, be aware that individuals have issues, positions, and interests. *Issues* are items that are specifically placed on the bargaining table for discussion. *Positions* are the individual's stand on the issues. For instance, salary may be an issue for discussion. The salary you hope to receive is your position. Finally, *interests* are the underlying concerns that are affected by the negotiation resolution. For instance, the reason that you might want a six-figure salary is that you are trying to buy a house in Vancouver, and that is your only hope of being able to make mortgage payments.

Negotiators who recognize the underlying interests of themselves and the other party may have more flexibility in achieving a resolution. For instance, in the example just given, an employer who offers you a mortgage at a lower rate than the bank does, or

negotiation A process in which two or more parties exchange goods or services and try to agree on the exchange rate for them.

In general, people negotiate more effectively within cultures than between them. Politeness and positivity characterize the typical conflict-avoidant negotiations in Japan such as those of labour union leader Hidekazu Kitagawa (right), shown here presenting wage and benefits demands to Ikuo Mori, president of Fuji Heavy Industries, maker of Subaru vehicles.

who provides you with an interest-free loan that can be used against the mortgage, may be able to address your underlying interests without actually meeting your salary position. You may be satisfied with this alternative, if you understand what your interest is.

Below we discuss bargaining strategies and how to negotiate.

Bargaining Strategies

There are two general approaches to negotiation: *distributive bargaining* and *integrative bargaining*.[54] These are compared in Exhibit 9-3.

Distributive Bargaining

Distributive bargaining is a negotiating strategy that operates under zero-sum (win–lose) conditions. That is, any gain I make is at your expense, and vice versa. You see a used car advertised for sale online. It appears to be just what you have been looking to buy. You go out to see the car. It's great, and you want it. The owner tells you the asking price. You don't want to pay that much. The two of you then negotiate over the price. Every dollar you can get the seller to cut from the car's price is a dollar you save, and

> Should you try to win at any cost when you bargain?

distributive bargaining Negotiation that seeks to divide up a fixed amount of resources; a win–lose solution.

EXHIBIT 9-3 Distributive vs. Integrative Bargaining		
Bargaining Characteristic	**Distributive Bargaining**	**Integrative Bargaining**
Available resources	Fixed amount of resources to be divided	Variable amount of resources to be divided
Primary motivations	I win, you lose	I win, you win
Primary interests	Opposed to each other	Convergent or congruent with each other
Focus of relationships	Short-term	Long-term

Source: Based on R. J. Lewicki and J. A. Litterer, *Negotiation* (Homewood, IL: Irwin, 1985), p. 280.

every dollar more the seller can get from you comes at your expense. So the essence of distributive bargaining is negotiating over who gets what share of a fixed pie. By **fixed pie**, we mean a set amount of goods or services to be divided up. When the pie is fixed, or the parties believe it is, they tend to bargain distributively.

A party engaged in distributive bargaining focuses on trying to get the opponent to agree to a specific target point, or to get as close to it as possible. Examples of this tactic are persuading your opponent of the impossibility of reaching his or her target point and the advisability of accepting a settlement near yours; arguing that your target is fair, while your opponent's is not; and attempting to get your opponent to feel emotionally generous toward you and thus accept an outcome close to your target point.

When engaged in distributive bargaining, one of the best things you can do is to make the first offer, and to make it an aggressive one. Making the first offer shows power; individuals in power are much more likely to make initial offers, speak first at meetings, and thereby gain the advantage. Another reason this is a good strategy is the anchoring bias (the tendency for people to fixate on initial information). Once that anchoring point is set, people fail to adequately adjust it based on subsequent information. A savvy negotiator sets an anchor with the initial offer, and scores of negotiation studies show that such anchors greatly favour the person who sets them.[55]

For example, say you have a job offer, and your prospective employer asks you what sort of starting salary you would want. You have just been given a gift—you have a chance to set the anchor, meaning that you should ask for the highest salary that you think the employer could reasonably offer. For most of us, asking for a million dollars is only going to make us look ridiculous, which is why we suggest being on the high end of what you think is *reasonable*. Too often, we err on the side of caution, being afraid of scaring off the employer, and thus settle for far too little. It *is* possible to scare off an employer, and it's true that employers do not like candidates to be overly aggressive in salary negotiations, but liking is not the same as respect or doing what it takes to hire or retain someone.[56] What happens much more often is that we ask for less than what we could have obtained, as the *Ethical Dilemma* on page 336 shows.

OB in the Street shows that in the context of eBay auctions, however, sellers who start with a low price on an item can end up getting a higher selling price.

OB IN THE **STREET**
A Low Anchor Value Can Reap Higher Returns on eBay

Should a seller use a high or a low starting bid in an eBay auction? In their analysis of auction results on eBay, a group of researchers found that *lower* starting bids generated higher final prices.[57] As just one example, Nikon digital cameras with ridiculously low starting bids (one penny) sold for an average of $312, whereas those with higher starting prices went for an average of $204.

What explains such a counterintuitive result? The researchers found that low starting bids attract more bidders, and this increased traffic generates more competing bidders, so in the end the price is higher. Although this may seem irrational, negotiation and bidding behaviour are not always rational, and as you have probably experienced firsthand, once you start bidding for something, you want to win, forgetting that for many auctions the one with the highest bid is often the loser (the so-called winner's curse).

fixed pie The belief that there is only a set amount of goods or services to be divided up between the parties.

If you are thinking of participating in an auction, consider the following two points. First, some buyers think sealed-bid auctions—where bidders submit a single bid in a concealed fashion—present an opportunity to get a "steal" because a price war cannot develop among bidders. However, evidence routinely indicates that sealed-bid auctions are bad for the winning bidder (and thus good for the seller) because the winning bid is higher than would otherwise be the case. Second, buyers sometimes think jumping bids—placing a bid higher than the auctioneer is asking—is a smart strategy because it drives away competing bidders early in the game. Again, this is a myth. Evidence indicates bid jumping is good at causing other bidders to follow suit, thus increasing the value of the winning bid. _____

Another distributive bargaining tactic is revealing a deadline. Negotiators who reveal deadlines speed concessions from their negotiating counterparts, making them reconsider their position. And even though negotiators don't *think* this tactic works, in reality, negotiators who reveal deadlines do better.[58]

Integrative Bargaining

In contrast to distributive bargaining, **integrative bargaining** assumes that one or more settlements exist that can create a win–win solution. In terms of intraorganizational behaviour, integrative bargaining is preferable to distributive bargaining. Why? Because the former builds long-term relationships and makes working together in the future easier. It bonds negotiators and allows both sides to leave the bargaining table feeling that they have achieved a victory. For instance, in union–management negotiations, both sides might sit down to figure out other ways to reduce costs within an organization, so that it's possible to have greater wage increases. Distributive bargaining, on the other hand, leaves one party a loser. It tends to build animosity and deepen divisions when people must work together on an ongoing basis. For a discussion on the role of unions in labour–management negotiations, see *Case Incident—The Pros and Cons of Collective Bargaining* on page 337.

Research shows that over repeated bargaining episodes, a "losing" party who feels positive about the negotiation outcome is much more likely to bargain cooperatively in subsequent negotiations. This points to the important advantage of integrative negotiations: Even when you "win," you want your opponent to feel positively about the negotiation.[59]

Why, then, don't we see more integrative bargaining in organizations? The answer lies in the conditions necessary for this type of negotiation to succeed. These include parties who are open with information and candid about their concerns, sensitivity by both parties to the other's needs, the ability to trust one another, and a willingness by both parties to maintain flexibility.[60] Because these conditions often don't exist in organizations, negotiations often take a win-at-any-cost dynamic.

There are ways to achieve more integrative outcomes. Individuals who bargain in teams reach more integrative agreements than those who bargain individually because more ideas are generated when more people are at the bargaining table.[61] Another way to achieve higher joint-gain settlements is to put more issues on the table. The more negotiable issues that are introduced into a negotiation, the more opportunity there is for "logrolling," where issues are traded because of the parties' differences in preferences. This approach creates better outcomes for each side than if each issue were negotiated individually.[62] Focus also on the underlying interests of both sides rather than on issues. In other words, it's better to concentrate on *why* an employee wants a raise rather than to focus just on the raise amount—some unseen potential for integrative outcomes may arise if both sides concentrate on what they really want rather than on specific items they're bargaining over. Typically, it's easier to concentrate on

integrative bargaining Negotiation that seeks one or more settlements that can create a win–win solution.

underlying interests when parties stay focused on broad, overall goals rather than on immediate outcomes of a specific decision.[63] Negotiations when both parties are focused on learning and understanding the other side tend to yield higher joint outcomes than those in which parties are more interested in their individual bottom-line outcomes.[64]

How does anxiety affect negotiating outcomes?

Compromise may be your worst enemy in negotiating a win–win agreement. Compromising reduces the pressure to bargain integratively. After all, if you or your opponent caves in easily, no one needs to be creative to reach a settlement. People then settle for less than they could have obtained if they had been forced to consider the other party's interests, trade off issues, and be creative.[65] Consider a classic example where two sisters are arguing over who gets an orange. Unknown to them, one sister wants the orange to drink the juice, whereas the other sister wants the orange peel to bake a cake. If one sister gives in and gives the other sister the orange, then they will not be forced to explore their reasons for wanting the orange, and thus they will never find the win–win solution: They could *each* have the orange because they want different parts of it! A poor compromise may sometimes be the result of negotiation anxiety. A 2011 study found that negotiators who feel anxious "expect lower outcomes, make lower first offers, respond more quickly to offers, exit bargaining situations earlier, and ultimately obtain worse outcomes."[66] If self-efficacy is high, this will moderate some of the harmful effects of anxiety.[67] So it's important to feel prepared and do what you can to reduce anxiety before negotiating a deal.

How to Negotiate

Exhibit 9-4 provides a simplified model of the negotiation process. It views negotiation as made up of five steps: (1) developing a strategy; (2) defining ground rules; (3) clarifying and justifying; (4) bargaining and problem solving; and (5) attaining closure and implementation.

Developing a Strategy

Before you start negotiating, you need to do your homework. What is the nature of the conflict? What is the history leading up to this negotiation? Who is involved, and what are their perceptions of the conflict? What do you want from the negotiation? What are *your* goals? It often helps to put your goals in writing and develop a range of outcomes—from "most hopeful" to "minimally acceptable"—to keep your attention focused.

You also want to prepare an assessment of what you think are the other party's goals.[68] What will they probably ask for? How entrenched are they likely to be in their position? What intangible or hidden interests may be important to them? On what terms might they be willing to settle? When you can anticipate your opponent's position, you are better equipped to counter arguments with the facts and figures that support your position. You might also be able to anticipate better negotiating options for yourself. You want to be sure, however, that the information that you consider regarding your opponent is relevant to the negotiation. A 2011 study found that too much of the wrong kind of information can make for worse bargaining outcomes. In some cases, the person with extraneous information stopped looking for mutually beneficial outcomes earlier than those who did not have this information.[69]

EXHIBIT 9-4 The Negotiation Process

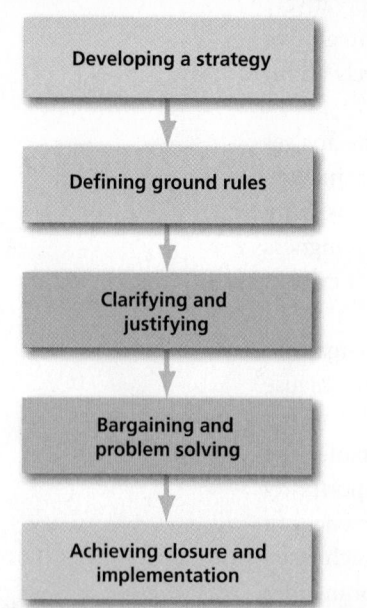

Developing a strategy

Defining ground rules

Clarifying and justifying

Bargaining and problem solving

Achieving closure and implementation

Source: Based on R. J. Lewicki, "Bargaining and Negotiation," *Exchange: The Organizational Behavior Teaching Journal* 6, no. 2 (1981), pp. 39–40.

EXHIBIT 9-5 Staking Out the Bargaining Zone

In determining goals, parties are well advised to consider their "target and resistance" points, as well as their *best alternative to a negotiated agreement* (**BATNA**).[70] The buyer and the seller are examples of two negotiators. Each has a *target point* that defines what he or she would like to achieve. Each also has a *resistance point*, which marks the lowest outcome that is acceptable—the point below which each would break off negotiations rather than accept a less favourable settlement. The area between these two points makes up each negotiator's aspiration range. As long as there is some overlap between the buyer's and seller's aspiration ranges, a **bargaining zone** exists where each side's aspirations can be met. Referring to Exhibit 9-5, if the buyer's resistance point is $450, and the seller's resistance point is $500, then the two may not be able to reach agreement because there is no overlap in their aspiration ranges.

One's BATNA represents the alternative that an individual will face if negotiations fail. For instance, during the BC Teachers' Federation and BC government negotiations, both parties wanted to avoid a legislated end to the strike, if possible. The government knew that legislation would cause even more animosity. The teachers knew that they would likely get a worse deal if the government imposed one than if they worked with the mediator to get a settlement. In the end, both sides must have concluded that what they had achieved through mediation was better than the alternative of a legislated end to the dispute.

As part of your strategy, you should determine not only your BATNA but also some estimate of the other side's as well.[71] If you go into your negotiation having a good idea of what the other party's BATNA is, even if you are not able to meet theirs, you might be able to get them to change it. Think carefully about what the other side is willing to give up. People who underestimate their opponent's willingness to give on key issues before the negotiation even starts end up with lower outcomes from a negotiation.[72]

You can practise your negotiating skills in the *Experiential Exercise* on page 335.

Defining Ground Rules

Once you have done your planning and developed a strategy, you are ready to begin defining the ground rules and procedures with the other party over the negotiation itself. Who will do the negotiating? Where will it take place? What time constraints, if any, will apply? To what issues will negotiation be limited? Will there be a specific procedure to follow if an impasse is reached? During this phase, the parties will also exchange their initial proposals or demands. *From Concepts to Skills* on pages 338–339 directly addresses some of the actions you should take to improve the likelihood that you can achieve a good agreement.

Clarifying and Justifying

After you have been presented your initial positions, you and the other party will explain, amplify, clarify, bolster, and justify your original demands. This step need not be confrontational. Rather, it's an opportunity for educating each other on the issues,

BATNA The *best alternative to a negotiated agreement*; the outcome an individual faces if negotiations fail.

bargaining zone The zone between each party's resistance point, assuming that there is overlap in this range.

OB IN ACTION
Tips for Getting to Yes

R. Fisher and W. Ury present four principles for win–win negotiations in their book *Getting to Yes*:[73]

→ **Separate** the **people from** the **problem**. Work on the issues at hand, rather than getting involved in personality issues between the parties.

→ Focus on **interests, not positions**. Try to identify what each person needs or wants, rather than coming up with an unmovable position.

→ Look for ways to achieve **mutual gains**. Rather than focusing on one "right" solution for your position, brainstorm for solutions that will satisfy the needs of both parties.

→ Use **objective criteria** to achieve a fair solution. Try to focus on fair standards, such as market value, expert opinion, norms, or laws to help guide decision making.

why they are important, and how each arrived at their initial demands. Provide the other party with any documentation that helps support your position.

Bargaining and Problem Solving

The essence of the negotiation process is the actual give and take in trying to hash out an agreement. A 2011 study found that those who used competing and collaborating (essentially a combination of the forcing and problem solving conflict resolution styles discussed earlier in the chapter) as part of their strategy to gain a higher starting salary were more successful (and received higher increases) than those who used compromising and accommodating strategies.[74] The study looked at the influence of individual differences and negotiation strategies on starting salary outcomes based on a sample of 149 newly hired employees in various industry settings. Results indicated that those who chose to negotiate increased their starting salaries by an average of $5000. Individuals who negotiated by using competing and collaborating strategies, characterized by an open discussion of one's positions, issues, and perspectives, further increased their salaries as compared with those who used compromising and accommodating strategies. Individual differences, including risk aversion and integrative attitudes, played a significant role in predicting whether individuals negotiated, and if so, what strategies they used.

OB in Action—Tips for Getting to Yes gives you further ideas on how to make negotiating work for you, based on the popular book *Getting to Yes*.[75]

Achieving Closure and Implementation

The final step in the negotiation process is formalizing your agreement and developing procedures necessary for implementing and monitoring it. For major negotiations—from labour–management negotiations to bargaining over lease terms—this will require hammering out the specifics in a formal contract. For most cases, however, closure of the negotiation process is nothing more formal than a handshake.

Individual Differences in Negotiation Effectiveness

5 Show how individual differences influence negotiations.

Are some people better negotiators than others? The answer is more complex than you might think. Three factors influence how effectively individuals negotiate: personality, moods/emotions, and gender.

Personality Traits in Negotiation

Can you predict an opponent's negotiating tactics if you know something about his or her personality? Because personality and negotiation outcomes are related but only weakly, the answer is, at best, "sort of." Most research has focused on the Big Five personality trait of agreeableness, for obvious reasons—agreeable individuals are cooperative, compliant, kind, and conflict-averse. We might think such characteristics make agreeable individuals easy prey in negotiations, especially distributive ones. The evidence suggests, however, that overall agreeableness is weakly related to negotiation outcomes. Why is this the case?

It appears that the degree to which agreeableness, and personality more generally, affects negotiation outcomes depends on the situation. The importance of being extraverted in negotiations, for example, will very much depend on how the other party reacts to someone who is assertive and enthusiastic. One complicating factor for agreeableness is that it has two facets: The tendency to be cooperative and compliant is one, but so is the tendency to be warm and empathetic.[76] It may be that while the former is a hindrance to negotiating favourable outcomes, the latter helps. Empathy, after all, is the ability to take the perspective of another person and to gain insight and understanding of them. We know so-called perspective-taking benefits integrative negotiations, so perhaps the null effect for agreeableness is due to the two tendencies pulling against one another. If this is the case, then the best negotiator is a competitive but empathetic one, and the worst is a gentle but empathetic one. *Focus on Ethics* indicates how empathy can help you be a more ethical negotiator.

FOCUS ON ETHICS

Using Empathy to Negotiate More Ethically

How can empathy make you a more ethical negotiator? You may have noticed that much of our advice for negotiating effectively depends on understanding the perspective and goals of the person with whom you are negotiating.[77] Preparing checklists of your negotiation partner's interests, likely tactics, and BATNA have all been shown to improve negotiation outcomes. Can these steps make you a more ethical negotiator as well? Studies suggest that they might.

Researchers asked respondents to indicate how much they tended to think about other people's feelings and emotions and to describe the types of tactics they engaged in during a negotiation exercise. More empathetic individuals consistently engaged in fewer unethical negotiation behaviours like making false promises and manipulating information and emotions. To put this in terms familiar to you from personality research, it appears that individuals who are higher in agreeableness will be more ethical negotiators.

When considering how to improve your ethical negotiation behaviour, follow these guidelines:

1. Try to understand your negotiation partner's perspective, not just by understanding cognitively what the other person wants, but by empathizing with the emotional reaction he or she will have to the possible outcomes.
2. Be aware of your own emotions, because many moral reactions are fundamentally emotional. One study found that engaging in unethical negotiation strategies increased feelings of guilt, so by extension, feeling guilty in a negotiation may mean that you are engaging in behaviour you will regret later.
3. Beware of empathizing so much that you work against your own interests. Just because you try to understand the motives and emotional reactions of the other side does not mean you have to assume that the other person is going to be honest and fair in return. So be on guard. _____

A 2012 study suggests that the type of negotiations matters as well. In this study, agreeable individuals reacted more positively and felt less stress (measured by their cortisol levels) in integrative negotiations than in distributive ones. Low levels of stress, in turn, made for more effective negotiation outcomes.[78] Similarly, in "hard-edged" distributive negotiations, where giving away information leads to a disadvantage, extraverted negotiators do less well because they tend to share more information than they should.[79]

Research also indicates that intelligence predicts negotiation effectiveness, but, as with personality, the effects are not especially strong.[80] In a sense, these weak links mean that you are not severely disadvantaged, even if you are an agreeable extravert, when it's time to negotiate. We can all learn to be better negotiators.[81]

Moods/Emotions in Negotiation

Do moods and emotions influence negotiation? They do, but the way they work depends on the emotions as well as the context. A negotiator who shows anger generally induces concessions from opponents, for instance, because the other negotiator believes no further concessions from the angry party are possible. One factor that governs this outcome, however, is power—you should show anger in negotiations only if you have at least as much power as your counterpart. If you have less, showing anger actually seems to provoke "hardball" reactions from the other side.[82] Another factor is how genuine your anger is—"faked" anger, or anger produced from so-called surface acting (see Chapter 2), is not effective, but showing anger that is genuine (so-called deep acting) does.[83] It also appears that having a history of showing anger, rather than sowing the seeds of revenge, actually induces more concessions because the other party perceives the negotiator as "tough."[84] Finally, culture seems to matter. For instance, one study found that when East Asian participants showed anger, it induced more concessions than if the negotiator expressing anger was from the United States or Europe, perhaps because of the stereotype of East Asians as refusing to show anger.[85]

Anxiety also appears to have an impact on negotiation. For example, one study found that individuals who experienced more anxiety about a negotiation used more deceptions in dealing with others.[86] Another study found that anxious negotiators expect lower outcomes, respond to offers more quickly, and exit the bargaining process more quickly, leading them to obtain worse outcomes.[87]

As you can see, emotions—especially negative ones—matter to negotiation. Even emotional unpredictability affects outcomes; researchers have found that negotiators who express positive and negative emotions in an unpredictable way extract more concessions because it makes the other party feel less in control.[88] As one negotiator put it, "Out of the blue, you may have to react to something you have been working on in one way, and then something entirely new is introduced, and you have to veer off and refocus."[89]

Finally, emotions play a major role in shaping perceptions.[90] Negative emotions allow us to oversimplify issues, lose trust, and put negative interpretations on the other party's behaviour.[91] In contrast, positive feelings increase our tendency to see potential relationships among elements of a problem, take a broader view of the situation, and develop innovative solutions.[92]

Gender Differences in Negotiation

Men and women behave similarly in many areas of organizational behaviour, but negotiation is not one of them. Men and women tend to negotiate differently, and these differences affect outcomes.

A popular stereotype is that women are more cooperative and pleasant in negotiations than are men. Although this stereotype is controversial, it has some merit. Men tend to place a higher value on status, power, and recognition, whereas women tend to place a higher value on compassion and altruism. Moreover, women tend to value relationship outcomes more than men, and men tend to value economic outcomes more than women.[93]

> Ever wonder if men and women negotiate differently?

These differences affect both negotiation behaviour and negotiation outcomes. Compared with men, women tend to behave in a less assertive, less self-interested, and more accommodating manner in negotiations. As a 2012 literature review concluded, women "are more reluctant to initiate negotiations, and when they do initiate negotiations, they ask for less, are more willing to accept [the] offer, and make more generous offers to their negotiation partners than men do."[94] A 2012 study of MBA students at Carnegie-Mellon University found that male MBA students took the step of negotiating their first offer 57 percent of the time, compared with 4 percent for female MBA students. The net result? A $4000 difference in starting salaries.[95]

However, the disparity goes even further than that. Because of the way women approach negotiation, other negotiators seek to exploit female negotiators by, for example, making lower salary offers. As a result, "female negotiators obtain poorer individual outcomes than male negotiators do, and two women negotiating together build less total value than do two male negotiators."[96]

This is not a "fix the woman" problem for two reasons. First, as is the case with any stereotype that has some validity, we always find individual variations. There are average differences between men and women in negotiation, but this hardly means that every man's behaviour is more assertive than every woman's in negotiation. Second, some men hold a gender double standard—when women behave stereotypically, men are more likely to take advantage of the cooperative behaviour, but when women behave assertively, their assertive behaviour is viewed more negatively than if the same behaviour were demonstrated by men.

So what can be done to change this troublesome state of affairs? First, organizational culture plays a role here. If an organization, even unwittingly, encourages a predominantly competitive model for negotiators, this will tend to increase gender-stereotypical behaviours (men negotiating competitively, women negotiating cooperatively), and it will also increase backlash when women go against stereotype. Men and women need to know that it's acceptable for each to show a full range of negotiating behaviours. Thus, a female negotiator who behaves competitively and a male negotiator who behaves cooperatively need to know that they are not violating expectations.

Second, at an individual level, women cannot directly control male stereotypes of women. Fortunately, such stereotypes are fading. However, women *can* control their own negotiating behaviour. Does this mean they should always behave aggressively and in a self-interested manner in negotiations? If economic outcomes are valued, then the answer, in general, is yes. And, of course, the shoe can be put on the other foot—if men value social outcomes, they should consider behaving in a more cooperative manner.

Research is less clear as to whether women can improve their outcomes even further by showing some gender-stereotypical behaviours. A 2012 article by Laura Kray, professor at the University of California, Berkeley, and colleagues suggested that female negotiators who were instructed to behave with "feminine charm" (be animated in body movements, make frequent eye contact with their partner, smile, laugh, be playful, and frequently compliment their partner) did better in negotiations than women not so instructed. These behaviours did not work for men, regardless of the gender of their negotiating partner.[97]

Other researchers disagree and argue that what can best benefit women is to break down gender stereotypes on the part of individuals who hold them.[98] It's possible this is a short-term/long-term situation: In the short term, women can gain an advantage in negotiation by being both assertive and flirtatious, but in the long term, their interests are best served by eliminating these sorts of sex role stereotypes.

Evidence also suggests that women's own attitudes and behaviours hurt them in negotiations. Managerial women demonstrate less confidence than men in anticipation of negotiating and are less satisfied with their performance afterward, even when their performance and the outcomes

Respected for her intelligence, confident negotiating skills, and successful outcomes, Christine Lagarde is the managing director of the International Monetary Fund (IMF). Prior to that she was the minister for the economy, finance, and employment in France, where she used her negotiating skills to boost French exports by 10 percent. She is also known for her much earlier work as a labour and anti-trust lawyer for the global law firm Baker & McKenzie, during which she negotiated with France's trade unions to change the country's labour laws, including ending the 35-hour limit on the workweek, to help boost the nation's sluggish economy.

Yuri Gripas/Landov

they achieve are similar to those of men.[99] Women are also less likely than men to see an ambiguous situation as an opportunity for negotiation. Women may unduly penalize themselves by failing to engage in negotiations that would be in their best interest. Some research suggests that women are less aggressive in negotiations because they are worried about backlash from others. This finding has an interesting qualifier: Women are more likely to engage in assertive negotiation when they are bargaining on behalf of someone else than when they are bargaining on their own behalf.[100] A 2011 study by professor Linda Schweitzer of the Sprott School of Business, Carleton University, and three colleagues found that women tend to have lower expectations about salaries and promotions as they enter the workforce, which may explain why they are less aggressive in salary negotiations.[101]

Third-Party Negotiations

6 Assess the roles and functions of third-party negotiations.

To this point, we have discussed bargaining in terms of direct negotiations. Occasionally, however, individuals or group representatives reach a stalemate and are unable to resolve their differences. In such cases, they may turn to alternative dispute resolution (ADR), where a third party helps both sides find a solution outside a courtroom. The three basic third-party roles are mediator, arbitrator, and conciliator.

Mediator

A **mediator** is a neutral third party who facilitates a negotiated solution by using reasoning and persuasion, suggesting alternatives, and the like. Mediators can be much more aggressive in proposing solutions than conciliators. Mediators are widely used in labour–management negotiations and in civil court disputes. British Columbia's Motor Vehicle Branch uses mediation to help settle accident claims. In Ontario, all disputes between companies and employees now go to mediation within 100 days. Pilot projects found that more than 60 percent of the disputes were partly or fully resolved within 60 days after the start of the mediation session.[102]

The overall effectiveness of mediated negotiations is fairly impressive. For example, a 2014 Mediate BC survey found that over 90 percent of mediations resolved all issues or helped the parties move toward resolution. The survey also found that the average satisfaction rate with the process was over 90 percent.[103] But the situation is the key to whether mediation will succeed; the conflicting parties must be motivated to bargain and resolve their conflict. Additionally, conflict intensity cannot be too high; mediation is most effective under moderate levels of conflict. Finally, perceptions of the mediator are important; to be effective, the mediator must be perceived as neutral and noncoercive.

Arbitrator

An **arbitrator** is a third party with the authority to dictate an agreement. Arbitration can be voluntary (requested by the parties) or compulsory (forced on the parties by law or contract).

The big advantage of arbitration over mediation is that it always results in a settlement. Whether there is a negative side depends on how "heavy-handed" the arbitrator appears. If one party is left feeling overwhelmingly defeated, that party is certain to be dissatisfied and the conflict may resurface at a later time.

Conciliator

A **conciliator** is a trusted third party who provides an informal communication link between the negotiator and the opponent. Conciliation is used extensively in international,

mediator A neutral third party who facilitates a negotiated solution by using reasoning, persuasion, and suggestions for alternatives.

arbitrator A third party to a negotiation who has the authority to dictate an agreement.

conciliator A trusted third party who provides an informal communication link between the negotiator and the opponent.

labour, family, and community disputes. In practice, conciliators typically act as more than mere communication conduits. They also engage in fact-finding, interpreting messages, and persuading disputants to develop agreements.

In Canada, the first step in trying to resolve a labour relations dispute can be to bring in a conciliation officer when agreement cannot be reached. This may be a good faith effort to resolve the dispute. Sometimes, however, a conciliator is used so that the union can reach a legal strike position or management can engage in a lockout. Provinces vary somewhat in how they set out the ability to engage in a strike after going through a conciliation process. For instance, in Nova Scotia, once the conciliation officer files a report that the dispute cannot be resolved through conciliation, there is a 14-day waiting period before either party can give 48 hours' notice of either a strike or a lockout.[104]

GLOBAL IMPLICATIONS

Below we consider (1) how conflict is handled in different cultures, (2) whether there are differences in negotiating styles across cultures, and (3) how the display of emotions affects negotiations in different cultures.

Conflict Resolution and Culture

Research suggests that differences across countries in conflict resolution strategies may be based on collectivistic tendencies and motives.[105] Collectivistic cultures see people as deeply embedded in social situations, whereas individualistic cultures see people as autonomous. As a result, collectivists are more likely to seek to preserve relationships and promote the good of the group as a whole. They will avoid direct expression of conflicts, preferring to use more indirect methods for resolving differences of opinion. Collectivists may also be more interested in demonstrations of concern and working through third parties to resolve disputes, whereas individualists will be more likely to confront differences of opinion directly and openly.

Some research supports this theory. Compared with collectivistic Japanese negotiators, individualistic US negotiators are more likely to see offers from their counterparts as unfair and reject them. Another study revealed that while US managers are more likely to use competing tactics when faced with a conflict, Chinese managers are more likely to use compromising and avoiding.[106] Interview data, however, suggest top management teams in Chinese high-technology firms prefer integration even more than compromising and avoiding.[107]

Cultural Differences in Negotiating Style

So what can we say about culture and negotiations? First, it appears that people generally negotiate more effectively within cultures than between them. For example, a Colombian is apt to do better negotiating with a Colombian than with a Sri Lankan. Second, it appears that in cross-cultural negotiations, it's especially important that the negotiators be high in openness. This point suggests that cross-cultural negotiators should rank high on openness to experience and avoid factors such as time pressures that tend to inhibit learning about and understanding the other party.[108]

Culture, Negotiations, and Emotions

As a rule, no one likes to face an angry counterpart in negotiations. However, East Asian negotiators may respond less favourably to anger than people from other cultures.[109]

Two separate studies found that East Asian negotiators were less likely to accept offers from negotiators who displayed anger during negotiations. Another study explicitly compared how US and Chinese negotiators react to an angry counterpart.

When confronted with an angry negotiator, Chinese negotiators increased their use of distributive negotiating tactics, whereas US negotiators decreased their use of these tactics.[110]

Why might East Asian and Chinese negotiators respond more negatively to angry negotiators? The authors of the research speculated that because their cultures emphasize respect and deference, they may be particularly likely to perceive angry behaviour as disrespectful, and thus deserving of uncooperative tactics in response.

Summary

LESSONS LEARNED

- A medium level of conflict often results in higher productivity than an absence of conflict.
- Negotiators should identify their BATNA (*best alternative to a negotiated agreement*).
- In relationships with long-term consequences, it's best to use a win–win strategy in bargaining.

While many people assume that conflict lowers group and organizational performance, this assumption is frequently incorrect. Conflict can be either constructive or destructive to the functioning of a group or unit. As shown in Exhibit 9-2, levels of conflict can be either too high or too low to be constructive. Either extreme hinders performance. An optimal level is one that prevents stagnation, stimulates creativity, allows tensions to be released, and initiates the seeds of change without being disruptive or preventing coordination of activities.

SNAPSHOT SUMMARY

Conflict Defined
- Functional vs. Dysfunctional Conflict
- Types of Conflict
- Loci of Conflict
- Sources of Conflict

Conflict Resolution
- Conflict Management Strategies Based on Dual Concern Theory
- What Can Individuals Do to Manage Conflict?

- Resolving Personality Conflicts
- Resolving Intercultural Conflicts

Conflict Outcomes

Negotiation
- Bargaining Strategies
- How to Negotiate

Individual Differences in Negotiation Effectiveness
- Personality Traits in Negotiation

- Moods/Emotions in Negotiation
- Gender Differences in Negotiation

Third-Party Negotiations
- Mediator
- Arbitrator
- Conciliator

MyManagementLab

Study, practise, and explore real business situations with these helpful resources:

- **Study Plan:** Check your understanding of chapter concepts with self-study quizzes.
- **Online Lesson Presentations:** Study key chapter topics and work through interactive assessments to test your knowledge and master management concepts.
- **Videos:** Learn more about the management practices and strategies of real companies.
- **Simulations:** Practise management decision-making in simulated business environments.

P **I** **A** PERSONAL INVENTORY ASSESSMENT

for **Review**

1. What is conflict?

2. What are the three types of conflict and the three loci of conflict?

3. What are the conditions that lead to conflict?

4. What are the differences between distributive and integrative bargaining?

5. How do individual differences influence negotiations?

6. What are the roles and functions of third-party negotiations?

for **Managers**

- Seek integrative solutions when your objective is to learn, when you want to merge insights from people with different perspectives, when you need to gain commitment by incorporating concerns into a consensus, and when you need to work through feelings that have interfered with a relationship.

- It's best to avoid an issue when it's trivial or symptomatic of other issues, when more important issues are pressing, when you perceive no chance of satisfying everyone's concerns, when people need to cool down and regain perspective, when gathering information, and when others can resolve the conflict more effectively.

- Consider compromising when goals are important but not worth potential disruption, when opponents with equal power are committed to mutually exclusive goals, and when you need temporary settlements to complex issues.

- Distributive bargaining can resolve disputes, but it often reduces the satisfaction of one or more negotiators because it's confrontational and focused on the short term. Integrative bargaining, in contrast, tends to provide outcomes that satisfy all parties and build lasting relationships.

- Make sure you set aggressive negotiating goals and try to find creative ways to achieve the objectives of both parties, especially when you value the long-term relationship with the other party. That does not mean sacrificing your self-interest; rather, it means trying to find creative solutions that give both parties what they really want.

for **You**

- It may seem easier, but avoiding conflict does not necessarily have a more positive outcome than working with someone to resolve the conflict.

- Trying to achieve a win–win solution in a conflict situation tends to lead to better relationships and greater trust.

- It's not always possible to resolve conflict on one's own. There are alternative dispute resolution options, including having someone help mediate the conflict.

- It's better to focus more on interests rather than positions when engaged in a negotiation. Doing so gives you the ability to arrive at more flexible solutions.

OB *at* **Work**

Conflict: Good or Bad?

  POINT

  COUNTERPOINT

Let's briefly review how stimulating conflict can provide benefits to the organization:[111]

- *Conflict is a means by which to bring about radical change.* It's an effective device by which management can drastically change the existing power structure, current interaction patterns, and entrenched attitudes. If there is no conflict, it means the real problems are not being addressed.

- *Conflict facilitates group cohesiveness.* While conflict increases hostility between groups, external threats tend to cause a group to pull together as a unit. Conflict with another group brings together those within each group. Such intragroup cohesion is a critical resource that groups draw on in good and especially in bad times.

- *Conflict improves group and organizational effectiveness.* Groups or organizations devoid of conflict are likely to suffer from apathy, stagnation, groupthink, and other debilitating diseases. In fact, more organizations probably fail because they have *too little* conflict, not because they have too much. Stagnation is the biggest threat to organizations, but since it occurs slowly, its ill effects often go unnoticed until it's too late. Conflict can break complacency—although most of us don't like conflict, it's often the last best hope of saving an organization.

- *Conflict brings about a slightly higher, more constructive level of tension.* Constructive levels of tension enhance the chances of solving the conflicts in a way satisfactory to all parties concerned. When the level of tension is very low, the parties may not be sufficiently motivated to do something about a conflict.

It may be true that conflict is an inherent part of any group or organization. It may not be possible to eliminate it completely. However, just because conflicts exist is no reason to glorify them. All conflicts are dysfunctional, and it's one of management's major responsibilities to keep conflict intensity as low as humanly possible. A few points will support this case:

- *The negative consequences from conflict can be devastating.* The list of negatives associated with conflict is awesome. The most obvious are increased turnover, decreased employee satisfaction, inefficiencies between work units, sabotage, labour grievances and strikes, and physical aggression. One study estimated that managing conflict at work costs the average employer nearly 450 days of management time a year.

- *Effective managers build teamwork.* A good manager builds a coordinated team. Conflict works against such an objective. A successful work group is like a successful sports team: Members all know their roles and support their teammates. When a team works well, the whole becomes greater than the sum of the parts. Management creates teamwork by minimizing internal conflicts and facilitating internal coordination.

- *Competition is good for an organization, but not conflict.* Competition and conflict should not be confused with each other. *Conflict* is behaviour directed against another party, whereas *competition* is behaviour aimed at obtaining a goal without interference from another party. Competition is healthy; it's the source of organizational vitality. Conflict, on the other hand, is destructive.

- *Conflict is avoidable.* It may be true that conflict is inevitable when an organization is in a downward spiral, but the goal of good leadership and effective management is to avoid the spiral to begin with.

PERSONAL **INVENTORY** ASSESSMENT

Strategies for Handling Conflict: Different people tend to rely on different strategies for handling conflict. Use this scale to determine your preferred strategy. Is there an alternative strategy that may be more effective in workplace situations?

Managing Interpersonal Conflict: This self-assessment is designed to help you better understand your preferred approaches to managing interpersonal conflict.

BREAKOUT **GROUP** EXERCISES

Form small groups to discuss the following topics, as assigned by your instructor:

1. You and 2 other students carpool to school every day. The driver has recently taken to playing a new radio station quite loudly. You do not like the music, or the loudness. Using one of the conflict-handling strategies outlined in Exhibit 9-1, indicate how you might go about resolving this conflict.

2. Using the example above, identify a number of BATNAs (*best alternative to a negotiated agreement*) available to you, and then decide whether you should continue carpooling.

3. Which conflict-handling strategy is most consistent with how you deal with conflict? Is your strategy effective? Why or why not?

EXPERIENTIAL EXERCISE

A Negotiation Role Play

This role play is designed to help you develop your negotiating skills. The class is to break into pairs. One person will play the role of Alex, the department supervisor. The other person will play C.J., Alex's boss.

The situation: Alex and C.J. work for hockey-equipment manufacturer Bauer. Alex supervises a research laboratory. C.J. is the manager of R & D. Alex and C.J. are former skaters who have worked for Bauer for more than 6 years. C.J. has been Alex's boss for 2 years.

One of Alex's employees has greatly impressed Alex. This employee is Lisa Roland. Lisa was hired 11 months ago. She is 24 years old and holds a master's degree in mechanical engineering. Her entry-level salary was $57 500 a year. She was told by Alex that, in accordance with corporation policy, she would receive an initial performance evaluation at 6 months and a comprehensive review after 1 year. Based on her performance record, Lisa was told she could expect a salary adjustment at the time of the 1-year review.

Alex's evaluation of Lisa after 6 months was very positive. Alex commented on the long hours Lisa was working, her cooperative spirit, the fact that others in the lab enjoyed working with her, and her immediate positive impact on the project she had been assigned. Now that Lisa's first anniversary is coming up, Alex has again reviewed Lisa's performance. Alex thinks Lisa may be the best new person the R & D group has ever hired. After only a year, Alex has ranked Lisa as the number 3 performer in a department of 11.

Salaries in the department vary greatly. Alex, for instance, has a basic salary of $93 800, plus eligibility for a bonus that might add another $7000 to $11 000 a year. The salary range of the 11 department members is $48 400 to $79 000. The lowest salary is a recent hire with a bachelor's degree in physics. The 2 people that Alex has rated above Lisa earn base salaries of $73 800 and $78 900. They are both 27 years old and have been at Bauer for 3 and 4 years, respectively. The median salary in Alex's department is $65 300.

Alex's role: You want to give Lisa a big raise. While she is young, she has proven to be an excellent addition to the department. You don't want to lose her. More important, she knows in general what other people in the department are earning, and she thinks she is underpaid. The company typically gives 1-year raises of 5 percent, although 10 percent is not unusual and 20 to 30 percent increases have been approved on occasion. You would like to get Lisa as large an increase as C.J. will approve.

C.J.'s role: All your supervisors typically try to squeeze you for as much money as they can for their people. You understand this because you did the same thing when you were a supervisor, but your boss wants to keep a lid on costs. He wants you to keep raises for recent hires generally in the range of 5 to 8 percent. In fact, he has sent a memo to all managers and supervisors stating this objective. However, your boss is also very concerned with equity and paying people what they are worth. You feel assured that he will support any salary recommendation you make, as long as it can be justified. Your goal, consistent with cost reduction, is to keep salary increases as low as possible.

The negotiation: Alex has a meeting scheduled with C.J. to discuss Lisa's performance review and salary adjustment. Take a couple of minutes to think through the facts in this exercise and to prepare a strategy. Then you have up to 15 minutes to conduct your negotiation. When your negotiation is complete, the class will compare the various strategies used and the outcomes that resulted.

ETHICAL **DILEMMA**

The Lowball Applicant

Consider this first-person account:

I am a human resources manager, so I interview people every day. Sometimes the managers in my company ask me to pre-screen candidates, which I do after discussing the job at length with the manager. I usually start the candidate screening with a few personality–job fit tests; then conduct an interview, following a list of job-specific questions the manager has given me; and finally discuss the job requirements, our company, and the pay/benefits. By that time in the process, the candidate usually has a good idea of the job and is eager to suggest a high level of pay at the top of the advertised bracket or, often, above the pay bracket. However, this isn't always the case.

One time in particular, an excellent candidate with outstanding qualifications surprised me by saying that since she wanted flextime, she would accept a rate below the pay bracket. Confused, I asked her if she wanted a reduction in hours below full time. She said no, she expected to work full time and only wanted to come in a little late and would leave a little late to make up the time. I guess she figured this was a concession worth slashing her salary for, but our company has flextime. In fact, she could have asked for five fewer hours per week, still been considered full time by our company policies, and negotiated for above the advertised pay grade.

I knew the manager would be highly interested in this candidate and that he could probably get her to work the longer full-time hours at a lower rate of pay. That outcome might be best for the company, or it might not. She obviously didn't fully understand the company policies in her favour, and she was unsophisticated about her worth in the marketplace. What should I have done?

Questions

1. If the human resources manager were to coach the applicant to request a higher salary, would the coaching work against the interests of the organization? Is it the responsibility of the human resources manager to put the organization's financial interests first?

2. What do you see as the potential downside of the human resources manager abstaining from discussing the pay issue further with the candidate?

3. If the candidate were hired at the reduced rate she proposed, how might the situation play out over the next year when she gets to know the organization and pay standards better?

CASE INCIDENTS

Choosing Your Battles

While much of this chapter has discussed methods for achieving harmonious relationships and getting out of conflicts, it's also important to remember that there are situations in which too little conflict can be a problem.[112] As we noted, in creative problem-solving teams, some

level of task conflict early in the process of formulating a solution can be an important stimulus to innovation.

However, the conditions must be right for productive conflict. In particular, individuals must feel psychologically safe in bringing up issues for discussion. If people fear that what they say is going to be held against them, they may be reluctant to speak up or rock the boat. Experts suggest that effective conflicts have three key characteristics: They should (1) speak to what is possible, (2) be compelling, and (3) involve uncertainty.

So how should a manager "pick a fight"? First, ensure that the stakes are sufficient to actually warrant a disruption. Second, focus on the future, and on how to resolve the conflict rather than on whom to blame. Third, tie the conflict to fundamental values. Rather than concentrating on winning or losing, encourage both parties to see how successfully exploring and resolving the conflict will lead to optimal outcomes for all. If managed successfully, some degree of open disagreement can be an important way for companies to manage simmering and potentially destructive conflicts.

However, not every organization follows these principles. CP Rail and the City of Vancouver have been at odds on what should happen to a rail line that runs down what is called the Arbutus Corridor on the west side of Vancouver. CP stopped using the line in the late 1990s, and over the years residents have used the area on either side of the railway tracks for award-winning community gardens as well as walking their dogs. CP wanted to develop the property for commercial and residential use. The city was opposed to this, and a 2006 Supreme Court of Canada judgment gave it the right to determine how the land would be used. The city would like to see the property, which is 11 kilometres long, used as a greenway and a future transit corridor.

CP owns the land and wants to develop it or sell it to the city. In 2014, CP grew tired of the impasse with Vancouver. No talks between the parties had taken place in years. The railway announced that it was going to reinstate train service, which it has the legal right to do, even though the city does not want this to happen. Rather than fighting this battle with the city, the railway decided to pick a battle with the gardeners who were using the private property. CP gave notice that it would begin tearing out gardens in August, at the height of harvest season. They then destroyed some of the gardens in mid-

August, hoping that pressure from the community about the loss of their gardens would spur the city into making some sort of settlement with the company. Instead, the move infuriated both gardeners and people living in the area because it was viewed as a bullying tactic. Many of the gardens had existed while BC Rail was still operating, and the company had not objected to them at the time.

To escalate further, CP informed people living in the area that it planned to spray herbicides along the line. CP director Mike LoVecchio wrote, "This work is to continue throughout August and September. Our goal is to have the entire line ready for train operations in the fall." Following these actions, the city entered into talks with CP, but the two parties could not agree on the price the city should pay the railway for the land. In October 2014, the city launched a constitutional challenge against the railway, which means that the issue will be tied up in court for quite some time. The city also applied for permanent injunctions to stop CP from doing any more damage to the remaining gardens or doing anything further to reactivate the rail line. In January 2015, the city lost its bid to halt CP's Arbutus corridor plan. However, the city launched another lawsuit to have the railway declared abandoned, to be heard later in 2015.

Questions

1. Can involving a third party in a dispute, much like CP Rail did with the community gardeners, ever result in a positive outcome?

2. How can negotiators use conflict management strategies to their advantage so that differences in interests lead to positive integrative solutions rather than dysfunctional conflicts?

3. Can you think of situations in your own life in which silence has worsened a conflict between parties? What might have been done differently to ensure that open communication facilitated collaboration instead?

The Pros and Cons of Collective Bargaining

Fewer employees in the private sector are unionized, compared with those who work in the public sector (16.4 vs. 71.4 percent in 2012).[113] Does being in a labour union make a difference for optimal wages and benefits?

On the positive side, by negotiating as a collective, public sector employees, who are more heavily unionized, are able to earn, on average, roughly 12 percent more than employees working in the mostly non-unionized

OB *at Work*

private sector. Unions also can protect the rights of workers against capricious actions by employers. Consider the following example:

> Lydia criticized the work of five of her co-workers. They were not amused and posted angry messages on a Facebook page. Lydia complained to her supervisor that the postings violated the employer's "zero tolerance" policy against "bullying and harassment." The employer investigated and, agreeing that its policy had been violated, fired the five.

Most of us would probably prefer not to be fired for Facebook posts. This is a protection unions can provide.

On the negative side, public-sector unions at times have been able to negotiate employment arrangements that are hard to sustain. According to the Fraser Institute, almost 90 percent of those employed by the Canadian government receive pension benefits as part of their total compensation. Only 24 percent of private sector employees have these benefits. This allowed government employees to retire about 2.5 years earlier than private sector employees between 2007 and 2011.

Further, it's often more difficult to fire a member of a public-sector union, even if performance is exceptionally poor. In 2011, 3.8 percent of private sector employees were fired. Only 0.6 percent of public sector employees were fired.

Reasonable people can disagree about the pros and cons of unions and whether they help or hinder an organization's ability to be successful. There is no dispute, however, that they often figure prominently in the study of workplace conflict and negotiation strategies.

Questions

1. Labour–management negotiations might be characterized as more distributive than integrative. Do you agree? Why do you think this is the case? What, if anything, would you do about it?

2. If unions have negotiated unreasonable agreements, what responsibility does management or the administration bear for agreeing to these terms? Why do you think they do agree?

3. If you were advising union and management representatives about how to negotiate an agreement, drawing from the concepts in this chapter, what would you tell them?

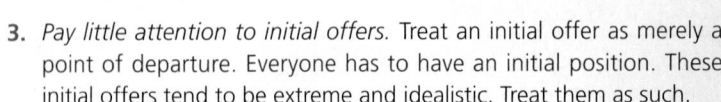

FROM CONCEPTS TO SKILLS

Negotiating

Once you have taken the time to assess your own goals, to consider the other party's goals and interests, and to develop a strategy, you are ready to begin actual negotiations. The following five suggestions should improve your negotiating skills:[114]

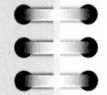

1. *Begin with a positive overture.* Studies on negotiation show that concessions tend to be reciprocated and lead to agreements. As a result, begin bargaining with a positive overture—perhaps a small concession—and then reciprocate your opponent's concessions.

2. *Address problems, not personalities.* Concentrate on the negotiation issues, not on the personal characteristics of your opponent. When negotiations get tough, avoid the tendency to attack your opponent. It's your opponent's ideas or position that you disagree with, not him or her personally. Separate the people from the problem, and don't personalize differences.

3. *Pay little attention to initial offers.* Treat an initial offer as merely a point of departure. Everyone has to have an initial position. These initial offers tend to be extreme and idealistic. Treat them as such.

4. *Emphasize win–win solutions.* Inexperienced negotiators often assume that their gain must come at the expense of the other party. As noted with integrative bargaining, that need not be the case. There are often win–win solutions. But assuming a zero-sum game means missed opportunities for trade-offs that could benefit both sides. So if conditions are supportive, look for an integrative solution. Frame options in terms of your opponent's interests, and look for solutions that can allow your opponent, as well as yourself, to declare a victory.

5. *Create an open and trusting climate.* Skilled negotiators are better listeners, ask more questions, focus their arguments more directly, are less defensive, and have learned to avoid words and phrases that can irritate an opponent (for example, "generous offer," "fair price," "reasonable arrangement"). In other words, they are better at creating the open and trusting climate necessary for reaching an integrative settlement.

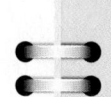 **Practising Skills**

As marketing director for Done Right, a regional home-repair chain, you have come up with a plan you believe has significant potential for future sales. Your plan involves a customer information service designed to help people make their homes more environmentally sensitive. Then, based on homeowners' assessments of their homes' environmental impact, your firm will be prepared to help them deal with problems or concerns they may uncover. You are really excited about the competitive potential of this new service. You envision pamphlets, in-store appearances by environmental experts, as well as contests for consumers and school kids. After several weeks of preparations, you make your pitch to your boss, Nick Castro. You point out how the market for environmentally sensitive products is growing and how this growing demand represents the perfect opportunity for Done Right. Nick seems impressed by your presentation, but he has expressed one major concern: He thinks your workload is already too heavy. He does not see how you are going to have enough time to start this new service and still be able to look after all of your other assigned marketing duties. You really want to start the new service. What strategy will you follow in your negotiation with Nick?

Reinforcing Skills

1. Negotiate with a team member or work colleague to handle a small section of work that you are not going to be able to get done in time for an important deadline.

2. The next time you purchase a relatively expensive item (such as an automobile, apartment lease, appliance, jewellery), attempt to negotiate a better price and gain some concessions such as an extended warranty, smaller down payment, maintenance services, or the like.

Workplace Bullying

Meredith Boucher, a former Walmart assistant manager at a store in Windsor, Ontario, was awarded $410 000 in damages by the Ontario Court of Appeal after successfully arguing that she was subjected to workplace bullying by her manager, Jason Pinnock.[1] Boucher described her experience to reporter Ioanna Roumeliotis on CBC's *The National* in July 2014:

He would start off and he would start, "Gong, gong, gong, gong!" [swinging his arms as if hitting a gong]. And then he'd be like, "This is a [expletive] gong show" [close to Boucher's face]

and then he'd start, "Di, di, di, di, di, di, di, di, di, di, di, di, di, di, di" [waving his hands wildly and getting very close to Boucher]. And he'd ... he'd just go off and he'd go crazy ... every day ... and he was doing it in front of everyone.

Boucher's harassment started after she refused to falsify temperature logs for refrigerated cases in the store. Pinnock targeted Boucher for six months, engaging in a variety of activities to demean her. Boucher complained to Walmart senior managers about Pinnock's behaviour several times, but they did nothing.

The Court of Appeal award reduced the original $1.4 million Boucher was awarded by a jury. However, the court found both Walmart and Pinnock liable, assigning fines to both parties. The jury heard testimony from Boucher that Pinnock called her "a [expletive] idiot" and made her count skids in front of co-workers to prove that she knew how to count.

Workplaces in many parts of Canada are required to address bullying. Bullying itself is not illegal, but some forms of it—for example, threats, assault, and harassment— are included in the Criminal Code.

What Is Happening in Our Workplaces?

Workplaces today are receiving highly critical reviews, being called everything from "uncivil" to "toxic."

Lynne Anderson and Christine Pearson, management professors from St. Joseph's University and the University of North Carolina, respectively, note that "historians may view the dawn of the twenty-first century as a time of thoughtless acts and rudeness: We tailgate, even in the slow lane; we dial wrong numbers and then slam the receiver on the innocent respondent; we break appointments with nonchalance."[2] The workplace has often been seen as one of the places where civility still ruled, with co-workers treating one another with a mixture of formality and friendliness, distance and politeness. However, with downsizing, re-engineering, budget cuts, pressures for increased productivity, autocratic work environments, and the use of part-time employees, there has been an increase in "uncivil and aggressive workplace behaviours."[3]

What does civility in the workplace mean? A simple definition of *workplace civility* is behaviour "involving politeness and regard for others in the workplace, within workplace norms for respect."[4] *Workplace incivility*, then, "involves acting with disregard for others in the workplace, in violation of workplace norms for respect."[5] Of course, different workplaces will have different norms for what determines mutual respect. For instance, in most restaurants, if the staff were rude to you when you were there for dinner, you would be annoyed, and perhaps even complain to the manager. However, at The Elbow Room Café in downtown Vancouver, if customers complain they are in a hurry, manager Patrick Savoie might well say, "If you're in a hurry, you should have gone to McDonald's."[6] Such a comeback is acceptable to the diners at The Elbow Room Café, because rudeness is its trademark.[7]

Most work environments are not expected to be characterized by such rudeness. However, this has been changing in recent years. Robert Warren, a University of Manitoba marketing professor, notes that "simple courtesy has gone by the board."[8]

Instead, we see workplaces characterized by workplace bullying, which can take the form of repetitive verbal abuse and offensive behaviour (including gestures) by one or more people that threaten, humiliate, or intimidate a person; it can also involve work interference that prevents a person from getting work done.[9]

What Do We Know About Workplace Bullying?

There are few statistics on workplace bullying in Canada. The Workplace Bullying Institute conducts the largest scientific study of bullying in the United States, and a 2014 study of 1000 adults found the following:[10]

- The percentage of respondents who have suffered abusive conduct at work is 27 percent.
- The percentage of respondents who have witnessed abusive conduct at work is 21 percent.
- A full 72 percent of respondents are aware that workplace bullying happens.
- Men are significantly more likely to engage in bullying behaviour than women (69 percent vs. 31 percent).
- Women who bully are significantly more likely to bully women rather than men (68 percent vs. 32 percent).
- Men who bully are more likely to target women rather than men (57 percent vs. 43 percent).
- Overall, 60 percent of bullying targets are women.

FACTBOX

What happens when employees experience rudeness in the workplace?

- "48% decreased their work effort,
- 47% decreased their time at work,
- 38% decreased their work quality,
- 66% said their performance declined,
- 80% lost work time worrying about the incident,
- 63% lost time avoiding the offender, and
- 78% said their commitment to the organization declined."[11]

The evidence suggests that rudeness, bullying, and violence are all on the rise. The victims of these negative behaviours are not just the ones who suffer, however.[12] Witnesses to bullying also suffer.[13]

While rudeness is on the rise, professor André Roberge at Laval University suggests that some of the rudeness is generational. He finds that "young clerks often lack both knowledge and civility. Employers are having to train young people in simple manners because that is not being done at home."[14] Professor Warren backs this up: "One of the biggest complaints I hear from businesses when I go to talk about graduates is the lack of interpersonal skills."[15]

Workplace Violence

Recently, researchers have suggested that incivility may be the beginning of more negative behaviours in the workplace, including aggression and violence.[16]

Kevin Douglas Addison chose a deadly way to exhibit the anger he felt toward his former employer. In April 2014, he took a shotgun and opened fire at his former place of employment, the Western Forest Products mill in Nanaimo, BC, killing two employees (one of them a foreman) and injuring two others. The mill had closed in 2008 and had re-opened in a smaller capacity in 2010. Co-workers speculated that financial problems as well as not being rehired when the mill re-opened may have led Addison to engage in the shooting. Roy Robertson, a retired mill employee, called Addison "an absolutely super nice guy. But me, you, anyone else can crack under pressure. I don't know his situation."[17]

Workplace violence, according to the International Labour Organization (ILO), includes

> any incident in which a person is abused, threatened or assaulted in circumstances relating to [his or her] work. These behaviours would originate from customers or co-workers at any level of the organization. This definition would include all forms of harassment, bullying, intimidation, physical threats, assaults, robbery and other intrusive behaviour.[18]

Few Canadian statistics on anger at work are available, although we do know that 53 percent of women and 47 percent of men reported experiencing workplace violence in 2004. About 17 percent of the incidents where violent victimization occurred happens in the workplace.[19] Glenn French, president and founder of the Toronto-based Canadian Initiative on Workplace Violence, suggests that these numbers underrepresent the true state of violence in Canada. He acknowledges that there is less gun violence in the workplace here than in the United States: "We do it the Canadian way: we don't kill you, we'll just make your life a living hell

by harassing and intimidating you on the job. The face of violence in Canada tends to be far more indirect than what we've seen [in the Western Forest Products mill in Nanaimo]."[20]

Sandra Robinson and Jennifer Berdahl, both professors at the Sauder School of Business at the University of British Columbia, have recently been looking at the effects of being ignored (ostracized) in the workplace. Their research found that while people tend to think that ostracism is less offensive than harassment, the people who are ostracized seem to suffer greater effects. "The experience of ostracism has a bigger impact on job dissatisfaction, on psychological well-being, on self-reported physical health, on intentions to quit the company," Robinson said.[21] The study found that ostracism was quite widespread: 71 percent of employees reported being ostracized in the previous six months, compared with 48 percent who reported being bullied.[22]

Those who are ostracized are more likely to quit their jobs within three years than those who have been bullied. Robinson concluded that because ostracism is less visible, it's harder to fight. "Victims of ostracism really feel they can't do anything about it. It's very difficult to call-out the absence of behaviour. A lot of people end up quitting for their own well-being."[23]

What Causes Incivility (and Worse) in the Workplace?

If employers and employees are acting with less civility toward each other, what is causing this to happen?

Managers and employees often have different views of the employee's role in the organization. Jeffrey Pfeffer, a professor of organizational behaviour at the Graduate School of Business

at Stanford University, notes that many companies don't really value their employees: "Most managers, if they're being honest with themselves, will admit it: When they look at their people, they see costs, they see salaries, they see benefits, they see overhead. Very few companies look at their people and see assets."[24]

Most employees, however, like to think that they are assets to their organization. The realization that they are simply costs and not valued members of an organization can cause frustration for employees.

In addition, "employers' excessive demands and top-down style of management are contributing to the rise of 'work rage,'" claims Gerry Smith, author of *Work Rage*.[25] He cites demands coming from a variety of sources: "overtime, downsizing, rapid technological changes, company restructuring and difficulty balancing the demands of job and home."[26] Smith worries about the consequences of these demands: "If you push people too hard, set unrealistic expectations and cut back their benefits, they're going to strike back."[27]

Smith's work supports the findings of studies that report the most common cause of anger and bullying is the actions of supervisors or managers.[28] Other common causes of anger identified by the researchers include lack of productivity by co-workers and others; tight deadlines; heavy workload; interaction with the public; and bad treatment. The inset *Do You Have a Bad Boss?* describes some of the bad behaviour of bosses.

A 2011 study found that how managers deal with displays of anger at work can do much to defuse tensions. Co-workers want to see the manager take some responsibility for a fellow employee's anger, rather than disciplining the employee, if the manager or the working conditions are the source of the anger.[29]

Do You Have a Bad Boss?

You know you have a bad boss if he or she . . . (percent reporting bosses who did this)[30]

. . . fails to keep promises (39%)

. . . fails to give credit when due (37%)

. . . gave you the "silent treatment" at least once in the past year (31%)

. . . makes negative comments about you behind your back to other employees or managers (25%)

. . . invades your personal privacy (24%)

. . . blames others to cover up mistakes or to minimize their own embarrassment (23%)

FACT**BOX**

- 40% of Canadians have experienced workplace bullying at least weekly for the last six months.
- 74% of employees say their managers make inappropriate comments.
- Only 3% of bullied people file lawsuits.
- 57% of employees say their managers bully or intimidate.
- 56% of reported bullying incidents were initiated by managers and 33% were initiated by co-workers.
- 77% of bullying cases involved single perpetrators.
- 23% of bullying cases involved multiple perpetrators.[34]

The Psychological Contract

Some researchers have looked at this frustration in terms of a breakdown of the psychological contract formed between employees and employers.

An employer and employee begin to develop psychological contracts as they are first introduced to each other in the hiring process.[31] These contracts continue over time as the employer and the employee come to understand each other's expectations about the amounts and quality of work to be performed and the types of rewards to be given. For instance, when an employee is continually asked to work late and/or be available at all hours through pagers and email, the employee may assume that doing so will result in greater rewards or faster promotion down the line. The employer may have had no such intention, and may even be thinking that the employee should be grateful simply to have a job. Later, when the employee does not get expected (though never promised) rewards, he or she is disappointed.

Sandra Robinson, an organizational behaviour professor at the Sauder School of Business at the University of British Columbia, and her colleagues have found that when a psychological contract is violated (perceptually or actually), the relationship between the employee and the employer is damaged. The result can be a loss of trust.[32] The breakdown in trust can cause employees to be less ready to accept decisions or obey rules.[33] The erosion of trust can also lead employees to take revenge on the employer. So they don't carry out their end of a task. Or they refuse to pass on messages. They engage in any number of subtle and not-so-subtle behaviours that affect the way work gets done—or prevents work from getting done.

Recent research on the psychological contract suggests that violations of implicit or explicit promises may not be necessary to affect employee intentions to stay with the organization and/or engage in citizenship behaviours. Professors Samantha Montes and David Zweig of the Rotman School of Management found that employees expect decent pay, developmental

opportunities, and support (whether or not employers promise to deliver such); and when they don't receive those things, their behaviour toward the organization becomes negative.[35]

The Toxic Organization

Pfeffer suggests that companies have become "toxic places to work."[36] He notes that companies, particularly in Silicon Valley, ask their employees to sign contracts on the first day of work indicating the employee's understanding that the company has the right to fire at will and for any reason. Some employers also ask their employees to choose between having a life and having a career. Pfeffer relates a joke people used to tell about Microsoft: "We offer flexible time—you can work any 18 hours you want."[37] This kind of attitude can be

---

toxic to employees, although it does not imply that Microsoft is a toxic employer. The inset *How to Deal with a Toxic Boss* gives tips, should you find yourself in that situation.

What does it mean to be a toxic organization? The inset *What Does a Toxic Organization Look Like?* describes one. The late professor Peter Frost of the Sauder School of Business at the University of British Columbia noted that there will always be pain in organizations, but that sometimes it becomes so intense or prolonged that conditions within the organization begin to break down. In other words, the situation becomes toxic. This is not dissimilar to what the liver or kidneys do when toxins become too intense in a human body.[39]

What causes organizations to be toxic? Like Pfeffer, Frost and Robinson identify a number of factors. Downsizing and organizational change are two main factors, particularly in recent years. Sometimes organizations experience unexpected events—such as the sudden death of a key manager, an unwise move by senior management, strong competition from a start-up company—that lead to toxicity. Other organizations are toxic throughout their system due to policies and prac-

tices that create distress. Such factors as unreasonable stretch goals or performance targets, or unrelenting internal competition, can create toxicity. There are also toxic managers who lead through insensitivity, vindictiveness, and failure to take responsibility, or they are control freaks or are unethical.

What Are the Effects of Incivility and Toxicity in the Workplace?

In general, researchers have found that the effects of workplace anger are sometimes subtle: a hostile work environment and the tendency to do only enough work to get by.[40]

Those who feel chronic anger in the workplace are more likely to report "feelings of betrayal by the organization, decreased feelings of loyalty, a decreased sense that respondent values and the organization's values are similar, a decreased sense that the employer treated the respondent with dignity and respect, and a decreased sense that employers had fulfilled promises made to respondents."[41] So do these feelings make a difference? Apparently so. Researchers have found that those who felt angry with their employers were less likely to put forth their best effort, more likely to be competitive toward other employees, and less likely to suggest "a quicker and better way to do their job."[42] All of these actions tend to decrease the productivity possible in the workplace.

It's not just those who work for an organization who are affected by incivility and toxicity. Poor service, from indifference to rudeness to outright hostility, characterizes many transactions in Canadian businesses. "Across the country, better business bureaus, provincial government consumer-help agencies and media ombudsmen report a lengthening litany of complaints

F A C E O F F

Manners are an over-romanticized concept. The big issue is not that employees need to be concerned about their manners. Rather, employers should be paying better wages.

The Golden Rule "Do unto others as you would have others do unto you," should still have a role in today's workplace. Being nice pays off.

about contractors, car dealers, repair shops, moving companies, airlines and department stores."[44] This suggests that customers and clients may well be feeling the impact of internal workplace dynamics.

Legislation to Prevent Bullying

The Canadian Criminal Code has no bullying offence, although depending on the circumstance, other charges could be made, such as criminal harassment, uttering threats, assault, and sexual assault. On a provincial level, only some provinces have adopted legislation directed at bullying. Others are still working out potential approaches.[45]

For instance, in 2012 WorkSafeBC started to accept mental disorder claims that were the results of "a cumulative series of significant work-related stressors." That was a major shift for the organization, which promotes workplace health and safety in British Columbia. Previously it had only processed claims for stress from traumatic events. Between 2012 and 2014, WorkSafeBC accepted 655 mental stress claims and paid out more than $10 million in damages. While the majority of claims were for traumatic incidents, about 30 percent were for workplace stress. "Forty-five to 50 people are applying for benefits

every week. That's an indication that there are problems in the workplace," says Jennifer Leyen, director of special care services for WorkSafeBC.[46]

WorkSafeBC requires employers in the province to have a policy in place to prevent bullying and harassment. It also reminds employers and employees what bullying includes: insults, sabotage, threats. However, bullying does not include negative work evaluations, discipline, or firing. Some experts find that this new policy is not enough, however. "It overlooks other issues like the damage caused by a constant thrum of low-level incivility—the eye rolling, the interruptions, the dismissiveness."[47]

RESEARCH EXERCISES

1. Look for data on violence and anger in the workplace in other countries. How do these data compare with the Canadian and American data presented here? What might you conclude about how violence and anger in the workplace are expressed in different cultures?

2. Identify three Canadian organizations that are trying to foster better and/or less toxic environments for their employees. What kind of effect is this having on the organizations' bottom lines?

YOUR PERSPECTIVE

1. Is it reasonable to suggest, as some researchers have, that young people today have not learned to be civil to others or do not place a high priority on doing so? Do you see this as one of the causes of incivility in the workplace?

2. What should be done about managers who create toxicity in the workplace while being rewarded because they achieve bottom-line results? Should bottom-line results justify their behaviour?

WANT TO KNOW MORE?

If you would like to read more on this topic, see P. K. Jonason, S. Slomski, and J. Partyka, "The Dark Triad at Work: How Toxic Employees Get Their Way," *Personality and Individual Differences*, February 2012, pp. 449–453; B. Schyns and J. Schilling, "How Bad Are the Effects of Bad Leaders? A Meta-Analysis of Destructive Leadership and Its Outcomes," *The Leadership Quarterly*, February 2013, pp. 138–158; Canadian Centre for Occupational Health and Safety, "Bullying in the Workplace," **www.ccohs.ca/oshanswers/psychosocial/bullying.html**; and L. Durré, *Surviving the Toxic Workplace* (New York: McGraw Hill, 2010).

Organizational Culture

How can organizers of "the Greatest Outdoor Show on Earth" deal effectively with challenges, including major crises? A strong organizational culture is part of the answer.

LEARNING OUTCOMES

After studying this chapter, you should be able to:

1. Describe the common characteristics of organizational culture.

2. Identify the functional effects of organizational culture on people and the organization.

3. Identify the factors that create and sustain an organization's culture.

4. Show how culture is transmitted to employees.

5. Identify the liabilities of organizational culture.

6. Demonstrate how an ethical organizational culture can be created.

7. Describe a positive organizational culture.

T he 10-day Calgary Stampede, held every July, is a celebration of Alberta's history and spirit. It showcases the people, animals, traditions, and values of the West.[1] The theme of the stampede is "We're Greatest Together," a sentiment that organizers try to have reflected in every aspect of their organizational culture. This culture was put to the test in 2013 when the Stampede grounds were flooded in the days just before the official opening, leaving organizers and thousands of volunteers scrambling to relocate key events and accommodate over a million visitors despite the flood waters. Calls for the Stampede to proceed no matter what were so widespread that "Come Hell or High Water" became the official rallying cry, song, and T-shirt of an entire city.

Hans-Peter Merten/Robert Harding World Imagery/Alamy

The teamwork, commitment, and persistence displayed while saving the show was so impressive that it's not surprising that the Calgary Stampede received the prestigious Waterstone Award for Canada's Top 10 Most Admired Corporate Cultures in 2013. The award is based on demonstrating a positive culture that is supported by and aligned with the organization's leadership, recruitment methods, reward systems, and manner of measuring organizational performance.

Commenting on the award, Susan Garnett, vice president of People Services for the Stampede, observed that the Calgary Stampede works with the community "to preserve and promote western heritage and values—and we do that all year long. This award as a most-admired corporate culture verifies what we already know—we are greatest together."

In this chapter, we show that every organization has a culture. We examine how that culture reveals itself and the impact it has on the attitudes and behaviours of members of that organization. An understanding of what makes up an organization's culture and how it is created, sustained, and learned enhances our ability to explain and predict the behaviour of people at work.

THE BIG IDEA

A strong organizational culture can guide individual decisions and help everyone work together toward the same goals.

 IS FOR **EVERYONE**

- What does organizational culture do?
- What kind of organizational culture would work best for you?
- Is culture the same as rules?

What Is Organizational Culture?

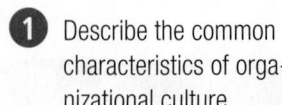

1 Describe the common characteristics of organizational culture.

When Henry Mintzberg, professor at McGill University and one of the world's leading management experts, was asked to compare organizational structure and corporate culture, he said, "Culture is the soul of the organization—the beliefs and values, and how they are manifested. I think of the structure as the skeleton, and as the flesh and blood. And culture is the soul that holds the thing together and gives it life force."[2]

Mintzberg's culture metaphor provides a clear image of how to think about culture. Culture provides stability to an organization and gives employees a clear understanding of "the way things are done around here." Culture sets the tone for how an organization operates and how individuals within the organization interact. Think of the different impressions you have when a receptionist tells you that "Ms. Dettweiler" will be available shortly, while at another organization you are told that "Emma" will be with you as soon as she gets off the phone. It's clear that in one organization the rules are more formal than in the other.

As we discuss organizational culture, you may want to remember that organizations differ considerably in the cultures they adopt. Consider the different cultures of Calgary-based WestJet Airlines and Montreal-based Air Canada. WestJet is viewed as having a "young, spunky, can-do environment, where customers will have more fun."[3] Air Canada, by contrast, is considered less helpful and friendly. One analyst even suggested that Air Canada staff "tend to make their customers feel stressed" by their confrontational behaviour.[4] Our discussion of culture should help you understand how these differences across organizations occur.

Learn About Yourself
Company Culture Assessment

As you start to think about different organizations where you might work, you will want to research their cultures. For instance, some organizations' cultures are admired more than others: Winnipeg-based Bison Transport, Calgary-based The Sovereign General Insurance Company, Vancouver-based 1-800-GOT-JUNK, and Toronto-based G Adventures are 4 of the 10 companies named "Most Admired Corporate Cultures" of 2013 in the Mid-Market category (revenues over $100 million to $500 million).[5] It's important to consider whether you are a good cultural match for a job. An organization that expects employees to work 15 hours a day may not be where you would like to work.

Definition of *Organizational Culture*

Organizational culture refers to a system of shared meaning held by members that distinguishes the organization from other organizations.[6] Seven primary characteristics capture the essence of an organization's culture:[7]

- *Innovation and risk-taking.* The degree to which employees are encouraged to be innovative and take risks.

- *Attention to detail.* The degree to which employees are expected to work with precision, analysis, and attention to detail.

- *Outcome orientation.* The degree to which management focuses on results, or outcomes, rather than on the techniques and processes used to achieve these outcomes.

- *People orientation.* The degree to which management decisions take into consideration the effect of outcomes on people within the organization.

- *Team orientation.* The degree to which work activities are organized around teams rather than individuals.

- *Aggressiveness.* The degree to which people are aggressive and competitive rather than easygoing and supportive.

- *Stability.* The degree to which organizational activities emphasize maintaining the status quo in contrast to growth.

organizational culture A system of shared meaning held by members that distinguishes the organization from other organizations.

EXHIBIT 10-1 Contrasting Organizational Cultures

Organization A	Organization B
• Managers must fully document all decisions. • Creative decisions, change, and risks are not encouraged. • Extensive rules and regulations exist for all employees. • Productivity is valued over employee morale. • Employees are encouraged to stay within their own department. • Individual effort is encouraged.	• Management encourages and rewards risk-taking and change. • Employees are encouraged to "run with" ideas, and failures are treated as "learning experiences." • Employees have few rules and regulations to follow. • Productivity is balanced with treating its people right. • Team members are encouraged to interact with people at all levels and functions. • Many rewards are team-based.

Each of these characteristics exists on a continuum from low to high.

When individuals consider their organization in terms of these seven characteristics, they get a composite picture of the organization's culture. This picture becomes the basis for feelings of shared understanding that members have about the organization, how things are done in it, and the way members are supposed to behave. Exhibit 10-1 demonstrates how these characteristics can be mixed to create highly diverse organizations. Organizational characteristics are even reflected in your classroom, as the *Experiential Exercise* on page 372 shows.

Some research has conceptualized culture into four different types based on the Competing Values Framework we described in Chapter 1:[8] the collaborative and cohesive *clan*, the innovative and adaptable *adhocracy*, the controlled and consistent *hierarchy*, and the competitive and customer-focused *market*. A review of 94 studies found that job attitudes were especially positive in clan-based cultures, innovation was especially strong in market cultures, and financial performance was especially good in market cultures.[9] Although the Competing Values Framework received some support, the review authors noted that further theoretical work is needed to ensure that it's consistent with the actual cultural values found in organizations.

Levels of Culture

Because organizational culture has multiple levels,[10] the metaphor of an iceberg has often been used to describe it.[11] However, a simmering volcano may better represent the layers of culture: Beliefs, values, and assumptions bubble below, producing observable aspects of culture at the surface. Exhibit 10-2 reminds us that culture is very visible at the level of **artifacts**. These are what you see, hear, and feel when you encounter an organization's culture. You may notice, for instance, that employees in two offices have very different dress policies, or one office displays great works of art while another posts company mottos on the wall. These visible artifacts emerge from the organization's culture.

Exhibit 10-2 also shows us that beliefs, values, and assumptions, unlike artifacts, are not always readily observable. Instead, we rely on the visible artifacts (material symbols, special language used, rituals carried out, and stories told to others) to help us uncover the organization's beliefs, values, and assumptions. **Beliefs** are the understandings of how objects and ideas relate to each other. **Values** are the stable, long-lasting beliefs about what is important. For instance, Winnipeg-based Palliser Furniture, a manufacturer of leather- and fabric-upholstered furniture, promotes the following corporate

artifacts Aspects of an organization's culture that you see, hear, and feel.

beliefs The understandings of how objects and ideas relate to each other.

values The stable, long-lasting beliefs about what is important.

EXHIBIT 10-2 Layers of Culture

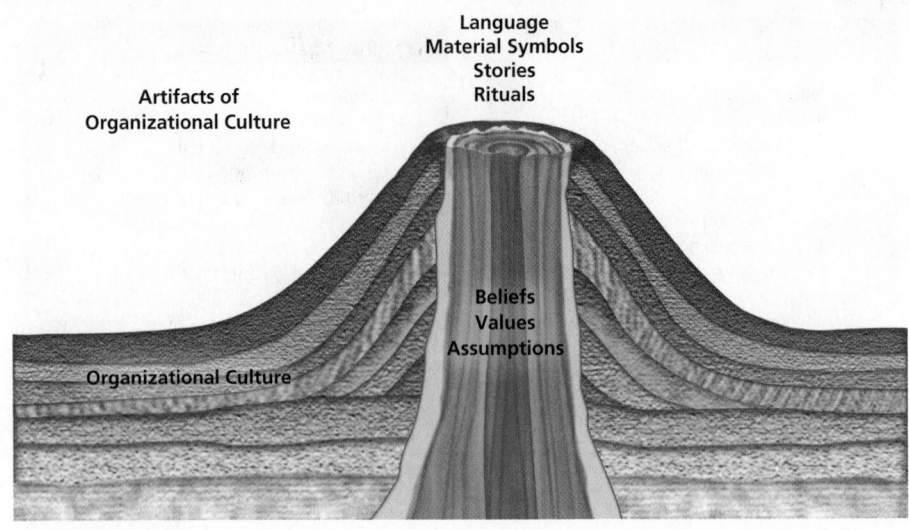

values: integrity, promoting people's dignity and value, respect for the environment, community support, and striving for excellence.[12] **Assumptions** are the taken-for-granted notions of how something should be. When basic assumptions are held by the entire group, members will have difficulty conceiving of another way of doing things. For instance, in Canada, some students hold a basic assumption that universities should not consider costs when setting tuition, and should keep tuition low for greater access by students. Beliefs, values, and assumptions, if we can uncover them, help us understand why organizations do the things that we observe.

Culture's Functions

2 Identify the functional effects of organizational culture on people and the organization.

Culture performs a number of functions within an organization:

- It has a boundary-defining role because it creates distinction between one organization and others.

- It conveys a sense of identity to organization members.

- It helps create commitment to something larger than an individual's self-interest.

- It enhances stability; it is the social glue that helps hold the organization together by providing standards for what employees should say and do.

- It serves as a control mechanism that guides and shapes the attitudes and behaviour of employees, and helps them make sense of the organization.

This last function is of particular interest to us.[13] Culture defines the rules of the game.

Today's trend toward decentralized organizations makes culture more important than ever, but ironically it also makes establishing a strong culture more difficult. When formal authority and control systems are reduced, culture's *shared meaning* can point everyone in the same direction. However, employees organized in teams may show greater allegiance to their team and its values than to the organization as a whole. In virtual organizations,

What does organizational culture do?

assumptions The taken-for-granted notions of how something should be.

the lack of frequent face-to-face contact makes establishing a common set of norms very difficult. Strong leadership that communicates frequently about common goals and priorities is especially important in innovative organizations.[14]

Culture Creates Climate

If you have worked with someone whose positive attitude inspired you to do your best, or with a lacklustre team that drained your motivation, you have experienced the effects of climate. **Organizational climate** refers to the shared perceptions organizational members have about their organization and work environment.[15] This aspect of culture is like team spirit at the organizational level. When everyone has the same general feelings about what is important or how well things are working, the effect of these attitudes will be more than the sum of the individual parts. One meta-analysis found that across dozens of different samples, psychological climate was strongly related to individuals' level of job satisfaction, involvement, commitment, and motivation.[16] A positive overall workplace climate has been linked to higher customer satisfaction and financial performance as well.[17]

Dozens of dimensions of climate have been studied, including innovation, creativity, communication, warmth and support, involvement, safety, justice, diversity, and customer service.[18] A person who encounters a positive climate for performance will think about doing a good job more often and will believe others support his or her success. Someone who encounters a positive climate for diversity will feel more comfortable collaborating with co-workers regardless of their demographic background. Climates can interact with one another to produce behaviour. For example, a positive climate for worker empowerment can lead to higher levels of performance in organizations that also have a climate for personal accountability.[19] Climate also influences the habits people adopt. If the climate for safety is positive, everyone wears safety gear and follows safety procedures even if individually they would not normally think very often about being safe—indeed, many studies have shown that a positive safety climate

Charles Platiau/Reuters

Employees of French video game publisher Ubisoft are shown working on an upcoming version of the *Just Dance* game at the firm's creative studio near Paris. Imaginative employees who work in teams on challenging projects at Ubisoft's 29 creative studios around the world share the positive climate of creative collaboration that reflects the diversity of team members.

> **Watch** on **MyManagementLab**
>
> Zappos: Motivating Employees through Company Culture

> **Watch** on **MyManagementLab**
>
> Blackbird Guitars: Organizational Culture

organizational climate The shared perceptions organizational members have about their organization and work environment.

decreases the number of documented injuries on the job.[20] WestJet sets the tone for its customers by making sure its employees have fun too, as *OB in the Workplace* shows.

OB IN THE **WORKPLACE**
WestJet Brings on the Fun

How does a company ensure its cultural climate is maintained and supported?   WestJet is a Canadian airline famous for its fun, customer-oriented corporate culture.[21] Both employees and guests are encouraged to actually enjoy flying—a goal that is reinforced by a casual working environment in which jokes and innocuous silliness are encouraged. Maintaining this positive and upbeat culture can be difficult, especially within a high-stress industry that experiences a great deal of uncertainty. WestJet management is well aware of the effects of the economy on its industry and ensures that, even in times of austerity, resources are provided to maintain its culture. WestJet has over 200 employee events a year that support and reinforce its culture. Employees who get it right are recognized through a "Kudos Corner"—an online program that allows peers and customers to acknowledge excellence when they see it.

Even WestJet's organizational structure supports its culture. For example, the company has a "WestJetters" committee of flight attendants who meet in order to, among other things, write jokes that can be used to amuse guests on flights. Devoting time and money to this sort of work may seem frivolous to some, but WestJet sees it as a crucial component of cultural maintenance. "Everybody's unique," says Don Bell, a WestJet founder and the airline's executive vice-president, "and if you embrace people's personalities rather than turn them into robots, and give them the guidelines and the working environment to blossom, it creates something that's very hard to reckon with."

WestJet has been able to demonstrate very clearly that a direct link exists between maintaining its fun, upbeat culture and high levels of customer satisfaction. Vince Molinaro, managing director of Leadership Solutions for Knightsbridge Human Capital Solutions, observed that "far too many organizations operate on the belief that you can have one set of principles and standards for employees, and another completely different set for customers. WestJet is demonstrating the power of alignment between employee and customer."

The Ethical Dimension of Culture

Organizational cultures are not neutral in their ethical orientation, even when they are not openly pursuing ethical goals. Over time, the **ethical work climate (EWC)**, or the shared concept of right and wrong behaviour in the workplace, develops as part of the organizational climate. The ethical climate reflects the true values of the organization and shapes the ethical decision-making of its members.

Researchers have developed ethical climate theory (ECT) and the ethical climate index (ECI) to categorize and measure the ethical dimensions of organizational cultures.[22] Of the nine identified climate categories, five have been found to be most prevalent in organizations: *instrumental, caring, independence, law and code,* and *rules.* Each explains the general mindset, expectations, and values of the managers and employees in relation to their organization. For instance, in an *instrumental* ethical climate, managers may frame their decision making around the assumption that employees (and companies) are motivated by self-interest (egoistic). Conversely, in a *caring* climate, managers may operate under the expectation that their decisions will positively affect the greatest number of stakeholders (employees, customers, suppliers) possible.

ethical work climate (EWC) The shared concept of right and wrong behaviour in the workplace that reflects the true values of the organization and shapes the ethical decision-making of its members.

Ethical climates of *independence* rely on each individual's personal moral ideas to dictate his or her workplace behaviour. *Law and code* climates require managers and employees to use an external standardized moral compass such as a professional code of conduct for norms, while *rules* climates tend to operate by internal standardized expectations from, perhaps, an organizational policy manual. Organizations often progress through different categories as they move through their business life cycle.

An organization's ethical climate powerfully influences the way its individual members feel they should behave, so much so that researchers have been able to predict organizational outcomes from the climate categories.[23]

The ECI is a new way researchers are seeking to understand the context of ethical drivers in organizations. By measuring the collective levels of moral sensitivity, judgment, motivation, and character of our organizations, we may be able to judge the strength of the influence our ethical climates have on us.[24]

Although ECT was first introduced more than 25 years ago, researchers have recently been studying ethics in organizations more closely to determine not only how ethical climates behave (through ECI, for instance, introduced in 2010) but also how they might be fostered, and even changed.[25] Eventually, we will be able to provide leaders with clear blueprints for designing effective ethical climates to improve the lives of an organization's members.

Do Organizations Have Uniform Cultures?

Organizational culture represents a perception of the organization that employees hold in common. We should, therefore, expect that individuals with different backgrounds or at different hierarchical levels will describe their organization's culture in similar terms.[26] That does not mean that an organization has no subcultures.

Most large organizations have a dominant culture and numerous subcultures.[27] A **dominant culture** expresses the **core values** a majority of members share and that give an organization its distinct personality.[28] **Subcultures** tend to develop in large organizations to reflect common problems, situations, or experiences faced by groups of members in the same department or location.

Internet retailer Zappos understands how organizational behaviour affects an organization's performance. According to the Zappos Insights website, employees are encouraged "to create fun and a little weirdness," which helps the firm maintain a positive work environment.

Ronda Churchill/Bloomberg/Getty Images

dominant culture A system of shared meaning that expresses the core values shared by a majority of the organization's members.

core values The primary or dominant values that are accepted throughout the organization.

subcultures Mini-cultures within an organization, typically defined by department designations and geographical separation.

If organizations were composed only of a variety of subcultures, organizational culture as an independent variable would be significantly less powerful. It is the "shared meaning" aspect of culture that makes it such a potent device for guiding and shaping behaviour. This is what allows us to say that the Zappos culture values customer care and dedication over speed and efficiency, and to use that information to better understand the behaviour of Zappos executives and employees.[29] But subcultures can influence members' behaviour too.

Strong vs. Weak Cultures

It is possible to differentiate between strong and weak cultures.[30] If most employees (responding to management surveys) have the same opinions about the organization's mission and values, the culture is strong; if opinions vary widely, the culture is weak.

In a **strong culture**, the organization's core values are both intensely held and widely shared.[31] The more members who accept the core values and the greater their commitment, the stronger the culture and the greater its influence on member behaviour. This is because the high degree of shared values and intensity create a climate of high behavioural control. American retailer Nordstrom has developed one of the strongest service cultures in the retailing industry. Nordstrom employees know what is expected of them, and these expectations go a long way in shaping their behaviour. Google and Procter & Gamble also have strong innovative cultures, and they are trying to learn how to be even better innovators from each other, as *Case Incident—Google and P&G Swap Employees* on page 374 shows.

A strong culture builds cohesiveness, loyalty, and organizational commitment. These qualities, in turn, lessen employees' tendency to leave the organization.[32] One study found that the more employees agreed on customer orientation in a service organization, the higher the profitability of the business unit.[33] Another study found that when team managers and team members disagreed about perceptions of organizational support, team members experienced more negative moods, and the performance of teams was lower.[34] These negative effects are especially strong when managers believe the organization provides more support than employees think it does.

Reading an Organization's Culture

The Calgary Stampede reinforces its culture of being "Great Together" in many ways.[35] It offers visitors specialized social media sites and GPS-enabled mobile applications that make it easy to invite and then locate friends, even in crowds of thousands. In addition, over 2300 community volunteers from all walks of life support the Stampede. Volunteers include high school students, seniors, and everyone in-between. There are 47 different volunteer committees, which offer a broad range of opportunities for people from a variety of backgrounds. A large number of volunteers return every year, helping to maintain some cultural continuity within the organization's open and welcoming environment.

The spirit of inclusiveness permeates right up the board level. Unlike many Canadian organizations, the Calgary Stampede has a significant number of female board members: 5 of 20 board members (or 25 percent) are women. This commitment to diversity at the most senior levels sets the tone for the rest of the organization, reinforcing the inclusive culture sought by Stampede organizers. Why does culture have such a strong influence on people's behaviour?

> What kind of organizational culture would work best for you?

As we noted in Exhibit 10-2, the artifacts of culture inform outsiders and employees about the underlying values and beliefs of the organization's culture. These artifacts, or physical manifestations of culture, include stories, rituals,

strong culture A culture in which the core values are intensely held and widely shared.

material symbols, and language. The extent to which organizations have artifacts of their culture indicates whether they have strong or weak cultures. *From Concepts to Skills* on pages 375–377 offers additional ideas on how to "read" an organization's culture.

Stories

When Toronto-based Bank of Montreal (BMO) decided several years ago to become a leader in customer service in the banking industry, it needed a way of communicating this message to the bank's employees. The decision: "Every meeting starts with a customer story." No matter what kind of meeting is being held, one staff member has to tell a recent story about an interaction with a customer—ranging from feel-good stories to horror stories of something that went wrong for the customer. By focusing on customer stories, employees know they need to pay attention to interactions so that they can share the stories. Susan Brown, a senior vice-president with BMO, explains the importance of the story focus for the bank: "If you want to change culture, a great way to do it is the customer story. It's part of the evolution of developing a customer-centric culture."[36]

Stories circulate through many organizations, anchoring the present in the past and legitimating current practices. They typically include narratives about the organization's founders, rule breaking, rags-to-riches successes, reductions in the workforce, relocation of employees, reactions to past mistakes, and organizational coping.[37] Employees also create their own narratives about how they came to either fit or not fit with the organization during the process of socialization, including first days on the job, early interactions with others, and first impressions of organizational life.[38]

Rituals

Rituals are repetitive sequences of activities that express and reinforce the key values of the organization; what goals are most important; and which people are important and which are expendable.[39]

Southwest Airlines is known for good customer service. However, legend has it that a woman who was a frequent flyer complained constantly about the service, dispiriting the customer service department. Finally, the head of customer relations asked Herb Kelleher, the founder, what they should do. Kelleher's response to the customer was brief: "Dear Mrs. X, We will miss you. Love, Herb." Employees were thrilled to get this kind of support from their CEO.

Justin Sullivan/Getty Images

rituals Repetitive sequences of activities that express and reinforce the key values of the organization; what goals are most important; and which people are important and which are expendable.

One well-known corporate ritual is Walmart's company chant. Begun by the company's founder, Sam Walton, as a way to motivate and unite his workforce, "Gimme a W, gimme an A, gimme an L, give me an M, A, R, T!" has become a company ritual that bonds Walmart employees and reinforces Walton's belief in the importance of his employees to the company's success. Similar corporate chants are used by IBM, Ericsson, Novell, Deutsche Bank, and PricewaterhouseCoopers.[40]

Material Symbols

The layout of corporate headquarters, the types of cars given to top executives, and the presence or absence of corporate aircraft are a few examples of **material symbols**. Others include the size of offices, the elegance of furnishings, executive perks, and dress code.[41] In addition, corporate logos, signs, brochures, and advertisements reveal aspects of the organization's culture.[42] These material symbols convey to employees, customers, and clients who is important, the degree of egalitarianism top management desires, and the kinds of behaviour that are appropriate (such as risk-taking, conservative, authoritarian, participative, individualistic, social). For instance, pictures of all Creo employees hang in the Burnaby, BC-based company's entrance lobby, which visibly conveys Creo's anti-hierarchical culture.

Companies differ in how much separation they make between their executives and employees. This plays out in how material benefits are distributed to executives. Some companies provide their top executives with chauffeur-driven limousines and, when they travel by air, unlimited use of the corporate jet. Other companies might pay for car and air transportation for top executives, only the car is a Chevrolet with no driver, and the jet seat is in the economy section of a commercial airliner. At Bolton, Ontario-based Husky Injection Molding Systems, a more egalitarian culture is favoured. Employees and management share the parking lot, dining room, and even washrooms. *Case Incident—Is*

THE CANADIAN PRESS/AP/Nam Y. Huh

material symbols What conveys to employees who is important, the degree of egalitarianism top management desires, and the kinds of behaviour that are appropriate.

At Walmart, culture is transmitted to employees through the daily ritual of the "Walmart cheer." The cheer is performed at both US and international stores. Employees are asked to do the cheer in every morning meeting. Shown here are employees of a Walmart store in Evergreen Park, Illinois, chanting the motivational cheer that helps preserve a small-family spirit and work environment within the world's largest retailer.

a 5S Culture for You? on page 374 discusses how the 5S method has been used to implement and sustain order in workspaces.

Language

Many organizations and subunits within them use language to help members identify with the culture, show their acceptance of it, and help preserve it. Baristas at Starbucks call drinks *short, tall, grande,* and *venti* instead of *small, medium, large,* and *extra-large,* and they know the difference between a half-decaf double tall almond skinny mocha and an iced short schizo skinny hazelnut cappuccino with wings.[43] Students and employees at Grant MacEwan College are informed by the philosophy of the college's namesake. Dr. Grant MacEwan, historian, writer, politician, and environmentalist, was never a formal part of the management of the organization. However, many phrases from his writing and creed have found their way into formal college publications and calendars, as well as informal communications, including his most well known, "I have tried to leave things in the vineyard better than I found them."[44]

Creating and Sustaining an Organization's Culture

Maintaining an organizational culture in the face of interference can be challenging.[45] The Calgary Stampede saw several challenges to its inclusive, community-spirited culture in its early years. The first Stampede was held in 1886 and included all members of the local community, including the five First Nations of Treaty No. 7: the Tsuu T'ina, Piikani, Stoney, Kainai, and Siksika. These bands held powwows and offered cultural displays during the Stampede, and their onsite "village" was a popular attraction. Efforts by the Department of Indian Affairs to suppress Aboriginal culture in 1912 meant that Aboriginals could not participate in the Stampede. Stampede organizers fought back hard, so that Aboriginal people would not be excluded. The organizers fought back again after the 1914 Indian Act made it illegal for Aboriginal people to participate in fairs and parades.

The Stampede's commitment to an inclusive culture has paid off. Some powwow organizers and participants are fourth-generation volunteers. By 2014 the village associated with the powwow doubled in size and featured an exhibit outlining partnerships between the city, local First Nations, and the Stampede. What role does culture play in creating high-performing organizations?

3 Identify the factors that create and sustain an organization's culture.

An organization's culture does not pop out of thin air, and once established, it rarely fades away. What influences the creation of a culture? What reinforces and sustains these forces once they are in place? Exhibit 10-3 summarizes how an organization's culture is established and sustained. We describe each part of this process next.

How a Culture Begins

An organization's current customs, traditions, and general way of doing things are largely due to what it has done before and how successful it was in doing it. This leads

EXHIBIT 10-3 How Organizational Cultures Form

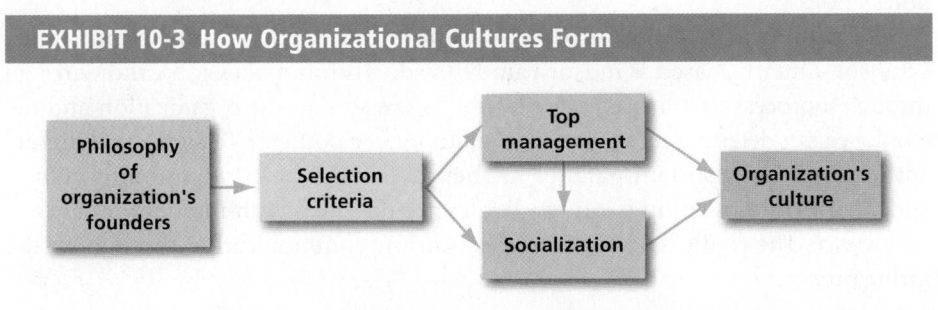

us to the ultimate source of an organization's culture: the founders.[46] Free of previous customs or ideologies, founders have a vision of what the organization should be, and the firm's small size makes it easy to impose that vision on all organizational members. In the case of the Calgary Stampede, early founders were willing to fight much larger political and legal systems, including the Indian Act itself, to ensure that Aboriginal people could participate in the event. This philosophy would have sent a very strong message to Stampede workers and volunteers, reinforcing their culture of inclusion in a time period not known for tolerance in general and certainly not distinguished by any widespread inclusion of Aboriginal cultures and people.

> Is culture the
> same as rules?

Culture creation occurs in three ways.[47] First, founders only hire and keep employees who think and feel the way they do. Second, they indoctrinate and socialize employees to their way of thinking and feeling. Finally, the founders' own behaviour encourages employees to identify with the founders and thereby internalize those beliefs, values, and assumptions. When the organization succeeds, the founders' personality becomes embedded in the culture.

The culture at Toronto-based PCL, the largest general contracting organization in Canada, is still strongly influenced by the vision of Ernest Poole, who founded the company in 1906. "Poole's rules," which include "Employ highest grade people obtainable" and "Encourage integrity, loyalty and efficiencies," still influence the way the company hires and trains its employees long after the founder's death.[48] Other contemporary examples of founders who have had an immeasurable impact on their organizations' cultures are the late Ted Rogers of Toronto-based Rogers Communications, Frank Stronach of Aurora, Ontario-based Magna International, and Richard Branson of UK-based Virgin Group.

Keeping a Culture Alive

Simulate on **MyManagementLab**

Organizational Culture

Once a culture is in place, practices within the organization maintain it by giving employees a set of similar experiences.[49] The selection process, performance evaluation criteria, training and career development activities, and promotion procedures ensure that those hired fit in with the culture, reward those who support it, and penalize (and even expel) those who challenge it. Three forces play a particularly important part in sustaining a culture: *selection* practices, the actions of *top management*, and *socialization* methods. Let's look at each.

Selection

4 Show how culture is transmitted to employees.

The explicit goal of the selection process is to identify and hire individuals who have the knowledge, skills, and abilities to perform successfully.

The final decision, because it's significantly influenced by the decision maker's judgment of how well the candidates will fit into the organization, identifies people whose values are essentially consistent with at least a good portion of the organization's values.[50]

Selection also provides information about the organization to applicants. Windsor, Ontario-based Windsor Family Credit Union makes job candidates go through a process that has as many as eight steps so that the organization and the employee can determine if they are a good fit for each other.[51] To signal that dignity and respect are important parts of Kitchener, Ontario-based Mennonite Savings and Credit Union's culture, job candidates are provided with interview questions in advance. The credit union encourages two-way communication throughout the hiring process.[52]

Careful hiring practices mean that those who perceive a conflict between their values and those of the organization can remove themselves from the applicant pool. Selection, therefore, becomes a two-way street: It allows the employer or applicant to avoid a mismatch and sustains organizational culture by selecting out those individuals who might attack or undermine the organization's core values.

Top Management

The actions of top management also have a major impact on the organization's culture.[53] Through words and behaviour, senior executives establish norms that filter through the organization about, for instance, whether risk-taking is desirable; how much freedom managers give their employees; what is appropriate dress; and what actions will pay off in terms of pay raises, promotions, and other rewards.

Socialization

No matter how effectively the organization recruits and selects new employees, they need help adapting to the prevailing culture. That help is **socialization**.[54] As a 2011 study suggests, socialization done well will develop a new employee's self-efficacy, hope, optimism, and resilience.[55]

> **socialization** The process that adapts new employees to an organization's culture.

New employees at the Japanese electronics company Sanyo are socialized through a particularly long training program. At their intensive five-month course, trainees eat and sleep together in company-subsidized dorms and are required to vacation together at company-owned resorts. They learn the Sanyo way of doing everything—from how to speak to managers to proper grooming and dress.[56] The company considers this program essential for transforming young employees, fresh out of school, into dedicated *kaisha senshi*, or corporate warriors.

Starbucks does not go to the extreme that Sanyo does, but it seeks the same outcome.[57] All new employees go through 24 hours of training. Classes cover everything necessary to transform new employees into brewing consultants. They learn the Starbucks philosophy, the company jargon, and even how to help customers make decisions about beans and grind, as well as about espresso machines. The result is employees who understand Starbucks' culture and who project an enthusiastic and knowledgeable image to customers.

An organization continues to socialize its employees throughout their career in the organization, which further contributes to sustaining the culture. As part of its continual socialization process, the CEO of Windsor Family Credit Union takes employees to breakfast quarterly to find out about their questions, concerns, and their work.[59] These breakfasts also provide an opportunity to ensure that employees understand the overall goals of the organization.

We can think of socialization as a process composed of three stages: prearrival, encounter, and metamorphosis.[60]

THE CANADIAN PRESS/Fred Lum/The Globe and Mail

Softchoice was a recipient of the Top 10 Most Admired Corporate Culture awards in 2013. The technology solutions and managed services provider understands how a strong organizational culture can lead to high performance. Sandy Fallon, senior vice-president of people, explains why: "Engagement is extremely important to us. At the same time, we want to make sure we measure our progress. How are we doing? What is the engagement level? We are always asking those questions and hearing back from employees."[58] One of the ways Softchoice keeps its employees engaged is by allowing them to bring their dogs to work, which reduces stress and encourages more interaction among employees.

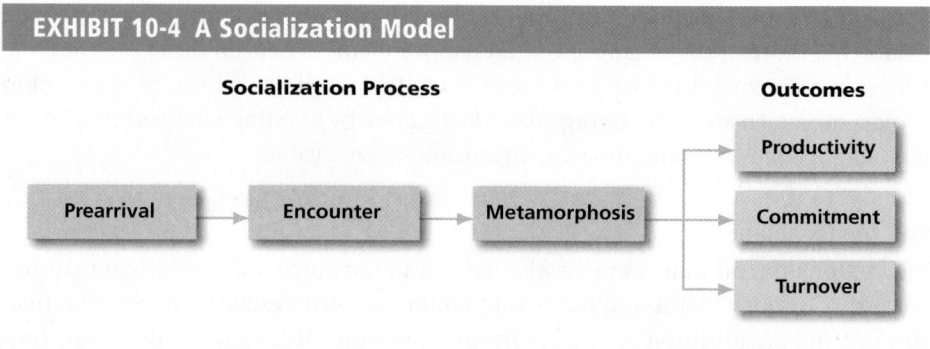

EXHIBIT 10-4 A Socialization Model

This process (illustrated in Exhibit 10-4) has an impact on the new employee's work productivity, commitment to the organization's objectives, and eventual decision to stay with the organization. *OB in the Workplace* discusses how TELUS starts to socialize future employees from the time they visit the company's Careers web page.

IN THE **WORKPLACE**
Making Culture Work

How early on should socialization take place? Leaders at Burnaby, BC-based TELUS recognize that in order for an organizational culture to work, that culture needs to be established early, preferably during the hiring process.[61] It also needs to be continually supported and reinforced.

TELUS prides itself on a culture focused on collaborative learning. This culture is heavily reinforced on its Careers web page. TELUS asks prospective candidates whether they build "spirited relationships." Prospective candidates are also informed that they should expect to "foster a strong collaborative network," and "continually drive their own learning." That learning is expected to begin immediately. Unlike most employers, TELUS offers job applicants tips about what specifically to include in their résumé and cover letter and how best to prepare for an interview with the company. It even offers a "Career Tools" page that helps job seekers identify their goals, outline their personal strengths, and match those goals and strengths with open positions within the organization.

This focus on learning is further reinforced after the hiring process. For example, collaboration tools and internal social networking sites are provided to all employees, and open door policies encourage the free flow of information between staff and management. Regular webinars are offered on a variety of topics and mentors and coaches assist with the learning process. Dan Pontefract, chief envisioner at TELUS, explains the company's approach: "the more open and collaborative you are with people, the healthier your culture becomes." A healthy, established culture that emphasizes ongoing learning helps TELUS stay ahead of the curve in a highly competitive, innovation-focused industry.

The Prearrival Stage The **prearrival stage** explicitly recognizes that each individual arrives with a set of values, attitudes, and expectations about both the work and the organization. One major purpose of a business school, for example, is to socialize business students to the attitudes and behaviours business firms want. Newcomers to high-profile organizations with a strong market position will make their own

prearrival stage The period of learning in the socialization process that occurs before a new employee joins the organization.

assumptions about what it must be like to work there.[62] What people know before they join the organization and how proactive their personality is are critical predictors of how well they adjust to a new culture.[63]

One way to capitalize on prehire characteristics in socialization is to use the selection process to inform prospective employees about the organization as a whole. We have also seen how the selection process ensures the inclusion of the "right type"—those who will fit in.

The Encounter Stage   Upon entering the organization, the new employee begins the **encounter stage** and confronts the possibility that expectations—of the job, co-workers, boss, and the organization in general—may differ from reality. If the employee's expectations are fairly accurate, the encounter stage merely reaffirms earlier perceptions.

However, this is often not the case. At the extreme, new members may become totally disillusioned with the realities of their job and resign. Proper recruiting and selection should significantly reduce the probability of that outcome, and so too should encouraging friendship ties in the organization—newcomers are more committed when friends and co-workers help them "learn the ropes."[64] A 2011 study by professor Alan Saks of the Rotman School of Management at the University of Toronto and professor Jamie Gruman of the School of Hospitality and Tourism Management at the University of Guelph demonstrates the benefits of orientation, training, and mentorship programs for new employees. These activities help employees adjust better because they make them feel happier, more confident that they will more likely fit with the organization, and therefore more engaged.[65]

Bloomberg/Getty Images

In a study conducted by the US Reputation Institute and *Canadian Business* magazine in 2014, Tim Hortons was rated as the company with the best corporate reputation in Canada, as well as coming in second in the world. The company has often fared well in this survey. However, in September 2014, Tim Hortons was bought by Burger King. Will this have an impact on Tim's culture going forward?[66]

encounter stage The stage in the socialization process in which a new employee sees what the organization is really like and confronts the possibility that expectations and reality may diverge.

EXHIBIT 10-5 Entry Socialization Options

Formal vs. Informal The more a new employee is segregated from the ongoing work setting and differentiated in some way to make explicit his or her newcomer's role, the more formal socialization is. Specific orientation and training programs are examples. Informal socialization puts the new employee directly into his or her job, with little or no special attention.

Individual vs. Collective New members can be socialized individually. This describes how it's done in many professional offices. They can also be grouped together and processed through an identical set of experiences, as in military boot camp.

Fixed vs. Variable This refers to the time schedule in which newcomers make the transition from outsider to insider. A fixed schedule establishes standardized stages of transition. This characterizes rotational training programs. It also includes probationary periods, such as the 8- to 10-year "associate" status accounting and law firms use before deciding whether to name a candidate as a partner. Variable schedules give no advance notice of their transition timetable. Variable schedules describe the typical promotion system, where individuals are not advanced to the next stage until they are "ready."

Serial vs. Random Serial socialization is characterized by the use of role models who train and encourage the newcomer. Apprenticeship and mentoring programs are examples. In random socialization, role models are deliberately withheld. The new employee is left on his or her own to figure things out.

Investiture vs. Divestiture Investiture socialization assumes that the newcomer's qualities and qualifications are the necessary ingredients for job success, so these qualities and qualifications are confirmed and supported. Divestiture socialization tries to strip away certain characteristics of the recruit. Fraternity and sorority "pledges" go through divestiture socialization to shape them into the proper role.

Sources: Based on J. Van Maanen, "People Processing: Strategies of Organizational Socialization," *Organizational Dynamics,* Summer 1978, pp. 19–36; and E. H. Schein, "Organizational Culture," *American Psychologist,* February 1990, p. 116.

The Metamorphosis Stage Finally, to work out any problems discovered during the encounter stage, the new employee changes or goes through the **metamorphosis stage**. The entry socialization options presented in Exhibit 10-5 are designed to bring about the desired metamorphosis. The more management relies on formal, collective, fixed, and serial socialization programs and emphasizes divestiture, the more likely that newcomers' differences and perspectives will be stripped away and replaced by standardized and predictable behaviours. These *institutional* practices are common in police departments, fire departments, and other organizations that value rule following and order. Programs that are informal, individual, variable, random, and emphasize investiture are more likely to give newcomers an innovative sense of their role and methods of working. Creative fields, such as research and development, advertising, and filmmaking, rely on these *individual* practices. Most research suggests that high levels of institutional practices encourage person–organization fit and high levels of commitment, whereas individual practices produce more role innovation.[67]

We can say that metamorphosis and the entry socialization process is complete when

- The new employee has become comfortable with the organization and his or her job

- The new employee has internalized the norms of the organization and the work group, and understands and accepts these norms

- The new employee feels accepted by his or her peers as a trusted and valued individual, is self-confident that he or she has the competence to complete the job successfully, and understands the system—not only his or her own tasks but also the rules, procedures, and informally accepted practices

- The new employee understands how he or she will be evaluated and knows what criteria will be used to measure and appraise his or her work; he or she knows what is expected and what constitutes a job "well done"

metamorphosis stage The stage in the socialization process in which a new employee adjusts to the values and norms of the job, work group, and organization.

Michael Christopher Brown/Magnum Photos

New employees at Broad Air Conditioning in Changsha, China, are indoctrinated in the company's military-style culture by going through a 10-day training session of boot camp, where they are divided into platoons and live in barracks. Boot camp prepares new hires for the military formality that prevails at Broad, where employees begin their work week standing in formation during a flag-raising ceremony of two company flags and the flag of China. All employees live in dorms on the company campus and receive free food and lodging. To motivate its workers, Broad has scattered throughout the campus 43 life-size bronze statues of inspirational leaders from Confucius to Jack Welch, the former CEO of GE.

As Exhibit 10-4 on page 360 shows, successful metamorphosis should have a positive impact on the new employee's productivity and commitment to the organization. It should also reduce the tendency to leave the organization.

Researchers have begun to examine how employee attitudes change during socialization by measuring those attitudes at several points over the first few months. One study has documented patterns of "honeymoons" and "hangovers" for new workers, showing that the period of initial adjustment is often marked by decreases in job satisfaction as their idealized hopes come into contact with the reality of organizational life.[68] Other research suggests that role conflict and role overload for newcomers rise over time and that workers with the largest increases in these role problems experience the largest decreases in commitment and satisfaction.[69] It may be that the initial adjustment period for newcomers presents increasing demands and difficulties, at least in the short term.

The Liabilities of Organizational Culture

Culture enhances organizational commitment and increases the consistency of employee behaviour.[70] These are clearly benefits to an organization. Culture is valuable to employees too, because it spells out how things are done and what is important. However, we should not ignore the potentially dysfunctional aspects of culture, especially of a strong culture, on an organization's effectiveness. Hewlett-Packard, once known as a premier computer manufacturer, has been rapidly losing market share and profits as the dysfunction of its top management team has trickled down, leaving employees disengaged, uncreative, unappreciated, and polarized.[71] A strong poisonous culture can also affect a company's bottom line, as the *Ethical Dilemma* on page 373 shows.

5 Identify the liabilities of organizational culture.

Below, we consider organizational culture's impact on change, diversity, and mergers and acquisitions.

Barrier to Change

Culture is a liability when the shared values do not agree with those that further the organization's effectiveness. For example, when an organization's environment is undergoing rapid change, its entrenched culture may no longer be appropriate.[72] Consistency of behaviour, an asset in a stable environment, may then burden the organization and make it difficult to respond to changes. For many organizations with strong cultures, practices that previously led to successes can lead to failure when those practices no longer match up well with environmental needs.[73]

Barrier to Diversity

Hiring new employees who differ from the majority in race, gender, disability, or other characteristics creates a paradox:[74] Management demonstrates support for the differences that these employees bring to the workplace, but newcomers who wish to fit in must accept the organization's core cultural values. Because diverse behaviours and unique strengths are likely to diminish as people attempt to assimilate, strong cultures can become liabilities when they effectively eliminate these advantages. A strong culture that condones prejudice, supports bias, or becomes insensitive to people who are different can undermine formal corporate diversity policies.

Barrier to Mergers and Acquisitions

Historically, when management looked at merger or acquisition decisions, the key factors were related to financial advantages or product synergy. In recent years, cultural compatibility has become a primary concern.[75] All things being equal, whether the merger or acquisition actually works seems to have much to do with how well the two organizations' cultures match up.

A survey by consulting firm A. T. Kearney revealed that 58 percent of mergers failed to reach their financial goals.[76] As one expert commented, "Mergers have an unusually high failure rate, and it's always because of people issues"—in other words, because of conflicting organizational cultures. The $183 billion merger between America Online (AOL) and Time Warner in 2001 was the largest in US corporate history.[77] It was also a disaster. Only one year later, the company suffered an astounding annual loss of $99 billion—what was then the largest financial loss in US history.[78] Culture clash is commonly argued to be one of the causes of AOL Time Warner's problems.

Strategies for Merging Cultures

Organizations can use several strategies when considering how to merge the cultures of two organizations:[79]

- *Assimilation.* The entire new organization is determined to take on the culture of one of the merging organizations. This strategy works best when one of the organizations has a relatively weak culture. However, if a culture is simply imposed on an organization, it rarely works.

- *Separation.* The organizations remain separate and keep their individual cultures. This strategy works best when the organizations have little overlap in the industries in which they operate.

- *Integration.* A new culture is formed by merging parts of each of the organizations. This strategy works best when aspects of each organization's culture need to be improved.

Changing Organizational Culture

The Calgary Stampede is about inclusion, but it's also about tradition.[80] It's a celebration of Western cowboy culture. That culture, however, has at times found itself at odds with modern sensibilities. Organizers have needed to find compromises that allow the Stampede to maintain western cultural traditions while still accommodating modern concerns. Nowhere was this more evident than in the chuckwagon race controversies.

In 1986 nine horses were killed in chuckwagon race accidents. That started an ongoing controversy, with some arguing that the races are cruel and should be banned and others arguing that all sport has some element of risk and chuckwagon races are a beloved tradition.

Stampede organizers have worked in cooperation with the Society for the Prevention of Cruelty to Animals to find a way to change their approach and encourage the development of a safety culture while still maintaining traditions. That has meant some changes to the rules such as altering the design of the wagons to lessen the possibility of entanglements and commencing random drug and alcohol testing on both horses and riders. Similar changes have been made in other events, particularly after six animals died in 2010. For example, in 2011 a no-time penalty rule was introduced for participants who make a dangerous tackle in the steer-wrestling event.

These rule changes can be poorly received by traditionalists who see them as interfering with the "purity" of the sport. Stampede organizers minimize this resistance by carefully explaining the anticipated safety impacts and by rigorous and consistent enforcement of the rules. Over time, the consistency of their messaging helps to broaden awareness and fosters the safety culture that they seek. Why has the Stampede been so successful in creating an organizational culture that enables change?

Changing an organization's culture is difficult and requires that many aspects of the organization change at the same time, especially the reward structure. Culture is such a challenge to change because it often represents the established mindset of employees and managers.

John Kotter, professor of leadership at Harvard Business School, has created a detailed approach to implementing change, which we discuss in Chapter 14.[81] Efforts directed at changing organizational culture do not usually yield immediate or dramatic results. Cultural change is actually a lengthy process—measured in years, not months. But we can ask the question, "Can culture be changed?" And the answer is, "Yes!" The evidence suggests that cultural change is most likely to occur when most or all of the following conditions exist:

- *A dramatic crisis.* A shock that undermines the status quo calls into question the relevance of the current culture. Examples of a crisis might be a surprising financial setback, the loss of a major customer, or a dramatic technological breakthrough by a competitor.

- *Turnover in leadership.* New top leadership, which can provide an alternative set of key values, may be perceived as more capable of responding to the crisis. Top leadership definitely refers to the organization's chief executive, but also might need to include all senior management positions.

- *Young and small organization.* The younger the organization, the less entrenched its culture will be. It's also easier for management to communicate its new values when the organization is small.

- *Weak culture.* The more widely held a culture is, and the higher the agreement among members on its values, the more difficult it will be to change. Weak cultures are more open to change than strong ones.

Below we discuss two specific kinds of cultural change: creating an ethical organizational culture and creating a positive organizational culture.

⊙ **Watch** on **MyManagementLab**

The Work Zone Role Plays— Organizational Culture

Creating an Ethical Organizational Culture

6 Demonstrate how an ethical organizational culture can be created.

The organizational culture most likely to shape high ethical standards among its members is high in risk tolerance, low to moderate in aggressiveness, and focuses on means as well as outcomes.[82] This type of culture takes a long-term perspective and balances the rights of multiple stakeholders, including the employees, stockholders, and the community. Managers are supported for taking risks and innovating, are discouraged from engaging in unbridled competition, and guided to pay attention not just to *what* goals are achieved but also to *how*.

If the culture is strong and supports high ethical standards, it should have a very powerful and positive influence on employee behaviour. However, examples of organizations that have failed to establish proper codes of ethical conduct can be found in the media nearly every day. Some actively deceive customers or clients. Others produce products that harm consumers or the environment, or they harass or discriminate against certain groups of employees. Others are more subtle and cover up or fail to report wrongdoing. The negative consequences of a systematic culture of unethical behaviour can be severe and include customer boycotts, fines, lawsuits, and government regulation of an organization's practices.

What can managers do to create a more ethical culture? They can adhere to the following principles:[83]

- *Be a visible role model.* Employees will look to the actions of top management as a benchmark for appropriate behaviour. Senior managers who take the ethical high road send a positive message.

- *Communicate ethical expectations.* Minimize ethical ambiguities by sharing an organizational code of ethics that states the organization's primary values and ethical rules that employees must follow.

- *Provide ethics training.* Set up seminars, workshops, and training programs to reinforce the organization's standards of conduct, to clarify what practices are permissible, and to address possible ethical dilemmas.

- *Visibly reward ethical acts and punish unethical ones.* Appraise managers on how their decisions measured against the organization's code of ethics. Review the means taken to achieve goals, as well as the ends themselves. Visibly reward those who act ethically and conspicuously punish those who do not.

- *Provide protective mechanisms.* Provide formal mechanisms so employees can discuss ethical dilemmas and report unethical behaviour without fear of reprimand. These might include ethics counsellors, ombudspersons, or ethics officers.

The work of setting a positive ethical climate has to start at the top of the organization.[84] A study of 195 managers demonstrated that when top management emphasizes strong ethical values, supervisors are more likely to practise ethical leadership. Positive ethical attitudes transfer down to line employees, who show lower levels of deviant behaviour and higher levels of cooperation and assistance. A study involving auditors found perceived pressure from organizational leaders to behave unethically was associated with increased intentions to engage in unethical practices.[85] Clearly the wrong type of organizational culture can negatively influence employees' ethical behaviour. Finally, employees whose ethical values are similar to those of their department are more likely to be promoted, so we can think of ethical culture as flowing from the bottom up as well.[86]

Creating a Positive Organizational Culture

7 Describe a positive organizational culture.

At first blush, creating a positive culture may sound hopelessly naive, or like a Dilbert-style conspiracy. The one thing that makes us believe this trend is here to stay is that there are signs that management practice and OB research are converging.

A **positive organizational culture** emphasizes building on employee strengths, rewards more often than it punishes, and emphasizes individual vitality and growth.[87] Let's consider each of these areas.

Building on Employee Strengths

Although a positive organizational culture does not ignore problems, it emphasizes showing employees how they can capitalize on their strengths. As management guru Peter Drucker said, "Most [employees] do not know what their strengths are. When you ask them, they look at you with a blank stare, or they respond in terms of subject knowledge, which is the wrong answer." Wouldn't it be better to be in an organizational culture that helped you discover your strengths and learn how to make the most of them?

Larry Hammond, CEO of Auglaize Provico, an agribusiness based in Ohio, used this approach when you would least expect it: during the darkest days of his business. In the midst of the firm's worst financial struggles, when it had to lay off one-quarter of its workforce, Hammond decided to try a different approach. Rather than dwell on what was wrong, he took advantage of what was right. "If you really want to [excel], you have to know yourself—you have to know what you're good at, and you have to know what you're not so good at," says Hammond. With the help of Gallup consultant Barry Conchie, Hammond focused on discovering and using employee strengths and helped turn the company around. "You ask Larry [Hammond] what the difference is, and he'll say that it's individuals using their natural talents," says Conchie.[88]

Rewarding More Often Than Punishing

Although most organizations are sufficiently focused on extrinsic rewards such as pay and promotions, they often forget about the power of smaller (and cheaper) rewards like praise. Part of creating a positive organizational culture is "catching employees doing something right." Many managers withhold praise because they are afraid employees will coast or because they think praise is not valued. Employees generally don't ask for praise, and managers usually don't realize the costs of failing to give it.

Consider Elzbieta Górska-Kolodziejczyk, a plant manager for International Paper's facility in Kwidzyn, Poland. Employees worked in a bleak windowless basement. Staffing became roughly one-third of its prior level, while production tripled. These challenges had done in the previous three managers. So when Górska-Kolodziejczyk took over, although she had many ideas about transforming the organization, at the top of her list was recognition and praise. She initially found it difficult to give praise to those who were not used to it, especially men. "They were like cement at the beginning," she said. "Like cement." Over time, however, she found they valued and even reciprocated praise. One day a department supervisor pulled her over to tell her she was doing a good job. "This I do remember, yes," she said.[89]

Emphasizing Vitality and Growth

No organization will get the best out of employees who see themselves as cogs in the machine. A positive culture realizes the difference between a job and a career. It supports not only what the employee contributes to organizational effectiveness, but also how the organization can make the employee more effective personally and professionally.

Limits of Positive Culture

Is a positive culture the answer to all organizational problems? Although companies have embraced aspects of a positive organizational culture, it's a new enough area that there is some uncertainty about how and when it works best.

positive organizational culture
A culture that emphasizes building on employee strengths, rewards more than punishes, and emphasizes individual vitality and growth.

Not all national cultures value being positive as much as Canadian and US cultures do, and, even within these countries, there surely are limits to how far we should go to preserve a positive culture. For example, Admiral, a British insurance company, has established a Ministry of Fun in its call centres to organize poem writing, foosball, conker (a British game involving chestnuts), and fancy dress days, while other companies in the insurance industry have maintained more serious cultures. When does the pursuit of a positive culture start to seem coercive or even Orwellian? As one critic notes, "Promoting a social orthodoxy of positiveness focuses on a particular constellation of desirable states and traits but, in so doing, can stigmatize those who fail to fit the template."[90] There may be benefits to establishing a positive culture, but an organization also needs to be objective and not pursue it past the point of effectiveness. See *Point/Counterpoint* on page 371 for additional thoughts on whether organizations should create a positive organizational culture.

GLOBAL IMPLICATIONS

We considered global cultural values (collectivism and individualism, power distance, and so on) in Chapter 3. Here, our focus is a bit narrower: How is organizational culture affected by a global context?

Organizational cultures often reflect national culture. The culture at AirAsia, a Malaysian-based airline, emphasizes openness and friendship. The carrier has a lot of parties, a participative management, and no private offices, reflecting Malaysia's relatively collectivistic culture. However, the culture of Air Canada does not reflect the same degree of informality. If Air Canada were to set up operations in Malaysia or merge with AirAsia, it would need to take these cultural differences into account. When an organization opens up operations in another country, it ignores the local culture at its own risk.

Three times a week, employees at the Canadian unit of Japanese video game maker Tecmo Koei begin the day by standing next to their desks, facing their boss, and saying "Good morning" in unison. Employees then deliver short speeches on topics that range from corporate principles to 3D game engines. Tecmo Koei also has employees punch a time clock and asks women to serve tea to top executive guests. Although these practices are consistent with Tecmo Koei's culture, they do not fit Canadian culture very well. "It's kind of like school," says one Canadian employee.[91]

The management of ethical behaviour is one area where national culture can rub up against corporate culture.[92] Canadian managers tend to endorse the supremacy of anonymous market forces and implicitly or explicitly view profit maximization as a moral obligation for business organizations. This worldview sees bribery, nepotism, and favouring personal contacts as highly unethical. Any action that deviates from profit maximization may indicate that inappropriate or corrupt behaviour may be occurring. In contrast, managers in developing economies are more likely to see ethical decisions as embedded in a social environment. That means doing special favours for family and friends is not only appropriate but possibly even an ethical responsibility. Managers in many nations also view capitalism skeptically and believe the interests of employees should be put on a par with the interests of shareholders.

Because culture strongly affects performance, organizations who have units in different countries need to construct and clearly communicate a multinational culture that focuses on corporate values. These values should be unique and separate from identifiable country norms, emphasize respect and tolerance for cultural differences, and address the issue of cultural identity. Globalization can be an opportunity to positively change organizational culture.

EXHIBIT 10-6 How Organizational Cultures Have an Impact on Employee Performance and Satisfaction

Summary

Exhibit 10-6 depicts organizational culture as an intervening variable. Employees form an overall subjective perception of the organization based on factors such as degree of risk tolerance, team emphasis , and support of people. This overall perception becomes, in effect, the organization's culture or personality and affects employee performance and satisfaction, with stronger cultures having greater impact.

SNAPSHOT SUMMARY

What Is Organizational Culture?

• Definition of *Organizational Culture*
• Levels of Culture
• Culture's Functions
• Culture Creates Climate
• The Ethical Dimension of Culture
• Do Organizations Have Uniform Cultures?
• Strong vs. Weak Cultures

Reading an Organization's Culture

• Stories
• Rituals
• Material Symbols
• Language

Creating and Sustaining an Organization's Culture

• How a Culture Begins
• Keeping a Culture Alive

The Liabilities of Organizational Culture

• Barrier to Change
• Barrier to Diversity
• Barrier to Mergers and Acquisitions

Changing Organizational Culture

• Creating an Ethical Organizational Culture
• Creating a Positive Organizational Culture

MyManagementLab   Study, practise, and explore real business situations with these helpful resources:

• **Study Plan:** Check your understanding of chapter concepts with self-study quizzes.
• **Online Lesson Presentations:** Study key chapter topics and work through interactive assessments to test your knowledge and master management concepts.
• **Videos:** Learn more about the management practices and strategies of real companies.
• **Simulations:** Practise management decision-making in simulated business environments.

 PERSONAL INVENTORY ASSESSMENT

OB at Work

for **Review**

1. What is organizational culture, and what are its common characteristics?

2. What are the functional effects of organizational culture on people and the organization?

3. What factors create and sustain an organization's culture?

4. How is culture transmitted to employees?

5. What are the liabilities of organizational culture?

6. How can an ethical organizational culture be created?

7. What is a positive organizational culture?

for **Managers**

- Realize that an organization's culture is relatively fixed in the short term. To effect change, involve top management and strategize a long-term plan.

- Hire individuals whose values align with those of the organization; these employees will tend to remain committed and satisfied. Not surprisingly, "misfits" have considerably higher turnover rates.

- Understand that employees' performance and socialization depend to a considerable degree on their knowing what to do and not do. Train your employees well and keep them informed of changes to their job roles.

- Be aware that your company's organizational culture may not be "transportable" to other countries. Understand the cultural relevance of your organization's norms before introducing new plans or initiatives overseas.

for **You**

- Increase your understanding of culture by looking for similarities and differences across groups and organizations. For instance, do you have two courses where the classroom environment differs considerably? What does this suggest about the underlying assumptions in teaching students? Similarly, compare customer service at two local coffee shops or sandwich shops. What does the employee behaviour suggest about each organization's culture?

- Carefully consider the culture of any organization at which you are thinking of being employed. You will feel more comfortable in cultures that share your values and expectations. You may find yourself reacting very negatively if an organization's culture (and values) does not match your own.

- Keep in mind that groups create mini-cultures of their own. When you work in a group on a student project, be aware of the values and norms that are being supported early on in the group's life. These will greatly influence the group's culture.

Organizations Should Strive to Create a Positive Organizational Culture

Organizations should do everything they can to establish a positive culture, because it works.[93] Scores of recent studies have shown that individuals who are in positive states of mind at work and in life lead happier, more productive, and more fulfilling lives. Given the accumulating evidence, researchers are now studying ways to make that happen.

In a recent *Harvard Business Review* article, Wharton faculty member Adam Grant discusses an interesting concept: *outsourcing inspiration*. What does he mean by that? Grant writes: "A growing body of research shows that end users—customers, clients, patients, and others who benefit from a company's products and services—are surprisingly effective in motivating people to work harder, smarter, and more productively."

Some examples of how this might work:

- A "buddy program" that introduces Alzheimer's patients to scientists working to develop treatments for the disease.
- Weekly team meetings that begin with stories about how the team has made a difference in customers' lives.
- Health care workers coming face to face with a patient whose story deeply touches them.

Of course, there are other ways of creating a positive organizational culture, including building on strengths and rewarding more than punishing.

Creating a positive organizational culture is not magic, but it tends to have extremely positive benefits for organizations that embrace it. *Outsourcing inspiration* is a great way for employees to feel appreciated, to experience empathy, and to see the impact of their work—all motivating outcomes that will lead organizations to be more effective and individuals more fulfilled in their work.

Many unanswered questions exist about the merits of using positive organizational scholarship to build positive organizational cultures. Let's focus on three.

What is a positive culture? The employment relationship can be amicable and even mutually beneficial. However, glossing over natural differences in interests with the frosting of positive culture is intellectually dishonest and potentially harmful. From time to time, any organization needs to undertake unpopular actions. Can anyone dismiss an employee positively (and honestly), or explain to someone why others received a raise? There is a danger in trying to sugarcoat. Positive relationships will develop—or not—on their own. We would be better off preaching that people, and organizational cultures, should be honest and fair rather than unabashedly positive.

Is practice ahead of science? Before we start beseeching organizations to build positive cultures, we should make sure these interventions work as we think they do. Many have unintended consequences, and we simply don't have enough research to support the claims put forth. As one reviewer noted, "Everyone wants to believe they could have greater control over their lives by simply changing the way they think. Research that supports this idea gets promoted loudly and widely." But it's not based on a mountain of evidence.

Is building a positive culture manipulative? Psychologist Lisa Aspinwall writes of "saccharine terrorism," where employees are coerced into positive mindsets by Happiness Coaches. You may think this an exaggeration, but companies like UBS, American Express, KPMG, FedEx, Adobe, and IBM use Happiness Coaches to do exactly that. As one critic noted, "Encouraging people to maintain a happy outlook in the face of less-than-ideal conditions is a good way of keeping citizens under control in spite of severe societal problems, or keeping employees productive while keeping pay and benefits low."

PERSONAL **INVENTORY** ASSESSMENT

Company Culture Assessment: Employees usually work best when there is alignment between the company culture and their own cultural preferences. Use this scale to assess which culture is the best fit for you.

BREAKOUT **GROUP** EXERCISES

Form small groups to discuss the following topics, as assigned by your instructor:

1. Choose 2 courses that you are taking this term, ideally in different faculties, and describe the culture of the classroom in each. What are the similarities and differences? What values about learning might you infer from your observations of culture?

2. Identify artifacts of culture in your current or previous workplace. From these artifacts, would you conclude that the organization had a strong or weak culture?

3. Have you or someone you know worked somewhere where the culture was strong? What was your reaction to that strong culture? Did you like that environment, or would you prefer to work where there is a weaker culture? Why?

EXPERIENTIAL EXERCISE

Rate Your Classroom Culture

Listed here are 14 statements. Using the 5-item scale (from Strongly Agree to Strongly Disagree), respond to each statement by circling the number that best represents your opinion.

	Strongly Agree	Agree	Neutral	Disagree	Strongly Disagree
1. I feel comfortable challenging statements made by my instructor.	5	4	3	2	1
2. My instructor heavily penalizes assignments that are not turned in on time.	1	2	3	4	5
3. My instructor believes that "it's final results that count."	1	2	3	4	5
4. My instructor is sensitive to my personal needs and problems.	5	4	3	2	1
5. A large portion of my grade depends on how well I work with others in the class.	5	4	3	2	1
6. I often feel nervous and tense when I come to class.	1	2	3	4	5
7. My instructor seems to prefer stability over change.	1	2	3	4	5
8. My instructor encourages me to develop new and different ideas.	5	4	3	2	1

9. My instructor has little tolerance for sloppy thinking.	1	2	3	4	5
10. My instructor is more concerned with how I came to a conclusion than with the conclusion itself.	5	4	3	2	1
11. My instructor treats all students alike.	1	2	3	4	5
12. My instructor frowns on class members helping each other with assignments.	1	2	3	4	5
13. Aggressive and competitive people have a distinct advantage in this class.	1	2	3	4	5
14. My instructor encourages me to see the world differently.	5	4	3	2	1

Scoring Key:

Calculate your total score by adding up the numbers you circled. Your score will fall between 14 and 70.

A high score (49 or above) describes an open, risk-taking, supportive, humanistic, team-oriented, easy-going, growth-oriented culture. A low score (35 or below) describes a closed, structured, task-oriented, individualistic, tense, and stability-oriented culture. Note that differences count, so a score of 60 is a more open culture than one that scores 50. Also, realize that one culture isn't preferable over another. The "right" culture depends on you and your preferences for a learning environment.

Form teams of 5 to 7 members each. Compare your scores. How closely do they align? Discuss and resolve any discrepancies. Based on your team's analysis, what type of student do you think would perform best in this class?

ETHICAL **DILEMMA**

A Bankrupt Culture

Like many newspapers, the *Chicago Tribune* is in trouble.[94] The paper was bought by real estate mogul Sam Zell in 2007, who promptly filed for bankruptcy. That did not surprise experts. What Zell did next did.

Zell hired Randy Michaels as the Tribune Company's CEO. Soon after Michaels arrived, he launched an attack on the Tribune's culture. In an informal meeting with a group of fellow Tribune executives, Michaels said, "Watch this" and offered the waitress $100 to show her breasts. The group was dumbfounded.

But Michaels hardly stopped there.

Michaels was fond of a culture that included "sexual innuendo, poisonous workplace banter, and profane invective." One press release announced the hiring of Kim Johnson, who, it was said, was "a former waitress at 'Knockers—The Place for Hot Racks and Cold Brews.'" Another executive reporting to Michaels sent links to raunchy websites in email messages. Michaels was heard loudly discussing with other executives he had brought with him the "sexual suitability of various employees."

When some complained about the change in the organization's culture, Michaels rewrote the employee handbook. "Working at Tribune means accepting that you might hear a word that you, personally, might not use," the new manual stated. "You might experience an attitude

you don't share. You might hear a joke that you don't consider funny. That is because a loose, fun, nonlinear atmosphere is important to the creative process." It then concluded, "This should be understood, should not be a surprise, and not considered harassment."

Eventually Michaels was forced out, but the damage had been done. The Tribune was in bankruptcy through 2012, and the company restructured In 2013. More than 5000 employees have lost their jobs. In retrospect, Zell has called his purchase "the deal from hell." It appears that he appointed a CEO to match the deal.

Questions

1. What does this story tell you about the effect of top management on organizational culture?

2. Denise Brown, a former member of the Tribune's management, said, "If you spoke up, you were portrayed as a sissy." How would you have reacted if you witnessed some of these behaviours?

3. How can you determine when a line has been crossed between a fun and informal culture, and one that is offensive and inappropriate?

CASE INCIDENTS

Is a 5S Culture for You?

Jay Scovie looked at his workspace.[95] He took pride in how nice and tidy he had made it look. As it turns out, his pride was misplaced. Sweeping visible clutter from your workspace by packing it into boxes hidden in a closet was not acceptable to his employer, Japanese manufacturer Kyocera. Scovie's habit drew the attention of Dan Brown, Kyocera's newly appointed inspector. "It became a topic of repeated conversation," Scovie said.

Why the obsession with order? Kyocera has joined a growing list of organizations that base their culture on 5S, a concept borrowed from lean manufacturing and based on five phases or principles:

1. *Sorting (Seiri).* Going through all tools, materials, and supplies so as to keep only what is essential.

2. *Straightening (Seiton).* Arranging tools, supplies, equipment, and parts in a manner that promotes maximum efficiency. For everything there should be a place, and everything should be in its place.

3. *Shining (Seiso).* Systematic cleaning to make the workplace and workspace as clean and neat as possible. At the end of the shift or workday, everything is left as it was when the workday started.

4. *Standardizing (Seiketsu).* Knowing exactly what your responsibilities are to keep the first three S's.

5. *Sustaining (Shitsuke).* Maintaining and reviewing standards, rigorous review, and inspection to ensure order does not slowly slip back into disorder or chaos.

Other companies are following Kyocera in making 5S an important part of their culture, including London,

Ontario-based 3M Canada, Markham, Ontario-based Steelcase, and St. Thomas, Ontario-based Waltec. Lawn mower manufacturer Toro organizes printer output according to 5S principles, and Virginia Mason Hospital in Seattle uses 5S to coordinate office space and arrange the placement of medical equipment, such as stethoscopes. Paul Levy, president and CEO of Beth Israel Deaconess Medical Center in Boston, has used 5S to reduce errors and time lost searching for equipment.

At Kyocera, Brown exercises some discretion—he asked one employee to remove a hook on her door while allowing another to keep a whale figurine on her desk. "You have to figure out how to balance being too picky with upholding the purpose of the program," he said. While Brown was happy with Scovie's desk (if not the closet), he wanted to look inside. Scovie tried to redirect the conversation but relented when Brown pressed. Inside one of Scovie's desk drawers was a box full of CDs, small electronic devices, and items Kyocera no longer makes. "Obviously, we're at the sorting stage here," Scovie told Brown.

Questions

1. What would you see as the value in Kyocera using 5S?

2. What are some advantages and disadvantages of trying to impose a similar culture in Canadian companies?

3. What might your response be to having to engage in the 5S principles in your workplace?

Google and P&G Swap Employees

The cultures of Google and Procter & Gamble (P&G) could not be more different.[96] P&G is notoriously controlled, disciplined, scalable, and rigid—so much so that employees call themselves "Proctoids." Google is just as famous for its laid-back, unstandardized, free-flowing culture.

So what would cause these two large, successful examples of strong—yet dissimilar—corporate culture to decide to socialize one another's employees? One reason clearly is

marketing: P&G sees more of its future marketing efforts occurring online, and Google, of course, is an ideal fit for that strategy. Google, for its part, sees P&G as the ultimate "heavy hitter" buyer for its ad space (P&G is the biggest advertiser in the world).

However, it also seems clear that this exchange is about more than marketing. After all, P&G and Google do business with plenty of organizations with which they don't swap employees. Both companies believe that by exposing key managers to a culture that emphasizes innovation, but in a wholly different way, they can push their own innovation even further.

Sometimes we learn the most from the ways in which we are different, and that is certainly the case here. In one of the early employee swaps, Denise Chudy, a Google sales-team leader, stunned P&G managers with recent data indicating online search for the word *coupons* was up 50 percent in the past year. P&G staffers see themselves as members of one of the world's most innovative and data-driven organizations, famous for tracking consumer preferences, product use, and buying behaviour. They are not easily stunned. To enter Google's own universe was a humbling, and challenging, learning experience.

Google's swapped employees are learning something, too. When poring over decades of marketing materials on P&G's Tide detergent and the firm's allegiance to bright orange packaging, Google employee Jen Bradburn wrote, "It's a help to know not to mess with the orange too much."

Differences, of course, are still apparent. When one P&G manager showed Google employees a 1954 ad for Tide, he proudly noted, "That's when you reached 70 percent to 80 percent of your audience with television." The Google team laughed in astonishment.

Questions

1. Do you think the employee swap between Google and P&G is a good idea for both companies? Why or why not? Why do so few companies do this?

2. One of the reasons P&G and Google agreed to the swap was to transmit the best aspects of the other company's culture to their own. Drawing from this chapter, describe how culture might be transmitted in such swaps.

3. Which culture—Google's or P&G's—do you think would fit you best? Why?

4. Would you enjoy an employee swap with a company with a very different culture? Why or why not?

FROM CONCEPTS TO SKILLS

How to "Read" an Organization's Culture

The ability to read and assess an organization's culture can be a valuable skill.[97]

If you are looking for a job, you will want to choose an employer whose culture is compatible with your values and in which you will feel comfortable. If you can accurately assess a prospective employer's culture before you make your decision, you may be able to save yourself a lot of grief and reduce the likelihood of making a poor choice. Similarly, you will undoubtedly have business transactions with numerous organizations during your professional career. You will be trying to sell a product or service, negotiate a contract, or arrange a joint venture, or you may merely be seeking out which individual in an organization controls certain decisions. The ability to assess another organization's culture can be a definite plus in successfully completing these pursuits.

For the sake of simplicity, we will approach the problem of reading an organization's culture from the point of view of a job applicant. We will assume you are interviewing for a job. Here is a list of things you can do to help learn about a potential employer's culture:

- Observe the physical surroundings. Pay attention to signs, pictures, style of dress, length of hair, degree of openness between offices, and office furnishings and arrangements.

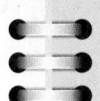

- With whom did you meet? Just the person who would be your immediate manager? Or potential colleagues, managers from other departments, or senior executives? Based on what they revealed, to what degree do people other than the immediate manager have input into the hiring decision?

- How would you characterize the style of the people you met? Formal? Casual? Serious? Jovial?

- Does the organization have formal rules and regulations printed in a human resource policy manual? If so, how detailed are these policies?

- Ask questions of the people you meet. The most valid and reliable information tends to come from asking the same questions of many people (to see how closely their responses align) and by talking with boundary spanners. *Boundary spanners* are employees whose work links them to the external environment and includes jobs such as human resources interviewer, salesperson, purchasing agent, labour negotiator, public relations specialist, and company lawyer.

Questions that will give you insights into organizational processes and practices might include the following:

- What is the background of the founders?

- What is the background of current senior managers? What are their functional specializations? Were they promoted from within or hired from outside?

- How does the organization integrate new employees? Is there an orientation program? Training? If so, could you describe these features?

- How does your manager define his or her job success? (Amount of profit? Serving customers? Meeting deadlines? Acquiring budget increases?)

- How would you define fairness in terms of reward allocations?

- Can you identify some people here who are on the "fast track"? What do you think has put them on the fast track?

- Can you identify someone who seems to be considered a deviant in the organization? How has the organization responded to this person?

- Can you describe a decision that someone made here that was well received?

- Can you describe a decision that did not work out well? What were the consequences for the decision maker?

- Could you describe a crisis or critical event that has occurred recently in the organization? How did top management respond? What was learned from this experience?

Practising Skills

After spending your first three years after college graduation as a freelance graphic designer, you are looking at pursuing a job as an account executive at a graphic design firm. You feel that the scope of assignments 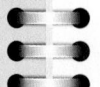 and potential for technical training far exceed what you would be able to do on your own, and you are looking to expand your skills and meet a brand-new set of challenges. However, you want to make sure you "fit" in to the organization where you are going to be spending more than eight hours every workday. What is the best way for you to find a place where you will be happy, and where your style and personality will be appreciated?

Reinforcing Skills

1. Do some comparisons of the atmosphere or feeling you get from various organizations. It will probably be easiest for you to do this exercise using restaurants, retail stores, or banks. Based on the atmosphere that you observe, what type of organizational culture do you think these organizations might have? If you can, interview three employees at each organization for their descriptions of their organization's culture.

2. Think about changes (major and minor) that you have dealt with over the past year. Perhaps these changes involved other people and perhaps they were personal. Did you resist the change? Did others resist the change? How did you overcome your resistance or the resistance of others to the change?

11

Leadership

Bryce Williams was elected as chief of the Tsawwassen First Nation when he was only 22 years old. Two years later, he has proven to be a strong leader focused on cultural and economic growth, including the construction of the second-largest mall in Canada. What makes a successful leader?

LEARNING OUTCOMES

After studying this chapter, you should be able to:

1 Contrast leadership and management.

2 Summarize the conclusions of trait theories of leadership.

3 Identify the central tenets and main limitations of behavioural theories of leadership.

4 Assess contingency theories of leadership by their level of support.

5 Contrast charismatic and transformational leadership.

6 Identify the leadership roles available to nonmanagers.

7 Define *authentic leadership*.

8 Discuss the requirements of ethical leadership.

9 Define *servant leadership*.

Although he is still young, 24-year-old Bryce Williams knows a great deal about leadership.[1] He is the elected chief of the Tsawwassen First Nation (TFN), the first urban self-governed nation in BC through a treaty signed in 2009. The treaty not only opened up enormous opportunities for economic development but also created concerns about cultural maintenance. Williams' commitment to balance led to his election as chief in 2012. When he was asked about his surprise win against older and more experienced candidates, Williams replied that "I think my people-first mentality is a big part of getting elected—and being involved with the community quite often and having that want and need to strengthen the culture."

CBC

Williams has the credibility that comes from being directly involved in cultural maintenance himself. He is a talented carver who teaches Coast Salish art to children in his community. As an elected leader he strives to help foster the creation of "culture-bearers" by supporting traditional arts such as weaving, dancing, singing, and carving. This support is carried out in a way that also leads to economic opportunity. For example, in January 2014 the TFN broke ground on two new destination shopping malls on Tsawwassen land. These mega malls will not only generate profits for the band but also help provide a forum for the display and sale of traditional arts products. "Obviously it's good to keep the culture alive, but you can't host programs and services when you don't have money to move those things forward, so they're both very important," observes Williams.

In this chapter, we review leadership studies to determine what makes an effective leader. We consider factors that affect one's ability to lead and examine inspirational leadership and self-management. Finally, we discuss contemporary issues in leadership.

THE BIG IDEA

Knowing how to lead well does not come naturally. Effective leadership requires an understanding of how to inspire individuals to achieve common goals.

OB IS FOR **EVERYONE**

- Have you ever wondered if there was one *right* way to lead?
- Can anyone be a leader?
- How do you manage yourself?

What Is Leadership?

1 Contrast leadership and management.

We define **leadership** as the ability to influence a group toward the achievement of a vision or set of goals. The source of this influence may be formal, such as that provided by managerial rank in an organization. But not all leaders are managers, nor are all managers leaders. Just because an organization provides its managers with certain formal rights is no assurance they will lead effectively. Nonsanctioned leadership—the ability to influence that arises outside the formal structure of the organization—is often as important or more important than formal influence. Leaders can emerge from within a group as well as by formal appointment.

Organizations need strong leadership *and* strong management for optimal effectiveness. We need leaders to challenge the status quo, create visions of the future, and inspire organizational members to achieve the visions. We also need managers to formulate detailed plans, create efficient organizational structures, and oversee day-to-day operations.

In our discussion of leadership, we will focus on two major tasks of those who lead in organizations: managing those around them to get the day-to-day tasks done, and inspiring others to do the extraordinary. It will become clear that successful leaders rely on a variety of interpersonal skills in order to encourage others to perform at their best. It will also become clear that, no matter the place in the hierarchy, from CEO to team leader, a variety of individuals can be called on to perform leadership roles.

Leadership as Supervision

When asked about what traits a chief should have, Bryce Williams says that a leader is someone who can be the "voice of the people."[2] He does not mean being loud or opinionated. In fact, during his nation's legislative assembly he is often silent, even during tense debates. He is listening, carefully absorbing everyone's viewpoint and perspective. Some people recall that prior chiefs had a different style, getting more involved and advocating strongly for one side of a debate. Steven Stark, a member of the legislature, observed that "Bryce is conservative. He watches. He is quiet but he uses his words wisely. He has that open ear." Listening carefully helps Williams find mutually beneficial solutions to problems. For example, when discussing a dispute with a local municipality over sewer lines, he observes that "there has to be relationship building there and we just have to find a way to work together so that we can … benefit all of our communities." So, what makes an effective leader?

In this section, we discuss theories of leadership that were developed before 1980. These early theories focused on the supervisory nature of leadership—that is, how individuals managed the day-to-day functioning of employees. The theories took different approaches in understanding how best to lead in a supervisory capacity. The three general types of theories that emerged were (1) trait theories, which propose leaders have a particular set of traits that makes them different from nonleaders; (2) behavioural theories, which propose that particular behaviours make for better leaders; and (3) contingency theories, which propose the situation has an effect on leaders. When you think about these theories, remember that although they have been considered "theories of leadership," they rely on an older understanding of what "leadership" means, and don't convey a distinction between leadership and supervision.

2 Summarize the conclusions of trait theories of leadership.

leadership The ability to influence a group toward the achievement of a vision or set of goals.

trait theories of leadership Theories that consider personal qualities and characteristics that differentiate leaders from nonleaders.

Trait Theories: Are Leaders Different from Others?

Have you ever wondered whether some fundamental personality difference makes some people "born leaders"? **Trait theories of leadership** focus on personal qualities and characteristics. The search for personality, social, physical, or intellectual attributes that differentiate leaders from nonleaders goes back to the earliest stages of leadership research. Trait theory emerged in the hope that if it were possible to identify the traits of leaders, it would be easier to select people to fill leadership roles. Being able to select good leaders is important because not all people know how to be good leaders, as *Focus on Research* shows.

FOCUS ON RESEARCH ## Bad Bosses Everywhere

Doesn't leadership come naturally? Although much is expected of leaders, what is surprising is how rarely they seem to meet the most basic definitions of effectiveness.[3] A recent study of 700 employees revealed that many believe their supervisors don't give credit when it's due, gossip about them behind their backs, and don't keep their word. The situation is so bad that for many employees, the study's lead author says, "They don't leave their company, they leave their boss."

Key findings of the study are as follows:

- 39 percent said their supervisor failed to keep promises.
- 37 percent said their supervisor failed to give credit when due.
- 31 percent said their supervisor gave them the "silent treatment" in the past year.
- 27 percent said their supervisor made negative comments about them to other employees or managers.
- 24 percent said their supervisor invaded their privacy.
- 23 percent said their supervisor blames others to cover up mistakes or minimize embarrassment.

Why do companies promote such people into leadership positions? One reason may be the Peter Principle. When people are promoted into one job (say, as a supervisor or coach) based on how well they did another (say, salesperson or player), that assumes that the skills of one role are the same as the other. The only time such people stop being promoted is when they reach their level of incompetence. Judging from the results of this study, that level of leadership incompetence is reached all too often.

A recent study found that lack of respect for a leader by employees—for instance, when employees feel that the leader is not the best person for the job—has a significant impact on whether employees will follow that leader. The researchers found that simply naming someone "the leader" did not by itself create effective leadership.[4] _____

Research efforts at isolating leadership traits resulted in a number of dead ends. A research review in the late 1960s identified nearly 80 leadership traits, but only 5 of these traits were common to 4 or more of the investigations.[5] By the 1990s, we could say that most "leaders are not like other people," but the particular traits that were isolated varied a great deal from review to review.[6] Identifying leadership traits remained a challenge.

A breakthrough came when researchers began organizing traits around the Big Five Personality Model (see Chapter 2).[7] Most of the dozens of traits in various leadership reviews fit under one of the Big Five (for example, ambition and energy are part of extraversion), giving strong support to certain traits as predictors of leadership.

A comprehensive review of the leadership literature, organized around the Big Five, found extraversion to be the most predictive trait of effective leadership.[8] However, extraversion is more strongly related to the way leaders emerge than to their effectiveness. Sociable and dominant people are more likely to assert themselves in group situations, but leaders need to make sure they are not too assertive. One study found that leaders who scored very high on assertiveness were less effective than those who scored moderately high.[9]

Unlike agreeableness and emotional stability, conscientiousness and openness to experience also showed strong and consistent relationships to leadership, although not quite as strong as extraversion. Overall, the trait approach does have something to offer. Leaders who like being around people and are able to assert themselves (extraverted), are disciplined and keep commitments they make (conscientious), and are creative and flexible (open) do have an advantage when it comes to leadership, suggesting that good leaders do have key traits in common.

One reason is that conscientiousness and extraversion are positively related to leaders' self-efficacy, which explained most of the variance in subordinates' ratings of leader performance.[10] People are more likely to follow someone who is confident that she is going in the right direction.

Another trait that may indicate effective leadership is emotional intelligence (EI), discussed in Chapter 2. Advocates of EI argue that without it, a person can have outstanding training, a highly analytical mind, a compelling vision, and an endless supply of terrific ideas but still not make a great leader. This may be especially true as individuals move up in an organization.[11] A core component of EI is empathy. Empathetic leaders can sense others' needs, listen to what followers say (and don't say), and read the reactions of others. A leader who effectively displays and manages emotions will find it easier to influence the feelings of followers by expressing genuine sympathy and enthusiasm for good performance, and by showing irritation when employees fail to perform.[12]

The link between EI and leadership effectiveness may be worth investigating in greater detail.[13] Recent research has demonstrated that people high in EI are more likely to emerge as leaders, even after taking cognitive ability and personality into account.[14] Based on the latest findings, we offer two conclusions. First, contrary to what we believed 20 years ago and thanks to the Big Five Personality Model, we can say that traits can predict leadership. Second, traits do a better job at predicting the emergence of leaders and the appearance of leadership than in distinguishing between *effective* and *ineffective* leaders.[15] The fact that an individual exhibits the right traits and that others consider that person to be a leader does not necessarily mean that the leader is successful at getting a group to achieve its goals. *Case Incident—Moving from Colleague to Supervisor* on page 408 considers the challenges one faces when moving from being a co-worker to taking on leadership responsibilities.

Behavioural Theories: Do Leaders Behave in Particular Ways?

Identify the central tenets and main limitations of behavioural theories of leadership.

The failures of early trait studies led researchers in the late 1940s through the 1960s to wonder whether there was something unique in the way that effective leaders behave. Trait research provides a basis for *selecting* the right people for leadership. In contrast, **behavioural theories of leadership** implied we could *train* people to be leaders.

The Ohio State Studies

The most comprehensive behavioural theories resulted from the Ohio State Studies in the late 1940s,[16] which sought to identify independent dimensions of leader behaviour. Beginning with more than a thousand dimensions, the studies narrowed the list to two that substantially accounted for most of the leadership behaviour described by employees: *initiating structure* and *consideration*.

Initiating structure is the extent to which a leader is likely to define and structure his or her role and those of employees in order to attain goals; it includes behaviour that attempts to organize work, work relationships, and goals. A leader high in initiating structure is someone who "assigns group members to particular tasks," "expects workers to maintain definite standards of performance," and "emphasizes the meeting of deadlines."[17]

Consideration is the extent to which a leader's job relationships are characterized by mutual trust, respect for employees' ideas, and regard for their feelings. A leader high

behavioural theories of leadership Theories that propose that specific behaviours differentiate leaders from nonleaders.

initiating structure The extent to which a leader is likely to define and structure his or her role and the roles of employees in order to attain goals.

consideration The extent to which a leader is likely to have job relationships characterized by mutual trust, respect for employees' ideas, and regard for their feelings.

PR NewsFoto/PespsiCo., Ray Hand/AP Images

Indra Nooyi, CEO and board chairman of PepsiCo, is described as fun-loving, sociable, agreeable, conscientious, emotionally stable, and open to experiences. Recognized as one of the most powerful women in business, Nooyi's personal qualities and traits have contributed to her job performance and success.

in consideration helps employees with personal problems, is friendly and approachable, treats all employees as equals, and expresses appreciation and support. In a recent survey, when asked to indicate the factors that most motivated them at work, 66 percent of employees mentioned appreciation.[18]

The Michigan Studies

Leadership studies at the University of Michigan's Survey Research Center had similar objectives to the Ohio State Studies: to locate behavioural characteristics of leaders that appeared related to performance effectiveness.[19] The Michigan group identified two behavioural types: **employee-oriented leaders**, who emphasized interpersonal relations by taking a personal interest in the needs of employees and accepting individual differences among them; and **production-oriented leader**, who emphasized the technical or task aspects of the job—focusing on accomplishing the group's task. These dimensions are closely related to the Ohio State dimensions. Employee-oriented leadership is similar to consideration, and production-oriented leadership is similar to initiating structure. In fact, most leadership researchers use the terms synonymously.[20]

At one time, the results of testing behavioural theories were thought to be disappointing. However, a review of 160 studies found the followers of leaders high in consideration were more satisfied with their jobs, were more motivated, and had more respect for their leaders. Initiating structure was more strongly related to higher levels of group and organization productivity and more positive performance evaluations.

RESEARCH FINDINGS: Behavioural Theories of Leadership

A 2011 study integrated the results of 59 previous studies in order to determine the impact of specific leader behaviours on leadership effectiveness, group performance, and employee job satisfaction.[21] Task-oriented behaviours explained 47.6 percent of the variance in group performance and 33.3 percent of the variance in overall leadership effectiveness. Change-oriented transformational leadership

employee-oriented leader A leader who emphasizes interpersonal relations.

production-oriented leader A leader who emphasizes the technical or task aspects of the job.

behaviours were also strongly associated with group performance and overall effectiveness, explaining 28.5 percent and 22.5 percent, respectively, of the variance in these areas. Consideration behaviours (such as providing emotional support) had a smaller but still significant impact on performance and leadership effectiveness (16.6 percent and 19.5 percent of total variance, respectively). Being supportive was associated with employee job satisfaction (21 percent of variance), but providing a reward structure had a greater impact, explaining 43.9 percent of the variance in employee job satisfaction. These results suggest that while all of these leader behaviours are important, task-oriented behaviours are essential to leadership effectiveness.

Contingency Theories: Does the Situation Matter?

4 Assess contingency theories of leadership by their level of support.

Some tough-minded leaders seem to gain a lot of admirers when they take over struggling companies and turn them around. However, predicting leadership success is more complex than isolating a few traits or behaviours. What works in very bad times and in very good times doesn't seem to translate into long-term success. When researchers looked at situational influences, it appeared that under condition *a*, leadership style *x* would be appropriate, whereas style *y* was more suitable for condition *b*, and style *z* for condition *c*. But what *were* conditions *a*, *b*, and *c*? We consider four situational theories below: the Fiedler contingency model, Hersey and Blanchard's Situational Leadership®, and path-goal theory.

> Have you ever wondered if there was one *right* way to lead?

Fiedler Contingency Model

◄◉► Simulate on **MyManagementLab**

Leadership

The first comprehensive contingency model for leadership was developed by Fred Fiedler.[22] The **Fiedler contingency model** proposes that effective group performance depends on the proper match between the leader's style and the degree to which the situation gives the leader control.

Fiedler created the *least preferred co-worker (LPC)* questionnaire to determine whether individuals were primarily interested in good personal relations with co-workers, and thus *relationship-oriented*, or primarily interested in productivity, and thus *task-oriented*. Fiedler assumed that an individual's leadership style is fixed. Therefore, if a situation requires a task-oriented leader and the person in that leadership position is relationship-oriented, either the situation has to be modified or the leader must be removed and replaced for optimum effectiveness to be achieved.

After assessing an individual's basic leadership style through an LPC questionnaire, the next step is to match the leader with the situation. Fiedler identified three contingency dimensions that determine the situation a leader faces. That situation will then affect the leader's effectiveness:

- *Leader–member relations.* The degree of confidence, trust, and respect members have for their leader.

- *Task structure.* The degree to which job assignments are procedurized (that is, structured or unstructured).

- *Position power.* The degree of influence a leader has over power-based activities such as hiring, firing, discipline, promotions, and salary increases.

The next step is to evaluate the situation in terms of these three variables. Fiedler stated that the better the leader–member relations, the more highly structured the job, and the stronger the position power, the more control the leader has. A very favourable situation (in which the leader has a great deal of control) might include a payroll manager who is well respected and whose employees have confidence in her

Fiedler contingency model A leadership theory that proposes that effective group performance depends on the proper match between the leader's style and the degree to which the situation gives the leader control.

(good leader–member relations); activities that are clear and specific—such as wage computation, cheque writing, and report filing (high task structure); and provision of considerable freedom to reward and punish employees (strong position power). An unfavourable situation might be that of the disliked chairperson of a volunteer United Way fundraising team. In this job, the leader has very little control.

Fiedler suggested that task-oriented leaders perform best in situations of high and low control, while relationship-oriented leaders perform best in moderate control situations.[23] In a high control situation, a leader can "get away" with task orientation, because the relationships are good, and followers are easily influenced.[24] In a low control situation (which is characterized by poor relations, ill-defined task, and low influence), task orientation may be the only thing that makes it possible to get something done. In a moderate control situation, being relationship-oriented may smooth the way to getting things done.

How would you apply Fiedler's findings? You would match leaders with the type of situation—in terms of leader–member relations, task structure, and position power—for which they were best suited. Because Fiedler views an individual's leadership style as fixed, there are only two ways to improve leader effectiveness.

First, you can change the leader to fit the situation—as a baseball manager puts a right- or left-handed pitcher into the game depending on the hitter. If a group situation rates highly unfavourable but is currently led by a relationship-oriented manager, the group's performance could be improved under a manager who is task-oriented. The second alternative is to change the situation to fit the leader, by restructuring tasks or increasing or decreasing the leader's power to control factors such as salary increases, promotions, and disciplinary actions.

Studies testing the overall validity of the Fiedler model find considerable evidence to support substantial parts of it.[25] But the logic underlying the LPC questionnaire is not well understood, and respondents' scores are not stable.[26] The contingency variables are also complex and difficult for practitioners to assess.[27]

Hersey and Blanchard's Situational Leadership®

Situational Leadership® (SL), focuses on followers. SL says successful leadership depends on selecting the right leadership style contingent on the followers' *readiness*, or the extent to which they are willing and able to accomplish a specific task. A leader should choose one of four behaviours, depending on follower readiness. This idea is illustrated in Exhibit 11-1.

If followers are *unable* and *unwilling* to do a task, the leader needs to give clear and specific directions; if they are *unable* and *willing*, the leader needs to display high task orientation to compensate for followers' lack of ability and high relationship orientation to get them to "buy into" the leader's desires. If followers are *able* and *unwilling*, the leader needs to use a supportive and participative style; if they are both *able* and *willing*, the leader does not need to do much.

SL has intuitive appeal. It acknowledges the importance of followers and builds on the logic that leaders can compensate for their limited ability and motivation. Yet research efforts to test and support the theory have generally been disappointing.[28] Why? Possible explanations include internal ambiguities and inconsistencies in the model itself as well as problems with research methodology in tests. So despite its intuitive appeal and wide popularity, any endorsement must be cautious for now.

Path-Goal Theory

Developed by University of Toronto professor Martin Evans in the late 1960s and subsequently expanded upon by Robert House (formerly at the University of Toronto, but now at the Wharton School of Business at the University of Pennsylvania), **path-goal theory** extracts elements from the Ohio State leadership research on initiating structure and consideration and the expectancy theory of motivation.[29] It says that it's the leader's

Situational Leadership® (SL) A leadership theory that focuses on the readiness of followers.

path-goal theory A leadership theory that says it is the leader's job to assist followers in attaining their goals and to provide the necessary direction and/or support to ensure that their goals are compatible with the overall objectives of the group or organization.

EXHIBIT 11-1 Hersey and Blanchard's Situational Leadership®

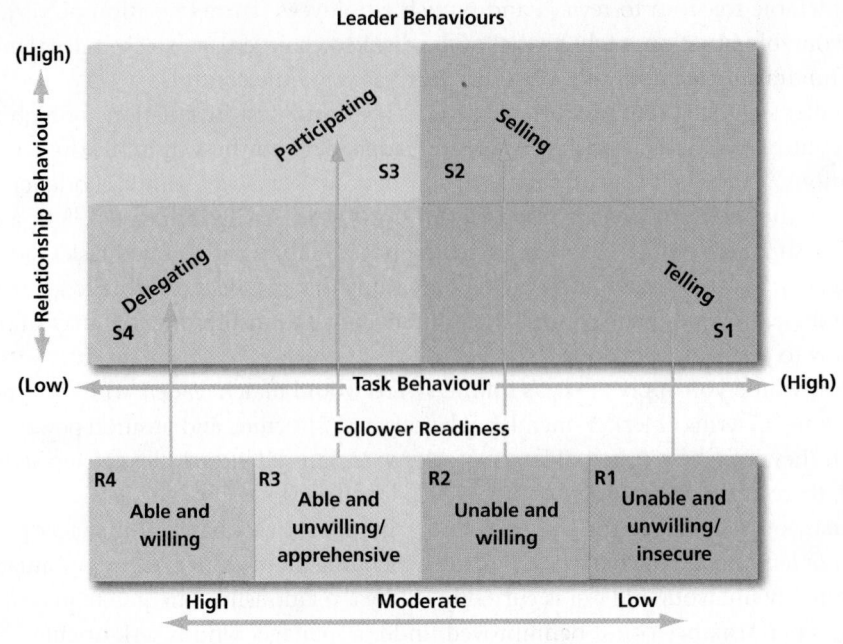

job to provide followers with the information, support, or other resources necessary to achieve their goals. (The term *path-goal* implies effective leaders clarify followers' paths to their work goals and make the journey easier by reducing roadblocks.)

According to this theory, leaders should follow three guidelines to be effective:[30]

- *Determine the outcomes subordinates want.* These might include good pay, job security, interesting work, and autonomy to do one's job.

- *Reward individuals with their desired outcomes* when they perform well.

- *Let individuals know what they need to do to receive rewards* (that is, the path to the goal), remove any barriers that would prevent high performance, and express confidence that individuals have the ability to perform well.

Path-goal theory identifies four leadership behaviours that might be used in different situations to motivate individuals:

- The *directive leader* lets followers know what is expected of them, schedules work to be done, and gives specific guidance as to how to accomplish tasks. This closely parallels the Ohio State dimension of initiating structure. This behaviour is best used when individuals have difficulty doing tasks or the tasks are ambiguous. It would not be very helpful when used with individuals who are already highly motivated, have the skills and abilities to do the task, and understand the requirements of the task.

- The *supportive leader* is friendly and shows concern for the needs of followers. This is essentially synonymous with the Ohio State dimension of consideration. This behaviour is often recommended when individuals are under stress, or otherwise show that they need to be supported.

- The *participative leader* consults with followers and uses their suggestions before making a decision. This behaviour is most appropriate when individuals need to buy in to decisions.

EXHIBIT 11-2 Path-Goal Theory

CONTINGENCY FACTORS

Environmental
- Task structure
- Formal authority system
- Work group

Leader Behaviour
- Directive
- Supportive
- Participative
- Achievement-oriented

Subordinate
- Locus of control
- Experience
- Perceived ability

Outcomes
- Performance
- Satisfaction

- The *achievement-oriented leader* sets challenging goals and expects followers to perform at their highest level. This behaviour works well with individuals who like challenges and are highly motivated. It would be less effective with less capable individuals, or those who are highly stressed from overwork.

As Exhibit 11-2 illustrates, path-goal theory proposes two types of contingency variables that affect the leadership behaviour–outcome relationship: environmental variables that are outside the control of the employee and variables that are part of the personal characteristics of the employee. The theory proposes that employee performance and satisfaction are likely to be positively influenced when the leader compensates for what is lacking in either the employee or the work setting. However, the leader who spends time explaining tasks when those tasks are already clear or when the employee has the ability and experience to handle them without interference is likely to be ineffective because the employee will see such directive behaviour as redundant or even insulting.

PERSONAL INVENTORY ASSESSMENT

Learn About Yourself
Leadership Style Indicator

RESEARCH FINDINGS: Path-Goal Theory

Testing path-goal theory has not been easy. A review of the evidence suggests mixed support, which indicates "that either effective leadership does not rest in the removal of roadblocks and pitfalls to employee path instrumentalities as path-goal theories propose or that the nature of these hindrances is not in accord with the proposition of the theories."[31] Another review found the lack of support to be "shocking and disappointing."[32] Some researchers believe that the theory is valid but incomplete and that even more attention should be focused on things that moderate the relationship between leader and follower behaviours. In a study of 162 workers in a document-processing organization, for example, researchers found workers' conscientiousness was related to higher levels of performance only when supervisors set goals and defined roles, responsibilities, and priorities.[33] Other studies have found that goal-focused leadership can lead to higher levels of emotional exhaustion for subordinates who are low in conscientiousness and emotional stability.[34] These studies demonstrate that leaders who set goals enable conscientious followers to achieve higher performance but may cause stress for workers who are low in conscientiousness.

One of the dangers of any theory of situational leadership is the assumption that the behaviour of the leader should adjust to meet followers' needs. It may be that leaders act on employees' perceived needs rather than their real needs. Recall from Chapter 2 that "perceptions are reality." A recent study found that "if managers view followers positively—that they are good citizens, industrious, enthusiastic—they will treat their employees positively. If they think of their employees negatively—that they are conforming, insubordinate and incompetent—they will treat them that way."[35] By extension, managers may not adopt the appropriate situational leadership behaviour if they have incorrect perceptions of their employees. *Case Incident—Leadership by Algorithm* on page 409 explores ways to learn how to adapt your leadership style to better fit the situation.

Substitutes for Leadership

The previous three theories argue that leaders are needed, but that leaders should consider the situation in determining which style of leadership to adopt. However, numerous studies collectively demonstrate that, in many situations, leaders' actions are irrelevant. Experience and training are among the *substitutes* that can replace the need for a leader's support or ability to create structure. Organizational characteristics such as explicit formalized goals, rigid rules and procedures, and cohesive work groups can also replace formal leadership, while indifference to organizational rewards can neutralize its effects. *Neutralizers* make it impossible for leader behaviour to make any difference to follower outcomes. These substitutes and neutralizers are shown in Exhibit 11-3.[36]

It's simplistic to think employees are guided to goal accomplishments solely by the actions of their leaders. We have introduced a number of variables—such as attitudes, personality, ability, and group norms—that affect employee performance and satisfaction. Leadership is simply another independent variable in our overall organizational behaviour (OB) model.

EXHIBIT 11-3 Substitutes and Neutralizers for Leadership

Characteristics of Individual	Effect on Leadership
Experience/training	Substitutes for task-oriented leadership
Professionalism	Substitutes for relationship-oriented and task-oriented leadership
Indifference to rewards	Neutralizes relationship-oriented and task-oriented leadership

Characteristics of Job	
Highly structured task	Substitutes for task-oriented leadership
Provides its own feedback	Substitutes for task-oriented leadership
Intrinsically satisfying	Substitutes for relationship-oriented leadership

Characteristics of Organization	
Explicit formalized goals	Substitutes for task-oriented leadership
Rigid rules and procedures	Substitutes for task-oriented leadership
Cohesive work groups	Substitutes for relationship-oriented and task-oriented leadership

Source: Based on S. Kerr and J. M. Jermier, "Substitutes for Leadership: Their Meaning and Measurement," *Organizational Behavior and Human Performance*, December 1978, p. 378.

Sometimes the difference between substitutes and neutralizers is fuzzy. If I am working on a task that is intrinsically enjoyable, theory predicts that leadership will be less important because the task itself provides enough motivation. But does that mean intrinsically enjoyable tasks neutralize leadership effects, or substitute for them, or both? Another problem is that while substitutes for leadership (such as employee characteristics, the nature of the task, and so forth) matter to performance, that does not necessarily mean that leadership does not matter to performance.[37]

Inspirational Leadership

Bryce Williams wants to create a new generation of "culture-bearers," a goal he takes very seriously.[38] As the leader of the Tsawwassen First Nation, he has begun realizing this goal in a number of ways. The mega malls being built on Tsawwassen lands are a good start, since they will create a convenient and high-profile location to market traditional arts and crafts. Williams' vision extends far beyond that, however. As a trained carver, he teaches Salish coastal art to Tsawwassen children at a weekly book and art club, helping to develop the talents of young artists. This contact also makes him accessible to local children and youth. Peggy McCleod, who facilitates the classes, says that "having that time the way they do every week, with one of the leaders, I think really goes a long way to speak to how valued they are." As for Williams, his perspective is very straightforward. "Part of being a Haida artist or a Coast Salish artist is being willing to pass on those traditions. It uplifts me to be able to pass along some of that knowledge." What does it take to be an inspirational leader?

5 Contrast charismatic and transformational leadership.

The leadership theories we have discussed above ignore the importance of the leader as a communicator who inspires others to act beyond their immediate self-interests. In this section, we present two contemporary leadership theories with a common theme. They view leaders as individuals who inspire followers through their words, ideas, and behaviours. These theories are charismatic leadership and transformational leadership.

Charismatic Leadership

The following individuals are often cited as being charismatic leaders: Frank Stronach of Aurora, Ontario-based Magna International; Mogens Smed, CEO of Calgary-based DIRTT (Doing It Right This Time) Environmental Solutions; Pierre Trudeau, the late prime minister; Michaëlle Jean, former Governor General; and Craig Kielburger, of Free The Children. So what do they have in common?

What Is Charismatic Leadership?

Max Weber, a sociologist, defined *charisma* (from the Greek for "gift") more than a century ago as "a certain quality of an individual personality, by virtue of which he or she is set apart from ordinary people and treated as endowed with supernatural, super-human, or at least specifically exceptional powers or qualities. These are not accessible to the ordinary person and are regarded as of divine origin or as exemplary, and on the basis of them the individual concerned is treated as a leader."[39] Weber argued that charismatic leadership was one of several ideal types of authority.

The first researcher to consider charismatic leadership in terms of OB was Robert House. According to House's **charismatic leadership theory**, followers make attributions of heroic or extraordinary leadership abilities when they observe certain behaviours, and tend to give these leaders power.[40] A number of studies have attempted to identify the characteristics of the charismatic leader and have documented four—they have a vision, they are willing to take personal risks to achieve that vision, they are sensitive to followers' needs, and they exhibit behaviours that are out of the ordinary (see Exhibit 11-4).[41]

charismatic leadership theory
A leadership theory that states that followers make attributions of heroic or extraordinary leadership abilities when they observe certain behaviours.

> **EXHIBIT 11-4 Key Characteristics of Charismatic Leaders**
>
> 1. *Vision and articulation.* Has a vision—expressed as an idealized goal—that proposes a future better than the status quo; and is able to clarify the importance of the vision in terms that are understandable to others.
>
> 2. *Personal risk.* Willing to take on high personal risk, incur high costs, and engage in self-sacrifice to achieve the vision.
>
> 3. *Sensitivity to followers' needs.* Perceptive of others' abilities and responsive to their needs and feelings.
>
> 4. *Unconventional behaviour.* Engages in behaviours that are perceived as novel and counter to norms.
>
> *Source:* Based on J. A. Conger and R. N. Kanungo, *Charismatic Leadership in Organizations* (Thousand Oaks, CA: Sage, 1998), p. 94.

Are the heroic qualities ascribed to charismatic leaders part of their DNA? *Point/Counterpoint* on page 406 considers the question.

How Charismatic Leaders Influence Followers

How do charismatic leaders actually influence followers? By articulating an appealing **vision**—a long-term strategy for how to attain a goal by linking the present with a better future for the organization. Desirable visions fit the times and circumstances and reflect the uniqueness of the organization.

A vision needs an accompanying **vision statement**, a formal articulation of an organization's vision or mission. Charismatic leaders may use vision statements to imprint on followers an overarching goal and purpose. They build followers' self-esteem and confidence with high performance expectations and the belief that followers can attain them.

Next, through words and actions, the leader conveys a new set of values and sets an example for followers to imitate. One study of Israeli bank employees showed, for example, that charismatic leaders were more effective because their employees personally identified with them.[42] Charismatic leaders also set a tone of cooperation and mutual support. A study of 115 government employees found they had a stronger sense of personal belonging at work when they had charismatic leaders, increasing their willingness to engage in helping and compliance-oriented behaviour.[43]

Finally, the charismatic leader engages in emotion-inducing and often unconventional behaviour to demonstrate courage and convictions about the vision. Followers "catch" the emotions their leader conveys.[44]

RESEARCH FINDINGS: Charismatic Leadership

Research shows impressive correlations between charismatic leadership and high performance and satisfaction among followers.[45] People working for charismatic leaders are motivated to exert extra work effort and, because they like and respect their leader, express greater satisfaction. It also appears that organizations with charismatic CEOs are more profitable. And charismatic professors enjoy higher course evaluations.[46]

Even in laboratory studies, when people are psychologically aroused, they are more likely to respond to charismatic leaders.[47] This may explain why charismatic leaders tend to surface in politics, religion, wartime, or a business firm that is in its infancy or facing a life-threatening crisis.

vision A long-term strategy for attaining a goal or goals.

vision statement A formal articulation of an organization's vision or mission.

The transformational leadership of Cisco CEO John Chambers has helped grow the company into the top global designer and maker of networking equipment, with record worldwide sales of US$46 billion a year. Chambers communicates his visionary strategy to employees, encourages them to be creative, and empowers them to make decisions.

People are especially receptive to charismatic leadership when they sense a crisis, when they are under stress, or when they fear for their lives. Charismatic leaders are able to reduce stress for their employees, perhaps because they help make work seem more meaningful and interesting.[48] Some people's personalities are especially susceptible to charismatic leadership.[49] Consider self-esteem. If a person lacks self-esteem and questions his or her self-worth, that person is more likely to absorb a leader's direction rather than establish his or her own way of leading or thinking.

A recent study found that it is possible for a person to learn how to communicate charismatically, which would then lead that person to be perceived more as a leader. People who are perceived to be charismatic show empathy, enthusiasm, and self-confidence; have good speaking and listening skills; and make eye contact.[50] To learn more about how to be charismatic yourself, see the *Experiential Exercise* on page 407.

The Dark Side of Charismatic Leadership

When organizations are in need of great change, charismatic leaders are often able to inspire their followers to meet the challenges of change. Be aware that a charismatic leader may become a liability to an organization once the crisis is over and the need for dramatic change subsides.[51] Why? Because then the charismatic leader's overwhelming self-confidence can be a disadvantage. He or she is unable to listen to others, becomes uncomfortable when challenged by aggressive employees, and begins to hold an unjustifiable belief in his or her "rightness" on issues. Some would argue that Toronto mayor Rob Ford's refusal to step down as mayor after incriminating evidence of drug use materialized would fit this description.

Charismatic leadership, by its very nature, silences criticism. Thus, employees follow the lead of their visionary CEOs unquestioningly. Professor David Leighton, of the Richard Ivey School of Business at the University of Western Ontario, notes that even boards of directors and auditors are reluctant to challenge these CEOs. He finds that Canada's "more balanced culture" is less likely to turn CEOs into heroes.[52]

A study of 29 companies that went from good to great (their cumulative stock returns were all at least three times better than the general stock market over 15 years) found that a key difference in successful charismatic leaders may be the *absence* of being ego-driven.[53] Although the leaders of these firms were fiercely ambitious and driven, their ambition was directed toward their company rather than themselves. They took responsibility for mistakes and poor results but gave credit for successes to other people. These individuals are called level 5 leaders because they have four basic leadership qualities—individual capability, team skills, managerial competence, and the ability to stimulate others to high performance—plus a fifth quality: a paradoxical blend of personal humility and professional will. **Level 5 leaders** channel their ego needs away from themselves and into the goal of building a great company while getting little notoriety in the business press.

Transformational Leadership

👁 Watch on MyManagementLab

Leading

A stream of research has focused on differentiating transformational from transactional leaders.[54] The Ohio and Michigan State studies, the Fiedler contingency model, and path-goal theory describe **transactional leaders**—those who guide their followers toward established goals by clarifying role and task requirements. **Transformational leaders** inspire followers to transcend their self-interests for the good of the organization, and can have an extraordinary effect on their followers.[55] Richard Branson of the Virgin Group is a good example of a transformational leader. He pays attention to the concerns and developmental needs of individual followers; changes followers' awareness of issues by helping them to look at old problems in new ways; and excites and inspires followers to put out extra effort to achieve group goals. A 2012 study suggests that transformational leaders are most effective when their followers are able to see the positive impact of their work through direct interaction with customers or other beneficiaries.[56] Exhibit 11-5 briefly identifies and defines the characteristics that differentiate transactional from transformational leaders.

level 5 leaders Leaders who are fiercely ambitious and driven, but their ambition is directed toward their company rather than themselves.

transactional leaders Leaders who guide or motivate their followers in the direction of established goals by clarifying role and task requirements.

transformational leaders Leaders who inspire followers to transcend their own self-interests and who are capable of having a profound and extraordinary effect on followers.

Transactional and transformational leadership complement each other; they are not opposing approaches to getting things done.[57] Transformational leadership *builds on* transactional leadership and produces levels of follower effort and performance that go beyond what transactional leadership alone can do. But the reverse is not true. So if you are a good transactional leader but do not have transformational qualities, you will likely only be a mediocre leader. The best leaders are transactional *and* transformational.

EXHIBIT 11-5 Characteristics of Transactional and Transformational Leaders

Transactional Leader

Contingent Reward: Contracts exchange of rewards for effort, promises rewards for good performance, recognizes accomplishments.

Management by Exception (active): Watches and searches for deviations from rules and standards, takes correct action.

Management by Exception (passive): Intervenes only if standards are not met.

Laissez-Faire: Abdicates responsibilities, avoids making decisions.

Transformational Leader

Idealized Influence: Provides vision and sense of mission, instills pride, gains respect and trust.

Inspirational Motivation: Communicates high expectations, uses symbols to focus efforts, expresses important purposes in simple ways.

Intellectual Stimulation: Promotes intelligence, rationality, and careful problem solving.

Individualized Consideration: Gives personal attention, treats each employee individually, coaches, advises.

Source: B. M. Bass, "From Transactional to Transformational Leadership: Learning to Share the Vision," *Organizational Dynamics,* Winter 1990, p. 22. Copyright © Elsevier.

EXHIBIT 11-6 Full Range of Leadership Model

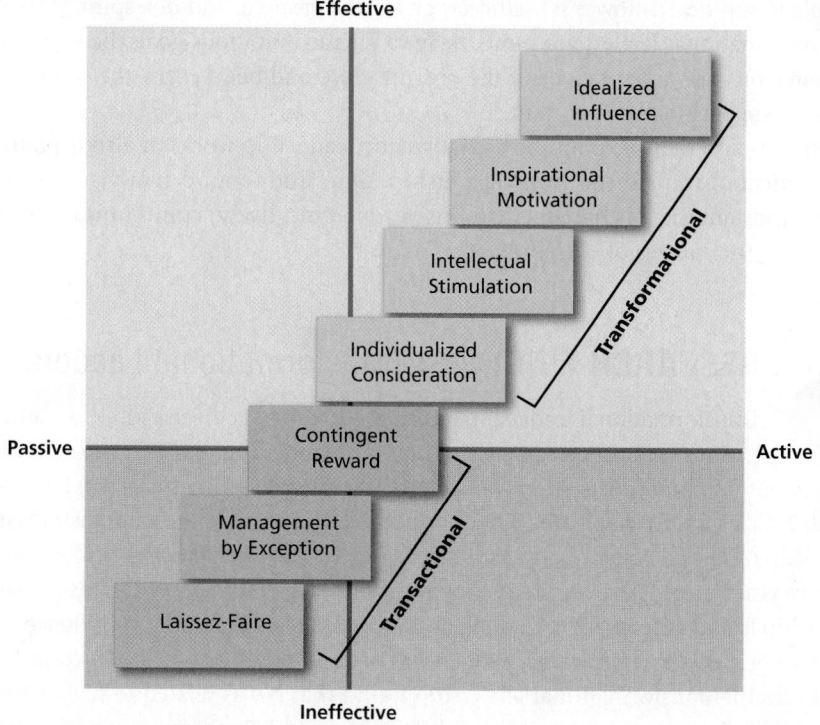

Full Range of Leadership Model

Exhibit 11-6 shows the full range of leadership model. Laissez-faire is the most passive and therefore the least effective of the leader behaviours.[58] Management by exception—active or passive—is slightly better than laissez-faire, but it's still considered ineffective. Management by exception leaders tend to be available only when there is a problem, which is often too late. Contingent reward leadership can be an effective style of leadership, but will not get employees to go above and beyond the call of duty.

Only with the four remaining leadership styles—all aspects of transformational leadership—are leaders able to motivate followers to perform above expectations and transcend their own self-interest for the sake of the organization. Individualized consideration, intellectual stimulation, inspirational motivation, and idealized influence (known as the "four *I*'s") all result in extra effort from employees, higher productivity, higher morale and satisfaction, higher organizational effectiveness, lower turnover, lower absenteeism, and greater organizational adaptability. Based on this model, leaders are generally most effective when they regularly use each of the four *I*'s.

How Transformational Leadership Works

Transformational leaders are more effective because they themselves are more creative and also because they encourage those who follow them to be creative, too.[59] In companies with transformational leaders, there is greater decentralization of responsibility, managers have more propensity to take risks, and compensation plans are geared toward long-term results, all of which facilitate corporate entrepreneurship.[60] One study of information technology workers in China found empowering leadership behaviour led to feelings of positive personal control among workers, which increased their creativity at work.[61] Another recent study indicated that abusive supervisors negatively affect creativity, not for just their direct reports but for entire teams.[62]

Companies with transformational leaders show greater agreement among top managers about the organization's goals, which yields superior organizational performance.[63] The

Israeli military have seen similar results, showing that transformational leaders improve performance by building consensus among group members.[64] Transformational leaders are able to increase follower self-efficacy, giving the group a "can do" spirit.[65] Followers of transformational leaders are more likely to pursue ambitious goals, be familiar with and agree on the strategic goals of the organization, and believe that the goals they are pursuing are personally important.[66]

Just as vision helps explain how charismatic leadership works, it also explains part of the effect of transformational leadership. One study found that vision was even more important than a charismatic (effusive, dynamic, lively) communication style in explaining the success of entrepreneurial firms.[67]

RESEARCH FINDINGS: Transformational Leadership

Transformational leadership has been supported at diverse job levels and occupations (school principals, marine commanders, ministers, presidents of MBA associations, military cadets, union shop stewards, schoolteachers, sales reps). One study of R & D firms found that teams whose project leaders scored high on transformational leadership produced better-quality products as judged one year later and were more profitable five years later.[68] Another study looking at employee creativity and transformational leadership found employees with transformational leaders had more confidence in their ability to be creative at work and higher levels of creative performance.[69] A review of 117 studies testing transformational leadership found that it was related to higher levels of individual follower performance, team performance, and organizational performance.[70]

Transformational leadership is not equally effective in all situations, however. It has a greater impact on the bottom line in smaller, privately held firms than in more complex organizations.[71] Transformational leadership may be more effective when leaders can directly interact with the workforce to make decisions than when they report to an external board of directors or deal with a complex bureaucratic structure. One study showed transformational leaders were more effective in improving group potency in teams higher in power distance and collectivism.[72]

A 2014 study also distinguished between an individual employee's perception of leadership behaviours and the collective perception shared by a group of followers. The researchers found that transformative leadership consistently increased the number of organizational citizenship behaviours engaged in by employees. That effect was significantly stronger when the group as a whole agreed that the leader's behaviours were empowering. If only some individuals felt empowered, the positive impact was lessened considerably.[73]

Transformational leadership theory is not perfect. There are concerns about whether contingent reward leadership is strictly a characteristic of transactional leaders only. And contrary to the full range of leadership model, the 4 *I*'s in transformational leadership are not always superior in effectiveness to transactional leadership (contingent reward leadership sometimes works as well as transformational leadership).

In summary, transformational leadership is more strongly correlated than transactional leadership with lower turnover rates, higher productivity, lower employee stress and burnout, and higher employee satisfaction.[74] Like charisma, it can be learned. One study of Canadian bank managers found that branches managed by those who underwent transformational leadership training performed significantly better than branches whose managers did not receive training.[75]

The Global Leadership and Organizational Behavior Effectiveness (GLOBE) research program—of 825 organizations in 62 countries—that we discussed in Chapter 3 links a number of elements of transformational leadership with effective leadership, regardless of country.[76] This conclusion is very important because it disputes the contingency view that leadership style needs to adapt to cultural differences.

What elements of transformational leadership appear universal? Vision, foresight, providing encouragement, trustworthiness, dynamism, positiveness, and proactiveness top the list. The GLOBE team concluded that "effective business leaders in any country are expected by their subordinates to provide a powerful and proactive vision to guide the company into the future, strong motivational skills to stimulate all employees to fulfill the vision, and excellent planning skills to assist in implementing the vision."[77] A vision is important in any culture, but the way it is formed and communicated may need to be adapted.

Contemporary Leadership Roles

Mentoring is an important aspect of leadership.[78] Chief Bryce Williams has always been happy to learn from others. In fact, it's part of what makes him a strong leader despite his youth. His grandfather had been a chief and his father had sat on council, so Williams was exposed to the political life early on. He also sat on the executive council for three years before running for chief. The mentoring and learning process did not end with his election. He still pays close attention to the opinions of his executive council, and he shares decision-making authority with his Tsawwassen First Nation legislative assembly, which is made up of 12 legislators and the chief. The legislative assembly meets at regular sessions, which are held over several weeks once or twice a year. Steven Stark observes that "we have a very unique team standing behind Bryce. He is young, but we knew that when we elected him. A lot of us talked about it, that Bryce isn't the only one that makes all the decisions." What can formal leaders do to help foster self-directed leadership in others?

> **6** Identify the leadership roles available to nonmanagers.

Transformational leadership theory focuses on heroic leaders, leaders at the top echelons of the organization, and also on individuals rather than teams. However, the notion of "leader at the top" does not adequately reflect what is happening in some workplaces today, where there is less hierarchy and more connections, both inside and outside of the organization. There is a need for more "distributed leadership." In this form, leadership is "distributed across many players, both within and across organizations, up and down the hierarchy, wherever information, expertise, vision, and new ways of working together reside."[79]

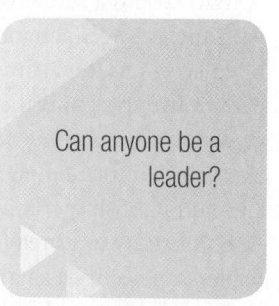

Can anyone be a leader?

The following sections aim to explain how leadership can be spread throughout the organization through mentoring, self-leadership, team leadership, online leadership, and leading without authority. Even if you are not a manager or someone thinking about leadership in a corporate situation, this discussion offers important insights into how you can take on a leadership role in an organization.

P I A

PERSONAL INVENTORY ASSESSMENT

Learn About Yourself
Personal Assessment of Management Skills

Mentoring

Many leaders take responsibility for developing future leaders through mentoring relationships. A **mentor** is a senior employee who sponsors and supports a less-experienced employee (a protégé). The mentoring role includes coaching, counselling, and sponsorship to help protégés develop skills, to provide support and help bolster protégés' self-confidence, and to lobby so that protégés get good assignments, promotions, and salary increases.[80] Successful mentors are good teachers. They present ideas clearly, listen well, and empathize with protégés' problems.

Traditional informal mentoring relationships develop when leaders identify a less experienced, lower-level employee who appears to have potential for future development.[81] The protégé will often be tested with a particularly challenging assignment. If he or she performs acceptably, the mentor will develop the relationship, informally

mentor A senior employee who sponsors and supports a less-experienced employee.

Ed Clark (right), who stepped down as CEO of TD Bank in October 2014, spotted something in Bharat Masrani (left) the first time he met him in 2002. Clark soon became Masrani's mentor and champion, providing him with a variety of career opportunities. The mentoring paid off, as Masrani became Clark's successor.

showing the protégé how the organization *really* works outside its formal structures and procedures.

Why would a leader want to be a mentor?[82] Many feel they have something to share with the younger generation and want to provide a legacy. Mentoring provides unfiltered access to the attitudes of employees, and protégés can be an excellent source of early warning signals that identify potential organizational problems.

Are all employees in an organization equally likely to participate in a mentoring relationship? Unfortunately, no.[83] However, research continues to indicate that employers should establish mentoring programs because they benefit both mentors and protégés. A recent study in Korea found that mentors achieved higher levels of transformational leadership abilities as a result of the process, while organizational commitment and well-being increased for both mentors and protégés.[84]

Although begun with the best intentions, these formal relationships are not as effective as informal ones.[85] Poor planning and design tend to be the reason. Mentor commitment is critical to a program's effectiveness; mentors must see the relationship as beneficial to themselves and the protégé. The protégé, too, must feel he or she has input into the relationship; someone who feels that it's foisted on him or her will just go through the motions.[86] Formal mentoring programs are also most likely to succeed if they appropriately match the work style, needs, and skills of protégé and mentor.[87]

You might assume that mentoring is valuable for objective outcomes such as compensation and job performance, but the research suggests the gains are primarily psychological. Research indicates that while mentoring can have an impact on career success, it's not as much of a contributing factor as ability and personality. It may *feel* nice to have a mentor, but it does not appear that having a mentor, or even having a good mentor who provides both support and advice, is critical to one's career. Mentors may be effective not because of the functions they provide but because of the resources they can obtain: A mentor connected to a powerful network can build relationships that will help the protégé advance. Network ties, whether built through a mentor or not, are a significant predictor of career success.[88] If a mentor is not well connected or not a very strong performer, the best mentoring advice in the world will not be very beneficial.

Self-Leadership (or Self-Management)

A growing trend in organizations is the focus on self-leadership, or self-management, where individuals and teams set goals, plan and implement tasks, evaluate performance, solve their own problems, and motivate themselves.[89] (Recall our discussion of self-managed teams in Chapter 6.)

Reduced levels of supervision, offices in the home, teamwork, and growth in service and professional employment have increased the demand for self-leadership. Self-management can also be a substitute or neutralizer for leadership from others.

Despite the lack of studies of self-management techniques in organizational settings, self-management strategies have been shown to be successful in nonorganizational settings.[91] Those who practise self-management look for opportunities to be more effective in the workplace and improve their career success and provide their own sense of reward and feedback after carrying out their accomplishments. Moreover, self-reinforced behaviour is often maintained at a higher rate than behaviour that is externally regulated.[92] *OB in Action—Engaging in Self-Leadership* indicates ways in which you can practise effective self-leadership.

How do leaders create self-leaders? The following approaches have been suggested:[93]

- *Model self-leadership.* Practise self-observation, setting challenging personal goals, self-direction, and self-reinforcement. Then display these behaviours, and encourage others to rehearse and then produce them.

- *Encourage employees to create self-set goals.* Support employees in developing quantitative, specific goals; having such goals is the most important part of self-leadership.

- *Encourage the use of self-rewards to strengthen and increase desirable behaviours.* By contrast, limit self-punishment only to occasions when the employee has been dishonest or destructive.

- *Create positive thought patterns.* Encourage employees to use mental imagery and self-talk to further stimulate self-motivation.

- *Create a climate of self-leadership.* Redesign the work to increase the natural rewards of a job and focus on these naturally rewarding features of work to increase motivation.

- *Encourage self-criticism.* Encourage individuals to be critical of their own performance.

The underlying assumptions behind self-leadership are that people are responsible, capable, and able to exercise initiative without the external constraints of bosses, rules, or regulations. Given the proper support, individuals can monitor and control their own behaviour.

Team Leadership

Leadership is increasingly taking place within a team context. As teams grow in popularity, the role of the leader in guiding team members takes on heightened importance.[94]

OB IN ACTION
Engaging in Self-Leadership

To engage in effective self-leadership:[90]

→ **Think horizontally, not vertically.** Vertical relationships in the organization matter, but peers can become trusted colleagues and have a great impact on your work.

→ Focus on **influence, not control.** Work with your colleagues, not for them. Be collaborative and share credit.

→ **Create opportunities**, don't wait for them. Rather than look for the right time, be more action oriented.

How do you manage yourself?

▣ Watch on **MyManagementLab**

The Work Zone Role Plays— Leadership

Also, because of its more collaborative nature, the role of team leader is different from the traditional leadership role performed by first-line supervisors.

Many leaders are not equipped to handle the change to team leader. As one prominent consultant noted, "Even the most capable managers have trouble making the transition because all the command-and-control type things they were encouraged to do before are no longer appropriate. There's no reason to have any skill or sense of this."[95] This same consultant estimated that "probably 15 percent of managers are natural team leaders; another 15 percent could never lead a team because it runs counter to their personality. [They are unable to sublimate their dominating style for the good of the team.] Then there's that huge group in the middle: team leadership doesn't come naturally to them, but they can learn it."[96]

Effective team leaders need to build commitment and confidence, remove obstacles, create opportunities, and be part of the team.[97] They have to learn skills such as the patience to share information, the willingness to trust others, the ability to give up authority, and an understanding of when to intervene. New team leaders may try to retain too much control at a time when team members need more autonomy, or they may abandon their teams at times when the teams need support and help.[98]

Roles of Team Leaders

A study of 20 organizations that reorganized themselves around teams found certain common responsibilities that all leaders had to assume. These included coaching, facilitating, training, communicating, handling disciplinary problems, and reviewing team/individual performance.[99] Many of these responsibilities apply to managers in general. A more meaningful way to describe the team leader's job is to focus on two priorities: managing the team's external boundary and facilitating the team process.[100] We have divided these priorities into four specific roles that team leaders play:

- *Liaisons with external constituencies.* Outsiders include upper management, other internal teams, customers, and suppliers. The leader represents the team to other constituencies, secures needed resources, clarifies others' expectations of the team, gathers information from the outside, and shares this information with team members.

- *Troubleshooters.* When the team has problems and asks for assistance, team leaders sit in on meetings and try to help resolve the problems. This rarely relates to technical or operational issues because the team members typically know more about the tasks being done than does the team leader. The leader contributes by asking penetrating questions, by helping the team discuss problems, and by getting needed resources from external constituencies. For instance, when a team in an aerospace firm found itself short-handed, its team leader took responsibility for getting more staff. He presented the team's case to upper management and got the approval through the company's human resources department.

- *Conflict managers.* When disagreements surface, team leaders help process the conflict. What is the source of the conflict? Who is involved? What are the issues? What resolution options are available? What are the advantages and disadvantages of each? By getting team members to address questions such as these, the leader minimizes the disruptive aspects of intrateam conflicts.

- *Coaches.* They clarify expectations and roles, teach, offer support, cheerlead, and do whatever else is necessary to help team members improve their work performance.

Online Leadership

How do you lead people who are physically separated from you and with whom you communicate electronically? This question needs attention from OB researchers.[101]

Today's managers and their employees are increasingly being linked by networks rather than geographical proximity. We propose that online leaders have to think carefully about what actions they want their digital messages to initiate. They confront unique challenges, the greatest of which appears to be developing and maintaining trust. **Identification-based trust**, based on a mutual understanding of each other's intentions and appreciation of the other person's wants and desires, is particularly difficult to achieve without face-to-face interaction.[102] Online negotiations can also be hindered because parties express lower levels of trust.[103]

Good leadership skills will soon include the ability to communicate support, trust, and inspiration through electronic communication and to accurately read emotions in others' messages. In electronic communication, writing skills are likely to become an extension of interpersonal skills.

Leading without Authority

Can you lead, even if you don't have the authority (or a formal appointment)? For instance, what if you wanted to convince the dean to introduce more relevant business courses, or you wanted to convince the president of the company where you work to use more environmentally friendly strategies in dealing with waste? How do you effectively lead in a student group, when everyone is a peer?

Leadership at the grassroots level does happen. Rosabeth Moss Kanter, in her book *The Change Masters*,[104] discusses examples of employees who saw something that needed changing and took on the responsibility to do so. Employees were more likely to do this when organizations permitted initiative at all levels of the organization, rather than making it a tool of senior executives only.

Leading without authority means exhibiting leadership behaviour even though you do not have a formal position or title. Neither Martin Luther King Jr. nor Nelson Mandela operated from a position of authority, yet each was able to inspire many to follow him in the quest for social justice. The workplace can be an opportunity for leading without authority as well. As Ronald Heifetz of the Harvard Kennedy School notes, "Leadership means taking responsibility for hard problems beyond anyone's expectations."[105] It also means not waiting for the coach's call.[106]

What are the benefits of leading without authority? Heifetz has identified three:[107]

- *Latitude for creative deviance.* It's easier to raise harder questions and look for less traditional solutions when a person is not locked into the trappings that go with authority.

- *Issue focus.* Individuals can focus on a single issue, rather than be concerned with the myriad issues that those in authority face.

- *Front-line information.* An individual is closer to the detailed experiences of some of the stakeholders and thus, more information is available.

Not all organizations support this type of leadership, and some have been known to actively suppress it. Still, you may want to reflect on the possibility of engaging in leadership behaviour because you see a need, rather than because you are required to act.

Contemporary Issues in Leadership

As an Aboriginal leader, Bryce Williams appreciates the need to be an authentic voice for his First Nation.[108] Steven Stark, a member of the legislature, notes that Williams' commitment to economic development does not undermine his enduring commitment to supporting Tsawwassen First Nation (TFN) culture. Stark is very blunt in his assessment of the need for authenticity. "You could talk white language all day long and sound very sophisticated, but if you don't have that native culture behind you and talk with the native tongue, you're not going

identification-based trust Trust based on a mutual understanding of each other's intentions and appreciation of each other's wants and desires.

to get very far." Stark had heard previous leaders talk about the importance of culture without following through. Williams came in and centred his election platform on cultural revitalization, and his cultural ties and commitment were the deciding factors for many TFN members. How important is authentic leadership?

What is authentic leadership? Is there an ethical dimension to leadership? What is servant leadership? In this section, we briefly address these contemporary issues in leadership.

Authentic Leadership

7 Define *authentic leadership*.

Campbell Soup's CEO Denise Morrison decided to lower sodium in the company's soup products simply because it was the right thing to do.[109] Kathleen Taylor, chair of the Royal Bank of Canada (RBC), believes that being a successful leader requires being authentic: "authentic leaders build meaningful relationships that yield far better results than command and control of the past."[110]

Authentic leaders know who they are, know what they believe in and value, and act on those values and beliefs openly and candidly. Their followers consider them to be ethical people. The primary quality produced by authentic leadership is trust. Authentic leaders share information, encourage open communication, and stick to their ideals. The result: People come to have faith in them.

There has been limited research on authentic leadership to date. However, recent research indicates that authentic leadership, especially when shared among top management team members, can create a positive energizing effect that heightened firm performance.[111] Authentic leadership is a promising way to think about ethics and trust in leadership because it focuses on the moral aspects of being a leader. Transformational or charismatic leaders can have a vision and communicate it persuasively, but sometimes the vision is wrong (as in the case of Hitler), or the leader is more concerned with his own needs or pleasures, as in the case of former Toronto mayor, Rob Ford.[112]

authentic leaders Leaders who know who they are, know what they believe in and value, and act on these values and beliefs openly and candidly. Their followers could consider them to be ethical people.

Ton Koene/ZUMA Press/Newscom

Entrepreneur Grace Liu (third from the right, in the first row) is an authentic leader. Shown here with her employees, Liu is co-founder and managing director of Asianera, a maker of hand-painted bone china. She built her successful business of high-quality porcelain and innovative design based on her strong personal core values of respecting the individual and operating with integrity.

Ethical Leadership

Researchers have begun to study the ethical implications in leadership.[113] Why now? One reason may be the growing interest in ethics throughout the field of management. Another reason may be that ethical lapses by business leaders are never absent from the headlines. Another may be the discovery that many past leaders—such as Martin Luther King Jr. and John F. Kennedy—suffered ethical shortcomings. Another reason may be the growing realization that although every member of an organization is responsible for ethical behaviour, many initiatives aimed at increasing organizational ethical behaviour are focused on the leaders. The role of the leader in creating the ethical expectations for all members is crucial.[114] A recent study of 2572 US Army soldiers underscored that ethical top leadership influences not only direct followers but also all organizational levels, because these top leaders create an ethical culture and expect lower-level leaders to behave along ethical guidelines.[115]

Ethics and leadership intersect in a number of ways. Transformational leadership has ethical implications since these leaders change the way followers think. Charisma, too, has an ethical component. Unethical leaders use their charisma to enhance power over followers, directed toward self-serving ends. Leaders who treat their followers with fairness, especially by providing honest, frequent, and accurate information, are seen as more effective.[116] Related to this is the concept of humbleness, another characteristic ethical leaders often exhibit as part of being authentic. Research indicates that leaders who model humility help followers to understand the growth process for their own development.[117] Leaders rated as highly ethical tend to have followers who engage in more organizational citizenship behaviours and who are more willing to bring problems to the leaders' attention.[118] Recent research also found that ethical leadership reduced interpersonal conflicts.[119]

Because top executives set the moral tone for an organization, they need to set high ethical standards, demonstrate them through their own behaviour, and encourage and reward integrity in others while avoiding abuses of power such as giving themselves large raises and bonuses while laying off employees. A recent research review found that role modelling by top leaders positively influenced managers throughout their organizations to behave ethically and fostered a climate that reinforced group-level ethical conduct. The findings suggest that organizations should invest in ethical leadership training programs, especially in industries with few ethical regulations. The researchers furthermore advised that ethical leadership training programs to teach cultural values should be mandated for leaders who take foreign assignments or manage multicultural work teams.[120]

For ethical leadership to be effective, it's not enough for the leader to simply possess high moral character. After all, no universal standard for ethical behaviour exists, and ethical norms vary by culture, by industry, and even sometimes within an organization. Leaders must be willing to express their ethical beliefs and persuade others to follow their standards. Followers must believe in both the leader and the overlying principles, even if they don't personally agree with every minor stance.

Leadership is not value-free. In assessing its effectiveness we need to address the *means* that a leader uses in trying to achieve goals, as well as the content of those goals. Scholars have tried to integrate ethical and charismatic leadership by advancing the idea of **socialized charismatic leadership**—leadership that conveys other-centred (not self-centred) values and models ethical conduct.[121] Socialized charismatic leaders are able to bring employee values in line with their own values through their words and actions.[122]

One researcher suggests that there are four cornerstones to a "moral foundation of leadership":[123]

- *Truth telling.* Leaders who tell the truth as they see it allow for a mutual, fair exchange to occur.

8 Discuss the requirements of ethical leadership.

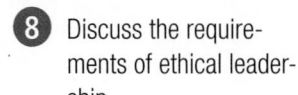

PERSONAL INVENTORY ASSESSMENT

Learn About Yourself
Ethical Leadership Assessment

socialized charismatic leadership Leadership that conveys values that are other-centred vs. self-centred and models ethical conduct.

Arthur Mola/AP Images

Craig Kielburger was just 12 years old when he read about a young Pakistani boy of the same age who was murdered while engaged in child labour, and rallied his classmates to become involved in stopping the practice. This work eventually led to the creation of Free The Children, an organization that now operates in 45 countries, trying to reduce the use of child labour. Kielburger is an example of someone showing ethical leadership at a very early age.

- *Promise keeping.* Leaders need to be careful of the commitments they make, and then careful of keeping those commitments.

- *Fairness.* Leaders who are equitable ensure that followers get their fair share for their contributions to the organization.

- *Respect for the individual.* Leaders who tell the truth, keep promises, and are fair show respect for followers. Respect means treating people with dignity.

Moral leadership comes from within the individual, and in general means treating people well, and with respect.

Do you think it would be ethical for a leader to go undercover in his or her organization to see how employees performed? The *Ethical Dilemma* on page 407 considers this question.

Servant Leadership

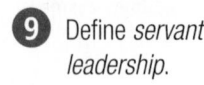

9 Define *servant leadership.*

Scholars have recently considered ethical leadership from a new angle by examining **servant leadership**.[124] Servant leaders go beyond their self-interest and focus on opportunities to help followers grow and develop. They don't use power to achieve ends; they emphasize persuasion. Characteristic behaviours include listening, empathizing, persuading, accepting stewardship, and actively developing followers' potential. A recent study of 126 CEOs found that servant leadership is negatively correlated with the trait of narcissism.[125] Because servant leadership focuses on serving the needs of others, research has focused on its outcomes for the well-being of followers.

What are the effects of servant leadership? One study of 123 supervisors found it resulted in higher levels of commitment to the supervisor, self-efficacy, and perceptions of justice, which all were related to organizational citizenship behaviour (OCB).[126] This relationship between servant leadership and follower OCB appears to be stronger

servant leadership A leadership style marked by going beyond the leader's own self-interest and instead focusing on opportunities to help followers grow and develop.

when followers are focused on being dutiful and responsible.[127] Second, servant leadership increases team potency (a belief that one's team has above-average skills and abilities), which in turn leads to higher levels of group performance.[128] Third, a study with a nationally representative sample found higher levels of OCB associated with a focus on growth and advancement, which in turn was associated with higher levels of creative performance.[129]

GLOBAL IMPLICATIONS

Most of the research discussed in this chapter was conducted in English-speaking countries. We know very little about how culture might influence the validity of the theories, particularly in Eastern cultures. However, a recent analysis of the GLOBE research program (see Chapter 3 for more details) has produced some useful preliminary insights about how to manage in Brazil, France, Egypt, and China.[130] Let's consider each.

- *Brazil.* Based on the values of Brazilian employees, a manager leading a team in Brazil would need to be team oriented, participative, and humane. Leaders high on consideration who emphasize participative decision making and have high LPC scores would be best suited to managing employees in this culture. As one Brazilian manager said in the study, "We do not prefer leaders who take self-governing decisions and act alone without engaging the group. That's part of who we are."

- *France.* French employees have a more bureaucratic view of leaders and are less likely to expect them to be humane and considerate than Canadian and American employees. A leader high on initiating structure (relatively task oriented) will do best and can make decisions in a relatively autocratic manner. A manager who scores high on consideration (people oriented) may find that style backfiring in France.

- *Egypt.* Employees in Egypt are more likely to value team-oriented and participative leadership than Canadian and American employees. However, Egypt is also a relatively high-power-distance culture, meaning status differences between leaders and followers are expected. To be participative yet demonstrate one's status, the leader should ask employees for their opinions, try to minimize conflicts, and not be afraid to take charge and make the final decision (after consulting team members).

- *China.* According to the GLOBE study, Chinese culture emphasizes being polite, considerate, and unselfish, but it also has a high performance orientation. These two factors suggest consideration and initiating structure may both be important. Although Chinese culture is relatively participative compared with the cultures of Canada and the United States, there are also status differences between leaders and employees. These findings suggest that a moderately participative style may work best with Chinese employees.

While the idea of charismatic leadership was developed based on North American observations, professors Dale Carl of the Faculty of Management at Ryerson University and Mansour Javidan at the Thunderbird School of Global Management in Arizona found that transformational leadership is expressed relatively similarly in a variety of countries, including Canada, Hungary, India, Turkey, Austria, Singapore, Sweden, and Venezuela. The transformational leadership traits that appear to be universal are vision, foresight, providing encouragement, trustworthiness, dynamism, positiveness, and proactiveness. The two concluded that "effective business leaders in any country are expected by their subordinates to provide a powerful and proactive vision to guide the company into the future, strong motivational skills to stimulate all employees to fulfill the vision, and excellent planning skills to assist in implementing the vision."[131]

A vision is important in any culture, then, but how it's formed and communicated may still need to vary by culture. A GE executive who used his US leadership style in Japan recalls, "Nothing happened. I quickly realized that I had to adapt my approach, to act more as a consultant to my colleagues and to adopt a team-based motivational decision-making process rather than the more vocal style which tends to be common in the West. In Japan the silence of a leader means far more than a thousand words uttered by somebody else."[132]

Summary

Leadership plays a central part in understanding group behaviour because it's the leader who usually directs us toward our goals. Knowing what makes a good leader should thus be valuable in improving group performance. The early search for a set of universal leadership traits failed. However, recent efforts using the Big Five Personality Model show strong and consistent relationships between leadership and extraversion, conscientiousness, and openness to experience. The behavioural approach's major contribution was narrowing leadership into task-oriented (initiating structure) and people-oriented (consideration) styles. By considering the situation in which the leader operates, contingency theories promised to improve on the behavioural approach, but only Fiedler's least preferred co-worker theory has fared well in leadership research. Research on charismatic and transformational leadership has made major contributions to our understanding of leadership effectiveness.

SNAPSHOT SUMMARY

What Is Leadership?

Leadership as Supervision
- Trait Theories: Are Leaders Different from Others?
- Behavioural Theories: Do Leaders Behave in Particular Ways?
- Contingency Theories: Does the Situation Matter?
- Substitutes for Leadership

Inspirational Leadership
- Charismatic Leadership
- Transformational Leadership

Contemporary Leadership Roles
- Mentoring
- Self-Leadership (or Self-Management)
- Team Leadership

- Online Leadership
- Leading without Authority

Contemporary Issues in Leadership
- Authentic Leadership
- Ethical Leadership
- Servant Leadership

OB *at* Work

for **Review**

1. How are leadership and management different from one another?

2. What are the conclusions of trait theories of leadership?

3. What are the central tenets and main limitations of behavioural theories of leadership?

4. What is Fiedler's contingency model? Has it been supported in research?

5. How do charismatic and transformational leadership compare and contrast? Are they valid?

6. What leadership roles are available to nonmanagers?

7. What is authentic leadership?

8. What are the requirements of ethical leadership?

9. What is servant leadership? How does it make a difference in organizations?

for **Managers**

■ For management positions, hire candidates who exhibit transformational leadership qualities and who have demonstrated vision and charisma.

■ Tests and interviews can help you identify people with leadership qualities.

■ Hire candidates whom you believe are ethical and trustworthy for management roles, and train current managers in your organization's ethical standards in order to increase leadership effectiveness.

■ Seek to develop trusting relationships with followers because, as organizations have become less stable and predictable, strong bonds of trust are replacing bureaucratic rules in defining expectations and relationships.

■ Consider investing in leadership training such as formal courses, workshops, rotating job responsibilities, coaching, and mentoring.

for **You**

■ It's easy to imagine that theories of leadership are more important to those who are leaders or who plan in the near future to become leaders. However, leadership opportunities occur throughout an organization. You have no doubt seen a student leader who did not necessarily have any formal authority be extremely successful.

■ Leaders are not born, they learn how to lead by paying attention to the situation and what needs to be done.

■ There is no one best way to lead. It's important to consider the situation and the needs of the people who will be led.

■ Sometimes no leader is needed— the individuals in the group simply work well enough together that each takes turns at leadership without appointing a formal leader.

OB *at* **Work**

Heroes Are Made, Not Born

We often ascribe heroic qualities to our leaders.[133] They are courageous in the face of great risk. They persevere when few would. They take action when most sit by. Heroes are exceptional people who display exceptional behaviour.

But some social psychologists question this conventional wisdom. They note that heroism can be found in many spheres of life, including in the behaviour of whistle-blowers, explorers, religious leaders, scientists, Good Samaritans, and those who beat the odds. At some time in our lives, we all show heroism when the situation allows us to. If we want to see more heroic behaviour, we need to create more situations that produce it.

Stanford psychologist Phil Zimbardo goes even further to argue that our romantic view that heroes are born is misplaced:

> The banality of evil is matched by the banality of heroism. Neither is the consequence of dispositional tendencies … Both emerge in particular situations at particular times, when situational forces play a compelling role in moving individuals across the line from inaction to action.

People exhibit brave behaviour every day. The workers who risked their lives to contain Japan's earthquake-ravaged nuclear reactors in 2011 are a great example. Thus, we err when we think leaders are uniquely positioned to behave heroically. We all can be heroes in the right situation.

Of course heroes are not like everyone else. That is what makes them heroes.

A generation of evidence from behavioural genetics reveals that "everything is genetic," meaning we have yet to discover an important human behaviour that does not have genetic origins. Although we are not aware of any such study with respect to heroism, it would be surprising if courageous behaviour were not at least partly genetic.

It's foolish to think courageous people are not exceptional because of who they are. Just as we know there is an entrepreneurial personality and a leader personality, there is a heroic personality. Research suggests, for example, that people who score high on conscientiousness are more likely to engage in courageous behaviour.

Not all leaders are heroes, but many have exhibited courageous behaviour. CEO Richard Branson may or may not be a hero, but when he launches his latest attempt to set the world record for an around-the-world balloon flight or sloop sailing, he exhibits the same courageous behaviour when he is leading conglomerate Virgin Group. Virgin Group now includes more than 400 companies, including Virgin Galactic, a space tourism company, and Virgin Fuels, whose goal is to revolutionize the industry by providing sustainable fuels for automobiles and aircraft. Same leader, same heroic behaviour—in work and in life.

Are we really to believe that Richard Branson and other courageous leaders are just like everyone else?

PERSONAL **INVENTORY** ASSESSMENT

Leadership Style Indicator: While leadership styles will often need to vary based on the situation, most people have a preference for one style or another. Use this scale to assess your personal leadership style preference.

Personal Assessment of Management Skills: This instrument is designed to assess your proficiency in the use of important personal and interpersonal skills that are relevant for managers.

Ethical Leadership Assessment: Since leaders set the tone for the entire organization, it's especially important that they engage in ethical behaviours. Use this scale to assess your ethical perspective on leadership roles.

BREAKOUT **GROUP** EXERCISES

Form small groups to discuss the following topics, as assigned by your instructor:

1. Identify an example of someone you think of as a good leader (currently or in the past). What traits did he or she have? How did these traits differ from those in someone you identify as a bad leader?

2. Identify a situation when you were in a leadership position (in a group, in the workplace, within your family, etcetera). To what extent were you able to use a contingency approach to leadership? What made that easier or more difficult for you?

3. When you have worked in student groups, how frequently have leaders emerged in the groups? What difficulties occur when leaders are leading peers? Are there ways to overcome these difficulties?

EXPERIENTIAL EXERCISE

Being Charismatic

From Concepts to Skills on pages 410–411 provides ideas on how to become charismatic. In this exercise, you will use that information to practise projecting charisma.[134]

1. The class should break into pairs.

2. Student A's task is to "lead" Student B through a new-student orientation to your college or university. The orientation should last about 10 to 15 minutes. Assume that Student B is new to your college or university and is unfamiliar with the campus. Student A should attempt to project himself or herself as charismatic.

3. Roles now reverse and Student B's task is to "lead" Student A in a 10- to 15-minute program on how to study more effectively for college or university exams. Take a few minutes to think about what has worked well for you, and assume that Student A is a new student interested in improving his or her study habits. Again, Student B should attempt to project himself or herself as charismatic.

4. When both role plays are complete, each pair should assess how well it did in projecting charisma and how it might improve.

ETHICAL **DILEMMA**

Undercover Leaders

The W Network television show *Undercover Boss Canada* features a leader working undercover in his or her own company to find out how the organization really works.[135] Here, we consider the ethical leadership lessons it might offer.

Executives from Mexx Canada, Calgary Transit, Sodexo Canada, and Mr. Lube have been featured on the show. Typically, the executive works undercover for a week. Then the employees with whom and under whom the leader has worked are summoned to company headquarters and rewarded, or punished, for their actions.

In one episode, Andy Clark, the founder and CEO of Edmonton-based Clark Builders, strapped on a tool belt for the first time in 30 years and added a moustache to work beside his employees. He wondered if, at 62 years old, he could keep up. He made a lot of rookie errors, but when he heard about the wife of one of his employees who was quite sick, he called a doctor friend to see if he could help with her cancer and offered to pay the full medical cost for treatment. He said he "just wanted to improve the quality of her life, however much she had left."

Some criticize the show for its faux realism. The CEOs know they are on camera, so every word and facial expression is for the cameras. Many employees know they are on camera, too. One critic commented, "Because the series' very existence requires cooperation from the executives that it purports to make suffer for their sins, it has to raise them higher, in the end, than it found them at the start."

Realistic or not, the series continues to be popular. And the effects on the bosses featured in the episodes—and their employees—are profound.

Lisa Lisson, president of Mississauga-based Fedex Canada, joined her employees on the front line to see how they worked. She says the company "prides itself on providing excellent service to our customers." Commenting on her experience, she said "I am so glad that I did this. I think it's important for presidents of companies to get to know their employees. They give their heart and soul to our company and we need to take time to really get to know who they are and tell them that we care about them. Because we do."

The idea has moved beyond television too. Recently, the Australian government created a program that places CEOs undercover in their own workplaces. One participating CEO, Phil Smith of clothing retailer Fletcher Jones, said tearfully, "I learnt a lot from this that I wouldn't have found out any other way."

Questions

1. Do you think it's ethical for a leader to go undercover in his or her organization? Why or why not?

2. Do you think leaders who work undercover are really changed as a result of their experiences?

3. Would you support a government program that gave companies incentives to send leaders undercover?

CASE INCIDENTS

Moving from Colleague to Supervisor

Cheryl Kahn, Rob Carstons, and Linda McGee have something in common.[136] They all were promoted within their organizations into management positions. As well, each found the transition a challenge.

Kahn was promoted to director of catering for the Glazier Group of restaurants. With the promotion, she realized that things would never be the same again. No longer would she be able to participate in water-cooler gossip or shrug off an employee's chronic lateness. She says she found her new role to be daunting. "At first I was like a bulldozer knocking everyone over, and that was not well received. I was saying, 'It's my way or the highway.' And was forgetting that my friends were also in transition." She admits that this style alienated just about everyone with whom she worked.

Carstons, a technical manager at IBM, talks about the uncertainty he felt after being promoted to a manager from a junior programmer. "It was a little bit challenging to be suddenly giving directives to peers, when just the day before you were one of them. You try to be careful not to offend anyone. It's strange walking into a room and the whole conversation changes. People don't want to be as open with you when you become the boss."

McGee is now president of Medex Insurance Services. She started as a customer-service representative with the company, then leapfrogged over colleagues in a series of promotions. Her fast rise created problems. Colleagues would say, "'Oh, here comes the big cheese now.' God only knows what they talked about behind my back."

Questions

1. A lot of new managers err in selecting the right leadership style when they move into management. Why do you think this happens?

2. If new managers don't know what leadership style to use, what does this say about leadership and leadership training?

3. Which leadership theories, if any, could help new leaders deal with this transition?

4. Do you think it's easier or harder to be promoted internally into a formal leadership position than to come into it as an outsider? Explain.

Leadership by Algorithm

Is there one right way to lead?[137] Research suggests not, the methods explored in this chapter text suggest not, and common sense suggests a "one size fits all" approach could be disastrous because organizations exist for diverse purposes and develop unique cultures. Leadership development programs generally teach a best-practices model, but experts suggest that individuals trained in leadership techniques that are contrary to their own natures risk losing the authenticity crucial to effective leadership. The real path to leadership may lie in algorithms.

If you have ever taken a strengths-based assessment such as the Harrison Assessment or Gallup's Clifton StrengthsFinder, you know that surveys aimed at discovering your personality, skills, and preferences result in a personal profile. This tool is helpful in leadership development, but algorithms can take your leadership development to the next level of personalization and application. They can take the results from each survey you complete, for instance, and use them to create a leadership program that matches your needs and abilities.

As the founder of TMBC and author of *StandOut*, Marcus Buckingham is an expert on creating leadership programs. He recommends the following steps:

Step 1. Find or develop the assessment tools. These might include a personality component, such as a Big Five inventory test, and will include other tests companies can resource or create according to what leadership characteristics they are seeking to monitor.

Step 2. Identify the top leaders in the organization and administer the test to them. Similarities in their profiles may not emerge across the broad spectrum of all top leaders. This step is not to determine what all the leaders have in common, but to group the top leaders into categories by their similar profiles.

Step 3. Interview the leaders within each profile category to learn about the techniques they use that work. Often these will be unique, unscripted, and revealingly correlated to the strengths in their assessment profile. Compile the techniques within each profile category.

Step 4. The results of top leader profile categories and their techniques can be used to create an algorithm, or tailored method, for developing leaders. Administer the assessment tests to developing leaders and determine their profile categories. The techniques from successful leaders can now be shared with the developing leaders who are most like them because they share the same profile category.

These steps provide a means for successful leaders to pass along to developing leaders techniques that are likely to feel authentic to the developing leaders and that encourage creativity. The techniques can be delivered in an ongoing process as short, personalized, interactive, and readily applicable tips and advice, for results no two-week leadership development course could achieve.

Questions

1. If you have participated in leadership development programs, how effective did you find them in (a) teaching you techniques and (b) giving you practical strategies you could use? What could they do better?

2. What are some potential negatives of using Buckingham's approach to leadership development?

3. Would you suggest applying Buckingham's steps to an organization in which you have worked? Why or why not?

FROM CONCEPTS TO SKILLS

Practising to Be Charismatic

In order to be charismatic in your leadership style, you need to engage in the following behaviours:[138]

1. *Project a powerful, confident, and dynamic presence.* This has both verbal and nonverbal components. Use a captivating and engaging voice tone. Convey confidence. Talk directly to people, maintain direct eye contact, and hold your body posture in a way that says you are sure of yourself. Speak clearly, avoid stammering, and avoid sprinkling your sentences with noncontent phrases such as "ahhh" and "you know."

2. *Articulate an overarching goal.* You need to share a vision for the future, develop an unconventional way of achieving the vision, and have the ability to communicate the vision to others.

   The vision is a clear statement of where you want to go and how you are going to get there. You need to persuade others that the achievement of this vision is in their self-interest.

   You need to look for fresh and radically different approaches to problems. The road to achieving your vision should be seen as novel, but also appropriate to the context.

   Charismatic individuals not only have a vision, but they are also able to get others to buy into it. The real power of Martin Luther King Jr. was not that he had a dream, but that he could articulate it in terms that made it accessible to millions.

3. *Communicate high performance expectations and confidence in others' ability to meet these expectations.* You need to demonstrate your confidence in people by stating ambitious goals for them individually and as a group. You then convey absolute belief that they will achieve their expectations.

4. *Be sensitive to the needs of followers.* Charismatic leaders get to know their followers individually. You need to understand their individual needs and develop intensely personal relationships with each. This is done through encouraging followers to express their points of view, being approachable, genuinely listening to and caring about followers' concerns, and asking questions so that followers can learn what is really important to them.

Practising Skills

You are a manufacturing manager in a large electronics plant.[139] The company's management is always searching for ways to increase efficiency. They recently installed new machines and set up a new simplified work system, but to the surprise of everyone—including you—the expected increase in production was not realized. In fact, production has begun to drop, quality has fallen off, and the number of employee resignations has risen.

You do not think that there is anything wrong with the machines. You have had reports from other companies that are using them, and they confirm your opinion. You have also had representatives from the firm that built the machines go over them, and they report that the machines are operating at peak efficiency.

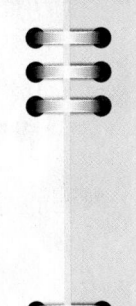

You know that some aspect of the new work system must be responsible for the change, but you are getting no help from your immediate team members—four first-line supervisors who report to you and who are each in charge of a section—or your supply manager. The drop in production has been variously attributed to poor training of the operators, lack of an adequate system of financial incentives, and poor morale. All of the individuals involved have deep feelings about this issue. Your team does not agree with you or with one another.

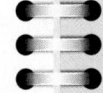

This morning you received a phone call from your division manager. He had just received your production figures for the past six months and was calling to express his concern. He indicated that the problem was yours to solve in any way that you think best, but that he would like to know within a week what steps you plan to take.

You share your division manager's concern with the falling productivity and know that your employees are also concerned. Using your knowledge of leadership concepts, which leadership style would you choose? And why?

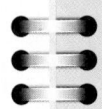

1. Think of a group or team to which you currently belong or of which you have been a part. What type of leadership style did the leader of this group appear to exhibit? Give some specific examples of the types of leadership behaviours he or she used. Evaluate the leadership style. Was it appropriate for the group? Why or why not? What would you have done differently? Why?

2. Observe two sports teams (either college/university or professional—one that you consider successful and the other unsuccessful). What leadership styles appear to be used in these team situations? Give some specific examples of the types of leadership behaviours you observe. How would you evaluate the leadership style? Was it appropriate for the team? Why or why not? To what degree do you think leadership style influenced the team's outcomes?

Reinforcing Skills

OB *at* **Work**

12 Decision Making, Creativity, and Ethics

A military veteran suffered discrimination by three police officers due to their poor decision making. How can people avoid common decision pitfalls and make good decisions?

LEARNING OUTCOMES

After studying this chapter, you should be able to:

1. Contrast the rational model of decision making with bounded rationality and intuition.

2. Describe common decision biases and errors.

3. Contrast the strengths and weaknesses of group decision making.

4. Compare the effectiveness of interacting, brainstorming, and the nominal group technique.

5. Define *creativity*, and describe the three-stage model of creativity.

6. Describe the four criteria used in making ethical decisions.

7. Define *corporate social responsibility*.

O n April 16, 2011, Billy-Joe Nachuk, a decorated military veteran suffering from posttraumatic stress disorder, made a courageous decision to socialize at the Keystone Motor Inn's restaurant and bar in Brandon, Manitoba.[1] Suffering from anxiety, he had avoided public spaces for two years, but now he had Gambler, a service dog trained to help him manage his symptoms. Despite explanations and the provision of official service dog certification papers, Keystone management complained about the presence of the dog to three on-duty police officers who were at the restaurant. One of the officers asked Nachuk about the dog, and he explained that it was a service dog. Because Nachuk was not blind, the officer did not believe

CBC News

Nachuk needed the dog. Despite further attempts by Nachuk to explain why he had a service dog, the officers would not listen and escorted him out of the bar.

Nachuk filed a human rights complaint for discrimination based on disability as a result of this incident. In April 2014, the Manitoba Human Rights Commission agreed that discrimination had taken place and awarded him damages. The Brandon Police Services have since addressed the issue with training. The question remains, How could three officers working together make the mutual decision that Nachuk's dog was not a "legitimate" service dog in the face of clear evidence otherwise, most notably his official service dog papers? What does this situation tell us about our own capacity for decision-making errors?

In this chapter, we describe how decisions in organizations are made, as well as how creativity is linked to decision making. We also look at the ethical and socially responsible aspects of decision making as part of our discussion. Decision making affects people at all levels of the organization, and it's engaged in by both individuals and groups. Therefore, we also consider the special characteristics of group decision making.

 **IS FOR EVERYONE**

- Do people really consider every alternative when making a decision?

- Is it okay to use intuition when making decisions?

- Why is it that we sometimes make bad decisions?

- Why are some people more creative than others?

- How can people make more ethical decisions?

How Should Decisions Be Made?

A **decision** is the choice made from two or more alternatives. Decision making happens at all levels of an organization. Business schools train students to follow rational decision-making models. While models have merit, they don't always describe how people make decisions. There are decision-making errors people commit in addition to the perceptual errors we discussed in Chapter 3.

Knowing how to make decisions is an important part of everyday life. Below we consider various decision-making models that apply to both individual and group choices. (Later in the chapter, we discuss special aspects of group decision making.) We start with the rational decision-making model, which describes decision making in the ideal world, a situation that rarely exists. We then look at alternatives to the rational model, and how decisions actually get made.

The Rational Decision-Making Process

1 Contrast the rational model of decision making with bounded rationality and intuition.

We often think that the best decision maker is the **rational** decision maker, who makes consistent, value-maximizing choices within specified constraints.[2] These choices are made following a six-step **rational decision-making model**.[3] Moreover, specific assumptions underlie this model.

The Six-Step Rational Model

◄●─[Simulate on **MyManagementLab**

Decision Making

The six steps in the rational decision-making model are presented in Exhibit 12-1.

First, the decision maker must *define the problem*. If you calculate your monthly expenses and find you are spending $50 more than your monthly earnings, you have defined a problem. Many poor decisions can be traced to the decision maker overlooking a problem or defining the wrong problem.

The decision maker then needs to *identify the criteria* that are relevant to making the decision. This step brings the decision maker's interests, values, and similar personal

decision The choice made from two or more alternatives.

rational Refers to choices that are consistent and value-maximizing within specified constraints.

rational decision-making model A six-step decision-making model that describes how individuals should behave in order to maximize some outcome.

EXHIBIT 12-1 Steps in the Rational Decision-Making Model

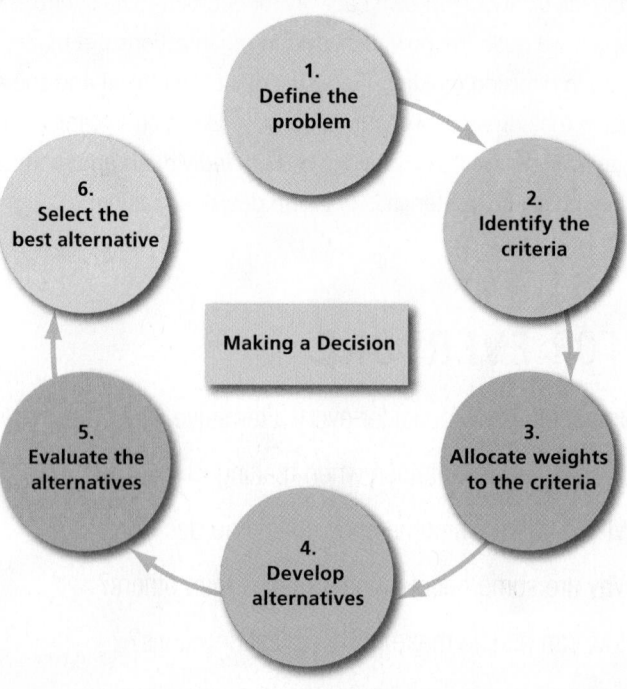

1. Define the problem
2. Identify the criteria
3. Allocate weights to the criteria
4. Develop alternatives
5. Evaluate the alternatives
6. Select the best alternative

Making a Decision

preferences into the process, because not all individuals will consider the same factors relevant for any particular decision.

To understand the types of criteria that might be used to make a decision, consider how Toronto-based Canadian Imperial Bank of Commerce (CIBC) handles the many sponsorship requests it receives each year. When it makes a decision about whether to support a request, the bank takes into account a number of criteria. Specifically, to be eligible for funding, a request must

- Be aligned to youth, community, or health
- Be for a Canadian organization, using funds in Canada
- Be for a registered charity with a Canada Revenue Agency Charitable Registration Number or a non-profit organization
- Have achievements and goals in line with CIBC's overall goals
- Address a community need
- Include planned and measureable outcomes, that can be evaluated
- Have audited financial statements, principled financial practices, and sustainable funding[4]

If the sponsorship request does not meet these criteria, it is not funded.

Because the criteria identified are rarely all equal in importance, the third step requires the decision maker to *allocate weights to the criteria*.

The fourth step requires the decision maker to *develop alternatives* that could succeed in resolving the problem.

The decision maker then critically *evaluates the alternatives*, using the previously established criteria and weights.

Finally, the decision maker *selects the best alternative* by evaluating each alternative against the weighted criteria and selecting the alternative with the highest total score.

Assumptions of the Model

The rational decision-making model assumes that the decision maker has complete information, is able to identify all the relevant options in an unbiased manner, and chooses the option with the highest utility.[5] Most decisions don't follow the rational model; people are usually content to find an acceptable or reasonable solution to a problem rather than an optimal one. Choices tend to be limited to the neighbourhood of the problem symptom and the current alternative.

How Do Individuals Actually Make Decisions?

It seems hard to comprehend how three trained police officers could overlook Billy-Joe Nachuk's explanation that his dog was a service dog, especially since he had the corresponding paperwork.[6] Stereotypes and biases may have played roles. One officer asked, "Why do you have a service dog, you aren't blind," suggesting stereotypical thinking about disability and service animals. The officers may have assumed that Nachuk was being difficult and presumptuous by bringing a dog into the building, and trying to challenge authority. What sorts of perceptual biases might affect the decisions people make?

Most decisions in the real world don't follow the rational model. As one expert in decision making has concluded, "Most significant decisions are made by judgment, rather than by a defined prescriptive model."[7] What is more, people are remarkably unaware of making suboptimal decisions.[8]

In the following sections, we indicate areas where the reality of decision making conflicts with the rational model.[9] None of these ways of making decisions should be considered *irrational*; they simply depart from the rational model when information is unavailable or too costly to collect.

Bounded Rationality in Considering Alternatives

Our limited information-processing capability makes it impossible to assimilate all the information necessary to optimize.[10] Most people respond to a complex problem by reducing it to a level they can readily understand. Many problems don't have an optimal solution because they are too complicated to fit the rational decision-making model, so people *satisfice*; they seek solutions that are satisfactory and sufficient.

> Do people really consider every alternative when making a decision?

When you considered which university or college to attend, did you look at *every* workable alternative? Did you carefully identify all the criteria that were important in your decision? Did you evaluate each alternative against the criteria in order to find the optimum school? The answer to these questions is probably no. But don't feel bad, because few people selected their educational institution this way.

Because the human mind cannot formulate and solve complex problems with full rationality, we operate within the confines of **bounded rationality**. We construct simplified models that extract the essential features from problems without capturing all their complexity.[11] We can then behave rationally within the limits of the simple model.

How does bounded rationality work for the typical individual? Once we have identified a problem, we begin to search for criteria and alternatives. But the criteria are unlikely to be exhaustive. We identify alternatives that are highly visible and that usually

Isao Moriyasu is president of DeNA, a Japanese Internet firm focused on social game platforms and social games. Shown here with the firm's new "comm" app, Moriyasu operates within the confines of bounded rationality in making complex decisions about acquiring other firms, expanding globally, and rapidly developing new services.

Yuriko Nakao/Reuters

bounded rationality Limitations on a person's ability to interpret, process, and act on information.

represent familiar criteria and tried-and-true solutions. Next, we begin reviewing the alternatives, focusing on choices that differ little from the current state until we identify one that is "good enough"—that meets an acceptable level of performance. That ends our search. So the solution represents a **satisficing** choice—the first *acceptable* one we encounter—rather than an optimal one.

Satisficing is not always bad—a simple process may frequently be more sensible than the traditional rational decision-making model.[12] To use the rational model, you need to gather a great deal of information about all the options, compute applicable weights, and then calculate values across a huge number of criteria. All these processes can cost time, energy, and money. If there are many unknown weights and preferences, the fully rational model may not be any more accurate than a best guess. Sometimes a fast-and-frugal process of solving problems might be your best option. Returning to your college or university choice, would it be best to fly around the country to visit dozens of potential campuses and pay application fees for all? It might be smarter to satisfice by finding a few colleges or universities that match most of your preferences and then focus your attention on differentiating among those.

Intuition

Perhaps the least rational way of making decisions is **intuitive decision making**, an unconscious process created from distilled experience.[13] Intuitive decision making occurs outside conscious thought; relies on holistic associations, or links between disparate pieces of information; is fast; and is affectively charged, meaning that it engages the emotions.[14]

> Is it okay to use intuition when making decisions?

While intuition is not rational, it's not necessarily wrong. Nor does it always contradict rational analysis; rather, the two can complement each other. Intuition can be a powerful force in decision making. Nor is it superstition, or the product of some magical or paranormal sixth sense. Intuition is complex and based on years of experience and learning. *OB in the Street* shows how intuition applies to grand master chess players.

OB IN THE STREET
Intuition Comes to the Chess Board

Can intuition really help you win a chess game?   Apparently so.[15] Novice chess players and grand masters were shown an actual, but unfamiliar, chess game with about 25 pieces on the board. After 5 or 10 seconds, the pieces were removed, and each subject was asked to reconstruct the pieces by position. On average, the grand master could put 23 or 24 pieces in their correct squares, while the novice was able to replace only 6. Then the exercise was changed. This time, the pieces were placed randomly on the board. Again, the novice got only about 6 correct, but so did the grand master! The second exercise demonstrated that the grand master did not have a better memory than the novice. What the grand master *did* have was the ability, based on the experience of having played thousands of chess games, to recognize patterns and clusters of pieces that occur on chessboards in the course of games. Studies also show that chess professionals can play 50 or more games simultaneously, making decisions in seconds, and exhibit only a moderately lower level of skill than when playing one game under tournament conditions, where decisions take half an hour or longer. The expert's experience allows him or her to recognize the pattern in a situation and draw on previously learned information associated with that pattern to arrive at a decision quickly. The result is that the intuitive decision maker can decide rapidly based on what appears to be very limited information.

satisficing To provide a solution that is both satisfactory and sufficient.

intuitive decision making An unconscious process created out of a person's many experiences.

As the example of the chess players shows, those who use intuition effectively often rely on their experiences to help guide and assess their intuitions. That may be why senior managers are more likely to turn to intuition when they are lacking full information, as *Focus on Research* shows.

Putting Intuition to Work in the Workplace

How do senior managers use intuition in their decision making? A study of 57 Australian senior executives who make marketing sponsorship decisions found that almost all of them used intuition to help guide their decisions at least some of the time.[16] Organizations that placed a high value on trust when selecting sponsorship opportunities were more likely to have managers who based their decisions on intuition. Not surprisingly, managers at organizations with highly formalized decision-making processes reported less use of intuition, although even they reported using it moderately frequently. Managers were more likely to rely on their intuition when the factors under consideration were vague or complex, or the benefits of sponsorship were largely nonmonetary and intangible. Uncertainty in the environment, it seems, increased their reliance on "gut feel." While intuition can help us make better decisions if we have the appropriate tacit knowledge, it's worthwhile to double-check to ensure that perceptual errors are not biasing our thought processes.

Does intuition contribute to effective decision making? Researchers are divided, but most experts are skeptical, in part because intuition is hard to measure and analyze. A recent study that examined people's ability to "use their gut" to make decisions found that not everyone's gut is reliable. For some, the physiological feeling that one associates with intuition works, but for others it does not.[17] Probably the best advice from one expert is this: "Intuition can be very useful as a way of setting up a hypothesis but is unacceptable as 'proof.'"[18] Use hunches based on experience to speculate, yes, but always make sure to test those hunches with objective data and rational analysis. Intuition is also part of spirituality, a burgeoning area of interest to OB scholars, as *OB on the Edge—Spirituality in the Workplace* on pages 448–453 demonstrates.

Judgment Shortcuts

2 Describe common decision biases and errors.

Decision makers engage in bounded rationality, but they also allow systematic biases and errors to creep into their judgments.[19] To minimize effort and avoid trade-offs, people tend to rely too heavily on experience, impulses, gut feelings, and convenient rules of thumb. Shortcuts can be helpful. However, they can lead to distortions of rationality, as *OB in the Street* shows.

> Why is it that we sometimes make bad decisions?

OB IN THE **STREET**
Penalty Kick Decisions

Should you stand still or leap into action? This is the classic question facing a goalie in a faceoff against a midfielder for a penalty kick.[20] Ofer H. Azar, a lecturer in the School of Management at Ben-Gurion University in Israel, finds that goalies often make the wrong decision.

Why? The goalie tries to anticipate where the ball will go after the kick. There is only a split second to do anything after the kick, so anticipating and acting seem like a good decision.

Azar became interested in studying goalie behaviour after realizing that the "incentives are huge" for the goalie to get it right. "Goalkeepers face penalty kicks regularly, so they are not only high-motivated decision makers, but also very experienced ones," he explains. That said, 80 percent of penalty kicks score, so goalies are in a difficult situation at that instant when the kick goes off.

Azar's study found that goalies rarely stayed in the centre of the net as the ball was fired (just 6.3 percent of the time). But staying in the centre is actually the best strategy. Goalies halted penalty kicks when staying in the centre 33.3 percent of the time. They were successful only 14.2 percent of the time when they moved left and only 12.6 percent of the time when they moved right.

Azar argues that the results show that there is a "bias for action," explaining that goalies think they will feel worse if they do *nothing* and miss, than if they do *something* and miss. This bias then clouds their judgment, encouraging them to move to one side or the other, rather than just staying in the centre, where the odds are actually more in their favour.

In what follows, we discuss some of the most common judgment shortcuts to alert you to mistakes that are often made when making decisions.

Overconfidence Bias

Recent research continues to conclude that we tend to be overconfident about our abilities and about the abilities of others; also, that we are usually not aware of this bias.[21] It's been said that "no problem in judgment and decision making is more prevalent and more potentially catastrophic than overconfidence."[22]

When we are given factual questions and asked to judge the probability that our answers are correct, we tend to be overly optimistic. This is known as **overconfidence bias**. In a study of confidence intervals (educated guesses about some characteristic of a population), when people said they were 90 percent confident that their answers were correct, their answers were correct only about 50 percent of the time—and experts were no more accurate in their estimation of confidence intervals than were novices.[23]

Individuals whose intellectual and interpersonal abilities are *weakest* are most likely to overestimate their performance and ability.[24] Also, a negative relationship exists between entrepreneurs' optimism and performance of their new ventures: the more optimistic, the less successful.[25] The tendency to be too confident about their ideas might keep some from planning how to avoid problems that arise. Overconfidence is most likely to surface when organizational members are considering issues or problems that are outside their area of expertise.[26]

Anchoring Bias

The **anchoring bias** is a tendency to fixate on initial information and fail to adequately adjust for subsequent information.[27] It occurs because the mind appears to give a disproportionate amount of emphasis to the first information it receives.[28] Anchors are widely used by people in professions where persuasion skills are important—such as advertising, management, politics, real estate, and law. For instance, in a mock jury trial, the plaintiff's attorney asked one set of jurors to make an award in the range of $15 million to $50 million. The plaintiff's attorney asked another set of jurors for an award in the range of $50 million to $150 million. Consistent with the anchoring bias, the median awards were $15 million and $50 million, respectively.[29]

Consider the role of anchoring in negotiations. Any time a negotiation takes place, so does anchoring. As soon as someone states a number, your ability to ignore that number

overconfidence bias Error in judgment that arises from being far too optimistic about one's own performance.

anchoring bias A tendency to fixate on initial information, from which one then fails to adequately adjust for subsequent information.

has been compromised. For instance, when a prospective employer asks how much you were making in your prior job, your answer typically anchors the employer's offer. You may want to keep this in mind when you negotiate your salary, but remember to set the anchor only as high as you realistically can. The more precise your anchor, the smaller the adjustment. Some research suggests that people think of making an adjustment after an anchor is set as rounding off a number. If you suggest a salary of $55 000, your boss will consider $50 000 to $60 000 a reasonable range for negotiation, but if you mention $55 650, your boss is more likely to consider $55 000 to $56 000 the range of likely values for negotiation.[30]

Confirmation Bias

The rational decision-making process assumes that we objectively gather information. But we don't. We *selectively* gather it. The **confirmation bias** represents a case of selective perception. We seek out information that reaffirms our past choices, and we discount information that contradicts them.[31] We also tend to accept at face value information that confirms our preconceived views, while we are skeptical of information that challenges these views. Therefore, the information we gather is typically biased toward supporting views we already hold. This confirmation bias influences where we go to collect evidence because we tend to seek out sources most likely to tell us what we want to hear. It also leads us to give too much weight to supporting information and too little to contradictory information.[32] We are most prone to confirmation bias when we believe we have good information and strongly hold our opinions. Fortunately, those who feel there is a strong need to be accurate in making a decision are less prone to confirmation bias.

Availability Bias

The **availability bias** is the tendency for people to base their judgments on information that is readily available.[33] Recent research indicates that a combination of readily available information and our previous direct experience with similar information is particularly impactful to our decision making. Events that evoke emotions, that are particularly vivid, or that have occurred more recently tend to be more available in our memory. As a result, we tend to overestimate unlikely events, such as being in an airplane crash, suffering complications from medical treatment, or getting fired.[34] The availability bias can also explain why managers, when doing annual performance appraisals, tend to give more weight to the recent behaviour of an employee than to that of six or nine months ago.

Escalation of Commitment

Some decision makers escalate commitment to a failing course of action.[35] **Escalation of commitment** refers to staying with a decision even when there is clear evidence that it's wrong. For example, a friend has been dating a man for about four years. Although she admits that things are not going well, she is determined to marry him anyway. Her justification: "I have a lot invested in the relationship!"

When is escalation of commitment most likely to occur? A 2012 study indicates that it tends to occur when individuals view themselves as responsible for the outcome. The fear of personal failure even biases the way we search for and evaluate information so that we choose only information that supports our dedication. We might, for example, weight opinions in favour of reinvestment as more credible than opinions for divestment.[36]

A 2012 meta-analysis revealed some interesting findings about what causes us to escalate our commitment after initial failure. First, it does not appear to matter whether we chose the failing course of action or it was assigned to us—we feel responsible and escalate commitment in either case. Second, the sharing of decision authority—such as when others review the choice we made—can lead to higher escalation of commitment

confirmation bias The tendency to seek out information that reaffirms past choices and to discount information that contradicts past judgments.

availability bias The tendency for people to base their judgments on information that is readily available to them rather than complete data.

escalation of commitment An increased commitment to a previous decision despite negative information.

because the original decision is more public (thus, individuals feel a stronger need to justify the original decision by continuing). Finally, awareness of sunk costs associated with the decision reduces escalation of commitment when individuals feel responsible (it gives them an "escape clause").[37]

Randomness Error

Most of us like to think we have some control over our world and our destiny. Our tendency to believe we can predict the outcome of random events is the **randomness error**.

Decision making suffers when we try to create meaning in random events, particularly when we turn imaginary patterns into superstitions.[38] These can be completely contrived, such as "I never make important decisions on Friday the 13th." They can also evolve from a certain pattern of behaviour that has been reinforced previously. For example, Mikaël Kingsbury, a world champion in moguls who won a silver medal at the Sochi Olympics while representing Canada, wears the same T-shirt under his ski clothing at every competition. The T-shirt says "It's good to be the King." He wore it the first time he won a medal in a World Cup event, and then started wearing it to every major competition. "Even if I do badly, it's still got some magic," he said.[39] Superstitious behaviour can be debilitating when it affects daily judgments or biases major decisions.

Risk Aversion

Mathematically, we should find a 50–50 flip of the coin for $100 to be worth as much as a sure promise of $50. After all, the expected value of the gamble over a number of trials is $50. However, nearly everyone but committed gamblers would rather have the sure thing than a risky prospect.[40] For many people, a 50–50 flip of a coin even for $200 might not be worth as much as a sure promise of $50, even though the gamble is mathematically worth twice as much! This tendency to prefer a sure thing over a risky outcome is **risk aversion**.

Risk aversion has important implications. To offset the risks inherent in a commission-based wage, companies pay commissioned employees considerably more than they do those on straight salaries. Risk-averse employees will stick with the established way of doing their jobs rather than take a chance on innovative methods. Sticking with a strategy that has worked in the past minimizes risk, but it will lead to stagnation. Ambitious people with power that can be taken away (most managers) appear to be especially risk averse, perhaps because they don't want to gamble everything they have worked so hard to achieve.[41] CEOs at risk of dismissal are also exceptionally risk averse, even when a riskier investment strategy is in their firms' best interests.[42]

Risk preference is sometimes reversed: People prefer to take chances when trying to prevent a negative outcome.[43] They would rather take a 50–50 gamble on losing $100 than accept the certain loss of $50. Thus they will risk losing a lot of money at trial rather than settle out of court. Trying to cover up wrongdoing instead of admitting a mistake, despite the risk of truly catastrophic press coverage or even jail time, is another example. Stressful situations can make risk preferences stronger. People will more likely engage in risk-seeking behaviour for negative outcomes, and risk-averse behaviour for positive outcomes, when under stress.[44]

Hindsight Bias

The **hindsight bias** is the tendency to believe falsely, after the outcome of an event is actually known, that we could have accurately predicted that outcome.[45] When we have accurate feedback on the outcome, we seem to be pretty good at concluding that it was obvious. As Malcolm Gladwell, author of *Outliers*, *The Tipping Point*, and *David and Goliath*, writes, "What is clear in hindsight is rarely clear before the fact. It's an obvious point, but one that nonetheless bears repeating."[46]

randomness error The tendency of individuals to believe that they can predict the outcome of random events.

risk aversion The tendency to prefer a sure gain of a moderate amount over a riskier outcome, even if the riskier outcome might have a higher expected payoff.

hindsight bias The tendency to believe falsely, after an outcome of an event is actually known, that one could have accurately predicted that outcome.

IN **ACTION**
Reducing Biases and Errors in Decision Making

→ **Focus on goals**. Clear goals make decision making easier and help you eliminate options that are inconsistent with your interests.

→ **Look for information that disconfirms** your **beliefs**. When we deliberately consider various ways we could be wrong, we challenge our tendencies to think we are smarter than we actually are.

→ **Don't create meaning** out of random events. Ask yourself if patterns can be meaningfully explained or whether they are merely coincidence. Don't attempt to create meaning out of coincidence.

→ **Increase** your **options**. The more alternatives you can generate, and the more diverse those alternatives, the greater your chance of finding an outstanding one.[47]

The hindsight bias reduces our ability to learn from the past. It lets us think that we are better predictors than we really are, and can make us falsely confident. If your actual predictive accuracy is only 40 percent, but you think it's 90 percent, you are likely to be less skeptical about your predictive skills.

OB in Action—Reducing Biases and Errors in Decision Making provides you with some ideas for improving your decision making.

Group Decision Making

The belief—characterized by juries—that two heads are better than one has long been accepted as a basic component of North American and many other countries' legal systems. Today, many decisions in organizations are made by groups, teams, or committees. In this section, we review group decision making and compare it with individual decision making.

Groups vs. the Individual

Decision-making groups may be widely used in organizations, but are group decisions preferable to those made by an individual alone? The answer to this depends on a number of factors we consider below.[48] See Exhibit 12-2 for a summary of our major points. *Point/Counterpoint* on page 441 also considers whether people are more creative when they work alone or with others.

3 Contrast the strengths and weaknesses of group decision making.

Strengths of Group Decision Making

Groups generate *more complete information and knowledge*. By combining the resources of several individuals, groups bring more input into the decision process. They offer *increased diversity of views*, which opens up the opportunity to consider more approaches and alternatives. Finally, groups lead to *increased acceptance of a solution*.[49] Group members who participated in making a decision are likely to support it enthusiastically and encourage others to accept it.

EXHIBIT 12-2 Group vs. Individual Decision Making

Criteria of Effectiveness	Groups	Individuals
More complete information	√	
Diversity of views	√	
Decision quality	√	
Accuracy	√	
Creativity	√	
Degree of acceptance	√	
Speed		√
Efficiency		√

Weaknesses of Group Decision Making

Group decisions are *time-consuming* because groups typically take more time to reach a solution. There are *conformity pressures*. The desire by group members to be accepted and considered an asset to the group can result in squashing any overt disagreement. Group discussion can be *dominated by one or a few members*. If they are low- and medium-ability members, the group's overall effectiveness will suffer. Finally, group decisions suffer from *ambiguous responsibility*. In an individual decision, it's clear who is accountable for the final outcome. In a group decision, the responsibility of any single member is watered down.

Effectiveness and Efficiency

Whether groups are more effective than individuals depends on how you define effectiveness. Group decisions are generally more *accurate* than the decisions of the average individual in a group, but they are less accurate than the judgments of the most accurate group member.[50] If decision effectiveness is defined in terms of *speed*, individuals are superior. If *creativity* is important, groups tend to be more effective than individuals. And if effectiveness means the degree of *acceptance* the final solution achieves, the nod again goes to the group.[51]

But we cannot consider effectiveness without also assessing efficiency. With few exceptions, group decision making consumes more work hours than an individual tackling the same problem alone. The exceptions tend to be the instances in which, to achieve comparable quantities of diverse input, the single decision maker must spend a great deal of time reviewing files and talking to other people. In deciding whether to use groups, then, consideration should be given to assessing whether increases in effectiveness are more than enough to offset the reductions in efficiency. The *Experiential Exercise* on page 442 gives you an opportunity to assess the effectiveness and efficiency of group decision making vs. individual decision making.

Groupthink and Groupshift

Two by-products of group decision making have the potential to affect the group's ability to appraise alternatives objectively and arrive at quality solutions: groupthink and groupshift.

Groupthink

Have you ever felt like speaking up in a meeting, classroom, or informal group, but decided against it? One reason may have been shyness. On the other hand, you may have been a victim of **groupthink**. Groupthink relates to norms. It describes situations in which group pressures for conformity deter the group from critically appraising unusual, minority, or unpopular views. Groupthink is a disease that attacks many groups and can dramatically hinder their performance. The individual's mental efficiency, reality testing, and moral judgment deteriorate as a result of group pressures.[52]

We have all seen the symptoms of the groupthink phenomenon:[53]

- *Illusion of invulnerability.* Group members become overconfident among themselves, allowing them to take extraordinary risks.

- *Assumption of morality.* Group members believe highly in the moral rightness of the group's objectives and do not feel the need to debate the ethics of their actions.

- *Rationalized resistance.* Group members rationalize any resistance to the assumptions they have made. No matter how strongly the evidence may contradict their basic assumptions, members behave so as to reinforce those assumptions continually.

◉−Watch on **MyManagementLab**

Decision Making (TWZ Role Play)

---

groupthink A phenomenon in which group pressures for conformity prevent the group from critically appraising unusual, minority, or unpopular views.

- *Peer pressure.* Group members apply direct pressure on those who momentarily express doubts about any of the group's shared views or who question the validity of arguments supporting the alternative favoured by the majority.

- *Minimized doubts.* Those group members who have doubts or hold differing points of view seek to avoid deviating from what appears to be group consensus by keeping silent about misgivings and even minimizing to themselves the importance of their doubts.

- *Illusion of unanimity.* If someone does not speak, it's assumed that he or she is in full agreement. In other words, abstention becomes viewed as a yes vote.

Groupthink can also take place among strategic decision-makers, as *OB in the Street* shows.

OB IN THE STREET
Groupthink at Target Canada

Why did a large, experienced retailer make so many basic errors when launching its Canadian outlets? In 2013, US-based Target brought its mass-merchandise stores to Canada, building over 100 stores in under a year.[54] Things did not go well over 2013 and 2014. The stores drastically underperformed, with customers complaining about poor selection, high prices, and empty store shelves. The retailer admits to poor planning, failing to research the prices charged by its Canadian competitors, and not making sure its supply chains would work properly.

Even with these difficulties, Target Chief Financial Officer John Mulligan said the retailer was in Canada for the long haul. Mulligan admitted that "we bit off way too much, too early. In retrospect we should've probably opened five to 10 stores [in 2013]—refined the operations, refined the supply chain, the technology, got our store teams trained. But again, that's all hindsight, we are where we are right now and we're focused on moving forward to fix this for our guests." Despite this statement, in 2015 the US parent company's CEO, Brian Cornell, announced that Target was pulling out of Canada and closing all 133 stores across the country.

Why did Target's Canadian management team choose to continue to open even more new stores in 2014 after its first stores opened with a strategy that was proving highly problematic? Groupthink is part of the answer. As one former employee stated: "[Key team members from the United States] were not guides or resources, as much as they were obstacles to progress. If it didn't come from/work in the U.S. then it was not a discussion point." The same employee added: "To . . . assume that the same 'playbook' used in the U.S. would work in Canada was incredible. The inability of the [key team members from the United States] to think and work beyond this led to us attempting to Xerox the U.S. store culture (for Team Members and Guests) instead of develop one that is tailored to Canadian tastes and attitudes."

Groupthink appears to be closely aligned with the conclusions psychologist Solomon Asch drew in his experiments with a lone dissenter, which we described in Chapter 6. Individuals who hold a position that is different from that of the dominant majority are under pressure to suppress, withhold, or modify their true feelings and beliefs. As members of a group, we find it more pleasant to be in agreement—to be a positive part of the group—than to be a disruptive force, even if disruption is necessary to improve the effectiveness of the group's decisions. Groups that are more focused on performance than on learning are especially likely to fall victim to groupthink and to suppress the opinions of those who do not agree with the majority.[55]

Do all groups suffer from groupthink? No. It seems to occur most often where there is a clear group identity, where members hold a positive image of their group, which they want to protect, and where the group perceives a collective threat to this positive image.[56] So groupthink is less a dissenter-suppression mechanism than a means for a group to protect its positive image. One study showed that those influenced by groupthink were more confident about their course of action early on.[57] Groups that believe too strongly in the correctness of their course of action are more likely to suppress dissent and encourage conformity than are groups that are more skeptical about their course of action.

What can managers do to minimize groupthink?[58]

- *Monitor group size.* People grow more intimidated and hesitant as group size increases, and, although there is no magic number that will eliminate group-think, individuals are likely to feel less personal responsibility when groups get larger than about 10.

- *Encourage group leaders to play an impartial role.* Leaders should actively seek input from all members and avoid expressing their own opinions, especially in the early stages of deliberation.

- *Appoint one group member to play the role of devil's advocate.* This member's role is to overtly challenge the majority position and offer divergent perspectives.

- *Stimulate active discussion of diverse alternatives to encourage dissenting views and more objective evaluations.* Group members might delay discussion of possible gains so they can first talk about the dangers or risks inherent in a decision. Requiring members to first focus on the negatives of an alternative makes the group less likely to stifle dissenting views and more likely to gain an objective evaluation.

While considerable anecdotal evidence indicates the negative implications of group-think in organizational settings, not much actual empirical work has been conducted in organizations in this area.[59] In fact, researchers on groupthink have been criticized for

THE CANADIAN PRESS/Ryan Remiorz

Young adults rioting in the streets of Vancouver after the Canucks' loss to the Boston Bruins in Game 7 of the 2011 NHL playoffs may have been affected by groupthink as they got carried away, smashing windows, looting, and setting fires. It is unlikely that everyone who participated in the riots had carefully planned out their activities in advance of the riots starting.

suggesting that its effect is uniformly negative[60] and for overestimating the link between the decision-making process and its outcome.[61] A study of groupthink using 30 teams from 5 large corporations suggests that elements of groupthink may affect decision making differently. For instance, the illusion of invulnerability, assumption of morality, and illusion of unanimity were positively associated with team performance.[62] The most recent research suggests that we should be aware of groupthink conditions that lead to poor decisions, while realizing that not all groupthink symptoms harm decision making.

Groupshift or Group Polarization

There are differences between group decisions and the individual decisions of group members.[63] What appears to happen often times in groups is that the discussion leads members toward a more extreme view of the position they already held. Conservative types become more cautious, and more aggressive types take on more risk. The group discussion tends to exaggerate the initial position of the group because participants have engaged in **groupshift**, a phenomenon in which the initial positions of individual group members become exaggerated because of the interactions of the group.

Group polarization is a special type of groupthink. A group's "polarized" decision reflects the dominant decision-making norm that develops during discussion. Whether the shift in the group's decision is toward greater caution or more risk depends on the dominant prediscussion norm.

Several explanations have been offered to account for the shift toward polarization in a group.[64] It has been argued, for instance, that the discussion makes members more comfortable with one another, and, thus, more willing to express extreme versions of their original positions. Another argument is that the group diffuses responsibility. Group decisions free any single member from accountability for the group's final choice, so greater risks can be taken. It's also likely that people take on extreme positions because they want to demonstrate how different they are from the outgroup.[65] People on the fringes of political or social movements take on ever-more extreme positions just to prove they are really committed to the cause, whereas those who are more cautious tend to take moderate positions to demonstrate how reasonable they are.

How should you use the findings on groupshift? Recognize that group decisions exaggerate the initial position of the individual members, that the shift has been shown more often to be toward greater risk, and that the direction in which a group will shift is a function of the members' prediscussion inclinations. *Case Incident—"If Two Heads Are Better Than One, Are Four Even Better?"* on page 446 considers the impact of groupshift on investment decisions.

Group Decision-Making Techniques

4 Compare the effectiveness of interacting, brainstorming, and the nominal group technique.

Groups can use a variety of techniques to make decisions. We outline three of them below.

Interacting Groups

The most common form of group decision making takes place in **interacting groups**. Members meet face to face and rely on both verbal and nonverbal interaction to communicate with one another. But as our discussion of groupthink demonstrated, interacting groups often censor themselves and pressure individual members toward conformity of opinion. *Brainstorming* and the *nominal group technique* can reduce many of the problems inherent in the traditional interacting group.

Brainstorming

Brainstorming uses an idea-generation process that specifically encourages any and all alternatives, in a criticism-free environment.

groupshift A phenomenon in which the initial positions of individual group members become exaggerated because of the interactions of the group.

interacting groups Typical groups in which members interact with one another face to face.

brainstorming An idea-generation process that specifically encourages any and all alternatives, while withholding any criticism of those alternatives.

In a typical brainstorming session, 6 to 12 people sit around a table. The group leader states the problem in a clear manner so that all participants understand it. Members then "free-wheel" as many alternatives as they can in a given period of time. To encourage group members to "think the unusual," no criticism is allowed, and all ideas are recorded for later discussion and analysis.

Brainstorming may indeed generate ideas—but not in a very efficient manner. Research consistently shows that individuals working alone generate more ideas than a group in a brainstorming session.[66] One reason for this is "production blocking." When people generate ideas in a group, many people are talking at once, which blocks the thought process and eventually impedes the sharing of ideas.[67] Another reason suggested by a 2011 study is fixation—group members start to fixate early on a limited number of solutions rather than continue to look for others.[68] One recent study suggests that goal-setting approaches might make brainstorming more effective.[69] The following technique goes further than brainstorming by offering methods that help groups arrive at a preferred solution.[70]

Nominal Group Technique

The **nominal group technique** restricts discussion or interpersonal communication during the decision-making process, hence the term *nominal* (which means "in name only"). Group members are all physically present, as in a traditional committee meeting, but they operate independently. Specifically, a problem is presented and then the group takes the following steps:

- Before any discussion takes place, each member independently writes down his or her ideas on the problem.

- After this silent period, each member presents one idea to the group. Group members take turns presenting a single idea until all ideas have been presented and recorded. No discussion takes place until all ideas have been recorded.

- The group discusses the ideas for clarity and evaluates them.

- Each group member silently and independently ranks the ideas. The idea with the highest aggregate ranking determines the final decision.

The steps of the nominal group technique are illustrated in Exhibit 12-3. The chief advantage of the technique is that it permits the group to meet formally but does not restrict independent thinking, as does the interacting group. Research generally shows that nominal groups outperform brainstorming groups.[71]

Each of these group decision techniques has its own strengths and weaknesses. The choice depends on what criteria you want to emphasize and the cost-benefit trade-off.

nominal group technique A group decision-making method in which individual members meet face to face to pool their judgments in a systematic but independent fashion.

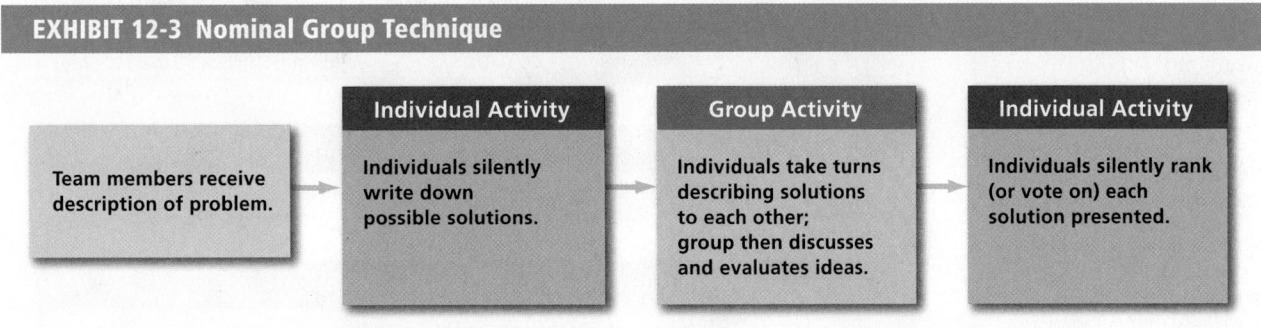

EXHIBIT 12-3 Nominal Group Technique

| Team members receive description of problem. | **Individual Activity** Individuals silently write down possible solutions. | **Group Activity** Individuals take turns describing solutions to each other; group then discusses and evaluates ideas. | **Individual Activity** Individuals silently rank (or vote on) each solution presented. |

EXHIBIT 12-4 Evaluating Group Effectiveness

Effectiveness Criteria	Type of Group			
	Interacting	Brainstorming	Nominal	Electronic
Number and quality of ideas	Low	Moderate	High	High
Social pressure	High	Low	Moderate	Low
Money costs	Low	Low	Low	High
Speed	Moderate	Moderate	Moderate	Moderate
Task orientation	Low	High	High	High
Potential for interpersonal conflict	High	Low	Moderate	Low
Commitment to solution	High	Not applicable	Moderate	Moderate
Development of group cohesiveness	High	High	Moderate	Low

Source: Based on J. K. Murnighan, "Group Decision Making: What Strategies Should You Use?" *Academy of Management Review,* February 1981, p. 61.

As Exhibit 12-4 indicates, an interacting group is good for achieving commitment to a solution, brainstorming develops group cohesiveness, and the nominal group technique is an inexpensive means for generating a large number of ideas.

Creativity in Organizational Decision Making

5 Define *creativity*, and describe the three-stage model of creativity.

Although the rational decision-making model will often improve decisions, a decision maker also needs **creativity**; that is, the ability to produce novel and useful ideas.[72] These ideas are different from what has been done before but are appropriate for the problem presented.

Why is creativity important to decision making? It allows the decision maker to more fully appraise and understand problems, including seeing problems others cannot see. Such thinking is becoming more important.

Although all aspects of organizational behaviour have complexities, that is especially true for creativity. To simplify, Exhibit 12-5 provides a **three-stage model of creativity** in organizations. The core of the model is *creative behaviour*, which has both *causes* (predictors of creative behaviour) and *outcomes* (innovation). In this section, we discuss the three stages of creativity, starting with the centre, creative behaviour.

PERSONAL INVENTORY ASSESSMENT

Learn About Yourself
Creative Style Indicator

creativity The ability to produce novel and useful ideas.

three-stage model of creativity The proposition that creativity involves three stages: causes (creative potential and creative environment), creative behaviour, and creative outcomes (innovation).

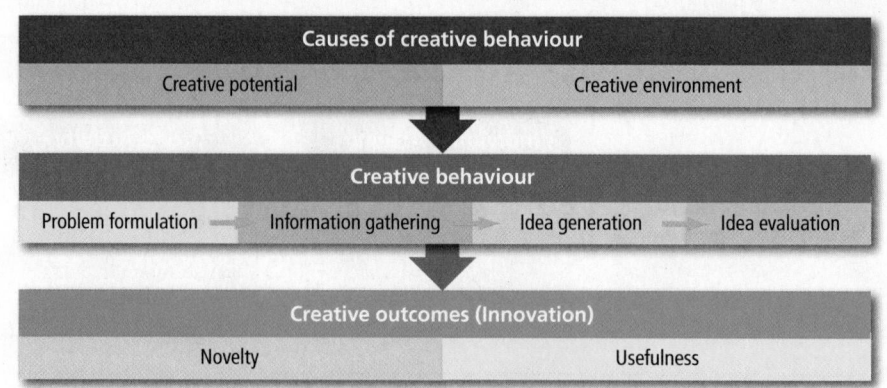

EXHIBIT 12-5 Three-Stage Model of Creativity in Organizations

Causes of creative behaviour

Creative potential | Creative environment

Creative behaviour

Problem formulation → Information gathering → Idea generation → Idea evaluation

Creative outcomes (Innovation)

Novelty | Usefulness

Creative Behaviour

Creative behaviour occurs in four steps, each of which leads to the next:

- *Problem formulation.* Any act of creativity begins with a problem that the behaviour is designed to solve. Thus, **problem formulation** is defined as the stage of creative behaviour in which we identify a problem or an opportunity that requires a solution as yet unknown. For example, Brendan Brazier believed at an early age that a plant-based diet could transform him into a professional athlete, so he set out to prove that by following such a diet. Brazier attributes "clean eating" to his seven-year career as an Ironman triathlete and two-time win of the Canadian 50-kilometre Ultra Marathon. He is also the formulator of a line of plant-based nutritional products through his company, Vega, as well as a bestselling author.[73]

- *Information gathering.* Given a problem, the solution is rarely directly at hand. We need time to learn more and to process that learning. Thus, **information gathering** is the stage of creative behaviour when possible solutions to a problem incubate in an individual's mind. Niklas Laninge of Hoa's Tool Shop, a Stockholm-based company that helps organizations become more innovative, argues that creative information gathering means thinking beyond usual routines and comfort zones. For example, have lunch with someone outside your field to discuss the problem. "It's so easy, and you're forced to speak about your business and the things that you want to accomplish in new terms. You can't use buzzwords because people don't know what you mean," Laninge says.[74]

- *Idea generation.* Once we have collected the relevant information, it's time to translate knowledge into ideas. Thus, **idea generation** is the process of creative behaviour in which we develop possible solutions to a problem from relevant information and knowledge. Increasingly, idea generation is collaborative. For example, when NASA engineers developed the idea for landing a spacecraft on Mars, they did so collaboratively. Before coming up with the Curiosity—an SUV-sized rover that lands on Mars from a sky crane—the team spent three days scribbling potential ideas on whiteboards.[75]

- *Idea evaluation.* Finally, it's time to choose from the ideas we have generated. Thus, **idea evaluation** is the process of creative behaviour in which we evaluate potential solutions to identify the best one. Sometimes the method of choosing can be innovative. When Dallas Mavericks owner Mark Cuban was unhappy with the basketball team's uniforms, he asked fans to help design and choose the best uniform. Cuban said, "What's the best way to come up with creative ideas? You ask for them. So we are going to crowd source the design and colors of our uniforms."[76] Generally, you want those who evaluate ideas to be different from those who generate them, to eliminate the obvious biases.

Case Incident—The Youngest Female Self-Made Billionaire on page 445 asks you to consider how the three-stage model of creativity applies to the success of Spanx owner Sara Blakely.

Causes of Creative Behaviour

Having defined creative behaviour, the main stage in the three-stage model, we now look back to the causes of creativity: creative potential and creative environment.

Creative Potential

Is there such a thing as a creative personality? Indeed. While creative genius—whether in science (Albert Einstein), art

> Why are some people more creative than others?

problem formulation The stage of creative behaviour that involves identifying a problem or an opportunity that requires a solution as yet unknown.

information gathering The stage of creative behaviour when possible solutions to a problem incubate in an individual's mind.

idea generation The process of creative behaviour that involves developing possible solutions to a problem from relevant information and knowledge.

idea evaluation The process of creative behaviour involving the evaluation of potential solutions to problems to identify the best one.

PERSONAL INVENTORY ASSESSMENT

Learn About Yourself
How Creative Are You?

(Pablo Picasso), or business (Steve Jobs)—is scarce, most people have some of the characteristics shared by exceptionally creative people. The more of these characteristics we have, the higher our creative potential.

Intelligence is related to creativity. Smart people are more creative because they are better at solving complex problems. However, intelligent individuals may also be more creative because they have greater "working memory"; that is, they can recall more information that is related to the task at hand.[77]

The Big Five personality trait of openness to experience (see Chapter 2) correlates with creativity, probably because open individuals are less conformist in action and more divergent in thinking.[78] Other traits of creative people include proactive personality, self-confidence, risk taking, tolerance for ambiguity, and perseverance.[79]

Expertise is the foundation for all creative work and thus is the single most important predictor of creative potential. Film writer, producer, and director Quentin Tarantino spent his youth working in a video rental store, where he built up an encyclopedic knowledge of movies. The potential for creativity is enhanced when individuals have abilities, knowledge, proficiencies, and similar expertise to their field of endeavour. You would not expect someone with minimal knowledge of programming to be very creative as a software engineer.

Creative Environment

Most of us have creative potential we can learn to apply, but as important as creative potential is, by itself it is not enough. We need to be in an environment where creative potential can be realized. What environmental factors affect whether creative potential translates into creative behaviours?

First and perhaps most important is *motivation*. If you are not motivated to be creative, it is unlikely that you will be. A 2013 review of 26 studies revealed that intrinsic motivation, or the desire to work on something because it's interesting, exciting,

Shahrzad Rafati, founder and CEO of Vancouver-based BroadbandTV, made *Fast Company*'s 2014 Most Creative People in Business 1000 list. When she was still an undergraduate computer science major at UBC, she came up with the idea of taking video uploaded to sites like YouTube and merging it with online advertising opportunities—bringing together both "pirates" and corporate content providers. Her company's MultiChannel Network (MCN) was ranked the third-largest on YouTube in 2014 with more than 1.6 billion monthly views.

Stuart Davis/PNG

satisfying, and challenging (discussed in more detail in Chapters 4 and 5), correlates fairly strongly with creative outcomes. This link is true regardless of whether we are talking about student creativity or employee creativity.[80]

It's also valuable to work in an environment that rewards and recognizes creative work. The organization should foster the free flow of ideas, including providing fair and constructive judgment. Freedom from excessive rules encourages creativity; employees should have the freedom to decide what work is to be done and how to do it. A 2012 study of 385 employees working for several drug companies in China revealed that both structural empowerment (in which the structure of the work unit allows sufficient employee freedom) and psychological empowerment (which lets the individual feel personally empowered) were related to employee creativity.[81]

Good leadership matters to creativity. A 2012 study of more than 100 teams working in a large bank revealed that when the leader behaved in a punitive, unsupportive manner, the teams were less creative.[82] By contrast, when leaders are encouraging in tone, run their units in a transparent fashion, and encourage the development of their employees, the individuals they supervise are more creative.[83]

As we learned in Chapter 6, more work today is being done in teams, and many people believe diversity will increase team creativity. Past research, unfortunately, has suggested that diverse teams are not more creative. More recently, however, a 2012 study of Dutch teams revealed that when team members were explicitly asked to understand and consider the point of view of the other team members (an exercise called perspective-taking), diverse teams *were* more creative than those with less diversity.[84] A 2012 study of 68 Chinese teams reported that diversity was positively related to team creativity only when the team's leader was inspirational and instilled members with confidence.[85] Another 2012 study in a multinational pharmaceutical company found that teams that comprised members with diverse business functions were more creative when they shared knowledge of one another's areas of expertise.[86] Collectively, these studies show that diverse teams *can* be more creative, but only under certain conditions.

Creative Outcomes (Innovation)

The final stage in our model of creativity is the outcome. Creative behaviour does not always produce a creative or innovative outcome. An employee might generate a creative idea and never share it. Management might reject a creative solution. Teams might squelch creative behaviours by isolating those who propose different ideas. A 2012 study showed that most people have a bias against accepting creative ideas because ideas create uncertainty. When people feel uncertain, their ability to see any idea as creative is blocked.[87]

We can define *creative outcomes* as ideas or solutions judged to be novel and useful by relevant stakeholders. Novelty itself does not generate a creative outcome if it is not useful. Thus, "off-the-wall" solutions are creative only if they help solve the problem. The usefulness of the solution might be self-evident (for example, the iPad), or it might be considered successful by stakeholders before the actual success can be known.[88]

An organization may harvest many creative ideas from its employees and call itself innovative. However, as one expert recently stated, "Ideas are useless unless used." Soft skills help translate ideas into results. A 2012 study found that among employees of a large agribusiness company, creative ideas were most likely to be implemented when the individual was motivated to translate the idea into practice—and when he or she had strong networking ability.[89] Another important factor is organizational climate; a 2013 study of health care teams found that team creativity translated into innovation only when the climate actively supported innovation.[90] These studies highlight an important fact: Creative ideas do not implement themselves; translating them into creative outcomes is a social process that requires use of other concepts addressed in this book, including power and politics (Chapter 8), leadership (Chapter 11), and motivation (Chapters 4 and 5).

From Concepts to Skills on pages 446–447 provides suggestions on how you can become more effective at solving problems creatively.

What About Ethics in Decision Making?

6 Describe the four criteria used in making ethical decisions.

The three police officers involved in Billy-Joe Nachuk's human rights complaint were on-duty, playing a formal role representing civil order and respect for the public.[91] As such, their actions hold greater ethical implications, a fact noted by the Manitoba Human Rights Commission when it released its decision. The actions of a single representative can undermine the public's perception of the ethics of an entire organization. For that reason, the commission noted that officers should be held to a higher standard of behaviour and should be a positive example of accommodation for people with disabilities—a standard that was not achieved by the three officers in their interaction with Nachuk. How does ethics influence decision making?

No contemporary examination of decision making would be complete without the discussion of ethics, because ethical considerations should be an important criterion in organizational decision making. **Ethics** is the study of moral values or principles that guide our behaviour and inform us whether actions are right or wrong. Ethical principles help us "do the right thing." In this section, we present four ways to ethically frame decisions and examine the factors that shape an individual's ethical decision-making behaviour. We also examine ways to encourage more ethical decisions. To learn more about your approach to ethical decision making, see the *Ethical Dilemma* on page 444.

Four Ethical Decision Criteria

An individual can use four criteria in making ethical choices.[92] The first is **utilitarianism**, in which decisions are made solely on the basis of their outcomes, ideally to provide the greatest good for the greatest number. This view dominates business decision making. It is consistent with goals such as efficiency, productivity, and high profits. By maximizing profits, for instance, business executives can argue that they are securing the greatest good for the greatest number—as they hand out dismissal notices to 15 percent of employees.

A second ethical criterion is to make decisions consistent with fundamental liberties and privileges as set forth in documents such as the Canadian Charter of Rights and Freedoms. An emphasis on *rights* in decision making means respecting and protecting the basic rights of individuals, such as the rights to privacy, free speech, and due process. This criterion protects **whistle-blowers** when they report unethical or illegal practices by their organizations to the media or to government agencies, using their right to free speech.

A third criterion is to impose and enforce rules fairly and impartially to ensure *justice* or an equitable distribution of benefits and costs. Union members typically favour this view. It justifies paying people the same wage for a given job, regardless of performance differences, and using seniority as the primary determination in making layoff decisions. A focus on justice protects the interests of the underrepresented and less powerful, but it can encourage a sense of entitlement that reduces risk-taking, innovation, and productivity.

A fourth ethical criterion is *care*. The ethics of care can be stated as follows: "The morally correct action is the one that expresses care in protecting the special relationships that individuals have with each other."[93] The care criterion suggests that we should be aware of the needs, desires, and well-being of those to whom we are closely connected. This perspective does remind us of the difficulty of being impartial in all decisions.

ethics The study of moral values or principles that guide our behaviour and inform us whether actions are right or wrong.

utilitarianism A decision focused on outcomes or consequences that emphasizes the greatest good for the greatest number.

whistle-blowers Individuals who report unethical practices by their employer to outsiders.

Leslie Ferenc/The Star/GetStock

Toronto-based Hospitality Workers Training Centre (HWTC) is a partnership between UNITE HERE (the hospitality workers' union) and major hotels in Toronto. The purpose of HWTC is to train people who face employment barriers in skills necessary for the hospitality industry, and then help them find work. Genevievea Scott, 27, shown here, was one of those trainees. Recently, HWTC opened Hawthorne, a restaurant in downtown Toronto, so that entrants and current workers could get skills training in the jobs involved in running a restaurant. Danielle Olsen, executive director of HWTC, shows that HWTC goes beyond utilitarian criteria when she says that "it is essential for us to balance the tension between Hawthorne's social mission and the economic reality of running a restaurant." HWTC clearly supports social justice as well.[94]

A focus on utilitarianism promotes efficiency and productivity, but it can sideline the rights of some individuals, particularly those with minority representation. The use of rights protects individuals from injury and is consistent with freedom and privacy, but it can create a legalistic environment that hinders productivity and efficiency. A focus on justice protects the interests of the underrepresented and less powerful, but it can encourage a sense of entitlement that reduces risk taking, innovation, and productivity.

Decision makers, particularly in for-profit organizations, feel comfortable with utilitarianism. The "best interests" of the organization and stockholders can justify a lot of questionable actions, such as large layoffs. But many critics feel this perspective needs to change. Public concern about individual rights and social justice suggests that managers should develop ethical standards based on nonutilitarian criteria. This presents a challenge because satisfying individual rights and social justice creates far more ambiguities than utilitarian effects on efficiency and profits. However, while raising prices, selling products with questionable effects on consumer health, closing down inefficient plants, laying off large numbers of employees, and moving production overseas to cut costs can be justified in utilitarian terms, a single ethical criterion may no longer be sufficient to judge how good a decision is.

People don't always follow ethical standards. To understand why, researchers are turning increasingly to **behavioural ethics**—an area of study that analyzes how people behave when confronted with ethical dilemmas. Their research tells us that while ethical standards exist collectively (society and organizations) and individually (personal ethics), individuals don't always follow ethical standards promulgated by their organizations, and we sometimes violate our own standards. Our ethical behaviour varies widely from one situation to the next. *Focus on Research* considers why people cheat, and what organizations can do to limit cheating.

behavioural ethics Analyzing how people actually behave when confronted with ethical dilemmas.

Why People Cheat

What makes individuals decide to cheat? We all have cheated at something.[95] We could assume that deciding to cheat is a product of cold hard calculus: Is the benefit of cheating worth the cost? Research shows, however, that cheating is less rational than expected. Several 2012 research projects yield the following insights about how organizations can stem cheating and other unethical behaviour:

- *Cheating happens away from the cash.* One study found that people steal more when they are a couple of steps removed from the cash. For example, one gallery's gift shop was hemorrhaging money, but the reason was that volunteers were helping themselves to merchandise, not the cash drawer. Similarly, when researchers put six packs of Coke and six $1 bills in dorm fridges, every Coke was gone within 72 hours, but none of the cash.
- *Cheating is contagious.* A study of high school students in upper-middle-class communities revealed that among the 93 percent who admitted to cheating, the top reason was the pervasiveness of cheating by others. A recent study of accounting undergraduates revealed that cheating was most likely among students who reported having recently seen cheating and having friends who cheated.
- *Moods affect cheating.* Research shows that people cheat more when they are angry or tired. This insight reveals another positive dividend of trying to reduce negative moods at work, as we discussed in Chapter 2.
- *Incentives matter.* Studies suggest that high-stakes outcomes create cheating as an inevitable consequence. Coaches, CEOs, and political leaders should still be held accountable, but it's helpful to understand circumstances in which expectations may seem attainable only by cheating.

Making Ethical Decisions

How might we increase ethical decision-making in organizations? First, sociologist James Q. Wilson proposed the *broken windows theory*—the idea that decayed and disorderly urban environments may facilitate criminal behaviour because they signal antisocial norms. Although controversial, the theory does fit with behavioural ethics research showing that seemingly superficial aspects of the environment—such as lighting, outward displays of wealth and status, and cleanliness—can affect ethical behaviour in organizations.[96] Managers must first realize that ethical behaviour can be affected by signals; for example, if signs of status and money are everywhere, an employee may perceive those, rather than ethical standards, to be of the highest importance. Second, managers should encourage conversations about moral issues; they may serve as a reminder and increase ethical decision making. A 2012 study found that simply asking business school students to think of an ethical situation had powerful effects when they were making ethical choices later.[97] Finally, we should be aware of our own moral "blind spots"—the tendency to see ourselves as more moral than we are and others as less moral than they are. Although smart people can be just as susceptible to moral blind spots as others, an environment that encourages open discussions and does not penalize people for coming forward is key to overcoming blind spots and increasing the ethicality of decision making.[98]

> How can people make more ethical decisions?

Behavioural ethics research stresses the importance of culture to ethical decision making. There are few global standards for ethical decision making,[99] as contrasts between Asia and the West illustrate. What is ethical in one culture may be unethical

Tara Walton/ZUMA Press/Newscom

After a garment factory building in Pakistan collapsed, killing and injuring thousands of people in April 2013, Galen Weston (right), chairman of Brampton, Ontario-based Loblaw Companies, said Loblaw would "be a 'force for good' in Bangladesh." Loblaw is Toronto-based Joe Fresh's parent corporation, and some of Joe Fresh's clothes were manufactured in the collapsed factory. Loblaw signed an agreement to monitor all factories worldwide for fire safety and structural soundness. It's the only Canadian company to have done so. Some labour rights activists have argued that more Canadian companies should take a more ethical approach to offshore production. Weston is shown here with Joe Mimran of Joe Fresh, speaking to the media one week after the building's collapse.[100]

in another. For example, because bribery is more common in countries such as China, a Canadian working in China might face a dilemma: Should I pay a bribe to secure business if it's an accepted part of that country's culture? Although some companies such as IBM explicitly address this issue, many don't. Without sensitivity to cultural differences in defining ethical conduct, organizations may encourage unethical conduct without even knowing it.

While the difference between an ethical and unethical decision is not always clear-cut, there are some questions you should consider. Exhibit 12-6 illustrates a decision

EXHIBIT 12-6 Is a Decision Ethical?

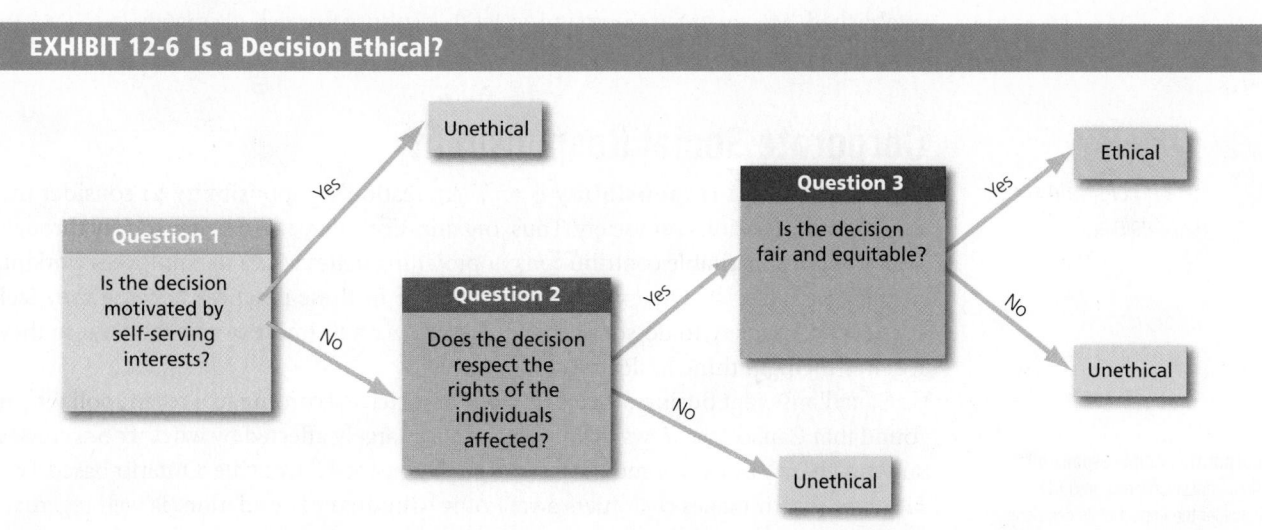

tree to guide ethical decision making.[101] This tree is built on three of the ethical decision criteria—utilitarianism, rights, and justice—presented above. The first question you need to answer addresses self-interest vs. organizational goals.

The second question concerns the rights of other parties. If the decision violates the rights of someone else (the person's right to privacy, for instance), then the decision is unethical.

The final question that needs to be addressed relates to whether the decision conforms to standards of fairness and equity. The department head who inflates the performance evaluation of a favoured employee and deflates the evaluation of a disfavoured employee—and then uses these evaluations to justify giving the former a big raise and nothing to the latter—has treated the disfavoured employee unfairly.

Unfortunately, the answers to the questions in Exhibit 12-6 are often argued in ways to make unethical decisions seem ethical. Powerful people, for example, can become very adept at explaining self-serving behaviours in terms of the organization's best interests. Similarly, they can persuasively argue that unfair actions are really fair and just. Our point is that immoral people can justify almost any behaviour. Those who are powerful, articulate, and persuasive are the most likely to be able to get away with unethical actions successfully. When faced with an ethical dilemma, try to answer the questions in Exhibit 12-6 truthfully. Organizations that don't foster a strong culture of ethics may find themselves facing disaster, as the story of now-bankrupt Montreal, Maine and Atlantic Railway (MMA), discussed in *OB in the Workplace*, shows.

OB IN THE **WORKPLACE**
The Ethics of Fostering a "Culture of Shortcuts"

How can an organization's culture contribute to a deadly disaster? The Transportation Safety Board of Canada's report about the Lac-Mégantic, Quebec, derailment that killed 47 people and obliterated part of the town indicated that MMA's lax attitude toward safety contributed to the disaster.[102] "The TSB found MMA was a company with a weak safety culture that did not have a functioning safety management system to manage risks," the agency said. The company's approach to safety represents a significant breach of ethics given the threat posed by a lack of appropriate standards in the rail industry. Gaps in training, employee monitoring, and maintenance were noted. One such gap, a failure to properly test the air brake system, contributed directly to the tragic events of July 6, 2013. From all indications, this "culture of shortcuts" was well established. Management's decision to let this culture flourish ultimately led MMA to disaster, bankruptcy, and ruin.

Corporate Social Responsibility

7 Define *corporate social responsibility*.

Corporate social responsibility is an organization's responsibility to consider the impact of its decisions on society. Thus, organizations may try to better society through such things as charitable contributions or providing better wages to employees working in offshore factories. Organizations may engage in these practices because they feel pressured by society to do so, or they may seek ways to improve society because they feel it is the right thing to do.

Canadians want businesses to give back to society, according to a recent poll which found that Canadians' views of corporations are largely affected by whether businesses support charitable causes and protect the environment.[103] Oakville, Ontario-based Tim Hortons, which makes customers aware of its Children's Foundation, is well regarded by Canadians.[104]

corporate social responsibility
An organization's responsibility to consider the impact of its decisions on society.

Not everyone agrees that organizations should engage in corporate social responsibility. For example, economist Milton Friedman remarked in *Capitalism and Freedom* that "few trends could so thoroughly undermine the very foundations of our free society as the acceptance by corporate officials of a social responsibility other than to make as much money for their stockholders as possible."[105]

Joel Bakan, professor of law at the University of British Columbia, author of *The Corporation*,[106] and co-director of the documentary of the same name, is more critical of organizations than Friedman. Bakan suggests that today's corporations have many of the same characteristics as a psychopathic personality (for example, self-interested, lacking empathy, manipulative, and reckless in their disregard of others). Bakan notes that even though companies have a tendency to act psychopathically, this is not why they are fixated on profits. Rather, their only legal responsibility is to maximize organizational profits for stockholders. He proposes changes in laws to encourage corporations to behave more socially responsibly.

Canadian senior executives have mixed feelings about the extent to which businesses should get involved in charitable giving, or forcing industry standards on foreign corporations. A 2011 poll found that 45 percent believe individual shareholders, not the company, should make personal decisions about giving to charity. Another 35 percent, however, felt corporations should donate to charities. One CEO explained, "Being a good corporate citizen means assisting those less fortunate—as long as it is done in the context of the entities' aims, objectives and employees' desires."[107] A 2011 poll conducted by COMPAS found that Canadian business leaders were not about imposing Canadian management values on Chinese employers, however. "We don't have the right to tell China how to run its economy," said one CEO. "We have the choice to buy, or not to buy."[108]

A recent survey found that Canadian and American MBA students are very interested in the subject of corporate social responsibility. Over 80 percent of respondents "believed business professionals should take into account social and environmental impacts when making decisions." Almost two-thirds of these respondents felt that corporate social responsibility should be part of core MBA classes, and 60 percent said "they would seek socially responsible employment."[109]

GLOBAL **IMPLICATIONS**

In this section, we consider global research on the three key areas we discussed in this chapter: decision making, creativity, and ethics.

Decision Making

The rational decision-making model makes no acknowledgment of cultural differences, nor does the bulk of OB research literature on decision making. A recent review of cross-cultural OB research covered 25 areas, but cultural influence on decision making was not among them. Another recent review identified 15 topics, but the result was the same: No research on culture and decision making.[110]

However, Indonesians, for instance, don't necessarily make decisions the same way Australians do. Therefore, we need to recognize that the cultural background of a decision maker can have a significant influence on the selection of problems, the depth of analysis, the importance placed on logic and rationality, and whether organizational decisions should be made autocratically by an individual manager or collectively in groups.[111]

Cultures differ in their time orientation, the importance of rationality, their belief in the ability of people to solve problems, and their preference for collective decision making. Differences in time orientation help us understand why managers in Egypt make decisions at a much slower and more deliberate pace than their US counterparts.

While rationality is valued in North America, that is not true elsewhere in the world. A North American manager might make an important decision intuitively but know it's important to appear to proceed in a rational fashion because rationality is highly valued in the West. In countries such as Iran, where rationality is not as paramount as other factors, efforts to appear rational are not necessary.

Some cultures emphasize solving problems, while others focus on accepting situations as they are. Canada falls in the first category; Thailand and Indonesia are examples of the second. Because problem-solving managers believe they can and should change situations to their benefit, Canadian managers might identify a problem long before their Thai or Indonesian counterparts would choose to recognize it as such. Decision making by Japanese managers is much more group-oriented than in Canada. The Japanese value conformity and cooperation. So before Japanese CEOs make an important decision, they collect a large amount of information, which they use in consensus-forming group decisions.

In short, there are probably important cultural differences in decision making, but unfortunately not yet much research to identify them.

Creativity

A 2013 nation-wide study suggests that countries scoring high on Hofstede's culture dimension of individuality (discussed in Chapter 3) are more creative.[112] Western countries such as the United States, Italy, and Belgium score high on individuality, and South American and Eastern countries such as China, Colombia, and Pakistan score low. Do these findings mean that Western cultures are more creative? Some evidence suggests that this is true. A 2013 study compared the creative projects of German and Chinese college students, some of whom were studying in their homeland, and some of whom were studying abroad. An independent panel of Chinese and German judges determined that the German students were most creative and that Asian German students were more creative than domestic Chinese students. These results suggested that the German culture was more creative.[113] However, even if some cultures are more creative on average, strong variations always occur within cultures. Put another way, millions of Chinese are more creative than their US counterparts.

Ethics

No global ethical standards exist,[114] as contrasts between Asia and the West illustrate.[115] Because bribery is commonplace in countries such as China, a Canadian working in China might face a dilemma: Should I pay a bribe to secure business if it's an accepted part of that country's culture? A manager of a large US company operating in China caught an employee stealing. Following company policy, she fired him and turned him over to the local authorities. Later, she was horrified to learn the employee had been summarily executed.[116]

Although ethical standards may seem ambiguous in the West, criteria defining right and wrong are actually much clearer there than in Asia, where few issues are black and white and most are grey. In Japan, people doing business together often exchange gifts, even expensive ones. This is part of Japanese tradition. When North American and European companies started doing business in Japan, most North American executives were not aware of the Japanese tradition of exchanging gifts and wondered whether this was a form of bribery. Most have come to accept this tradition now, and have even set different limits on gift giving in Japan than in other countries.[117]

Global organizations must establish ethical principles for decision makers in countries such as India and China and modify them to reflect cultural norms if they want to uphold high standards and consistent practices. Having agreements among countries to police bribery may not be enough, however. The 34 countries of the Organisation for Economic Co-operation and Development (OECD) entered into an agreement to tackle corporate bribery in 1997. However, a 2011 study by Berlin-based Transparency International found that 21 of the OECD countries are "doing little or nothing" to enforce the agreement. Canada came under strong criticism for being "the only G7 country in the little or no enforcement category." The United States and Germany rated highest on number of cases filed. Transparency International noted that Canada needed to enforce more of its laws in this area.[118]

Summary

An understanding of the way people make decisions can help us explain and predict behaviour, but few important decisions are simple or unambiguous enough for the rational decision-making model's assumptions to apply. We find individuals looking for solutions that satisfice rather than optimize, injecting biases into the decision process, and relying on intuition. Managers should encourage creativity in employees and teams to create a route to innovative decision-making. Individuals are more likely to make ethical decisions when the culture in which they work supports ethical decision making.

LESSONS LEARNED

- Individuals often short-cut the decision-making process and do not consider all options.
- Intuition leads to better results when supplemented with evidence and good judgment.
- Exceptional creativity is rare, but expertise in a subject and a creative environment encourage novel and useful creative outcomes.

SNAPSHOT SUMMARY

How Should Decisions Be Made?
- The Rational Decision-Making Process

How Do Individuals Actually Make Decisions?
- Bounded Rationality in Considering Alternatives
- Intuition
- Judgment Shortcuts

Group Decision Making
- Groups vs. the Individual
- Groupthink and Groupshift
- Group Decision-Making Techniques

Creativity in Organizational Decision Making
- Creative Behaviour
- Causes of Creative Behaviour

- Creative Outcomes (Innovation)

What About Ethics in Decision Making?
- Four Ethical Decision Criteria
- Making Ethical Decisions

Corporate Social Responsibility

MyManagementLab   Study, practise, and explore real business situations with these helpful resources:

- **Study Plan:** Check your understanding of chapter concepts with self-study quizzes.
- **Online Lesson Presentations:** Study key chapter topics and work through interactive assessments to test your knowledge and master management concepts.
- **Videos:** Learn more about the management practices and strategies of real companies.
- **Simulations:** Practise management decision-making in simulated business environments.

P I A PERSONAL INVENTORY ASSESSMENT

OB at Work

for Review

1. What is the rational model of decision making? How is it different from bounded rationality and intuition?

2. What are some common decision biases or errors people make?

3. What are the strengths and weaknesses of group (versus individual) decision making?

4. How effective are interacting, brainstorming, and the nominal group technique?

5. What is creativity, and what is the three-stage model of creativity?

6. What are the four criteria used in making ethical decisions, and how do they differ?

7. What is corporate social responsibility?

for Managers

- Adjust your decision-making approach to the national culture you are operating in and to the criteria your organization values. If you operate in a country that does not value rationality, don't feel compelled to follow the rational decision-making model or to try to make your decisions appear rational. Adjust your decision-making approach to ensure compatibility with the organizational culture.

- Be aware of biases. Then try to minimize their impact. *OB in Action— Reducing Biases and Errors in Decision Making* on page 422 offers some suggestions.

- Combine rational analysis with intuition. These are not conflicting approaches to decision making. By using both, you can actually improve your decision-making effectiveness.

- Try to enhance your creativity. Actively look for novel solutions to problems, attempt to see problems in new ways, use analogies, and hire creative talent. Try to remove work and organizational barriers that might impede your creativity.

for You

- In some decision situations, consider following the rational decision-making model. Doing so will ensure that you review a wider variety of options before committing to a particular decision.

- Analyze the decision situation and be aware of your biases. We all bring biases to the decisions we make.

- Combine rational analysis with intuition. As you gain experience, you should feel increasingly confident in imposing your intuitive processes on top of your rational analysis.

- Use creativity-stimulation techniques. You can improve your overall decision-making effectiveness by searching for innovative solutions to problems. This can be as basic as telling yourself to think creatively and to look specifically for unique alternatives.

- When making decisions, think about their ethical implications. A quick way to do this is to ask yourself: Would I be embarrassed if this action were printed on the front page of the newspaper?

People Are More Creative When They Work Alone

POINT

I know groups are all the rage.[119] Businesses are knocking down walls and cubicles to create more open, "collaborative" environments. "Self-managing teams" are replacing the traditional middle manager. Students in universities are constantly working on group projects, and even young children are finding themselves learning in small groups.

I also know *why* groups are all the rage. Work, they say, has become too complex for individuals to perform alone. Groups are better at brainstorming and coming up with creative solutions to complicated problems. Groups also produce higher levels of commitment and satisfaction—so long as group members develop feelings of cohesiveness and trust one another.

For every group that comes up with a creative solution, I'll show you twice as many individuals who would come up with a better solution had they only been left alone. Consider creative geniuses like Leonardo DaVinci, Isaac Newton, and Pablo Picasso. Or, more recently, Steve Wozniak, the co-founder of Apple Computer. All were introverts who toiled by themselves. According to Wozniak, "I'm going to give you some advice that might be hard to take. That advice is: Work alone . . . not on a committee. Not on a team."

Enough anecdotal evidence. Research has also shown that groups can kill creativity. One study found that computer programmers at companies that give them privacy and freedom from interruptions outperformed their counterparts at companies that forced more openness and collaboration. Or consider Adrian Furnham, an organizational psychologist whose research led him to conclude that "business people must be insane to use brainstorming groups." People slack off in groups, and they're afraid to communicate any ideas that might make them sound dumb. These problems don't exist when people work alone. So take Picasso's advice: "Without great solitude, no serious work is possible."

COUNTERPOINT

I will grant your point that there are circumstances in which groups can hinder creative progress, but if the right conditions are put in place, groups are simply much better at coming up with novel solutions to problems than are individuals. Using strategies such as the nominal group technique, generating ideas electronically rather than face-to-face, and ensuring that individuals do not evaluate others' ideas until all have been generated are just a few ways you can set up groups for creative success.

The fact of the matter is that problems *are* too complex these days for individuals to effectively perform alone. Consider the Rovers launched by NASA to roam around Mars collecting data. An accomplishment like that is made possible only by a group, not a lone individual. Steve Wozniak's collaboration with Steve Jobs is what really made Apple sail as a company.

In addition, the most influential research is conducted by teams of academics, rather than individuals. Indeed, if you look at recent Nobel Prize winners in areas such as economics, physics, and chemistry, the majority have been won by academics who collaborated on the research.

So if you want creativity, two heads are in fact better than one.

OB *at Work*

Creative Style Indicator: Creativity takes different forms. Use this scale to assess your own creative style when approaching problems at work.

How Creative Are You?: Some occupations require high levels of creativity, while others focus more on following rules. Use this scale to determine how creative you are. This information can help guide career decisions.

BREAKOUT **GROUP** EXERCISES

Form small groups to discuss the following topics, as assigned by your instructor:

1. Apply the rational decision-making model to deciding where your group might eat dinner this evening. How closely were you able to follow the rational model in making this decision?

2. The company that makes your favourite snack product has been accused of being weak in its social responsibility efforts. What impact will this have on your purchase of any more products from that company?

3. You have seen a classmate cheat on an exam or an assignment. Do you do something about this or ignore it?

EXPERIENTIAL EXERCISE

Wilderness Survival

You are a member of a hiking party. After reaching base camp on the first day, you decide to take a quick sunset hike by yourself. After a few exhilarating miles, you decide to return to camp. On your way back, you realize that you are lost. You have shouted for help, to no avail. It is now dark, and getting cold.

Your Task

Without communicating with anyone else in your group, read the following scenarios and choose the best answer. Keep track of your answers on a sheet of paper. You have 10 minutes to answer the 10 questions.

1. The first thing you decide to do is to build a fire. However, you have no matches, so you use the bow and drill method. What is the bow and drill method?

   a. A dry, soft stick is rubbed between one's hands against a board of supple green wood.

   b. A soft green stick is rubbed between one's hands against a hardwood board.

   c. A straight stick of wood is quickly rubbed back and forth against a dead tree.

   d. Two sticks (one being the bow, the other the drill) are struck to create a spark.

2. It occurs to you that you can also use the fire as a distress signal. How do you form the international distress signal?

   a. 2 fires

   b. 4 fires in a square

   c. 4 fires in a cross

   d. 3 fires in a line

3. You are very thirsty. You go to a nearby stream and collect some water in the small metal cup you have in your backpack. How long should you boil the water?

    a. 15 minutes

    b. 1 minute

    c. A few seconds

    d. It depends on the altitude.

4. You are very hungry, so you decide to eat what appear to be edible berries. When performing the universal edibility test, what should you do?

    a. Do not eat for 2 hours before the test.

    b. If the plant stings your lip, confirm the sting by holding it under your tongue for 15 minutes.

    c. If nothing bad has happened 2 hours after digestion, eat half a cup of the plant and wait again.

    d. Separate the plant into its basic components and eat each component, one at a time.

5. Next, you decide to build a shelter for the evening. In selecting a site, what do you *not* have to consider?

    a. It must contain material to make the type of shelter you need.

    b. It must be free of insects, reptiles, and poisonous plants.

    c. It must be large enough and level enough for you to lie down comfortably.

    d. It must be on a hill so you can signal rescuers and keep an eye on your surroundings.

6. In the shelter that you built, you notice a spider. You heard from a fellow hiker that black widow spiders populate the area. How do you identify a black widow spider?

    a. Its head and abdomen are black; its thorax is red.

    b. It is attracted to light.

    c. It runs away from light.

    d. It is dark with a red or orange marking on the female's abdomen.

7. After getting some sleep, you notice that the night sky has cleared, so you decide to try to find your way back to base camp. You believe you should travel north and can use the North Star for navigation. How do you locate the North Star?

    a. Hold your right hand up as far as you can and look between your index and middle fingers.

    b. Find Sirius and look 60 degrees above it and to the right.

    c. Look for the Big Dipper and follow the line created by its cup end.

    d. Follow the line of Orion's belt.

8. You come across a fast-moving stream. What is the best way to cross it?

    a. Find a spot downstream from a sandbar, where the water will be calmer.

    b. Build a bridge.

    c. Find a rocky area, because the water will be shallow and you will have hand- and footholds.

    d. Find a level stretch where it breaks into a few channels.

9. After walking for about an hour, you feel several spiders in your clothes. You don't feel any pain, but you know some spider bites are painless. Which of these spider bites is painless?

    a. Black widow

    b. Brown recluse

    c. Wolf spider

    d. Harvestman (daddy longlegs)

10. You decide to eat some insects. Which insects should you avoid?

    a. Adults that sting or bite

    b. Caterpillars and insects that have a pungent odour

    c. Hairy or brightly coloured ones

    d. All the above

Group Task

Break into groups of 5 or 6 people. Now imagine that your whole group is lost. Write down your own answers first, and then compile your group's answers by reaching consensus approach to reach each decision. Once the group comes to an agreement, write the group decisions down on the same sheet of paper that you used for your individual answers. You will have approximately 20 minutes for the group task.

Scoring Your Answers

Your instructor will provide you with the correct answers, which are based on expert judgments in these situations. Once you have received the answers, calculate (A) your individual score; (B) your group's score; (C) the average individual score in the group; and (D) the best individual score in the group. Write these down and consult with your group to ensure that these scores are accurate.

(A) Your individual score _____

(B) Your group's score _____

(C) Average individual score in group _____

(D) Best individual score in group _____

Discussion Questions

1. How did your group (B) perform relative to yourself (A)?

2. How did your group (B) perform relative to the average individual score in the group (C)?

3. How did your group (B) perform relative to the best individual score in the group (D)?

4. Compare your results with those of other groups. Did some groups do a better job of outperforming individuals than others?

5. What do these results tell you about the effectiveness of group decision making?

6. What can groups do to make group decision making more effective?

7. What circumstances might cause a group to perform worse than its best individual?

ETHICAL **DILEMMA**

Five Ethical Decisions: What Would You Do?

Assume that you are a middle manager in a company with about 1000 employees. How would you respond to each of the following situations?[120]

1. You are negotiating a contract with a potentially very large customer whose representative has hinted that you could almost certainly be assured of getting his business if you gave him and his wife an all-expenses-paid cruise to the Caribbean. You know the representative's employer would not approve of such a "payoff," but you have the discretion to authorize such an expenditure. What would you do?

2. You have an autographed CD by Sam Roberts and put it up for sale on eBay. So far, the highest bid is $74.50. A friend has offered you $100 for the CD, commenting that he could get $150 for it on

eBay in a year. You know this is highly unlikely. Should you sell your friend the CD for what he offered ($100)? Do you have an obligation to tell your friend you have listed your CD on eBay?

3. Your company policy on reimbursement for meals while travelling on company business is that you will be repaid for your out-of-pocket costs, which are not to exceed $80 a day. You don't need receipts for these expenses—the company will take your word. When travelling, you tend to eat at fast-food places and rarely spend in excess of $20 a day. Most of your colleagues submit reimbursement requests in the range of $55 to $60 a day regardless of what their actual expenses are. How much would you request for your meal reimbursements?

4. You are the manager at a gaming company, and you are responsible for hiring a group to outsource the production of a highly anticipated new game. Because your company is a giant in the industry, numerous companies are trying to get the bid. One of them offers you some kickbacks if you give that firm the bid, but ultimately, it is up to your bosses to decide on the company. You don't mention the incentive, but you push upper management to give the bid to the company that offered you the kickback. Is withholding the truth as bad as lying? Why or why not?

5. You have discovered that one of your closest friends at work has stolen a large sum of money from the company. Would you do nothing? Go directly to an executive to report the incident before talking about it with the offender? Confront the individual before taking action? Make contact with the individual with the goal of persuading that person to return the money?

CASE INCIDENTS

The Youngest Female Self-Made Billionaire

Picture this.[121] The billionaire owner and founder stands in the conference room trying on bras while the CEO stands behind her, adjusting the straps. The floor is littered with underwear. The owner takes off one bra and puts on another. Five executives in the conference room barely blink.

Welcome to Sara Blakely's company, Spanx. In just a few years, Spanx has become to slimming underwear what JELL-O is to gelatin and Kleenex is to facial tissue: So dominant is the brand that its name is synonymous with the category.

At 42, Blakely is not the youngest billionaire in the world. However, she is the youngest female self-made billionaire. Like many stories of entrepreneurial success, hers is part gritty determination, part inspiration, and part circumstance. The grit was easy to see early on. As a child growing up in Clearwater Beach, Florida, she lured friends into doing her chores by setting up a competition. At 16, Blakely was so intent on success that she listened to self-help guru Wayne Dyer's recordings incessantly. Friends refused to ride in her car. "No! She's going to make us listen to that motivational crap!" Blakely recalls they said.

After twice failing to get into law school, Blakely started her first business in 1990, running a kids' club at the Clearwater Beach Hilton. It worked until the Hilton's general manager found out. Later, while working full-time in sales, Blakely began learning how to start a business. Her inspiration for Spanx came while she was cold-calling customers as a sales manager for an office supply company. She hated pantyhose. "It's Florida, it's hot, I'm carrying copy machines," she noted.

At the Georgia Tech library, Blakely researched every pantyhose patent ever filed. She wrote her patent application by following a textbook she read in Barnes & Noble. Then she worked on marketing, manufacturing, and financing, treating each as its own project. After numerous rejections, she finally found mill owners in North Carolina willing to finance the manufacturing. "At the end of the day, the guy ended up just wanting to help me," Blakely said. "He didn't even believe in the idea."

For a time, Blakely relied on US stores such as Neiman Marcus to set up her table and on word-of-mouth to get the news out to the public. Her big break came when she sent samples to Oprah Winfrey's stylist. Harpo Productions called to say that Winfrey would name Spanx her favourite product of the year and warned Blakely to get her website ready. She did not have a website.

Billions of dollars in sales later, Blakely has no plans to slow down. Spanx is sold in 54 countries, and Blakely wants to double international sales in three years. She says: "The biggest risk in life is not risking. Every risk you take in life is in direct proportion to the reward. If I'm afraid of something, it's the next thing I have to go do. That's just the way I've been."

Questions

1. Does hindsight bias affect the factors to which you might attribute Blakely's success? Why or why not?

2. Use the three-stage model of creativity to analyze Blakely's decision making. What can you learn from her story that might help you be more creative in the future?

"If Two Heads Are Better Than One, Are Four Even Better?"

Maggie Becker, age 24, is a marketing manager for a small chain of shops in Halifax. Recently, Maggie's wealthy uncle passed away and left her, his only niece, $100 000. Maggie considers her current salary adequate to meet her current living expenses, so she would like to invest the money so that when she buys a house she will have a nice nest egg on which to draw.

One of Maggie's neighbours, Brian, is a financial adviser. Brian told Maggie that the array of investment options is virtually endless. She asked him to present her with two of the best options, and this is what he offered her:

1. A very low-risk AAA bond fund. With this option, based on the information Brian provided, Maggie estimates that after five years she stands virtually zero chance of losing money, with an expected gain of approximately $7000.

2. A moderate-risk mutual fund. Based on the information Brian provided her, Maggie estimates that with this option she stands a 50 percent chance of making $40 000 but also a 50 percent chance of losing $20 000.

Maggie prides herself on being rational and objective in her thinking. However, she is unsure of what to do in this case. Brian refuses to help her, telling her that she has already limited herself by asking for only two options. While driving to her parents' house for the weekend, Maggie finds herself vacillating between the two options. Her older brother is also visiting the folks this weekend, so Maggie decides to gather her family around the table after dinner, lay out the two options, and go with their decision. "You know the old saying—two heads are better than one," she says to herself, "so four heads should be even better."

Questions

1. Has Maggie made a good decision about the way she is going to make the decision?

2. Which investment would you choose? Why?

3. Which investment do you think most people would choose?

4. Based on what you have learned about groupshift, which investment do you think Maggie's family will choose?

FROM CONCEPTS TO SKILLS

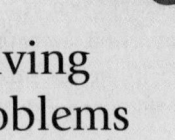

Solving Problems Creatively

You can be more effective at solving problems creatively if you use the following 10 suggestions:[122]

1. *Think of yourself as creative.* Research shows that if you think you cannot be creative, you won't be. Believing in your ability to be creative is the first step in becoming more creative.

2. *Pay attention to your intuition.* Every individual has a subconscious mind that works well. Sometimes answers will come to you when you least expect them. Listen to that "inner voice." In fact, most creative people will keep a notepad near their bed and write down ideas when the thoughts come to them.

3. *Move away from your comfort zone.* Every individual has a comfort zone in which certainty exists. But creativity and the known often do not mix. To be creative, you need to move away from the status quo and focus your mind on something new.

4. *Determine what you want to do.* This includes such things as taking time to understand a problem before beginning to try to resolve it, getting all the facts in mind, and trying to identify the most important facts.

5. *Think outside the box.* Use analogies whenever possible (for example, could you approach your problem like a fish out of water and look at what the fish does to cope? Or can you use the things you have to do to find your way when it's foggy to help you solve your problem?). Use

different problem-solving strategies, such as verbal, visual, mathematical, or theatrical. Look at your problem from a different perspective, or ask yourself what someone else, such as your grandmother, might do if faced with the same situation.

6. *Look for ways to do things better.* This may involve trying consciously to be original, not worrying about looking foolish, keeping an open mind, being alert to odd or puzzling facts, thinking of unconventional ways to use objects and the environment, discarding usual or habitual ways of doing things, and striving for objectivity by being as critical of your own ideas as you would be of someone else's.

7. *Find several right answers.* Being creative means continuing to look for other solutions even when you think you have solved the problem. A better, more creative solution just might be found.

8. *Believe in finding a workable solution.* Like believing in yourself, you also need to believe in your ideas. If you don't think you can find a solution, you probably won't.

9. *Brainstorm with others.* Creativity is not an isolated activity. Bouncing ideas off of others creates a synergistic effect.

10. *Turn creative ideas into action.* Coming up with creative ideas is only part of the process. Once the ideas are generated, they must be implemented. Keeping great ideas in your mind, or on papers that no one will read, does little to expand your creative abilities.

Every time the phone rings, your stomach clenches and your palms start to sweat. And it's no wonder! As sales manager for Brinkers, a machine tool parts manufacturer, you are besieged by calls from customers who are upset about late deliveries. Your boss, Carter Hererra, acts as both production manager and scheduler. Every time your sales representatives negotiate a sale, it's up to Carter to determine whether production can actually meet the delivery date the customer specifies. Carter invariably says, "No problem." The good thing about this is that you make a lot of initial sales. The bad news is that production hardly ever meets the shipment dates that Carter authorizes. Moreover, he does not seem to be all that concerned about the aftermath of late deliveries. He says: "Our customers know they're getting outstanding quality at a great price. Just let them try to match that anywhere. It can't be done. So even if they have to wait a couple of extra days or weeks, they're still getting the best deal they can." Somehow the customers don't see it that way, and they let you know about their unhappiness. Then it's up to you to try to soothe the relationship. You know this problem has to be taken care of, but what possible solutions are there? After all, how are you going to keep from making your manager angry or making the customers angry? Use your knowledge of creative problem-solving to come up with solutions.

Practising Skills

1. Take 20 minutes to list as many words as you can using the letters in the word *brainstorm*. (There are at least 95.) If you run out of listings before time is up, it's okay to quit early. But try to be as creative as you can.

Reinforcing Skills

2. List on a piece of paper some common terms that apply to both water and finance. How many were you able to come up with?

StockLite/Shutterstock

Spirituality in the Workplace

One fall day, Kira Leskew, who was owner of Etobicoke, Ontario-based Amberwood Doors, found herself screaming into the phone.[1] The customer at the other end of the line was upset because a part had not been delivered on time, but Leskew attacked the customer rather than admit fault.

She was so upset when she hung up the phone that she retreated to her car to try some meditation. "Using breathing to calm down, I went into feel space," she explains. "Essentially I paid attention to how I felt, and named my emotions: I felt hurt, upset, let down and embarrassed. Within a few minutes, I had a realization of what was really bothering me: I was breaking my word to my customer." After she calmed down, Leskew called her customer to deal with the issue more graciously.

Leskew has since offered mindful meditation sessions to her employees, and most have taken the four one-hour sessions given over two months. She said the sessions paid off with a "notable increase in teamwork, respect and support."

What Is Spirituality?

Workplace spirituality is *not* about organized religious practices. It's not about God or theology. This point was made clear in a recent study of 275 natural and social scientists at elite universities. About 25 percent "said they have a spirituality that is consistent with science, although they are not formally religious."[2]

Workplace spirituality recognizes that people have an inner life that nourishes and is nourished by meaningful work in the context of community.[3] Organizations that promote a spiritual culture recognize that people seek to find meaning and purpose in their work and desire to connect with other human beings as part of a community. Many of the topics we have discussed—ranging from job design (designing work that is meaningful to employees) to transformational leadership (leadership practices that emphasize a higher-order purpose and self-transcendent goals) are well matched to the concept of organizational spirituality. When a company emphasizes its commitment to paying suppliers in developing countries a fair (above-market) price for their goods to facilitate community development—as do Vancouver-based Maiwa, Halifax-based Fibres of Life, Hudson, Quebec-based Pure Art, and Whitehorse-based Bean North Café—it is encouraging a more spiritual culture.[4]

Blake Ashforth of Arizona State University and Michael Pratt of the University of Illinois propose that workplace spirituality has three major dimensions:

- *Transcendence of self:* a connection to something greater than one's self, and encompassing other people and things

- *Holism and harmony:* integration of self in such a way that it informs one's behaviour

- *Growth:* self-development, self-actualization and achieving one's hopes and potential

When pursued together, these three dimensions lead to connection, coherence, and completeness.[5]

Why Spirituality Now?

As we noted in our discussion of emotions in Chapter 3, there is controversy over whether feelings should be displayed in the workplace. At the same time, employers are showing more concern about an employee's inner life. Just as the study of emotions improves our understanding of organizational behaviour, an awareness of spirituality can help us better understand employee behaviour in the twenty-first century. Similarly, organizations that are concerned with spirituality are more likely to directly address problems created by conflicts that occur in everyday life.[6]

Of course, employees have always had an inner life. So why has the search for meaning and purposefulness in work surfaced now? We summarize the reasons in the inset *Reasons for the Growing Interest in Spirituality*.

Spirituality and Mindfulness

Recently, mindfulness has become part of the discussion on spirituality in the workplace. Ellen J. Langer, Harvard professor of psychology, has been studying mindfulness for much of her academic career. She defines mindfulness as "the process of actively noticing new things. When you do that, it puts you in the present. It makes you more sensitive to context and perspective. It's the essence of engagement."[7]

Reasons for the Growing Interest in Spirituality

- Spirituality acts as a counterbalance to the pressures and stress of a turbulent pace of life. Contemporary lifestyles—single-parent families, geographical mobility, the temporary nature of jobs, new technologies that create distance between people—underscore the lack of community many people feel and increase the need for involvement and connection.

- Formalized religion has not worked for many people, and they continue to look for anchors to replace lack of faith and to fill a growing feeling of emptiness.

- Job demands have made the workplace dominant in many people's lives, yet they continue to question the meaning of work.

- More people desire to integrate personal life values with their professional life.

- An increasing number of people are finding that the pursuit of more material acquisitions leaves them unfulfilled.

workplace spirituality The recognition that people have an inner life that nourishes and is nourished by meaningful work that takes place in the context of community.

Advantages to Mindfulness

- It's easier to pay attention.
- You remember more of what you've done.
- You're more creative.
- You're able to take advantage of opportunities when they present themselves.
- You avert the danger not yet arisen.
- You like people better, and people like you better, because you're less evaluative.
- You're more charismatic.[8]

Mindfulness means staying aware in the present and not simply accepting that "this is the way we have always done things." Langer explains how to make this possible: "When you're mindful, rules, routines, and goals guide you; they don't govern you."[9] The inset *Advantages to Mindfulness* presents Langer's reasons to be mindful.

What is Langer's advice about being mindful? "Life consists only of moments, nothing more than that. So if you make the moment matter, it all matters. You can be mindful, you can be mindless. You can win, you can lose. The worst case is to be mindless and lose. So when you're doing anything, be mindful, notice new things, make it meaningful to you, and you'll prosper."[10]

Meditation is one of the ways to become more mindful. Professor Jamie Gruman, at the College of Business and Economics at the University of Guelph, who studies meditation in the workplace, notes that "research shows people who meditate suffer from less stress, are less rigid in their thinking and are less likely to have overly emotional reactions to difficulties. All of these things are qualities of effective working and management decision making."[11]

Research also shows that engaging in meditation helps people be more creative;[12] and that just three successive days of 25 minutes of mindfulness meditation can effectively reduce stress.[13] Fifteen minutes of mindful meditation was found to be helpful in stopping individuals from thinking about sunk costs when making decisions (a bias we described in Chapter 12), making them more able to focus on the present and make clearer decisions.[14]

Mindful meditation is easy to practice, "doesn't require a rigid schedule," and can easily become part of one's work routine, notes Maria Gonzalez, president of Toronto-based Argonauta Strategic Alliances Consulting.[15] Her clients include BMO Financial Group, Ontario's Hydro One and the Conference Board of Canada. She is also the author of *Mindful Leadership*.[16] Business meetings are a good example of why mindfulness is needed. "In many conversations, neither side is fully there for the discussion. It's become a constant that people are trying to multitask and holding their BlackBerrys under the table at meetings and never focusing on the issue at hand," says Gonzalez.[17]

Characteristics of a Spiritual Organization

Spiritual organizations are concerned with helping people develop and reach their full potential. This is analogous to Abraham Maslow's description of self-actualization that we discussed in relation to motivation in Chapter 4. Similarly, organizations concerned with spirituality are more likely to directly address problems created by work–life conflicts.[18]

The Vancouver Island Health Authority recognizes that spiritual care can be helpful to those faced with stressful health care decisions.[19] Consequently, Nanaimo Regional General Hospital offers staff, patients, and patients' families access to spiritual health services that match their belief perspectives.

At Montreal-based Aliments Ouimet-Cordon Bleu, a processed-foods company, CEO J. Robert Ouimet has installed meditation rooms in all of his factories. He took this idea from a conversation he had with Mother Teresa. "There is no talking or eating allowed—only silence. The idea is to give the workplace a feeling of serenity and a sense of higher purpose," he explains. Ouimet wants his workplace to be a place not only where goods are produced but also where employees find their lives enriched. Ouimet's goal is to make it possible for his employees to discover their essential values, some of which are "solidarity and brotherhood, peace and serenity, humility and reconciliation between people."[20] To

do this he has developed Integrated System of Management Activities (ISMA), which include, among others, "a gesture, personal testimonials, a room for silence and reflection, annual personal bilateral meetings, the community meal, a monthly spiritual support group...." He believes that these "soulful initiatives" increase "not only human happiness and well-being, but company profitability as well." A 2011 study backs him up: "Mindfulness meditation has been reported to enhance numerous mental abilities, including rapid memory recall," says a co-author of the study.[21]

London, Ontario-based 3M Canada also provides a quiet room for meditation and reflection, which was one of the factors cited in explaining why it was chosen as one of Canada's top 100 employers for 2014.[22] Calgary-based Shell Canada provides a meditation and reflection centre so that its employees can have a more mindful, calming experience at work.[23]

What differentiates spiritual organizations from their nonspiritual counterparts? Although research on this question is only preliminary, our review identified four cultural characteristics that tend to be evident in spiritual organizations.[24]

Strong Sense of Purpose

Spiritual organizations build their cultures around a meaningful purpose. While profits may be important, they are not the primary value of these organizations. People want to be inspired by a purpose that they believe is important and worthwhile.

Charllotte Kwon, owner and CEO of Vancouver-based Maiwa Handprints, pays the artisans from developing countries who provide textiles for her retail stores substantially more than what others pay them.

She wants to protect craftspeople, so that they can continue to produce their artwork. She also wanted to make sure that their traditional arts will survive. "I don't want to lose traditional dyes made with specific recipes that are rarely written down. Without care, that information could be lost forever."[25] She also notes that she does not need to pay the artisans minimum prices to survive: "I live okay. I don't need anything more."[26]

Trust and Respect

Spiritual organizations are characterized by mutual trust, honesty, and openness. Managers are not afraid to admit mistakes. Steve Reaume, dealer principal of Windsor-based Reaume Chevrolet Buick GMC, a company founded by his grandfather, attributes the success of the business to the trust his family has built in the community. The company displays "A Tradition of Trust . . . since 1931" banner in its showroom and on its website. Reaume explains the company's approach: "Generation after generation we've been earning people's trust. Treating customers right, every time, is all it takes."[27] Trust is also a big part of how Reaume treats its workforce and fosters employee loyalty.

Humanistic Work Practices

The practices embraced by spiritual organizations include flexible work schedules, group- and organization-based rewards, narrowing of pay and status differentials, guarantees of individual employee rights, employee empowerment, and job security. Hewlett-Packard, for instance, has handled temporary downturns through voluntary attrition and shortened workweeks (shared by all), and it has handled longer-term declines through early retirements and buyouts.

FACTBOX

- 64% of Canadians consider themselves spiritual.
- 71% of Canadians attend religious services at least sometimes.
- 50% of Canadians report that they are religious.
- 60% of Canadians think that public schools should be doctrine-free.[28]

Toleration of Employee Expression

Finally, spiritual organizations don't stifle employee emotions. They allow people to be themselves—to express their moods and feelings without guilt or fear of reprimand. Employees at Calgary-based WestJet Airlines, for instance, are encouraged to express their sense of humour on the job, to act spontaneously, and to make their work fun.

At Aliments Ouimet-Cordon Bleu, employees are encouraged to have annual one-on-one meetings with their managers where employees can express any and all frustrations without worrying that something negative will happen to them. When Ouimet first introduced this practice, employees were reluctant to voice their concerns. As Ouimet notes, "Over time, a sense of trust developed."[29] Ouimet's employees are also encouraged to engage in "gestures of reconciliation," where they apologize to one another when interpersonal conflicts arise. Ouimet says he sets the example by apologizing when he has "blown a gasket."

Organizational Models for Fostering Spirituality

- *Religion-based organization:* The organization's practices are consistent with biblical teachings; there is an emphasis on prayer as a primary form of intrafirm communication; employees are expected to accept core Christian principles as guides to decision making.

- *Evolutionary organization:* Spiritual openness is encouraged; the guiding texts are a mixture of Christian scriptures and philosophical works (Kant, Neibuhr, Buber); there is an emphasis on serving the customer, preserving the environment, and respecting stakeholders.

- *Recovering organization:* The organization models itself after the 12-step program of Alcoholics Anonymous; spirituality is discussed in ways that are acceptable to the largest number of people. The 12-step program emphasizes confession (of failures), acceptance of God's will and guidance, and reliance on the help of others. This model is infrequently found in the business world.

- *Socially responsible organization:* Social concerns and values are part of everyday business activities; the organization emphasizes the expression of the individual's "whole person" and soul; customers, suppliers, and other stakeholders are expected to bond more readily to the firm; spirituality and soul are explicit core business principles.

- *Values-based organization:* The organization firmly rejects all notions of religious doctrine; it favours nonreligious and nonspiritual secular values or virtues (e.g., awareness, consciousness, dignity, honesty, openness, respect, integrity, and, above all, trust); values are guides for policy setting and decision making throughout the firm. The Golden Rule is the prime business principle.

- *Best-practice model:* The organization combines parts of all of the above models; it emphasizes values-based secular orientation; it adds an openly expressed spiritual dimension; it emphasizes the importance of "a higher power," periodic moral audits, and a broadly inclusive approach to stakeholders."[30]

The inset *Organizational Models for Fostering Spirituality* describes models for spiritually based organizations.

Achieving a Spiritual Organization

Many organizations have grown interested in spirituality but have had difficulty putting its principles into practice. Several types of practices can facilitate a spiritual workplace,[31] including those that support work–life balance. Leaders can demonstrate values, attitudes, and behaviours that trigger intrinsic motivation and a sense of calling through work. Encouraging employees to consider how their work provides a sense of purpose through community building can also help achieve a spiritual workplace.

Criticisms of Spirituality

Critics of organizations that embrace spiritual values have focused on three issues. First is the question of scientific foundation. What, really, is workplace spirituality? Is it just a new management buzzword? Second, are spiritual organizations legitimate? Third is the question of economics: Are spirituality and profits compatible?

First, as you might imagine, comparatively little research exists on workplace spirituality.[32] We don't know whether the concept will have staying power. Do the cultural characteristics just identified really separate spiritual organizations? Spirituality has been defined so broadly in some sources that practices from job rotation to corporate retreats at meditation centres have been identified as spiritual practices. Do employees of so-called spiritual organizations perceive that they work in spiritual organizations? Although research suggests support for workplace spirituality, the questions we have just posed need to be answered before the concept gains full credibility.

On the second question, dealing with the legitimacy of spiritual organizations, an emphasis on spirituality can clearly make some employees uneasy. Critics have argued that secular institutions, especially business firms, have no business imposing spiritual values on employees. This criticism is undoubtedly valid when spirituality is defined as bringing religion and God into the workplace.[33] However, the criticism seems less stinging when the goal is limited to helping employees find meaning and purpose in their work lives. If the concerns listed in the inset *Reasons for the Growing Interest in Spirituality* on page 449 truly characterize a large segment of the workforce, maybe the time is right for more organizations to help employees find meaning and purpose in their work and to use the workplace as a source of community.

Finally, whether spirituality and profits are compatible objectives is certainly relevant for managers and investors in business. The evidence, although limited, indicates that they are. In one study, organizations that provided their employees with opportunities for spiritual development outperformed those that did not.[34] Other studies reported that spirituality in organizations was positively related to creativity, employee satisfaction,

team performance, and organizational commitment.[35]

The cynic will say that all of this caring stuff is in fact merely good public relations. Even so, the results at both WestJet and Aliments Ouimet-Cordon Bleu suggest that a caring organization is good for the bottom line. WestJet is strongly committed to providing the lowest airfares, on-time service, and a pleasant experience for customers. WestJet employees have one of the lowest turnover rates in the airline industry, the company consistently has the lowest labour costs per miles flown of any major airline, and it has proven itself to be the most consistently profitable airline in Canada.[36] Jacques Gingras, a production manager at Aliments Ouimet-Cordon Bleu, says Ouimet's practices really help the bottom line. "Obviously, people can't go to the silence rooms whenever they want, because we're running an assembly line. But they communicate well and respect one another. It makes the operation run more smoothly."[37]

RESEARCH EXERCISES

1. Look for data on companies that foster spirituality in the workplace in Canada and the United States. Can you draw any inferences about whether incorporating spirituality in the workplace is becoming a trend?

2. Identify three Canadian organizations or CEOs that have encouraged more openness toward spirituality in their organizations. What, if any, commonalities exist in these organizations?

YOUR PERSPECTIVE

1. Have you ever tried meditation? If yes, did it help you achieve more clarity in your thinking? If not, what are your views on this practice?

2. What does spirituality mean to you?

WANT TO KNOW MORE?

In 2013 three of the top-selling books by Canadian authors, based on international sales, were on spirituality. *A New Earth: Awakening to Your Life's Purpose*, by Vancouver's Eckhart Tolle topped the list. Another book of Tolle's, the spiritual guide *The Power of Now*, placed sixth on the list of top-sellers. *The Shack*, by William Paul Young, placed third on the bestseller list.

Revitalization Saint-Pierre is a nonprofit that is fighting poverty and helping regenerate its neighbourhood. How has embedding community participation in its organizational structure contributed to its success?

LEARNING OUTCOMES

After studying this chapter, you should be able to:

1 Identify the six elements of an organization's structure.

2 Describe the characteristics of a bureaucracy.

3 Describe the characteristics of a matrix organization.

4 Describe the characteristics of a virtual organization.

5 Understand why managers would want to create a boundaryless organization.

6 Demonstrate how organizational structures differ, and contrast mechanistic and organic structural models.

7 Analyze the behavioural implications of different organizational designs.

David Marshall, Revitalisation Saint-Pierre

David Marshall, director of Montreal-based Revitalization Saint-Pierre, is committed to keeping control of the agency in the hands of neighbourhood citizens.[1] The organization's funding comes from the municipality, private donations, and revenue from agency-run businesses, while decision-making authority stays in the hands of community members. All strategic and most tactical decisions are made by committee. These committees have 6 to 20 members and at least 50 percent of members must be local citizens.

Four key priorities were established to enhance the area's development when the agency began in 2003: the revitalization of "main street," increased access to outdoor sports facilities, the creation of a community festival, and the creation of a general store that would stock low-cost fruits and vegetables. By facilitating the engagement and commitment of local volunteers in these priorities, Revitalization Saint-Pierre has avoided the "volunteer fatigue" that is common among many service agencies.

The theme of this chapter is that organizations have different structures, determined by specific forces, and that these structures have a bearing on employee attitudes and behaviour. Organizations need to think carefully about the best way to organize how people inside and outside the organization are connected to one another. These connections form the basis for organizational structure.

THE BIG IDEA

Organizational structure determines what gets done in an organization, and who does it.

 IS FOR **EVERYONE**

- What happens when a person performs the same task over and over again?

- What happens when a person reports to two bosses?

- Can an organization really have no boundaries?

- So what does *technology* mean?

What Is Organizational Structure?

1 Identify the six elements of an organization's structure.

An **organizational structure** defines how job tasks are formally divided, grouped, and coordinated. Managers need to address six key elements when they design their organization's structure: work specialization, departmentalization, chain of command, span of control, centralization and decentralization, and formalization.[2] Exhibit 13-1 presents all of these elements as answers to an important structural question.

Work Specialization

We use the term **work specialization**, or *division of labour*, to describe the degree to which tasks in the organization are subdivided into separate jobs. The essence of work specialization is that, rather than an entire job being completed by one individual, it's broken down into a number of steps, with each step being completed by a separate individual. In essence, individuals specialize in doing part of an activity rather than the entire activity.

> What happens when a person performs the same task over and over again?

Specialization can be efficient. Employee skills at performing a task improve through repetition. Less time is spent in changing tasks, in putting away tools and equipment from a prior step in the work process, and in preparing for another. It's easier and less costly to find and train employees to do specific and repetitive tasks. This is especially true of highly sophisticated and complex operations. For example, could Montreal-based Bombardier produce even one Canadian regional jet a year if one person had to build the entire plane alone? Not likely! Finally, work specialization increases efficiency and productivity by encouraging the creation of special inventions and machinery.

However, specialization can lead to boredom, fatigue, stress, low productivity, poor quality, increased absenteeism, and high turnover, so it is not always the best way to organize employees. Giving employees a variety of activities to do, allowing them to do a whole and complete job, and putting them into teams with interchangeable skills can result in significantly higher output and increased employee satisfaction.

Most managers today recognize that specialization provides economies in certain types of jobs but problems when it's carried too far. High work specialization helps McDonald's make and sell hamburgers and fries efficiently, and aids medical specialists

organizational structure How job tasks are formally divided, grouped, and coordinated.

work specialization The degree to which tasks in the organization are subdivided into separate jobs.

EXHIBIT 13-1 Six Key Questions That Managers Need to Answer in Designing the Proper Organizational Structure	
The Key Question	**The Answer Is Provided By**
1. To what degree are tasks subdivided into separate jobs?	*Work specialization*
2. On what basis will jobs be grouped together?	*Departmentalization*
3. To whom do individuals and groups report?	*Chain of command*
4. How many individuals can a manager efficiently and effectively direct?	*Span of control*
5. Where does decision-making authority lie?	*Centralization and decentralization*
6. To what degree will there be rules and regulations to direct employees and managers?	*Formalization*

Work is specialized at the Russian factories that manufacture the wooden nesting dolls called *matryoshkas*. At this factory outside Moscow, individuals specialize in doing part of the doll production, from the craftsmen who carve the dolls to the painters who decorate them. Work specialization brings efficiency to doll production, as some 50 employees can make 100 *matryoshkas* every two days.

working in hospitals. Other companies, on the other hand, have achieved success by reducing specialization.

Wherever job roles can be broken down into specific tasks or projects, specialization is possible. This opens the potential for employers to use online platforms to assign multiple workers to tasks from a broader functional role like marketing.[3] Thus, whereas specialization of yesteryear focused on breaking manufacturing tasks into specific duties within the same plant, today's specialization breaks complex tasks into specific elements by technology, by expertise, and often globally. Yet the core principle is the same.

Departmentalization

Once jobs are divided up through work specialization, they must be grouped so that common tasks can be coordinated. The basis on which jobs are grouped together is called **departmentalization**. One of the concerns related to departmental groups is that they can become *silos* within an organization. Often, departments start protecting their own turf and not interacting well with other departments, which can lead to a narrow vision with respect to organizational goals.

Functional Departmentalization

One of the most popular ways to group activities is by *functions* performed. For example, a manufacturing company might separate engineering, accounting, manufacturing, human resource, and purchasing specialists into common departments. Similarly, a hospital might have departments devoted to research, patient care, accounting, and so forth. The major advantage to functional groupings is obtaining efficiencies from putting people with common skills and orientations together into common units.

Product Departmentalization

Tasks can also be departmentalized by the type of *product* the organization produces. Procter & Gamble groups each major product—such as Tide, Pampers, Charmin,

departmentalization The basis on which jobs are grouped together.

THE CANADIAN PRESS/Graham Hughes

The Carillon Generating Station on the Ottawa River (shown here) is one of Montreal-based Hydro-Québec's hydroelectric power stations. Hydro-Québec organizes its operations by functions so that the company can be more responsive to growth outside Quebec. It has four divisions: Hydro-Québec Production, Hydro-Québec TransÉnergie, Hydro-Québec Distribution, and Hydro-Québec Équipement et services partagés/Société d'énergie de la Baie James.

and Pringles—under an executive who has complete global responsibility for it. The major advantage to this type of grouping is increased accountability for product performance, since all activities related to a specific product line are under the direction of a single manager.

Geographical Departmentalization

Another way to departmentalize is on the basis of geography, or territory. The sales function, for instance, may be divided regionally with departments for British Columbia, the Prairies, Central Canada, and Atlantic Canada. Each of these regions is, in effect, a department organized around geography. If an organization's customers are scattered over a large geographical area and have similar needs based on their location, then this form of departmentalization can be valuable.

Process Departmentalization

Some companies organize departments by the processing that occurs. For example, an aluminum tubing manufacturer might have the following departments: casting; press; tubing; finishing; and inspecting, packing, and shipping. This is an example of process departmentalization, because each department specializes in one specific phase in the production of aluminum tubing. Since each process requires different skills, this method offers a basis for the homogeneous categorizing of activities.

Process departmentalization can be used for processing customers, as well as products. For example, in some provinces, you may go through a series of steps handled by several departments before receiving your driver's licence: (1) validation by a motor vehicles division; (2) processing by the licensing department; and (3) payment collection by the treasury department.

Customer Departmentalization

Yet another way to departmentalize is on the basis of the particular type of customer the organization seeks to reach. Microsoft, for example, is organized around four customer markets: consumers, large corporations, software developers, and small businesses. Customers in each department have a common set of problems and needs best met by having specialists for each.

Large organizations may use all the forms of departmentalization we have described. A major Japanese electronics firm organizes each of its divisions along functional lines, its manufacturing units around processes, sales around seven geographical regions, and each sales region into four customer groupings. In a strong recent trend among organizations of all sizes, rigid functional departmentalization is increasingly complemented by teams that cross traditional departmental lines. As we described in Chapter 6, as tasks have become more complex, and more diverse skills are needed to accomplish those tasks, management has turned to cross-functional teams.

Chain of Command

While the chain of command was once a basic cornerstone in the design of organizations, it has far less importance today.[4] But contemporary managers should still consider its implications, particularly for industries that deal with potential life-or-death situations. The **chain of command** is the continuous line of authority that extends from upper organizational levels to the lowest level and clarifies who reports to whom. It helps employees answer questions such as, "Who do I go to if I have a problem?" and "To whom do I report?"

We cannot discuss the chain of command without also discussing authority and unity of command. **Authority** refers to the rights inherent in a managerial position to give orders and expect them to be obeyed. To facilitate coordination, each managerial position is given a place in the chain of command, and each manager is given a degree of authority in order to meet his or her responsibilities. The principle of **unity of command** helps preserve the concept of an unbroken line of authority. It says a person should have one and only one superior to whom he or she is directly responsible. If the unity of command is broken, an employee might have to cope with conflicting demands or priorities from several superiors, as is often the case in organization charts' dotted-line reporting relationships.

Because managers have limited time and knowledge, they may choose to delegate some of their responsibilities to other employees. **Delegation** is the assignment of authority to another person to carry out specific duties, allowing the employee to make some of the decisions. Delegation is an important part of a manager's job, as it can ensure that the right people are part of the decision-making process. Through delegation, employees are being empowered to make decisions that previously were reserved for management. *From Concepts to Skills* on pages 484–485 presents strategies to be a better delegator.

Times change, and so do the basic tenets of organizational design. A low-level employee today can access information in seconds that was available only to top managers a generation ago. Operating employees are empowered to make decisions previously reserved for management. Add the popularity of self-managed and cross-functional teams as well as the creation of new structural designs that include multiple bosses, and you can see why authority and unity of command may appear to hold less relevance. *Point/Counterpoint* on page 480 considers whether management as we know it is an outdated concept.

Many organizations still find they can be most productive by enforcing the chain of command. Indeed, one survey of more than 1000 managers found that 59 percent of them agreed with the statement, "There is an imaginary line in my company's organizational chart. Strategy is created by people above this line, while strategy is executed by people below the line."[5] However, this same survey found that lower-level employees' buy-in to the organization's strategy was inhibited because they did not participate in the setting of the strategy but relied on those at the top of the hierarchy to do so.

PERSONAL INVENTORY ASSESSMENT

Learn About Yourself
Delegation Self-Assessment

---

chain of command The continuous line of authority that extends from upper organizational levels to the lowest level and clarifies who reports to whom.

authority The rights inherent in a managerial position to give orders and to expect the orders to be obeyed.

unity of command The idea that a subordinate should have only one superior to whom he or she is directly responsible.

delegation Assignment of authority to another person to carry out specific duties, allowing the employee to make some of the decisions.

Sometimes lower-level employees don't follow the chain of command and engage in creative deviance that results in very successful ideas, as *Case Incident—Creative Deviance: Bucking the Hierarchy?* on page 483 shows.

Span of Control

Span of control refers to the number of employees who report to a manager. This number will vary by organization, and by unit within an organization, and is determined by the number of employees a manager can efficiently and effectively direct. In an assembly-line factory, a manager may be able to direct numerous employees, because the work is well defined and controlled by machinery. A sales manager, by contrast, might have to give one-on-one supervision to individual sales reps, and, therefore, fewer would report to the sales manager. All things being equal, the wider or larger the span, the more efficient the organization. An example can illustrate the validity of this statement.

Assume that we have two organizations, both of which have approximately 4100 operative-level employees. As Exhibit 13-2 illustrates, if one has a uniform span of 4 and the other a span of 8, the wider span would have 2 fewer levels and approximately 800 fewer managers. If the average manager earned $56 000 a year, the wider span would save about $45 million a year in management salaries. Obviously, wider spans are more efficient in terms of cost. However, at some point when supervisors no longer have time to provide the necessary leadership and support, a wider span reduces effectiveness and has a negative effect on employee performance.

Narrow or small spans have their advocates. By keeping the span of control to 5 or 6 employees, a manager can maintain close control.[6] But narrow spans have three major drawbacks. First, as already described, they are expensive because they add levels of management. Second, they make vertical communication in the organization more complex. The added levels of hierarchy slow down decision making and tend to isolate upper management. Third, narrow spans of control encourage overly tight supervision and discourage employee autonomy.

The trend in recent years has been toward wider spans of control.[7] Wider spans of control are consistent with recent efforts by companies to reduce costs, cut overhead, speed up decision making, increase flexibility, get closer to customers, and empower employees. However, to ensure that performance does not suffer because of these wider

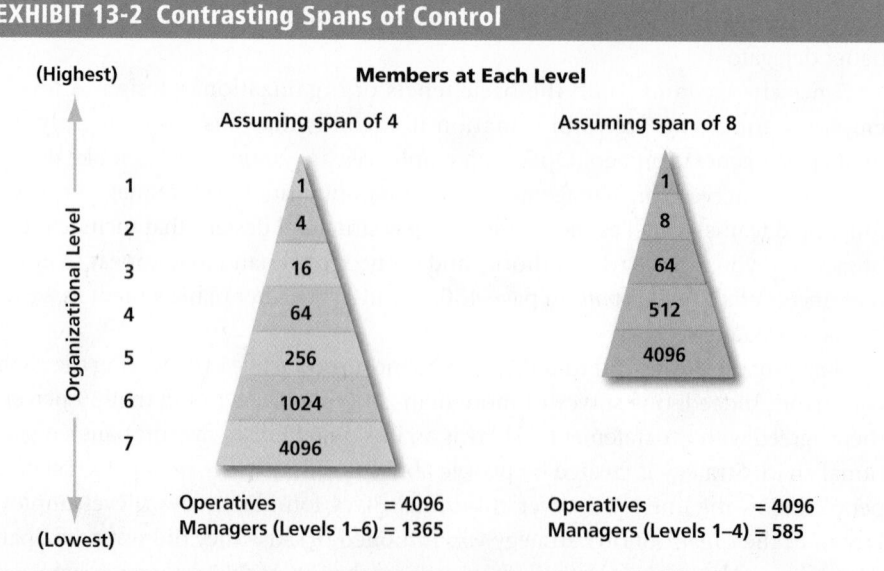

EXHIBIT 13-2 Contrasting Spans of Control

(Highest)

Members at Each Level

Organizational Level

Assuming span of 4

Level	Members
1	1
2	4
3	16
4	64
5	256
6	1024
7	4096

Assuming span of 8

Level	Members
1	1
2	8
3	64
4	512
5	4096

Operatives   = 4096
Managers (Levels 1–6) = 1365

Operatives   = 4096
Managers (Levels 1–4) = 585

(Lowest)

span of control The number of employees that report to a manager.

spans, organizations have been investing heavily in employee training. Managers recognize that they can handle a wider span when employees know their jobs inside and out or can turn to their co-workers when they have questions.

Centralization and Decentralization

Centralization refers to the degree to which decision making is concentrated at a single point in the organization. In centralized organizations, top managers make all the decisions, and lower-level managers merely carry out their directives. In organizations at the other extreme, decentralized decision making is pushed down to the managers closest to the action or even to work groups.

The concept of centralization includes only formal authority; that is, the rights inherent in one's position. An organization characterized by centralization is inherently different structurally from one that is decentralized. In an organization characterized by **decentralization**, employees can act more quickly to solve problems, more people provide input into decisions, and employees are less likely to feel alienated from those who make decisions that affect their work lives. Decentralized departments make it easier to address customer concerns as well. A 2013 study suggests that the effects of centralization and decentralization can be predicted: Centralized organizations are better for avoiding commission errors (bad choices), while decentralized organizations are better for avoiding omission errors (lost opportunities).[8]

Management efforts to make organizations more flexible and responsive have produced a recent trend toward decentralized decision making by lower-level managers, who are closer to the action and typically have more detailed knowledge about problems than top managers. Big retailers such as Hudson's Bay have given store managers considerably more discretion in choosing what merchandise to stock. Doing so allows the stores to compete more effectively against local merchants. When Procter & Gamble empowered small groups of employees to make many decisions about new-product development independent of the usual hierarchy, it was able to rapidly increase the proportion of new products ready for market.[9] Research investigating a large number of Finnish organizations demonstrated that companies with decentralized research and development offices in multiple locations were better at producing innovation than companies that centralized all research and development in a single office.[10]

Decentralization is often necessary for companies with offshore sites because localized decision making is needed to respond to each region's profit opportunities, client base, and specific laws, while centralized oversight is needed to hold regional managers accountable. Failure to successfully balance these priorities can harm not only the company, but also its relationships with foreign governments, as in the groundbreaking 2013 case brought by Argentina's government against Britain's HSBC Holdings bank for wrongdoing at its Argentine subsidiary. According to reports, the local HSBC headquarters in Buenos Aires aided Argentine companies to evade taxes and launder money through phantom accounts.[11] Perhaps in this situation tighter corporate oversight could have made these activities impossible.

Formalization

Formalization refers to the degree to which jobs within the organization are standardized. In organizations that are highly formalized, there are explicit job descriptions, lots of organizational rules, and clearly defined procedures covering work processes. Employees can be expected always to handle the same input in exactly the same way, resulting in a consistent and uniform output where there is high formalization. Where formalization is low, job behaviours are relatively nonprogrammed, and employees have a great deal of freedom to exercise discretion in their work. Formalization not only eliminates the possibility of employees engaging in alternative behaviours but also removes the need for employees to consider alternatives.

centralization The degree to which decision making is concentrated at a single point in the organization.

decentralization The degree to which decision making is distributed to lower-level employees.

formalization The degree to which jobs within the organization are standardized.

Greg Wood/Getty Images

Hospitals benefit from standardized work processes and procedures common to bureaucratic structure because they help employees perform their jobs efficiently. The nursing staff in the maternity ward of a New Zealand hospital adhere to formal rules and regulations in providing care to moms and newborns.

McDonald's is an example of a company where employee routines are highly formalized. Employees are instructed in such things as how to greet the customer (smile, be sincere, make eye contact), ask for and receive payment (state amount of order clearly and loudly, announce the amount of money the customer gives to the employee, count change out loud and efficiently), and thank the customer (give a sincere thank you, make eye contact, ask customer to come again). McDonald's includes this information in training and employee handbooks, and managers are given a checklist of these behaviours so that they can observe their employees to ensure that the proper procedures are followed.[12]

The degree of formalization can vary widely among organizations and within organizations. Publishing representatives who call on college and university professors to inform them of their company's new publications have a great deal of freedom in their jobs. They have only a general sales pitch, which they tailor as needed, and rules and procedures governing their behaviour may be little more than the requirement to submit a weekly sales report and suggestions on what to emphasize about forthcoming titles. At the other extreme, clerical and editorial employees in the same publishing houses may need to be at their desks by 8 a.m. and follow a set of precise procedures dictated by management.

Common Organizational Designs

We now turn to describing some of the more common organizational designs: the *simple structure*, the *bureaucracy*, and the *matrix structure*.

The Simple Structure

simple structure An organizational design characterized by a low degree of departmentalization, wide spans of control, authority centralized in a single person, and little formalization.

What do a small retail store, a start-up electronics firm run by a hard-driving entrepreneur, and an airline "war room" in the midst of a company-wide pilots' strike have in common? They probably all use the **simple structure**.

The simple structure is said to be characterized most by what it is *not* rather than by what it is. The simple structure is not elaborate.[13] It has a low degree of departmentalization, wide spans of control, authority centralized in a single person, and little formalization. It is a "flat" organization; it usually has only two or three vertical levels, a loose body of employees, and one individual in whom the decision-making authority is centralized.

Most companies start as a simple structure, and many innovative technology-based firms with short expected lifespans, such as cellphone app development firms, remain compact by design.[14] The simple structure is most widely adopted in small businesses in which the manager and the owner are one and the same, such as the local corner grocery store.

The strength of the simple structure lies in its simplicity. It's fast, flexible, and inexpensive to maintain, and accountability is clear. One major weakness is that it's difficult to maintain in anything other than small organizations. It becomes increasingly inadequate as an organization grows because its low formalization and high centralization tend to create information overload at the top. As size increases, decision making typically becomes slower and can eventually come to a standstill as the single executive tries to continue making all the decisions. This often proves to be the undoing of many small businesses. If the structure is not changed and made more elaborate, the firm often loses momentum and can eventually fail. The simple structure's other weakness is that it's risky—everything depends on one person. One serious illness can literally destroy the organization's information and decision-making centre.

The Family Business

Family businesses employ 6 million people in Canada and represent about 60 percent of the country's gross domestic product.[15] Some of the most prominent family businesses in Canada over the past 50 years include Montreal, Quebec-based Seagram

Mississauga, Ontario-based Furlani's Food Corporation uses a "family business" mentality to govern its approach to employees. The business is run in a non-hierarchical manner and no formal or impersonal human resources processes dictate employee behaviour. Employees are encouraged to share ideas openly, which keeps morale high. For a recent improvement project, employees from different levels and areas collaborated to make the process go smoothly.

Company (the Bronfman family), Calgary, Alberta-based Shaw Communications (the Shaw family), Montreal, Quebec-based Birks jewellers (the Birk family), Saint John, New Brunswick-based J.D. Irving (the Irving family), and Florenceville, New Brunswick-based McCain Foods (the McCain family). Not all family businesses are as large as these, however, and many have relatively simple structures.

Family businesses have more complex dynamics than nonfamily businesses, because they face both family/personal relations and business/management relations. These companies generally have shareholders (family members and perhaps others), although the businesses may be public companies listed on the stock exchange. For instance, of the companies mentioned above, Seagram Company and Shaw Communications are public companies. Shaw Communications has an interesting structure—only family members have voting shares.

Unlike nonfamily businesses, family businesses must manage the conflicts found within families, as well as the normal business issues that arise for any business. As John Davis of Harvard Business School notes, "In a family business, the business, the family, and the ownership group all need governance." Good governance structures can help family businesses manage the conflicts that may arise. Good governance includes "a sense of direction, values to live by or work by, and well-understood and accepted policies that tell organization members how they should behave."[16]

One area in which governance can play a key role is in CEO succession. Family businesses need to figure out rules of succession for when the CEO retires, and also rules for who in the family gets to work in the business. Succession in family-owned businesses often does not work "because personal and emotional factors determine who the next leader will be," rather than suitability.[17] For instance, a father may want his first-born son to take over the business, even if one of the daughters might make a better CEO. The issues become more complex when second- and third-generation family members become involved in the family business. So what makes family businesses unique? Founders of family businesses seek to "build businesses that are also family institutions."[18] As a result, there is added pressure on the business, which needs to balance business needs and family needs. Family businesses may have different goals than nonfamily businesses as well, emphasizing the importance of family values in maintaining and growing the business rather than wealth maximization.

The Bureaucracy

2 Describe the characteristics of a bureaucracy.

Standardization! That is the key concept underlying all bureaucracies. Consider the bank where you keep your chequing account, the department store where you buy your clothes, or the government offices that collect your taxes, enforce health regulations, or provide local fire protection. They all rely on standardized work processes for coordination and control.

Bureaucracy is a dirty word in many people's minds. However, it does have advantages. Its primary strength is its ability to perform standardized activities in a highly efficient manner. Putting like specialties together in functional departments results in economies of scale, minimum duplication of people and equipment, and employees who can speak "the same language" among their peers.

A **bureaucracy** is characterized by highly routine operating tasks achieved through specialization, strictly formalized rules and regulations, tasks that are grouped into functional departments, centralized authority, narrow spans of control, and decision making that follows the chain of command.

bureaucracy An organizational design with highly routine operating tasks achieved through specialization, formalized rules and regulations, tasks that are grouped into functional departments, centralized authority, narrow spans of control, and decision making that follows the chain of command.

Strengths of Bureaucracy

German sociologist Max Weber, writing in the early 1900s, described bureaucracy as an alternative to the traditional administrative form. In the traditional model, leaders could be quite arbitrary, with authority based on personal relations. There were no general rules, and no separation between the leader's "private" and "public" business. Bureaucracy solved some of the problems of leaders who took advantage of their situation.

The primary strength of the bureaucracy lies in its ability to perform standardized activities in a highly efficient manner. Bureaucracies can get by nicely with less talented—and, hence, less costly—middle- and lower-level managers. Rules and regulations substitute for managerial discretion. Standardized operations, coupled with high formalization, allow decision making to be centralized. There is little need for innovative and experienced decision makers below the level of senior executives. In short, bureaucracy is an effective structure for ensuring consistent application of policies and practices and for ensuring accountability.

Weaknesses of Bureaucracy

Bureaucracy is not without its problems. Listen in on a dialogue among four executives in one company: "You know, nothing happens in this place until we *produce* something," said the production executive. "Wrong," commented the research and development manager. "Nothing happens until we *design* something!" "What are you talking about?" asked the marketing executive. "Nothing happens here until we *sell* something!" The exasperated accounting manager responded, "It doesn't matter what you produce, design, or sell. No one knows what happens until we *tally up the results*!" This conversation highlights that bureaucratic specialization can create conflicts in which functional-unit goals override the overall goals of the organization. Each department acts like a silo, focusing more on what it perceives as its own value and contribution to the organization. Each silo fails to understand that departments are really interdependent, with each having to perform well for the company as a whole to survive. The conflict that can happen among functional units means that sometimes functional unit goals can override the overall goals of the organization.

Bureaucracy can sometimes lead to power being concentrated in the hands of just a few people, with others expected to follow their orders unquestioningly. The *Ethical Dilemma* on page 482 illustrates what can happen when someone higher in the authority chain pressures someone below him or her to perform unethical tasks.

The other major weakness of a bureaucracy is something we have all experienced: obsessive concern with following the rules. When cases arise that don't precisely fit the rules, there is no room for modification. The bureaucracy is efficient only as long as employees confront problems that they have previously encountered and for which programmed decision rules have already been established. *Case Incident—"I Detest Bureaucracy"* on page 483 lets you consider alternatives to bureaucracy and how you might feel about these alternatives.

The Matrix Structure

Another popular organizational design option is the **matrix structure**. You will find it being used in advertising agencies, aerospace firms, research and development laboratories, construction companies, hospitals, government agencies, universities, management consulting firms, and entertainment companies.[19] It combines two forms of departmentalization: functional and product. Companies that use matrix-like structures include Boeing, BMW, IBM, and Procter & Gamble.

The strength of functional departmentalization is putting like specialists together, which minimizes the number necessary while allowing the pooling and sharing of specialized resources across products. Its major disadvantage is the difficulty of coordinating the tasks of diverse functional specialists on time and within budget. Product departmentalization has exactly the opposite benefits and disadvantages. It facilitates coordination among specialties to achieve on-time completion and meet budget targets. It provides clear responsibility for all activities related to a product but with duplication

 3 Describe the characteristics of a matrix organization.

matrix structure An organizational design that combines functional and product departmentalization; it has a dual chain of command.

EXHIBIT 13-3 Matrix Structure for a Faculty of Business Administration

Academic departments \ Programs	Undergraduate	Master's	PhD	Research	Executive development	Community service
Accounting						
Administrative studies						
Finance						
Information and decision sciences						
Marketing						
Organizational behaviour						
Quantitative methods						

of activities and costs. The matrix attempts to gain the strengths of each, while avoiding their weaknesses.

The most obvious structural characteristic of the matrix is that it breaks the unity-of-command concept. Employees in the matrix have two bosses—their functional department managers and their product managers.

Exhibit 13-3 shows the matrix structure used in a faculty of business administration. The academic departments of accounting, administrative studies, finance, and so forth are functional units. Specific programs (that is, products) are overlaid on the functions. Thus, members in a matrix structure have a dual chain of command: to their functional department and to their product groups. A professor of accounting who is teaching an undergraduate course reports to the director of undergraduate programs, as well as to the chair of the accounting department.

Advantages of a Matrix Structure

The strength of the matrix is its ability to foster coordination when the organization has a number of complex and interdependent activities. Information permeates the organization and more quickly reaches those people who need it. Furthermore, the matrix reduces "bureaupathologies." The dual lines of authority reduce tendencies of departmental members to become so busy protecting their little worlds that the organization's overall goals become secondary.[20] A matrix also achieves economies of scale and facilitates the allocation of specialists by providing both the best resources and an effective way of ensuring their efficient deployment.

Disadvantages of a Matrix Structure

The major disadvantages of the matrix lie in the confusion it creates, its tendency to foster power struggles, and the stress it places on individuals.[21] Without the unity-of-command concept, ambiguity about who reports to whom is significantly increased and often leads to conflict. It's not unusual for product managers to fight over getting the best specialists assigned to their products. Bureaucracy reduces the potential for power grabs by defining the rules of the

> What happens when a person reports to two bosses?

game. When those rules are "up for grabs," power struggles between functional and product managers result. For individuals who desire security and absence of ambiguity, this work climate can be stressful. Reporting to more than one manager introduces role conflict, and unclear expectations introduce role ambiguity. The comfort of bureaucracy's predictability is replaced by insecurity and stress.

New Design Options

David Marshall, director of Revitalization Saint-Pierre, says that one of the best things about having committees dominated by Saint-Pierre residents is the ease with which the agency can identify service gaps and respond to evolving needs.[22] "Having the people who actually use our services deciding where to focus our attention helps keep us relevant," he explains. "It also fosters creativity and innovation." For example, in 2003, access to affordable, fresh food was identified as an issue, resulting in the creation of a general store and community kitchen. Soon, members of the food security committee noticed that some residents still could not afford adequate nutrition. The committee created a policy giving people the opportunity to exchange work hours worked in the store for fresh, healthy food.

In 2013, the food security committee identified four other Montreal neighbourhoods that lacked access to high quality, affordable food. A mobile store was developed for summer 2014, and it was a resounding success. In what situations could new forms of organization be effective?

Senior managers in a number of organizations have been developing new structural options with fewer layers of hierarchy and more emphasis on opening the boundaries of the organization.[23] In this section, we describe two such designs: the *virtual organization* and the *boundaryless organization*. We also discuss how efforts to reduce bureaucracy and increase strategic focus have made downsizing routine.

The Virtual Organization

Why own when you can rent? That question captures the essence of the **virtual organization** (also sometimes called the *network organization* or *modular organization*).[24] The virtual organization can take several different forms, depending on its degree of centralization. In some instances, a small, core organization outsources major business functions. In this case, the core organization would have more of the control. In more extreme forms, the virtual organization "is a continually evolving network of independent companies—suppliers, customers, even competitors—linked together to share skills, costs, and access to one another's markets."[25] In this case, participants give up some of their control and act more interdependently. Thus, virtual organizations may not have a central office, an organizational chart, or a hierarchy. Typically, the organizations come together to exploit specific opportunities or attain specific strategic objectives.

4 Describe the characteristics of a virtual organization.

The prototype of the virtual structure is today's movie-making organization. In Hollywood's golden era, movies were made by huge, vertically integrated corporations. Studios such as MGM, Warner Brothers, and 20th Century Fox owned large movie lots and employed thousands of full-time specialists—set designers, camera people, film editors, directors, and even actors. Today, most movies are made by a collection of individuals and small companies who come together and make films project by project.[26] This structural form allows each project to be staffed with the talent best suited to its demands rather than just the people employed by the studio. It minimizes bureaucratic overhead because there is no lasting organization to maintain. As well, it lessens long-term risks and their costs because there is no long term—a team is assembled for a finite period and then disbanded.

About one in nine Canadian companies engages in some sort of alliance. These alliances take many forms, ranging from precompetitive consortia to coproduction,

virtual organization A continually evolving network of independent companies—suppliers, customers, even competitors—linked together to share skills, costs, and access to one another's markets.

EXHIBIT 13-4 A Virtual Organization

Independent research and development consulting firm

Advertising agency

Executive group

Factories in South Korea

Commissioned sales representatives

cross-equity arrangements, and equity joint ventures with separate legal entities.[27] Amazon.ca partners with Canada Post in such an arrangement. Orders placed on Amazon.ca's website are fulfilled and shipped by Assured Logistics, which is part of Canada Post. Assured Logistics operates a Toronto-area warehouse that stores books, music, and movies so that they can be shipped when ordered, thus eliminating the need for Amazon to set up its own warehouse facility in Canada. Newman's Own, the food products company founded by Paul Newman, sells hundreds of millions of dollars in food every year yet employs only 28 people. This is possible because it outsources almost everything: manufacturing, procurement, shipping, and quality control.

What is going on here? A quest for maximum flexibility. These virtual organizations have created networks of relationships that allow them to contract out manufacturing, distribution, marketing, or any other business function management feels others can do better or more cheaply. The virtual organization stands in sharp contrast to the typical bureaucracy and concentrates on what it does best, which is typically design or marketing.

Exhibit 13-4 shows a virtual organization in which management outsources all the primary functions of the business. The core of the organization is a small group of executives whose job is to oversee directly any activities done in house and to coordinate relationships with the other organizations that manufacture, distribute, and perform other crucial functions for the virtual organization. The dotted lines represent the relationships typically maintained under contracts. In essence, managers in virtual structures spend most of their time coordinating and controlling external relations, typically by way of computer-network links.

The major advantage of the virtual organization is its flexibility, which allows individuals with an innovative idea and little money to successfully compete against more established organizations. Virtual organizations also save a great deal of money by eliminating permanent offices and hierarchical roles.[28]

The drawbacks of virtual organizations have become increasingly clear as their popularity has grown.[29] They are in a state of perpetual flux and reorganization, which means roles, goals, and responsibilities are unclear, setting the stage for political behaviour. Cultural alignment and shared goals can be lost because of the low degree of interaction among members. Team members who are geographically dispersed and communicate infrequently find it difficult to share information and knowledge, which can limit innovation and slow response time. Sometimes, as with Vancouver-based Lululemon's shipments of unintentionally see-through yoga pants, the consequences of having geographically remote managers can be embarrassing and even financially harmful to the company.[30] Ironically, some virtual organizations are less adaptable and innovative than those with well-established communication and collaboration networks. A leadership presence that reinforces the organization's purpose and facilitates communication is thus especially valuable.

The Boundaryless Organization

5 Understand why managers would want to create boundaryless organizations.

boundaryless organization An organization that seeks to eliminate the chain of command, have limitless spans of control, and replace departments with empowered teams.

General Electric's former chairman, Jack Welch, coined the term **boundaryless organization** to describe his idea of what he wanted GE to become: a "family grocery store."[31] That is, in spite of GE's monstrous size (2013 revenues were over $150 billion), Welch wanted to eliminate vertical and horizontal boundaries within it and break down external barriers between the company and its customers and suppliers. The boundaryless organization seeks to eliminate the chain of command, have limitless spans of control, and replace departments with empowered teams. Although GE has not yet achieved this boundaryless state—and probably never will—it has made significant progress toward that end. So have other companies, such as Hewlett-Packard, AT&T, Motorola, and 3M.

OB in the Workplace explores some of the issues involved in creating a global virtual workplace.

OB IN THE **WORKPLACE**
The World Is My Corporate Headquarters

What does it mean to be a virtual company? Neither Automattic Inc., with 123 employees working in 26 countries nor Kalypso LP, with 150 employees around the globe has a corporate headquarters or, truly, an office of any sort.[32] The implications of this new understanding of what it means to be a global virtual business are logistical, structural, and human.

On the logistics end of getting work done, office-less companies utilize every technology available, from Skype to blogs. Sensitive information is limited to phone discussions, though the difficulty of scheduling virtual meetings can be tricky across a number of time zones. When needed and at least annually, employees fly to designated intermediate spots for face-to-face time. Employees live where they want or where a strategic company presence for clients is desired.

The office-less company is not a good fit for every industry. The complete decentralization of the organization's physical structure dictates a nonhierarchical organization chart. High employee autonomy and empowerment to make decisions means supervision must be very light in order for the company to compete and take advantage of business opportunities specific to one employee's region, which the rest of the company cannot see.

With hiring possibilities worldwide, the company must also be clear about who can recruit new candidates and how to fit them into the organizational structure. Though the office-less company sounds like a good opportunity to maximize the worldwide talent pool, it presents challenges on a human level. According to Bill Poston, founding-partner of Kalypso, the office-less company does not work for people "who are uncomfortable with ambiguity." With the technology available, workers are not isolated, but the necessary lack of hierarchy means some workers may feel underappreciated.

The office-less company is still a rarity in the world, but its popularity is growing. It's very possible that truly global corporations of the future will need to consider a decentralization strategy that includes either many headquarters—or no headquarters at all.

The boundaryless organization breaks down barriers internally by flattening the hierarchy, creating cross-hierarchical teams (which include top executives, middle managers, supervisors, and operative employees), and using participative decision-making practices and 360-degree performance appraisals (where peers and others above and below the employee evaluate his or her performance). Another way management can cut through barriers is to use lateral transfers, rotating people into and out of different functional areas. This approach turns specialists into generalists.

Can an organization really have no boundaries?

One of the drawbacks of boundaryless organizations is that they are difficult to manage. It's difficult to overcome the political and authority boundaries inherent in many organizations. It can also be time-consuming and difficult to manage the coordination necessary with so many different stakeholders. That said, the well-managed boundaryless organization offers the best talents of employees across several different

BMW Group operates as a boundaryless organization in designing, developing, and producing its BMW, Rolls-Royce, and Mini cars. The automaker's plant, shown here in Jakarta, Indonesia, is part of BMW's flexible global production network that responds quickly to fluctuations in customer demands and market requirements.

organizations; enhances cooperation across functions, divisions, and external groups; and potentially offers much quicker response time to the environment.

The Leaner Organization: Organization Downsizing

The goal of the new organizational forms we have described is to improve agility by creating a lean, focused, and flexible organization. *Downsizing* is a systematic effort to make an organization leaner by closing locations, reducing staff, or selling off business units that do not add value.

The radical shrinking of Waterloo-based BlackBerry was a case of downsizing due to loss of market share and changes in consumer demand. The company started large layoffs in mid-2011, which continued until mid-2014 when the company's CEO, John Chen, wrote the following in a memo to employees: "We have completed the restructuring notification process, and the work force reduction that began three years ago is now behind us."[33] Forty percent of BlackBerry's employees were laid off between September 2013 and May 2014 alone. The downsizing was the result of difficulties in producing an innovative smartphone that could compete with products made by Apple and Samsung.

Other firms downsize to direct all their efforts toward their core competencies. American Express claims to have been doing this in a series of layoffs over more than a decade: 7700 jobs in 2001; 6500 jobs in 2002; 7000 jobs (10 percent of its workforce) in 2008; and 4000 jobs in 2009. The 2013 cut of 5400 jobs (8.5 percent of the remaining workforce) represents "its biggest retrenchment in a decade."[34] Each layoff has been accompanied by a restructuring to reflect changing customer preferences, away from personal customer service and toward online customer service. According to CEO Ken Chennault, these "restructuring initiatives" are "designed to make American Express more nimble, more efficient and more effective in using our resources to drive growth … and to maintain marketing and promotion investments."[35]

Some companies focus on lean management techniques to reduce bureaucracy and speed decision making. For example, Starbucks adopted lean initiatives in 2009, which encompassed all levels of management and also focused on faster barista techniques and manufacturing processes. Customers have generally applauded the shortened wait times and product consistency at this well-run corporation. Starbucks continues to reap returns from its lean initiatives, posting notable revenue gains each quarter.[36]

Despite the advantages of being a lean organization, the impact of downsizing on organizational performance has been a source of controversy.[37] Reducing the size of the workforce has an immediately positive outcome in the form of lower wage costs. Companies downsizing to improve strategic focus often see positive effects on stock prices after the announcement. On the other hand, among companies that only cut employees but don't restructure, profits and stock prices usually decline. Part of the problem is the effect of downsizing on employee attitudes. Those who remain often feel worried about future layoffs and may be less committed to the organization.[38] Stress reactions can lead to increased sickness absences, lower concentration on the job, and lower creativity. In companies that don't invest much in their employees, downsizing can also lead to more voluntary turnover, so vital human capital is lost. The result is a company that is more anemic than lean.

Companies can reduce negative impacts by preparing in advance, thus alleviating some employee stress and strengthening support for the new strategic direction.[39] The following are some effective strategies for downsizing. Most are closely linked to the principles for organizational justice we discussed in Chapter 4:

- *Investment.* Companies that downsize to focus on core competencies are more effective when they invest in high-involvement work practices afterward.

- *Communication.* When employers make efforts to discuss downsizing with employees early, employees are less worried about the outcomes and feel the company is taking their perspective into account.

- *Participation.* Employees worry less if they can participate in the process in some way. In some companies, voluntary early retirement programs or severance packages can help achieve leanness without layoffs.

- *Assistance.* Severance, extended health care benefits, and job search assistance demonstrate a company cares about its employees and honours their contributions.

Companies that make themselves lean can be more agile, efficient, and productive—but only if they make cuts carefully and help employees through the process.

Why Do Structures Differ?

We have described organizational designs ranging from the highly structured bureaucracy to the amorphous boundaryless organization. The other designs we discussed exist somewhere in-between.

Exhibit 13-5 recaps our discussions by presenting two extreme models of organizational design. One we will call the **mechanistic model**. It's generally synonymous with the bureaucracy in that it has highly standardized processes for work, high formalization, and more managerial hierarchy. The other extreme, the **organic model**, looks a lot like the boundaryless organization. It's flat, has fewer formal procedures for making decisions, has multiple decision makers, and favours flexible practices.[40]

With these two models in mind, let's ask a few questions: Why are some organizations structured along more mechanistic lines, whereas others follow organic characteristics? What forces influence the choice of design? In the following pages, we present the major causes, or determinants, of an organization's structure: strategy, organizational size, technology, and environment.[41] The *Experiential Exercise* on page 481

 Demonstrate how organizational structures differ, and contrast mechanistic and organic structural models.

mechanistic model A structure characterized by high specialization, rigid departmentalization, a clear chain of command, narrow spans of control, a limited information network, and centralization.

organic model A structure that is flat, uses cross-functional and cross-hierarchical teams, possesses a comprehensive information network, has wide spans of control, and has low formalization.

EXHIBIT 13-5 Mechanistic vs. Organic Models

The Mechanistic Model

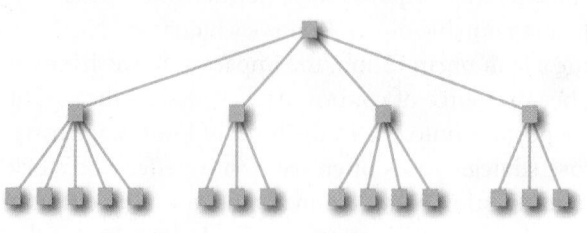

The Organic Model

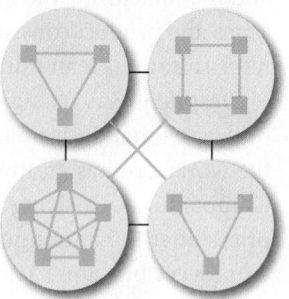

- High specialization
- Rigid departmentalization
- Clear chain of command
- Narrow spans of control
- Centralization
- High formalization

- Cross-functional teams
- Cross-hierarchical teams
- Free flow of information
- Wide spans of control
- Decentralization
- Low formalization

gives you the opportunity to create different organizational structures and see how they can affect productivity.

Organizational Strategy

◄●┤Simulate on MyManagementLab

Organizational Structure

●┤Watch on MyManagementLab

Rudi's Bakery: Organizational Structure

●┤Watch on MyManagementLab

ZipCar: Organizational Structure

Because structure is a means to help management achieve its objectives, and objectives are derived from the organization's overall strategy, it's only logical that structure follow strategy.[42] If management significantly changes the organization's strategy, the structure must change to accommodate.[43] Most current strategy frameworks focus on three strategy dimensions—innovation, cost minimization, and imitation—and the structural design that works best with each.[44]

Innovation Strategy

To what degree does an organization introduce major new products or services? An **innovation strategy** strives to achieve meaningful and unique innovations. Obviously, not all firms pursue innovation. Apple and 3M do, but it certainly is not a strategy pursued by McDonald's. Innovative firms will use competitive pay and benefits to attract top candidates and motivate employees to take risks. Some degree of mechanistic structure can actually benefit innovation. Well-developed communication channels, policies for enhancing long-term commitment, and clear channels of authority all may make it easier for rapid change to occur smoothly.

Cost-Minimization Strategy

innovation strategy A strategy that emphasizes the introduction of major new products and services.

cost-minimization strategy A strategy that emphasizes tight cost controls, avoidance of unnecessary innovation or marketing expenses, and price cutting.

imitation strategy A strategy of moving into new products or new markets only after their viability has already been proven.

An organization pursuing a **cost-minimization strategy** tightly controls costs, refrains from incurring unnecessary innovation or marketing expenses, and cuts prices in selling a basic product. This would describe the strategy pursued by Walmart, as well as the sellers of generic grocery products. Cost-minimizing organizations pursue fewer policies meant to develop commitment among their workforce.

Imitation Strategy

Organizations following an **imitation strategy** try to both minimize risk and maximize opportunity for profit, moving into new products or new markets only after innovators have proven their viability. Mass-market fashion manufacturers like H&M that copy designer styles follow this strategy, as do firms such as Hewlett-Packard and Caterpillar.

EXHIBIT 13-6 The Strategy–Structure Relationship	
Strategy	**Structural Option**
Innovation	*Organic:* A loose structure; low specialization, low formalization, decentralized
Cost minimization	*Mechanistic:* Tight control; extensive work specialization, high formalization, high centralization
Imitation	*Mechanistic and organic:* Mix of loose with tight properties; tight controls over current activities and looser controls for new undertakings

They follow smaller and more innovative competitors with superior products, but only after competitors have demonstrated that the market is there. Italy's Moleskine, a small maker of fashionable notebooks, is another example of imitation strategy, but in the reverse; looking to open more retail shops around the world, it's employing the expansion strategies of larger, successful fashion companies Salvatore Ferragamo and Brunello Cucinelli.[45]

Exhibit 13-6 describes the structural option that best matches each strategy. Innovators need the flexibility of the organic structure, while cost minimizers seek the efficiency and stability of the mechanistic structure. Imitators combine the two structures. They use a mechanistic structure in order to maintain tight controls and low costs in their current activities, but create organic subunits in which to pursue new undertakings.

Organizational Size

An organization's size significantly affects its structure.[46] Organizations that employ 2000 or more people tend to have more specialization, more departmentalization, more vertical levels, and more rules and regulations than do small organizations. However, size becomes less important as an organization expands. Why is this? At around 2000 employees an organization is already fairly mechanistic. An additional 500 employees will not have much impact. But adding 500 employees to an organization that has only 300 members is likely to significantly shift it toward a more mechanistic structure.

Technology

Technology describes the way an organization transfers its inputs into outputs. Every organization has at least one technology for converting financial, human, and physical resources into products or services. Ford Motor Company uses an assembly-line process to make its vehicles. Universities may use a number of instruction technologies to teach students—the formal lecture method, case-analysis, experiential exercises, programmed learning and online instruction and distance learning. Regardless, organizational structures adapt to their technology.

Variations in Technology

Numerous studies have examined the technology–structure relationship.[47] What differentiates technologies is their *degree of routineness*. Routine activities are characterized by automated and standardized operations, such as an assembly line, where one might affix a car door to a car at set intervals, automated transaction processing of sales transactions, and printing and binding of this book. Nonroutine activities are customized and require frequent revision and updating. They include furniture restoring, custom shoemaking, genetic research, and the writing and

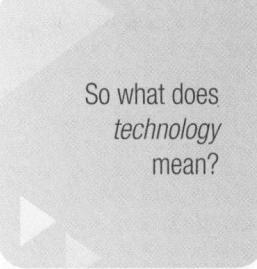

So what does *technology* mean?

technology The way in which an organization transfers its inputs into outputs.

editing of this book. In general, organizations engaged in nonroutine activities tend to prefer organic structures, while those performing routine activities prefer mechanistic structures.

Environment

An organization's **environment** includes outside institutions or forces that can affect the organization's performance, such as suppliers, customers, competitors, government regulatory agencies, and public pressure groups. Some organizations face dynamic environments—rapidly changing government regulations affecting their business, new competitors, difficulties in acquiring raw materials, continually changing product preferences by customers, and so on. Other organizations face relatively static environments—few forces in their environment are changing. Dynamic environments create significantly more uncertainty for managers than do static ones. To minimize uncertainty in key market arenas, managers may broaden their structure to sense and respond to threats. Most companies, including Pepsi and WestJet Airlines, have added social networking departments to their structure so as to respond to negative information posted on blogs. Or companies may form strategic alliances with other companies; for example, Microsoft and Yahoo! joined forces to better compete with Google in the online search provider arena.

Any organization's environment has three dimensions: capacity, volatility, and complexity.[48]

The *capacity* of an environment refers to the degree to which it can support growth. Rich and growing environments generate excess resources, which can buffer the organization in times of relative scarcity.

Volatility describes the degree of instability in an environment. A dynamic environment with a high degree of unpredictable change makes it difficult for management to make accurate predictions. Because information technology changes at such a rapid pace, for instance, more organizations' environments are becoming volatile.

Finally, *complexity* is the degree of heterogeneity and concentration among environmental elements. Simple environments—like the tobacco industry, where the methods of production, competitive and regulatory pressures, and the like haven't changed in quite some time—are homogeneous and concentrated. Environments characterized by heterogeneity and dispersion—like the broadband industry—are complex and diverse, with numerous competitors.

Exhibit 13-7 summarizes our definition of the environment along its three dimensions. The arrows in this figure are meant to indicate movement toward higher

EXHIBIT 13-7 Three-Dimensional Model of the Environment

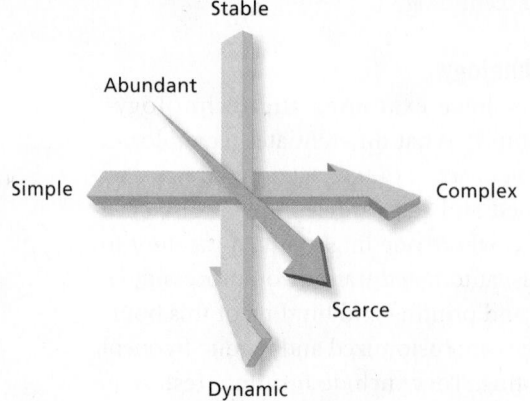

Stable

Abundant

Simple

Complex

Scarce

Dynamic

uncertainty. Organizations that operate in environments characterized as scarce, dynamic, and complex face the greatest degree of uncertainty because they have high unpredictability, little room for error, and a diverse set of elements in the environment to monitor constantly.

Given this three-dimensional definition of *environment*, we can offer some general conclusions about environmental uncertainty and structural arrangements. The more scarce, dynamic, and complex the environment, the more organic a structure should be. The more abundant, stable, and simple the environment, the more mechanistic a structure should be.

Organizational Designs and Employee Behaviour

We opened this chapter by implying that an organization's structure can have significant effects on its members. What might those effects be?

A review of the evidence leads to a pretty clear conclusion: You cannot generalize! Not everyone prefers the freedom and flexibility of organic structures. Different factors stand out in different structures as well. In highly formalized, heavily structured, mechanistic organizations, the level of fairness in formal policies and procedures is a very important predictor of satisfaction. In more personal, individually adaptive organic organizations, employees value interpersonal justice more.[49] Some people are most productive and satisfied when work tasks are standardized and ambiguity minimized—that is, in mechanistic structures. So any discussion of the effect of organizational design on employee behaviour has to address individual differences. To do so, let's consider employee preferences for work specialization, span of control, and centralization.[50] *Focus on Research* looks at the impact of working from home on employee behaviour.

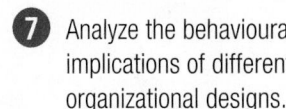 Analyze the behavioural implications of different organizational designs.

PERSONAL INVENTORY ASSESSMENT

Learn About Yourself
Cognitive Style Indicator

FOCUS ON RESEARCH   ## Working from Home

Are there advantages to companies that let employees work from home? Employees who work from home even part of the time report they are happier, and as we saw in Chapter 3, happier employees are likely to be more productive than their dissatisfied counterparts.[51] From an organization's perspective, companies are realizing gains of five to seven extra work hours a week for each employee working from home. There are also cost savings, from reduced overhead for office space and utilities to elimination of unproductive social time. Employers of a home-based workforce can establish work teams and organizational reporting relationships with little attention to office politics, opening the potential to more objectively assign roles and responsibilities. These may be some of the reasons organizations have increasingly endorsed the concept of telecommuting.

Although we can all think of jobs that may never be conducive to working from home (such as many in the service industry), not all positions that *could* be based from home *should* be. Research indicates the success of a work-from-home position depends on the job's structure even more than on its tasks. The amount of interdependence needed between employees within a team or in a reporting relationship sometimes requires *epistemic interdependence*, which is each employee's ability to predict what other employees will do. Organization consultants pay attention to how employee roles relate in the *architecture* of the organization chart, realizing that intentional relationship building is key. Thus, while an employee may complete the tasks of a job well by working alone from home, the benefits of teamwork can be lost.

The success of a work-from-home program depends on the individual, the job, and the culture of the organization. Work from home can be satisfying for employees and efficient for organizations, but research suggests that there are limits.

The evidence generally indicates that work specialization contributes to higher employee productivity—but at the price of reduced job satisfaction. However, work specialization is not an unending source of higher productivity. Problems start to surface, and productivity begins to suffer, when the human diseconomies of doing repetitive and narrow tasks overtake the economies of specialization. As the workforce has become more highly educated and desirous of jobs that are intrinsically rewarding, we seem to reach the point at which productivity begins to decline as a function of specialization more quickly than in the past. While decreased productivity often prompts companies to add oversight and inspection roles, the better answer may be to reorganize work functions and accountability.[52] There is still a segment of the workforce that prefers the routine and repetitiveness of highly specialized jobs. Some individuals want work that makes minimal intellectual demands and provides the security of routine; for them, high work specialization is a source of job satisfaction. The question, of course, is whether they represent 2 percent of the workforce or 52 percent. Given that some self-selection operates in the choice of careers, we might conclude that negative behavioural outcomes from high specialization are most likely to surface in professional jobs occupied by individuals with high needs for personal growth and diversity.

It's probably safe to say that no evidence supports a relationship between span of control and employee satisfaction or performance. Although it's intuitively attractive to argue that large spans might lead to higher employee performance because they provide more distant supervision and more opportunity for personal initiative, the research fails to support this notion. Some people like to be left alone; others prefer the security of a boss who is quickly available at all times. Consistent with several of the contingency theories of leadership discussed in Chapter 11, we would expect factors such as employees' experiences and abilities and the degree of structure in their tasks to explain when wide or narrow spans of control are likely to contribute to their performance and job satisfaction. However, some evidence indicates that a manager's job satisfaction increases as the number of employees supervised increases.

We find fairly strong evidence linking centralization and job satisfaction. In general, less centralized organizations have a greater amount of autonomy. Autonomy appears positively related to job satisfaction. But, again, while one employee may value freedom, another may find autonomous environments frustratingly ambiguous.

Our conclusion: To maximize employee performance and satisfaction, managers must take into account individual differences, such as experience, personality, and the work task. Culture should factor in, too.

We can draw one obvious insight: Other things being equal, people don't select employers randomly. They are attracted to, are selected by, and stay with organizations that suit their personal characteristics.[53] Job candidates who prefer predictability are likely to seek out and take employment in mechanistic structures, and those who want autonomy are more likely to end up in an organic structure. So the effect of structure on employee behaviour is undoubtedly reduced when the selection process facilitates proper matching of individual characteristics with organizational characteristics. Furthermore, companies should strive to establish, promote, and maintain the unique identity of their structures since skilled employees may quit as a result of dramatic changes.[54]

GLOBAL IMPLICATIONS

When we think about how culture influences how organizations are to be structured, several questions come to mind. First, does culture really matter to organizational structure? Second, do employees in different countries vary in their perceptions of different types of organizational structures? Finally, how do cultural considerations fit with our discussion of the boundaryless organization? Let's tackle each question in turn.

Culture and Organizational Structure

Does culture really affect organizational structure? The answer might seem obvious—yes!—but there are reasons it may not matter as much as you think. The US model of business has been very influential on organizational structures in other countries. Moreover, US and Canadian structures themselves have been influenced by structures in other countries (especially Japan, Great Britain, and Germany). However, cultural concerns still might be important. Bureaucratic structures still dominate in many parts of Europe and Asia. One management expert argues that US management often places too much emphasis on individual leadership, which may be jarring in countries where decision making is more decentralized.[55]

Culture and Employee Structure Preferences

Research suggests that national culture influences the preference for structure.[56] Organizations that operate with people from high power-distance cultures, such as Greece, France, and most of Latin America, find that their employees are much more accepting of mechanistic structures than are employees from low power-distance countries. So consider cultural differences along with individual differences when predicting how structure will affect employee performance and satisfaction.

Learn About Yourself
Organizational Structure Assessment

Culture and the Boundaryless Organization

When fully operational, the boundaryless organization also breaks down barriers created by geography. Today most large US companies and some Canadian companies see themselves as global corporations and many, such as Coca-Cola and McDonald's, do as much business overseas as in North America, and some struggle to incorporate geographical regions into their structure. In other cases, the boundaryless organization approach is need-based. Such is the case with Chinese companies, which have made 93 acquisitions in the oil and gas industry since 2008 to meet the forecasted demand their resources in China cannot meet.[57] The boundaryless organization provides one solution because it considers geography more of a tactical, logistical issue than a structural one. In short, the goal of the boundaryless organization is to break down cultural barriers.

One way to do so is through strategic alliances. Firms such as NEC Corporation, Boeing, and Apple each have strategic alliances or joint partnerships with dozens of companies. These alliances blur the distinction between one organization and another as employees work on joint projects. Research from 119 international joint ventures (IJVs) in China indicates that these partnerships allow firms to learn from one another and obtain higher new product performance especially where a strong learning culture exists.[58] Moreover, some companies allow customers to perform functions previously done by management. Some AT&T units receive bonuses based on customer evaluations of the teams that serve them. Finally, telecommuting is blurring organizational boundaries. The security analyst with Merrill Lynch who does his job from his ranch in Alberta or the software designer in Winnipeg who works for a Waterloo firm are just two of the millions of employees who work outside the physical boundaries of their employers' premises.

Culture and the Impact of Downsizing

The changing landscape of organizational structure designs has implications for the individual progressing on a career path. Recent research interviews with managers in Japan, the United Kingdom, and the United States indicate that employees who have weathered downsizing and resulting hybrid organizational structures consider their

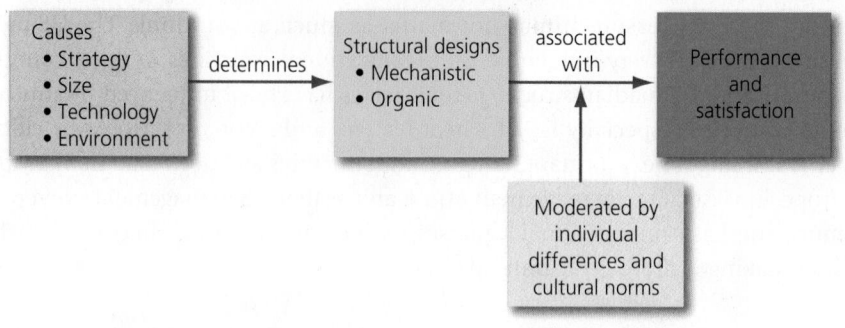

EXHIBIT 13-8 Organizational Structure: Its Determinants and Outcomes

future career prospects diminished. While this may or may not be true, it shows that organizational structure does affect the employee and thus must be carefully designed.[59]

Summary

The theme of this chapter is that an organization's internal structure contributes to explaining and predicting behaviour. That is, in addition to individual and group factors, the structure has a bearing on employee attitudes. What is the basis for this argument? To the degree that an organization's structure reduces ambiguity for employees and clarifies concerns such as "What am I supposed to do?" "How am I supposed to do it?" "To whom do I report?" and "To whom do I go if I have a problem?" it shapes their attitudes and facilitates and motivates them to higher levels of performance. Exhibit 13-8 summarizes what we have discussed.

SNAPSHOT SUMMARY

What Is Organizational Structure?
- Work Specialization
- Departmentalization
- Chain of Command
- Span of Control
- Centralization and Decentralization
- Formalization

Common Organizational Designs
- The Simple Structure
- The Bureaucracy
- The Matrix Structure

New Design Options
- The Virtual Organization
- The Boundaryless Organization

- The Leaner Organization: Organization Downsizing

Why Do Structures Differ?
- Organizational Strategy
- Organizational Size
- Technology
- Environment

Organizational Designs and Employee Behaviour

MyManagementLab   Study, practise, and explore real business situations with these helpful resources:

- **Study Plan:** Check your understanding of chapter concepts with self-study quizzes.
- **Online Lesson Presentations:** Study key chapter topics and work through interactive assessments to test your knowledge and master management concepts.
- **Videos:** Learn more about the management practices and strategies of real companies.
- **Simulations:** Practise management decision-making in simulated business environments.

P I A PERSONAL INVENTORY ASSESSMENT

for **Review**

1. What are the six key elements that define an organization's structure?

2. What are the characteristics of a bureaucracy, and how does it differ from a simple structure?

3. What are the characteristics of a matrix organization?

4. What are the characteristics of a virtual organization?

5. Why would managers create a boundaryless organization?

6. Why do organizational structures differ, and what is the difference between a mechanistic structure and an organic structure?

7. What are the behavioural implications of different organizational designs?

for **Managers**

- Specialization can make operations more efficient, but remember that excessive specialization can create employee dissatisfaction and reduce motivation.

- Avoid designing rigid hierarchies that overly limit employees' empowerment and autonomy.

- Balance the advantages of virtual and boundaryless organizations against the potential pitfalls before adding flexible workplace options.

- Downsize your organization to realize major cost savings, and focus the company around core competencies—but only if necessary because downsizing can have a significant negative impact on employee morale.

- Consider the scarcity, dynamism, and complexity of the environment, and balance the organic and mechanistic elements when designing an organizational structure.

for **You**

- Think about the type of organizational structure that suits you best when you look for a job. You may prefer a structured workplace, like that of a mechanistic organization. Or you may prefer a much less structured workplace, like that of an organic organization.

- If you decide to start your own company, know the different structural considerations so that you can create an organization that meets your needs as both a business person and a person with additional interests.

- As a manager or as an entrepreneur, consider how much responsibility (centralization/decentralization) you want to take for yourself compared with how much you are willing to share with others in the organization.

OB *at* *Work*

The End of Management

Management—at least as we know it—is dying.[60] Formal organizational structures are giving way to flatter, less bureaucratic, less formal structures. And that's a good thing.

Today, leaders are celebrated for triumphing *over* structure rather than for working well within it. Innovative companies such as Apple, Google, Facebook, Twitter, and Groupon were born and now thrive thanks not to a multilayered bureaucracy, but to an innovative idea that was creatively executed by a flexible group of people freely collaborating. Management in those companies exists to facilitate, rather than control.

The new wave of eliminating job titles is a prime indicator of companies learning to structure for innovation. This trend is a reflection of the changes in job scope that have come with increased technological savvy. For instance, the fact that most managers do their own keyboarding has dramatically changed the job of the office secretary of generations before. The scope of what managers do has broadened to include typing, taking notes, and managing their own files/schedules, while the scope of what secretaries (or administrative assistants) do has broadened to include making social media posts and assuming technical duties. The most innovative firms have questioned whether they need job titles at all, instead emphasizing collaboration throughout the organization.

The best companies have eliminated offices altogether and encourage employees to mingle and form teams according to their project interests. This suits younger workers who never did want offices, who aspire to work *with* the top players rather than *report to* them, and who value flexible hours and work from home options. Job titles are gone, roles are ambiguous, and reporting relationships morph by project.

The talent is ready for the elimination of management as we know it. The successful corporation of the future will have a flatter organizational structure and accountability based on performance.

There is no "right size fits all" approach to organizational structure. How flat, informal, and collaborative an organization should be depends on many factors, but no matter what, management structure is needed. Let's consider two cases.

People lauded how loosely and informally Warren Buffett structured his investment firm, Berkshire Hathaway. Buffett spends most of his day reading and talking informally "with highly gifted people whom he trusts and who trust him." This sounded wonderful until it was discovered Buffett's CFO and heir apparent David Sokol was on the take. Sokol made $3 million when he successfully lobbied for Berkshire Hathaway to acquire a firm in which he had secretly acquired a significant stake. His insider manoeuvres discovered, Sokol was forced to resign. Wouldn't Buffett have known Sokol was compromised if he supervised more closely or had structures in place to check such "freedom"? It's hard to argue with Berkshire Hathaway's past successes, but they don't prove the company is ideally structured.

Berkshire Hathaway is a cautionary example of the perils of a structure that is *too* flat and informal. For the benefits of a formal structure, look no further than Honeywell International. CEO David Cote seems relaxed and fun-loving (witness his Harley-Davidson rides and office attire of leather bomber jacket and jeans), but his hard-hitting work ethic is legendary. As the leader of a global technology and manufacturing conglomerate, Cote keeps a tight rein on the four industry divisions and 132 000 employees.

Cote's control focus does not end at the executive suite, thanks to a formal organizational structure with job titles, security clearances, role descriptions … the works, at all levels on the organization chart. At the factories, job titles are painted literally on the *floor* to indicate who needs to be present—and standing—at organizational meetings monitored with a clock hand that turns red when 15 minutes is up. Not only did Cote successfully merge three disparate company cultures and more than 250 factories, but the new Honeywell has climbed up the *Fortune* 500 ranks and pulls in $37.1 billion in annual sales. The company's profits have increased faster than sales, in part due to Cote's insistence on freezing raises and hiring only two to three employees for every four to five who exit.

The examples of Berkshire Hathaway and Honeywell illustrate the strong need for management structure in an ever-changing, diverse, worldwide marketplace.

PERSONAL **INVENTORY** ASSESSMENT

Delegation Self-Assessment: Most employees, whether leaders or team members, need to delegate work from time to time. Use this scale to assess your ability to delegate effectively.

Cognitive Style Indicator: Cognitive style can profoundly influence both task preferences and organizational structure preferences. Use this scale to determine your preferred cognitive style.

Organizational Structure Assessment: Personality and cultural factors can influence which organizational structure you prefer. Use this scale to determine what type of organizational structure would be the best fit for you.

BREAKOUT **GROUP** EXERCISES

Form small groups to discuss the following topics, as assigned by your instructor:

1. Describe the structure of an organization in which you worked. Was the structure appropriate for the tasks being done?

2. Have you ever worked in an organization with a structure that seemed inappropriate to the task? What would have improved the structure?

3. You are considering opening up a coffee bar with several of your friends. What kind of structure might you use? After the coffee bar becomes successful, you decide that expanding the number of branches might be a good idea. What changes to the structure might you make?

EXPERIENTIAL EXERCISE

Words-in-Sentences Company

Overview: You are a small company that

1. manufactures words; and

2. packages them into meaningful English-language sentences.[61]

Market research has established that sentences of at least 3 words but not more than 6 words are in demand. Therefore, packaging, distribution, and sales should be set up for **3- to 6-word sentences.**

Time: Approximately 30 minutes. (Note: A production run takes 10 minutes. While the game is more effective if 2 [or more] production runs are completed, even 1 production run will generate effective discussion about how organizational structure affects performance.)

Group Task: Your group must design and participate in running a W-I-S company. You will be competing with other companies in your industry. The success of your company will depend on (a) your objectives, (b) planning, (c) organizational structure, and (d) quality control. You should design your organization to be as efficient as possible during each 10-minute production run. After the first production run, you will have an opportunity to reorganize your company if you want.

Raw Materials: For each production run, you will be given a **"raw material phrase."** The letters found in the phrase serve as the raw materials available to produce new words in sentences. For example, if the raw material phrase is "organizational behaviour is fun," you could produce the words and sentence "Nat ran to a zoo." One way to think of your raw material phrase is to take all the letters appearing in the phrase and write them down as many times as they appear in the phrase. Thus, for the phrase "organizational behaviour is fun" you have: a-4; b-1; c-0; d-0; e-1; f-1; g-1; h-1; i-4; j-0; k-0; l-1; m-0; n-3; o-3; p-0; q-0; r-2; s-1; t-1; u-2; v-1; w-0; x-0; y-0; z-1, for a total of 28 raw material letters.

OB *at* **Work**

Production Standards:	There are several rules that have to be followed in producing "words-in-sentences." **If these rules are not followed, your output will not meet production specifications and will not pass quality-control inspection.**

1. A letter may appear only as often in a manufactured word as it appears in the raw material phrase; for example, "organizational behaviour is fun" has 1 letter *l* and 1 letter *e*. Thus "steal" is legitimate, but not "teller." It has too many *l*'s and *e*'s.

2. Raw material letters can be used again in different manufactured words.

3. A manufactured **word** may be used only **once** during a production run; once a word—for example, "the"—is used in a sentence, it is out of stock for the rest of the production run. No other sentence may use the word "the."

4. A new word may not be made by adding *s* to form the plural of an already used manufactured word.

5. Sentences must make grammatical and logical sense.

6. All words must be in the English language.

7. Names and places are acceptable.

8. Slang is not acceptable.

9. Writing must be legible. Any illegible sentence will be disqualified.

10. Only sentences that have a minimum of 3 words and a maximum of 6 words will be considered.

Directions:

Step 1 Production Run 1. The instructor will place a raw material phrase on the board or overhead. When the instructor announces, "Begin production," you are to manufacture as many words as possible and package them in sentences for delivery to the Quality Control Review Board. You will have 10 minutes.

Step 2 When the instructor announces "Stop production," you will have 30 seconds to deliver your output to the Quality Control Review Board. Output received after 30 seconds does not meet the delivery schedule and will not be counted. You may use up to 2 sheets of paper, and each sheet of paper must identify your group.

Step 3 Your output should be delivered by your quality-control representative, who will work with the other representatives to evaluate the performance of each of the groups.

Measuring Performance: The output of your W-I-S company is measured by the total number of acceptable words that are packaged in sentences of 3 to 6 words only.

Quality Control: If any word in a sentence does not meet the standards set forth above, all the words in the sentence will be rejected. The Quality Control Review Board (composed of 1 member from each company) is the final arbiter of acceptability. In the event of a tie vote on the Review Board, a coin toss will determine the outcome.

Step 4 While the output is being evaluated, you should make plans for organizing the second production run.

Step 5 Production Run 2.

Step 6 The results are presented.

Step 7 Discussion.

ETHICAL **DILEMMA**

Just Following Orders

Betty Vinson took a job as a mid-level accountant for $50 000 a year with a small long-distance company that grew up to become a giant telecom five years later.[62]

Hard-working and diligent, within two years Ms Vinson was promoted to a senior manager in the corporate accounting division. In her new job, she helped compile quarterly results, along with 10 employees who reported to her. Soon after taking the new position, her bosses asked her to make false accounting entries. At first, she said "no." But continued pressure led her to finally cave in. Her decision to make the false entries came after the company's chief financial officer assured her that he would assume all responsibility.

Over the course of six quarters, Ms Vinson made illegal entries to bolster the company's profits at the request of her superiors. At the end of 18 months, she had helped falsify at least $3.7 billion in profits. Of course, the whole scheme unravelled, in what became the largest fraud case in corporate history.

Ms Vinson pleaded guilty to two criminal counts of conspiracy and securities fraud, charges that carry a maximum sentence of 15 years in prison. She was sentenced to five months in prison and five months of house arrest.

What would you have done had you been in Ms Vinson's job? Is "just following orders" an acceptable excuse for breaking the law? If your livelihood is on the line, do you say "no" to a powerful boss? What can organizations do to lessen the chance that employees might capitulate to unethical pressures imposed by their boss?

CASE INCIDENTS

Creative Deviance: Bucking the Hierarchy?

One of the major functions of an organizational hierarchy is to increase standardization and control for top managers.[63] Using the chain of command, managers can direct the activities of subordinates toward a common purpose. If the right person with a creative vision is in charge of a hierarchy, the results can be phenomenal. Until Steve Jobs's passing in October 2011, Apple had used a strongly top-down creative process in which most major decisions and innovations flowed directly through Jobs and then were delegated to subteams as specific assignments to complete.

Then there is creative deviance, in which individuals create extremely successful products despite being told by senior management to stop working on them. The electrostatic displays used in more than half of Hewlett-Packard's instruments, the tape slitter that was one of the most important process innovations in 3M's history, and Nichia's development of multi-billion-dollar LED bright lighting technology were all officially rejected by the management hierarchy. In all of these cases, an approach like Apple's would have shut down some of the most successful products these companies ever produced. Doing "business as usual" can become such an imperative in a hierarchical organization that new ideas are seen as threats rather than opportunities for development.

It's not immediately apparent why top-down decision making works so well for one highly creative company like Apple, while hierarchy nearly ruined innovations at several other organizations. It may be that Apple's structure is actually quite simple, with relatively few layers and a great deal of responsibility placed on each individual for his or her own outcomes. Or it may be that Apple simply had a very unique leader who was able to rise above the conventional strictures of a CEO to create a culture of constant innovation.

Questions

1. Do you think it's possible for an organization to deliberately create an "anti-hierarchy" to encourage employees to engage in more acts of creative deviance? What steps might a company take to encourage creative deviance?

2. What are the dangers of an approach that encourages creative deviance?

3. Why do you think a company such as Apple is able to be creative with a strongly hierarchical structure, whereas other companies find hierarchy limiting?

4. Do you think Apple's success has been entirely dependent upon Steve Jobs's role as head of the hierarchy? What are the potential liabilities of a company that is so strongly connected to the decision-making of a single individual?

"I Detest Bureaucracy"

Greg Strakosch, founder and CEO of interactive media company TechTarget, hates bureaucracy.[64] So he has created a workplace where his 600 employees are free to come and go as they please. There are no set policies mandating working hours or detailing sick, personal, or vacation days. Employees are free to take as much vacation as they want and to work the hours when they are most productive—even if it's between midnight and 4 a.m. If you need a day off to take your kid to camp? No problem. Strakosch says ideas like setting a specific number of sick days "strike me as arbitrary and dumb." He trusts his employees to act responsibly.

OB *at* **Work**

Strakosch is quick to state that "this isn't a country club." A painstaking hiring process is designed to weed out all but the most autonomous. Managers set ambitious quarterly goals, and employees are given plenty of independence to achieve them. However, there is little tolerance for failure. As TechTarget's website states, there is a 100 percent focus on results. Employees are fired for underachieving.

Moreover, while hours are flexible, employees frequently put in at least 50 hours a week. In addition, regardless of hours worked, employees are required to remain accessible via email, cellphone, instant messaging, or laptop.

Strakosch's approach seems to be working. TechTarget became a public company in May 2007 with a $100 million IPO and has grown to become the leading online media company for the technology sector. In May 2014, the company was recognized as one of the "Best Places to Work," the seventh time it has been so recognized.

Questions

1. What type of organizational structure does TechTarget have?

2. Why does this type of structure work at TechTarget?

3. How transferable is this structure to other organizations?

4. Would you want to work at TechTarget? Why or why not?

FROM CONCEPTS TO SKILLS

Delegating Authority

Managers get things done through other people. Because there are limits to any manager's time and knowledge, effective managers need to understand how to delegate. *Delegation* is the assignment of authority to another person to carry out specific duties. It allows an employee to make some of the decisions. Delegation should not be confused with participation. In participative decision making, there is a sharing of authority. In delegation, employees make decisions on their own.

A number of actions differentiate the effective delegator from the ineffective delegator. You can become a more effective delegator if you use the following five suggestions:[65]

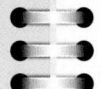

1. *Clarify the assignment.* The place to begin is to determine what is to be delegated and to whom. You need to identify the person most capable of doing the task, then determine if he or she has the time and motivation to do the job.

   Assuming that you have a willing and able employee, it is your responsibility to provide clear information on what is being delegated, the results you expect, and any time or performance expectations you hold.

   Unless there is an overriding need to adhere to specific methods, you should delegate only the end results. That is, get agreement on what is to be done and the end results expected, but let the employee decide on the means.

2. *Specify the employee's range of discretion.* Every act of delegation comes with constraints. You are delegating authority to act, but not unlimited authority. What you are delegating is authority to act on certain issues and, on those issues, within certain parameters. You need to specify what those parameters are so employees know, in no uncertain terms, the range of their discretion.

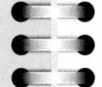

3. *Allow the employee to participate.* One of the best sources for determining how much authority will be necessary to accomplish a task is the employee who will be held accountable for that task. If you allow employees to participate in determining what is delegated, how much authority is needed to get the job done, and the standards by which they will be judged, you increase employee motivation, satisfaction, and accountability for performance.

4. *Inform others that delegation has occurred.* Delegation should not occur in a vacuum. Not only do you and the employee need to know specifically what has been delegated and how much authority has been granted, but anyone else who may be affected by the delegation act also needs to be informed.

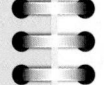

5. *Establish feedback controls.* The establishment of controls to monitor the employee's progress increases the likelihood that important problems

will be identified early and that the task will be completed on time and to the desired specifications. For instance, agree on a specific time for completion of the task, and then set progress dates when the employee will report back on how well he or she is doing and any major problems that have surfaced. This can be supplemented with periodic spot checks to ensure that authority guidelines are not being abused, organization policies are being followed, and proper procedures are being met.

Practising Skills

You are the director of research and development for a large pharmaceutical manufacturer. You have six people who report directly to you: Sue (your secretary), Dale (laboratory manager), Todd (quality standards manager), Linda (patent coordination manager), Ruben (market coordination manager), and Marjorie (senior projects manager). Dale is the most senior of the five managers and is generally acknowledged as the chief candidate to replace you if you are promoted or leave.

You have received your annual instructions from the CEO to develop next year's budget for your area. The task is relatively routine, but takes quite a bit of time. In the past, you have always done the annual budget yourself. But this year, because your workload is exceptionally heavy, you have decided to try something different. You are going to assign budget preparation to one of your subordinate managers. The obvious choice is Dale. Dale has been with the company longest, is highly dependable, and, as your probable successor, is most likely to gain from the experience. The budget is due on your boss's desk in eight weeks. Last year it took you about 30 to 35 hours to complete. However, you have done a budget many times before. For a novice, it might take double that amount of time.

The budget process is generally straightforward. You start with last year's budget and modify it to reflect inflation and changes in departmental objectives. All the data that Dale will need are in your files, online, or can be obtained from your other managers.

You have just walked over to Dale's office and informed him of your decision. He seemed enthusiastic about doing the budget, but he also has a heavy workload. He told you, "I'm regularly coming in around 7 a.m. and it's unusual for me to leave before 7 p.m. For the past five weekends, I've even come in on Saturday mornings to get my work done. I can do my best to try to find time to do the budget." Specify exactly what you would say to Dale and the actions you would take if Dale agrees to do the budget.

Reinforcing Skills

1. Watch a classic movie that has examples of "managers" delegating assignments. Pay explicit attention to the incidence of delegation. Was delegating done effectively? What was good about the practice? How might it have been improved? Movies with delegation examples include *The Godfather*, *The Firm*, *Star Trek*, *Office Space*, *Nine-to-Five*, and *Working Girl*.

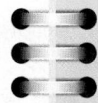

2. The next time you have to do a group project for a class, pay explicit attention to how tasks are delegated. Does someone assume a leadership role? If so, note how closely the delegation process is followed. Is delegation different in project or study groups than in typical work groups?

Organizational Change

Hudson's Bay has struggled for years to find its niche. In the highly competitive retail market, how can the retailer adapt to ensure it stays relevant and profitable?

LEARNING OUTCOMES

After studying this chapter, you should be able to:

1 Identify the forces for change.

2 Compare the four main approaches to managing organizational change.

3 Describe the sources of resistance to change.

4 Describe two ways to create a culture for change.

Throughout much of the early 2000s, Hudson's Bay (HBC) was struggling with both sales and its identity.[1] As Anthony Stokan, a Toronto-based retail consultant, explained in March 2006, "You've got an organization that has been grovelling to turn around for a decade and the shopping opportunities for the average Canadian consumer have never been more extraordinary." The retail operation had just been involved in a hostile takeover by Jerry Zucker, who took the company private, named himself CEO, and dismissed a number of senior executives. The battle to turn around HBC's fortunes began.

Lucas Oleniuk/ZUMA Press/Newscom

Zucker's vision was a more customer-service oriented department store. By taking the company private, he "liberated HBC from the relentless focus of 'the street' on quarterly performance and allowed necessary changes to occur." However, before Zucker could complete the turnaround, he passed away in 2008. HBC was then acquired by another equity firm, whose new board comprised experienced international retailers who committed to continuing Zucker's vision of excellent customer service and developing a new direction for HBC.

One of those international retailers was Bonnie Brooks, who was appointed president and CEO of HBC in 2008. Would Brooks be able to change HBC in a way that would support the company's viability over the long term?

HBC is just one of many organizations that needs to reinvent itself if it is to survive in a challenging business environment. Engaging in any kind of change in an organization is not easy. In this chapter, we examine the forces for change, managing change, and contemporary change issues.

THE BIG IDEA

Change is inevitable, and being able to adapt to change will help the process go more smoothly.

IS FOR **EVERYONE**

- Are there positive approaches to change?
- How do you respond to change?
- What makes organizations resist change?

Forces for Change

1 Identify the forces for change.

No company today is in a particularly stable environment. Even those with dominant market share must change, sometimes radically. The Future Shop store that opened in Cornwall, Ontario, in mid-November 2014 is a sign of the changes happening to big box stores.[2] The store is small, less than one-third the size of the average Future Shop store. A large warehouse attached to the store caters to online shoppers who then go to the store to pick up their items. Fewer customers show up to browse merchandise. Instead, they do their research online. Enticing them to pick up merchandise ordered online is intended to get people into the store, so that perhaps they will buy more. The Internet has changed the way people shop, and big box stores are having to change the way they interact with customers.

"Change or die!" is the rallying cry among today's managers worldwide. Exhibit 14-1 summarizes six distinct forces that act as stimulants for change.

In a number of places in this book, we have discussed the changing *nature of the workforce*. Almost every organization must adjust to a multicultural environment, demographic changes, immigration, and outsourcing.

Technology is changing jobs and organizations. It is not hard to imagine the very idea of an office becoming an antiquated concept in the near future.

The Canadian housing and financial sectors have experienced extraordinary *economic shocks* in recent years, although not to the extent that they have in the United States. The financial turbulence that began in 2008 has eroded the average employee's retirement account considerably, forcing many employees to postpone their anticipated retirement date and, in some cases, making it harder for younger people to find jobs.

EXHIBIT 14-1 Forces for Change	
Force	**Examples**
Nature of the workforce	More cultural diversity
	Aging population
	Many new entrants with inadequate skills
Technology	Faster, cheaper, and more mobile computers
	Online music sharing
	Deciphering of the human genetic code
Economic shocks	Rise and fall of dot-com stocks
	Record low interest rates
	Turbulent financial markets
Competition	Global competitors
	Mergers and consolidations
	Growth of e-commerce
Social trends	Internet chat rooms
	Retirement of Baby Boomers
	Rise of discount and "big box" retailers
World politics	Global financial crises
	Opening of markets in China
	Government shakeups around the world
	Extreme weather

Andrew Francis Wallace/ZUMA Press/Newscom

Michael Medline, the new CEO of Canadian Tire, recognizes that his company has had a poor digital presence in recent years. He plans to change that quickly by introducing more consumer email alerts to help his customers, including letting them know that items they might need (for example, shovels when it's snowing) are on sale.

Meanwhile, spending has dropped, and many Canadian retailers are still suffering the consequences today.

Competition has changed. Competitors are as likely to come from across the ocean as from across town. Successful organizations will be fast on their feet, capable of developing new products rapidly and getting them to market quickly. In other words, they will be flexible and will require an equally flexible and responsive workforce.

Social trends don't remain static either. Consumers who are otherwise strangers now meet and share product information in chat rooms and blogs. Companies must continually adjust product and marketing strategies to be sensitive to changing social trends. For example, consumers, employees, and organizational leaders are increasingly sensitive to environmental concerns. As a result, "green" practices have quickly become expected rather than optional.

Not even globalization's strongest proponents could have imagined how *world politics* would change in recent years. We have seen a major set of financial crises that have rocked global markets, Japan's fall into recession in 2014, a dramatic rise in the power and influence of China, intense shakeups in governments around the world, and the societal effects of extreme weather. Throughout the industrialized world, businesses—particularly in the banking and financial sectors—have come under new scrutiny.

Opportunities for Change

Organizations have many opportunities to engage in change. They can change their motivation structures or redesign jobs. They may engage in corporate social responsibility. They may organize more around teams or share more leadership by empowering employees. They may create flatter structures, or move to more modular structures. Sometimes the entire culture of the organization needs to change for organizational change to be successful, as *Case Incident—Starbucks Returns to Its Roots*

EXHIBIT 14-2 Organizational Targets for Change

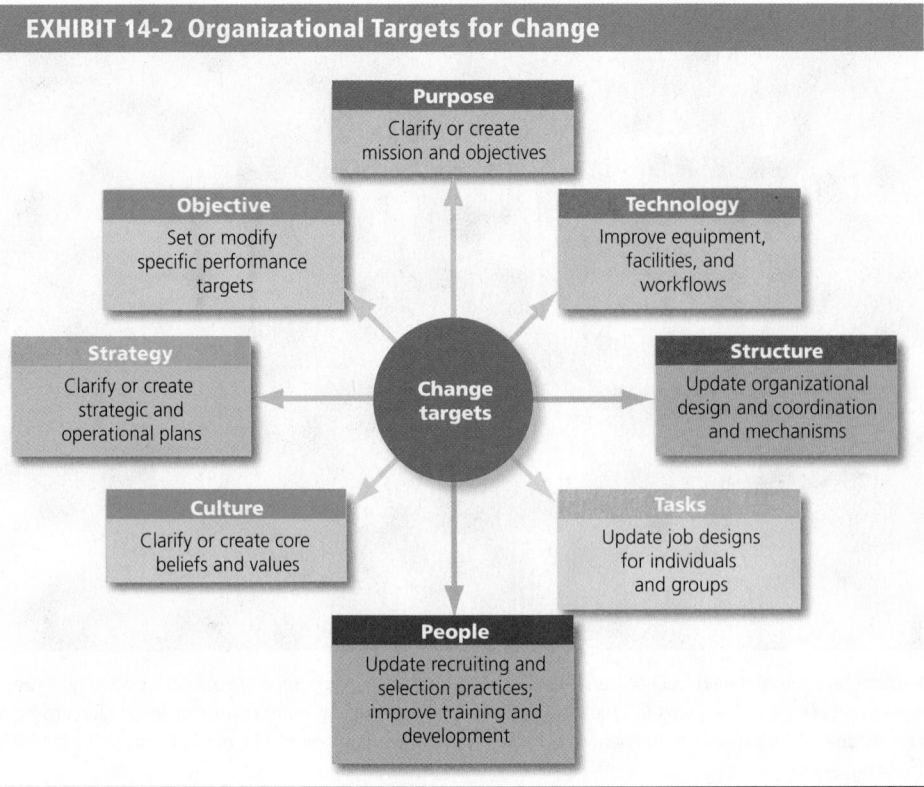

Source: J. R. Schermerhorn Jr., J. G. Hunt, and R. N. Osborn, *Organizational Behavior*, 9th ed., 2005, p. 363, Figure 16.1. Copyright © 2005 John Wiley & Sons, Inc.

on page 512 shows. Exhibit 14-2 summarizes the range of change targets available to organizations.

As we discussed the workplace in this book, and talked about possible change, we might have implied that change happens easily, perhaps overnight, and does not require careful thought or planning. This implication exists because we did not discuss how these changes actually happen in the workplace, what has to be done to achieve change, and how difficult change actually is. We wanted you to understand what changes were possible before we actually discussed how to carry them out.

Change Agents

Who is responsible for managing change activities in an organization? The answer is **change agents**.[3] They see a future for the organization that others have not identified, and they are able to motivate, invent, and implement this vision. Change agents can be managers or nonmanagers, employees of the organization or outside consultants.[4]

In some instances, internal management will hire the services of outside consultants to provide advice and assistance with major change efforts. Because they are from the outside, these individuals can offer an objective perspective often unavailable to insiders. Outside consultants, however, are disadvantaged because they usually have an inadequate understanding of the organization's history, culture, operating procedures, and personnel. Outside consultants also may be prone to initiating more drastic changes—which can be a benefit or a disadvantage—because they don't have to live with the repercussions after the change is implemented. In contrast, internal staff specialists or managers, when acting as change agents, may be more thoughtful (and possibly more cautious) because they have to live with the consequences of their actions.

change agents People who act as catalysts and assume the responsibility for managing change activities.

THE CANADIAN PRESS/Chris Young

John Betts, president of Toronto-based McDonald's Canada, is always looking for new ideas to reinvent his company. When he wanted to get Canadians to think about McDonald's as a great place to buy coffee, the company offered free coffee for two weeks, which brought in large numbers of customers to try the coffee, and increased coffee sales considerably.

Approaches to Managing Change

In 2008, when Bonnie Brooks was appointed president and CEO of HBC, many retail analysts were saying that "Hudson's Bay Co. was too broken to fix."[5] Brooks liked the challenge. She had spent the previous 11 years, including the last 5 as president, at Hong Kong-based Lane Crawford Joyce Group, which had more than 500 stores in Asia. Brooks was internationally recognized for her work in turning around the Lane Crawford stores.

Brooks took what others saw as Hudson's Bay's misfortune—too much real estate—and turned it into a benefit. Rather than selling off stores, like Sears Canada had done, Brooks turned to creating stores within stores at Hudson's Bay. Top Shop (a British fashion retailer), Coach, Burberry, and Kleinfeld Bridal were encouraged to open stores in Hudson's Bay. She attracted new designers for The Room, a higher end assortment of women's clothing. Brooks noted that Hudson's Bay was in the right place to do this: "There is no other store in Canada that could provide that [kind of shopping experience]. Sears wouldn't be able to attract those brands and Holt Renfrew wouldn't have the space."

Customers also bought into the changes. Five years into Brooks' term, Joe Thacker, chief strategist at Toronto-based Fusion Retail Analytics, said the following: "The turnaround, I think, is real. Those numbers aren't coming from industry growth. That's all coming from market share gains." What has made Brooks' approach to change successful?

2 Compare the four main approaches to managing organizational change.

To this point, we have discussed the kinds of changes organizations can make. Assuming that an organization has uncovered a need for change, how does it engage in the change process? We turn to four approaches to managing change: Lewin's classic three-step model of the change process, Kotter's eight-step plan for implementing change, action research, and appreciative inquiry.

Lewin's Three-Step Model

Kurt Lewin argued that successful change in organizations should follow three steps, which are illustrated in Exhibit 14-3: **unfreezing** the status quo, **moving** to a new state, and **refreezing** the new change to make it permanent.[6]

unfreezing Change efforts to overcome the pressures of both individual resistance and group conformity.

moving Efforts to get employees involved in the change process.

refreezing Stabilizing a change intervention by balancing driving and restraining forces.

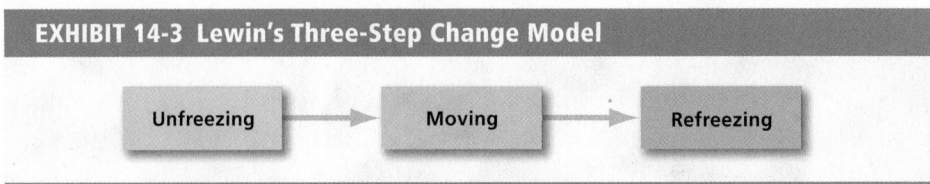

EXHIBIT 14-3 Lewin's Three-Step Change Model

Unfreezing → Moving → Refreezing

The status quo can be considered to be an equilibrium state. To move from this equilibrium—to overcome the pressures of both individual resistance and group conformity—unfreezing must happen in one of three ways. (See Exhibit 14-4.) The **driving forces**, which direct behaviour away from the status quo, can be increased. The **restraining forces**, which hinder movement from the existing equilibrium, can be decreased. A third alternative is to *combine the first two approaches*. Companies that have been successful in the past are likely to encounter restraining forces because people question the need for change.[7] Similarly, research shows that companies with strong cultures excel at incremental change but are overcome by restraining forces against radical change.[8]

The value of this model can be seen through the example of a large oil company that decided to consolidate its three regional marketing offices in Winnipeg, Calgary, and Vancouver into a single regional office in Calgary. The decision was made in Toronto, and the people affected had no say whatsoever in the choice. The reorganization meant transferring more than 150 employees, eliminating some duplicate managerial positions, and instituting a new hierarchy of command.

The oil company's management could expect employee resistance to the consolidation and outlined its alternatives. Those in Winnipeg or Vancouver may not want to transfer to another city, pull children out of school, make new friends, adapt to new co-workers, or undergo the reassignment of responsibilities. Positive incentives such as pay increases, liberal moving expenses, and low-cost mortgage funds for new homes in Calgary might encourage employees to accept the change. Management might also unfreeze acceptance of the status quo by removing restraining forces. It could counsel employees individually, hearing and clarifying each employee's specific concerns and apprehensions. Assuming that most of the fears are unjustified, the counsellor could assure the employees that there was nothing to fear and then demonstrate, through tangible evidence, that restraining forces are unwarranted. If resistance is extremely high, management may have to resort to both reducing resistance and increasing the attractiveness of the alternative if the unfreezing is to be successful.

driving forces Forces that direct behaviour away from the status quo.

restraining forces Forces that hinder movement away from the status quo.

Research on organizational change has shown that, to be effective, the actual change has to happen quickly.[9] Organizations that build up to change do less well than those that get to and through the moving stage quickly.

Once the consolidation change has been implemented, to be successful the new situation must be refrozen so that it can be sustained over time. Without this last step, change likely will be short-lived and employees will try to go back to the previous equilibrium state. The objective of refreezing, then, is to stabilize the new situation by balancing the driving and restraining forces.

How could the oil company's management refreeze its consolidation change? By systematically replacing temporary forces with permanent ones. Management might impose a new bonus system tied to the specific changes desired. The formal rules and regulations governing behaviour of those affected by the change should also be revised to reinforce the new situation. Over time, of course, the work group's own norms will evolve to sustain the new equilibrium. But until that point is reached, management will have to rely on more formal mechanisms.

EXHIBIT 14-4 Unfreezing the Status Quo

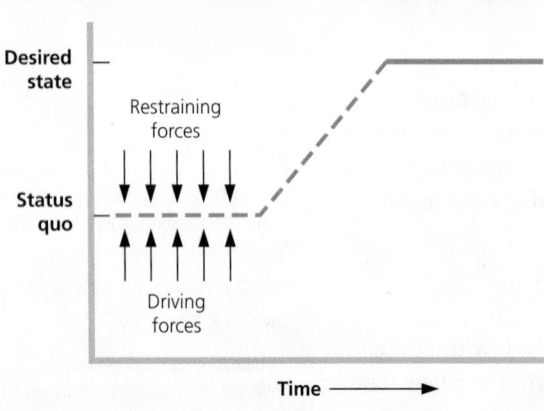

Desired state

Restraining forces

Status quo

Driving forces

Time →

A key feature of Lewin's three-step model is its conception of change as an episodic activity. For a debate about whether organizational change today is an episodic activity or an ongoing and at times chaotic process, see *Point/Counterpoint* on page 509.

Kotter's Eight-Step Plan for Implementing Change

John Kotter of Harvard Business School built on Lewin's three-step model to create a more detailed approach for implementing change.[10]

Kotter began by listing common failures that occur when managers try to initiate change. These include the inability to create a sense of urgency about the need for change; failure to create a coalition for managing the change process; the absence of a vision for change and inability to effectively communicate that vision; not removing obstacles that could impede the achievement of the vision; failure to provide short-term and achievable goals; the tendency to declare victory too soon; and/or not anchoring the changes in the organization's culture.

Kotter then established eight sequential steps to overcome these problems. These steps are listed in Exhibit 14-5.

Notice how Exhibit 14-5 builds on Lewin's model. Kotter's first four steps essentially represent the "unfreezing" stage. Steps 5 through 7 represent "moving." The final step works on "refreezing." Kotter's contribution lies in providing managers and change agents with a more detailed guide for successfully implementing change.

Action Research

Action research refers to a change process based on the systematic collection of data and then selection of a change action based on what the analyzed data indicate.[11] Its value is in providing a scientific method for managing planned change. Action research consists of five steps: diagnosis, analysis, feedback, action, and evaluation.

The change agent, often an outside consultant in action research, begins by gathering information about problems, concerns, and needed changes from members of the organization. This *diagnosis* is analogous to the physician's search to find specifically what ails a patient. In action research, the change agent asks questions, reviews records, interviews employees, and listens to their concerns.

EXHIBIT 14-5 Kotter's Eight-Step Plan for Implementing Change

1. Establish a sense of urgency by creating a compelling reason for why change is needed.

2. Form a coalition with enough power to lead the change.

3. Create a new vision to direct the change and strategies for achieving the vision.

4. Communicate the vision throughout the organization.

5. Empower others to act on the vision by removing barriers to change and encouraging risk-taking and creative problem-solving.

6. Plan for, create, and reward short-term "wins" that move the organization toward the new vision.

7. Consolidate improvements, reassess changes, and make necessary adjustments in the new programs.

8. Reinforce the changes by demonstrating the relationship between new behaviours and organizational success.

Source: Based on J. P. Kotter, *Leading Change* (Boston: Harvard Business School Press, 1996).

action research A change process based on the systematic collection of data and then selection of a change action based on what the analyzed data indicate.

Diagnosis is followed by *analysis*. What problems do people key in on? What patterns do these problems seem to take? The change agent organizes this information into primary concerns, problem areas, and possible actions.

Action research requires the people who will participate in any change program to help identify the problem and determine the solution. So the third step—*feedback*—requires sharing with employees what has been found from the first and second steps. The employees, with the help of the change agent, develop action plans for bringing about any needed change.

Now the *action* part of action research is set in motion. The employees and the change agent carry out the specific actions they have identified to correct the problems.

The final step, consistent with the scientific underpinnings of action research, is *evaluation* of the action plan's effectiveness, using the initial data gathered as a benchmark.

Action research provides at least two specific benefits for an organization. First, it is problem-focused. The change agent objectively looks for problems, and the type of problem determines the type of change action. While this may seem intuitively obvious, many change activities are not handled this way. Rather, they are solution-centred. The change agent has a favourite solution—for example, implementing flextime, teams, or a process re-engineering program—and then seeks out problems that his or her solution fits. Second, because action research involves employees so thoroughly in the process, it reduces resistance to change. Once employees have actively participated in the feedback stage, the change process typically takes on a momentum of its own under their sustained pressure to bring it about.

Appreciative Inquiry

Most organizational change approaches are problem centred. They identify a problem or set of problems, then look for a solution. **Appreciative inquiry (AI)** accentuates the positive.[12] Rather than looking for problems to fix, this approach seeks to identify the unique qualities and special strengths of an organization, which can then be built on to improve performance. That is, it focuses on an organization's successes rather than on its problems.

> Are there positive approaches to change?

The appreciative inquiry process (see Exhibit 14-6) consists of four steps, or "Four *D*'s," often played out in a large-group meeting over a two- or three-day time period, and overseen by a trained change agent:

- *Discovery.* Identify what people think are the strengths of the organization. Employees recount times they felt the organization worked best or when they specifically felt most satisfied with their jobs.

- *Dreaming.* Employees use information from the discovery phase to speculate on possible futures for the organization, such as what the organization will be like in five years.

appreciative inquiry (AI) An approach to change that seeks to identify the unique qualities and special strengths of an organization, which can then be built on to improve performance.

EXHIBIT 14-6 The "Four *D*'s" of Appreciative Inquiry

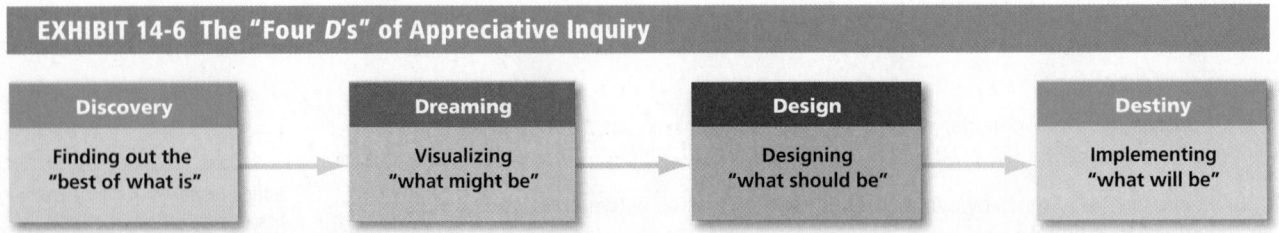

Discovery	Dreaming	Design	Destiny
Finding out the "best of what is"	Visualizing "what might be"	Designing "what should be"	Implementing "what will be"

Source: Based on D. L. Cooperrider and D. Whitney, *Collaborating for Change: Appreciative Inquiry* (San Francisco: Berrett-Koehler, 2000).

- *Design.* Based on the dream articulation, participants focus on finding a common vision of how the organization will look, and agree on its unique qualities.

- *Destiny.* In this final step, participants discuss how the organization is going to fulfill its dream, and they typically write action plans and develop implementation strategies.

AI has proven to be an effective change strategy in organizations such as Toronto-based Orchestras Canada, Ajax, Ontario-based Nokia Canada, Burnaby, BC-based TELUS, Calgary-based EnCana, and Toronto-based CBC.

Nokia Canada employees consider the future, envision the perfect solutions to the future, and then identify what needs to happen to get to the future as envisioned. Of their AI work, general manager Nathalie Le Prohon says, "It's very unstructured, very open to innovation and imagination, and very powerful as a tool for developing new thought leadership, new ways to approach business problems."[13]

TELUS's Go East division in Calgary has used AI to increase positive ideas among customer-care employees. Barbara Armstrong, a senior manager, explains the positive impact of the process: "The fact that [front-line workers] are being heard completely changes the way they view things."[14]

The use of AI in organizations is relatively recent, and it has not yet been determined when it is most appropriately used for organizational change.[15] However, it does give us the opportunity of viewing change from a much more positive perspective.

Resistance to Change

> Like any change agent, Bonnie Brooks faced resistance as she started to implement changes at Hudson's Bay.[16] Not all of senior management agreed with what she was doing. But she was not deterred, and she explained how she made the changes happen. "The key is being enthusiastic, painting a picture that people can grasp and understand and generating enough excitement, motivation. Once the senior management team got behind the concept of our reinvention, I think my surprise was actually the speed with which we made the transformation." What other tactics might Brooks have used to help break down resistance to change?

3 Describe the sources of resistance to change.

◉ Watch on **MyManagementLab**

Organizational Change (TWZ Role Play)

Our egos are fragile, and we often see change as threatening. One recent study showed that even when employees are shown data that suggest they need to change, they latch on to whatever data they can find that suggest they are okay and don't need to change.[17] Employees who have negative feelings about a change cope by not thinking about it, increasing their use of sick time, or quitting. All these reactions can sap the organization of vital energy when it's most needed.[18] Resistance to change can be positive if it leads to open discussion and debate.[19] These responses are usually preferable to apathy or silence and can indicate that members of the organization are engaged in the process, providing change agents an opportunity to explain the change effort. Change agents can also use resistance to modify the change to fit the preferences of other members of the organization. When they treat resistance only as a threat, rather than a point of view to be discussed, they may increase dysfunctional conflict.

Resistance to change does not necessarily surface in standardized ways. It can be overt, implicit, immediate, or deferred. It is easiest for management to deal with resistance when it is overt and immediate, such as complaints, a work slowdown, or a strike threat. The greater challenge is managing resistance that is implicit or deferred. These responses—loss of loyalty to the organization, loss of motivation to work, increased errors or mistakes, increased absenteeism—are more difficult to recognize. Deferred actions also cloud the link between the change and the reaction to it and may surface weeks, months, or even years later. Or a single change that in and of itself might have little impact becomes "the straw that breaks the camel's back" because resistance to earlier changes has been deferred and stockpiled.

Let's look at the sources of resistance. For analytical purposes, we have categorized them by individual and organizational sources. In the real world, the sources often overlap.

Individual Resistance

Individual sources of resistance to change reside in basic human characteristics such as perceptions, personalities, and needs. Exhibit 14-7 summarizes four reasons why individuals may resist change:[20]

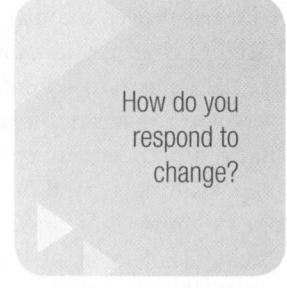

How do you respond to change?

- *Self-interest*. People worry that they will lose something of value if change happens. Thus, they look after their own self-interests rather than those of the total organization.

- *Misunderstanding and lack of trust*. People resist change when they don't understand the nature of the change and fear that the cost of change will outweigh any potential gains for them. This often occurs when they don't trust those initiating the change.

PERSONAL INVENTORY ASSESSMENT

Learn About Yourself
What's My Comfort with Change?

- *Different assessments*. People resist change when they see it differently than their managers do and think the costs outweigh the benefits, even for the organization. Managers may assume that employees have the same information that they do, but this is not always the case.

- *Low tolerance for change*. People resist change because they worry that they do not have the skills and behaviour required of the new situation. They may feel that they are being asked to do too much, too quickly.

In addition to the above, individuals sometimes worry that being asked to change may indicate that what they have been doing in the past was somehow wrong. Managers should not overlook the effects of peer pressure on an individual's response to change. As well, the manager's attitude (positive or negative) toward the change and his or her relationship with employees will affect an individual's response to change.

EXHIBIT 14-7 Sources of Individual Resistance to Change

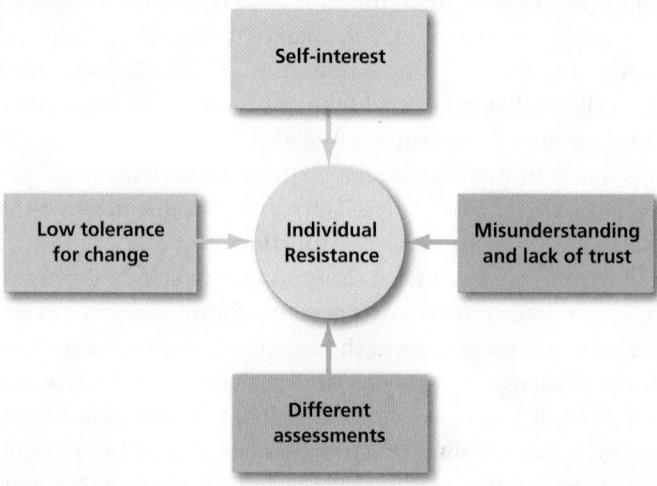

Source: Based on J. P. Kotter and L. A. Schlesinger, "Choosing Strategies for Change," *Harvard Business Review*, July–August 2008, pp. 107–109.

The *Ethical Dilemma* on page 511 looks at one employee's resistance to a change in the workplace and asks you to consider whether the plan for implementing that change might have been part of the problem.

Cynicism

Employees often feel cynical about the change process, particularly if they have been through several rounds of "change," and nothing appears (to them) to have changed. One study identified sources of cynicism in the change process of a large unionized manufacturing plant.[21] The major elements contributing to the cynicism were as follows:

- Feeling uninformed about what was happening
- Lack of communication and respect from one's manager
- Lack of communication and respect from one's union representative
- Lack of opportunity for meaningful participation in decision making

The researchers also found that employees with negative personalities were more likely to be cynical about change. While organizations might not be able to change an individual's personality, they certainly have the ability to provide greater communication and respect, as well as opportunities to participate in decision making. The researchers found that cynicism about change led to such outcomes as lower commitment, less satisfaction, and reduced motivation to work hard.

Organizational Resistance

Organizations, by their very nature, are conservative.[22] They actively resist change. You don't have to look far to see evidence of this phenomenon. Government agencies want to continue doing what they have been doing for years, whether the need for their service changes or remains the same. Organized religions are deeply entrenched in their history. Attempts to change church doctrine require great persistence and patience. Educational institutions, which exist to open minds and challenge established ways of thinking, are themselves extremely resistant to change. Most school systems are using essentially the same teaching technologies today as they were 50 years ago. Similarly, most business firms appear highly resistant to change. *Case Incident—When Companies Fail to Change* on page 513 considers how the failure to innovate has left a number of once leading-edge companies at the back of the pack.

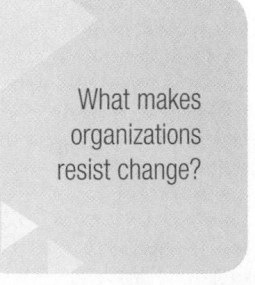

What makes organizations resist change?

Six major sources of organizational resistance (shown in Exhibit 14-8) are as follows:[23]

- *Structural inertia.* Organizations have built-in mechanisms—such as their selection processes and formalized regulations—to produce stability. When an organization is confronted with change, this structural inertia acts as a counterbalance to sustain stability.

- *Limited focus of change.* Organizations are made up of a number of interdependent subsystems. One cannot be changed without affecting the others. So limited changes in subsystems tend to be nullified by the larger system.

- *Group inertia.* Even if individuals want to change their behaviour, group norms may act as a constraint.

- *Threat to expertise.* Changes in organizational patterns may threaten the expertise of specialized groups.

EXHIBIT 14-8 Sources of Organizational Resistance to Change

Threat to established resource allocations → Organizational Resistance

Structural inertia → Organizational Resistance

Threat to established power relationships → Organizational Resistance

Limited focus of change → Organizational Resistance

Threat to expertise → Organizational Resistance

Group inertia → Organizational Resistance

Canada's Yellow Pages Group is a company that has faced significant change. The company has diversified from print directories to aggressively develop and market online directories and direct marketing services for businesses. Despite this high degree of organizational change, Yellow Pages Group has been named a top employer repeatedly. By emphasizing its strong culture of continuous improvement and attracting employees that share its values, the company is able to reduce organizational resistance to change.

- *Threat to established power relationships.* Any redistribution of decision-making authority can threaten long-established power relationships within the organization.

- *Threat to established resource allocations.* Groups in the organization that control sizable resources often see change as a threat. They tend to be content with the way things are.

The *Experiential Exercise* on page 510 asks you to identify how power relationships are affected by organizational change.

Overcoming Resistance to Change

Not all change is good. Research has shown that sometimes an emphasis on making speedy decisions can lead to bad decisions. Sometimes the line between resisting needed change and falling into a "speed trap" is a fine one indeed.[24] What is more, sometimes in the "fog of change," those who are initiating change fail to realize the full magnitude of the effects they are causing or to estimate their true costs to the organization. Thus, although the perspective generally taken is that rapid, transformational change is good, this is not always the case. Change agents need to carefully think through the full implications.

Eight tactics can be used by change agents to deal with resistance to change.[25] Let's review them briefly.

- *Education and communication.* Communicating the logic of a change can reduce resistance on two levels. First, it fights the effects of misinformation and poor communication: If employees receive the full facts and get any misunderstandings cleared up, resistance should subside. Second, communication can be helpful in "selling" the need for change. Research shows that change is more likely when the need for change is packaged properly.[26] A study of German companies revealed that changes are most effective when a company communicates its rationale, balancing various stakeholder (shareholders, employees, community, customers) interests, vs. a rationale based on shareholder interests only.[27] Similarly, a study of a changing organization in the Philippines found that formal change information sessions decreased employees' anxiety about the change, while providing high-quality information about the change increased their commitment to it.[28]

- *Participation and involvement.* It's difficult for individuals to resist a change decision in which they have participated. Assuming that the participants have the expertise to make a meaningful contribution, their involvement can reduce resistance, obtain commitment, and increase the quality of the change decision. However, against these advantages are the negatives: potential for a poor solution and great consumption of time.

- *Building support and commitment.* When employees' fear and anxiety are high, employee counselling and therapy, new-skills training, or a short paid leave of absence may facilitate adjustment. When managers or employees have low emotional commitment to change, they favour the status quo and resist it.[29] Employees are also more accepting of changes when they are committed to the organization as a whole.[30] So firing up employees and emphasizing their commitment to the organization overall can also help them emotionally commit to the change rather than embrace the status quo.

- *Developing positive relationships.* People are more willing to accept changes if they trust the managers implementing them.[31] One study surveyed 235 employees from a large housing corporation in the Netherlands that was experiencing a merger. Those who had a more positive relationship with their supervisors, and who felt that the work environment supported development, were much more positive about the change process.[32] A 2011 set of studies found that individuals whose personalities made them more resistant to change felt more positive about a change if they trusted the change agent.[33] This research suggests that if managers are able to facilitate positive relationships, they may be able to overcome resistance to change even among those who ordinarily don't like changes.

- *Implementing changes fairly.* One way organizations can minimize the negative impact of change is to make sure the change is implemented fairly. As we learned in Chapter 4, procedural fairness becomes especially important when employees perceive an outcome as negative, so it's crucial that employees see the reason for the change and perceive its implementation as consistent and fair.[34]

- *Manipulation and co-optation.* The term *manipulation* refers to covert influence attempts. Twisting and distorting facts to make them more attractive, withholding undesirable information, and creating false rumours to get employees to accept a change are all examples of manipulation. If management threatens to close a manufacturing plant whose employees are resisting an across-the-board pay cut, and if the threat is actually untrue, management is using manipulation. *Co-optation,* on the other hand, is a form of both manipulation and participation. It seeks to "buy off" the leaders of a resistance group by giving them a key role, seeking their advice not to find a better solution but to get their endorsement. Both manipulation and co-optation are relatively inexpensive ways to gain the support of adversaries, but they can backfire if the targets become aware they are being tricked or used. Once that is discovered, the change agent's credibility may drop to zero.

- *Selecting people who accept change.* Research suggests that the ability to easily accept and adapt to change is related to personality—some people simply have more positive attitudes about change than others.[35] Such individuals are open to experience, take a positive attitude toward change, are willing to take risks, and are flexible in their behaviour. One study of managers in the United States, Europe, and Asia found that those with a positive self-concept and high risk tolerance coped better with organizational change. A study of 258 police officers found that those who were higher in growth-needs, internal locus of control, and internal work motivation had more positive attitudes about organizational change efforts.[36] Individuals higher in general mental ability are also better able to learn and adapt to changes in the workplace.[37] In sum, an impressive body of evidence shows organizations can facilitate change by selecting people predisposed to accept it.

  It's also important for change agents to be aware of how adaptable workplace teams are to change. Studies have shown that teams with a collective orientation to learning about and mastering tasks are better able to adapt to changing environments.[38] This research suggests that it may be necessary to consider not only individual motivation but also group motivation when planning to implement changes.

- *Explicit and implicit coercion.* Coercion is the application of direct threats or force upon the resisters. If management really is determined to close a manufacturing plant whose employees do not accept a pay cut, the company is using coercion. Other examples are threats of transfer, loss of promotions, negative performance evaluations, and a poor letter of recommendation. The advantages and drawbacks of coercion are approximately the same as those for manipulation and co-optation.

As you read *OB in the Workplace*, consider which of the above steps staff at Rockwood Institution used to help inmates introduce changes into their lives.

 # IN THE **WORKPLACE**
Habitat for Humanity and Rockwood Institution Partner to Change Lives

How can prison inmates be encouraged to learn new skills and influence their community in positive ways? Recidivism rates among released offenders are higher when those offenders don't perceive any other lifestyle options that would enable them to effectively support themselves and their loved ones.[39] At Rockwood Institution in Manitoba, Assistant Warden Shannon Plowman has found an effective formula to change recidivism rates by partnering with Linda Peters, the vice president of Program Delivery for Habitat for Humanity. Their program, which is financially supported by Public Safety Canada and Human Resources and Skills Development Canada, gives minimum-security inmates with poor job prospects the opportunity to learn marketable construction skills in a safe and supportive environment.

At Rockwood, inmates who participate in the Habitat for Humanity specialized work program are provided with formal instruction on tool use and construction basics. Then, under professional supervision, they apply those skills to building a ready-to-transport house on the grounds of the correctional facility. The homes are then relocated to appropriate sites and are provided to needy families on the Habitat for Humanity waiting list. Eligible program "graduates" can also do supervised work in the broader community, receiving day passes to help on Habitat for Humanity builds in nearby

Winnipeg and surrounding communities. These day passes are highly desirable, viewed as a privilege and reward. Upon release, some people even find transitional employment with Habitat for Humanity, working there for several months to help develop an employment history and contacts in the construction industry.

This program manages change well. It focuses on providing education and fostering participation and direct involvement. Parole officers try to recommend new participants who are already open to changing their lives and most "graduates" advocate for the program to other inmates. Support and commitment to the program are increased by allowing some participants to meet the families receiving the new homes, something that inmates report as being a transformative experience in their lives. One participant stated that "I never realized I could be proud for good things I was doing. Before I was always admired for being scary and fighting, it surprises me how proud I am of working on this house."

Rockwood officials and Habitat for Humanity staff work together to create an environment that enables, supports, and then reinforces and rewards positive change. It is a model many for-profit companies could learn from. _____

From Concepts to Skills on pages 513–515 provides additional tips for carrying out organizational change.

The Politics of Change

No discussion of resistance to change would be complete without a brief mention of the politics of change. Because change invariably threatens the status quo, it inherently implies political activity.[40]

Politics suggests that the demand for change is more likely to come from outside change agents, employees who are new to the organization (who have less invested in the status quo), or managers who are slightly removed from the main power structure. Managers who have spent their entire careers with a single organization and eventually achieve a senior position in the hierarchy are often major impediments to change. It's a very real threat to their status and position. Yet they may be expected to implement change to demonstrate that they are not merely caretakers. By acting as change agents, they can convey to stockholders, suppliers, employees, and customers that they are addressing problems and adapting to a dynamic environment. Of course, as you might guess, when forced to introduce change, these long-time power holders tend to implement incremental change. Radical change is too threatening. This explains why boards of directors that recognize the need for rapid and radical change frequently turn to outside candidates for new leadership.[41] *OB in Action* provides some tips for keeping the pace of change going quickly.

OB IN ACTION
How to Speed Up the Pace of Change

→ Compel executives to **confront reality** and **agree on ground rules** for working together.

→ **Limit change initiatives** to two or three.

→ **Move ahead quickly** and dialogue with those not on board.

→ Get **all employees engaged**. Explain how changes are relevant to them personally.

→ Offer appropriate **rewards and incentives**.

→ **Celebrate milestones**.

→ **Anticipate** and **defuse** postlaunch blues and midcourse overconfidence.[42]

Creating a Culture for Change

In 2013, Hudson's Bay (HBC) announced that Bonnie Brooks' term as president would end in January 2014 and that she would become the vice-chairman to assist Richard Baker (who had become CEO of HBC in 2012) with corporate strategy.[43] Liz Rodbell, president of HBC's Lord & Taylor chain, was appointed to replace Brooks as president. Brooks was not only the president of Hudson's Bay but also its voice. Noted for her "low, smoky voice," she starred in a number of radio ads, announcing that something was on sale. Rodbell became the new "voice" of Hudson's Bay ads as of the 2014 holiday season. Will customers respond as favourably to Rodbell as they did Brooks?

When Brooks' new position was announced, concern among investors led HBC's stock price to drop three points immediately afterward. What would this reaction mean for the changes already underway in the company (such as the purchase of Saks Fifth Avenue)? Brooks expressed confidence that change would continue at HBC, and that she would still be a part of that change. As she describes her new role: "My main interest is the challenge of change, and the challenge of taking on projects that aren't for the faint of heart."

Has Brooks' emphasis on change over five years as president been enough to create a culture of continuous change within HBC that will continue to keep the retailer relevant to customers? How can HBC compete successfully with Nordstrom, a recent entrant to the Canadian retail market, and La Maison Simons, which is expanding beyond Quebec?

④ Describe two ways to create a culture for change.

We have considered how organizations can *adapt* to change. But recently, some OB scholars have focused on a more proactive approach—how organizations can *embrace* change by transforming their cultures. In this section we review two such approaches: stimulating an innovative culture and creating a learning organization.

Stimulating a Culture of Innovation

How can an organization become more innovative? Although there is no guaranteed formula, certain characteristics surface again and again when researchers study innovative organizations.[44] We consider the characteristics as structural, cultural, and human resources. Change agents should consider introducing these characteristics into their organization if they want to create an innovative climate. Let's start by clarifying what we mean by innovation.

Definition of *Innovation*

Change refers to making things different. **Innovation**, a more specialized kind of change, is a new idea applied to initiating or improving a product, process, or service.[45] So all innovations involve change, but not all changes necessarily involve new ideas or lead to significant improvements. Innovations can range from small incremental improvements, such as tablet computers, to radical breakthroughs, such as Nissan's electric Leaf car.

Sources of Innovation

Structural variables have been the most studied potential source of innovation.[46] A comprehensive review of the structure–innovation relationship leads to the following conclusions:[47]

- *Organic structures positively influence innovation.* Because they are lower in vertical differentiation, formalization, and centralization, organic organizations facilitate the flexibility, adaptation, and cross-fertilization that make the adoption of innovations easier.

- *Long tenure in management is associated with innovation.* Managerial tenure apparently provides legitimacy and knowledge of how to accomplish tasks and obtain desired outcomes.

- *Innovation is nurtured when there are slack resources.* Having an abundance of resources allows an organization to afford to purchase innovations, bear the cost of instituting innovations, and absorb failures.

- *Interunit communication is high in innovative organizations.*[48] Innovative organizations are high users of committees, task forces, cross-functional teams, and other mechanisms that facilitate interaction across departmental lines.

innovation A new idea applied to initiating or improving a product, process, or service.

Wang qiming/Imaginechina/AP Images

Baidu, a Chinese company that made the first search engine designed specifically for the Chinese language, has built a culture that fosters innovation. Baidu describes its culture as simple and reliable, where candour and trust are valued, politicking is taboo, and an organic structure promotes the cross-fertilization of ideas.

Innovative organizations tend to have similar *cultures*. They encourage experimentation. They reward both successes and failures. They celebrate mistakes. Unfortunately, in too many organizations, people are rewarded for the absence of failures rather than for the presence of successes. Such cultures extinguish risk-taking and innovation. People will suggest and try new ideas only when they feel such behaviours exact no penalties. Managers in innovative organizations recognize that failures are a natural by-product of venturing into the unknown. 3M is known for its culture of innovation, as *OB in the Workplace* describes.

PERSONAL INVENTORY ASSESSMENT

Learn About Yourself
Innovative Attitude Scale

IN THE **WORKPLACE**
3M Is a Leader in Innovation

What does it take to be a leader in innovation? Many organizations strive to achieve the standard of innovation reached by 3M, the company responsible for the development of waterproof sandpaper, masking tape, and Post-it® notes.[49] 3M has developed a reputation for sustained innovation over a long period of time, even though it is a large organization with over $30 billion in global sales, over 80 000 employees worldwide, and operations in more than 70 countries. It has a stated objective that 30 percent of its sales are to come from products less than four years old. In one year alone, 3M launched more than 200 new products.

In 2014, two of its technologies won Edison Awards, a global competition for exceptional creativity and ingenuity. The company won a silver award for its Petrifilm™ *Salmonella* Express System—a test method for the rapid detection and biochemical confirmation of salmonella in food. It also won a bronze for its Two-Phase Immersion Cooling Technology using 3M™ Novec™ Engineered Fluid—a cooling technology for hardware in data centres that can be used to significantly reduce energy costs.

Why is 3M such a successful innovator? The company encourages its employees to take risks—and rewards the failures, as well as the successes. 3M's management has the patience to see ideas through to successful products. It invests nearly 7 percent of company sales revenue in research and development, yet management tells its R & D people that not everything will work. It also fosters a culture that allows people to defy their managers. For instance, each new employee and his or her manager take a one-day orientation class where, among other things, stories are told of victories won by employees despite the opposition of their boss.

All of 3M's scientists and managers are challenged to "keep current." Idea champions are created and encouraged by allowing scientists and engineers to spend up to 15 percent of their time on projects of their own choosing. If a 3M scientist comes up with a new idea but finds resistance within the researcher's own division, he or she can apply for a $70 000 grant from an internal venture-capital fund to further develop the idea.

Within the *human resources* category, innovative organizations actively promote the training and development of their members so that they keep current, offer high job security so employees don't fear getting fired for making mistakes, and encourage individuals to become champions of change. Once a new idea is developed, **idea champions** actively and enthusiastically promote the idea, build support for it, overcome resistance to it, and ensure that it's implemented.[50] Champions have common personality characteristics: extremely high self-confidence, persistence, energy, and a tendency to take risks. They also display characteristics associated with transformational leadership. They inspire and energize others with their vision of the potential of an innovation and through their strong personal conviction in their mission. Idea champions are good at gaining the commitment of others, and their jobs provide considerable decision-making discretion. This autonomy helps them introduce and implement innovations in organizations.[51]

Creating a Learning Organization

Another way an organization can proactively manage change is to make continuous growth part of its culture—to become a learning organization.[52]

What Is a Learning Organization?

Just as individuals learn, so too do organizations. A **learning organization** is an organization that has developed the continuous capacity to adapt and change. "All organizations learn, whether they consciously choose to or not—it is a fundamental requirement for their sustained existence."[53] Some organizations just do it better than others.

Most organizations engage in what has been called **single-loop learning**.[54] When errors are detected, the correction process relies on past routines and present policies. This type of learning has been likened to a thermostat, which, once set at 17°C, simply turns on and off to keep the room at the set temperature. It does not question whether the temperature should be set at 17°C. In contrast, learning organizations use **double-loop learning**. They correct errors by modifying the organization's objectives, policies, and standard routines. Double-loop learning challenges deeply rooted assumptions and norms within an organization. It provides opportunities for radically different solutions to problems and dramatic jumps in improvement. To draw on the thermostat analogy, a thermostat using double-loop learning would try to determine whether the correct policy is 17°C, and whether changes might be necessitated by the change in season.

Exhibit 14-9 summarizes the five basic characteristics of a learning organization. It's one in which people put aside their old ways of thinking, learn to be open with each other, understand how their organization really works, form a plan or vision on which everyone can agree, and then work together to achieve that vision.[55]

idea champions Individuals who actively and enthusiastically promote an idea, build support for it, overcome resistance to it, and ensure that the idea is implemented.

learning organization An organization that has developed the continuous capacity to adapt and change.

single-loop learning A process of correcting errors using past routines and present policies.

double-loop learning A process of correcting errors by modifying the organization's objectives, policies, and standard routines.

EXHIBIT 14-9 Characteristics of a Learning Organization

1. The organization has a shared vision that everyone agrees on.

2. People discard their old ways of thinking and the standard routines they use for solving problems or doing their jobs.

3. Members think of all organizational processes, activities, functions, and interactions with the environment as part of a system of interrelationships.

4. People openly communicate with each other (across vertical and horizontal boundaries) without fear of criticism or punishment.

5. People suppress their personal self-interest and fragmented departmental interests to work together to achieve the organization's shared vision.

Source: Based on P. M. Senge, *The Fifth Discipline* (New York: Doubleday, 1990).

Proponents of the learning organization envision it as a remedy for three fundamental problems of traditional organizations: fragmentation, competition, and reactiveness.[56] First, *fragmentation* based on specialization creates "walls" and "chimneys" that separate different functions into independent and often warring fiefdoms. Second, an overemphasis on *competition* often undermines collaboration. Managers compete to show who is right, who knows more, or who is more persuasive. Divisions compete when they ought to cooperate and share knowledge. Team leaders compete to show who the best manager is. Third, *reactiveness* misdirects management's attention to problem solving rather than creation. The problem solver tries to make something go away, while a creator tries to bring something new into being. An emphasis on reactiveness pushes out innovation and continuous improvement and, in its place, encourages people to run around "putting out fires."

Managing Learning

What can managers do to make their firms learning organizations? Here are some suggestions:

- *Establish a strategy.* Managers need to make their commitment to change, innovation, and continuous improvement explicit.

- *Redesign the organization's structure.* The formal structure can be a serious impediment to learning. Flattening the structure, eliminating or combining departments, and increasing the use of cross-functional teams reinforces interdependence and reduces boundaries.

- *Reshape the organization's culture.* To become a learning organization, managers must demonstrate by their actions that taking risks and admitting failures are desirable traits. That means rewarding people who take chances and make mistakes. Managers also need to encourage functional conflict. "The key to unlocking real openness at work," says one expert on learning organizations, "is to teach people to give up having to be in agreement. We think agreement is so important. Who cares? You have to bring paradoxes, conflicts, and dilemmas out in the open, so collectively we can be more intelligent than we can be individually."[57]

GLOBAL IMPLICATIONS

A number of change issues we have discussed in this chapter are culture-bound. To illustrate, let's briefly look at five questions:

- *Do people believe change is possible?* Remember that cultures vary in terms of beliefs about their ability to control their environment. In cultures in which people believe that they can dominate their environment, individuals will take a proactive view of change. This, for example, would describe Canada and the United States. In many other countries, such as Iran and Saudi Arabia, people see themselves as subjugated to their environment and thus will tend to take a passive approach toward change.

- *If change is possible, how long will it take to bring it about?* A culture's time orientation can help us answer this question. Societies that focus on the long term, such as Japan, will demonstrate considerable patience while waiting for positive outcomes from change efforts. In societies with a short-term focus, such as Canada and the United States, people expect quick improvements and will seek change programs that promise fast results.

- *Is resistance to change greater in some cultures than in others?* Resistance to change will be influenced by a society's reliance on tradition. Italians, as an example, focus on the past, whereas Canadians emphasize the present. Italians, therefore, should generally be more resistant to change efforts than their Canadian counterparts.

- *Does culture influence how change efforts will be implemented?* Power distance can help with this issue. In high power distance cultures, such as Malaysia and Panama, change efforts will tend to be autocratically implemented by top management. In contrast, low power distance cultures value democratic methods. We would predict, therefore, a greater use of participation in countries such as Austria and Denmark.

- *Do successful idea champions do things differently in different cultures?* The evidence indicates that the answer is yes.[58] People in collectivistic cultures, in contrast to individualistic cultures, prefer appeals for cross-functional support for innovation efforts; people in high power distance cultures prefer

Four Seasons Hotels and Resorts operates 92 properties in 38 countries around the world. Managing change in this company would normally be very complex because of the cultural diversity of its employees. However, it's made easier by the fact that all employees, such as those shown here at the Caprice restaurant in the Four Seasons Hotel in Hong Kong, China, share a common service culture and a set of common corporate values. As a result, Four Seasons has won awards as the employer of choice in many of the countries in which it operates.

champions to work closely with those in authority to approve innovative activities before work is conducted on them; and the higher the uncertainty avoidance of a society, the more champions should work within the organization's rules and procedures to develop the innovation. These findings suggest that effective managers will alter their organization's championing strategies to reflect cultural values. So, for instance, while idea champions in Russia might succeed by ignoring budgetary limitations and working around confining procedures, idea champions in Greece, Portugal, Guatemala, and other cultures high in uncertainty avoidance will be more effective by closely following budgets and procedures.

Summary

The need for change has been implied throughout this text. For instance, think about attitudes, motivation, work teams, communication, leadership, organizational structures, and organizational cultures. Change was an integral part in our discussion of each. If environments were perfectly static, if employees' skills and abilities were always up to date, and if tomorrow were always exactly the same as today, organizational change would have little or no relevance to managers. But the real world is turbulent, requiring organizations and their members to undergo dynamic change if they are to perform at competitive levels.

LESSONS LEARNED

- Individuals resist change; breaking down that resistance is important.
- Change requires unfreezing the status quo, moving to a new state, and making the new change permanent.
- Innovative cultures reward both successes and failures so that people are not afraid to make mistakes.

SNAPSHOT SUMMARY

Forces for Change
- Opportunities for Change
- Change Agents

Approaches to Managing Change
- Lewin's Three-Step Model
- Kotter's Eight-Step Plan for Implementing Change

- Action Research
- Appreciative Inquiry

Resistance to Change
- Individual Resistance
- Organizational Resistance
- Overcoming Resistance to Change
- The Politics of Change

Creating a Culture for Change
- Stimulating a Culture of Innovation
- Creating a Learning Organization

MyManagementLab   Study, practise, and explore real business situations with these helpful resources:

- **Study Plan:** Check your understanding of chapter concepts with self-study quizzes.
- **Online Lesson Presentations:** Study key chapter topics and work through interactive assessments to test your knowledge and master management concepts.
- **Videos:** Learn more about the management practices and strategies of real companies.
- **Simulations:** Practise management decision-making in simulated business environments.

P I A PERSONAL INVENTORY ASSESSMENT

for **Review**

1. What are the forces for change?
2. What are the four main approaches to managing organizational change?
3. What forces act as sources of resistance to change?
4. How can managers create a culture for change?

for **Managers**

- Consider that, as a manager, you are a change agent in your organization. The decisions you make and your role-modelling behaviour will help shape the organization's change culture.
- Your management policies and practices will determine the degree to which the organization learns and adapts to changing environmental factors.
- People resist change because change can be stressful. Low to moderate amounts of stress enable many people to perform their jobs better by increasing their work intensity, alertness, and ability to react. Therefore, don't hesitate to introduce change just because stress might be induced.

for **You**

- Not everyone is comfortable with change, but you should realize that change is a fact of life. It is difficult to avoid and can result in negative consequences when it is avoided.
- If you need to change something in yourself, be aware of the importance of creating new systems to replace the old. Saying you want to be healthier without specifying that you intend to go to the gym three times a week or eat five servings of fruits and vegetables a day means that change likely will not occur. It's important to specify goals and behaviours as part of change.
- Consider focusing on positive aspects of change, rather than negative ones. For instance, instead of noting that you did not study hard enough, acknowledge the effort you put into studying and how that helped your performance, and then set positive goals as a result.

Organizational Change Is Like Sailing Calm Waters

POINT

Organizational change is an episodic activity.[59] That is, it starts at some point, proceeds through a series of steps, and culminates in some outcome that those involved hope is an improvement over the starting point. It has a beginning, a middle, and an end.

Lewin's three-step model represents a classic illustration of this perspective. Change is seen as a break in the organization's equilibrium. The status quo has been disturbed, and change is necessary to establish a new equilibrium state. The objective of refreezing is to stabilize the new situation by balancing the driving and restraining forces.

Some experts have argued that organizational change should be thought of as balancing a system made up of five interacting variables within the organization—people, tasks, technology, structure, and strategy. A change in any one variable has repercussions on one or more of the others. This perspective is episodic in that it treats organizational change as essentially an effort to sustain an equilibrium. A change in one variable begins a chain of events that, if properly managed, requires adjustments in the other variables to achieve a new state of equilibrium.

Another way to conceptualize the episodic view of change is to think of managing change as analogous to captaining a ship. The organization is like a large ship travelling across the calm Mediterranean Sea to a local port. The ship's captain has made this exact trip hundreds of times before with the same crew. Every once in a while, however, a storm will appear, and the crew has to respond. The captain will make the appropriate adjustments—that is, implement changes—and, having manoeuvred through the storm, will return to calm waters. Like this ship's voyage, managing an organization should be seen as a journey with a beginning and an end, and implementing change as a response to a break in the status quo that is needed only occasionally.

COUNTERPOINT

The episodic approach for handling organizational change has become obsolete. Developed in the 1950s and 1960s, it reflects the environment of those times treating change as the occasional disturbance in an otherwise peaceful world. However, it bears little resemblance to today's environment of constant and chaotic change.

If you want to understand what it's like to manage change in today's organizations, think of it as equivalent to permanent whitewater rafting. The organization is not a large ship, but more akin to a 40-foot raft. Rather than sailing a calm sea, this raft must traverse a raging river made up of an uninterrupted flow of whitewater rapids. To make things worse, the raft is manned by 10 people who have never worked together or travelled the river before, much of the trip is in the dark, the river is dotted with unexpected turns and obstacles, the exact destination of the raft is not clear, and at irregular intervals the raft needs to pull to shore, where some new crew members are added and others leave. Change is a natural state, and managing it is a continual process. That is, managers never get the luxury of escaping the whitewater rapids.

The stability and predictability characterized by the episodic perspective no longer captures the world we live in. Disruptions in the status quo are not occasional, temporary, and followed by a return to an equilibrium state. There is, in fact, no equilibrium state. Managers today face constant change, bordering on chaos. They are being forced to play a game they have never played before, governed by rules that are created as the game progresses.

OB *at* **Work**

What's My Comfort with Change?: Some people deal well with change while others do not. Use this scale to determine your own comfort with change. This information can help in career selection, since some occupations and industries experience more change than others.

Leading Positive Change: Change leaders require a complex mix of skills and abilities. Use this scale to assess your ability to lead positive change within an organization.

Innovation Attitude Scale: What is your attitude toward innovation? Use this scale to help determine if you would work well in occupations and industries that require high levels of innovation.

BREAKOUT **GROUP** EXERCISES

Form small groups to discuss the following topics, as assigned by your instructor:

1. Identify a local company that you think needs to undergo change. What factors suggest that change is necessary?

2. Have you ever tried to change the behaviour of someone you worked with (for instance, someone in one of your project groups)? How effective were you in getting change to occur? How would you explain this?

3. Identify a recent change that your college or university introduced, and its effects on the students. Did the students accept the change or fight it? How would you explain this?

EXPERIENTIAL EXERCISE

Power and the Changing Environment

Objectives

1. To describe the forces for change influencing power differentials in organizational and interpersonal relationships.

2. To understand the effect of technological, legal/political, economic, and social changes on the power of individuals within an organization.[60]

The Situation

Your organization manufactures golf carts and sells them to country clubs, golf courses, and consumers. Your team is faced with the task of assessing how environmental changes will affect individuals' organizational power. Read each of the five scenarios and then, for each, identify the 5 members in the organization whose power will increase most in light of the environmental condition(s).

Advertising expert (m)	Accountant–CGA (m)	Product designer (m)
Chief financial officer (f)	General manager (m)	In-house counsel (m)
Securities analyst (m)	Marketing manager (f)	Public relations expert (m)
Operations manager (f)	Computer programmer (f)	Human resources manager (f)
Corporate trainer (m)	Industrial engineer (m)	Chemist (m)
(m) = male (f) = female		

1. New computer-aided manufacturing technologies are being introduced in the workplace during the upcoming 2 to 18 months.

2. New federal emissions standards are being legislated by the government.

3. Sales are way down; the industry appears to be shrinking.

4. The company is planning to go international in the next 12 to 18 months.

5. The Canadian Human Rights Commission is applying pressure to balance the male–female population in the organization's upper hierarchy by threatening to publicize the predominance of men in upper management.

The Procedure

1. Divide the class into teams of 3 to 4 students each.

2. Teams should read each scenario and identify the 5 members whose power will increase most in light of the external environmental condition described.

3. Teams should then address the question: Assuming that the 5 environmental changes are taking place at once, which 5 members of the organization will now have the most power?

4. After 20 to 30 minutes, representatives of each team will be selected to present and justify their conclusions to the entire class. Discussion will begin with scenario 1 and proceed through to scenario 5. Then the class will look at what might happen if all 5 environmental changes happened at once.

ETHICAL **DILEMMA**

Changes at the Television Station

A local television station had been experiencing a ratings decline for several years.[61] In 2014, the station switched some of its programming. That has explained some of the ratings decline. However, in recent months, the ratings have continued to slide. Eventually, the station manager, Lucien Stone, decided he had to make a change to the local newscast.

After meeting with the programming manager, Stone called a meeting of the employees and announced his intention to "spice things up" during the 5 p.m. and 10 p.m. local news. The 30-minute broadcasts would still include the traditional "top stories," "sports," and "weather" segments. However, on slow news days, more attention-getting material would be used. Stone also indicated some programming decisions would probably be revisited. "The days of *Little House on the Prairie* are over," he said.

Madison Devereaux, 29, had been the chief meteorologist since 2012. After receiving a degree in meteorology, she joined the station and quickly worked her way up the ranks, impressing viewers and management alike with her extensive knowledge and articulate, professional, mistake-free delivery.

Although she was religious, Devereaux was not one to express her religious beliefs in the newsroom. Most of those at the station were not even aware that she closely practised a religion.

Devereaux was troubled by the announced changes to the programming but did not speak up at the time. One Monday during a pre-production meeting, she learned that on Thursday of that week, one of the reporters, Sam Berkshow, would present a segment called "Dancing Around the Economy," which would focus on how local strip clubs were doing well despite the sluggish economy.

Devereaux did not think it was appropriate to air the segment during the 5 p.m. newscast and asked both her producer and Stone to reconsider the piece, or at least air it in the 10 p.m. time slot. When they refused, she asked whether she could take the day off when the segment aired. Stone again refused. This was "sweeps week" (when ratings are calculated), Stone wanted to air the story, and Devereaux's contract prohibited her from taking time off during sweeps week.

When Devereaux did not show up for work that Thursday, the station fired her, arguing that she had breached her contract.

For her part, Devereaux said, "I'm not angry with the station, but I am sorry about the changes that have taken place."

Questions

1. Do you think either party behaved unethically in this case? If so, why?

2. If you share Devereaux's view on the segment, would you have handled the situation differently? How?

3. Drawing on Kotter's eight-step plan for implementing change, how might the station have handled its planned change differently?

CASE INCIDENTS

Starbucks Returns to Its Roots

You are probably so used to seeing Starbucks coffee shops everywhere that you might not realize the company went from just 11 stores in the United States in 1987 to 18 000 locations in 60 countries and earning more than $3.6 billion in quarterly revenue in 2014.[62] Canada has the second-highest number of stores in the world (the United States is first), but it has the highest density, at 39.54 stores per million people, greater than the United States, which is in second place at 36.25 stores per million people.

This incredibly rapid growth sprang from the company's ability to create a unique experience for customers who wanted to buy its distinct brand of lattes and mochas wherever they found themselves. At Starbucks' core, there is also a culture of treating each customer as a valued guest who should feel comfortable relaxing and taking in the ambience of the store. Whether you were in its first Canadian location in Vancouver or its location in St. John's, Newfoundland, you knew what to expect at Starbucks.

This uniform culture was truly put to the test in the face of massive expansion, however, and by 2006 Starbucks' chairman and former CEO Howard Schultz knew something had gone wrong. He noted that "As I visited hundreds of Starbucks stores in cities around the world, the entrepreneurial merchant in me sensed that something intrinsic to Starbucks' brand was missing. An aura. A spirit. The stores were lacking a certain soul." Starbucks' performance had become lacklustre, with hundreds of planned store openings being cancelled and hundreds more stores being closed.

So, Schultz took the dramatic step of coming back as CEO and engaging in a company-wide effort to change the corporate culture back to what it had been before the expansion. All Starbucks stores were closed

for a single afternoon as part of a training effort of the baristas. Quality control was a primary mission; baristas were instructed to pour every glass of espresso like honey from a spoon to preserve the flavour. This emphasis on quality over speed ran counter to the principles of mass production, but it was just what the company needed to ensure it could retain its culture. Espresso machines that obscured the customers' view were replaced with lower-profile machines that allowed baristas to look directly at guests while making beverages. And "assembly-line production," like making several drinks at once, was discouraged in favour of slowly making each drink for each customer.

Schultz is convinced his efforts to take the culture back to its roots as a neighbourhood coffee shop—one entranced with the "romance of coffee" and treating every customer as an old friend—have saved the company.

Questions

1. What factors are most likely to change when a company grows very rapidly, as Starbucks did? How can these changes threaten the culture of an organization?

2. Why might this type of radical change process be easier for Starbucks to implement than it would be for other companies?

3. A great deal of the return to its original culture has been credited to Howard Schultz, who acted as an idea champion. Explain how Schultz's efforts to change Starbucks' culture fit with our discussion of approaches to managing change earlier in the chapter.

When Companies Fail to Change

The Triniton TV, transistor radio, Walkman, and VCR are the stuff of time capsules nowadays, but not long ago they were cutting-edge technology.[63] Japan was at the pinnacle of the home consumer electronics industry from the 1970s to the 1990s, introducing new innovations to the world each year. Now those same Japanese firms are at the back of the pack and struggling to stay in the game. Japanese electronics production has fallen by more than 41 percent, and Japan's global market share of electronics goods and services has decreased by more than half since 2000. Sony, for example, did not earn any profits between 2008 and 2012, and then was falling behind again in 2014. What happened?

The simple answer is failure to innovate. While firms outside Japan pioneered digital technology and conquered the Internet, Japanese firms stuck to semiconductors and hardware. But the deeper issue is the refusal of Japanese managers to adapt to the changing global environment and to change their organizations accordingly. For instance, Sony mastered the technology needed for a digital music player years before Apple introduced the iPod in 2001, but its engineers resisted the change. Sony's divisions would not cooperate with one another fast enough to compete in this market or in the new market for flat-screen TVs. Even now, Sony has not managed to change its organization to reflect current global thinking in the industry. For instance, they and other Japanese firms make a larger number of products than most of their global competitors. Former Sony executive Yoshiaki Sakito said,

"Sony makes too many models, and for none of them can they say, 'This contains our best, most cutting-edge technology.' Apple, on the other hand, makes one amazing phone in just two colors and says, 'This is the one.'" Sony was attempting to adjust its behaviour by fall 2014, by realizing that it had too many models of smartphone. The plan is to focus on premium phones.

For Japanese electronics companies to survive, they must change. They were once able to structure their organizations around abundant, inexpensive labour to keep costs down and prices competitive, but that is no longer the case. One complicating factor is that Japan is an ancient country of many traditions, with a low birth rate and an aging population. The country's culture will make it even more difficult to realign to globalization. It now must change to foster innovation, which may involve a cultural as much as an organizational transformation.

Questions

1. What made the Japanese electronics industry initially successful?

2. Why is the Japanese electronics industry no longer a success story?

3. What types of organizational changes would you advise Japanese electronics managers to consider?

4. How do you think Japanese demographic trends have been a factor in the innovation problem?

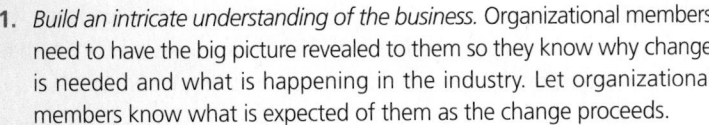

FROM CONCEPTS TO SKILLS

Carrying Out Organizational Change

An After Action Review is a nonhierarchical team debriefing process that helps participants in and those responsible for a project understand what went well, what went wrong, and how performance can be improved.[64] Seven disciplines embedded in the After Action Review can help create effective change:

1. *Build an intricate understanding of the business.* Organizational members need to have the big picture revealed to them so they know why change is needed and what is happening in the industry. Let organizational members know what is expected of them as the change proceeds.

2. *Encourage uncompromising straight talk.* Communication cannot be based on hierarchy, but must allow everyone to contribute freely to the discussion.

3. *Manage from the future.* Rather than setting goals that are directed toward a specific future point in time (and thus encouraging everyone to stop when the goal is achieved), manage from the perspective of always looking toward the future and future needs.

4. *Harness setbacks.* When things do not go as planned, and there are setbacks, it's natural to blame yourself, others, or bad luck. Instead, teach everyone to view setbacks as learning opportunities and opportunities for improvement.

5. *Promote inventive accountability.* While employees know what the specific targets and goals are, they should also be encouraged in the change process to be inventive and take initiative when new opportunities arise.

6. *Understand the quid pro quo.* When organizations undergo change processes, employees are put under a lot of stress and strain. Organizations must ensure that employees are rewarded for their efforts. To build appropriate commitment, organizations must develop four levels of incentives:

   a. Reward and recognition for effort

   b. Training and skill development that will make the employee marketable

   c. Meaningful work that provides intrinsic satisfaction

   d. Communication about where the organization is going and some say in the process for employees

7. *Create relentless discomfort with the status quo.* People are more willing to change when the current situation looks less attractive than the new situation.

These points indicate that effective change is a comprehensive process, requiring a lot of commitment from both the organization's leaders and its members.

Practising Skills

You are the nursing supervisor at a local hospital that employs both emergency room and floor nurses. Each of these teams of nurses tends to work almost exclusively with others doing the same job. In your professional reading, you have come across the concept of cross-training nursing teams and giving them more varied responsibilities, which in turn has been shown to improve patient care while lowering costs. You call the two team leaders, Sue and Scott, into your office to explain that you want the nursing teams to move to this approach. To your surprise, they are both opposed to the idea. Sue says she and the other emergency room (ER) nurses feel they are needed in the ER, where they fill the most vital

role in the hospital. They work special hours when needed, do whatever tasks are required, and often work in difficult and stressful circumstances. They think the floor nurses have relatively easy jobs for the pay they receive. Scott, the leader of the floor nurse team, tells you that his group believes the ER nurses lack the special training and extra experience that the floor nurses bring to the hospital. The floor nurses claim they have the heaviest responsibilities and do the most exacting work. Because they

have ongoing contact with patients and families, they believe they should not be called away from vital floor duties to help the ER nurses complete their tasks. What should you do about your idea to introduce more cross-training for the nursing teams?

Reinforcing Skills

1. Think about a change (major and minor) that you have dealt with over the last year. Perhaps the change involved other people, and perhaps it was personal. Did you resist the change? Did others resist the change? How did you overcome your resistance or the resistance of others to the change?

2. Interview a manager at three different organizations about a change he or she implemented. What was the manager's experience in implementing the change? How did the manager manage resistance to the change?

ADDITIONAL CASES

The Additional Cases present key concepts examined in the text. The following table indicates the chapters that apply to the major topic areas addressed in each case.

Cases	Chapters													
	1	2	3	4	5	6	7	8	9	10	11	12	13	14
Case 1: The Personality Problem		✓	✓							✓				
Case 2: The Path to Fraud			✓									✓		
Case 3: Auditing, Attitudes, and Absenteeism			✓	✓	✓			✓		✓		✓	✓	
Case 4: Bad Faith Bargaining? Government Power and Negotiations with the Public Service							✓	✓				✓		
Case 5: Gender-Based Harassment among the Royal Canadian Mounted Police								✓		✓	✓			✓
Case 6: Disability Accommodations and Promotions at Bunco			✓							✓				
Case 7: Promotion from Within			✓	✓	✓		✓	✓						
Case 8: Repairing Jobs That Fail to Satisfy		✓	✓		✓									
Case 9: Boundaryless Organizations						✓				✓			✓	✓
Case 10: Trouble at City Zoo					✓		✓			✓	✓		✓	✓

Case 1: The Personality Problem

Learning Goals

In this case, you will have an opportunity to assess the positive and negative traits associated with a personality type that is often encountered in highly competitive, performance-oriented settings. You should consider the role of organizational culture in supporting and reinforcing behaviours associated with this personality type. Use that insight to suggest strategies that could help maximize the benefits of this personality type while minimizing its liabilities.

Major Topic Areas

- Personality (Chapter 2)
- Organizational culture (Chapter 10)
- Work attitudes (Chapter 3)

The Scenario

Jasmine Patel, director of Human Resources at Vertical Horizon, sits at her desk thinking about what to do next.[1] She is wondering how to handle the disruptive behaviour of a high-performing sales representative, Rhett Stark.

Vertical Horizon is a software company in the Kitchener-Waterloo high-tech corridor. It started out developing programming tools that help large teams of software developers work together effectively. Now it was moving into other areas such as web content management. Since the company was in the midst of adding to its product line, it was very important that the sales representatives support the transition. If sales of the new product line were too low, the entire company could fold.

The sales team consists of 12 outside (field) sales representatives and 6 inside representatives who provide support to the outside representatives. Each inside representative is responsible for generating leads and otherwise supporting the two outside sales representatives assigned to them. In addition, the sales team includes a sales manager who can be consulted on a daily basis for advice and a vice-president (VP) of Sales who is responsible for strategic initiatives.

Most of the sales representatives, as well as the sales manager and the VP of Sales, are relatively new to the organization. As a result, they often consult with Rhett for advice about the company's products, its customers, and sales strategies. Rhett is an outside sales representative who has been with the company for over eight years, a long time in the software world. His natural charisma combined with his strong product knowledge and excellent customer service has helped him exceed his sales quota quarter after quarter. Rhett is charming, bold, and highly self-confident. He is a gifted leader who has a natural ability to draw people to him. People feel special around Rhett.

One co-worker says: "when he talks to you, he makes you feel like you are the most important and interesting person in the world." Although Rhett's personality has helped him become a successful sales representative, it has its downside.

Rhett is the ringleader of a group of sales representatives who often work late and then go out partying together. This behaviour has been supported by the VP of Sales, who feels that the time spent bonding after work makes for a strong team. The nights the sales representatives have spent together clubbing and bar hopping has created cohesion within the work group, but it has also had some negative effects. Jasmine overheard two male members of the sales team discussing marital problems that had arisen as a result of their late nights out. "What bothered me," one said to the other, "is that when I told Rhett that my wife was upset about it, he just laughed and walked away. I know it's my own responsibility, but you would think he would be more sympathetic."

A high-performing sales representative named Malcolm spoke to Jasmine privately about Rhett and made a similar point: "It's pretty clear that Rhett has a lot of informal power around here," he said. "Everyone, even management, listens to him and does what he says. I'm worried because I'm not part of his 'pack.' I don't drink or go out with Rhett's group. Rhett makes fun of me behind my back. He insults me in front of others, and no one dares say anything about it. Given his informal power in this department, how can I ever expect a fair chance at a promotion?"

Worrisome, too, is Rhett's behaviour with his inside sales representative, Aisha. Aisha recently asked to meet with Jasmine to discuss a few "issues." She told Jasmine: "Rhett

delegates work to me and then interferes by micro-managing it. When a project goes well, he takes the credit for it; when a project goes badly, he blames me publicly. I'm often asked to go beyond my duties to help Rhett; he even thinks it's okay to call me late at night and on weekends. If I don't do what Rhett asks, he says I'm being difficult and questioning his authority. Most of the time, I feel like I'm here only to meet his needs and not those of the other sales representative I'm assigned to. The thing is, Rhett's in charge of my performance review."

Jasmine has no authority to tell Rhett how to live his life outside the workplace, but it's clear that he is negatively affecting other employees in the department. He also appears to be completely unconcerned about his impact on other employees. Jasmine suspects that Rhett is a narcissist, and perhaps Machiavellian too. But he is the company's best sales representative by far. How can she manage this difficult personality and help create a healthier work environment?

Discussion Questions

1. Do you think that Rhett is Machiavellian and a narcissist? Why or why not?

2. Assuming that Rhett is Machiavellian and a narcissist, what is the most effective way to minimize the negative effect he can have on other employees?

3. How has the organization's culture contributed to the toxic subculture that seems to be developing in the sales department? What can management do to foster an organizational culture that is supportive of all employees, positive, and high performing?

Case 2: The Path to Fraud

Learning Goals

In this case, you will have an opportunity to evaluate a decision-making process that ultimately led to an employee engaging in unethical and illegal behaviour. Consider which factors contributed to Julie's decision to engage in fraud. How did organizational variables combine with external pressures to influence her decision? Use that insight to make recommendations about what the insurance company could, and should, do to prevent similar situations from unfolding in the future.

Major Topic Areas

- Decision-making and ethics (Chapter 12)

- Work values and attitudes (Chapter 3)

- Corporate social responsibility (Chapter 12)

The Scenario

Julie Smith trembled uncontrollably as the judge ordered her to stand up for sentencing.[1] It was really happening. She would be sent to prison. All this time, no matter how many warnings she got from her lawyer, a part of her had never really believed that it would come to this. "A four month sentence to be served in a minimum security facility followed by two years of probation," thundered the judge, "and you will pay full restitution." Julie fell back into her chair and began to cry. How would her six-year-old son cope while she was imprisoned? She had not even told anyone in her family what was happening because she was so embarrassed and humiliated. How had she ended up here?

In mid-2007, Julie started working as an accounts payable clerk for a large insurance company. Her job consisted primarily of processing invoices but as a member of the wider finance department she had many opportunities to observe and learn the company's audit procedures. Julie viewed the work in accounts payable as repetitive and tedious, and she was aware that she did not have the discretion or authority to make her own decisions. Everything at this company was done VERY strictly by the book. Despite these limitations, however, Julie enjoyed her job and the company of her co-workers and colleagues, and she felt that her employer treated her well.

In early 2008, Julie made a lateral move to the department that administered corporate commercial accounts. Large corporations bought insurance policies as protection from lawsuits and were required to pay a flat rate per term regardless of the number of claims made against them. Julie oversaw more than 500 corporate policies. When one of the corporate clients experienced a loss, Julie would process the claims for legal fees, compensation, and related incidentals. Examples of common losses included compensation paid out due to slips and falls, safety violations, and other lawsuits. Julie processed an average of 13 to 15 claims per week. When the compensation was less than $10 000, Julie simply created, signed, and issued the cheque herself. Claims over $10 000 required a second signature, but she could ask anybody in the office to sign, so this was rarely a problem.

After several months on the job, Julie noticed that the corporate clients did not receive reports about claims made against their accounts. Since corporate clients paid a flat fee regardless of how many cases were processed, the corporate clients had little incentive to actively monitor claims activities.

Although she enjoyed her job and her co-workers, Julie, a single mother with a toddler, struggled to make ends meet. She earned $24 000 per year. Her expenses had exceeded her income ever since her son was born. Daycare was so expensive, but she had no choice but to use it if she was planning to work full-time. Worse, the small savings account that she inherited upon her mother's death a few years ago was nearly empty. She had only a high school education, and she had been very lucky to land the job at the insurance company in the first place. Her options for increasing her income were limited, and her son's father had never been involved in parenting or provided any type of financial support. In fact, Julie doubted she would be able to locate him, even if she tried. As she worried and considered her limited alternatives, Julie thought about her work tasks again, remembered that her company's internal audit process examined corporate commercial accounts only every six years, and came up with an idea for some relief.

Julie's son was enrolled in a private, at-home, daycare service. She was friends with Marie, the person who operated the home daycare, and they had shared a lot of laughs together. Julie usually paid for daycare on a bi-weekly basis using a personal cheque. Until the day she didn't. Three weeks after her initial flash of "inspiration," a different kind of cheque was handed over to Marie, one with the insurance company's name featured as payer instead of Julie's name. "That's weird," commented Marie, "what is up with this?" "Oh, I was embarrassed to tell you," said Julie, looking down at her feet. "I'm having some financial difficulties and my employer has decided to help me out, so the cheques for daycare will come from the company from now on." Although this sounded a little strange to Marie, she figured that the issue was personal, shrugged, and accepted Julie's cheque.

Julie left the daycare feeling euphoric. Her idea had actually worked! Three weeks previously, she had created a "loss" in the system with Marie's name ascribed to it. Julie selected one of the very large corporate commercial accounts against which to submit the claim, a company that was seldom, if ever, reviewed. She was well aware of the most common types of losses experienced, and so it was not difficult to come up with a scenario and dollar value that would not attract attention. She simply entered Marie's name as the claimant, approved the claim, and in due course a cheque was issued.

The plan had worked so well the first time that Julie executed it again. And again. And again. A little over eight months passed and, in that time, she created eight different claims under Marie's name. She added it up one day and realized that she had netted $12 000 from her "side activities." Julie reflected on how easy it had all been. She worried that she would be tempted to do it over and over again, and not just for daycare expenses. This was not the person she wanted to be. She decided that the only solution was to remove herself from temptation. She asked for, and received, a transfer to another department.

While Julie was celebrating her transfer and the fact that she would no longer be tempted, a problem emerged. The cheque for the last claim she had invented came back to her, because she had not filled in a field that coded the claim for the accounting system. Normally she could have fixed the oversight in a few seconds, but because she had been transferred, she no longer had access to the system. The person who replaced Julie asked her for a copy of the paperwork to back up the claim before filling in the missing information. Julie was unable to provide any. Not long after this incident, Julie arrived at work one morning to find herself called into a private room. Management informed her that they knew about the fraudulent claims, fired her, and advised her to get a lawyer. One month later, a police officer came to her home, and she was formally charged with fraud over $5000.

Now here she was, in court, being sentenced. She feared that her little boy would not understand why she would not return home that night. She had not told anybody about what was happening, in denial that she might actually go to jail. She felt numb all over and just prayed that her new boyfriend would be willing to take care of her son until she was released.

If not, her son would become a ward of the state and be sent to a foster home; a thought that once again reduced Julie to despair. All she had ever wanted was to be able to look after her son properly. How had it come to this?

Discussion Questions

1. What does this case teach us about ethical decision-making behaviours?

2. Did the workplace environment or corporate culture contribute to Julie's ability to rationalize her fraudulent activities? Did these factors contribute to her decision to stop committing fraud? Based on your understanding of how work attitudes develop, explain how organizational factors may have contributed to her activities and subsequent decisions.

3. What can employers do to create an environment that encourages ethical behaviour?

Case 3: Auditing, Attitudes, and Absenteeism

Learning Goals

In this case, you will have an opportunity to evaluate whether an ethical lapse in an employee's behaviour should be considered as an isolated incident or a symptom of broader problems within the corporate culture. You will also be asked to consider which factors contributed to the decision by Peter's direct reports to simply go along with his directions. Other issues to consider include the following: How might factors such as poor socialization or communication have contributed to the behaviour of Peter's direct reports? What would theories of motivation suggest? Should the organization have used a more formalized structure? Use your own insight to make recommendations about what the organization could, and should, do to prevent similar situations from developing in the future.

Major Topic Areas

- Work attitudes (Chapter 3)
- Organizational culture and socialization (Chapter 10)
- Power and group dynamics (Chapter 8)
- Motivation (Chapters 4 and 5)
- Ethical decision-making (Chapter 12)
- Organizational structure (Chapter 13)

The Scenario

"You've got to be kidding" said Sanjay, shaking his head, "is he there right now?" "Yes," said Bianca, "if we drive over there you can see for yourself." "What the heck," exclaimed Sanjay, "let's go."[1] The pair left their office tower and drove the 10 minute distance to Peter's house. Bianca was right. Peter was supposed to be out at a client site overseeing an audit, but his car was parked in his driveway, and he could be seen clearly through his large, living room window. "Well, this is awkward," sighed Sanjay. "What do we do now?"

Sanjay and Bianca were senior managers at one of Canada's top four professional audit firms. Their team was responsible for performing audits for a broad range of corporate clients. The firm had a very traditional and formalized structure, like the other large players in their industry. Recent graduates were hired as "students in accounts" during which time they were expected to complete their professional exams and work toward their chartered accountant (CA) designation. Upon passing their CA exams, they could compete to become junior auditors in the firm. If they chose to stay with the firm, they could then expect to progress to a supervisory role and finally, in six to seven years become a senior manager. The best and brightest auditors stood to become future partners in the firm. Many graduates, however, simply worked at the company long enough to achieve their CA designation, which requires a minimum of two years' experience working in an auditing firm. The culture this process created was coined "up or out," since that is exactly what happened. Employees moved up (i.e., they were promoted) or out (i.e., left the company). There was no shame in leaving, though; in fact, it was anticipated that most employees would remain only long enough to get their designations and then move on.

Peter had joined the firm a few years ago and had progressed to a supervisory role. Recently, Peter had come to the conclusion that the path to partner was not right for him, and he began applying for jobs with other companies. But his decision to apply for jobs elsewhere created a dilemma. He was not comfortable telling his employer he was looking for work elsewhere, and he was also concerned that if his employer knew that he was contemplating leaving the firm, his current assignments and standing would be negatively affected. To make matters worse, Peter had no idea how long it would take to find a new job, and he also had no idea how to manage organizing time off to participate in interviews.

Peter reviewed his work tasks and responsibilities and came up with what he perceived to be a viable solution to his dilemma. He began telling the people under his supervision that their current client did not require their presence on Fridays, and they should work at home instead. Peter encouraged them to use the time to work on things like file reviews or even just to relax. The members of Peter's team did not question his instructions, even though it was highly unusual to be allowed, and even encouraged, to work from home. Even full partners seldom worked from home. The clients themselves did not question the team's absence on Fridays either (one suspects that the average worker is not terribly disappointed when he/she discovers that the audit team is absent for a day). This arrangement allowed Peter to tell his manager that he was conducting on-site audits on Fridays, when he was actually scheduling and attending a series of job interviews on those days.

The situation continued for a couple of months before a few of Peter's direct reports became uncomfortable enough to say something. They approached Bianca, who drove past Peter's house the following Friday to see for herself whether or not he was there. When she confirmed that he was at home, instead of "on-site," she returned to the office to discuss the situation with Sanjay. Now here the two of them were, standing on Peter's front step, wondering how to handle the situation. Sanjay knocked on the door. Peter answered, but as soon as he saw Sanjay and Bianca, his face turned red. They asked him what was going on and were stunned when Peter began to cry.

After Peter regained his composure, the three of them returned to the office to discuss the situation. Sanjay and Bianca learned that the reason for the absences on Fridays was so that Peter could attend job interviews. Once Sanjay and Bianca heard all of the details, they asked Peter to step out of the office while they discussed the situation in more detail. "The irony," remarked Sanjay, once they were alone, "is that if Peter had just told us what was happening, we would have been happy to give him time off to go to interviews. We recently completed his performance evaluation, and although he is a solid accountant, he just isn't partner material. He doesn't have a future here anyway. It's not that he is a bad auditor, but others are better. I would have been happy to help him find a good placement." "That's all well and good," said Bianca, "but it isn't even Peter I'm worried about. He supervised several different teams over the couple of months he was doing this. Why did it take so long for any of them to let us know what he was doing? I know the work still got done and the clients were satisfied, and I know that everyone likes to be friendly around here and hang out together, but these people are auditors for goodness sake! I would have expected better. Do you think this might be a symptom of a bigger problem with our corporate culture? And if so, what should we do about it?"

Discussion Questions

1. Why do you think Peter's direct reports kept quiet about the "work from home" directive for as long as they did? Why did some of them eventually decide to inform management?

2. Do you think this situation would have happened if the organization had a more formal structure in place? Why or why not?

3. Do you think the lapse in Peter's ethical behaviour indicates a broader problem with the firm's corporate culture? Why or why not? If yes, what should management do now to try to change its corporate culture?

Case 4: Bad Faith Bargaining? Government Power and Negotiations with the Public Service

Learning Goals

In this case, you will have an opportunity to assess the impact of federal government policy on labour relations in the public sector. You will be asked to consider what strategies and tactics may contribute to the escalation of conflict and how the situation could be handled moving forward to lessen the intensity and emotional nature of the conflict. You will also be asked to consider issues of power and ethics. Do you believe the federal government is acting ethically in the case? What about the unions?

Major Topic Areas

- Power and politics (Chapter 8)
- Conflict and negotiation (Chapter 9)
- Ethics (Chapter 12)

The Scenario

Bargaining between unions and management in the public sector can be not only newsworthy but also highly controversial.[1]

In 1967, the Canadian government gave federal public servants collective bargaining rights. Those rights gave public service unions the right to choose whether to settle contract disputes by arbitration or by strike.

Treasury Board President Tony Clement, who is currently responsible for federal labour issues, changed those rights in 2013 when he introduced sweeping reforms to the Public Service Labour Relations Act. The new rules for collective bargaining seem to favour the government.

In the federal public service, unions were once able to decide whether they wanted to settle their disputes by arbitration (a process in which an arbitrator imposes a decision on the parties in a dispute) or conciliation (a process in which a settlement is recommended and is backed by the right to strike). The new rules give the federal government, rather than the federal unions, the power to decide whether individual disputes are solved by arbitration or conciliation. Federal public service unions are concerned that the government can force them into conciliation (and a possible strike), even if their members believe arbitration would resolve a dispute. Ultimately, the new rules for collective bargaining have decreased the power of unions that represent federal public servants and make it more likely that affected union members will agree to concessions if they consider strike action undesirable.

The federal government has also placed limits on the factors that arbitrators and conciliation boards can consider when they provide decisions on disputes for federal unions. They are required to focus on two factors: the federal government's "fiscal circumstances relative to its budgetary policies" and the ability to recruit and retain employees. The labour board had previously concluded that those two preconditions favoured the federal government to an excessive degree; despite this conclusion, Clement made the preconditions law a few months later.

In 2014, Clement announced that the federal government would revamp the public service's sick leave policy.[2] Under the new collective bargaining rules, federal public service unions are seriously limited in resolving any disputes over sick leave.

Under the federal government's existing sick leave policy, federal public servants receive 15 days of paid sick leave per year. Unused days can be carried over to subsequent years (a process known as "banking") and then be used as needed. In some cases, employees may end up with many weeks "banked." This can help them get through a prolonged illness or major injuries, since it takes 65 days to become eligible for long-term disability payments. Clement points out that the existing sick leave policy creates significant liabilities on the government balance sheet, since the government needs to account for the potential use of banked sick days. In early 2014, banked sick leave was valued at $5.2 billion.[3] At the same time, a report by the Parliamentary Budget Office indicates that it costs the government very little to pay sick leave to federal servants. For example, "the report found that sick leave can range from a low of 0.16 per cent of total [federal] departmental spending to 2.74 per cent on the high end of the scale."[4]

Clement also cited absenteeism as an issue related to the existing sick leave policy, since workers with large amounts of banked sick leave time might use sick days for purposes other than those originally intended. Sick leave policy is also associated with an equity issue. Since employees need to wait 65 days to get long-term disability payments, the net effect is that long-term employees (ones who have had time to bank many days) have a much better safety net than junior employees. Clement believes that replacing the sick leave policy with a short-term disability plan would ensure that everyone's health needs are met in a consistent and fair manner, while mitigating the problems associated with the existing policy. He feels so strongly about it that he began negotiations with insurance providers before finalizing the new policy with the federal public service unions, a step that was very poorly received.

As a result, 17 federal public service unions have signed a "solidarity pledge," agreeing that they will not surrender their current sick leave benefits. Many of those unions have three-year contracts that expire in December 2014, setting the stage for conflict and unrest over this (and likely other) issues. Will a bruising battle lie ahead?

Discussion Questions

1. Do the new collective bargaining rules for federal public service unions introduced by the federal government represent an abuse of government power? Why or why not?

2. Have any negotiation or communication errors been made by the government or by the unions in relation to federal sick leave reform? If yes, what are they?

3. How could the government, as an employer, proceed to develop a more trusting relationship with employees under the new rules for collective bargaining? What could they do to better manage labour relations moving forward?

Case 5: Gender-Based Harassment among the Royal Canadian Mounted Police

Learning Goals

In this case, you will have an opportunity to evaluate how organizational culture influences the way power is used and ethical decisions are made within the Royal Canadian Mounted Police (RCMP). Consider why the RCMP developed such a widespread problem with gender-based harassment allegations. Did the RCMP leadership contribute to the problem and, if so, how can they help to resolve it?

Major Topic Areas

- Workplace harassment and bullying (Chapter 8)
- Organizational culture (Chapter 10)
- Organizational change (Chapter 14)
- Leadership (Chapter 11)

The Scenario

In December 2006, the BC Court of Appeal upheld the decision by the BC Supreme Court to award Nancy Sulz $950 000 in damages for severe, long-term harassment experienced while she worked for Canada's RCMP.[1] The sexual harassment she endured starting in 1995 led to her request for a medical discharge from the RCMP in 2000, due to major depressive disorder. Her harasser, Staff Sergeant Donald Smith, has continued to enjoy a successful career with the force. Sulz was not the first person to complain about him; another female officer made similar allegations in the late 1980s but ultimately did not pursue them.

Four female RCMP officers alleged that they were sexually assaulted by Sergeant Robert Blundell during undercover operations that took place in Calgary between 1994 and 1997. Their internal complaints were dismissed and ignored, a problem that went all the way up to then-Commissioner Giuliano Zaccardelli. The officers reported that after filing complaints, they were "considered rats and whistleblowers and subject to harassing ridicule."[2] The four officers felt that "the lack of response signaled to the rank and file of the RCMP that silence, cover-up, and minimization are the preferred method of dealing with harassment within the RCMP."[3]

The officers chose to file a lawsuit against the RCMP in Calgary's Court of Queen's Bench in September 2003 because of the RCMP's lack of response. "We have done everything we can do within the force to address the problems and issues," the four reported in a formal statement. "They have not been

satisfactorily resolved, and we've had to take this step as a last resort."[4] At the time of filing their case, two of the alleged victims were on stress leave and the other two reported losing career opportunities within the force. One lost her role as a hostage negotiator, and the other has not been assigned to undercover operations since making the allegations. The alleged perpetrator of the sexual assaults, meanwhile, lost one day of pay and was later promoted. The case was settled out of court in 2007, with the terms kept secret.[5] However, in December 2011, *The Fifth Estate* reported that two of the complainants continue to feel they were let down by the RCMP in the matter. "That seems to be the way of the RCMP, that's kind of like the toothless tiger. There's never any accountability," said Victoria Cliffe, one of the four complainants.[6]

Janet Merlo, of Nanaimo, BC, would no doubt understand the frustration the four Calgary RCMP officers experienced. She received a medical discharge from the RCMP due to post-traumatic stress disorder that was a direct result of ongoing workplace harassment and bullying. She was allegedly subjected to frequent sexual remarks and unwanted invitations from her immediate supervisor. Co-workers also left sex toys and pornography on her desk. It took two years after Merlo's initial complaint for the organization to respond. The response thanked Merlo for her letter and noted: "As you are aware the RCMP does not take these allegations lightly and, in fact, has an obligation to provide a harassment free environment for all of our employees."[7] Merlo was advised that the matter had been investigated but no action would be taken. Subsequently, Merlo initiated legal proceedings, but she was unable to continue due to the high costs involved.[8] Heli Kijanen, of Thunder Bay, Ontario, who quit her job with the RCMP in 2011 due to incessant harassment, has experienced the same challenges trying to get justice.

Other court cases are proceeding. Officer Elisabeth Couture, of Surrey, BC, made a claim through civilian courts against three male RCMP colleagues for systematically targeting her and creating a climate of fear in the workplace. Staff Sgt. Travis Pearson found himself in criminal court due to allegations that he raped Officer Susan Gastaldo, of Burnaby, BC, in his home and then actively stalked her children in order to intimidate her into silence. An unidentified former RCMP officer testified at his trial that Pearson had also attempted to rape her under very similar circumstances, but she was too intimidated to report it at the time.[9]

In November 2011, Corporal Catherine Galliford, of Langley, BC, another RCMP officer and victim of ongoing workplace sexual harassment, decided she had had enough. She used the media to give her voice weight and expose the extent and severity of the harassment experienced by many of the 2613 female RCMP officers, a small minority in a force of 22 000. It was not long before other women, inspired by Galliford, also came forward to tell their stories, resulting in the beginnings of a class action lawsuit against the RCMP for its failure to address widespread gender-based harassment and bullying. RCMP leadership has little reason to be surprised. An internal study conducted in 1996 found that 6 out of 10 female Mounties had been sexually harassed at work and that more than 10 percent reported unwanted touching by male colleagues.

Unfortunately, that same leadership has done a very poor job of responding to complaints or addressing the cultural issues that underlie them. Questioned after Galliford had gone public, Krista Carle, one of the four Calgary RCMP officers who filed a complaint against Blundell, said the following about her formal complaint: "there was an internal review and nothing came of it. There was a memo that went out to colleagues and staff about how there was an incident with someone placing inappropriate material on someone's desk. Everyone knew it was me, so it was almost like I got blamed for getting the guys in trouble. And they never found out who put the porn on my desk."[10] Carle was discharged from the RCMP with post-traumatic stress disorder that she attributes to 19 years of unremitting sexual harassment and general bullying.

Paul Champ, a lawyer who has been involved in RCMP cases, says that "the process often takes years because the RCMP often does not treat complaints as a priority. . . . Most complaints are dismissed out of hand or dismissed with no remedy offered to the complainant other than 'we talked to him about it.'"[11]

Recognition of the scope of the problem led Bob Paulson, the new RCMP Commissioner, to make an unprecedented formal statement acknowledging that the continued existence of the force itself was at risk. He needed to "clear-cut problems that have taken root deeply. Too many Mounties believe their authority entitles them to misuse power. . . . The Mounties are one or two more earth-shattering heartbreaks away from losing all credibility. I tell you, one day there is

going to be the removal of the Stetson (the RCMP's emblematic hat and symbol of the force) if we don't get this right."[12]

Steps have been taken. An external labour relations expert was retained to review the RCMP's existing harassment policy, and a new code of conduct was introduced in April 2014.[13] Some are skeptical that these efforts will help to change a long entrenched culture. Officer Elisabeth Couture believes that "management at the local level routinely turns a blind eye to harassment as it's occurring. You can have all the staff workshops on the issue that you want, but unless detachment supervisors deal with incidents in a forceful and unequivocal manner it won't matter."[14]

The RCMP's female officers who have experienced harassment, both past and present, are not waiting around to see if these efforts to effect change within the RCMP will be successful. By July 2014, a class action lawsuit was launched by over 330 women.[15] Lawyer Alexander Zaitzeff, who is representing Janet Merlo, reports that "the stories are consistent. The stories are common in terms of harassment, bullying, and oftentimes, sexual issues. The calls are sad, hugely sad. The stories are terrible. Many serving members are unable to work because they are petrified in light of their experiences."[16] Lawyers are also quick to point out the impact that these gender-biased attitudes may have on perceived injustice in the broader community. For instance, a lack of perceived sensitivity may inhibit female members of the public from reporting sexual assaults or stalking incidents. With the class action lawsuit proceeding, the RCMP leadership will need to carefully consider how to restore its reputation and credibility among both female staff and the broader community.

Discussion Questions

1. What aspects of the organizational culture in the RCMP may have contributed to its problems with widespread sexual harassment allegations?

2. Do the alleged claims of sexual harassment point to a leadership problem? Why or why not?

3. Devise a plan to manage a culture change at the RCMP. What resistance might you encounter and how could you overcome it?

Case 6: Disability Accommodations and Promotions at Bunco

Learning Goals

In this case, you will have to decide whether to promote an employee who has a disability. You will need to consider whether the particular disability presents a legally and morally

defensible reason against promotion to a management role. If you choose to promote the employee, what can you do to help ensure his success? If you do *not* promote him, how can you explain and justify your decision, while helping the person to maintain positive work attitudes?

Major Topic Areas

- Diversity (disability) (Chapter 3)

- Work attitudes (Chapter 3)

- Recruitment and selection (Chapter 10)

The Scenario

Nicholas, the director of finance at Bunco Canada, sat wearily at his desk, sighed deeply, and rubbed his eyes.[1] He wondered whether an external search for the company's newly created accounting manager role was the right choice. Had Nicholas' decision been reasonable and fair?

Paul had worked for Nicholas as a staff accountant for 14 years. Paul was a Certified Management Accountant (CMA) and was the senior accountant responsible for external financial reporting.

Paul was a consistent and reliable employee who, due to his long tenure, knew a lot about the organization. He had, at some point in his career, performed most accounting functions at Bunco, including plant costing, budgeting, analysis, and financial planning, and so he understood the details of each role extremely well. Paul got along well with the junior staff (most of whom had been with the company for more than 10 years) and was considered a key member of the accounting team. He frequently acted as an informal adviser to other members of his team, put in overtime, and engaged in special projects, including process improvements and database optimization. In fact, he had become the sole subject matter expert on some critical financial applications needed for monthly reporting. In the past four years, however, Paul had required special accommodations from Bunco for Crohn's disease.

Crohn's disease is an incurable inflammatory bowel disease that results in sporadic and unpredictable bouts of moderate to severe pain, fever, diarrhea, gas, vomiting, and rectal bleeding.[2] Sufferers of Crohn's may experience brief or extended remissions that last months or even years, and then relapse without obvious triggers, although many patients with Crohn's disease report that stress significantly worsens symptoms and can trigger flare-ups.[3] There is no cure for the disease, but anti-inflammatory and immune-modulator medication, surgery, and careful attention to diet can control symptoms and minimize relapses for some people.[4]

Canadian courts recognize Crohn's disease as a legitimate disability for employment-related purposes. Employers are required to accommodate Crohn's disease as long as that accommodation does not result in excessive hardship to them. "Duty to reasonably accommodate" means that an employer must take all reasonable measures to enable a disabled employee to keep working. In addition to making physical accommodations such as providing laptops, wheelchair ramps, etc., employers can also be required to revise job responsibilities and performance appraisal criteria.

When he was first diagnosed with Crohn's four years ago, Paul had discussed several concerns with Nicholas. "Nicholas, I don't know how long it will take me to get this under control. It's not like I can't work at all. I'll go for a couple hours and be fine, but then. . . I don't think anyone wants me running to the washrooms here. Besides it's humiliating. I need some privacy. When the pain flares up it's all I can focus on. Maybe I could just work from home on a laptop on my bad days, play it by ear a little bit?"

Nicholas replied: "Well I don't see a problem with you working from home sometimes, but are you sure that's what you want? I spoke to an HR representative about this yesterday, and she pointed out that we have a corporate policy that prohibits laptop use for everyone except senior management and sales, but under the circumstances, I'm pretty sure I can get one approved for you. I was wondering if going on long-term disability might be a better solution for you to get yourself well though, assuming that we can get the insurance company to support the claim. Your health has to be your first priority. That said, I don't really know what we'll do if you leave!"

Paul was reluctant to seek long-term disability, because he did not want to give up so much of his life to the disease. It was also unclear whether the claim would be accepted by Bunco's insurer. After another discussion with an HR representative, Nicholas decided that a laptop should be issued to Paul and that he should be permitted to work at home on his bad days. Nicholas trusted him not to abuse the privilege so felt no need to document the decision further. An informal "handshake agreement" was readily accepted by Paul.

Accommodation Implemented: The First Few Years

Paul and Nicholas explained the situation to co-workers in a regularly scheduled staff meeting, and, initially, everyone was supportive of the new arrangement. As more time passed, however, Nicholas became worried. He had anticipated the occasional absence, but over the first few months of the new arrangement, Paul consistently worked two days in the office and then had to go home for two to three days, meaning he was absent more than 50 percent of the time. Although Paul did respond to email, Nicholas felt that he had underestimated the ongoing impact that Paul's absence might have on the team over the long term. Nicholas was being inundated with daily questions from staff that would normally have been routed to Paul. Despite the difficulties adjusting, Nicholas felt strongly that accommodating Paul was the right thing to do, so he said nothing. About five months after the initial discussion and the purchase of a laptop for use by Paul, Paul's symptoms decreased, and he was able to work in the office about 85 percent of the time for the next 18 months.

About two years ago, Crohn's-related relapses and problems returned for Paul. At the same time, due to growth in market-share and a new acquisition, the demands on the accounting department had increased significantly. Budget constraints did not allow for the hiring of additional staff. Everyone had to work a little harder and be willing to work significantly more overtime, often until 11:00 p.m. or midnight for several days in a row.

As previously mentioned, bouts of Crohn's disease are often triggered by stress. Since month's- and year's ends were particularly stressful times, Paul would often experience attacks then, just when he was needed most in the office. He was frequently absent during these key times, missing more than half of the month's ends over six months. Other accounting employees, who previously had supported Paul's accommodations, began to murmur their resentment among themselves.

One day Nicholas overheard several colleagues talk about him, when they did not realize he was in the area. "It would really make my life easier if I could work from home," one said. Another asked, Couldn't he control his Crohn's with diet, if he really tried to? I think he just doesn't want to be stuck here all evening for a week like us suckers!" "I don't think he can control it *that* much," another voice chimed. A fourth person responded, "even so, it does make for a convenient excuse doesn't it; he could fake it on any given day, and nobody would even know the difference. I bet he took off this afternoon because he heard they're bringing in pizza for dinner AGAIN." "It's not even fair," a fifth voice complained, "if he can phone and email his work in why can't we? My ex is furious that I missed my night with the kids; I'll be paying for that one for a while."

Nicholas worried about the worsening morale among what had previously been a very close team. Furthermore, Paul had been significantly late submitting his external financial reports on several occasions, and his lack of availability had hampered other people's ability to complete interdependent tasks. Since his relapse began 18 months ago, the department had been late in submitting its monthly financial reports to head office seven times! The department still complied with deadlines imposed by the Securities and Exchange Commission (SEC), but it missed many internal deadlines. While not all of the department's late filings could be directly attributed to Paul's condition (and absences), he had certainly contributed to the problem.

That said, Nicholas knew that Paul had limited control over the Crohn's disease, so Nicholas did not mention his concerns to Paul or document performance problems. If anyone else said anything to Paul directly, Nicholas was unaware of it.

Nicholas ended up doing little more than hope that Paul would experience a remission and that the situation would improve.

The Accounting Manager Role

Meanwhile the changes continued apace at Bunco. Ongoing growth and further acquisitions-in-process meant that Nicholas acquired significant new responsibilities. Part of that transition included Nicholas taking on a more strategic role in financial management and physically relocating to the company's executive headquarters in Toronto. This meant that he would no longer be around day to day to manage the accounting department at the northern packaging facility. It was also no longer adequate for the department to adopt a flat organizational structure, with staff accountants formally reporting to the director. An accounting manager position would need to be created.

As director, Nicholas was responsible for financial strategy, identifying opportunities for cost reduction and revenue growth, foreign exchange strategy, ameliorating controls, and managing transition teams for new acquisitions. In turn, the new accounting manager would be responsible for much of what Nicholas had previously done. This included advising senior executives, including the CEO, about monthly financial results and projected year-end performance, as well as overall responsibility for costing and management accounting. This position required ongoing communication with various parts of the company, including occasional travel to the head office. The most important part of the accounting manager role, however, involved managing the team at the northern facility. This included assigning tasks and providing daily guidance, advice, and social support to junior staff.

Under normal circumstances, Paul would have been the natural choice for promotion to this new accounting manager position. He wanted it; indeed, he felt it was owed to him in return for his long years of service. He was the most senior person in the department and, other than Nicholas, Paul had the highest level of formal accounting education. The other members of the department did not qualify for the role, as they were not CMAs. Paul had also created many of the spreadsheets and systems that were an integral component of the company's financial reporting system. The new role, however, would come with a significantly increased stress load, since it involved management responsibilities and a much higher political profile in the organization. Could Paul really handle the stress, given his disability? Also, if he did experience a flare-up, how could he manage a team of people from home, when multiple questions came up each day? Reports to head office were already being sent late with alarming frequency, damaging the northern branch's reputation within the company. Would this situation become worse under Paul's direction?

Fourteen months earlier, Nicholas had carefully considered his options vis-à-vis filling the future account manager position. He tried to discuss his concerns with his HR department but discovered that promotions were legal and ethical grey areas when it came to disability accommodation. Under a subset of law regarding duty to accommodate, employers were not able to deny promotions based on inability to perform a job without first proving undue hardship, but what did that really mean? The concept was largely untested in the courtroom. An HR staff member suggested that Paul be asked to participate in a detailed medical assessment to prove that he could not complete the essential operational requirements of the job. This suggestion did not sit well with Nicholas. A medical assessment could be regarded as invasive, and the procedure would lead to Paul being expected to share a great deal of confidential medical information. Furthermore, as with any management job, it was hard to distinguish the *essential* aspects of the job from the secondary ones. Presenting and defending monthly financial reports, for example, was a key part of the job. It was also very stressful, as the reports were examined and questioned in detail by powerful senior executives. Since stress was a trigger for flare-ups of Crohn's disease, could Paul handle the pressure? What about travel to head office? This was also stressful, and travel might well prove impossible for Paul.

Was it fair to expect Paul to try, given his medical condition? Nicholas' biggest concern, however, was that Paul would not always be physically available to the staff. Nicholas felt that the physical presence of a manager in the office was central to the orderly flow of information, completion of daily tasks, and maintenance of a supportive and collegial environment. He did not know if he could truly justify calling that physical presence "essential," but his gut told him it was.

Under pressure to decide whether to fill the new position internally or externally, Nicholas was not sure that he was making the right choice, but he decided to launch an external search for an account manager, instead of promoting Paul.

Discussion Questions

1. Should Nicholas have promoted Paul? Why or why not?

2. a. What are Nicholas' legal responsibilities to Paul in this situation?

   b. What are Nicholas' ethical responsibilities to Paul in this situation? How does that balance with Nicholas' responsibilities to Paul's co-workers?

3. If Paul were to be promoted, what strategies could Nicholas use to help Paul achieve success in his new role?

Case 7: Promotion from Within

Learning Goals

This case will allow you to evaluate the impact of (in)effective employee relations on motivation and job performance. Pay particular attention to issues of perceived equity and also to expectation setting and how they each relate to motivation. Is this company's approach to internal recruitment likely to cause ongoing problems for them? If so, why?

Major Topic Areas

- Motivation (Chapters 4 and 5)
- Work attitudes (Chapter 3)
- Communication (Chapter 7)
- Politics (Chapter 8)

The Scenario

The two interviewers leaned forward across the table and looked at Elisa intently. "We are very impressed with your résumé and your recently completed MBA," the HR manager

stated, "but the client training role that we have available is entry level. With your 10 years of sales and training experience and your education, you seem rather overqualified and we are concerned."

Elisa shifted slightly in her seat then turned on her best smile as she answered the interviewer. "I do understand that I am overqualified for this job," she responded, "I have also heard that Kium Solutions is a really great place to work and I know your CEO has some really interesting ideas for moving the company forward. I think I could do a lot of good here and I am willing to start in an entry level job to get in the door as long as there are other opportunities down the road." The interviewers glanced at each other and nodded. "Well that works for us," responded the HR manager. "You can start now and I am quite confident that something more challenging that better matches your qualifications will come up within a year or so." "That sounds great," said Elisa. "I look forward to coming on board."

Fifteen months later, Elisa was still in the entry level training role, which saw her travelling to different client sites each day to train their new employees on how to use Kium's document management systems. Elisa was the first person with a degree in education who had served in the client trainer role. Her formal knowledge about teaching and learning had helped her make substantial improvements to the existing client training program. Elisa's manager had commented several times about the significant increases in client satisfaction ratings that they had observed. Clients were especially impressed that Elisa was so readily available to them—she even gave them her personal cellphone number. If they had a software question or problem at 9:00 p.m. or on a Saturday, Elisa would answer her phone and cheerfully help, something that was neither expected nor required. Elisa was sure that she had done everything she could to impress her new employers. As a result, she was particularly excited when her co-worker pointed out the new job that had been posted to the internal recruitment webpage (a special website for jobs posted internally with the intent of promoting from within).

The posting was for a newly created position, director of Training. Previously, the company only had client trainers (an entry level job) and HR generalists who took care of all employee training. The new directorship would report to the VP of Sales, making it a highly prestigious position within the corporate hierarchy. The director would be responsible for improving initial staff orientation and the training received by new hires in the Sales department. Kium relied on its salesforce to grow its business. The director of Training would therefore be fulfilling an important role in the organization. Elisa could not be more delighted. After all, she had an MBA and a degree in adult education, plus she had over a decade of experience selling software solutions (although for companies other than Kium). In fact, it was her desire to get away from never-ending sales quotas and broaden her career choices that led her to pursue an MBA. Given her many qualifications and her record of strong performance, Elisa was confident that she would be a competitive candidate for the role.

Elisa sent in her résumé and, at the end of the application period, she was not the least bit surprised when she was called for an interview with the VP of Sales.

Elisa knew that she would have to explain why she was well qualified for the job. To prepare for the inter-view, she reread the strategic goals, vision, and mission of the company and thought carefully about how she could contribute. She even had her boyfriend ask her mock interview questions so that she could practise her answers. On the morning of her interview, although she felt prepared, she was also nervous. Then disappointment struck. The assistant to the VP of Sales called to say that the VP of Sales was no longer interested in interviewing her. After reviewing her résumé, he realized that she did not have enough direct experience in sales at Kium.

Elisa was stunned, wondering what on earth had happened. She could not believe that she would not even be given an opportunity to explain why she would be a good candidate for the job. She sent an email to the VP's assistant explaining her qualifications, but the assistant again confirmed that Elisa would not be permitted to interview for the job. Ultimately, Elisa went home an hour early that day, still distressed and bewildered. At 5:17 p.m. her cellphone rang. She saw that it was an important client who had recently purchased an expensive and complex solution from Kium. Just days ago, Elisa had promised the CEO at the client company that she would be there to answer questions and support their roll-out every step of the way. She looked again at the call display and at the time. She quietly looked away and let the call go to voicemail. The client could wait until Monday.

Discussion Questions

1. How would you explain the abrupt change in Elisa's customer service behaviour? Outline what has happened to her motivation using expectancy and equity theories.

2. Could Elisa's employer have anticipated the impact that cancelling the directorship interview might have on her future performance? What should her employer have done differently?

3. Elisa raised concern about being shut out of the directorship interview to the HR manager. What could the HR manager do now to help improve Elisa's motivation? Explain why your idea would be effective.

Case 8: Repairing Jobs That Fail to Satisfy

Learning Goals

Companies often divide up work as a way to improve efficiency, but specialization can lead to negative consequences. FlowFix is a company that for years has effectively used specialization to reduce costs relative to that of its competitors, but rising customer complaints suggest that the firm's strong position may be slipping. After reading the case, suggest some ways the company can create more interesting work for employees while improving customer satisfaction rates. You will also need to tackle the problem of how to find people qualified and ready to perform the multiple responsibilities required in FlowFix's jobs.

Major Topic Areas

- Job design (Chapter 5)
- Job satisfaction (Chapter 3)
- Personality (Chapter 2)
- Emotional labour (Chapter 2)

The Scenario

FlowFix is a mid-sized residential and commercial plumbing maintenance firm that operates in the Greater Vancouver area. It has been a major regional player in plumbing for decades. Tyron Johnson has been the senior executive at FlowFix for about two years. He used to work for a newer competing chain, Lightning Plumber, which has been drawing away more and more customers from FlowFix. Although his job at FlowFix pays more, Tyron is not happy with the way things are going. He has noticed the work environment is not as vital or energetic as the environment he saw at Lightning Plumber.

Tyron thinks the problem is that employees are not motivated to provide the type of customer service Lightning Plumber employees offer. He recently sent surveys to customers to collect information about customer service performance, and the data confirmed his fears. Although 60 percent of respondents said they were satisfied with their experience and would use FlowFix again, 40 percent felt their experience was not good, and 30 percent said they would use a competitor the next time they had a plumbing problem.

Tyron is wondering whether FlowFix's job design might be contributing to its problems in retaining customers. FlowFix has about 110 employees who are divided into one of four basic job categories: plumbers, plumber's assistants, order processors, and billing representatives. This structure is designed to keep costs as low as possible. Plumbers, who are licensed, make very high wages, whereas plumber's assistants make about one-quarter of what a licensed plumber makes. Using plumber's assistants is therefore a very cost-effective strategy that enables FlowFix to easily undercut the competition when it comes to price. Order processors make even less than plumber's assistants but about the same as billing processors. All work is specialized, but employees are often dependent on those in other job categories to perform at their most efficient level.

Like most plumbing companies, FlowFix gets a lot of residential business from people who consult the Internet. Corporate clients also use the company's online interface to make nonroutine maintenance requests. Customers either call in to describe a plumbing problem or submit an online request for plumbing services, receiving a return call with the information required to solve the problem within 24 hours.

In both scenarios, FlowFix's order processors determine from the customer's description of the problem whether a plumber or a plumber's assistant should make the service call. The job is then assigned accordingly, and a service representative goes to the location. When the job has been completed, the information is relayed to a billing representative. The billing representative forwards the invoice to the service rep via cellphone, and the service rep then presents a bill to the customer for payment by credit card, debit card, or cash (corporate clients remit payment via monthly invoices rather than on-the-spot).

The Problem

Although specialization cuts costs significantly, Tyron is worried about customer dissatisfaction. According to his survey, about 25 percent of customer contacts ended in no service call because customers were confused by the diagnostic questions the order processors asked or because the order processors did not have sufficient knowledge or skill to explain the situation. That means fully one in four people who call FlowFix to hire a plumber were worse than dissatisfied: they did not become customers at all! The remaining 75 percent of calls that did end in a customer service encounter resulted in other problems.

The most frequent complaints, Tyron discovered via the customer surveys, were about response time and cost, especially when the wrong person was sent to a job. A plumber's assistant cannot complete a more technically complicated job. If a plumber's assistant arrives onsite and cannot do the work, the appointment must be rescheduled (with a licensed plumber) and the customer's time and the staff's time have been wasted. The resulting delay often caused customers to decline further contact with FlowFix—many of them decided to move forward with Lightning Plumber instead.

"When I arrive at a job I can't take care of," says plumber's assistant Kiera Fritz, "the customer gets ticked off. They thought they were getting a licensed plumber, since they were calling for a plumber. Telling them they have to have someone else come out doesn't go over well."

On the other hand, when a plumber responds to a job easily handled by a plumber's assistant, the customer is still charged at the plumber's higher rate. Licensed plumber Philip Wong also does not like being in the position of giving customers bad news. "If I get called out to do something like snake a drain, the customer isn't expecting a hefty bill. I'm caught between a rock and a hard place—I don't set the rates or make the appointments, but I'm the one who gets it from the customer." Plumbers also resent being sent to do such simple work.

Louisa Gomez is one of FlowFix's order processors. She is also frustrated when the wrong person is sent to a job but feels she and the other order processors are doing the best they can. "We have a questionnaire we're supposed to follow with the calls to find out what the problem is and who needs to take the job," she explains. "The customers don't know that we have a standard form, so they think we can answer all their questions. Most of us don't know any more about plumbing than the caller. If they don't use the terms on the questionnaire, we don't understand what they're talking about. A plumber would, but we're not plumbers; we just take the calls."

Customer service issues also involve the billing representatives. They are the ones who are responsible for continuing to contact customers about payment. "It's not my fault the wrong guy was sent," says Susan MacArthur. "If two guys went out, that's two trips. If a plumber did the work, you pay plumber rates. Some of these customers don't get that I didn't take their first call, and so I get yelled at." The billing representatives also complain that they see only the tail end of the process, so they don't know what the original call entailed. The job is fairly impersonal, and much of the work involves recording customer complaints. Remember—40 percent of customers are not satisfied, and it's the billing representatives who take the brunt of customers' negative reactions on the phone.

All employees have to engage in emotional labour and it is not clear that they have the skills or personality traits to complete the customer interaction component of their jobs. FlowFix's employees are not trained to provide customer service, and they see their work mostly in technical, or mechanical, terms. Quite a few are actually anxious about speaking directly with customers. The order processors and billing representatives realize customer service is part of their job, but they also find dealing with negative feedback from customers and co-workers taxing.

A couple of months ago, a human resource management consultant was hired to survey FlowFix employees about their job attitudes. The results, shown below on a scale of 1 to 5, indicated that FlowFix employees were less satisfied than employees in comparable jobs. The table below provides a breakdown of respondents' satisfaction levels across a number of categories.

The Proposed Solution

The company is in trouble, and as revenues shrink and the cost savings that were supposed to be achieved by dividing up work fail to materialize, a change seems to be in order.

Tyron proposes using cash rewards to improve performance among employees. He thinks if employees were paid based on work outcomes, they'd work harder to satisfy customers. Because it's not easy to measure how satisfied people are with the initial call-in, Tyron would like to give the order processors a small reward for every 20 calls successfully completed. For the hands-on work, he would like to have each billing representative collect information about customer satisfaction for each completed call. If no complaints are made and the job is handled promptly, a moderate cash reward would be given to the plumber or plumber's assistant. If the customer indicates real satisfaction with the service, a larger cash reward would be provided.

Tyron also wants to find a way to hire people who are a better fit with the company's new goals. The current hiring procedure relies on unstructured interviews, and Tyron has realized that he, his senior office manager, and his most experienced lead plumber are not very consistent when interviewing. Furthermore, they often rely on their gut instinct when making hiring decisions. Tyron thinks it would be better if hiring methods were standardized and customer service skills were evaluated during that process to help them identify recruits who can actually succeed in the job.

Discussion Questions

1. Although it's clear employees are not especially satisfied with their work, do you think this is a reason for concern? Does research suggest satisfied workers are actually better at their jobs? Are any other behavioural outcomes associated with job satisfaction?

	FlowFix Plumbers	FlowFix Plumber's Assistants	FlowFix Office Employees	Average Plumber	Average Office Employees
I am satisfied with the work I am asked to do.	3.7	2.5	2.5	4.3	3.5
I am satisfied with my working conditions.	3.8	2.4	3.7	4.1	4.2
I am satisfied with my interactions with co-workers.	3.5	3.2	2.7	3.8	3.9
I am satisfied with my interactions with my supervisor.	2.5	2.3	2.2	3.5	3.4

The information that appears above about "average plumbers" and "average office employees" is taken from the consultant's records of similar companies and published industry data about skilled tradespeople. The comparatively low averages for FlowFix employees are not exactly surprising given some of the complaints FlowFix employees have made. Tyron is worried about these results, but has not been able to formulate a solution. The traditional FlowFix culture has been focused on minimizing costs, and the "soft stuff" like employee satisfaction has not been a major issue.

2. Using the job characteristics model, explain why the present system of job design may be contributing to employee dissatisfaction. Describe some ways you could help employees feel more satisfied with their work by redesigning their jobs.

3. Tyron has a somewhat vague idea about how to implement the cash rewards system. Describe some of the specific ways you would make the reward system work better, while keeping morale high, based on the case.

4. Explain the advantages and disadvantages of using financial incentives in a program of this nature. What, if any, potential problems might arise if people are given money for achieving customer satisfaction goals? What other types of incentives might be considered?

5. Create a specific plan to assess whether the reward system is working. What are the dependent variables that should change if the system works? How will you go about measuring success?

6. What types of hiring recommendations would you make to find people better suited for these jobs? Which Big Five Personality Model traits would be useful for the customer service responsibilities and emotional labour?

Case 9: Boundaryless Organizations

Learning Goals

The multinational organization is an increasingly common and important part of the economy. This case takes you into the world of a cutting-edge music software business seeking success across three very different national and organizational cultures. Its managers need to make important decisions about how to structure work processes so that employees can be satisfied and productive doing very different tasks.

Major Topic Areas

- Organizational structure and boundaryless organizations (Chapter 13)

- Organizational culture (Chapter 10)

- Diversity and teams (Chapter 6)

- Organizational socialization (Chapter 10)

- Organizational change (Chapter 14)

The Scenario

Newskool Grooves is a transnational company that develops music software used to compose music, play recordings in clubs, and produce albums. Founder and CEO Gerd Finger is, understandably, the company's biggest fan. "I started this company from nothing, from just me, my ideas, and my computer. I love music—love playing music, love writing programs for making music, love listening to music—and the money is nice, too." Finger says he never wanted to work for someone else, to give away his ideas and let someone else profit from them. He wanted to keep control over them, and their image. "Newskool Grooves is always ahead of the pack. In this business, if you can't keep up, you're out. And we are the company everyone else must keep up with. Everyone knows when they get something from us, they're getting only the best and the newest."

The company headquarters are in Berlin, the nerve centre for the organization, where new products are developed and the organizational strategy is established. Newskool outsources a great deal of its coding work to programmers in Bangalore, India. Its marketing efforts are increasingly based in its Toronto offices. This division of labour is at least partially based on technical expertise and cost issues. The German team excels at design and production tasks. Because most of Newskool's customers are English speakers, the Toronto office has been the best group to write ads and market products. The Bangalore offices are filled with outstanding programmers who don't require the very high rates of compensation you would find in German or Canadian offices. The combination of high-tech software, rapid reorganization, and outsourcing makes Newskool the very definition of a boundaryless organization.

Finger also makes the final decision on all hiring for the company and places a heavy emphasis on independent work styles. "Why would I want to put my company in the hands of people I can't count on?" he asks with a laugh. "They have to believe in what we're doing here, really understand our direction and be able to go with it. I'm not the babysitter, I'm not the school master handing out homework. School time is over. This is the real world."

The Work Culture

Employees want to work at Newskool Grooves because it's cutting edge. Newskool's core market is dance musicians and DJs—people who appreciate that while relatively expensive, Newskool is a very high-quality and innovative brand. Newskool sees itself as a trendsetter, and this strategy has tended to pay off. While competitors develop similar products and therefore need to continually lower their prices to compete with one another, Newskool has kept revenues high by creating completely new products that don't face this type of price competition.

Unfortunately, computer piracy has eroded Newskool's ability to make money with just software-based music tools, and it has had to move into the production of hardware, such as drum machines and amplifiers that incorporate its computer technology. Making this massive market change might be challenging for some companies, but for an organization that reinvents itself every two to three years like Newskool does, the bigger fight is a constant war against stagnation and rigidity.

The organization has a very decentralized structure. With only 115 employees, the original management philosophy of allowing all employees to participate in decision making and innovation is still the lifeblood of the company's culture. One developer notes, "At Newskool, they want you to be part of the process. If you are a person who wants to do what you're told at work, you're in trouble. Most times, they can't tell you what they want you to do next—they don't even know what comes next! That's why they hire employees who are creative, people who can try to make the next thing happen. It's challenging, but a lot of us think it's very much an exciting environment."

The Boundaryless Environment

Because so much of the work can be performed on computers, Finger decided early to allow employees to work outside the office. The senior management in Berlin and Toronto are both quite happy with this arrangement. Because some marketing work does require face-to-face contact, the Toronto office has weekly in-person meetings. Employees who like Newskool are happiest when they can work through the night and sleep most of the day, firing up their computers to get work done at the drop of a hat. Project discussions often happen via social networking on the company's intranet.

The Bangalore offices have been less eager to work with the boundaryless model. Managers say their computer programmers find working with so little structure rather uncomfortable. They are more used to the idea of a strong leadership structure and well-defined work processes. "When I started," says one manager, "Gerd said getting in touch with him would be no problem, getting in touch with Toronto would be no problem. We're small, we're family, he said. Well, it is a problem. When I call Toronto, they say to wait until their meeting day. I can't always wait until they decide to get together. I call Gerd—he says, 'Figure it out.' Then when I do, he says it isn't right and we have to start again. If he just told me in the first place, we would have done it."

Some recent events have also shaken up the company's usual way of doing business. Developers in the Berlin office had a major communications breakdown about their hardware DJ controller, which required many hours of discussion to resolve. It seems that people who seldom met face to face had all made progress—but had moved in opposite directions. To test and design the company's hardware products, employees apparently need to do more than send each other code; sometimes they need to collaborate face to face. Some spirited disagreements have been voiced within the organization about how to move forward in this new environment.

At the same time, the Toronto office was experiencing challenges in its ability to execute its marketing plans. According to Marketing Director Sandra Pelham, "Now that we were producing hardware—real instruments—we finally thought, 'All right, this is something we can work with!' We had a whole slate of musicians and DJs and producers to contact for endorsements, but Gerd said, 'No way.' He didn't want customers who only cared that a celebrity liked us. He scrapped the whole campaign. He says we're all about creativity and doing our own thing—until we don't want to do things his way."

Although the organization is not without problems, there is little question Newskool has been a standout success in the computer music software industry. While many companies are failing, Newskool is using its market power to push forward the next generation of electronic music-making tools. As Finger puts it, "Once the rest of the industry has gotten together and figured out how they're all going to cope with change, they'll look around and see that we're already three miles ahead of them down the road to the future."

Discussion Questions

1. Identify some of the problems likely to occur in a boundaryless organization such as Newskool Grooves. What are the advantages of boundaryless organizations?

2. Consider some of the cultural issues that will affect a company operating in various parts of the world. What actions would you take to ensure that Newskool's different offices work effectively with one another?

3. Based on what you know about motivation, personality, and organizational culture, what types of people are likely to be satisfied in each functional area of the company? Use concepts from the job characteristics model to describe what might need to change to increase employee satisfaction in all areas.

4. What types of human resources practices need to be implemented in this sort of organization? What principles of selection and hiring are likely to be effective? Which Big Five personality traits and abilities might Newskool supervisors want to use for selection?

Case 10: Trouble at City Zoo

Learning Goals

In this case, you will have an opportunity to assess how to restore trust among employees who have low morale. You should consider how organizational culture has led to the problems faced at the zoo. You will determine whether the organizational structure should be changed and also whether new reward systems should be put in place.

Major Topic Areas

- Communication (Chapter 7)
- Organizational design (Chapter 13)
- Leadership (Chapter 11)
- Organizational culture (Chapter 10)
- Job design (Chapter 5)
- Change management (Chapter 14)
- Resistance to change (Chapter 14)

The Scenario

City Zoo has been an important visitor destination for generations of children.[1] Locally, provincially, and nationally, City Zoo has had a remarkable reputation for providing a high quality environment for its animals while enabling children of all ages to learn about animals and see them in natural environments. The zoo operates with a dedicated staff, as well as a large number of volunteers. Over half of its revenues come from a special tax levy on city property owners who vote on whether to renew the levy during city elections held every three years.

Despite its sterling reputation, the zoo went through a year of unpleasant publicity in 2014, after the board of directors dismissed head veterinarian Tim Bernardino. Newspaper reports of the dismissal suggested that Bernardino had been dismissed for speaking up about harm to some of the zoo's animals. The publicity forced zoo management to respond to many tough questions regarding its practices and operations regarding both animals and staff. City Council acted swiftly in the face of continued negative press coverage of the zoo, feeling a responsibility to the taxpayers. In order to answer all of the questions raised by the press, council created a special Citizens' Task Force to review the zoo's finances and operations, including animal care.

It is February 2015, and Emma Breslin has just been hired by the board of directors to take over as executive director of the zoo. She is reviewing the many concerns raised by the task force and wondering how she might restore employees' and the public's confidence in the zoo. She will be meeting with the board in two weeks to present her recommendations for moving forward. The board has asked her to act quickly because city residents will vote on the next tax levy in just three months. A "no" vote would substantially reduce the zoo's revenues for the next several years. (Exhibit 1 outlines the revenues and expenses of the zoo for fiscal year 2014.)

Background

The City Zoological Gardens got its start in 1905, when Samantha Fraser donated a hedgehog to the city's Parks Board. Building on that first donation, the zoo has grown to be one of the most comprehensive zoological institutions in the country. The zoo's African Savannah recreates the look of Africa's plains and jungles. The Savannah houses the world-famous Hippoquarium, the first natural hippo habitat to be created in a zoo. The zoo includes exhibits for Siberian tigers, Asian sloth bears, and the endangered African wild dogs. The zoo has also renovated the Aviary and the Primate Forest. More recent improvements include a new parking lot and gift shop. The zoo is a top tourist attraction for the city, and the number of annual visitors to the zoo has nearly tripled from 1982 (364 000 visitors) to 2013 (more than 1 million visitors). In the past five years, the zoo has twice been ranked as one of the top 10 zoos in North America for children and families. It was also voted one of the top five zoos in North America in the "North America's Favorite Zoo" contest sponsored by Microsoft. The zoo's vision and mission statements (see Exhibit 2) are widely credited with helping the zoo achieve these awards.

Until 1982, the zoo was run by the city. That year, ownership was transferred to the City Zoological Society, a private nonprofit organization. Because of its dedication, the Society was able to introduce a number of improvements that the city had not been able to accomplish. The zoo has since doubled in size and now contributes significantly to the local economy. A recent study by a local university found that the zoo generates almost $8 in local economic activity for each tax dollar it receives.

The zoo employs 157 full-time staff members and more than 550 part-time and seasonal employees. There are also more than 300 volunteers who assist with programs, events, and community outreach. Donors and members provide financial support for animal conservation and educational programming.

EXHIBIT 1   City Zoo Revenues and Expenses, Fiscal Year 2014

Public Support

	Property Tax Levy Receipts	$6 466 860
	Grants	$174 780
	Education Program Revenue	$344 110
	Total Public Support	**$6 985 750**

Development Revenue

	Membership	$3 903 420
	Friends of the Zoo	$214 397
	Annual Fundraising	$130 852
	Corporate Support	$302 952
	Development Events	$391 565
	Total Development Revenue	**$4 943 186**

Earned Revenue

	Admissions	$3 253 355
	Advanced Sales	$337 908
	Gross Revenue From Concessions and Gift Shop Operations	$7 153 483
	Rides, Parking, and Tours	$1 560 727
	Facility Rentals	$116 520
	Total Earned Revenue	**$12 421 993**
	Other Revenue	**$34 956**
Total Public Support and Revenue		**$24 385 885**

Expenses

	Cost of Goods Sold	$2 448 164
	Wages and Benefits	$13 900 524
	Supplies, Maintenance, and Utilities	$4 387 642
	Professional Services	$2 246 560
	Other Expenses	$714 487
	Conservation—Project Support	$45 093
	Animal Purchases	$76 542
	Special Exhibits	$293 630
Total Operating Expenses		**$24 112 642**
Excess (Deficit)		**$273 243**

The Ministry of Natural Resources Inquiries

The 2010 Inquiry   In December 2009, Medusa, a female sloth bear mistakenly believed to be pregnant, was put into isolation, where it died. Zoo officials later admitted that they had misunderstood how to properly care for sloth bears. Tim French, the curator of Large Mammals at the time, made the decision to put the bear in isolation on his own, without reporting this to his supervisors. The bear's zookeeper, Melissa Fox, who reported to French, objected to his decision, but no one would listen to her, including acting head veterinarian Wynona Singh (who was in charge while Dr. Bernardino was away on research). Fox's daily notes, which she was required to file with her supervisor, described her worries about the bear. Fox finally became so upset with the bear's condition that she asked to be transferred to another part of the zoo. French resigned after the bear's death.

Vision Statement
To be one of the world's outstanding zoological institutions.

Mission Statement
Our mission is to provide excellent animal management, educational programs, and scientific activities and to provide visitors with an enjoyable, educational, and family-oriented experience.

Objectives to achieve mission statement:

- Animal exhibits that reflect natural habitats
- Educational programs to help visitors understand the relationships of wildlife and the environment
- Refuges for rare and endangered species to protect and propagate them
- Scientific programs that contribute to greater understanding of animals and their habitats
- A clean, safe, and pleasant facility for visitors and employees
- A broad base of community support and involvement
- Operating on a sound business basis

As a result of the investigation, the zoo was fined $1500 by the Ministry of Natural Resources for violating federal animal welfare regulations. The zoo also agreed to create an animal reporting system so that employees could raise any concerns they had about animal welfare, although nothing ever resulted from this agreement.

The 2013 Inquiry In February 2013, the Ministry of Natural Resources began an investigation of animal deaths that had occurred at the zoo over the past several years:

- Cupid, a hippopotamus, died in the summer of 2012 at the age of 49. While the veterinary staff raised some questionable circumstances concerning the death, zoo officials dismissed the animal's death as "old age."
- George, a 14-year-old giraffe, died in 2010 from tetanus three weeks after he was gored by a kudu when the two were put in an enclosure together.
- Medusa, the female sloth bear, died in December 2009.

Zoo officials were puzzled about why the Ministry of Natural Resources had decided to investigate these deaths. "Initially, my gut reaction was that the Ministry of Natural Resources was just stepping things up because of what had transpired at that other zoo," a zoo spokesperson said. The spokesperson was referring to several suspicious animal deaths, including an orangutan euthanized by mistake, at a large zoo in another part of the country.

As the Ministry of Natural Resources investigation progressed, however, many zoo staff became nervous about the way it was being conducted. Inspectors did not reveal the exact reason for their inspection, but they asked specific questions about the giraffe and the hippopotamus. The inspectors requested to speak to some employees, while refusing to speak with others. Zoo officials later said the surprise inspection was "unusual, unprecedented, and aggressive."

"As you can imagine, it was a very upsetting and confusing time. We've never had this kind of inspection, and the frustrating thing was they would not tell us what they were inspecting for," said William Lau, the zoo's executive director.

Before the Ministry of Natural Resources could issue a report, zoo officials decided to conduct their own internal investigation into the deaths of George, the giraffe, and Cupid, the hippopotamus. Officials were concerned that someone at the zoo had made a call to the Ministry of Natural Resources that led to the surprise inspection. Lau claimed that the investigation was not a "witch hunt," and that officials were not trying to find out if anyone had acted as a whistle-blower. "We simply want to understand what the Ministry of Natural Resources is worried about," he said.

The Ministry of Natural Resources issued a report on its investigation the following month. In it, the inspectors noted that the zoo had ignored the warnings of Dr. Tim Bernardino, City Zoo's head veterinarian, about animal care. "From the review of numerous documents and interviews, it is clear that these veterinary recommendations from the attending veterinarian [Dr. Bernardino] have not been addressed in a reasonable time. The licensee [the City Zoo] has failed to provide the attending veterinarian with adequate authority to ensure the provision of adequate veterinary care," the report stated.

Zoo Management

Board of Directors

The board of directors oversees City Zoo's business affairs and strategic plan, but day-to-day operations are left in the hands of the executive director. There are 18 people on the board. Each board member serves a three-year term. The term can be renewed up to two times, if the board member is nominated by the Nominating Committee and approved by the board of directors. The board in recent years has been mostly hands-off, allowing the executive director a great deal of latitude in running the zoo.

Executive Director

The executive director is effectively the CEO of the zoo, carrying out the strategic plan of the board. William (Bill) Lau was appointed executive director in 1989. Under his leadership, the zoo expanded considerably, won numerous awards, and significantly increased its revenues.

Lau did a good job of raising the zoo profile externally, particularly in leading fundraising efforts that brought numerous exotic animals to the zoo. He was not necessarily seen as a good internal leader, however. The board's Executive Management Committee reported at a March 13, 2011, board meeting that the zoo's work environment was characterized by numerous disagreements. The minutes of this meeting showed that the board discussed "'open warfare' between managers; back-biting and rude behaviour during meetings; and problems in managers' relationships with Mr. Lau." The minutes also reported that "Working with Bill is experienced by some as difficult, intimidating, or scary." Some staff had complained that Lau frequently yelled at staff and failed to acknowledge their value. "There is a fear of repercussion, and some people are afraid they will be . . . seen as stupid, belittled in meetings, [and] blamed and shamed in front of others," the minutes state.

Chief Operating Officer

The chief operating officer (COO) is second in command at the zoo, reporting to the executive director. The COO respon-sibilities include most of the operational functions of the zoo: finance, human resources, maintenance and horticul-ture, interpretive services, and education. The Department of Veterinary Care was the only nonoperational function that also reported to the COO. All other animal-related departments, including the curators, reported to the executive director.

In early 2011, the zoo hired Robert (Bob) Stellenbosch to be the new COO. Unlike the COO he replaced, Stellenbosch had no animal-care experience in his previous positions. Before coming to the zoo, he had been executive director of the National Funeral Directors Association for 14 years. Prior to that, he had been executive director of the Provincial Bankers Association. Nevertheless, veterinary care still fell under Stellenbosch's mandate, and the head veterinarian reported to him. Stellenbosch did not see this as a problem. As Stellenbosch pointed out, he often had to oversee "departments in areas I know very little about. The secret [is] having a strong line of communication with the people who report to you."

The zoo's executive director also did not see Stellenbosch's lack of animal-care experience as a problem. "We were looking for anybody with a background that could run a zoo on a day-to-day basis. We didn't find anybody with an animal background who could do that. We chose Bob Stellenbosch because he was the best candidate," Lau said.

Caring for the Animals

Three sets of employees work closely with the animals: veteri-narians, curators, and zookeepers.

The Veterinarians

Dr. Tim Bernardino   Dr. Tim Bernardino, director of Animal Health and Nutrition at City Zoo, was the zoo's head veteri-narian, and had been a zoo employee for 22 years. Eight full- and part-time employees in the animal health and nutrition department reported to him. Veterinarians are responsible for the health care program for the animals, and they also maintain all health records. Bernardino was also the "attending veterinarian" for the zoo, a position that carries with it the responsibility to communicate on a regular basis with the Ministry of Natural Resources. Part of this respon-sibility involved bringing questionable animal deaths to the attention of the Ministry of Natural Resources.

Bernardino was well respected by the international veteri-narian community, and well-liked by the zookeepers. He was known to deeply care for all of the animals in the zoo, and kept up with the latest literature on the best ways to manage and display animals to maximize their comfort and well-being.

Bernardino's performance as head veterinarian was gener-ally applauded by senior management. He had received glowing ratings in his annual performance reviews throughout his career. For instance, at the end of 2013, Bernardino received one of his best performance reviews ever. Robert Stellenbosch, his direct supervisor, wrote that Bernardino main-tained "the highest quality of work!" He also wrote that "Tim is well respected throughout the zoo." Stellenbosch praised the veterinarian's technical skills, his dependability, and his tremendous work ethic.

There were occasional negative comments in his reviews, although these did not seem to weigh heavily in his overall evaluations. For instance, in his 2009 review a former super-visor wrote, "Tim can be intense and inflexible, causing strained relations with fellow employees." Still, the supervisor noted that Bernardino "gets along reasonably well" with other zoo employees. In his 2013 review, the veterinarian was specifically asked to "focus more on people skills in the depart-ment and with curators." The review also noted that "Tim is strong in his beliefs, and sometimes needs to temper that once a final decision is made."

The negative performance appraisal comments were related to Bernardino's relationships with the curators and zookeepers. He was well respected by the zookeepers, and maintained good relations with them because their observa-tions of the animals helped the animals stay healthy. However, some of the curators felt that Bernardino empowered the zookeepers too much, so that the zookeepers would some-times go around their curators to make complaints about animal care. Bernardino worried that some of the zookeepers were disciplined by their curators when they spoke with him about their concerns regarding the animals. "People don't feel free to be open. Discussions don't happen. [There is] control of information, control of communications, control of decision making [by the curators]," he said.

Beth Else, curator of Conservation and Research, saw it differently. "I think he empowered the keepers to go around the supervisors and go to him when they didn't get the answer that they liked," she said, echoing comments of the other curators.

Despite his generally good reviews, Bernardino also felt that he was "alienated from the decision-making process . . . with the curatorial staff and with other administrators." He sometimes complained the curators were given more weight than the veterinary staff in decision making about the animals, even when the health of the animals was in question. He also felt that his role as attending veterinarian, where he was accountable to the Ministry of Natural Resources, was "not well defined or understood by those in the zoo community."

Bernardino's reviews took a turn for the worse after the Ministry of Natural Resources released the report of its 2013 surprise investigation. Just two months later, in May 2013, Stellenbosch gave Bernardino, in writing, a reprimand about his performance. "We need to have team players, and you need to work through these issues in a more professional, less 'attacking' manner," the COO's warning stated. Bernardino was also told that he lacked "team attitude, professionalism, and judgment."

This warning was closely followed by the announcement that Bernardino would share the "attending veterinarian" position with two others: his subordinate, veterinarian Wynona Singh, and Mammals curator Randi Walker. Although Walker was also a veterinarian, she was not licensed to practise as one in the province. In August 2013, Bernardino was told that he would no longer serve as an "attending veterinarian," and that Singh would be the sole "attending veterinarian." At about the same time, Bernardino received a written reprimand, in which he was accused of "steadily undermining animal curator Dr. Walker, poor communication skills, and intimidating other employees."

Dr. Wynona Singh Dr. Wynona Singh, who reported to Dr. Bernardino, had been a full-time veterinarian at the zoo since 1999. She first joined the zoo in 1989 as a part-time veterinarian. Singh was the veterinarian on call when the giraffe died in 2010 and the sloth bear died in 2009, although she was not implicated in either death.

Bernardino and Singh often butted heads. In his 2012 evaluation of her, Bernardino recommended that she receive no salary increase. In January 2013, Bernardino told the zoo's human resources director that "if she doesn't improve and we keep her, I'm out of here."

Bernardino was reflecting on a survey of her performance he had conducted with the veterinary and animal food staff. Only 29 percent of them gave her favourable ratings, while 61 percent noted that she had big communication problems. The zookeepers specifically complained that Singh did not relate well to them and was not always open to their concerns. This led Bernardino to tell her that she "had to continue to improve some management skills, including communication." Despite negative reviews from her immediate staff and subordinates, Singh received high marks from the curators and associate curators, who indicated their full and unambiguous support of her.

The Curators and Zookeepers

Curators make recommendations such as what animals to acquire, whether animals should be bred, and whether animals should be lent to other zoos for either breeding or display purposes. Curators are also responsible for the designing and planning of animal exhibits, including coming up with ideas for new exhibits that might be of interest to the public. Although curators are responsible for the overall well-being of the animals, they are certainly aware of the marketing and public relations functions of animal exhibits.

The general curator at a zoo oversees the entire animal collection and animal management and is responsible for strategic collection planning. Zoos also have animal curators who manage a specific section of the animal collection. City Zoo had four area curators: curator of Fishes, curator of Reptiles, curator of Birds, and curator of Mammals. Some areas also had associate curators, such as the assistant curator of Large Mammals and the assistant curator of Small Mammals.

Senior zookeepers and zookeepers (also called *keepers*) report to the curators and work with individual animals, feeding them, handling them, keeping their cages clean, and looking after their welfare on a day-to-day basis. Keepers often work with the same animals for a number of years, so they can grow quite attached to their animals. Keepers can feel that they understand more about the welfare of their animals than the curators.

At City Zoo there was significant tension between the curators and the keepers. The keepers complained that curators did not listen to their concerns, and curators complained that the keepers often went around them to share concerns about animals with Dr. Bernardino. The curators felt that the keepers should raise all concerns with them, rather than with the veterinarian.

Randi Walker Randi Walker was curator of Mammals at the zoo. The Mammals department's 22 full-time employees (including 14 zookeepers) took care of the zoo's apes, great cats, bears, elephants, and all hoofed animals. This was the largest animal department at the zoo, and was twice the size of the next largest department, the Birds department. All of the deaths investigated by the Ministry of Natural Resources had happened in Walker's unit.

The assistant curator of Large Mammals and the assistant curator of Small Mammals worked under Walker. The assistant curators were two of the most liked curators at the zoo. They had excellent animal-care backgrounds, were very aware of the zoo's communication problems, and knew how to work effectively with the other employees. They were also respected by the zookeepers and other curators.

Although curators do not usually have veterinary training, Walker had completed her veterinary studies. However, she was not licensed to practise veterinary medicine in the province. Her background may have led to her difficult relationship with Bernardino. Sometimes she tried to second guess him, and other times she attempted to overrule his decisions.

Walker was particularly uncomfortable with the relationship that Bernardino had with the Mammals zookeepers. She felt that his close relationship to them undermined her. "There are communication problems with mammal keepers and [Mammals curator Randi Walker]," one keeper said. "Some people can talk; other people, if they open their mouth, she jumps on them. That's the underlying thing why people talk to Dr. Tim."

Gorilla keeper Dale Petiniot noted that while she had no problem discussing issues with Walker, sometimes keepers needed to discuss issues with a neutral third party. "It's not always that we're justified, but sometimes you need to talk about things, and you don't have a next step, other than the vet," Ms. Petiniot said.

When zoo officials, responding to the Ministry of Natural Resources' surprise investigation, tried to investigate the death of George the giraffe, they quickly discovered that most employees in the Mammals department would simply not talk about the event, saying that they feared retribution by Walker. Even though zoo officials offered immunity from any disciplinary action in exchange for clarification about what had happened, no one came forth to take responsibility for putting the two animals together. "Nobody claimed responsibility," Andy Yang, curator of Reptiles and head of the internal investigation, said.

The report of the internal investigation concluded, "The apparent failure of the mammal keeper staff to inform, discuss, and plan this introduction with the veterinary staff prior to any action was unacceptable and compromised the welfare of the giraffe." Yang's committee made a pointed observation regarding the Mammals department: "There are significant communication problems in the Mammals department that need attention. These communications problems have negatively affected animal welfare."

Xavier Tolson, a human resources consultant hired by the zoo at the end of 2013 to analyze workplace problems in the Mammals department, reached many of the same conclusions. "I do not believe I have ever seen a department as dysfunctional as the Mammals department" at City Zoo. He noted that there was a lot of conflict between the head curator and the zookeepers.

Tolson suggested that the keepers had a tendency to try to bully Walker into seeing their point of view about animal concerns.

Although most of her subordinates were critical of Walker's performance, managers at the most senior levels in the zoo were strongly supportive of her. She was always deferential to their views, and they felt she was right not to cave in to employee concerns.

The Biological Program Committee

In most zoos, the general curator oversees the work of the curators, zookeepers, and veterinarians and attempts to resolve any issue that might come up among the three groups. However, City Zoo had no general curator. When the zoo hired Robert Stellenbosch as COO in 2011, he was unable to serve as general curator, a role his predecessor had filled, because he had no previous animal experience.

Shortly after Stellenbosch was hired, Lau announced that the newly created Biological Program Committee (BPC) would perform the duties normally handled by the general curator. The committee consisted of the curators of Mammals, Birds, Reptiles, and Fishes, an animal behaviour specialist, and members of the zoo's veterinary staff. Only the four curators and the animal behaviour specialist had voting rights on the committee, however. The curators took turns chairing the monthly committee, rotating the position every few months. No one else was allowed to chair the committee.

Not everyone was happy with the new management committee meetings. Bernardino, who had had a very good relationship with the former general curator, felt that his authority was diminished because of the BPC structure. Bernardino also objected that he was not able to rotate into the role of committee chair. He complained that the curators did not pay enough attention to animal-care issues. He also complained that the curators treated members of the veterinary staff who were on the committee like second-class citizens. After trying to get along with the new management structure for about six months, Bernardino took his concerns about the BPC to the executive director. Lau dismissed the veterinarian's concerns, suggesting that communication among committee members was good, except for some "troublemakers," which Bernardino took to be a reference to himself.

Beth Else, curator of Conservation and Research at the zoo, noticed a change in Bernardino's demeanour after the creation of the BPC. "It seemed in the past that Tim relied on gentle persuasion to bring people over to his way of thinking. In recent years, particularly in the past year, Tim has been more of a disruptive influence at the zoo," Else said. "I don't want to give the impression that I think Tim is malicious, because I don't," Else said. "Tim, in his own mind, thinks he is doing what is right."

Other employees must have agreed with Else that Bernardino was trying to do the right things at the zoo. On February 23, 2014, the zoo staff voted on nominees for "Outstanding Employee" of the year. Bernardino received the most votes.

Shockwaves at the Zoo

Head Veterinarian Fired

On February 28, 2014, City Zoo dismissed Bernardino from his $102 000-a-year position as head veterinarian. The executive director said that the dismissal had nothing to do with the 2013 Ministry of Natural Resources inspection, or with issues about animal care. "There is no question in my mind that he raised the level of animal care here at the zoo," Lau explained. "And while I do have a problem with the way Bernardino dealt with the Ministry of Natural Resources in the past, the termination was a result of our concerns over Dr. Bernardino's administrative and management skills that we had worked with him to address over the last several years."

Bernardino's dismissal created shockwaves both inside and outside of the zoo. The local newspaper contacted several well-known veterinarians throughout the country to find out what they could do about Bernardino. All of the contacted veterinarians spoke with great regard for the dismissed veterinarian. Reporters also uncovered previous performance reviews of Bernardino, which indicated that Bernardino had performed exceptionally in his work with the animals. Reporters concluded from their investigation that "The firing of Dr. Bernardino in late February was the culmination of a year-long struggle between him and zoo administrators beginning, it appears, with the veterinarian's frank comments last year during a routine animal-care inspection by the Ministry of Natural Resources. Those comments led to an admonition by the Ministry of Natural Resources that the zoo failed to heed warnings about its animal-care practices."

The intense press coverage prompted the city to start its own investigation of zoo administration. City Council felt an obligation to protect taxpayers' money, and recognized that public confidence in the zoo was at an all-time low because of all the negative publicity. Council appointed a 14-member Citizens' Task Force in mid-March. The mandate of the task force was to review zoo finances and operations, including animal care, and to issue a report within 100 days.

As the task force was getting underway, more scandal struck the zoo. The local newspaper reported that Executive Director William Lau had traded in the Jeep he had been given at zoo expense for a luxury Volvo, also paid for by the zoo. Similarly, COO Robert Stellenbosch had traded in his Dodge for a luxury Volvo. The two Volvos were costing taxpayers $1200 per month.

Members of the public were outraged by this news, coming just two weeks after Bernardino's firing. One long-standing zoo member emailed the local newspaper that he was disgusted with zoo administrators: "The firing of the whistleblowing vet is enough to make one wonder if the chimpanzees could not do a better job of running the place. If anything would make me stop supporting the zoo, it is the attitude of the zoo director and [chief operating officer]. To rent Volvos for themselves, to be so wasteful with the dollars of the taxpayers is tantamount to being part of the low-down reptile exhibit."

A Settlement and Resignations at the Top

After his dismissal, Bernardino approached the board of directors, requesting that they meet with him and give him back his job. The board was feeling under siege because of all the negative publicity. Bernardino's dismissal seemed to mobilize community sentiment toward the veterinarian, and against the zoo's senior management.

In an effort to quiet speculation by community members about zoo leadership, the board of directors made a settlement with Dr. Bernardino on May 1, 2014. The agreement reinstated him to his position of director of Animal Health and Nutrition of the zoo effective immediately, although he would serve in this role only as a "consultant," on an "as-needed basis." The agreement stated that Bernardino was not allowed to be on zoo grounds while performing his job, and could not enter the zoo as a private citizen for six months. The agreement prohibited him from discussing "his opinions as to the welfare of the animals at the Zoo, the circumstances of his termination or reinstatement of employment, his opinions regarding personnel at the Zoo, or any other matters pertaining to the Zoo" with anyone unless subpoenaed.

Bernardino's consulting position was to last for 18 months. He would be paid $105 000, plus health and retirement benefits during that time. Under the settlement, he would also receive $42 815 in back pay, benefits, and attorney's fees. The board agreed to remove all negative evaluations that were added to his file in 2013. Bernardino agreed that he would not file claims of wrongful discharge or breach of contract against the zoo.

Two weeks after the settlement with Bernardino, the zoo board announced that Executive Director William Lau would retire immediately, after 25 years at the zoo. The board also announced that COO Robert Stellenbosch would resign once a new management team was in place.

The Findings of the Citizens' Task Force

The Citizens' Task Force presented its findings to City Council at a public meeting held on July 8, 2014. The task force divided its presentation into three parts: a discussion of the employee survey they had commissioned; a presentation of what they had learned about the politics of zookeeping; and a discussion of other observations about how the zoo operated.

Employee Survey The Citizens' Task Force asked Maynard & Associates, a Toronto-based employee relations consulting firm, to determine employee morale. Exhibit 3 summarizes the results of the survey, including separate results for the Mammals department. Maynard & Associates have collected

		EXHIBIT 3 Employee Attitude Survey of City Zoo, and Some Comparisons				
			Percentage of Employees Who Agree or Strongly Agree with Statement			
Category	*Question*		*City Zoo*	*Mammals Department*	*Other Zoos*	*Other Organizations*
Pay	My compensation is satisfactory and fair compared with that of other employees who work here.		80	81	82	75
	My compensation is satisfactory and fair compared with what I would earn at similar companies.		81	81	82	74
Recognition	My supervisor recognizes and provides positive feedback for work well done.		63	57	68	72
Supervision	My supervisor treats me fairly.		43	43	63	63
	My supervisor helps me perform my work effectively.		41	39	70	70
Communication	I feel comfortable expressing my ideas to my supervisor and other leaders in the company.		41	35	71	73
	Leaders communicate pertinent information to employees.		51	48	55	74
Empowerment	I am free to make decisions that affect my work without consulting with my supervisor.		55	45	67	69
	My ideas are used when managers make decisions that affect the company.		49	41	65	70
Job Satisfaction	Overall, the company is a good place to work.		68	60	70	77
Management	The managers here are honest, fair, and ethical.		45	39	76	79
Participation	Managers seek employee input into the way work is done here.		53	45	68	77
Teamwork	Employees work together as a team here.		59	53	79	79
	Teamwork is encouraged here.		55	50	75	75
Training	I receive adequate job-related training to do my job.		85	83	81	76
	There are plenty of opportunities here to learn additional skills.		85	78	81	74
Work Demands	The workload is fair and reasonable.		75	74	73	79

baseline data as a result of their many employee surveys, and those data are also included.

On many dimensions, City Zoo employees were more critical than the average employee in Maynard's surveys. Zoo employees complained about the lack of effective leadership, poor communication, and the scarcity of teamwork. Only half of the employees said there was open and honest communication at the zoo, and many employees noted that this lack of communication led to rumours and myths that spread throughout the zoo.

Employees said that they did not feel that they could talk freely to their supervisors about job-related problems, and they gave low marks to supervisors for resolving employee problems. Employees also gave low marks to supervisors for letting employees know what was expected of them. Supervisors were also criticized for not considering differing opinions, and a number of employees noted that they feared punishment if they expressed contrary opinions. Employees also expressed the expectation many employees placed on each other that "if you are not with us; you are against us," which created a lot of divisiveness across the zoo.

Despite the low morale uncovered by the survey, results indicated that employees loved working at the zoo, were fairly paid, and felt that they had been trained appropriately to do their jobs. However, they wanted to see an end to the political, communication, and leadership problems that dominated day-to-day work at the zoo.

The Politics of Zookeeping   Three members of the Citizens' Task Force were asked to discuss the events that had occurred at City Zoo with respected members of the zoo community throughout North America. Dr. Christopher Bondar, the associate veterinarian at the Central Canada Zoo, suggested that it was not surprising that there were tensions between zoo management and the veterinarians. "The zoo business in general, because people's emotions tend to run high about animals and their welfare and because it is a small community, tends to have a lot of politics," said Dr. Bondar, who added that he has not encountered such problems at his own zoo. It can be hard to understand all of the politics at zoos because "so many businesses are about paperwork or industry or goods that don't spawn the type of passion people have for living animals."

Members of the task force spoke with Dr. Philip Robinson, a former director of veterinary services at the San Diego Zoo, and author of the book *Life at the Zoo: Behind the Scenes with the Animal Doctors*, and asked him about the relationship between curators and veterinarians. "The perception that [veterinarians] should stick to sick animals and leave the other issues to the other people on

staff—traditionally, this is sort of a turf battle that has more to do with management style than anything that benefits the animals," he told them.

Other experts supported Dr. Robinson's position. They told the task force that it is crucial for veterinarians to interact with keepers to understand the needs of individual animals. "If the curator says to the keeper, 'You only tell me what's happening,' then the veterinarian is sort of between a rock and a hard place to know when the animal is on the road to a problem, or already is there and has the problem," said Randolph Stuart, the executive director of the Canadian Association of Zoo Veterinarians. "That's why most vets will keep a good rapport with keepers."

Experts in the area of zoo administration suggested that many zoo administrators don't appreciate the passion that veterinarians bring to their work. Veterinarians are chiefly concerned with animal welfare, while the zoo administration is also concerned with fundraising, providing an experience for zoo visitors, running successful gift shops and snack bars, and making sure parking lots are adequately designed for visitor load.

Dr. Mark Cornwall, the director of animal health and attending veterinarian at the Maple Leaf Zoo stressed the need for good communication among all zoo employees. The Maple Leaf Zoo was sued by an employee under whistle-blower protection legislation. The employee was demoted and harassed after she complained to government officials about unsafe conditions at the zoo. "Everybody kind of learned something from that," said Dr. Cornwall. "Animal welfare comes first," he said. "Zoo veterinarians are really the ones who are in charge of that. Veterinarians tend to champion those causes because that is what they are expected to do. You have different perspectives and opinions on those things, but the key is to sit down with all the folks." He added, "Zoos are complicated organisms and organizations. Open communication can improve the situation, however."

Other Issues Raised by the Task Force   During its presentation, the Citizens' Task Force identified a number of other issues of concern, and they briefly reviewed these for council.

- *Organizational culture.* The task force found that lack of trust was a big issue among staff. They also found a "culture of fear" and noted that even though retaliation was often subtle, it was definitely there. In particular, keepers were afraid to admit actions or mistakes, even when immunity was offered. The task force expressed concern that many of the zookeepers were too focused on their own specific job duties and did not "see or support the 'big picture' of the zoo as both a wildlife conservation facility and a business."

- *Relationship among curators, veterinarians, and zookeepers.* Some curators were found to be good at managing animals but weak at managing people. The keepers complained that curators did not always respond in a timely manner to their proposals and suggestions for improving animal care. Veterinarians had some of the same complaints as the keepers— that curators did not always see the need to consult with veterinarians on animal management issues. The task force also noted that some keepers and curators held grudges that they might not be able to put behind them.

  Curators complained that veterinarians undermined them through direct contact with the keepers. However, the task force noted that there was no defined communication path for keepers to raise concern with the veterinary staff. Moreover, experts throughout the zoo veterinary world stressed the importance of open communication between keepers and veterinarians so that vets can fulfill their obligations under the Fish and Wildlife Conservation Act.

  The task force concluded that there was a lack of communication among keepers, veterinarians, and curators that led to questionable care standards for the animals. Because departments of the zoo did not work closely together, there was not a good system of checks and balances to maintain appropriate care.

- *The biological program committee.* The Citizens' Task Force was particularly critical of the BPC, suggesting that many of the zoo's problems resulted from the creation of the BPC. The BPC created a mutual admiration society for the curators, and allowed the curators to overlook the concerns of keepers and the veterinarian staff. The board also found that there was no real accountability for decisions because of the committee structure.

- *Organizational structure.* The task force raised a number of questions about the current structure of the zoo, noting that communication issues, lack of teamwork, and lack of coordination were all factors that resulted in animal deaths, and were likely related to the current structure. During their investigation, they had asked Lau whether all individuals directly involved with animal care had reported to him. He claimed they did, until a member of the task force, pointing to the

organizational chart (see Exhibit 4), noted that the veterinarians and veterinarian technicians reported to the COO.

"It was largely the size of the group, and the number of people reporting to different people. We were trying to divide the zoo up so that neither Bob nor I [had too many]," Lau explained. "Money being what it is, we didn't want another high management position."

- *Employee conduct.* The task force found that there was a "lack of consistency, uniformity, accountability, and decisiveness in the enforcement of standards of conduct across departments" and that the Employee Relations department was not good at enforcing standards of conduct. A number of employees complained that those who worked hard were often expected to compensate for employees who underperformed.

  Employees are disciplined through a "five step" process. An employee can be terminated if he or she receives five written infractions within a 12-month period. The task force found this process so burdensome that employees were almost never terminated. In fact, Jennifer Fisher, employee relations director, told the task force that "no animal keepers or other non-managerial employees had been fired in the past 20 years."

A New Executive Director Takes Over

Emma Breslin began her position as the new executive director last week, nine months after the previous executive director retired.

Breslin's previous position was as executive director for the past 10 years at Maritimes Zoo, a smaller zoo with 51 employees, a general curator, and two contract veterinarians. Breslin had been hired by Maritimes Zoo to reunite a divided staff. She is known as a consensus leader, and at Maritimes Zoo she increased communication, improved supervisory skills, and taught employees to value each other's contributions to the successful operation of the zoo. Breslin was also successful in raising awareness among the community about why financial support from the public was so important to the zoo.

Breslin faces a large public relations problem as she begins her new job. She knows that much of the zoo's revenue is dependent upon public support. The next tax levy vote is three months from now. The zoo also raises significant revenue through the "Friends of the Zoo" program, an annual subscription program where people donate money to the zoo.

EXHIBIT 4   Organizational Chart of City Zoo, January 2014

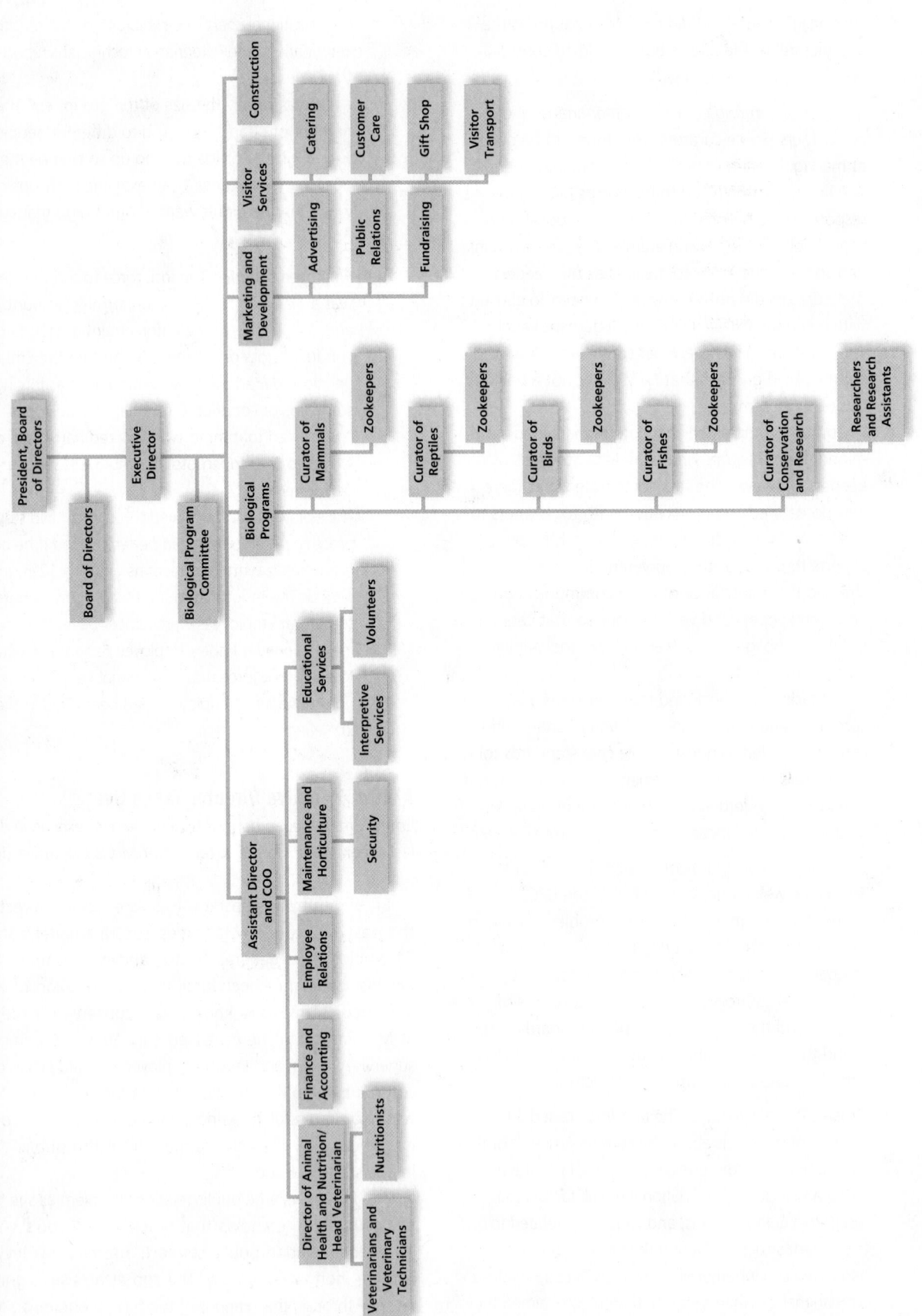

She needs to restore community trust. At the same time, she needs to grow zoo attendance levels, which have fallen in the past six months, and develop a strategic plan for the zoo.

Breslin also faces a very divided and demoralized staff. She has reviewed what was written in the press and familiarized herself with the Citizens' Task Force review. She knows she needs to bring some peace and stability to employee relations. Her most difficult task will be to unite the staff. She needs to build staff morale and gain their trust. She wonders how she will accomplish these goals over the next year. The outline of what she intends to do over the next six months to get things back on track is to be presented to the board in two weeks.

Discussion Questions

1. What can Emma Breslin do to restore trust and morale among the employees?

2. Should Breslin promote Wynona Singh to head (and attending) veterinarian or hire someone from outside?

3. What changes to the organizational structure could Breslin make to help foster a more positive work environment?

4. How might trust be restored among community members so that a positive outcome for the tax levy might occur?

ENDNOTES

Chapter 1

1 Opening vignette based on T. Tedesco, "Boardroom Culture Choking Lululemon," *National Post*, June 12, 2014, p. FP1; Z. Mcknight, "A Rare Look Behind the Luon Curtain," *Vancouver Sun*, August 17, 2013, p. D3; and M. Straus, "Labour Woes in Asia the Latest Snag for Lululemon," *Globe and Mail*, June 23, 2013.

2 See, for example, C. Heath and S. B. Sitkin, "Big-B versus Big-O: What Is *Organizational* about Organizational Behavior?" *Journal of Organizational Behavior* 22 (2001), pp. 43–58. For a review of what one eminent researcher believes *should* be included in organizational behaviour, based on survey data, see J. B. Miner, "The Rated Importance, Scientific Validity, and Practical Usefulness of Organizational Behavior Theories: A Quantitative Review," *Academy of Management Learning & Education* 2, no. 3 (September 2003), pp. 250–268.

3 Statistics Canada, *Canada Year Book 2010 Edition* (Ottawa: Minister of Industry, 2010); and Industry Canada, "Key Small Business Statistics—August 2013," modified September 10, 2013, http://www.ic.gc.ca/eic/site/061.nsf/eng/02804.html.

4 C. R. Farquhar and J. A. Longair, *Creating High-Performance Organizations with People*, Report R164–96 (Ottawa: The Conference Board of Canada, 1996).

5 American Management Association, "2012 Critical Skills Survey," January 30, 2013, http://www.amanet.org/uploaded/2012-Critical-Skills-Survey.pdf.

6 W. Immen, "People Skills Win Out, Survey Finds," *Globe and Mail*, October 23, 2009, p. B15.

7 See, for example, C. Penttila, "Hiring Hardships," *Entrepreneur*, October 2002, pp. 34–35.

8 These companies were named in the 100 Top Employers for 2014. See http://www.canadastop100.com/national/.

9 I. S. Fulmer, B. Gerhart, and K. S. Scott, "Are the 100 Best Better? An Empirical Investigation of the Relationship Between Being a 'Great Place to Work' and Firm Performance," *Personnel Psychology*, Winter 2003, pp. 965–993.

10 S. E. Humphrey, J. D. Nahrgang, and F. P. Morgeson, "Integrating Motivational, Social, and Contextual Work Design Features: A Meta-analytic Summary and Theoretical Extension of the Work Design Literature," *Journal of Applied Psychology* 92, no. 5 (2007), pp. 1332–1356.

11 E. R. Burris, "The Risks and Rewards of Speaking Up: Managerial Responses to Employee Voice," *Academy of Management Journal* 55, no. 4 (2012), pp. 851–875.

12 Families and Work Institute, *The 2002 National Study of the Changing Workforce* (New York: Author, 2002).

13 T. L. Miller, C. L. Wesley II, and D. E. Williams, "Educating the Minds of Caring Hearts: Comparing the Views of Practitioners and Educators on the Importance of Social Entrepreneurship Competencies," *Academy of Management Learning & Education* 2, no. 3 (2012), pp. 349–370.

14 H. Aguinis and A. Glavas, "What We Know and Don't Know About Corporate Social Responsibility: A Review and Research Agenda," *Journal of Management* (July 2012), pp. 932–968.

15 Vignette based on M. Straus, "Supplier of Too-Sheer Yoga Pants Insists It Stuck to Lululemon Design," *Globe and Mail*, March 19, 2013, http://www.theglobeandmail.com/globe-investor/supplier-of-too-sheer-yoga-pants-insists-it-stuck-to-lululemon-design/article9948948/; M. Lustrin and F. Patinkin, "Lululemon Founder Chip Wilson Blames Women's Bodies for Yoga Pant Problems, *ABC News*, November 7, 2013, http://abcnews.go.com/US/lululemon-founder-chip-wilson-blames-womens-bodies-yoga/story?id=20815278; and "Lululemon Pants Don't Work for Some Women: Founder," *Bloomberg TV*, November 5, 2013, http://www.bloomberg.com/video/lululemon-pants-don-t-work-for-some-women-founder-ATKjgs7jQduIr_ou1z8XYg.html.

16 M. Warner, "Organizational Behavior Revisited," *Human Relations*, October 1994, pp. 1151–1166.

17 Based on W. Chuang and B. Lee, "An Empirical Evaluation of the Overconfidence Hypothesis," *Journal of Banking and Finance*, September 2006, pp. 2489–2515; and A. R. Drake, J. Wong, and S. B. Salter, "Empowerment, Motivation, and Performance: Examining the Impact of Feedback and Incentives on Nonmanagement Employees," *Behavioral Research in Accounting* 19 (2007), pp. 71–89.

18 D. M. Rousseau and S. McCarthy, "Educating Managers from an Evidence-Based Perspective," *Academy of Management Learning & Education* 6, no. 1 (2007), pp. 84–101; and S. L. Rynes, T. L. Giluk, and K. G. Brown, "The Very Separate Worlds of Academic and Practitioner Periodicals in Human Resource Management: Implications for Evidence-Based Management," *Academy of Management Journal* 50, no. 5 (2007), pp. 987–1008.

19 J. and S. Welch, "When to Go with Your Gut," *LinkedIn*, November 12, 2013, https://www.linkedin.com/pulse/article/20131112125301-86541065-when-to-go-with-your-gut.

20 J. Surowiecki, "The Fatal-Flaw Myth," *New Yorker*, July 31, 2006, p. 25.

21 A. McAfee and E. Brynjolfsson, "Big Data: The Management Revolution," *Harvard Business Review* (October 2012), pp. 59–68.

22 N. Bloom, R. Sadun, and J. Van Reenan, "How Three Essential Practices Can Address Even the Most Complex Global Practices," *Harvard Business Review*, November 2012, pp. 77–82.

23 M. J. Mauboussin, "Most Companies Use the Wrong Metrics. Don't Be One of Them," *Harvard Business Review* (October 2012), pp. 46–56.

24 Vignette based on Z. Mcknight, "A Rare Look at the Luon Empire of Lululemon," *Vancouver Sun*, August 17, 2013, p. D3, http://o.canada.com/business/a-rare-look-at-the-luon-empire-of-lululemon.

25 D. Flavelle, "Rona Sees Growth Here: Home Reno Sales Flat during Make-or-Break Season but Canadian Retailer Keeps Faith in Diversification," *Toronto Star*, April 20, 2011, p. B1; and N. Van Praet, "Rona Shares Rise To Price Offered By Lowe's Two Years Ago," *Financial Post*, August 27, 2014.

26 Based on "Yum! Restaurants China," Yum! Brands, http://www.yum.com/brands/china.asp

27 See, for example, R. R. Thomas Jr., "From Affirmative Action to Affirming Diversity," *Harvard Business Review*, March–April 1990, pp. 107–117; B. Mandrell and S. Kohler-Gray, "Management Development That Values Diversity," *Personnel*, March 1990, pp. 41–47; J. Dreyfuss, "Get Ready for the New Work Force," *Fortune*, April 23, 1990, pp. 165–181; and I. Wielawski, "Diversity Makes Both Dollars and Sense," *Los Angeles Times*, May 16, 1994, p. II3.

28 Based on http://www.eluta.ca/jobs-at-sasktel#diversity:diversity-more; http://www.sasktel.com/wps/wcm/connect/content/home/about-sasktel/news/2012/sasktel-connects-8-more-first-nations-to-hs-internet; http://itac.ca/itaconline/aug09_online_full.html; and http://www.ammsa.com/publications/windspeaker/aboriginal-people-will-make-nearly-one-quarter-saskatchewan%E2%80%99s-population.

29 June 2011 figures, as reported at http://www.statcan.gc.ca/subjects-sujets/labour-travail/lfs-epa/t110708a2-eng.htm.

30 See, for example, M. Workman and W. Bommer, "Redesigning Computer Call Center Work: A Longitudinal Field Experiment," *Journal of Organizational Behavior*, May 2004, pp. 317–337.

31 See, for example, V. S. Major, K. J. Klein, and M. G. Ehrhart, "Work Time, Work Interference with Family, and Psychological Distress," *Journal of Applied Psychology*, June 2002, pp. 427–436; D. Brady, "Rethinking the Rat Race," *BusinessWeek*, August 26, 2002, pp. 142–143; and J. M. Brett and L. K. Stroh, "Working 61 Plus Hours a Week: Why Do Managers Do It?" *Journal of Applied Psychology*, February 2003, pp. 67–78.

32 E. J. Hirst, "Burnout on the Rise," *Chicago Tribune*, October 19, 2012, http://articles.chicagotribune.com/2012-10-29/business/ct-biz-1029-employee-burnout-20121029_1_employee-burnout-herbert-freudenberger-employee-stress.

33 S. Shellenbarger, "Single and Off the Fast Track," *Wall Street Journal*, May 23, 2012, pp. D1, D3.

34 M. Mithel, "What Women Want," *Business Today*, March 8, 2013, http://businesstoday.intoday.in/story/careers-work-life-balance-women/1/193135.html.

35 Based on C. Atchison, "Secrets of Canada's Best Bosses," *PROFIT*, February 16, 2011, http://www.profitguide.com/manage-grow/leadership/secrets-of-canada%E2%80%99s-best-bosses-30084.

36 D. S. Ones and S. Dilchert, "Environmental Sustainability at Work: A Call to Action," *Industrial and Organizational Psychology* 5 (2012), pp. 444–466.

37 C. Hymowitz, "CEOs Value Pragmatists with Broad, Positive Views," *Wall Street Journal*, January 27, 2003.

38 F. Luthans and C. M. Youssef, "Emerging Positive Organizational Behavior," *Journal of Management*, June 2007, pp. 321–349; C. M. Youssef and F. Luthans, "Positive Organizational Behavior in the Workplace: The Impact of Hope, Optimism, and Resilience," *Journal of Management* 33, no. 5 (2007), pp. 774–800; J. E. Dutton and S. Sonenshein, "Positive Organizational Scholarship," in *Encyclopedia of Positive Psychology*, ed. C. Cooper and J. Barling (Thousand Oaks, CA: Sage, 2007); A. M. Saks and J. A. Gruman, "Organizational Socialization and Positive Organizational Behaviour: Implications for Theory, Research, and Practice," *Canadian Journal of Administrative Sciences* 28, no. 1 (2011), pp. 4–16; and E. K. Loway, "Positive Organizational Scholarship," *Canadian Journal of Administrative Sciences* 28, no. 1 (2011), pp. 1–3.

39 L. M. Roberts, G. Spreitzer, J. Dutton, R. Quinn, E. Heaphy, and B. Barker, "How to Play to Your Strengths," *Harvard Business Review*, January 2005, pp. 1–6; and L. M. Roberts, J. E. Dutton, G. M. Spreitzer, E. D. Heaphy, and R. E. Quinn, "Composing the Reflected Best-Self Portrait: Becoming Extraordinary in Work Organizations," *Academy of Management Review* 30, no. 4 (2005), pp. 712–736.

40 D. M. Mayer, M. Kuenzi, R. Greenbaum, M. Bardes, and R. Salvador, "How Low Does Ethical Leadership Flow? Test of a Trickle-Down Model," *Organizational Behavior and Human Decision Processes* 108, no. 1 (2009), pp. 1–13; and A. Ardichvili, J. A. Mitchell, and D. Jondle, "Characteristics of Ethical Business Cultures," *Journal of Business Ethics* 85, no. 4 (2009), pp. 445–451.

41 D. W. Organ, *Organizational Citizenship Behavior: The Good Soldier Syndrome* (Lexington, MA: Lexington Books, 1988), p. 4.

42 M. G. Ehrhart and S. E. Naumann, "Organizational Citizenship Behavior in Work Groups: A Group Norms Approach," *Journal of Applied Psychology* 89, no. 6 (2004), pp. 960–974.

43 "Corporate Culture," *Canadian HR Reporter* 17, no. 21 (2004), pp. 7–11.

44 See, for example, P. M. Podsakoff, S. B. MacKenzie, J. B. Paine, and D. G. Bachrach, "Organizational Citizenship Behaviors: A Critical Review of the Theoretical and Empirical Literature and Suggestions for Future Research," *Journal of Management* 26, no. 3 (2000), pp. 543–548; and S. W. Whiting, P. M. Podsakoff, and J. R. Pierce, "Effects of Task Performance, Helping, Voice, and Organizational Loyalty on Performance Appraisal Ratings," *Journal of Applied Psychology* 93, no. 1 (2008), pp. 125–139.

45 L. Nguyen, "Canadian Economy Loses $16.6B Annually Due to Absenteeism," *Toronto Star*, September 23, 2013.

46 W. Hoge, "Sweden's Cradle-to-Grave Welfare Starts to Get Ill," *International Herald Tribune*, September 25, 2002, p. 8.

47 See, for example, M. C. Sturman and C. O. Trevor, "The Implications of Linking the Dynamic Performance and Turnover Literatures," *Journal of Applied Psychology* 86, no. 4 (August 2001), pp. 684–696.

48 M. Casey-Campbell and M. L. Martens, "Sticking It All Together: A Critical Assessment of the Group Cohesion-Performance Literature," *International Journal of Management Reviews* 11, no. 2 (2008), pp. 223–246.

49 A. J. Rucci, S. P. Kirn, and R. T. Quinn, "The Employee–Customer–Profit Chain at Sears," *Harvard Business Review*, January–February 1998, pp. 83–97.

50 Based on C. Duhigg and K. Bradsher, "How U.S. Lost Out on iPhone Work," *New York Times*, January 22, 2013, pp. A1, A22–A23; H. Gao, "How the Apple Confrontation Divides China," *Atlantic*, April 8, 2013, http://www.theatlantic.com/china/archive/2013/04/how-the-apple-confrontation-divides-china/274764/; and A. Satariano, "Apple Slowdown Threatens $30 Billion Global Supplier Web," *Bloomberg*, http://www.bloomberg.com/news/2013-04-18/apple-slowdown-threatens-30-billion-global-supplier-web-tech.html.

51 Based on P. Coy, M. Conlin, and M. Herbst, "The Disposable Worker," *Bloomberg Businessweek*, January 7, 2010, http://www.businessweek.com; S. Tully, "Fortune 500: Profits Bounce Back," *Fortune*, May 3, 2010, pp. 140–144; D. Ariely, "You Are What You Measure," *Harvard Business Review*, June 2010, p. 38; and M. Straus, "Labour Woes in Asia the Latest Snag for Lululemon," *Globe and Mail*, June 23, 2013.

52 R. E. Quinn, *Beyond Rational Management: Mastering the Paradoxes and Competing Demands of High Performance* (San Francisco: Jossey-Bass, 1991); R. E. Quinn, S. R. Faerman, M. P. Thompson, and M. R. McGrath, *Becoming a Master Manager: A Competency Framework* (New York: Wiley, 1990); and K. Cameron and R. E. Quinn, *Diagnosing and Changing Organizational Culture: Based on the Competing Values Framework* (Reading, MA: Addison Wesley Longman, 1999).

53 R. E. Quinn, S. R. Faerman, M. P. Thompson, and M. R. McGrath, *Becoming a Master Manager: A Competency Framework* (New York: Wiley, 1990).

54 D. Maley, "Canada's Top Women CEOs," *Maclean's*, October 20, 1997, pp. 52 passim.

55 Written by Nancy Langton and Joy Begley, copyright 1999. (The events described are based on an actual situation, although the participants, as well as the centre, have been disguised.)

Chapter 2

1 Opening vignette based on D. Eng, "Freshii's Fresh Take on Fast Food," *Fortune*, April 11, 2013, http://fortune.com/2013/04/11/freshiis-fresh-take-on-fast-food/; M. Brandau, "Freshii CEO Discusses Move into China," *Restaurant News*, January 3, 2013, http://nrn.com/international/freshii-ceo-discusses-move-china; "Freshii CEO: How 'Undercover Boss' Changed My Business," *Business Insider*, March 7, 2013, http://www.bullfax.com/?q=node-freshii-ceo-how-undercover-boss-changed-my-business; and

K. Martonik, "Freshii CEO Matthew Corrin on Undercover Boss," *Fransmart* (blog), March 14, 2013, http://fransmart.com/blog/55/Freshii-CEO-Matthew-Corrin-on-Undercover-Boss.html.

2   B. Nyhan and J. Reifler, "When Corrections Fail: The Persistence of Political Misperceptions," *Political Behavior* 32, no. 2 (2010), pp. 303–330.

3   D. Wood, P. Harms, and S. Vazire, "Perceiver Effects as Projective Tests: What Your Perceptions of Others Say About You," *Journal of Personality and Social Psychology* 99, no. 1 (2010), pp. 174–190.

4   H. H. Kelley, "Attribution in Social Interaction," in *Attribution: Perceiving the Causes of Behavior*, ed. E. Jones, D. Kanouse, H. Kelley, N. Nisbett, S. Valins, and B. Weiner (Morristown, NJ: General Learning Press, 1972); and M. J. Martinko, P. Harvey, and M. T. Dasborough, "Attribution Theory in the Organizational Sciences: A Case of Unrealized Potential," *Journal of Organizational Behavior* 32, no. 1 (2011), pp. 144–149.

5   See L. Ross, "The Intuitive Psychologist and His Shortcomings," in *Advances in Experimental Social Psychology*, vol. 10, ed. L. Berkowitz (Orlando, FL: Academic Press, 1977), pp. 174–220; and A. G. Miller and T. Lawson, "The Effect of an Informational Option on the Fundamental Attribution Error," *Personality and Social Psychology Bulletin*, June 1989, pp. 194–204.

6   M. J. Young, M. W. Morris, and V. M. Scherwin, "Managerial Mystique: Magical Thinking in Judgments of Managers' Vision, Charisma, and Magnetism," *Journal of Management* 39, no. 4 (May 2013), pp. 1044–1061.

7   Columbia Business School, "Dynamics behind Magical Thinking and Charismatic Leadership Revealed," *ScienceDaily*, July 15, 2011.

8   N. Epley and D. Dunning, "Feeling 'Holier Than Thou': Are Self-Serving Assessments Produced by Errors in Self- or Social Predictions?" *Journal of Personality and Social Psychology* 79, no. 6 (2000), pp. 861–875.

9   M. C. Frame, K. J. Roberto, A. E. Schwab, and C. T. Harris, "What Is Important on the Job? Differences across Gender, Perspective, and Job Level," *Journal of Applied Social Psychology* 40, no. 1 (January 2010), pp. 36–56.

10   Based on N. Hall, "Lawyer Awarded $100,000 by B.C. Human Rights Tribunal for Discrimination," *Vancouver Sun*, July 18, 2011; and *Gichuru v. The Law Society of British Columbia* (No. 9), 2011 BCHRT 185, https://www.canlii.org/en/bc/bchrt/doc/2011/2011bchrt185/2011bchrt185.html.

11   See K. R. Murphy, R. A. Jako, and R. L. Anhalt, "Nature and Consequences of Halo Error: A Critical Analysis," *Journal of Applied Psychology*, April 1993, pp. 218–225; P. Rosenzweig, *The Halo Effect* (New York: Free Press, 2007); I. Dennis, "Halo Effects in Grading Student Projects," *Journal of Applied Psychology* 92, no. 4 (2007), pp. 1169–1176; and C. E. Naquin and R. O. Tynan, "The Team Halo Effect: Why Teams Are Not Blamed for Their Failures," *Journal of Applied Psychology*, April 2003, pp. 332–340.

12   S. E. Asch, "Forming Impressions of Personality," *Journal of Abnormal and Social Psychology*, July 1946, pp. 258–290.

13   "UVic Grad Student Launches First Nations Music Website," *Times Colonist* (Victoria), October 23, 2011.

14   See, for example, G. N. Powell, "The Good Manager: Business Students' Stereotypes of Japanese Managers versus Stereotypes of American Managers," *Group & Organization Management*, March 1992, pp. 44–56; C. Ostroff and L. E. Atwater, "Does Whom You Work with Matter? Effects of Referent Group Gender and Age Composition on Managers' Compensation," *Journal of Applied Psychology*, August 2003, pp. 725–740; M. E. Heilman, A. S. Wallen, D. Fuchs, and M. M. Tamkins, "Penalties for Success: Reactions to Women Who Succeed at Male Gender-Typed Tasks," *Journal of Applied Psychology*, June 2004, pp. 416–427; and R. A. Posthuma and M. A. Campion, "Age Stereotypes in the Workplace: Common Stereotypes, Moderators, and Future Research Directions," *Journal of Management* 35, no. 1 (2009), pp. 158–188.

15   J. L. Eberhardt, P. G. Davies, V. J. Purdic-Vaughns, and S. L. Johnson, "Looking Deathworthy: Perceived Stereotypicality of Black Defendants Predicts Capital-Sentencing Outcomes," *Psychological Science* 17, no. 5 (2006), pp. 383–386.

16   Based on A. C. Kay, M. V. Day, M. P. Zanna, and A. D. Nussbaum, "The Insidious (and Ironic) Effects of Positive Stereotypes," *Journal of Experimental Social Psychology* 49 (2013), pp. 287–291; J. O. Sly and S. Cheryan, "When Compliments Fail to Flatter: American Individualism and Responses to Positive Stereotypes," *Journal of Personality and Social Psychology* 104 (2013), pp. 87–102; M. J. Tagler, "Choking Under the Pressure of a Positive Stereotype: Gender Identification and Self-Consciousness Moderate Men's Math Test Performance," *Journal of Social Psychology* 152 (2012), pp. 401–416; M. A. Beasley and M. J. Fischer, "Why They Leave: The Impact of Stereotype Threat on the Attrition of Women and Minorities from Science, Math and Engineering Majors," *Social Psychology of Education* 15 (2012), pp. 427–448; and A. Krendl, I. Gainsburg, and N. Ambady, "The Effects of Stereotypes and Observer Pressure on Athletic Performance," *Journal of Sport & Exercise Psychology* 34 (2012), pp. 3–15.

17   J. D. Remedios, A. L. Chasteen, and J. D. Paek, "Not All Prejudices Are Experienced Equally: Comparing Experiences of Racism and Sexism in Female Minorities," *Group Processes & Intergroup Relations*, June 11, 2011, published online before print, http://ir.lib.uwo.ca/cgi/viewcontent.cgi?article=1952&context=etd.

18   K. A. Martin, A. R. Sinden, and J. C. Fleming, "Inactivity May Be Hazardous to Your Image: The Effects of Exercise Participation on Impression Formation," *Journal of Sport & Exercise Psychology* 22, no. 4 (December 2000), pp. 283–291.

19   F. Yuan and R. W. Woodman, "Innovative Behavior in the Workplace: The Role of Performance and Image Outcome Expectations," *Academy of Management Journal* 53, no. 2 (2010), pp. 323–342.

20   J. K. Harter, F. L. Schmidt, J. W. Asplund, E. A. Killham, and S. Agrawal, "Causal Impact of Employee Work Perceptions on the Bottom Line of Organizations," *Perspectives on Psychological Science* 5, no. 4 (2010), pp. 378–389.

21   Y. H. Kim, C. Y. Chiu, and Z. Zou, "Know Thyself: Misperceptions of Actual Performance Undermine Achievement Motivation, Future Performance, and Subjective Well-Being," *Journal of Personality and Social Psychology* 99, no. 3 (2010), pp. 395–409.

22   H. G. Heneman III and T. A. Judge, *Staffing Organizations* (Middleton, WI: Mendota House, 2006).

23   J. Willis and A. Todorov, "First Impressions: Making Up Your Mind after a 100ms Exposure to a Face," *Psychological Science*, July 2006, pp. 592–598.

24   N. Eisenkraft, "Accurate by Way of Aggregation: Should You Trust Your Intuition-Based First Impressions?" *Journal of Experimental Social Psychology*, March 2013, pp. 277–279.

25   See, for example, K. F. E. Wong and J. Y. Y. Kwong, "Effects of Rater Goals on Rating Patterns: Evidence from an Experimental Field Study," *Journal of Applied Psychology* 92, no. 2 (2007), pp. 577–585; and S. E. DeVoe and S. S. Iyengar, "Managers' Theories of Subordinates: A Cross-Cultural Examination of Manager Perceptions of Motivation and Appraisal of Performance," *Organizational Behavior and Human Decision Processes*, January 2004, pp. 47–61.

26   D. B. McNatt and T. A. Judge, "Boundary Conditions of the Galatea Effect: A Field Experiment and Constructive Replication," *Academy of Management Journal*, August 2004, pp. 550–565; O. B. Davidson and D. Eden, "Remedial Self-Fulfilling Prophecy: Two Field Experiments to Prevent Golem Effects among Disadvantaged Women," *Journal of Applied Psychology*, June 2000, pp. 386–398; D. Eden, "Self-Fulfilling Prophecies in Organizations," in *Organizational Behavior: The State of the Science*, 2nd ed., ed. J. Greenberg (Mahwah, NJ: Lawrence Erlbaum, 2003), pp. 91–122; and G. Natanovich and D. Eden, "Pygmalion Effects among

Outreach Supervisors and Tutors: Extending Sex Generalizability," *Journal of Applied Psychology* 93, no. 6 (2008), pp. 1382–1389.

27 See, for example, K. F. E. Wong and J. Y. Y. Kwong, "Effects of Rater Goals on Rating Patterns: Evidence from an Experimental Field Study," *Journal of Applied Psychology* 92, no. 2 (2007), pp. 577–585; and S. E. DeVoe and S. S. Iyengar, "Managers' Theories of Subordinates: A Cross-Cultural Examination of Manager Perceptions of Motivation and Appraisal of Performance," *Organizational Behavior and Human Decision Processes*, January 2004, pp. 47–61.

28 Vignette based on L. Evans, "When Founding a Company with No Experience Isn't A Huge Mistake," *FastCompany.com*, May 15, 2014, http://www.fastcompany.com/3030569/hit-the-ground-running/when-founding-a-company-with-no-experience-isnt-a-huge-mistake; "Freshii Founder's 5-Part Operating Manifesto," *Inc.*, March 28, 2013, http://www.inc.com/matthew-corrin/freshii-operating-manifesto.html; and "Toronto through the Eyes of Freshii Founder Matthew Corrin," *BlogTO*, http://www.blogto.com/people/2009/09/toronto_through_the_eyes_of_freshii_founder_matthew_corrin/, September 13, 2009.

29 G. W. Allport, *Personality: A Psychological Interpretation* (New York: Holt, Rinehart and Winston, 1937), p. 48.

30 K. I. van der Zee, J. N. Zaal, and J. Piekstra, "Validation of the Multicultural Personality Questionnaire in the Context of Personnel Selection," *European Journal of Personality* 17 (2003), pp. S77–S100.

31 S. A. Birkeland, T. M. Manson, J. L. Kisamore, M. T. Brannick, and M. A. Smith, "A Meta-analytic Investigation of Job Applicant Faking on Personality Measures," *International Journal of Selection and Assessment* 14, no. 14 (2006), pp. 317–335.

32 T. A. Judge, C. A. Higgins, C. J. Thoresen, and M. R. Barrick, "The Big Five Personality Traits, General Mental Ability, and Career Success across the Life Span," *Personnel Psychology* 52, no. 3 (1999), pp. 621–652.

33 See R. Illies, R. D. Arvey, and T. J. Bouchard, "Darwinism, Behavioral Genetics, and Organizational Behavior: A Review and Agenda for Future Research," *Journal of Organizational Behavior* 27, no. 2 (2006), pp. 121–141; and W. Johnson, E. Turkheimer, I. I. Gottesman, and T. J. Bouchard, Jr., "Beyond Heritability: Twin Studies in Behavioral Research," *Current Directions in Psychological Science* 18, no. 4 (2009), pp. 217–220.

34 B. Benyamin, B. Pourcain, O. S. Davis, G. Davies, N. K. Hansell, M. J. Brion, R. M. Kirkpatrick, R. A. M. Cents, S. Franić, M. B. Miller, C. M. A. Haworth, E. Meaburn, T. S. Price, D. M. Evans, N. Timpson, J. Kemp, S. Ring, W. McArdle, S. E. Medland, J. Yang, S. E. Harris, D. C. Liewald, P. Scheet, X. Xiao, J. J. Hudziak, E. J. C. de Geus, Wellcome Trust Case Control Consortium 2 (WTCCC2), V. W. V. Jaddoe, J. M. Starr, F. C. Verhulst, C. Pennell, H. Tiemeier, W. G. Iacono, L. J. Palmer, G. W. Montgomery, N. G. Martin, D. I. Boomsma, D. Posthuma, M. McGue, M. J. Wright, G. Davey Smith, I. J. Deary, R. Plomin, and P. M. Visscher, "Childhood Intelligence Is Heritable, Highly Polygenic and Associated with FNBP1L," *Molecular Psychiatry* 19 (2014), pp. 253–258.

35 O. S. P. Davis, G. Band, M. Pirinen, C. M. A. Haworth, E. L. Meaburn, Y. Kovas, N. Harlaar, S. J. Docherty, K. B. Hanscombe, M. Trzaskowski, Charles J. C. Curtis, A. Strange, C. Freeman, C. Bellenguez, Z. Su, R. Pearson, D. Vukcevic, C. Langford, P. Deloukas, S. Hunt, E. Gray, S. Dronov, S. C. Potter, A. Tashakkori-Ghanbaria, S. Edkins, S. J. Bumpstead, J. M. Blackwell, E. Bramon, M. A. Brown, J. P. Casas, A. Corvin, A. Duncanson, J. A. Z. Jankowski, H. S. Markus, C. G. Mathew, C. N. A. Palmer, A. Rautanen, S. J. Sawcer, R. C. Trembath, A. C. Viswanathan, N. W. Wood, I. Barroso, L. Peltonen, P. S. Dale, S. A. Petrill, L. S. Schalkwyk, I. W. Craig, C. M. Lewis, T. S. Price, The Wellcome Trust Case Control Consortium, P. Donnelly, R. Plomin, and C. A. Spencer, "The Correlation between Reading and Mathematics Ability at Age Twelve Has a Substantial Genetic Component,"

Nature Communications 5 (2014), p. 4204, http://www.nature.com/ncomms/2014/140708/ncomms5204/full/ncomms5204.html.

36 S. Srivastava, O. P. John, and S. D. Gosling, "Development of Personality in Early and Middle Adulthood: Set Like Plaster or Persistent Change?" *Journal of Personality and Social Psychology*, May 2003, pp. 1041–1053; and B. W. Roberts, K. E. Walton, and W. Viechtbauer, "Patterns of Mean-Level Change in Personality Traits across the Life Course: A Meta-analysis of Longitudinal Studies," *Psychological Bulletin* 132, no. 1 (2006), pp. 1–25.

37 S. E. Hampson and L. R. Goldberg, "A First Large Cohort Study of Personality Trait Stability over the 40 Years between Elementary School and Midlife," *Journal of Personality and Social Psychology* 91, no. 4 (2006), pp. 763–779.

38 See A. H. Buss, "Personality as Traits," *American Psychologist*, November 1989, pp. 1378–1388; and D. G. Winter, O. P. John, A. J. Stewart, E. C. Klohnen, and L. E. Duncan, "Traits and Motives: Toward an Integration of Two Traditions in Personality Research," *Psychological Review*, April 1998, pp. 230–250.

39 See, for instance, G. W. Allport and H. S. Odbert, "Trait Names, A Psycholexical Study," *Psychological Monographs* 47, no. 211 (1936); and R. B. Cattell, "Personality Pinned Down," *Psychology Today*, July 1973, pp. 40–46.

40 R. B. Kennedy and D. A. Kennedy, "Using the Myers-Briggs Type Indicator in Career Counseling," *Journal of Employment Counseling*, March 2004, pp. 38–44.

41 See, for instance, D. J. Pittenger, "Cautionary Comments Regarding the Myers-Briggs Type Indicator," *Consulting Psychology Journal: Practice and Research*, Summer 2005, pp. 210–221; L. Bess and R. J. Harvey, "Bimodal Score Distributions and the Myers-Briggs Type Indicator: Fact or Artifact?" *Journal of Personality Assessment*, February 2002, pp. 176–186; R. M. Capraro and M. M. Capraro, "Myers-Briggs Type Indicator Score Reliability across Studies: A Meta-analytic Reliability Generalization Study," *Educational and Psychological Measurement*, August 2002, pp. 590–602; and R. C. Arnau, B. A. Green, D. H. Rosen, D. H. Gleaves, and J. G. Melancon, "Are Jungian Preferences Really Categorical? An Empirical Investigation Using Taxometric Analysis," *Personality and Individual Differences*, January 2003, pp. 233–251.

42 M. R. Barrick and M. K. Mount, "Yes, Personality Matters: Moving On to More Important Matters," *Human Performance* 18, no. 4 (2005), pp. 359–372.

43 W. Fleeson and P. Gallagher, "The Implications of Big Five Standing for the Distribution of Trait Manifestation in Behavior: Fifteen Experience-Sampling Studies and a Meta-analysis," *Journal of Personality and Social Psychology* 97, no. 6 (2009), pp. 1097–1114.

44 J. B. Hirsh and J. B. Peterson, "Predicting Creativity and Academic Success with a 'Fake-Proof' Measure of the Big Five," *Journal of Research in Personality* 42 (2008), pp. 1323–1333.

45 "New Fake-Proof Personality Test Created," *ScienceDaily*, October 8, 2008, http://www.-sciencedaily.-com/-releases/-2008/-10/-081007102849.-htm.

46 See, for instance, M. R. Barrick and M. K. Mount, "The Big Five Personality Dimensions and Job Performance: A Meta-analysis," *Personnel Psychology*, Spring 1991, pp. 1–26; G. M. Hurtz and J. J. Donovan, "Personality and Job Performance: The Big Five Revisited," *Journal of Applied Psychology*, December 2000, pp. 869–879; J. Hogan and B. Holland, "Using Theory to Evaluate Personality and Job-Performance Relations: A Socioanalytic Perspective," *Journal of Applied Psychology*, February 2003, pp. 100–112; and M. R. Barrick and M. K. Mount, "Select on Conscientiousness and Emotional Stability," in *Handbook of Principles of Organizational Behavior*, ed. E. A. Locke (Malden, MA: Blackwell, 2004), pp. 15–28.

47 M. K. Mount, M. R. Barrick, and J. P. Strauss, "Validity of Observer Ratings of the Big Five Personality Factors," *Journal of Applied Psychology*, April 1994, p. 272. Additionally confirmed by G. M. Hurtz and J. J. Donovan, "Personality and Job Performance: The

Big Five Revisited," *Journal of Applied Psychology* 85 (2000), pp. 869–879; and M. R. Barrick, M. K. Mount, and T. A. Judge, "The FFM Personality Dimensions and Job Performance: Meta-analysis of Meta-analyses," *International Journal of Selection and Assessment* 9 (2001), pp. 9–30.

48 S. J. Motowidlo, M. P. Martin, and A. E. Crook, "Relations between Personality, Knowledge, and Behavior in Professional Service Encounters," *Journal of Applied Social Psychology* 43, no. 9 (2013), pp. 1851–1861.

49 A. E. Poropat, "A Meta-analysis of the Five-Factor Model of Personality and Academic Performance," *Psychological Bulletin* 135, no. 2 (2009), pp. 322–338.

50 F. L. Schmidt and J. E. Hunter, "The Validity and Utility of Selection Methods in *Personnel Psychology*: Practical and Theoretical Implications of 85 Years of Research Findings," *Psychological Bulletin*, September 1998, p. 272.

51 A. M. Cianci, H. J. Klein, and G. H. Seijts, "The Effect of Negative Feedback on Tension and Subsequent Performance: The Main and Interactive Effects of Goal Content and Conscientiousness," *Journal of Applied Psychology* 95, no. 4 (2010), pp. 618–630.

52 H. Le, I. Oh, S. B. Robbins, R. Ilies, E. Holland, and P. Westrick, "Too Much of a Good Thing: Curvilinear Relationships between Personality Traits and Job Performance," *Journal of Applied Psychology* 96, no. 1 (2011), pp. 113–133.

53 T. Bogg and B. W. Roberts, "Conscientiousness and Health-Related Behaviors: A Meta-analysis of the Leading Behavioral Contributors to Mortality," *Psychological Bulletin* 130, no. 6 (2004), pp. 887–919.

54 G. J. Feist, "A Meta-analysis of Personality in Scientific and Artistic Creativity," *Personality and Social Psychology Review* 2, no. 4 (1998), pp. 290–309; C. Robert and Y. H. Cheung, "An Examination of the Relationship Between Conscientiousness and Group Performance on a Creative Task," *Journal of Research in Personality* 44, no. 2 (2010), pp. 222–231; and M. Batey, T. Chamorro-Premuzic, and A. Furnham, "Individual Differences in Ideational Behavior: Can the Big Five and Psychometric Intelligence Predict Creativity Scores?" *Creativity Research Journal* 22, no. 1 (2010), pp. 90–97.

55 R. J. Foti and M. A. Hauenstein, "Pattern and Variable Approaches in Leadership Emergence and Effectiveness," *Journal of Applied Psychology*, March 2007, pp. 347–355.

56 L. I. Spirling and R. Persaud, "Extraversion as a Risk Factor," *Journal of the American Academy of Child and Adolescent Psychiatry* 42, no. 2 (2003), p. 130.

57 B. Weiss and R. S. Feldman, "Looking Good and Lying to Do It: Deception as an Impression Management Strategy in Job Interviews," *Journal of Applied Social Psychology* 36, no. 4 (2006), pp. 1070–1086.

58 J. A. LePine, J. A. Colquitt, and A. Erez, "Adaptability to Changing Task Contexts: Effects of General Cognitive Ability, Conscientiousness, and Openness to Experience," *Personnel Psychology* 53 (2000), pp. 563–595.

59 S. Clarke and I. Robertson, "An Examination of the Role of Personality in Accidents Using Meta-analysis," *Applied Psychology: An International Review* 57, no. 1 (2008), pp. 94–108.

60 R. Ilies, I. S. Fulmer, M. Spitzmuller, and M. D. Johnson, "Personality and Citizenship Behavior: The Mediating Role of Job Satisfaction," *Journal of Applied Psychology* 94, no. 4 (2009), pp. 945–959.

61 J. F. Rauthmann, "The Dark Triad and Interpersonal Perception: Similarities and Differences in the Social Consequences of Narcissism, Machiavellianism, and Psychopathy," *Social Psychological and Personality Science* 3 (2012), pp. 487–496.

62 P. K. Jonason, S. Slomski, and J. Partyka, "The Dark Triad at Work: How Toxic Employees Get Their Way," *Personality and Individual Differences* 52 (2012), pp. 449–453.

63 E. H. O'Boyle, D. R. Forsyth, G. C. Banks, and M. A. McDaniel, "A Meta-analysis of the Dark Triad and Work Behavior: A Social

Exchange Perspective," *Journal of Applied Psychology* 97 (2012), pp. 557–579.

64 L. Zhang, and M. A. Gowan, "Corporate Social Responsibility, Applicants' Individual Traits, and Organizational Attraction: A Person–Organization Fit Perspective," *Journal of Business and Psychology* 27 (2012), pp. 345–362.

65 D. N. Hartog and F. D. Belschak, "Work Engagement and Machiavellianism in the Ethical Leadership Process," *Journal of Business Ethics* 107 (2012), pp. 35–47.

66 J. J. Sosik, J. U. Chun, and W. Zhu, "Hang On to Your Ego: The Moderating Role of Leader Narcissism on Relationships between Leader Charisma and Follower Psychological Empowerment and Moral Identity," *Journal of Business Ethics*, February 12, 2013; and B. M. Galvin, D. A. Waldman, and P. Balthazard, "Visionary Communication Qualities as Mediators of the Relationship between Narcissism and Attributions of Leader Charisma," *Personnel Psychology* 63, no. 3 (2010), pp. 509–537.

67 C. Andreassen, H. Ursin, H. Eriksen, and S. Pallesen, "The Relationship of Narcissism with Workaholism, Work Engagement, and Professional Position," *Social Behavior and Personality* 40, no. 6 (2012), pp. 881–890.

68 K. A. Byrne and D. A. Worthy, "Do Narcissists Make Better Decisions? An Investigation of Narcissism and Dynamic Decision-Making Performance," *Personality and Individual Differences*, July 2013, pp. 112–117.

69 B. J. Hoffman, S. E. Strang, K. W. Kuhnert, W. K. Campbell, C. L. Kennedy, and A. LoPilato, "Leader Narcissism and Ethical Context: Effects on Ethical Leadership and Leader Effectiveness," *Journal of Leadership & Organizational Studies* 20 (2013), pp. 25–37.

70 M. Maccoby, "Narcissistic Leaders: The Incredible Pros, the Inevitable Cons," *Harvard Business Review*, January–February 2000, pp. 69–77, http://www.maccoby.com/Articles/NarLeaders.shtml.

71 A. Chatterjee and D. C. Hambrick, "Executive Personality, Capability Cues, and Risk Taking: How Narcissistic CEOs React to Their Successes and Stumbles," *Administrative Science Quarterly* 56 (2011), pp. 202–237.

72 C. J. Resick, D. S. Whitman, S. M. Weingarden, and N. J. Hiller, "The Bright-Side and Dark-Side of CEO Personality: Examining Core Self-Evaluations, Narcissism, Transformational Leadership, and Strategic Influence," *Journal of Applied Psychology* 94, no. 6 (2009), pp. 1365–1381.

73 C. Carpenter, "Narcissism on Facebook: Self-Promotional and Anti-Social Behavior," *Personality and Individual Differences* 52 (2012), pp. 482–486.

74 L. L. Meier and N. K. Semmer, "Lack of Reciprocity and Strain: Narcissism as a Moderator of the Association Between Feeling Under-benefited and Irritation," *Work & Stress* 26 (2012), pp. 56–67.

75 E. H. O'Boyle, D. R. Forsyth, G. C. Banks, and M. A. McDaniel, "A Meta-analysis of the Dark Triad and Work Behavior: A Social Exchange Perspective," *Journal of Applied Psychology* 97, no. 3 (2012), p. 558.

76 A. Reece, A. Girkan, and T. Chamorro-Premuzic, "Greed Is Good? Assessing the Relationship between Entrepreneurship and Subclinical Psychopathy," *Personality and Individual Differences* (in press), http://dx.doi.org/10.1016/j.paid.2012.10.013.

77 B. Wille, F. De Fruyt, and B. De Clercq, "Expanding and Reconceptualizing Aberrant Personality at Work: Validity of Five-Factor Model Aberrant Personality Tendencies to Predict Career Outcomes," *Personnel Psychology* 66 (2013), pp. 173–223.

78 P. K. Jonason, S. Slomski, and J. Partyka, "The Dark Triad at Work: How Toxic Employees Get Their Way," *Personality and Individual Differences* 52 (2012), pp. 449–453; and H. M. Baughman, S. Dearing, E. Giammarco, and P. A. Vernon, "Relationships between Bullying Behaviours and the Dark Triad: A Study with Adults," *Personality and Individual Differences* 52 (2012), pp. 571–575.

79 T. A. Judge and J. E. Bono, "A Rose by Any Other Name . . . Are Self-Esteem, Generalized Self-Efficacy, Neuroticism, and Locus of Control Indicators of a Common Construct?" in *Personality Psychology in the Workplace*, ed. B. W. Roberts and R. Hogan, pp. 93–118 (Washington, DC: American Psychological Association); and A. M. Grant and A. Wrzesniewski "I Won't Let You Down . . . or Will I? Core Self-Evaluations, Other-Orientation, Anticipated Guilt and Gratitude, and Job Performance," *Journal of Applied Psychology* 95, no. 1 (2010), pp. 108–121.

80 A. Erez and T. A. Judge, "Relationship of Core Self-Evaluations to Goal Setting, Motivation, and Performance," *Journal of Applied Psychology* 86, no. 6 (2001), pp. 1270–1279.

81 A. N. Salvaggio, B. Schneider, L. H. Nishi, D. M. Mayer, A. Ramesh, and J. S. Lyon, "Manager Personality, Manager Service Quality Orientation, and Service Climate: Test of a Model," *Journal of Applied Psychology* 92, no. 6 (2007), pp. 1741–1750; B. A. Scott and T. A. Judge, "The Popularity Contest at Work: Who Wins, Why, and What Do They Receive?" *Journal of Applied Psychology* 94, no. 1 (2009), pp. 20–33; and T. A. Judge and C. Hurst, "How the Rich (and Happy) Get Richer (and Happier): Relationship of Core Self-Evaluations to Trajectories in Attaining Work Success," *Journal of Applied Psychology* 93, no. 4 (2008), pp. 849–863.

82 A. M. Grant and A. Wrzesniewksi, "I Won't Let You Down . . . or Will I? Core Self-Evaluations, Other-Orientation, Anticipated Guilt and Gratitude, and Job Performance," *Journal of Applied Psychology* 95, no. 1 (2010), pp. 108–121.

83 U. Malmendier and G. Tate, "CEO Overconfidence and Corporate Investment," *Journal of Finance* 60, no. 6 (December 2005), pp. 2661–2700.

84 See M. Snyder, *Public Appearances/Private Realities: The Psychology of Self-Monitoring* (New York: W. H. Freeman, 1987); and S. W. Gangestad and M. Snyder, "Self-Monitoring: Appraisal and Reappraisal," *Psychological Bulletin*, July 2000, pp. 530–555.

85 F. J. Flynn and D. R. Ames, "What's Good for the Goose May Not Be as Good for the Gander: The Benefits of Self-Monitoring for Men and Women in Task Groups and Dyadic Conflicts," *Journal of Applied Psychology* 91, no. 2 (2006), pp. 272–281; and M. Snyder, *Public Appearances/Private Realities: The Psychology of Self-Monitoring* (New York: W. H. Freeman, 1987).

86 H. Oh and M. Kilduff, "The Ripple Effect of Personality on Social Structure: Self-monitoring Origins of Network Brokerage," *Journal of Applied Psychology* 93, no. 5 (2008), pp. 1155–1164; and A. Mehra, M. Kilduff, and D. J. Brass, "The Social Networks of High and Low Self-Monitors: Implications for Workplace Performance," *Administrative Science Quarterly*, March 2001, pp. 121–146.

87 D. V. Day, D. J. Schleicher, A. L. Unckless, and N. J. Hiller, "Self-Monitoring Personality at Work: A Meta-analytic Investigation of Construct Validity," *Journal of Applied Psychology*, April 2002, pp. 390–401.

88 Based on S. Hirschmüller, B. Egloff, S. Nestler, and D. Mitja, "The Dual Lens Model: A Comprehensive Framework for Understanding Self–Other Agreement of Personality Judgments at Zero Acquaintance," *Journal of Personality and Social Psychology* 104 (2013), pp. 335–353.

89 J. M. Crant, "Proactive Behavior in Organizations," *Journal of Management* 26, no. 3 (2000), p. 436.

90 P. D. Converse, Patrick J. Pathak, A. M. DePaul-Haddock, T. Gotlib, and M. Merbedone, "Controlling Your Environment and Yourself: Implications for Career Success," *Journal of Vocational Behavior* 80 (2012), pp. 148–159.

91 J. M. Crant, "Proactive Behavior in Organizations," *Journal of Management* 26, no. 3 (2000), p. 436.

92 See, for instance, R. C. Becherer and J. G. Maurer, "The Proactive Personality Disposition and Entrepreneurial Behavior among Small Company Presidents," *Journal of Small Business Management*, January 1999, pp. 28–36.

93 S. E. Seibert, J. M. Crant, and M. L. Kraimer, "Proactive Personality and Career Success," *Journal of Applied Psychology*, June 1999, pp. 416–427; S. E. Seibert, M. L. Kraimer, and J. M. Crant, "What Do Proactive People Do? A Longitudinal Model Linking Proactive Personality and Career Success," *Personnel Psychology*, Winter 2001, p. 850; F. J. Flynn and D. R. Ames, "What's Good for the Goose May Not Be as Good for the Gander: The Benefits of Self-Monitoring for Men and Women in Task Groups and Dyadic Conflicts," *Journal of Applied Psychology* 91, no. 2 (2006), pp. 272–281; and J. D. Kammeyer-Mueller and C. R. Wanberg, "Unwrapping the Organizational Entry Process: Disentangling Multiple Antecedents and Their Pathways to Adjustment," *Journal of Applied Psychology* 88, no. 5 (2003), pp. 779–794.

94 Vignette based on A. Fass, "Freshii Founder's 5-Part Operating Manifesto," *Inc.*, March 28, 2013, http://www.inc.com/matthew-corrin/freshii-operating-manifesto.html.

95 See, for instance, C. D. Fisher and N. M. Ashkanasy, "The Emerging Role of Emotions in Work Life: An Introduction," *Journal of Organizational Behavior*, Special Issue (2000), pp. 123–129; N. M. Ashkanasy, C. E. J. Hartel, and W. J. Zerbe, eds., *Emotions in the Workplace: Research, Theory, and Practice* (Westport, CT: Quorum Books, 2000); N. M. Ashkanasy and C. S. Daus, "Emotion in the Workplace: The New Challenge for Managers," *Academy of Management Executive*, February 2002, pp. 76–86; and N. M. Ashkanasy, C. E. J. Hartel, and C. S. Daus, "Diversity and Emotion: The New Frontiers in Organizational Behavior Research," *Journal of Management* 28, no. 3 (2002), pp. 307–338.

96 See, for example, L. L. Putnam and D. K. Mumby, "Organizations, Emotion and the Myth of Rationality," in *Emotion in Organizations*, ed. S. Fineman (Thousand Oaks, CA: Sage, 1993), pp. 36–57; and J. Martin, K. Knopoff, and C. Beckman, "An Alternative to Bureaucratic Impersonality and Emotional Labor: Bounded Emotionality at the Body Shop," *Administrative Science Quarterly*, June 1998, pp. 429–469.

97 B. E. Ashforth and R. H. Humphrey, "Emotion in the Workplace: A Reappraisal," *Human Relations*, February 1995, pp. 97–125.

98 S. G. Barsade and D. E. Gibson, "Why Does Affect Matter in Organizations?" *Academy of Management Perspectives*, February 2007, pp. 36–59.

99 See N. H. Frijda, "Moods, Emotion Episodes and Emotions," in *Handbook of Emotions*, ed. M. Lewis and J. M. Haviland (New York: Guilford Press, 1993), pp. 381–403.

100 H. M. Weiss and R. Cropanzano, "Affective Events Theory," in *Research in Organizational Behavior*, vol. 18, ed. B. M. Staw and L. L. Cummings (Greenwich, CT: JAI Press, 1996), pp. 17–19.

101 See P. Ekman and R. J. Davidson, eds., *The Nature of Emotions: Fundamental Questions* (Oxford, UK: Oxford University Press, 1994).

102 N. H. Frijda, "Moods, Emotion Episodes and Emotions," in *Handbook of Emotions*, ed. M. Lewis and J. M. Haviland (New York: Guilford Press, 1993), pp. 381–403.

103 See P. Ekman and R. J. Davidson, eds., *The Nature of Emotions: Fundamental Questions* (Oxford, UK: Oxford University Press, 1994).

104 Based on K. Sanford and A. J. Grace, "Emotion and Underlying Concerns during Couples' Conflict: An Investigation of within-Person Change," *Personal Relationships* 18, no. 1 (2011), pp. 96–109; and Baylor University, "Exploring How Partners Perceive Each Other's Emotion during a Relationship Fight," *ScienceDaily*, December 16, 2010, http://www.sciencedaily.com/releases/2010/12/101216161514.htm.

105 See J. A. Morris and D. C. Feldman, "Managing Emotions in the Workplace," *Journal of Managerial Issues* 9, no. 3 (1997), pp. 257–274; S. Mann, *Hiding What We Feel, Faking What We Don't: Understanding the Role of Your Emotions at Work* (New York: HarperCollins, 1999); and S. M. Kruml and D. Geddes,

"Catching Fire without Burning Out: Is There an Ideal Way to Perform Emotion Labor?" in *Emotions in the Workplace*, ed. N. M. Ashkanasy, C. E. J. Hartel, and W. J. Zerbe (New York: Quorum Books, 2000), pp. 177–188.

106. P. Ekman, W. V. Friesen, and M. O'Sullivan, "Smiles When Lying," in *What the Face Reveals: Basic and Applied Studies of Spontaneous Expression Using the Facial Action Coding System (FACS)*, ed. P. Ekman and E. L. Rosenberg (London: Oxford University Press, 1997), pp. 201–216.

107. A. Grandey, "Emotion Regulation in the Workplace: A New Way to Conceptualize Emotional Labor," *Journal of Occupational Health Psychology* 5, no. 1 (2000), pp. 95–110; and R. Cropanzano, D. E. Rupp, and Z. S. Byrne, "The Relationship of Emotional Exhaustion to Work Attitudes, Job Performance, and Organizational Citizenship Behavior," *Journal of Applied Psychology*, February 2003, pp. 160–169.

108. A. R. Hochschild, "Emotion Work, Feeling Rules, and Social Structure," *American Journal of Sociology*, November 1979, pp. 551–575; W.-C. Tsai, "Determinants and Consequences of Employee Displayed Positive Emotions," *Journal of Management* 27, no. 4 (2001), pp. 497–512; M. W. Kramer and J. A. Hess, "Communication Rules for the Display of Emotions in Organizational Settings," *Management Communication Quarterly*, August 2002, pp. 66–80; and J. M. Diefendorff and E. M. Richard, "Antecedents and Consequences of Emotional Display Rule Perceptions," *Journal of Applied Psychology*, April 2003, pp. 284–294.

109. R. C. Solomon, "Back to Basics: On the Very Idea of 'Basic Emotions,'" *Journal for the Theory of Social Behaviour* 32, no. 2 (2002), pp. 115–144.

110. C. M. Brotheridge and R. T. Lee, "Development and Validation of the Emotional Labour Scale," *Journal of Occupational and Organizational Psychology* 76, no. 3 (September 2003), pp. 365–379.

111. U. R. Hulsheger, H. J. E. M. Alberts, A. Feinholdt, and J. W. B. Lang, "Benefits of Mindfulness at Work: The Role of Mindfulness in Emotion Regulation, Emotional Exhaustion, and Job Satisfaction," *Journal of Applied Psychology*, March 2013, pp. 310–325.

112. J. P. Trougakos, D. J. Beal, S. G. Green, and H. M. Weiss, "Making the Break Count: An Episodic Examination of Recovery Activities, Emotional Experiences, and Positive Affective Displays," *Academy of Management Journal* 51, no. 1 (2008), pp. 131–146.

113. J. M. Diefendorff, R. J. Erickson, A. A. Grandey, and J. J. Dahling, "Emotional Display Rules as Work Unit Norms: A Multilevel Analysis of Emotional Labor among Nurses," *Journal of Occupational Health Psychology* 16 (2011), pp. 170–186.

114. S. Brassen, M. Gamer, and C. Büchel, "Anterior Cingulate Activation Is Related to a Positivity Bias and Emotional Stability in Successful Aging," *Biological Psychiatry* 70, no. 2 (2011), pp. 131–137.

115. A. R. Damasio, *Descartes' Error: Emotion, Reason, and the Human Brain* (New York: Quill, 1994).

116. N. M. Ashkanasy and C. S. Daus, "Emotion in the Workplace: The New Challenge for Managers," *Academy of Management Executive*, February 2002, pp. 76–86.

117. Based on D. R. Caruso, J. D. Mayer, and P. Salovey, "Emotional Intelligence and Emotional Leadership," in *Multiple Intelligences and Leadership*, ed. R. E. Riggio, S. E. Murphy, and F. J. Pirozzolo (Mahwah, NJ: Lawrence Erlbaum, 2002), p. 70.

118. This section is based on D. Goleman, *Emotional Intelligence* (New York: Bantam, 1995); P. Salovey and D. Grewal, "The Science of Emotional Intelligence," *Current Directions in Psychological Science* 14, no. 6 (2005), pp. 281–285; P. Salovey and D. Grewal, "The Science of Emotional Intelligence," *Current Directions in Psychological Science* 14, no. 6 (2005), pp. 281–285; M. Davies, L. Stankov, and R. D. Roberts, "Emotional Intelligence: In Search of

an Elusive Construct," *Journal of Personality and Social Psychology*, October 1998, pp. 989–1015; and D. Geddes and R. R. Callister, "Crossing the Line(s): A Dual Threshold Model of Anger in Organizations," *Academy of Management Review* 32, no. 3 (2007), pp. 721–746.

119. E. H. O'Boyle, R. H. Humphrey, J. M. Pollack, T. H. Hawver, and P. A. Story, "The Relation between Emotional Intelligence and Job Performance: A Meta-analysis," *Journal of Organizational Behavior* 32, no. 5 (2011), pp. 788–818.

120. R. Gilkey, R. Caceda, and C. Kilts, "When Emotional Reasoning Trumps IQ," *Harvard Business Review*, September 2010, p. 27.

121. M. Maccoby, "To Win the Respect of Followers, Leaders Need Personality Intelligence," *Ivey Business Journal* 72, no. 3 (2008); J. Reid, "The Resilient Leader: Why EQ Matters," *Business Journal* 72, no. 3 (2008); and P. Wieand, J. Birchfield, and M. C. Johnson III, "The New Leadership Challenge: Removing the Emotional Barriers to Sustainable Performance in a Flat World," *Ivey Business Journal* 72, no. 4 (2008).

122. M. Seo and L. F. Barrett, "Being Emotional During Decision Making—Good or Bad? An Empirical Investigation," *Academy of Management Journal* 50, no. 4 (2007), pp. 923–940.

123. P. Wieand, J. Birchfield, and M. C. Johnson III, "The New Leadership Challenge: Removing the Emotional Barriers to Sustainable Performance in a Flat World," *Ivey Business Journal* 72, no. 4 (2008), http://iveybusinessjournal.com/topics/leadership/the-new-leadership-challenge-removing-the-emotional-barriers-to-sustainable-performance-in-a-flat-world#.VCxlNyItCWg.

124. C. Cherniss, "The Business Case for Emotional Intelligence," *Consortium for Research on Emotional Intelligence in Organizations*, 1999, http://www.eiconsortium.org/reports/business_case_for_ei.html.

125. F. J. Landy, "Some Historical and Scientific Issues Related to Research on Emotional Intelligence," *Journal of Organizational Behavior* 26, no. 4 (June 2005), pp. 411–424.

126. K. S. Law, C. Wong, and L. J. Song, "The Construct and Criterion Validity of Emotional Intelligence and Its Potential Utility for Management Studies," *Journal of Applied Psychology* 89, no. 3 (2004), pp. 483–496.

127. D. L. Van Rooy and C. Viswesvaran, "Emotional Intelligence: A Meta-analytic Investigation of Predictive Validity and Nomological Net," *Journal of Vocational Behavior* 65, no. 1 (August 2004), pp. 71–95.

128. R. Bar-On, D. Tranel, N. L. Denburg, and A. Bechara, "Exploring the Neurological Substrate of Emotional and Social Intelligence," *Brain* 126, no. 8 (August 2003), pp. 1790–1800.

129. P. A. Vernon, K. V. Petrides, D. Bratko, and J. A. Schermer, "A Behavioral Genetic Study of Trait Emotional Intelligence," *Emotion* 8, no. 5 (2008), pp. 635–642.

130. E. A. Locke, "Why Emotional Intelligence Is an Invalid Concept," *Journal of Organizational Behavior* 26, no. 4 (June 2005), pp. 425–431.

131. J. D. Mayer, R. D. Roberts, and S. G. Barsade, "Human Abilities: Emotional Intelligence," *Annual Review of Psychology* 59 (2008), pp. 507–536; H. A. Elfenbein, "Emotion in Organizations: A Review and Theoretical Integration," *Academy of Management Annals* 1 (2008), pp. 315–386; and D. L. Joseph and D. A. Newman, "Emotional Intelligence: An Integrative Meta-analysis and Cascading Model," *Journal of Applied Psychology* 95 (2010), pp. 54–78.

132. J. M. Conte, "A Review and Critique of Emotional Intelligence Measures," *Journal of Organizational Behavior* 26, no. 4 (2005), pp. 433–440; and M. Davies, L. Stankov, and R. D. Roberts, "Emotional Intelligence: In Search of an Elusive Construct," *Journal of Personality and Social Psychology* 75, no. 4 (1998), pp. 989–1015.

133. T. Decker, "Is Emotional Intelligence a Viable Concept?" *Academy of Management Review* 28, no. 2 (2003), pp. 433–440; and M. Davies, L. Stankov, and R. D. Roberts, "Emotional Intelligence: In

Search of an Elusive Construct," *Journal of Personality and Social Psychology* 75, no. 4 (1998), pp. 989–1015.

134 D. L. Joseph and D. A. Newman, "Emotional Intelligence: An Integrative Meta-analysis and Cascading Model," *Journal of Applied Psychology* 95 (2010), pp. 54–78.

135 Based on D. Iliescu, A. Ilie, D. Ispas, and A. Ion, "Emotional Intelligence in Personnel Selection: Applicant Reactions, Criterion, and Incremental Validity," *International Journal of Selection and Assessment*, September 2012, pp. 347–358; R. Sharma, "Measuring Social and Emotional Intelligence Competencies in the Indian Context," *Cross Cultural Management* 19 (2012), pp. 30–47; and S. Sharma, M. Gangopadhyay, E. Austin, and M. K. Mandal, "Development and Validation of a Situational Judgment Test of Emotional Intelligence," *International Journal of Selection and Assessment*, March 2013, pp. 57–73.

136 S. L. Robinson and R. J. Bennett, "A Typology of Deviant Workplace Behaviors: A Multidimensional Scaling Study," *Academy of Management Journal*, April 1995, p. 556.

137 S. L. Robinson and R. J. Bennett, "A Typology of Deviant Workplace Behaviors: A Multidimensional Scaling Study," *Academy of Management Journal*, April 1995, pp. 555–572.

138 Based on A. G. Bedeian, "Workplace Envy," *Organizational Dynamics*, Spring 1995, p. 50.

139 A. G. Bedeian, "Workplace Envy," *Organizational Dynamics*, Spring 1995, p. 54.

140 S. C. Douglas, C. Kiewitz, M. Martinko, P. Harvey, Y. Kim, and J. U. Chun, "Cognitions, Emotions, and Evaluations: An Elaboration Likelihood Model for Workplace Aggression," *Academy of Management Review* 33, no. 2 (2008), pp. 425–451.

141 K. Lee and N. J. Allen, "Organizational Citizenship Behavior and Workplace Deviance: The Role of Affect and Cognition," *Journal of Applied Psychology* 87, no. 1 (2002), pp. 131–142; and T. A. Judge, B. A. Scott, and R. Ilies, "Hostility, Job Attitudes, and Workplace Deviance: Test of a Multilevel Model," *Journal of Applied Psychology* 91, no. 1 (2006), pp. 126–138.

142 Based on R. L. Hotz, "Too Important to Smile Back: The 'Boss Effect,'" *Wall Street Journal*, October 16, 2012, p. D2; E. Kim and D. J. Yoon, "Why Does Service with a Smile Make Employees Happy? A Social Interaction Model," *Journal of Applied Psychology* 97 (2012), pp. 1059–1967; and K. Weintraub, "But How Do You Really Feel? Someday the Computer May Know," *New York Times*, October 16, 2012, p. D3.

143 S. L. Koole, "The Psychology of Emotion Regulation: An Integrative Review," *Cognition and Emotion* 23 (2009), pp. 4–41; H. A. Wadlinger and D. M. Isaacowitz, "Fixing Our Focus: Training Attention to Regulate Emotion," *Personality and Social Psychology Review* 15 (2011), pp. 75–102.

144 D. H. Kluemper, T. DeGroot, and S. Choi, "Emotion Management Ability: Predicting Task Performance, Citizenship, and Deviance," *Journal of Management*, May 2013, pp. 878–905.

145 B. A. Scott, C. M. Barnes, and D. T. Wagner, "Chameleonic or Consistent? A Multilevel Investigation of Emotional Labor Variability and Self-Monitoring," *Academy of Management Journal* 55, no. 4 (2012), pp. 905–926.

146 T. L. Webb, E. Miles, and P. Sheeran, "Dealing with Feeling: A Meta-analysis of the Effectiveness of Strategies Derived from the Process Model of Emotion Regulation," *Psychological Bulletin* 138, no. 4 (2012), pp. 775–808; S. Srivastava, M. Tamir, K. M. McGonigal, O. P. John, and J. J. Gross, "The Social Costs of Emotional Suppression: A Prospective Study of the Transition to College," *Journal of Personality and Social Psychology* 96 (2009), pp. 883–897; Y. Liu, L. M. Prati, P. L. Perrewé, and R. A. Brymer, "Individual Differences in Emotion Regulation, Emotional Experiences at Work, and Work-Related Outcomes: A Two-Study Investigation," *Journal of Applied Social Psychology* 40 (2010), pp. 1515–1538; and H. A. Wadlinger and D. M. Isaacowitz,

"Fixing Our Focus: Training Attention to Regulate Emotion," *Personality and Social Psychology Review* 15 (2011), pp. 75–102.

147 E. Halperin, R. Porat, M. Tamir, and J. J. Gross, "Can Emotion Regulation Change Political Attitudes in Intractable Conflicts? From the Laboratory to the Field," *Psychological Science*, January 2013, pp. 106–111.

148 F. Nils and B. Rimé, "Beyond the Myth of Venting: Social Sharing Modes Determine the Benefits of Emotional Disclosure," *European Journal of Social Psychology* 42 (2012), pp. 672–681; and J. D. Parlamis, "Venting as Emotion Regulation: The Influence of Venting Responses and Respondent Identity on Anger and Emotional Tone," *International Journal of Conflict Management* 23 (2012), pp. 77–96.

149 J. V. Wood, S. A. Heimpel, L. A. Manwell, and E. J. Whittington, "This Mood Is Familiar and I Don't Deserve to Feel Better Anyway: Mechanisms Underlying Self-Esteem Differences in Motivation to Repair Sad Moods," *Journal of Personality and Social Psychology* 96 (2009), pp. 363–380.

150 S. L. Koole, "The Psychology of Emotion Regulation: An Integrative Review," *Cognition and Emotion* 23 (2009), pp. 4–41.

151 L. K. Barber, P. G. Bagsby, and D. C. Munz, "Affect Regulation Strategies for Promoting (or Preventing) Flourishing Emotional Health," *Personality and Individual Differences* 49 (2010), pp. 663–666.

152 S.-C. S. Chi and S.-G. Liang, "When Do Subordinates' Emotion-Regulation Strategies Matter? Abusive Supervision, Subordinates' Emotional Exhaustion, and Work Withdrawal," *The Leadership Quarterly*, February 2013, pp. 125–137.

153 R. H. Humphrey, "How Do Leaders Use Emotional Labor?" *Journal of Organizational Behavior*, July 2012, pp. 740–744.

154 Based on "Affective Computing," *MIT*, accessed October 1, 2014, http://affect.media.mit.edu/; "Affective Computing and Intelligent Interaction" (paper presented at IEEE Computer Society Annual Conference, Geneva, Switzerland, September 2013), http://ieeexplore.ieee.org/xpl/mostRecentIssue.jsp?reload=true&punumber=6679936; and K. Weintraub, "But How Do You Really Feel? Someday the Computer May Know," *New York Times*, October 16, 2012, p. D3.

155 C. West, "How Culture Affects the Way We Think," *APS Observer* 20, no. 7 (2007), pp. 25–26.

156 T. Masuda, R. Gonzalez, L. Kwan, and R. E. Nisbett, "Culture and Aesthetic Preference: Comparing the Attention to Context of East Asians and Americans," *Personality and Social Psychology Bulletin* 34, no. 9 (2008), pp. 1260–1275.

157 D. C. Park, "Developing a Cultural Cognitive Neuroscience of Aging," in *Handbook of Cognitive Aging*, ed. S. M. Hofer and D. F. Alwin (Thousand Oaks, CA: Sage, 2008), pp. 352–367.

158 Q. Wang, "On the Cultural Constitution of Collective Memory," *Memory* 16, no. 3 (2008), pp. 305–317.

159 See, for example, D. S. Krull, M. H.-M. Loy, J. Lin, C.-F. Wang, S. Chen, and X. Zhao, "The Fundamental Attribution Error: Correspondence Bias in Individualistic and Collectivist Cultures," *Personality and Social Psychology Bulletin*, October 1999, pp. 1208–1219; and F. F. T. Chiang and T. A. Birtch, "Examining the Perceived Causes of Successful Employee Performance: An East-West Comparison," *International Journal of Human Resource Management* 18, no. 2 (2007), pp. 232–248.

160 S. Nam, "Cultural and Managerial Attributions for Group Performance," unpublished doctoral dissertation, University of Oregon. Cited in R. M. Steers, S. J. Bischoff, and L. H. Higgins, "Cross-Cultural Management Research," *Journal of Management Inquiry*, December 1992, pp. 325–326.

161 T. Menon, M. W. Morris, C. Y. Chiu, and Y. Y. Hong, "Culture and the Construal of Agency: Attribution to Individual versus Group Dispositions," *Journal of Personality and Social Psychology* 76 (1999), pp. 701–717; and R. Friedman, W. Liu, C. C. Chen, and

S. S. Chi, "Causal Attribution for Interfirm Contract Violation: A Comparative Study of Chinese and American Commercial Arbitrators," *Journal of Applied Psychology* 92, no. 3 (2007), pp. 856–864.

162 J. Spencer-Rodgers, M. J. Williams, D. L. Hamilton, K. Peng, and L. Wang, "Culture and Group Perception: Dispositional and Stereotypic Inferences About Novel and National Groups," *Journal of Personality and Social Psychology* 93, no. 4 (2007), pp. 525–543.

163 J. D. Brown, "Across the (Not So) Great Divide: Cultural Similarities in Self-Evaluative Processes," *Social and Personality Psychology Compass* 4, no. 5 (2010), pp. 318–330.

164 A. Zhang, C. Reyna, Z. Qian, and G. Yu, "Interpersonal Attributions of Responsibility in the Chinese Workplace: A Test of Western Models in a Collectivistic Context," *Journal of Applied Social Psychology* 38, no. 9 (2008), pp. 2361–2377; and A. Zhang, F. Xia, and C. Li, "The Antecedents of Help Giving in Chinese Culture: Attribution, Judgment of Responsibility, Expectation Change and the Reaction of Affect," *Social Behavior and Personality* 35, no. 1 (2007), pp. 135–142.

165 See, for example, R. R. McCrae and P. T. Costa Jr., "Personality Trait Structure as a Human Universal," *American Psychologist*, May 1997, pp. 509–516; S. Yamagata, A. Suzuki, J. Ando, Y. Ono, K. Yutaka, N. Kijima, K. Yoshimura, F. Ostendorf, A. Angleitner, R. Riemann, F. M. Spinath, W. J. Livesley, and K. L. Jang, "Is the Genetic Structure of Human Personality Universal? A Cross-Cultural Twin Study from North America, Europe, and Asia," *Journal of Personality and Social Psychology* 90, no. 6 (2006), pp. 987–998; H. C. Triandis and E. M. Suh, "Cultural Influences on Personality," in *Annual Review of Psychology*, vol. 53, ed. S. T. Fiske, D. L. Schacter, and C. Zahn-Waxler (Palo Alto, CA: Annual Reviews, 2002), pp. 133–160; R. R. McCrae and J. Allik, *The Five-Factor Model of Personality across Cultures* (New York: Kluwer Academic/Plenum, 2002); and R. R. McCrae, P. T. Costa Jr., T. A. Martin, V. E. Oryol, A. A. Rukavishnikov, I. G. Senin, M. Hřebíčková, and T. Urbánek, "Consensual Validation of Personality Traits across Cultures," *Journal of Research in Personality* 38, no. 2 (2004), pp. 179–201.

166 A. T. Church and M. S. Katigbak, "Trait Psychology in the Philippines," *American Behavioral Scientist*, September 2000, pp. 73–94.

167 J. F. Salgado, "The Five Factor Model of Personality and Job Performance in the European Community," *Journal of Applied Psychology*, February 1997, pp. 30–43.

168 G. Van Hoye and H. Lootens, "Coping with Unemployment: Personality, Role Demands, and Time Structure," *Journal of Vocational Behavior* 82 (2013), pp. 85–95.

169 G. Chen, J. Farh, E. M. Campbell-Bush, Z. Wu, and X. Wu, "Teams as Innovative Systems: Multilevel Motivational Antecedents of Innovation in R&D Teams," *Journal of Applied Psychology* 98, no. 6 (2013), pp. 1018–1027.

170 Z. Zhang, M. Wang, and J. Shi, Junqi, "Leader-Follower Congruence in Proactive Personality and Work Outcomes: The Mediating Role of Leader-Member Exchange," *Academy of Management Journal* 55 (2012), pp. 111–130.

171 M. Eid and E. Diener, "Norms for Experiencing Emotions in Different Cultures: Inter- and International Differences," *Journal of Personality and Social Psychology* 81, no. 5 (2001), pp. 869–885.

172 S. Oishi, E. Diener, and C. Napa Scollon, "Cross-Situational Consistency of Affective Experiences across Cultures," *Journal of Personality and Social Psychology* 86, no. 3 (2004), pp. 460–472; and J. Leu, J. Wang, and K. Koo, "Are Positive Emotions Just as 'Positive' across Cultures?" *Emotion* 11, no. 4 (2011).

173 M. Eid and E. Diener, "Norms for Experiencing Emotions in Different Cultures: Inter- and International Differences," *Journal of Personality and Social Psychology* 81, no. 5 (2001), pp. 869–885.

174 O. Burkeman, "The Power of Negative Thinking," *New York Times*, August 5, 2012, p. 9.

175 E. Jaffe, "Positively Negative," *Observer*, November 2012, pp. 13–17, http://www.psychologicalscience.org/index.php/publications/observer/2012/november-12/positively-negative.html.

176 M. Eid and E. Diener, "Norms for Experiencing Emotions in Different Cultures: Inter- and International Differences," *Journal of Personality and Social Psychology* 81, no. 5 (2001), pp. 869–885.

177 B. Mesquita, "Emotions in Collectivist and Individualist Contexts," *Journal of Personality and Social Psychology* 80, no. 1 (2001), pp. 68–74.

178 B. Plasait, *l'accueil des touristes dans les grands centres de transit* (Paris, France: Collection Rapports officiels, Editions Documentation Française, 2004).

179 B. E. Ashforth and R. H. Humphrey, "Emotion in the Workplace: A Reappraisal," *Human Relations*, February 1995, p. 104; and D. Rubin, "Grumpy German Shoppers Distrust the Wal-Mart Style," *Seattle Times*, December 30, 2001, p. A15.

180 S. Nelton, "Emotions in the Workplace," *Nation's Business*, February 1996, p. 25.

181 Based on J. M. Twenge, W. K. Campbell, and E. C. Freeman, "Generational Differences in Young Adults' Life Goals, Concern for Others, and Civic Orientation, 1966–2009," *Journal of Personality and Social Psychology* 102 (2012), pp. 1045–1062; J. Jin and J. Rounds, "Stability and Change in Work Values: A Meta-analysis of Longitudinal Studies," *Journal of Vocational Behavior* 80 (2012), pp. 326–339; S. W. Lester, R. L. Standifer, N. J. Schultz, and J. M. Windsor, "Actual Versus Perceived Generational Differences at Work: An Empirical Examination," *Journal of Leadership & Organizational Studies* 19 (2012), pp. 341–354; Conference Board of Canada, "Canadian Organizations Need to Separate Facts from Stereotypes to Capitalize on Future Workforce," news release, September 9, 2014; M. Hemmadi "How Are Millennials Responding to a Tough Job Market? Lowering Their Expectations," *Canadian Business*, September 22, 2014, http://www.canadianbusiness.com/blogs-and-comment/millennials-lowered-expectations-job-market/); and J. Nelson, "Millennials Value Workplace Culture: Study," *Globe and Mail*, May 6, 2014.

182 Exercise based on M.-A. Reinard and N. Schwartz, "The Influence of Affective States on the Presence of Lie Detection," *Journal of Experimental Psychology* 18 (2012), pp. 377–389.

183 Based on S. Shellenbarger, "Thinking Happy Thoughts at Work," *Wall Street Journal*, January 27, 2010, p. D2; S. Sharma and D. Chatterjee, "Cos Are Keenly Listening to 'Happiness Coach,'" *Economic Times*, July 16, 2010, http://articles.economictimes.indiatimes.com; J. Smith, *The Executive Happiness Coach*, accessed May 3, 2011, http://www.lifewithhappiness.com; and S. Sonnentag and A. M. Grant, "Doing Good at Work Feels Good at Home, But Not Right Way: When and Why Perceived Prosocial Impact Predicts Positive Affect," *Personnel Psychology* 65 (2012), pp. 495–530.

184 Based on T. A. Judge, B. A. Livingston, and C. Hurst, "Do Nice Guys—and Gals—Really Finish Last? The Joint Effects of Sex and Agreeableness on Income," *Journal of Personality and Social Psychology* 102 (2012), pp. 390–407; J. B. Bernerth, S. G. Taylor, H. J. Walker, and D. S. Whitman, "An Empirical Investigation of Dispositional Antecedents and Performance-Related Outcomes of Credit Scores," *Journal of Applied Psychology* 97 (2012), pp. 469–478; J. Carpenter, D. Doverspike, and R. F. Miguel, "Public Service Motivation as a Predictor of Attraction to the Public Sector," *Journal of Vocational Behavior* 80 (2012), pp. 509–523; and A. Neal, G. Yeo, A. Koy, and T. Xiao, "Predicting the Form and Direction of Work Role Performance from the Big 5 Model of Personality Traits," *Journal of Organizational Behavior* 33 (2012), pp. 175–192.

185 Based on P. Ekman, *Telling Lies: Clues to Deceit in the Marketplace, Politics, and Marriage* (New York: W. W. Norton & Co., 2009); D. Jones, "It's Written All Over Their Faces," *USA Today*, February 25, 2008, pp. 1B–2B; N. O. Rule and N. Ambady, "The Face of

Success," *Psychological Science* 19, no. 2 (2008), pp. 109–111; and R. Reisenzein, M. Studtmann, and G. Horstmann, "Coherence between Emotion and Facial Expression: Evidence from Laboratory Experiments," *Emotion Review*, January 2013, pp. 16–23.

186 Based on V. P. Richmond, J. C. McCroskey, and S. K. Payne, *Nonverbal Behavior in Interpersonal Relations*, 2nd ed. (Englewood Cliffs, NJ: Prentice Hall, 1991), pp. 117–138; and L. A. King, "Ambivalence over Emotional Expression and Reading Emotions in Situations and Faces," *Journal of Personality and Social Psychology*, March 1998, pp. 753–762.

Chapter 3

1 Opening vignette based on "TD Bank Group and Corus Entertainment Come Together in Support of Frontier College," news release, July 24, 2014; and Corus Entertainment, "Employee Engagement: Corporate Social Responsibility," accessed October 8, 2014, http://www.corusent.com/home/Corporate/CorporateSocialResponsibility/EmployeeEngagement/tabid/2566/Default.aspx.

2 M. Rokeach, *The Nature of Human Values* (New York: Free Press, 1973), p. 5.

3 See, for example, B. Meglino and E. Ravlin, "Individual Values in Organizations," *Journal of Management* 24, no. 3 (1998), pp. 351–389.

4 M. Rokeach and S. J. Ball-Rokeach, "Stability and Change in American Value Priorities, 1968–1981," *American Psychologist*, May 1989, pp. 775–784.

5 M. Rokeach, *The Nature of Human Values* (New York: Free Press, 1973), p. 6.

6 M. Rokeach, *The Nature of Human Values* (New York: Free Press, 1973), p. 56.

7 M. Rokeach, *The Nature of Human Values* (New York: Free Press, 1973), p. 56.

8 K. Hodgson, *A Rock and a Hard Place: How to Make Ethical Business Decisions When the Choices Are Tough* (New York: AMACOM, 1992), pp. 66–67.

9 K. Hodgson, "Adapting Ethical Decisions to a Global Marketplace," *Management Review* 81, no. 5 (May 1992), pp. 53–57. Reprinted by permission.

10 Vignette based on Corus Entertainment, "Employee Engagement: Corporate Social Responsibility," accessed October 8, 2014, http://www.corusent.com/home/Corporate/CorporateSocialResponsibility/EmployeeEngagement/tabid/2566/Default.aspx.

11 G. Hofstede, *Culture's Consequences: International Differences in Work-Related Values* (Beverly Hills, CA: Sage, 1980); G. Hofstede, *Cultures and Organizations: Software of the Mind* (London: McGraw-Hill, 1991); G. Hofstede, "Cultural Constraints in Management Theories," *Academy of Management Executive* 7, no. 1 (1993), pp. 81–94; G. Hofstede and M. F. Peterson, "National Values and Organizational Practices," in *Handbook of Organizational Culture and Climate*, ed. N. M. Ashkanasy, C. M. Wilderom, and M. F. Peterson (Thousand Oaks, CA: Sage, 2000), pp. 401–416; and G. Hofstede, *Culture's Consequences: Comparing Values, Behaviors, Institutions, and Organizations Across Nations*, 2nd ed. (Thousand Oaks, CA: Sage, 2001). For criticism of this research, see B. McSweeney, "Hofstede's Model of National Cultural Differences and Their Consequences: A Triumph of Faith—A Failure of Analysis," *Human Relations* 55, no. 1 (2002), pp. 89–118.

12 G. Hofstede, "Dimensionalizing Cultures: The Hofstede Model in Context," Online Readings in Psychology and Culture, Unit 2, 2011, http://scholarworks.gvsu.edu/orpc/vol2/iss1/8.

13 G. Hofstede, "Dimensionalizing Cultures: The Hofstede Model in Context," Online Readings in Psychology and Culture, Unit 2, 2011, http://scholarworks.gvsu.edu/orpc/vol2/iss1/8.

14 G. Hofstede and M. H. Bond, "The Confucius Connection: From Cultural Roots to Economic Growth," *Organizational Dynamics*, Spring 1988, pp. 12–13.

15 G. Hofstede, G. J. Hofstede, and M. Minkov, *Cultures and Organizations, Software of the Mind*, 3rd rev. ed. (New York: McGraw-Hill, 2010), p. 35.

16 See A. Harzing and G. Hofstede, "Planned Change in Organizations: The Influence of National Culture," in *Research in the Sociology of Organizations, Cross Cultural Analysis of Organizations*, vol. 14, ed. P. A. Bamberger, M. Erez, and S. B. Bacharach (Greenwich, CT: JAI Press, 1996), pp. 297–340. The five usual criticisms and Hofstede's responses (in parentheses) are (1) surveys are not a suitable way to measure cultural differences (answer: they should not be the only way); (2) nations are not the proper units for studying cultures (answer: they are usually the only kind of units available for comparison); (3) a study of the subsidiaries of one company cannot provide information about entire national cultures (answer: what was measured were differences among national cultures, and any set of functionally equivalent samples can supply information about such differences); (4) the IBM data are old and therefore obsolete (answer: the dimensions found are assumed to have century-old roots; they have been validated against all kinds of external measurements; and recent replications show no loss of validity); and (5) four or five dimensions are not enough (answer: additional dimensions should be statistically independent of the dimensions defined earlier; they should be valid on the basis of correlations with external measures; and candidates are welcome to apply).

17 V. Taras, B. L. Kirkman, and P. Steel, "Examining the Impact of Culture's Consequences: A Three-Decade, Multilevel, Meta-analytic Review of Hofstede's Cultural Value Dimensions," *Journal of Applied Psychology* 95, no. 5 (2010), pp. 405–439.

18 M. Javidan and R. J. House, "Cultural Acumen for the Global Manager: Lessons from Project GLOBE," *Organizational Dynamics* 29, no. 4 (2001), pp. 289–305; and R. J. House, P. J. Hanges, M. Javidan, and P. W. Dorfman, eds., *Leadership, Culture, and Organizations: The GLOBE Study of 62 Societies* (Thousand Oaks, CA: Sage, 2004).

19 J. P. Meyer, D. J. Stanley, T. A. Jackson, K. J. McInnis, E. R. Maltin, and L. Sheppard, "Affective, Normative, and Continuance Commitment Levels Across Cultures: A Meta-analysis," *Journal of Vocational Behavior* 80, no. 2 (2012), pp. 225–245.

20 B. Meglino, E. C. Ravlin, and C. L. Adkins, "A Work Values Approach to Corporate Culture: A Field Test of the Value Congruence Process and Its Relationship to Individual Outcomes," *Journal of Applied Psychology* 74 (1989), pp. 424–432.

21 B. Z. Posner, J. M. Kouzes, and W. H. Schmidt, "Shared Values Make a Difference: An Empirical Test of Corporate Culture," *Human Resource Management* 24 (1985), pp. 293–310; and A. L. Balazas, "Value Congruency: The Case of the 'Socially Responsible' Firm," *Journal of Business Research* 20 (1990), pp. 171–181.

22 C. A. O'Reilly, J. Chatman, and D. Caldwell, "People and Organizational Culture: A Q-Sort Approach to Assessing Person-Organizational Fit," *Academy of Management Journal* 34 (1991), pp. 487–516.

23 C. Enz and C. K. Schwenk, "Performance and Sharing of Organizational Values" (paper presented at the annual meeting of the Academy of Management, Washington, DC, 1989).

24 See, for example, *The Multigenerational Workforce* (Alexandria, VA: Society for Human Resource Management, 2009); and M. Adams, *Sex in the Snow* (Toronto: Penguin, 1997).

25 J. Timm, "Leadership Q&A: Robert Dutton," *Canadian Business*, June 22, 2011.

26 K. W. Smola and C. D. Sutton, "Generational Differences: Revisiting Generational Work Values for the New Millennium," *Journal of Organizational Behavior* 23 (2002), pp. 363–382; and

K. Mellahi and C. Guermat, "Does Age Matter? An Empirical Examination of the Effect of Age on Managerial Values and Practices in India," *Journal of World Business* 39, no. 2 (2004), pp. 199–215.

27 B. Hite, "Employers Rethink How They Give Feedback," *Wall Street Journal*, October 13, 2008, p. B5.

28 Statistics Canada, "Census of Population," *The Daily*, February 11, 2003.

29 E. Parry and P. Urwin, "Generational Differences in Work Values: A Review of Theory and Evidence," *International Journal of Management Reviews* 13, no. 1 (2011), pp. 79–96.

30 J. M. Twenge, S. M. Campbell, B. J. Hoffman, and C. E. Lance, "Generational Differences in Work Values: Leisure and Extrinsic Values Increasing, Social and Intrinsic Values Decreasing," *Journal of Management* 36, no. 5 (2010), pp. 1117–1142.

31 Based on P. Loriggio, "Teen Who Won Google Prize Juggles School Work with Science Fair," *Maclean's*, December 27, 2013; and A. Kingston, "Get Ready for Generation Z," *Maclean's*, July 15, 2014.

32 Statistics Canada, Immigration and Ethnocultural Diversity in Canada (Catalogue no. 99-010-X2011001) (Ottawa: Statistics Canada, 2013).

33 Statistics Canada, *Immigration and Ethnocultural Diversity in Canada* (Catalogue no. 99-010-X2011001) (Ottawa: Statistics Canada, 2013).

34 Statistics Canada, *Immigration and Ethnocultural Diversity in Canada* (Catalogue no. 99-010-X2011001) (Ottawa: Statistics Canada, 2013).

35 Statistics Canada, "2011 Census of Population: Linguistic Characteristics of Canadians," *The Daily*, October 24, 2012.

36 Statistics Canada, "2011 Census of Population: Linguistic Characteristics of Canadians," *The Daily*, October 24, 2012.

37 E. Thompson, "Canadians Hearing, Seeing Racism: Poll," *Toronto Sun*, March 16, 2010.

38 "American vs. Canadian Youth: Lifestyles, Values Differ," *MarketingCharts*, November 19, 2009, http://www.marketingcharts.com/television/american-vs-canadian-youth-lifestyles-values-differ-10588/

39 "The choice in Quebec," *Maclean's*, October 30, 1995, pp. 18–33.

40 R. N. Kanungo and J. K. Bhatnagar, "Achievement Orientation and Occupational Values: A Comparative Study of Young French and English Canadians," *Canadian Journal of Behavioural Science* 12 (1978), pp. 384–392; M. W. McCarrey, S. Edwards, and R. Jones, "Personal Values of Canadian Anglophone and Francophone Employees and Ethnolinguistic Group Membership, Sex and Position Level," *Journal of Psychology* 104 (1978), pp. 175–184; M. W. McCarrey, S. Edwards, and R. Jones, "The Influence of Ethnolinguistic Group Membership, Sex, and Position Level on Motivational Orientation of Canadian Anglophone and Francophone Employees," *Canadian Journal of Behavioural Science* 9 (1977), pp. 274–282; M. W. McCarrey, Y. Gasse, and L. F. Moore, "Work Value Goals and Instrumentalities: A Comparison of Canadian West-Coast Anglophone and Quebec City Francophone Managers," *International Review of Applied Psychology* 33 (1984), pp. 291–303; and S. C. Jain and D. A. Ralston, "The North American Free Trade Agreement: An Overview," in *NAFTA: A Three-Way Partnership for Free Trade and Growth*, ed. S. C. Jain and D. A. Ralston (Storrs, CT: University of Connecticut, 1996), pp. 3–7.

41 M. Major, M. McCarrey, P. Mercier, and Y. Gasse, "Meanings of Work and Personal Values of Canadian Anglophone and Francophone Middle Managers," *Canadian Journal of Administrative Sciences*, September 1994, pp. 251–263.

42 R. N. Kanungo and J. K. Bhatnagar, "Achievement Orientation and Occupational Values: A Comparative Study of Young French and English Canadians," *Canadian Journal of Behavioural Science* 12 (1978), pp. 384–392.

43 V. Mann-Feder and V. Savicki, "Burnout in Anglophone and Francophone Child and Youth Workers in Canada: A Cross-Cultural Comparison," *Child & Youth Care Forum* 32, no. 6 (2003), p. 345.

44 R. N. Kanungo and J. K. Bhatnagar, "Achievement Orientation and Occupational Values: A Comparative Study of Young French and English Canadians," *Canadian Journal of Behavioural Science* 12 (1978), pp. 384–392.

45 V. Mann-Feder and V. Savicki, "Burnout in Anglophone and Francophone Child and Youth Workers in Canada: A Cross-Cultural Comparison," *Child & Youth Care Forum* 32, no. 6 (2003), pp. 337–354.

46 N. J. Adler and J. L. Graham, "Cross-Cultural Interaction: The International Comparison Fallacy?" *Journal of International Business Studies* 20 (1989), pp. 515–537.

47 N. J. Adler, J. L. Graham, and T. S. Gehrke, "Business Negotiations in Canada, Mexico, and the United States," *Journal of Business Research* 15 (1987), pp. 411–429.

48 H. C. Jain, J. Normand, and R. N. Kanungo, "Job Motivation of Canadian Anglophone and Francophone Hospital Employees," *Canadian Journal of Behavioural Science*, April 1979, pp. 160–163; and R. N. Kanungo, G. J. Gorn, and H. J. Dauderis, "Motivational Orientation of Canadian Anglophone and Francophone Managers," *Canadian Journal of Behavioural Science*, April 1976, pp. 107–121.

49 M. Major, M. McCarrey, P. Mercier, and Y. Gasse, "Meanings of Work and Personal Values of Canadian Anglophone and Francophone Middle Managers," *Canadian Journal of Administrative Sciences*, April 2009, pp. 251–263.

50 K. L. Gibson, S. J. Mckelvie, and A. F. De Man, "Personality and Culture: A Comparison of Francophones and Anglophones in Québec," *Journal of Social Psychology* 148, no. 2 (2008), pp. 133–165.

51 G. Bouchard, F. Rocher, and G. Rocher, *Les Francophones Québécois* (Montreal: Bowne de Montréal, 1991).

52 K. L. Gibson, S. J. Mckelvie, and A. F. De Man, "Personality and Culture: A Comparison of Francophones and Anglophones in Québec," *Journal of Social Psychology* 148, no. 2 (2008), pp. 133–165.

53 C. P. Egri, D. A. Ralston, C. S. Murray, and J. D. Nicholson, "Managers in the NAFTA Countries: A Cross-Cultural Comparison of Attitudes toward Upward Influence Strategies," *Journal of International Management* 6, no. 2 (2000), pp. 149–171.

54 C. P. Egri, D. A. Ralston, C. S. Murray, and J. D. Nicholson, "Managers in the NAFTA Countries: A Cross-Cultural Comparison of Attitudes toward Upward Influence Strategies," *Journal of International Management* 6, no. 2 (2000), p. 164. See also R. Dheer, T. Lenartowicz, M. F Peterson, and M. Petrescu, "Cultural Regions of Canada and United States: Implications for International Management Research," *International Journal of Cross Cultural Management*, July 30, 2014 (published online before print); and J. P. Cannon, P. M. Doney, M. R. Mullen, and K. J. Petersen, "Building Long-Term Orientation In Buyer–Supplier Relationships: The Moderating Role of Culture," *Journal of Operations Management* 28, no. 6 (November 2010), pp. 506–521.

55 G. Hamilton, "B.C. First Nation Logging Firm Wins National Award," *Vancouver Sun*, July 14, 2011, p. C2.

56 G. Hamilton, "B.C. First Nation Logging Firm Wins National Award," *Vancouver Sun*, July 14, 2011, p. C2.

57 L. Redpath and M. O. Nielsen, "A Comparison of Native Culture, Non-Native Culture and New Management Ideology," *Canadian Journal of Administrative Sciences* 14, no. 3 (1997), p. 327.

58 G. C. Anders and K. K. Anders, "Incompatible Goals in Unconventional Organizations: The Politics of Alaska Native Corporations," *Organization Studies* 7 (1986), pp. 213–233;

G. Dacks, "Worker-Controlled Native Enterprises: A Vehicle for Community Development in Northern Canada?" *Canadian Journal of Native Studies* 3 (1983), pp. 289–310; and L. P. Dana, "Self-Employment in the Canadian Sub-Arctic: An Exploratory Study," *Canadian Journal of Administrative Sciences* 13 (1996), pp. 65–77.

59 L. Redpath and M. O. Nielsen, "A Comparison of Native Culture, Non-Native Culture and New Management Ideology," *Canadian Journal of Administrative Sciences* 14, no. 3 (1997), p. 327.

60 R. B. Anderson, "The Business Economy of the First Nations in Saskatchewan: A Contingency Perspective," *Canadian Journal of Native Studies* 2 (1995), pp. 309–345.

61 E. Struzik, "'Win-Win Scenario' Possible for Resource Industry, Aboriginals," *Edmonton Journal*, April 6, 2003, p. A12.

62 High Level Woodlands website, accessed October 8, 2014, http://www.highlevelwoodlands.com.

63 "Closing the Circle from Research to Action," accessed October 8, 2014, http://www.umce.ca/foresterie/sfmn/nouvelles/LUM-Webb.pdf.

64 D. C. Natcher and C. G. Hickey, "Putting the Community Back into Community-Based Resource Management: A Criteria and Indicators Approach to Sustainability," *Human Organization* 61, no. 4 (2002), pp. 350–363.

65 Discussion based on L. Redpath and M. O. Nielsen, "A Comparison of Native Culture, Non-Native Culture and New Management Ideology," *Canadian Journal of Administrative Sciences* 14, no. 3 (1997), pp. 327–339.

66 Discussion based on L. Redpath and M. O. Nielsen, "A Comparison of Native Culture, Non-Native Culture and New Management Ideology," *Canadian Journal of Administrative Sciences* 14, no. 3 (1997), pp. 327–339.

67 D. Grigg and J. Newman, "Five Ways to Foster Bonds, Win Trust in Business," *Ottawa Citizen*, April 23, 2003, p. F12.

68 T. Chui, K. Tran, and J. Flanders, "Chinese Canadians: Enriching the Cultural Mosaic," *Canadian Social Trends*, no. 76, Spring 2005, pp. 26–34.

69 Statistics Canada, "Canada's Visible Minority Population in 2017," *The Daily*, March 22, 2005.

70 I. Y. M. Yeung and R. L. Tung, "Achieving Business Success in Confucian Societies: The Importance of Guanxi (Connections)," *Organizational Dynamics*, Special Report, 1998, pp. 72–83.

71 I. Y. M. Yeung and R. L. Tung, "Achieving Business Success in Confucian Societies: The Importance of Guanxi (Connections)," *Organizational Dynamics*, Special Report, 1998, p. 73.

72 A. Barsky, S. A. Kaplan, and D. J. Beal, "Just Feelings? The Role of Affect in the Formation of Organizational Fairness Judgments," *Journal of Management*, January 2011, pp. 248–279; S. J. Breckler, "Empirical Validation of Affect, Behavior, and Cognition as Distinct Components of Attitude," *Journal of Personality and Social Psychology*, May 1984, pp. 1191–1205; J. A. Mikels, S. J. Maglio, A. E. Reed, and L. J. Kaplowitz, "Should I Go with My Gut? Investigating the Benefits of Emotion-Focused Decision Making," *Emotion*, August 2011, pp. 743–753; and A. J. Rojas Tejada, O. M. Lozano Rojas, M. Navas Luque, and P. J. Pérez Moreno, "Prejudiced Attitude Measurement Using the Rasch Scale Model," *Psychological Reports*, October 2011, pp. 553–572.

73 M. Riketta, "The Causal Relation between Job Attitudes and Performance: A Meta-analysis of Panel Studies," *Journal of Applied Psychology* 93, no. 2 (2008), pp. 472–481.

74 D. P. Moynihan and S. K. Pandey, "Finding Workable Levers over Work Motivation: Comparing Job Satisfaction, Job Involvement, and Organizational Commitment," *Administration & Society* 39, no. 7 (2007), pp. 803–832.

75 For problems with the concept of job satisfaction, see R. Hodson, "Workplace Behaviors," *Work and Occupations*, August 1991, pp. 271–290; and H. M. Weiss and R. Cropanzano, "Affective Events Theory: A Theoretical Discussion of the Structure, Causes and Consequences of Affective Experiences at Work," in *Research in Organizational Behavior*, vol. 18, ed. B. M. Staw and L. L. Cummings (Greenwich, CT: JAI Press, 1996), pp. 1–3.

76 J. Morrissy, "Canadian Workers among Most Dissatisfied in World," *Vancouver Sun*, June 25, 2011.

77 J. Barling, E. K. Kelloway, and R. D. Iverson, "High-Quality Work, Job Satisfaction, and Occupational Injuries," *Journal of Applied Psychology* 88, no. 2 (2003), pp. 276–283; and F. W. Bond and D. Bunce, "The Role of Acceptance and Job Control in Mental Health, Job Satisfaction, and Work Performance," *Journal of Applied Psychology* 88, no. 6 (2003), pp. 1057–1067.

78 Y. Georgellis and T. Lange, "Traditional versus Secular Values and the Job-Life Satisfaction Relationship Across Europe," *British Journal of Management* 23 (2012), pp. 437–454.

79 S. E. Humphrey, J. D. Nahrgang, and F. P. Morgeson, "Integrating Motivational, Social, and Contextual Work Design Features: A Meta-analytic Summary and Theoretical Extension of the Work Design Literature," *Journal of Applied Psychology* 92, no. 5 (2007), pp. 1332–1356; and D. S. Chiaburu and D. A. Harrison, "Do Peers Make the Place? Conceptual Synthesis and Meta-analysis of Coworker Effect on Perceptions, Attitudes, OCBs, and Performance," *Journal of Applied Psychology* 93, no. 5 (2008), pp. 1082–1103.

80 E. Diener, E. Sandvik, L. Seidlitz, and M. Diener, "The Relationship between Income and Subjective Well-Being: Relative or Absolute?" *Social Indicators Research* 28 (1993), pp. 195–223.

81 E. Diener, E. Sandvik, L. Seidlitz, and M. Diener, "The Relationship between Income and Subjective Well-Being: Relative or Absolute?" *Social Indicators Research* 28 (1993), pp. 195–223.

82 E. Diener, E. Sandvik, L. Seidlitz, and M. Diener, "The Relationship between Income and Subjective Well-Being: Relative or Absolute?" *Social Indicators Research* 28 (1993), pp. 195–223.

83 R. E. Silverman, "Work as Labor or Love?" *Wall Street Journal*, October 18, 2012, p. D3.

84 T. A. Judge and C. Hurst, "The Benefits and Possible Costs of Positive Core Self-Evaluations: A Review and Agenda for Future Research," in *Positive Organizational Behavior*, ed. D. Nelson and C. L. Cooper (London, UK: Sage, 2007), pp. 159–174.

85 T. A. Judge, C. J. Thoresen, J. E. Bono, and G. K. Patton, "The Job Satisfaction–Job Performance Relationship: A Qualitative and Quantitative Review," *Psychological Bulletin*, May 2001, pp. 376–407.

86 T. A. Judge, C. J. Thoresen, J. E. Bono, and G. K. Patton, "The Job Satisfaction–Job Performance Relationship: A Qualitative and Quantitative Review," *Psychological Bulletin*, May 2001, pp. 376–407; and T. Judge, S. Parker, A. E. Colbert, D. Heller, and R. Ilies, "Job Satisfaction: A Cross-Cultural Review," in *Handbook of Industrial, Work, & Organizational Psychology*, vol. 2, ed. N. Anderson, D. S. Ones, H. K. Sinangil, and C. Viswesvaran (Thousand Oaks, CA: Sage, 2001), p. 41.

87 C. Ostroff, "The Relationship between Satisfaction, Attitudes, and Performance: An Organizational Level Analysis," *Journal of Applied Psychology*, December 1992, pp. 963–974; A. M. Ryan, M. J. Schmit, and R. Johnson, "Attitudes and Effectiveness: Examining Relations at an Organizational Level," *Personnel Psychology*, Winter 1996, pp. 853–882; and J. K. Harter, F. L. Schmidt, and T. L. Hayes, "Business-Unit Level Relationship between Employee Satisfaction, Employee Engagement, and Business Outcomes: A Meta-analysis," *Journal of Applied Psychology*, April 2002, pp. 268–279.

88 D. W. Organ, *Organizational Citizenship Behavior: The Good Soldier Syndrome* (Lexington, MA: Lexington Books, 1988), p. 4.

89 D. W. Organ, *Organizational Citizenship Behavior: The Good Soldier Syndrome* (Lexington, MA: Lexington Books, 1988); C. A. Smith, D. W. Organ, and J. P. Near, "Organizational Citizenship Behavior: Its Nature and Antecedents," *Journal of Applied Psychology*, 1983, pp. 653–663.

90 J. Farh, C. Zhong, and D. W. Organ, "Organizational Citizenship Behavior in the People's Republic of China," *Academy of Management Proceedings*, August 2000, pp. D1–D6.

91 J. M. George and A. P. Brief, "Feeling Good-Doing Good: A Conceptual Analysis of the Mood at Work–Organizational Spontaneity Relationship," *Psychological Bulletin* 112 (2002), pp. 310–329; S. Wagner and M. Rush, "Altruistic Organizational Citizenship Behavior: Context, Disposition and Age," *Journal of Social Psychology* 140 (2002), pp. 379–391; and J. R. Spence, D. L. Ferris, D. J. Brown, and D. Heller, "Understanding Daily Citizenship Behaviors: A Social Comparison Perspective," *Journal of Organizational Behavior* 32, no. 4 (2011), pp. 547–571.

92 P. E. Spector, *Job Satisfaction: Application, Assessment, Causes, and Consequences* (Thousand Oaks, CA: Sage, 1997), pp. 57–58.

93 P. M. Podsakoff, S. B. MacKenzie, J. B. Paine, and D. G. Bachrach, "Organizational Citizenship Behaviors: A Critical Review of the Theoretical and Empirical Literature and Suggestions for Future Research," *Journal of Management* 26, no. 3 (2000), pp. 513–563.

94 B. J. Hoffman, C. A. Blair, J. P. Maeriac, and D. J. Woehr, "Expanding the Criterion Domain? A Quantitative Review of the OCB Literature," *Journal of Applied Psychology* 92, no. 2 (2007), pp. 555–566; and J. A. LePine, A. Erez, and D. E. Johnson, "The Nature and Dimensionality of Organizational Citizenship Behavior: A Critical Review and Meta-analysis," *Journal of Applied Psychology*, February 2002, pp. 52–65.

95 S. L. Blader and T. R. Tyler, "Testing and Extending the Group Engagement Model: Linkages between Social Identity, Procedural Justice, Economic Outcomes, and Extrarole Behavior," *Journal of Applied Psychology* 94, no. 2 (2009), pp. 445–464; J. Fahr, P. M. Podsakoff, and D. W. Organ, "Accounting for Organizational Citizenship Behavior: Leader Fairness and Task Scope Versus Satisfaction," *Journal of Management*, December 1990, pp. 705–722; and M. A. Konovsky and D. W. Organ, "Dispositional and Contextual Determinants of Organizational Citizenship Behavior," *Journal of Organizational Behavior*, May 1996, pp. 253–266.

96 D. S. Chiaburu and D. A. Harrison, "Do Peers Make the Place? Conceptual Synthesis and Meta-analysis of Coworker Effect on Perceptions, Attitudes, OCBs, and Performance," *Journal of Applied Psychology* 93, no. 5 (2008), pp. 1082–1103; and J. R. Spence, D. L. Ferris, D. J. Brown, and D. Heller, "Understanding Daily Citizenship Behaviors: A Social Comparison Perspective," *Journal of Organizational Behavior* 32, no. 4 (2011), pp. 547–571.

97 R. Ilies, I. S. Fulmer, M. Spitzmuller, and M. D. Johnson, "Personality and Citizenship Behavior: The Mediating Role of Job Satisfaction," *Journal of Applied Psychology* 94 (2009), pp. 945–959.

98 R. Ilies, B. A. Scott, and T. A. Judge, "The Interactive Effects of Personal Traits and Experienced States on Intraindividual Patterns of Citizenship Behavior," *Academy of Management Journal* 49 (2006), pp. 561–575.

99 See, for example, E. Naumann and D. W. Jackson Jr., "One More Time: How Do You Satisfy Customers?" *Business Horizons*, May–June 1999, pp. 71–76; D. J. Koys, "The Effects of Employee Satisfaction, Organizational Citizenship Behavior, and Turnover on Organizational Effectiveness: A Unit-Level, Longitudinal Study," *Personnel Psychology*, Spring 2001, pp. 101–114; J. Griffith, "Do Satisfied Employees Satisfy Customers? Support-Services Staff Morale and Satisfaction among Public School Administrators, Students, and Parents," *Journal of Applied Social Psychology*, August 2001, pp. 1627–1658; and C. Vandenberghe, K. Bentein, R. Michon, J. Chebat, M. Tremblay, and J. Fils, "An Examination of the Role of Perceived Support and Employee Commitment in Employee-Customer Encounters," *Journal of Applied Psychology* 92, no. 4 (2007), pp. 1177–1187.

100 http://about.zappos.com/our-unique-culture/zappos-core-values/deliver-wow-through-service.

101 E. A. Locke, "The Nature and Causes of Job Satisfaction," in *Handbook of Industrial and Organizational Psychology*, ed. M. D. Dunnette (Chicago: Rand McNally, 1976), p. 1331; K. D. Scott and G. S. Taylor, "An Examination of Conflicting Findings on the Relationship between Job Satisfaction and Absenteeism: A Meta-analysis," *Academy of Management Journal*, September 1985, pp. 599–612; and R. Steel and J. R. Rentsch, "Influence of Cumulation Strategies on the Long-Range Prediction of Absenteeism," *Academy of Management Journal*, December 1995, pp. 1616–1634.

102 J. P. Hausknecht, N. J. Hiller, and R. J. Vance, "Work-Unit Absenteeism: Effects of Satisfaction, Commitment, Labor Market Conditions, and Time," *Academy of Management Journal* 51, no. 6 (2008), pp. 1123–1245.

103 W. Hom and R. W. Griffeth, *Employee Turnover* (Cincinnati, OH: South-Western Publishing, 1995); R. W. Griffeth, P. W. Hom, and S. Gaertner, "A Meta-analysis of Antecedents and Correlates of Employee Turnover: Update, Moderator Tests, and Research Implications for the Next Millennium," *Journal of Management* 26, no. 3 (2000), p. 479.

104 D. Liu, T. R. Mitchell, T. W. Lee, B. C. Holtom, and T. R. Hinkin, "When Employees Are Out of Step with Coworkers: How Job Satisfaction Trajectory and Dispersion Influence Individual- and Unit-Level Voluntary Turnover," *Academy of Management Journal* 55, no. 6 (2012), pp. 1360–1380.

105 T. H. Lee, B. Gerhart, I. Weller, and C. O. Trevor, "Understanding Voluntary Turnover: Path-Specific Job Satisfaction Effects and the Importance of Unsolicited Job Offers," *Academy of Management Journal* 51, no. 4 (2008), pp. 651–671.

106 K. Jiang, D. Liu, P. F. McKay, T. W. Lee, and T. R. Mitchell, "When and How Is Job Embeddedness Predictive of Turnover? A Meta-analytic Investigation," *Journal of Applied Psychology* 97 (2012), pp. 1077–1096.

107 P. E. Spector, S. Fox, L. M. Penney, K. Bruursema, A. Goh, and S. Kessler, "The Dimensionality of Counterproductivity: Are All Counterproductive Behaviors Created Equal?" *Journal of Vocational Behavior* 68, no. 3 (2006), pp. 446–460; and D. S. Chiaburu and D. A. Harrison, "Do Peers Make the Place? Conceptual Synthesis and Meta-analysis of Coworker Effect on Perceptions, Attitudes, OCBs, and Performance," *Journal of Applied Psychology* 93, no. 5 (2008), pp. 1082–1103.

108 See D. Farrell, "Exit, Voice, Loyalty, and Neglect as Responses to Job Dissatisfaction: A Multidimensional Scaling Study," *Academy of Management Journal*, December 1983, pp. 596–606; C. E. Rusbult, D. Farrell, G. Rogers, and A. G. Mainous III, "Impact of Exchange Variables on Exit, Voice, Loyalty, and Neglect: An Integrative Model of Responses to Declining Job Satisfaction," *Academy of Management Journal*, September 1988, pp. 599–627; M. J. Withey and W. H. Cooper, "Predicting Exit, Voice, Loyalty, and Neglect," *Administrative Science Quarterly*, December 1989, pp. 521–539; J. Zhou and J. M. George, "When Job Dissatisfaction Leads to Creativity: Encouraging the Expression of Voice," *Academy of Management Journal*, August 2001, pp. 682–696; J. B. Olson-Buchanan and W. R. Boswell, "The Role of Employee Loyalty and Formality in Voicing Discontent," *Journal of Applied Psychology*, December 2002, pp. 1167–1174; and A. Davis-Blake, J. P. Broschak, and E. George, "Happy Together? How Using Nonstandard Workers Affects Exit, Voice, and Loyalty among Standard Employees," *Academy of Management Journal* 46, no. 4 (2003), pp. 475–485.

109 A. J. Nyberg and R. E. Ployhart, "Context-Emergent Turnover (CET) Theory: A Theory of Collective Turnover," *Academy of Management Review* 38 (2013), pp. 109–131.

110 R. B. Freeman, "Job Satisfaction as an Economic Variable," *American Economic Review*, January 1978, pp. 135–141.

111 K. Holland, "Inside the Minds of Your Employees," *New York Times*, January 28, 2007, p. B1; and "Study Sees Link between

Morale and Stock Price," *Workforce Management*, February 27, 2006, p. 15.

112 P. Brown, "The Workplace as a Solar System," *New York Times*, October 28, 2006, p. B5.

113 E. White, "How Surveying Workers Can Pay Off," *Wall Street Journal*, June 18, 2007, p. B3.

114 G. J. Blau and K. R. Boal, "Conceptualizing How Job Involvement and Organizational Commitment Affect Turnover and Absenteeism," *Academy of Management Review*, April 1987, p. 290.

115 O. N. Solinger, W. van Olffen, and R. A. Roe, "Beyond the Three-Component Model of Organizational Commitment," *Journal of Applied Psychology* 93 (2008), pp. 70–83.

116 N. J. Allen and J. P Meyer, "The Measurement and Antecedents of Affective, Continuance, and Normative Commitment to the Organization," *Journal of Occupational Psychology* 63 (1990), pp. 1–18; and J. P. Meyer, N. J. Allen, and C. A. Smith, "Commitment to Organizations and Occupations: Extension and Test of a Three-Component Conceptualization," *Journal of Applied Psychology* 78 (1993), pp. 538–551.

117 M. Riketta, "Attitudinal Organizational Commitment and Job Performance: A Meta-analysis," *Journal of Organizational Behavior*, March 2002, pp. 257–266.

118 T. A. Wright and D. G. Bonett, "The Moderating Effects of Employee Tenure on the Relation between Organizational Commitment and Job Performance: A Meta-analysis," *Journal of Applied Psychology*, December 2002, pp. 1183–1190.

119 T. W. H. Ng, D. C. Feldman, and S. S. K. Lam, "Psychological Contract Breaches, Organizational Commitment, and Innovation-Related Behaviors: A Latent Growth Modeling Approach," *Journal of Applied Psychology* 95 (2010), pp. 744–751.

120 See, for example, W. Hom, R. Katerberg, and C. L. Hulin, "Comparative Examination of Three Approaches to the Prediction of Turnover," *Journal of Applied Psychology*, June 1979, pp. 280–290; H. Angle and J. Perry, "Organizational Commitment: Individual and Organizational Influence," *Work and Occupations*, May 1983, pp. 123–146; J. L. Pierce and R. B. Dunham, "Organizational Commitment: Pre-Employment Propensity and Initial Work Experiences," *Journal of Management*, Spring 1987, pp. 163–178; and T. Simons and Q. Roberson, "Why Managers Should Care About Fairness: The Effects of Aggregate Justice Perceptions on Organizational Outcomes," *Journal of Applied Psychology* 88, no. 3 (2003), pp. 432–443.

121 Y. Gong, K. S. Law, S. Chang, and K. R. Xin, "Human Resources Management and Firm Performance: The Differential Role of Managerial Affective and Continuance Commitment," *Journal of Applied Psychology* 94, no. 1 (2009), pp. 263–275.

122 A. A. Luchak and I. R. Gellatly, "A Comparison of Linear and Nonlinear Relations between Organizational Commitment and Work Outcomes," *Journal of Applied Psychology* 92, no. 3 (2007), pp. 786–793.

123 See, for example, J. M. Diefendorff, D. J. Brown, and A. M. Kamin, "Examining the Roles of Job Involvement and Work Centrality in Predicting Organizational Citizenship Behaviors and Job Performance," *Journal of Organizational Behavior*, February 2002, pp. 93–108.

124 Based on G. J. Blau and K. R. Boal, "Conceptualizing How Job Involvement and Organizational Commitment Affect Turnover and Absenteeism," *Academy of Management Review*, April 1987, p. 290.

125 G. Chen and R. J. Klimoski, "The Impact of Expectations on Newcomer Performance in Teams as Mediated by Work Characteristics, Social Exchanges, and Empowerment," *Academy of Management Journal* 46, no. 5 (2003), pp. 591–607; A. Ergeneli, G. Saglam, and S. Metin, "Psychological Empowerment and Its Relationship to Trust in Immediate Managers," *Journal of Business Research*, January 2007, pp. 41–49; and S. E. Seibert, S. R. Silver, and W. A. Randolph, "Taking Empowerment to the Next Level: A Multiple-Level Model of Empowerment, Performance, and Satisfaction," *Academy of Management Journal* 47, no. 3 (2004), pp. 332–349.

126 B. J. Avolio, W. Zhu, W. Koh, and P. Bhatia, "Transformational Leadership and Organizational Commitment: Mediating Role of Psychological Empowerment and Moderating Role of Structural Distance," *Journal of Organizational Behavior* 25, no. 8 (2004), pp. 951–968.

127 M. Singh and A. Sarkar, "The Relationship Between Psychological Empowerment and Innovative Behavior," *Journal of Personnel Psychology* 2 (2012), pp. 127–137.

128 D. A. Kaplan, "Salesforce's Happy Workforce," *Fortune*, February 6, 2012, pp. 101–112.

129 L. Rhoades, R. Eisenberger, and S. Armeli, "Affective Commitment to the Organization: The Contribution of Perceived Organizational Support," *Journal of Applied Psychology* 86, no. 5 (2001), pp. 825–836.

130 C. Vandenberghe, K. Bentein, R. Michon, J. Chebat, M. Tremblay, and J. Fils, "An Examination of the Role of Perceived Support and Employee Commitment in Employee–Customer Encounters," *Journal of Applied Psychology* 92, no. 4 (2007), pp. 1177–1187; and P. Eder and R. Eisenberger, "Perceived Organizational Support: Reducing the Negative Influence of Coworker Withdrawal Behavior," *Journal of Management* 34, no. 1 (2008), pp. 55–68.

131 J. Farh, R. D. Hackett, and J. Liang, "Individual-Level Cultural Values as Moderators of Perceived Organizational Support—Employee Outcome Relationships in China: Comparing the Effects of Power Distance and Traditionality," *Academy of Management Journal* 50, no. 3 (2007), pp. 715–729.

132 D. R. May, R. L. Gilson, and L. M. Harter, "The Psychological Conditions of Meaningfulness, Safety and Availability and the Engagement of the Human Spirit at Work," *Journal of Occupational and Organizational Psychology* 77, no. 1 (2004), pp. 11–37.

133 B. L. Rich, J. A. Lepine, and E. R. Crawford, "Job Engagement: Antecedents and Effects on Job Performance," *Academy of Management Journal* 53, no. 3 (2010), pp. 617–635; and J. B. James, S. McKechnie, and J. Swanberg, "Predicting Employee Engagement in an Age-Diverse Retail Workforce," *Journal of Organizational Behavior* 32, no. 2 (2011), pp. 173–196.

134 "Building a Better Workforce," *PROFIT*, February 16, 2011, http://www.profitguide.com/manage-grow/human-resources/building-a-better-workforce-30073.

135 "Building a Better Workforce," *PROFIT*, February 16, 2011, http://www.profitguide.com/manage-grow/human-resources/building-a-better-workforce-30073.

136 J. Wright, "Trust and Confidence Key to Building a Better Workplace," HRVoice.org, May 8, 2013.

137 S. Crabtree, "Worldwide, 13% of Employees Are Engaged at Work," *Gallup World*, October 8, 2013; and http://www.molsoncoors.com/en/Responsibility/What%20Matters%20To%20Us/Employees%20Community/Our%20Employees/Engagement.aspx.

138 http://www.molsoncoors.com/en/Responsibility/What%20Matters%20To%20Us/Employees%20Community/Our%20Employees/Engagement.aspx.

139 Based on C. Chase, "Butler Charles MacPherson Is Taking Ford of Canada's Service Advisors to School," *Driving*, August 8, 2014, http://driving.ca/ford/auto-news/news/how-a-butler-is-helping-to-improve-fords-customer-service; H. Kafoury, "Creating Customer Loyalty, One Employee at a Time; Engaging Workers Can Start with Mutual Respect between Management and Staff," *Gazette* (Montreal), January 21, 2014, p. B2; and J. Lofaro, "Charles the Butler in Ottawa to Train Ford Employees Proper Etiquette," *Metro* (Ottawa),

August 6, 2014, http://metronews.ca/news/ottawa/1119408/charles-the-butler-in-ottawa-to-train-ford-employees-proper-etiquette/.

140 "Employee Engagement," *Workforce Management*, February 2013, p. 19; and "The Cornerstone OnDemand 2013 U.S. Employee Report," *Cornerstone OnDemand*, 2013, http://www.cornerstone-ondemand.com/resources/research/survey-2013.

141 W. B. Schaufeli, A. B. Bakker, and W. van Rhenen, "How Changes in Job Demands and Resources Predict Burnout, Work Engagement, and Sickness Absenteeism," *Journal of Organizational Behavior* 30, no. 7 (2009), pp. 893–917; E. R. Crawford, J. A. LePine, and B. L. Rich, "Linking Job Demands and Resources to Employee Engagement and Burnout: A Theoretical Extension and Meta-analytic Test," *Journal of Applied Psychology* 95, no. 5 (2010), pp. 834–848; and D. Xanthopoulou, A. B. Bakker, E. Demerouti, and W. B. Schaufeli, "Reciprocal Relationships Between job Resources, Personal Resources, and Work Engagement," *Journal of Vocational Behavior* 74, no. 3 (2009), pp. 235–244.

142 B. L. Rich, J. A. LePine, and E. R. Crawford, "Job Engagement: Antecedents and Effects on Job Performance," *Academy of Management Journal* 53, no. 3 (2010), pp. 617–635.

143 M. Tims, A. B. Bakker, and D. Xanthopoulou, "Do Transformational Leaders Enhance Their Followers' Daily Work Engagement?" *Leadership Quarterly* 22, no. 1 (2011), pp. 121–131; and F. O. Walumbwa, P. Wang, H. Wang, J. Schaubroeck, and B. J. Avolio, "Psychological Processes Linking Authentic Leadership to Follower Behaviors," *Leadership Quarterly* 21, no. 5 (2010), pp. 901–914.

144 Y. Brunetto, S. T. T. Teo, K. Shacklock, and R. Farr-Wharton, "Emotional Intelligence, Job Satisfaction, Well-being and Engagement: Explaining Organisational Commitment and Turnover Intentions in Policing," *Human Resource Management Journal* 22, no. 4 (2012), pp. 428–441.

145 P. Petrou, E. Demerouti, M. C. W. Peeters, W. B. Schaufeli, and Jørn Hetland, "Crafting a Job on a Daily Basis: Contextual Correlates and the Link to Work Engagement," *Journal of Organizational Behavior*, November 2012, pp. 1120–1141.

146 A. B. Bakker, "An Evidence-Based Model of Work Engagement," *Current Directions in Psychological Science* 20, no. 4 (August 2011), pp. 265–269.

147 See, for example, B. L. Rich, J. A. LePine, and E. R. Crawford, "Job Engagement: Antecedents and Effects on Job Performance," *Academy of Management Journal* 53, no. 3 (2010), pp. 617–635; and M. S. Christian, A. S. Garza, and J. E. Slaughter, "Work Engagement: A Quantitative Review and Test of Its Relations with Task and Contextual Performance," *Personnel Psychology* 64, no. 1 (2011), pp. 89–136.

148 J. M. George, "The Wider Context, Costs, and Benefits of Work Engagement," *European Journal of Work and Organizational Psychology* 20, no. 1 (2011), pp. 53–59; and J. R. B. Halbesleben, J. Harvey, and M. C. Bolino, "Too Engaged? A Conservation of Resources View of the Relationship between Work Engagement and Work Interference with Family," *Journal of Applied Psychology* 94, no. 6 (2009), pp. 1452–1465.

149 Vignette based on Corus Entertainment, *Corporate Social Responsibility Report, 2013*, accessed October 8, 2014, http://files.corusent.com/finances/documents/csr/coruscsr_2013.pdf; and "Corus Entertainment Inc.," Eluta.com, accessed October 8, 2014, http://www.eluta.ca/jobs-at-corus-entertainment#diversity:diversity-more.

150 Corus Entertainment, "Accessibility & Diversity," accessed October, 2014 http://www.corusent.com/home/Corporate/AboutCorus/AccessibilityDiversity/tabid/2572/Default.aspx.

151 N. Girouard, D. Stack, and M. O'Neill-Gilbert, "Ethnic Differences during Social Interactions of Preschoolers in Same-Ethnic and Cross-Ethnic Dyads," *European Journal of Developmental Psychology* 8, no. 2 (2011), pp. 185–202.

152 R. A. Roe and P. Ester, "Values and Work: Empirical Findings and Theoretical Perspective," *Applied Psychology: An International Review* 48 (1999), pp. 1–21.

153 A. Chapin, "Special Report: Diversity Knocks," *Canadian Business*, October 7, 2010.

154 D. A. Thomas and R. J. Ely, "Making Differences Matter: A New Paradigm for Managing Diversity," *Harvard Business Review*, September 1996, pp. 79–90; C. L. Holladay and M. A. Quiñones, "The Influence of Training Focus and Trainer Characteristics on Diversity Training Effectiveness," *Academy of Management Learning and Education* 7, no. 3 (2008), pp. 343–354; and R. Anand and M. Winters, "A Retrospective View of Corporate Diversity Training from 1964 to the Present," *Academy of Management Learning and Education* 7, no. 3 (2008), pp. 356–372.

155 L. Legault, J. Gutsell, and M. Inzlicht, "Ironic Effects of Anti-Prejudice Messages," *Psychological Science*, July 6, 2011, http://www.psychologicalscience.org/index.php/news/releases/ironic-effects-of-anti-prejudice-messages.html.

156 Q. M. Roberson and C. K. Stevens, "Making Sense of Diversity in the Workplace: Organizational Justice and Language Abstraction in Employees' Accounts of Diversity-Related Incidents," *Journal of Applied Psychology* 91 (2006), pp. 379–391; and D. A. Harrison, D. A. Kravitz, D. M. Mayer, L. M. Leslie, and D. Lev-Arey, "Understanding Attitudes toward Affirmative Action Programs in Employment: Summary and Meta-analysis of 35 Years of Research," *Journal of Applied Psychology* 91 (2006), pp. 1013–1036.

157 A. Kalev, F. Dobbin, and E. Kelly, "Best Practices or Best Guesses? Assessing the Efficacy of Corporate Affirmative Action and Diversity Policies," *American Sociological Review* 71, no. 4 (2006), pp. 589–617.

158 For more examples, see D. Jermyn, "45 of Canada's Most Welcoming Places to Work," *Globe and Mail*, February 21, 2011, p. B14.

159 A. Pomeroy, "Cultivating Female Leaders," *HR Magazine*, February 2007, pp. 44–50.

160 Based on P. Jeffery, "A Call to Action," *FP Magazine*, June 21, 2011.

161 L. Nguyen, "Banana Peel Thrown at Flyers' Wayne Simmonds Called a Wake-Up Call to NHL for More Ethnic Diversity," *Vancouver Sun*, September 23, 2011.

162 P. C. Earley and E. Mosakowski, "Cultural Intelligence," *Harvard Business Review*, October 2004, pp. 139–146.

163 S. S. Ramalu, R. C. Rose, N. Kumar, and J. Uli, "Doing Business in Global Arena: An Examination of the Relationship between Cultural Intelligence and Cross-Cultural Adjustment," *Asian Academy of Management Journal* 15, no. 1 (2010), pp. 79–97.

164 M. Gorji and H. Ghareseflo, "The Survey of Relationship between Cultural Intelligence and Emotional Intelligence with Employee's Performance," *International Proceedings of Economics Development & Research* 25 (2011), p. 175.

165 J. Sanchez-Burks, F. Lee, R. Nisbett, I. Choi, S. Zhao, and J. Koo, "Conversing across Cultures: East-West Communication Styles in Work and Nonwork Contexts," *Journal of Personality and Social Psychology* 85, no. 2 (2003), pp. 363–372.

166 P. C. Earley and E. Mosakowski, "Cultural Intelligence," *Harvard Business Review*, October 2004, pp. 139–146.

167 M. J. Gelfand, M. Erez, and Z. Aycan, "Cross-Cultural Organizational Behavior," *Annual Review of Psychology* 58 (2007), pp. 479–514; and A. S. Tsui, S. S. Nifadkar, and A. Y. Ou, "Cross-National, Cross-Cultural Organizational Behavior Research: Advances, Gaps, and Recommendations," *Journal of Management*, June 2007, pp. 426–478.

168 World Business Culture, "Doing Business in South Korea," accessed June 24, 2013, http://www.worldbusinessculture.com/Business-in-South-Korea.html.

169 C. Osborne, "South Korea Hits 100% Mark in Wireless Broadband," *CNET*, July 23, 2012, http://www.cnet.com/news/south-korea-hits-100-mark-in-wireless-broadband/.

170 Based on E. Snape, C. Lo, and T. Redman, "The Three-Component Model of Occupational Commitment: A Comparative Study of Chinese and British Accountants," *Journal of Cross-Cultural Psychology*, November 2008, pp. 765–781; and Y. Cheng and M. S. Stockdale, "The Validity of the Three-Component Model of Organizational Commitment in a Chinese Context," *Journal of Vocational Behavior*, June 2003, pp. 465–489.

171 E. Bellman, "Reversal of Fortune Isolates India's Brahmins," *Wall Street Journal*, December 29, 2007, p. A4.

172 A. Sippola and A. Smale, "The Global Integration of Diversity Management: A Longitudinal Case Study," *International Journal of Human Resource Management* 18, no. 11 (2007), pp. 1895–1916.

173 Based on "If You Started a Job and You Didn't Like It, How Long Would You Stay?" *USA Today*, June 11, 2012, p. 1B; O. Gough and S. Arkani, "The Impact of the Shifting Pensions Landscape on the Psychological Contract," *Personnel Review* 40, no. 2 (2011), pp. 173–184; "Loyalty Gap Widens," *USA Today*, May 16, 2012, p. 1B; P. Korkki, "The Shifting Definition of Worker Loyalty," *New York Times*, April 24, 2011, p. BU8; and "Is Workplace Loyalty an Outmoded Concept?" *Financial Times*, March 8, 2011, http://www.ft.com.

174 This exercise is based on M. Allen, "Here Comes the Bribe," *Entrepreneur*, October 2000, p. 48.

175 Reconstructed, based on H. Sokoloff, "Firing of Teacher Upheld for His Opinions on Race," *National Post*, March 13, 2002, pp. A1, A11.

176 Based on J. Zaslow, "From Attitude to Gratitude: This Is No Time for Complaints," *Wall Street Journal*, March 4, 2009, p. D1; A. M. Wood, S. Joseph, and J. Maltby, "Gratitude Uniquely Predicts Satisfaction with Life: Incremental Validity above the Domains and Facets of the Five Factor Model," *Personality and Individual Differences* 45, no. 1 (2008), pp. 49–54; and R. A. Emmons, "Gratitude, Subjective Well-Being, and the Brain," in *The Science of Subjective Well-Being*, ed. M. Eid and R. J. Larsen (New York: Guilford Press, 2008), pp. 469–489.

OB on the Edge: Stress at Work

1 Based on J. O'Kane, "Canada's Work-Life Balance More Off-Kilter Than Ever," *Globe and Mail*, October 25, 2012; D. Hansen, "Worker Who Felt 'Thrown Away' Wins," *Vancouver Sun*, August 16, 2006; and S. Kiume, "Trouble in jPod," *World of Psychology* (blog), accessed October 9, 2014, http://psychcentral.com/blog/archives/2007/02/28/trouble-in-jpod/.

2 Based on Statistics Canada, "Perceived Life Stress, Quite a Lot, by Sex, by Province and Territory," last modified June 12, 2014, http://www.statcan.gc.ca/tables-tableaux/sum-som/l01/cst01/health107b-eng.htm.

3 L. Nguyen, "Canadian Economy Loses $16.6B Annually Due to Absenteeism," *Toronto Star*, September 23, 2013.

4 K. MacQueen, "Workplace Stress Costs Us Dearly, and Yet Nobody Knows What It Is or How to Deal with It," *Maclean's*, October 15, 2007.

5 J. O'Kane, "Canada's Work-Life Balance More Off-Kilter Than Ever," *Globe and Mail*, October 25, 2012.

6 J. O'Kane, "Canada's Work-Life Balance More Off-Kilter Than Ever," *Globe and Mail*, October 25, 2012.

7 Based on Statistics Canada, "Perceived Life Stress, Quite a Lot, by Sex, by Province and Territory," last modified June 12, 2014, http://www.statcan.gc.ca/tables-tableaux/sum-som/l01/cst01/health107b-eng.htm.

8 V. Galt, "Productivity Buckling under the Strain of Stress, CEOs Say," *Globe and Mail*, June 9, 2005, p. B1.

9 "Canadian Workers among Most Stressed," *Worklife Report* 14, no. 2 (2002), pp. 8–9.

10 "Canadian Workers among Most Stressed," *Worklife Report* 14, no. 2 (2002), pp. 8–9.

11 Adapted from R. S. Schuler, "Definition and Conceptualization of Stress in Organizations," *Organizational Behavior and Human Performance*, April 1980, p. 189. For an updated review of definitions, see C. L. Cooper, P. J. Dewe, and M. P. O'Driscoll, *Organizational Stress: A Review and Critique of Theory, Research, and Applications* (Thousand Oaks, CA: Sage, 2002).

12 See, for example, M. A. Cavanaugh, W. R. Boswell, M. V. Roehling, and J. W. Boudreau, "An Empirical Examination of Self-Reported Work Stress among U.S. Managers," *Journal of Applied Psychology*, February 2000, pp. 65–74.

13 S. Shellenbarger, "When Stress Is Good for You," *Wall Street Journal*, January 24, 2012, pp. D1, D5.

14 S. Shellenbarger, "When Stress Is Good for You," *Wall Street Journal*, January 24, 2012, pp. D1, D5.

15 N. P. Podsakoff, J. A. LePine, and M. A. LePine, "Differential Challenge-Hindrance Stressor Relationships with Job Attitudes, Turnover Intentions, Turnover, and Withdrawal Behavior: A Meta-analysis," *Journal of Applied Psychology* 92, no. 2 (2007), pp. 438–454; and J. A. LePine, M. A. LePine, and C. L. Jackson, "Challenge and Hindrance Stress: Relationships with Exhaustion, Motivation to Learn, and Learning Performance," *Journal of Applied Psychology*, October 2004, pp. 883–891.

16 L. W. Hunter and S. M. B. Thatcher, "Feeling the Heat: Effects of Stress, Commitment, and Job Experience on Job Performance," *Academy of Management Journal* 50, no. 4 (2007), pp. 953–968.

17 J. C. Wallace, B. D. Edwards, T. Arnold, M. L. Frazier, and D. M. Finch, "Work Stressors, Role-Based Performance, and the Moderating Influence of Organizational Support," *Journal of Applied Psychology* 94, no. 1 (2009), pp. 254–262.

18 K. Kensing, "The Most Stressful Jobs of 2014," accessed October 9, 2014, http://www.careercast.com/jobs-rated/most-stressful-jobs-2014.

19 J. de Jonge and C. Dormann, "Stressors, Resources, and Strain at Work: A Longitudinal Test of the Triple-Match Principle," *Journal of Applied Psychology* 91, no. 5 (2006), pp. 1359–1374; K. Daniels, N. Beesley, A. Cheyne, and V. Wimalasiri, "Coping Processes Linking the Demands-Control-Support Model, Affect and Risky Decisions at Work," *Human Relations* 61, no. 6 (2008), pp. 845–874; and M. van den Tooren and J. de Jonge, "Managing Job Stress in Nursing: What Kind of Resources Do We Need?" *Journal of Advanced Nursing* 63, no. 1 (2008), pp. 75–84.

20 This section is adapted from C. L. Cooper and R. Payne, *Stress at Work* (London, UK: Wiley, 1978); S. Parasuraman and J. A. Alutto, "Sources and Outcomes of Stress in Organizational Settings: Toward the Development of a Structural Model," *Academy of Management Journal* 27, no. 2 (June 1984), pp. 330–350; and P. M. Hart and C. L. Cooper, "Occupational Stress: Toward a More Integrated Framework," in *Handbook of Industrial, Work and Organizational Psychology*, vol. 2, ed. N. Anderson, D. S. Ones, H. K. Sinangil, and C. Viswesvaran (London, UK: Sage, 2001), pp. 93–114.

21 E. A. Rafferty and M. A. Griffin, "Perceptions of Organizational Change: A Stress and Coping Perspective," *Journal of Applied Psychology* 71, no. 5 (2007), pp. 1154–1162.

22 H. Garst, M. Frese, and P. C. M. Molenaar, "The Temporal Factor of Change in Stressor-Strain Relationships: A Growth Curve Model on a Longitudinal Study in East Germany," *Journal of Applied Psychology*, June 2000, pp. 417–438.

23 See, for example, M. L. Fox, D. J. Dwyer, and D. C. Ganster, "Effects of Stressful Job Demands and Control of Physiological and Attitudinal Outcomes in a Hospital Setting," *Academy of Management Journal*, April 1993, pp. 289–318.

24 G. W. Evans and D. Johnson, "Stress and Open-Office Noise," *Journal of Applied Psychology*, October 2000, pp. 779–783.

25 T. M. Glomb, J. D. Kammeyer-Mueller, and M. Rotundo, "Emotional Labor Demands and Compensating Wage Differentials," *Journal of Applied Psychology*, August 2004, pp. 700–714; and A. A. Grandey, "When 'The Show Must Go On': Surface Acting and Deep Acting as Determinants of Emotional Exhaustion and Peer-Rated Service Delivery," *Academy of Management Journal*, February 2003, pp. 86–96.

26 S. Lim, L. M. Cortina, and V. J. Magley, "Personal and Workgroup Incivility: Impact on Work and Health Outcomes," *Journal of Applied Psychology* 93, no. 1 (2008), pp. 95–107; N. T. Buchanan and L. F. Fitzgerald, "Effects of Racial and Sexual Harassment on Work and the Psychological Well-Being of African American Women," *Journal of Occupational Health Psychology* 13, no. 2 (2008), pp. 137–151; C. R. Willness, P. Steel, and K. Lee, "A Meta-analysis of the Antecedents and Consequences of Workplace Sexual Harassment," *Personnel Psychology* 60, no. 1 (2007), pp. 127–162; and B. Moreno-Jiménez, A. Rodríguez-Muñoz, J. C. Pastor, A. I. Sanz-Vergel, and E. Garrosa, "The Moderating Effects of Psychological Detachment and Thoughts of Revenge in Workplace Bullying," *Personality and Individual Differences* 46, no. 3 (2009), pp. 359–364.

27 V. S. Major, K. J. Klein, and M. G. Ehrhart, "Work Time, Work Interference with Family, and Psychological Distress," *Journal of Applied Psychology*, June 2002, pp. 427–436; see also P. E. Spector, C. L. Cooper, S. Poelmans, T. D. Allen, M. O'Driscoll, J. I. Sanchez, O. L. Siu, P. Dewe, P. Hart, L. Lu, L. F. R. De Moraes, G. M. Ostrognay, K. Sparks, P. Wong, and S. Yu, "A Cross-National Comparative Study of Work-Family Stressors, Working Hours, and Well-Being: China and Latin America versus the Anglo World," *Personnel Psychology*, Spring 2004, pp. 119–142.

28 D. L. Nelson and C. Sutton, "Chronic Work Stress and Coping: A Longitudinal Study and Suggested New Directions," *Academy of Management Journal*, December 1990, pp. 859–869.

29 J. B. Avey, F. Luthans, and S. M. Jensen, "Psychological Capital: A Positive Resource for Combating Employee Stress and Turnover," *Human Resource Management*, September–October 2009, pp. 677–693.

30 Sun Life Financial, *Sun Life-Buffett National Wellness Survey 2013*, 2013, http://www.sunlife.ca; G. Marr, "Nay-cation? Why Canadians Are Leaving Vacation Days On the Table," *Financial Post*, March 18, 2014; and L. Nguyen, "Canadian Economy Loses $16.6B Annually Due to Absenteeism," *Toronto Star*, September 23, 2013.

31 H. Selye, *The Stress of Life*, rev. ed. (New York: McGraw-Hill, 1976); and Q. Hu, W. B. Schaufeli, and T. W. Taris, "The Job Demands–Resources Model: An Analysis of Additive and Joint Effects of Demands and Resources," *Journal of Vocational Behavior* 79, no. 1 (2011), pp. 181–190.

32 R. S. Schuler, "Definition and Conceptualization of Stress in Organizations," *Organizational Behavior and Human Performance*, April 1980, p. 191; and R. L. Kahn and P. Byosiere, "Stress in Organizations," *Organizational Behavior and Human Performance*, April 1980, pp. 604–610.

33 J. Schaubroeck, J. R. Jones, and J. L. Xie, "Individual Differences in Utilizing Control to Cope with Job Demands: Effects on Susceptibility to Infectious Disease," *Journal of Applied Psychology*, April 2001, pp. 265–278.

34 M. Kivimäki, J. Head, J. E. Ferrie, E. Brunner, M. G. Marmot, J. Vahtera, and M. J. Shipley, "Why Is Evidence on Job Strain and Coronary Heart Disease Mixed? An Illustration of Measurement Challenges in the Whitehall II Study," *Psychosomatic Medicine* 68, no. 3 (2006), pp. 398–401.

35 M. Borritz, K. B. Christensen, U. Bültmann, R. Rugulies, T. Lund, I Andersen, E. Villadsen, F. Didreichsen, and T. S. Krisensen, "Impact on Burnout and Psychosocial Work Characteristics on Future Long-Term Sickness Absence, Prospective Results of the Danish PUMA Study among Human Service Workers," *Journal of Occupational and Environmental Medicine* 52, no. 10 (2010), pp. 964–970.

36 R. Ilies, N. Dimotakis, and I. E. DePater, "Psychological and Physiological Reactions to High Workloads: Implications for Well-Being," *Personnel Psychology* 63, no. 2 (2010), pp. 407–463.

37 C. L. Cooper and J. Marshall, "Occupational Sources of Stress: A Review of the Literature Relating to Coronary Heart Disease and Mental Ill Health," *Journal of Occupational Psychology* 49, no. 1 (1976), pp. 11–28.

38 J. R. Hackman and G. R. Oldham, "Development of the Job Diagnostic Survey," *Journal of Applied Psychology*, April 1975, pp. 159–170; "Burnout among Finnish Employees," *Journal of Occupational Health Psychology* 16, no. 3 (2011), pp. 345–360; E. R. Crawford, J. A. LePine, and B. L. Rich, "Linking Job Demands and Resources to Employee Engagement and Burnout: A Theoretical Extension and Meta-analytic Test," *Journal of Applied Psychology* 95, no. 5 (2010), pp. 834–848; and G. A. Chung-Yan, "The Nonlinear Effects of Job Complexity and Autonomy on Job Satisfaction, Turnover, and Psychological Well-Being," *Journal of Occupational Health Psychology* 15, no. 3 (2010), pp. 237–251.

39 L. L. Meier, N. K. Semmer, A. Elfering, and N. Jacobshagen, "The Double Meaning of Control: Three-Way Interactions between Internal Resources, Job Control, and Stressors at Work," *Journal of Occupational Health Psychology* 13, no. 3 (2008), pp. 244–258.

40 E. M. de Croon, J. K. Sluiter, R. W. B. Blonk, J. P. J. Broersen, and M. H. W. Frings-Dresen, "Stressful Work, Psychological Job Strain, and Turnover: A 2-Year Prospective Cohort Study of Truck Drivers," *Journal of Applied Psychology*, June 2004, pp. 442–454; R. Cropanzano, D. E. Rupp, and Z. S. Byrne, "The Relationship of Emotional Exhaustion to Work Attitudes, Job Performance, and Organizational Citizenship Behaviors," *Journal of Applied Psychology*, February 2003, pp. 160–169; and S. Diestel and K. Schmidt, "Costs of Simultaneous Coping with Emotional Dissonance and Self-Control Demands at Work: Results from Two German Samples," *Journal of Applied Psychology* 96, no. 3 (2011), pp. 643–653.

41 J. L. Xie and G. Johns, "Job Scope and Stress: Can Job Scope Be Too High?" *Academy of Management Journal*, October 1995, pp. 1288–1309.

42 S. J. Motowidlo, J. S. Packard, and M. R. Manning, "Occupational Stress: Its Causes and Consequences for Job Performance," *Journal of Applied Psychology*, November 1987, pp. 619–620.

43 See J. B. Halbesleben, "Sources of Social Support and Burnout: A Meta-analytic Test of the Conservation of Resources Model," *Journal of Applied Psychology* 91, no. 5 (2006), pp. 1134–1145; N. Bolger and D. Amarel, "Effects of Social Support Visibility on Adjustment to Stress: Experimental Evidence," *Journal of Applied Psychology* 92, no. 3 (2007), pp. 458–475; and C. Fernet, M. Gagné, and S. Austin, "When Does Quality of Relationships with Coworkers Predict Burnout over Time? The Moderating Role of Work Motivation," *Journal of Organizational Behavior* 31 (2010), pp. 1163–1180.

44 R. J. Burke, A. M. Richardson, and M. Mortinussen, "Workaholism among Norwegian Managers: Work and Well-Being Outcomes," *Journal of Organizational Change Management* 7 (2004), pp. 459–470; and W. B. Schaufeli, T. W. Taris, and W. van Rhenen, "Workaholism, Burnout, and Work Engagement: Three of a Kind or Three Different Kinds of Employee Well-Being?" *Applied Psychology: An International Review* 57, no. 2 (2008), pp. 173–203.

45 T. H. Macan, "Time Management: Test of a Process Model," *Journal of Applied Psychology*, June 1994, pp. 381–391.

46 See, for example, G. Lawrence-Ell, *The Invisible Clock: A Practical Revolution in Finding Time for Everyone and Everything* (Seaside Park,

NJ: Kingsland Hall, 2002); and B. Tracy, *Time Power* (New York: AMACOM, 2004).

47 R. W. Renn, D. G. Allen, and T. M. Huning, "Empirical Examination of Individual-Level Personality-Based Theory of Self-Management Failure," *Journal of Organizational Behavior* 32, no. 1 (2011), pp. 25–43; and P. Gröpel and P. Steel, "A Mega-Trial Investigation of Goal Setting, Interest Enhancement, and Energy on Procrastination," *Personality and Individual Differences* 45, no. 5 (2008), pp. 406–411.

48 S. A. Devi, "Aging Brain: Prevention of Oxidative Stress by Vitamin E and Exercise," *Scientific World Journal* 9 (2009), pp. 366–372. See also P. Salmon, "Effects of Physical Exercise on Anxiety, Depression, and Sensitivity to Stress: A Unifying Theory," *Clinical Psychology Review* 21, no. 1 (2001), pp. 33–61.

49 K. M. Richardson and H. R. Rothstein, "Effects of Occupational Stress Management Intervention Programs: A Meta-analysis," *Journal of Occupational Health Psychology* 13, no. 1 (2008), pp. 69–93.

50 V. C. Hahn, C. Binnewies, S. Sonnentag, and E. J. Mojza, "Learning How to Recover From Job Stress: Effects of a Recovery Training Program on Recovery, Recovery-Related Self-Efficacy, and Well-Being," *Journal of Occupational Health Psychology* 16, no. 2 (2011), pp. 202–216; and C. Binnewies, S. Sonnentag, and E. J. Mojza, "Recovery during the Weekend and Fluctuations in Weekly Job Performance: A Week-Level Study Examining Intra-Individual Relationships," *Journal of Occupational and Organizational Psychology* 83, no. 2 (2010), pp. 419–441.

51 S. Gordon, "The Benefits of Office Wellness Programs," *Globe and Mail*, September 6, 2012.

52 J. Lee, "How to Fight That Debilitating Stress in Your Workplace," *Vancouver Sun*, April 5, 1999, p. C3. Reprinted with permission.

53 S. Gordon, "The Benefits of Office Wellness Programs," *Globe and Mail*, September 6, 2012.

54 Sun Life Financial, *Sun Life-Buffett National Wellness Survey 2013*, 2013, http://www.sunlife.ca.

55 "Cdn Employers Not Measuring Wellness Outcomes: Survey," *Benefits Canada*, May 4, 2011, http://www.benefitscanada.com/news/cnd-employers-not-measuring-wellness-outcomes-survey-16510.

56 P. M. Wright, "Operationalization of Goal Difficulty as a Moderator of the Goal Difficulty-Performance Relationship," *Journal of Applied Psychology*, June 1990, pp. 227–234; E. A. Locke and G. P. Latham, "Building a Practically Useful Theory of Goal Setting and Task Motivation: A 35-Year Odyssey," *American Psychologist* 57, no. 9 (2002), pp. 705–717; K. L. Langeland, C. M. Johnson, and T. C. Mawhinney, "Improving Staff Performance in a Community Mental Health Setting: Job Analysis, Training, Goal Setting, Feedback, and Years of Data," *Journal of Organizational Behavior Management*, 1998, pp. 21–43.

57 E. R. Greenglass and L. Fiksenbaum, "Proactive Coping, Positive Affect, and Well-Being: Testing for Mediation Using Path Analysis," *European Psychologist* 14, no. 1 (2009), pp. 29–39; and P. Miquelon and R. J. Vallerand, "Goal Motives, Well-Being, and Physical Health: Happiness and Self-Realization as Psychological Resources under Challenge," *Motivation and Emotion* 30, no. 4 (2006), pp. 259–272.

58 M. M. Butts, R. J. Vandenberg, D. M. DeJoy, B. S. Schaffer, and M. G. Wilson, "Individual Reactions to High Involvement Work Processes: Investigating the Role of Empowerment and Perceived Organizational Support," *Journal of Occupational Health Psychology* 14, no. 2 (2009), pp. 122–136.

59 S. Greengard, "It's About Time," *Industry Week*, February 7, 2000, pp. 47–50; and S. Nayyar, "Gimme a Break," *American Demographics*, June 2002, p. 6.

60 See, for example, B. Leonard, "Health Care Costs Increase Interest in Wellness Programs," *HR Magazine*, September 2001, pp. 35–36; and "Healthy, Happy and Productive," *Training*, February 2003, p. 16.

61 K. M. Richardson and H. R. Rothstein, "Effects of Occupational Stress Management Intervention Programs: A Meta-analysis," *Journal of Occupational Health Psychology* 13, no. 1 (2008), pp. 69–93.

62 Based on S. Martin, "Money Is the Stressor for Americans," *Monitor on Psychology*, December 2008, pp. 28–29; *Helicobacter pylori and Peptic Ulcer Disease*, Centers for Disease Control and Prevention, U.S. Department of Health and Human Services; and M. Maynard, "Maybe the Toughest Job Aloft," *New York Times*, August 15, 2006, pp. C1, C6.

Chapter 4

1 Opening vignette based on J. Graham, "McMorris's Fractured Rib Won't Derail Sochi Dreams," *Globe and Mail*, January 28, 2014, p. S3; and C. Bane, "Mark McMorris Breaks Rib In Slope Crash," *X Games*, January 25, 2014, http://xgames.espn.go.com/snowboarding/article/10351911/mark-mcmorris-breaks-rib-slope-style-finals.

2 See, for example, G. P. Latham and C. C. Pinder, "Work Motivation Theory and Research at the Dawn of the Twenty-First Century," *Annual Review of Psychology* 56 (2005), pp. 485–516; and C. C. Pinder, *Work Motivation in Organizational Behavior*, 2nd ed. (London, UK: Psychology Press, 2008).

3 S. Crabtree, "Worldwide, 13% of Employees Are Engaged at Work," *Gallup World*, October 8, 2013, http://www.gallup.com/poll/165269/worldwide-employees-engaged-work.aspx.

4 "The 2014 Wasting Time at Work Survey: Everything You've Always Wanted to Know About Wasting Time in the Office," *Salary.com*, accessed October 10, 2014, http://www.salary.com.

5 See, for example, T. R. Mitchell, "Matching Motivational Strategies with Organizational Contexts," in *Research in Organizational Behavior*, vol. 19, ed. L. L. Cummings and B. M. Staw (Greenwich, CT: JAI Press, 1997), pp. 60–62.

6 D. Gregor, *The Human Side of Enterprise* (New York: McGraw-Hill, 1960). For an updated analysis of Theory X and Theory Y constructs, see R. J. Summers and S. F. Cronshaw, "A Study of McGregor's Theory X, Theory Y and the Influence of Theory X, Theory Y Assumptions on Causal Attributions for Instances of Worker Poor Performance," in *Organizational Behavior*, ed. S. L. McShane, ASAC Conference Proceedings, vol. 9, part 5, Halifax, 1988, pp. 115–123.

7 K. W. Thomas, *Intrinsic Motivation at Work* (San Francisco: Berrett-Koehler, 2000); and K. W. Thomas, "Intrinsic Motivation and How It Works," *Training*, October 2000, pp. 130–135.

8 A. Kohn, *Punished by Rewards* (Boston: Houghton Mifflin, 1993).

9 Based on D. Albarracin, I. Senay, and K. Noguchi, "Will We Succeed? The Science of Self-motivation," *Psychological Science*, April 2010; and "Will We Succeed? The Science of Self-Motivation," *ScienceDaily*, June 1, 2010, http://www.sciencedaily.com/releases/2010/05/100528092021.htm.

10 A. H. Maslow, *Motivation and Personality* (New York: Harper and Row, 1954).

11 C. Conley, *Peak: How Great Companies Get Their Mojo from Maslow* (San Francisco: Jossey-Bass, 2007).

12 See, for example, E. E. Lawler III and J. L. Suttle, "A Causal Correlation Test of the Need Hierarchy Concept," *Organizational Behavior and Human Performance* 7, no. 2 (1972), pp. 265–287; D. T. Hall and K. E. Nougaim, "An Examination of Maslow's Need Hierarchy in an Organizational Setting," *Organizational Behavior and Human Performance* 3, no. 1 (1968), pp. 12–35;

and J. Rauschenberger, N. Schmitt, and J. E. Hunter, "A Test of the Need Hierarchy Concept by a Markov Model of Change in Need Strength," *Administrative Science Quarterly* 25, no. 4 (1980), pp. 654–670.

13 L. Tay and E. Diener, "Needs and Subjective Well-Being around the World," *Journal of Personality and Social Psychology*, June 20, 2011, published online before print, http://academic.udayton.edu/jackbauer/Readings%20595/Tay%20Diener%2011%20needs%20WB%20world%20copy.pdf.

14 D. T. Kenrick, V. Griskevicius, S. L. Neuberg, and M. Schaller, "Renovating the Pyramid of Needs: Contemporary Extensions Built on Ancient Foundations," *Perspectives on Psychological Science* 5, no. 3 (2010), pp. 292–314.

15 F. Herzberg, B. Mausner, and B. Snyderman, *The Motivation to Work* (New York: Wiley, 1959).

16 R. J. House and L. A. Wigdor, "Herzberg's Dual-Factor Theory of Job Satisfaction and Motivations: A Review of the Evidence and Criticism," *Personnel Psychology*, Winter 1967, pp. 369–389; D. P. Schwab and L. L. Cummings, "Theories of Performance and Satisfaction: A Review," *Industrial Relations*, October 1970, pp. 403–430; R. J. Caston and R. Braito, "A Specification Issue in Job Satisfaction Research," *Sociological Perspectives*, April 1985, pp. 175–197; and J. Phillipchuk and J. Whittaker, "An Inquiry into the Continuing Relevance of Herzberg's Motivation Theory," *Engineering Management Journal* 8, no. 1 (1996), pp. 15–20.

17 R. J. House and L. A. Wigdor, "Herzberg's Dual-Factor Theory of Job Satisfaction and Motivations: A Review of the Evidence and Criticism," *Personnel Psychology*, Winter 1967, pp. 369–389; D. P. Schwab and L. L. Cummings, "Theories of Performance and Satisfaction: A Review," *Industrial Relations*, October 1970, pp. 403–430; and R. J. Caston and R. Braito, "A Specification Issue in Job Satisfaction Research," *Sociological Perspectives*, April 1985, pp. 175–197.

18 D. C. McClelland, *The Achieving Society* (New York: Van Nostrand Reinhold, 1961); J. W. Atkinson and J. O. Raynor, *Motivation and Achievement* (Washington, DC: Winston, 1974); D. C. McClelland, *Power: The Inner Experience* (New York: Irvington, 1975); and M. J. Stahl, *Managerial and Technical Motivation: Assessing Needs for Achievement, Power, and Affiliation* (New York: Praeger, 1986).

19 D. C. McClelland, *The Achieving Society* (New York: Van Nostrand Reinhold, 1961).

20 D. C. McClelland and D. G. Winter, *Motivating Economic Achievement* (New York: The Free Press, 1969); and J. B. Miner, N. R. Smith, and J. S. Bracker, "Role of Entrepreneurial Task Motivation in the Growth of Technologically Innovative Firms: Interpretations from Follow-up Data," *Journal of Applied Psychology*, October 1994, pp. 627–630.

21 D. C. McClelland, *Power: The Inner Experience* (New York: Irvington, 1975); D. C. McClelland and D. H. Burnham, "Power Is the Great Motivator," *Harvard Business Review*, March–April 1976, pp. 100–110; and R. E. Boyatzis, "The Need for Close Relationships and the Manager's Job," in *Organizational Psychology: Readings on Human Behavior in Organizations*, 4th ed., ed. D. A. Kolb, I. M. Rubin, and J. M. McIntyre (Upper Saddle River, NJ: Prentice Hall, 1984), pp. 81–86.

22 D. G. Winter, "The Motivational Dimensions of Leadership: Power, Achievement, and Affiliation," in *Multiple Intelligences and Leadership*, ed. R. E. Riggio, S. E. Murphy, and F. J. Pirozzolo (Mahwah, NJ: Lawrence Erlbaum, 2002), pp. 119–138.

23 J. B. Miner, *Studies in Management Education* (New York: Springer, 1965).

24 Vignette based on C. Bane, "Mark McMorris Breaks Rib in Slope Crash," *X Games*, January 25, 2014, http://xgames.espn.go.com/snowboarding/article/10351911/mark-mcmorris-breaks-rib-slope-style-finals; and K. Gillespie, "Canadian Slopestyle Star Is One

Fierce Competitor," *Waterloo Region Record*, January 31, 2014, p. D4.

25 V. H. Vroom, *Work and Motivation* (New York: Wiley, 1964).

26 For criticism, see H. G. Heneman III and D. P. Schwab, "Evaluation of Research on Expectancy Theory Prediction of Employee Performance," *Psychological Bulletin* 78, no. 1 (1972), pp. 1–9; T. R. Mitchell, "Expectancy Models of Job Satisfaction, Occupational Preference and Effort: A Theoretical, Methodological and Empirical Appraisal," *Psychological Bulletin* 81, no. 12 (1974), pp. 1053–1077; and W. Van Eerde and H. Thierry, "Vroom's Expectancy Models and Work-Related Criteria: A Meta-analysis," *Journal of Applied Psychology* 81, no. 5 (1996), pp. 575–586. For support, see L. W. Porter and E. E. Lawler III, *Managerial Attitudes and Performance* (Homewood, IL: Irwin, 1968); and J. J. Donovan, "Work Motivation," in *Handbook of Industrial, Work & Organizational Psychology*, vol. 2, ed. N. Anderson, D. S. Ones, H. K. Sinangil, and C. Viswesvaran (Thousand Oaks, CA: Sage, 2001), pp. 56–59.

27 Based on J. Nocera, "The Anguish of Being an Analyst," *New York Times*, March 4, 2006, pp. B1, B12.

28 See, for example, H. G. Heneman III and D. P. Schwab, "Evaluation of Research on Expectancy Theory Prediction of Employee Performance," *Psychological Bulletin*, July 1972, pp. 1–9; T. R. Mitchell, "Expectancy Models of Job Satisfaction, Occupational Preference and Effort: A Theoretical, Methodological and Empirical Appraisal," *Psychological Bulletin*, November 1974, pp. 1053–1077; and L. Reinharth and M. A. Wahba, "Expectancy Theory as a Predictor of Work Motivation, Effort Expenditure, and Job Performance," *Academy of Management Journal*, September 1975, pp. 502–537.

29 See, for example, L. W. Porter and E. E. Lawler III, *Managerial Attitudes and Performance* (Homewood, IL: Richard D. Irwin, 1968); D. F. Parker and L. Dyer, "Expectancy Theory as a Within-Person Behavioral Choice Model: An Empirical Test of Some Conceptual and Methodological Refinements," *Organizational Behavior and Human Performance*, October 1976, pp. 97–117; H. J. Arnold, "A Test of the Multiplicative Hypothesis of Expectancy-Valence Theories of Work Motivation," *Academy of Management Journal*, April 1981, pp. 128–141; and W. Van Eerde and H. Thierry, "Vroom's Expectancy Models and Work-Related Criteria: A Meta-analysis," *Journal of Applied Psychology*, October 1996, pp. 575–586.

30 P. C. Earley, *Face, Harmony, and Social Structure: An Analysis of Organizational Behavior across Cultures* (New York: Oxford University Press, 1997); R. M. Steers and C. Sanchez-Runde, "Culture, Motivation, and Work Behavior," in *Handbook of Cross-Cultural Management*, ed. M. Gannon and K. Newman (London: Blackwell, 2001), pp. 190–215; and H. C. Triandis, "Motivation and Achievement in Collectivist and Individualistic Cultures," in *Advances in Motivation and Achievement*, vol. 9, ed. M. Maehr and P. Pintrich (Greenwich, CT: JAI Press, 1995), pp. 1–30.

31 C. Gabelica, P. Van den Bossche, M. Segers, and W. Gijselaersa, "Feedback, a Powerful Lever in Teams: A Review," *Educational Research Review*, June 2012, pp. 123–144.

32 S. Huang, Y. Zhang, and S. M. Broniarczyk, "So Near and Yet So Far: The Mental Representation of Goal Progress," *Journal of Personality and Social Psychology* 103, no. 2 (2012), pp. 225–241.

33 B. D. Cawley, L. M. Keeping, and P. E. Levy, "Participation in the Performance Appraisal Process and Employee Reactions: A Meta-analytic Review of Field Investigations," *Journal of Applied Psychology*, August 1998, pp. 615–633; and P. E. Levy and J. R. Williams, "The Social Context of Performance Appraisal: A Review and Framework for the Future," *Journal of Management* 30, no. 6 (2004), pp. 881–905.

34 List directly quoted from R. Kreitner and A. Kinicki, *Organizational Behavior*, 6th ed. (New York: McGraw-Hill/Irwin, 2004), p. 335 (emphasis added).

35 E. A. Locke, "Toward a Theory of Task Motivation and Incentives," *Organizational Behavior and Human Performance*, May 1968, pp. 157–189.

36 P. C. Earley, P. Wojnaroski, and W. Prest, "Task Planning and Energy Expended: Exploration of How Goals Influence Performance," *Journal of Applied Psychology*, February 1987, pp. 107–114.

37 "KEYGroup Survey Finds Nearly Half of All Employees Have No Set Performance Goals," *IPMA-HR Bulletin*, March 10, 2006, p. 1; S. Hamm, "SAP Dangles a Big, Fat Carrot," *BusinessWeek*, May 22, 2006, pp. 67–68; and "P&G CEO Wields High Expectations but No Whip," *USA Today*, February 19, 2007, p. 3B.

38 See, for example, S. J. Carroll and H. L. Tosi, *Management by Objectives: Applications and Research* (New York: Macmillan, 1973); and R. Rodgers and J. E. Hunter, "Impact of Management by Objectives on Organizational Productivity," *Journal of Applied Psychology*, April 1991, pp. 322–336.

39 E. A. Locke and G. P. Latham, *A Theory of Goal Setting and Task Performance* (Englewood Cliffs, NJ: Prentice Hall, 1980).

40 E. A. Locke, K. N. Shaw, L. M. Saari, and G. P. Latham, "Goal Setting and Task Performance," *Psychological Bulletin*, January 1981, pp. 125–152; and A. J. Mento, R. P. Steel, and R. J. Karren, "A Meta-analytic Study of the Effects of Goal Setting on Task Performance: 1966–1984," *Organizational Behavior and Human Decision Processes*, February 1987, pp. 52–83.

41 R. E. Wood, A. J. Mento, and E. A. Locke, "Task Complexity as a Moderator of Goal Effects: A Meta-analysis," *Journal of Applied Psychology*, August 1987, pp. 416–425.

42 P. M. Wright, "Operationalization of Goal Difficulty as a Moderator of the Goal Difficulty-Performance Relationship," *Journal of Applied Psychology*, June 1990, pp. 227–234; E. A. Locke and G. P. Latham, "Building a Practically Useful Theory of Goal Setting and Task Motivation: A 35-Year Odyssey," *American Psychologist* 57, no. 9 (2002), pp. 705–717.

43 P. M. Wright, J. R. Hollenbeck, S. Wolf, and G. C. McMahan, "The Effects of Varying Goal Difficulty Operationalizations on Goal Setting Outcomes and Processes," *Organizational Behavior and Human Decision Processes*, January 1995, pp. 28–43.

44 K. L. Langeland, C. M. Johnson, and T. C. Mawhinney, "Improving Staff Performance in a Community Mental Health Setting: Job Analysis, Training, Goal Setting, Feedback, and Years of Data," *Journal of Organizational Behavior Management*, 1998, pp. 21–43.

45 J. M. Ivancevich and J. T. McMahon, "The Effects of Goal Setting, External Feedback, and Self-Generated Feedback on Outcome Variables: A Field Experiment," *Academy of Management Journal*, June 1982, pp. 359–372; and E. A. Locke, "Motivation through Conscious Goal Setting," *Applied and Preventive Psychology* 5 (1996), pp. 117–124.

46 E. A. Locke and G. P. Latham, *A Theory of Goal Setting and Task Performance* (Englewood Cliffs, NJ: Prentice Hall, 1990).

47 K. Dewettinck and H. van Dijk, "Linking Belgian Employee Performance Management System Characteristics with Performance Management System Effectiveness: Exploring the Mediating Role of Fairness," *International Journal of Human Resource Management*, February 1, 2013, pp. 806–825; and M. Erez, P. C. Earley, and C. L. Hulin, "The Impact of Participation on Goal Acceptance and Performance: A Two-Step Model," *Academy of Management Journal* 28, no. 1 (1985), pp. 50–66.

48 T. S. Bateman and B. Bruce, "Masters of the Long Haul: Pursuing Long-Term Work Goals," *Journal of Organizational Behavior*, October 2012, pp. 984–1006; and E. A. Locke, "The Motivation to Work: What We Know," *Advances in Motivation and Achievement* 10 (1997), pp. 375–412.

49 H. J. Klein, M. J. Wesson, J. R. Hollenbeck, P. M. Wright, and R. D. DeShon, "The Assessment of Goal Commitment: A Measurement Model Meta-analysis," *Organizational Behavior and Human Decision Processes* 85, no. 1 (2001), pp. 32–55.

50 J. E. Bono and A. E. Colbert, "Understanding Responses to Multi-Source Feedback: The Role of Core Self-evaluations," *Personnel Psychology*, Spring 2005, pp. 171–203; and S. A. Jeffrey, A. Schulz, and A. Webb, "The Performance Effects of an Ability-Based Approach to Goal Assignment," *Journal of Organizational Behavior Management* 32 (2012), pp. 221–241.

51 A. M. O'Leary-Kelly, J. J. Martocchio, and D. D. Frink, "A Review of the Influence of Group Goals on Group Performance," *Academy of Management Journal*, October 1994, pp. 1285–1301; and T. Tammemagi, D. O'Hora, and K. A. Maglieri, "The Effects of a Goal Setting Intervention on Productivity and Persistence in an Analogue Work Task," *Journal of Organizational Behavior Management*, March 1, 2013, pp. 31–54.

52 K. D. Vohs, J. K. Park, and B. J. Schmeichel, "Self-Affirmation Can Enable Goal Disengagement," *Journal of Personality and Social Psychology* 104, no. 1 (2013), pp. 14–27.

53 G. P. Latham and E. A. Locke, "Enhancing the Benefits and Overcoming the Pitfalls of Goal Setting," *Organizational Dynamics* 35, no. 6 (2006), pp. 332–340; L. D. Ordóñez, M. E. Schweitzer, A. D. Galinsky, and M. Bazerman, "Goals Gone Wild: The Systematic Side Effects of Overprescribing Goal Setting," *Academy of Management Perspectives* 23, no.1 (2009), pp. 6–16; and E. A. Locke and G. P. Latham, "Has Goal Setting Gone Wild, or Have Its Attackers Abandoned Good Scholarship?" *Academy of Management Perspectives* 23, no. 1 (2009), pp. 17–23.

54 S. J. Perry, L. A. Witt, L. M. Penney, and L. Atwater, "The Downside of Goal-Focused Leadership: The Role of Personality in Subordinate Exhaustion," *Journal of Applied Psychology* 95, no. 6 (2010), pp. 1145–1153.

55 K. Lanaj, C. D. Chang, and R. E. Johnson, "Regulatory Focus and Work-Related Outcomes: A Review and Meta-analysis," *Psychological Bulletin* 138, no. 5 (2012), pp. 998–1034.

56 K. Lanaj, C. D. Chang, and R. E. Johnson, "Regulatory Focus and Work-Related Outcomes: A Review and Meta-analysis," *Psychological Bulletin* 138, no. 5 (2012), pp. 998–1034.

57 A. Bandura, *Self-Efficacy: The Exercise of Control* (New York: Freeman, 1997). See also M. Salanová, S. Llorens, and W. Schaufeli, "'Yes, I Can, I Feel Good, and I Just Do It!' On Gain Cycles and Spirals of Efficacy Beliefs, Affect, and Engagement," *Applied Psychology: An International Review* 60, no. 2 (2011), pp. 255–285.

58 A. D. Stajkovic and F. Luthans, "Self-Efficacy and Work-Related Performance: A Meta-analysis," *Psychological Bulletin*, September 1998, pp. 240–261; and A. Bandura, "Cultivate Self-Efficacy for Personal and Organizational Effectiveness," in *Handbook of Principles of Organizational Behavior*, ed. E. Locke (Malden, MA: Blackwell, 2004), pp. 120–136.

59 M. Salanova, S. Llorens, and W. B. Schaufeli, "'Yes I Can, I Feel Good, and I Just Do It!' On Gain Cycles and Spirals of Efficacy Beliefs, Affect, and Engagement," *Applied Psychology: An International Review* 60, no. 2 (2011), pp. 255–285.

60 P. Tierney and S. M. Farmer, "Creative Self-Efficacy Development and Creative Performance Over Time," *Journal of Applied Psychology* 96, no. 2 (2011), pp. 277–293.

61 A. Bandura and D. Cervone, "Differential Engagement in Self-Reactive Influences in Cognitively-Based Motivation," *Organizational Behavior and Human Decision Processes*, August 1986, pp. 92–113.

62 A. Bandura, *Self-Efficacy: The Exercise of Control* (New York: Freeman, 1997).

63 D. Eden, "Self-Fulfilling Prophecies in Organizations," in *Organizational Behavior: The State of the Science*, 2nd ed., ed. J. Greenberg (Mahwah, NJ: Lawrence Erlbaum, 2003), pp. 91–122.

64 R. C. Rist, "Student Social Class and Teacher Expectations: The Self-Fulfilling Prophecy in Ghetto Education," *Harvard Educational Review* 70, no. 3 (2000), pp. 266–301.

65 D. Eden, "Self-Fulfilling Prophecies in Organizations," in *Organizational Behavior: The State of the Science*, 2nd ed., ed. J. Greenberg (Mahwah, NJ: Lawrence Erlbaum, 2003), pp. 91–122.

66 C. L. Holladay and M. A. Quiñones, "Practice Variability and Transfer of Training: The Role of Self-Efficacy Generality," *Journal of Applied Psychology* 88, no. 6 (2003), pp. 1094–1103.

67 E. C. Dierdorff, E. A. Surface, and K. G. Brown, "Frame-of-Reference Training Effectiveness: Effects of Goal Orientation and Self-Efficacy on Affective, Cognitive, Skill-Based, and Transfer Outcomes," *Journal of Applied Psychology* 95, no. 6 (2010), pp. 1181–1191; and R. Grossman, and E. Salas, "The Transfer of Training: What Really Matters," *International Journal of Training and Development* 15, no. 2 (2011), pp. 103–120.

68 T. A. Judge, C. L. Jackson, J. C. Shaw, B. Scott, and B. L. Rich, "Self-Efficacy and Work-Related Performance: The Integral Role of Individual Differences," *Journal of Applied Psychology* 92, no. 1 (2007), pp. 107–127.

69 T. A. Judge, C. L. Jackson, J. C. Shaw, B. Scott, and B. L. Rich, "Self-Efficacy and Work-Related Performance: The Integral Role of Individual Differences," *Journal of Applied Psychology* 92, no. 1 (2007), pp. 107–127.

70 K. M. Eddington, C. Majestic, and P. J. Silvia, "Contrasting Regulatory Focus and Reinforcement Sensitivity: A Daily Diary Study of Goal Pursuit and Emotion," *Personality and Individual Differences*, August 2012, pp. 335–340.

71 B. F. Skinner, *Contingencies of Reinforcement* (East Norwalk, CT: Appleton-Century-Crofts, 1971).

72 J. A. Mills, *Control: A History of Behavioral Psychology* (New York: New York University Press, 2000).

73 F. Luthans and R. Kreitner, *Organizational Behavior Modification and Beyond*, 2nd ed. (Glenview, IL: Scott, Foresman, 1985); and A. D. Stajkovic and F. Luthans, "A Meta-analysis of the Effects of Organizational Behavior Modification on Task Performance, 1975–95," *Academy of Management Journal*, October 1997, pp. 1122–1149.

74 Vignette based on C. Blatchford, "First Day, First Scandal; 'Ridiculous' Judging Forces McMorris into Slopestyle Semifinals," *Windsor Star*, February 7, 2014, p. B2; and K. Gillespie, "Slopestylers Not Worried Over Judging Concerns," *Toronto Star*, February 9, 2014, p. S5.

75 J. S. Adams, "Inequity in Social Exchanges," in *Advances in Experimental Social Psychology*, ed. L. Berkowitz (New York: Academic Press, 1965), pp. 267–300.

76 P. S. Goodman, "An Examination of Referents Used in the Evaluation of Pay," *Organizational Behavior and Human Performance*, October 1974, pp. 170–195; S. Ronen, "Equity Perception in Multiple Comparisons: A Field Study," *Human Relations*, April 1986, pp. 333–346; R. W. Scholl, E. A. Cooper, and J. F. McKenna, "Referent Selection in Determining Equity Perception: Differential Effects on Behavioral and Attitudinal Outcomes," *Personnel Psychology*, Spring 1987, pp. 113–127; T. P. Summers and A. S. DeNisi, "In Search of Adams' Other: Reexamination of Referents Used in the Evaluation of Pay," *Human Relations*, June 1990, pp. 497–511; S. Werner and N. P. Mero, "Fair or Foul? The Effects of External, Internal, and Employee Equity on Changes in Performance of Major League Baseball Players," *Human Relations*, October 1999, pp. 1291–1312; and R. W. Griffeth and S. Gaertner, "A Role for Equity Theory in the Turnover Process: An Empirical Test," *Journal of Applied Social Psychology*, May 2001, pp. 1017–1037.

77 See, for example, E. Walster, G. W. Walster, and W. G. Scott, *Equity: Theory and Research* (Boston: Allyn and Bacon, 1978); and J. Greenberg, "Cognitive Reevaluation of Outcomes in Response to Underpayment Inequity," *Academy of Management Journal*, March 1989, pp. 174–184.

78 P. S. Goodman and A. Friedman, "An Examination of Adams' Theory of Inequity," *Administrative Science Quarterly*, September 1971, pp. 271–288; R. P. Vecchio, "An Individual-Differences Interpretation of the Conflicting Predictions Generated by Equity Theory and Expectancy Theory," *Journal of Applied Psychology*, August 1981, pp. 470–481; R. T. Mowday, "Equity Theory Predictions of Behavior in Organizations," in *Motivation and Work Behavior*, 6th ed., ed. R. Steers, L. W. Porter, and G. Bigley (New York: McGraw-Hill, 1996), pp. 111–131; R. W. Griffeth and S. Gaertner, "A Role for Equity Theory in the Turnover Process: An Empirical Test," *Journal of Applied Social Psychology*, May 2001, pp. 1017–1037; and L. K. Scheer, N. Kumar, and J.-B. E. M. Steenkamp, "Reactions to Perceived Inequity in U.S. and Dutch Interorganizational Relationships," *Academy of Management* 46, no. 3 (2003), pp. 303–316.

79 See, for example, R. C. Huseman, J. D. Hatfield, and E. W. Miles, "A New Perspective on Equity Theory: The Equity Sensitivity Construct," *Academy of Management Journal* 12, no. 2 (1987), pp. 222–234; K. S. Sauley and A. G. Bedeian, "Equity Sensitivity: Construction of a Measure and Examination of Its Psychometric Properties," *Journal of Management* 26, no. 5 (2000), pp. 885–910; and J. A. Colquitt, "Does the Justice of One Interact with the Justice of Many? Reactions to Procedural Justice in Teams," *Journal of Applied Psychology* 89, no. 4 (2004), pp. 633–646.

80 C. O. Trevor, G. Reilly, and B. Gerhart, "Reconsidering Pay Dispersion's Effect on the Performance of Interdependent Work: Reconciling Sorting and Pay Inequality," *Academy of Management Journal*, June 2012, pp. 585–610.

81 C. O. Trevor, G. Reilly, and B. Gerhart, "Reconsidering Pay Dispersion's Effect on the Performance of Interdependent Work: Reconciling Sorting and Pay Inequality," *Academy of Management Journal*, June 2012, pp. 585–610.

82 See, for example, R. Cropanzano, J. H. Stein, and T. Nadisic, *Social Justice and the Experience of Emotion* (New York: Routledge/Taylor and Francis Group, 2011).

83 G. S. Leventhal, "What Should Be Done with Equity Theory? New Approaches to the Study of Fairness in Social Relationships," in *Social Exchange: Advances in Theory and Research*, ed. K. Gergen, M. Greenberg, and R. Willis (New York: Plenum, 1980), pp. 27–55.

84 J. Brockner and B. M. Wiesenfeld, "An Integrative Framework for Examining Reactions to Decisions: Interactive Effects of Outcomes and Procedures," *Psychological Bulletin* 120 (1996), pp. 189–208.

85 R. Folger and D. P. Skarlicki, "Fairness as a Dependent Variable: Why Tough Times Can Lead to Bad Management," in *Justice in the Workplace: From Theory to Practice*, ed. R. Cropanzano (Mahway, NJ: Erlbaum, 2001), pp. 97–118.

86 C. R. Wanberg, L. W. Bunce, and M. B. Gavin, "Perceived Fairness of Layoffs Among Individuals Who Have Been Laid Off," *Personnel Psychology* 52 (1999), pp. 59–84.

87 J. C. Shaw, E. Wild, and J. A. Colquitt, "To Justify or Excuse? A Meta-Analytic Review of the Effects of Explanations," *Journal of Applied Psychology* 88, no. 3 (2003), pp. 444–458.

88 R. J. Bies, "Are Procedural and Interactional Justice Conceptually Distinct?" in *Handbook of Organizational Justice*, ed. J. Greenberg and J. A. Colquitt (Mahwah, NJ: Erlbaum, 2005), pp. 85–112; and B. A. Scott, J. A. Colquitt, and E. L. Paddock, "An Actor-Focused Model of Justice Rule Adherence and Violation: The Role of Managerial Motives and Discretion," *Journal of Applied Psychology* 94, no. 3 (2009), pp. 756–769.

89 G. A. Van Kleef, A. C. Homan, B. Beersma, D. V. Knippenberg, B. V. Knippenberg, and F. Damen, "Searing Sentiment or Cold Calculation? The Effects of Leader Emotional Displays on Team Performance Depend on Follower Epistemic Motivation," *Academy of Management Journal* 52, no. 3 (2009), pp. 562–580.

90 J. M. Robbins, M. T. Ford, and L. E. Tetrick, "Perceived Unfairness and Employee Health: A Meta-analytic Integration," *Journal of Applied Psychology* 97, no. 2 (2012), pp. 235–272.

91 J. A. Colquitt, B. A. Scott, J. B. Rodell, D. M. Long, C. P. Zapata, D. E. Conlon, and M. J. Wesson, "Justice at the Millennium, A Decade Later: A Meta-analytic Test of Social Exchange and Affect-Based Perspectives," *Journal of Applied Psychology* 98, no. 2 (2013), pp. 199–236.

92 B. A. Scott, J. A. Colquitt, and E. L. Paddock, "An Actor-Focused Model of Justice Rule Adherence and Violation: The Role of Managerial Motives and Discretion," *Journal of Applied Psychology* 94, no. 3 (2009), pp. 756–769.

93 B. A. Scott, J. A. Colquitt, and E. L. Paddock, "An Actor-Focused Model of Justice Rule Adherence and Violation: The Role of Managerial Motives and Discretion," *Journal of Applied Psychology* 94, no. 3 (2009), pp. 756–769.

94 K. Leung, K. Tong, and S. S. Ho, "Effects of Interactional Justice on Egocentric Bias in Resource Allocation Decisions," *Journal of Applied Psychology* 89, no. 3 (2004), pp. 405–415; and L. Francis-Gladney, N. R. Manger, and R. B. Welker, "Does Outcome Favorability Affect Procedural Fairness as a Result of Self-Serving Attributions," *Journal of Applied Social Psychology* 40, no. 1 (2010), pp. 182–194.

95 L. J. Barclay and D. P. Skarlicki, "Healing the Wounds of Organizational Injustice: Examining the Benefits of Expressive Writing," *Journal of Applied Psychology* 94, no. 2 (2009), pp. 511–523.

96 E. Deci and R. Ryan, eds., *Handbook of Self-Determination Research* (Rochester, NY: University of Rochester Press, 2002); R. Ryan and E. Deci, "Self-Determination Theory and the Facilitation of Intrinsic Motivation, Social Development, and Well-Being," *American Psychologist* 55, no. 1 (2000), pp. 68–78; and M. Gagné and E. L. Deci, "Self-Determination Theory and Work Motivation," *Journal of Organizational Behavior* 26, no. 4 (2005), pp. 331–362.

97 E. L. Deci, R. Koestner, and R. M. Ryan, "A Meta-analytic Review of Experiments Examining the Effects of Extrinsic Rewards on Intrinsic Motivation," *Psychological Bulletin* 125, no. 6 (1999), pp. 627–668; N. Houlfort, R. Koestner, M. Joussemet, A. Nantel-Vivier, and N. Lekes, "The Impact of Performance-Contingent Rewards on Perceived Autonomy and Competence," *Motivation & Emotion* 26, no. 4 (2002), pp. 279–295; G. J. Greguras and J. M. Diefendorff, "Different Fits Satisfy Different Needs: Linking Person-Environment Fit to Employee Commitment and Performance Using Self-Determination Theory," *Journal of Applied Psychology* 94, no. 2 (2009), pp. 465–477; and M. P. Moreno-Jiménez and M. C. H. Villodres, "Prediction of Burnout in Volunteers," *Journal of Applied Social Psychology* 40, no. 7 (2010), pp. 1798–1818. This work studies the personal experience of volunteering and several antecedent and consequent variables. We studied the effect of the amount of time dedicated to the organization, motivation, social support, integration in the organization, self-efficacy, and characteristics of the work on a consequent variable of the volunteering experience; that is, burnout, with its three components of efficacy, cynicism, and exhaustion. The statistical analysis shows that the time dedicated to volunteering and the extrinsic motivations (that is, social and career) predicts higher levels of burnout, whereas intrinsic motivations (that is, values and understanding), life satisfaction, and integration in the organization are negatively related to burnout.

98 R. Eisenberger and L. Rhoades, "Incremental Effects of Reward on Creativity," *Journal of Personality and Social Psychology* 81, no. 4 (2001), pp. 728–741; and R. Eisenberger, W. D. Pierce, and J. Cameron, "Effects of Reward on Intrinsic Motivation—Negative, Neutral, and Positive: Comment on Deci, Koestner, and Ryan (1999)," *Psychological Bulletin* 125, no. 6 (1999), pp. 677–691.

99 M. Burgess, M. E. Enzle, and R. Schmaltz, "Defeating the Potentially Deleterious Effects of Externally Imposed Deadlines: Practitioners' Rules-of-Thumb," *Personality and Social Psychology Bulletin* 30, no. 7 (2004), pp. 868–877.

100 K. Byron and S. Khazanchi, "Rewards and Creative Performance: A Meta-analytic Test of Theoretically Derived Hypotheses," *Psychological Bulletin* 138, no. 4 (2012), pp. 809–830.

101 K. M. Sheldon, A. J. Elliot, and R. M. Ryan, "Self-Concordance and Subjective Well-Being in Four Cultures," *Journal of Cross-Cultural Psychology* 35, no. 2 (2004), pp. 209–223.

102 K. M. Sheldon, A. J. Elliot, and R. M. Ryan, "Self-Concordance and Subjective Well-Being in Four Cultures," *Journal of Cross-Cultural Psychology* 35, no. 2 (2004), pp. 209–223.

103 J. E. Bono and T. A. Judge, "Self-Concordance at Work: Toward Understanding the Motivational Effects of Transformational Leaders," *Academy of Management Journal* 46, no. 5 (2003), pp. 554–571.

104 L. M. Graves, M. N. Ruderman, P. J. Ohlott, and Todd J. Webber, "Driven to Work and Enjoyment of Work: Effects on Managers' Outcomes," *Journal of Management* 38, no. 5 (2012), pp. 1655–1680.

105 J. P. Meyer, T. E. Becker, and C. Vandenberghe, "Employee Commitment and Motivation: A Conceptual Analysis and Integrative Model," *Journal of Applied Psychology* 89, no. 6 (2004), pp. 991–1007.

106 K. W. Thomas, E. Jansen, and W. G. Tymon Jr., "Navigating in the Realm of Theory: An Empowering View of Construct Development," in *Research in Organizational Change and Development*, vol. 10, ed. W. A. Pasmore and R. W. Woodman (Greenwich, CT: JAI Press, 1997), pp. 1–30.

107 This section based on C. Michaelson, "Meaningful Motivation for Work Motivation Theory," *Academy of Management Review* 30, no. 2 (2005), pp. 235–238; and R. M. Steers, R. T. Mowday, and D. L. Shapiro, "Response to Meaningful Motivation for Work Motivation Theory," *Academy of Management Review* 30, no. 2 (2005), p. 238.

108 C. Michaelson, "Meaningful Motivation for Work Motivation Theory," *Academy of Management Review* 30, no. 2 (2005), p. 237.

109 N. J. Adler, *International Dimensions of Organizational Behavior*, 4th ed. (Cincinnati, OH: South-Western Publishing, 2002), p. 174.

110 G. Hofstede, "Motivation, Leadership, and Organization: Do American Theories Apply Abroad?" *Organizational Dynamics*, Summer 1980, p. 55.

111 G. Hofstede, "Motivation, Leadership, and Organization: Do American Theories Apply Abroad?" *Organizational Dynamics*, Summer 1980, p. 55.

112 D. F. Crown, "The Use of Group and Groupcentric Individual Goals for Culturally Heterogeneous and Homogeneous Task Groups: An Assessment of European Work Teams," *Small Group Research* 38, no. 4 (2007), pp. 489–508; J. Kurman, "Self-Regulation Strategies in Achievement Settings: Culture and Gender Differences," *Journal of Cross-Cultural Psychology* 32, no. 4 (2001), pp. 491–503; and M. Erez and P. C. Earley, "Comparative Analysis of Goal-Setting Strategies across Cultures," *Journal of Applied Psychology* 72, no. 4 (1987), pp. 658–665.

113 C. Sue-Chan and M. Ong, "Goal Assignment and Performance: Assessing the Mediating Roles of Goal Commitment and Self-Efficacy and the Moderating Role of Power Distance," *Organizational Behavior and Human Decision Processes* 89, no. 2 (2002), pp. 1140–1161.

114 R. Fischer and P. B. Smith, "Reward Allocation and Culture: A Meta-analysis," *Journal of Cross-Cultural Psychology* 34, no. 3 (2003), pp. 251–268.

115 F. F. T. Chiang and T. Birtch, "The Transferability of Management Practices: Examining Cross-National Differences in Reward Preferences," *Human Relations* 60, no. 9 (2007), pp. 1293–1330; A. E. Lind, T. R. Tyler, and Y. J. Huo, "Procedural Context and

Culture: Variation in the Antecedents of Procedural Justice Judgments," *Journal of Personality and Social Psychology* 73, no. 4 (1997), pp. 767–780; and M. J. Gelfand, M. Erez, and Z. Aycan, "Cross-Cultural Organizational Behavior," *Annual Review of Psychology* 58 (2007), pp. 479–514.

116 J. K. Giacobbe-Miller, D. J. Miller, and V. I. Victorov, "A Comparison of Russian and U.S. Pay Allocation Decisions, Distributive Justice Judgments, and Productivity under Different Payment Conditions," *Personnel Psychology* 51, no. 1 (1998), pp. 137–163.

117 M. C. Bolino and W. H. Turnley, "Old Faces, New Places: Equity Theory in Cross-Cultural Contexts," *Journal of Organizational Behavior* 29, no. 1 (2008), pp. 29–50.

118 Based on S. E. DeVoe and S. S. Iyengar, "Managers' Theories of Subordinates: A Cross-Cultural Examination of Manager Perceptions of Motivation and Appraisal of Performance," *Organizational Behavior and Human Decision Processes*, January 2004, pp. 47–61.

119 I. Harpaz, "The Importance of Work Goals: An International Perspective," *Journal of International Business Studies*, First Quarter 1990, pp. 75–93.

120 G. E. Popp, H. J. Davis, and T. T. Herbert, "An International Study of Intrinsic Motivation Composition," *Management International Review*, January 1986, pp. 28–35.

121 R. Fischer and P. B. Smith, "Reward Allocation and Culture: A Meta-analysis," *Journal of Cross-Cultural Psychology* 34, no. 3 (2003), pp. 251–268.

122 F. T. Chiang and T. Birtch, "The Transferability of Management Practices: Examining Cross-National Differences in Reward Preferences," *Human Relations* 60, no. 9 (2007), pp. 1293–1330; A. E. Lind, T. R. Tyler, and Y. J. Huo, "Procedural Context and Culture: Variation in the Antecedents of Procedural Justice Judgments," *Journal of Personality and Social Psychology* 73, no. 4 (1997), pp. 767–780; and M. J. Gelfand, M. Erez, and Z. Aycan, "Cross-Cultural Organizational Behavior," *Annual Review of Psychology* 58 (2007), pp. 479–514.

123 Based on E. A. Locke and G. P. Latham, "Building a Practically Useful Theory of Goal Setting and Task Motivation," *American Psychologist* 57 (2002), pp. 705–771; A. Tugend, "Expert's Advice to the Goal-Oriented: Don't Overdo It," *New York Times*, October 6, 2012, p. B5; and C. Richards, "Letting Go of Long-Term Goals," *New York Times*, August 4, 2012.

124 Based on A. Ellin, "Failure Is Not an Option," *New York Times*, April 15, 2012, pp. 13–14.

125 Based on J. McFarland, "Major CEO Pay Increases in the Cards Again," *Globe and Mail*, June 1, 2014, http://www.theglobeandmail.com/report-on-business/careers/management/executive-compensation/pay-is-on-the-rise-for-canadas-top-executives/article18940701/; "CEO vs Average Pay in Canada: All in a Day's Work?" Canadian Centre for Policy Alternatives, January 2, 2014, https://www.policyalternatives.ca/ceo; J. Bizjak, M. Lemmon, and T. Nguyen, "Are All CEOs Above Average? An Empirical Analysis of Compensation Peer Groups and Pay Design," *Journal of Financial Economics* 100, no. 3 (2011), pp. 538–555; R. Foroohar, "Stuffing Their Pockets: For CEOs, A Lucrative Recession" *Newsweek*, September 13, 2010; A. Kleinman, "Mark Zuckerberg $1 Salary Puts Him in Elite Group of $1 CEOs," *Huffington Post*, April 29, 2013; and G. Morgenson, "If Shareholders Say 'Enough Already,' the Board May Listen," *New York Times*, April 6, 2013.

126 Based on "Quebecor Plays Hardball with Defiant Union: Vidéotron 'Ready to Listen': Aims to Sell Cable Installation Operations," *Financial Post (National Post)*, March 5, 2002, p. FP6; and S. Silcoff, "Quebecor and Union in Showdown over Costs," *Financial Post (National Post)*, February 28, 2002, p. FP3.

127 Based on S. P. Robbins and D. A. DeCenzo, *Fundamentals of Management*, 4th ed. (Upper Saddle River, NJ: Prentice Hall, 2004), p. 85.

Chapter 5

1 Opening vignette based on D. Baer, "How Hootsuite CEO Ryan Holmes Is Building a Yoga-Loving Maple-Syrup Mafia," *Fast Company*, accessed October 10, 2014, http://www.fastcompany.com/3019055/bottom-line/how-hootsuite-ceo-ryan-holmes-is-building-a-yoga-loving-maple-syrup-mafia; and R. Holmes, "2 Ways to Keep Company Culture Alive during Rapid Expansion," *Hootsuite* (blog), accessed October 10, 2014, http://blog.hootsuite.com/ryan-holmes-linkedin-1/.

2 D. W. Krueger, "Money, Success, and Success Phobia," in *The Last Taboo: Money as a Symbol and Reality in Psychotherapy and Psychoanalysis*, ed. D. W. Krueger (New York: Brunner/Mazel, 1986), pp. 3–16.

3 J. Nelson, "Payday Woes," *Canadian Business*, April 8, 2011.

4 T. R. Mitchell and A. E. Mickel, "The Meaning of Money: An Individual-Difference Perspective," *Academy of Management*, July 1999, pp. 568–578.

5 T. A. Judge, R. F. Piccolo, J. C. Podsakoff, and B. L. Rich, "The Relationship between Pay Satisfaction and Job Satisfaction," *Journal of Vocational Behavior* 77 (2010), 157–167.

6 R. Fischer and D. Boer, "What Is More Important for National Well-Being: Money or Autonomy? A Meta-analysis of Well-Being, Burnout, and Anxiety across 63 Societies," *Journal of Personality and Social Psychology*, July 2011, pp. 164–184.

7 S. A. Hewlett, L. Sherbin, and K. Sumberg, "How Gen Y & Boomers Will Reshape Your Agenda," *Harvard Business Review*, July/August 2009, pp. 71–76.

8 This paragraph is based on T. R. Mitchell and A. E. Mickel, "The Meaning of Money: An Individual-Difference Perspective," *Academy of Management*, July 1999, pp. 568–578. The reader may want to refer to the myriad of references cited in the article.

9 S. A. Hewlett, L. Sherbin, and K. Sumberg "How Gen Y & Boomers Will Reshape Your Agenda," *Harvard Business Review*, July/August 2009, pp. 71–76.

10 Vignette based on R. Holmes, "2 Ways to Keep Company Culture Alive during Rapid Expansion," *Hootsuite* (blog), accessed October 10, 2014, http://blog.hootsuite.com/ryan-holmes-linkedin-1/; and A. Kritsch, "5 Secrets for a Better Work-Life Balance: Inside Hootsuite Culture," *Hootsuite* (blog), accessed October 10, 2014, http://blog.hootsuite.com/5-secrets-for-a-better-work-life-balance/.

11 E. White, "Opportunity Knocks, and It Pays a Lot Better," *Wall Street Journal*, November 13, 2006, p. B3.

12 D. A. McIntyre and S. Weigley, "8 Companies That Most Owe Workers a Raise," *USA Today*, May 13, 2013, http://www.usatoday.com/story/money/business/2013/05/12/8-companies-that-most-owe-workers-a-raise/2144013/.

13 M. Sabramony, N. Krause, J. Norton, and G. N. Burns "The Relationship between Human Resource Investments and Organizational Performance: A Firm-Level Examination of Equilibrium Theory," *Journal of Applied Psychology* 93, no. 4 (2008), pp. 778–788.

14 H. Shaw, "Walmart Canada Stung As Retail Competition Heats Up," *Financial Post*, November 14, 2013.

15 Based on J. R. Schuster and P. K. Zingheim, "The New Variable Pay: Key Design Issues," *Compensation & Benefits Review*, March–April 1993, p. 28; K. S. Abosch, "Variable Pay: Do We Have the Basics in Place?" *Compensation & Benefits Review*, July–August 1998, pp. 12–22; and K. M. Kuhn and M. D. Yockey, "Variable Pay as a Risky Choice: Determinants of the Relative Attractiveness of Incentive Plans," *Organizational Behavior and Human Decision Processes*, March 2003, pp. 323–341.

16 "Canada's General Motors Workers to Get Up to 16 Per Cent of Salary in Bonuses," *Canadian Press*, February 14, 2011.

17 "Canada's General Motors Workers to Get Up to 16 Per Cent of Salary in Bonuses," *Canadian Press*, February 14, 2011.

18 J. Ratner, "Dofasco Boss Took Home Biggest Pay," *National Post*, February 1, 2006, p. WK3.

19 "Canada's General Motors Workers to Get Up to 16 Per Cent of Salary in Bonuses," *Canadian Press*, February 14, 2011.

20 "2010 Global Salary Increase & Variable Pay Budget Trends," accessed October 14, 2014, http://www.compensationforce.com/2010/02/2010-global-salary-increase-variable-pay-budget-trends.html.

21 B. Wysocki, Jr., "Chilling Reality Awaits Even the Employed," *Wall Street Journal*, November 5, 2001, p. A1.

22 G. D. Jenkins Jr., N. Gupta, A. Mitra, and J. D. Shaw, "Are Financial Incentives Related to Performance? A Meta-analytic Review of Empirical Research," *Journal of Applied Psychology* 83, no. 5 (1998), pp. 777–787; and S. L. Rynes, B. Gerhart, and L. Parks, "Personnel Psychology: Performance Evaluation and Pay for Performance," *Annual Review of Psychology* 56, no. 1 (2005), pp. 571–600.

23 G. D. Jenkins Jr., N. Gupta, A. Mitra, and J. D. Shaw, "Are Financial Incentives Related to Performance? A Meta-analytic Review of Empirical Research," *Journal of Applied Psychology*, October 1998, pp. 777–787; and S. L. Rynes, B. Gerhart, and L. Parks, "Personnel Psychology: Performance Evaluation and Pay for Performance," *Annual Review of Psychology* 56, no. 1 (2005), pp. 571–600.

24 "Many Companies Fail to Achieve Success with Pay-for-Performance Programs," *Hewitt & Associates News and Information*, June 9, 2004; and J. Pfeffer, *What Were They Thinking? Unconventional Wisdom About Management* (Boston: Harvard Business School Press, 2007).

25 S. Halzack, "Companies Look to Bonuses Instead of Salary Increases in an Uncertain Economy," *Washington Post*, November 6, 2012, http://www.washingtonpost.com/business/economy/companies-look-to-bonuses-instead-of-salary-increases-in-an-uncertain-economy/2012/11/06/52a7ec12-2751-11e2-9972-71bf64ea091c_story.html.

26 C. M. Barnes, J. Reb, and D. Ang, "More Than Just the Mean: Moving to a Dynamic View of Performance-Based Compensation," *Journal of Applied Psychology* 97, no. 3 (2012), pp. 711–718.

27 E. J. Castilla and S. Benard, "The Paradox of Meritocracy in Organizations," *Administrative Science Quarterly* 55, no. 4 (2010), pp. 543–576.

28 "Bonus Pay in Canada," *Manpower Argus*, September 1996, p. 5; E. White, "Employers Increasingly Favor Bonuses to Raises," *Wall Street Journal*, August 28, 2006, p. B3; and J. S. Lublin, "Boards Tie CEO Pay More Tightly to Performance," *Wall Street Journal*, February 21, 2006, pp. A1, A14.

29 D. Alexander, "Bonus Pools At Canada's Big Banks Rise Least Since 2010," *FP Street*, December 10, 2013, http://business.financialpost.com/2013/12/10/bonus-pools-at-canadas-big-banks-rise-least-since-2010/.

30 Based on R. Curran, "Did Bonuses Help to Fuel Meltdown?" *Post. IE online*, September 21, 2008; and V. Bajaj, A. R. Sorkin, and M. J. de la Merced, "As Goldman and Morgan Shift, a Wall St. Era Ends," *New York Times*, September 21, 2008, http://dealbook.nytimes.com/2008/09/21/goldman-morgan-to-become-bank-holding-companies/.

31 S. S. Wiltermuth and F. Gino, "'I'll Have One of Each': How Separating Rewards into (Meaningless) Categories Increases Motivation," *Journal of Personality and Social Psychology*, January 2013, pp. 1–13.

32 G. E. Ledford Jr., "Paying for the Skills, Knowledge, and Competencies of Knowledge Workers," *Compensation & Benefits Review*, July–August 1995, pp. 55–62; B. Murray and B. Gerhart, "An Empirical Analysis of a Skill-Based Pay Program and Plant Performance Outcomes," *Academy of Management Journal*, February 1998, pp. 68–78; J. R. Thompson and C. W. LeHew, "Skill-Based Pay as an Organizational Innovation," *Review of Public Personnel Administration*, Winter 2000, pp. 20–40; and J. D. Shaw, N. Gupta, A. Mitra, and G. E. Ledford Jr., "Success and Survival of Skill-Based Pay Plans," *Journal of Management*, February 2005, pp. 28–49.

33 A. Mitra, N. Gupta, and J. D. Shaw, "A Comparative Examination of Traditional and Skill-Based Pay Plans," *Journal of Managerial Psychology* 26, no. 4 (2011), pp. 278–296.

34 E. C. Dierdorff and E. A. Surface, "If You Pay for Skills, Will They Learn? Skill Change and Maintenance under a Skill-Based Pay System," *Journal of Management* 34, no. 4 (2008), pp. 721–743.

35 See, for example, D. O. Kim, "Determinants of the Survival of Gainsharing Programs," *Industrial & Labor Relations Review* 53, no. 1 (1999), pp. 21–42; "Why Gainsharing Works Even Better Today Than in the Past," *HR Focus*, April 2000, pp. 3–5; L. R. Gomez-Mejia, T. M. Welbourne, and R. M. Wiseman, "The Role of Risk Sharing and Risk Taking Under Gainsharing," *Academy of Management Review* 25, no. 3 (2000), pp. 492–507; M. Reynolds, "A Cost-Reduction Strategy That May Be Back," *Healthcare Financial Management*, January 2002, pp. 58–64; M. R. Dixon, L. J. Hayes, and J. Stack, "Changing Conceptions of Employee Compensation," *Journal of Organizational Behavior Management* 23, no. 2–3 (2003), pp. 95–116; and I. M. Leitman, R. Levin, M. J. Lipp, L. Sivaprasad, C. J. Karalakulasingam, D. S. Bernard, P. Friedmann, and D. J. Shulkin, "Quality and Financial Outcomes from Gainsharing for Inpatient Admissions: A Three-Year Experience," *Journal of Hospital Medicine* 5, no. 9 (2010), pp. 501–517.

36 T. M. Welbourne and C. J. Ferrante, "To Monitor or Not to Monitor: A Study of Individual Outcomes from Monitoring One's Peers under Gainsharing and Merit Pay," *Group & Organization Management* 33, no. 2 (2008), pp. 139–162.

37 Whole Foods, "Form 10-K for Fiscal Year Ended September 29, 2013," p. 7, http://www.sec.gov/Archives/edgar/data/865436/000086543613000134/wfm10k2013.htm.

38 "Mark Zuckerberg Reaped $2.3 Billion on Facebook Stock Options," *Huffington Post*, April 26, 2013, http://www.huffingtonpost.com/2013/04/26/zuckerberg-stock-options_n_3166661.html.

39 N. Chi and T. Han, "Exploring the Linkages between Formal Ownership and Psychological Ownership for the Organization: The Mediating Role of Organizational Justice," *Journal of Occupational and Organizational Psychology* 81, no. 4 (2008), pp. 691–711.

40 See K. M. Young, ed., *The Expanding Role of ESOPs in Public Companies* (New York: Quorum, 1990); J. L. Pierce and C. A. Furo, "Employee Ownership: Implications for Management," *Organizational Dynamics*, Winter 1990, pp. 32–43; J. Blasi and D. L. Druse, *The New Owners: The Mass Emergence of Employee Ownership in Public Companies and What It Means to American Business* (Champaign, IL: Harper Business, 1991); F. T. Adams and G. B. Hansen, *Putting Democracy to Work: A Practical Guide for Starting and Managing Worker-Owned Businesses* (San Francisco: Berrett-Koehler, 1993); and A. A. Buchko, "The Effects of Employee Ownership on Employee Attitudes: An Integrated Causal Model and Path Analysis," *Journal of Management Studies*, July 1993, pp. 633–656.

41 N. Lees, "Trendy Yogurt Store Set to Open," *Edmonton Journal*, July 11, 2012, p. C1.

42 A. A. Buchko, "The Effects of Employee Ownership on Employee Attitudes: An Integrated Causal Model and Path Analysis," *Journal of Management Studies*, July 1993, pp. 633–656; and R. P. Garrett, "Does Employee Ownership Increase Innovation?" *New England Journal of Entrepreneurship* 13, no. 2 (2010), pp. 37–46.

43 K. Vermond, "Worker as Shareholder: Is It Worth It?" *Globe and Mail*, March 29, 2008, p. B21.

44 J. L. Pierce and C. A. Furo, "Employee Ownership: Implications for Management," *Organizational Dynamics*, Winter 1990, pp. 32–43; and S. Kaufman, "ESOPs' Appeal on the Increase," *Nation's Business*, June 1997, p. 43.

45 See data in D. Stamps, "A Piece of the Action," *Training*, March 1996, p. 66.

46 X. Zhang, K. M. Bartol, K. G. Smith, M. D. Pfarrer, and D. M. Khanin, "CEOs on the Edge: Earnings Manipulation and Stock-Based Incentive Misalignment," *Academy of Management Journal* 51, no. 2 (2008), pp. 241–258.

47 C. G. Hanson and W. D. Bell, *Profit Sharing and Profitability: How Profit Sharing Promotes Business Success* (London, UK: Kogan Page, 1987); M. Magnan and S. St-Onge, "Profit Sharing and Firm Performance: A Comparative and Longitudinal Analysis" (paper presented at the 58th annual meeting of the Academy of Management, San Diego, CA, August 1998); and D. D'Art and T. Turner, "Profit Sharing, Firm Performance, and Union Influence in Selected European Countries," *Personnel Review* 33, no. 3 (2004), pp. 335–350.

48 A. Bayo-Moriones and M. Larraza-Kintana, "Profit-Sharing Plans and Affective Commitment: Does the Context Matter?" *Human Resource Management* 48, no. 2 (2009), pp. 207–226.

49 E. P. Lazear, "Performance Pay and Productivity," *American Economic Review* 90, no. 5 (December 2000), pp. 1346–1361. See also S. Oah, and J.-H. Lee. "Effects of Hourly, Low-Incentive, and High-Incentive Pay on Simulated Work Productivity: Initial Findings with a New Laboratory Method," *Journal of Organizational Behavior Management* 31, no. 1 (2011), pp. 21–42.

50 C. B. Cadsby, F. Song, and F. Tapon, "Sorting and Incentive Effects of Pay for Performance: An Experimental Investigation," *Academy of Management Journal* 50, no. 2 (2007), pp. 387–405.

51 See, for example, M. W. Barringer and G. T. Milkovich, "A Theoretical Exploration of the Adoption and Design of Flexible Benefit Plans: A Case of Human Resource Innovation," *Academy of Management Review*, April 1998, pp. 305–324; D. Brown, "Everybody Loves Flex," *Canadian HR Reporter*, November 18, 2002, p. 1; J. Taggart, "Putting Flex Benefits through Their Paces," *Canadian HR Reporter*, December 2, 2002, p. G3; and N. D. Cole and D. H. Flint, "Perceptions of Distributive and Procedural Justice in Employee Benefits: Flexible versus Traditional Benefit Plans," *Journal of Managerial Psychology* 19, no. 1 (2004), pp. 19–40.

52 D. A. DeCenzo and S. P. Robbins, *Human Resource Management*, 7th ed. (New York: Wiley, 2002), pp. 346–348.

53 P. Stephens, "Flex Plans Gain in Popularity," *CA Magazine*, January/February 2010, p. 10.

54 D. Lovewell, "Flexible Benefits: Benefits on Offer," *Employee Benefits*, March 2010, p. S15.

55 Our definition of a formal recognition system is based on S. E. Markham, K. D. Scott, and G. H. McKee, "Recognizing Good Attendance: A Longitudinal, Quasi-Experimental Field Study," *Personnel Psychology*, Autumn 2002, p. 641.

56 S. J. Peterson and F. Luthans, "The Impact of Financial and Nonfinancial Incentives on Business Unit Outcomes over Time," *Journal of Applied Psychology* 91, no. 1 (2006), pp. 156–165.

57 R. J. Long and J. L. Shields, "From Pay to Praise? Non-Case Employee Recognition in Canadian and Australian Firms," *International Journal of Human Resource Management* 21, no. 8 (2010), pp. 1145–1172.

58 A. D. Stajkovic and F. Luthans, "Differential Effects of Incentive Motivators on Work Performance," *Academy of Management Journal* 4, no. 3 (2001), p. 587. See also F. Luthans and A. D. Stajkovic, "Provide Recognition for Performance Improvement," in *Handbook of Principles of Organizational Behavior*, ed. E. A. Locke (Malden, MA: Blackwell, 2004), pp. 166–180.

59 B. Scudamore, "Pump up Employee Passion," *PROFIT*, October 13, 2010, http://www.profitguide.com/manage-grow/human-resources/pump-up-employee-passion-29964.

60 Hewitt Associates, "Employers Willing to Pay for High Performance," news release, September 8, 2004.

61 "Building a Better Workforce," *PROFIT*, February 16, 2011, http://www.profitguide.com/manage-grow/human-resources/building-a-better-workforce-30073.

62 See also D. A. Johnson and A. M. Dickinson, "Employee-of-the-Month Programs: Do They Really Work?" *Journal of Organizational Behavior Management* 30, no. 4 (2010), pp. 308–324.

63 S. Kerr, "On the Folly of Rewarding A, While Hoping for B," *Academy of Management Executive* 9, no. 1 (1995), pp. 7–14.

64 "More on the Folly," *Academy of Management Executive* 9, no. 1 (1995), pp. 15–16.

65 M. Parker, "Strategies for Creating a Culture of Innovation," *Canadian Business Online*, August 29, 2007.

66 Based on L. Pope and J. Harvey-Berino, "Burn and Earn: A Randomized Controlled Trial Incentivizing Exercise during Fall Semester for College First-Year Students," *Preventive Medicine* 56, no. 3–4 (March 2013), pp. 197–201.

67 A. Kohn, *Punished by Rewards* (Boston: Houghton Mifflin, 1999), p. 181.

68 A. Kohn, *Punished by Rewards* (Boston: Houghton Mifflin, 1993), p. 186. See also Peter R. Scholtes, "An Elaboration of Deming's Teachings on Performance Appraisal," in *Performance Appraisal: Perspectives on a Quality Management Approach*, ed. Gary N. McLean, Susan R. Damme, and Richard A. Swanson (Alexandria, VA: American Society for Training and Development, 1990); H. H. Meyer, E. Kay, and J. R. P. French Jr., "Split Roles in Performance Appraisal," *Harvard Business Review*, 1965, excerpts reprinted in "HBR Retrospect," *Harvard Business Review*, January–February 1989, p. 26; W.-U. Meyer, M. Bachmann, U. Biermann, M. Hempelmann, F.-O. Ploeger, and H. Spiller, "The Informational Value of Evaluative Behavior: Influences of Praise and Blame on Perceptions of Ability," *Journal of Educational Psychology* 71, 1979, pp. 259–268; and A. Halachmi and M. Holzer, "Merit Pay, Performance Targetting, and Productivity," *Review of Public Personnel Administration* 7 (1987), pp. 80–91.

69 A. S. Blinder, "Introduction," in *Paying for Productivity: A Look at the Evidence*, ed. A. S. Blinder (Washington, DC: Brookings Institution, 1990).

70 A. Kohn, *Punished by Rewards* (Boston: Houghton Mifflin, 1999), p. 187.

71 D. Tjosvold, *Working Together to Get Things Done: Managing for Organizational Productivity* (Lexington, MA: Lexington Books, 1986); P. R. Scholtes, *The Team Handbook: How to Use Teams to Improve Quality* (Madison, WI: Joiner Associates, 1988); and A. Kohn, *No Contest: The Case Against Competition*, rev. ed. (Boston: Houghton Mifflin, 1992).

72 E. L. Deci, "Applications of Research on the Effects of Rewards," in *The Hidden Costs of Rewards: New Perspectives on the Psychology of Human Motivation*, ed. M. R. Lepper and D. Green (Hillsdale, NJ: Erlbaum, 1978).

73 S. E. Perry, *San Francisco Scavengers: Dirty Work and the Pride of Ownership* (Berkeley, CA: University of California Press, 1978).

74 A. Kohn, *Punished by Rewards* (Boston: Houghton Mifflin, 1999), p. 192.

75 T. H. Naylor, "Redefining Corporate Motivation, Swedish Style," *Christian Century*, May 30–June 6, 1990, pp. 566–570; R. A. Karasek, T. Thorell, J. E. Schwartz, P. L. Schnall, C. F. Pieper, and J. L. Michela, "Job Characteristics in Relation to the Prevalence of Myocardial Infarction in the US Health Examination Survey (HES) and the Health and Nutrition Examination Survey (HANES)," *American Journal of Public Health* 78 (1988), pp. 910–916; and D. P. Levin, "Toyota Plant in Kentucky Is Font of Ideas for the U.S.," *New York Times*, May 5, 1992, pp. A1, D8.

76 M. Bosquet, "The Prison Factory," reprinted from *Le Nouvel Observateur* in *Working Papers for a New Society*, Spring 1973, pp. 20–27; J. Holusha, "Grace Pastiak's 'Web of Inclusion,'" *New York Times*, May 5, 1991, pp. F1, F6; J. Simmons and W. Mares,

Working Together: Employee Participation in Action (New York: New York University Press, 1985); D. I. Levine and L. D'Andrea Tyson, "Participation, Productivity, and the Firm's Environment," in *Paying for Productivity: A Look at the Evidence*, ed. A. S. Blinder (Washington, DC: Brookings Institution, 1990); and W. F. Whyte, "Worker Participation: International and Historical Perspectives," *Journal of Applied Behavioral Science* 19 (1983), pp. 395–407.

77 Based on "At Starbucks, Baristas Told No More Than Two Drinks," *Wall Street Journal*, October 13, 2010, http://online.wsj.com/articles/SB10001424052748704164004575548403514060736.

78 J. R. Hackman and G. R. Oldham, "Motivation through the Design of Work: Test of a Theory," *Organizational Behavior and Human Performance*, August 1976, pp. 250–279.

79 Payscale, "The Most and Least Meaningful Jobs, 2014," accessed October 14, 2014, http://www.payscale.com/data-packages/most-and-least-meaningful-jobs/full-list.

80 J. R. Hackman, "Work Design," in *Improving Life at Work*, ed. J. R. Hackman and J. L. Suttle (Santa Monica, CA: Goodyear, 1977), p. 129.

81 Based on M. Gagné and D. Bhave, "Autonomy in the Workplace: An Essential Ingredient to Employee Engagement and Well-Being in Every Culture?" in *Human Autonomy in Cross-Cultural Context: Perspectives on the Psychology of Agency, Freedom, and Well-Being*, ed. V. I. Chirkov, R. M. Ryan, and K. M. Sheldon (Berlin, Germany: Springer, 2011); and "Freedom's Just Another Word for Employee Satisfaction," *Concordia University*, January 24, 2011, http://www.concordia.ca/cunews/main/releases/2011/01/24/freedoms-just-another-word-for-employee-satisfaction.html.

82 D. A. Light, "Human Resources: Recruiting Generation 2001," *Harvard Business Review*, July–August 1998, pp. 13–16.

83 See "Job Characteristics Theory of Work Redesign," in *Theories of Organizational Behavior*, ed. J. B. Miner (Hinsdale, IL: Dryden Press, 1980), pp. 231–266; B. T. Loher, R. A. Noe, N. L. Moeller, and M. P. Fitzgerald, "A Meta-analysis of the Relation of Job Characteristics to Job Satisfaction," *Journal of Applied Psychology*, May 1985, pp. 280–289; S. J. Behson, E. R. Eddy, and S. J. Lorenzet, "The Importance of the Critical Psychological States in the Job Characteristics Model: A Meta-analytic and Structural Equations Modeling Examination," *Current Research in Social Psychology*, May 2000, pp. 170–189; T. A. Judge, "Promote Job Satisfaction through Mental Challenge," in *Handbook of Principles of Organizational Behavior*, ed. E. A. Locke, pp. 75–89 (Hoboken, NJ: Wiley-Blackwell, 2003); S. E. Humphrey, J. D. Nahrgang, and F. P. Morgeson, "Integrating Motivational, Social, and Contextual Work Design Features: A Meta-analytic Summary and Theoretical Extension of the Work Design Literature," *Journal of Applied Psychology* 92, no. 5 (2007), pp. 1332–1356; R. F. Piccolo, R. Greenbaum, D. N. D. Hartog, and R. Folger, "The Relationship between Ethical Leadership and Core Job Characteristics," *Journal of Organizational Behavior* 31, no. 2/3 (2010), pp. 259–278; D. J. Holman, C. M. Axtell, C. A. Sprigg, P. Totterdell, and T. D. Wall, "The Mediating Role of Job Characteristics in Job Redesign Interventions: A Serendipitous Quasi-Experiment," *Journal of Organizational Behavior* 31, no. 1 (2010), pp. 84–105; and M. Gagné and D. Bhave, "Autonomy in the Workplace: An Essential Ingredient to Employee Engagement and Well-Being in Every Culture?" in *Human Autonomy in Cross-Cultural Context: Perspectives on the Psychology of Agency, Freedom, and Well-Being*, ed. V. I. Chirkov, R. M. Ryan, and K. M. Sheldon (Berlin, Germany: Springer, 2011).

84 T. A. Judge, S. K. Parker, A. E. Colbert, D. Heller, and R. Ilies, "Job Satisfaction: A Cross-Cultural Review," in *Handbook of Industrial, Work and Organizational Psychology*, vol. 2, ed. N. Anderson and D. S. Ones (Thousand Oaks, CA: Sage Publications, 2002), pp. 25–52.

85 See, for example, J. R. Hackman and G. R. Oldham, *Work Redesign* (Reading, MA: Addison Wesley, 1980); J. B. Miner, *Theories of Organizational Behavior* (Hinsdale, IL: Dryden Press, 1980), pp. 231–266; R. W. Griffin, "Effects of Work Redesign on Employee Perceptions, Attitudes, and Behaviors: A Long-Term Investigation," *Academy of Management Journal*, June 1991, pp. 425–435; and G. Johns, "Some Unintended Consequences of Job Design," *Journal of Organizational Behavior* 31, no. 2/3 (2010), pp. 361–369.

86 J. R. Hackman, "Work Design," in *Improving Life at Work*, ed. J. R. Hackman and J. L. Suttle (Santa Monica, CA: Goodyear, 1977), p. 129.

87 J. P. Wanous, "Individual Differences and Reactions to Job Characteristics," *Journal of Applied Psychology*, October 1974, pp. 616–622; and H. P. Sims and A. D. Szilagyi, "Job Characteristic Relationships: Individual and Structural Moderators," *Organizational Behavior and Human Performance*, June 1976, pp. 211–230.

88 B. Ingram, "Island Health Care Model Shift Criticized By Nurses, *Nanaimo Daily News*, January 15, 2014, p. A5.

89 F. Pomeroy, "Workplace Change: A Union Perspective," *Canadian Business Review* 22, no. 2 (1995), pp. 17–19.

90 Skytrax website review of Singapore Airlines, accessed May 31, 2013, http://www.airlinequality.com/Airlines/SQ.htm.

91 T. Silver, "Rotate Your Way to Higher Value," *Baseline*, March/April 2010, p. 12; and J. J. Salopek, "Coca-Cola Division Refreshes Its Talent with Diversity Push on Campus," *Workforce Management Online*, March 2011.

92 A. Christini and D. Pozzoli, "Workplace Practices and Firm Performance in Manufacturing: A Comparative Study of Italy and Britain," *International Journal of Manpower* 31, no. 7 (2010), pp. 818–842; and K. Kaymaz, "The Effects of Job Rotation Practices on Motivation: A Research on Managers in the Automotive Organizations," *Business and Economics Research Journal* 1, no. 3 (2010), pp. 69–86.

93 J. R. Hackman and G. R. Oldham, *Work Redesign* (Reading, MA: Addison-Wesley, 1980).

94 A. M. Grant, J. E. Dutton, and B. D. Rosso, "Giving Commitment: Employee Support Programs and the Prosocial Sensemaking Process," *Academy of Management Journal* 51, no. 5 (2008), pp. 898–918.

95 See, for example, J. R. Hackman and G. R. Oldham, *Work Redesign* (Reading, MA: Addison-Wesley, 1980); J. B. Miner, *Theories of Organizational Behavior* (Hinsdale, IL: Dryden Press, 1980), pp. 231–266; R. W. Griffin, "Effects of Work Redesign on Employee Perceptions, Attitudes, and Behaviors: A Long-Term Investigation," *Academy of Management Journal* 34, no. 2 (1991), pp. 425–435; and J. L. Cotton, *Employee Involvement* (Newbury Park, CA: Sage, 1993), pp. 141–172.

96 R. D. Pritchard, M. M. Harrell, D. DiazGrandos, and M. J. Guzman, "The Productivity Measurement and Enhancement System: A Meta-analysis," *Journal of Applied Psychology* 93, no. 3 (2008), pp. 540–567.

97 F. P. Morgeson, M. D. Johnson, M. A. Campion, G. J. Medsker, and T. V. Mumford, "Understanding Reactions to Job Redesign: A Quasi-Experimental Investigation of the Moderating Effects of Organizational Contact on Perceptions of Performance Behavior," *Personnel Psychology* 39 (2006), pp. 333–363.

98 F. W. Bond, P. E. Flaxman, and D. Bunce, "The Influence of Psychological Flexibility on Work Redesign: Mediated Moderation of a Work Reorganization Intervention," *Journal of Applied Psychology* 93, no. 3 (2008), pp. 645–654.

99 A. M. Grant, "Leading with Meaning: Beneficiary Contact, Prosocial Impact, and the Performance Effects of Transformational Leadership," *Academy of Management Journal*, 55 (2012), pp. 458–476; and A. M. Grant and S. K. Parker, "Redesigning Work Design Theories: The Rise of Relational and Proactive Perspectives," *Annals of the Academy of Management* 3, no. 1 (2009), pp. 317–375.

100 Y. N. Turner, I. Hadas-Halperin, and D. Raveh, "Patient Photos Spur Radiologist Empathy and Eye for Detail" (paper presented at the annual meeting of the Radiological Society of North America, November 2008).

101 A. M. Grant, E. M. Campbell, G. Chen, K. Cottone, D. Lapedis, and K. Lee, "Impact and the Art of Motivation Maintenance: The Effects of Contact with Beneficiaries on Persistence Behavior," *Organizational Behavior and Human Decision Processes* 103, no. 1 (2007), pp. 53–67.

102 A. M. Grant, "The Significance of Task Significance: Job Performance Effects, Relational Mechanisms, and Boundary Conditions," *Journal of Applied Psychology* no. 93 (2008), pp. 108–124.

103 L. Duxbury and C. Higgins, "Revisiting Work-Life Issues in Canada: The 2012 National Study on Balancing Work and Caregiving in Canada," accessed October 14, 2014, http://www.healthyworkplaces.info/wp-content/uploads/2012/11/2012-National-Work-Long-Summary.pdf.

104 Society for Human Resource Management, *2012 Employee Benefits* (Alexandria, VA: Author, 2012).

105 T. Kato, "Work and Family Practices in Japanese Firms: Their Scope, Nature, and Impact on Employee Turnover," *International Journal of Human Resource Management* 20, no. 2 (2009), pp. 439–456; and P. Mourdoukoutas, "Why Do Women Fare Better in the German World of Work than in the US?" *Forbes*, March 25, 2013, http://www.forbes.com/sites/panosmourdoukoutas/2013/03/25/why-do-women-fare-better-in-the-german-world-of-work-than-in-the-us/.

106 R. Waring, "Sunday Dialogue: Flexible Work Hours," *New York Times*, January 19, 2013, http://www.nytimes.com/2013/01/20/opinion/sunday/sunday-dialogue-flexible-work-hours.html?pagewanted=all&_r=0.

107 See, for example, D. A. Ralston and M. F. Flanagan, "The Effect of Flextime on Absenteeism and Turnover for Male and Female Employees," *Journal of Vocational Behavior*, April 1985, pp. 206–217; D. A. Ralston, W. P. Anthony, and D. J. Gustafson, "Employees May Love Flextime, but What Does It Do to the Organization's Productivity?" *Journal of Applied Psychology*, May 1985, pp. 272–279; D. R. Dalton and D. J. Mesch, "The Impact of Flexible Scheduling on Employee Attendance and Turnover," *Administrative Science Quarterly*, June 1990, pp. 370–387; B. B. Baltes, T. E. Briggs, J. W. Huff, J. A. Wright, and G. A. Neuman, "Flexible and Compressed Workweek Schedules: A Meta-analysis of Their Effects on Work-Related Criteria," *Journal of Applied Psychology* 84, no. 4 (1999), pp. 496–513; K. M. Shockley and T. D. Allen, "When Flexibility Helps: Another Look at the Availability of Flexible Work Arrangements and Work-Family Conflict," *Journal of Vocational Behavior* 71, no. 3 (2007), pp. 479–493; and J. G. Grzywacz, D. S. Carlson, and S. Shulkin, "Schedule Flexibility and Stress: Linking Formal Flexible Arrangements and Perceived Flexibility to Employee Health," *Community, Work, and Family* 11, no. 2 (2008), pp. 199–214.

108 D. Keevil, *The Flexible Workplace Study: Asking the Experts About Flexible Policies and Workplace Performance* (Halifax: Halifax YWCA in cooperation with Status of Women Canada, 1996).

109 L. Duxbury and G. Haines, "Predicting Alternative Work Arrangements from Salient Attitudes: A Study of Decision Makers in the Public Sector," *Journal of Business Research*, August 1991, pp. 83–97.

110 J. E. Fast and J. A. Frederick, "Working Arrangements and Time Stress," *Canadian Social Trends*, Winter 1996, pp. 14–19.

111 A. Sisco and R. Nelson, *From Vision to Venture: An Account of Five Successful Aboriginal Businesses* (Ottawa: The Conference Board of Canada, 2008).

112 S. Schieman and M. Young, "Is There a Downside to Schedule Control for the Work-Family Interface?" *Journal of Family Issues* 31, no. 10 (2010), pp. 1391–1414.

113 K. M. Shockley and T. D. Allen, "Investigating the Missing Link in Flexible Work Arrangement Utilization: An Individual Difference Perspective," *Journal of Vocational Behavior* 76, no. 1 (2010), pp. 131–142.

114 T. Grant, "Job Sharing," *Globe and Mail*, May 16, 2009, p. B14.

115 Society for Human Resource Management, *2008 Employee Benefits* (Alexandria, VA: Author, 2008).

116 T. Grant, "Job Sharing," *Globe and Mail*, May 16, 2009, p. B1.

117 T. Grant, "Job Sharing," *Globe and Mail*, May 16, 2009, p. B1.

118 D. Hodges, "New Nunavut: Canada's Newest Territory Faces the Daunting Task of Creating a New Health Bureaucracy While Dealing with Traditional Recruitment Problems in the Arctic," *Medical Post*, November 13, 2001, p. 31.

119 See, for example, E. J. Hill, M. Ferris, and V. Martinson, "Does It Matter Where You Work? A Comparison of How Three Work Venues (Traditional Office, Virtual Office, and Home Office) Influence Aspects of Work and Personal/ Family Life," *Journal of Vocational Behavior* 63, no. 2 (2003), pp. 220–241; B. Williamson, "Managing Virtual Workers," *Bloomberg Businessweek*, July 16, 2009, http://www.businessweek.com/stories/2009-07-15/managing-virtual-workers; and B. A. Lautsch and E. E. Kossek, "Managing a Blended Workforce: Telecommuters and Non-Telecommuters," *Organizational Dynamics* 40, no. 1 (2010), pp. 10–17.

120 B. Belton, "Best Buy Copies Yahoo, Reins in Telecommuting," *USA Today*, March 6, 2013, http://www.usatoday.com/story/money/business/2013/03/06/best-buy-telecommuting-ban-yahoo/1966667/.

121 J. Berkow, "Telework: The New Labour Force Norm," *Postmedia News*, July 7, 2011.

122 G. Karstens-Smith, "Remote Work an Escape When Trapped by Gridlock," *Toronto Star*, May 29, 2014, p. B1.

123 "Canadian Studies on Telework," *InnoVisions Canada*, http://www.ivc.ca/studies/canada/.

124 J. Budak, "Work-Life: Better Working through Living," *Canadian Business*, April 5, 2011.

125 Cited in R. W. Judy and C. D'Amico, *Workforce 2020* (Indianapolis, IL: Hudson Institute, 1997), p. 58.

126 D. Bradbury, "Nothing to Fear from Teleworking," *Financial Post*, March 16, 2010, http://www.financialpost.com/story.html?id=2689687; V. Galt, "Telecommute—and Save the Environment," *Globe and Mail*, April 27, 2007, http://www.ivc.ca/media/articles/savetheenvironment.html.

127 M. E. Roloff, "Why Teleworkers Are More Satisfied with Their Jobs Than Are Office-Based Workers: When Less Contact Is Beneficial," *Journal of Applied Communication Research* 38, no. 4 (2010), pp. 336–361.

128 E. E. Kossek, B. A. Lautsch, S. C. Eaton, "Telecommuting, Control, and Boundary Management: Correlates of Policy Use and Practice, Job Control, and Work-Family Effectiveness," *Journal of Vocational Behavior* 68, no. 2 (2006), pp. 347–367.

129 J. Kotkin, "Marissa Mayer's Misstep and the Unstoppable Rise of Telecommuting," *Forbes*, March 26, 2013.

130 J. M. Stanton and J. L. Barnes-Farrell, "Effects of Electronic Performance Monitoring on Personal Control, Task Satisfaction, and Task Performance," *Journal of Applied Psychology*, December 1996, pp. 738–745; and L. Taskin and F. Bridoux, "Telework: A Challenge to Knowledge Transfer in Organizations," *International Journal of Human Resource Management* 21, no. 13 (2010), pp. 2503–2520.

131 See, for example, P. Brotherton, "For Teleworkers, Less Is Definitely More," *T1D* 65 (March 2011), p. 29; and M. Virick, N. DaSilva, and K. Arrington, "Moderators of the Curvilinear Relation Between Extent of Telecommuting and Job and Life Satisfaction: The Role of Performance Outcome Orientation and Worker Type," *Human Relations* 63, no. 1 (2010), pp. 137–154.

132 J. Welch and S. Welch, "The Importance of Being There," *BusinessWeek*, April 16, 2007, p. 92; Z. I. Barsness, K. A. Diekmann, and M. L. Seidel, "Motivation and Opportunity: The Role of Remote Work, Demographic Dissimilarity, and Social Network Centrality in Impression Management," *Academy of Management Journal* 48, no. 3 (2005), pp. 401–419.

133 P. Glavin, S. Schieman, and S. Reid, "Boundary-Spanning Work Demands and Their Consequences for Guilt and Psychological Distress," *Journal of Health and Social Behavior* 52, no. 1 (2011), pp. 43–57.

134 F. P. Morgeson and S. E. Humphrey, "The Work Design Questionnaire (WDQ): Developing and Validating a Comprehensive Measure for Assessing Job Design and the Nature of Work," *Journal of Applied Psychology* 91, no. 6 (2006), pp. 1321–1339; S. E. Humphrey, J. D. Nahrgang, and F. P. Morgeson, "Integrating Motivational, Social, and Contextual Work Design Features: A Meta-analytic Summary and Theoretical Extension of the Work Design Literature," *Journal of Applied Psychology* 92, no. 5 (2007), pp. 1332–1356; and R. Takeuchi, D. P. Lepak, H. Wang, and K. Takeuchi, "An Empirical Examination of the Mechanisms Mediating Between High-Performance Work Systems and the Performance of Japanese Organizations," *Journal of Applied Psychology* 92, no. 4 (2007), pp. 1069–1083.

135 Vignette based on A. Kritsch, "5 Secrets for a Better Work-Life Balance: Inside Hootsuite Culture," *Hootsuite* (blog), accessed October 10, 2014, http://blog.hootsuite.com/5-secrets-for-a-better-work-life-balance/.

136 See, for example, the increasing body of literature on empowerment, such as D. P. Ashmos, D. Duchon, R. R. McDaniel Jr., and J. W. Huonker, "What a Mess! Participation as a Simple Managerial Rule to 'Complexify' Organizations," *Journal of Management Studies* 39, no. 2 (2002), pp. 189–206; S. E. Seibert, S. R. Silver, and W. A. Randolph, "Taking Empowerment to the Next Level: A Multiple-Level Model of Empowerment, Performance, and Satisfaction," *Academy of Management Journal* 47, no. 3 (2004), pp. 332–349; M. M. Butts, R. J. Vandenberg, D. M. DeJoy, B. S. Schaffer, and M. G. Wilson, "Individual Reactions to High Involvement Work Processes: Investigating the Role of Empowerment and Perceived Organizational Support," *Journal of Occupational Health Psychology* 14, no. 2 (2009), pp. 122–136; R. Park, E. Applebaum, and D. Kruse, "Employee Involvement and Group Incentives in Manufacturing Companies: A Multi-Level Analysis," *Human Resource Management Journal* 20, no. 3 (2010), pp. 227–243; D. C. Jones, P. Kalmi, and A. Kauhanen, "How Does Employee Involvement Stack Up? The Effects of Human Resource Management Policies in a Retail Firm," *Industrial Relations* 49, no. 1 (2010), pp. 1–21; and M. T. Maynard, L. L. Gilson, and J. E. Mathieu, "Empowerment—Fad or Fab? A Multilevel Review of the Past Two Decades of Research," *Journal of Management* 38, no. 4 (2012), pp. 1231–1281.

137 J. J. Caughron and M. D. Mumford, "Embedded Leadership: How Do a Leader's Superiors Impact Middle-Management Performance?" *Leadership Quarterly*, June 2012, pp. 342–353.

138 See, for example, K. L. Miller and P. R. Monge, "Participation, Satisfaction, and Productivity: A Meta-analytic Review," *Academy of Management Journal*, December 1986, pp. 727–753; J. A. Wagner III, "Participation's Effects on Performance and Satisfaction: A Reconsideration of Research Evidence," *Academy of Management Review*, April 1994, pp. 312–330; C. Doucouliagos, "Worker Participation and Productivity in Labor-Managed and Participatory Capitalist Firms: A Meta-analysis," *Industrial and Labor Relations Review*, October 1995, pp. 58–77; J. A. Wagner III, C. R. Leana, E. A. Locke, and D. M. Schweiger, "Cognitive and Motivational Frameworks in U.S. Research on Participation: A Meta-analysis of Primary Effects," *Journal of Organizational Behavior* 18 (1997), pp. 49–65; E. A. Locke, M. Alavi, and J. A. Wagner III, "Participation in Decision Making: An Information Exchange Perspective," in *Research in Personnel and Human Resource Management*, vol. 15, ed. G. R. Ferris (Greenwich, CT: JAI Press,

1997), pp. 293–331; and J. A. Wagner III and J. A. LePine, "Effects of Participation on Performance and Satisfaction: Additional Meta-analytic Evidence," *Psychological Reports*, June 1999, pp. 719–725.

139 D. K. Datta, J. P. Guthrie, and P. M. Wright, "Human Resource Management and Labor Productivity: Does Industry Matter?" *Academy of Management Journal* 48, no. 1 (2005), pp. 135–145; C. M. Riordan, R. J. Vandenberg, and H. A. Richardson, "Employee Involvement Climate and Organizational Effectiveness" *Human Resource Management* 44, no. 4 (2005), pp. 471–488.

140 J. L. Cotton, *Employee Involvement* (Newbury Park, CA: Sage, 1993), pp. 141–172.

141 See, for example, M. Gilman and P. Marginson, "Negotiating European Works Council: Contours of Constrained Choice," *Industrial Relations Journal*, March 2002, pp. 36–51; J. T. Addison and C. R. Belfield, "What Do We Know About the New European Works Council? Some Preliminary Evidence from Britain," *Scottish Journal of Political Economy*, September 2002, pp. 418–444; and B. Keller, "The European Company Statute: Employee Involvement—and Beyond," *Industrial Relations Journal*, December 2002, pp. 424–445.

142 J. L. Cotton, *Employee Involvement* (Newbury Park, CA: Sage, 1993), pp. 141–172.

143 J. L. Cotton, *Employee Involvement* (Newbury Park, CA: Sage, 1993), pp. 141–172.

144 N. Nohria, B. Groysberg, and L.-E. Lee, "Employee Motivation: A Powerful New Model," *Harvard Business Review* 86, July–August 2008, pp. 78–84.

145 P. R. Lawrence and N. Nohria, *Driven: How Human Nature Shapes Our Choices* (San Francisco: Jossey-Bass, 2002).

146 S. Miller, "Companies Worldwide Rewarding Performance with Variable Pay," *Society for Human Resource Management*, March 1, 2010, http://www.shrm.org/hrdisciplines/compensation/articles/pages/variableworld.aspx.

147 S. Miller, "Asian Firms Offer More Variable Pay Than Western Firms," *Society for Human Resource Management*, March 28, 2012, http://www.shrm.org/hrdisciplines/compensation/articles/pages/asianvariablepay.aspx.

148 P. Stephens, "Flex Plans Gain in Popularity," *CA Magazine*, January/February 2010, p. 10.

149 S. Hemsley, "Flexible Benefits Schemes Receiving Surprisingly Low Take-up," *HR Magazine UK*, June 5, 2013, http://www.hrmagazine.co.uk/hr/features/1077403/flexible-benefits-schemes-receiving-surprisingly-low.

150 R. S. Schuler and N. Rogovsky, "Understanding Compensation Practice Variations across Firms: The Impact of National Culture," *Journal of International Business Studies* 29, no. 1 (First Quarter 1998), pp. 159–177.

151 M. Erez, "Culture and Job Design," *Journal of Organizational Behavior* 31, no. 2/3 (2010), pp. 389–400.

152 B. M. Meglino and A. M. Korsgaard, "The Role of Other Orientation in Reactions to Job Characteristics," *Journal of Management*, February 2007, pp. 57–83.

153 M. F. Peterson and S. A. Ruiz-Quintanilla, "Cultural Socialization as a Source of Intrinsic Work Motivation," *Group & Organization Management*, June 2003, pp. 188–216.

154 P. Peters and L. den Dulk, "Cross Cultural Differences in Managers' Support for Home-Based Telework: A Theoretical Elaboration," *International Journal of Cross Cultural Management*, December 2003, pp. 329–346.

155 See, for example, A. Sagie and Z. Aycan, "A Cross-Cultural Analysis of Participative Decision-Making in Organizations," *Human Relations*, April 2003, pp. 453–473; and J. Brockner, "Unpacking Country Effects: On the Need to Operationalize the Psychological Determinants of Cross-National Differences," in *Research in Organizational Behavior*, vol. 25, ed. R. M. Kramer and B. M. Staw (Oxford, UK: Elsevier, 2003), pp. 336–340.

156 C. Robert, T. M. Probst, J. J. Martocchio, R. Drasgow, and J. J. Lawler, "Empowerment and Continuous Improvement in the United States, Mexico, Poland, and India: Predicting Fit on the Basis of the Dimensions of Power Distance and Individualism," *Journal of Applied Psychology*, October 2000, pp. 643–658.

157 Z. X. Chen and S. Aryee, "Delegation and Employee Work Outcomes: An Examination of the Cultural Context of Mediating Processes in China," *Academy of Management Journal* 50, no. 1 (2007), pp. 226–238.

158 G. Huang, X. Niu, C. Lee, and S. J. Ashford, "Differentiating Cognitive and Affective Job Insecurity: Antecedents and Outcomes," *Journal of Organizational Behavior* 33, no. 6 (2012), pp. 752–769.

159 Based on J. Surowiecki, "Face Time," *New Yorker*, March 18, 2013, http://www.newyorker.com/magazine/2013/03/18/face-time; and L. Taskin and F. Bridoux, "Telework: A Challenge to Knowledge Transfer in Organizations," *International Journal of Human Resource Management* 21, no. 13 (2010), pp. 2503–2520.

160 This exercise is based on W. P. Ferris, "Enlivening the Job Characteristics Model," in *Proceedings of the 29th Annual Eastern Academy of Management Meeting*, ed. C. Harris and C. C. Lundberg (Baltimore, MD: May 1992), pp. 125–128.

161 Based on J. McFarland, "Major CEO Pay Increases in the Cards Again," *Globe and Mail*, June 1, 2014, http://www.theglobeandmail.com/report-on-business/careers/management/executive-compensation/pay-is-on-the-rise-for-canadas-top-executives/article18940701/; T. Tedesco, "U.S. CEO Pay Leaves Canadians in Dust; Up 9% in a Year," *National Post*, May 30, 2014, p. A1; "Canada's CEOs Ring in New Year with a Bang," *Canadian Centre for Policy Alternatives*, January 2, 2014, https://www.policyalternatives.ca/newsroom/news-releases/canada%E2%80%99s-ceos-ring-new-year-bang#sthash; E. Chemi and A. Giorgi, "The Pay-for-Performance Myth," *Bloomberg Businessweek*, July 22, 2014, http://www.businessweek.com/articles/2014-07-22/for-ceos-correlation-between-pay-and-stock-performance-is-pretty-random; "How They Performed," *Financial Post Magazine*, November 2013, p. 43; "Gimme Gimme: Greed, the Most Insidious of Sins, Has Once Again Embraced a Decade," *Financial Post*, September 28/30, 1996, pp. 24–25; and I. McGugan, "A Crapshoot Called Compensation," *Canadian Business*, July 1995, pp. 67–70.

162 Based on P. Coy, "The Leisure Gap," *Bloomberg Businessweek*, July 23–29, 2012, pp. 8–10; A. B. Krueger and A. I. Mueller, "Time Use, Emotional Well-Being, and Unemployment: Evidence from Longitudinal Data," *American Economic Review*, May 2012, pp. 594–599; and L. Kwoh, "More Firms Offer Option to Swap Cash for Time," *Wall Street Journal*, September 26, 2012, p. B6; and N. Macdonald, "Who Needs a Break? Canadians Do. We're the Fourth-Hardest Workers in the World," *Maclean's*, July 1, 2009.

163 Based on V. S. Chib, B. DeMartino, S. Shimojo, and J. P. O'Doherty, "Neural Mechanisms Underlying Paradoxical Performance for Monetary Incentives Are Driven by Loss Aversion," *Neuron* 74 (2012), pp. 582–594; N. Fleming, "The Bonus Myth" *New Scientist* 210 (2011), pp. 40–43; D. Woodward, "Perking Up the Workplace," *Director*, February 2011, pp. 33–34; S. Ladika, "Are Wellness Incentives Bad for Your Company's Health?" *Workforce Management*, February 2013, p. 6; and G. G. Scott, "How to Create a Motivating Environment," *Nonprofit World* 28 (September/October 2010), p. 9.

164 Based on J. R. Hackman, "Work Design," in *Improving Life at Work*, ed. J. R. Hackman and J. L. Suttle (Santa Monica, CA: Goodyear, 1977), pp. 132–133.

Chapter 6

1 Opening vignette based on http://www.cirquedusoleil.com; "Cirque du Soleil on Teamwork and Creativity," *Business Banter*, June 28, 2011, http://businessbanter.wordpress.com/2011/06/28/cirque-du-soleil-on-teamwork-and-creativity/; G. Collins, "Run Away to the Circus? No Need. It's Staying Here," *New York Times*, April 29, 2009, p. C1; and A. Tesolin, "Igniting the Creative Spark at Cirque du Soleil—Arupa Tesolin Interviews Lyn Heward Creative Leader at Cirque," SelfGrowth.com, http://www.selfgrowth.com/articles/Igniting_the_Creative_Spark_at_Cirque_du_Soleil.html.

2 J. R. Katzenback and D. K. Smith, *The Wisdom of Teams: Creating the High-Performance Organization* (New York: Harper Business, 1999), p. 45.

3 J. R. Katzenback and D. K. Smith, *The Wisdom of Teams: Creating the High-Performance Organization* (New York: Harper Business, 1999), p. 214.

4 See, for example, D. Tjosvold, *Team Organization: An Enduring Competitive Advantage* (Chichester, UK: Wiley, 1991); S. A. Mohrman, S. G. Cohen, and A. M. Mohrman Jr., *Designing Team-Based Organizations* (San Francisco: Jossey-Bass, 1995); P. MacMillan, *The Performance Factor: Unlocking the Secrets of Teamwork* (Nashville, TN: Broadman and Holman, 2001); and E. Salas, C. A. Bowers, and E. Edens, eds., *Improving Teamwork in Organizations: Applications of Resource Management Training* (Mahwah, NJ: Erlbaum, 2002).

5 J. Mathieu, M. T. Maynard, T. Rapp, and L. Gilson, "Team Effectiveness 1997–2007: A Review of Recent Advancements and a Glimpse into the Future," *Journal of Management* 34, no. 3 (2008), pp. 410–476.

6 J. H. Shonk, *Team-Based Organizations* (Homewood, IL: Business One Irwin, 1992); and M. A. Verespej, "When Workers Get New Roles," *IndustryWeek*, February 3, 1992, p. 11.

7 See, for example, C. C. Manz and H. P. Sims Jr., *Business without Bosses: How Self-Managing Teams Are Building High Performance Companies* (New York: Wiley, 1993); J. R. Barker, "Tightening the Iron Cage: Concertive Control in Self-Managing Teams," *Administrative Science Quarterly*, September 1993, pp. 408–437; and S. G. Cohen, G. E. Ledford Jr., and G. M. Spreitzer, "A Predictive Model of Self-Managing Work Team Effectiveness," *Human Relations*, May 1996, pp. 643–676.

8 See, for example, J. L. Cordery, W. S. Mueller, and L. M. Smith, "Attitudinal and Behavioral Effects of Autonomous Group Working: A Longitudinal Field Study," *Academy of Management Journal*, June 1991, pp. 464–476; R. A. Cook and J. L. Goff, "Coming of Age with Self-Managed Teams: Dealing with a Problem Employee," *Journal of Business and Psychology*, Spring 2002, pp. 485–496; and C. W. Langfred, "Too Much of a Good Thing? Negative Effects of High Trust and Individual Autonomy in Self-Managing Teams," *Academy of Management Journal*, June 2004, pp. 385–399.

9 A. Mehra, M. Kilduff, and D. J. Brass, "At the Margins: A Distinctiveness Approach to the Social Identity and Social Networks of Underrepresented Groups," *Academy of Management Journal* 41, no. 4 (1998), pp. 441–452.

10 B. H. Bradley, B. E. Postlethwaite, A. C. Klotz, M. R. Hamdani, and K. G. Brown, "Reaping the Benefits of Task Conflict in Teams: The Critical Role of Team Psychological Safety Climate," *Journal of Applied Psychology*, 97, no. 1 (2012), pp. 151–158.

11 G. L. Stewart, S. H. Courtright, and M. R. Barrick, "Peer-Based Control in Self-Managing Teams: Linking Rational and Normative Influence with Individual and Group Performance," *Journal of Applied Psychology* 97, no. 2 (2012), pp. 435–447.

12 J. Devaro, "The Effects of Self-Managed and Closely Managed Teams on Labor Productivity and Product Quality: An Empirical Analysis of a Cross-Section of Establishments," *Industrial Relations* 47, no. 4 (2008), pp. 659–698.

13 A. Shah, "Starbucks Strives for Instant Gratification with Via Launch," *PRWeek*, December 2009, p. 15.

14 "Cross-Functional Obstacles," *Training*, May 1994, pp. 125–126.

15 See, for example, M. E. Warkentin, L. Sayeed, and R. Hightower, "Virtual Teams versus Face-to-Face Teams: An Exploratory Study of a Web-Based Conference System," *Decision Sciences*, Fall 1997, pp. 975–993; A. M. Townsend, S. M. DeMarie, and A. R. Hendrickson, "Virtual Teams: Technology and the Workplace of the Future," *Academy of Management Executive*, August 1998, pp. 17–29; D. Duarte and N. T. Snyder, *Mastering Virtual Teams: Strategies, Tools, and Techniques* (San Francisco: Jossey-Bass, 1999); M. L. Maznevski and K. M. Chudoba, "Bridging Space over Time: Global Virtual Team Dynamics and Effectiveness," *Organization Science*, September–October 2000, pp. 473–492; and J. Katzenbach and D. Smith, "Virtual Teaming," *Forbes*, May 21, 2001, pp. 48–51.

16 "Virtual Teams a First in Canada," *Financial Post*, January 19, 2011, http://business.financialpost.com/2011/01/19/mba-virtual-teams-a-first-in-canada/. Material reprinted with the express permission of: National Post, a division of Postmedia Network Inc.

17 R. S. Gajendran and A. Joshi, "Innovation in Globally Distributed Teams: The Role of LMX, Communication Frequency, and Member Influence on Team Decisions," *Journal of Applied Psychology* 97, no. 6 (2012), pp. 1252–1261.

18 J. R. Mesmer-Magnus, L. A. DeChurch, M. Jimenez-Rodriguez, J. Wildman, and M. Shuffler, "A Meta-analytic Investigation of Virtuality and Information Sharing in Teams," *Organizational Behavior and Human Decision Processes* 115, no. 2 (2011), pp. 214–225.

19 Based on P. Tilstone, "Cut Carbon . . . and Bills," *Director*, May 2009, p. 54; L. C. Latimer, "6 Strategies for Sustainable Business Travel," *Greenbiz*, February 11, 2011, http://www.greenbiz.com/blog/2011/02/11/6-strategies-sustainable-business-travel; and F. Gebhart, "Travel Takes a Big Bite Out of Corporate Expenses," *Travel Market Report*, May 30, 2013, http://www.travelmarketreport.com/articles/Travel-Takes-Big-Bite-Out-of-Corporate-Expenses.

20 A. Malhotra, A. Majchrzak, and B. Rosen, "Leading Virtual Teams," *Academy of Management Perspectives*, February 2007, pp. 60–70; and J. M. Wilson, S. S. Straus, and B. McEvily, "All in Due Time: The Development of Trust in Computer Mediated and Face-to-Face Teams," *Organizational Behavior and Human Decision Processes* 19 (2006), pp. 16–33.

21 C. Joinson, "Managing Virtual Teams," *HR Magazine*, June 2002, p. 71. Reprinted with the permission of *HR Magazine*, published by the Society for Human Resource Management, Alexandria, VA.

22 P. Balkundi and D. A. Harrison, "Ties, Leaders, and Time in Teams: Strong Inference About Network Structure's Effects on Team Viability and Performance," *Academy of Management Journal* 49, no. 1 (2006), pp. 49–68; G. Chen, B. L. Kirkman, R. Kanfer, D. Allen, and B. Rosen, "A Multilevel Study of Leadership, Empowerment, and Performance in Teams," *Journal of Applied Psychology* 92, no. 2 (2007), pp. 331–346; L. A. DeChurch and M. A. Marks, "Leadership in Multiteam Systems," *Journal of Applied Psychology* 91, no. 2 (2006), pp. 311–329; A. Srivastava, K. M. Bartol, and E. A. Locke, "Empowering Leadership in Management Teams: Effects on Knowledge Sharing, Efficacy, and Performance," *Academy of Management Journal* 49, no. 6 (2006), pp. 1239–1251; and J. E. Mathieu, K. K. Gilson, and T. M. Ruddy, "Empowerment and Team Effectiveness: An Empirical Test of an Integrated Model," *Journal of Applied Psychology* 91, no. 1 (2006), pp. 97–108.

23 Vignette based on E. Syracopoulos, "#FocusFriday: How Cirque du Soleil's Graphics Team Stays Focused Off Stage," *Xerox* (blog), July 29, 2011, http://simplifywork.blogs.xerox.com/2011/07/29/focusfriday-how-cirque-du-soleils-graphics-team-stays-focused-off-stage/#.VD75TyItCWg; and http://www.cirquedusoleil.com.

24 Based on Ed Tait, "Bombers Believe in Willy," *Winnipeg Free Press*, August 5, 2014, p. D1; "Talent, Teamwork Fuel Bombers Turnaround," *Brandon Sun*, August 6, 2014; G. Lawless, "They've Got a Marquee Man, Now Bombers' Task Is a Talent Hunt to Fill Supporting Roles," *Winnipeg Free Press*, October 29, 2014; and "Coach Will Keep Tabs On Players' Effort," *Winnipeg Free Press*, October 30, 2014, p. D3.

25 See M. F. Peterson, P. B, Smith, A. Akande, S. Ayestaran, S. Bochner, V. Callan, N. Guk Cho, J. C. Jesuino, M. D'Amorim, P.-H. Francois, K. Hofmann, P. L. Koopman, K. Leung, T. K. Lim, and S. Mortaz, "Role Conflict, Ambiguity, and Overload: A 21-Nation Study," *Academy of Management Journal*, April 1995, pp. 429–452.

26 See, for example, F. T. Amstad, L. L. Meier, U. Fasel, A. Elfering, and N. K. Semmer, "A Meta-analysis of Work-Family Conflict and Various Outcomes with a Special Emphasis on Cross-Domain versus Matching-Domain Relations," *Journal of Occupational Health Psychology* 16, no. 2 (2011), pp. 151–169.

27 M. A. Hogg and D. J. Terry, "Social Identity and Self-Categorization Processes in Organizational Contexts," *Academy of Management Review* 25, no. 1 (2000), pp. 121–140.

28 D. Vora and T. Kostova. "A Model of Dual Organizational Identification in the Context of the Multinational Enterprise," *Journal of Organizational Behavior* 28 (2007), pp. 327–350.

29 C. Reade, "Dual Identification in Multinational Corporations: Local Managers and Their Psychological Attachment to the Subsidiary versus the Global Organization," *International Journal of Human Resource Management*, 12, no. 3 (2001), pp. 405–424.

30 E. H. Schein, *Organizational Psychology*, 3rd ed. (Englewood Cliffs, NJ: Prentice Hall, 1980), p. 145.

31 For a recent review of the research on group norms, see J. R. Hackman, "Group Influences on Individuals in Organizations," in *Handbook of Industrial & Organizational Psychology*, vol. 3, 2nd ed., ed. M. D. Dunnette and L. M. Hough (Palo Alto, CA: Consulting Psychologists Press, 1992), pp. 235–250.

32 Adapted from P. S. Goodman, E. Ravlin, and M. Schminke, "Understanding Groups in Organizations," in *Research in Organizational Behavior*, vol. 9, ed. L. L. Cummings and B. M. Staw (Greenwich, CT: JAI Press, 1987), p. 159.

33 Submitted by Don Miskiman, Chair and U-C Professor of Management, Malaspina University College, Nanaimo, BC. With permission.

34 D. C. Feldman, "The Development and Enforcement of Group Norms," *Academy of Management Journal*, January 1984, pp. 47–53; and K. L. Bettenhausen and J. K. Murnighan, "The Development of an Intragroup Norm and the Effects of Interpersonal and Structural Challenges," *Administrative Science Quarterly*, March 1991, pp. 20–35.

35 D. C. Feldman, "The Development and Enforcement of Group Norms," *Academy of Management Journal*, January 1984, pp. 47–53; and K. L. Bettenhausen and J. K. Murnighan, "The Development of an Intragroup Norm and the Effects of Interpersonal and Structural Challenges," *Administrative Science Quarterly*, March 1991, pp. 20–35.

36 C. A. Kiesler and S. B. Kiesler, *Conformity* (Reading, MA: Addison Wesley, 1969).

37 S. E. Asch, "Effects of Group Pressure upon the Modification and Distortion of Judgments," in *Groups, Leadership and Men*, ed. H. Guetzkow (Pittsburgh, PA: Carnegie Press, 1951), pp. 177–190; and S. E. Asch, "Studies of Independence and Conformity: A Minority of One Against a Unanimous Majority," *Psychological Monographs: General and Applied* 70, no. 9 (1956), pp. 1–70.

38 S. L. Robinson and A. M. O'Leary-Kelly, "Monkey See, Monkey Do: The Influence of Work Groups on the Antisocial Behavior of Employees," *Academy of Management Journal* 41 (1998), pp. 658–672.

39 J. M. George, "Personality, Affect and Behavior in Groups," *Journal of Applied Psychology* 78 (1993), pp. 798–804; and J. M. George and L. R. James, "Personality, Affect, and Behavior in Groups Revisited: Comment on Aggregation, Levels of Analysis, and a Recent Application of Within and Between Analysis," *Journal of Applied Psychology* 78 (1993), pp. 798–804.

40 Vignette based on "Backstage at Cirque du Soleil's New Show, Which Both Defies Logic and Is Utterly Real," *Globe and Mail*, August 22, 2014, http://www.theglobeandmail.com/arts/cirque-du-soleils-30th-anniversary-show-manages-both-to-defy-logic-and-be-utterly-real/article20169022/.

41 B. W. Tuckman, "Developmental Sequences in Small Groups," *Psychological Bulletin*, June 1965, pp. 384–399; B. W. Tuckman and M. C. Jensen, "Stages of Small-Group Development Revisited," *Group and Organizational Studies*, December 1977, pp. 419–427; and M. F. Maples, "Group Development: Extending Tuckman's Theory," *Journal for Specialists in Group Work*, Fall 1988, pp. 17–23.

42 J. F. George and L. M. Jessup, "Groups over Time: What Are We Really Studying?" *International Journal of Human-Computer Studies* 47, no. 3 (1997), pp. 497–511.

43 R. C. Ginnett, "The Airline Cockpit Crew," in *Groups That Work (and Those That Don't)*, ed. J. R. Hackman (San Francisco: Jossey-Bass, 1990).

44 C. J. G. Gersick, "Time and Transition in Work Teams: Toward a New Model of Group Development," *Academy of Management Journal*, March 1988, pp. 9–41; C. J. G. Gersick, "Marking Time: Predictable Transitions in Task Groups," *Academy of Management Journal*, June 1989, pp. 274–309; E. Romanelli and M. L. Tushman, "Organizational Transformation as Punctuated Equilibrium: An Empirical Test," *Academy of Management Journal*, October 1994, pp. 1141–1166; B. M. Lichtenstein, "Evolution or Transformation: A Critique and Alternative to Punctuated Equilibrium," in *Academy of Management Best Paper Proceedings*, ed. D. P. Moore (National Academy of Management Conference, Vancouver, 1995), pp. 291–295; and A. Seers and S. Woodruff, "Temporal Pacing in Task Forces: Group Development or Deadline Pressure?" *Journal of Management* 23, no. 2 (1997), pp. 169–187.

45 C. J. G. Gersick, "Time and Transition in Work Teams: Toward a New Model of Group Development," *Academy of Management Journal*, March 1988, pp. 9–41; and M. J. Waller, J. M. Conte, C. B. Gibson, and M. A. Carpenter, "The Effect of Individual Perceptions of Deadlines on Team Performance," *Academy of Management Review*, October 2001, pp. 586–600.

46 C. J. G. Gersick, "Time and Transition in Work Teams: Toward a New Model of Group Development," *Academy of Management Journal*, March 1988, pp. 9–41; and C. J. G. Gersick, "Marking Time: Predictable Transitions in Task Groups," *Academy of Management Journal*, June 1989, pp. 274–309.

47 M. M. Kazmer, "Disengaging from a Distributed Research Project: Refining a Model of Group Departures," *Journal of the American Society for Information Science and Technology*, April 2010, pp. 758–771.

48 K. L. Bettenhausen, "Five Years of Groups Research: What We Have Learned and What Needs to be Addressed," *Journal of Management* 17, 1991, pp. 345–381; and R. A. Guzzo and G. P. Shea, "Group Performance and Intergroup Relations in Organizations," in *Handbook of Industrial and Organizational Psychology*, vol. 3, 2nd ed., ed. M. D. Dunnette and L. M. Hough (Palo Alto, CA: Consulting Psychologists Press, 1992), pp. 269–313.

49 A. Chang, P. Bordia, and J. Duck, "Punctuated Equilibrium and Linear Progression: Toward a New Understanding of Group Development," *Academy of Management Journal* 46, no. 1 (2003), pp. 106–117; and S. G. S. Lim and J. K. Murnighan, "Phases, Deadlines, and the Bargaining Process," *Organizational Behavior and Human Decision Processes* 58 (1994), pp. 153–171.

50 Vignette based on A. Tesolin, "Igniting the Creative Spark at Cirque du Soleil—Arupa Tesolin Interviews Lyn Heward Creative Leader at Cirque," SelfGrowth.com, http://www.selfgrowth.com/articles/Igniting_the_Creative_Spark_at_Cirque_du_Soleil.html; and M. Baghai and J. Quigley, "Cirque du Soleil: A Very Different Vision of Teamwork," *Fast Company*, February 4, 2011.

51 See, for example, D. L. Gladstein, "Groups in Context: A Model of Task Group Effectiveness," *Administrative Science Quarterly*, December 1984, pp. 499–517; J. R. Hackman, "The Design of Work Teams," in *Handbook of Organizational Behavior*, ed. J. W. Lorsch (Englewood Cliffs, NJ: Prentice Hall, 1987), pp. 315–342; M. A. Campion, G. J. Medsker, and C. A. Higgs, "Relations between Work Group Characteristics and Effectiveness: Implications for Designing Effective Work Groups," *Personnel Psychology*, 1993; and R. A. Guzzo and M. W. Dickson, "Teams in Organizations: Recent Research on Performance and Effectiveness," in *Annual Review of Psychology*, vol. 47, ed. J. T. Spence, J. M. Darley, and D. J. Foss, 1996, pp. 307–338.

52 D. E. Hyatt and T. M. Ruddy, "An Examination of the Relationship between Work Group Characteristics and Performance: Once More into the Breech," *Personnel Psychology*, Autumn 1997, p. 555.

53 This model is based on M. A. Campion, E. M. Papper, and G. J. Medsker, "Relations between Work Team Characteristics and Effectiveness: A Replication and Extension," *Personnel Psychology*, Summer 1996, pp. 429–452; D. E. Hyatt and T. M. Ruddy, "An Examination of the Relationship between Work Group Characteristics and Performance: Once More into the Breech," *Personnel Psychology*, Autumn 1997, pp. 553–585; S. G. Cohen and D. E. Bailey, "What Makes Teams Work: Group Effectiveness Research from the Shop Floor to the Executive Suite," *Journal of Management* 23, no. 3 (1997), pp. 239–290; G. A. Neuman and J. Wright, "Team Effectiveness: Beyond Skills and Cognitive Ability," *Journal of Applied Psychology*, June 1999, pp. 376–389; and L. Thompson, *Making the Team* (Upper Saddle River, NJ: Prentice Hall, 2000), pp. 18–33.

54 See M. Mattson, T. V. Mumford, and G. S. Sintay, "Taking Teams to Task: A Normative Model for Designing or Recalibrating Work Teams" (paper presented at the National Academy of Management Conference, Chicago, August 1999); and G. L. Stewart and M. R. Barrick, "Team Structure and Performance: Assessing the Mediating Role of Intrateam Process and the Moderating Role of Task Type," *Academy of Management Journal*, April 2000, pp. 135–148.

55 E. M. Stark, "Interdependence and Preference for Group Work: Main and Congruence Effects on the Satisfaction and Performance of Group Members," *Journal of Management* 26, no. 2 (2000), pp. 259–279; and J. W. Bishop, K. D. Scott, and S. M. Burroughs, "Support, Commitment, and Employee Outcomes in a Team Environment," *Journal of Management* 26, no. 6 (2000), pp. 1113–1132.

56 D. Aarts, "Canada's Smartest Employers 2014," *PROFIT*, November 7, 2013, http://www.profitguide.com/manage-grow/human-resources/meet-canadas-smartest-employers-2014-59150/2.

57 W. G. Dyer, R. H. Daines, and W. C. Giauque, *The Challenge of Management* (New York: Harcourt Brace Jovanovich, 1990), p. 343.

58 J. R. Hackman, *Leading Teams* (Boston: Harvard Business School Press, 2002).

59 S. A. Haslam and S. Reicher, "Stressing the Group: Social Identity and the Unfolding Dynamics of Responses to Stress," *Journal of Applied Psychology* 91, no. 5 (2006), pp. 1037–1052; S. Reicher and S. A. Haslam, "Rethinking the Psychology of Tyranny: The BBC Prison Study," *British Journal of Social Psychology* 45, no. 1 (2006), pp. 1–40; and P. G. Zimbardo, "On Rethinking the Psychology of Tyranny: The BBC Prison Study," *British Journal of Social Psychology* 45, no. 1 (2006), pp. 47–53.

60 For a review of the research on group norms, see J. R. Hackman, "Group Influences on Individuals in Organizations," in M. D. Dunnette and L. M. Hough (eds.), *Handbook of Industrial & Organizational Psychology*, 2nd ed., vol. 3 (Palo Alto, CA: Consulting Psychologists Press, 1992), pp. 235–250. For a more recent discussion, see M. G. Ehrhart and S. E. Naumann, "Organizational Citizenship Behavior in Work Groups: A Group Norms Approach," *Journal of Applied Psychology*, December 2004, pp. 960–974.

61 W. Immen, "The More Women in Groups, the Better," *Globe and Mail*, April 27, 2005, p. C3; and J. L. Berdahl and C. Anderson, "Men, Women, and Leadership Centralization in Groups over Time," *Group Dynamics: Theory, Research, and Practice* 9, no. 1 (2005), pp. 45–57.

62 R. I. Beekun, "Assessing the Effectiveness of Sociotechnical Interventions: Antidote or Fad?" *Human Relations*, October 1989, pp. 877–897.

63 S. G. Cohen, G. E. Ledford, and G. M. Spreitzer, "A Predictive Model of Self-Managing Work Team Effectiveness," *Human Relations*, May 1996, pp. 643–676.

64 D. R. Ilgen, J. R. Hollenbeck, M. Johnson, and D. Jundt, "Teams in Organizations: From Input-Process-Output Models to IMOI Models," *Annual Review of Psychology* 56, no. 1 (2005), pp. 517–543.

65 B. A. De Jong, and K. T. Dirks, "Beyond Shared Perceptions of Trust and Monitoring in Teams: Implications of Asymmetry and Dissensus," *Journal of Applied Psychology* 97, no. 2 (2012), pp. 391–406.

66 P. L. Schindler and C. C. Thomas, "The Structure of Interpersonal Trust in the Workplace," *Psychological Reports*, October 1993, pp. 563–573.

67 Based on D. L. Ferrin and N. Gillespie, "Trust Differences Across National-Societal Cultures: Much To Do, or Much Ado About Nothing," in *Organizational Trust: A Cultural Perspective*, ed. M. N. K. Sanders, D. Skinner, G. Dietz, N. Gillespie, and Roy J. Lewicki (New York: Cambridge University Press, 2010), pp. 42–86; and J. Lauring and J. Selmer, "Openness to Diversity, Trust and Conflict in Multicultural Organizations," *Journal of Management & Organization*, November 2012, pp. 795–806.

68 See C.-H. Chuang, S. Chen, and C.-W. Chuang, "Human Resource Management Practices and Organizational Social Capital: The Role of Industrial Characteristics," *Journal of Business Research*, May 2013, pp. 678–687; F. Aime, C. J. Meyer, and S. E. Humphrey, "Legitimacy of Team Rewards: Analyzing Legitimacy as a Condition for the Effectiveness of Team Incentive Designs," *Journal of Business Research* 63, no. 1 (2010), pp. 60–66; P. A. Bamberger and R. Levi, "Team-Based Reward Allocation Structures and the Helping Behaviors of Outcome-Interdependent Team Members," *Journal of Managerial Psychology* 24, no. 4 (2009), pp. 300–327; and M. J. Pearsall, M. S. Christian, and A. P. J. Ellis, "Motivating Interdependent Teams: Individual Rewards, Shared Rewards, or Something in Between?" *Journal of Applied Psychology* 95, no. 1 (2010), pp. 183–191.

69 K. Merriman, "Low-Trust Teams Prefer Individualized Pay," *Harvard Business Review* 86, November 2008, p. 32.

70 J. Pfeffer and N. Langton, "The Effect of Wage Dispersion on Satisfaction, Productivity, and Working Collaboratively: Evidence from College and University Faculty," *Administrative Science Quarterly* 38 (1993), pp. 382–407.

71 M. Bloom, "The Performance Effects of Pay Dispersion on Individuals and Organizations," *Academy of Management Journal* 42 (1999), pp. 25–40.

72 B. Beersma, J. R. Hollenbeck, D. E. Conlon, S. E. Humphrey, H. Moon, and D. R. Ilgen, "Cutthroat Cooperation: The Effects of Team Role Decisions on Adaptation to Alternative Reward Structures," *Organizational Behavior and Human Decision Processes* 108, no. 1 (2009), pp. 131–142; and M. D. Johnson, S. E. Humphrey, D. R. Ilgen, D. Jundt, and C. J. Meyer, "Cutthroat Cooperation: Asymmetrical Adaptation to Changes in Team Reward Structures," *Academy of Management Journal* 49, no. 1 (2006), pp. 103–119.

73 R. R. Hirschfeld, M. H. Jordan, H. S. Feild, W. F. Giles, and A. A. Armenakis, "Becoming Team Players: Team Members' Mastery of Teamwork Knowledge as a Predictor of Team Task Proficiency and Observed Teamwork Effectiveness," *Journal of Applied Psychology* 91,

no. 2 (2006), pp. 467–474; and K. R. Randall, C. J. Resick, and L. A. DeChurch, "Building Team Adaptive Capacity: The Roles of Sensegiving and Team Composition," *Journal of Applied Psychology* 96, no. 3 (2011), pp. 525–540.

74 Moon, J. R. Hollenbeck, and S. E. Humphrey, "Asymmetric Adaptability: Dynamic Team Structures as One-Way Streets," *Academy of Management Journal* 47, no. 5 (October 2004), pp. 681–695; A. P. J. Ellis, J. R. Hollenbeck, and D. R. Ilgen, "Team Learning: Collectively Connecting the Dots," *Journal of Applied Psychology* 88, no. 5 (October 2003), pp. 821–835; C. L. Jackson and J. A. LePine, "Peer Responses to a Team's Weakest Link: A Test and Extension of LePine and Van Dyne's Model," *Journal of Applied Psychology* 88, no. 3 (June 2003), pp. 459–475; and J. A. LePine, "Team Adaptation and Postchange Performance: Effects of Team Composition in Terms of Members' Cognitive Ability and Personality," *Journal of Applied Psychology* 88, no. 1 (February 2003), pp. 27–39.

75 S. T. Bell, "Deep-Level Composition Variables as Predictors of Team Performance: A Meta-analysis," *Journal of Applied Psychology* 92, no. 3 (2007), pp. 595–615; and M. R. Barrick, G. L. Stewart, M. J. Neubert, and M. K. Mount, "Relating Member Ability and Personality to Work-Team Processes and Team Effectiveness," *Journal of Applied Psychology*, June 1998, pp. 377–391.

76 K. Tasa, G. J. Sears, and A. C. H. Schat, "Personality and Teamwork Behavior in Context: The Cross-Level Moderating Role of Collective Efficacy," *Journal of Organizational Behavior* 32, no. 1 (2011), pp. 65–85.

77 T. A. O'Neill and N. J. Allen, "Personality and the Prediction of Team Performance," *European Journal of Personality* 25, no. 1 (2011), pp. 31–42.

78 A. Ellis, J. R. Hollenbeck, D. R. Ilgen, C. O. Porter, B. West, and H. Moon, "Team Learning: Collectively Connecting the Dots," *Journal of Applied Psychology* 88 (2003), pp. 821–835; C. O. L. H. Porter, J. R. Hollenbeck, and D. R. Ilgen, "Backing up Behaviors in Teams: The Role of Personality and Legitimacy of Need," *Journal of Applied Psychology* 88, no. 3 (June 2003), pp. 391–403; A. Colquitt, J. R. Hollenbeck, and D. R. Ilgen, "Computer-Assisted Communication and Team Decision-Making Performance: The Moderating Effect of Openness to Experience," *Journal of Applied Psychology* 87, no. 2 (April 2002), pp. 402–410; J. A. LePine, J. R. Hollenbeck, D. R. Ilgen, and J. Hedlund, "The Effects of Individual Differences on the Performance of Hierarchical Decision Making Teams: Much More Than G," *Journal of Applied Psychology* 82 (1997), pp. 803–811; C. L. Jackson and J. A. LePine, "Peer Responses to a Team's Weakest Link," *Journal of Applied Psychology* 88, no. 3 (2003), pp. 459–475; and M. R. Barrick, G. L. Stewart, J. M. Neubert, and M. K. Mount, "Relating Member Ability and Personality to Work-Team Processes and Team Effectiveness," *Journal of Applied Psychology* 83, no. 3 (1998), pp. 377–391.

79 M. R. Barrick, G. L. Stewart, M. J. Neubert, and M. K. Mount, "Relating Member Ability and Personality to Work-Team Processes and Team Effectiveness," *Journal of Applied Psychology*, June 1998, p. 388; and S. E. Humphrey, J. R. Hollenbeck, C. J. Meyer, and D. R. Ilgen, "Trait Configurations in Self-Managed Teams: A Conceptual Examination of the Use of Seeding for Maximizing and Minimizing Trait Variance in Teams," *Journal of Applied Psychology* 92, no. 3 (2007), pp. 885–892.

80 S. E. Humphrey, F. P. Morgeson, and M. J. Mannor, "Developing a Theory of the Strategic Core of Teams: A Role Composition Model of Team Performance," *Journal of Applied Psychology* 94, no. 1 (2009), pp. 48–61.

81 E. Sundstrom, K. P. Meuse, and D. Futrell, "Work Teams: Applications and Effectiveness," *American Psychologist*, February 1990, pp. 120–133.

82 See, for example, M. Sashkin and K. J. Kiser, *Putting Total Quality Management to Work* (San Francisco: Berrett-Koehler, 1993); and J. R. Hackman and R. Wageman, "Total Quality Management: Empirical,

Conceptual and Practical Issues," *Administrative Science Quarterly*, June 1995, pp. 309–342.

83 K. Y. Williams and C. A. O'Reilly III, "Demography and Diversity in Organizations: A Review of 40 Years of Research," in *Research in Organizational Behavior*, vol. 20, ed. B. M. Staw and L. L. Cummings (Stamford, CT: Jai Press, 1998), pp. 77–140; and A. Joshi, "The Influence of Organizational Demography on the External Networking Behavior of Teams," *Academy of Management Review*, July 2006, pp. 583–595.

84 A. Joshi and H. Roh, "The Role of Context in Work Team Diversity Research: A Meta-analytic Review," *Academy of Management Journal* 52, no. 3 (2009), pp. 599—627; S. K. Horwitz and I. B. Horwitz, "The Effects of Team Diversity on Team Outcomes: A Meta-analytic Review of Team Demography," *Journal of Management* 33, no. 6 (2007), pp. 987–1015; and S. T. Bell, A. J. Villado, M. A. Lukasik, L. Belau, and A. L. Briggs, "Getting Specific about Demographic Diversity Variable and Team Performance Relationships: A Meta-analysis," *Journal of Management* 37, no. 3 (2011), pp. 709–743.

85 S. J. Shin and J. Zhou, "When Is Educational Specialization Heterogeneity Related to Creativity in Research and Development Teams? Transformational Leadership as a Moderator," *Journal of Applied Psychology* 92, no. 6 (2007), pp. 1709–1721; and K. J. Klein, A. P. Knight, J. C. Ziegert, B. C. Lim, and J. L. Saltz, "When Team Members' Values Differ: The Moderating Role of Team Leadership," *Organizational Behavior and Human Decision Processes* 114, no. 1 (2011), pp. 25–36.

86 J. Shin, T. Kim, J. Lee, and L. Bian, "Cognitive Team Diversity and Individual Team Member Creativity: A Cross-Level Interaction," *Academy of Management Journal* 55, no. 1 (2012), pp. 197–212.

87 W. E. Watson, K. Kumar, and L. K. Michaelsen, "Cultural Diversity's Impact on Interaction Process and Performance: Comparing Homogeneous and Diverse Task Groups," *Academy of Management Journal*, June 1993, pp. 590–602; P. C. Earley and E. Mosakowski, "Creating Hybrid Team Cultures: An Empirical Test of Transnational Team Functioning," *Academy of Management Journal*, February 2000, pp. 26–49; and S. Mohammed and L. C. Angell, "Surface- and Deep-Level Diversity in Workgroups: Examining the Moderating Effects of Team Orientation and Team Process on Relationship Conflict," *Journal of Organizational Behavior*, December 2004, pp. 1015–1039.

88 D. Coutu, "Why Teams Don't Work" *Harvard Business Review*, May 2009, pp. 99–105. The evidence in this section is described in L. Thompson, *Making the Team* (Upper Saddle River, NJ: Prentice Hall, 2000), pp. 65–67. See also L. A. Curral, R. H. Forrester, and J. F. Dawson, "It's What You Do and the Way That You Do It: Team Task, Team Size, and Innovation-Related Group Processes," *European Journal of Work & Organizational Psychology* 10, no. 2 (June 2001), pp. 187–204; R. C. Liden, S. J. Wayne, and R. A. Jaworski, "Social Loafing: A Field Investigation," *Journal of Management* 30, no. 2 (2004), pp. 285–304; and J. A. Wagner, "Studies of Individualism–Collectivism: Effects on Cooperation in Groups," *Academy of Management Journal* 38, no. 1 (February 1995), pp. 152–172.

89 "Is Your Team Too Big? Too Small? What's the Right Number?" *Knowledge@Wharton*, June 14, 2006, pp. 1–5; see also A. M. Carton and J. N. Cummings, "A Theory of Subgroups in Work Teams," *Academy of Management Review* 37, no. 3 (2012), pp. 441–470.

90 See, for example, D. R. Comer, "A Model of Social Loafing in Real Work Groups," *Human Relations*, June 1995, pp. 647–667; S. M. Murphy, S. J. Wayne, R. C. Liden, and B. Erdogan, "Understanding Social Loafing: The Role of Justice Perceptions and Exchange Relationships," *Human Relations*, January 2003, pp. 61–84; and R. C. Liden, S. J. Wayne, R. A. Jaworski, and N. Bennett, "Social Loafing: A Field Investigation," *Journal of Management*, April 2004, pp. 285–304.

91 W. Moede, "Die Richtlinien der Leistungs-Psychologie," *Industrielle Psychotechnik* 4 (1927), pp. 193–207. See also D. A. Kravitz and B. Martin, "Ringelmann Rediscovered: The Original Article," *Journal of Personality and Social Psychology*, May 1986, pp. 936–941.

92 See, for example, J. A. Shepperd, "Productivity Loss in Performance Groups: A Motivation Analysis," *Psychological Bulletin*, January 1993, pp. 67–81; and S. J. Karau and K. D. Williams, "Social Loafing: A Meta-analytic Review and Theoretical Integration," *Journal of Personality and Social Psychology*, October 1993, pp. 681–706.

93 A. W. Delton, L. Cosmides, M. Guemo, T. E. Robertson, and J. Tooby, "The Psychosemantics of Free Riding: Dissecting the Architecture of a Moral Concept," *Journal of Personality and Social Psychology* 102, no. 6 (2012), pp. 1252–1270.

94 D. E. Hyatt and T. M. Ruddy, "An Examination of the Relationship between Work Group Characteristics and Performance: Once More into the Breech," *Personnel Psychology*, Autumn 1997, p. 555; and J. D. Shaw, M. K. Duffy, and E. M. Stark, "Interdependence and Preference for Group Work: Main and Congruence Effects on the Satisfaction and Performance of Group Members," *Journal of Management* 26, no. 2 (2000), pp. 259–279.

95 J. A. LePine, R. F. Piccolo, C. L. Jackson, J. E. Mathieu, and J. R. Saul, "A Meta-analysis of Teamwork Processes: Tests of a Multidimensional Model and Relationships with Team Effectiveness Criteria," *Personnel Psychology* 61 (2008), pp. 273–307.

96 I. D. Steiner, *Group Processes and Productivity* (New York: Academic Press, 1972).

97 J. A. LePine, R. F. Piccolo, C. L. Jackson, J. E. Mathieu, and J. R. Saul, "A Meta-analysis of Teamwork Processes: Tests of a Multidimensional Model and Relationships with Team Effectiveness Criteria," *Personnel Psychology* 61 (2008), pp. 273–307; and J. E. Mathieu and T. L. Rapp, "Laying the Foundation for Successful Team Performance Trajectories: The Roles of Team Charters and Performance Strategies," *Journal of Applied Psychology* 94, no. 1 (2009), pp. 90–103.

98 J. E. Mathieu and W. Schulze, "The Influence of Team Knowledge and Formal Plans on Episodic Team Process–Performance Relationships," *Academy of Management Journal* 49, no. 3 (2006), pp. 605–619.

99 A. N. Pieterse, D. van Knippenberg, and W. P. van Ginkel, "Diversity in Goal Orientation, Team Reflexivity, and Team Performance," *Organizational Behavior and Human Decision Processes* 114, no. 2 (2011), pp. 153–164.

100 A. Gurtner, F. Tschan, N. K. Semmer, and C. Nagele, "Getting Groups to Develop Good Strategies: Effects of Reflexivity Interventions on Team Process, Team Performance, and Shared Mental Models," *Organizational Behavior and Human Decision Processes* 102 (2007), pp. 127–142; M. C. Schippers, D. N. Den Hartog, and P. L. Koopman, "Reflexivity in Teams: A Measure and Correlates," *Applied Psychology: An International Review* 56, no. 2 (2007), pp. 189–211; and C. S. Burke, K. C. Stagl, E. Salas, L. Pierce, and D. Kendall, "Understanding Team Adaptation: A Conceptual Analysis and Model," *Journal of Applied Psychology* 91, no. 6 (2006), pp. 1189–1207.

101 A. N. Pieterse, D. van Knippenberg, and W. P. van Ginkel, "Diversity in Goal Orientation, Team Reflexivity, and Team Performance," *Organizational Behavior and Human Decision Processes* 114, no. 2 (2011), pp. 153–164.

102 E. Weldon and L. R. Weingart, "Group Goals and Group Performance," *British Journal of Social Psychology*, Spring 1993, pp. 307–334.

103 K. Tasa, S. Taggar, and G. H. Seijts, "The Development of Collective Efficacy in Teams: A Multilevel and Longitudinal Perspective," *Journal of Applied Psychology* 92, no. 1 (2007), pp. 17–27; C. B. Gibson, "The Efficacy Advantage: Factors Related to the Formation

of Group Efficacy," *Journal of Applied Social Psychology*, October 2003, pp. 2153–2086; and D. I. Jung and J. J. Sosik, "Group Potency and Collective Efficacy: Examining Their Predictive Validity, Level of Analysis, and Effects of Performance Feedback on Future Group Performance," *Group & Organization Management*, September 2003, pp. 366–391.

104 A. W. Richter, G. Hirst, D. van Knippenberg, and M. Baer, "Creative Self-Efficacy and Individual Creativity in Team Contexts: Cross-Level Interactions with Team Informational Resources," *Journal of Applied Psychology* 97, no. 6 (2012), pp. 1282–1290.

105 For some of the controversy surrounding the definition of cohesion, see J. Keyton and J. Springston, "Redefining Cohesiveness in Groups," *Small Group Research*, May 1990, pp. 234–254.

106 L. L. Greer, "Group Cohesion: Then and Now," *Small Group Research*, December 2012, pp. 655–661; B. Mullen and C. Cooper, "The Relation between Group Cohesiveness and Performance: An Integration," *Psychological Bulletin*, March 1994, pp. 210–227; S. M. Gully, D. J. Devine, and D. J. Whitney, "A Meta-analysis of Cohesion and Performance: Effects of Level of Analysis and Task Interdependence," *Small Group Research*, November 1995, pp. 497–520; and P. M. Podsakoff, S. B. MacKenzie, and M. Ahearne, "Moderating Effects of Goal Acceptance on the Relationship between Group Cohesiveness and Productivity," *Journal of Applied Psychology*, December 1997, pp. 974–983.

107 A. Chang and P. Bordia, "A Multidimensional Approach to the Group Cohesion-Group Performance Relationship," *Small Group Research*, August 2001, pp. 379–405.

108 Paragraph based on R. Kreitner and A. Kinicki, *Organizational Behavior*, 6th ed. (New York: Irwin, 2004), pp. 459–461.

109 R. Kreitner and A. Kinicki, *Organizational Behavior*, 6th ed. (New York: Irwin, 2004), p. 460. Reprinted by permission of McGraw Hill Education.

110 S. Mohammed, L. Ferzandi, and K. Hamilton, "Metaphor No More: A 15-Year Review of the Team Mental Model Construct," *Journal of Management* 36, no. 4 (2010), pp. 876–910.

111 A. P. J. Ellis, "System Breakdown: The Role of Mental Models and Transactive Memory on the Relationships between Acute Stress and Team Performance," *Academy of Management Journal* 49, no. 3 (2006), pp. 576–589.

112 S. W. J. Kozlowski and D. R. Ilgen, "Enhancing the Effectiveness of Work Groups and Teams," *Psychological Science in the Public Interest*, December 2006, pp. 77–124; and B. D. Edwards, E. A. Day, W. Arthur Jr., and S. T. Bell, "Relationships among Team Ability Composition, Team Mental Models, and Team Performance," *Journal of Applied Psychology* 91, no. 3 (2006), pp. 727–736.

113 K. M. Eisenhardt, J. L. Kahwajy, and L. J. Bourgeois III, "How Management Teams Can Have a Good Fight," *Harvard Business Review*, July–August 1997, p. 78.

114 J. Farh, C. Lee, and C. I. C. Farh, "Task Conflict and Team Creativity: A Question of How Much and When," *Journal of Applied Psychology* 95, no. 6 (2010), pp. 1173–1180.

115 K. J. Behfar, R. S. Peterson, E. A. Mannix, and W. M. K. Trochim, "The Critical Role of Conflict Resolution in Teams: A Close Look at the Links between Conflict Type, Conflict Management Strategies, and Team Outcomes," *Journal of Applied Psychology* 93, no. 1 (2008), pp. 170–188.

116 K. M. Eisenhardt, J. L. Kahwajy, and L. J. Bourgeois III, "How Management Teams Can Have a Good Fight," *Harvard Business Review*, July–August 1997, p. 78.

117 K. A. Jehn, S. Rispens, and S M. B. Thatcher, "The Effects of Conflict Asymmetry on Work Group and Individual Outcomes," *Academy of Management Journal* 53, no. 3 (2010), pp. 596–616.

118 K. Jehn, "A Multimethod Examination of the Benefits and Detriments of Intragroup Conflict," *Administrative Science Quarterly*, June 1995, pp. 256–282.

119 K. H. Price, D. A. Harrison, and J. H. Gavin, "Withholding Inputs in Team Contexts: Member Composition, Interaction Processes, Evaluation Structure, and Social Loafing," *Journal of Applied Psychology* 91, no. 6 (2006), pp. 1375–1384.

120 C. E. Naquin and R. O. Tynan, "The Team Halo Effect: Why Teams Are Not Blamed for Their Failures," *Journal of Applied Psychology*, April 2003, pp. 332–340.

121 D. Brown, "Innovative HR Ineffective in Manufacturing Firms," *Canadian HR Reporter*, April 7, 2003, pp. 1–2.

122 E. R. Crawford and J. A. LePine, "A Configural Theory of Team Processes: Accounting for the Structure of Taskwork and Teamwork," *Academy of Management Review*, January 2013, pp. 32–48; and A. B. Drexler and R. Forrester, "Teamwork—Not Necessarily the Answer," *HR Magazine*, January 1998, pp. 55–58.

123 "Watson Wyatt's Global Work Studies," *WatsonWyatt.com*, http://www.watsonwyatt.com/research/featured/workstudy.asp.

124 C. E. Nicholls, H. W. Lane, and M. Brehm Brechu, "Taking Self-Managed Teams to Mexico," *Academy of Management Executive* 13, no. 3 (1999), pp. 15–27.

125 W. E. Watson, K. Kumar, and L. K. Michaelsen, "Cultural Diversity's Impact on Interaction Process and Performance: Comparing Homogeneous and Diverse Task Groups," *Academy of Management Journal*, June 1993, pp. 590–602; P. C. Earley and E. Mosakowski, "Creating Hybrid Team Cultures: An Empirical Test of Transnational Team Functioning," *Academy of Management Journal*, February 2000, pp. 26–49; and S. Mohammed and L. C. Angell, "Surface- and Deep-Level Diversity in Workgroups: Examining the Moderating Effects of Team Orientation and Team Process on Relationship Conflict," *Journal of Organizational Behavior*, December 2004, pp. 1015–1039.

126 W. E. Watson, K. Kumar, and L. K. Michaelsen, "Cultural Diversity's Impact on Interaction Process and Performance: Comparing Homogeneous and Diverse Task Groups," *Academy of Management Journal*, June 1993, pp. 590–602.

127 D. F. Crown, "The Use of Group and Groupcentric Individual Goals for Culturally Heterogeneous and Homogeneous Task Groups: An Assessment of European Work Teams," *Small Group Research* 38, no. 4 (2007), pp. 489–508.

128 Based on D. Man and S. S. K. Lam, "The Effects of Job Complexity and Autonomy on Cohesiveness in Collectivist and Individualistic Work Groups: A Cross-Cultural Analysis," *Journal of Organizational Behavior*, December 2003, pp. 979–1001.

129 Based on S. I. Tannenbaum, J. Mathieu, E. Salas, and D. Cohen, "Teams Are Changing: Are Research and Practice Evolving Fast Enough," *Industrial and Organizational Psychology* 5 (2012), pp. 2–24; and R. Ashkenas, "How to Empower Your Team for Non-Negotiable Results," *Forbes*, April 24, 2013, http://www.forbes.com/sites/ronashkenas/2013/04/24/how-to-empower-your-team-with-non-negotiable-results/.

130 Based on E. Bernstein, "Speaking Up Is Hard to Do: Researchers Explain Why," *Wall Street Journal*, February 7, 2012, p. D1; and H. Leroy, B. Dierynck, F. Anseel, T. Simons, J. R. Halbesleben, D. McCaughey, G. T. Savage, and L. Sels, "Behavioral Integrity for Safety, Priority of Safety, Psychological Safety, and Patient Safety: A Team-Level Study," *Journal of Applied Psychology*, November 2012, pp. 1273–1281.

131 Based on C. Hymowitz, "IBM Combines Volunteer Service, Teamwork to Cultivate Emerging Markets," *Wall Street Journal*, August 4, 2008, p. B6; S. Gupta, "Mine the Potential of Multicultural Teams," *HR Magazine*, October 2008, pp. 79–84; H. Aguinis and K. Kraiger, "Benefits of Training and Development for Individuals and Teams, Organizations, and Society," *Annual Review of Psychology* 60, no. 1 (2009), pp. 451–474; and K. Gurchiek, "Global Training Sought for Leaders of Multicultural Teams," *Society for Human Resource Management*, September 15, 2011, http://www.shrm.org/about/news/pages/trainmulticulturalteams.aspx.

132 Based on ROBBINS, STEPHEN P.; HUNSAKER, PHILLIP L., TRAINING IN INTERPERSONAL SKILLS: TIPS FOR MANAGING PEOPLE AT WORK, 2nd Ed., © 1996, pp. 168–184. Reprinted and Electronically reproduced by permission of Pearson Education, Inc., Upper Saddle River, New Jersey.

OB on the Edge: Trust

1 Based on B. MacLellan, "Turning 20, and Still a Young and Independent Agency," *Environics*, August 14th, 2014, http://environicspr.com/us/2014/08/turning-20-still-young-independent-agency/; "Stitches of Laughter Help Create Tight-Knit Team," *Globe and Mail*, April 17 2014; and G. Marr, "Sabbaticals Boost Job Satisfaction," *Gazette* (Montreal), August 18, 2012, p. F14.

2 See, for example, K. T. Dirks and D. L. Ferrin, "Trust in Leadership: Meta-analytic Findings and Implications for Research and Practice," *Journal of Applied Psychology*, August 2002, pp. 611–628; the special issue on trust in an organizational context, B. McEvily, V. Perrone, A. Zaheer, guest editors, *Organization Science*, January–February 2003; and R. Galford and A. S. Drapeau, *The Trusted Leader* (New York: Free Press, 2003).

3 F. K. Sonnenberg, "Trust Me, Trust Me Not," *IndustryWeek*, August 16, 1993, pp. 22–28; and L. T. Hosmer, "Trust: the Connecting Link between Organizational Theory and Philosophical Ethics," *Academy of Management Review*, April 1995, pp. 379–403.

4 "A Lack of Trust and Confidence: Majority of Canadian Employees Don't Believe Their Senior Leaders," *CNW*, news release, October 18, 2012, http://www.hrvoice.org/wp-content/uploads/2013/05/BABW-Infographic.jpg.

5 "A Lack of Trust and Confidence: Majority of Canadian Employees Don't Believe Their Senior Leaders," *CNW*, news release, October 18, 2012, http://www.hrvoice.org/wp-content/uploads/2013/05/BABW-Infographic.jpg.

6 J. Pollack, "Do Your Employees Trust You? Behaviour Survey Finds Lack of Trust in Senior Leaders as Top Reason for Quitting," *Telegraph-Journal*, May 30, 2009, p. E1.

7 D. M. Rousseau, S. B. Sitkin, R. S. Burt, and C. Camerer, "Not So Different After All: A Cross-Discipline View of Trust," *Academy of Management Review*, July 1998, pp. 393–404; and J. A. Simpson, "Psychological Foundations of Trust," *Current Directions in Psychological Science* 16, no. 5 (2007), pp. 264–268.

8 J. B. Rotter, "Interpersonal Trust, Trustworthiness, and Gullibility," *American Psychologist*, January 1980, pp. 1–7.

9 J. D. Lewis and A. Weigert, "Trust as a Social Reality," *Social Forces*, June 1985, p. 970.

10 J. K. Rempel, J. G. Holmes, and M. P. Zanna, "Trust in Close Relationships," *Journal of Personality and Social Psychology*, July 1985, p. 96.

11 G. M. Granovetter, "Economic Action and Social Structure: The Problem of Embeddedness," *American Journal of Sociology*, November 1985, p. 491.

12 R. C. Mayer, J. H. Davis, and F. D. Schoorman, "An Integrative Model of Organizational Trust," *Academy of Management Review*, July 1995, p. 712.

13 C. Johnson-George and W. Swap, "Measurement of Specific Interpersonal Trust: Construction and Validation of a Scale to Assess Trust in a Specific Other," *Journal of Personality and Social Psychology*, September 1982, p. 1306.

14 R. C. Mayer, J. H. Davis, and F. D. Schoorman, "An Integrative Model of Organizational Trust," *Academy of Management Review*, July 1995, pp. 709–734; and J. A. Colquitt, B. A. Scott, and J. A. LePine, "Trust, Trustworthiness, and Trust Propensity: A Meta-analytic Test of Their Unique Relationships with Risk Taking and Job Performance," *Journal of Applied Psychology* 92, no. 4 (2007), pp. 909–927.

15 Cited in D. Jones, "Do You Trust Your CEO?" *USA Today*, February 12, 2003, p. 7B.

16 K. T. Dirks and D. L. Ferrin, "Trust in Leadership: Meta-analytic Findings and Implications for Organizational Research," *Journal of Applied Psychology* 87 (2002), pp. 611–628.

17 J. A. Simpson, "Foundations of Interpersonal Trust," in *Social Psychology: Handbook of Basic Principles*, 2nd ed., ed. A. W. Kruglanski and E. T. Higgins (New York: Guilford, 2007), pp. 587–607.

18 J. A. Simpson, "Foundations of Interpersonal Trust," in *Social Psychology: Handbook of Basic Principles*, 2nd ed., ed. A. W. Kruglanski and E. T. Higgins (New York: Guilford, 2007), pp. 587–607.

19 Based on J. R. Detert and E. R. Burris, "Leadership Behavior and Employee Voice: Is the Door Really Open?" *Academy of Management Journal* 50, no. 4 (2007), pp. 869–884; and J. A. Colquitt, B. A. Scott, and J. A. LePine, "Trust, Trustworthiness, and Trust Propensity: A Meta-analytic Test of Their Unique Relationships with Risk Taking and Job Performance," *Journal of Applied Psychology* 92, no. 4 (2007), pp. 909–927.

20 This section is based on D. E. Zand, *The Leadership Triad: Knowledge, Trust, and Power* (New York: Oxford University Press, 1997), pp. 122–134; and A. M. Zak, J. A. Gold, R. M. Ryckman, and E. Lenney, "Assessments of Trust in Intimate Relationships and the Self-Perception Process," *Journal of Social Psychology*, April 1998, pp. 217–228.

21 D. L. Shapiro, A. D. Boss, S. Salas, S. Tangirala, and M. A. Von Glinow, "When Are Transgressing *Leaders* Punitively Judged? An Empirical Test," *Journal of Applied Psychology* 96, no. 2 (2011), pp. 412–422.

22 D. L. Ferrin, P. H. Kim, C. D. Cooper, and K. T. Dirks, "Silence Speaks Volumes: The Effectiveness of Reticence in Comparison to Apology and Denial for Responding to Integrity- and Competence-Based Trust Violations," *Journal of Applied Psychology* 92, no. 4 (2007), pp. 893–908.

23 M. E. Schweitzer, J. C. Hershey, and E. T. Bradlow, "Promises and Lies: Restoring Violated Trust," *Organizational Behavior and Human Decision Processes* 101 (2006), pp. 1–19.

24 B. A. De Jong and T. O. M. Elfring, "How Does Trust Affect the Performance of Ongoing Teams? The Mediating Role of Reflexivity, Monitoring, and Effort," *Academy of Management Journal* 53, no. 3 (2010), pp. 535–549.

25 H. Zhao, S. J. Wayne, B. C. Glibkowski, and J. Bravo, "The Impact of Psychological Contract Breach on Work-Related Outcomes: A Meta-analysis," *Personnel Psychology* 60 (2007), pp. 647–680.

26 T. Davis and M. J. Landa, "The Trust Deficit," *Worklife Report* 4 (1999), pp. 6–7.

27 Adapted from J. O'Toole and W. Bennis, "What's Needed Next: A Culture of Candor," *Harvard Business Review*, June 2009, pp. 54–61.

28 L. Prusak and D. Cohen, "How to Invest in Social Capital," *Harvard Business Review*, June 2001, pp. 86–93.

29 L. Prusak and D. Cohen, "How to Invest in Social Capital," *Harvard Business Review*, June 2001, pp. 86–93.

30 K. T. Dirks, "Trust in Leadership and Team Performance: Evidence from NCAA Basketball," *Journal of Applied Psychology* 85 (2000), pp. 1004–1012.

31 Based on F. Bartolome, "Nobody Trusts the Boss Completely—Now What?" *Harvard Business Review*, March–April 1989, pp. 135–142; and P. Pascarella, "15 Ways to Win People's Trust," *IndustryWeek*, February 1, 1993, pp. 47–51.

32 FactBox based on Edelman Insights, 2014 Edelman Trust Barometer: Canadian Findings, January 30, 2014, http://www.slideshare.net/EdelmanInsights/2014-edelman-trust-barometer-canada-results.

33   B. A. De Jong and T. O. M. Elfring, "How Does Trust Affect the Performance of Ongoing Teams? The Mediating Role of Reflexivity, Monitoring, and Effort," *Academy of Management Journal* 53, no. 3 (2010), pp. 535–549.

34   Adapted from R. M. Kramer, "Rethinking Trust," *Harvard Business Review*, June 2009, p. 71.

35   C. W. Langfred, "Too Much of a Good Thing? Negative Effects of High Trust and Individual Autonomy in Self-Managing Teams," *Academy of Management Journal* 47, no. 3 (June 2004), pp. 385–399.

36   N. L. Carter and J. Mark Weber, "Not Pollyannas: Higher Generalized Trust Predicts Lie Detection Ability," *Social Psychological and Personality Science* 1, no. 3 (2010), pp. 274–279.

37   Based on information in R. M. Kramer, "Rethinking Trust," *Harvard Business Review*, June 2009, pp. 69–77.

38   R. M. Kramer, "Rethinking Trust," *Harvard Business Review*, June 2009, p. 71.

39   R. M. Kramer, "When Paranoia Makes Sense," *Harvard Business Review*, July 2002, pp. 62–69.

40   R. M. Kramer, "Rethinking Trust," *Harvard Business Review*, June 2009, p. 77.

Chapter 7

1   Opening vignette based on "Globe-Trotting Developers Locate Palette in Kitchener," *Exchange*, March–April 2014, p. 15; T. Pender, "Palette's Old-Fashioned Button, Dial Are Shortcuts for Tedious Computing Tasks," *Waterloo Region Record*, January 11, 2014, p. D12; C. Chu, "Palette—A Freeform Interface That Controls Any Software," *Kickstarter.com*, accessed October 17, 2014, https://www.kickstarter.com/projects/cchu/palette-a-freeform-interface-that-controls-any-sof; and http://www.haxlr8r.com/about/.

2   "Employers Cite Communication Skills, Honesty/Integrity as Key for Job Candidates," *IPMA-HR Bulletin*, March 23, 2007, p. 1.

3   J. Langan-Fox, "Communication in Organizations: Speed, Diversity, Networks, and Influence on Organizational Effectiveness, Human Health, and Relationships," in *Handbook of Industrial, Work and Organizational Psychology*, vol. 2, ed. N. Anderson, D. S. Ones, H. K. Sinangil, and C. Viswesvaran (Thousand Oaks, CA: Sage, 2001), p. 190.

4   J. C. McCroskey, J. A. Daly, and G. Sorenson, "Personality Correlates of Communication Apprehension," *Human Communication Research*, Spring 1976, pp. 376–380.

5   See R. L. Daft and R. H. Lengel, "Information Richness: A New Approach to Managerial Behavior and Organization Design," in *Research in Organizational Behavior*, vol. 6, ed. B. M. Staw and L. L. Cummings (Greenwich, CT: JAI Press, 1984), pp. 191–233; R. E. Rice and D. E. Shook, "Relationships of Job Categories and Organizational Levels to Use of Communication Channels, Including Electronic Mail: A Meta-analysis and Extension," *Journal of Management Studies*, March 1990, pp. 195–229; R. E. Rice, "Task Analyzability, Use of New Media, and Effectiveness," *Organization Science*, November 1992, pp. 475–500; S. G. Straus and J. E. McGrath, "Does the Medium Matter? The Interaction of Task Type and Technology on Group Performance and Member Reaction," *Journal of Applied Psychology*, February 1994, pp. 87–97; and J. Webster and L. K. Trevino, "Rational and Social Theories as Complementary Explanations of Communication Media Choices: Two Policy-Capturing Studies," *Academy of Management Journal*, December 1995, pp. 1544–1572.

6   D. K. Denton, "Engaging Your Employees in Times of Uncertainty," *International Journal of Productivity and Quality Management* 7, no. 2 (2011), pp. 202–208.

7   I. Austen, "Telling Tales Out of School, on YouTube," *New York Times*, November 27, 2006; and D. Rogers, "Quebec Students Suspended for Posting Teacher's Outburst Online," *Ottawa Citizen*, November 25, 2006.

8   P. Brent, "How to Arm, Not Alarm, Your Staff in Crisis," *Canadian Business*, March 14, 2011, p. 68.

9   "Virtual Pink Slips Start Coming Online," *Vancouver Sun*, July 3, 1999, p. D15.

10   Vignette based on C. Chu, "Palette—A Freeform Interface That Controls Any Software," *Kickstarter.com*, accessed October 17, 2014, https://www.kickstarter.com/projects/cchu/palette-a-freeform-interface-that-controls-any-sof.

11   K. Savitsky, B. Keysar, N. Epley, T. Carter, and A. Swanson, "The Closeness-Communication Bias: Increased Egocentrism among Friends versus Strangers," *Journal of Experimental Social Psychology* 47, no. 1 (2011), pp. 269–273.

12   M. Richtel, "Lost in E-mail, Tech Firms Face Self-Made Beast," *New York Times*, June 14, 2008.

13   M. Richtel, "Lost in E-Mail, Tech Firms Face Self-Made Beast," *New York Times*, June 14, 2008.

14   M. Richtel, "Lost in E-mail, Tech Firms Face Self-Made Beast," *New York Times*, June 14, 2008, pp. A1, A14; and M. Johnson, "Quelling Distraction," *HR Magazine*, August 2008, pp. 43–46.

15   W. R. Boswell and J. B. Olson-Buchanan, "The Use of Communication Technologies After Hours: The Role of Work-Attitudes and Work-Life Conflict," *Journal of Management* 33, no. 4 (2007), pp. 592–610.

16   P. Briñol, R. E. Petty, and J. Barden, "Happiness Versus Sadness as a Determinant of Thought Confidence in Persuasion: A Self-Validation Analysis," *Journal of Personality and Social Psychology* 93, no. 5 (2007), pp. 711–727.

17   R. C. Sinclair, S. E. Moore, M. M. Mark, A. S. Soldat, and C. A. Lavis, "Incidental Moods, Source Likeability, and Persuasion: Liking Motivates Message Elaboration in Happy People," *Cognition and Emotion* 24, no. 6 (2010), pp. 940–961; and V. Griskevicius, M. N. Shiota, and S. L. Neufeld, "Influence of Different Positive Emotions on Persuasion Processing: A Functional Evolutionary Approach," *Emotion* 10, no. 2 (2010), pp. 190–206.

18   J. Sandberg, "The Jargon Jumble," *Wall Street Journal*, October 24, 2006, p. B1.

19   E. W. Morrison and F. J. Milliken, "Organizational Silence: A Barrier to Change and Development in a Pluralistic World," *Academy of Management Review* 25, no. 4 (2000), pp. 706–725; and B. E. Ashforth and V. Anand, "The Normalization of Corruption in Organizations," *Research in Organizational Behavior* 25 (2003), pp. 1–52.

20   F. J. Milliken, E. W. Morrison, and P. F. Hewlin, "An Exploratory Study of Employee Silence: Issues That Employees Don't Communicate Upward and Why," *Journal of Management Studies* 40, no. 6 (2003), pp. 1453–1476.

21   This paragraph is based on J. O'Toole and W. Bennis, "What's Needed Next: A Culture of Candor," *Harvard Business Review*, June 2009, pp. 54–61.

22   M. Gladwell, *Outliers* (New York: Bay Bay Books, 2008), p. 184.

23   S. Tangirala and R. Ramunujam, "Employee Silence on Critical Work Issues: The Cross-Level Effects of Procedural Justice Climate," *Personnel Psychology* 61, no. 1 (2008), pp. 37–68; and F. Bowen and K. Blackmon, "Spirals of Silence: The Dynamic Effects of Diversity on Organizational Voice," *Journal of Management Studies* 40, no. 6 (2003), pp. 1393–1417.

24   L. S. Rashotte, "What Does That Smile Mean? The Meaning of Nonverbal Behaviors in Social Interaction," *Social Psychology Quarterly*, March 2002, pp. 92–102.

25   R. L. Birdwhistell, *Introduction to Kinesics* (Louisville, KY: University of Louisville Press, 1952).

26   J. Fast, *Body Language* (Philadelphia, PA: M. Evan, 1970), p. 7.

27 A. Mehrabian, *Nonverbal Communication* (Chicago: Aldine-Atherton, 1972).

28 N. M. Henley, "Body Politics Revisited: What Do We Know Today?" in *Gender, Power, and Communication in Human Relationships*, ed. P. J. Kalbfleisch and M. J. Cody (Hillsdale, NJ: Erlbaum, 1995), pp. 27–61.

29 E. T. Hall, *The Hidden Dimension*, 2nd ed. (Garden City, NY: Anchor Books/Doubleday, 1966).

30 B. M. Depaulo, D. A. Kashy, S. E. Kirkendol, M. M. Wyer, and J. A. Epstein, "Lying in Everyday Life," *Journal of Personality and Social Psychology* 70, No. 5 (1996), pp. 979–995; and K. B. Serota, T. R. Levine, and F. J. Boster, "The Prevalence of Lying in America: Three Studies of Self-Reported Lies," *Human Communication Research* 36, no. 1. (2010), pp. 2–25.

31 B. M. Depaulo, D. A. Kashy, S. E. Kirkendol, M. M. Wyer, and J. A. Epstein, "Lying in Everyday Life," *Journal of Personality and Social Psychology* 70, No. 5 (1996), pp. 979–995; and C. E. Naguin, T. R. Kurtzberg, and L. Y. Belkin, "The Finer Points of Lying Online: E-Mail Versus Pen and Paper," *Journal of Applied Psychology* 95, no. 2 (2010), pp. 387–394.

32 A. Vrij, P. A. Granhag, and S. Porter, "Pitfalls and Opportunities in Nonverbal and Verbal Lie Detection," *Psychological Science in the Public Interest* 11, no. 3 (2010), pp. 89–121.

33 Vignette based on A. Anwar, "When Long Distance Makes the Startup More Complicated," *National Post*, August 5, 2014, p. FP6.

34 R. L. Simpson, "Vertical and Horizontal Communication in Formal Organizations," *Administrative Science Quarterly*, September 1959, pp. 188–196; and B. Harriman, "Up and Down the Communications Ladder," *Harvard Business Review*, September–October 1974, pp. 143–151.

35 P. Dvorak, "How Understanding the 'Why' of Decisions Matters," *Wall Street Journal*, March 19, 2007, p. B3.

36 T. Neeley and P. Leonardi, "Effective Managers Say the Same Thing Twice (or More)," *Harvard Business Review*, May 2011, pp. 38–39.

37 A. DiPaula, M. Bacica, and J. Winram, "To Be Believed Is to Be Heard," *Leadership*, Summer 2014, http://sentisresearch.com/wp-content/uploads/2014/07/BCHRMA-Summer-2014.pdf.

38 "Building a Better Workforce," *PROFIT*, February 16, 2011, http://www.profitguide.com/manage-grow/human-resources/building-a-better-workforce-30073.

39 H. A. Richardson and S. G. Taylor, "Understanding Input Events: A Model of Employees' Responses to Requests for Their Input," *Academy of Management Review* 37 (2012), pp. 471–491.

40 B. Amble, "Managers Ignoring the People Who Matter," *Management-issues.com*, September 18, 2006, http://www.management-issues.com/news/3593/manages-ignoring-the-people-who-matter/.

41 "Building a Better Workforce," *PROFIT*, February 16, 2011, http://www.profitguide.com/manage-grow/human-resources/building-a-better-workforce-30073.

42 J. R. Detert and L. K. Treviño, "Speaking Up to Higher-Ups: How Supervisors and Skip-Level Leaders Influence Employee Voice," *Organization Science* 21, no. 1 (2010), pp. 249–270.

43 E. Nichols, "Hyper-Speed Managers," *HR Magazine*, April 2007, pp. 107–110.

44 See, for example, N. B. Kurland and L. H. Pelled, "Passing the Word: Toward a Model of Gossip and Power in the Workplace," *Academy of Management Review*, April 2000, pp. 428–438; and G. Michelson, A. van Iterson, and K. Waddington, "Gossip in Organizations: Contexts, Consequences, and Controversies," *Group and Organization Management* 35, no. 4 (2010), pp. 371–390.

45 G. Van Hoye and F. Lievens, "Tapping the Grapevine: A Closer Look at Word-of-Mouth as a Recruitment Source," *Journal of Applied Psychology* 94, no. 2 (2009), pp. 341–352.

46 See, for example, J. W. Newstrom, R. E. Monczka, and W. E. Reif, "Perceptions of the Grapevine: Its Value and Influence," *Journal of Business Communication*, Spring 1974, pp. 12–20; and S. J. Modic, "Grapevine Rated Most Believable," *IndustryWeek*, May 15, 1989, p. 14.

47 K. Davis cited in R. Rowan, "Where Did That Rumor Come From?" *Fortune*, August 13, 1979, p. 134.

48 Based on L. Hirschhorn, "Managing Rumors," in *Cutting Back*, ed. L. Hirschhorn (San Francisco: Jossey-Bass, 1983), pp. 54–56.

49 R. L. Rosnow and G. A. Fine, *Rumor and Gossip: The Social Psychology of Hearsay* (New York: Elsevier, 1976).

50 See, for example, J. G. March and G. Sevon, "Gossip, Information and Decision Making," in *Decisions and Organizations*, ed. J. G. March (Oxford, UK: Blackwell, 1988), pp. 429–442; M. Noon and R. Delbridge, "News from Behind My Hand: Gossip in Organizations," *Organization Studies* 14, no. 1 (1993), pp. 23–36; and N. DiFonzo, P. Bordia, and R. L. Rosnow, "Reining in Rumors," *Organizational Dynamics*, Summer 1994, pp. 47–62.

51 T. J. Grosser, V. Lopez-Kidwell, and G. Labianca, "A Social Network Analysis of Positive and Negative Gossip in Organizational Life," *Group and Organization Management* 35, no. 2 (2010), pp. 177–212.

52 M. Feinberg, R. Willer, J. Stellar, and D. Keltner, "The Virtues of Gossip: Reputational Information Sharing as Prosocial Behavior," *Journal of Personality and Social Psychology* 102 (2012), pp. 1015–1030.

53 J. K. Bosson, A. B. Johnson, K. Niederhoffer, and W. B. Swann Jr., "Interpersonal Chemistry through Negativity: Bonding by Sharing Negative Attitudes About Others," *Personal Relationships* 13 (2006), pp. 135–150.

54 L. Hirschhorn, "Managing Rumors," in *Cutting Back*, ed. L. Hirschhorn (San Francisco: Jossey-Bass, 1983), pp. 54–56; and D. K. Denton, "Engaging Your Employees in Times of Uncertainty," *International Journal of Productivity and Quality Management* 7, no. 2 (2011), pp. 202–208.

55 N. Bilton, "Disruptions: Life's Too Short for So Much E-mail," *New York Times*, July 8, 2012, http://bits.blogs.nytimes.com/2012/07/08/life%E2%80%99s-too-short-for-so-much-e-mail/.

56 R. E. Silverman, "How to Be a Better Boss in 2013," *Wall Street Journal*, January 2, 2013, pp. B1, B4.

57 B. Gates, "How I Work: Bill Gates," *Fortune*, April 17, 2006, http://money.cnn.com/2006/03/30/news/newsmakers/gates_howi-work_fortune/.

58 "Executive Summary," *Messagemind*, 2012, http://www.message-mind.com/resources-executive.php.

59 G. J. Mark, S. Voida, and A. V. Cardello, "'A Pace Not Dictated by Electrons': An Empirical Study of Work Without Email," *Proceedings of the SIGCHI Conference on Human Factors in Computing Systems* (Austin, TX: ACM, 2012), pp. 555–564, https://www.ics.uci.edu/~gmark/Home_page/Research_files/CHI%202012.pdf.

60 "Overloaded Canadians Trash 42% of All E-Mails: Study," *Ottawa Citizen*, June 26, 2008, p. D5.

61 Based on A. Anwar, "When Long Distance Makes the Startup More Complicated," *National Post*, August 5, 2014, p. FP6.

62 Based on S. Proudfoot, "1 in 3 Workers Admit to Improper E-mail; Stories of Career-Killing Gaffes Leave Many Unfazed, Study Finds," *Edmonton Journal*, June 25, 2008, p. A1; E. Church, "Employers Read E-mail as Fair Game," *Globe and Mail*, April 14, 1998, p. B16; and J. Kay, "Someone Will Watch Over Me: Think Your Office E-mails Are Private? Think Again," *National Post Business*, January 2001, pp. 59–64.

63 E. Church, "Employers Read E-mail as Fair Game," *Globe and Mail*, April 14, 1998, p. B16.

64. B. Roberts, "Social Media Gets Strategic," *HR Magazine*, October 2012, pp. 30–38.

65. Gartner Inc. website, http://www.gartner.com/technology/topics/social-media.jsp, accessed May 29, 2013.

66. The Associated Press, "Number of Active Users at Facebook Over the Years," *Yahoo! News*, May 1, 2013, http://news.yahoo.com/number-active-users-facebook-over-230449748.html.

67. "Facebook Quarterly Earnings Slides: Q1 2013," *Facebook*, accessed October 17, 2014, http://files.shareholder.com/downloads/AMDA-NJ5DZ/2462702744x0x659143/b4c0beda-da0a-4f8e-9735-9852ef08adb1/FB_Q113_InvestorDeck_FINAL.pdf.

68. "About Tumblr.com," *Tumblr*, accessed October 14, 2014, https://www.tumblr.com/about; and "14 Surprising Statistics About WordPress Usage," *ManageWP Blog*, February 7, 2014, https://managewp.com/14-surprising-statistics-about-wordpress-usage.

69. S. Adams, "Less Than a Third of Top CEOs Are on Social Media," *Forbes*, http://www.forbes.com/sites/susanadams/2013/08/07/less-than-a-third-of-top-ceos-are-on-social-media/.

70. L. Kwoh and M. Korn, "140 Characters of Risk: CEOs on Twitter," *Wall Street Journal*, September 26, 2012, pp. B1, B8.

71. M. Richtel, "Lost in E-mail, Tech Firms Face Self-Made Beast," *New York Times*, June 14, 2008, pp. A1, A14; and M. Johnson, "Quelling Distraction," *HR Magazine*, August 2008, pp. 43–46.

72. See M. Munter, "Cross-Cultural Communication for Managers," *Business Horizons*, May–June 1993, pp. 75–76; and H. Ren and B. Gray, "Repairing Relationship Conflict: How Violation Types and Culture Influence the Effectiveness of Restoration Rituals," *Academy of Management Review* 34, no. 1 (2009), pp. 105–126.

73. See E. T. Hall, *Beyond Culture* (Garden City, NY: Anchor Press/Doubleday, 1976); W. L. Adair, "Integrative Sequences and Negotiation Outcome in Same- and Mixed-Culture Negotiations," *International Journal of Conflict Management* 14, no. 3–4 (2003), pp. 1359–1392; W. L. Adair and J. M. Brett, "The Negotiation Dance: Time, Culture, and Behavioral Sequences in Negotiation," *Organization Science* 16, no. 1 (2005), pp. 33–51; E. Giebels and P. J. Taylor, "Interaction Patterns in Crisis Negotiations: Persuasive Arguments and Cultural Differences," *Journal of Applied Psychology* 94, no. 1 (2009), pp. 5–19; and M. G. Kittler, D. Rygl, and A. Mackinnon, "Beyond Culture or Beyond Control? Reviewing the Use of Hall's High-/Low-Context Concept," *International Journal of Cross-Cultural Management* 11, no. 1 (2011), pp. 63–82.

74. M. C. Hopson, T. Hart, and G. C. Bell, "Meeting in the Middle: Fred L. Casmir's Contributions to the Field of Intercultural Communication," *International Journal of Intercultural Relations*, November 2012, pp. 789–797.

75. "Charting a New Course," *National Post*, February 4, 2014

76. M. C. Hopson, T. Hart, and G. C. Bell, "Meeting in the Middle: Fred L. Casmir's Contributions to the Field of Intercultural Communication," *International Journal of Intercultural Relations*, November 2012, pp. 789–797; J. Lauring and J. Selmer, "International Language Management and Diversity Climate in Multicultural Organizations," *International Business Review*, April 2012, pp. 156–166; and L. Louhiala-Salminen and A. Kankaaranta, "Language as an Issue in International Internal Communication: English or Local Language? If English, what English?" *Public Relations Review*, June 2012, pp. 262–269.

77. Based on S. F. Gale, "Policies Must Score a Mutual Like," *Workforce Management*, August 2012; R. Huggins and S. Ward, "Countries with the Highest Percentage of Adults Who Use Social Networking Sites," *USA Today*, February 8, 2012, p. 1A; A. L. Kavanaugh, E. A. Fox, S. D. Sheetz, S. Yang, L. T. Li, D. J. Soemaker, A. Natsev, and L. Xie, "Social Media Use by Government: From the Routine to the Critical," *Government Information Quarterly*, October 2012, pp. 480–491; and S. Johnson, "Those Facebook Posts Could Cost You a Job," *San Jose Mercury News*, January 16, 2012, http://www.mercurynews.com/business/ci_19754451.

78. Based on E. Bernstein, "Reply All: The Button Everyone Loves to Hate," *Wall Street Journal*, March 8, 2011, pp. D1, D4; A. Bryant, "No Need to Hit The 'Send' Key. Just Talk to Me," *New York Times*, August 29, 2010, p. 2; and R. E. Silverman, "Ban 'Reply to All,'" *Wall Street Journal*, January 2, 2013, pp. B1, B4.

79. Based on B. Acohido, "Social-Media Tools Boost Productivity," *USA Today*, August 13, 2012, p. 1B; S. Dutta, "What's Your Personal Social Media Strategy," *Harvard Business Review*, November 2010, pp. 127–130; G. Connors, "10 Social Media Commandments for Employers," *Workforce Management*, February 2010, http://www.workforce.com/articles/10-social-media-commandments-for-employers; and L. Kwoh and M. Korn, "140 Characters of Risk: CEOs on Twitter," *Wall Street Journal*, September 26, 2012, pp. B1, B8.

80. Based on A. A. Buchko, K. J. Buchko, and J. M Meyer, "Is There Power in PowerPoint? A Field Test of the Efficacy of PowerPoint on Memory and Recall of Religious Sermons," *Computers in Human Behavior*, March 2012, pp. 688–695; "Full Text of Iran's Proposals to Six World Powers in Moscow," *FARS News Agency* (Tehran), http://english.farsnews.com/newstext.php?nn=9103085486; and B. Parks, "Death to PowerPoint," *Bloomberg Businessweek*, September 3–9, 2012, pp. 83–85.

81. Based on S. P. Robbins and P. L. Hunsaker, *Training in Interpersonal Skills: TIPs for Managing People at Work*, 2nd ed. (Upper Saddle River, NJ: Prentice Hall, 1996), Chapter 3; and data in R. C. Huseman, J. M. Lahiff, and J. M. Penrose, *Business Communication: Strategies and Skills* (Chicago: Dryden Press, 1988), pp. 380, 425.

Chapter 8

1. Opening vignette based on D. Peat, "Mayor Rob Ford Admits He 'Embarrassed' Council," *Toronto Sun*, August 28, 2014; "Mayor Subpoenaed In Lisi Extortion Case," *Globe and Mail*, September 6, 2014, p. A13; R. Doolittle, "So You Wanna See This Video?" *Globe and Mail*, September 6, 2014, p. F4; and J. Warmington, "Rob Ford: I Will Run Again For Mayor," *Toronto Sun*, October 27, 2014.

2. R. M. Kanter, "Power Failure in Management Circuits," *Harvard Business Review*, July–August 1979, p. 65.

3. Based on B. M. Bass, *Bass & Stogdill's Handbook of Leadership*, 3rd ed. (New York: Free Press, 1990).

4. D. H. Gruenfeld, M. E. Inesi, J. C. Magee, and A. D. Galinsky, "Power and the Objectification of Social Targets," *Journal of Personality and Social Psychology* 95, no. 1 (2008), pp. 111–127; A. D. Galinsky, J. C. Magee, D. H. Gruenfeld, J. A. Whitson, and K. A. Liljenquist, "Power Reduces the Press of the Situation: Implications for Creativity, Conformity, and Dissonance," *Journal of Personality and Social Psychology* 95, no. 6 (2008), pp. 1450–1466; and J. C. Magee and C. A. Langner, "How Personalized and Socialized Power Motivation Facilitate Antisocial and Prosocial Decision-Making," *Journal of Research in Personality* 42, no. 6 (2008), pp. 1547–1559.

5. R. M. Kanter, "Power Failure in Management Circuits," *Harvard Business Review*, July–August 1979, p. 65.

6. "Power Outage: A Loss of Social Power Distorts How Money Is Represented," *ScienceDaily*, July 26, 2010, http://www.sciencedaily.com/releases/2010/06/100607151320.htm.

7. G. A. Van Kleef, A. C. Homan, C. Finkenauer, S. Gundemir, and E. Stamkou, "Breaking the Rules to Rise to Power: How Norm Violators Gain Power in the Eyes of Others," *Social Psychological and Personality Science*, January 26, 2011, published online before print, http://selfteachingresources.pbworks.com/f/Breaking+the+Rules+to+Rise+to+Power+−+How+Norm+Violators+Gain+Power+in+the+Eyes+of+Others.pdf.

8. J. Lammers, D. A. Stapel, and A. Galinsky, "Power Increases Hypocrisy: Moralizing in Reasoning, Immunity and Behavior," *Psychological Science* 21, no. 5 (2010), pp. 737–744.

9 S. Prashad, "Fill Your Power Gap," *Globe and Mail*, July 23, 2003, p. C3.

10 Based on E. Inesi, S. Botti, D. Dubois, D. D. Rucker, and A. D. Galinsky, "Power and Choice: Their Dynamic Interplay in Quenching the Thirst for Personal Control," *Psychological Science*, June 2011, published online before print; and Association for Psychological Science, "Power and Choice Are Interchangeable: It's All About Controlling Your Life," *ScienceDaily*, April 28, 2011, http://www.sciencedaily.com/releases/2011/04/110426111419.htm.

11 M. Gee, "The Next Few Weeks Promise to Be a Corker," *Globe and Mail*, September 2, 2014, p. A5.

12 J. R. P. French Jr. and B. Raven, "The Bases of Social Power," in *Studies in Social Power*, ed. D. Cartwright (Ann Arbor, MI: University of Michigan, Institute for Social Research, 1959), pp. 150–167; B. H. Raven, "The Bases of Power: Origins and Recent Developments," *Journal of Social Issues*, Winter 1993, pp. 227–251; and G. Yukl, "Use Power Effectively," in *Handbook of Principles of Organizational Behavior*, ed. E. A. Locke (Malden, MA: Blackwell, 2004), pp. 242–247.

13 E. A. Ward, "Social Power Bases of Managers: Emergence of a New Factor," *Journal of Social Psychology*, February 2001, pp. 144–147.

14 S. R. Giessner and T. W. Schubert, "High in the Hierarchy: How Vertical Location and Judgments of Leaders' Power Are Interrelated," *Organizational Behavior and Human Decision Processes* 104, no. 1 (2007), pp. 30–44.

15 S. Milgram, *Obedience to Authority* (New York: Harper and Row, 1974).

16 G. Yukl, H. Kim, and C. M. Falbe, "Antecedents of Influence Outcomes," *Journal of Applied Psychology* 81, no. 3 (1996), pp. 309–317.

17 P. P. Carson, K. D. Carson, and C. W. Roe, "Social Power Bases: A Meta-analytic Examination of Interrelationships and Outcomes," *Journal of Applied Social Psychology* 23, no. 14 (1993), pp. 1150–1169.

18 C. M. Falbe and G. Yukl, "Consequences for Managers of Using Single Tactics and Combinations of Tactics," *Academy of Management Journal* 35, 1992, pp. 638–652.

19 Cited in J. R. Carlson, D. S. Carlson, and L. L. Wadsworth, "The Relationship between Individual Power Moves and Group Agreement Type: An Examination and Model," *SAM Advanced Management Journal* 65, no. 4 (2000), pp. 44–51.

20 Vignette based on "Ward 2 (Etobicoke North)," *CBC News*, October 26, 2014, http://www.cbc.ca/news/canada/toronto/torontovotes/ward-2-etobicoke-north-1.2800492; and "Toronto Election: Rob Ford Will Return to Council," *CBC News*, October 27, 2014.

21 R. E. Emerson, "Power-Dependence Relations," *American Sociological Review* 27 (1962), pp. 31–41.

22 Thanks are due to an anonymous reviewer for supplying this insight.

23 H. Mintzberg, *Power in and Around Organizations* (Englewood Cliffs, NJ: Prentice Hall, 1983), p. 24.

24 This section adapted from G. Yukl, C. M. Falbe, and J. Y. Youn, "Patterns of Influence Behavior for Managers," *Group & Organization Studies* 18, no. 1 (March 1993), p. 7.

25 G. Yukl, *Leadership in Organizations*, 5th ed. (Upper Saddle River, NJ: Prentice Hall, 2002), pp. 141–174; G. R. Ferris, W. A. Hochwarter, C. Douglas, F. R. Blass, R. W. Kolodinksy, and D. C. Treadway, "Social Influence Processes in Organizations and Human Resource Systems," in *Research in Personnel and Human Resources Management*, vol. 21, ed. G. R. Ferris and J. J. Martocchio (Oxford, UK: JAI Press/Elsevier, 2003), pp. 65–127; and C. A. Higgins, T. A. Judge, and G. R. Ferris, "Influence Tactics and Work Outcomes: A Meta-analysis," *Journal of Organizational Behavior*, March 2003, pp. 89–106.

26 C. M. Falbe and G. Yukl, "Consequences for Managers of Using Single Influence Tactics and Combinations of Tactics," *Academy of Management Journal*, July 1992, pp. 638–653.

27 R. E. Petty and P. Briñol, "Persuasion: From Single to Multiple to MetaCognitive Processes," *Perspectives on Psychological Science* 3, no. 2 (2008), pp. 137–147.

28 I. Stern and J. D. Westphal, "Stealthy Footsteps to the Boardroom: Executives' Backgrounds, Sophisticated Interpersonal Influence Behavior, and Board Appointments," *Administrative Science Quarterly* 55, no. 2 (2010), pp. 278–319; and G. Yukl, *Leadership in Organizations*, 5th ed. (Upper Saddle River, NJ: Prentice Hall, 2002), pp. 141–174.

29 N. K. Grant, L. R. Fabrigar, and Heidi Lim, "Exploring the Efficacy of Compliments as a Tactic for Securing Compliance," *Basic & Applied Social Psychology* 32, no. 3 (2010), pp. 226–233.

30 C. M. Falbe and G. Yukl, "Consequences for Managers of Using Single Influence Tactics and Combinations of Tactics," *Academy of Management Journal*, July 1992, pp. 638–653.

31 A. W. Kruglanski, A. Pierro, and E. T. Higgins, "Regulatory Mode and Preferred Leadership Styles: How Fit Increases Job Satisfaction," *Basic and Applied Social Psychology* 29, no. 2 (2007), pp. 137–149; and A. Pierro, L. Cicero, and B. H. Raven, "Motivated Compliance with Bases of Social Power," *Journal of Applied Social Psychology* 38, no. 7 (2008), pp. 1921–1944.

32 G. R. Ferris, D. C. Treadway, P. L. Perrewé, R. L. Brouer, C. Douglas, and S. Lux, "Political Skill in Organizations," *Journal of Management*, June 2007, pp. 290–320; K. J. Harris, K. M. Kacmar, S. Zivnuska, and J. D. Shaw, "The Impact of Political Skill on Impression Management Effectiveness," *Journal of Applied Psychology* 92, no. 1 (2007), pp. 278–285; W. A. Hochwarter, G. R. Ferris, M. B. Gavin, P. L. Perrewé, A. T. Hall, and D. D. Frink, "Political Skill as Neutralizer of Felt Accountability–Job Tension Effects on Job Performance Ratings: A Longitudinal Investigation," *Organizational Behavior and Human Decision Processes* 102 (2007), pp. 226–239; and D. C. Treadway, G. R. Ferris, A. B. Duke, G. L. Adams, and J. B. Tatcher, "The Moderating Role of Subordinate Political Skill on Supervisors' Impressions of Subordinate Ingratiation and Ratings of Subordinate Interpersonal Facilitation," *Journal of Applied Psychology* 92, no. 3 (2007), pp. 848–855.

33 M. C. Andrews, K. M. Kacmar, and K. J. Harris, "Got Political Skill? The Impact of Justice on the Importance of Political Skills for Job Performance." *Journal of Applied Psychology* 94, no. 6 (2009), pp. 1427–1437.

34 C. Anderson, S. E. Spataro, and F. J. Flynn, "Personality and Organizational Culture as Determinants of Influence," *Journal of Applied Psychology* 93, no. 3 (2008), pp. 702–710.

35 Vignette based on G. McArthur, "Toronto Mayor Rob Ford Arranged Meeting between Client of Family Firm, Water Officials," *Globe and Mail*, November 24, 2014; and "Stop Abusing Your Office," *Toronto Star*, June 8, 2014, p. A12.

36 Y. Cho and N. J. Fast, "Power, Defensive Denigration, and the Assuaging Effect of Gratitude Expression," *Journal of Experimental Social Psychology* 48 (2012), pp. 778–782.

37 M. Pitesa and S. Thau, "Masters of the Universe: How Power and Accountability Influence Self-Serving Decisions under Moral Hazard," *Journal of Applied Psychology* 98 (2013), pp. 550–558; and N. J. Fast, N. Sivanathan, D. D. Mayer, and A. D. Galinsky, "Power and Overconfident Decision-Making," *Organizational Behavior and Human Decision Processes* 117 (2012), pp. 249–260.

38 J. K. Maner, M. T. Gaillot, A. J. Menzel, and J. W. Kunstman, "Dispositional Anxiety Blocks the Psychological Effects of Power," *Personality and Social Psychology Bulletin* 38 (2012), pp. 1383–1395.

39 J. Tierney, "A Serving of Gratitude May Save the Day," *International New York Times*, November 21, 2011, http://www.nytimes

.com/2011/11/22/science/a-serving-of-gratitude-brings-healthy-dividends.html?_r=0.

40 N. J. Fast, N. Halevy, and A. D. Galinsky, "The Destructive Nature of Power Without Status," *Journal of Experimental Social Psychology* 48 (2012), pp. 391–394.

41 T. Seppälä, J. Lipponen, A. Bardi, and A. Pirttilä-Backman, "Change-Oriented Organizational Citizenship Behaviour: An Interactive Product of Openness to Change Values, Work Unit Identification, and Sense of Power," *Journal of Occupational and Organizational Psychology* 85 (2012), pp. 136–155.

42 K. A. DeCelles, D. S. DeRue, J. D. Margolis, and T. L. Ceranic, "Does Power Corrupt or Enable? When and Why Power Facilitates Self-Interested Behavior," *Journal of Applied Psychology* 97 (2012), pp. 681–689.

43 "Building a Better Workforce," *PROFIT*, February 16, 2011, http://www.profitguide.com/manage-grow/human-resources/building-a-better-workforce-30073.

44 "Canada's 10 Most Admired Corporate Cultures," *National Post*, February 3, 2014, JV1– JV8, http://www.waterstonehc.com/sites/default/files/news/files/CMACC-%20Feb%203,%202014.pdf.

45 This is the definition given by R. Forrester, "Empowerment: Rejuvenating a Potent Idea," *Academy of Management Executive*, August 2000, pp. 67–80.

46 R. E. Quinn and G. M. Spreitzer, "The Road to Empowerment: Seven Questions Every Leader Should Consider," *Organizational Dynamics*, Autumn 1997, p. 38.

47 R. Quinn, and G. Spreitzer, "The Road to Empowerment: Seven Questions Every Leaders Should Consider," *Center for Effective Organizations*, February 1999, http://ceo.usc.edu/pdf/G973315.pdf.

48 C. Argyris, "Empowerment: The Emperor's New Clothes," *Harvard Business Review*, May–June 1998.

49 J. Schaubroeck, J. R. Jones, and J. L. Xie, "Individual Differences in Utilizing Control to Cope with Job Demands: Effects on Susceptibility to Infectious Disease," *Journal of Applied Psychology* 86, no. 2 (2001), pp. 265–278.

50 "Delta Promotes Empowerment," *Globe and Mail*, May 31, 1999, Advertising Supplement, p. C5.

51 R. Sutton, "How to Be a Good Boss in a Bad Economy," *Harvard Business Review*, June 2009, pp. 42–50.

52 D. Keltner, D. H. Gruenfeld, and C. Anderson, "Power, Approach, and Inhibition," *Psychological Review* 110, no. 2 (2003), pp. 265–284.

53 T. Lee and C. M. Brotheridge, "When the Prey Becomes the Predator: Bullying as Predictor of Reciprocal Bullying, Coping, and Well-Being," working paper, University of Regina, Regina, 2005.

54 N. J. Fast and S. Chen, "When the Boss Feels Inadequate: Power, Incompetence, and Aggression," *Psychological Science* 20, no. 11 (2009), pp. 1406–1413.

55 University of California-Berkeley, "Bosses Who Feel Inadequate Are More Likely to Bully," *ScienceDaily*, October 15, 2009, http://www.sciencedaily.com/releases/2009/10/091014102209.htm.

56 M. S. Hershcovis and J. Barling, "Comparing the Outcomes of Sexual Harassment and Workplace Aggression: A Meta-analysis" (paper presented at the Seventh International Conference on Work, Stress and Health, Washington, DC, March 8, 2008).

57 Quebec Labour Standards, s. 81.18, "Psychological Harassment at Work."

58 "Resources: Bullying and Harassment Prevention Tool Kit," *WorkSafe BC*, accessed October 21, 2014, http://www2.worksafebc.com/Topics/BullyingAndHarassment/Resources.asp?reportID=37260.

59 S. Stecklow, "Sexual-Harassment Cases Plague U.N.," *Wall Street Journal*, May 21, 2009, p. A1.

60 *Janzen v. Platy Enterprises Ltd.*, [1989] 10 CHRR D/6205 SCC.

61 R. Ilies, N. Hauserman, S. Schwochau, and J. Stibal, "Reported Incidence Rates of Work-Related Sexual Harassment in the United States," *Personnel Psychology* 56, no. 3 (2003), pp. 607–631; A. B. Malamut and L. R. Offermann, "Coping with Sexual Harassment: Personal, Environmental, and Cognitive Determinants," *Journal of Applied Psychology*, December 2001, pp. 1152–1166; L. M. Cortina and S. A. Wasti, "Profiles in Coping: Responses to Sexual Harassment Across Persons, Organizations, and Cultures," *Journal of Applied Psychology*, February 2005, pp. 182–192; and J. W. Kunstman, "Sexual Overperception: Power, Mating Motives, and Biases in Social Judgment," *Journal of Personality and Social Psychology* 100, no. 2 (2011), pp. 282–294.

62 F. Krings and S. Facchin, "Organizational Justice and Men's Likelihood to Sexually Harass: The Moderating Role of Sexism and Personality," *Journal of Applied Psychology* 94, no. 2 (2009), pp. 501–510.

63 Based on "The Dos and Don'ts of Office Romances," *Toronto Star*, August 2, 2012, http://www.thestar.com/life/2012/08/02/the_dos_and_donts_of_office_romances.html; H. Levitt, "What Tangled Webs We Weave," *Financial Post*, May 23, 2012, http://business.financialpost.com/2012/05/23/what-tangled-webs-we-weave/; and *Reichard v. Kuntz*, [2011] ONSC 7460 (CanLII), para. 50.

64 A. M. Dionisi, J. Barling, and K. E. Dupré, "Revisiting the Comparative Outcomes of Workplace Aggression and Sexual Harassment," *Journal of Occupational Health Psychology* 17 (2012), pp. 398–408.

65 M. B. Nielsen and S. Einarsen, "Prospective Relationships between Workplace Sexual Harassment and Psychological Distress," *Occupational Medicine* 62 (2012), pp. 226–228.

66 C. Bass, "University Bans Faculty-Student Sex," *Yale Alumni Magazine*, March/April 2010, https://www.yalealumnimagazine.com/articles/2740/university-bans-faculty-student-sex.

67 "Human Rights Policies and Procedures, Part IV," *Carleton.ca*, accessed October 21, 2014, http://www.carleton.ca/equity/human-rights/policy/human-rights-policies-and-procedures-part-2/.

68 C. Hill and E. Silva, *Drawing the Line: Sexual Harassment on Campus* (Washington, DC: American Association of University Women, 2005).

69 "Western University Student Newspaper Pens 'Guide on How to Sexually Harass' TAs (TWEETS)," *Huffington Post*, August 26, 2014, http://www.huffingtonpost.ca/2014/08/26/western-university-gazette-seduce-ta_n_5718759.html.

70 H. Burnett-Nichols, "Don't Touch, Do Tell," *University Affairs*, March 8, 2010, http://www.universityaffairs.ca/dont-touch-do-tell.aspx.

71 Based on J. L. Berdahl and K. Aquino, "Sexual Behavior at Work: Fun or Folly?" *Journal of Applied Psychology* 94, no. 1 (2009), pp. 34–47; and C. Boyd, "The Debate over the Prohibition of Romance in the Workplace," *Journal of Business Ethics* 97, no. 2 (2010), pp. 325–338.

72 Vignette based on D. Dale, "Rob Ford: 'Yes, I Have Smoked Crack Cocaine,'" *Toronto Star*, November 5, 2013.

73 S. A. Culbert and J. J. McDonough, *The Invisible War: Pursuing Self-Interest at Work* (New York: Wiley, 1980), p. 6.

74 H. Mintzberg, *Power in and Around Organizations* (Englewood Cliffs, NJ: Prentice Hall, 1983), p. 26.

75 T. Cole, "Who Loves Ya?" *Report on Business Magazine*, April 1999, p. 54.

76 S. B. Bacharach and E. J. Lawler, "Political Alignments in Organizations," in *Power and Influence in Organizations*, ed. R. M.

Kramer and M. A. Neale (Thousand Oaks, CA: Sage, 1998), pp. 68–69.

77 D. Farrell and J. C. Petersen, "Patterns of Political Behavior in Organizations," *Academy of Management Review*, July 1982, p. 405. For a thoughtful analysis of the academic controversies underlying any definition of organizational politics, see A. Drory and T. Romm, "The Definition of Organizational Politics: A Review," *Human Relations*, November 1990, pp. 1133–1154; and R. S. Cropanzano, K. M. Kacmar, and D. P. Bozeman, "Organizational Politics, Justice, and Support: Their Differences and Similarities," in *Organizational Politics, Justice and Support: Managing Social Climate at Work*, ed. R. S. Cropanzano and K. M. Kacmar (Westport, CT: Quorum Books, 1995), pp. 1–18.

78 J. Pfeffer, *Power in Organizations* (Marshfield, MA: Pittman, 1981).

79 A. Drory and T. Romm, "The Definition of Organizational Politics: A Review," *Human Relations*, November 1990, pp. 1133–1154.

80 G. R. Ferris, G. S. Russ, and P. M. Fandt, "Politics in Organizations," in *Impression Management in Organizations*, ed. R. A. Giacalone and P. Rosenfeld (Newbury Park, CA: Sage, 1989), pp. 143–170; and K. M. Kacmar, D. P. Bozeman, D. S. Carlson, and W. P. Anthony, "An Examination of the Perceptions of Organizational Politics Model: Replication and Extension," *Human Relations*, March 1999, pp. 383–416.

81 K. M. Kacmar and R. A. Baron, "Organizational Politics: The State of the Field, Links to Related Processes, and an Agenda for Future Research," in *Research in Personnel and Human Resources Management*, vol. 17, ed. G. R. Ferris (Greenwich, CT: JAI Press, 1999); and M. Valle and L. A. Witt, "The Moderating Effect of Teamwork Perceptions on the Organizational Politics-Job Satisfaction Relationship," *Journal of Social Psychology*, June 2001, pp. 379–388.

82 G. R. Ferris, D. D. Frink, M. C. Galang, J. Zhou, K. M. Kacmar, and J. L. Howard, "Perceptions of Organizational Politics: Prediction, Stress-Related Implications, and Outcomes," *Human Relations*, February 1996, pp. 233–266; K. M. Kacmar, D. P. Bozeman, D. S. Carlson, and W. P. Anthony, "An Examination of the Perceptions of Organizational Politics Model; Replication and Extension," *Human Relations*, March 1999, p. 388; and J. M. L. Poon, "Situational Antecedents and Outcomes of Organizational Politics Perceptions," *Journal of Managerial Psychology* 18, no. 2 (2003), pp. 138–155.

83 C. Kiewitz, W. A. Hochwarter, G. R. Ferris, and S. L. Castro, "The Role of Psychological Climate in Neutralizing the Effects of Organizational Politics on Work Outcomes," *Journal of Applied Social Psychology*, June 2002, pp. 1189–1207; and J. M. L. Poon, "Situational Antecedents and Outcomes of Organizational Politics Perceptions," *Journal of Managerial Psychology* 18, no. 2 (2003), pp. 138–155.

84 K. M. Kacmar, D. P. Bozeman, D. S. Carlson, and W. P. Anthony, "An Examination of the Perceptions of Organizational Politics Model," *Human Relations* 52, no. 3 (1999), p. 389.

85 K. M. Kacmar, D. P. Bozeman, D. S. Carlson, and W. P. Anthony, "An Examination of the Perceptions of Organizational Politics Model," *Human Relations* 52, no. 3 (1999), pp. 383–416.

86 K. M. Kacmar, D. G. Bachrach, K. J. Harris, and S. Zivnuska, "Fostering Good Citizenship Through Ethical Leadership: Exploring the Moderating Role of Gender and Organizational Politics," *Journal of Applied Psychology* 96 (2011), pp. 633–642.

87 Based on R. W. Allen, D. L. Madison, L. W. Porter, P. A. Renwick, and B. T. Mayes, "Organizational Politics: Tactics and Characteristics of Its Actors," *California Management Review*, Fall 1979, pp. 77–83.

88 Based on M. Thompson, "How to Work with Your Startup Frenemies," *VentureBeat*, December 22, 2012, from http://venturebeat.com/; and N. L. Mead and J. K. Maner, "On Keeping Your Enemies Close: Powerful Leaders Seek Proximity to Ingroup Power

Threats," *Journal of Personality and Social Psychology* 102 (2012), pp. 576–591.

89 See, for example, W. L. Gardner and M. J. Martinko, "Impression Management in Organizations," *Journal of Management*, June 1988, pp. 321–338; M. C. Bolino and W. H. Turnley, "More Than One Way to Make an Impression: Exploring Profiles of Impression Management," *Journal of Management* 29, no. 2 (2003), pp. 141–160; S. Zivnuska, K. M. Kacmar, L. A. Witt, D. S. Carlson, and V. K. Bratton, "Interactive Effects of Impression Management and Organizational Politics on Job Performance," *Journal of Organizational Behavior*, August 2004, pp. 627–640; and M. C. Bolino, K. M. Kacmar, W. H. Turnley, and J. B. Gilstrap, "A Multi-Level Review of Impression Management Motives and Behaviors," *Journal of Management* 34, no. 6 (2008), pp. 1080–1109.

90 M. Snyder and J. Copeland, "Self-Monitoring Processes in Organizational Settings," in *Impression Management in the Organization*, ed. R. A. Giacalone and P. Rosenfeld (Hillsdale, NJ: Lawrence Erlbaum, 1989), p. 11; M. C. Bolino and W. H. Turnley, "More Than One Way to Make an Impression: Exploring Profiles of Impression Management," *Journal of Management* 29, no. 2 (2003), pp. 141–160; and W. H. Turnley and M. C. Bolino, "Achieved Desired Images While Avoiding Undesired Images: Exploring the Role of Self-Monitoring in Impression Management," *Journal of Applied Psychology*, April 2001, pp. 351–360.

91 M. R. Leary and R. M. Kowalski, "Impression Management: A Literature Review and Two-Component Model," *Psychological Bulletin*, January 1990, p. 40.

92 W. L. Gardner and M. J. Martinko, "Impression Management in Organizations," *Journal of Management*, June 1988, p. 333.

93 J. Ham and R. Vonk, "Impressions of Impression Management: Evidence of Spontaneous Suspicion of Ulterior Motivation," *Journal of Experimental Social Psychology* 47, no. 2 (2011), pp. 466–471; and W. M. Bowler, J. R. B. Halbesleben, and J. R. B. Paul, "If You're Close with the Leader, You Must Be a Brownnose: The Role of Leader–Member Relationships in Follower, Leader, and Coworker Attributions of Organizational Citizenship Behavior Motives," *Human Resource Management Review* 20, no. 4 (2010), pp. 309–316.

94 C. Lebherz, K. Jonas, and B. Tomljenovic, "Are We Known by the Company We Keep? Effects of Name Dropping on First Impressions," *Social Influence* 4, no. 1 (2009), pp. 62–79.

95 J. R. B. Halbesleben, W. M. Bowler, M. C. Bolino, and W. H Turnley, "Organizational Concern, Prosocial Values, or Impression Management? How Supervisors Attribute Motives to Organizational Citizenship Behavior," *Journal of Applied Social Psychology* 40, no. 6 (2010), pp. 1450–1489.

96 A. P. J. Ellis, B. J. West, A. M. Ryan, and R. P. DeShon, "The Use of Impression Management Tactics in Structural Interviews: A Function of Question Type?" *Journal of Applied Psychology*, December 2002, pp. 1200–1208.

97 C. K. Stevens and A. L. Kristof, "Making the Right Impression: A Field Study of Applicant Impression Management during Job Interviews," *Journal of Applied Psychology* 80 (1995), pp. 587–606; L. A. McFarland, A. M. Ryan, and S. D. Kriska, "Impression Management Use and Effectiveness across Assessment Methods," *Journal of Management* 29, no. 5 (2003), pp. 641–661; C. A. Higgins and T. A. Judge, "The Effect of Applicant Influence Tactics on Recruiter Perceptions of Fit and Hiring Recommendations: A Field Study," *Journal of Applied Psychology* 89, no. 4 (2004), pp. 622–632; and W. C. Tsai, C. C. Chen, and S. F. Chiu, "Exploring Boundaries of the Effects of Applicant Impression Management Tactics in Job Interviews," *Journal of Management*, February 2005, pp. 108–125.

98 D. C. Gilmore and G. R. Ferris, "The Effects of Applicant Impression Management Tactics on Interviewer Judgments," *Journal of Management*, December 1989, pp. 557–564.

99   C. K. Stevens and A. L. Kristof, "Making the Right Impression: A Field Study of Applicant Impression Management during Job Interviews," *Journal of Applied Psychology* 80 (1995), pp. 587–606.

100 C. A. Higgins, T. A. Judge, and G. R. Ferris, "Influence Tactics and Work Outcomes: A Meta-analysis," *Journal of Organizational Behavior,* March 2003, pp. 89–106.

101 C. A. Higgins, T. A. Judge, and G. R. Ferris, "Influence Tactics and Work Outcomes: A Meta-analysis," *Journal of Organizational Behavior,* March 2003, pp. 89–106.

102 K. J. Harris, K. M. Kacmar, S. Zivnuska, and J. D. Shaw, "The Impact of Political Skill on Impression Management Effectiveness," *Journal of Applied Psychology* 92, no. 1 (2007), pp. 278–285; and D. C. Treadway, G. R. Ferris, A. B. Duke, G. L. Adams, and J. B. Thatcher, "The Moderating Role of Subordinate Political Skill on Supervisors' Impressions of Subordinate Ingratiation and Ratings of Subordinate Interpersonal Facilitation," *Journal of Applied Psychology* 92, no. 3 (2007), pp. 848–855.

103 R. Westwood, "Order of Canada Winner Lied About Ph.D," *Macleans.ca,* September 26, 2013, http://www.macleans.ca/general/an-order-of-lies/; and "Louis LaPierre Stripped of Order of Canada," *CBC News,* June 13, 2014, http://www.cbc.ca/news/canada/new-brunswick/louis-lapierre-stripped-of-order-of-canada-1.2675141.

104 C. Robert, T. M. Probst, J. J. Martocchio, F. Drasgow, and J. J. Lawler, "Empowerment and Continuous Improvement in the United States, Mexico, Poland, and India: Predicting Fit on the Basis of the Dimensions of Power Distance and Individualism," *Journal of Applied Psychology* 85 (2000), pp. 643–658.

105 W. A. Randolph and M. Sashkin, "Can Organizational Empowerment Work in Multinational Settings?" *Academy of Management Executive,* February 2002, pp. 102–115.

106 M. Gagné and D. Bhave, "Autonomy in the Workplace: An Essential Ingredient to Employee Engagement and Well-Being in Every Culture?" in *Human Autonomy in Cross-Cultural Context: Perspectives on the Psychology of Agency, Freedom, and Well-Being,* ed. V. I. Chirkov, R. M. Ryan, and K. M. Sheldon (Berlin, Germany: Springer, 2011).

107 Concordia University, "Freedom's Just Another Word for Employee Satisfaction," *ScienceDaily,* January 24, 2011, http://www.concordia.ca/cunews/main/releases/2011/01/24/freedoms-just-another-word-for-employee-satisfaction.html.

108 P. P. Fu and G. Yukl, "Perceived Effectiveness of Influence Tactics in the United States and China," *Leadership Quarterly,* Summer 2000, pp. 251–266; O. Branzei, "Cultural Explanations of Individual Preferences for Influence Tactics in Cross-Cultural Encounters," *International Journal of Cross Cultural Management,* August 2002, pp. 203–218; G. Yukl, P. P. Fu, and R. McDonald, "Cross-Cultural Differences in Perceived Effectiveness of Influence Tactics for Initiating or Resisting Change," *Applied Psychology: An International Review,* January 2003, pp. 66–82; and P. P. Fu, T. K. Peng, J. C. Kennedy, and G. Yukl, "Examining the Preferences of Influence Tactics in Chinese Societies: A Comparison of Chinese Managers in Hong Kong, Taiwan, and Mainland China," *Organizational Dynamics* 33, no. 1 (2004), pp. 32–46.

109 P. P. Fu and G. Yukl, "Perceived Effectiveness of Influence Tactics in the United States and China," *Leadership Quarterly,* Summer 2000, pp. 251–266.

110 S. J. Heine, "Making Sense of East Asian Self-Enhancement," *Journal of Cross-Cultural Psychology,* September 2003, pp. 596–602.

111 E. Szabo, "Meaning and Context of Participation in Five European Countries," *Management Decision* 44, no. 2 (2006), pp. 276–289.

112 P. P. Fu, T. K. Peng, J. C. Kennedy, and G. Yukl, "A Comparison of Chinese Managers in Hong Kong, Taiwan, and Mainland China," *Organizational Dynamics,* February 2004, pp. 32–46.

113 See T. Romm and A. Drory, "Political Behavior in Organizations: A Cross-Cultural Comparison," *International Journal of Value Based Management* 1 (1988), pp. 97–113; and E. Vigoda, "Reactions to Organizational Politics: A Cross-Cultural Examination in Israel and Britain," *Human Relations,* November 2001, pp. 1483–1518.

114 J. L. T. Leong, M. H. Bond, and P. P. Fu, "Perceived Effectiveness of Influence Strategies in the United States and Three Chinese Societies," *International Journal of Cross Cultural Management,* May 2006, pp. 101–120.

115 Y. Miyamoto and B. Wilken, "Culturally Contingent Situated Cognition: Influencing Other People Fosters Analytic Perception in the United States but Not in Japan," *Psychological Science* 21, no. 11 (2010), pp. 1616–1622.

116 Based on B. Burrough and B. McLean, "The Hunt for Steve Cohen," *Vanity Fair,* June 2013, http://www.vanityfair.com/business/2013/06/steve-cohen-insider-trading-case; C. Anderson, R. Willer, G. J. Kilduff, and C. E. Brown, "The Origins of Deference: When Do People Prefer Lower Status?" *Journal of Personality and Social Psychology* 102 (2012), pp. 1077–1088; C. Anderson, M. W. Kraus, A. D. Galinsky, and D. Keltner, "The Local-Ladder Effect: Social Status and Subjective Well-Being," *Psychological Science* 23, no. 7 (2012), pp. 764–771; and S. Kennelly, "Happiness Is About Respect, Not Riches," *Greater Good,* July 13, 2012, http://greatergood.berkeley.edu/article/item/happiness_is_about_respect_not_riches.

117 This exercise was inspired by one found in Judith R. Gordon, *Organizational Behavior,* 2nd ed. (Englewood Cliffs, NJ: Prentice Hall, 1992), pp. 499–502.

118 Based on J. Sancton, "Milgram at McDonald's," *Bloomberg Businessweek,* September 2, 2012, pp. 74–75; and A. Wolfson, "'Compliance' Re-Creates McDonald's Strip-Search Ordeal," *USA Today,* September 1, 2012, http://usatoday30.usatoday.com/news/nation/story/2012-09-01/Compliance-strip-search-hoax/57509182/1.

119 Based on M. L. Tushman, W. K. Smith, and A. Binns, "The Ambidextrous CEO," *Harvard Business Review,* June 2011, pp. 74–79; and S. Bogan, "Find Your Focus," *Financial Planning,* February 2011, p. 72.

120 Based on M. G. McIntyre, "Disgruntlement Won't Advance Your Career," *Pittsburgh Post-Gazette,* September 23, 2012; and S. Shellenbarger, "What to Do with a Workplace Whiner," *Wall Street Journal,* September 12, 2012, pp. D1, D3.

121 Based on S. P. Robbins and P. L. Hunsaker, *Training in Interpersonal Skills: Tips for Managing People at Work,* 2nd ed. (Upper Saddle River, NJ: Prentice Hall, 1996), pp. 131–134.

Chapter 9

1   Opening vignette based on G. Hoekstra, "B.C. Teachers Losing Public Support as Strike Drags On," *Vancouver Sun,* August 29, 2014; T. Sherlock, "Mediator Meets with Teachers Union President, Government Negotiator Today," *Vancouver Sun,* August 28, 2014; and C. Kilian, "Why Clark Refuses to Hear What Supreme Court Tells Her (Twice)," *TheTyee.ca,* January 29, 2014.

2   See, for example, C. F. Fink, "Some Conceptual Difficulties in the Theory of Social Conflict," *Journal of Conflict Resolution,* December 1968, pp. 412–460. For an updated review of the conflict literature, see J. A. Wall Jr. and R. R. Callister, "Conflict and Its Management," *Journal of Management* 21, no. 3 (1995), pp. 515–558.

3   L. L. Putnam and M. S. Poole, "Conflict and Negotiation," in *Handbook of Organizational Communication: An Interdisciplinary Perspective,* ed. F. M. Jablin, L. L. Putnam, K. H. Roberts, and L. W. Porter (Newbury Park, CA: Sage, 1987), pp. 549–599.

4   K. W. Thomas, "Conflict and Negotiation Processes in Organizations," in *Handbook of Industrial and Organizational Psychology,* 2nd ed., vol. 3, ed. M. D. Dunnette and L. M. Hough (Palo Alto, CA: Consulting Psychologists Press, 1992), pp. 651–717.

5   For a comprehensive review of this approach, also called the *interactionist approach*, see C. De Dreu and E. Van de Vliert, eds., *Using Conflict in Organizations* (London, UK: Sage, 1997).

6   J. Yang and K. W. Mossholder, "Decoupling Task and Relationship Conflict: The Role of Intragroup Emotional Processing," *Journal of Organizational Behavior* 25, no. 5 (August 2004), pp. 589–605; and N. Gamero, V. González-Romá, and J. M. Peiró, "The Influence of Intra-Team Conflict on Work Teams' Affective Climate: A Longitudinal Study," *Journal of Occupational and Organizational Psychology* 81, no. 1 (2008), pp. 47–69.

7   N. Halevy, E. Y. Chou, and A. D. Galinsky, "Exhausting or Exhilarating? Conflict as Threat to Interests, Relationships and Identities," *Journal of Experimental Social Psychology* 48 (2012), pp. 530–537.

8   F. R. C. de Wit, L. L. Greer, and K. A. Jehn, "The Paradox of Intragroup Conflict: A Meta-Analysis," *Journal of Applied Psychology* 97 (2012), pp. 360–390.

9   J. Farh, C. Lee, and C. I. C. Farh, "Task Conflict and Team Creativity: A Question of How Much and When," *Journal of Applied Psychology* 95, no. 6 (2010), pp. 1173–1180.

10 B. H. Bradley, A. C. Klotz, B. F. Postlethwaite, and K. G. Brown, "Ready to Rumble: How Team Personality Composition and Task Conflict Interact to Improve Performance," *Journal of Applied Psychology* 98 (2013), pp. 385–392.

11 B. H. Bradley, B. F. Postlethwaite, A. C. Klotz, M. R. Hamdani, and K. G. Brown, "Reaping the Benefits of Task Conflict in Teams: The Critical Role of Team Psychological Safety Climate," *Journal of Applied Psychology* 97 (2012), pp. 151–158.

12 G. A. Van Kleef, W. Steinel, and A. C. Homan, "On Being Peripheral and Paying Attention: Prototypicality and Information Processing in Intergroup Conflict," *Journal of Applied Psychology* 98 (2013), pp. 63–79.

13 S. Benard, "Cohesion from Conflict: Does Intergroup Conflict Motivate Intragroup Norm Enforcement and Support for Centralized Leadership?" *Social Psychology Quarterly* 75 (2012), pp. 107–130.

14 This section is based on S. P. Robbins, *Managing Organizational Conflict: A Nontraditional Approach* (Englewood Cliffs, NJ: Prentice Hall, 1974), pp. 31–55; and J. A. Wall Jr. and R. R. Callister, "Conflict and Its Management," *Journal of Management* 21, no. 3 (1995), pp. 517–523.

15 R. S. Peterson and K. J. Behfar, "The Dynamic Relationship between Performance Feedback, Trust, and Conflict in Groups: A Longitudinal Study," *Organizational Behavior and Human Decision Processes*, September–November 2003, pp. 102–112.

16 See K. A. Jehn, "A Multimethod Examination of the Benefits and Detriments of Intragroup Conflict," *Administrative Science Quarterly*, June 1995, pp. 256–282.

17 T. M. Glomb and H. Liao, "Interpersonal Aggression in Work Groups: Social Influence, Reciprocal, and Individual Effects," *Academy of Management Journal* 46, no. 4 (2003), pp. 486–496; and V. Venkataramani and R. S. Dalal, "Who Helps and Who Harms? Relational Aspects of Interpersonal Helping and Harming in Organizations," *Journal of Applied Psychology* 92, no. 4 (2007), pp. 952–966.

18 R. Friedman, C. Anderson, J. Brett, M. Olekalns, N. Goates, and C. C. Lisco, "The Positive and Negative Effects of Anger on Dispute Resolution: Evidence from Electronically Mediated Disputes," *Journal of Applied Psychology*, April 2004, pp. 369–376.

19 Vignette based on G. Hoekstra, "B.C. Teachers Losing Public Support as Strike Drags On," *Vancouver Sun*, August 29, 2014; and T. Sherlock, "Mediator Meets with Teachers Union President, Government Negotiator Today," *Vancouver Sun*, August 28, 2014.

20 D. Tjosvold, "Cooperative and Competitive Goal Approach to Conflict: Accomplishments and Challenges," *Applied Psychology: An International Review* 47, no. 3 (1998), pp. 285–342.

21 K. W. Thomas, "Conflict and Negotiation Processes in Organizations," in *Handbook of Industrial and Organizational Psychology*, 2nd ed., vol. 3, ed. M. D. Dunnette and L. M. Hough (Palo Alto, CA: Consulting Psychologists Press, 1992), pp. 651–717.

22 C. K. W. De Dreu, A. Evers, B. Beersma, E. S. Kluwer, and A. Nauta, "A Theory-Based Measure of Conflict Management Strategies in the Workplace," *Journal of Organizational Behavior* 22, no. 6 (September 2001), pp. 645–668. See also D. G. Pruitt and J. Rubin, *Social Conflict: Escalation, Stalemate and Settlement* (New York: Random House, 1986).

23 C. K. W. De Dreu, A. Evers, B. Beersma, E. S. Kluwer, and A. Nauta, "A Theory-Based Measure of Conflict Management Strategies in the Workplace," *Journal of Organizational Behavior* 22, no. 6 (September 2001), pp. 645–668.

24 R. A. Baron, "Personality and Organizational Conflict: Effects of the Type A Behavior Pattern and Self-Monitoring," *Organizational Behavior and Human Decision Processes*, October 1989, pp. 281–296; A. Drory and I. Ritov, "Effects of Work Experience and Opponent's Power on Conflict Management Styles," *International Journal of Conflict Management* 8 (1997), pp. 148–161; R. J. Sternberg and L. J. Soriano, "Styles of Conflict Resolution," *Journal of Personality and Social Psychology*, July 1984, pp. 115–126; and R. J. Volkema and T. J. Bergmann, "Conflict Styles as Indicators of Behavioral Patterns in Interpersonal Conflicts," *Journal of Social Psychology*, February 1995, pp. 5–15.

25 Based on S. P. Robbins, *Managing Organizational Conflict: A Nontraditional Approach* (Upper Saddle River, NJ: Prentice Hall, 1974), pp. 59–89.

26 Based on K. W. Thomas, "Toward Multidimensional Values in Teaching: The Example of Conflict Behaviors," *Academy of Management Review*, July 1977, p. 487; and C. K. W. De Dreu, A. Evers, B. Beersma, E. S. Kluwer, and A. Nauta, "A Theory-Based Measure of Conflict Management Strategies in the Workplace," *Journal of Organizational Behavior* 22, no. 6 (September 2001), pp. 645–668.

27 "Managers Spend More Than 6 Hours per Week Handling Staff Conflicts: Survey," *HR Reporter*, March 23, 2011.

28 R. D. Ramsey, "Interpersonal Conflicts," *SuperVision* 66, no. 4 (April 2005), pp. 14–17.

29 R. Kreitner and A. Kinicki, *Organizational Behavior*, 6th ed. (New York: McGraw-Hill, 2004), p. 492, Table 14-1. Reprinted by permission of McGraw Hill Education.

30 "Negotiating South of the Border," *Harvard Management Communication Letter* 2, no. 8 (August 1999), p. 12.

31 F. W. Swierczek, "Culture and Conflict in Joint Ventures in Asia," *International Journal of Project Management* 12, no. 1 (1994), pp. 39–47.

32 P. S. Kirkbride, S. Tang, and R. I. Westwood, "Chinese Conflict Preferences and Negotiation Behavior: Cultural and Psychological Influences," *Organization Studies* 12, no. 3 (1991), pp. 365–386; S. Tang and P. Kirkbride, "Development of Conflict Management Skills in Hong Kong: An Analysis of Some Cross-Cultural Implications," *Management Education and Development* 17, no. 3 (1986), pp. 287–301; P. Trubisky, S. Ting-Toomey, and S. L. Lin, "The Influence of Individualism-Collectivism and Self-monitoring on Conflict Styles," *International Journal of Intercultural Relations* 15 (1991), pp. 65–84; and K. I. Ohbuchi and Y. Takahashi, "Cultural Styles of Conflict Management in Japanese and Americans: Passivity, Covertness, and Effectiveness of Strategies," *Journal of Applied Social Psychology* 24 (1994), pp. 1345–1366.

33 P. S. Kirkbride, S. Tang, and R. I. Westwood, "Chinese Conflict Preferences and Negotiation Behavior: Cultural and Psychological

Influences," *Organization Studies* 12 (1991), pp. 365–386; and F. W. Swierczek, "Culture and Conflict in Joint Ventures in Asia," *International Journal of Project Management* 12 (1994), pp. 39–47.

34 C. L. Wang, X. Lin, A. K. K. Chan, and Y. Shi, "Conflict Handling Styles in International Joint Ventures: A Cross-Cultural and Cross-National Comparison," *Management International Review* 45, no. 1 (2005), pp. 3–21.

35 M. A. Rahim, "A Measure of Styles of Handling Interpersonal Conflict," *Academy of Management Journal* 26 (1983), pp. 368–376; and C. H. Tinsley, "Model of Conflict Resolution in Japanese, German, and American Cultures," *Journal of Applied Psychology* 83 (1998), pp. 316–323.

36 R. T. Moran, J. Allen, R. Wichman, T. Ando, and M. Sasano, "Japan," in *Global Perspectives on Organizational Conflict*, ed. M. A. Rahim and A. A. Blum (Westport, CT: Praeger 1994), pp. 33–52.

37 D. C. Barnlund, *Communicative Styles of Japanese and Americans: Images and Realities* (Belmont, CA: Wadsworth 1989); and K. I. Ohbuchi and Y. Takahashi, "Cultural Styles of Conflict Management in Japanese and Americans: Passivity, Covertness, and Effectiveness of Strategies," *Journal of Applied Social Psychology* 24 (1994), pp. 1345–1366.

38 Z. Ma, "Chinese Conflict Management Styles and Negotiation Behaviours: An Empirical Test," *International Journal of Cross Cultural Management*, April 2007, pp. 101–119.

39 K. Leung, "Some Determinants of Reactions to Procedural Models for Conflict Resolution: A Cross-National Study," *Journal of Personality and Social Psychology* 53 (1987), pp. 898–908; K. Leung and E. A. Lind, "Procedure and Culture: Effects of Culture, Gender, and Investigator Status on Procedural Preferences," *Journal of Personality and Social Psychology* 50 (1986), pp. 1134–1140; M. W. Morris, K. Y. Williams, K. Leung, R. Larrick, M. T. Mendoza, D. Bhatnagar, J. Li, M. Kondo, J. Luo, and J. Hu, "Conflict Management Style: Accounting for Cross-National Differences," *Journal of International Business Studies* 29 (1998), pp. 729–747; and F. W. Swierczek, "Culture and Conflict in Joint Ventures in Asia," *International Journal of Project Management* 12 (1994), pp. 39–47.

40 J. S. Black and M. Mendenhall, "Resolving Conflicts with the Japanese: Mission Impossible?" *Sloan Management Review* 34 (1993), pp. 49–59.

41 Vignette based on T. Sherlock, "Mediator Meets with Teachers Union President, Government Negotiator Today," *Vancouver Sun*, August 28, 2014.

42 B. A. Nijstad and S. C. Kaps, "Taking the Easy Way Out: Preference Diversity, Decision Strategies, and Decision Refusal in Groups," *Journal of Personality and Social Psychology* 94, no. 5 (2008), pp. 860–870.

43 Based on D. Tjosvold, *Learning to Manage Conflict: Getting People to Work Together Productively* (New York: Lexington Books, 1993), pp. 12–13.

44 M. E. Zellmer-Bruhn, M. M. Maloney, A. D. Bhappu, and R. Salvador, "When and How Do Differences Matter? An Exploration of Perceived Similarity in Teams," *Organizational Behavior and Human Decision Processes* 107, no. 1 (2008), pp. 41–59.

45 See T. H. Cox, S. A. Lobel, and P. L. McLeod, "Effects of Ethnic Group Cultural Differences on Cooperative Behavior on a Group Task," *Academy of Management Journal*, December 1991, pp. 827–847; and D. van Knippenberg, C. K. W. De Dreu, and A. C. Homan, "Work Group Diversity and Group Performance: An Integrative Model and Research Agenda," *Journal of Applied Psychology*, December 2004, pp. 1008–1022.

46 R. Ilies, M. D. Johnson, T. A. Judge, and J. Keeney, "A Within-Individual Study of Interpersonal Conflict as a Work Stressor: Dispositional and Situational Moderators," *Journal of Organizational Behavior* 32, no. 1 (2011), pp. 44–64.

47 K. J. Behfar, R. S. Peterson, E. A. Mannix, and W. M. K. Trochim, "The Critical Role of Conflict Resolution in Teams: A Close Look at the Links between Conflict Type, Conflict Management Strategies, and Team Outcomes," *Journal of Applied Psychology* 93, no. 1 (2008), pp. 170–188; A. G. Tekleab, N. R. Quigley, and P. E. Tesluk, "A Longitudinal Study of Team Conflict, Conflict Management, Cohesion, and Team Effectiveness," *Group and Organization Management* 34, no. 2 (2009), pp. 170–205; and E. Van de Vliert, M. C. Euwema, and S. E. Huismans, "Managing Conflict with a Subordinate or a Superior: Effectiveness of Conglomerated Behavior," *Journal of Applied Psychology* 80 (1995), pp. 271–281.

48 A. Somech, H. S. Desivilya, and H. Lidogoster, "Team Conflict Management and Team Effectiveness: The Effects of Task Interdependence and Team Identification," *Journal of Organizational Behavior* 30, no. 3 (2009), pp. 359–378.

49 See J. A. Wall Jr. and R. R. Callister, "Conflict and Its Management," *Journal of Management* 21, no. 3 (1995), pp. 523–526 for evidence supporting the argument that conflict is almost uniformly dysfunctional. See also P. J. Hinds and D. E. Bailey, "Out of Sight, Out of Sync: Understanding Conflict in Distributed Teams," *Organization Science*, November–December 2003, pp. 615–632.

50 K. A. Jehn, L. Greer, S. Levine, and G. Szulanski, "The Effects of Conflict Types, Dimensions, and Emergent States on Group Outcomes," *Group Decision and Negotiation* 17, no. 6 (2005), pp. 777–796.

51 M. E. Zellmer-Bruhn, M. M. Maloney, A. D. Bhappu, and R. Salvador, "When and How Do Differences Matter? An Exploration of Perceived Similarity in Teams," *Organizational Behavior and Human Decision Processes* 107, no. 1 (2008), pp. 41–59.

52 Vignette based on V. Palmer, "Tried-and-true Ready Method Yields a Breakthrough," *Vancouver Sun*, September 17, 2014; and A. Woo, "BCTF Members Ratify New Six-Year Contract, Ending B.C. Teachers' Strike," *Globe and Mail*, September 19, 2014, http://politics.theglobeandmail.com/2014/09/19/bctf-members-ratify-tentative-agreement/.

53 J. A. Wall Jr., *Negotiation: Theory and Practice* (Glenview, IL: Scott, Foresman, 1985).

54 This model is based on R. J. Lewicki, "Bargaining and Negotiation," *Exchange: The Organizational Behavior Teaching Journal* 6, no. 2 (1981), pp. 39–40; and B. S. Moskal, "The Art of the Deal," *IndustryWeek*, January 18, 1993, p. 23.

55 J. C. Magee, A. D. Galinsky, and D. H. Gruenfeld, "Power, Propensity to Negotiate, and Moving First in Competitive Interactions," *Personality and Social Psychology Bulletin*, February 2007, pp. 200–212.

56 H. R. Bowles, L. Babcock, and L. Lei, "Social Incentives for Gender Differences in the Propensity to Initiative Negotiations: Sometimes It Does Hurt to Ask," *Organizational Behavior and Human Decision Processes* 103 (2007), pp. 84–103.

57 Based on G. Ku, A. D. Galinsky, and J. K. Murnighan, "Starting Low but Ending High: A Reversal of the Anchoring Effect in Auctions," *Journal of Personality and Social Psychology* 90, June 2006, pp. 975–986; K. Sherstyuk, "A Comparison of First Price Multi-Object Auctions," *Experimental Economics* 12, no. 1 (2009), pp. 42–64; and R. M. Isaac, T. C. Salmon, and A. Zillante, "A Theory of Jump Bidding in Ascending Auctions," *Journal of Economic Behavior & Organization* 62, no. 1 (2007), pp. 144–164.

58 D. A. Moore, "Myopic Prediction, Self-Destructive Secrecy, and the Unexpected Benefits of Revealing Final Deadlines in Negotiation," *Organizational Behavior and Human Decision Processes*, July 2004, pp. 125–139.

59 J. R. Curhan, H. A. Elfenbein, and H. Xu, "What Do People Value When They Negotiate? Mapping the Domain of Subjective Value in Negotiation," *Journal of Personality and Social Psychology* 91, no. 3 (2007), pp. 493–512.

60 K. W. Thomas, "Conflict and Negotiation Processes in Organizations," in *Handbook of Industrial and Organizational Psychology*, 2nd ed., vol. 3, ed. M. D. Dunnette and L. M. Hough (Palo Alto, CA: Consulting Psychologists Press, 1992), pp. 651–717.

61 P. M. Morgan and R. S. Tindale, "Group vs. Individual Performance in Mixed-Motive Situations: Exploring an Inconsistency," *Organizational Behavior and Human Decision Processes*, January 2002, pp. 44–65.

62 C. E. Naquin, "The Agony of Opportunity in Negotiation: Number of Negotiable Issues, Counterfactual Thinking, and Feelings of Satisfaction," *Organizational Behavior and Human Decision Processes*, May 2003, pp. 97–107.

63 M. Giacomantonio, C. K. W. De Dreu, and L. Mannetti, "Now You See It, Now You Don't: Interests, Issues, and Psychological Distance in Integrative Negotiation," *Journal of Personality and Social Psychology* 98, no. 5 (2010), pp. 761–774.

64 F. S. Ten Velden, B. Beersma, and C. K. W. De Dreu, "It Takes One to Tango: The Effect of Dyads' Epistemic Motivation Composition in Negotiation," *Personality and Social Psychology Bulletin* 36, no. 11 (2010), pp. 1454–1466.

65 C. K. W. De Dreu, L. R. Weingart, and S. Kwon, "Influence of Social Motives on Integrative Negotiation: A Meta-analytic Review and Test of Two Theories," *Journal of Personality and Social Psychology*, May 2000, pp. 889–905.

66 A. W. Brooks and M. E. Schweitzer, "Can Nervous Nelly Negotiate? How Anxiety Causes Negotiators to Make Low First Offers, Exit Early, and Earn Less Profit," *Organizational Behavior and Human Decision Processes* 115, no. 1 (2011), p. 43.

67 A. W. Brooks and M. E. Schweitzer, "Can Nervous Nelly Negotiate? How Anxiety Causes Negotiators to Make Low First Offers, Exit Early, and Earn Less Profit," *Organizational Behavior and Human Decision Processes* 115, no. 1 (2011), pp. 43–54.

68 D. Malhotra and M. Bazerman, "Investigative Negotiation," *Harvard Business Review*, September 2007, pp. 72–78.

69 S. S. Wiltermuth and M. A. Neale, "Too Much Information: The Perils of Nondiagnostic Information in Negotiations," *Journal of Applied Psychology* 96, no. 1 (2011), pp. 192–201.

70 R. Fisher and W. Ury, *Getting to Yes: Negotiating Agreement without Giving In*, 2nd ed. (New York: Penguin, 1991).

71 M. H. Bazerman and M. A. Neale, *Negotiating Rationally* (New York: Free Press, 1992), pp. 67–68.

72 R. P. Larrick and G. Wu, "Claiming a Large Slice of a Small Pie: Asymmetric Disconfirmation in Negotiation," *Journal of Personality and Social Psychology* 93, no. 2 (2007), pp. 212–233.

73 R. Fisher and W. Ury, *Getting to Yes: Negotiating Agreement without Giving In*, 2nd ed. (New York: Penguin, 1991).

74 M. Marks and C. Harold, "Who Asks and Who Receives in Salary Negotiation," *Journal of Organizational Behavior* 32, no. 3 (2011), pp. 371–394.

75 R. Fisher and W. Ury, *Getting to Yes; Negotiating Agreement without Giving In*, 2nd ed. (New York: Penguin, 1991).

76 T. A. Judge, B. A. Livingston, and C. Hurst, "Do Nice Guys—and Gals—Really Finish Last? The Joint Effects of Sex and Agreeableness on Income," *Journal of Personality and Social Psychology* 102 (2012), pp. 390–407.

77 Based on T. R. Cohen, "Moral Emotions and Unethical Bargaining: The Differential Effects of Empathy and Perspective Taking in Deterring Deceitful Negotiation," *Journal of Business Ethics* 94, no. 4 (2010), pp. 569–579; and R. Volkema, D. Fleck, and A. Hofmeister, "Predicting Competitive-Unethical Negotiating Behavior and Its Consequences," *Negotiation Journal* 26, no. 3 (2010), pp. 263–286.

78 N. Dimotakis, D. E. Conlon, and R. Ilies, "The Mind and Heart (Literally) of the Negotiator: Personality and Contextual Determinants of Experiential Reactions and Economic Outcomes in Negotiation," *Journal of Applied Psychology* 97 (2012), pp. 183–193.

79 E. T. Amanatullah, M. W. Morris, and J. R. Curhan, "Negotiators Who Give Too Much: Unmitigated Communion, Relational Anxieties, and Economic Costs in Distributive and Integrative Bargaining," *Journal of Personality and Social Psychology* 95, no. 3 (2008), pp. 723–738; and D. S. DeRue, D. E. Conlon, H. Moon, and H. W. Willaby, "When Is Straightforwardness a Liability in Negotiations? The Role of Integrative Potential and Structural Power," *Journal of Applied Psychology* 94, no. 4 (2009), pp. 1032–1047.

80 B. Barry and R. A. Friedman, "Bargainer Characteristics in Distributive and Integrative Negotiation," *Journal of Personality and Social Psychology*, February 1998, pp. 345–359.

81 A. Zerres, J. Hüffmeier, P. A. Freund, K. Backhaus, and G. Hertel, "Does It Take Two to Tango? Longitudinal Effects of Unilateral and Bilateral Integrative Negotiation Training," *Journal of Applied Psychology* 98 (2013), pp. 478–491.

82 G. Lelieveld, E. Van Dijk, I. Van Beest, and G. A. Van Kleef, "Why Anger and Disappointment Affect Other's Bargaining Behavior Differently: The Moderating Role of Power and the Mediating Role of Reciprocal Complementary Emotions," *Personality and Social Psychology Bulletin* 38 (2012), pp. 1209–1221.

83 S. Côté, I. Hideg, and G. A. van Kleef, "The Consequences of Faking Anger in Negotiations," *Journal of Experimental Social Psychology* 49 (2013), pp. 453–463.

84 G. A. Van Kleef and C. K. W. De Dreu, "Longer-Term Consequences of Anger Expression in Negotiation: Retaliation or Spillover?" *Journal of Experimental Social Psychology* 46, no. 5 (2010), pp. 753–760.

85 H. Adam and A. Shirako, "Not All Anger Is Created Equal: The Impact of the Expresser's Culture on the Social Effects of Anger in Negotiations," *Journal of Applied Psychology* 98, no. 5 (2013), pp. 735–798.

86 M. Olekalns and P. L Smith, "Mutually Dependent: Power, Trust, Affect, and the Use of Deception in Negotiation," *Journal of Business Ethics* 85, no. 3 (2009), pp. 347–365.

87 A. W. Brooks and M. E. Schweitzer, "Can Nervous Nellie Negotiate? How Anxiety Causes Negotiators to Make Low First Offers, Exit Early, and Earn Less Profit," *Organizational Behavior and Human Decision Processes* 115, no. 1 (2011), pp. 43–54.

88 M. Sinaceur, H. Adam, G. A. Van Kleef, and A. D. Galinsky, "The Advantages of Being Unpredictable: How Emotional Inconsistency Extracts Concessions in Negotiation," *Journal of Experimental Social Psychology* 49 (2013), pp. 498–508.

89 K. Leary, J. Pillemer, and M. Wheeler, "Negotiating with Emotion," *Harvard Business Review*, January–February 2013, pp. 96–103.

90 A. M. Isen, A. A. Labroo, and P. Durlach, "An Influence of Product and Brand Name on Positive Affect: Implicit and Explicit Measures," *Motivation & Emotion*, March 2004, pp. 43–63.

91 A. M. Isen, A. A. Labroo, and P. Durlach, "An Influence of Product and Brand Name on Positive Affect: Implicit and Explicit Measures," *Motivation & Emotion*, March 2004, pp. 43–63.

92 P. J. D. Carnevale and A. M. Isen, "The Influence of Positive Affect and Visual Access on the Discovery of Integrative Solutions in Bilateral Negotiations," *Organizational Behavior and Human Decision Processes*, February 1986, pp. 1–13; and C. Montes, D. Rodriguez, and G. Serrano, "Affective Choice of Conflict Management Styles," *International Journal of Conflict Management* 23 (2012), pp. 6–18.

93 P. D. Trapnell and D. L. Paulhus, "Agentic and Communal Values: Their Scope and Measurement," *Journal of Personality Assessment* 94 (2012), pp. 39–52.

94 C. T. Kulik and M. Olekalns, "Negotiating the Gender Divide: Lessons from the Negotiation and Organizational Behavior Literatures," *Journal of Management* 38 (2012), pp. 1387–1415.

95 C. Suddath, "The Art of Haggling," *Bloomberg Businessweek*, November 26, 2012, p. 98.

96 C. T. Kulik and M. Olekalns, "Negotiating the Gender Divide: Lessons from the Negotiation and Organizational Behavior Literatures," *Journal of Management* 38 (2012), pp. 1387–1415.

97 L. J. Kray, C. C. Locke, and A B. Van Zant, "Feminine Charm: An Experimental Analysis of Its Costs and Benefits in Negotiations," *Personality and Social Psychology Bulletin* 38 (2012), pp. 1343–1357.

98 S. de Lemus, R. Spears, M. Bukowski, M. Moya, and J. Lupiáñez, "Reversing Implicit Gender Stereotype Activation as a Function of Exposure to Traditional Gender Roles," *Social Psychology* 44 (2013), pp. 109–116.

99 D. A. Small, M. Gelfand, L. Babcock, and H. Gettman, "Who Goes to the Bargaining Table? The Influence of Gender and Framing on the Initiation of Negotiation," *Journal of Personality and Social Psychology* 93, no. 4 (2007), pp. 600–613; and C. K. Stevens, A. G. Bavetta, and M. E. Gist, "Gender Differences in the Acquisition of Salary Negotiation Skills: The Role of Goals, Self-Efficacy, and Perceived Control," *Journal of Applied Psychology* 78, no. 5 (October 1993), pp. 723–735.

100 E. T. Amanatullah and M. W. Morris, "Negotiating Gender Roles: Gender Differences in Assertive Negotiating Are Mediated by Women's Fear of Backlash and Attenuated When Negotiating on Behalf of Others," *Journal of Personality and Social Psychology* 98, no. 2 (2010), pp. 256–267.

101 L. Schweitzer, E. Ng, S. Lyons, and L. Kuron, "Exploring the Career Pipeline: Gender Differences in Pre-Career Expectations," *Relations Industrielles/Industrial Relations* 66, no. 3 (2011), pp. 422–444.

102 C. Olsheski, "Resolving Disputes Has Just Become More Efficient," *Financial Post (National Post)*, August 16, 1999, p. D9.

103 Mediate BC, "Mediator Survey 2014," *Mediate BC*, October 14, 2014, http://www.mediatebc.com/PDFs/MBC-Survey-Summary-Final.aspx.

104 Conciliation and Labour Tribunals Division, Nova Scotia Labour and Advanced Education, *Conciliation: A Guide for Employer and Union Committees* (Halifax: Author, 2012), http://novascotia.ca/lae/conciliation/docs/Conciliation_Guide_WEB.pdf.

105 H. R. Markus and S. Kitayama, "Culture and the Self: Implications for Cognition, Emotion, and Motivation," *Psychological Review* 98, no. 2 (1991), pp. 224–253; and H. Ren and B. Gray, "Repairing Relationship Conflict: How Violation Types and Culture Influence the Effectiveness of Restoration Rituals," *Academy of Management Review* 34, no. 1 (2009), pp. 105–126.

106 M. J. Gelfand, M. Higgins, L. H. Nishii, J. L. Raver, A. Dominguez, F. Murakami, S. Yamaguchi, and M. Toyama, "Culture and Egocentric Perceptions of Fairness in Conflict and Negotiation," *Journal of Applied Psychology*, October 2002, pp. 833–845; and Z. Ma, "Chinese Conflict Management Styles and Negotiation Behaviours: An Empirical Test," *International Journal of Cross Cultural Management*, April 2007, pp. 101–119.

107 P. P. Fu, X. H. Yan, Y. Li, E. Wang, and S. Peng, "Examining Conflict-Handling Approaches by Chinese Top Management Teams in IT Firms," *International Journal of Conflict Management* 19, no. 3 (2008), pp. 188–209.

108 L. A. Liu, R. Friedman, B. Barry, M. J. Gelfand, and Z. Zhang, "The Dynamics of Consensus Building in Intracultural and Intercultural Negotiations," *Administrative Science Quarterly* 57 (2012), pp. 269–304.

109 Based on S. Kopelman and A. S. Rosette, "Cultural Variation in Response to Strategic Emotions in Negotiations," *Group Decision and Negotiation* 17, no. 1 (2008), pp. 65–77; and M. Liu, "The Intrapersonal and Interpersonal Effects of Anger on Negotiation Strategies: A Cross-Cultural Investigation," *Human Communication Research* 35, no. 1 (2009), pp. 148–169.

110 M. Liu, "The Intrapersonal and Interpersonal Effects of Anger on Negotiation Strategies: A Cross-Cultural Investigation," *Human Communication Research* 35, no. 1 (2009), pp. 148–169; and H. Adam, A. Shirako, and W. W. Maddux, "Cultural Variance in the Interpersonal Effects of Anger in Negotiations," *Psychological Science* 21, no. 6 (2010), pp. 882–889.

111 Point was influenced by E. Van de Vliert, "Escalative Intervention in Small-Group Conflicts," *Journal of Applied Behavioral Science*, Winter 1985, pp. 19–36; Counterpoint is based on Q. Reade, "Workplace Conflict Is Time-Consuming Problem for Business," *PersonnelToday.com*, September 30, 2004, http://www.personnel-today.co.uk.

112 Based on S. A. Joni and D. Beyer, "How to Pick a Good Fight," *Harvard Business Review*, December 2009, pp. 48–57; and B. H. Bradley, B. E. Postlewaite, A. C. Klotz, M. R. Hamdani, and K. G. Brown, "Reaping the Benefits of Task Conflict in Teams: The Critical Role of Team Psychological Safety Climate," *Journal of Applied Psychology*, Advance publication (July 4, 2011), doi:10.1037/a0024200. CP Rail content based on "Community Gardens Ripped Up Along Arbutus Corridor," *CBC.ca*, August 14, 2014; "Arbutus Corridor: Herbicide Spraying Suspended While CP and City Talk," *CBC.ca*, August 27, 2014, http://www.cbc.ca/news/canada/british-columbia/arbutus-corridor-herbicide-spraying-suspended-while-cp-and-city-talk-1.2748266; "Vancouver Taking Battle over Arbutus Corridor to Court," *CTV News Vancouver*, October 3, 2014, http://bc.ctvnews.ca/vancouver-taking-battle-over-arbutus-corridor-to-court-1.2038606#ixzz3I3ulUapj; and J. Lee, "CP Rail Temporarily Halts Arbutus Corridor Work, *Vancouver Sun*, November 4, 2014, http://www.vancouversun.com/news/metro/Rail+temporarily+halts+Arbutus+spur+work/10352423/story.html.

113 Based on D. Galarneau and T. Sohn, "Long-Term Trends in Unionization," *Statistics Canada*, last modified April 28, 2014, http://www.statcan.gc.ca/pub/75-006-x/2013001/article/11878-eng.htm; and Fraser Institute, "Government Employees in Canada Earn 12 Per Cent More, on Average, Than Equivalent Private-Sector Workers," news release, April 4, 2013, http://www.fraserinstitute.org/research-news/news/news-releases/Government-employees-in-Canada-earn-12-per-cent-more,-on-average,-than-equivalent-private-sector-workers/.

114 These suggestions are based on J. A. Wall Jr. and M. W. Blum, "Negotiations," *Journal of Management*, June 1991, pp. 278–282; and J. S. Pouliot, "Eight Steps to Success in Negotiating," *Nation's Business*, April 1999, pp. 40–42.

OB on the Edge: Workplace Bullying

1 Based on CBC, "A Look at the High Cost of Bullies in the Workplace," *The National*, July 20, 2014; C. Pearson, "Record Workplace Bullying Award Against Walmart Reduced on Appeal," *Windsor Star*, May 27, 2014.

2 L. M. Anderson and C. M. Pearson, "Tit for Tat? The Spiraling Effect of Incivility in the Workplace," *Academy of Management Review* 24, no. 3 (1999), pp. 452–471.

3 L. M. Anderson and C. M. Pearson, "Tit for Tat? The Spiraling Effect of Incivility in the Workplace," *Academy of Management Review* 24, no. 3 (1999), pp. 452–471. For further discussion of this, see R. A. Baron and J. H. Neuman, "Workplace Violence and Workplace Aggression: Evidence on Their Relative Frequency and Potential Causes," *Aggressive Behavior* 22 (1996), pp. 161–173; C. C. Chen and W. Eastman, "Towards a Civic Culture for Multicultural Organizations," *Journal of Applied Behavioral Science* 33 (1997), pp. 454–470; J. H. Neuman and R. A. Baron, "Aggression in the Workplace," in *Antisocial Behavior in*

Organizations, ed. R. A. Giacalone and J. Greenberg (Thousand Oaks, CA: Sage, 1997), pp. 37–67.

4   L. M. Anderson and C. M. Pearson, "Tit for Tat? The Spiraling Effect of Incivility in the Workplace," *Academy of Management Review* 24, no. 3 (1999), pp. 452–471.

5   L. M. Anderson and C. M. Pearson, "Tit for Tat? The Spiraling Effect of Incivility in the Workplace," *Academy of Management Review* 24, no. 3 (1999), pp. 452–471.

6   R. Corelli, "Dishing Out Rudeness: Complaints Abound as Customers Are Ignored, Berated," *Maclean's*, January 11, 1999, p. 44.

7   See Urbanspoon reviews for The Elbow Room, 2013 and 2014, http://www.urbanspoon.com/r/14/180579/restaurant/Yaletown/The-Elbow-Room-Cafe-Vancouver.

8   R. Corelli, "Dishing Out Rudeness: Complaints Abound as Customers Are Ignored, Berated," *Maclean's*, January 11, 1999, p. 44.

9   "Definition of Workplace Bullying," *Workforce Bullying Institute*, http://www.workplacebullying.org/individuals/problem/definition/.

10 "2014 WBI U.S. Workplace Bullying Survey," Workplace Bullying Institute, February 2014, http://www.workplacebullying.org/wbiresearch/wbi-2014-us-survey/.

11 C. Porath and C. Pearson, "The Price of Incivility Lack of Respect: Hurts Morale and the Bottom Line," *Harvard Business Review*, January–February 2013, p. 117.

12 A. M. Hansen and R. Persson, "Frequency of Bullying at Work, Physiological Response, and Mental Health," *Journal of Psychosomatic Research* 70, no. 1 (January 2011), pp. 19–27.

13 B. L. Lovell and R. T. Lee, "Impact of Workplace Bullying on Emotional and Physical Well-Being: A Longitudinal Collective Case Study," *Journal of Aggression, Maltreatment & Trauma* 20, no. 3 (April 2011), pp. 344–357.

14 R. Corelli, "Dishing Out Rudeness: Complaints Abound as Customers Are Ignored, Berated," *Maclean's*, January 11, 1999, p. 44.

15 R. Corelli, "Dishing Out Rudeness: Complaints Abound as Customers Are Ignored, Berated," *Maclean's*, January 11, 1999, p. 44.

16 R. A. Baron and J. H. Neuman, "Workplace Violence and Workplace Aggression: Evidence on Their Relative Frequency and Potential Causes," *Aggressive Behavior* 22 (1996), pp. 161–173; C. MacKinnon, *Only Words* (New York: Basic Books, 1994); J. Marks, "The American Uncivil Wars," *U.S. News & World Report*, April 22, 1996, pp. 66–72; and L. P. Spratlen, "Workplace Mistreatment: Its Relationship to Interpersonal Violence," *Journal of Psychosocial Nursing* 32, no. 12 (1994), pp. 5–6.

17 K. MacQueen and C. McKenna, "Workplace Rampage," *Maclean's*, May 8, 2014.

18 W. M. Glenn, "An Employee's Survival Guide: An ILO Survey of Workplaces in 32 Countries Ranked Argentina the Most Violent, Followed by Romania, France and Then, Surprisingly, Canada," *Occupational Health & Safety*, April–May 2002, p. 28 passim.

19 D. Flavelle, "Managers Cited for Increase in 'Work Rage,'" *Vancouver Sun*, April 11, 2000, pp. D1, D11; and "Profile of Violent Workplace Victimization Incidents," *Statistics Canada*, 2007, http://www.statcan.gc.ca/pub/85f0033m/2007013/findings-resultats/4054152-eng.htm.

20 K. MacQueen and C. McKenna, "Workplace Rampage," *Maclean's*, May 8, 2014, http://www.macleans.ca/news/canada/the-shootings-at-western-forest-in-nanaimo-point-to-a-bigger-problem/.

21 E. Ellis, "Today's Jobs Can Be Hard on Your Head," *Vancouver Sun*, June 25, 2014, p. D1.

22 J. O'Reilly, S. L. Robinson, J. L. Berdahl, and S. Banki, "Is Negative Attention Better Than No Attention? The Comparative Effects of Ostracism and Harassment at Work," *Organizational Science*, April 4, 2014. Published online.

23 E. Ellis, "Today's Jobs Can Be Hard on Your Head," *Vancouver Sun*, June 25, 2014, p. D1.

24 A. M. Webber, "Danger: Toxic Company," *Fast Company*, November 1998, pp. 152–157.

25 D. Flavelle, "Managers Cited for Increase in 'Work Rage,'" *Vancouver Sun*, April 11, 2000, pp. D1, D11; and G. Smith, *Work Rage* (Toronto: HarperCollins Canada, 2000).

26 "Work Rage," *BCBusiness Magazine*, January 2001, p. 23.

27 D. Flavelle, "Managers Cited for Increase in 'Work Rage,'" *Vancouver Sun*, April 11, 2000, pp. D1, D11.

28 A. Skogstad, T. Torsheim, S. Einarsen, and L.J. Hauge, "Testing the Work Environment Hypothesis of Bullying on a Group Level of Analysis: Psychosocial Factors as Precursors of Observed Workplace Bullying," *Applied Psychology: An International Review* 60, no. 3 (July 2011), pp. 475–495.

29 D. Geddes, and L. T. Stickney, "The Trouble with Sanctions: Organizational Responses to Deviant Anger Displays at Work," *Human Relations* 64, no. 2 (February 2011), pp. 201–230.

30 B. Ray, "Who's Afraid of the Big Bad Boss? Plenty of Us, New FSU Study Shows," *FSU News*, December 4, 2006, https://www.fsu.edu/news/2006/12/04/bad.boss/.

31 H. Levinson, *Emotional Health in the World of Work* (Boston: South End Press, 1964); and E. Schein, *Organizational Psychology* (Englewood Cliffs, NJ: Prentice Hall, 1980).

32 E. W. Morrison and S. L. Robinson, "When Employees Feel Betrayed: A Model of How Psychological Contract Violation Develops," *Academy of Management Journal* 22 (1997), pp. 226–256; S. L. Robinson, "Trust and Breach of the Psychological Contract," *Administrative Science Quarterly* 41 (1996), pp. 574–599; and S. L. Robinson, M. S. Kraatz, and D. M. Rousseau, "Changing Obligations and the Psychological Contract: A Longitudinal Study," *Academy of Management Journal* 37 (1994), pp. 137–152. A recent study suggests that perceptions of the psychological contract vary by culture: D. C. Thomas, S. R. Fitzsimmons, E. C. Ravlin, K. Au, B. Z. Ekelund, and C. Barzantny, "Psychological Contracts across Cultures," *Organization Studies* 31, no. 11 (2010), pp. 1437–1458.

33 T. R. Tyler and P. Dogoey, "Trust in Organizational Authorities: The Influence of Motive Attributions on Willingness to Accept Decisions," in *Trust in Organizations*, ed. R. M. Kramer and T. R. Tyler (Thousand Oaks, CA: Sage, 1996), pp. 246–260.

34 D. Abma, "Bad Managers a Problem in Canadian Workplaces: Survey," *Financial Post*, January 19, 2011; and "2014 WBI U.S. Workplace Bullying Survey," *Workplace Bullying Institute*, February 2014, http://www.workplacebullying.org/wbiresearch/wbi-2014-us-survey/.

35 S. Montes and D. Zweig, "Do Promises Matter? An Exploration of the Role of Promises in Psychological Contract Breach," *Journal of Applied Psychology* 94, no. 5 (2009), pp. 1243–1260.

36 A. M. Webber, "Danger: Toxic Company," *Fast Company*, November 1998, pp. 152–157.

37 A. M. Webber, "Danger: Toxic Company," *Fast Company*, November 1998, pp. 152–157.

38 Based on A. McKee, "Neutralize Your Toxic Boss," *HBR Blog Network*, September 24, 2008, http://blogs.hbr.org/2008/09/neutralize-your-toxic-boss/; and "Toxic Bosses: How to Live with the S.O.B.," *BusinessWeek*, August 13, 2008, http://www.businessweek.com/stories/2008-08-13/toxic-bosses-how-to-live-with-the-s-dot-o-dot-b-dot.

39   P. Frost, *Toxic Emotions at Work* (Cambridge, MA: Harvard Business School Press, 2003).

40   "Men More Likely to Be Rude in Workplace, Survey Shows," *Vancouver Sun*, August 16, 1999, p. B10.

41   D. E. Gibson and S. G. Barsade, "The Experience of Anger at Work: Lessons from the Chronically Angry" (paper presented at the annual meetings of the Academy of Management, Chicago, August 11, 1999).

42   D. E. Gibson and S. G. Barsade, "The Experience of Anger at Work: Lessons from the Chronically Angry" (paper presented at the annual meetings of the Academy of Management, Chicago, August 11, 1999).

43   R. Bacal, "Toxic Organizations—Welcome to the Fire of an Unhealthy Workplace," *Work 911.com*, 2000, http://work911 .com/articles/toxicorgs.htm.

44   R. Corelli, "Dishing Out Rudeness: Complaints Abound as Customers Are Ignored, Berated," *Maclean's*, January 11, 1999, p. 44.

45   L. Panjvani, "An Overview of Anti-bullying Legislation and Alternatives in Canada," *LawNow*, July 1, 2013, http://www .lawnow.org/an-overview-of-anti-bullying-legislation-and-alternatives-in-canada.

46   E. Ellis, "Today's Jobs Can Be Hard on Your Head," *Vancouver Sun*, June 25, 2014, p. D1.

47   E. Ellis, "Today's Jobs Can Be Hard on Your Head," *Vancouver Sun*, June 25, 2014, p. D1.

Chapter 10

1   Opening vignette based on Calgary Stampede, "Calgary Stampede Among Most Admired Corporate Cultures and Alberta's Top Employers," news release, February 5, 2014, http://news. calgarystampede.com/News/Latest-News/Release-Details/2014/ Calgary-Stampede-Among-Canadas-Most-Admired-Corporate-Cultures-/default.aspx; and "The Stampede That Almost Never Was Due to Flood Wraps-Up," *Canadian Press*, July 14, 2013, http://www.huffingtonpost.ca/2013/07/14/calgary-stampede-2013-flood-wrap-up_n_3596529.html.

2   "Organization Man: Henry Mintzberg Has Some Common Sense Observations About the Ways We Run Companies," *Financial Post*, November 22/24, 1997, pp. 14–16.

3   K. McArthur, "Air Canada Tells Employees to Crack a Smile More Often," *Globe and Mail*, March 14, 2002, pp. B1, B2.

4   K. McArthur, "Air Canada Tells Employees to Crack a Smile More Often," *Globe and Mail*, March 14, 2002, pp. B1, B2.

5   http://www.waterstonehc.com/news-events/news/announcing-canadas-10-most-admired-corporate-cultures-2013.

6   See, for example, H. S. Becker, "Culture: A Sociological View," *Yale Review*, Summer 1982, pp. 513–527; and E. H. Schein, *Organizational Culture and Leadership* (San Francisco: Jossey-Bass, 1985), p. 168.

7   This seven-item description is based on C. A. O'Reilly III, J. Chatman, and D. F. Caldwell, "People and Organizational Culture: A Profile Comparison Approach to Assessing Person-Organization Fit," *Academy of Management Journal*, September 1991, pp. 487–516; and J. A. Chatman and K. A. Jehn, "Assessing the Relationship between Industry Characteristics and Organizational Culture: How Different Can You Be?" *Academy of Management Journal*, June 1994, pp. 522–553. For a description of other popular measures, see A. Xenikou and A. Furnham, "A Correlational and Factor Analytic Study of Four Questionnaire Measures of Organizational Culture," *Human Relations*, March 1996, pp. 349–371. For a review of cultural dimensions, see N. M. Ashkanasy, C. P. M. Wilderom, and M. F. Peterson, eds., *Handbook*

8   *of Organizational Culture and Climate* (Thousand Oaks, CA: Sage, 2000), pp. 131–145.

8   K. S. Cameron, R. E. Quinn, J. DeGraff, and A. V. Thakor, *Competing Values Leadership: Creating Value in Organizations* (Cheltenham, UK and Northampton, MA: Edward Elgar, 2006).

9   C. A. Hartnell, A. Y. Ou, and A. Kinicki, "Organizational Culture and Organizational Effectiveness: A Meta-analytic Investigation of the Competing Values Framework's Theoretical Suppositions," *Journal of Applied Psychology*, January 17, 2011, published online before print. doi:10.1037/a0021987.

10   E. Schein, "Coming to a New Awareness of Organizational Culture," *Sloan Management Review*, Winter 1984, pp. 3–16; E. Schein, *Organizational Culture and Leadership*, 2nd ed. (San Francisco: Jossey-Bass, 1992); and E. Schein, "What Is Culture?" in *Reframing Organizational Culture*, ed. P. J. Frost, L. F. Moore, M. R. Louis, C. C. Lundberg, and J. Martin (Newbury Park, CA: Sage, 1991), pp. 243–253.

11   T. G. Stroup Jr., "Leadership and Organizational Culture: Actions Speak Louder Than Words," *Military Review* 76, no. 1 (January–February 1996), pp. 44–49; B. Moingeon and B. Ramanantsoa "Understanding Corporate Identity: The French School of Thought," *European Journal of Marketing* 31, no. 5/6 (1997), pp. 383–395; A. P. D. Van Luxemburg, J. M. Ulijn, and N. Amare, "The Contribution of Electronic Communication Media to the Design Process: Communicative and Cultural Implications," *IEEE Transactions on Professional Communication* 45, no. 4 (December 2002), pp. 250–264; L. D. McLean, "Organizational Culture's Influence on Creativity and Innovation: A Review of the Literature and Implications for Human Resource Development," *Advances in Developing Human Resources* 7, no. 2 (May 2005), pp. 226–246; and V. J. Friedman and A. B. Antal, "Negotiating Reality: A Theory of Action Approach to Intercultural Competence," *Management Learning* 36, no. 1 (2005), pp. 69–86.

12   See "Palliser Furniture—High Quality Leather Furniture," accessed November 3, 2014, http://www.transitionsfurniture.com/palliser-furniture/.

13   See C. A. O'Reilly and J. A. Chatman, "Culture as Social Control: Corporations, Cultures, and Commitment," in *Research in Organizational Behavior*, vol. 18, ed. B. M. Staw and L. L. Cummings (Greenwich, CT: JAI Press, 1996), pp. 157–200.

14   Y. Ling, Z. Simsek, M. H. Lubatkin, and J. F. Veiga, "Transformational Leadership's Role in Promoting Corporate Entrepreneurship: Examining the CEO-TMT Interface," *Academy of Management Journal* 51, no. 3 (2008), pp. 557–576; and A. Malhotra, A. Majchrzak, and B. Rosen, "Leading Virtual Teams," *Academy of Management Perspectives* 21, no. 1 (2007), pp. 60–70.

15   D. Denison, "What Is the Difference between Organizational Culture and Organizational Climate? A Native's Point of View on a Decade of Paradigm Wars," *Academy of Management Review* 21 (1996) pp. 519–654; and L. R. James, C. C. Choi, C. E. Ko, P. K. McNeil, M. K. Minton, M. A. Wright, and K. Kim, "Organizational and Psychological Climate: A Review of Theory and Research," *European Journal of Work and Organizational Psychology* 17, no. 1 (2008), pp. 5–32.

16   J. Z. Carr, A. M. Schmidt, J. K. Ford, and R. P. DeShon, "Climate Perceptions Matter: A Meta-analytic Path Analysis Relating Molar Climate, Cognitive and Affective States, and Individual Level Work Outcomes," *Journal of Applied Psychology* 88, no. 4 (2003), pp. 605–619.

17   M. Schulte, C. Ostroff, S. Shmulyian, and A. Kinicki, "Organizational Climate Configurations: Relationships to Collective Attitudes, Customer Satisfaction, and Financial Performance," *Journal of Applied Psychology* 94, no. 3 (2009), pp. 618–634.

18   See, for example, D. S. Pugh, J. Dietz, A. P. Brief, and J. W. Wiley, "Looking Inside and Out: The Impact of Employee and

Community Demographic Composition on Organizational Diversity Climate," *Journal of Applied Psychology* 93, no. 6 (2008), pp. 1422–1428; K. H. Ehrhart, L. A. Witt, B. Schneider, and S. J. Perry, "Service Employees Give as They Get: Internal Service as a Moderator of the Service Climate-Service Outcomes Link," *Journal of Applied Psychology* 96, no. 2 (2011), pp. 423–431; and A. Simha and J. B. Cullen, "Ethical Climates and Their Effects on Organizational Outcomes: Implications from the Past and Prophecies for the Future," *Academy of Management Perspectives*, November 2011, pp. 20–34.

19 J. C. Wallace, P. D. Johnson, K. Mathe, and J. Paul, "Structural and Psychological Empowerment Climates, Performance, and the Moderating Role of Shared Felt Accountability: A Managerial Perspective," *Journal of Applied Psychology* 96, no. 3 (2011), pp. 840–850.

20 J. M. Beus, S. C. Payne, M. E. Bergman, and W. Arthur, "Safety Climate and Injuries: An Examination of Theoretical and Empirical Relationships," *Journal of Applied Psychology* 95, no. 4 (2010), pp. 713–727.

21 Based on "West Jet, a True Example of Customer-Centric Culture," *Knightsbridge Thought Leadership Newsletter*, accessed August 15, 2014, http://www.knightsbridge.com/sitecore/content/Knightsbridge/home/ThoughtLeadership/onPeopleNewsletter/Articles/FEAT%201_Sept2011_WestJet.

22 A. Simha and J. B. Cullen, "Ethical Climates and Their Effects on Organizational Outcomes: Implications from the Past and Prophecies for the Future," *Academy of Management*, November 2012, pp. 20–34.

23 A. Simha and J. B. Cullen, "Ethical Climates and Their Effects on Organizational Outcomes: Implications from the Past and Prophecies for the Future," *Academy of Management*, November 2012, pp. 20–34.

24 A. Arnaud, "Conceptualizing and Measuring Ethical Work Climate Development and Validation of the Ethical Climate Index," *Business & Society*, June 2010, pp. 345–458.

25 A. Arnaud and M. Schminke, "The Ethical Climate and Context of Organizations: A Comprehensive Model," *Organization Science*, November–December 2012, pp. 1767–1780.

26 The view that there will be consistency among perceptions of organizational culture has been called the "integration" perspective. For a review of this perspective and conflicting approaches, see D. Meyerson and J. Martin, "Cultural Change: An Integration of Three Different Views," *Journal of Management Studies*, November 1987, pp. 623–647; and P. J. Frost, L. F. Moore, M. R. Louis, C. C. Lundberg, and J. Martin, eds., *Reframing Organizational Culture* (Newbury Park, CA: Sage, 1991).

27 See J. M. Jermier, J. W. Slocum Jr., L. W. Fry, and J. Gaines, "Organizational Subcultures in a Soft Bureaucracy: Resistance Behind the Myth and Facade of an Official Culture," *Organization Science*, May 1991, pp. 170–194; S. A. Sackmann, "Culture and Subcultures: An Analysis of Organizational Knowledge," *Administrative Science Quarterly*, March 1992, pp. 140–161; R. F. Zammuto, "Mapping Organizational Cultures and Subcultures: Looking Inside and across Hospitals" (paper presented at the 1995 National Academy of Management Conference, Vancouver, BC, August 1995); and G. Hofstede, "Identifying Organizational Subcultures: An Empirical Approach," *Journal of Management Studies*, January 1998, pp. 1–12.

28 D. A. Hoffman and L. M. Jones, "Leadership, Collective Personality, and Performance," *Journal of Applied Psychology* 90, no. 3 (2005), pp. 509–522.

29 T. Hsieh, "Zappos's CEO on Going to Extremes for Customers," *Harvard Business Review*, July/August 2010, pp. 41–45.

30 See, for example, G. G. Gordon and N. DiTomaso, "Predicting Corporate Performance from Organizational Culture," *Journal of Management Studies*, November 1992, pp. 793–798; and J. B.

Sorensen, "The Strength of Corporate Culture and the Reliability of Firm Performance," *Administrative Science Quarterly*, March 2002, pp. 70–91.

31 Y. Wiener, "Forms of Value Systems: A Focus on Organizational Effectiveness and Cultural Change and Maintenance," *Academy of Management Review*, October 1988, p. 536; and B. Schneider, A. N. Salvaggio, and M. Subirats, "Climate Strength: A New Direction for Climate Research," *Journal of Applied Psychology* 87 (2002), pp. 220–229.

32 R. T. Mowday, L. W. Porter, and R. M. Steers, *Employee-Organization Linkages: The Psychology of Commitment, Absenteeism, and Turnover* (New York: Academic Press, 1982); C. Vandenberghe, "Organizational Culture, Person-Culture Fit, and Turnover: A Replication in the Health Care Industry," *Journal of Organizational Behavior*, March 1999, pp. 175–184; and M. Schulte, C. Ostroff, S. Shmulyian, and A. Kinicki, "Organizational Climate Configurations: Relationships to Collective Attitudes, Customer Satisfaction, and Financial Performance," *Journal of Applied Psychology* 94, no. 3 (2009), pp. 618–634.

33 J. W. Grizzle, A. R. Zablah, T. J. Brown, J. C. Mowen, and J. M. Lee, "Employee Customer Orientation in Context: How the Environment Moderates the Influence of Customer Orientation on Performance Outcomes," *Journal of Applied Psychology* 94, no. 5 (2009), pp. 1227–1242.

34 M. R. Bashshur, A. Hernández, and V. González-Romá, "When Managers and Their Teams Disagree: A Longitudinal Look at the Consequences of Differences in Perceptions of Organizational Support," *Journal of Applied Psychology* 96, no. 3 (2011), pp. 558–573.

35 Vignette based on "Getting Involved," *Calgary Stampede*, accessed August 15, 2014, http://corporate.calgarystampede.com/getting-involved/volunteering; and "Organization Overview: Board of Directors," *Calgary Stampede*, accessed August 15, 2014, http://corporate.calgarystampede.com/about/organization-overview/board-of-directors.

36 R. Spence, "Telling Stories Makes for Happy Endings," *National Post (Financial Post)*, April 20, 2009, pp. FP4.

37 D. M. Boje, "The Storytelling Organization: A Study of Story Performance in an Office-Supply Firm," *Administrative Science Quarterly*, March 1991, pp. 106–126; and M. Ricketts and J. G. Seiling, "Language, Metaphors, and Stories: Catalysts for Meaning Making in Organizations," *Organization Development Journal*, Winter 2003, pp. 33–43.

38 A. J. Shipp and K. J. Jansen, "Reinterpreting Time in Fit Theory: Crafting and Recrafting Narratives of Fit in Medias Res," *Academy of Management Review* 36, no. 1 (2011), pp. 76–101.

39 A. M. Pettigrew, "On Studying Organizational Cultures," *Administrative Science Quarterly*, December 1979, p. 576. See also K. Kamoche, "Rhetoric, Ritualism, and Totemism in Human Resource Management," *Human Relations*, April 1995, pp. 367–385.

40 V. Matthews, "Starting Every Day with a Shout and a Song," *Financial Times*, May 2, 2001, p. 11; and M. Gimein, "Sam Walton Made Us a Promise," *Fortune*, March 18, 2002, pp. 121–130.

41 A. Rafaeli and M. G. Pratt, "Tailored Meanings: On the Meaning and Impact of Organizational Dress," *Academy of Management Review*, January 1993, pp. 32–55.

42 Thanks to an anonymous reviewer for adding these.

43 M. Pendergast, *Uncommon Grounds: The History of Coffee and How It Transformed Our World* (New York: Basic Books, 1999), p. 369.

44 Thanks to a reviewer for this story.

45 Vignette based on M. Foran, *Icon, Brand, Myth: The Calgary Stampede* (Edmonton: Athabasca University Press, 2008); and M. Toneguzzi, "Indian Village Headed for Bigger Home," *Calgary Herald*, July 13, 2011.

46 E. H. Schein, "The Role of the Founder in Creating Organizational Culture," *Organizational Dynamics*, Summer 1983, pp. 13–28; and Y. L. Zhao, O. H. Erekson, T. Wang, and M. Song, "Pioneering Advantages and Entrepreneurs' First-Mover Decisions: An Empirical Investigation for the United States and China," *Journal of Product Innovation Management*, December 2012, pp. 190–210.

47 E. H. Schein, "Leadership and Organizational Culture," in *The Leader of the Future*, ed. F. Hesselbein, M. Goldsmith, and R. Beckhard (San Francisco: Jossey-Bass, 1996), pp. 61–62.

48 "PCL's Biggest Investment: Its People," *National Post*, September 2, 2008, p. FP10.

49 See, for example, J. R. Harrison and G. R. Carroll, "Keeping the Faith: A Model of Cultural Transmission in Formal Organizations," *Administrative Science Quarterly*, December 1991, pp. 552–582.

50 B. Schneider, H. W. Goldstein, and D. B. Smith, "The ASA Framework: An Update," *Personnel Psychology*, Winter 1995, pp. 747–773; D. M. Cable and T. A. Judge, "Interviewers' Perceptions of Person-Organization Fit and Organizational Selection Decisions," *Journal of Applied Psychology*, August 1997, pp. 546–561; M. L. Verquer, T. A. Beehr, and S. H. Wagner, "A Meta-analysis of Relations between Person-Organization Fit and Work Attitudes," *Journal of Vocational Behavior*, December 2003, pp. 473–489; and W. Li, Y. Wang, P. Taylor, K. Shi, and D. He, "The Influence of Organizational Culture on Work-Related Personality Requirement Ratings: A Multilevel Analysis," *International Journal of Selection and Assessment* 16, no. 4 (2008), pp. 366–384.

51 "Building a Better Workforce," *PROFIT*, February 16, 2011, http://www.profitguide.com/manage-grow/human-resources/building-a-better-workforce-30073.

52 "Building a Better Workforce," *PROFIT*, February 16, 2011, http://www.profitguide.com/manage-grow/human-resources/building-a-better-workforce-30073.

53 D. C. Hambrick and P. A. Mason, "Upper Echelons: The Organization as a Reflection of Its Top Managers," *Academy of Management Review*, April 1984, pp. 193–206; M. A. Carpenter, M. A. Geletkanycz, and W. G. Sanders, "Upper Echelons Research Revisited: Antecedents, Elements, and Consequences of Top Management Team Composition," *Journal of Management* 30, no. 6 (2004), pp. 749–778, and H. Wang, A. S. Tsui, and K. R. Xin, "CEO Leadership Behaviors, Organizational Performance, and Employees' Attitudes," *The Leadership Quarterly* 22, no. 1 (2011), pp. 92–105.

54 See, for example, J. P. Wanous, *Organizational Entry*, 2nd ed. (New York: Addison Wesley, 1992); G. T. Chao, A. M. O'Leary-Kelly, S. Wolf, H. J. Klein, and P. D. Gardner, "Organizational Socialization: Its Content and Consequences," *Journal of Applied Psychology*, October 1994, pp. 730–743; B. E. Ashforth, A. M. Saks, and R. T. Lee, "Socialization and Newcomer Adjustment: The Role of Organizational Context," *Human Relations*, July 1998, pp. 897–926; D. A. Major, "Effective Newcomer Socialization into High-Performance Organizational Cultures," in *Handbook of Organizational Culture & Climate*, ed. N. M. Ashkanasy, C. P. M. Wilderom, and M. F. Peterson (Thousand Oaks, CA: Sage, 2000), pp. 355–368; and D. M. Cable and C. K. Parsons, "Socialization Tactics and Person-Organization Fit," *Personnel Psychology*, Spring 2001, pp. 1–23.

55 A. M. Saks and J. A. Gruman, "Organizational Socialization and Positive Organizational Behaviour: Implications for Theory, Research, and Practice," *Canadian Journal of Administrative Sciences* 28, no. 1 (2011), pp. 4–16.

56 J. Impoco, "Basic Training, Sanyo Style," *U.S. News & World Report*, July 13, 1992, pp. 46–48.

57 B. Filipczak, "Trained by Starbucks," *Training*, June 1995, pp. 73–79; and S. Gruner, "Lasting Impressions," *Inc.*, July 1998, p. 126.

58 "Canada's 10 Most Admired Corporate Cultures," *National Post*, February 3, 2014, p. JV3, http://www.waterstonehc.com/sites/default/files/news/files/CMACC-%20Feb%203,%202014.pdf.

59 "Building a Better Workforce," *PROFIT*, February 16, 2011, http://www.profitguide.com/manage-grow/human-resources/building-a-better-workforce-30073.

60 J. Van Maanen and E. H. Schein, "Career Development," in *Improving Life at Work*, ed. J. R. Hackman and J. L. Suttle (Santa Monica, CA: Goodyear, 1977), pp. 58–62.

61 Based on S. Dutton, "TELUS: A Pervasive Learning Culture," *Business to Community*, August 9, 2014, http://www.business2community.com/human-resources/telus-pervasive-learning-culture-keeps-employees-tuned-engaged-0967431#!bAwMv1; "Why TELUS: Career Development," *TELUS*, accessed August 20, 2014, http://about.telus.com/community/english/careers/why_telus/career_development; and "Why TELUS: Culture," *TELUS*, accessed August 20, 2014, http://about.telus.com/community/english/careers/why_telus/culture.

62 C. J. Collins, "The Interactive Effects of Recruitment Practices and Product Awareness on Job Seekers' Employer Knowledge and Application Behaviors," *Journal of Applied Psychology* 92, no. 1 (2007), pp. 180–190.

63 J. D. Kammeyer-Mueller and C. R. Wanberg, "Unwrapping the Organizational Entry Process: Disentangling Multiple Antecedents and Their Pathways to Adjustment," *Journal of Applied Psychology* 88 (2003), pp. 779–794; E. W. Morrison, "Longitudinal Study of the Effects of Information Seeking on Newcomer Socialization," *Journal of Applied Psychology* 78 (2003), pp. 173–183; and M. Wangm Y. Zhan, E. McCune, and D. Truxillo, "Understanding Newcomers' Adaptability and Work-Related Outcomes: Testing the Mediating Roles of Perceived P-E Fit Variables," *Personnel Psychology* 64, no. 1 (2011), pp. 163–189.

64 E. W. Morrison, "Newcomers' Relationships: The Role of Social Network Ties During Socialization," *Academy of Management Journal* 45 (2002), pp. 1149–1160.

65 A. M. Saks and J. A. Gruman, "Getting Newcomers Engaged: The Role of Socialization Tactics," *Journal of Managerial Psychology* 26 (2011), pp. 383–402.

66 "Canada's Best Brands 2014: Canadians Name Their Favourite Companies," *Canadian Business*, May 14, 2014, http://www.canadianbusiness.com/lists-and-rankings/best-brands/2014-introduction/.

67 T. N. Bauer, T. Bodner, B. Erdogan, D. M. Truxillo, and J. S. Tucker, "Newcomer Adjustment during Organizational Socialization: A Meta-analytic Review of Antecedents, Outcomes, and Methods," *Journal of Applied Psychology* 92, no. 3 (2007), pp. 707–721.

68 W. R. Boswell, A. J. Shipp, S. C., Payne, and S. S. Culbertson, "Changes in Newcomer Job Satisfaction Over Time: Examining the Pattern of Honeymoons and Hangovers," *Journal of Applied Psychology* 94, no. 4 (2009), pp. 844–858.

69 C. Vandenberghe, A. Panaccio, K. Bentein, K. Mignonac, and P. Roussel, "Assessing Longitudinal Change of and Dynamic Relationships Among Role Stressors, Job Attitudes, Turnover Intention, and Well-Being in Neophyte Newcomers," *Journal of Organizational Behavior* 32, no. 4 (2011), pp. 652–671.

70 J. E. Sheridan, "Organizational Culture and Employee Retention," *Academy of Management Journal*, December 1992, pp. 1036–1056.

71 J. Bandler and D. Burke, "How HP Lost Its Way," *Fortune*, May 21, 2012, pp. 147–164.

72 J. B. Sorensen, "The Strength of Corporate Culture and the Reliability of Firm Performance," *Administrative Science Quarterly*, March 2002, pp. 70–91.

73 See, for example, D. Miller, "What Happens after Success: The Perils of Excellence," *Journal of Management Studies*, May 1994, pp. 11–38.

74 See T. Cox Jr., *Cultural Diversity in Organizations: Theory, Research & Practice* (San Francisco: Berrett-Koehler, 1993), pp. 162–170; L. Grensing-Pophal, "Hiring to Fit Your Corporate Culture," *HR Magazine*, August 1999, pp. 50–54; and D. L. Stone, E. F. Stone-Romero, and K. M. Lukaszewski, "The Impact of Cultural Values on the Acceptance and Effectiveness of Human Resource Management Policies and Practices," *Human Resource Management Review* 17, no. 2 (2007), pp. 152–165.

75 S. Cartwright and C. L. Cooper, "The Role of Culture Compatibility in Successful Organizational Marriages," *Academy of Management Executive*, May 1993, pp. 57–70; R. A. Weber and C. F. Camerer, "Cultural Conflict and Merger Failure: An Experimental Approach," *Management Science*, April 2003, pp. 400–412; and I. H. Gleibs, A. Mummendey, and P. Noack, "Predictors of Change in Postmerger Identification During a Merger Process: A Longitudinal Study," *Journal of Personality and Social Psychology* 95, no. 5 (2008), pp. 1095–1112.

76 P. Gumbel, "Return of the Urge to Merge," *Time Europe Magazine*, July 13, 2003, http://www.time.com/time/europe/magazine/article/0,13005,901030721-464418,00.html.

77 P. Grainge, *Brand Hollywood: Selling Entertainment in a Global Media Age* (New York: Routledge), p. 130.

78 P. Grainge, *Brand Hollywood: Selling Entertainment in a Global Media Age* (New York: Routledge), p. 131.

79 K. W. Smith, "A Brand-New Culture for the Merged Firm," *Mergers and Acquisitions* 35, no. 6 (June 2000), pp. 45–50.

80 Vignette based on S. Fisher, "Stampede Tightens Race Rules," *Calgary Sun*, February 15, 2011, p. 10; and L. Storry, "Safety Rules Beefed Up for Calgary Stampede Events," *Calgary Herald*, February 24, 2011, http://www2.canada.com/calgaryherald/news/story.html?id=00227e33-899b-4ce8-8245-9eb5bccf27c3.

81 J. P. Kotter, "Leading Changes: Why Transformation Efforts Fail," *Harvard Business Review*, March–April 1995, pp. 59–67; and J. P. Kotter, *Leading Change* (Boston: Harvard Business School Press, 1996).

82 See B. Victor and J. B. Cullen, "The Organizational Bases of Ethical Work Climates," *Administrative Science Quarterly*, March 1988, pp. 101–125; R. L. Dufresne, "An Action Learning Perspective on Effective Implementation of Academic Honor Codes," *Group & Organization Management*, April 2004, pp. 201–218; and A. Ardichvili, J. A. Mitchell, and D. Jondle, "Characteristics of Ethical Business Cultures," *Journal of Business Ethics* 85, no. 4 (2009), pp. 445–451.

83 J. P. Mulki, J. F. Jaramillo, and W. B. Locander, "Critical Role of Leadership on Ethical Climate and Salesperson Behaviors," *Journal of Business Ethics* 86, no. 2 (2009), pp. 125–141; M. Schminke, M. L. Ambrose, and D. O. Neubaum, "The Effect of Leader Moral Development on Ethical Climate and Employee Attitudes," *Organizational Behavior and Human Decision Processes* 97, no. 2 (2005), pp. 135–151; and M. E. Brown, L. K. Treviño, and D. A. Harrison, "Ethical Leadership: A Social Learning Perspective for Construct Development and Testing," *Organizational Behavior and Human Decision Processes* 97, no. 2 (2005), pp. 117–134.

84 D. M. Mayer, M. Kuenzi, R. Greenbaum, M. Bardes, and S. Salvador, "How Low Does Ethical Leadership Flow? Test of a Trickle-Down Model," *Organizational Behavior and Human Decision Processes* 108, no. 1 (2009), pp. 1–13.

85 B. Sweeney, D. Arnold, and B. Pierce, "The Impact of Perceived Ethical Culture of the Firm and Demographic Variables on Auditors' Ethical Evaluation and Intention to Act Decisions," *Journal of Business Ethics* 93, no. 4 (2010), pp. 531–551.

86 M. L. Gruys, S. M. Stewart, J. Goodstein, M. N. Bing, and A. C. Wicks, "Values Enactment in Organizations: A Multi-Level Examination," *Journal of Management* 34, no. 4 (2008), pp. 806–843.

87 D. L. Nelson and C. L. Cooper, eds., *Positive Organizational Behavior* (London, UK: Sage, 2007); K. S. Cameron, J. E. Dutton, and R. E. Quinn, eds., *Positive Organizational Scholarship: Foundations of a New Discipline* (San Francisco: Berrett-Koehler, 2003); and F. Luthans and C. M. Youssef, "Emerging Positive Organizational Behavior," *Journal of Management*, June 2007, pp. 321–349.

88 J. Robison, "Great Leadership Under Fire," *Gallup Leadership Journal*, March 8, 2007, pp. 1–3.

89 R. Wagner and J. K. Harter, *12: The Elements of Great Managing* (New York: Gallup Press, 2006).

90 S. Fineman, "On Being Positive: Concerns and Counterpoints," *Academy of Management Review* 31, no. 2 (2006), pp. 270–291.

91 P. Dvorak, "A Firm's Culture Can Get Lost in Translation," *Wall Street Journal*, April 3, 2006, pp. B1, B3; K. Kranhold, "The Immelt Era, Five Years Old, Transforms GE," *Wall Street Journal*, September 11, 2006, pp. B1, B3; and S. McCartney, "Teaching Americans How to Behave Abroad," *Wall Street Journal*, April 11, 2006, pp. D1, D4.

92 D. J. McCarthy and S. M. Puffer, "Interpreting the Ethicality of Corporate Governance Decision in Russia: Utilizing Integrative Social Contracts Theory to Evaluate the Relevance of Agency Theory Norms," *Academy of Management Review* 33, no. 1 (2008), pp. 11–31.

93 Based on B. Azar, "Positive Psychology Advances, with Growing Pains," *Monitor on Psychology*, April 2011, pp. 32–36; A. Grant, "How Customers Can Rally Your Troops," *Harvard Business Review*, June 2011, http://hbr.org/2011/06/how-customers-can-rally-your-troops/ar/1; and J. McCarthy, "5 Big Problems with Positive Thinking (And Why You Should Do It Anyway)," *Positive Psychology*, October 5, 2010, http://psychologyofwellbeing.com/201010/5-big-problems-with-positive-thinking-and-why-you-should-do-it-anyway.html.

94 D. Carr, "At Debt-Ridden Tribune, a Culture Run Amok," *New York Times*, October 6, 2010, pp. A1, A22; E. Lee, "Tribune CEO Says Protest Over Koch Newspaper Sale Is Premature," *Bloomberg*, May 16, 2013, http://www.bloomberg.com/news/2013-05-15/tribune-ceo-says-furor-over-possible-newspaper-sale-is-premature.html; M. Oneal and P. Rosenthal, "Tribune Co. CEO Randy Michaels Resigns Amid Accusations of Crass Behavior," *Chicago Tribune*, October 22, 2010, http://articles.chicagotribune.com/2010-10-22/business/ct-biz-tribune-ceo-randy-michaels-resigns-oct22_1_randy-michaels-don-liebentritt-gerry-spector; P. Whoriskey, "Former Tribune, Times Mirror Executives, Editors Sue Shareholders," *Washington Post*, June 2, 2011, http://www.washingtonpost.com; and D. Lieberman, "Tribune Restructuring Will Slash 700 Newspaper-Related Jobs," *Deadline Hollywood*, November 20, 2013, http://deadline.com/2013/11/tribune-restructuring-will-slash-about-700-newspaper-related-jobs-640013/.

95 J. Jargon, "Neatness Counts at Kyocera and Others in the 5S Club," *Wall Street Journal*, October 27, 2008, pp. A1, A15; R. Gapp, R. Fisher, and K. Kobayashi, "Implementing 5S within a Japanese Context: An Integrated Management System," *Management Decision* 46, no. 4 (2008), pp. 565–579; and R. Hough, "5S Implementation Methodology," *Management Services* 52, no. 2 (2008), pp. 44–45.

96 Based on E. Byron, "A New Odd Couple: Google, P&G Swap Workers to Spur Innovation," *Wall Street Journal*, November 19, 2008, pp. A1, A18; A. G. Lafley, "P&G's Innovation Culture," *Strategy+Business*, August 28, 2008, pp. 1–7; and "P&G, Google Swap Workers for Research," *Silicon Valley/San Jose Business Journal*, November 20, 2008, http://www.bizjournals.com/sanjose/stories/2008/11/17/daily51.html?page=all.

97 Ideas in this feature were influenced by A. L. Wilkins, "The Culture Audit: A Tool for Understanding Organizations," *Organizational Dynamics*, Autumn 1983, pp. 24–38; H. M. Trice and J. M. Beyer, *The Cultures of Work Organizations* (Englewood Cliffs, NJ: Prentice Hall, 1993), pp. 358–362; H. Lancaster, "To Avoid a Job Failure, Learn the Culture of a Company First," *Wall Street Journal*, July 14, 1998, p. B1; and M. Belliveau, "4 Ways to Read a Company," *Fast Company*, October 1998, p. 158.

Chapter 11

1   Opening vignette based on P. Holdsworth and E. Riva-Guerra, "Young B.C. Chief Balances Major Development with Tradition," *CBC News*, April 23, 2014, http://www.cbc.ca/news/aboriginal/young-b-c-chief-balances-major-development-with-tradition-1.2618187; "Construction of Tsawwassen First Nation Mega Mall Begins," *CBC News*, January 24, 2014, http://www.cbc.ca/news/canada/british-columbia/construction-of-tsawwassen-first-nation-mega-malls-begins-1.2510438; and K. Hilderman, "Chief Bryce Williams, Tsawwassen First Nation," *BC Business*, July 2, 2013, http://www.bcbusiness.ca/people/chief-bryce-williams-tsawwassen-first-nation.

2   Vignette based on P. Holdsworth and E. Riva-Guerra, "Young B.C. Chief Balances Major Development with Tradition," *CBC News*, April 23, 2014, http://www.cbc.ca/news/aboriginal/young-b-c-chief-balances-major-development-with-tradition-1.2618187; and K. Hilderman, "Chief Bryce Williams, Tsawwassen First Nation," *BC Business*, July 2, 2013, http://www.bcbusiness.ca/people/chief-bryce-williams-tsawwassen-first-nation.

3   Based on D. Fost, "Survey Finds Many Workers Mistrust Bosses," *San Francisco Chronicle*, January 3, 2007, http://www.sfgate.com; and T. Weiss, "The Narcissistic CEO," *Forbes*, August 29, 2006, http://www.forbes.com.

4   C. C. Eckel, E. Fatas, and R. Wilson, "Cooperation and Status in Organizations," *Journal of Public Economic Theory* 12, no. 4 (2010), pp. 737–762.

5   J. G. Geier, "A Trait Approach to the Study of Leadership in Small Groups," *Journal of Communication*, December 1967, pp. 316–323.

6   S. A. Kirkpatrick and E. A. Locke, "Leadership: Do Traits Matter?" *Academy of Management Executive*, May 1991, pp. 48–60; and S. J. Zaccaro, R. J. Foti, and D. A. Kenny, "Self-Monitoring and Trait-Based Variance in Leadership: An Investigation of Leader Flexibility across Multiple Group Situations," *Journal of Applied Psychology*, April 1991, pp. 308–315.

7   See T. A. Judge, J. E. Bono, R. Ilies, and M. Werner, "Personality and Leadership: A Review" (paper presented at the 15th Annual Conference of the Society for Industrial and Organizational Psychology, New Orleans, 2000); and T. A. Judge, J. E. Bono, R. Ilies, and M. W. Gerhardt, "Personality and Leadership: A Qualitative and Quantitative Review," *Journal of Applied Psychology*, August 2002, pp. 765–780.

8   T. A. Judge, J. E. Bono, R. Ilies, and M. Werner, "Personality and Leadership: A Review" (paper presented at the 15th Annual Conference of the Society for Industrial and Organizational Psychology, New Orleans, 2000).

9   D. R. Ames and F. J. Flynn, "What Breaks a Leader: The Curvilinear Relation between Assertiveness and Leadership," *Journal of Personality and Social Psychology* 92, no. 2 (2007), pp. 307–324.

10 K. Ng, S. Ang, and K. Chan, "Personality and Leader Effectiveness: A Moderated Mediation Model of Leadership Self-Efficacy, Job Demands, and Job Autonomy," *Journal of Applied Psychology* 93, no. 4 (2008), pp. 733–743.

11 This section is based on D. Goleman, "What Makes a Leader?" *Harvard Business Review*, November–December 1998, pp. 93–102; J. M. George, "Emotions and Leadership: The Role of Emotional Intelligence," *Human Relations*, August 2000, pp. 1027–1055; C.-S. Wong and K. S. Law, "The Effects of Leader and Follower Emotional Intelligence on Performance and Attitude: An Exploratory Study," *Leadership Quarterly*, June 2002, pp. 243–274; and D. R. Caruso and C. J. Wolfe, "Emotional Intelligence and Leadership Development," in *Leader Development for Transforming Organizations: Growing Leaders for Tomorrow*, ed. D. David and S. J. Zaccaro (Mahwah, NJ: Lawrence Erlbaum, 2004), pp. 237–263.

12 R. H. Humphrey, J. M. Pollack, and T. H. Hawver, "Leading with Emotional Labor," *Journal of Managerial Psychology* 23 (2008), pp. 151–168.

13 F. Walter, M. S. Cole, and R. H. Humphrey, "Emotional Intelligence: Sine Qua Non of Leadership or Folderol?" *Academy of Management Perspectives*, February 2011, pp. 45–59.

14 S. Côté, P. N. Lopez, P. Salovey, and C. T. H. Miners, "Emotional Intelligence and Leadership Emergence in Small Groups," *Leadership Quarterly* 21 (2010), pp. 496–508.

15 T. A. Judge, J. E. Bono, R. Ilies, and M. Werner, "Personality and Leadership: A Review" (paper presented at the 15th Annual Conference of the Society for Industrial and Organizational Psychology, New Orleans, 2000); R. G. Lord, C. L. DeVader, and G. M. Alliger, "A Meta-analysis of the Relation between Personality Traits and Leadership Perceptions: An Application of Validity Generalization Procedures," *Journal of Applied Psychology*, August 1986, pp. 402–410; and J. A. Smith and R. J. Foti, "A Pattern Approach to the Study of Leader Emergence," *Leadership Quarterly*, Summer 1998, pp. 147–160.

16 R. M. Stogdill and A. E. Coons, eds., *Leader Behavior: Its Description and Measurement*, Research Monograph no. 88 (Columbus: Ohio State University, Bureau of Business Research, 1951). This research is updated in C. A. Schriesheim, C. C. Cogliser, and L. L. Neider, "Is It 'Trustworthy'? A Multiple-Levels-of-Analysis Reexamination of an Ohio State Leadership Study, with Implications for Future Research," *Leadership Quarterly*, Summer 1995, pp. 111–145; and T. A. Judge, R. F. Piccolo, and R. Ilies, "The Forgotten Ones? The Validity of Consideration and Initiating Structure in Leadership Research," *Journal of Applied Psychology*, February 2004, pp. 36–51.

17 R. M. Stogdill and A. E. Coons, eds., *Leader Behavior: Its Description and Measurement*, Research Monograph no. 88 (Columbus: Ohio State University, Bureau of Business Research, 1951), pp. 48, 154.

18 D. Akst, "The Rewards of Recognizing a Job Well Done," *Wall Street Journal*, January 31, 2007, p. D9.

19 R. Kahn and D. Katz, "Leadership Practices in Relation to Productivity and Morale," in *Group Dynamics: Research and Theory*, 2nd ed., ed. D. Cartwright and A. Zander (Elmsford, NY: Row, Paterson, 1960).

20 T. A. Judge, R. F. Piccolo, and R. Ilies, "The Forgotten Ones? The Validity of Consideration and Initiating Structure in Leadership Research," *Journal of Applied Psychology*, February 2004, pp. 36–51.

21 S. Derue, J. Nahrgang, N. Wellman, and S. Humphrey. "Trait and Behavioral Theories of Leadership: An Integration and Meta-analytic Test of their Relative Validity," *Personnel Psychology* 64 (2011), pp. 7–52.

22 F. E. Fiedler, *A Theory of Leadership Effectiveness* (New York: McGraw-Hill, 1967).

23 Cited in R. J. House and R. N. Aditya, "The Social Scientific Study of Leadership: Quo Vadis?" *Journal of Management* 23, no. 3 (1997), p. 422.

24 G. Johns and A. M. Saks, *Organizational Behaviour*, 5th ed. (Toronto: Pearson Education Canada, 2001), pp. 278–279.

25 L. H. Peters, D. D. Hartke, and J. T. Pohlmann, "Fiedler's Contingency Theory of Leadership: An Application of the Meta-Analysis Procedures of Schmidt and Hunter," *Psychological Bulletin*, March 1985, pp. 274–285; C. A. Schriesheim, B. J. Tepper, and L. A. Tetrault, "Least Preferred Coworker Score, Situational Control, and Leadership Effectiveness: A Meta-analysis of Contingency Model Performance Predictions," *Journal of Applied Psychology*, August 1994, pp. 561–573; and R. Ayman, M. M. Chemers, and F. Fiedler, "The Contingency Model of Leadership Effectiveness: Its Levels of Analysis," *Leadership Quarterly*, Summer 1995, pp. 147–167.

26 See, for example, R. W. Rice, "Psychometric Properties of the Esteem for the Least Preferred Coworker (LPC) Scale," *Academy of Management Review*, January 1978, pp. 106–118; C. A. Schriesheim, B. D. Bannister, and W. H. Money, "Psychometric Properties of the LPC Scale: An Extension of Rice's Review," *Academy of Management Review*, April 1979, pp. 287–290; and

J. K. Kennedy, J. M. Houston, M. A. Korgaard, and D. D. Gallo, "Construct Space of the Least Preferred Coworker (LPC) Scale," *Educational & Psychological Measurement*, Fall 1987, pp. 807–814.

27 See E. H. Schein, *Organizational Psychology*, 3rd ed. (Upper Saddle River, NJ: Prentice Hall, 1980), pp. 116–117; and B. Kabanoff, "A Critique of Leader Match and Its Implications for Leadership Research," *Personnel Psychology*, Winter 1981, pp. 749–764.

28 See, for example, C. F. Fernandez and R. P. Vecchio, "Situational Leadership Theory Revisited: A Test of an Across-Jobs Perspective," *Leadership Quarterly* 8, no. 1 (1997), pp. 67–84; C. L. Graeff, "Evolution of Situational Leadership Theory: A Critical Review," *Leadership Quarterly* 8, no. 2 (1997), pp. 153–170; and R. P. Vecchio and K. J. Boatwright, "Preferences for Idealized Styles of Supervision," *Leadership Quarterly*, August 2002, pp. 327–342.

29 M. G. Evans, "The Effects of Supervisory Behavior on the Path-Goal Relationship," *Organizational Behavior and Human Performance* 5 (1970), pp. 277–298; M. G. Evans, "Leadership and Motivation: A Core Concept," *Academy of Management Journal* 13 (1970), pp. 91–102; R. J. House, "A Path-Goal Theory of Leader Effectiveness," *Administrative Science Quarterly*, September 1971, pp. 321–338; R. J. House and T. R. Mitchell, "Path-Goal Theory of Leadership," *Journal of Contemporary Business*, Autumn 1974, p. 86; M. G. Evans, "Leadership," in *Organizational Behavior*, ed. S. Kerr (Columbus, OH: Grid Publishing, 1979); R. J. House, "Retrospective Comment," in *The Great Writings in Management and Organizational Behavior*, 2nd ed., ed. L. E. Boone and D. D. Bowen (New York: Random House, 1987), pp. 354–364; and M. G. Evans, "*Fuhrungstheorien, Weg-ziel-theorie,*" in *Handworterbuch Der Fuhrung*, 2nd ed., ed. A. Kieser, G. Reber, and R. Wunderer, trans. G. Reber (Stuttgart, Germany: Schaffer Poeschal Verlag, 1995), pp. 1075–1091.

30 G. R. Jones, J. M. George, C. W. L. Hill, and N. Langton, *Contemporary Management* (Toronto: McGraw-Hill Ryerson, 2002), p. 392.

31 J. C. Wofford and L. Z. Liska, "Path-Goal Theories of Leadership: A Meta-analysis," *Journal of Management* 19, no. 4 (1993), pp. 857–876.

32 P. M. Podsakoff, S. B. MacKenzie, and M. Ahearne, "Searching for a Needle in a Haystack: Trying to Identify the Illusive Moderators of Leadership Behaviors," *Journal of Management* 21 (1995), pp. 423–470.

33 A. E. Colbert and L. A. Witt, "The Role of Goal-Focused Leadership in Enabling the Expression of Conscientiousness," *Journal of Applied Psychology*, 94, no. 3 (2009), pp. 790–796.

34 S. J. Perry, L. A. Witt, L. M. Penney, and L. Atwater, "The Downside of Goal-Focused Leadership: The Role of Personality in Subordinate Exhaustion," *Journal of Applied Psychology* 95, no. 6 (2010), pp. 1145–1153.

35 T. Sy, "What Do You Think of Followers? Examining the Content, Structure, and Consequences of Implicit Followership Theories," *Organizational Behavior and Human Decision Processes* 113, no. 2 (2010), pp. 73–84.

36 S. Kerr and J. M. Jermier, "Substitutes for Leadership: Their Meaning and Measurement," *Organizational Behavior and Human Performance*, December 1978, pp. 375–403; J. P. Howell and P. W. Dorfman, "Substitutes for Leadership: Test of a Construct," *Academy of Management Journal*, December 1981, pp. 714–728; J. P. Howell, P. W. Dorfman, and S. Kerr, "Leadership and Substitutes for Leadership," *Journal of Applied Behavioral Science* 22, no. 1 (1986), pp. 29–46; J. P. Howell, D. E. Bowen, P. W. Dorfman, S. Kerr, and P. M. Podsakoff, "Substitutes for Leadership: Effective Alternatives to Ineffective Leadership," *Organizational Dynamics*, Summer 1990, pp. 21–38; P. M. Podsakoff, B. P. Niehoff, S. B. MacKenzie, and M. L. Williams, "Do Substitutes for Leadership Really Substitute for Leadership? An Empirical Examination of Kerr and Jermier's Situational Leadership Model," *Organizational*

Behavior and Human Decision Processes, February 1993, pp. 1–44; P. M. Podsakoff and S. B. MacKenzie, "An Examination of Substitutes for Leadership within a Levels-of-Analysis Framework," *Leadership Quarterly*, Fall 1995, pp. 289–328; P. M. Podsakoff, S. B. MacKenzie, and W. H. Bommer, "Transformational Leader Behaviors and Substitutes for Leadership as Determinants of Employee Satisfaction, Commitment, Trust, and Organizational Citizenship Behaviors," *Journal of Management* 22, no. 2 (1996), pp. 259–298; P. M. Podsakoff, S. B. MacKenzie, and W. H. Bommer, "Meta-analysis of the Relationships between Kerr and Jermier's Substitutes for Leadership and Employee Attitudes, Role Perceptions, and Performance," *Journal of Applied Psychology*, August 1996, pp. 380–399; and J. M. Jermier and S. Kerr, "'Substitutes for Leadership: Their Meaning and Measurement'—Contextual Recollections and Current Observations," *Leadership Quarterly* 8, no. 2 (1997), pp. 95–101.

37 S. D. Dionne, F. J. Yammarino, L. E. Atwater, and L. R. James, "Neutralizing Substitutes for Leadership Theory: Leadership Effects and Common-Source Bias," *Journal of Applied Psychology* 87 (2002), pp. 454–464; and J. R. Villa, J. P. Howell, P. W. Dorfman, and D. L. Daniel, "Problems with Detecting Moderators in Leadership Research Using Moderated Multiple Regression," *Leadership Quarterly* 14 (2002), pp. 3–23.

38 Vignette based on P. Holdsworth and E. Riva-Guerra, "Young B.C. Chief Balances Major Development with Tradition," *CBC News*, April 23, 2014, http://www.cbc.ca/news/aboriginal/young-b-c-chief-balances-major-development-with-tradition-1.2618187; and "Construction of Tsawwassen First Nation Mega Mall Begins," *CBC News*, January 24, 2014, http://www.cbc.ca/news/canada/british-columbia/construction-of-tsawwassen-first-nation-mega-malls-begins-1.2510438.

39 M. Weber, *The Theory of Social and Economic Organization*, trans. A. M. Henderson and T. Parsons (New York: The Free Press, 1947).

40 J. A. Conger and R. N. Kanungo, "Behavioral Dimensions of Charismatic Leadership," in *Charismatic Leadership*, ed. J. A. Conger and R. N. Kanungo (San Francisco: Jossey-Bass, 1988), p. 79; and A.-K. Samnani and P. Singh, "When Leaders Victimize: The Role of Charismatic Leaders in Facilitating Group Pressures," *Leadership Quarterly* 24, no. 1, February 2013, pp. 189–202.

41 J. A. Conger and R. N. Kanungo, *Charismatic Leadership in Organizations* (Thousand Oaks, CA: Sage, 1998); and R. Awamleh and W. L. Gardner, "Perceptions of Leader Charisma and Effectiveness: The Effects of Vision Content, Delivery, and Organizational Performance," *Leadership Quarterly*, Fall 1999, pp. 345–373.

42 R. Kark, B. Shamir, and G. Chen, "The Two Faces of Transformational Leadership: Empowerment and Dependency," *Journal of Applied Psychology* 88, no. 2 (2003), pp. 246–255.

43 D. N. Den Hartog, A. H. B. De Hoogh, and A. E. Keegan, "The Interactive Effects of Belongingness and Charisma on Helping and Compliance," *Journal of Applied Psychology* 92, no. 4 (2007), pp. 1131–1139.

44 A. Erez, V. F. Misangyi, D. E. Johnson, M. A. LePine, and K. C. Halverson, "Stirring the Hearts of Followers: Charismatic Leadership as the Transferal of Affect," *Journal of Applied Psychology* 93, no. 3 (2008), pp. 602–615. For reviews on the role of vision in leadership, see S. J. Zaccaro, "Visionary and Inspirational Models of Executive Leadership: Empirical Review and Evaluation," in *The Nature of Executive Leadership: A Conceptual and Empirical Analysis of Success*, ed. S. J. Zaccaro (Washington, DC: American Psychological Association, 2001), pp. 259–278; and M. Hauser and R. J. House, "Lead through Vision and Values," in *Handbook of Principles of Organizational Behavior*, ed. E. A. Locke (Malden, MA: Blackwell, 2004), pp. 257–273.

45 D. A. Waldman, B. M. Bass, and F. J. Yammarino, "Adding to Contingent-Reward Behavior: The Augmenting Effect of

Charismatic Leadership," *Group & Organization Studies*, December 1990, pp. 381–394; and S. A. Kirkpatrick and E. A. Locke, "Direct and Indirect Effects of Three Core Charismatic Leadership Components on Performance and Attitudes," *Journal of Applied Psychology*, February 1996, pp. 36–51.

46 A. H. B. de Hoogh, D. N. den Hartog, P. L. Koopman, H. Thierry, P. T. van den Berg, and J. G. van der Weide, "Charismatic Leadership, Environmental Dynamism, and Performance," *European Journal of Work & Organizational Psychology*, December 2004, pp. 447–471; S. Harvey, M. Martin, and D. Stout, "Instructor's Transformational Leadership: University Student Attitudes and Ratings," *Psychological Reports*, April 2003, pp. 395–402; and D. A. Waldman, M. Javidan, and P. Varella, "Charismatic Leadership at the Strategic Level: A New Application of Upper Echelons Theory," *Leadership Quarterly*, June 2004, pp. 355–380.

47 J. C. Pastor, M. Mayo, and B. Shamir, "Adding Fuel to Fire: The Impact of Followers' Arousal on Ratings of Charisma," *Journal of Applied Psychology* 92, no. 6 (2007), pp. 1584–1596.

48 A. H. B. De Hoogh and D. N. Den Hartog, "Neuroticism and Locus of Control as Moderators of the Relationships of Charismatic and Autocratic Leadership with Burnout," *Journal of Applied Psychology* 94, no. 4 (2009), pp. 1058–1067.

49 F. Cohen, S. Solomon, M. Maxfield, T. Pyszczynski, and J. Greenberg, "Fatal Attraction: The Effects of Mortality Salience on Evaluations of Charismatic, Task-Oriented, and Relationship-Oriented Leaders," *Psychological Science*, December 2004, pp. 846–851; and M. G. Ehrhart and K. J. Klein, "Predicting Followers' Preferences for Charismatic Leadership: The Influence of Follower Values and Personality," *Leadership Quarterly*, Summer 2001, pp. 153–179.

50 K. Levine, R. Muenchen, and A. Brooks, "Measuring Transformational and Charismatic Leadership: Why Isn't Charisma Measured?" *Communication Monographs* 77, no. 4 (2010), pp. 576–591.

51 J. A. Conger, *The Charismatic Leader: Behind the Mystique of Exceptional Leadership* (San Francisco: Jossey-Bass, 1989); R. Hogan, R. Raskin, and D. Fazzini, "The Dark Side of Charisma," in *Measures of Leadership*, ed. K. E. Clark and M. B. Clark (West Orange, NJ: Leadership Library of America, 1990); D. Sankowsky, "The Charismatic Leader as Narcissist: Understanding the Abuse of Power," *Organizational Dynamics*, Spring 1995, pp. 57–71; and J. O'Connor, M. D. Mumford, T. C. Clifton, T. L. Gessner, and M. S. Connelly, "Charismatic Leaders and Destructiveness: An Historiometric Study," *Leadership Quarterly*, Winter 1995, pp. 529–555.

52 G. Pitts, "Scandals Part of Natural Cycles of Excess," *Globe and Mail*, June 28, 2002, pp. B1, B5.

53 J. Collins, "Level 5 Leadership: The Triumph of Humility and Fierce Resolve," *Harvard Business Review*, January 2001, pp. 67–76; J. Collins, "Good to Great," *Fast Company*, October 2001, pp. 90–104; J. Collins, "The Misguided Mix-up," *Executive Excellence*, December 2002, pp. 3–4; and H. L. Tosi, V. F. Misangyi, A. Fanelli, D. A. Waldman, and F. J. Yammarino, "CEO Charisma, Compensation, and Firm Performance," *The Leadership Quarterly* 15 (2004), pp. 405–420.

54 See, for example, B. M. Bass, B. J. Avolio, D. I. Jung, and Y. Berson, "Predicting Unit Performance by Assessing Transformational and Transactional Leadership," *Journal of Applied Psychology*, April 2003, pp. 207–218; and T. A. Judge and R. F. Piccolo, "Transformational and Transactional Leadership: A Meta-analytic Test of Their Relative Validity," *Journal of Applied Psychology*, October 2004, pp. 755–768.

55 N.-W. Chi, Y.-Y. Chung, and W.-C. Tsai, "How Do Happy Leaders Enhance Team Success? The Mediating Roles of Transformational Leadership, Group Affective Tone, and Team Processes," *Journal of Applied Social Psychology* 41, no. 6 (2011), pp. 1421–1454.

56 A. M. Grant, "Leading with Meaning: Beneficiary Contact, Prosocial Impact, and the Performance Effects of Transformational Leadership," *Academy of Management Journal* 55 (2012), pp. 458–476.

57 B. M. Bass, "Leadership: Good, Better, Best," *Organizational Dynamics*, Winter 1985, pp. 26–40; and J. Seltzer and B. M. Bass, "Transformational Leadership: Beyond Initiation and Consideration," *Journal of Management*, December 1990, pp. 693–703.

58 T. R. Hinkin and C. A. Schriescheim, "An Examination of 'Nonleadership': From Laissez-Faire Leadership to Leader Reward Omission and Punishment Omission," *Journal of Applied Psychology* 93, no. 6 (2008), pp. 1234–1248.

59 S. J. Shin and J. Zhou, "Transformational Leadership, Conservation, and Creativity: Evidence from Korea," *Academy of Management Journal*, December 2003, pp. 703–714; V. J. García-Morales, F. J. Lloréns-Montes, and A. J. Verdú-Jover, "The Effects of Transformational Leadership on Organizational Performance Through Knowledge and Innovation," *British Journal of Management* 19, no. 4 (2008), pp. 299–313; and S. A. Eisenbeiss, D. van Knippenberg, and S. Boerner, "Transformational Leadership and Team Innovation: Integrating Team Climate Principles," *Journal of Applied Psychology* 93, no. 6 (2008), pp. 1438–1446.

60 Y. Ling, Z. Simsek, M. H. Lubatkin, and J. F. Veiga, "Transformational Leadership's Role in Promoting Corporate Entrepreneurship: Examining the CEO-TMT Interface," *Academy of Management Journal* 51, no. 3 (2008), pp. 557–576.

61 X. Zhang and K. M. Bartol, "Linking Empowering Leadership and Employee Creativity: The Influence of Psychological Empowerment, Intrinsic Motivation, and Creative Process Engagement," *Academy of Management Journal* 53, no. 1 (2010), pp. 107–128.

62 D. Liu, H. Liao, and R. Loi, "The Dark Side of Leadership: A Three-Level Investigation of the Cascading Effect of Abusive Supervision on Employee Creativity," *Academy of Management Journal* 55 (2012), pp. 1187–1212.

63 A. E. Colbert, A. E. Kristof-Brown, B. H. Bradley, and M. R. Barrick, "CEO Transformational Leadership: The Role of Goal Importance Congruence in Top Management Teams," *Academy of Management Journal* 51, no. 1 (2008), pp. 81–96.

64 D. Zohar and O. Tenne-Gazit, "Transformational Leadership and Group Interaction as Climate Antecedents: A Social Network Analysis," *Journal of Applied Psychology* 93, no. 4 (2008), pp. 744–757.

65 F. O. Walumbwa, B. J. Avolio, and W. Zhu, "How Transformational Leadership Weaves Its Influence on Individual Job Performance: The Role of Identification and Efficacy Beliefs," *Personnel Psychology* 61, no. 4 (2008), pp. 793–825.

66 J. E. Bono and T. A. Judge, "Self-Concordance at Work: Toward Understanding the Motivational Effects of Transformational Leaders," *Academy of Management Journal*, October 2003, pp. 554–571; Y. Berson and B. J. Avolio, "Transformational Leadership and the Dissemination of Organizational Goals: A Case Study of a Telecommunication Firm," *Leadership Quarterly*, October 2004, pp. 625–646; and J. Schaubroeck, S. S. K. Lam, and S. E. Cha, "Embracing Transformational Leadership: Team Values and the Impact of Leader Behavior on Team Performance," *Journal of Applied Psychology* 92, no. 4 (2007), pp. 1020–1030.

67 J. R. Baum, E. A. Locke, and S. A. Kirkpatrick, "A Longitudinal Study of the Relation of Vision and Vision Communication to Venture Growth in Entrepreneurial Firms," *Journal of Applied Psychology*, February 2000, pp. 43–54.

68 R. T. Keller, "Transformational Leadership, Initiating Structure, and Substitutes for Leadership: A Longitudinal Study of Research

and Development Project Team Performance," *Journal of Applied Psychology* 91, no. 1 (2006), pp. 202–210.

69 Y. Gong, J. Huang, and J. Farh, "Employee Learning Orientation, Transformational Leadership, and Employee Creativity: The Mediating Role of Employee Creative Self-Efficacy," *Academy of Management Journal* 52, no. 4 (2009), pp. 765–778.

70 G. Wang, I. Oh, S. H. Courtright, and A. E. Colbert, "Transformational Leadership and Performance across Criteria and Levels: A Meta-analytic Review of 25 Years of Research," *Group and Organization Management* 36, no. 2 (2011), pp. 223–270.

71 Y. Ling, Z. Simsek, M. H. Lubatkin, and J. F. Veiga, "The Impact of Transformational CEOs on the Performance of Small- to Medium-Sized Firms: Does Organizational Context Matter?" *Journal of Applied Psychology* 93, no. 4 (2008), pp. 923–934.

72 J. Schaubroeck, S. S. K. Lam, and S. E. Cha, "Embracing Transformational Leadership: Team Values and the Impact of Leader Behavior on Team Performance," *Journal of Applied Psychology* 92, no. 4 (2007), pp. 1020–1030.

73 S. Auh, B. Mengue, and Y. Jung, "Unpacking the Relationship between Empowering Leadership and Service-Oriented Citizenship Behaviors: a Multilevel Approach," *Journal of the Academy of Marketing Science* 42 (2014), pp. 558–579.

74 H. Hetland, G. M. Sandal, and T. B. Johnsen, "Burnout in the Information Technology Sector: Does Leadership Matter?" *European Journal of Work and Organizational Psychology* 16, no. 1 (2007), pp. 58–75; and K. B. Lowe, K. G. Kroeck, and N. Sivasubramaniam, "Effectiveness Correlates of Transformational and Transactional Leadership: A Meta-analytic Review of the MLQ Literature," *Leadership Quarterly*, Fall 1996, pp. 385–425.

75 See, for example, J. Barling, T. Weber, and E. K. Kelloway, "Effects of Transformational Leadership Training on Attitudinal and Financial Outcomes: A Field Experiment," *Journal of Applied Psychology*, December 1996, pp. 827–832; T. Dvir, D. Eden, and B. J. Avolio, "Impact of Transformational Leadership on Follower Development and Performance: A Field Experiment," *Academy of Management Journal*, August 2002, pp. 735–744; and R. A. Hassan, B. A. Fuwad, and A. I. Rauf, "Pre-Training Motivation and the Effectiveness of Transformational Leadership Training: An Experiment," *Academy of Strategic Management Journal* 9, no. 2 (2010), pp. 1–8.

76 R. J. House, M. Javidan, P. Hanges, and P. Dorfman, "Understanding Cultures and Implicit Leadership Theories Across the Globe: An Introduction to Project GLOBE," *Journal of World Business*, Spring 2002, pp. 3–10.

77 D. E. Carl and M. Javidan, "Universality of Charismatic Leadership: A Multi-Nation Study" (paper presented at the National Academy of Management Conference, Washington, DC, August 2001), p. 29.

78 Vignette based on P. Holdsworth and E. Riva-Guerra, "Young B.C. Chief Balances Major Development with Tradition," *CBC News*, April 23, 2014, http://www.cbc.ca/news/aboriginal/young-b-c-chief-balances-major-development-with-tradition-1.2618187; and K. Hilderman, "Chief Bryce Williams, Tsawwassen First Nation," *BC Business*, July 2, 2013, http://www.bcbusiness.ca/people/chief-bryce-williams-tsawwassen-first-nation.

79 D. Ancona, E. Backman, and H. Bresman, "X-Teams: New Ways of Leading in a New World," *Ivey Business Journal* 72, no. 3 (May–June 2008), http://iveybusinessjournal.com/topics/the-organization/x-teams-new-ways-of-leading-in-a-new-world#.VFla-yItCWg.

80 See, for example, L. J. Zachary, *The Mentor's Guide: Facilitating Effective Learning Relationships* (San Francisco: Jossey-Bass, 2000); M. Murray, *Beyond the Myths and Magic of Mentoring: How to Facilitate an Effective Mentoring Process*, rev. ed. (New York: Wiley, 2001); and F. Warner, "Inside Intel's Mentoring Movement," *Fast Company*, April 2002, pp. 116–120.

81 B. R. Ragins and J. L. Cotton, "Easier Said Than Done: Gender Differences in Perceived Barriers to Gaining a Mentor," *Academy of Management Journal* 34, no. 4 (1993), pp. 939–951; C. R. Wanberg, E. T. Welsh, and S. A. Hezlett, "Mentoring Research: A Review and Dynamic Process Model," in *Research in Personnel and Human Resources Management*, vol. 22, ed. G. R. Ferris and J. J. Martocchio (Greenwich, CT: Elsevier Science, 2003), pp. 39–124; and T. D. Allen, "Protégé Selection by Mentors: Contributing Individual and Organizational Factors," *Journal of Vocational Behavior* 65, no. 3 (2004), pp. 469–483.

82 T. D. Allen, M. L. Poteet, J. E. A. Russell, and G. H. Dobbins, "A Field Study of Factors Related to Supervisors' Willingness to Mentor Others," *Journal of Vocational Behavior* 50, no. 1 (1997), pp. 1–22; S. Aryee, Y. W. Chay, and J. Chew, "The Motivation to Mentor among Managerial Employees in the Maintenance Career Stage: An Interactionist Perspective," *Group and Organization Management* 21, no. 3 (1996), pp. 261–277; L. T. Eby, A. L. Lockwood, and M. Butts, "Perceived Support for Mentoring: A Multiple Perspectives Approach," *Journal of Vocational Behavior* 68, no. 2 (2006), pp. 267–291; and T. D. Allen, E. Lentz, and R. Day, "Career Success Outcomes Associated with Mentoring Others: A Comparison of Mentors and Nonmentors," *Journal of Career Development* 32, no. 3 (2006), pp. 272–285.

83 See, for example, D. A. Thomas, "The Impact of Race on Managers' Experiences of Developmental Relationships: An Intra-Organizational Study," *Journal of Organizational Behavior*, November 1990, pp. 479–492; K. E. Kram and D. T. Hall, "Mentoring in a Context of Diversity and Turbulence," in *Managing Diversity*, ed. E. E. Kossek and S. A. Lobel (Cambridge, MA: Blackwell, 1996), pp. 108–36; M. N. Ruderman and M. W. Hughes-James, "Leadership Development across Race and Gender," in *The Center for Creative Leadership Handbook of Leadership Development*, ed. C. D. McCauley, R. S. Moxley, and E. Van Velsor (San Francisco: Jossey-Bass, 1998), pp. 291–335; and B. R. Ragins and J. L. Cotton, "Mentor Functions and Outcomes: A Comparison of Men and Women in Formal and Informal Mentoring Relationships," *Journal of Applied Psychology*, August 1999, pp. 529–550.

84 J. U. Chun, J. J. Sosik, and N. Y. Yun, "A Longitudinal Study of Mentor and Protégé Outcomes in Formal Mentoring Relationships," *Journal of Organizational Behavior*, November 12, 2012, pp. 35–49.

85 B. R. Ragins and J. L. Cotton, "Mentor Functions and Outcomes: A Comparison of Men and Women in Formal and Informal Mentoring Relationships," *Journal of Applied Psychology*, August 1999, pp. 529–550; and C. M. Underhill, "The Effectiveness of Mentoring Programs in Corporate Settings: A Meta-analytical Review of the Literature," *Journal of Vocational Behavior* 68, no. 2 (2006), pp. 292–307.

86 T. D. Allen, E. T. Eby, and E. Lentz, "The Relationship between Formal Mentoring Program Characteristics and Perceived Program Effectiveness," *Personnel Psychology* 59 (2006), pp. 125–153; T. D. Allen, L. T. Eby, and E. Lentz, "Mentorship Behaviors and Mentorship Quality Associated with Formal Mentoring Programs: Closing the Gap between Research and Practice," *Journal of Applied Psychology* 91, no. 3 (2006), pp. 567–578; and M. R. Parise and M. L. Forret, "Formal Mentoring Programs: The Relationship of Program Design and Support to Mentors' Perceptions of Benefits and Costs," *Journal of Vocational Behavior* 72, no. 2 (2008), pp. 225–240.

87 L. T. Eby and A. Lockwood, "Protégés' and Mentors' Reactions to Participating in Formal Mentoring Programs: A Qualitative Investigation," *Journal of Vocational Behavior* 67, no. 3 (2005), pp. 441–458; G. T. Chao, "Formal Mentoring: Lessons Learned from Past Practice," *Professional Psychology: Research and Practice* 40, no. 3 (2009), pp. 314–320; and C. R. Wanberg, J. D. Kammeyer-Mueller, and M. Marchese, "Mentor and Protégé Predictors and

Outcomes of Mentoring in a Formal Mentoring Program," *Journal of Vocational Behavior* 69 (2006), pp. 410–423.

88 M. K. Feeney and B. Bozeman, "Mentoring and Network Ties," *Human Relations* 61, no. 12 (2008), pp. 1651–1676; N. Bozionelos, "Intra-Organizational Network Resources: How They Relate to Career Success and Organizational Commitment," *Personnel Review* 37, no. 3 (2008), pp. 249–263; and S. A. Hezlett and S. K. Gibson, "Linking Mentoring and Social Capital: Implications for Career and Organization Development," *Advances in Developing Human Resources* 9, no. 3 (2007), pp. 384–412.

89 C. C. Manz and H. P. Sims Jr., *The New SuperLeadership: Leading Others to Lead Themselves* (San Francisco: Berrett-Koehler Publishers, 2001).

90 J. Kelly and S. Nadler, "Leading from Below," *Wall Street Journal*, March 3, 2007, pp. R4, R10.

91 A. Bandura, "Self-Reinforcement: Theoretical and Methodological Considerations," *Behaviorism* 4 (1976), pp. 135–155; P. W. Corrigan, C. J. Wallace, and M. L. Schade, "Learning Medication Self-Management Skills in Schizophrenia; Relationships with Cognitive Deficits and Psychiatric Symptom," *Behavior Therapy*, Winter 1994, pp. 5–15; A. S. Bellack, "A Comparison of Self-Reinforcement and Self-Monitoring in a Weight Reduction Program," *Behavior Therapy* 7 (1976), pp. 68–75; T. A. Eckman, W. C. Wirshing, and S. R. Marder, "Technique for Training Schizophrenic Patients in Illness Self-Management: A Controlled Trial," *American Journal of Psychiatry* 149 (1992), pp. 1549–1555; J. J. Felixbrod and K. D. O'Leary, "Effect of Reinforcement on Children's Academic Behavior as a Function of Self-Determined and Externally Imposed Contingencies," *Journal of Applied Behavior Analysis* 6 (1973), pp. 141–150; A. J. Litrownik, L. R. Franzini, and D. Skenderian, "The Effects of Locus of Reinforcement Control on a Concept Identification Task," *Psychological Reports* 39 (1976), pp. 159–165; P. D. McGorry, "Psychoeducation in First-Episode Psychosis: A Therapeutic Process," *Psychiatry*, November 1995, pp. 313–328; G. S. Parcel, P. R. Swank, and M. J. Mariotto, "Self-Management of Cystic Fibrosis: A Structural Model for Educational and Behavioral Variables," *Social Science and Medicine* 38 (1994), pp. 1307–1315; and G. E. Speidel, "Motivating Effect of Contingent Self-Reward," *Journal of Experimental Psychology* 102 (1974), pp. 528–530.

92 D. B. Jeffrey, "A Comparison of the Effects of External Control and Self-Control on the Modification and Maintenance of Weight," *Journal of Abnormal Psychology* 83 (1974), pp. 404–410.

93 C. C. Manz and H. P. Sims Jr., *The New SuperLeadership: Leading Others to Lead Themselves* (San Francisco: Berrett-Koehler, 2001).

94 See, for example, J. H. Zenger, E. Musselwhite, K. Hurson, and C. Perrin, *Leading Teams: Mastering the New Role* (Homewood, IL: Business One Irwin, 1994); and M. Frohman, "Nothing Kills Teams Like Ill-Prepared Leaders," *IndustryWeek*, October 2, 1995, pp. 72–76.

95 See, for example, M. Frohman, "Nothing Kills Teams Like Ill-Prepared Leaders," *IndustryWeek*, October 2, 1995, p. 93.

96 See, for example, M. Frohman, "Nothing Kills Teams Like Ill-Prepared Leaders," *IndustryWeek*, October 2, 1995, p. 100.

97 J. R. Katzenbach and D. K. Smith, *The Wisdom of Teams: Creating the High-Performance Organization* (Boston: Harvard Business School Press, 1993).

98 N. Steckler and N. Fondas, "Building Team Leader Effectiveness: A Diagnostic Tool," *Organizational Dynamics*, Winter 1995, p. 20.

99 R. S. Wellins, W. C. Byham, and G. R. Dixon, *Inside Teams* (San Francisco: Jossey-Bass, 1994), p. 318.

100 N. Steckler and N. Fondas, "Building Team Leader Effectiveness: A Diagnostic Tool," *Organizational Dynamics*, Winter 1995, p. 21.

101 L. A. Hambley, T. A. O'Neill, and T. J. B. Kline, "Virtual Team Leadership: The Effects of Leadership Style and Communication Medium on Team Interaction Styles and Outcomes," *Organizational Behavior and Human Decision Processes* 103 (2007), pp. 1–20; and B. J. Avolio and S. S. Kahai, "Adding the 'E' to E-Leadership: How It May Impact Your Leadership," *Organizational Dynamics* 31, no. 4 (2003), pp. 325–338.

102 S. J. Zaccaro and P. Bader, "E-Leadership and the Challenges of Leading E-Teams: Minimizing the Bad and Maximizing the Good," *Organizational Dynamics* 31, no. 4 (2003), pp. 381–385.

103 C. E. Naquin and G. D. Paulson, "Online Bargaining and Interpersonal Trust," *Journal of Applied Psychology*, February 2003, pp. 113–120.

104 R. M. Kanter, *The Change Masters, Innovation and Entrepreneurship in the American Corporation* (New York: Simon and Schuster, 1983).

105 R. A. Heifetz, *Leadership without Easy Answers* (Cambridge, MA: Harvard University Press, 1996), p. 205.

106 R. A. Heifetz, *Leadership without Easy Answers* (Cambridge, MA: Harvard University Press, 1996), p. 205.

107 R. A. Heifetz, *Leadership without Easy Answers* (Cambridge, MA: Harvard University Press, 1996), p. 188.

108 Vignette based on P. Holdsworth and E. Riva-Guerra, "Young B.C. Chief Balances Major Development with Tradition," *CBC News*, April 23, 2014, http://www.cbc.ca/news/aboriginal/young-b-c-chief-balances-major-development-with-tradition-1.2618187.

109 See B. J. Avolio, W. L. Gardner, F. O. Walumbwa, F. Luthans, and D. R. May, "Unlocking the Mask: A Look at the Process by Which Authentic Leaders Impact Follower Attitudes and Behaviors," *Leadership Quarterly*, December 2004, pp. 801–823; W. L. Gardner and J. R. Schermerhorn Jr., "Performance Gains Through Positive Organizational Behavior and Authentic Leadership," *Organizational Dynamics*, August 2004, pp. 270–281; and M. M. Novicevic, M. G. Harvey, M. R. Buckley, J. A. Brown-Radford, and R. Evans, "Authentic Leadership: A Historical Perspective," *Journal of Leadership and Organizational Behavior* 13, no. 1 (2006), pp. 64–76.

110 "Expect to Make a Difference, Be an Authentic Leader and Have Integrity," *York University*, October 22, 2014, http://yfile .news.yorku.ca/2014/10/22/expect-to-make-a-difference-be-an-authentic-leader-have-integrity/.

111 K. M. Hmieleski, M. S. Cole, and R. A. Baron, "Shared Authentic Leadership and New Venture Performance," *Journal of Management*, September 2012, pp. 1476–1499.

112 R. Ilies, F. P. Morgeson, and J. D. Nahrgang, "Authentic Leadership and Eudaemonic Wellbeing: Understanding Leader-Follower Outcomes," *Leadership Quarterly* 16 (2005), pp. 373–394.

113 This section is based on E. P. Hollander, "Ethical Challenges in the Leader–Follower Relationship," *Business Ethics Quarterly*, January 1995, pp. 55–65; J. C. Rost, "Leadership: A Discussion About Ethics," *Business Ethics Quarterly*, January 1995, pp. 129–142; L. K. Treviño, M. Brown, and L. P. Hartman, "A Qualitative Investigation of Perceived Executive Ethical Leadership: Perceptions from Inside and Outside the Executive Suite," *Human Relations*, January 2003, pp. 5–37; and R. M. Fulmer, "The Challenge of Ethical Leadership," *Organizational Dynamics* 33, no. 3 (2004), pp. 307–317.

114 J. Stouten, M. van Dijke, and D. De Cremer, "Ethical Leadership: An Overview and Future Perspectives," *Journal of Personnel Psychology* 11 (2012), pp. 1–6.

115 J. M. Schaubroeck, S. T. Hannah, B. J. Avolio, S. W. J. Kozlowski, et al., "Embedding Ethical Leadership within and across Organization Levels," *Academy of Management Journal* 55 (2012), pp. 1053–1078.

116 D. van Knippenberg, D. De Cremer, and B. van Knippenberg, "Leadership and Fairness: The State of the Art," *European Journal of Work and Organizational Psychology* 16, no. 2 (2007), pp. 113–140.

117 B. P. Owens and D. R. Hekman, "Modeling How to Grow: An Inductive Examination of Humble Leader Behaviors, Contingencies, and Outcomes," *Academy of Management Journal* 55 (2012), pp. 787–818.

118 K. M. Kacmar, D. G. Bachrach, K. J. Harris, and S. Zivnuska, "Fostering Good Citizenship through Ethical Leadership: Exploring the Moderating Role of Gender and Organizational Politics," *Journal of Applied Psychology* 96, no. 3 (May 2011), pp. 633–642; and F. O. Walumbwa and J. Schaubroeck, "Leader Personality Traits and Employee Voice Behavior: Mediating Roles of Ethical Leadership and Work Group Psychological Safety," *Journal of Applied Psychology* 94, no. 5 (2009), pp. 1275–1286.

119 D. M. Mayer, K. Aquino, R. L. Greenbaum, and M. Kuenzi, "Who Displays Ethical Leadership, and Why Does It Matter? An Examination of Antecedents and Consequences of Ethical Leadership," *Academy of Management Journal* 55 (2012), pp. 151–171.

120 S. A. Eisenbeiss and S. R. Giessner, "The Emergence and Maintenance of Ethical Leadership in Organizations," *Journal of Personnel Psychology* 11 (2012), pp. 7–19.

121 M. E. Brown and L. K. Treviño, "Socialized Charismatic Leadership, Values Congruence, and Deviance in Work Groups," *Journal of Applied Psychology* 91, no. 4 (2006), pp. 954–962.

122 M. E. Brown and L. K. Treviño, "Leader-Follower Values Congruence: Are Socialized Charismatic Leaders Better Able to Achieve It?" *Journal of Applied Psychology* 94, no. 2 (2009), pp. 478–490.

123 J. G. Clawson, *Level Three Leadership* (Upper Saddle River, NJ: Prentice Hall, 1999), pp. 46–49.

124 D. van Dierendonck, "Servant Leadership: A Review and Synthesis," *Journal of Management* 37, no. 4 (2011), pp. 1228–1261.

125 S. J. Peterson, F. M. Galvin, and D. Lange, "CEO Servant Leadership: Exploring Executive Characteristics and Firm Performance," *Personnel Psychology* 65 (2012), pp. 565–596.

126 F. Walumbwa, C. A. Hartnell, and A. Oke, "Servant Leadership, Procedural Justice Climate, Service Climate, Employee Attitudes, and Organizational Citizenship Behavior: A Cross-Level Investigation," *Journal of Applied Psychology* 95, no. 3 (2010), pp. 517–529.

127 D. De Cremer, D. M. Mayer, M. van Dijke, B. C. Schouten, and M. Bardes, "When Does Self-Sacrificial Leadership Motivate Prosocial Behavior? It Depends on Followers' Prevention Focus," *Journal of Applied Psychology* 2009, no. 4 (2009), pp. 887–899.

128 J. Hu and R. C. Liden, "Antecedents of Team Potency and Team Effectiveness: An Examination of Goal and Process Clarity and Servant Leadership," *Journal of Applied Psychology*, 96, no. 4 (July 2011), pp. 851–862.

129 M. J. Neubert, K. M. Kacmar, D. S. Carlson, L. B. Chonko, and J. A. Roberts, "Regulatory Focus as a Mediator of the Influence of Initiating Structure and Servant Leadership on Employee Behavior," *Journal of Applied Psychology* 93, no. 6 (2008), pp. 1220–1233.

130 M. Javidan, P. W. Dorfman, M. S. de Luque, and R. J. House, "In the Eye of the Beholder: Cross Cultural Lessons in Leadership from Project GLOBE," *Academy of Management Perspectives*, February 2006, pp. 67–90.

131 D. E. Carl and M. Javidan, "Universality of Charismatic Leadership: A Multi-Nation Study" (paper presented at the National Academy of Management Conference, Washington, DC, August 2001), p. 29; and R. J. House, M. Javidan, P. Hanges, and P. Dorfman, "Understanding Cultures and Implicit Leadership Theories across the Globe: An Introduction to Project GLOBE," *Journal of World Business*, Spring 2002, pp. 3–10.

132 N. Beccalli, "European Business Forum Asks: Do Companies Get the Leaders They Deserve?" *European Business Forum*, 2003, http://

www.pwcglobal.com/extweb/pwcpublications.nsf/DocID/D1EC3 380F589844585256D7300346A1B.

133 Based on Z. E. Franco, K. Blau, and P. G. Zimbardo, "Heroism: A Conceptual Analysis and Differentiation Between Heroic Action and Altruism," *Review of General Psychology* 15, no. 2 (2011), pp. 99–113; O. Dorell, "At Nuke Plant, Heroes Emerge," *USA Today*, March 25, 2011, pp. 1A, 2A; G. R. Goethals and S. C. Allison, "Making Heroes: The Construction of Courage, Competence, and Virtue," *Advances in Experimental Psychology* 46 (2012), pp. 183–235; L. J. Walker, J. A. Frimer, and W. L. Dunlop, "Varieties of Moral Personality: Beyond the Banality of Heroism," *Journal of Personality* 78, no. 3 (2010), pp. 907–942; and J. Lehrer, "Are Heroes Born, or Can They Be Made?" *Wall Street Journal*, December 11, 2010, p. C12.

134 This exercise is based on J. M. Howell and P. J. Frost, "A Laboratory Study of Charismatic Leadership," *Organizational Behavior and Human Decision Processes*, April 1989, pp. 243–269.

135 Based on episodes of *Undercover Boss Canada*; K. Kern, "The Fakery of CEOs Undercover," *Bloomberg Businessweek*, February 15, 2010, pp. 78–79. K. Jones, "CEOs Go Undercover Over Workplace Safety," SafetyAtWorkBlog, February 5, 2011, http://safetyatworkblog.wordpress.com/; and D. Kaplan, "'Undercover Boss' a Life-Changing Experience for Sporting Goods Mogul Mitchell Modell," March 1, 2013, http://www.nydailynews.com/entertainment/tv-movies/undercover-boss-life-changer-modell-ceo-article-1.1276376.

136 Based on D. Koeppel, "A Tough Transition: Friend to Supervisor," *New York Times*, March 16, 2003, p. BU-12.

137 Based on M. Buckingham, "Leadership Development in the Age of the Algorithm," *Harvard Business Review*, June 2012, pp. 86–94; M. D. Watkins, "How Managers Become Leaders," *Harvard Business Review*, June 2012, pp. 64–72; and J. M. Podolny, "A Conversation with James G. March on Learning About Leadership," *Academy of Management Learning & Education* 10 (2011), pp. 502–506.

138 Based on J. M. Howell and P. J. Frost, "A Laboratory Study of Charismatic Leadership," *Organizational Behavior and Human Decision Processes*, April 1989, pp. 243–269.

139 Based on V. H. Vroom, "A New Look at Managerial Decision Making," *Organizational Dynamics*, Spring 1973, pp. 66–80. With permission.

Chapter 12

1 Opening vignette based on Manitoba Human Rights Commission, Adjudicated Decision between Billy-Joe Nachuk and Brandon Police Services, April 30, 2014, http://www.manitobahumanrights.ca/publications/legal/decision_nachuk.html.

2 See H. A. Simon, "Rationality in Psychology and Economics," *Journal of Business*, October 1986, pp. 209–224; and A. Langley, "In Search of Rationality: The Purposes Behind the Use of Formal Analysis in Organizations," *Administrative Science Quarterly*, December 1989, pp. 598–631.

3 For a review of the rational decision-making model, see E. F. Harrison, *The Managerial Decision Making Process*, 5th ed. (Boston: Houghton Mifflin, 1999), pp. 75–102.

4 CIBC, "Donations and Sponsorship Funding Guidelines," accessed November 7, 2014, https://www.cibc.com/ca/inside-cibc/community-matters/funding-guidelines.html.

5 J. G. March, *A Primer on Decision Making* (New York: The Free Press, 2009); and D. Hardman and C. Harries, "How Rational Are We?" *Psychologist*, February 2002, pp. 76–79.

6 Vignette based on Manitoba Human Rights Commission, Adjudicated Decision between Billy-Joe Nachuk and Brandon Police Services, April 30, 2014, http://www.manitobahumanrights.ca/publications/legal/decision_nachuk.html.

7   M. H. Bazerman and D. A. Moore, *Judgment in Managerial Decision Making*, 7th ed. (Hoboken, NJ: Wiley, 2008).

8   J. E. Russo, K. A. Carlson, and M. G. Meloy, "Choosing an Inferior Alternative," *Psychological Science* 17, no. 10 (2006), pp. 899–904.

9   See, for example, L. R. Beach, *The Psychology of Decision Making* (Thousand Oaks, CA: Sage, 1997).

10 D. Kahneman, "Maps of Bounded Rationality: Psychology for Behavioral Economics," *The American Economic Review* 93, no. 5 (2003), pp. 1449–1475; and J. Zhang, C. K. Hsee, and Z. Xiao, "The Majority Rule in Individual Decision Making," *Organizational Behavior and Human Decision Processes* 99 (2006), pp. 102–111.

11 See H. A. Simon, *Administrative Behavior*, 4th ed. (New York: The Free Press, 1997); and M. Augier, "Simon Says: Bounded Rationality Matters," *Journal of Management Inquiry*, September 2001, pp. 268–275.

12 G. Gigerenzer, "Why Heuristics Work," *Perspectives on Psychological Science* 3, no. 1 (2008), pp. 20–29; and A. K. Shah and D. M. Oppenheimer, "Heuristics Made Easy: An Effort-Reduction Framework," *Psychological Bulletin* 134, no. 2 (2008), pp. 207–222.

13 See T. Gilovich, D. Griffin, and D. Kahneman, *Heuristics and Biases: The Psychology of Intuitive Judgment* (New York: Cambridge University Press, 2002).

14 E. Dane and M. G. Pratt, "Exploring Intuition and Its Role in Managerial Decision Making," *Academy of Management Review* 32, no. 1 (2007), pp. 33–54.

15 Based on P. D. Brown, "Some Hunches About Intuition," *New York Times*, November 17, 2007, p. B5.

16 Based on D. Delaney, C. Guilding, and L. McManus, "The Use of Intuition in the Sponsorship Decision Making Process," *Contemporary Management Research* 10, no. 1 (2014), pp. 33–60.

17 B. D. Dunn and H. C. Galton, "Listening to Your Heart: How Interoception Shapes Emotion Experience and Intuitive Decision Making," *Psychological Science* 21, no. 12 (December 2010), pp. 1835–1844.

18 C. Akinci and E. Sadler-Smith, "Intuition in Management Research: A Historical Review," *International Journal of Management Reviews* 14 (2012), pp. 104–122.

19 S. P. Robbins, *Decide & Conquer: Making Winning Decisions and Taking Control of Your Life* (Upper Saddle River, NJ: Financial Times/Prentice Hall, 2004), p. 13.

20 Based on P. Cohen, "Stand Still: Use Penalty-Kick Wisdom to Make Your Decisions," *National Post*, March 8, 2008, p. FW9.

21 S. Ludwig and J. Nafziger, "Beliefs about Overconfidence," *Theory and Decision*, April 2011, pp. 475–500.

22 S. Plous, *The Psychology of Judgment and Decision Making* (New York: McGraw-Hill, 1993), p. 217.

23 C. R. M. McKenzie, M. J. Liersch, and I. Yaniv, "Overconfidence in Interval Estimates: What Does Expertise Buy You," *Organizational Behavior and Human Decision Processes* 107 (2008), pp. 179–191.

24 J. Kruger and D. Dunning, "Unskilled and Unaware of It: How Difficulties in Recognizing One's Own Incompetence Lead to Inflated Self-Assessments," *Journal of Personality and Social Psychology*, November 1999, pp. 1121–1134.

25 K. M. Hmieleski and R. A. Baron, "Entrepreneurs' Optimism and New Venture Performance: A Social Cognitive Perspective," *Academy of Management Journal* 52, no. 3 (2009), pp. 473–488.

26 J. Kruger and D. Dunning, "Unskilled and Unaware of It: How Difficulties in Recognizing One's Own Incompetence Lead to Inflated Self-Assessments," *Journal of Personality and Social Psychology*, November 1999, pp. 1121–1134.

27 See, for example, A. Tversky and D. Kahneman, "Judgment under Uncertainty: Heuristics and Biases," *Science*, September 1974, pp. 1124–1131.

28 J. S. Hammond, R. L. Keeney, and H. Raiffa, *Smart Choices* (Boston: HBS Press, 1999), p. 191.

29 R. Hastie, D. A. Schkade, and J. W. Payne, "Juror Judgments in Civil Cases: Effects of Plaintiff's Requests and Plaintiff's Identity on Punitive Damage Awards," *Law and Human Behavior*, August 1999, pp. 445–470.

30 C. Janiszewski and D. Uy, "Precision of the Anchor Influences the Amount of Adjustment," *Psychological Science* 19, no. 2 (2008), pp. 121–127.

31 See R. S. Nickerson, "Confirmation Bias: A Ubiquitous Phenomenon in Many Guises," *Review of General Psychology*, June 1998, pp. 175–220; and E. Jonas, S. Schultz-Hardt, D. Frey, and N. Thelen, "Confirmation Bias in Sequential Information Search after Preliminary Decisions," *Journal of Personality and Social Psychology*, April 2001, pp. 557–571.

32 B. Nyhan and J. Reifler, "When Corrections Fail: The Persistence of Political Misperceptions," *Political Behavior* 32, no. 2 (2010), pp. 303–330.

33 See A. Tversky and D. Kahneman, "Availability: A Heuristic for Judging Frequency and Probability," in *Judgment under Uncertainty: Heuristics and Biases*, ed. D. Kahneman, P. Slovic, and A. Tversky (Cambridge, UK: Cambridge University Press, 1982), pp. 163–178; and B. J. Bushman and G. L. Wells, "Narrative Impressions of Literature: The Availability Bias and the Corrective Properties of Meta-analytic Approaches," *Personality and Social Psychology Bulletin*, September 2001, pp. 1123–1130.

34 T. Pachur, R. Hertwig, and F. Steinmann, "How Do People Judge Risks: Availability Heuristic, Affect Heuristic, or Both?" *Journal of Experimental Psychology: Applied* 18 (2012), pp. 314–330; and A. Tversky and D. Kahneman, "Availability: A Heuristic for Judging Frequency and Probability," in *Judgment Under Uncertainty: Heuristics and Biases*, ed. D. Kahneman, P. Slovic, and A. Tversky (Cambridge, UK: Cambridge University Press, 1982), pp. 163–178.

35 See B. M. Staw, "The Escalation of Commitment to a Course of Action," *Academy of Management Review*, October 1981, pp. 577–587; and H. Moon, "Looking Forward and Looking Back: Integrating Completion and Sunk-Cost Effects within an Escalation-of-Commitment Progress Decision," *Journal of Applied Psychology*, February 2001, pp. 104–113.

36 T. Schultze, F. Pfeiffer, and S. Schulz-Hardt, "Biased Information Processing in the Escalation Paradigm: Information Search and Information Evaluation as Potential Mediators of Escalating Commitment," *Journal of Applied Psychology* 97 (2012), pp. 16–32.

37 D. J. Sleesman, D. E. Conlon, G. McNamara, and J. E. Miles, "Cleaning Up the Big Muddy: A Meta-analytic Review of the Determinants of Escalation of Commitment," *Academy of Management Journal* 55 (2012), pp. 541–562.

38 See, for example, A. James and A. Wells, "Death Beliefs, Superstitious Beliefs and Health Anxiety," *British Journal of Clinical Psychology*, March 2002, pp. 43–53.

39 K. Gillespie, "Canadian Athletes' Superstitious Ways," *Toronto Star*, January 24, 2014.

40 See, for example, D. J. Keys and B. Schwartz, "Leaky Rationality: How Research on Behavioral Decision Making Challenges Normative Standards of Rationality," *Psychological Science* 2, no. 2 (2007), pp. 162–180; and U. Simonsohn, "Direct Risk Aversion: Evidence from Risky Prospects Valued Below Their Worst Outcome," *Psychological Science* 20, no. 6 (2009), pp. 686–692.

41 J. K. Maner, M. T. Gailliot, D. A. Butz, and B. M. Peruche, "Power, Risk, and the Status Quo: Does Power Promote Riskier or More Conservative Decision Making," *Personality and Social Psychology Bulletin* 33, no. 4 (2007), pp. 451–462.

42 A. Chakraborty, S. Sheikh, and N. Subramanian, "Termination Risk and Managerial Risk Taking," *Journal of Corporate Finance* 13, (2007), pp. 170–188.

43 D. Kahneman and A. Tversky, "Prospect Theory: An Analysis of Decisions under Risk," *Econometrica* 47, no. 2 (1979), pp. 263–291; and P. Bryant and R. Dunford, "The Influence of Regulatory Focus on Risky Decision-Making," *Applied Psychology: An International Review* 57, no. 2 (2008), pp. 335–359.

44 A. J. Porcelli and M. R. Delgado, "Acute Stress Modulates Risk Taking in Financial Decision Making," *Psychological Science* 20, no. 3 (2009), pp. 278–283.

45 R. L. Guilbault, F. B. Bryant, J. H. Brockway, and E. J. Posavac, "A Meta-analysis of Research on Hindsight Bias," *Basic and Applied Social Psychology*, September 2004, pp. 103–117; and L. Werth, F. Strack, and J. Foerster, "Certainty and Uncertainty: The Two Faces of the Hindsight Bias," *Organizational Behavior and Human Decision Processes*, March 2002, pp. 323–341.

46 M. Gladwell, "Connecting the Dots," *New Yorker*, March 10, 2003.

47 S. P. Robbins, *Decide & Conquer: Making Winning Decisions and Taking Control of Your Life* (Upper Saddle River, NJ: Financial Times/Prentice Hall, 2004), pp. 164–168.

48 See N. R. F. Maier, "Assets and Liabilities in Group Problem Solving: The Need for an Integrative Function," *Psychological Review*, April 1967, pp. 239–249; G. W. Hill, "Group versus Individual Performance: Are N+1 Heads Better Than One?" *Psychological Bulletin*, May 1982, pp. 517–539; M. D. Johnson and J. R. Hollenbeck, "Collective Wisdom as an Oxymoron: Team-Based Structures as Impediments to Learning," in *Research Companion to the Dysfunctional Workplace: Management, Challenges and Symptoms*, ed. J. Langan-Fox, C. L. Cooper, and R. J. Klimoski (Northampton, MA: Edward Elgar Publishing, 2007), pp. 319–331; and R. F. Martell and M. R. Borg, "A Comparison of the Behavioral Rating Accuracy of Groups and Individuals," *Journal of Applied Psychology*, February 1993, pp. 43–50.

49 See, for example, W. C. Swap and Associates, *Group Decision Making* (Newbury Park, CA: Sage, 1984).

50 "Group Judgments," *Psychological Bulletin*, January 1997, pp. 149–167; and B. L. Bonner, S. D. Sillito, and M. R. Baumann, "Collective Estimation: Accuracy, Expertise, and Extroversion as Sources of Intra-Group Influence," *Organizational Behavior and Human Decision Processes* 103 (2007), pp. 121–133.

51 See, for example, W. C. Swap and Associates, *Group Decision Making* (Newbury Park, CA: Sage, 1984).

52 I. L. Janis, *Groupthink: Psychological Studies of Policy Decisions and Fiascoes*, 2nd ed. (Boston: Houghton Mifflin, 1982); W. Park, "A Review of Research on Groupthink," *Journal of Behavioral Decision Making*, July 1990, pp. 229–245; C. P. Neck and G. Moorhead, "Groupthink Remodeled: The Importance of Leadership, Time Pressure, and Methodical Decision Making Procedures," *Human Relations*, May 1995, pp. 537–558; and J. N. Choi and M. U. Kim, "The Organizational Application of Groupthink and Its Limits in Organizations," *Journal of Applied Psychology*, April 1999, pp. 297–306.

53 From Janis. Groupthink, 2E. © 1982 Wadsworth, a part of Cengage Learning, Inc.

54 Based on L. Nguyen, "Target Corp. Regrets Opening So Many Stores So Quickly in Canada," *Canadian Press*, August 20, 2014, http://www.ctvnews.ca/business/target-corp-regrets-opening-so-many-stores-so-quickly-in-canada-1.1967662; M. Healy, "Same-Store Sales at Target Canada Tumble 11% in Second Quarter," *CBC News*, August 20, 2014, http://www.cbc.ca/news/business/same-store-sales-at-target-canada-tumble-11-in-second-quarter-1.2741617; "Why Was Target Canada Such a Disaster?" *Abbotsford Today*, May 26, 2014, http://www.abbotsfordtoday.ca/why-was-target-canada-such-a-disaster/; and P. Evans, "Target Closes All 133 Stores in Canada, Gets Creditor Protection," *CBC News*, January 15, 2015.

55 G. Park and R. P. DeShon, "A Multilevel Model of Minority Opinion Expression and Team Decision-Making Effectiveness," *Journal of Applied Psychology* 95, no. 5 (2010), pp. 824–833.

56 M. E. Turner and A. R. Pratkanis, "Mitigating Groupthink by Stimulating Constructive Conflict," in *Using Conflict in Organizations*, ed. C. De Dreu and E. Van de Vliert (London: Sage, 1997), pp. 53–71.

57 J. A. Goncalo, E. Polman, and C. Maslach, "Can Confidence Come Too Soon? Collective Efficacy, Conflict, and Group Performance over Time," *Organizational Behavior and Human Decision Processes* 113, no. 1 (2010), pp. 13–24.

58 See N. R. F. Maier, *Principles of Human Relations* (New York: Wiley, 1952); N. Richardson Ahlfinger and J. K. Esser, "Testing the Groupthink Model: Effects of Promotional Leadership and Conformity Predisposition," *Social Behavior & Personality* 29, no. 1 (2001), pp. 31–41; and S. Schultz-Hardt, F. C. Brodbeck, A. Mojzisch, R. Kerschreiter, and D. Frey, "Group Decision Making in Hidden Profile Situations: Dissent as a Facilitator for Decision Quality," *Journal of Personality and Social Psychology* 91, no. 6 (2006), pp. 1080–1093.

59 J. N. Choi and M. U. Kim, "The Organizational Application of Groupthink and Its Limitations in Organizations," *Journal of Applied Psychology* 84 (1999), pp. 297–306.

60 J. Longley and D. G. Pruitt, "Groupthink: A Critique of Janis' Theory," in *Review of Personality and Social Psychology*, ed. L. Wheeler (Newbury Park, CA: Sage, 1980), pp. 507–513; and J. A. Sniezek, "Groups under Uncertainty: An Examination of Confidence in Group Decision Making," *Organizational Behavior & Human Decision Processes* 52, 1992, pp. 124–155.

61 C. McCauley, "The Nature of Social Influence in Groupthink: Compliance and Internalization," *Journal of Personality and Social Psychology* 57 (1989), pp. 250–260; P. E. Tetlock, R. S. Peterson, C. McGuire, S. Chang, and P. Feld, "Assessing Political Group Dynamics: A Test of the Groupthink Model," *Journal of Personality and Social Psychology* 63 (1992), pp. 781–796; S. Graham, "A Review of Attribution Theory in Achievement Contexts," *Educational Psychology Review* 3 (1991), pp. 5–39; and G. Moorhead and J. R. Montanari, "An Empirical Investigation of the Groupthink Phenomenon," *Human Relations* 39 (1986), pp. 399–410.

62 J. N. Choi and M. U. Kim, "The Organizational Application of Groupthink and Its Limitations in Organizations," *Journal of Applied Psychology* 84 (1999), pp. 297–306.

63 See D. J. Isenberg, "Group Polarization: A Critical Review and Meta-analysis," *Journal of Personality and Social Psychology*, December 1986, pp. 1141–1151; J. L. Hale and F. J. Boster, "Comparing Effect Coded Models of Choice Shifts," *Communication Research Reports*, April 1988, pp. 180–186; and P. W. Paese, M. Bieser, and M. E. Tubbs, "Framing Effects and Choice Shifts in Group Decision Making," *Organizational Behavior & Human Decision Processes*, October 1993, pp. 149–165.

64 R. D. Clark III, "Group-Induced Shift toward Risk: A Critical Appraisal," *Psychological Bulletin*, October 1971, pp. 251–270.

65 Z. Krizan and R. S. Baron, "Group Polarization and Choice-Dilemmas: How Important Is Self-Categorization?" *European Journal of Social Psychology* 37, no. 1 (2007), pp. 191–201.

66 N. W. Kohn and S. M. Smith, "Collaborative Fixation: Effects of Others' Ideas on Brainstorming," *Applied Cognitive Psychology* 25, no. 3 (May/June 2011), pp. 359–371.

67 N. L. Kerr and R. S. Tindale, "Group Performance and Decision-Making," *Annual Review of Psychology* 55 (2004), pp. 623–655.

68 N. W. Kohn and S. M. Smith, "Collaborative Fixation: Effects of Others' Ideas on Brainstorming," *Applied Cognitive Psychology* 25, no. 3 (May/June 2011), pp. 359–371; and S. M. Smith, "The Constraining Effects of Initial Ideas," in *Group Creativity*, ed. P. B. Paulus and B. A. Nijstad (New York: Oxford University Press, 2003), pp. 15–31.

69 R. C. Litchfield, "Brainstorming Reconsidered: A Goal-Based View," *Academy of Management Review* 33, no. 3 (2008), pp. 649–668.

70 See A. L. Delbecq, A. H. Van deVen, and D. H. Gustafson, *Group Techniques for Program Planning: A Guide to Nominal and Delphi Processes* (Glenview, IL: Scott, Foresman, 1975); and P. B. Paulus and H.-C. Yang, "Idea Generation in Groups: A Basis for Creativity in Organizations," *Organizational Behavior and Human Decision Processing*, May 2000, pp. 76–87.

71 C. Faure, "Beyond Brainstorming: Effects of Different Group Procedures on Selection of Ideas and Satisfaction with the Process," *Journal of Creative Behavior* 38 (2004), pp. 13–34.

72 T. M. Amabile, "A Model of Creativity and Innovation in Organizations," in *Research in Organizational Behavior*, vol. 10, ed. B. M. Staw and L. L. Cummings (Greenwich, CT: JAI Press, 1988), p. 126; and J. E. Perry-Smith and C. E. Shalley, "The Social Side of Creativity: A Static and Dynamic Social Network Perspective," *Academy of Management Review*, January 2003, pp. 89–106.

73 B. Brazier, "Brendan Brazier on Holistic Nutrition," *Ask Men*, n.d., http://ca.askmen.com/sports/foodcourt/brendan-brazier-on-holistic-nutrition.html; and "Is Your Art Killing You?" *InvestorIdeas.com*, May 13, 2013, http://www.investorideas.com/news/2013/renewable-energy/05134.asp.

74 G. Anderson, "Three Tips to Foster Creativity at Your Startup," *ArcticStartup*, May 8, 2013, http://www.arcticstartup.com/2013/05/08/three-tips-to-foster-creativity-at-your-startup.

75 E. Millar, "How Do Finnish Kids Excel without Rote Learning and Standardized Testing?" *Globe and Mail*, May 9, 2013, http://www.theglobeandmail.com/report-on-business/economy/canada-competes/how-do-finnish-kids-excel-without-rote-learning-and-standardized-testing/article11810188/.

76 Z. Harper, "Mark Cuban Wants You to Design the New Dallas Mavericks Uniforms," CBSSports.com, May 13, 2013, http://www.cbssports.com/nba/eye-on-basketball/22230801/mark-cuban-wants-you-to-design-the-new-dallas-mavericks-uniforms.

77 C. K. W. De Dreu, B. A. Nijstad, M. Baas, I. Wolsink, and M. Roskes, "Working Memory Benefits Creative Insight, Musical Improvisation, and Original Ideation Through Maintained Task-Focused Attention," *Personality and Social Psychology Bulletin* 38 (2012), pp. 656–669.

78 S. M. Wechsler, C. Vendramini, and T. Oakland, "Thinking and Creative Styles: A Validity Study," *Creativity Research Journal* 24 (April 2012), pp. 235–242.

79 Y. Gong, S. Cheung, M. Wang, and J. Huang, "Unfolding the Proactive Processes for Creativity: Integration of the Employee Proactivity, Information Exchange, and Psychological Safety Perspectives," *Journal of Management* 38 (2012), pp. 1611–1633.

80 S. N. de Jesus, C. L. Rus, W. Lens, and S. Imaginário, "Intrinsic Motivation and Creativity Related to Product: A Meta-Analysis of the Studies Published Between 1990–2010," *Creativity Research Journal* 25 (2013), pp. 80–84.

81 L. Sun, Z. Zhang, J. Qi, and Z. X. Chen, "Empowerment and Creativity: A Cross-Level Investigation," *Leadership Quarterly* 23 (2012), pp. 55–65.

82 D. Liu, H. Liao, and R. Loi, "The Dark Side of Leadership: A Three-Level Investigation of the Cascading Effect of Abusive Supervision on Employee Creativity," *Academy of Management Journal* 55 (2012), pp. 1187–1212.

83 J. B. Avey, F. L. Richmond, and D. R. Nixon, "Leader Positivity and Follower Creativity: An Experimental Analysis," *Journal of Creative Behavior* 46 (2012), pp. 99–118; and A. Rego, F. Sousa, C. Marques, M. E. Cunha, "Authentic Leadership Promoting Employees' Psychological Capital and Creativity," *Journal of Business Research* 65 (2012), pp. 429–437.

84 I. J. Hoever, D. van Knippenberg, W. P. van Ginkel, and H. G. Barkema, "Fostering Team Creativity: Perspective Taking as Key to Unlocking Diversity's Potential," *Journal of Applied Psychology* 97 (2012), pp. 982–996.

85 S. J. Shin, T. Kim, J. Lee, and L. Bian, "Cognitive Team Diversity and Individual Team Member Creativity: A Cross-Level Interaction," *Academy of Management Journal* 55 (2012), pp. 197–212.

86 A. W. Richter, G. Hirst, D. van Knippenberg, and M. Baer, "Creative Self-Efficacy and Individual Creativity in Team Contexts: Cross-Level Interactions with Team Informational Resources," *Journal of Applied Psychology* 97 (2012), pp. 1282–1290.

87 J. S. Mueller, S. Melwani, and J. A. Goncalo, "The Bias against Creativity: Why People Desire but Reject Creative Ideas," *Psychological Science* 23 (2012), pp. 13–17.

88 T. Montag, C. P. Maertz, and M. Baer, "A Critical Analysis of the Workplace Creativity Criterion Space," *Journal of Management* 38 (2012), pp. 1362–1386.

89 M. Baer, "Putting Creativity to Work: The Implementation of Creative Ideas in Organizations," *Academy of Management Journal* 55 (2012), pp. 1102–1119.

90 A. Somech and A. Drach-Zahavy, "Translating Team Creativity to Innovation Implementation: The Role of Team Composition and Climate for Innovation," *Journal of Management* 39 (2013), pp. 684–708.

91 Vignette based on Manitoba Human Rights Commission, Adjudicated Decision between Billy-Joe Nachuk and Brandon Police Services, April 30, 2014, http://www.manitobahumanrights.ca/publications/legal/decision_nachuk.html.

92 P. L. Schumann, "A Moral Principles Framework for Human Resource Management Ethics," *Human Resource Management Review* 11 (Spring–Summer 2001), pp. 93–111; M. G. Velasquez, *Business Ethics*, 4th ed. (Upper Saddle River, NJ: Prentice Hall, 1998), Chapter 2; and G. F. Cavanagh, D. J. Moberg, and M. Valasquez, "The Ethics of Organizational Politics," *Academy of Management Journal*, June 1981, pp. 363–374.

93 P. L. Schumann, "A Moral Principles Framework for Human Resource Management Ethics," *Human Resource Management Review* 11 (Spring–Summer 2001), pp. 93–111.

94 B. Reuber, "Toronto Restaurant Balances Social Mission with Economic Return," *Globe and Mail*, October 17, 2014, http://www.theglobeandmail.com/report-on-business/small-business/sb-growth/sustainability/toronto-restaurant-balances-social-mission-with-economic-return/article21125089/.

95 Based on R. A. Bernardi, C. A. Banzhoff, A. M. Martino, and K. J. Savasta, "Challenges to Academic Integrity: Identifying the Factors Associated with the Cheating Chain," *Accounting Education* 21 (2012), pp. 247–263; M. K. Galloway, "Cheating in Advantaged High Schools: Prevalence, Justifications, and Possibilities for Change," *Ethics & Behavior* 22 (2012), pp. 378–399; and M. H. Bazerman and A. E. Tenbrunsel, *Blind Spots: Why We Fail to Do What's Right and What to Do about It* (Princeton, NJ: Princeton University Press, 2012).

96 L. L. Shu and F. Gino, "Sweeping Dishonesty Under the Rug: How Unethical Actions Lead to Forgetting of Moral Rules," *Journal of Personality and Social Psychology* 102 (2012), pp. 1164–1177.

97 B. C. Gunia, L. Wang, L. Huang, J. Wang, and J. K. Murnighan, "Contemplation and Conversation: Subtle Influences on Moral Decision Making," *Academy of Management Journal* 55 (2012), pp. 13–33.

98 R. F. West, R. J. Meserve, and K. E. Stanovich, "Cognitive Sophistication Does Not Attenuate the Bias Blind Spot," *Journal of Personality and Social Psychology* 103 (2012), pp. 506–519.

99 T. Jackson, "Cultural Values and Management Ethics: A 10-Nation Study," *Human Relations*, October 2001, pp. 1267–1302; see also J. B. Cullen, K. P. Parboteeah, and M. Hoegl, "Cross-National Differences in Managers' Willingness to Justify Ethically Suspect Behaviors: A Test of Institutional Anomie Theory," *Academy of Management Journal*, June 2004, pp. 411–421.

100 J. Sisler, "Joe Fresh Continuing Garment Business in Bangladesh in Year After Tragedy," *CBC.ca*, April 10, 2014, http://www.cbc.ca/news/world/joe-fresh-continuing-garment-business-in-bangladesh-in-year-after-tragedy-1.2606120.

101 This discussion is based on G. F. Cavanagh, D. J. Moberg, and M. Valasquez, "The Ethics of Organizational Politics," *Academy of Management Journal*, June 1981, pp. 363–374.

102 Vignette based on "Lac Mégantic: TSB Finds Company Had Weak Safety Culture," *CBC.ca*, August 19, 2014, http://www.cbc.ca/news/canada/montreal/lac-m%C3%A9gantic-tsb-finds-company-had-weak-safety-culture-1.2739921; and I. Peritz, "Lac-Mégantic Deaths Were Avoidable, Coroner's Report Says," *Globe and Mail*, October 8, 2014, http://www.theglobeandmail.com/news/national/lac-megantic-deaths-were-avoidable-coroners-report-says/article20982746/.

103 J. Castaldo, "Those Emotional Canadians!" *Canadian Business*, May 10, 2010, pp. 32–33.

104 M. McClearn, "Brands We Trust: On a First-Name Basis," *Canadian Business*, April 7, 2011.

105 M. Friedman, *Capitalism and Freedom* (Chicago: University of Chicago Press, 1962).

106 J. Bakan, *The Corporation* (Toronto: Big Picture Media Corporation, 2003).

107 J. Nelson, "The CEO Poll: Should Companies Give to Charity?" *Canadian Business*, April 7, 2011.

108 J. Castaldo, "The CEO Poll: The Trouble with Outsourcing," *Canadian Business*, April 7, 2011.

109 Net Impact, "Survey Shows MBA Students Believe Business Should Be Agent of Social Change," *Greenbiz.com*, October 25, 2006, http://www.greenbiz.com/news/2006/10/25/survey-shows-mba-students-believe-business-should-be-agent-social-change.

110 M. J. Gelfand, M. Erez, and Z. Aycan, "Cross-Cultural Organizational Behavior," *Annual Review of Psychology*, January 2007, pp. 479–514; and A. S. Tsui, S. S. Nifadkar, and A. Y. Ou, "Cross-National, Cross-Cultural Organizational Behavior Research: Advances, Gaps, and Recommendations," *Journal of Management*, June 2007, pp. 426–478.

111 N. J. Adler, *International Dimensions of Organizational Behavior*, 4th ed. (Cincinnati, OH: South-Western Publishing, 2002), pp. 182–189.

112 T. Rinne, D. G. Steel, and J. Fairweather, "The Role of Hofstede's Individualism in National-Level Creativity," *Creativity Research Journal* 25 (2013), pp. 129–136.

113 X. Yi, W. Hu, H. Scheithauer, and W. Niu, "Cultural and Bilingual Influences on Artistic Creativity Performances: Comparison of German and Chinese Students," *Creativity Research Journal* 25 (2013), pp. 97–108.

114 T. Jackson, "Cultural Values and Management Ethics: A 10-Nation Study," *Human Relations*, October 2001, pp. 1267–1302; see also J. B. Cullen, K. P. Parboteeah, and M. Hoegl, "Cross-National Differences in Managers' Willingness to Justify Ethically Suspect Behaviors: A Test of Institutional Anomie Theory," *Academy of Management Journal*, June 2004, pp. 411–421.

115 W. Chow Hou, "To Bribe or Not to Bribe?" *Asia, Inc.*, October 1996, p. 104.

116 P. Digh, "Shades of Gray in the Global Marketplace," *HR Magazine*, April 1997, p. 91.

117 T. Donaldson, "Values in Tension: Ethics Away from Home," *Harvard Business Review*, September–October 1996, pp. 48–62.

118 Transparency International, *Annual Report 2011* (Berlin, Germany: Author, 2012), http://www.transparency.org/content/download/61106/978536.

119 Based on S. Cain, "The Rise of the New Groupthink," *New York Times*, January 15, 2012, pp. 1, 6; and C. Faure, "Beyond Brainstorming: Effects of Different Group Procedures on Selection of Ideas and Satisfaction with the Process," *Journal of Creative Behavior* 38 (2004), pp. 13–34.

120 Several of these scenarios are based on D. R. Altany, "Torn between Halo and Horns," *IndustryWeek*, March 15, 1993, pp. 15–20.

121 Based on J. Mulkerrins, "All Spanx to Sara," *Daily Mail*, April 6, 2013, http://www.dailymail.co.uk/home/you/article-2303499/Meet-Spanx-creator-Sarah-Blakely.html; C. O'Connor, "American Booty," *Forbes*, March 26, 2012, pp. 172–178; and R. Tulshyan, "Spanx's Sara Blakely: Turning $5,000 into $1 Billion with Panties," *CNN.com*, December 5, 2012, http://edition.cnn.com/2012/12/04/business/sara-blakely-spanx-underwear/.

122 Based on J. Calano and J. Salzman, "Ten Ways to Fire Up Your Creativity," *Working Woman*, July 1989, p. 94; J. V. Anderson, "Mind Mapping: A Tool for Creative Thinking," *Business Horizons*, January–February 1993, pp. 42–46; M. Loeb, "Ten Commandments for Managing Creative People," *Fortune*, January 16, 1995, pp. 135–136; and M. Henricks, "Good Thinking," *Entrepreneur*, May 1996, pp. 70–73.

OB on the Edge: Spirituality in the Workplace

1 Vignette based on W. Immen, "Meditation Finds an Ommm in the Office," *Globe and Mail*, November 27, 2012, http://www.theglobeandmail.com/report-on-business/small-business/sb-managing/human-resources/meditation-finds-an-ommm-in-the-office/article5684202/.

2 Rice University, "More Than 20 Percent of Atheist Scientists Are 'Spiritual,' Study Finds," *ScienceDaily*, May 5, 2011, http://www.sciencedaily.com/releases/2011/05/110505124039.htm; and E. H. Ecklund and E. Long, "Scientists and Spirituality," *Sociology of Religion* 72, no. 3 (2011), pp. 253–274.

3 D. P. Ashmos and D. Duchon, "Spirituality at Work: A Conceptualization and Measure," *Journal of Management Inquiry*, June 2000, p. 139; and E. Poole, "Organisational Spirituality: A Literature Review," *Journal of Business Ethics* 84, no. 4 (2009), pp. 577–588.

4 L. W. Fry and J. W. Slocum, "Managing the Triple Bottom Line through Spiritual Leadership," *Organizational Dynamics* 37, no. 1 (2008), pp. 86–96.

5 B. E. Ashforth and M. G. Pratt, "Institutionalized Spirituality: An Oxymoron?" in *Handbook of Workplace Spirituality and Organizational Performance*, ed. R. A. Giacalone and C. L. Jurkiewicz (Armonk, NY: M. E. Sharpe, 2010), pp. 44–58; and A. M. Saks, "Workplace Spirituality and Employee Engagement," *Journal of Management, Spirituality & Religion* 8, no. 4 (2011), pp. 317–340.

6 V. Ligo, "Configuring a Christian Spirituality of Work," *Theology Today*, 2011, pp. 441–466.

7 A. Beard, "Mindfulness in the Age of Complexity," *Harvard Business Review*, March 2014, pp. 68–73, https://hbr.org/2014/03/mindfulness-in-the-age-of-complexity.

8 A. Beard, "Mindfulness in the Age of Complexity," *Harvard Business Review*, March 2014, pp. 68–73, https://hbr.org/2014/03/mindfulness-in-the-age-of-complexity.

9 A. Beard, "Mindfulness in the Age of Complexity," *Harvard Business Review*, March 2014, pp. 68–73, https://hbr.org/2014/03/mindfulness-in-the-age-of-complexity.

10 A. Beard, "Mindfulness in the Age of Complexity," *Harvard Business Review*, March 2014, pp. 68–73, https://hbr.org/2014/03/mindfulness-in-the-age-of-complexity.

11 W. Immen, "Meditation Finds an Ommm in the Office," *Globe and Mail*, November 27, 2012, http://www.theglobeandmail.com/report-on-business/small-business/sb-managing/

human-resources/meditation-finds-an-ommm-in-the-office/article5684202/.

12 L. S. Colzato, A. Szapora, D. Lippelt, and B. Hommel, "Prior Meditation Practice Modulates Performance and Strategy Use in Convergent- and Divergent-Thinking Problems," *Mindfulness*, October 2014.

13 J. D. Creswell, L. E. Pacilio, E. K. Lindsay, K. W. Brown, "Brief Mindfulness Meditation Training Alters Psychological and Neuroendocrine Responses to Social Evaluative Stress," *Psychoneuroendocrinology* 44 (June 2014), pp. 1–12.

14 A. C. Hafenbrack, Z. Kinias, S. G. Barsade, "Debiasing the Mind through Meditation: Mindfulness and the Sunk-Cost Bias," *Psychological Science* 25, no. 2 (2013), pp. 369–376.

15 W. Immen, "Meditation Finds an Ommm in the Office," *Globe and Mail*, November 27, 2012, http://www.theglobeandmail.com/report-on-business/small-business/sb-managing/human-resources/meditation-finds-an-ommm-in-the-office/article5684202/.

16 M. Gonzalez, *Mindful Leadership: The 9 Ways to Self-Awareness, Transforming Yourself, and Inspiring Others* (Mississauga: John Wiley and Sons, 2012).

17 W. Immen, "Meditation Finds an Ommm in the Office," *Globe and Mail*, November 27, 2012, http://www.theglobeandmail.com/report-on-business/small-business/sb-managing/human-resources/meditation-finds-an-ommm-in-the-office/article5684202/.

18 W. Duggleby, D. Cooper, and K. Penz, "Hope, Self-Efficacy, Spiritual Well-Being and Job Satisfaction," *Journal of Advanced Nursing* 65, no. 11 (November 2009), pp. 2376–2385.

19 Information based on "About Us," *Vancouver Island Health Authority*, accessed November 27, 2014, http://www.viha.ca/spiritual_care/about/.

20 L. W. Fry, L. L. Matherly, and J.-R. Ouimet, "The Spiritual Leadership Balanced Scorecard Business Model: The Case of the Cordon Bleu-Tomasso Corporation," *Journal of Management, Spirituality & Religion* 7, no. 4 (2010), pp. 283–314.

21 S. McGreevey, "Turn Down the Volume," *Harvard Gazette*, April 22, 2011, http://news.harvard.edu/gazette/story/2011/04/%E2%80%98turn-down-the-volume%E2%80%99/.

22 "The Best Canadian Companies to Work for in 2014," *Business Review Canada*, November 25, 2013, http://www.businessreviewcanada.ca/leadership/10/The-best-Canadian-companies-to-work-for-in-2014.

23 "Canadians Are Impatient, But Seek Serenity: Trend Part 1," *JWT Canada*, February 10, 2014, https://www.jwt.com/en/canada/thinking/canadiansareimpatientbutseekserenitytrendpart1/.

24 This section is based on I. I. Mitroff and E. A. Denton, *A Spiritual Audit of Corporate America: A Hard Look at Spirituality, Religion, and Values in the Workplace* (San Francisco: Jossey-Bass, 1999); E. H. Burack, "Spirituality in the Workplace," *Journal of Organizational Change Management* 12, no. 3 (1999), pp. 280–291; and C. L. Jurkiewicz and R. A. Giacalone, "A Values Framework for Measuring the Impact of Workplace Spirituality on Organizational Performance," *Journal of Business Ethics* 49, no. 2 (2004), pp. 129–142.

25 D. McDonald, "A Colourful Commitment to Craft Leads to UFV Honorary Degree for Charllotte Kwon," *UFV Today*, June 11, 2014.

26 A. Daniels, "Textile Importer Defends Artisans' Rights," *Vancouver Sun*, May 1, 2000, pp. C8, C10.

27 "Get to Know Our Management Team," *Reaume Chev/Buick/GMC*, accessed November 27, 2014, http://www.reaumechev.com/contact-us-our-managers.

28 R. Johnson, "Polling Religion in Canada," *National Post*, December 21, 2012 (based on a 2012 Forum Research poll, commissioned exclusively for the *National Post*).

29 M. Conlin, "Religion in the Workplace: The Growing Presence of Spirituality in Corporate America," *BusinessWeek*, November 1, 1999, pp. 151–158; and P. Paul, "A Holier Holiday Season," *American Demographics*, December 2001, pp. 41–45.

30 I. I. Mitroff and E. A. Denton, *A Spiritual Audit of Corporate America: A Hard Look at Spirituality, Religion, and Values in the Workplace* (San Francisco: Jossey-Bass, 1999).

31 See, for example, B. S. Pawar, "Workplace Spirituality Facilitation: A Comprehensive Model," *Journal of Business Ethics* 90, no. 3 (2009), pp. 375–386; and L. Lambert, *Spirituality Inc.: Religion in the American Workplace* (New York: New York University Press, 2009).

32 M. C. McKee, "Workplace Spirituality," *Workplace Review*, November 2006, http://www.smu.ca/academic/sobey/workplacereview/nov2006/WorkplaceSpirituality.pdf.

33 M. Conlin, "Religion in the Workplace: The Growing Presence of Spirituality in Corporate America," *BusinessWeek*, November 1, 1999, pp. 151–158; and P. Paul, "A Holier Holiday Season," *American Demographics*, December 2001, pp. 41–45.

34 J.-C. Garcia-Zamor, "Workplace Spirituality and Organizational Performance," *Public Administration Review*, May–June 2003, pp. 355–363; and L. W. Fry, S. T. Hannah, M. Noel, and F. O. Walumbwa, "Impact of Spiritual Leadership on Unit Performance," *Leadership Quarterly* 22, no. 2 (2011), pp. 259–270.

35 A. Rego and M. Pina e Cunha, "Workplace Spirituality and Organizational Commitment: An Empirical Study," *Journal of Organizational Change Management* 21, no. 1 (2008), pp. 53–75; and R. W. Kolodinsky, R. A. Giacalone, and C. L. Jurkiewicz, "Workplace Values and Outcomes: Exploring Personal, Organizational, and Interactive Workplace Spirituality," *Journal of Business Ethics* 81, no. 2 (2008), pp. 465–480.

36 Cited in A. M. Saks, "Workplace Spirituality and Employee Engagement," *Journal of Management, Spirituality & Religion* 8, no. 4 (2011), pp. 317–340.

37 P. Preville, "For God's Sake," *Canadian Business*, June 25–July 9, 1999, p. 61.

Chapter 13

1 Opening vignette based on information gathered during a phone interview with agency Director David Marshall, August 28, 2014. The text was verified and approved by David Marshall on September 16, 2014. The agency website can be found here: http://ville.montreal.qc.ca/portal/page?_pageid=8197,90563764&_dad=portal&_schema=PORTAL.

2 See, for example, R. L. Daft, *Organization Theory and Design*, 6th ed. (Cincinnati, OH: South Western College, 1998).

3 J. Schramm, "A Cloud of Workers," *HR Magazine*, March 2013, p. 80.

4 C. Hymowitz, "Managers Suddenly Have to Answer to a Crowd of Bosses," *Wall Street Journal*, August 12, 2003, p. B1.

5 "How Hierarchy Can Hurt Strategy Execution," *Harvard Business Review*, July–August 2010, pp. 74–75.

6 See, for example, L. Urwick, *The Elements of Administration* (New York: Harper and Row, 1944), pp. 52–53.

7 J. Child and R. G. McGrath, "Organizations Unfettered: Organizational Form in an Information-Intensive Economy," *Academy of Management Journal*, December 2001, pp. 1135–1148.

8 F. A. Csascar, "Organizational Structure as a Determinant of Performance: Evidence from Mutual Funds," *Strategic Management Journal*, June 2013, pp. 611–632.

9 B. Brown and S. D. Anthony, "How P&G Tripled Its Innovation Success Rate," *Harvard Business Review*, June 2011, pp. 64–72.

10   A. Leiponen and C. E. Helfat, "Location, Decentralization, and Knowledge Sources for Innovation," *Organization Science* 22, no. 3 (2011), pp. 641–658.

11   K. Parks, "HSBC Unit Charged in Argentine Tax Case," *Wall Street Journal*, March 19, 2013, p. C2; and "HSBC Raided in Laundering Investigation," *Buenos Aires Herald*, August 14, 2014, http://www.buenosairesherald.com/article/167055/hsbc-raided-in-laundering-investigation.

12   G. Morgan, *Images of Organization* (Newbury Park, CA: Sage, 1986), p. 21.

13   H. Mintzberg, *Structure in Fives: Designing Effective Organizations* (Englewood Cliffs, NJ: Prentice Hall, 1983), p. 157.

14   A. Murray, "Built Not to Last," *Wall Street Journal*, March 18, 2013, p. A11.

15   Alberta Business Family Institute, "ABFI Offers Valuable Programs, Services, and Advice," accessed November 25, 2014, http://business.ualberta.ca/centres/family-business.

16   J. Davis, "Governing the Family-Run Business," *Harvard Business School Working Knowledge*, September 4, 2001.

17   D. Miller, L. Steier, and I. Le Breton-Miller, "Lost in Time: Intergenerational Succession, Change, and Failure in Family Business," *Journal of Business Venturing*, July 2003, pp. 513–531.

18   J. J. Chrisman, J. H. Chua, and L. P. Steier, "An Introduction to Theories of Family Business," *Journal of Business Venturing*, July 2003, pp. 441–448.

19   K. Knight, "Matrix Organization: A Review," *Journal of Management Studies*, May 1976, pp. 111–130; and L. R. Burns and D. R. Wholey, "Adoption and Abandonment of Matrix Management Programs: Effects of Organizational Characteristics and Interorganizational Networks," *Academy of Management Journal*, February 1993, pp. 106–138.

20   See, for example, M. Bidwell, "Politics and Firm Boundaries: How Organizational Structure, Group Interests, and Resources Affect Outsourcing," *Organization Science*, November–December 2012, pp. 1622–1642.

21   See, for example, S. M. Davis and P. R. Lawrence, "Problems of Matrix Organization," *Harvard Business Review*, May–June 1978, pp. 131–142.

22   Vignette based on information gathered during a phone interview with agency Director David Marshall, August 28, 2014. The text was verified and approved by David Marshall on September 16, 2014. The agency website can be found here: http://ville.montreal.qc.ca/portal/page?_pageid=8197,90563764&_dad=portal&_schema=PORTAL.

23   N. Anand and R. L. Daft, "What Is the Right Organization Design?" *Organizational Dynamics* 36, no. 4 (2007), pp. 329–344.

24   See, for example, R. E. Miles and C. C. Snow, "The New Network Firm: A Spherical Structure Built on Human Investment Philosophy," *Organizational Dynamics*, Spring 1995, pp. 5–18; D. Pescovitz, "The Company Where Everybody's a Temp," *New York Times Magazine*, June 11, 2000, pp. 94–96; B. Hedberg, G. Dahlgren, J. Hansson, and N. Olve, *Virtual Organizations and Beyond* (New York: Wiley, 2001); N. S. Contractor, S. Wasserman, and K. Faust, "Testing Multitheoretical, Multilevel Hypotheses About Organizational Networks: An Analytic Framework and Empirical Example," *Academy of Management Review* 31, no. 3 (2006), pp. 681–703; and Y. Shin, "A Person-Environment Fit Model for Virtual Organizations," *Journal of Management*, October 2004, pp. 725–743.

25   G. G. Dess, A. M. A. Rasheed, K. J. McLaughlin, and R. Priem, "The New Corporate Architecture," *Academy of Management Executive*, August 1995, pp. 7–18.

26   J. Bates, "Making Movies and Moving On," *Los Angeles Times*, January 19, 1998, p. A1.

27   "Why Do Canadian Companies Opt for Cooperative Ventures?" *Micro: The Micro-Economic Research Bulletin* 4, no. 2 (1997), pp. 3–5.

28   J. Schramm, "At Work in a Virtual World," *HR Magazine*, June 2010, p. 152.

29   C. B. Gibson and J. L. Gibbs, "Unpacking the Concept of Virtuality: The Effects of Geographic Dispersion, Electronic Dependence, Dynamic Structure, and National Diversity on Team Innovation," *Administrative Science Quarterly* 51, no. 3 (2006), pp. 451–495; and H. M. Latapie and V. N. Tran, "Subculture Formation, Evolution, and Conflict Between Regional Teams in Virtual Organizations," *Business Review*, Summer 2007, pp. 189–193.

30   A. Poon and K. Tally, "Yoga-Pants Supplier Says Lululemon Stretches Truth," *Wall Street Journal*, March 20, 2013, p. B1.

31   "GE: Just Your Average Everyday $60 Billion Family Grocery Store," *IndustryWeek*, May 2, 1994, pp. 13–18.

32   Based on T. Johns and L. Gratton, "The Third Wave of Virtual Work," *Harvard Business Review*, January–February 2013, pp. 66–73; R. E. Silverman, "Step Into the Office-Less Company," *Wall Street Journal*, September 15, 2012, p. B6; and R. E. Silverman, "Tracking Sensors Invade the Workplace," *Wall Street Journal*, March 7, 2013, p. B1.

33   D. Friend, "BlackBerry CEO John Chen Says Years of Layoffs Are Finally Over," *Canadian Press*, August 5, 2014.

34   S. Brady, "American Express Kicks Off 2013 with Biggest Layoffs in Four Years," *Brand Channel*, January 10, 2013, http://www.brandchannel.com/home/post/American-Express-Layoffs-011013.aspx.

35   S. Brady, "American Express Kicks Off 2013 with Biggest Layoffs in Four Years," *Brand Channel*, January 10, 2013, http://www.brandchannel.com/home/post/American-Express-Layoffs-011013.aspx; and R. Sidel and A. R. Johnson, "Travel Cuts at AmEx Point to End of Era," *Wall Street Journal*, January 13, 2013, http://online.wsj.com/article/SB100014241278873245957045782394938433 99684.html#articleTabs%3Darticle.

36   "Starbucks Reports 13% Rise in Profit," *New York Times*, January 24, 2013, http://www.nytimes.com/2013/01/25/business/starbucks-earnings-increased-13-in-latest-quarter.html?_r=0.

37   See J. P. Guthrie and D. K. Datta, "Dumb and Dumber: The Impact of Downsizing on Firm Performance as Moderated by Industry Conditions," *Organization Science* 19, no. 1 (2008), pp. 108–123; and K. P. De Meuse, T. J. Bergmann, P. A. Vanderheiden, and C. E. Roraff, "New Evidence Regarding Organizational Downsizing and a Firm's Financial Performance: A Long-Term Analysis," *Journal of Managerial Issues* 16, no. 2 (2004), pp. 155–177.

38   See, for example, C. O. Trevor and A. J. Nyberg, "Keeping Your Headcount When All About You Are Losing Theirs: Downsizing, Voluntary Turnover Rates, and the Moderating Role of HR Practices," *Academy of Management Journal* 51, no. 2 (2008), pp. 259–276; S. Moore, L. Grunberg, and E. Greenberg, "Surviving Repeated Waves of Organizational Downsizing: The Recency, Duration, and Order Effects Associated with Different Forms of Layoff Contact," *Anxiety, Stress & Coping: An International Journal* 19, no. 3 (2006), pp. 309–329; T. M. Probst, S. M. Stewart, M. L. Gruys, and B. W. Tierney, "Productivity, Counterproductivity and Creativity: The Ups and Downs of Job Insecurity," *Journal of Occupational and Organizational Psychology* 80, no. 3 (2007), pp. 479–497; and J. E. Ferrie, M. J. Shipley, M. G. Marmot, P. Martikainen, S. Stansfeld, and G. D. Smith, "Job Insecurity in White-Collar Workers: Toward an Explanation of Associations with Health," *Journal of Occupational Health Psychology* 6, no. 1 (2001), pp. 26–42.

39   C. D. Zatzick and R. D. Iverson, "High-Involvement Management and Workforce Reduction: Competitive Advantage or Disadvantage?" *Academy of Management Journal* 49, no. 5 (2006), pp. 999–1015; A. Travaglione and B. Cross, "Diminishing the Social Network in Organizations: Does There Need to Be Such a

Phenomenon as 'Survivor Syndrome' After Downsizing?" *Strategic Change* 15, no. 1 (2006), pp. 1–13; and J. D. Kammeyer-Mueller, H. Liao, and R. D. Arvey, "Downsizing and Organizational Performance: A Review of the Literature from a Stakeholder Perspective," *Research in Personnel and Human Resources Management* 20 (2001), pp. 269–329.

40 T. Burns and G. M. Stalker, *The Management of Innovation* (London: Tavistock, 1961); and J. A. Courtright, G. T. Fairhurst, and L. E. Rogers, "Interaction Patterns in Organic and Mechanistic Systems," *Academy of Management Journal*, December 1989, pp. 773–802.

41 This analysis is referred to as a contingency approach to organization design. See, for example, J. M. Pennings, "Structural Contingency Theory: A Reappraisal," in *Research in Organizational Behavior*, vol. 14, ed. B. M. Staw and L. L. Cummings (Greenwich, CT: JAI Press, 1992), pp. 267–309; J. R. Hollenbeck, H. Moon, A. P. J. Ellis, B. J. West, D. R. Ilgen, L. Sheppard, C. O. L. H. Porter, and J. A. Wagner III, "Structural Contingency Theory and Individual Differences: Examination of External and Internal Person-Team Fit," *Journal of Applied Psychology*, June 2002, pp. 599–606; and A. Drach-Zahavy and A. Freund, "Team Effectiveness under Stress: A Structural Contingency Approach," *Journal of Organizational Behavior* 28, no. 4 (2007), pp. 423–450.

42 The strategy-structure thesis was originally proposed in A. D. Chandler Jr., *Strategy and Structure: Chapters in the History of the Industrial Enterprise* (Cambridge, MA: MIT Press, 1962). For an updated analysis, see T. L. Amburgey and T. Dacin, "As the Left Foot Follows the Right? The Dynamics of Strategic and Structural Change," *Academy of Management Journal*, December 1994, pp. 1427–1452.

43 The strategy–structure thesis was originally proposed in A. D. Chandler Jr., *Strategy and Structure: Chapters in the History of the Industrial Enterprise* (Cambridge, MA: MIT Press, 1962). For an updated analysis, see T. L. Amburgey and T. Dacin, "As the Left Foot Follows the Right? The Dynamics of Strategic and Structural Change," *Academy of Management Journal*, December 1994, pp. 1427–1452.

44 See R. E. Miles and C. C. Snow, *Organizational Strategy, Structure, and Process* (New York: McGraw-Hill, 1978); D. C. Galunic and K. M. Eisenhardt, "Renewing the Strategy-Structure-Performance Paradigm," in *Research in Organizational Behavior*, vol. 16, ed. B. M. Staw and L. L. Cummings (Greenwich, CT: JAI Press, 1994), pp. 215–255; I. C. Harris and T. W. Ruefli, "The Strategy/Structure Debate: An Examination of the Performance Implications," *Journal of Management Studies*, June 2000, pp. 587–603; and S. M. Toh, F. P. Morgeson, and M. A. Campion, "Human Resource Configurations: Investigating Fit with the Organizational Context," *Journal of Applied Psychology* 93, no. 4 (2008), pp. 864–882.

45 M. Mesco, "Moleskine Tests Appetite for IPOs," *Wall Street Journal*, March 19, 2013, p. B8.

46 See, for example, P. M. Blau and R. A. Schoenherr, *The Structure of Organizations* (New York: Basic Books, 1971); D. S. Pugh, "The Aston Program of Research: Retrospect and Prospect," in *Perspectives on Organization Design and Behavior*, ed. A. H. Van de Ven and W. F. Joyce (New York: Wiley, 1981), pp. 135–166; R. Z. Gooding and J. A. Wagner III, "A Meta-analytic Review of the Relationship between Size and Performance: The Productivity and Efficiency of Organizations and Their Subunits," *Administrative Science Quarterly*, December 1985, pp. 462–481; and A. C. Bluedorn, "Pilgrim's Progress: Trends and Convergence in Research on Organizational Size and Environments," *Journal of Management*, Summer 1993, pp. 163–192.

47 See C. Perrow, "A Framework for the Comparative Analysis of Organizations," *American Sociological Review*, April 1967, pp. 194–208; J. Hage and M. Aiken, "Routine Technology, Social Structure, and Organizational Goals," *Administrative Science Quarterly*, September 1969, pp. 366–377; C. C. Miller, W. H. Glick, Y. Wang, and G. P. Huber, "Understanding Technology-Structure Relationships: Theory Development and Meta-analytic Theory Testing," *Academy of Management Journal*, June 1991, pp. 370–399; and W. D. Sine, H. Mitsuhashi, and D. A. Kirsch, "Revisiting Burns and Stalker: Formal Structure and New Venture Performance in Emerging Economic Sectors," *Academy of Management Journal* 49, no. 1 (2006), pp. 121–132.

48 G. G. Dess and D. W. Beard, "Dimensions of Organizational Task Environments," *Administrative Science Quarterly*, March 1984, pp. 52–73; E. A. Gerloff, N. K. Muir, and W. D. Bodensteiner, "Three Components of Perceived Environmental Uncertainty: An Exploratory Analysis of the Effects of Aggregation," *Journal of Management*, December 1991, pp. 749–768; and O. Shenkar, N. Aranya, and T. Almor, "Construct Dimensions in the Contingency Model: An Analysis Comparing Metric and Non-Metric Multivariate Instruments," *Human Relations*, May 1995, pp. 559–580.

49 C. S. Spell and T. J. Arnold, "A Multi-Level Analysis of Organizational Justice and Climate, Structure, and Employee Mental Health," *Journal of Management* 33, no. 5 (2007), pp. 724–751; and M. L. Ambrose and M. Schminke, "Organization Structure as a Moderator of the Relationship Between Procedural Justice, Interactional Justice, Perceived Organizational Support, and Supervisory Trust," *Journal of Applied Psychology* 88, no. 2 (2003), pp. 295–305.

50 See, for example, L. W. Porter and E. E. Lawler III, "Properties of Organization Structure in Relation to Job Attitudes and Job Behavior," *Psychological Bulletin*, July 1965, pp. 23–51; L. R. James and A. P. Jones, "Organization Structure: A Review of Structural Dimensions and Their Conceptual Relationships with Individual Attitudes and Behavior," *Organizational Behavior and Human Performance*, June 1976, pp. 74–113; C. S. Spell and T. J. Arnold, "A Multi-Level Analysis of Organizational Justice Climate, Structure, and Employee Mental Health," *Journal of Management* 33, no. 5 (2007), pp. 724–751; and J. D. Shaw and N. Gupta, "Job Complexity, Performance, and Well-Being: When Does Supplies-Values Fit Matter?" *Personnel Psychology* 57, no. 4 (2004), pp. 847–879.

51 Based on P. Puranam, M. Raveendran, and T. Knudsen, "Organization Design: The Epistemic Interdependence Perspective," *Academy of Management Review* 37, no. 3 (2012), pp. 419–440; and R. E. Silverman and Q. Fottrell, "The Home Office in the Spotlight," *Wall Street Journal*, February 27, 2013, p. B6.

52 T. Martin, "Pharmacies Feel More Heat," *Wall Street Journal* (March 16–17, 2013), p. A3.

53 See, for example, B. Schneider, H. W. Goldstein, and D. B. Smith, "The ASA Framework: An Update," *Personnel Psychology* 48, no. 4 (1995), pp. 747–773; and R. E. Ployhart, J. A. Weekley, and K. Baughman, "The Structure and Function of Human Capital Emergence: A Multilevel Examination of the Attraction-Selection-Attrition Model," *Academy of Management Journal* 49, no. 4 (2006), pp. 661–677.

54 J. B. Stewart, "A Place to Play for Google Staff," *New York Times*, March 16, 2013, p. B1.

55 P. Dvorak, "Making U.S. Management Ideas Work Elsewhere," *Wall Street Journal*, May 22, 2006, p. B3.

56 See, for example, B. K. Park, J. A. Choi, M. Koo, S. Sul, and I. Choi, "Culture, Self, and Preference Structure: Transitivity and Context Independence Are Violated More by Interdependent People," *Social Cognition*, February 2013, pp. 106–118.

57 J. Scheck, L. Moloney, and A. Flynn, "Eni, CNPC Link Up in Mozambique," *Wall Street Journal*, March 15, 2013, p. B3.

58 Z. Yao, Z. Yang, G. Fisher, C. Ma, and E. Fang "Knowledge Complementarity, Knowledge Absorption Effectiveness, and New Product Performance: The Exploration of International Joint

Ventures in China," *International Business Review*, February 2013, pp. 216–227.

59 J. Hassard, J. Morris, and L. McCann, "'My Brilliant Career'? New Organizational Forms and Changing Managerial Careers in Japan, the UK, and USA," *Journal of Management Studies*, May 2012, pp. 571–599.

60 Based on A. Bryant, "Structure? The Flatter the Better," *New York Times*, January 17, 2010, p. BU2; "Honeywell International: From Bitter to Sweet," *Economist*, April 14, 2012, http://www.economist.com/node/21552631; A. Efrati and S. Morrison, "Chief Seeks More Agile Google," *Wall Street Journal*, January 22, 2011, pp. B1, B4; H. El Nasser, "What Office? Laptops Are Workspace," *USA Today*, June 6, 2012; *Fortune* 500 rankings, http://money.cnn.com/magazines/fortune/fortune500/2012/full_list/; "Honeywell | Company Structure Information from ICIS," *ICIS.com*, accessed November 12, 2014, http://www.icis.com/v2/companies/9145292/honeywell/structure.html; K. Linebaugh, "Honeywell's Hiring Is Bleak," *Wall Street Journal*, March 6, 2013, p. B3; A. Murray, "The End of Management," *Wall Street Journal*, August 21, 2010, p. W3; A. R. Sorkin, "Delegator in Chief," *New York Times*, April 24, 2011, p. B4; and S. Tully, "How Dave Cote Got Honeywell's Groove Back," *CNN Money*, May 14, 2012, http://management.fortune.cnn.com/2012/05/14/500-honeywell-cote/.

61 The source of this exercise is unknown.

62 Based on S. Pulliam, "A Staffer Ordered to Commit Fraud Balked, Then Caved," *Wall Street Journal*, June 23, 2003, p. A1; and E. McClam, "Ex-WorldCom Exec Gets Prison, House Arrest," *USA Today*, August 5, 2005, http://usatoday30.usatoday.com/money/industries/telecom/2005-08-05-vinson_x.htm.

63 Based on C. Mainemelis, "Stealing Fire: Creative Deviance in the Evolution of New Ideas," *Academy of Management Review* 35, no. 4 (2010), pp. 558–578; and A. Lashinsky, "Inside Apple," *Fortune*, May 23, 2011, pp. 125–134.

64 Based on P. J. Sauer, "Open-Door Management," *Inc.*, June 2003, p. 44; and "Not Just Jobs. Opportunities," TechTarget.com, accessed November 12, 2014, http://www.techtarget.com/html/job_opps.htm.

65 Based on S. P. Robbins and P. L. Hunsaker, *Training in Interpersonal Skills*, 3rd ed. (Upper Saddle River, NJ: Prentice Hall, 2003), pp. 95–98.

Chapter 14

1 Opening vignette based on "Zucker Shakes Up HBC," *National Post*, March 10, 2006; and HBC, "Our History: People: Builders: A History of HBC Ownership," accessed November 25, 2014, http://www.patrimoinehbc.ca/hbcheritage/history/people/builders/a-history-of-hbc-ownership.

2 M. Strauss, "Retail Reboot: How E-Commerce Is Forcing an Industry Transformation," *Globe and Mail*, November 14, 2014.

3 See, for example, K. H. Hammonds, "Practical Radicals," *Fast Company*, September 2000, pp. 162–174; and P. C. Judge, "Change Agents," *Fast Company*, November 2000, pp. 216–226.

4 A. Finder, P. D. Healy, and K. Zernike, "President of Harvard Resigns, Ending Stormy 5-Year Tenure," *New York Times*, February 22, 2006, pp. A1, A19.

5 Vignette based on M. Strauss, "Five Years in, the Turnaround 'Is Real' at Hudson's Bay," *Globe and Mail*, June 12, 2013; "Leadership," HBC, accessed November 25, 2014, http://investor.hbc.com/management.cfm; and F. Kopun, "Bonnie Brooks, President of HBC, Talks About Her Newest Challenge," *Toronto Star*, July 19, 2013.

6 K. Lewin, *Field Theory in Social Science* (New York: Harper and Row, 1951).

7 P. G. Audia, E. A. Locke, and K. G. Smith, "The Paradox of Success: An Archival and a Laboratory Study of Strategic

Persistence Following Radical Environmental Change," *Academy of Management Journal*, October 2000, pp. 837–853.

8 J. B. Sorensen, "The Strength of Corporate Culture and the Reliability of Firm Performance," *Administrative Science Quarterly*, March 2002, pp. 70–91.

9 J. Amis, T. Slack, and C. R. Hinings, "The Pace, Sequence, and Linearity of Radical Change," *Academy of Management Journal*, February 2004, pp. 15–39; and E. Autio, H. J. Sapienza, and J. G. Almeida, "Effects of Age at Entry, Knowledge Intensity, and Imitability on International Growth," *Academy of Management Journal*, October 2000, pp. 909–924.

10 J. P. Kotter, "Leading Changes: Why Transformation Efforts Fail," *Harvard Business Review*, March–April 1995, pp. 59–67; and J. P. Kotter, *Leading Change* (Boston: Harvard Business School Press, 1996).

11 See, for example, C. Eden and C. Huxham, "Action Research for the Study of Organizations," in *Handbook of Organization Studies*, ed. S. R. Clegg, C. Hardy, and W. R. Nord (London: Sage, 1996); and L. S. Lüscher and M. W. Lewis, "Organizational Change and Managerial Sensemaking: Working through Paradox," *Academy of Management Journal* 51, no. 2 (2008), pp. 221–240.

12 See, for example, G. R. Bushe, "Advances in Appreciative Inquiry as an Organization Development Intervention," *Organizational Development Journal*, Summer 1999, pp. 61–68; D. L. Cooperrider and D. Whitney, *Collaborating for Change: Appreciative Inquiry* (San Francisco: Berrett-Koehler, 2000); R. Fry, F. Barrett, J. Seiling, and D. Whitney, eds., *Appreciative Inquiry & Organizational Transformation: Reports from the Field* (Westport, CT: Quorum, 2002); J. K. Barge and C. Oliver, "Working with Appreciation in Managerial Practice," *Academy of Management Review*, January 2003, pp. 124–142; and D. van der Haar and D. M. Hosking, "Evaluating Appreciative Inquiry: A Relational Constructionist Perspective," *Human Relations*, August 2004, pp. 1017–1036.

13 R. Rabinovitch, "Training and Development," *Canadian HR Reporter* 17, no. 10 (May 17, 2004), pp. 7–10.

14 D. Sankey, "New Tool Solves Firms' Problems," *Calgary Herald*, July 12, 2003, p. CR1F.

15 G. R. Bushe, "Advances in Appreciative Inquiry as an Organization Development Intervention," *Organization Development Journal* 17, no. 2 (Summer 1999), pp. 61–68.

16 Vignette based on F. Kopun, "Bonnie Brooks, President of HBC, Talks About Her Newest Challenge," *Toronto Star*, July 19, 2013.

17 P. G. Audia and S. Brion, "Reluctant to Change: Self-Enhancing Responses to Diverging Performance Measures," *Organizational Behavior and Human Decision Processes* 102 (2007), pp. 255–269.

18 M. Fugate, A. J. Kinicki, and G. E. Prussia, "Employee Coping with Organizational Change: An Examination of Alternative Theoretical Perspectives and Models," *Personnel Psychology* 61, no. 1 (2008), pp. 1–36.

19 J. D. Ford, L. W. Ford, and A. D'Amelio, "Resistance to Change: The Rest of the Story," *Academy of Management Review* 33, no. 2 (2008), pp. 362–377.

20 J. P. Kotter and L. A. Schlesinger, "Choosing Strategies for Change," *Harvard Business Review*, July–August 2008, pp. 130–139.

21 A. E. Reichers, J. P. Wanous, and J. T. Austin, "Understanding and Managing Cynicism About Organizational Change," *Academy of Management Executive* 11 (1997), pp. 48–59.

22 R. H. Hall, *Organizations: Structures, Processes, and Outcomes*, 4th ed. (Englewood Cliffs, NJ: Prentice Hall, 1987), p. 29.

23 D. Katz and R. L. Kahn, *The Social Psychology of Organizations*, 2nd ed. (New York: Wiley, 1978), pp. 714–715.

24 M. T. Hannan, L. Pólos, and G. R. Carroll, "The Fog of Change: Opacity and Asperity in Organizations," *Administrative Science Quarterly*, September 2003, pp. 399–432.

25 J. P. Kotter and L. A. Schlesinger, "Choosing Strategies for Change," *Harvard Business Review*, March–April 1979, pp. 106–114.

26 J. E. Dutton, S. J. Ashford, R. M. O'Neill, and K. A. Lawrence, "Moves That Matter: Issue Selling and Organizational Change," *Academy of Management Journal*, August 2001, pp. 716–736.

27 P. C. Fiss and E. J. Zajac, "The Symbolic Management of Strategic Change: Sensegiving via Framing and Decoupling," *Academy of Management Journal* 49, no. 6 (2006), pp. 1173–1193.

28 A. E. Rafferty and S. L. D. Restubog, "The Impact of Change Process and Context on Change Reactions and Turnover During a Merger," *Journal of Management* 36, no. 5 (2010), pp. 1309–1338.

29 Q. N. Huy, "Emotional Balancing of Organizational Continuity and Radical Change: The Contribution of Middle Managers," *Administrative Science Quarterly*, March 2002, pp. 31–69; D. M. Herold, D. B. Fedor, and S. D. Caldwell, "Beyond Change Management: A Multilevel Investigation of Contextual and Personal Influences on Employees' Commitment to Change," *Journal of Applied Psychology* 92, no. 4 (2007), pp. 942–951; and G. B. Cunningham, "The Relationships among Commitment to Change, Coping with Change, and Turnover Intentions," *European Journal of Work and Organizational Psychology* 15, no. 1 (2006), pp. 29–45.

30 R. Peccei, A. Giangreco, and A. Sebastiano, "The Role of Organizational Commitment in the Analysis of Resistance to Change: Co-predictor and Moderator Effects," *Personnel Review* 40, no. 2 (2011), pp. 185–204.

31 J. P. Kotter, "Leading Change: Why Transformational Efforts Fail," *Harvard Business Review*, January 2007, pp. 96–103.

32 K. van Dam, S. Oreg, and B. Schyns, "Daily Work Contexts and Resistance to Organisational Change: The Role of Leader-Member Exchange, Development Climate, and Change Process Characteristics," *Applied Psychology: An International Review* 57, no. 2 (2008), pp. 313–334.

33 S. Oreg and N. Sverdlik, "Ambivalence toward Imposed Change: The Conflict between Dispositional Resistance to Change and the Orientation toward the Change Agent," *Journal of Applied Psychology* 96, no. 2 (2011), pp. 337–349.

34 D. B. Fedor, S. Caldwell, and D. M. Herold, "The Effects of Organizational Changes on Employee Commitment: A Multilevel Investigation," *Personnel Psychology* 59 (2006), pp. 1–29.

35 S. Oreg, "Personality, Context, and Resistance to Organizational Change," *European Journal of Work and Organizational Psychology* 15, no. 1 (2006), pp. 73–101.

36 S. M. Elias, "Employee Commitment in Times of Change: Assessing the Importance of Attitudes toward Organizational Change," *Journal of Management* 35, no. 1 (2009), pp. 37–55.

37 J. W. B. Lang and P. D. Bliese, "General Mental Ability and Two Types of Adaptation to Unforeseen Change: Applying Discontinuous Growth Models to the Task-Change Paradigm," *Journal of Applied Psychology* 94, no. 2 (2009), pp. 411–428.

38 C. O. L. H. Porter, J. W. Webb, and C. I. Gogus, "When Goal Orientations Collide: Effects of Learning and Performance Orientation on Team Adaptability in Response to Workload Imbalance," *Journal of Applied Psychology* 95, no. 5 (2010), pp. 935–943.

39 Based on original research conducted by Dr. Katherine Breward, University of Winnipeg, as yet unpublished; and Habitat for Humanity, "Habitat for Humanity Manitoba Partners with Rockwood Institution to Build a Home in Winnipeg," news release, December 18, 2013, http://www.habitat.mb.ca/PDF/media/2013/Habitat%20Rockwood%20Home%20Dedication%20Press%20RELEASE.PDF.

40 See J. Pfeffer, *Managing with Power: Politics and Influence in Organizations* (Boston: Harvard Business School Press, 1992), pp. 7, 318–320; and D. Knights and D. McCabe, "When 'Life Is but a Dream': Obliterating Politics through Business Process Reengineering?" *Human Relations*, June 1998, pp. 761–798.

41 See, for example, A. Karaevli, "Performance Consequences for New CEO 'Outsiderness': Moderating Effects of Pre- and Post-Succession Contexts," *Strategic Management Journal* 28, no. 7 (2007), pp. 681–706.

42 R. H. Miles, "Accelerating Corporate Transformations (Don't Lose Your Nerve!)," *Harvard Business Review*, January/February 2010, pp. 68–75.

43 Vignette based on M. Strauss and B. Marotte, "Executive Shuffle at HBC as Brooks Takes New Role," *Globe and Mail*, June 18, 2013; F. Kopun, "Bonnie Brooks, President of HBC, Talks About Her Newest Challenge," *Toronto Star*, July 19, 2013; and S. Krashinsky, "Hudson's Bay Takes a Chance on a New Voice to Sell Its Brand," *Globe and Mail*, November 13, 2014.

44 See, for example, F. Yuan and R. W. Woodman, "Innovative Behavior in the Workplace: The Role of Performance and Image Outcome Expectations," *Academy of Management Journal* 53, no. 2 (2010), pp. 323–342.

45 See, for example, A. Van de Ven, "Central Problems in the Management of Innovation," *Management Science* 32 (1986), pp. 590–607; and R. M. Kanter, "When a Thousand Flowers Bloom: Structural, Collective and Social Conditions for Innovation in Organizations," in *Research in Organizational Behavior*, vol. 10, ed. B. M. Staw and L. L. Cummings (Greenwich, CT: JAI Press, 1988), pp. 169–211.

46 F. Damanpour, "Organizational Innovation: A Meta-analysis of Effects of Determinants and Moderators," *Academy of Management Journal*, September 1991, p. 557.

47 F. Damanpour, "Organizational Innovation: A Meta-analysis of Effects of Determinants and Moderators," *Academy of Management Journal*, September 1991, pp. 555–590.

48 See also P. R. Monge, M. D. Cozzens, and N. S. Contractor, "Communication and Motivational Predictors of the Dynamics of Organizational Innovation," *Organization Science*, May 1992, pp. 250–274.

49 Based on "The Drought Is Over at 3M," *BusinessWeek*, November 7, 1994, pp. 140–141; T. A. Stewart, "3M Fights Back," *Fortune*, February 5, 1996, pp. 94–99; T. D. Schellhardt, "David in Goliath," *Wall Street Journal*, May 23, 1996, p. R14; "Who We Are," *3M*, accessed November 26, 2014, http://solutions.3mcanada.ca/wps/portal/3M/en_CA/about-3M/information/about/us/; and "3M Earns Top Honors at 2014 Edison Awards," news release, May 1, 2014, http://news.3m.com/press-release/company/3m-earns-top-honors-2014-edison-awards.

50 J. M. Howell and C. A. Higgins, "Champions of Change," *Business Quarterly*, Spring 1990, pp. 31–32; and D. L. Day, "Raising Radicals: Different Processes for Championing Innovative Corporate Ventures," *Organization Science*, May 1994, pp. 148–172.

51 J. M. Howell and C. A. Higgins, "Champions of Change," *Business Quarterly*, Spring 1990, pp. 31–32.

52 See, for example, T. B. Lawrence, M. K. Mauws, B. Dyck, and R. F. Kleysen, "The Politics of Organizational Learning: Integrating Power into the 4I Framework," *Academy of Management Review*, January 2005, pp. 180–191.

53 D. H. Kim, "The Link between Individual and Organizational Learning," *Sloan Management Review*, Fall 1993, p. 37.

54 C. Argyris and D. A. Schon, *Organizational Learning* (Reading, MA: Addison-Wesley, 1978).

55 L. Berghman, P. Matthyssens, S. Streukens, and K. Vandenbempt, "Deliberate Learning Mechanisms for Stimulating Strategic Innovation Capacity," *Long Range Planning* (February–April 2013), pp. 39–71; and B. Dumaine, "Mr. Learning Organization," *Fortune*, October 17, 1994, p. 148.

56 F. Kofman and P. M. Senge, "Communities of Commitment: The Heart of Learning Organizations," *Organizational Dynamics,* Autumn 1993, pp. 5–23.

57 B. Dumaine, "Mr. Learning Organization," *Fortune,* October 17, 1994, p. 154.

58 M. Cerne, M. Jaklic, and M. Skerlavaj, "Decoupling Management and Technological Innovations: Resolving the Individualism-Collectivism Controversy," *Journal of International Management,* June 2013, pp. 103–117; and S. Shane, S. Venkataraman, and I. MacMillan, "Cultural Differences in Innovation Championing Strategies," *Journal of Management* 21, no. 5 (1995), pp. 931–952.

59 For contrasting views on episodic and continuous change, see K. E. Weick and R. E. Quinn, "Organizational Change and Development," in *Annual Review of Psychology,* vol. 50, ed. J. T. Spence, J. M. Darley, and D. J. Foss (Palo Alto, CA: Annual Reviews, 1999), pp. 361–386. Counterpoint based on R. Thomas, D. S. Leisa, and C. Hardy, "Managing Organizational Change: Negotiating Meaning and Power-Resistance Relations," *Organization Science* 22, no. 1 (2011), pp. 22–41; and P. B. Vaill, *Managing as a Performing Art: New Ideas for a World of Chaotic Change* (San Francisco: Jossey-Bass, 1989).

60 Adapted from J. E. Barbuto Jr., "Power and the Changing Environment," *Journal of Management Education,* April 2000, pp. 288–296.

61 Based on C. Edelhart, "Weatherman's Stand Against Story Costs Job," *Californian,* May 16, 2011, http://www.bakersfieldcalifornian.com/local/x1898679505/Weathermans-stand-against-story-costs-job; and K. T. Phan, "ABC Affiliate Fires Christian over Strip Club Segment," *Fox News,* May 10, 2011, http://nation.foxnews.com/firing/2011/05/10/abc-affiliate-fires-christian-over-strip-club-segment.

62 Based on M. Babad, "How Starbucks Has Conquered Canada," *Globe and Mail,* May 27 2014, http://www.hoovers.com/company-information/cs/company-profile.STARBUCKS_CORPORATION.824509ef484db9e9.html; H. Schultz, "How Starbucks Got Its Mojo Back," *Newsweek,* March 21, 2011, http://www.newsweek.com/how-starbucks-got-its-mojo-back-66183; A. Ignatius, "We Had to Own the Mistakes," *Harvard Business Review,* July/August 2010, pp. 108–115; and R. Baker, "Starbucks Demonstrates 'Power of Brand,'" *Marketing Week,* April 28, 2011, http://www.marketingweek.com/2011/04/28/starbucks-demonstrates-power-of-brand/.

63 Based on A. Lawson, "Sony Issues New Profit Warning Hit By Massive Smartphone Losses," *Independent,* September 17, 2014; H. Hiyama, "Sony Break-Up Call Shines Light on Electronics Industry Problems," *Japan Today,* June 7, 2013, http://www.japantoday.com/category/opinions/view/sony-break-up-call-shines-light-on-electronic-industry-problems; R. Katz, "How Japan Blew Its Lead in Electronics," *Wall Street Journal,* March 23, 2012, p. A15; and H. Tabuchi, "How the Parade Passed Sony By," *New York Times,* April 15, 2012, pp. B1, B7.

64 Based on R. Pascale, M. Millemann, and L. Gioja, "Changing the Way We Change," *Harvard Business Review,* November–December 1997, pp. 127–139. The actual names of the points based on the After Action Review are taken from the article, although the summaries are provided by the authors of this book. See also "After Action Review," *Knowledge Sharing Tools and Methods Toolkit,* accessed November 26, 2014, http://www.kstoolkit.org/After+Action+Review.

Additional Cases: 1

1 Note that this case is based largely on actual events occurring at a Canadian company. At the request of the individuals directly involved, however, the employee names and the company name have been disguised.

Additional Cases: 2

1 This is a true story about a female employee in a Canadian company. The names of the people involved have been disguised.

However, the events are truthful and accurate. This case is based on an interview with "Julie" conducted after her release from jail. The interview took place on December 27, 2011.

Additional Cases: 3

1 This case is based on a real Canadian company. At the request of the owners, the employee names and the company name have been disguised.

Additional Cases: 4

1 This case is based largely on an extended feature news story written by K. More, "Public Service Bargaining: a Bruising Battle Lies Ahead," *Ottawa Citizen,* July 18, 2014, http://ottawacitizen.com/news/national/public-service-bargaining-a-bruising-battle-lies-ahead.

2 A. Thomson, "Tony Clement, Treasury Board President, Proposes Changes to Public Servants' Sick Leave," *Huffington Post Canada,* August 2, 2014, http://www.huffingtonpost.ca/2014/02/08/tony-clement-sick-leave_n_4752463.html.

3 K. May, "Tony Clement Wants to Cut Public Servants' Sick Days to Five," *Ottawa Citizen,* September 11, 2014, http://ottawacitizen.com/news/national/clement-wants-to-cut-public-servants-sick-days-to-five.

4 T. Pedwell, "PBO Sick Leave Report: No 'Incremental' Costs to Taxpayers," *Huffington Post Canada,* July 16, 2014, http://www.huffingtonpost.ca/2014/07/16/pbo-sick-leave-report_n_5590817.html.

Additional Cases: 5

1 S. Kari, S. "Ex-constable Must Again Prove RCMP Harassment," *Globe and Mail,* December 20, 2011, http://www.theglobeandmail.com/news/national/ex-constable-must-again-prove-rcmpharassment/article151366/.

2 S. Stewart, A. Hoffman, and P. Waldie, "Female Mounties Allege Harassment Not Investigated to Protect RCMP," *Canadian Press,* December 20, 2011, http://www.theglobeandmail.com/news/national/female-mounties-allege-harassment-not-investigatedto-protect-rcmp/article1016726/.

3 S. Stewart, A. Hoffman, and P. Waldie, "Female Mounties Allege Harassment Not Investigated to Protect RCMP," *Canadian Press,* December 20, 2011, http://www.theglobeandmail.com/news/national/female-mounties-allege-harassment-not-investigatedto-protect-rcmp/article1016726/.

4 S. Stewart, A. Hoffman, and P. Waldie, "Female Mounties Allege Harassment Not Investigated to Protect RCMP," *Canadian Press,* December 20, 2011, http://www.theglobeandmail.com/news/national/female-mounties-allege-harassment-not-investigatedto-protect-rcmp/article1016726/.

5 "More B.C. Mounties Complain of Harassment," *CBC News,* November 8, 2011, http://www.cbc.ca/news/canada/britishcolumbia/story/2011/11/08/bc-rcmp-harassment.html.

6 "Lawyer 'Stunned' RCMP Brass Came in to Settle Harassment Case," *CBC News,* December 9, 2011, http://www.cbc.ca/news/canada/story/2011/12/09/rcmp-allegations-blundell.html.

7 G. Mason, "RCMP Took Two Years to Respond to Officer's Sexual Harassment Complaint," *Globe and Mail,* December 5, 2011, http://www.theglobeandmail.com/news/national/britishcolumbia/gary_mason/rcmp-took-two-years-to-respond-toofficers-sexual-harassment-complaint/article2261049/.

8 G. Mason, "Former Mountie Paints Picture of Near Daily Harassment," *Globe and Mail,* December 8, 2011, http://www.theglobeandmail.com/news/national/former-mountie-paintspicture-of-near-daily-harassment/article2259072/.

9 S. Cooper, "Alleged Mountie Harassment Made RCMP Staffer Fear for Family's Lives Court Hears," *National Post,* November 18,

2011, http://news.nationalpost.com/2011/11/18/allegedmountie-harassment-made-rcmp-staffer-fear-for-familys-livescourt-hears/.

10 V. Luk, "RCMP Sexual Harassment Claims Deepen after Second Female Mountie Comes Forward," *National Post*, November 10, 2011, http://news.nationalpost.com/2011/11/10/rcmp-sexualharassment-claims-deepen-after-second-female-mountie-slamsforce/.

11 V. Luk, "RCMP Sexual Harassment Claims Deepen after Second Female Mountie Comes Forward," *National Post*, November 10, 2011, http://news.nationalpost.com/2011/11/10/rcmp-sexualharassment-claims-deepen-after-second-female-mountie-slamsforce/.

12 C. Freeze, "Top Mountie Delivers Candid, Scathing View of Force at the Brink," *Globe and Mail*, December 20, 2011, http://www.theglobeandmail.com/news/politics/top-mountie-deliverscandid-scathing-view-of-force-at-the-brink/article2277241/.

13 D. Leblanc, "RCMP Introduce New Code of Conduct," *Globe and Mail*, April 26, 2014, http://www.theglobeandmail.com/news/politics/rcmp-introduce-new-code-of-conduct/article18237170/.

14 G. Mason, "RCMP Took Two Years to Respond to Officer's Sexual Harassment Complaint," *Globe and Mail*, December 5, 2011, http://www.theglobeandmail.com/news/national/britishcolumbia/gary_mason/rcmp-took-two-years-to-respond-toofficers-sexual-harassment-complaint/article2261049/.

15 A. Woo, "Sexual Harassment Claims Against RCMP Reach 336," *Globe and Mail*, July 18, 2014, http://www.theglobeandmail.com/news/british-columbia/sexual-harassment-claims-against-rcmp-reach-336/article19669218/.

16 I. Bailey, "Lawyers Preparing Possible Class Action Lawsuit against RCMP," *Globe and Mail*, December 21, 2011, http://www.theglobeandmail.com/news/national/lawyers-preparingpossible-class-action-suit-against-rcmp/article2278817/.

Additional Cases: 6

1 This case is an abbreviated version of a published case that appeared in the *Case Research Journal*. See K. Breward, "Disability Accommodations and Promotions at Bunco," *Case Research Journal* 30, no. 1 (2010), pp. 65–72. Reprinted with permission.

2 National Digestive Diseases Information Clearinghouse (NDDIC), Digestive Diseases *National Institute of Health* publication number 06-3410. Bethesda, MD: Author, 2006. http://digestive.niddk.nih.gov/ddiseases/pubs/crohns/#stress.

3 National Digestive Diseases Information Clearinghouse (NDDIC), Digestive Diseases *National Institute of Health*, publication number 06-3410 (Bethesda, MD: Author, 2006). http://digestive.niddk.nih.gov/ddiseases/pubs/crohns/#stress.

4 "Crohn's Disease," *MedicineNet.com*, accessed December 3, 2014, http://www.medicinenet.com/crohns_disease/article.htm.

Additional Cases: 10

1 This case was prepared by Nancy Langton, Sauder School of Business. This case is based on an actual set of events, although all names have been changed. © 2006 by Nancy Langton. Case sources: "Zoo Mulls Qualities Sought in Next Director," *toledoblade.com*, September 9, 2005, http://toledoblade.com; S. Eder, "Zoo Task Force Sets 100-Day Target for Submitting Investigation Report," *toledoblade.com*, March 25, 2005; S. Eder, "Experience with Animals Lacking for Operations Chief," *toledoblade.com*, March 13, 2005; S. Eder, "Reichard Held in High Esteem by Fellow Zoo Veterinarians," *toledoblade.com*, March 9, 2005; M Greenwell, "Zoo Sees New Job As Way to Fix Problems," *toledoblade.com*, June 23, 2005; J. Laidman, "Employee Relations Top Zoo Leaders' List," *toledoblade.com*, May 22, 2005; J. Laidman, "Embattled Zoo Leaders Quit," *toledoblade.com*, May 5, 2005; J. Laidman, "Clash of Philosophies, Loss of Animals Triggered Turmoil," *toledoblade.com*, March 13, 2005; J. Laidman, "Fired Zoo Veterinarian's File Mostly Positive, with a Few Concerns," *toledoblade.com*, March 9, 2005; J. Laidman, "Toledo Zoo Veterinarian Blames Firing on His Warnings to USDA," *toledoblade.com*, March 8, 2005; J. Laidman, "Feds Probe 2 Animal Deaths at Toledo Zoo," *toledoblade.com*, February 24, 2004; J. Laidman and T. Vezner, "Staff Offers Criticism, Praise in Zoo Survey," *toledoblade.com*, May 27, 2005; J. Laidman and T. Vezner, "Vet's Deal Isn't First to Silence Ex-Official," *toledoblade.com*, May 2, 2005; J. Laidman and T. Vezner, "Internal Battles Plunge Zoo into a Caldron of Discontent," *toledoblade.com*, March 20, 2005; S. H. Staelin, "Zoo Board Tackles Challenges," *toledoblade.com*, April 16, 2005; T. Vezner, "Zoo Names Chief Veterinarian, Ignoring Task Force's Proposal," *toledoblade.com*, December 17, 2005; T. Vezner, "Consultant Hired to Oversee Zoo Administration," *toledoblade.com*, July 20, 2005; T. Vezner, "Zoo's Ex-Vet on Hand for Report," *toledoblade.com*, July 9, 2005; T. Vezner, "Zoo Task Force Report Demands Broad Changes," *toledoblade.com*, July 7, 2005; T. Vezner and J. Laidman, "Flurry of Changes Leaves Workers Reeling," *toledoblade.com*, May 6, 2005; T. Vezner, "Settlement Bars Zoo Vet from Speaking to Panel," *toledoblade.com*, May 1, 2005; T. Vezner, "Zoo Task Force's Questions for Dennler Hit Time Limit," *toledoblade.com*, April 1, 2005; T. Vezner, "Inquiry in 2004 Disclosed Problems," *toledoblade.com*, March 27, 2005; Lucas County Commissioners Special Citizens Task Force for the Zoo, Final Report, July 8, 2005, http://www.co.lucas.oh.us/ commissioners/Final_Report_Zoo_Task_Force.pdf; http://www.toledozoo.org, accessed January 17, 2006; and http://www.doctortim.org, accessed January 17, 2006.

GLOSSARY/SUBJECT INDEX

The page on which a key term is defined is printed in boldface.

boards of directors, and diversity, 106

body movements, 254

bonus. An individual-based incentive plan that rewards employees for recent performance rather than historical performance. 15f, **170**–171

books on OB, 28

bookselling industry, 11

boss effect, 64

boundaryless organization. An organization that seeks to eliminate the chain of command, have limitless spans of control, and replace departments with empowered teams. **468**–470, 477

bounded rationality. Limitations on a person's ability to interpret, process, and act on information. **416**–417

brainstorming. An idea-generation process that specifically encourages any and all alternatives, while withholding any criticism of those alternatives. **426**–427

broken windows theory, 434

bullying in the workplace, 287

bureaucracy. An organizational design with highly routine operating tasks achieved through specialization, formalized rules and regulations, tasks that are grouped into functional departments, centralized authority, narrow spans of control, and decision making that follows the chain of command. **464**–465

burnout, 60

butlers, 101–102

C

Canada
    ESOPs in, 172
    global competition, 16
    harassment, 287
    job redesign, 182
    labour relations dispute, 331
    multiculturalism, 88
    values, Canadian *vs.* American, 88, 89f
    values in Canadian workplace, 84–92, 85f

capacity, 474

Capitalism and Freedom (Friedman), 437

care, 432

caring, 352

case studies, 10f

cases and case incidents
    Apple Goes Global, 30–31
    Attaching the Carrot to the Stick, 198–199
    Auditing, Attitudes, and Absenteeism, 519–520
    Bad Faith Bargaining?, 520–521
    Barry's Peer Becomes His Boss, 304–305
    Boundaryless Organizations, 530–531
    Can You Read Emotions from Faces?, 75
    Choosing Your Battles, 336–337
    On the Costs of Being Nice, 74–75

Creative Deviance: Bucking the Hierarchy?, 483

Delegate Power, or Keep It Close?, 304

Disability Accommodations and Promotions at Bunco, 523–526

Equity and Executive Pay, 161

Era of the Disposable Worker?, 31

Gender-Based Harassment among the Royal Canadian Mounted Police, 522–523

Google and P&G Swap Employees, 374–375

"I Detest Bureaucracy," 483–484

IBM's Multicultural Multinational Teams, 237

"If Two Heads Are Better than One, Are Four Even Better?", 446

Is a 5S Culture for You?, 374

Leadership by Algorithm, 409

Motivation for Leisure, 198

Moving from Colleague to Supervisor, 408–409

The Path to Fraud, 517–519

The Personality Problem, 516–517

PowerPoint Purgatory, 271–272

Promotion from Within, 526–527

Pros and Cons of Collective Bargaining, 337–338

Repairing Jobs That Fail to Satisfy, 527–530

Starbucks Returns to Its Roots, 512

Thinking Your Way to a Better Job, 116

Tongue-Tide in Teams, 236–237

Trouble at City Zoo, 532–543

Using Social Media to Your Advantage, 270–271

Wage Reduction Proposal, 162

When Companies Fail to Change, 513

You Cannot Do That, 115

Youngest Female Self-made Billionaire, 445

centralization. The degree to which decision making is concentrated at a single point in the organization. **461**

CEO compensation, 197–198

chain, 257

chain of command. The continuous line of authority that extends from upper organizational levels to the lowest level and clarifies who reports to whom. **459**–460

challenge stressors, 120

chameleon, 108

change
    action research, 493–494
    appreciative inquiry (AI), 494–495, 494f
    approaches to change management, 491–495
    change agents, 490, 493, 495
    culture for change, 501–505
    culture of innovation, 502–504
    forces for change, 488–490, 488f
    global context, 505–507

Kotter's eight-step plan for implementing change, 493, 493f
    learning organization, 504–505
    Lewin's three-step model, 491–493, 492f
    limited focus of change, 497
    low tolerance for change, 496
    opportunities for change, 489–490
    in organizational culture, 365–368
    organizational culture as barrier to, 364
    point/counterpoint, 509
    politics of change, 501
    resistance to change, 495–501
    selection of people who accept change, 500
    targets for change, 490f

change agents. People who act as catalysts and assume the responsibility for managing change activities. **490**, 493, 495

The Change Masters (Kanter), 399

channel. The medium through which a message travels. 248, **248**–251, 249f

channel richness. The amount of information that can be transmitted during a communication episode. **249**, 249f, 251

charismatic leadership, 389–392, 390f, 410–411

charismatic leadership theory. A leadership theory that states that followers make attributions of heroic or extraordinary leadership abilities when they observe certain behaviours. **389**

cheating, 434

chess, and intuition, 417

China, 91–92

choice, 153, 178, 276–277

co-optation, 499

coalitions, 282

code of ethics, 366

coercion, 500

coercive power. Power that is based on fear. **277**, 279

cognitive component. The opinion or belief segment of an attitude. **92**

cognitive CQ, 107

cognitive evaluation theory. Offering extrinsic rewards (for example, pay) for work effort that was previously rewarding intrinsically will tend to decrease the overall level of a person's motivation. **151**

cohesiveness. The degree to which team members are attracted to one another and are motivated to stay on the team. **228**–229, 229f, 231–232

collaboration, 177

collective socialization, 362f

collective turnover, 98

collectivism. A national culture attribute that describes a tight social framework in which people expect others in groups of which they are a part to look after them and protect them. **81**, 317, 331

commitment, 279, 499

NAME AND ORGANIZATION INDEX

LIST OF CANADIAN COMPANIES

Prince Edward Island

Quebec